MANAGEMENT

6TH EDITION

MANAGEMENT
6TH EDITION

Don Hellriegel

College of Business Administration and
Graduate School of Business
Texas A&M University

John W. Slocum, Jr.

Edwin L. Cox School of Business
Southern Methodist University

Addison-Wesley Publishing Company

Reading, Massachusetts ▼ Menlo Park, California ▼
New York ▼ Don Mills, Ontario ▼ Wokingham,
England ▼ Amsterdam ▼ Bonn ▼ Sydney ▼
Singapore ▼ Tokyo ▼ Madrid ▼ San Juan ▼
Paris ▼ Milan

Executive Editor: Barbara Rifkind

Sponsoring Editor: Beth Toland

Development Manager: Sue Gleason

Managing Editor: Mary Clare McEwing

Senior Production Supervisor: Peter Petraitis

Art and Design Director: Marshall Henrichs

Interior Designer: B B & K

Cover and Interior Photos: Marshall Henrichs

Production Services Manager: Sarah McCracken

Technical Art Consultant: Dick Morton

Computer Graphics Development: John Cornell

Illustrators: Eastern Rainbow

Photo Researcher: Darcy Lanham

Associate Editor: Christine O'Brien

Copyeditor: Jane Hoover

Feature Writers: Ann Hall/Michael Kirkpatrick

Proofreaders: Phyllis Coyne/Cecilia Thurlow

Layout Artists: Nancy McJennett/Nancy Blodgett

Production Coordinator: Jason Jordan

Production Assistant: Jean Castro

Permissions Editor: Mary Dyer

Manufacturing Supervisor: Roy Logan

Product Manager: Angie Davis

Promotions Supervisor: Eileen Spingler

Compositor & Color Separator: York Graphic Services

Printer: Von Hoffmann

Library of Congress Cataloging-in-Publication Data

Hellriegel, Don.
    Management / Don Hellriegel, John W. Slocum, Jr.—6th ed.
      p.   cm.
    Includes bibliographical references and index.
    ISBN 0-201-52600-X
    1. Management.   I. Slocum, John W.   II. Title.
HD31.H447   1991
  658.4—dc20   91-22706
                                            CIP

1 2 3 4 5 6 7 8 9 10 - VH - 95 94 93 92 91

Credits: Appear on last page of the book and constitutes a continuation of the copyright page.

PREFACE

Our vision for the sixth edition of *Management* is to create a sense of excitement for problems and actual choices experienced by managers of the 1990s, to achieve lasting learning by our primary audience: the student. **We wanted to create the experience of managing and of being managed in the nineties.** This vision drove every aspect of the revision—from content to pedagogical features to design to the learning package that accompanies the text. With this vision, we have created the conditions for learning management competencies and skills, as well as given readers the experience of being a manager and of being managed. This vision addresses the call for management educators to both ''teach it like it is'' and ''teach it like it should be'' in the real world. The authors, the editorial team at Addison-Wesley, and all of the reviewers were committed to achieving these goals.

We will try to capture the reasons for our excitement in this revision in the following sections. In a sense, this is like trying to capture a striking piece of artwork by describing it in a memo. Our enthusiasm can only truly be captured by engaging yourself in one of the chapters.

What's New in the Sixth Edition?

Our preface would go on for many pages if we attempted to list everything that's new in the sixth edition. Here are a few highlights:

- ▶ Every chapter has been thoroughly revised, including the deletion and addition of content, to give students the experience of being a manager and of being managed with respect to the focus of that particular chapter.

- ▶ The organization of the book is sufficiently flexible to allow the instructor to cover chapters in various sequences. For specifics, please see Chapter 1. It presents the strategy and organization of the whole book.

- ▶ There is a complete new chapter on entrepreneurship and small business. Of course, issues and examples related to entrepreneurship and small business are also introduced throughout the book. The management information systems chapter has been completely recast as a chapter on information management technologies.

- ▶ A variety of topics have been either introduced in this edition or more consistently presented in a variety of chapters—including creativity, innovation, organizational cultures, teams, diversity in the workplace, ethical decision making, global management, quality management, services management, total quality control, network organizations, employee empowerment, transformational leadership, and the list goes on.

- ▶ A new, unique section called *Experiencing Management* provides four competency-building features at the end of each chapter. In contrast, the fifth edition typically had one management case at the end of each chapter. With 22 chapters, the Experiencing Management section literally creates 88 opportunities for students to solve real problems and to make real choices for enhancing their learning.

Features

To give students the experience of managing and of being managed in the nineties, each chapter includes a set of special features.

Design In its design, the book conveys state-of-the-art management for today and the future. For example, the state-of-the-art presentation graphics in the text demonstrate some of the possibilities for managers with new information management technologies. The book cover and other in-text design features help to create the feeling of a manager's desktop. And the photos, with their extended captions, are an additional source of real-world applications.

Experiencing Management Each chapter ends with a section called *Experiencing Management*. It provides four separate competency-building activities:

- ▶ *Skill-Building Exercise* A diagnostic instrument or a quiz that helps the student evaluate his or her current skills, behaviors, and knowledge. Some of the skill-building exercises ask students to draw upon their observations or experiences in organizations.

- ▶ *Manager's Memo* An in-basket exercise, a simulated memo, or a letter to which the reader must respond by answering some challenging questions.

- ▶ *In the News* Helps prospective managers to appreciate and learn to interpret the way the media present current management events or issues. This competency-building exercise involves analyzing a clipping from the *Wall Street Journal* or *New York Times*. All but one appeared in 1991 issues.

▶ *Management Case* A broader perspective is taken in the management cases. They deal with larger situations and sets of problems. Questions are presented to guide discussion toward the specific learning goals associated with the case.

Video Case Each part opens with a story based on the MacNeil/Lehrer Business Reports video that relates to that part's topics. These stories make for good reading whether or not readers have seen the video.

Chapter Opener The chapter opener provides a roadmap for the chapter. Each chapter begins with a statement of *What You Will Learn*. This includes the five to seven learning goals of the chapter and a concluding Skill Development goal, which indicates the managerial competencies that should be developed through the chapter. A complete chapter outline follows.

Manager's Viewpoint At the beginning of each chapter, there is a profile of a manager or organization, written and designed to capture the theme of the chapter. The first paragraphs after the Manager's Viewpoint specifically link it to the topics of the chapter. Often, the Manager's Viewpoint is referred back to within the body of the chapter.

Insight Each chapter includes more than 30 real-world examples of organizations, managers, and problem situations. About five of these per chapter—the *Insights*—are of substantial length, to provide a deeper appreciation of the real-world situation. Insights portray service, manufacturing, large, small, mom-and-pop, multinational, and for profit or not-for-profit organizations.

Global Link It has become commonplace to speak of the ''global village.'' Yet, this expression aptly describes the new world today's managers inhabit. In addition to an early chapter on global management (Chapter 4), each chapter has a *Global Link* to provide international examples throughout the book. Global and international issues are also woven into the text itself, as indicated by the global icons 🌐 in the margins.

Ethics In addition to a major revision of Chapter 5 on ethics and social responsibility in management, we introduce ethical issues and dilemmas in a number of chapters, again highlighted with a marginal icon 🔒.

Summary A reader-friendly summary is provided for each chapter. This summary is organized to match the sequence of learning goals presented at the beginning of the chapter.

Questions for Discussion and Application Most of the discussion and application questions that appear at the end of each chapter are new or rewritten to capture the vision of developing managerial competencies and skills. Within this section, we've added questions from the perspective of *From Where You Sit*. These questions require the reader to use his or her own experiences to answer a question related to the chapter content.

Manager's Vocabulary An understanding of certain key terms and concepts is essential to the development of management competencies. Together, they form an indispensable vocabulary for managers. Within the text, we identify key terms and concepts with bold-face type and define them. In addition, we fully define the terms in the text's margins. We list them in the new Glossary at the end of the book.

Complete Supplements Package

The supplements have been designed to be consistent with the vision of creating the experience of being a manager and of being managed. The supplements carry out the goal of providing real problems and managerial choices for effective learning.

For the Student

Student Resource Manual with Media Guide and Integrative Cases This supplement contains the following elements for each chapter:

▶ Chapter objectives and outline

▶ Chapter highlights

▶ Matching exercises and answers

▶ Completion questions and answers

▶ Multiple-choice questions and answers

It also includes a special feature: the Media Guide—a field guide to popular business and management media, including periodicals, television, and emerging electronic sources. The Integrative Cases are a selection of longer cases that bring together many concepts.

Experiencing Management Experiential exercises prepared by Marshall Sashkin on perforated worksheets for the student's convenience.

How to Pack Your Career Parachute This free supplementary booklet is designed to help students prepare for the job market.

For the Instructor

Annotated Instructor's Edition The Annotated Instructor's Edition (AIE), contains all of the same material as the student edition, as well as annotations in the margins to help busy instructors prepare for and conduct class:

- ▶ Learning objectives
- ▶ Real-world examples
- ▶ Chapter-end questions
- ▶ Teaching tips
- ▶ Video cross-references
- ▶ Enrichment modules
- ▶ Ethics and international examples
- ▶ Classroom questions
- ▶ Transparencies
- ▶ Software cross-references

The front section of the AIE provides a description of each annotation, suggestions for using the AIE in the classroom, a detailed overview of the pedagogical features, detailed descriptions with sample pages of each supplement, a general review of teaching tips, and chapter-by-chapter outlines.

Instructor's Resource Manual The Instructor's Resource Manual (IRM) provides tips on using each supplement, suggestions for using the IRM, a lecture note converter to guide instructors through Hellriegel/Slocum, chapter-by-chapter lecture notes with enrichment modules, chapter-by-chapter answers/responses to all questions in each chapter, film and video suggestions, and 150 transparency masters from both the main text and other sources.

Transparencies A set of 125 full-color acetates—some from outside the text—is provided free upon adoption. A set of 150 transparency masters is included in the Instructor's Resource Manual.

Printed Test Item File The printed Test Item File contains 2300 test items, all of which include the correct answer and a page reference to the textbook. Each chapter contains approximately 50 multiple-choice, 20 matching, 30 true/false, and 5 essay questions.

Computerized Test Item File All questions from the printed test item file are contained in the computerized version for the the IBM-PC. Users may add/edit questions on screen, create multiple versions of exams, and instantly generate make-up tests. Answer keys are included.

Software/Video Library

The MacNeil/Lehrer Business Reports Video Library The MacNeil/Lehrer Business Reports Video Library provides adopters with a collection of current MacNeil/Lehrer Business Reports keyed to part-opening cases in the text and designed to enhance the classroom learning experience. The video library is provided free to each adopting school.

The Video Guide Along with recommendations for how to integrate the videotapes with specific chapters or topics, the Video Guide provides for each videotape:

- ▶ Recognizable companies and people featured
- ▶ A brief overview
- ▶ Key objectives for students
- ▶ Detailed summary that reviews the content of each videotape
- ▶ Relevant essay questions with answers
- ▶ Activities that include either group exercises or a brief quiz on issues covered

The Complete Manager Software The Complete Manager, an in-basket simulation for IBM-PC computers, is currently used by numerous Fortune 500 companies for management training and executive development programs. Our edition of The Complete Manager, produced by Strategic Management Group, Inc., has been specifically developed to accompany Hellriegel/Slocum. It is designed as a management development tool intended to educate students on leadership, teamwork, quality control, strategic issues, ethics, social responsibility, and other management issues. All topics are page-referenced to the textbook, and students can request on-line assistance with decisions.

Acknowledgments

Authors don't simply go off to their islands to write textbooks. Without the help, cajoling, and diverse perspectives of many individuals, this book would not have achieved its vision. This vision and its implementation were in turn nurtured by the strategic and chapter-by-chapter insights of two superb faculty members and teachers: David S. Fearon of Central Connecticut State University and Peggy A. Golden of the University of Louisville. In addition to their numerous suggestions, they challenged us with probing questions to make us rethink issues.

We would like to give special thanks to Dean A. Benton Cocanougher of the College of Business Administration and Graduate School of Business at Texas A&M University as well as President Ken Pye and Provost Ruth Morgan at Southern Methodist University for their personal support and encouragement. Our thanks to them for creating an environment that made this incredible book project possible. For their outstanding help with many critical tasks and manuscript preparation, we would like to express our gratitude to Argie Butler of Texas A&M University and Billie Boyd of Southern Methodist University.

Many individuals at Addison-Wesley worked hard with the goal of making this a better book. Because of them, it is a much better book than it would have been. Those most directly involved at Addison-Wesley include: Beth Toland, the sponsoring editor for this project; Sue Gleason, the development editor whose astute insights, professionalism and personal care are woven into the entire book; Mary Beth Jones, who kept the flow of correspondence and feedback loops on track; Jane Hoover and Connie Day, whose copy editing improved the flow and readability of the manuscript while preserving technical accuracy; Peter Petraitis, who orchestrated the production process to obtain a finished product on time; John Cornell and Dick Morton, who are chiefly responsible for this edition's state-of-technology art program; Darcy Lanham, who obtained the many photos that tell interesting stories; Christine O'Brien and Jason Jordan, who primarily orchestrated and coordinated the many supplements to this textbook; Ann Hall, who researched and developed the questions for the *In The News* feature included in the *Experiencing Management* section; Marshall Henrichs, who directed the development of the forward looking design; Michael A. Kirkpatrick, who wrote the video cases that appear between each major section; and Mary Dyer, who guided and helped us with the permissions.

Of course, we want to express a special debt to our colleagues and friends at Texas A&M University and Southern Methodist University for creating the community of colleagues that encourages and sustains our professional development. We give special thanks to our families for their empathy and understanding in ''letting us go'' for over a year to devote evenings and weekends on our ''authors' islands.'' With the completion of this text, we can almost sense the thrill of once again being able to spend a weekend with our families. If we had known what would be involved in developing this edition, we are not sure we would ever have undertaken it.

Because ignorance is bliss, we engaged in an odyssey to create a book, with others, that achieves its vision of giving students the experience of being a manager and of being managed.

Many reviewers also made numerous suggestions and comments on one or more chapters. Although there were different views about what to include, modify, or delete, their comments and suggestions resulted in substantial improvements in this edition. In fact, the improvements and changes are so significant that we considered, at one point, calling this a first edition. In any event, we are grateful to each of them. They are:

Suhail Abboushi, *Duquesne University*
Charna Blumberg, *University of Texas, Arlington*
James Buckenmeyer, *Southeast Missouri State University*
Albert Cabral, *Nazareth College of Rochester*
Martha Crumpacker, *Washburn University of Topeka*
Tammy J. Davis, *Georgia Southern College*
John Hall, *University of Florida*
Bruce Johnson, *Gustavus Adolphus College*
Marvin Karlins, *University of South Florida*
James W. Klingler, *Villanova University*
John P. Loveland, *New Mexico State University*
John D. Overby, *University of Tennessee, Martin*
E. Leroy Plumlee, *Western Washington University*
Charles B. Schrader, *Iowa State University*
Charlotte D. Sutton, *Auburn University*
Fred Ware, *Valdosta State College*

We also wish to thank the following reviewers of previous editions, whose comments have contributed to cumulative improvement in this edition:

Janet S. Adams, *Kennesaw College*
Raymond E. Alie, *Western Michigan University*
John R. Anstey, *University of Nebraska*
Debra A. Arvanites, *Villanova University*
Jay B. Barney, *Texas A&M University*
Stephen J. Carroll, *University of Maryland*
John Castellano, *College of Boca Raton*
William T. Fisher, *University of Connecticut*
William Flannery, *University of Texas, San Antonio*
Robert Gatewood, *University of Georgia*
Virginia Geurin, *University of North Carolina, Charlotte*
Robert L. Goldberg, *Northeastern University*
Jatinder N. D. Gupta, *Ball State University*
C. N. Hetzner, *University of Rhode Island*
Ellen Jackofsky, *Southern Methodist University*
Bruce H. Kemelgor, *University of Louisville*
Jeff Kerr, *University of Miami*
Lee Krajewski, *Ohio State University*
W. Anthony Kulisch, *University of the Pacific*
Edward K. Marlow, *Eastern Illinois University*
James C. McElroy, *Iowa State University*

Walter B. Newsom, *Mississippi State University*
dt Ogilvie, *University of Texas*
James G. Pesek, *Clarion University*
Larry Ritzman, *Boston College*
Doug Roberts, *LTV*
Stuart A. Rosencrantz, *Eastern Illinois University*
Marion Sobol, *Southern Methodist University*
Harry Sutherland, *Brooklyn Union Gas Company*

Heidi Vernon-Wortzel, *Northeastern University*
Jeff Weekley, *Greyhound Lines, Inc.*
Charles W. West, Jr., *University of North Carolina, Wilmington*
David A. Wilkerson, *Indiana State University*

D. H.
J. W. S.

DON HELLRIEGEL

Don Hellriegel is Professor of Management in the Department of Management and Jenna and Calvin R. Guest Professor of Business Administration in the College of Business Administration and Graduate School of Business at Texas A&M University. He received his B.S. and M.B.A. from Kent State University and Ph.D. in 1969 from the University of Washington. At Texas A&M since 1975, he has served as head of the Department of Management, interim executive vice chancellor for Academic Programs, and interim dean of the College of Business Administration. He has held a number of positions in the Academy of Management, including president, and was elected a fellow in 1980. He has served as associate editor and editor of the *Academy of Management Review,* and as a member of the Academy's Board of Governors from 1980 to 1989. He has co-authored five books and has published in a variety of journals.

JOHN W. SLOCUM, JR.

John W. Slocum, Jr. holds the O. Paul Corley Professorship in Organizational Behavior and Administration in the Edwin L. Cox School of Business, Southern Methodist University. Dr. Slocum, 39th president of the Academy of Management, was editor of the *Academy of Management Journal* and is currently editor of *Organization Sciences.* He is a fellow in the Academy of Management and Decision Sciences Institute. He has been awarded the Nicolas Saglo and Rotunda Outstanding Teaching Awards at SMU. He has served as a consultant to organizations such as Westinghouse, IBM, NASA, LTV, Brooklyn Union Gas Company, and Allstate. He has authored or co-authored more than five books and more than 96 articles for professional journals. Like his colleague and co-author, Dr. Slocum received an M.B.A. from Kent State University (1964) and a Ph.D. in organizational behavior from the University of Washington (1967).

BRIEF CONTENTS

CONTENTS

CHAPTER 4 GLOBAL FORCES AND MANAGEMENT 104

Software/Video Library

The MacNeil/Lehrer Business Reports Video Library
The MacNeil/Lehrer Business Reports Video Library provides adopters with a collection of current MacNeil/Lehrer Business Reports keyed to part-opening cases in the text and designed to enhance the classroom learning experience. The video library is provided free to each adopting school.

The Video Guide
Along with recommendations for how to integrate the video-tapes with specific chapters or topics, the Video Guide provides for each videotape:
- Recognizable companies and people featured
- A brief overview
- Key objectives for students
- Detailed summary that reviews the content of each videotape
- Relevant essay questions with answers
- Activities that include either group exercises or a brief quiz on issues covered

The Complete Manager Software
The Complete Manager, an in-basket simulation for IBM-PC computers, is currently used by numerous Fortune 500 companies for management training and executive development programs. Our edition of The Complete Manager, produced by Strategic Management Group, Inc., has been specifically developed to accompany Hellriegel/Slocum. It is designed as a management development tool intended to educate managers on leadership, organizational teamwork, ethics, social responsibility, and other management issues. All topics are page-referenced to the textbook, and students can request on-line assistance with decisions.

Part One

MANAGEMENT:

AN OVERVIEW

Gary Goldberg

One of the most important things a manager can do is create an atmosphere that inspires and encourages employees to be their most productive. This often-preached but rarely practiced philosophy is taken seriously by Gary Goldberg, founder of Ubu Productions, who notes that a big part of his job is making sure his employees are happy.

Goldberg, whose company is responsible for the television situation comedy, "Family Ties"—one of the most profitable TV shows ever created—didn't develop his management style in graduate school. During the late 1960s, Goldberg, a college dropout, actually lived in a cave in Greece with Diana Meehan, now his wife, and his dog, Ubu. Far from being a prospective businessman, Goldberg was a hippie with strong communal values.

In fact, Goldberg's move into television was almost an accident. After his experience in Greece, he returned to the states, went back to college and took a writing class. There, a professor told him he'd probably make a good TV scriptwriter. The idea fascinated Goldberg, even though he didn't own a television and hadn't looked at one in years. He bought himself a used set and started watching it. After getting a foot in the door at MTM Productions, his scriptwriting became more and more successful. Several years later, when someone showed an interest in his script for "Family Ties," he was given a chance to develop the show for Paramount.

Goldberg's past has clearly shaped both his managerial style and his creative impulses. (In fact, much of the humor in "Family Ties" stems from the philosophical conflict of two ex-hippies raising their conservative son.) All in all, Goldberg's style *appears* casual and relaxed. He kids around with his employees and often puts his arm around them as he goads and encourages them. He is unorthodox in other ways, too. For instance, it's not unusual to see Goldberg playing basketball with his staff in the middle of a working day. All of this helps foster a positive atmosphere for writing and directing. Moreover, Goldberg hangs around the set until a show is taped, lavishing praise on the actors and encouraging everyone. He clearly loves what he does, and his enthusiasm is contagious.

But Goldberg also backs up the "touchy-feely" management style with practicalities. Like a good commune leader, he makes sure the wealth is shared: all of his employees earn top dollar. Moreover, he helped set up a day care center for employees at Paramount. The result: his staff is tremendously loyal.

Goldberg clearly wants to have fun at work, and he wants the same for his staff. "Gary, I firmly believe, is successful because that was never his intention," says the show's star, Michael J. Fox. "He's happy creatively and that's almost all he's ever wanted." The atmosphere is one reason why Fox stayed with the show, even after becoming a movie superstar. If Fox had left, the show might have been jeopardized, if not canceled.

Goldberg is also efficient, a must in TV land. Taping "Family Ties" cost $750,000 an episode, and during one six-year stretch, Goldberg never had to pay his staff overtime, which shows that he can be a demanding, bottom-line boss. If the wealth is shared, so is the responsibility. To work for him, "you have to be responsible," he says. "I don't want to be there saying, 'Did you do this? Did you do that?'" In other words, when he delegates responsibility, he expects results.

Goldberg concedes that, because his staff has fun, it may not always look like they work hard, but he insists that isn't the case. And the results back him up.

What are the pros and cons of Goldberg's management style? In what ways is Goldberg's management style similar to that of a typical manager?

▶ 3

Chapter 1

MANAGEMENT TODAY

Bill Gates

What You Will Learn

1 The importance of organizations and their management in our lives.

2 The basic levels and types of management.

3 Different managerial functions and roles.

4 The types of work managers spend most of their time doing.

5 The four basic types of managerial skills and their relative importance.

6 Skill Development: How to evaluate your satisfaction with management as a career.

// I'd get bored if things just stayed

the same. //

Bill Gates

Microsoft

Bill Gates: Managing for the Nineties at Microsoft

If you spend any time at all at Microsoft Corporation, it doesn't take long to sense the imprint Bill Gates has made on the company he founded fifteen years ago, after leaving Harvard. His slang (fondly dubbed "Gatespeak") can be heard somewhere in nearly every conversation on Microsoft's wooded "campus" near Seattle. Some of the younger managers carry their Gates impressions almost to the point of caricature, giving their vowels the same singsong accent their thirty-four-year-old chairman does.

But Microsoft doesn't rest solely on the shoulders of its charismatic, still-young leader. All along, Gates has depended on a crew of strong professional managers. And, despite his reputation as the ultimate computer nerd, Microsoft's growth testifies to his own skills as a manager and a leader.

Granted, Microsoft—more than any other company to emerge from the personal computer revolution—embodies one person's vision. Its clarity of purpose, competitiveness, and tenacity emanate from Gates. In spite of his company's rapid growth, he has found an effective way to keep communicating that vision directly. In a business that thrives on creativity and innovation, his personal qualities have helped him keep the magic going into the nineties—well after Microsoft's initial success in the seventies.

The presence of a visionary leader is certainly one strength that companies of the nineties need in order to succeed. But, aside from Gates himself, where do Microsoft's strengths lie? In five basic principles: competitive positioning, global activity, teamwork, motivation, and communication. You'll see these five principles again and again, as you make your way through the hundreds of examples in this book.

1. *Competitive positioning.* One strength is Microsoft's current position in a volatile, hotly competitive industry. That position comes from the dominance of DOS (disk operating system), the software that IBM chose to control the workings of its first PC (personal computer). The Microsoft position is supported by the ongoing success of software packages like Microsoft Word. And it continues to find support from hot new products like Microsoft Windows 3.0, a graphics program designed to make PCs look and act as user friendly as Macintoshes.

2. *Global activity.* Gates also took Microsoft abroad long before its competitors. Microsoft products dominate nearly every foreign market they are in, generating even more sales and profits overseas than at home.

3. *Teamwork.* One key to Microsoft's success is Gates's ability to build and work with teams. Though the technologies all carry the Gates imprint, he and his managers break them down into specific business goals that can be handled by small, independent "business units." The groups are small enough—some of them as small as thirty people—for Gates to sit around a table and chat with key members, injecting his ideas in person. Although Gates delegates freely, his grasp of the details enables him to understand the forest and its trees. He is as likely to check the math in meeting handouts as he is to clarify fuzzy marketing strategies.

Says Gates, "I remember how much fun it is to be small, and the business units help preserve that feeling." Many evenings, long after other managers have left, Gates is still dropping in on the business units to see what's really happening there. Says Gates, "When I feel good at the end of the day, it's because I find a product group that is doing better than I expected, or because I contributed a good idea that ends up in a product."

4. *Motivation*. Microsoft works its employees hard, but they seem to love it. Many voluntarily put in seventy-five-hour weeks. Turnover is low, even though employees don't earn enormous salaries. The reason: the company is so generous with stock options that some employees are now worth millions. Also, the promotion plan for programmers is like that in a law firm. Each programmer is rated at one of six levels between 10 and 15. "When you hit 13, it's like making partner," says Gates. "We have a big ceremony and everything." While some programmers also perform some management chores, they don't have to be managers to climb the scale. All of this inspires tremendous loyalty.

5. *Communication*. Gates encourages employees to communicate with him directly through the company's electronic mail system, and dozens do each day. He tries to respond to each message the same day he gets it. (He also communicates with his parents via E-mail, although his mother admits that "he doesn't always answer *me* right away.")

Does Microsoft have weaknesses amid all of its strengths? Even Gates's biggest fans see a few worries on the horizon. As of this writing, rival Apple Computer was still pursuing a copyright suit, which holds that Microsoft Windows is too much like the Mac operating system for comfort. And the Federal Trade Commission (FTC) was rumored to be investigating Microsoft for anticompetitive practices, because of its historically close relationship with IBM.

Gates's response to such challenges? "I'd get bored if things just stayed the same."[1]

Even if you aren't planning to be a manager for a global software giant, following in Bill Gates's footsteps, these are challenging and exciting times for managers and for the people who report to them. Effective and innovative management like Gates's is critical to any organization's overall success. Even successful, established corporations such as American Express, Procter & Gamble, General Electric, and Westinghouse now demand that their managers become more innovative to meet the challenges that lie ahead. When Lou Gerstner became president of Travel Related Services at American Express, Visa and MasterCard were cutting into that company's profits, a trend Gerstner felt he had to reverse. He began by challenging two longstanding corporate beliefs: that there should be only one card, the green card, and that it had limited potential for growth and innovation. To broaden the customer base and encourage new ways of thinking about American Express, Gerstner quickly offered two new cards: Platinum and a revolving-credit card called Optima. He also used new ad campaigns to target two markets that American Express had neglected: college students and women. In addition, in 1988 American Express started a direct-mail merchandise program for all its cardholders. Cardholders can now use their cards to buy a variety of products, such as watches, luggage, clothing, jewelry, and furs, through the mail. What has been the result of such innovation? Since 1978 at Travel Related Services sales have increased more than 500 percent, and profits are up 28 percent.[2]

In addition to becoming more innovative, managers in the 1990s must expand their focus. United States firms are rapidly becoming part of a much broader—often global—economic community. Consider the astounding political and economic reforms in eastern Europe in late 1989 and the coming of the European Community in 1992. Managers of both U.S. and global corporations have yet to feel the full repercussions from these changes. One result of reform in the Soviet Union is that McDonald's opened its first restaurant in Moscow on January 31, 1990, with the capacity to serve 30,000 customers a day.

Today's managers also face expanding public relations duties. They must be able to respond quickly to crises that may create image problems. Consider the tragic day in 1989 when the oil tanker *Exxon Valdez* spilled 10.4 million gallons of crude oil in Alaska's Prince William Sound, killing thousands of birds and other wild creatures. Although this event took place thousands of miles from Exxon's corporate headquarters in Dallas, Texas, it immediately affected management decisions there. Exxon's CEO, Lawrence Rawl, was besieged by reporters who portrayed the world's third-largest industrial company as uncaring, incompetent, and penny pinching.[3] In today's broader economic community, managers can't assume that their organization's image will never be tarnished, that money will always be available for expansion, that other nations' governments will be stable, or that consumers will be satisfied with less than top quality.

organization Any structured group of people brought together to achieve certain goals that the individuals alone could not achieve.

But let's back up and talk about the immediate world in which you will operate. So far, we've cited examples of managers in large organizations. That's because organizations are the setting for all managers. Managers don't exist outside of them. An **organization** is any structured group of people brought together to achieve certain goals that individuals could not reach alone. Although alike in their need to achieve specific goals, organizations differ with respect to what those goals are. For example, a goal at American Airlines is to improve the company's profitability relative to that of other airlines. At Polaroid a goal is to create innovative cameras, whereas at Domino's Pizza a goal is to deliver hot pizza to customers in less than thirty minutes. Organizations differ in many other ways, too. Some are large and others small; some provide services and others are product-oriented. Some organizations, such as the armed forces, spend millions of dollars on recruiting members and develop methods to make sure they abide by formal rules. Others, such as the local PTA, spend little money to attract members and impose few controls on their behavior.

Organizations have been with us throughout history, so why are they, their goals, and their managers so important *today?* Because during the past fifty years, all developed nations have become societies of organizations, and the United States is no exception. Each of you could write your autobiography as a series of experiences with organizations, both large and small: hospitals, schools, sports teams, governments, banks, stores, clubs, and community groups. Some have been well managed, and others not.

In this book we look at organizations of all types and sizes and how their managers set and achieve goals. Our primary purposes are to help you understand how managers accomplish organizational goals and to teach you some of the skills you will need to be an effective manager in the 1990s. We haven't tried to cover every issue a manager might face—just those confronting *most* managers, regardless of their background or their organization's objectives or size.

MANAGEMENT AND MANAGERS

manager A person who allocates human and material resources and directs the operations of a department or an entire organization.

We've been talking about managers for several pages, so it's time to clarify exactly what the term means. A **manager** is a person who allocates human and material resources and directs the operations of a department or an entire organization.

Managers represent only a fraction of the employees in large firms. Most employees do nonmanagerial work. Receptionists, computer programmers, machine operators, secretaries, graphic designers, and maintenance people—all are important, but they aren't managers. What sets managers apart? Simply put, the difference is that *managers are evaluated on how well others do their jobs.* Furthermore, it is the responsibility of managers to try to determine and plan for the most effective and efficient way to achieve the organization's goals. For American Airlines to reach its overall profitability goal, for example, its managers have established five plans: (1) to reduce costs by buying fuel-efficient aircraft; (2) to reduce personnel by hiring only those who are most needed; (3) to restructure the route system to build up an efficient hub-and-spoke pattern of connecting airports, with about 80 percent of all traffic coming through Dallas–Fort Worth; (4) to maintain American's number 1 position in customer service; and (5) to expand marketing efforts by using customers for targeted promotions of vacations, car rentals, hotels, and the like.[4] These plans are specific to American Airlines, but all managers face similar challenges. That is, they must find ways to motivate employees and to increase their company's overall productivity, efficiency, service, quality, and innovativeness.

Managers achieve an organization's or department's objectives for the most part by arranging for others to do things—not by performing all the tasks themselves. **Management,** then, is planning, organizing, leading, and controlling the people working in an organization and the ongoing set of tasks and activities they perform. The organization's goals give direction to these tasks and activities.

The term *manager* covers many types of people. These include managers of small businesses, chief executive officers of multinational corporations, plant managers, and production supervisors—generalists and specialists. We refer to all of these types of managers throughout this book. Managers are also found in not-for-profit organizations, such as government agencies and religious groups, and trade associations, such as the American Snowmobile Association and the Professional Golfers Association.

management Planning, organizing, leading, and controlling the people working in an organization and the ongoing set of tasks and activities they perform.

Levels of Management

Managers are classified by their level within the organization. For example, entrepreneur Ray Kroc opened his first restaurant in Des Plaines, Illinois, on April 15, 1955, and his cash register rang up sales of $366.12 for the day. After this initial success he was able to convince others to join him. He became president and chief executive officer of McDonald's, a management position he held for more than twenty-five years. In 1991 the franchise system he founded had sales of more than $14 billion, was the biggest owner of commercial real estate in America, and employed more than 80,000 people to work in its more than 11,000 stores. In contrast, Jonnie Tsang is a manager of a McDonald's restaurant in Hong Kong with twenty-five employees.[5] Although both men can be called managers, their jobs aren't the same. The objectives, tasks, and responsibilities of the store manager are much different from those of the CEO.

Figure 1.1 shows the three basic management levels. We'll define the levels with a broad brush here, returning to add detail later in the chapter and throughout the book.

first-line manager Manager directly responsible for the production of goods or services.

First-Line Managers **First-line managers** are directly responsible for the production of goods or services. They can be called sales managers, section chiefs, or production supervisors. Employees who report to them do the organization's basic production work—whether of goods or of services. For example, a first-line manager at Bethlehem Steel supervises employees who make steel, operate and maintain machines, and write shipping orders. The sales manager at a local Toyota dealership supervises the salespeople who sell cars to customers.

This level of management is the link between the production or operations of each department and the rest of the organization. However, first-line managers in most companies spend little time with higher management or with people from other organizations. Most of their time is spent side by side with the people they supervise. First-line managers often lead hectic work lives full of interruptions. They communicate and solve problems within their own work areas. They work on the "firing line," where the action is. Jonnie Tsang, the McDonald's manager in Hong Kong, is a first-line manager.

Middle Managers Small organizations can function successfully with only one level of management. As an organization grows, however, so do its problems. Some managers at larger organizations must focus on coordinating employee activities,

When Thermo King Corp. introduced a new cooling unit to the refrigerated trucking industry, *training* became a key responsibility for first-line managers like Gina Williamson (left).

FIGURE 1.1

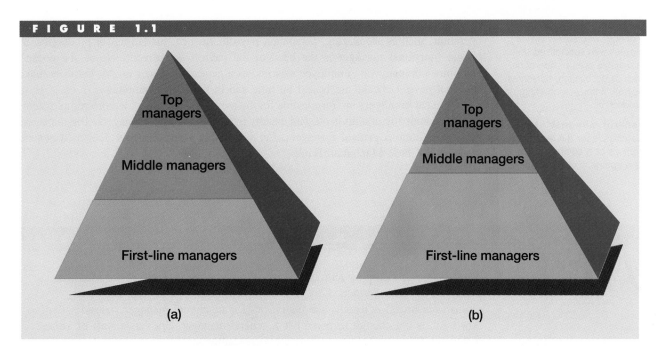

Basic Management Levels (a) The three basic management levels are traditionally presented as a pyramid, to reflect the higher proportion of lower-level managers in most organizations. (b) Many companies have "flattened" their structure to cut costs by eliminating many middle-management jobs in the late 1980s and early 1990s.

middle manager A manager who receives broad, overall strategies and policies from top managers and translates them into specific objectives and plans for first-line managers to implement.

top manager A manager who is responsible for the overall direction and operations of an organization.

determining which products or services to provide, and deciding how to market these products or services to customers. These are the problems of **middle managers.** They receive broad, overall strategies and policies from top managers and translate them into specific objectives and plans for first-line managers to implement. Middle managers typically hold such titles as department head, plant manager, and safety director. They are responsible for directing and coordinating the activities of first-line managers and, at times, such nonmanagerial personnel as clerks, receptionists, and staff assistants.

Top Managers **Top managers** are responsible for the overall direction and operations of an organization. Michael Eisner of Walt Disney Company and Sandra Kurtzig, founder and president of ASK Computers, are such managers. Typical titles of top managers are chief executive officer (CEO), president, chairman, division president, and executive vice-president. Top managers develop objectives, policies, and strategies for the entire organization. They set the goals that are handed down through the hierarchy, eventually reaching each worker.

Top managers often represent their organizations in community affairs, business deals, and government negotiations. They spend most of their time talking with other top managers in the company and with people outside the company. For example, Robert Crandall, president of American Airlines, spends a great deal of time explaining American's position on a variety of issues to his staff, to people from the Federal Aviation Administration (FAA), and to local government and community groups.

Functional and General Managers

Our brief descriptions of the three management levels can help you understand the jobs different managers perform. However, in large organizations managers are also distinguished by the *scope* of the activities they manage.

functional manager
Manager who supervises employees with specialized skills in a single area of operation, such as accounting, personnel, payroll, finance, marketing, or production.

general manager Manager responsible for the overall operations of a complex unit such as a company or a division.

Functional managers supervise employees with specialized skills in a single area of operation, such as accounting, personnel, payroll, finance, marketing, or production. A typical functional manager is the head of the payroll department. He or she doesn't determine companywide employee salaries, as a general manager might, but does make sure that payroll checks are issued on time and in the correct amounts.

General managers are responsible for the overall operations of a more complex unit, such as a company or a division, and usually oversee functional managers. Top managers are, by definition, general managers. Let's see what Anne Benbow does as a general manager at Chase Manhattan Bank.

MANAGERIAL FUNCTIONS AND ROLES

Now that you've learned something about various types of managers, let's consider what managers do—their managerial functions—and how they do it—the managerial roles they play. Managerial functions and roles are merely one way of describing a manager's job. Functions and roles may overlap somewhat, but you need to understand both to appreciate the nature and scope of management.

Managerial Functions

The successful manager does a good job of carrying out four basic managerial functions: planning, organizing, leading, and controlling. Most managers perform these functions simultaneously—rather than in a rigid, preset order—to achieve company objectives.

FIGURE 1.2

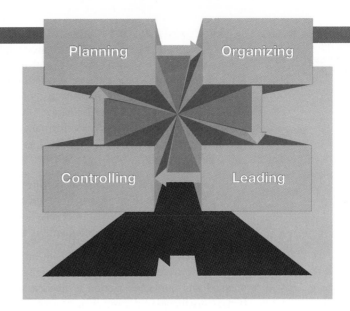

Basic Managerial Functions
Planning defines objectives and ways to reach them. Organizing creates a structure of relationships for carrying out plans. Leading motivates the people in the organization to do the job. Controlling monitors performance and either corrects it to match the original plans or alters the plans themselves.

planning The managerial function of defining goals and objectives for future performance and deciding on ways to reach them.

organizing The managerial function of creating a structure of relationships among employees that will enable them to carry out management's plans and meet overall objectives.

leading The managerial function of communicating with and motivating others to perform the tasks necessary to achieve the organization's objectives.

This point is illustrated graphically in Figure 1.2. In this section we will briefly examine these four functions without looking at their interrelationships. Throughout this text frequent references to the interrelationships among them will help to explain exactly how managers do their jobs.

Planning **Planning** means defining goals and objectives for future performance and deciding on ways to reach them. Managers at Frito-Lay, Boeing, Coca-Cola, and Shell, among others, plan for three reasons: (1) to establish objectives (directions) for the organization, such as increased profit, expanded market share, and social responsibility; (2) to identify and commit the organization's resources to achieve those objectives; and (3) to decide which activities are necessary to achieve them. We'll discuss the planning function in more detail in Chapters 6 through 9.

Organizing Once managers have prepared plans, they must translate those relatively abstract ideas into reality. Sound organization is essential to this effort. **Organizing** is the process of creating a structure of relationships among employees that will enable them to carry out management's plans and meet overall objectives. By organizing effectively, managers can better coordinate human and material resources. An organization's success depends largely on management's ability to utilize those resources efficiently and effectively.

The organizing process involves setting up departments and job descriptions. In this sense, staffing proceeds directly from the planning and organizing functions. For example, the National Aeronautics and Space Administration (NASA) uses a different kind of structure than does Hallmark Cards. At NASA, scientists, engineers, propulsion experts, computer programmers, and other professionals manage the space program in project teams. Printing greeting cards at Hallmark requires an efficient assembly line and workers who do repetitive tasks. NASA's specialists are not required to work on assembly lines, and Hallmark's assembly-line workers are not expected to write computer programs. We'll look at the organizing function in more depth in Chapters 10 through 12.

Leading After management has made plans, created a structure, and hired the right personnel, someone must lead the organization. Some managers call this process *directing* or *influencing*. Whatever it's called, **leading** involves communicating with and motivating others to perform the tasks necessary to achieve the organization's objectives. And leading isn't done only after planning and organizing end; it is crucial to those functions, too. Chapters 13 through 17 focus on leading.

controlling The process by which a person, group, or organization consciously monitors performance and takes corrective action.

Controlling **Controlling** is the process by which a person, group, or organization consciously monitors performance and takes corrective action. Walt Disney Company's CEO, Michael Eisner, and the managers below him use cost controls to achieve profit goals. First they gather production information (for example, the number of hotel rooms built or the cost of making a movie); then they analyze this information in light of performance (the number of hotel rooms occupied or the movie's financial success). Performance is expected to justify expenditure; if it doesn't, corrective action is taken. Thus the process of controlling is self-regulating and often cyclical:

► Managers set standards of performance.
► They measure current performance against those standards.
► They take action to correct any deviations.
► They may adjust the standards if necessary.

Just as a thermostat sends signals to a heating system that room temperature is too high or too low, so a control system sends signals to managers that things aren't working as planned and corrective action is needed. Chapters 18 through 20 present and discuss typical organizational control processes.

Now that you have some idea of the four managerial functions, the Global Link shows how they are carried out in a somewhat unusual setting: the South Korean chaebol. A **chaebol** is a business group consisting of large, globally diversified companies owned and managed by family members.

chaebol A South Korean business group consisting of large, globally diversified companies owned and managed by family members.

Managerial Roles

role An organized set of behaviors, which for managers may fall into the category of interpersonal, informational, or decisional.

Managers perform the four basic managerial functions while playing a variety of managerial roles. A **role** is an organized set of behaviors. Henry Mintzberg studied a variety of managerial jobs to arrive at the ten most common roles of managers. These fall into three categories: interpersonal, informational, and decisional (see Figure 1.3).[7]

Before discussing each of the managerial roles, we need to make four points: (1) every manager's job consists of some combination of these roles; (2) these roles often

---

FIGURE 1.3

The Manager's Roles

The ten managerial roles can be played at different times by the same manager and to different degrees depending on the level of management.

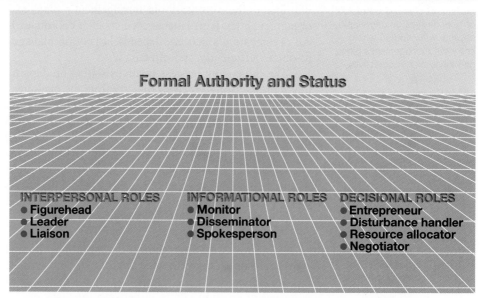

Reprinted by permission of the *Harvard Business Review*. Exhibit from "The Manager's Job: Folklore and Fact" by Henry Mintzberg (July–August 1975). Copyright © 1975 by the President and Fellows of Harvard College; all rights reserved.

GLOBAL Link

MANAGING IN A SOUTH KOREAN CHAEBOL

The economic growth of South Korea has often been called "the Miracle of the Han River." Over the past three decades, South Korea has achieved remarkable economic growth. Exports in 1964 were $100 million; by the end of 1990, over $50 billion.

One reason for Korean success is the growth of chaebols, such as Hyundai, Samsung, Lucky-Goldstar, Daewoo, Ssangyong, and Hyosung. These organizations share several characteristics that set them apart from U.S. organizations.

First, the founder and his relatives own all of a chaebol's businesses. Many Korean managers still hold the Confucian belief that the eldest son should inherit most of the family property and responsibility. Thus, seniority is the basis for salary and promotion decisions in most Korean chaebols. And employees who aren't family members don't hold top managerial positions.

Second, the CEO, typically the founder, assumes personal responsibility for every aspect of the chaebol's performance. According to Confucius, the son must show love, respect, and absolute obedience to the father. Responsibility and decision making are centralized in chaebols to ensure this sort of family obedience. In fulfilling his responsibility, Hyundai's chairman Ju-Yung Chung set aside precisely thirty minutes every morning, from 6:00 to 6:30, to receive phone calls from overseas managers. He asked them a series of questions and made decisions on the spot. No manager dared to question his decisions. To show respect, managers stand at attention when a chairman walks into the room and sit only when they are told to do so.

Third, most successful chaebols are founded by men with a clear vision of what businesses they wanted to be in. Hyundai manufactures steel, cars, ships, and heavy equipment. Chairman Chung chose his product lines carefully and implemented highly developed business plans to ensure their success.

Fourth, chaebols enjoy close relationships with government. The Korean government assists chaebols by providing preferential loans and interest rates, authorizing licensing arrangements, and including certain chaebols in its five-year economic plans. To gain these benefits, top managers in the chaebols need to be "connected" in the right places. That is, they must support the political party in power, make donations to the right causes, and participate in government-sponsored events, such as by providing resources when Seoul hosted the summer Olympic Games in 1988.

Finally, women in chaebols are assigned mostly to low-level managerial jobs, with little hope for advancement or job security. This practice follows from the Confucian tradition that women must obey men.

Considering the short history of Korean chaebols, it is easy to understand the prime role of the founder. As in many small U.S. businesses, the founder originally performed all four managerial functions—planning, organizing, leading, and controlling. As the chaebols grow and mature, however, more managers will be needed. Because much of the recruiting of new employees is based not on ability but on family connections, the issue of family control will no doubt become more important. Will new employees plan and lead chaebols into the twenty-first century?

Sources: Adapted from S. Yoo & S. M. Lee, "Management Style and Practice of Korean Chaebols," *California Management Review,* Summer 1987: 95–110; R. M. Steers, Y. K. Shin, & G. R. Ungson, *The Chaebol: Korea's New Industrial Might* (New York: Harper Business, 1989); D. Lei & J. W. Slocum, Jr., "Global Strategic Alliances: Payoffs and Pitfalls," *Organizational Dynamics,* Winter 1991, 44–62.

influence the characteristics of managerial work (discussed in the next section); (3) these roles are highly interrelated; and (4) the relative importance of each role varies considerably by managerial level and function.

Interpersonal Roles Interpersonal roles involve—as you might expect—relationships between people. Managers relate directly to other people in their roles as figureheads, leaders, and liaisons.

In the **figurehead role,** the most basic and simplest of all managerial roles, the manager represents the organization at ceremonial and symbolic functions. The mayor who presents a local hero with a key to the city, the supervisor who attends the wedding of a machine operator, the sales manager who takes an important customer to lunch—all are performing duties of the figurehead role necessary to an organization's image and success. Although figurehead duties may not seem important, they are expected of managers because they symbolize management's concern for employees, customers, and the community.

The **leader role** involves responsibility for directing and coordinating the activities of subordinates in order to accomplish organizational objectives. Some aspects of the leader role have to do with staffing: hiring, promoting, and firing. Other aspects involve motivating subordinates to meet the organization's needs. Still other aspects relate to projecting a vision with which employees can identify. Steve Jobs at Apple Computer and Edwin Land at Polaroid had visions that employees could rally behind. Jobs led his firm into the personal computer industry with his dream of designing a product that "would make a difference" in the world. He created a new industry because he thought people should have a device that could provide them with the same information large corporations and governments had access to. Land focused on innovations in a single-product market, instant photography. His motto was "Don't do anything that someone else can do." This vision inspired employees to explore new products; during Land's tenure at Polaroid more than 2000 products and processes were created and patented.[8]

The **liaison role** refers to managers' dealings with people outside the organization. These people include clients, government officials, customers, and suppliers. In the liaison role, the manager seeks support from people who can affect the organization's success.

Informational Roles Effective managers build networks of contacts. The many contacts made while performing figurehead and liaison roles give managers access to important information. Because of these contacts, managers are the nerve centers of their organizations. Three roles—monitor, disseminator, and spokesperson—comprise the information aspects of managerial work.

The **monitor role** involves seeking, receiving, and screening information. Like radar units, managers scan their environments for information that may affect their organization. Because much of the information received is oral (from gossip and hearsay, as well as from formal meetings), managers must test it and decide whether to use it.

In the **disseminator role,** the manager shares information with subordinates and other members of the organization. Some managers pass along special, or "privileged," information to certain subordinates who would not ordinarily have access to it and who can be trusted not to let it go further. In practice, passing information along to subordinates can be time-consuming and nonproductive. Successful managers do a good job deciding which and how much information will be useful.

Finally, in the **spokesperson role,** managers send information to others, especially those outside the organization, about the official position of the company. The spokesperson role is growing in importance—at least in part because the press and public are demanding more information. Many companies, in fact, have created a department of public information to handle such demands.

figurehead role The interpersonal role played by managers when they represent the organization at ceremonial and symbolic functions.

leader role The interpersonal role that managers play when they direct and coordinate the activities of subordinates to accomplish organizational objectives.

liaison role The interpersonal role played by managers when they deal with people outside the organization.

monitor role The informational role played by managers when they seek, receive, and screen information that may affect the organization.

disseminator role The informational role that managers play when they share knowledge or data with subordinates and other members of the organization.

spokesperson role The informational role managers play when they provide others, especially those outside the organization, with information that is to be taken as the official position of the organization.

Michael Eisner, Disney's CEO, plays the *entrepreneur role* whenever he provides the inspiration for a new project like Euro Disneyland, planned for a 1992 opening in France. Before turning things around at Disney, Eisner was known throughout the entertainment industry as an unusually creative chief executive.

As an example of a mishandled spokesperson role, let's once again consider the case of Lawrence Rawl and the Exxon oil spill. When the president and CEO of Exxon faced the press concerning that event, he found out how crucial the spokesperson role can be. When interviewed on programs such as CBS's "This Morning" and PBS's "MacNeil/Lehrer News Hour," Rawl claimed that it wasn't his job to know details of the cleanup plan. As CEO, Rawl might legitimately not know the details, but his going on the offensive and attacking the Coast Guard and government, accusing them of delaying the cleanup, made it appear that he was hiding something from the media. The result was a public relations nightmare for Exxon as the media continually publicized images of oil-drenched dead birds, rocks coated with viscous crude, and other examples of environmental spoilage. What Rawl learned from this incident was that the spokesperson role requires managers to acknowledge the public's legitimate interest in their organization's actions.

Decisional Roles Managers use the information they receive to decide when and how to commit their organization to new objectives and actions. Decisional roles are perhaps the most important of the three classes of roles. As entrepreneurs, disturbance handlers, resource allocators, and negotiators, managers are at the core of the organization's decision-making system.

entrepreneur role The decisional role played by managers when they design and implement a new project, enterprise, or even a business.

The **entrepreneur role** involves designing and starting a new project or enterprise. When Sam Walton founded Wal-Mart in 1962 and Sam's Wholesale Clubs in 1983, his main objective was to offer quality goods at low prices. To achieve the low-price objective, Wal-Mart keeps inventory low, has few managerial levels, and locates its stores mostly in small towns. Over a period of ten years, Wal-Mart has become the largest discounter in the United States. It has more than 1400 stores in twenty-seven states and over $32 billion in annual sales. As an entrepreneur, Walton was a designer and initiator of change in the discount retail industry.[9] The entrepreneur role can also be played within an existing organization. For instance, Arthur Fry at 3M played this role when he invented Post-it self-stick notes.

disturbance handler role The decisional role played by managers when they deal with problems and changes beyond their immediate control, such as a strike or a supplier's bankruptcy.

Managers play the **disturbance handler role** when dealing with problems and changes beyond their immediate control. Typical problems include strikes by labor, bankruptcy of major suppliers, and breaking of contracts by customers. Sometimes disturbances arise because a poor manager ignores a situation until it turns into a crisis. However, even good managers can't possibly anticipate all the results of their decisions or control the actions of others. In the summer of 1990, Saddam Hussein of Iraq invaded Kuwait. Oil prices skyrocketed overnight. Seeing Iraq's invasion of Kuwait as a threat to global peace, President Bush played a disturbance handler role in the Persian Gulf.

resource allocator role
The decisional role managers play when they choose among competing demands for money, equipment, personnel, and so forth.

negotiator role The decisional role played by managers when they meet with individuals or groups to discuss differences and reach some agreement.

The **resource allocator role** involves choosing among competing demands for money, equipment, personnel, and a manager's time. Managers have to ask themselves questions like these: What portion of the budget should be earmarked for advertising and what portion for improving an existing product line? Should a second shift of workers be added or overtime be paid to handle new orders? Disney's Eisner, for example, tried to buy the rights to Miss Piggy, Kermit the Frog, and other Muppets for a reported $150 million, instead of spending those funds on more new hotels.

Closely linked to the resource allocator role is the **negotiator role.** In this role, managers meet with individuals or groups to discuss differences and reach an agreement. Negotiations are an integral part of a manager's job. They are especially tough, though, when a manager must deal with people or groups (such as unions or political action committees) who don't share all of the manager's objectives.

We have discussed the ten managerial roles separately and pointed out that in reality, they are interdependent and sometimes played out simultaneously. As CEO at Perot Systems, H. Ross Perot certainly plays multiple roles. Some of these are identified in brackets in the following description of his activities.

H. ROSS PEROT, COMPANY BUILDER

*I*NSIGHT

"Perot Systems will become the premier computer services and communications firm in the world," pledged H. Ross Perot to the cofounders who joined him in creating Perot Systems in 1988 [leader role]. That same year the first company Perot had founded, Electronic Data Systems Corporation (EDS), a computer systems company, earned $323 million in profits on $4.44 billion in sales. Perot had sold EDS to General Motors in 1984 for $2.5 billion [negotiator role].

An almost stereotypical entrepreneur, Perot began by selling newspapers at the age of 12. He studied leadership at the U.S. Naval Academy and received technical training from IBM. Perot was 32 years old when he launched EDS [entrepreneur role].

It should come as no surprise, then, that Perot is a long-time champion of the open marketplace, where companies compete for customers by offering quality products and services at the best possible prices. By doing this, Perot convinced another entrepreneur, Herman Lay of Frito-Lay, Inc., to become EDS's first customer in 1962. Years later Perot Systems would beat out five competitors when Perot signed on its first customer, McGraw-Hill [liaison role].

Perot has been described as more of a leader than a manager. How does he describe good leadership? "Just treat people the way you'd want to be treated." He says this golden rule is timeless because human nature doesn't change. Thus, motivating and rewarding employees has had top priority at both EDS and Perot Systems. Perot has experimented with stock issues, equitable pay, and challenging assignments. He freely delegates responsibility to subordinates, emphasizing that they, too, are expected to

1. do the job for the customer,
2. make money at it, and
3. teach someone else to do it along the way.

Observers believe that Perot's real strengths lie in his organizational abilities. He organized EDS to be so flexible and responsive that it could be restructured in a matter of days [resource allocator role]. Key personnel could be replaced with no noticeable impact on customers.

After the sale of EDS to General Motors, Perot sought to change GM's corporate culture—from a closed, highly bureaucratic structure to a more open, less bureaucratic one—from within [leader role]. He argued against using committees and consultants to help with the change. He challenged management to treat dealers, employees, and customers with respect [spokesperson role]. He stood his ground against corporate dining rooms, chauffeured limousines, and executive bonuses. Ultimately, however, he found that he couldn't adjust to GM's corporate politics. In 1987 Perot accepted $750 million for his remaining shares of EDS stock [negotiator role].

Resuming a company-building career, Perot set clear goals for Perot Systems: $100 million in aftertax profits within ten years, employee ownership, and independence (no possibility of sale or merger). Consistent with Perot's beliefs, each employee is a team member, a full partner. By definition, team members take risks and take initiative, make decisions and make mistakes. Promotion is based solely on merit, not on length of service. Perot doesn't allow compromise on ethical standards, either: Team members may not bring discredit on the company, exercise discrimination, look down on others, become corporate politicians, move ahead at someone else's expense, or use illegal drugs. Finally, Perot emphasizes, "We will have *fun* participating in a great adventure—building our company."[10]

As this Insight illustrates, managerial roles coexist, often being played all at once by the same manager. The relative importance of each role varies from one level of management to the next and from one organization to the next. The personality, achievements, and ambitions of a manager will also affect the relative importance of each role. The following section describes how what managers do can vary according to their level in the organization.

WHAT MANAGERS REALLY DO

Among the thousands of books and articles written about managers, relatively few examine what they actually do. These few give the impression that managers spend most of their time in air-conditioned offices reading reports and attending meetings, rushing to and from airports, entertaining important customers, and solving complicated problems.

To some extent this impression may be accurate for top managers. Is it true for first-line and middle managers? A recent survey of more than 1400 managers, summarized in Table 1.1, was designed to answer the question.[11] These managers were able to identify seven major tasks performed by all managers. Let's take a few moments to see how the day-to-day work of managers differs at the three levels of management.

Principal Duties of First-Line Managers

Newly appointed first-line managers have much to learn—and also to unlearn. For example, a recently promoted production worker must learn to let others do the work he or she has been used to doing and to put aside thoughts about how much better and faster he or she did it. The manager must instead gain satisfaction from the accomplishments of others. New first-line managers learn to plan and schedule the work formerly laid out for them and not wait for orders. In the process they must also learn how their group fits into the total organization and how to share staff services with other managers.

What's Really Important in Different Management Jobs*

Key Management Tasks	Level of Management		
	First-line	*Middle*	*Top*
Managing individual performance	63	56	45
Instructing subordinates	40	36	27
Planning and allocating resources	47	66	61
Coordinating groups	39	51	54
Managing group/department performance	22	48	43
Monitoring business environment	13	20	34
Representing one's staff	51	55	53

*Numbers give percentages of managers who said task was important.
Source: Adapted from A. I. Kraut, P. R. Pegrego, D. D. McKenna, and M. D. Dunnette, "The Role of the Manager: What's Really Important in Different Management Jobs," *Academy of Management Executive,* 1989, *3*: 286–293.

First-line managers usually need strong technical skills to teach subordinates and supervise their day-to-day tasks. Effective first-line managers learn to "lean on" their technical expertise. Sometimes, though, a first-line manager is a recent college graduate (like yourself), responsible for the work of both hourly workers and professionals. This type of first-line manager is likely to have less hands-on experience. This isn't a problem if the manager has good interpersonal skills, which include the abilities to communicate with diverse types of people, to coach and counsel subordinates, and to provide constructive feedback.

In Table 1.1 you can see that managing individual performance was rated the single most important managerial task performed by first-line managers. Motivating and disciplining subordinates, keeping track of performance and providing feedback, and improving communications and individual productivity are all vital parts of that task.

Since most of you will start your managerial careers as first-line managers, the following Insight will give you a look at how a typical first-line manager spends her day.

I N S I G H T   Barbara Goldberg graduated from Brown University with a degree in economics three years ago. She is employed by Procter & Gamble (P & G) as a unit manager in the Boston area and works between fifty-five and sixty hours a week. She is required to call on major grocery store chains, such as A & P, and to supervise five salespeople. Twenty percent of her time is spent calling on the major chains' headquarters, and the rest is spent making calls at individual stores with her subordinates. One of her goals is to develop each subordinate so that he or she can step into a unit manager position after two or three years' selling experience.

At 7:15 A.M. Goldberg leaves her apartment and drives to the headquarters of the A & P chain. She checks the warehouse stock of the two products she represents: Folgers coffee and Citrus Hill orange juice. She then holds a meeting with two A & P buyers to review pricing, shelving, merchandising, and distribution for the past three months. In the lobby she jots down follow-up notes, calls her office for voice mail, and decides which phone calls to return. She also has to plan how she will work with her salesperson at her next stop.

She drives to a nearby supermarket to meet with John Remington, one of her salespeople. They pick up a weekly order sheet so that they can keep track of competitors' merchandising efforts. They have a coffee session with the store manager as they walk through the store. They check the allocation of shelf space, as well as positioning and pricing for the top twenty sizes and varieties of Folgers coffee. They compare P & G's prices to those of its competitors and replace a missing price tag. Remington rearranges both the Folgers and the Citrus Hill orange juice displays. Goldberg compliments him on the displays of P & G products.

By 11:00 A.M. Goldberg has arrived at her next supermarket. She and the salesperson take thirty minutes for lunch and then continue making calls. This day she will make eight calls with her salespeople before returning home after 6:00 P.M.

That evening Goldberg plans for the next day's meeting with another one of her salespeople by reviewing his call reports. She also arranges to have lunch with someone to coordinate her activities on the United Way Fund drive. She calls three other salespeople to cover problems that have arisen over product promotions and reviews their call reports from the previous day. On Sunday she organizes her schedule and headquarters presentations for the following week. She keeps in touch with her boss through biweekly reports and phone calls.[12]

What have we learned from following Goldberg around for a day? First, she puts in long hours doing her job. Second, she has to plan, organize, and decide what to do. Her schedule gives her freedom to arrange her day in a way that best suits her abilities. Third, she spends time with her salespeople and gives them feedback on their performance. Fourth, she plays many different roles, including those of leader, liaison, spokesperson, disseminator, and resource allocator.

Principal Duties of Middle Managers

Many middle managers began their careers as first-line managers. Typically, a middle manager has spent several years as a first-line manager, gaining knowledge about the business and learning technical skills. Even so, promotion from first-line to middle management is often difficult and sometimes traumatic. The percentages in Table 1.1 show that there is, in fact, a greater difference between first-line and middle than between middle and top management tasks.

The heavier emphases on managing group performance and on allocating resources represent the most important differences between first-line and middle managers. The middle manager is often involved in reviewing the work plans of various groups, helping them set priorities, and negotiating and coordinating their activities. Middle managers are involved in establishing target dates for work or services to be performed; developing evaluation criteria for performance; deciding which projects should be given money, personnel, and materials; and translating top management's general objectives into specific operational plans, schedules, and procedures.

Two ways middle managers accomplish their duties are through the delegation of authority to carry out top management's decisions and the coordination of schedules and resources with other managers. The major roles these managers play are interpersonal and informational because they face problems that are people-centered, rather than technical. Middle managers often spend about 80 percent of their time talking on the phone, attending committee meetings, and preparing reports.

Middle managers are also removed from the technical aspects of production work. Lacking hands-on experience, many of them must develop new skills to cope with top management's demands. One important skill is the ability to negotiate successfully with first-line managers to gain acceptance of top management's objectives. Another is the ability to achieve compromise and consensus in order to win support. Attending meetings with other middle managers and top managers demands oral communications skills that are better developed than those of first-line managers. And, finally, middle managers must be adept at developing their subordinates, opening lines of communication for them, and making them visible to other middle managers and to top managers.

Principal Duties of Top Managers

Pressures and demands on top managers can be intense. Tightly scheduled workdays, heavy travel requirements, and work weeks of sixty or more hours are common. During a typical day a top manager disposes of thirty-six pieces of mail, handles five telephone calls an hour, and goes to eight meetings. A true break is a luxury: Coffee is swallowed on the run, and lunch is often eaten during meetings with other managers, business associates, community representatives, or government officials. When there is some free time, eager subordinates vie for a share of it.

A top manager may spend days *and* nights working for the company. One night is spent working late at the office and another entertaining business associates. On other nights the typical top manager goes to his or her home, not to relax, but to use it as a branch office. Many recreational activities and social events are arranged for business purposes. Thus, the top manager seldom stops thinking about the job or playing the roles it demands. Such an approach to time management may succeed in getting the work done, but it also creates stress in most families. The following Insight shows how one top manager spends his day.

HOW A TOP MANAGER MANAGES A DAY

INSIGHT

So you think *your* job is impossible? Let's follow Robert Lutz, Chrysler's chief operating executive, for a day. He's in charge of ensuring that Chrysler plants make 10,000 cars and trucks every day and convincing people to buy them. He's also responsible for designing cars that won't be on the market until the twenty-first century.

Lutz arrives in his office at 8:04 A.M. and meets with a group of people who are spearheading the development of the Dodge Viper, a two-seat, ten-cylinder sports car. Lutz wants the car to go into production, but he must be able to guarantee that the company can manufacture 10,000 of them for less than $30,000 each.

At 10:00 A.M. the meeting breaks up, but Lutz stays around to clean up some details and review his notes. At 10:25 he runs to his car, a Dodge Spirit, fastens a radar detector to the windshield, and drives seven miles through traffic to Chrysler's Styling Dome, where he meets the vice-president for design. Their discussion ranges from the padding on steering wheels to the clay models of Chrysler's new 1993 midsize car, code-named LH.

At 12:01 P.M. Lutz leaves the meeting and drives two blocks to Chrysler's executive office building. He has a luncheon meeting with the heads of the Chrysler/Plymouth, Dodge, and Jeep/Eagle divisions and a controller. During lunch they discuss General Motors's continuing decline in sales and Chrysler's lag. Lutz wants each division head to cut advertising expenses. After some heated debate, he gets his way.

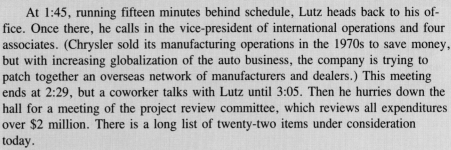

At 1:45, running fifteen minutes behind schedule, Lutz heads back to his office. Once there, he calls in the vice-president of international operations and four associates. (Chrysler sold its manufacturing operations in the 1970s to save money, but with increasing globalization of the auto business, the company is trying to patch together an overseas network of manufacturers and dealers.) This meeting ends at 2:29, but a coworker talks with Lutz until 3:05. Then he hurries down the hall for a meeting of the project review committee, which reviews all expenditures over $2 million. There is a long list of twenty-two items under consideration today.

The meeting adjourns at 4:30 P.M., and Lutz drops in on his boss for a thirty-minute off-the-record chat. At 5:00 he returns to his office, where the head of the Chrysler/Plymouth division has been waiting half an hour to see him. Lutz tries to hold regular informal meetings with each of the nine vice-presidents who report to him. This meeting is to discuss further the cut in advertising.

At 5:25, the meeting concluded, Lutz turns to his paperwork. Awaiting him are piles of correspondence arranged in folders. For the next two hours he highlights important figures in statistical reports. He finally arrives home around 8:00 P.M.[13]

Time Spent on the Managerial Functions

Figure 1.4 compares the distribution of time in a typical day among the four basic managerial functions by first-line, middle, and top managers. Note that first-line managers spend relatively little time planning and organizing. These functions are performed to a greater degree by middle and top managers. On the other hand, first-line managers spend 50 percent of their time leading (directing the actions of employees who actually do production work or deliver services) and 25 percent of their time controlling (making sure parts arrive, settling disputes among employees, scheduling vacations and overtime, and inspecting products). Middle managers, in contrast, spend much of their time planning, organizing, and leading to enable first-line managers and their subordinates to work as efficiently as possible. Ordering parts, dealing with customer complaints, and voicing first-line managers' concerns to top management are activities performed by middle managers. Top managers spend most of their day (over 75 percent) planning and leading. Although middle managers spend almost half of their time leading, this time is focused on their subordinates. Top managers spend the bulk of their leading time with key people and organizations external to their own organization. Note that middle and top managers spend little time *directly* controlling the behavior of others.

THE CHANGING WORLD OF WORK

Since you may become a manager shortly, let's consider what that job will be like in the 1990s. The entire work force that you will manage has already been born, and over two-thirds of those people are already working in organizations. As you think about managing these people, there are two important issues to consider: the changing nature of the work force and the changing face of organizations. These factors will change the duties of managers.

A Distribution of Managerial Time by Function

A typical manager's day can vary considerably depending on level in the organization.

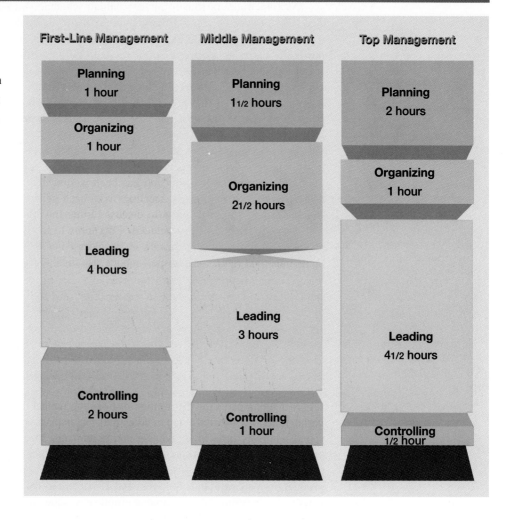

First-Line Management

Planning
1 hour

Organizing
1 hour

Leading
4 hours

Controlling
2 hours

Middle Management

Planning
1 1/2 hours

Organizing
2 1/2 hours

Leading
3 hours

Controlling
1 hour

Top Management

Planning
2 hours

Organizing
1 hour

Leading
4 1/2 hours

Controlling
1/2 hour

The Changing Nature of the Work Force

Relative to other generations, there will be fewer of you entering the job market than in the past. In contrast, the baby boom generation (those born between 1946 and 1961) created a huge work-force influx. Thus, in the 1960s and 1970s, organizations could be highly selective in their hiring practices. In the late 1970s, for instance, about 3 million people entered the 18–24 year old age group each year. In 1990 there were only 1.3 million new workers in this age group. During the next five years, this number will shrink even further. One problem this presents is that you will have to get more work done with fewer people. For your organization to survive, you will have to foster an environment that increases productivity per worker.[14]

The skills of entry-level employees will present you with another challenge. When the labor supply was high, organizations could be highly selective, retaining the skilled and not hiring the undereducated. In the future, organizations may have to hire workers who need remedial work in simple math and writing. In 1990 organizations spent more than $220 billion on training. Why? A higher skill level is required to perform many jobs, such as monitoring and maintaining computerized equipment.

The surging influx of women and minority groups into the work force is something else you will need to be aware of. Between 1988 and 2000, women will account for 58 percent of the growth in the U.S. labor force and minorities for over 49 percent—

compared with 45 and over 43 percent in 1988. The problem for both of these groups has been that there are few women and minorities in managerial positions. At MCI, for example, where 42 percent of the 20,400 employees are female, in 1990 women still held only 12 percent of the top 350 management jobs—and that was double the number of three years earlier. Organizations are having trouble finding, promoting, and retaining good women managers. Many of the most capable women get fed up with organizational life when they fail to advance into top management. Twenty years after women first entered managerial ranks, very few have broken through the middle ranks to top management positions. A recent study by the editors of *Fortune* magazine found that less than 4 percent of the organizations surveyed had women in top management positions. Similarly, a study of *Fortune*'s top 1000 organizations found that less than 4 percent of their top management positions were held by African-Americans, Asians, and Hispanics. Further, more than half of the minority group workers who will be entering the work force will be coming from school systems that haven't adequately prepared them with the skills necessary for advancement within organizations.

dual-career couple Any couple in which both the husband and the wife are employed.

Another issue that must be addressed by management in the 1990s is child care. Many of the women entering the work force have or will have children. A recent survey by the Society for Human Resource Management reported that only 10 percent of U.S. organizations provide childcare assistance, a shortage made even more acute by the increasing number of **dual-career couples** (both husband and wife work).[15]

The Changing Face of Organizations

Between 1990 and 2000, the number of people aged 35 to 47 will increase by 38 percent, and the number between 48 and 53 will increase by 67 percent. What this means for you is that there will be increased competition for the high-level management jobs traditionally held by people in those age groups. In 1987, 1 manager in 20 was promoted into a top management position; in 2001, the ratio is expected to be 1 in 50. The traditional lure of promotion as an incentive to work long, hard hours appears to be weakening.[16]

downsizing The process of letting employees go in an attempt to improve an organization's efficiency.

Another force working to change organizations is mergers and acquisitions, which have affected an estimated 15 million workers. One management tactic popular during the 1980s was downsizing an organization after a merger. **Downsizing** is the process of letting employees go in an attempt to improve an organization's efficiency. A recent survey by the American Management Association (AMA) showed that almost 40 percent of the largest organizations in the United States plan to reduce their work force by downsizing. As a result, people are becoming concerned more with simply holding onto their jobs than with doing their work.[17]

The focus for tomorrow's organizations will be on service, not manufacturing. In 1990 the service sector accounted for more than 67 percent of the nation's gross national product and 71 percent of its employment. Traditionally, service-oriented organizations have recruited people with low skill levels and have provided little in the way of training. The possibility of ''electronic offices'' means that eventually many people will be able to work out of their homes instead of commuting to an office.[18] Your task will be to manage people who may not have the skills needed to perform their jobs and whom you may not even see on a daily basis. How will you motivate people you can't talk with face to face?

The Changing Duties of Management

All of these trends will affect you as you launch your career. Your challenge will be to lead and be managed during times that will see an older and more culturally diversified work force, changes within and to organizations, and redefined product-service mixes. The following paragraphs sketch the effects of these broad changes on the duties of first-line, middle, and top managers.

First-Line Managers in the 1990s The first-line manager's job will change in several ways. First, because of downsizing, these managers must assume greater responsibility for the work of their departments. At Murata Business Systems, which makes fax machines, specialists in the areas of quality control, human resources, and industrial engineering provide guidance and support. The first-line manager can't be expected to be expert in every one of these areas but should be able to coordinate and organize the efforts of the specialists to get the job done. Second, the workers that first-line managers supervise will be less satisfied with authoritative management. They will expect more job satisfaction and will want to participate in decisions affecting their work. **Quality circles,** where workers and first-line managers discuss ways to improve the way their jobs are done, are already being used by organizations ranging from manufacturers of cars and airplanes to banks and fast-food restaurants.[19] Employees want to make their jobs more creative, challenging, and fun. Third, the work itself will change. The design and manufacture of products are being changed to meet new market requirements, global competition, increased energy-efficiency standards, and more stringent safety and health regulations. In addition, robots will increasingly displace people who perform routine or dangerous jobs. Robots, in turn, create new technical or software-related jobs that require greater skill and knowledge. Employees in service organizations will deal more and more with words and symbols rather than materials and products. First-line managers must adapt to all these changing aspects of work as readily as, if not quicker than, the employees they supervise.

Middle Managers in the 1990s Middle managers will face a different set of challenges. Managers will talk about improving efficiency, quality, productivity, and service, using fewer people. A wave of corporate mergers, acquisitions, divestitures, and leveraged buyouts (LBOs) has made entire levels of management redundant. (A **leveraged buyout** is the acquisition of a company, financed through borrowing, by a small group of investors.) Middle managers have been the hardest hit. From 1984 to 1990, as a result of downsizing, an estimated 500,000 middle managers at more than 300 corporations lost their jobs or were eased out with special early-retirement incentives. For example, IBM restructured its organization and announced that more than 10,000 employees—many at the middle-management level—would be let go. With survival a key issue, it's no wonder many middle managers are feeling powerless and anxious.[20]

Top Managers in the 1990s Top managers must strive to make their companies competitive in a global economy. Globalization will increasingly require **joint ventures** (those partnerships in which two or more firms create another business to produce a product or service) and cooperative management arrangements, such as that between General Motors and Toyota to build Toyota Corollas in Fremont, California. For example, Thomson, S.A. of France recently formed a joint venture with JVC of Japan.[21] Thomson hopes to learn skills vital to competing in consumer electronics, such as manufacturing technologies in optical and compact discs, from its Japanese partner. JVC, in turn, hopes to acquire from Thomson the marketing skills needed to compete in fragmented European markets. In order to accommodate these new global arrangements, organizational structures that resemble a network of relationships, rather than the traditional organizational hierarchy, will be common. Top managers will also be required to streamline their organizations. This means fewer layers of management and fewer middle managers. The first step in this process is for top managers to develop a clear vision for their organization. They will work closer to the customer to learn customer preferences and how to cater to them. Finally, top managers are increasingly being held accountable to society for their organization's actions with respect to issues ranging from wellness to air and water pollution to hiring practices. Planning and implementing new programs related to these issues will consume much of top managers' time and energy.

quality circle Meeting at which workers and first-line managers discuss how to improve the way their jobs are done.

leveraged buyout The acquisition of a company, financed through borrowing, by a small group of investors.

joint venture A partnership between two (or more) firms to create another business to produce a product or service.

Now you've learned about basic levels of management, what managers do, and what the 1990s hold in store for them. But you may still be wondering exactly what it takes to be an effective manager. Are there basic managerial skills you can develop? (**Skills** are abilities related to performance that are not necessarily inborn.) For the purpose of our discussion here, we will separate managerial skills into four groups: technical, interpersonal, conceptual, and communication.[22] In practice, however, it may be difficult to tell where one skill begins and another ends. Throughout this book, both within chapters and in Skill-Building Exercises at the end of each chapter, we will focus on the basic skills you should develop to be more effective as both a manager and a subordinate.

The relative mix of skills required depends on the manager's level, responsibilities, and functions. For example, skills needed by the manager of a local 7-Eleven store are likely to be quite different from those needed by the regional vice-president of Southland Corporation, which operates all 7-Eleven stores. As you will see, the store manager probably needs relatively high technical and interpersonal skills, whereas the regional vice-president needs higher conceptual, interpersonal, and communication skills.

Technical Skills

Technical skills involve the ability to apply specific methods, procedures, and techniques in a specialized field. You can imagine the technical skills needed by design engineers, market researchers, accountants, and computer programmers. Their skills are concrete and can usually be taught in college courses or on-the-job training programs. Managers use technical skills to varying degrees. They are highly concerned with identifying and developing the technical skills needed by others in the organization.

Interpersonal Skills

Interpersonal skills include the abilities to lead, motivate, manage conflict, and work with others. Whereas technical skills involve working with things (techniques or physical

skills Abilities related to performance that are not necessarily inborn and that fall into four groups for managers: technical, interpersonal, conceptual, and communication.

technical skills The ability to apply specific methods, procedures, and techniques in a specialized field.

interpersonal skills The abilities to lead, motivate, manage conflict, and work with others.

Thinking up ways to enliven Convex Computer's annual company picnic is only one of CEO Bob Paluck's uses of *interpersonal skills*. One year, Bob slid face-first into six washtubs of raspberry Jell-O. The annual bash is a reflection of Paluck's ''work hard, play hard'' motto, which so far seems to be paying off in high employee morale, motivation, and productivity.

objects), interpersonal skills focus on working with people. Because every organization's most valuable resource is people, interpersonal skills are a key part of every manager's job, regardless of level (from supervisor to vice-president) or function (from production to marketing and finance).

A manager with excellent interpersonal skills encourages participation in decision making and lets subordinates express themselves without fear of humiliation. A manager with good interpersonal skills likes other people and is liked by them. Managers who lack effective interpersonal skills can be rude, abrupt, and unsympathetic, making others feel inadequate and resentful.

Conceptual Skills

conceptual skills Thinking and planning abilities that depend heavily on the ability to view the organization as a whole made up of interrelated parts.

Conceptual skills involve viewing the organization as a whole and applying one's planning and thinking abilities. Managers with good conceptual skills are able to see how the organization's various departments and functions relate to one another, how changes in one department can affect other departments. They use conceptual skills to diagnose and assess different types of management problems that might result.

Conceptual skills are among the most difficult to develop because they involve the way one thinks. To use conceptual skills well requires thinking in terms of (1) relative priorities, rather than ironclad objectives and criteria, (2) relative chances and probabilities, rather than certainties, and (3) rough correlations and overall patterns, rather than clear-cut, cause-and-effect relationships. Conceptual skills are especially important to the manager's decisional roles of entrepreneur, disturbance handler, resource allocator, and negotiator—all of which require an ability to scan the environment for trends.

Conceptual skills are needed by all managers, but especially top managers. They must perceive changes in the organization's environment and respond to them promptly by making the right decisions. For example, Citicorp is widely regarded as one of the most innovative banks in the world. It pioneered the negotiable certificate of deposit, was one of the first to use automated teller machines, has issued more credit cards than any other bank, and is the world's largest private foreign lender. All because Walter B. Wriston, Citicorp's recently retired CEO, had the foresight to steer the bank toward innovative ways of thinking about the problems that would be facing the world's economy in the 1990s.[23]

communication skills The abilities to send and receive information, thoughts, feelings, and attitudes.

Communication Skills

Communication skills are the abilities to send and receive information, thoughts, feelings, and attitudes. The ten managerial roles assume that managers have at least basic written, oral, and nonverbal (facial expressions, body posture) communication skills. Because managers spend a large portion of their time communicating, recruiters look for people who can communicate effectively. A common complaint is that professional programs in universities spend too much time developing students' technical skills and not enough time developing their communication skills. In fact, the importance of good communication skills cannot be stressed enough. At a time when organizations increasingly expect employees to work with minimal supervision and to show more initiative, competent communication skills are becoming a must.

The need to productively employ workers of both sexes and varied cultural and ethnic backgrounds puts a further premium on communication. Managing diversity, after all, isn't just adapting to the new realities of the U.S. labor force; it also means ensuring that all workers contribute their best ideas and efforts in an intensely competitive global arena. But it isn't always easy to evaluate the qualifications and performance of workers whose cultural backgrounds and languages are unfamiliar to you. The following Insight lists some pitfalls to avoid in communicating with a diverse group of people.

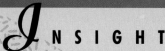

OK

1. In the United States, calling attention to one's achievements at work is considered a virtue and a sign of a professional attitude. Asian society, however, holds that a person should not call attention to professional achievements. Thus, when an American manager asks an Asian about his or her accomplishments, that person may be reluctant to answer.

2. Accents reveal very little about a person's education, level of understanding, or ability to understand English. Most Japanese experience difficulty in distinguishing and pronouncing the English *l* and *r* sounds. Similarly, persons from Arabic countries tend to confuse the English *g* and *j*, and Koreans have difficulty with the English *b* and *v*. None of these instances constitutes a basis for judging employment qualifications or performance.

3. The ambiguous *yes*: In Asian languages and cultures, it is common to answer *any* question at first with yes. The real answer comes later.

4. In the United States, workers who think for themselves and act independently are thought of as self-starters. In parts of Asia, the Hispanic countries, and much of Europe, however, to start something without having been specifically told to do so is considered a violation of authority.[24]

Relative Importance of Managerial Skills

The relative importance of the four types of managerial skills at each level of management is shown in Figure 1.5. Note that communication skills are equally important at all management levels. In fact, basic communication skills are necessary to competently utilize the other types of skills: interpersonal, technical, and conceptual. A manager's best ideas and intentions will have little impact if they cannot be communicated effectively to others.

As illustrated in Figure 1.5, the most striking difference among the levels of management is the shift from emphasis on technical skills to emphasis on conceptual skills. This is often a very difficult transition for managers. First-line managers may get promoted into middle management positions because they have excellent technical skills. These new

FIGURE 1.5

Relative Importance of Managerial Skills by Management Level

Interpersonal and communication skills are of equal importance to all levels of management. Technical skills are relatively more important to first-line managers, and conceptual skills to top managers.

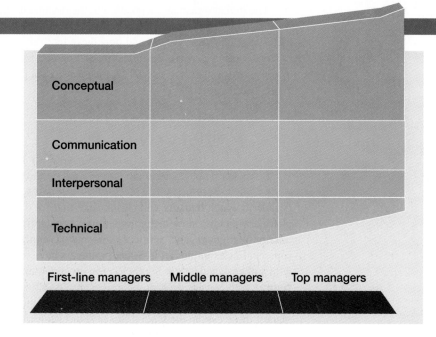

Importance of Managerial Skills in 1990 and 2000

Managerial Skill	Behavior	Year[1]	
		1990	*2000*
Technical	▶ Computer literacy	3	7
	▶ Marketing and sales	50	48
	▶ Production	21	9
Interpersonal	▶ Emphasize ethics	74	85
	▶ Manage human resources	41	53
	▶ Reassign or terminate unsatisfactory employees	34	71
Conceptual	▶ Formulate strategy	68	78
	▶ Convey strong sense of vision	75	98
	▶ Plan for management succession	56	85
	▶ Understand international economics and politics	10	19
Communication	▶ Communicate frequently with customers	41	78
	▶ Communicate frequently with employees	59	89
	▶ Handle media and public speaking	16	13
	▶ Sensitive to cultural differences	10	40

[1] Percentage reflects the number of managers who think each behavior is important.
Sources: Adapted from L. B. Korn, "How the Next CEO Will Be Different," *Fortune,* May 22, 1989, 157–161; B. Dumaine, "What Leaders of Tomorrow See," *Fortune,* July, 3, 1989, 48–62; and D. Anderson, "Building Tomorrow's Leaders," *GE Plastics,* January, 1, 1990, 14–15.

managers often make the mistake of relying on their technical skills, rather than learning new conceptual skills and developing their interpersonal skills. It is frequently because of this inattention to acquiring the necessary skills that middle managers fail to get promoted to top positions.

The higher a manager's position in the organization, the more he or she is involved in making complex decisions. Top managers need conceptual abilities to recognize important factors in their business and how these interrelate. Many of the responsibilities of top managers, such as resource allocation and overall business strategy, require a broad view. Without conceptual skills, managers cannot take actions that are in the best interests of the entire organization.

Skills for Managers in the Year 2000

With the coming of a single European market in 1992 and the blossoming of the Pan-Pacific market, managers in the twenty-first century will need to have a different mix of skills if they are to be more successful than today's managers. The 1990s promise to be a decade in which markets will shrink (like that for oil) and expand overnight (like that for pharmaceuticals), new technologies will constantly change ways of manufacturing and distributing goods and services, and new competition will pop up from unexpected sources. For example, all U.S. car producers have entered into some form of joint venture with either Japanese or South Korean manufacturers.[25] Chrysler's Diamond-Star joint venture with Mitsubishi Motors is an example. Mitsubishi manufactures low-cost engines, transmissions, and accelerators, and Chrysler provides the styling and distribution base to market these cars in the United States. Ford Motor Company and Mazda worked together for six years to design and manufacture the 1991 Ford Escort.

Table 1.2 indicates the relative importance of managerial skills at the beginning and end of the 1990s. These data were taken from surveys conducted by *Fortune* magazine, General Electric Company, and others.

The ability to provide visionary leadership will be the most highly valued managerial skill in the year 2000. This means creating a vision with which people can identify and to which they can commit.[26] The frequency of communication with both customers and employees will rise dramatically. With more lines of business all over the globe, managers will have to spend more time building consensus to meet the organization's objectives. Because of leveraged buyouts (LBOs), corporate downsizing, and the need for greater efficiency, employees will often have to be reassigned to unfamiliar organizational areas; and unsatisfactory performers will have to be fired as companies cut costs to improve their operations and meet the financial objectives of stockholders.

In order to cope with increasing globalization, managers will have to expand their communication skills by learning to speak either Japanese or German and becoming familiar with the history and economics of other countries. Organizations will need to establish high-level training programs that expose middle managers to the company's long-range plans. This will enable middle managers to deal more effectively with multinational joint ventures and to recognize the broad social and economic implications of their own decisions. Training programs will also show top managers how to conduct productive meetings with customers and to handle customers' concerns. Top managers, such as Jim Steffel at Fleetline and Ann Flavin at Optigraphics, frequently visit customers at their places of business to learn first-hand their views on service and quality.

Management—A Dynamic Process

The *process* of obtaining and organizing resources and of achieving objectives through other people—that is, managing—is dynamic rather than static. You can begin to get a sense of this dynamic nature in Figure 1.6.

Managerial thought evolves whenever new theories are presented or new practices are tried. If the theories seem to have merit or the practices appear to succeed, their use spreads to more and more organizations until, over a period of time, they become accepted ways of managing. The adoption of Japanese quality control methods by many U.S. firms is an example of evolution in management thought. In 1950 Edward Deming's total quality control method was rejected by U.S. companies but found a warm reception in Japan. Deming's method is more fully described in Chapter 20, but its essence is that poor quality is unacceptable. Data should be gathered to spot errors during the production process, not at its end. Employees should be rewarded for spotting quality problems, not punished. To honor his contributions to their industries, the Japanese created the Deming Prize, awarded annually to the Japanese company that has attained the highest level of quality. An increasing number of U.S. firms, such as Ford Motor Company, Whirlpool, and Texas Instruments, are now using Deming's ideas to improve their quality.[27]

Furthermore, many U.S. managers are eager to experiment with new solutions to urgent problems created by various internal and external forces. In recent years managerial decision making has felt the impact of a series of external forces: high rates of inflation (environmental force); the explosion in computer technology, fueled by development and production of the silicon chip (environmental force); changing oil prices and limits on production (international force); serious competition from imports in terms of quality, price, and market share (international force); and public policy, expressed in laws and regulations aimed at improving the physical environment and the health and safety of consumers and workers (ethical and social forces).

Managers of companies affected by such forces face immediate challenges to traditional ways of thinking, planning, and acting. If they can't adjust their decision making to

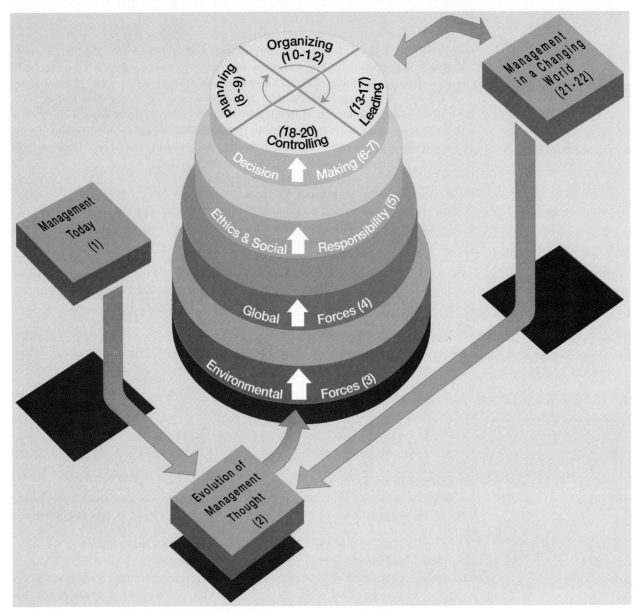

Management as a Dynamic Process

The number in parentheses identifies the chapter in this text where the topic is presented.

these new realities, their companies will be unable to compete successfully and will decline. Perhaps the best example of an industry's response to external forces is that of U.S. automakers. Their recent joint ventures with Japanese and South Korean competitors have led managers to rethink company objectives and ways of doing business. Ford and Mazda undertook broad restructuring of their decision-making processes. Chrysler and Mitsubishi built a whole new company. These organizations experienced change at all levels and in most internal functions to some degree; these changes, in turn, affected suppliers and the suppliers' decision-making processes.

Thus constant change gives management a dynamic dimension. The success of managers and their companies depends largely on how well they can accommodate change.

1. Organizations are essential to a society. People working together in an organized way can accomplish much that individuals working alone cannot. In fact, organizations are so much a part of our society that they touch our daily lives directly and indirectly in countless ways.

   Effective management is essential to the effectiveness of an organization. Managers establish organizational objectives, then direct subordinates, whom they depend on to achieve those objectives. Managers acquire and allocate the human and material resources without which organizations could not exist.

2. The three basic levels of management are first-line, middle, and top. First-line managers are directly responsible for the production of goods and services. They supervise workers and solve specific problems. Middle managers coordinate the work of several first-line managers or direct the operations of a functional department. They translate top management's strategies into specific objectives and programs for implementation. Top managers establish overall organizational objectives and strategies and direct the activities of a whole organization or a major segment of it.

   Managers are also distinguished by the scope of their jobs. Functional managers work in a particular department, such as accounting, marketing, or human resources. General managers are responsible for the overall operations of an organization.

3. The managerial functions—planning, organizing, leading, and controlling—define what managers do. The managerial roles—interpersonal, informational, decisional—define how managers do their jobs. Managerial functions and roles go hand in hand: Managers perform the functions while playing one or more roles.

4. Managers at different levels divide their time among the managerial functions quite differently. First-line managers spend about three-fourths of their time leading and controlling and the rest planning and organizing. Middle managers spend about two-thirds of their time organizing and leading and the rest planning and controlling. Top managers spend most of their time planning and leading and very little time directly organizing and controlling the work of others.

5. The four types of managerial skills are technical, interpersonal, conceptual, and communication. Technical skills are most important to first-line managers, who have to deal directly with specific methods of production. Interpersonal skills are important at all levels of management, because managing is the process of motivating other people in order to get something done. Conceptual skills are especially important to top managers, who have to think in more abstract terms and see parts in relation to the whole. Communication skills are important to all managers. Such skills enable managers to lead and motivate and to make changes in the organization's goals.

QUESTIONS FOR DISCUSSION AND APPLICATION

1. How might someone be both a functional and a general manager?

2. Who performs the four managerial functions in a chaebol? How does this arrangement differ from that at your local bank?

3. What are some differences between managerial roles and functions?

4. What are the ten managerial roles? Which roles does Bill Gates of Microsoft play?

5. **From Where You Sit.** How might knowing some of the challenges your first-line supervisor is facing help you on the job?

6. **From Where You Sit.** Contrast the typical daily routine of a job you've held with that of a first-line manager.

7. **From Where You Sit.** How can you build each of the four types of managerial skills on your first job?

8. Peter Drucker once said, ''An effective manager is a maniac on a mission.'' Relate his statement to the management roles and skills discussed in this chapter.

9. Look at the skills mix in Table 1.2. What additional skills, beyond those discussed in the text, do you think managers will need in the year 2000? Which ones will become less important? Why?

Will You Find Management Fulfilling?

Professionals or specialists who have managerial potential are usually able to think beyond the confines of their previous job roles. Intuitively, they have a human-relations orientation and understand that solutions are ultimately achieved through people.

This orientation is an important success factor in management. To find out how you rate as a "people person," indicate your agreement or disagreement with the following statements.

AGREE DISAGREE

1. The most important reward for an employee is more money.

2. Leadership ability is inborn; there is not much one can do to develop it.

3. Most professionals are interested in working on projects that bring them recognition among their peers.

4. An effective manager is able to size up an employee the first time she meets him or her.

5. Lack of challenge accounts for most employee loafing and grumbling.

6. Long acquaintance with employees enables a manager to predict what they will do in a given situation.

7. An employee's attitudes toward a company are difficult or impossible to change.

8. Employee output does not depend on what attitudes he or she has toward management and the company.

9. A manager should not praise staff members often for good work, because they will become difficult to handle and insist on salary raises.

10. A manager should not be expected to coach and train employees; most of her energies should go into running her department.

11. The most effective way to get increased performance from employees is to instill in them a fear that they may lose their jobs at any time.

12. A team of employees can always solve problems better than a single employee working alone.

13. Paying attention to the personality traits of each staff member goes a long way toward staving off morale problems.

14. High salaries and generous fringe benefits are the two most important motivating factors for employees.

15. In making a decision concerning an employee's work, a manager should usually have him or her participate in the decision making.

16. Employees will not have much respect for a manager who asks them for suggestions.

17. Self-understanding is just as important as understanding others.

18. A manager should not show too much friendliness and consideration toward staff members; they might think that she is ''soft.''

19. A manager should make sure that an efficient and capable employee stays in her department.

20. Close supervision of staff members produces the best results.

21. When employees have problems, they should try to solve them as best they can, rather than take up the manager's time.

22. A manager can do little to improve employee morale because she has to work within strict company rules and policies.

23. Recognizing the contributions of each employee individually is very important, rather than giving praise to the team as a whole.

24. Employees require individualized attention.

25. To serve as a source of information is one of the most important managerial functions.

26. Staff should be kept well informed about the objectives of the company and the rationale behind upper management's actions.

Interpretation. According to the latest human-relations theories and the most successful managerial practices, the ''correct'' responses to the 26 statements are as follows: (A = Agree; D = Disagree)

1. D	5. A	9. D	13. A	17. A	21. D	25. A
2. D	6. D	10. D	14. D	18. D	22. D	26. A
3. A	7. D	11. D	15. A	19. D	23. A	
4. D	8. D	12. D	16. D	20. D	24. A	

To claim that you are able to think in terms of managerial principles, you should have answered at least 80 percent of these questions correctly.

– MEMORANDUM –

To: Management students
From: Barry J. Gibbons, CEO, Burger King
Re: Malcolm Baldridge National Quality Award

Since I took over in 1988 as CEO of this $77 billion business, I've faced quite a number of challenges. The fast-food market is glutted with outlets; a teen labor shortage is causing me to redesign my kitchens for more automated cooking; and an aging baby-boom population is concerned about nutrition.

I had to downsize the organization, eliminating two management levels and 550 middle managers, to improve our profitability.

I had to give restaurant managers decision-making responsibility. Before my arrival, top managers made all decisions. Restaurant managers can now order supplies directly, via computer, from the lowest-priced supplier. I've asked my restaurant managers to take risks and have given each of them $25,000 to finance their new ideas.

I've installed a toll-free number—staffed by 45 customer service agents—so customers can call and complain about botched orders.

I changed Burger King's menu. We've phased out the salad bar, which proved too costly and was difficult to maintain, in favor of pre-packaged salads served with Paul Newman's salad dressing. We've test-marketed pizzas because 200 McDonald's are offering them.

And we're sponsoring promotions, based on popular cartoon characters such as the Teenage Mutant Ninja Turtles and the Simpsons, to attract children to our Kid's Club.

Several of my staff have suggested that Burger King apply for the Malcolm Baldridge National Quality Award. The objective of this award is to recognize corporations that have demonstrated concern for quality in both products and services. Here are the key criteria:

1. *Leadership.* Does the company integrate quality values and practices into its public responsibilities?

2. *Information.* Is the company gathering the right information in order to determine the quality of its products and services?

3. *Human Resource Utilization.* Does the company do a good job of developing its employees to realize their full potential and achieve full participation, quality leadership, and personal growth?

4. *Quality Assurance Results.* How do the company's products and services stack up against the competition? What improvements have been made to ensure quality?

5. *Customer Satisfaction.* Are customers satisfied with the services?

What we would like you to do is write a memo to the authors of this book indicating how Burger King measures up to these criteria.

At Procter & Gamble, Change Under Artzt Isn't Just Cosmetic

By Alecia Swasy

Just after New Year's day, investment bankers for Revlon Inc. chairman Ronald O. Perelman began quietly looking for someone to buy the glitzy cosmetics company. Within days, Procter & Gamble Co. came calling. Just a month later, P&G's relatively new chairman, Edwin Artzt, was meeting personally with Mr. Perelman, and P&G now appears the front-runner in an international competition for Revlon.

This hardly seems like the stodgy soap maker of Cincinnati. But P&G's aggressive interest in Revlon is just the latest move by Mr. Artzt to put his own stamp on the formal, slow-moving company.

In fact, Mr. Artzt has been on the warpath since he was named to P&G's top spot. He has told managers of faltering brands, like Citrus Hill orange juice, to get results or he'll sell the business. He has cut spending for once-sacred projects, like the fat substitute olestra, to focus on best-sellers like superconcentrated Tide detergent and Pert Plus shampoo. And he is clearing out managers who don't perform.

"I certainly don't want to have a short trigger with people and not give them a chance," he says. "But sure I've cleared out deadwood. Probably some of it was still breathing when it was cleared out."

P&G wasn't doing all that badly before Mr. Artzt took the helm. In fact, when the low-key John G. Smale stepped down in late 1989 after an 18% profit surge that fiscal year, Mr. Artzt was thought by many to be only a caretaker replacement.

But Mr. Artzt is confronting a maturing market for many of the company's staple products, such as diapers and detergents, while at the same time P&G's competitors have become more aggressive.

In response, Mr. Artzt wants to turn P&G into more of a fast-moving global marketer, particularly in high-growth areas such as cosmetics and health-care products. . . .

The eldest son of musicians, the 60-year-old Mr. Artzt won a basketball scholarship to the University of Oregon, where he studied journalism. After working as a sportswriter and a theater critic in Hollywood, he answered a newspaper ad for a P&G sales job. . . .

It was work thousands of miles from Cincinnati that eventually won Mr. Artzt the CEO post. He is credited with reviving P&G's struggling overseas operations, from which the company will soon be deriving more than half of its sales. In Japan, for example, he turned a money-losing operation into a big profit center by tailoring diapers and detergents to local tastes. . . .

"When he gets numbers he doesn't like, he'll be stalking the floors to find the people who produced them," says one manager, who notes that Mr. Artzt is a frequent visitor these days to the food and beverage division. "If you see Ed coming down the hall, look out." . . .

Mr. Artzt describes his management style as "helpful and supportive." On a Harvard recruiting trip, he singled out a P&G intern, recalling in detail her summer projects.

But he yells and curses when he's angry. At a recent cocktail party, Mr. Artzt chastised a junior manager, according to observers. "When are you going to fix your ad copy?" he demanded.

That hands-on approach unnerves some subordinates, but what challenges them the most is his demand for speed. As international chief, Mr. Artzt pushed for quick expansion of P&G's Always sanitary napkins. Within 31 months, the product was in 31 countries. Now it's the No. 1 or No. 2 brand in major markets, giving P&G about 12% of the $8 billion global market.

Today, product launches that once took years may take only months. Being quick is essential now that smaller competitors like Kimberly-Clark Corp. are moving faster. P&G's launch of ultra-thin diapers in the mid-1980s was supposed to give it a three- to five-year lead time, but Kimberly-Clark caught up within months. . . .

A clear priority is building what he calls "world brands." He points to Pert Plus, a combination shampoo-conditioner that's now the world's best-selling brand. Launched first in the U.S., Pert Plus is being rolled out quickly around the globe, although often under different labels. It's sold as Vidal Sassoon in Britain, for example, and Rejoy in Japan. "We'll definitely have more of our brands become world brands," Mr. Artzt says.

Wall Street Journal, March 5, 1991.

1. Discuss the managerial roles that Edwin L. Artzt is filling in this article. Is he emphasizing the interpersonal, informational, and decisional roles equally?

2. What effects might his decisions on clearing deadwood and turning around faltering brands have on middle management? on first-line management?

3. Which of Artzt's skills would be useful to you if you were a middle manager? Which of his skills would be detrimental?

THE MANAGER OF TOMORROW — TODAY

Tomorrow's manager comes from two distinct generations of managers. The first is the stereotypical grey-flannel executive of the 1950s and early 1960s, the manager who obeyed authority. This manager worked in an overwhelmingly white-male organization, took orders from top management, and was given little incentive to show initiative. Evolving out of the turbulence of the times, the manager of the 1970s and 1980s operated in a more fast-paced, cutthroat environment, in which top managers praised individual achievement amidst great technological and demographic change.

In the 1990s, emphasis will be increasingly placed on team building and managing a work force with multiple ethnic and cultural backgrounds. The goal for organizations isn't simply to hire culturally diverse individuals who have a variety of talents, viewpoints, and skills, but to put these individuals together on a winning team, able to make appeals to a more value-conscious consumer who wants greater personalization of products and services.

Ken Chenault, president of American Express's Consumer Card Group, USA, is typical of this new breed of manager. He has been described as a capable manager who studies the competition, knows the market conditions, maps out a vision, leads a team of culturally diverse managers, *and* makes a profit. Division vice-presidents who report to Chenault talk about his ability to create visions that inspire them, his use of the latest management techniques, and his ability to build teams and communicate with all of his subordinates. He is approachable, confident, and diplomatic. As one person put it, ''He can get all the horses to run as fast as they can and in the same direction.''

No manager can move with speed in today's marketplace without information. Spotting trends among the hundreds of facts the company maintains on individual cardmembers enables Chenault to guide his teams in

the development of new products and services. He also spends a great deal of time talking to customers, from whom he has gotten many good ideas for innovations. In fact, the Optima Card, the American Express revolving credit card, came from such discussions with customers.

One customer-oriented innovation is Genesis, a computer-driven technology that will provide one-call customer service. It will include a database of detailed information on the 22 million American Express cardholders. Genesis will provide fast customer service— prompt, round-the-clock attention to billing and the product needs of cardholders—for members located around the world. It's Chenault's responsibility to furnish the resources, human and capital, to make Genesis work. He must also forge a successful relationship between its marketing and operations functions.

Unlike many top managers in the 1980s, who viewed themselves as generals whose sole job was to give orders to subordinates, Chenault stays close to the action. Walking through the halls, he warmly greets fellow employees. He often works eighty-five hours a week, many of them on the road and in the air. But even with this hectic schedule, he makes time for his wife and son and heads up social projects: In 1989 he cosponsored fund-raising campaigns for Virginia Governor L. Douglas Wilder and Atlanta Mayor Maynard Jackson.

Like all top managers who must develop successful strategies for the next century, Chenault is a global manager. The consolidation of the European economy in 1992 and the decline of communism in Eastern Europe represents an expansion opportunity for American Express, which currently serves more than 130 countries. As chairperson of the company's Worldwide Card Committee, Chenault helps set policies and develop business strategies for the card business worldwide.

1. What managerial functions seem most important in Ken Chenault's workday? How would you expect these to change?

2. What managerial roles does Chenault play? How do these enable him to build teams?

3. What managerial skills does Chenault seem to have developed? How have these helped him at American Express?

4. How will the changing nature of the work force affect companies like American Express?

Chapter 2

THE EVOLUTION OF MANAGEMENT THOUGHT

Haymarket riot

What You Will Learn

1 The three branches of the traditional viewpoint of management: bureaucratic, scientific, and administrative.

2 The behavioral viewpoint's contribution to management.

3 How the systems viewpoint uses quantitative techniques to manage organizations.

4 The place of the contingency viewpoint in modern management.

5 **Skill Development:** Why studying the evolution of management thought can give you insights into managing today.

Chapter Outline

Manager's Viewpoint
A Good Year for Management—1886

The Traditional Viewpoint
Bureaucratic Management
Global Link: Egyptian Bureaucracy
Insight: United Parcel Service—A Working Bureaucracy
Scientific Management
Administrative Management
Assessing the Traditional Viewpoint

The Behavioral Viewpoint
Follett's Contributions
Barnard's Contributions
The Hawthorne Studies
Insight: Tandem Computers—People at Work
Assessing the Behavioral Viewpoint

The Systems Viewpoint
Basic Concepts of the Systems Viewpoint
System Types and Levels
Insight: Federal Express—An Open System
Quantitative Techniques
Assessing the Systems Viewpoint

The Contingency Viewpoint
Contingency Variables
Insight: The Woodward Studies
Assessing the Contingency Viewpoint

The Continuing Evolution of Management Thought

Experiencing Management
Skill-Building Exercise: How Bureaucratic Is Your Organization?

Manager's Memo

In the News

Management Case:
Two Plants at General Motors

A Good Year for Management—1886

During the thirty years following the Civil War, the United States emerged as a leading industrial nation. This shift from an agrarian to an urban society was abrupt and, for many Americans, meant drastic adjustment. Never before in the nation's history had so many individuals made so much money so quickly. By the end of the century there had arisen a new corporate capitalism ruled by a prosperous professional class. Captains of industry freely wielded mergers and acquisitions and engaged in cutthroat competition as they created huge monopolies in the oil, meat, steel, sugar, and tobacco industries. The federal government did nothing to interfere with these monopolies. On the one hand, new technology born of the war effort offered the promise of progress and growth; on the other, rapid social change and a growing disparity between rich and poor caused increasing conflict and instability.

The year 1886 was a watershed, marking several turning points in the course of business and management history. In that year engineer Henry R. Towne (1844–1924), cofounder of the Yale Lock Company, presented a paper titled "The Engineer as an Economist" to the American Society of Mechanical Engineers. In this paper Towne stated:

> There are many good mechanical engineers. There are also many good "businessmen," but the two are rarely combined in one person. But this combination of qualities . . . is essential to the management of industrial works, and has its highest effectiveness if united in one person . . . and the management of works has become a matter of such great and far-reaching importance as perhaps to justify its classification also as one of the modern arts.

No special group concerned with management practices existed in 1886. Towne therefore proposed that the American Society of Mechanical Engineers create an Economic Section to act as a clearinghouse and forum for "shop management" and "shop accounting." Shop management would deal with the subjects of organization, responsibility, reports, and the "executive management" of industrial works, mills, and factories. Shop accounting would treat the nuts and bolts of time and wage systems, cost determination and allocation, bookkeeping methods, and manufacturing accounting. The society would develop a body of literature, record members' experiences, and provide a forum for exchanging managers' ideas.

Other events in 1886 influenced the development of modern management thought and practice. During this boom period in American business history, employers generally regarded labor as a commodity to be purchased as cheaply as possible and maintained at minimal expense. Thus it was also a peak period of labor unrest—during 1886 over 600,000 employees were out of work because of strikes and lockouts. On May 4, 1886 a group of anarchist labor leaders led a demonstration in Chicago's Haymarket Square in support of an eight-hour work day. During the demonstration someone threw a bomb, killing seven bystanders. The Haymarket Affair was a setback for organized labor, because many people came to equate unionism with anarchism.

In his pioneering study in 1886 of labor history, *The Labor Movement in*

America, Richard T. Ely advocated a less radical approach to labor-management relations. Ely cautioned labor to work within the existing economic and political system. One union that followed Ely's advice was the American Federation of Labor (AFL), organized in 1886 by Samuel Gompers and Adolph Strasser. A conservative, "bread and butter" union, the AFL avoided politics and industrial unionism and organized skilled workers along craft lines (as carpenters, plumbers, bricklayers, and so forth). Like other early unions, the AFL protected its members from unfair management practices. Gompers's goal was to increase labor's bargaining power within the existing capitalistic framework. Under his leadership the AFL dominated the American labor scene for almost half a century.

Chicago in 1886 was also the birthplace of an aspiring mail order business called Sears, Roebuck and Company. From the very beginning Sears, founded by railroad station agent Richard W. Sears, who sold watches to farmers in his area, characterized the mass distribution system that promoted America's economic growth. For the first time affordable fine goods were available to both rural and urban consumers. Today Sears also operates thousands of retail stores, as well as offering a wide range of financial and real estate services. Also in 1886 the first Coca-Cola was served in Atlanta. This scarcely noticed event launched an enterprise that grew into a gigantic multinational corporation. Other companies that began in 1886 and remain in operation today include Avon Products, Cosmopolitan Magazine, Johnson & Johnson, Munsingwear, Upjohn, and Westinghouse.

Thus 1886 marked the origins of the study of modern management thought and practice, the successful organization of labor, and several well-known, large-scale enterprises. Even as these events were unfolding, a new symbol of American optimism and opportunity took final form on an island in New York harbor: The Statue of Liberty was dedicated in October 1886.[1]

Why are we harking back to century-old events in a book that claims to teach management for the 1990s? Part of our rationale is learning from the past. It is humbling to recall that management is an exceedingly young profession. In earlier, preindustrial society, men and women paced their work according to the sun, the seasons, and the demand for what they produced. Small communities encouraged personal, often familial, relationships between employers and employees. The explosive growth of urban industries—the factory system, in particular—changed the face of the American workplace forever. Workers in cities were forced to adapt to the formal structure and rules of the factory setting and to labor long hours for employers they never saw. Many were poorly educated and needed considerable oral instruction and hands-on training in unfamiliar tasks.

The emergence of the first large-scale business enterprises in the United States and western Europe raised issues and created challenges that previously had applied only to government organizations. Businesses needed the equivalent of government leaders—managers—to hire and train the right employees and to lead and motivate them. Managers were also needed to develop plans and design work units and, while doing so, make a profit—never a requirement for governments! In this chapter we briefly examine how management thought has evolved since 1886 to meet those needs.

Theorists over the past century have developed numerous models to answer the same basic management question: What is the best way to manage an organization? The reason we continue to study those models today is that they still apply to the manager's job. The following sections discuss the four most widely accepted viewpoints of management that have evolved since about 1886: traditional (or classical), behavioral, systems, and contingency. These viewpoints are based on different assumptions about the behavior of people in organizations, the key objectives of an organization, the types of problems faced, and the solutions to those problems. Figure 2.1 shows when each viewpoint emerged and began to gain popularity. As you can see, all four of these viewpoints still influence managers' thinking. In fact, one important source of disagreement among today's managers is the degree of emphasis that should be placed on each of them. Thus a major purpose

Even today, at organizations like American Airlines, *traditional bureaucratic management* techniques help handle thousands of telephone reservations daily at the Dallas-Fort Worth International Airport.

FIGURE 2.1

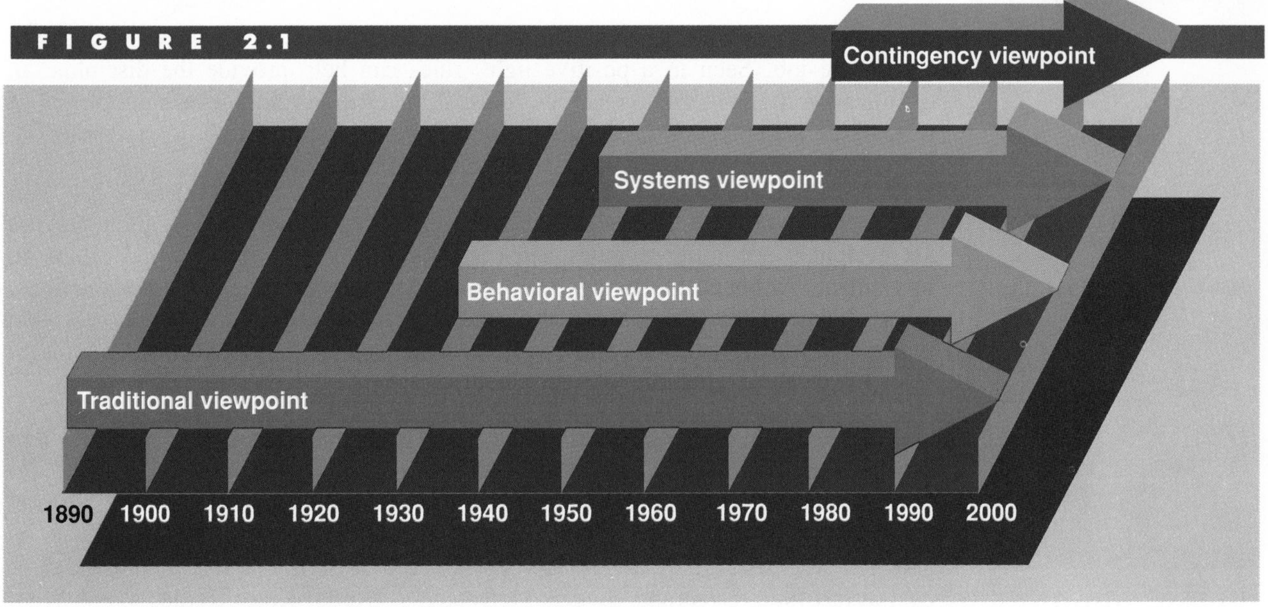

Contingency viewpoint

Systems viewpoint

Behavioral viewpoint

Traditional viewpoint

1890 1900 1910 1920 1930 1940 1950 1960 1970 1980 1990 2000

History of Management Thought

Each arrow shows when a major management viewpoint emerged and began to gain momentum. The influence of each continues into the 1990s.

of this chapter is to show you not only how each viewpoint has contributed to the historical evolution of modern management thought, but also how each can be used effectively in different circumstances—even into the 1990s.

THE TRADITIONAL VIEWPOINT

traditional viewpoint The oldest of the four major viewpoints of management; stresses the manager's role in a strict hierarchy and focuses on efficient and consistent job performance.

The oldest and perhaps most widely accepted viewpoint on management is called the **traditional (classical) viewpoint.** It is split into three main branches: bureaucratic management, scientific management, and administrative management. All three emerged during roughly the same time period—the late 1890s through the early 1900s, when engineers were seeking to make organizations run like well-oiled machines. The founders of these three branches came from Germany, the United States, and France, respectively.

Bureaucratic Management

bureaucratic management A traditional management system that relies on rules, set hierarchy, a clear division of labor, and firm procedures and that focuses on the overall organizational structure.

Bureaucratic management is a system that relies on rules, a set hierarchy, a clear division of labor, and firm procedures. Max Weber (1864–1920), a German social historian, is most closely associated with bureaucratic management (so named because Weber based his work on studies of Germany's governmental bureaucracy). Although Weber was one of the first theorists to deal with the problems of organizations, he was not widely recognized until his work was translated into English in 1947. He was primarily concerned with the broad social and economic issues facing society; his writings on bureaucracy represent only part of his total contribution.[2]

Bureaucratic management provides a rational blueprint of how an entire organization should operate. It prescribes seven characteristics: a formal system of rules, impersonality, division of labor, hierarchical structure, a detailed authority structure, lifelong career commitment, and rationality. Together these characteristics represent a formal, somewhat rigid method of managing. Let's take a look at this method, setting aside for the moment all the negative connotations the term *bureaucratic* has today and focusing on the system's strengths—consistency and predictability.

Max Weber

Rules   Rules are formal guidelines for the behavior of all employees while they are on the job. Seen in a positive light, rules can help provide the discipline an organization needs if it is to reach its goals. Adherence to rules ensures uniformity of procedures and operations and helps to maintain organizational stability, regardless of individual managers' or employees' personal desires.

Impersonality   Reliance on rules leads to impersonality. That is, all employees are evaluated according to rules and objective data, such as sales and return on investment. Although the term *impersonality* can also have negative connotations, Weber believed that this characteristic guarantees fairness for all employees—an impersonal superior does not allow subjective personal or emotional considerations to color his or her evaluations of subordinates.

Division of Labor   The **division of labor** is the process of dividing duties into simpler, more specialized tasks, enabling the organization to use personnel and job-training resources efficiently. Managers and employees are assigned and perform duties based on specialization and personal expertise. Unskilled employees can be assigned tasks that are relatively easy to learn and do. For example, employee turnover at fast food restaurants such as McDonald's, Burger King, Hardee's, and Wendy's is over 100 percent a year. However, because of division of labor, most jobs can be learned quickly and require only unskilled labor. Thus high turnover doesn't result in a major training problem.

Hierarchical Structure   Most organizations have a pyramid-shaped hierarchical structure, as illustrated in Figure 2.2. A **hierarchical structure** ranks jobs according to the amount of power and authority (the right to decide) given to each. Typically, power and authority increase at each higher level, up to the top of the hierarchy. Each lower-level position is under the control and direction of a higher-level position. According to Weber, a well-defined hierarchy helps control the behavior of employees by making clear to each exactly where he or she stands in relation to every other employee.

Authority Structure   A system based on rules, impersonality, division of labor, and a hierarchical structure is tied together by an **authority structure,** which determines who has the right to make decisions of varying importance at different levels within the organization. Weber identified three types of authority structures: traditional, charismatic, and rational-legal.

   Traditional authority is based on tradition or custom. The divine right of kings and the magical influence of tribal witch doctors are examples of traditional authority.

   Charismatic authority is evident when subordinates suspend their own judgment and comply voluntarily with a leader because of special personal qualities or abilities they perceive in that individual. Social, political, and religious movements are often headed by charismatic leaders (Jesus, Joan of Arc, Gandhi, Martin Luther King). Managers in business organizations seldom rely solely on charismatic authority, but some, such as Steven Jobs, Mary Kay Ash, and Walt Disney, have used their charisma to motivate and influence subordinates.

   Rational-legal authority is based on impersonal laws and rules that apply to all employees. A superior is obeyed because of the position he or she occupies within the organization's hierarchy. This authority depends on employees' acceptance of the organization's rules.

Lifelong Career Commitment   In a bureaucratic management system employment is viewed as a lifelong career commitment. That is, both the employee and the company view themselves as being committed to each other over the working life of the employee. Traditionally, Japanese and Korean organizations have hired workers with the expectation—by both parties—that a permanent bond was being forged. In general, lifelong career commitment means that job security is guaranteed as long as

division of labor   The process of dividing duties into simpler, more specialized tasks to promote efficiency.

hierarchical structure   The organizational structure that determines the amount of power and authority given to each position within the organization.

authority structure   The organizational structure that determines the rights to make decisions of varying importance at different levels within the organization.

traditional authority   An authority structure, defined by Max Weber, based on tradition or custom.

charismatic authority   The authority exerted by a person because of special qualities or powers others perceive in him or her.

rational-legal authority   An authority structure, defined by Max Weber, based on impersonal rules and laws that apply to all employees.

FIGURE 2.2

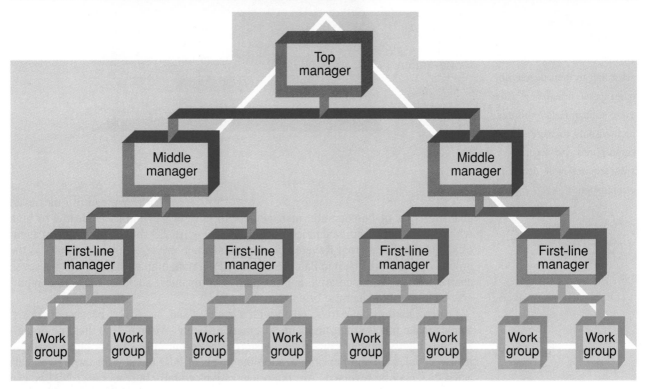

Hierarchical Organization Structure

Max Weber pointed out that organizations tend to have a pyramid-shaped structure, with positions arranged in a hierarchy of power and authority.

the employee is technically qualified and performs satisfactorily. Entrance requirements, such as level of education and experience, ensure that hiring is based on technical qualifications rather than patronage (for example, family connections). The organization uses job security, tenure, step-by-step salary increases, and pensions to ensure that employees satisfactorily perform assigned duties. Promotion is granted when an employee demonstrates the technical competence required to handle the demands of the next higher position. It is assumed that organizational level corresponds closely with expertise. Bureaucratic organizations, such as the civil service, often rely on the results of written and oral exams, amount of formal education, and previous work experience to determine management rank.

Rationality The last characteristic of bureaucratic management is rationality. Rational managers are those who use the most efficient possible means to achieve the organization's objectives. Managers in a bureaucratic management system run the organization logically and "scientifically," with all decisions leading directly to achieving the organization's objectives. When activities are goal-directed, the organization uses its financial and human resources efficiently. In addition, rationality allows general organizational objectives to be broken down into more specific objectives for each part of the organization. At Xerox, for example, the overall corporate objectives are to provide customers with copying machines and services of superior quality at a fair price and to earn enough profit to maintain the company's growth. An objective of its research and development (R&D) department is to pursue new xerographic technology and to transform technological breakthroughs into high-quality products and services. If all departments in the company reach their individual objectives, the corporation reaches its overall objectives.[3]

FIGURE 2.3

Continuum of Bureaucratic Orientation

Organizations can be ranked according to their degree of bureaucratic orientation. However, a diagram like this can be used only for very general comparisons. An accurate view requires more detailed examination.

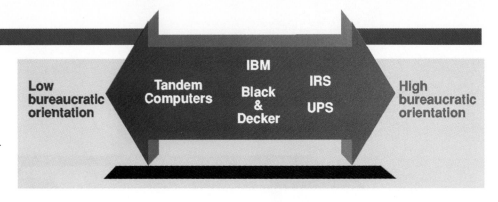

Ranking Organizations by Bureaucratic Orientation We can use the seven characteristics of bureaucratic management to rank organizations from low to high with respect to their bureaucratic orientation. As Figure 2.3 shows, government agencies, such as the Internal Revenue Service, and some private companies, such as the ground operations of United Parcel Service (UPS), rank high with respect to the seven characteristics. Some creative and innovative companies, such as Tandem Computers, have low bureaucratic orientation.

Such rankings have to be taken with a grain of salt, however, because inconsistencies make precise measurement extremely difficult. We may find that one organization is highly bureaucratic in its division of labor but only slightly bureaucratic in its use of rules. In another organization the levels of bureaucracy for these two characteristics may be reversed. Are the organizations equally bureaucratic? No one can say with certainty. Furthermore, the degree of bureaucracy within an organization may vary considerably among departments and divisions. For example, Black & Decker, like IBM, falls near the middle of the bureaucratic continuum, but its manufacturing plants, which produce standardized household goods (such as blenders, toasters, toaster ovens, and irons), tend to be more bureaucratic than its R&D departments, whose creativity would be stifled by too many rules.

Benefits of Bureaucracy The expected benefits of bureaucratic management are efficiency and consistency. A bureaucracy functions best when many routine tasks need to be done. Then lower-level employees can handle the bulk of the work by simply following rules. The fruits of their labor should be of standard (high) quality and produced at the rate necessary to meet organizational goals.

Some Drawbacks of Bureaucracy The same characteristics of bureaucratic management that can increase one organization's efficiency can lead to great inefficiency in a different organization. The following are five often unanticipated drawbacks of bureaucratic management.[4]

1. *Rigid rules and red tape.* Rigid adherence to rules and routines for their own sake is a major complaint of employees in many organizations. Such a system leaves little room for individual freedom and creativity, while fostering low motivation, entrenched ''career'' employees, high turnover among the best employees, and shoddy work. A significant amount of time and money can be wasted, as is made clear by the Global Link's account of how bureaucracy works in Egypt.

2. *Protection of authority.* A bureaucratic organization may encourage managers to perform at minimum productivity, while protecting and expanding their own authority. So at Wang, they're attacking bureaucracy head on. Wang believes that no one can afford to work in a maze of corporate buck-passers. How did Wang beat bureaucracy? By downsizing their entire organization. They have 21 percent fewer vice presidents today than on July 1, 1989; 25 percent fewer directors; 36 percent fewer managers, and 55 percent fewer first-line managers.

GLOBAL Link

EGYPTIAN BUREAUCRACY

Dealing with automobile or college registration may seem to you like a wrestling match with red tape, but it's nothing compared to the challenge for companies that try to do business in Egypt. There it takes up to thirty-four signatures to ship an order overseas, eleven different transactions to transfer a car from one person to another, and four days and twelve signatures to clear a shipment of books from the post office. General Motors spent more than three years getting all the necessary approvals to build a truck plant in Egypt. Compounding the frustration and delay is the fact that civil servants in Egypt work as little as two hours a day. It's been estimated that they spend only 15 percent of the workday doing government work—devoting the rest of their time to reading newspapers and chatting with co-workers.

Mr. Marzouk is president of Diea Company, which wanted to ship 48,000 white, blue, yellow, and red T-shirts from Cairo to a client in Frankfurt, West Germany. To ease the shipment through the Egyptian bureaucracy, he sent his crack red-tape handler to collect signatures of approval and stamps from the government agency in charge of cotton exports, the customs office, and the bank. When the approval sheet came back in sextuplicate, stamped five times per page, it was time for the required site visit by the government's quality control team—an additional two-day delay. Marzouk then personally walked the shipment through customs himself. He estimates that he spends $16 on tips for each shipment out of the country. At the cargo desk an inspector opened three of the ninety-six boxes to make sure they really contained T-shirts. Another inspector examined the T-shirts and determined that the selling price was high enough to satisfy government requirements. (If the selling price were too low, the government would levy a penalty on the firm.) After five hours Marzouk finally left the cargo dock knowing that his T-shirts would make it to West Germany.

Source: Adapted from B. Rosewicz, ''Factory Owner Joins Egypt's Export Push, but Runs into Hurdles: Bureaucracy, Inefficiency, Poor Quality Take Toll,'' *Wall Street Journal*, November 11, 1985, 1, 21.

3. *Slow decision making.* Large, complex organizations depend heavily on timely decisions. In a highly bureaucratic organization adherence to rules and procedures may come to take precedence over effective, timely decision making. When that happens, rules take on a life of their own. Formality and ritual delay decisions at every management level until all red tape has been cleared, petty insistence on power and status privileges has been satisfied, and any chance of error in judgment has been minimized.

4. *Incompatibility with changing technology.* Advancing technology may make bureaucratic management inappropriate. For example, people working on AIDS research face unique problems in attempting to find a cure for this disease. Bureaucratic rules are much less useful when the nature of the task itself continually changes and new procedures have to be experimented with.

5. *Incompatibility with professional values.* More and more professionals are being hired by bureaucratic organizations to fill important decision-making positions. Their professional values (such as advancing scientific knowledge, serving professional organizations, and finding innovative solutions to problems) may be incompatible with the bureaucratic need for efficiency, order, and consistency. Furthermore, bureaucratic authority is related to hierarchical position, but the professional sees authority as stemming from personal competence or technical knowledge.[5]

Assessing Bureaucratic Management Not all bureaucratically managed organizations are inefficient and unprofitable. In fact, bureaucratic management is still widely and effectively used. This approach is most effective when (1) large amounts of standard information have to be processed and an efficient processing method has been found (as in banks, insurance companies, the IRS, and traffic courts); (2) the needs of the customer are known and aren't likely to change (as in the registration of drivers in most states); (3) the technology is routine and stable, so employees can be easily and quickly taught how to operate machines (as at Domino's Pizza or Burger King and in toll booths); (4) the organization has to coordinate the activities of numerous employees in order to deliver a standardized service or product to the customer (as is done by the IRS and the U.S. Postal Service).[6]

United Parcel Service (UPS) provides an excellent example of how bureaucracy can lead to efficiency.

UNITED PARCEL SERVICE—A WORKING BUREAUCRACY

INSIGHT United Parcel Service (UPS) can deliver a small package anywhere in the United States for $2 to $3. The company views its prices as competitive with those of the U.S. Postal Service, Federal Express, and Purolator Courier. Unlike the Postal Service, however, UPS must pay taxes on real estate, income, and fuel. It can't subsidize package delivery with revenue from first-class letters. Nevertheless, UPS makes an excellent profit on its revenues of more than $12.4 billion.

Why has UPS been so successful in its ground operations? Two important reasons are automation and bureaucracy. Automation is evident in its 100 mechanized centers that sort at least 40,000 packages an hour. Employees who operate sorting machines handle 1124 packages an hour and are allowed no more than one mistake per 2500 packages. The more than 152,000 employees at UPS handle millions of packages a day. Yet the organization is so efficient that it can send a truck to pick up a package from a customer's home or business and deliver packages door to door—and still make money.

The bureaucratic organization at UPS results in efficiency. Each manager is given several bound policy books about company rules and is expected to refer to them regularly. For example, drivers are instructed to walk to a customer's door at a brisk pace of three feet per second. They should knock so as not to lose valuable seconds searching for the doorbell. Jobs at UPS centers are broken down in a clearly defined division of labor. Employees perform the specialized duties of drivers, loaders, clerks, washers, sorters, and property maintenance personnel. The hierarchy of authority is clearly defined: Eight levels extend from the washer at a local center up to the company president.

Technical qualifications are UPS's criteria for hiring and promotion. Company policy says, "A leader does not have to remind others of authority by use of a title. Knowledge, performance, and capacity should be adequate evidence of position and leadership." Special favors are forbidden. Each employee sets performance targets and has an equal opportunity to succeed. Promotions and salary increments are based on objective performance criteria, not on background or position in the organization.

Finally, UPS relies on extensive written records and has installed a computer system to help with record keeping. Recorded operating costs and production figures are compared to those of competitors. Daily worksheets specifying performance quotas are kept on every employee and department. Employees' daily achievements are accumulated on a weekly and monthly basis.

UPS pays its drivers $15 an hour, and, with overtime, many of them earn between $35,000 and $40,000 a year. In return for this salary UPS expects maximum performance, and it monitors employees accordingly. For example, one UPS manager watching a driver make deliveries and seeing any waste of seconds will point out the inefficiency at once. According to the manager, a mere thirty seconds wasted at each stop can snowball into big delays by day's end. UPS drivers, with nicknames like Ace, Hammer, Slick, and Rocket Shoes, take pride in meeting rules established by the company: "We used to joke that a good driver could get to his stop and back to the truck before the seat belt stopped swaying."[7]

Scientific Management

As you learned at the beginning of this chapter, manufacturing firms had become larger and much more complex by the end of the last century. As a result, not all managers could be directly involved with production; some began to spend more of their time administratively—planning, scheduling, and staffing. Also, managers were hard-pressed to keep up with advances in the new, machine-oriented production technology. The distancing of management from the physical production of goods created a need for production operations specialists who could solve the personnel and productivity problems that accompanied rapid industrialization and threatened operating efficiency.

scientific management A traditional management system that focuses on individual worker–machine relationships in manufacturing plants.

Frederick W. Taylor The stage was set for Frederick Winslow Taylor (1856–1915) to do his pioneering work in scientific management. Whereas bureaucratic management looks at broad organizational structures and work systems, **scientific management** focuses on individual worker-machine relationships in manufacturing plants. Its philosophy is that management practices should be based on proven fact and observation, not on hearsay or guesswork.[8]

Taylor, an American mechanical engineer influenced by Towne, started out as a foreman at Midvale Steel Company in Philadelphia. He believed that increased productivity ultimately depended on finding ways to make workers more efficient. One of Taylor's goals was to study and define precisely all aspects of the worker-machine relationship by using objective, scientific techniques.

When Taylor worked as a consultant to Bethlehem Steel, for example, he made a science of shoveling. Through observation and experimentation he looked for answers to such questions as these:

1. Will a first-class worker do more work per day with a shovelful of five, ten, fifteen, twenty, thirty, or forty pounds?
2. What kinds of shovels work best with which materials?
3. How quickly can a shovel be pushed into a pile of coal and pulled out properly loaded?
4. How long does it take to swing a shovel backwards and throw the load a given horizontal distance at a given height?

As Taylor accumulated answers to his questions, he developed views on how to increase the total amount shoveled per day. He started a program that matched workers, shovel sizes, materials, and so forth for each job. After the third year his program reduced the number of shovelers needed from 600 to 140, while the average number of tons shoveled per worker per day rose from 16 to 50. Workers' earnings also increased from $1.15 to $1.88 a day.

time-and-motion study A study that identifies and measures a worker's physical movements, analyzes the results, and deletes movements that slow down production.

Taylor analyzed work flows, supervisory techniques, and worker fatigue using time-and-motion studies. A **time-and-motion study** involves identifying and measuring a worker's physical movements when performing a task and then analyzing the results. Movements that slow down production are dropped. One goal of a time-and-motion study is to make a job highly routine and efficient. Eliminating wasted physical effort and specifying an exact sequence of activities reduce the amount of time, money, and effort needed to produce a product.

Taylor came to believe that there was *one best way* to perform any task. Like Weber, he thought that an organization operated best with definite, predictable methods, logically determined and set down as rules. Taylor was convinced that efficiency could be increased by having workers perform routine tasks that didn't require them to make decisions. Performance objectives expressed quantitatively (such as number of units produced per shift) addressed a problem that had begun to trouble managers—how to judge whether an employee had put in a fair day's work.

functional foremanship System developed by Taylor to link each foreman's area of specialization to that foreman's scope of authority.

Another of Taylor's ideas was based on his principle of specialization. He viewed expertise as the only source of authority and argued that a single foreman could not be expert at all the tasks supervised. Thus he proposed that each foreman's particular area of specialization be made an area of authority. Taylor called his solution **functional foremanship,** a system that assigned eight foremen to each work area. Four of the foremen would handle planning, production scheduling, time-and-motion studies, and discipline. The other four would deal with such matters as machinery maintenance, machine speed, feeding material into the machine, and production on the shop floor.

As far as what would motivate employees to work to their fullest capacity, Taylor believed that money was the answer. He supported the individual piecework system as the basis for pay. If workers met a certain production standard, they were to be paid at a standard wage rate. Workers who produced more than the standard were to be paid at a higher rate for all the pieces they produced, not just for those exceeding the standard. Taylor felt that workers would be rational; they would follow management's orders to produce more in response to financial incentives that allowed them to earn more money. Managers should, Taylor argued, use financial incentives if they were convinced that increases in productivity would more than offset higher employee earnings.

Lillian and Frank Gilbreth

The Gilbreths Frank (1868–1924) and Lillian (1878–1972) Gilbreth formed an unusual husband-and-wife engineering team who made significant contributions to scientific management. Frank used a revolutionary new tool—motion pictures—to study the structure of tasks. For instance, he identified eighteen individual motions that a bricklayer uses to lay bricks. By changing the task's structure, he was able to reduce the eighteen motions to five, which resulted in a more than 200 percent increase in the worker's overall productivity. Today's industrial engineers have combined Frank Gilbreth's methods with Taylor's to redesign jobs for greater efficiency.

Lillian Gilbreth, who carried on Frank's work (*and* raised their twelve children) after his death, was more concerned with the human side of industrial engineering. She championed the idea that workers should have standard days, scheduled rest breaks, and normal lunch periods. Her work influenced Congress to establish child labor laws and to develop rules for protecting workers from unsafe conditions.

Henry Gantt Taylor's associate Henry Gantt (1861–1919) focused on ''control'' systems for production scheduling. His Gantt charts are still widely used today to plan project timelines and have been adapted for computer scheduling applications. The **Gantt chart** is a progress report in visual form that identifies various stages of work that must be carried out in order to complete a project and sets a deadline for each stage. Gantt also established quota systems and bonuses for workers who exceeded their quotas.

Gantt chart A visual progress report that identifies individual work stages in a project's execution and a deadline for completion of each stage.

Assessing Scientific Management Taylor and other proponents of scientific management would recognize the acceptance of their ideas today at companies such as Control Data, Thyssen, USX, Nippon Oil, Kodak, and Honda. These firms make finished products faster and cheaper than Taylor could ever have dreamed, in part by taking for granted his idea that managers cannot expect employees without proper skills and training to do their jobs properly. Taylor's work has led today's managers to improve their employee selection and training processes and to seek the one best way to perform each task.

Unfortunately, most proponents of scientific management misread the human side of work. When Taylor and Frank Gilbreth formulated their principles and methods, they believed that workers were motivated primarily by a desire to earn money to satisfy their economic and physical needs. They failed to recognize that workers also have social needs and that working conditions and job satisfaction are often more important than money. For example, workers have struck in protest over working conditions, the speedup of an assembly line, or harassment by management—even when there was a fair financial incentive system in place. Managers today cannot assume that workers are interested only in higher wages. Dividing jobs into their simplest tasks and setting clear rules for accomplishing those tasks won't always lead to a quality product, high morale, and an effective organization. Today's workers want to participate in decisions that affect their performance. They want to be independent and to hold jobs that allow them self-fulfillment.

Administrative Management

administrative management A traditional management system that focuses on managers and their actions rather than on overall organizational structure or workers.

Administrative management focuses on the manager, rather than on bureaucratic management's overall organizational structure or scientific management's worker. This management approach evolved early in this century and is most closely identified with Henri Fayol (1841–1925), a French industrialist, whose most important writings on management weren't translated into English until 1930. Fayol credited his success as a manager to the methods he used, rather than to his personal qualities. He felt strongly that, to be successful, managers had only to understand the basic managerial functions—planning, organizing, leading, and controlling—and to apply certain management principles to them. He was the first person to group managers' functions this way.[9]

Like the other traditionalists, Fayol emphasized structure, believing that it is necessary if all important tasks are to be performed. He also believed that if people are to work together, they need a clear definition of what they're trying to accomplish and that individuals' tasks should mesh with the organization's objectives.

Fayol developed the following fourteen management principles and argued that managers should receive formal training in their application:

1. *Division of labor.* The more people specialize, the more efficiently they can perform their work.

2. *Authority.* Managers have the right, the authority, to give orders in order to get things done.

3. *Discipline.* Members of an organization need to respect the rules and agreements that govern it.

4. *Unity of command.* Each employee must receive instructions about a particular operation from only one person in order to avoid conflicting instructions and the resulting confusion.

5. *Unity of direction.* The efforts of employees working on a particular project should be coordinated and directed by only one manager in order to avoid conflicting policies and procedures.

6. *Subordination of individual interest to the common good.* The interests of individual employees should not take precedence over the interests of the entire organization.

7. *Remuneration.* Pay for work done should be fair to both the employee and the employer.

8. *Centralization.* Managers should retain final responsibility but should also give their subordinates enough authority to do their jobs properly.

9. *Scalar chain.* A single uninterrupted line of authority (often represented by the neat boxes and lines of an organization chart) should run from rank to rank from top management to the lowest-level position in the company.

10. *Order.* Materials and people should be in the right place at the right time. In particular, people should be in the jobs or positions best suited to them.

11. *Equity.* Managers should be both friendly and fair to their subordinates.

12. *Stability and tenure of staff.* A high rate of employee turnover is not efficient.

Characteristics of Traditional Management

Bureaucratic	Scientific	Administrative
Characteristics Rules Impersonality Division of labor Hierarchy Authority structure Lifelong career commitment Rationality	**Characteristics** Training in routines and rules "One best way" Financial motivation	**Characteristics** Defining of management functions Division of labor Hierarchy Authority Equity
Focus Whole organization	**Focus** Worker	**Focus** Manager
Benefits Consistency Efficiency	**Benefits** Productivity Efficiency	**Benefits** Clear structure Rules
Drawbacks Rigidity Slowness	**Drawbacks** Overlooks social needs	**Drawbacks** Doesn't consider environment Overemphasizes rational behavior of managers

13. *Initiative.*   Subordinates should be given the freedom to formulate and carry out their plans.

14. *Esprit de corps.*   Promoting team spirit gives the organization a sense of unity.

Managers still use many of Fayol's principles today, although organizations seldom apply them in exactly the same way. Situations vary and so, too, does the application of principles. At Standard Steel, for example, the maintenance superintendent has to take orders from the plant manager, the chief engineer, and the production manager—violating the unity of command principle. At the same mill, however, the maintenance superintendent has the authority to set priorities for plant maintenance, which illustrates the initiative principle.

Assessing the Traditional Viewpoint

Traditional management's three branches—bureaucratic, scientific, and administrative—still have their proponents, are often written about, and continue to find effective application—even in the 1990s. Let's summarize what the branches have in common and some drawbacks of the traditional viewpoint. Table 2.1 highlights the points discussed.

All three branches emphasize the formal aspects of organization.[10] Traditionalists were concerned with the formal relations among an organization's departments, tasks, and structural elements. Weber, Taylor, the Gilbreths, Gantt, and Fayol replaced seat-of-the-pants management practices with sound theoretical and scientific principles. Managers began to stress division of labor, hierarchical authority, rules, and decisions that would maximize economic rewards.

The traditional viewpoint of management stresses the manager's role in a hierarchy. In bureaucratic management there is a strong relationship between expertise and organizational level. Because of their higher position and presumed greater expertise, superiors are to be obeyed by subordinates. Administrative and scientific management's emphasis on logical structure and strict division of labor are based on similar reasoning.

Although the traditionalists' may have recognized that people had feelings and were influenced by their friends at work, their overriding focus was on efficient and effective job performance. Taylor considered the human side to the extent that he thought that eliminating bad feelings between workers and management and providing workers with a financial incentive would increase productivity. Job security, career progression, and protection of workers from employers' whims were considered important by the traditional management theorists, but they did not recognize informal or social relationships among employees at work. Taylor and Frank Gilbreth focused instead on well-written rules intended to ensure efficient performance—the primary standard against which employees were to be judged.

In assessing the work of the traditional theorists, you need to keep in mind that they were influenced by the economic conditions facing them at the time. The United States was moving toward becoming an industrial nation, unions were forming to protect workers' rights, and more laws were being passed to improve unsafe working conditions. Organizations operated in a relatively stable environment with few competitors. Much traditionalist thinking may still be found in today's most technologically advanced corporations. For example, Fayol's principles are widely used today as basic building blocks for management at Nestlé, Procter & Gamble, and other global corporations.

THE BEHAVIORAL VIEWPOINT

During the 1920s and 1930s the United States and other industrialized nations experienced radical social and cultural changes. Mass production triggered a second industrial revolution in the United States. Assembly lines were releasing a flood of inexpensive goods— cars, appliances, and clothing—into an increasingly consumer-oriented society. The country's overall standard of living rose, and working conditions in many industries improved. While productivity increased dramatically, the average work week declined from seventy hours to less than fifty. Hard-pressed to satisfy consumer demand, factories eagerly tried to attract workers from the farms to the cities by making industrial employment more appealing than it was during Taylor's tenure at Midvale Steel.

During the Great Depression the federal government began to play a more influential role in people's lives. By the time Franklin D. Roosevelt took office in 1933, the national economy was hovering on the brink of collapse. To provide employment the government undertook temporary public works projects—constructing dams, roads, and public buildings and laying out national parks. It also created government agencies, such as the Social Security Administration, to assist the aged, the unemployed, and the disabled.

In one of the era's most dramatic changes, unskilled workers increased their ability to influence management decisions by forming powerful labor unions. During the 1930s Congress added to the unions' power with legislation that deterred management from restricting union activities, legalized collective bargaining, and required management to bargain with unions. As a result the American Federation of Labor (AFL) grew rapidly, and the Congress of Industrial Organizations (CIO) was formed. In 1937 the autoworkers and steelworkers won their first big contracts. Eventually professionals and skilled workers, as well as unskilled laborers, united to bargain for better pay, increased benefits, and improved working conditions. Following the Depression and World War II, a new wave of optimism swept the American economy. Organized labor enjoyed its greatest success from the 1950s through the 1970s.

Against this backdrop of change and reform, managers were forced to recognize the human aspect of their task. They were now leading workers who did not appear to exhibit what traditional management theorists had thought was rational behavior. That is, workers weren't always performing up to their physiological capabilities, as Taylor had predicted

behavioral viewpoint One of the four major viewpoints of management, which focuses on helping managers deal effectively with the human side of organizations.

human relations viewpoint Another name for the *behavioral viewpoint*.

rational people would do. Nor were effective managers consistently following Fayol's fourteen principles. By exploring these inconsistencies, those who favored a behavioral viewpoint of management gained recognition. The **behavioral (human relations) viewpoint** focuses on helping managers to deal more effectively with the human side of organizations. Rather than focusing strictly on the functions of managers, it looks at *how* managers do what they do; that is, how they lead subordinates and communicate with them.

Follett's Contributions

In the early decades of this century, Mary Parker Follett (1868–1933) made important contributions to the behavioral viewpoint of management. She believed that management is a flowing, continuous process, not a static one. If a problem has been solved, she felt, the process that managers used to solve it probably generates new problems. She stressed (1) involving workers in solving problems and (2) the dynamics of management, rather than static principles. Both of these ideas contrasted sharply with the views of Weber, Taylor, and Fayol.[11]

Follett studied how managers did their jobs by observing them at work. Based on these observations she concluded that coordination is vital to effective management. She developed four principles of coordination for managers to apply:

1. Coordination is best achieved when the people responsible for making a decision are in direct contact.
2. Coordination during the early stages of planning and project implementation is essential.
3. Coordination should address all the factors in a situation.
4. Coordination must be worked at continuously.

Follett believed that the people closest to the action should be able to make the best decisions. For example, she was convinced that first-line managers are in the best position to coordinate production tasks. By increasing communication among themselves and with workers, these managers can make better decisions. Furthermore, they should not only plan and coordinate workers' activities, but also involve workers in the process. Simply because managers have told workers to do something a certain way, Follett argued, they should not assume that workers will do it. She argued further that it is the job of managers at all levels to set up a good working relationship with their subordinates. One way to do this is to involve subordinates in the decision-making process whenever they will be affected by the decision. Drawing on psychology and sociology, Follett also urged managers to recognize that each person is a collection of beliefs, emotions, and feelings.

Follett also felt that managers should help find ways to resolve interdepartmental conflict. Properly handled, conflict can stimulate and integrate managerial and production efforts. The best way to resolve conflict is for managers to communicate directly with each other and with workers. As part of this process, managers and workers should try to understand each other's views and the situations each faces.

Barnard's Contributions

Chester Barnard (1886–1961) studied economics at Harvard but failed to graduate because he never finished a course in laboratory science. He was hired at AT&T, and in 1927 he became president of New Jersey Bell. Barnard made two significant contributions to management that are detailed in his book *The Functions of the Executive*.[12]

Barnard viewed organizations as social systems that require employee cooperation if they are to be effective. Therefore people should continually communicate with one another. According to Barnard, managers' major roles are to communicate with employees and to motivate them to expend their fullest effort toward the organization's goals.

Barnard also believed that successful management depends on maintaining good relations with people outside the organization and others with whom managers deal regularly. By stressing the dependence of the organization on investors, suppliers, customers, and other outside interests, he introduced the idea that managers have to examine the organization's external environment and adjust its internal structure to maintain a balance between the two.

Another significant contribution of Barnard is the **acceptance theory of authority.** This theory of ''buy in'' states that employees have free will and thus will choose whether or not to follow management's orders. They will follow a manager's orders if they (1) understand what is required, (2) believe that the orders are consistent with the goals of the organization, and (3) see a positive benefit to themselves in carrying them out.

acceptance theory of authority Barnard's theory, which states that employees will choose to follow management's orders if they understand what is required, believe the orders to be consistent with organizational goals, and see positive benefit to themselves in carrying them out.

The Hawthorne Studies

The strongest support for the behavioral viewpoint emerged from studies carried out between 1924 and 1933 at Western Electric Company's Hawthorne plant in Chicago.[13] The Hawthorne Illumination Tests, begun in November 1924 and conducted in three departments of the plant, were initially developed and directed by Hawthorne engineers. They divided employees into two groups: a test group, whom they subjected to deliberate changes in lighting, and a control group, for whom lighting remained constant throughout the experiment. When lighting conditions for the test group were improved, the group's productivity also increased, as expected. The engineers were mystified, though, when there was a similar jump in productivity on reducing the test group's lighting to the point of twilight. To compound the mystery, the control group's output kept rising, even though its lighting condition didn't change. Western Electric called in Elton Mayo, a Harvard professor, to investigate these peculiar and puzzling results.

Mayo and his Harvard colleagues Fritz Roethlisberger and William Dickson devised a new experiment. They placed two groups of six women each in separate rooms. The researchers changed various conditions for the test group and left conditions unchanged for the control group. The changes included shortening the test group's coffee breaks, allowing it to choose its own rest periods, and letting it have a say in other suggested changes. Once again, output of the workers increased in both the test group and the control group. The researchers felt they could rule out financial incentives as a factor because they hadn't changed the payment schedule for either group.

Mayo finally concluded that the increases in productivity weren't caused by a physical event but by a complex emotional chain reaction. Because employees in both groups had been singled out for special attention, they had developed a group pride that motivated them to improve their performance. The sympathetic supervision they received further reinforced that motivation. These experimental results led to Mayo's first important discovery: When employees are given special attention, productivity is likely to change regardless of whether working conditions change. This phenomenon became known as the **Hawthorne effect.**

However, an important question remained unanswered: Why should a little special attention and the formation of group bonds produce such strong reactions? To find the answer Mayo interviewed workers, which led to his most significant finding: Informal work groups—the social environment of employees—greatly influence productivity. Many Western Electric employees found their lives inside and outside the factory dull and meaningless. Their workplace friends, chosen in part because of mutual antagonism toward ''the bosses,'' gave meaning to their working lives. Thus peer pressure, rather than management demands, had the strongest influence on employee productivity.[14]

The writings of Mayo, Roethlisberger, and Dickson influenced the basic conclusions that emerged from the Hawthorne studies and helped outline the behavioral viewpoint of management.[15] These theorists believed that individual work behavior is rarely a result of simple cause-and-effect relationships based on scientific principles, as the traditionalists believed. Instead it is determined by a complex set of factors. The informal work group

Hawthorne effect The fact that when workers receive special attention, their productivity is likely to improve whether or not working conditions actually change.

Holiday Corporation's Phil Satre, Mike Rose, Steve Boilenbach, and Mike Meeks get an *informal* head start on a busy day of meetings with a 7:30 breakfast at corporate headquarters.

develops its own set of norms to mediate between the needs of individuals and the work setting. The social structure of such informal groups is maintained through symbols of prestige and power. Managers need to consider the personal context (such as family situation and friendships) in order to understand each employee's unique needs and sources of satisfaction. Awareness of employee feelings and encouragement of employee participation in decision making can reduce resistance to change.

Tandem Computers has applied many behavioral concepts to the management of its employees. The following Insight reveals how incorporating these ideas can affect morale and productivity in a high-tech company today.

I N S I G H T Tandem Computers was founded in 1974 by four employees who left Hewlett-Packard. Tandem designs, develops, manufactures, markets, and supports computer systems for the on-line processing of transactions. These systems are used for electronic funds transfers, ATMs, travel reservations, credit card verifications, and the like. In 1990 Tandem's sales were over $1.6 billion, and it employed more than 9500 people worldwide.

Every Friday afternoon Tandem stages weekly ''beer busts.'' These events provide an opportunity for all employees to gather and socialize with their bosses and co-workers. Managers and subordinates are able to get to know one another better during this informal gathering than through the typical business day.

There are no time clocks or name badges at Tandem; managers often don't know exactly how long people work. According to Jim Treybig, one of the company's founders, ''We don't want to pay people for attendance, but for output.'' Its employees have flexible working hours, a swimming pool that is open before 6:00 A.M. and after 8:00 P.M., a volleyball court complete with showers and locker rooms, and an open-door policy that invites employees to drop in for a talk with their managers anytime.

The company devotes a lot of time to hiring the right people and making sure they are committed to Tandem and its goals. New employees go through up to twenty hours of interviewing, and a manager will never hire a candidate his or her people don't think is good. All new employees go through a two-day communications course.

Have these efforts paid off? Tandem's employee turnover rate is 7 percent, compared to an industry norm of 25 percent. A recent survey of all Tandem employees indicated that 83 percent believe that advancement opportunities are greater at Tandem than at any other place they have worked. Nearly all managerial promotions are from within, as opposed to hiring middle-level managers from other companies. The same survey indicated that 98 percent of the employees believe that Tandem is the best place they have *ever* worked. For one thing, all Tandem employees are stockholders. And stockholders' equity has increased nearly seventy-five times during the last decade.[16]

Assessing the Behavioral Viewpoint

The behavioral viewpoint goes beyond the traditionalists' mechanical view of the work world in stressing the importance of group dynamics and the manager's leadership style. It emphasizes the employee's human and social needs and the influence of the organization's social environment on the quality and quantity of work produced. These are the basic assumptions of the behavioral viewpoint:

1. Workers are motivated by social needs and get a sense of identity through their associations with one another.
2. Workers are more responsive to the social forces exerted by their peers than to management's financial incentives and rules.
3. Workers respond to managers who can help them satisfy their needs.
4. Managers need to coordinate the work of their subordinates democratically in order to improve efficiency.

These assumptions don't always hold in practice, of course. Improving working conditions and managers' human relations skills won't always increase productivity. Economic aspects of work are still important to the employee, as Taylor believed. The major union contracts negotiated in recent years, for instance, focus on job security and wage incentives. And, although employees enjoy working with co-workers who are friendly, low salaries tend to lead to absenteeism and turnover. The negative effects of clumsy organizational structure, poor communication, and routine or boring tasks won't be overcome by the presence of pleasant co-workers. The human aspect of the job in the 1990s is even more complex than was imagined by those advocating the behavioral viewpoint in the 1930s.[17]

THE SYSTEMS VIEWPOINT

During World War II the British assembled a team of mathematicians, physicists, and other professionals to solve wartime problems. These professionals formed the first operations research (OR) group. They were initially responsible for analyzing the makeup, routes, and speeds of convoys and probable submarine locations. The team achieved significant breakthroughs by developing ways to analyze complex systems problems that couldn't be handled solely by intuition or experience. The British and Americans further developed this approach (called *systems analysis*) throughout the war and applied it to many problems of war production and military logistics. Later, systems analysis became an accepted tool in the Department of Defense (DOD) and the space program as well as throughout private industry.

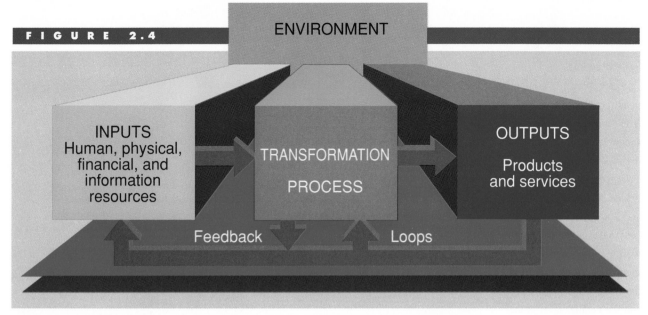

FIGURE 2.4

ENVIRONMENT

INPUTS
Human, physical, financial, and information resources

TRANSFORMATION PROCESS

OUTPUTS
Products and services

Feedback   Loops

Basic Systems View of Organization

An input at a fast food restaurant is the customer's order. The counterperson assembles the customer's order [transformation process] and presents it to the customer [output]. If the customer is dissatisfied with the system, he or she might complain to the restaurant's manager [feedback].

system An association of interrelated and interdependent parts.

systems viewpoint One of four major viewpoints of management, which represents an approach to solving problems within the framework of systematic output followed by feedback.

inputs The physical, human, material, financial, and information resources that enter the transformation process and leave it as outputs, according to the systems viewpoint of management.

transformation process The technology used to convert inputs (physical, human, material, financial, and information resources) into outputs, according to the systems viewpoint of management.

outputs The results of the transformation process, according to the systems viewpoint of management.

feedback Any form of information about a system's status and performance, according to the systems viewpoint of management.

Basic Concepts of the Systems Viewpoint

A **system** is an association of interrelated and interdependent parts. Just as the human body is a system with organs, muscles, bones, a nervous system, and a consciousness that links all the parts together, an organization is a system with many departments that are linked by people working together. A systems-oriented manager makes decisions only after identifying other managers or departments that might be affected by the decision.

The **systems viewpoint** of management represents an approach to solving problems by diagnosing them within a framework of what are called the system's inputs, transformation processes, and outputs, in the light of feedback (see Figure 2.4).[18] The system involved may be an individual, a work group, a department, or an entire organization.

Inputs are the physical, human, material, financial, and information resources that enter the transformation process. At a university, for example, inputs include students, faculty, money, and buildings. **Transformation processes** comprise the technologies used to convert inputs into outputs. Transformation processes at a university include technologies such as lectures, reading assignments, lab experiments, term papers, and tests. **Outputs** are the original inputs (human, physical, material, information, and financial resources) now in a changed condition. Outputs at a university include the graduating students. For a system to operate effectively, it must also provide for feedback. **Feedback** is any form of information about a system's status and performance. One form of feedback at a university is graduates' ability to get jobs. In an organization feedback may take the form of marketing surveys, financial reports, production records, performance appraisals, and the like. Management's role in the systems viewpoint is to ease the transformation process by planning, organizing, leading, and controlling the system.

System Types and Levels

There are two types of systems: closed and open. A **closed system** does not interact with its environment. Most production departments operate as closed systems—they produce

FIGURE 2.5

System Levels

The global level is a multinational organization such as BAT Industries. The organization level is the tobacco division of BAT Industries. The group level consists of brands such as Kool, Kent, and Lucky Strike. The organismic level is the people who work for, say, the Kool group. The organic level is those individuals' body parts, and the cellular level is the parts' individual cells.

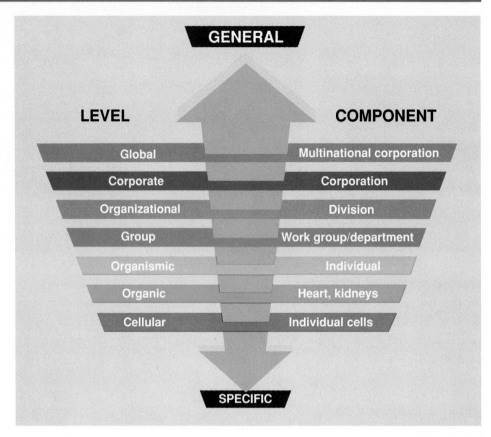

LEVEL	COMPONENT
Global	Multinational corporation
Corporate	Corporation
Organizational	Division
Group	Work group/department
Organismic	Individual
Organic	Heart, kidneys
Cellular	Individual cells

closed system A system that does not interact with its environment, according to the systems viewpoint of management.

open system A system that interacts with its external environment, according to the systems viewpoint of management.

subsystem One of possibly many lower levels within a larger system.

standardized products in an uninterrupted process. An **open system** interacts with the external environment. Managers in a marketing department, for example, constantly try to respond to changes in customers' desires. They monitor what competitors are doing, then develop ways in which their organization can deliver better quality and service at a lower price.

We can also think of a person, group, or organization as a **subsystem** of a larger system. For example, subsystems at Panasonic include its marketing, human resources, production, accounting, and finance departments. Panasonic is a subsystem of its parent corporation, Matsushita. Matsushita is a subsystem of Japan's overall economic subsystem (sales of over $42 billion), which is part of the world's economic system. Figure 2.5 illustrates systems and subsystems in the world economy. We call each a level of the overall system. Note that each level represents a successively simpler part of the overall system. One system's output is another system's input.

A manager turns his or her attention to a given system or subsystem depending on the problem that needs to be solved. For example, Robert L. Crandall, president and CEO of American Airlines, looked for innovative ways to increase employee productivity. He created separate task forces to study the competition, to work with the unions representing American's employees, and to determine how to increase customer satisfaction. In essence, Crandall was studying the problem by considering the effects of different levels of the U.S. economic system on American Airlines.

How can a manager use a systems viewpoint to integrate diverse aspects of one business? The management at one large service business—Federal Express—uses systems concepts to achieve that organization's goals. Basic systems concepts are noted in brackets. Federal Express is an open system because the entire organization interacts daily with customers (external environment).

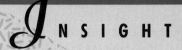

INSIGHT

Federal Express Corporation was founded in 1971 by Frederick Smith and started operations in 1972. Smith realized that ours is an information society in which time is of the essence. Over half of all working Americans earn their living by processing information. Business has become increasingly more urgent. Logistical systems to support this fast-paced economy have become integral parts of it.

Smith anticipated that growing service and computer industries that relied on rapid information delivery would support a small-package express business. He developed a system to provide overnight door-to-door delivery service for high-priority packages and documents. Service is provided Monday through Saturday, with packages and documents routed through 145 airports in the United States and certain points in Canada, Puerto Rico, Europe, and the Far East [open system]. Local offices are maintained at or near airports in more than 300 cities and employ customer service agents, handlers, loaders, and a staff of couriers who pick up and deliver packages [outputs]. The company now handles more than 850,000 packages per day and has an annual sales volume [outputs] of more than $4 billion.

Federal's innovative use of a computer system for tracking packages from their origin to their destination is critical to its success. This sophisticated computer system also allows messages [inputs] to be left for the courier even when the delivery vehicle isn't occupied. In addition, this system enables Federal to locate a customer's shipment any time it passes through six electronic gates during transit [transformation] and to accurately bill the customer. Automatic sorting systems based on computer and optical character recognition are used to provide efficient customer service.

Federal owns and operates more than 175 aircraft [transformation]. The company also operates more than 17,000 computer- and radio-dispatched vans that pick up and deliver shipments. These aircraft and vehicles are important subsystems of the company's air-ground transportation system. The company's aircraft operate in a hub-and-spoke pattern, with Memphis as the hub. Each weekday evening aircraft carry packages [inputs] for delivery from cities throughout the United States to Memphis, where they are sorted [transformation] between midnight and 2:00 A.M. and reloaded onto aircraft. They are then flown to cities by early morning, and delivered to customers [outputs] by the company's couriers by 10:30 A.M.[19]

FedEx system moves the mail at the Memphis Superhub.

Quantitative Techniques

While advocates of systems analysis were suggesting that managers look at inputs, transformation processes, and outputs before making a decision, others were creating quantitative techniques to aid in managerial decision making. Quantitative techniques have four basic characteristics:

1. *The primary focus is on decision making.* The solution identifies direct actions that managers can take.

2. *Alternatives are based on economic criteria.* Alternative actions are presented in terms of measurable criteria such as costs, revenues, return on investment, and tax implications.

3. *Mathematical models are used.* Situations are simulated and problems are analyzed by means of mathematical models.

4. *Computers are essential.* Computers are used to solve complex mathematical models that would be too costly and time-consuming to process manually.

Boeing Computer Services equipped 1600 workstations throughout the company with *customized solid-modeling software* that can help reduce design errors and shorten flow times from design to production.

The range of quantitative decision-making tools available to management has expanded greatly during the past two decades. Today's managers have inventory decision models, statistical decision theory, linear programming, and software to solve complex problems. Many tools are at their fingertips thanks to software that can be run on desk-top computers. In the past systems analysis had not been used by small businesses, such as retail stores, medical offices, mom-and-pop restaurants, and farmers. Today many of these small businesses own their own computers. Ready-to-use software packages, such as DBase IV and Lotus 1-2-3, enable small-business managers to set up programs to handle accounts payable, accounts receivable, and inventory control. A medical office system will do patient scheduling and create and maintain a data base for patients' medical records. In the largest companies groups of management scientists tackle a broad range of business problems by devising their own sophisticated mathematical models.[20]

Gambling casinos such as Caesar's Palace, Bally's, and Harrah's in Atlantic City spend millions on complimentary services (including food, rooms, and transportation) for high rollers. To reduce the cost of these services and improve the odds of these people's playing—and, therefore, losing—in their houses, casino managers employ sophisticated information systems that provide analyses on customers, including their game preferences, betting patterns, and food choices. Similarly, Hertz uses information systems to attract customers. Available in several languages (including English, French, German, Italian, and Spanish), the Hertz destination printout specifies expressways, exits, turns, and time duration of the trip. In some cities the computer prints a grid structure on a map to present information geographically.

Assessing the Systems Viewpoint

Systems analysis and quantitative techniques have been used primarily in the management of production processes and in the technical planning and decision-making areas of management. These techniques have not yet reached the stage where they can be used effectively to deal with the human aspects of management. Variables representing behavioral considerations and human values are difficult—if not impossible—to build into a mathematical model. Since these subjective variables must be taken into account in any business, large or small, judgments about people will continue to be vital in managerial decision making into the 1990s.

Research and development continues to expand the application of information systems in business. (Chapter 19 fully explores how this will happen.) Systems analysis is helping computer experts develop hardware as well as software with humanlike intelligence. They are trying to design computers capable of processing languages and reasoning. When machines can reason, they, like us, will be able to learn from past experience and apply what they have learned to solve new problems. As will be shown in Chapter 19, systems analysis is already having a major impact on manufacturing via the use of computer-aided design (CAD) and computer-aided manufacturing (CAM).

Organizations will no doubt continue to develop more sophisticated systems in order to increase productivity. Such systems will require organizations to change many aspects of their day-to-day existence. These changes will not come without struggle and difficulty. Yet it seems clear that for organizations to survive as we move through the 1990s, there will be a critical need for sophisticated systems to help managers make decisions.

THE CONTINGENCY VIEWPOINT

The **contingency viewpoint** (sometimes called the *contingency* or *situational approach*), summarized in Figure 2.6, was developed in the mid-1960s by managers and others who tried unsuccessfully to apply traditional and systems concepts to real managerial problems. For example, why did providing workers with a bonus for being on time decrease

Blending of Management Viewpoints

The management viewpoints all tend to influence one another in management practice. The contingency viewpoint uses facets of the others as needed.

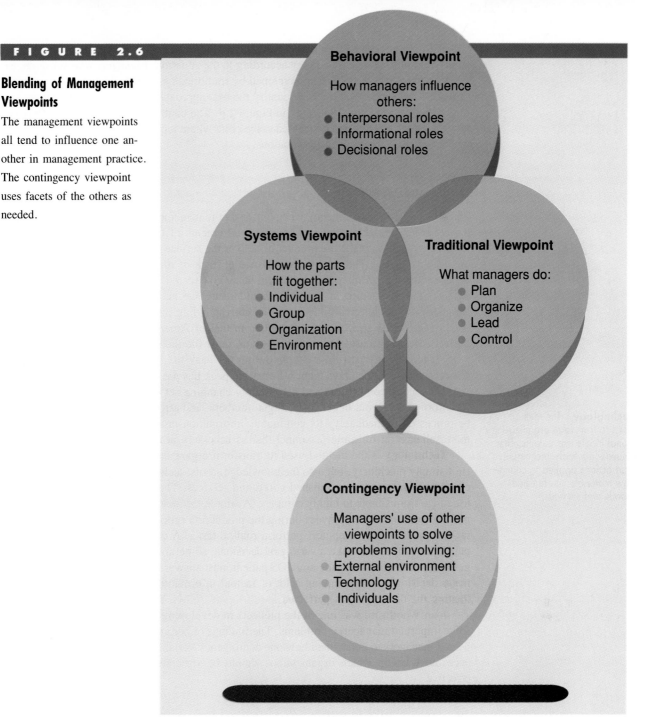

Behavioral Viewpoint

How managers influence others:
- Interpersonal roles
- Informational roles
- Decisional roles

Systems Viewpoint

How the parts fit together:
- Individual
- Group
- Organization
- Environment

Traditional Viewpoint

What managers do:
- Plan
- Organize
- Lead
- Control

Contingency Viewpoint

Managers' use of other viewpoints to solve problems involving:
- External environment
- Technology
- Individuals

contingency viewpoint
One of the four viewpoints of management, which contends that different situations require different practices and allows the use of the other viewpoints separately or in combination to deal with various problems.

lateness at one Marriott hotel and have little impact at another? Proponents of the contingency viewpoint contend that different situations require different practices. As one manager put it, the contingency viewpoint really means "it all depends."

The contingency viewpoint recognizes the possibility of using the other three management viewpoints independently or in combination, as necessary to deal with various situations. However, this viewpoint doesn't give managers free rein to indulge their personal biases and whims. Rather managers are expected to determine which methods are likely to be more effective than others in a given situation. Applying the contingency viewpoint requires the development of conceptual skills. Managers must be able to diagnose and understand a situation thoroughly—to determine which approach is most likely to be successful—before making a decision. The manager's interpersonal and communications skills are essential for actually implementing the decision.

The contingency viewpoint holds that the effectiveness of different managerial styles, guidelines, or techniques will vary according to the situation. Managers who subscribe to this viewpoint use the concepts developed by traditionalists, behavioralists, and systems analysts—but go beyond them to identify the best approach for each particular situation. This blending process is illustrated in Figure 2.6. The contingency viewpoint, because of its very nature, hasn't been developed to the point where it offers detailed prescriptions for the best way to manage in *all* situations.

Contingency Variables

The essence of the contingency viewpoint is that management practices should be consistent with key variables that include the requirements of the external environment, the technology used to make the product or deliver the service, and the people who work for the organization.[21] The relative importance of each of these contingency variables depends on the type of managerial problem being considered. For example, in designing an organization's structure, a manager should recognize and allow for the nature of the company's external environment and the corresponding information-processing requirements. The IRS's structure is different from that of American Airlines. The IRS has a fairly stable set of customers, most of whom must file their tax returns by April 15 each year. It hires many part-time people during the peak tax season to process returns and answer questions, then lays them off after the peak has passed. American Airlines, however, has many competitors and a constantly changing set of customers whose demands for information (about ticket costs, flight numbers, and arrival and departure times) must be processed immediately. Its continuous information-processing requirements call for more reliance on full-time personnel than is necessary at the IRS.

technology The method used to transform organizational inputs into outputs. The knowledge, tools, techniques, and actions applied to change raw materials into finished goods and services.

Technology is the method used to transform organizational inputs into outputs.[22] It isn't simply machinery, but also the knowledge, tools, techniques, and actions applied to change raw materials into finished goods and services. The technologies that employees use range from simple to highly complex. A simple technology involves routine decision-making rules to help employees during the production process. IRS clerks who keyboard tax information into computers perform routine tasks. A complex technology is one requiring employees to make a variety of decisions, sometimes with limited information to guide them. A doctor treating an AIDS patient must answer numerous questions and make many decisions without having a lot of factual information because the technology for treating the disease is not perfected.

Joan Woodward was one of the pioneers in developing the contingency viewpoint to solve important managerial problems. The findings of her group of researchers in England helped managers to understand how one contingency variable—technology—could influence the ways in which organizations should be structured in order to become more effective.

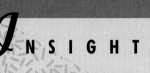

1. *Small-batch technology.* Firms using small-batch technology are job-shop operations where highly skilled workers apply their knowledge and skills to produce custom-made products. Custom home builders use this technology to build finely crafted new homes.

2. *Mass-production technology.* Firms using mass-production technology manufacture standardized goods on an assembly line. They use standardized parts and standard ways of producing the product. Companies employing this type of technology include automobile manufacturers (GM, Ford, Hyundai, Nissan), soft drink bottlers (PepsiCo, Dr Pepper/7-UP), and fast-food outlets (Wendy's, McDonald's, Long John Silver's).

3. *Continuous-process technology.* Continuous-process technology is highly automated and programmed. Machines handle the production process almost entirely, and output is highly predictable. Firms using this type of technology include petroleum refineries (Texaco, Shell, and Exxon), chemical plants (Dow Chemical and Du Pont), nuclear power plants, and large breweries (Coors and Miller). It is very expensive to stop production in such firms. Excess output is stored for later consumption, and companies lower their prices to stimulate demand for their products if necessary.

Studying the technology employed by effective firms, Woodward found a fairly consistent relationship between certain organizational characteristics and type of technology. These relationships are shown in the table. Firms using mass-production methods are more effective operating under bureaucratic management. Numerous rules and highly formalized communication systems are needed to coordinate and control these firms' production of standard outputs. However, firms using small-batch and continuous-process technologies have little or no need for bureaucratic methods. The study's conclusion was that a firm choosing an organizational design that complements its technology is more likely to be successful than a firm choosing a design that doesn't fit its technology.[23]

Woodward's Findings

Organizational Characteristic	Technology		
	Small-Batch	Mass-Production	Continuous-Process
Number of hierarchical levels	3	4	6
Number of rules and regulations	Few	Many	Few
Amount of verbal communication between workers and managers	High	Low	High
Amount of written communication between workers and managers	Low	High	Low
Bureaucratic orientation	Low	High	Low

Source: Adapted from Joan Woodward, *Industrial Organization: Theory and Practice,* 2nd ed. London: Oxford University Press, 1980.

Assessing the Contingency Viewpoint

The contingency viewpoint of management is useful because of its diagnostic approach, which clearly departs from the one-best-way approach of the traditionalists. The contingency viewpoint encourages managers to analyze and understand situational differences and to choose the solution best suited to the firm and the individual in each situation.[24]

Critics argue that the contingency viewpoint is really nothing new. They say it is merely a meshing of techniques from the other viewpoints of management. The contingency viewpoint does draw heavily from the other approaches. However, it is flexible, applying principles and tools from those approaches selectively and where most appropriate. It says that a manager should rely on absolute principles from the traditional, behavioral, and systems viewpoints only after properly diagnosing the realities of the situation. Such a diagnosis looks at the nature of a situation and the means by which a manager can influence it.

THE CONTINUING EVOLUTION OF MANAGEMENT THOUGHT

In the 1990s can we look forward to new management viewpoints—beyond the contingency approach? The answer is yes. In fact, in the 1980s new answers to the longstanding question of how best to manage for productivity and quality came from other cultures in management's global arena, most notably from Japan.

As was mentioned at the end of Chapter 1, Edward Deming's total quality control method was embraced by Japanese companies in the 1950s. It subsequently spread to their American counterparts. However, it isn't only a focus on quality that distinguishes the Japanese management style. That style also resembles bureaucratic management in its concept of lifelong employment and behavioral management in its use of group decision making. In Japanese firms everyone from managers to production workers is involved in a drawn-out process of decision making and problem solving. Whether or not Japanese management suits the individualistic orientation of U.S. firms is open to debate. And whether or not it is a new viewpoint of management may be questionable. But it does demonstrate that the body of management thought continues to grow and evolve—today more than ever in a context of global cross-fertilization.

CHAPTER SUMMARY

1. There are three branches of the traditional viewpoint: bureaucratic management, scientific management, and administrative management. Max Weber developed a theory of bureaucratic management that stresses the need for a strict hierarchy governed by clearly defined regulations and lines of authority. His theory contains seven principles: a formal system of rules, impersonality, division of labor, a hierarchical structure, a detailed authority structure, lifelong career commitment, and rationality.

    Scientific management theorists tried to find ways to make workers more productive. Frederick Taylor believed that management's job was to make individual workers more efficient. This was accomplished by improving worker-machine relationships, based on time-and-motion studies. Frank and Lillian Gilbreth also studied how to make workers more efficient. Frank focused on the various physical motions workers used, and Lillian emphasized the welfare of workers. Henry Gantt believed that workers' performance could be charted and thus improved through setting deadlines.

    Administrative management theorists focused on developing principles that managers, rather than workers, could use to become more effective. Henry Fayol outlined four functions—planning, organizing, leading, and controlling—that he believed all successful managers use in their work.

2. The behavioral viewpoint emphasizes employees' human and social needs. One of its first proponents, Mary Parker Follett, believed that it is management's job to coordinate the efforts of all employees toward a common organizational objective. Chester Barnard's contribution was similar to Follett's. He held, in part, that a

manager does not have the authority to tell a worker what to do unless the worker *accepts* that authority. Studies conducted at the Hawthorne plant of the Western Electric Company led to the conclusion that social and human factors can be more important than physical and financial factors in influencing productivity.

3. The systems viewpoint looks at organizations as a series of inputs, transformation processes, and outputs. A system may either be open or closed. Systems analysis advocates that managers use quantitative techniques to solve problems.

4. The contingency viewpoint, or the situational approach, is the most modern management viewpoint. In essence, managers who follow this approach can use any other viewpoint depending on the circumstances at the time. There are three key contingency variables—environment, technology, and people—that managers should consider before making a decision.

5. New management viewpoints continue to evolve, some of them based on incorporating the Japanese style of management in the U.S. culture.

QUESTIONS FOR DISCUSSION AND APPLICATION

1. What are the similarities and differences among the three branches of the traditional viewpoint?

2. How does UPS use ideas from bureaucratic management to increase its effectiveness?

3. Discuss some of the problems of bureaucratic organizations as indicated in the Global Link feature on Egyptian bureaucracy.

4. **From Where You Sit:** How likely is it that you will work for a manager using one of the types of traditional viewpoint?

5. What was Mary Parker Follett's advice to managers? Is it still useful today?

6. How do Barnard's management theories differ from those of Weber?

7. Why has Tandem Computers been so successful in its application of the behavioral viewpoint?

8. **From Where You Sit:** From an employee's point of view, do you agree with the second basic assumption of the behavioral viewpoint?

9. Identify the inputs, transformation processes, and outputs for your bank.

10. What types of problems does systems analysis tend to solve?

11. **From Where You Sit:** How has technology affected the registration process at your school?

12. **From Where You Sit:** How might the practice of management change further in the 1990s?

13. Visit a local department store and observe clerks' behaviors. What management viewpoint do many of these illustrate?

How Bureaucratic Is Your Organization?

In this Skill Building Exercise you are to focus on either your university or an organization for which you currently work in a full- or part-time capacity or for which you have worked in the past. Please circle the letter on the scale indicating the degree to which you agree or disagree with each statement. There is no "right" answer; simply respond according to how you see the organization being managed.

Strongly Agree (SA)	Agree (A)	Neutral (N)	Disagree (D)	Strongly Disagree (SD)

1. People in this organization are urged to be innovative.
   SA   A   N   D   SD

2. There are a lot of rules to follow in this organization.
   SA   A   N   D   SD

3. People who pay attention to details are likely to get ahead in this organization.
   SA   A   N   D   SD

4. A person has a secure job in this organization.
   SA   A   N   D   SD

5. Precision in one's work is valued by the organization.
   SA   A   N   D   SD

6. This company operates with a stable set of competitors.
   SA   A   N   D   SD

7. People in this organization are urged to take risks and experiment with new ways of doing things.
   SA   A   N   D   SD

8. Jobs in this organization are very predictable.
   SA   A   N   D   SD

9. There are few rules in this organization.
   SA   A   N   D   SD

10. Employees are very careful in performing their work.
    SA   A   N   D   SD

11. Employees are treated impersonally by managers in this organization.
    SA   A   N   D   SD

12. Lines of authority are closely followed in this organization.

SA   A   N   D   SD

13. Job opportunities in this organization are limited to employees who play by the rules.

SA   A   N   D   SD

14. Being highly organized is expected and rewarded in this organization.

SA   A   N   D   SD

15. Being people-oriented is a characteristic of this organization.

SA   A   N   D   SD

16. People are not constrained by many rules in this organization.

SA   A   N   D   SD

Scoring. On the scoring grid, circle the number that corresponds to your response to each of the 16 questions. Add the numbers in each column. Enter the total for each column on the line below. Add the column totals and enter as a total score. This is your organization's score.

Question	Strongly Agree	Agree	Neutral	Disagree	Strongly Disagree
1	5	4	3	2	1
2	5	4	3	2	1
3	5	4	3	2	1
4	5	4	3	2	1
5	5	4	3	2	1
6	1	2	3	4	5
7	5	2	3	2	1
8	1	4	3	2	1
9	5	4	3	2	1
10	5	4	3	2	1
11	5	4	3	2	1
12	5	4	3	3	5
13	5	2	3	4	—
14	1	2	—	—	
15	1				
16					

Scores: —   —   —   —   —   TOTAL SCORE = ____

Interpretation. A high score (90–64 points) indicates that your organization has many of the features characteristic of the bureaucratic viewpoint. A low score (32–16 points) indicates that your organization has more features usually associated with the behavioral, or human relations, viewpoint. A score in the middle range (63–33 points) indicates that your organization incorporates features of both the bureaucratic and the behavioral viewpoints.

To: Maryann Kern, Vice-President, Manufacturing
From: Michael Jordan, President
Subject: Worker Performance and Quality

Congratulations! You have met this year's goal of a 20 percent increase in the sales of integrated circuits and have done so without adding personnel. Although this is impressive, Maryann, some problems have come to my attention that we need to discuss.

As you know, chip manufacturing must be done in spotless conditions. Some of our largest customers, however, are complaining that our quality has gone down. For instance, Stonebriar Computers is threatening to either switch manufacturers or make their own circuits unless we do something about our quality.

Our personnel department has also informed me that manufacturing has spent more than $240,000 on training new people this year. Since your department added no personnel, I must assume that this money was spent training new people who replaced those who quit. Has turnover increased since you instituted those new rules sometime last year? Could there be a link between the new rules and the increased turnover? Since quality seems to be an issue with some of our customers, perhaps our workers are becoming bored with their routine tasks. What do you think?

I would like you to develop some ideas for reducing turnover and improving quality before our next monthly management meeting. Let's plan to discuss your ideas at that meeting.

Assume that you are the vice-president of manufacturing and have to write a response to the president. Consider the management viewpoints described in this chapter, and look at ways that each can shed light on the problems outlined in this memo.

New England Banker, Sticking to Old Ways, Avoided Rivals' Woes

BY RON SUSKIND

WORCESTER, Mass.—Hard by Lake Quinsigamond, condominiums rise like 10 stories of folly. Built with a small bank's $10 million loan, the complex now has walls decorated with auction stickers.

A few blocks away stands a half-empty, pastel shopping center. The original lender, excited to lend $4 million at the prime rate plus five percentage points, overlooked survey reports showing the land soft and difficult to build on. That bank failed. So did one that lent another $1.5 million to finish the project.

Down the road a mile, a cluster of town houses sports a marina with year-round, all-weather docks, but the developer couldn't make it through a real-estate market suddenly turned frigid. Another local bank took a $3 million cold shower.

All these bank-wrecking loans have one thing in common: Woodbury C. Titcomb, chairman of Peoples Bancorp of Worcester. But he didn't make the loans—he turned them all down.

"Some incredibly foolish loan requests crossed my desk in the past few years," says Mr. Titcomb, not exactly gloating but recalling with satisfaction his competitors' errors. "Well, maybe I'm overstating it. The banks that eventually made those loans didn't think they were foolish. Some of those banks, of course, aren't around anymore."

To Mr. Titcomb, avoiding bad loans is just so much common sense: Be prudent, anticipate what could go wrong and, above all, don't lend just because another bank might make the loan. But for years, Mr. Titcomb's stodginess was ridiculed by rivals, chastised by analysts and even questioned by his own directors.

Today, he is the envy of New England bankers. Peoples is solidly profitable while many local lenders are staggered by losses. It has bought two failed banks in the past two years—increasing its assets to $900 million from $570 million—and is picking over the region's mounting rubble for bargains. The savings bank's stock is higher than the price at which it was first offered to the public in 1986; that's true of only five of 63 publicly traded savings banks in New England, almost all of which went public in the mid-1980s, according to SNL Securities, a bank consulting firm.

"When everybody was lending money like mad, they all laughed at crazy Woodie, the guy with the buggy whip being passed by all those fast cars," says First Albany Corp. analyst Don Kauth. "Now he is one of the few healthy banks around, and they're calling him a genius."

Not everyone agrees that his Spartan practices have always been appropriate, however. "Because of Woodie's conservatism, Peoples just missed the train in terms of earnings and profits in the '80s," says Clealand Blair, president of C.B. Blair Builders Inc. "Overall, I think Woodie falls into the category of nothing ventured, nothing gained."

Mr. Titcomb responds that such a philosophy is fine for businessmen but not for bankers. He also notes his bank's generally steady earnings.

Mr. Titcomb, robust at 67, is among the last of a lost tribe: the maniacally frugal Yankee banker, the kind that, over two centuries, built the nation's strongest banking culture. That culture, with its strict norms ranging from cash-flow analysis to dress code, was largely swept away by the swift currents of the 1980s. Many are wondering how it all changed so fast. . . .

1. How would you describe the management viewpoint of Woodbury C. Titcomb?
2. Would he be successful in a different industry? Why or why not?
3. What are the drawbacks of his management approach?

TWO PLANTS AT GENERAL MOTORS

Van Nuys has been considered one of GM's more troubled plants, primarily because of union problems. Workers there in the 1980s felt little responsibility and little accountability for their on-the-job behavior. As a result, costs at Van Nuys were very high in comparison to those at other GM plants. The general manager found that workers operated in a vacuum: They did the job they were told to do without relating it to the finished car. They didn't know who did what to a car after it left their immediate area or how much it cost GM to have their co-workers repair any defects they created. Workers were treated like robots and acted like them, believing that they came to work and just put parts on a car. If they saw a defect, they didn't tell anyone; if the car was shipped out that way, tough luck. It was a vicious circle that really hurt GM where it could least afford to be hurt—in the area of quality.

The Fremont plant, which would be the site of the joint venture between GM and Toyota, resembled the Van Nuys plant in many ways. Daily absenteeism ran more than 20 percent, beer bottles littered the parking lot, and even the slightest union-management dispute had to go to the bargaining table. When GM and Toyota decided in the mid-1980s to run the plant jointly, Toyota announced that it didn't want anyone who wouldn't work under a new agreement. The new agreement's operating philosophy had seven points:

1. There would be a never-ending search for perfection.
2. The reduction of costs would be continuously pursued.
3. All employees' potential would be fully developed.
4. Mutual trust would be established between the union and management.
5. Teams of workers would monitor their own performance.
6. Every employee would be treated as a manager.
7. There would be job security for all employees.

The union agreed to reduce the number of job classifications from 183 to 4. Employees began to receive training by fellow hourly employees in Japan. Each team member was trained to do all jobs in the team. And if a defect was spotted along the line, the team had permission to stop the line and fix it.

What were the results? Employee morale is high and has remained high. Prospective employees are interviewed by workers who explain the goals of the system in great detail. Turnover, absenteeism, and the number of grievances filed have dropped. In addition, after three months the cars rolled off the assembly line with virtually no defects. It cost $750 less to build a car in Fremont than in other GM plants. The amount of space dedicated to rework in other GM plants is 12 percent, compared to 7 percent at the Fremont plant. This leaves Fremont more space for production. The automobiles it builds—first the Chevrolet Nova and Toyota Corolla FX, now replaced by Chevrolet's Geo Prizm and Toyota's four-door Corolla—are comparable in quality to cars built in Japan.

1. What management viewpoint seems to be followed at the Van Nuys plant?
2. What viewpoint seems to be followed at the Fremont plant?
3. Why is the Fremont plant more effective than the Van Nuys plant? What lessons should GM learn from this experience?

Part Two

ENVIRONMENTAL

FORCES

Glass Ceiling

Nearly 500,000 Americans work for Japanese companies located in the United States, and that number promises to increase as the Japanese continue to have success in this country. But Americans who want to work for a Japanese company in the United States should be forewarned: Cultural clashes between American workers and Japanese management have led not only to misunderstandings, but also to lawsuits.

The United States and Japan view employment in entirely different ways. Japanese employees tend to see the company they work for as family and expect to remain there for a lifetime. Moreover, there's a stricter sense of conformity in the Japanese workplace than in a U.S. company. Here, we often place more value on an individual's performance than on the team's. We also assume that a U.S. manager—by capitalizing on his or her performance—may reach the top by moving to another firm.

In an effort to eliminate the misunderstandings that stem from cultural differences, Panasonic has hired a consultant to teach its New Jersey workers about Japanese business culture. Panasonic hopes not to repeat the mistakes made by Kyocera, a Japanese company that once laid off 350 of its American workers after promising them lifelong jobs and telling them they were part of a family.

But Kyocera did lay off its American workers, and it did so abruptly—just as an American company might. The laid-off workers sued. Robert Rothman, who represented the fired employees, said the sense of betrayal was greater than in an American company because "an American company would have never represented to its workers that they had lifetime employment."

And then there's the case of Kent Cooper. Cooper used to be a manager for a Japanese company he will not name because he, too, sued. After nine months with the firm, he was promoted to vice president and, shortly after that, abruptly fired. He was told that his work was "exceptional," but the company let him go because they didn't see a long-term match between them, even though Cooper received a memo shortly before he was let go which stated, "don't worry about your job security."

Why were these Americans fired? Kenichi Ohmae, a management consultant, thinks that the problem isn't so much with Japanese companies as with U.S. workers who don't make a lifetime commitment to one company. And unless that kind of commitment is shown, he says, Japanese companies who need to cut costs will lay off American workers before Japanese. In addition, real power in a Japanese company comes by developing personal relationships with those in the firm—a great difficulty for U.S. managers because of the language and cultural barriers. Moreover, most Japanese business relationships are developed after hours, when executives are expected to both socialize and network. When an American executive is finished for the day, he or she usually goes straight home.

Despite efforts like Panasonic's, the two cultures still clash. For instance, Leo Smith, a Panasonic manager, once convinced his Japanese boss to do away with evaluation letters and replace them with face-to-face meetings. His boss agreed with the strategy, until the Japanese managers complained. Soon after, Smith was told, "I must have my letters," and without further conversation, Panasonic continued to use letters to evaluate its employees.

How can understanding the broader environment of their firm help Americans working for a Japanese company get promoted? Why is individual performance less important then group performance within a Japanese company? Do U.S. companies overemphasize individualism?

Chapter 3

ENVIRONMENTAL FORCES

AND MANAGEMENT

Anthony Frank

What You Will Learn

1 The nature of the general environment facing organizations, including the economic system, the political system, demographics, and culture.

2 How four basic cultural values influence managerial decisions and behavior.

3 How an organization's task environment directly affects its success.

4 How five competitive forces directly affect organizations in an industry.

5 Why technological forces have become increasingly important in planning strategic actions.

6 Five political strategies used by managers to cope with external political forces.

7 **Skill Development:** How to monitor and diagnose the external environment of any organization you become a part of.

Chapter Outline

The World of the U.S. Postal Service

Anthony M. Frank

U.S. Postal Service

A blizzard of mail—160 billion pieces—is delivered by the U.S. Postal Service each year. That's about 226 million pieces every twelve hours, which is Federal Express's total for an entire year. Customers can buy stamps and ship parcels at over 40,000 locations, some of them on wheels. Even in this era of private mail services and faxing, the Postal Service still does business with every American company and just about every American citizen. But few outfits catch as much flak. One reason for the flak is that about 0.04 percent of U.S. mail never gets delivered—61,000 missing pieces a year. Anthony M. Frank, head of the Postal Service, tells this self-deprecating one-liner: "If it's neither snow nor rain nor heat nor gloom of night, what the devil is wrong with the place?"

In one interview Frank commented on the key environmental forces facing the Postal Service:

Some seventy special-interest groups lobby us all the time. Still, I can't find anyone who is concerned with the overall health of the Postal Service. Magazine publishers are interested primarily in second-class mail. That is comparable to trying to have a healthy left rear hoof on a cow. But somebody had better start thinking about the whole cow, because you can't have a healthy hoof on a sick cow.

I need a lobby and I need it now. Our unions are very smart and spend about $2 million a year on lobbying. I'm not allowed to spend money on lobbying. I hope business people will do it for us.

My doomsday scenario? That Congress would give other deliverers access to the mailboxes. Now only mail carriers have such access. That would erode the Postal Service's profitable businesses, especially second- and third-class mail, which provide 25 percent of our operating income. Aside from obvious self-interest, I'm not sure I like the idea of lots of grubby fingers being able to get into mailboxes.

Let me give you an example. Some of the major magazines and catalogue companies are already experimenting with alternate delivery. They are hanging things on doorknobs. If the private sector starts eroding our business, we would have to raise the rates on everything, especially second- and third-class mail. This would drive out more business and lead to even higher prices.[1]

environment All external forces and the influences, direct and indirect, they have on the decisions and actions of an organization.

Like the managers of the U.S. Postal Service, all managers have to deal with a variety of groups and forces in the environment—from customers to competitors and from regulatory agencies to suppliers. What do we mean by environmental forces? Simply put, managers don't work in a vacuum-like closed system. An organization's **environment** consists of all the external fores and the influences, direct and indirect, they have on the decisions and actions of the organization. Of course, the specific kinds of environmental forces vary with time and type of industry. But, as we demonstrate in this chapter, a variety of environmental forces are central to the success or failure of *all* organizations.

The long-term effectiveness of the U.S. Postal Service, for instance, will be influenced by its managers' ability to deal with environmental opportunities and threats, such as alternative delivery services.

How can managers best deal with their environment? There are no pat answers to this question. However, managers can pursue two basic approaches: (1) position the organization so that its own capabilities provide the best *defense* against an environmental threat, such as the Postal Service's effort to get groups to lobby Congress on its behalf; and (2) take the *offensive* by attempting to change or take advantage of the environment, such as improving the Postal Service to better compete or to change false stereotypes through advertising and public relations. In brief, managers must develop both reactive (strong defense) and proactive (strong offense) strategies for taking advantage of environmental opportunities and reducing environmental threats.

We have chosen to be selective about which environmental forces to address in this chapter. For example, the international arena is certainly a key part of most managers' environment—today more than ever. We will touch only briefly on international forces here, however, because Chapter 4 is devoted to this important topic. Also, various groups in our society are pressing for new forms and higher levels of ethical behavior by managers and for increased social responsibility for organizations. We allude to these forces here, but all of Chapter 5 is devoted to ethics and social responsibility in management. Throughout this book environmental forces and their management are discussed wherever they are relevant to the topic of a chapter.

This chapter, then, begins with an introduction to the basic features of organizational environments: the general and the task environments. We present a diagnostic framework of types of task environments, which you can add to your growing toolkit of managerial skills. Most of the chapter is devoted to four of the key environmental forces that must be monitored and diagnosed because of their direct or indirect importance: cultural forces, competitive forces, technological forces, and political-legal forces.

THE GENERAL ENVIRONMENT

general environment
Those external factors, such as inflation rate and population demographics, that usually affect indirectly all or most organizations in the economy (also called the macroenvironment).

The **general environment,** sometimes called the *macroenvironment,* includes those external factors that usually affect all or most organizations in an economy. Take a look at the two outer rings in Figure 3.1. The general environment includes such broad factors as the type of economic system (for example, free enterprise, socialist, communist) and economic conditions (general prosperity, recession, depression); type of political system (democracy, dictatorship, monarchy); the natural resources (water, forests, oil, coal, soil); demographics (ages, genders, races, education levels represented in the work force); and cultural forces (values, language, religious influences). Some definitions of the general environment also include political-legal forces and technological forces (see the next two rings in the figure). We will treat these as part of the task environment, because they increasingly have direct impact on the day-to-day decisions managers make. First, let's briefly consider some of the impacts of the economic and political systems (especially in creating a renewed environmentalism), demographics, and cultural forces on most organizations in the United States.

Economic and Political Systems

The United States has an economic system of regulated free enterprise. Privately controlled markets based on supply and demand prevail over governmental control of production and prices. Free market competition, private contracts, profit incentives, technological advancement, and free labor (with collective bargaining rights) are essential elements in such a system. The government (part of the political system) acts as a watchdog over

FIGURE 3.1

Environmental Forces Affecting Management

The general environment includes the broad economic, political, and cultural systems shown in the two outermost rings. The task environment includes political-legal forces and also the progressively more direct influences of technological and competitive forces, shown in the innermost rings.

business, providing direction in such areas as antitrust, monetary policy, human rights, defense, and environmental matters. Public (government) ownership of enterprises is the exception to the rule, rather than the norm. There is no centrally planned economy as has been the case in the Soviet Union.[2] Particularly challenging economic and political forces may include fluctuating inflation rates, unemployment rates, tax rates, and interest rates; environmental regulations (with respect to air, water, and ground); and safety regulations covering both the workplace and goods produced.

Political and economic forces in the United States have led to a renewed environmentalism. Domestic environmental consciousness appears to be on the rise. A 1981 *New York Times*/CBS poll found that only 4 percent of the U.S. population agreed that "environmental improvements must be made regardless of cost." In 1989, a full 79 percent accepted this rather strong statement. National environmental groups are showing new signs of maturity. The National Resources Defense Council has abandoned some of its earlier views, considered by some to be "fanatic and utopian," and has displayed a greater understanding of the tradeoffs that have to be made, a greater willingness to move from confrontation to collaboration, in order to improve the environment.[3]

Alyeska Pipeline Service Co. routinely computer-checks the Alaska pipeline for damage.

This renewed environmentalism poses numerous economic and political challenges to business. With the passage of the U.S. Clean Air Act in 1990, response to these challenges is now more a requirement than a choice. Companies now make environmental considerations part of their decision making from the beginning, not simply something added as a reaction to disciplinary measures. They now think long term, although that may mean profits will suffer in the short term. Here are a few of the proactive and reactive steps organizations can take in heeding the call of renewed environmentalism:

▶ *Cut back on environmentally unsafe operations.* Du Pont, the leading producer of CFCs (chlorofluorocarbons), has announced that it will voluntarily pull out of this $750 million business by 2000, if not sooner.

▶ *Compensate for environmentally risky endeavors.* Applied Energy Services, a power plant management firm, donated $2 million in 1988 for tree planting in Guatemala to compensate for a coal-fired plant it was building in Connecticut. Oxygen generated by the trees is meant to offset carbon dioxide and carbon monoxide emissions that might lead to global warming.

▶ *Try to prevent confrontation with state or federal pollution control agencies.* W. R. Grace faces expensive and time-consuming lawsuits, because of its toxic dumps; and violations by Browning-Ferris, Waste Management, and Louisiana-Pacific have damaged their reputations.

▶ *Comply early with government regulations.* Since compliance costs increase over time, the companies that act early on will have lower costs. This will enable them to increase their market share and profit and to win a competitive advantage. Thus it is 3M's goal to meet government requirements for replacing or improving underground storage tanks by 1993 instead of 1998, the deadline for doing so.

▶ *Promote new manufacturing technologies.* Louisville Gas and Electric has taken the lead in installing smokestack scrubbers; Consolidated Natural Gas, in using clean burning technologies; and Nucor, in developing state-of-the-art steel mills. Pittsburgh Gas & Electric has agreed to rely on a combination of smaller-scale generating facilities, such as windmills and cogeneration plants, and aggressive conservation efforts. It has canceled plans to build large coal-burning and nuclear power plants.

▶ *Recycle wastes.* 3M is recycling and reusing solvents it once spewed into the atmosphere. Other firms with active recycling programs are Safety-Kleen (solvents and motor oil), Wellman (plastics), Jefferson Smurfit (paper), and Nucor (steel).[4]

Demographics

demographics The characteristics of people composing work groups, organizations, countries, or specific markets.

Demographics are the characteristics of people composing work groups, organizations, countries, or specific markets, such as individuals between the ages of 18 and 25.[5] Changing demographics play an important role in marketing, human resources management, finance, and other areas. Let's consider a few of the broad demographic changes that will be seen in the United States by the year 2000.

From 1985 to 2000 the Hispanic and Asian populations will each grow by 48 percent, the black population will grow by 28 percent, and the white population by only 5.6 percent. As a result, non-Hispanic whites will fall from 78 to 73 percent of the total population by 2000.

Women have dramatically increased their representation in occupations and industries in which they were once rarely found, such as business, engineering, and the law. The female share of the work force will reach 47 percent in 2000, up from about 44 percent in 1986. Many professional schools, such as business schools, have up to 50 percent female students. They represented only about 25 percent of enrollment ten years ago. By 2000 the number and percentage of women in middle- and top-level management positions is expected to rise dramatically.[6]

Finally, the U.S. work force is aging. The average age of workers will jump from 32 in 1990 to about 40 by the turn of the century. At that point nearly half of the labor force will come under the protection of the Age Discrimination in Employment Act. This act provides protection against age discrimination in employment to those ages 40 and older. The projected population increase for ages 45 and over is 30 percent, but it's only 2 percent for the 18-to-44 age group.[7]

Employers are likely to face new pressures from an increasingly diverse work force. The recognition of this trend is expressed in the label *managing diversity*. Some organizations are providing training to encourage employees to be more tolerant of language, age, race, and ethnic differences, to identify and reject racial and gender preferences in hiring and promotion, and to be responsive to the handicapped. The changing demographics make it no longer feasible for management to impose an ''Anglo-male'' culture.[8]

The following Insight portrays how some organizations have responded to one demographic change—the growing Hispanic population in the United States.

U.S. HISPANICS IN THE MARKETPLACE

*I*NSIGHT

''Corporate America has rediscovered the Hispanic market . . . a lot of major corporations are targeting advertising to Hispanics,'' says Lisa Navarrete, spokesperson for the National Council of La Raza.

In New York City's bus and subway systems, a growing number of ads for familiar products are in Spanish, and all safety instructions are in both English and Spanish. Hispanic food has become popular in major cities, where a variety of restaurants—Mexican, Cuban, Salvadoran, and others—reflect the local Hispanic communities. Mexican food tops the list. Thirty-eight million households eat Mexican foods, sales of which rose 60 percent between 1982 and 1990. Kraft's Velveeta cheese now comes in a spicy Mexican version, and jalapeño-flavored potato chips are sold nationally. Farmers in New Mexico report doubling their crops of chiles between 1977 and 1990.

Of course, the effort to target any market can have its pitfalls. Borden advertised ice cream using the Mexican slang word *nieve,* which literally means ''snow.'' The campaign worked fine in California and Texas, where there is a large Mexican-American population. But Cubans and Puerto Ricans in the East, unfamiliar with Mexican slang, thought the company was actually selling snow.

Univision, the largest Spanish-language television network, is estimated to reach 17 million Hispanics, with at least 5 million regular viewers. Formerly known as the Spanish International Network, it has been joined by a second Spanish network, Telemundo, with more than 3.3 million regular viewers.[9]

Cultural Forces

Underlying a society and surrounding an organization are various cultural forces, which often are not as visible as other general environmental forces. For our purposes **culture** can be defined as the shared characteristics (such as language, religion, level of economic development)[10] and values that distinguish the members of one group of people from those of another.[11] A *value* is a basic belief about a condition that has considerable importance and meaning to individuals and is relatively stable over time.[12] A **value system** consists of multiple beliefs that are compatible and supportive of one another. For example, beliefs in free enterprise and individual rights are mutually supportive.

Managers need to appreciate the significance of values and value systems, both their own and those of others. Values can have a big effect on how a manager does the following:

culture The shared characteristics (such as language, religion, heritage) and values that distinguish one group of people from another.

value system Multiple beliefs (values) that are compatible and supportive of one another.

► *Views other people and groups, thus influencing interpersonal relationships.* One male manager believes women are inferior, belong in the home, and should simply follow orders; another male manager sees women as equals who should be recognized, consulted, and promoted based on their contributions.

► *Perceives situations and problems.* One manager believes that conflict and competition can be managed and used constructively; another thinks they should be avoided altogether.

► *Goes about solving problems.* One manager believes that group decision making can be effective, another believes in always making decisions independently.

► *Determines what is and is not ethical behavior.* One manager believes that ethics means doing only what is absolutely required by law; another sees ethics as going well beyond minimum legal requirements.

► *Leads and controls employees.* One manager believes in sharing information and using controls based on mutual trust; another thinks subordinates are not to be trusted and controls should emphasize impersonal rules, close supervision, and a rigid chain of command.[13]

By diagnosing a culture's values, a manager or other employee can understand and predict others' expectations and avoid a number of cultural pitfalls. Otherwise one risks inadvertently antagonizing fellow employees, customers, or other groups by breaking a sacred taboo (showing the bottom of one's shoe to a Saudi) or ignoring a time-honored custom (preventing an employee from attending an important religious service).

The framework of work-related values outlined here and expanded on in Chapter 4 has been used in a number of studies. This framework was developed by Geert Hofstede, currently the Director of the Institute for Research on Intercultural Cooperation in the Netherlands, while he was an organizational research scientist at IBM.[14] The data reported here is based on his surveying 116,000 IBM employees in fifty countries. A number of subsequent studies have found his framework to be valuable. Hofstede's project uncovered some intriguing differences among countries in terms of four value dimensions: power distance, uncertainty avoidance, individualism (versus collectivism), and masculinity (versus femininity).[15] The following discussion focuses on Hofstede's ranking of four nations—Canada, France, Mexico, and the United States—with respect to each dimension. These rankings are based on the *dominant* value orientation in each country, with a ranking of 1 for the lowest and 50 for the highest position (relative to all fifty countries in the survey) on each value dimension. Figure 3.2 provides a composite of the rankings of Canada, France, Mexico, and the United States.

power distance Hofstede's value dimension that measures the degree to which influence and control are unequally distributed among individuals within a particular group.

Power distance is the degree to which influence and control are unequally distributed among individuals and institutions within a particular culture. If most people in a society support an unequal distribution, the nation is ranked high on the power distance dimension. In high-ranked societies, such as those of Mexico, France, India, and the Philippines, membership in a particular class or caste is critical to an individual's opportunity for advancement. Societies with lower rankings on power distance play down inequality. Individuals in the United States, Canada, Sweden, and Austria can achieve prestige, wealth, and social status, regardless of family background.

Managers operating in countries ranking low in power distance are expected to be generally supportive of equal rights and equal opportunity. For example, managers in Canada and the United States typically support participative management. In contrast, managers in Mexico, France, and India (ranked relatively high in power distance) have little use for the U.S. and Canadian style of participative management. United States and Canadian managers try not to set themselves too much apart from subordinates by appearing to be superior or unique. In the countries with high power distance, however, a more autocratic management style is not only more common but is expected by employees.

uncertainty avoidance Hofstede's value dimension that measures the degree to which individuals or societies attempt to avoid the ambiguity, riskiness, and indefiniteness of the future.

Uncertainty avoidance is the degree to which members of a society attempt to avoid the ambiguity, riskiness, and indefiniteness of the future. Individuals in cultures ranked low in this dimension are generally secure and don't expend a great deal of energy trying to avoid or minimize ambiguous situations. In cultures with high uncertainty avoidance,

FIGURE 3.2

Relative Ranking of Four Countries on Four Value Dimensions

You can see where each country stands relative to the others by reading the height of its curve above each value dimension. For instance, Mexico ranks highest in power distance, whereas the United States ranks highest in individualism.

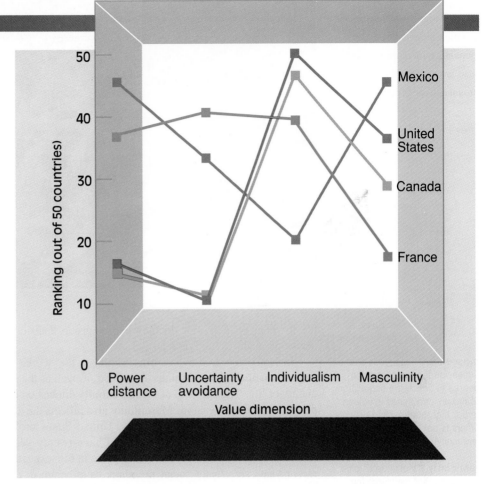

Source: Developed from G. Hofstede, *Culture's Consequences: International Differences in Work-Related Values* (Beverly Hills, Calif.: Sage, 1980).

individuals often try to make the future more predictable by establishing institutions that foster security. In organizations, high uncertainty avoidance is often associated with built-in career stability (job security), numerous rules governing behavior, intolerance of deviant ideas and behavior, belief in absolute truths, and overreliance on expertise.

United States and Canadian employees and managers ranked low on uncertainty avoidance, sharing a relatively high tolerance for uncertainty compared with workers and managers in France or Mexico. Thus Canadian and U.S. managers are more likely to be receptive to changing rules, open competition, and new ideas.

Individualism is a combination of the degree to which society expects people to take care of themselves and their immediate families and the degree to which individuals believe they are masters of their own destiny. The opposite of individualism is **collectivism,** which refers to a tight social framework in which group (family, clan, organization) members focus on the common welfare and feel strong loyalty toward one another.

United States and Canadian employees ranked very high in individualism, a result that agrees with the frequent characterization of these two countries as ''I'' societies rather than ''we'' societies. A strong sense of individualism supports and maintains a free and competitive (market-based) economic system. High individualism is also consistent with the individual merit and incentive pay systems so favorably viewed in the United States and Canada. Conversely, group incentives and strong seniority systems are likely to be found in countries with low individualism (high collectivism), such as Mexico and Japan. Managers and employees in a high-individualism culture move from organization to organization more frequently. They don't believe that their organizations are solely responsi-

individualism Hofstede's value dimension that measures the extent to which a culture expects people to take care of themselves and/or individuals believe they are masters of their own destiny (the opposite of *collectivism*).

collectivism Hofstede's value dimension that measures the tendency of group members to focus on the common welfare and feel loyalty toward one another (the opposite of *individualism*).

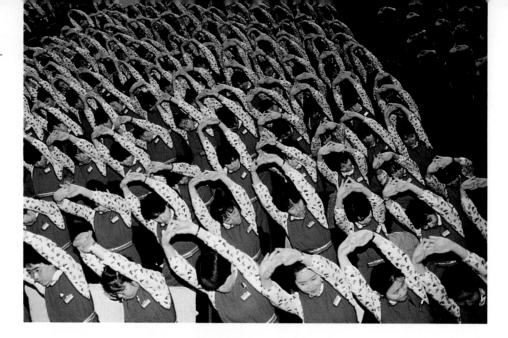

Japan's high *collectivism orientation* helps explain the popularity of morning exercise groups like this one at Itoyokado supermarket.

masculinity Hofstede's value dimension that measures the degree to which the acquisition of money and things is valued and a high quality of life for others is not (the opposite of *femininity*).

femininity Hofstede's value dimension that measures the tendency to be nurturing and people-oriented (the opposite of *masculinity*).

ble for their welfare, nor do they expect group decisions to be of higher quality than decisions made by individuals.

In Hofstede's framework **masculinity** is the degree to which assertiveness and the acquisition of money and things are valued, as well as the degree of indifference to others' quality of life. The opposite of the masculinity dimension is **femininity,** a more nurturing, people-oriented dimension. Masculinity also reflects the division of labor among men and women in a society. Canada and the United States probably rank lower today on the masculinity dimension than they would have twenty years ago, largely because of the societal changes that have been taking place in role expectations for males and females. In recent years significant social pressures have begun to change stereotyped notions that men should be assertive and women should be nurturing or that gender roles should be clearly differentiated.

In high-masculinity cultures, such as Mexico's, Japan's, Austria's, and Italy's, women are still not often found in managerial jobs. Men dominate most settings, and an organization's right to influence the private lives of its employees is widely accepted. One researcher has observed that Mexico, for example, rigidly defines gender-role expectations: The woman is expected to be supportive of and dependent on males—not to do for herself, but to yield to the wishes of others, caring for their needs before her own. A common belief in Muslim countries is that women are the inferior gender and should be subordinates instead of managers.[16]

In later chapters we will use the four work-related value dimensions discussed here as a means of understanding differences and similarities in cultures. We will also apply these value dimensions to understanding and managing differences among employees in a single work setting.[17]

THE TASK ENVIRONMENT

task environment The external forces, such as customers or labor unions, that have a direct effect on an organization.

In contrast to the general environment with its relatively indirect influences, the **task environment** includes all those external forces and groups that have *direct* influence on an organization's growth, success, and survival.[18] It normally includes an organization's customers or clients, competitors, suppliers, stockholders, government regulators, pressure groups, and labor unions (if unionized). Recall from the Manager's Viewpoint feature that some of the powerful groups in the task environment of the U.S. Postal Service include numerous special-interest customer lobbies (such as magazine and catalog publishers), the U.S. Congress (as regulators), and postal labor unions.

Managers and employees—from the manager and checkout clerk at the local supermarket to the director and mail carrier at the U.S. Postal Service—are finding it more and more necessary to focus on groups in the task environment. All levels of management need to expend much time and effort diagnosing the changing needs and expectations of these external groups as well as developing proactive and reactive approaches to managing them.[19] For example, in order to better service customers, Fred Brown, of Fred Brown Mazda/BMW in Bryan, Texas, has delegated to service representatives the authority to assess a customer's problem and take whatever corrective action is needed, on the spot. These and other service policies resulted in his dealership's receiving BMW Corporation's Most Outstanding U.S. Dealership of the Year Award in 1989.

Refer again to Figure 3.1. The task environment *always* includes competitive and technological forces, shown in the innermost rings. Although this book treats political-legal forces as part of the task environment, we recognize that they can be viewed as part of the general environment, depending on the situation and the perspective taken. For example, labor unions may be part of an organization's task or general environment. The United Auto Workers are part of the task environment for, and *directly* affect, Ford, General Motors, and Chrysler. (In turn, the management of these firms *directly* affects the United Auto Workers.) But unions are not part of the task environment for nonunion firms such as IBM, Hewlett-Packard, and Fred Brown Mazda/BMW. Unions *indirectly* affect them, however, as part of the general environment. Indirect effects might include successful union efforts to obtain legislation benefiting all workers, union and nonunion alike.

Managers must constantly evaluate the task environment as they diagnose issues and weigh decisions. The task environment has an important bearing on organizational planning, organizational structure, human resources management issues, and control decisions. But monitoring the complexities of the environmental forces shown in Figure 3.1 can be difficult for managers, because of their numerous day-to-day responsibilities. A number of organizations have special positions or departments—for example, marketing research, planning, public affairs, and purchasing—with primary responsibility for helping managers keep track of these environmental forces.

Types of Task Environments

Figure 3.3 provides a beginning framework for diagnosing and classifying the task environment. This framework classifies an organization's task environment on two dimensions—simple-complex and stable-changing.

The *simple-complex dimension* refers to whether the factors in the task environment are few and similar to one another or numerous and different. A construction firm that builds standardized residential housing would have a relatively simple environment. In contrast, a firm that builds customized homes, office buildings, and shopping centers is likely to face a more complex environment.

The *stable-changing dimension* refers to whether the factors in the task environment remain the same or vary over time. For decades AT&T could count on the Federal Communications Commission (FCC) for well-defined and stable regulations that gave AT&T a virtual monopoly in interstate telephone services. After the FCC deregulated some service areas, AT&T was faced with new competitors, such as MCI and Sprint. A manager who applied the grid shown in Figure 3.3 to such a situation would probably diagnose a need for significant changes in AT&T's organizational structure and marketing practices.

Four basic types of task environments—simple/stable, simple/changing, complex/stable, and complex/changing—are derived from classifying a firm's environmental factors along the simple-complex and stable-changing dimensions. An example of an organization facing a simple/stable environment is a local soft drink distributor. Soft drink distributors may have many customers, but the services they provide are typically quite standardized—primarily delivering the right number of bottles and cans to each customer.

Basic Types of Task Environments

All task environments are definitely not the same. One way of diagnosing an organization's environmental situation is positioning it on a grid of simple-complex and stable-changing dimensions.

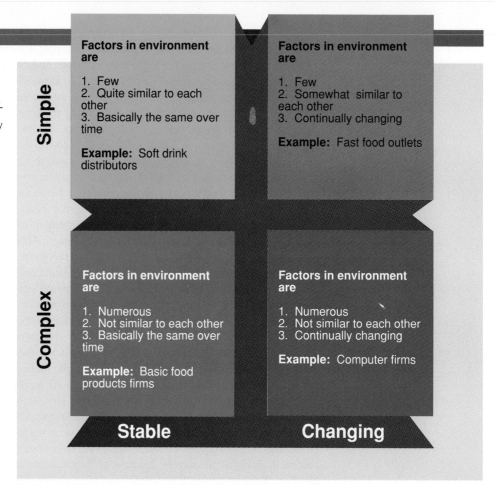

Simple

Factors in environment are

1. Few
2. Quite similar to each other
3. Basically the same over time

Example: Soft drink distributors

Factors in environment are

1. Few
2. Somewhat similar to each other
3. Continually changing

Example: Fast food outlets

Complex

Factors in environment are

1. Numerous
2. Not similar to each other
3. Basically the same over time

Example: Basic food products firms

Factors in environment are

1. Numerous
2. Not similar to each other
3. Continually changing

Example: Computer firms

Stable   **Changing**

Source: Adapted from R. Duncan, ''What Is the Right Organization Structure: Decision Tree Analysis Provides the Answer,'' *Organizational Dynamics,* Winter 1979, p. 63.

Most soft drink distributors deal with only a couple of national firms, such as Pepsi and Coca-Cola. They distribute the types of soft drinks Pepsi or Coke provides, and the franchiser (Pepsi or Coke) undertakes most of the marketing efforts. Thus the task environment is relatively simple and stable over time for such distributors.

The simple/changing and complex/stable environments fall between the two extremes. Local fast-food outlets, such as McDonald's and Burger King, seem to exist in a simple/changing environment. They offer limited menus and have standardized and simple procedures for preparing and serving the food. Their customers don't expect and can't receive much personal treatment. However, the menus, restaurant decor, and marketing tactics are constantly being tinkered with to adjust to changes in consumer preferences and to keep up with competition. On the other hand, Heinz, Campbell's, and other basic food products firms seem to operate in a complex/stable environment. For example, the basic line of Campbell's soups—chicken noodle, tomato, and cream of mushroom—hasn't changed for decades. However, the production and distribution processes for getting these soups onto grocery shelves are quite complex. To carry them out successfully, many suppliers, customers, and governmental regulations must be managed.

Not surprisingly, organizations in a simple/stable environment face the least amount of uncertainty, and those in a complex/changing environment face the most. **Environmental uncertainty** refers to the ambiguity and unpredictability of some external factors.[20] Organizations such as computer manufacturers (lower right-hand corner of Figure 3.3) face a **turbulent environment,** one that is very complex, includes many forces that are constantly changing, and is both ambiguous and unpredictable for managers. In his book *Managing in Turbulent Times,* Peter Drucker concluded: ''Some time during the 1970s, the longest period of continuity in economic history came to an end. At some time during the last ten years, we moved into turbulence.''[21]

environmental uncertainty The element of risk due to the ambiguity or unpredictability of certain factors external to an organization (such as government regulation).

turbulent environment An external environment that is very complex, includes many forces that are constantly changing, and is both ambiguous and unpredictable.

Turbulent environments are not limited to large corporations. Consider the competitive, regulatory, and technological turbulence faced by physicians who run their own practices. Their task environment has changed rapidly and become very complex over the past ten years, as described in the following Insight.

I N S I G H T

Two environmental forces have created a major threat to physicians who have their own practices. These are the persistent pressure of the federal government and private employers to control the growth of medical expenditures and the rapidly increasing growth in the number of new physicians.

Uncertainty and change arise as the relatively powerless physicians are forced to agree to whatever fee constraints are associated with federal and state cost-reduction programs and laws. Agreeing to each new constraint is preferable, after all, to the possible loss of patients and income if doctors didn't comply. Along with government's establishment of fee schedules, third-party payers such as Blue Cross have created added financial pressures. Before 1980 third-party payers were supportive of physicians; physicians were ''partners'' in establishing the fees for services provided. But that's no longer the case. Today insurance companies' reimbursement programs often reward physicians for keeping patient services and expenses below target levels. Physicians may be financially penalized for exceeding those limits by an insurer's refusal to reimburse for services actually provided. In some instances a physician's acceptance of a third-party payer's terms is necessary for gaining access to patients.

Competition is also increasing in physicians' task environment. Between 1960 and 1990 the number of physicians in the United States more than doubled, going from 259,000 to over 550,000. The U.S. population, however, hasn't increased proportionately. Competitive organizations providing health care are also proliferating. There are now health maintenance organizations (HMOs), independent practice associations (IPAs), competitive bidding, ambulatory care centers, outpatient clinics, and large group practices.

The turbulence in the physicians' environment is compounded by a reduction in total patient visits (both at offices and during hospital rounds), an increase in the number of group practices, and a decline in real income for physicians in small practices. Also, there has been explosive growth and change in the technology affecting the provision of health care (new drugs, new diagnostic procedures, new specialties, and new cures). And, if all of this weren't enough, the constant threat of lawsuits and liability claims from clients (customers) has skyrocketed. Clearly the task environment of physicians in small practices is turbulent.[22]

A CLOSER LOOK AT THE TASK ENVIRONMENT

The remainder of this chapter addresses the three major forces in the task environment that organizations must monitor, diagnose, and manage on a continuing basis. We begin in the innermost ring of Figure 3.1 and move outward—from competitive forces to technological forces to political-legal forces. In the next chapter we address competitive, political, and cultural forces from an international perspective. Competitive forces are closest to management in Figure 3.1 because they have the greatest day-to-day impact on organizations. Most middle-level and top managers (as well as professionals such as market researchers, planning analysts, purchasing agents, and sales representatives) spend considerable time and energy monitoring, diagnosing, and figuring out how to deal with competitive forces.

Competitive Forces

Organizations in any industry are directly affected by at least five competitive forces: competitors, new entrants, substitute goods and services, customers, and suppliers. The combined strength of these forces affects the long-term profitability of firms in any industry.[23] Managers must therefore monitor and diagnose each of these as well as their combined strength before making decisions about future courses of action.

Competitors Aside from customers, competitors are the single most important day-to-day force facing managers and other employees of an organization. Bruce D. Henderson, founder and chairman of the Boston Consulting Group, comments:

> For virtually all competitors their critical environment constraint is their actions in relation to competitors. Therefore any change in the environment that affects any competitor will have consequences that require some degree of adaptation. This requires continual change and adaptation by all competitors merely to maintain relative position.[24]

Rivalry among competitors produces strategies such as price cutting, advertising promotions, enhanced customer service or warranties, and improvements in product or service quality. Competitors use these strategies to try to improve their relative positions in an industry or to respond to actions by others. For example, when one firm cuts prices, other firms often quickly follow. All may end up worse off, because lower profits or even losses may result. On the other hand, advertising may increase demand for a product and an industry as a whole, leaving all firms better off.

The Global Link describes new levels of competitive rivalry being experienced by European airlines. The deregulation and resulting increased competitiveness of U.S. airlines is being felt around the world.

New Entrants The threat or reality of increased competition within an industry depends on the relative difficulty with which new firms begin to compete with established firms. In an industry with low barriers to entry, such as the fast food industry, competition will be fierce. The airline industry is a particularly interesting case because it has had both high and low barriers to entry over the past ten years. Economies of scale, product differentiation, capital requirements, and government regulation are four common factors that need to be diagnosed in assessing barriers to entry. Let's see how they have affected airline competition.

economy of scale The decrease in per-unit costs as the volume of goods and/or services produced increases.

Economies of scale refer to decreases in per-unit costs as the volume of goods and services produced by a firm increases. The potential for economies of scale in the airline industry is substantial. For example, an airline cannot fill all available space in a McDonnell-Douglas DC-10 with passengers; the bottom portion of the plane would contain an enormous amount of empty space, even if all the passengers were to bring extra baggage. Most costs associated with flying a DC-10 from Dallas to Honolulu are the same, whether this space is filled with revenue-generating cargo or left empty. By carrying both passengers and freight, American Airlines takes advantage of the economies of scale made possible by the DC-10.

product differentiation Something unique in terms of quality, price, design, brand image, or customer service that gives a product an edge over the competition.

Product differentiation is the creation of something unique in terms of quality, price, design, brand image, or customer service to give one firm's product an edge over another firm's. Its frequent-flyer program is one way American Airlines tried to

GLOBAL Link

WORLDWIDE AIRLINE COMPETITION

Swift changes are sweeping over—and shaking up—the world's fifty biggest passenger airlines. U.S. megacarriers, turned loose by deregulation more than a decade ago, are spreading their wings across the oceans and encouraging worldwide industry changes. The Europeans are responding to the challenge, and the Asians are gaining ground rapidly.

Not long ago Europe's carriers divided up the routes in the home territory among themselves. They set high prices and split the profits. The European Community is pushing toward its own deregulation in 1992, and already the industry has vastly changed. British Airways has been rejuvenated. New airlines have joined the battle for customers. European airlines have had to learn how to compete in pricing and service, in an environment where efficiency and safety are mandatory.

To increase efficiency, European carriers, including British Airways, Lufthansa, and Air France, have signed up with two new computer reservation systems that provide flight schedules to travel agents. One is linked to United Airlines' Apollo system, the other to Texas Air's System One. Believing that only the strongest will survive, many airlines have placed orders for costly new planes and are planning to increase marketing budgets. Smaller carriers are looking for allies: Belgium's Sabena is planning to sell shares to British Airways and KLM, and Swissair and SAS are forming a partnership and buying each other's shares. Even heavyweights such as Air France and Lufthansa are signing agreements to sell their services jointly in Europe and around the world. Freer and stiffer competition is clearly in the air for most of the world's airlines.

Source: Developed from W. Woods, "Revolution in the Air," *Fortune,* January 1, 1990, 49–58; C. Power, "Off We Go into the Hazy Blue Yonder," *Business Week,* September 18, 1989, 26–28; W. Woods, "Taking Off Overseas," *Fortune,* September 24, 1990, 52–53.

L. L. Bean, a leading direct-mail firm that sells sporting equipment and clothes, reflects the importance of customer power in its statement of beliefs about customers.

WHAT IS A CUSTOMER?

A CUSTOMER IS THE MOST IMPORTANT PERSON EVER IN THIS COMPANY - IN PERSON OR BY MAIL.

A CUSTOMER IS NOT DEPENDENT ON US, WE ARE DEPENDENT ON HIM.

A CUSTOMER IS NOT AN INTERRUPTION OF OUR WORK, HE IS THE PURPOSE OF IT.

WE ARE NOT DOING A FAVOR BY SERVING HIM, HE IS DOING US A FAVOR BY GIVING US THE OPPORTUNITY TO DO SO.

A CUSTOMER IS NOT SOMEONE TO ARGUE OR MATCH WITS WITH. NOBODY EVER WON AN ARGUMENT WITH A CUSTOMER.

A CUSTOMER IS A PERSON WHO BRINGS US HIS WANTS. IT IS OUR JOB TO HANDLE THEM PROFITABLY TO HIM AND TO OURSELVES.

L. L. BEAN, INC.
FREEPORT, MAINE

Source: L. L. Bean Annual Report, 1989.

differentiate its service. Members qualify for free tickets after flying a certain number of miles and in addition receive hotel and car rental discounts and other travel benefits.

Capital requirements are the dollars needed to finance equipment, supplies, advertising, research and development, and the like. The capital requirements for starting a major long-haul airline run to tens of millions of dollars. The cost of opening an exercise studio (with no special equipment) might be $50,000 or less.

Government regulation is a barrier to entry if it bars or severely restricts potential new entrants to an industry. Prior to deregulation of the airline industry in 1978, the interstate airlines made up a cartel administered by the Civil Aeronautics Board (CAB), which set fares and controlled routes. From 1945 to 1975 the air-carrier industry grew three times faster than the economy in general, yet no new trunk carriers entered the industry nor did any existing carriers file for bankruptcy.[25] After deregulation fourteen new nonunion airlines emerged. These new airlines—with their lower labor, maintenance, and capital costs—immediately began to compete with the eleven established trunk airlines (such as American, TWA, and Delta) by cutting prices. The price wars and other forms of competition stimulated by deregulation were followed by a number of airline failures (Braniff) and mergers (People's Express and New York Air into Continental). With fewer domestic carriers, there have been calls from some politicians and consumer groups for reregulation of the airlines.[26]

Substitute Goods and Services In a general sense, all organizations compete with other organizations that are producing **substitute goods or services,** goods or services that can easily replace theirs. For example, the introduction of desktop publishing systems by IBM, Apple, and others has enabled companies to use their personal computers to produce brochures, catalogs, timetables, and the like. Desktop printing systems thus substitute for the services of printing firms at a fraction of their cost. Many organizations, such as Westinghouse, Xerox, and the U.S. State Depart-

substitute good or service
A good or service that can easily replace another.

ment, commonly use electronic mail as a substitute for interoffice memos or the U.S. Postal Service. Electronic surveillance systems have drastically reduced the need for people to personally check all parts of a plant and its surroundings. Electronic systems thus substitute for security guards.

Customers Customers for goods or services naturally try to force down prices, obtain more or higher-quality products (while holding price constant), and increase competition among sellers by playing one against the other. Customers' bargaining power is likely to be relatively great under the following circumstances:

▶ *The customer purchases a large volume relative to the supplier's total sales.* Sears, Kmart, and Wal-Mart have clout because their large-volume purchases account for a sizable percentage of some suppliers' total sales.

▶ *The product or service represents a significant expenditure by the customer.* Customers are generally motivated to cut a cost that constitutes a large portion of their total costs. An individual will spend much more time and effort to obtain a rock-bottom price on a new car than on a car wash, a cheeseburger, or a paperback book.

▶ *Customers pose a realistic threat of backward integration.* **Backward integration** is the purchase of one or more of its suppliers by a larger organization as a cost-cutting strategy. General Motors and Ford have used the threat of manufacturing their own parts or acquiring the companies that do as a way to get lower prices and better quality from suppliers.

▶ *Customers have readily available alternatives for the same services or products.* For example, a consumer may not have a strong preference between Wendy's and Mc-Donald's, a Ford truck and a Chevrolet truck, or Visa and American Express.

Auto service customers can choose from among a host of firms that service cars, including MasterCare, Goodyear, Jiffy Lube, PepBoys, and Sears. Customer power is reflected in changes introduced by MasterCare auto service centers in 1990.

backward integration The purchase of one or more of its suppliers by a larger organization as a cost-cutting strategy.

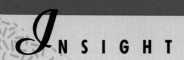

MASTERCARE

𝓘 **N S I G H T**

Recently MasterCare auto service centers, the $1-billion-a-year chain owned by Bridgestone/Firestone, started linking employees' pay to customer retention at outlets in Columbus, Ohio, and Memphis, Tennessee. Surveys of 4000 car owners in these cities showed that they despised MasterCare's high-pressure sales tactics. Says senior vice-president John Rooney: "We purported to be the premium provider of auto services in the United States, but we failed. We found we were rude, that mechanics left grease on car seats, and all sorts of things that irritated customers."

Customers told the company that honest, courteous service is twice as important to them as the price of a repair job. So now each month Rooney has an outside firm randomly poll fifty customers from each store, asking them whether they received good service and plan to return to MasterCare. Employees who keep customers loyal get bonuses equal to about 10 percent of their salaries. Even the mechanics' pay depends on the survey scores. Says Rooney: "It's not just the smoothness of the salesman that's important. It's also the quality of the work." MasterCare centers using the new pay system have raised customer retention 25 percent and lowered employee turnover about 40 percent. The latter is vital given the nationwide shortage of mechanics.[27]

Suppliers The bargaining power of suppliers often depends on how much they can raise prices above their costs or reduce the quality of goods and services they provide to organizations before losing them as customers. However, Boeing dominates the commercial aircraft business, with 54 percent of the world market, because of its reputation for quality, not because of low prices. Its supplier power comes primarily from technological leadership, high quality, and excellent service. Of course, Boeing's prices are probably lower than they would be if it didn't face competition from two major rivals: Airbus Industrie and McDonnell-Douglas Corporation.[28]

Not all suppliers or customers will have equal power.[29] For example, Boeing, in its role as customer, now combines orders for similar parts for various jet models to get prices from suppliers that are more competitive than those given when it bought the items separately. In its role as supplier, Boeing used to have to fill 600 or more requests from commercial airline customers for alterations to basic specifications. Now that is has an established reputation, its bargaining power with airlines is considerably greater, and customers have less of a free hand in designing their planes. As an accommodation, Boeing has a catalog from which customers can select some option packages.[30]

Copyrights and patents generally serve to increase supplier power over defined periods of time. The prices of movie tickets and videos of popular films are higher than they might otherwise be because of copyright protection. This protection prevents suppliers from copying and distributing a film or video without permission and payment of a royalty. In general, high supplier power under free and open markets tends to be short-lived, as is demonstrated by the personal computer industry.

Interconnecting Elements of a Usable Technology

Usable technologies involve complex interdependencies among various types of hardware, software, and brainware. These interdependencies are especially pronounced in today's fast-changing information technology.

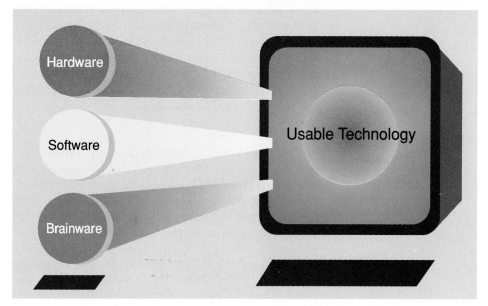

Technological Forces

technology The knowledge, tools, techniques, and actions used to transform materials, information, and other inputs into finished goods or services.

In Chapter 2 we defined the transformation process as the technology that changes organizational inputs into outputs. Technology isn't simply machines, of course. **Technology** is the knowledge, tools, techniques, and actions used to transform materials, information, and other inputs into finished goods and services.[32] A technology can be as simple as making coffee or as complicated as American Airlines' computer-based SABRE reservation system.

As suggested in Figure 3.4, usable technologies include three elements: hardware, software, and brainware. **Hardware** is the physical/logical means (machines, equipment) for carrying out tasks to achieve objectives. Hardware refers not only to the physical components, but to their logical layout as well. **Software** is the collection of rules, guidelines, and algorithms necessary for using the hardware properly—the know-how to carry out tasks to achieve objectives. **Brainware** is the objectives, the application, and the justification of hardware/software deployment—the know-what and know-why, what technology to employ, when, and why.

hardware The physical components and their logical layout that are the means for carrying out a task to achieve an objective.

Let's consider how these three elements of technology are represented in the automobile. An automobile has clearly identifiable hardware: a particular physical arrangement of parts that distinguishes it from, say, a motorcycle. It's supported by other hardware, such as roads, bridges, traffic signals, and auto facilities. An automobile's software consists of rules and guidelines covering its operation under different conditions, including driver's training manuals, owner's manuals, maintenance schedules, road maps, and rules and laws of driving conduct. Finally, an automobile's brainware consists of decisions on where to go, which route to take, and when and why to go there—decisions that can come only from human knowledge and objectives. This brainware is supported by other brainware: police, engineers who design new roads, policy makers who decide which roads to repair or build, specialists who repair the autos, and so on. One cannot define the automobile as a technology without referring to all three elements at the same time.[33]

software The collection of rules, guidelines, and algorithms necessary for using particular hardware properly.

brainware The objectives, the application, and the justification of hardware/software deployment, or what to employ, when, and why.

Impact of Technology Technological forces play an increasingly central role in creating and changing an organization's task environment. Technological change eliminates the present and helps to create the future. New technologies force organizations to reconsider their purposes and methods of operation or face extinction.[34]

The United States and several other industrial societies have become information societies. This shift was made possible by the explosion in computer-based and other information technologies. One example is the personal computer and its integration with mainframe computers and telecommunications systems to form supernets. Through them, firms can collect, process, and transmit vast amounts of data quickly and economically. For instance, Kodak now supplies photographic dealers with a microcomputer and software system that enables the dealers to order Kodak products directly, rather than through wholesalers.[35] The management of information technology is woven into various chapters, and all of Chapter 19 is devoted to this critical topic.

Role in Strategy Computer-based information technologies are now central to most organizations, which is one reason we include technological forces as part of the task environment. Inadequate information technologies can be a major factor in limiting strategic options. For example, a computer services supplier was delayed in responding to a competitor's price "unbundling" (meaning that the competitor began to price each service feature independently) because of limitations in its billing and accounting systems. A large office equipment company couldn't switch over from its time-consuming practice of special bids to a streamlined menu of standard contracts because of design limitations in its central order-processing system. A brokerage company couldn't satisfy its clients' repeated requests for an integrated picture of their holdings because the information from its equity, bond, and commodity account management systems couldn't be easily combined. Finally, because of weaknesses in its inventory management systems, a major communications company couldn't match its physical inventory with the responsible organizational units. As a result, management had great difficulty bringing inventory costs under control.[36]

On the positive side, information technology creates strategic options simply not feasible with older technologies:

▶ Computer-aided design linked to versatile, computer-controlled machines permits short production runs of custom designs with economies of scale approaching those of traditional large-scale manufacturing facilities.

▶ Consumers can comparison shop via home computers and "electronic shopping malls" more easily than using the Yellow Pages and telephones.

▶ Through on-line, real-time cash management systems, managers can determine profit and loss on a daily basis. This was impossible with manual methods and earlier stages of computer technology.

▶ Retail banking customers can perform a vast number of banking functions from remote locations, including shopping centers, apartment building lobbies, corporate offices, out-of-state banks, and their homes, using personal computers or ATMs.[37]

Political-Legal Forces

Societies often resolve conflicts over values and beliefs through their legal and political systems. For instance, in the United States and Canada the concepts of individual freedom, freedom of the press, property rights, and free enterprise are widely accepted. But these countries' legislative bodies, regulatory agencies, interest groups, and courts operate—often in conflict with one another—to define and influence the day-to-day interpretation of these values.

Many political and legal forces directly influence the way organizations operate. Changes in political forces have been especially significant over the past twenty-five years. Political changes will continue to affect organizations in the 1990s. In order to achieve organizational objectives, managers must diagnose these forces and come up with useful ways to anticipate, respond to, or avoid the environmental disturbances they cause.

For many organizations, such as telephone companies, banks, and public utilities, government regulation is a central component of the task environment. Consider how two

FIGURE 3.5

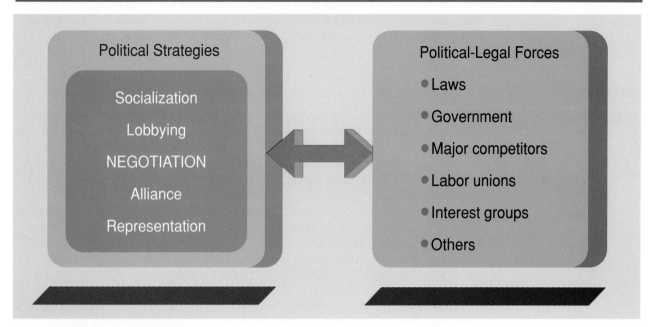

Managerial Political Strategies

Managers use five major political strategies in various combinations to meet the challenges posed by the political-legal forces in their environments. These forces in turn affect the choice of strategies.

of the five federal credit laws affect credit customers and creditors each time they do business in the United States:

The Equal Credit Opportunity Act entitles the customer to be considered for credit without regard to race, color, age, sex, or marital status. Although the act does not guarantee the customer will get credit, it does ensure that the credit grantor applies tests of credit-worthiness fairly and impartially.

The Truth in Lending Act says that credit grantors must reveal the "true" cost of using credit—for instance, the annual interest rate the customer will be paying. In the case of a revolving charge account, the customer must also be told the monthly interest rate and the minimum monthly payment.

Political-legal forces operating on an organization extend beyond laws and government institutions. They include the entire complex of task environment components—individuals, groups, and institutions—with the power to influence the organization's survival and growth: major competitors, major customers, shareholders, labor unions, consumer groups, minority groups, environmental groups, and foreign governments.[38] All of these elements can directly influence and be influenced by managers' decisions.

Managers use five major political strategies to cope with the political factors operating in their environments. Figure 3.5 identifies these five strategies: negotiation, lobbying, alliance, representation, and socialization. These strategies are not mutually exclusive. They are usually used in some combination, and each strategy often contains elements of the others. Negotiation, probably the most important political strategy, is shown at the center of the left-hand side of Figure 3.5. It affects the other four strategies, because each contains some degree of negotiation.

negotiation The process by which two or more individuals or groups having common and conflicting interests or objectives present and discuss proposals in an attempt to reach an agreement.

Negotiation Arriving at an agreement between two or more parties about the exchange of goods or services or about expected behaviors involves negotiation. **Negotiation** is the process by which two or more individuals or groups having both common and conflicting objectives present and discuss proposals in an attempt to reach an agreement.[39] Negotiation can take place only when the two parties believe that some form of agreement is both possible and mutually beneficial. The negotiation process can be time-consuming and complex, as the following Insight shows.

Paul Ravesies, retired president of ARCO International Oil and Gas Company, reviews his experience in negotiating with officials of the People's Republic of China:

A fundamental characteristic of Chinese negotiating is the effort to identify a sympathetic counterpart in the foreign team and cultivate a personal relationship. The purpose is to generate a sense of "friendship" with the intention of manipulating feelings of goodwill, obligation, guilt, or dependence to achieve the negotiating objective. "Friendship" to the Chinese way of thinking implies the obligation to provide support and assistance to one's "friends."

The Chinese view negotiations as an effort to reconcile the principles and objectives of the two sides and to test the foreign team's commitment to a relationship with the People's Republic of China. They do *not* see negotiation as a highly technical, impersonal process of haggling over details, in which the two sides initially take maximum positions and then seek to move to a point of convergence through incremental compromise.

Chinese officials are skilled at having long discussions that explore the limits of your views and flexibility. They resist exposing their own position until your stand is fully known and your patience has been well-tested. On the other hand, the Chinese are most gracious hosts. They often try to develop a positive atmosphere for talks through meticulously orchestrating hospitality, banquets, sightseeing, press conferences, plays, toasts, and courtesy meetings with very senior officials.

They may seek to minimize confrontation through subtle and indirect presentation of their position. When they seek to prevent the breakdown of a negotiating session, they may resort to stalling tactics or reach a partial agreement while reserving their position on important issues where they do not want to compromise.[40]

lobbying An attempt to influence government decisions by providing relevant officials with information on the anticipated effects of legislation or regulatory rulings.

Lobbying **Lobbying** is an attempt to influence government decisions by providing officials with information on the anticipated effects of legislation or regulatory rulings. The U.S. Congress and regulatory agencies such as the Securities and Exchange Commission (SEC), the Federal Communications Commission (FCC), and the Interstate Commerce Commission (ICC) are the targets of continual lobbying efforts by organizations affected by their decisions.[41] Organizations whose stability, survival, and growth are directly influenced by government decisions typically use their top managers to lobby for them. Anthony Frank personally lobbies Congress on legislation intended to influence the U.S. Postal Service. Of course, major users of the U.S. Postal Service also lobby Anthony Frank and Congress to obtain more favorable postal regulations or to ward off proposed unfavorable changes.

Only the largest organizations—for example, American Airlines, NBC, AT&T, and Exxon—can afford to lobby on their own behalf. The most common form of lobbying is by associations representing the interests of a group of individuals or organizations.[42] Approximately 4000 national lobbying organizations maintain staffs in Washington, D.C. An additional 75,000 state and local associations and organizations occasionally lobby Washington's decision makers. Two of the largest associations representing business interests are the National Chamber of Commerce, with about 36,000 business and organizational members, and the National Association of Manufacturers, with about 16,000 member corporations.[43] The American Association of Retired Persons (AARP), with over 30 million members, is the largest U.S. association representing individual interests. AARP has a paid staff of 1300, with headquarters in the heart of the nation's capital. The AARP lobbies on behalf of U.S. citizens aged 50 and over.[44]

alliance The uniting of two or more organizations, groups, or individuals to achieve common objectives with respect to a particular issue.

Alliances An **alliance** is a unified effort involving two or more organizations, groups, or individuals to achieve common objectives on a particular issue.[45] Alliances typically form around issues of economic self-interest, especially those created to influence government actions.[46] Economic issues that motivate the formation of alliances include government policy (for example, the control of raw materials or taxes), foreign relations (for example, the control of foreign sales or investment in overseas plants), and labor relations (for example, the control of salaries and benefits paid industrywide, such as within the construction industry or the National Football League). The alliance strategy is often used to:

▶ Oppose or support legislation, nomination of heads of regulatory agencies, and regulations issued by such agencies.

▶ Improve competitiveness of two or more organizations through collaboration. Corning Glass uses its twenty-three joint ventures with such foreign partners as Siemens (Germany), Samsung (Korea), Asahi Chemical (Japan), and Giba-Geigy (Switzerland) to penetrate and thrive in a growing number of related high-technology markets.[47]

▶ Promote particular products or services, such as oranges, computers, and electricity. For example, the Edison Electric Institute promotes both the use and conservation of electrical energy.

▶ Construct facilities beyond the resources of any one organization, such as nuclear power plants.

▶ Represent the interests of specific groups, such as women, the elderly, minorities, and particular industries.

An alliance both broadens and limits managerial power. When an alliance makes it possible to attain objectives that a single individual or organization would be unable to attain, it broadens managerial power. When an alliance requires a commitment to making certain decisions jointly in the future, it limits managerial power. Members of OPEC periodically negotiate the price to be charged for oil. These agreements are intended to broaden OPEC's power by generating more revenue for its members. However, to be successful in this endeavor OPEC must also limit the amount of oil that each country is allowed to produce.

A *joint venture,* which typically involves two or more firms becoming partners to form a separate entity, is a common example of a strategic alliance. The partners get from one another some competence that allows them to move more quickly toward their objectives. For example, CBS formed a number of joint ventures in the 1980s: with IBM and Sears to develop and market videotex, an electronic information system; with Twentieth Century–Fox to develop videotapes; and with Columbia Pictures (Coca-Cola) and Home Box Office (Time, Inc.) to develop motion pictures. Digital Equipment Corporation (DEC) strengthened itself in the manufacturing automation market by developing an alliance with Allen-Bradley, an industrial controls company.[48]

representation Membership in an outside organization for the purpose of furthering the interests of the member's organization.

Representation **Representation** refers to membership in an outside organization, intended to serve the interests of the member's organization or group. Representation strategy is often subtle and indirect. School administrators, for example, often receive paid time off and the use of school resources to participate in voluntary community associations that might support the school system, such as the PTA, Chamber of Commerce, Elks, Kiwanis, Moose, Rotary, and United Way. A more direct form of representation, often based on some legal requirement, occurs when a specific group selects representatives to give it a voice in an organization's decisions. Union members elect officers to represent them to management.

Corporate boards of directors, the top-level policy approval groups of firms, are elected by shareholders and are legally required to represent their interests. The National Association of Corporate Directors, however, suggest a much broader representation role for board members. Board members should also ensure that:

> Long-term strategic objectives and plans are established and that proper management structure (organization, systems, and people) is in place to achieve these objectives, while at the same time making sure that the structure functions to maintain the corporation's integrity, reputation, and responsibility to its various constituencies.[49]

The board's responsibility to monitor and control the actions of the chief executive officer and other top officers is particularly essential to its representing the interests of shareholders and other groups.[50]

socialization The process by which people learn the beliefs and values held by an organization (or the broader society).

Socialization **Socialization** is the process by which people come to believe in the values held by an organization or the broader society. The assumption is that people who accept and act in accordance with these basic values are less likely to sympathize with positions that threaten the organization or the political system. The so-called American business creed stresses the idea that a decentralized, privately owned, free, and competitive system in which price is the major regulatory or control system should be continued; citizens should oppose government actions interfering with or threatening this system. Most U.S. and Canadian businesspeople subscribe to these beliefs and act on them.

Socialization includes formal and informal attempts by organizations to mold new employees, so they will accept certain desired attitudes and ways of dealing with others and their jobs. At its headquarters in Armonk, New York, IBM each year reintroduces thousands of its managers to the company's values and philosophy. Xerox uses its training facility in Leesburg, Virginia to influence the attitudes of new managers. Of course, top management's attempts can be either offset or reinforced by the expectations of and pressures exerted by fellow workers or other groups.

All of the political strategies we've reviewed are subject to cultural forces. In the United States and Canada the relative importance placed on individualism limits the extent to which organizations can use the socialization strategy. Too much or what may be seen as the "wrong kind" of socialization is likely to be met with resistance and charges of invasion of privacy or violation of individual rights.

The overriding purpose of this chapter is to help you develop your diagnostic and monitoring skills with respect to the external environment. We have discussed and given examples of the various reactive and proactive approaches managers and other employees can use in coping with general environmental forces (such as culture) and task environmental forces (competition, technology, and political-legal forces). Environmental forces create both opportunities and threats and will challenge all of the skills and competencies you acquire.

CHAPTER SUMMARY

1. The general environment includes those external factors that usually affect all or most organizations in the economy, either directly or indirectly. It includes such broad factors as type of economic system and current economic conditions, type of political system, natural resources, demographics of the population, and cultural forces. Cultural forces, primarily working through value systems, shape the viewpoints and decision-making processes of managers and other employees. Hofstede's work-related value framework has four dimensions: power distance, uncertainty avoidance, individualism, and masculinity.

2. The task environment includes all those external factors and groups—customers, competitors, technology, regulatory agencies, laws, and so forth—that *directly* influence an organization's growth, success, and survival. Environmental forces are increasingly turbulent and global in scope, requiring managers and other employees to constantly monitor and diagnose the type of task environment they are facing.

3. Managers and other employees must assess and act on the effects of five competitive forces in the task environment: competitors, new entrants, substitute goods and services, customers, and suppliers.

   ▶ Organizations must compete successfully with their rivals in terms of price, quality, and customer satisfaction—or fail.

   ▶ New entrants into a market have to overcome the barriers of economies of scale, product differentiation, capital requirements, and government regulation in order to begin competing successfully.

   ▶ Organizations have to compete with those producing substitute goods and services, for instance movie theaters' competing with rental videos.

   ▶ In a free enterprise system customer power ultimately reigns and determines the effectiveness or ineffectiveness of managerial decisions and actions.

   ▶ Supplier power ultimately depends on providing high quality and service at a reasonable cost.

4. Technological forces in the task environment refer to the rapid changes in the specific knowledge, tools, and techniques used to transform materials, information, and other inputs into particular goods or services. Usable technologies include three interconnecting elements: hardware, software, and brainware.

5. Political-legal forces, which used to be in the background, now often directly influence the way organizations operate. Five political strategies managers use in coping with political-legal forces in the task environment are negotiation, lobbying, alliances, representation, and socialization.

   ▶ Managers often negotiate to obtain agreement on a policy, procedure, or contract when there is no agreement initially.

   ▶ Top management and associations regularly lobby legislatures and regulatory agencies to obtain preferential treatment or to minimize the negative impact of some action.

   ▶ Managers form alliances, bringing together organizations and groups having common interests in order to achieve certain objectives they could not have achieved individually.

   ▶ Managers often become active in associations outside the organization to represent the organization's interest and to project a positive image.

   ▶ Socialization can be indirect, such as building support among the general public for the free enterprise system and reduced government involvement, or direct, such as molding the attitudes of employees so they see and do things the organization's way.

QUESTIONS FOR DISCUSSION AND APPLICATION

1. What are some of the problems that U.S. women and minorities will face in their first managerial jobs? Would these problems be the same in other countries? Explain.

2. **From Where You Sit:** How would you describe your values in terms of Hofstede's four value dimensions? (The following Skill-Building Exercise should be helpful in assessing your value orientations.)

3. How and where do general and task environments overlap?

4. **From Where You Sit:** Referring to Figure 3.3, how would you diagnose and classify the task environment of your university or college as a whole? What factors need to be considered in making this diagnosis?

5. **From Where You Sit:** In what ways could it be fun for you to work for organizations in unregulated markets?

6. **From Where You Sit:** How would you assess the five basic competitive forces that affect one of the automobile dealerships near your residence? The hospital closest to you?

7. What technological forces are operating to fundamentally change industrial societies?

8. **From Where You Sit:** Identify three technological developments that are likely to affect the job you will have five years from now. Explain.

9. Which of the five political strategies have the greatest potential for leading to unethical behaviors? Why?

10. Should business groups (such as the Business Roundtable, the U.S. Chamber of Commerce, and the National Association of Manufacturers) be allowed to lobby before Congress or regulatory agencies? Explain.

11. **From Where You Sit:** How would you react to formal organizational socialization like IBM's? Does that tell you anything about the type of organization you would prefer?

12. **From Where You Sit:** Reread the Manager's Viewpoint feature at the beginning of this chapter. How are you a part of the U.S. Postal Service's general and task environments?

Values Survey

Instructions: Please indicate the degree to which you agree or disagree with each statement in the survey. Indicate your response by placing one of the numbers (1 through 5) in the blank at the beginning of the statement. Use the following scale.

1	2	3	4	5
Strongly Disagree	Disagree	Neither Agree nor Disagree	Agree	Strongly Agree

1. A person's behavior is controlled by an "I" consciousness.

2. One's involvement with organizations is not based on moral principles or purposes.

3. Identity is based in the individual.

4. Only those who depend on themselves get ahead in life.

5. One should live one's life independent of others as much as possible.

6. Survival of the group is not very important in an organization.

7. Superiors are different from me.

8. People should not be expected to spend their free time working on community projects.

9. Powerful people should try to look as powerful as possible.

10. Working with a group is less desirable than working alone.

11. People at higher power levels feel more threatened and less prepared to trust people.

12. It is undesirable to have a job where all work together and one doesn't get individual credit.

13. The use of power should be subject only to judgments of strong and weak.

14. Other people are a potential threat to one's power and rarely can be trusted.

15. In the long run, the societies most likely to prosper are those that give individuals maximum freedom to pursue their own personal ends rather than those that stress the obligations of individuals to work for the good of society.

16. Subordinates think superiors are different from themselves.

17. The independent spirit—rejecting all aid, needing no one, self-reliant, and free—is human nature at its best.

18. Powerful people should try to look more powerful than they are.

19. The use of power in organizations should not be subject to judgments of moral and immoral.

20. ☐ In learning course materials, it is more efficient to study by oneself than to work with other students.

21. ☐ The use of power in organizations should not be subject to judgments between good and evil.

22. ☐ If I were to work in a factory, I would rather do something entirely on my own than be part of a work team.

23. ☐ Conflicts between individual and group interests should be resolved in favor of the individual.

24. ☐ Power is a basic fact of society that precedes issues of good or evil. Its legitimacy is irrelevant.

25. ☐ The uncertainty inherent in life is not easily accepted.

26. ☐ I am not willing to take many risks in life.

27. ☐ There is a need for many written rules and regulations.

28. ☐ I have a great concern with security in life.

29. ☐ There should be as many rules as necessary in order to reduce risks.

30. ☐ The uncertainty inherent in life is felt as a continuous threat that must be fought.

31. ☐ I expect to be rewarded according to my accomplishments, irrespective of what others in my work group do.

32. ☐ Favors I receive from others in my work group make it necessary to give favors in return.

Scoring and Interpretation

Add up the points for your responses to the statements indicated under each of the following three value categories.

Individualism. The extent to which individuals believe they should take care of themselves and their immediate families and the extent to which individuals believe they are masters of their own destiny. The opposite of individualism is collectivism. Add the points for your responses to statements 1, 3, 4, 5, 6, 8, 10, 12, 15, 17, 20, 22, 23, 31, and 32, and put your TOTAL here _____. Scores of 60 to 75 may suggest a high degree of individualism. Scores of 15 to 30 may suggest a high degree of collectivism.

Power Distance. The extent to which individuals accept the socially determined unequal distribution of power among individuals and institutions within a particular culture. Add the points for your responses to statements 2, 7, 9, 11, 13, 14, 16, 18, 19, 21, and 24, and put your TOTAL here _____. Scores of 44 to 55 may suggest a strong belief in the unequal distribution of power among individuals and institutions within a particular culture. In contrast, low power distance may be suggested by scores of 11 to 22.

Uncertainty Avoidance. The extent to which individuals feel threatened by ambiguous and risky situations as well as try to avoid or reduce such situations. Add the points for your responses to statements 25, 26, 27, 28, 29, and 30, and put your TOTAL here _____. Scores of 24 to 30 may suggest a strong belief in uncertainty avoidance (for instance, a desire to avoid risky situations). Scores of 6 to 12 may suggest low uncertainty avoidance (an acceptance and tolerance of risky situations).

TO: Management Students

FROM: Donald N. Frey, CEO and Chairman of the
             Board (ret.), Bell and Howell Company

SUBJECT: Reflections on the Future

The past four decades have been among the most eventful in the history of the United States, economically, politically, and technologically. The dominant position the United States occupied ten years after World War II has given way to a more complicated, more mulitcultural, more multipolar, more challenging environment.

Like Ulysses in Greek mythology, we cannot go backward to the way things were; we can only go forward. I have no doubt of our nation's ability to go forward successfully if we are determined to do so — or even of its ability to overcome the competitive burden imposed by the enormous federal budget deficits of recent years. Many U.S. companies have set admirable examples of how to compete in an increasingly global and technology-driven environment.

The years just ahead will likely determine whether it is the destiny of the United States to be a leader or a follower in the family of nations. To a remarkable and unprecedented extent, the dynamic interrelationship between business and technology will determine that destiny. And if U.S. business is not hamstrung by impatient investors who demand results now at the expense of long-term corporate growth and development, the future of our companies and of our country is bright indeed.

Question: After thinking about the implications of this memo, you sit down to draft a response on the five key steps Canadian and U.S. managers need to take to ensure that their organizations remain economic leaders within their global industries. What will you say?

Kodak Zooms In on Pro Photographers

By Joan E. Rigdon

Gil Ford has had some unexpected visitors at his door: service representatives from Eastman Kodak Co.

Mr. Ford, owner of a photo lab in Jackson, Miss., and president of the Professional Photographers of America, for years felt ignored by the photographic giant. But now, he says, Kodak service representatives are treating him like royalty. They even gave one of his employees Super Bowl tickets this year. "They realize that we spend a lot of money on their products," Mr. Ford says.

This close attention is part of a change of emphasis at Kodak. In the early '80s, the company watched as droves of professional photographers defected to innovative Fuji Photo Film Co. Now Kodak is spending millions to woo them back, and often succeeding.

Many professional photographers who defected complaining of limited product innovations and shoddy processing say Kodak has solved some technical problems while introducing new niche products. Moreover, the once-standoffish company is deluging them with phone calls, visits, even offers to bankroll certain documentary photography shoots.

Jacques Cochin, a Parisian fashion photographer, says, "Now we have better films, better sponsoring and better communication." He especially likes Kodak's new passport card, which gives him perks such as cut-rate overnight courier service.

The battle, however, is hardly over. Fuji is fighting back with new products. It recently rolled out Velvia, a bright color slide film especially effective for outdoor shooting. It's also offering a new developing paper for portraits and wedding pictures: the paper presents warmer colors and takes twice as long to fade as Kodak's competing paper.

The professional market, with $1.4 billion in annual sales, is only a small part of the total $11.3 billion photography market. But it's a prized segment that's often a trend setter and showplace for technological prowess. Some films targeted to the professional market are later marketed with success to amateurs. Fuji's Reala color negative film, which the company says captures colors the way the human eye does, was introduced to the pros in 1989, but has been selling well to amateurs since last summer.

Kodak still controls the bulk of the professional market, an estimated $1 billion. But about seven years ago, what had been a virtual monopoly for the company began to erode. Fuji made inroads starting in 1984 when it handed out free film to professional photographers shooting the Olympic Games, of which it was a sponsor.

Rising defections shook Kodak enough for the company to form a professional photography division during a 1985 restructuring.

Professionals say they quickly noticed a change. "It used to be the big yellow giant that didn't listen," says Clyde Mueller, photo editor at the Standard-Examiner newspaper in Ogden, Utah. "Now it does."

Indeed, feedback from professionals prompted new products, such as T-Max, a fast black-and-white film good for taking sharp pictures in dim light, and new film canisters that are easier to open.

Kodak's new emphasis on old-fashioned service may be helping the most.

1. How does Bruce Henderson's quote on competition (page xxx) relate to Kodak and Fuji?
2. List the steps Kodak took to meet Fuji's challenge.
3. What might Fuji do to keep Kodak from gaining ground?

MISSOURI BOOK SERVICES

In the 1970s Missouri Book Services (MBS), the owner of several college bookstores, decided to enter the used textbook business. Such firms buy and sell used books, primarily through campus bookstores. As a new entrant to the field, MBS had few books to sell and few employees available to help bookstores staff the year-end buy-backs during which books are repurchased from students. With few books and little clout with bookstores, MBS seemed destined to remain an also-ran in a sleepy industry. Instead, they have become a major player, using information technology (IT) to transform the used book business.

The college bookstore managers that MBS serves face a remarkably intensive information-processing burden each semester. They have to correlate book selections from faculty, place orders with publishers and used book companies, shelve books for the first day of school, sell them to the students, pay the publishers, and handle returns. At a medium-sized college this process may involve thousands of students and books, hundreds of faculty, titles, and courses, and dozens of publishers and used book companies. At the end of the semester the managers have to decide which books to buy back from students and at what prices. For these managers the consequences of errors are serious, the pace hectic, and the results spotty.

Information-processing support for campus bookstores was nonexistent in the 1970s. Most operated with crude manual filing systems. Seeing the problem firsthand in their own bookstores, MBS developed TEXTAID, a computer system that store managers can use to administer the entire textbook management process. MBS chose to provide the software free of charge if the bookstore agreed to sell MBS a certain number of used books each year. MBS, thereby guaranteed a source of books, quickly became a dominant player in the industry. To stem a hemorrhaging market share, competitors were forced to follow MBS's lead.

MBS took what was essentially a commodity product and used IT to extensively augment it and embed it in a cluster of supporting services. Their customers, the college bookstore managers, faced an information-intensive task with no source of information-processing support. By offering such support, MBS radically differentiated itself from competitors. Moreover, the required customer investments in hardware and training ensure that, once committed to MBS's system, a given bookstore will probably remain as its customer (and supplier) for some time.

Several elements of MBS's strategy can be generalized. First, MBS uses IT to augment not only its own product but also other resources that are used in conjunction with its product—new textbooks are also managed by the TEXTAID system. Second, MBS provides support not just to its actual customer, the college administrator or bookstore manager who pays the bills, but also to other stakeholders, such as the bookstores' customers—students. Students are provided with a computer-generated bid for books they wish to sell back to the bookstore, thus giving some credibility to what had previously been perceived as a dubious process. Third, TEXTAID focuses on more than just economic needs. Students wish to be served quickly and treated fairly. The bookstore manager wants to be relieved of his or her fear that the right books will not be in stock when they're needed. Also, the manager is driven by a need to do a job well and perhaps to have more time to spend at home. By focusing on the diverse needs of the various stakeholders, the system forms a community around the firm's product, ensures commitment, offers few inroads to competitors, and thereby extends the sustainability of its competitive advantage.[53]

1. What general environmental factors indirectly influenced the growth of Missouri Book Services (MBS)?

2. Identify the probable role of the following competitive forces in the growth of MBS: competitors, new entrants, substitute goods and services, customers, and suppliers.

3. How important was information technology in creating the strategic options available to MBS? Explain.

4. Which of the political strategies appear to have been most important in the growth of MBS? Explain.

Chapter 4

GLOBAL FORCES AND MANAGEMENT

**Honeywell Company Car
in U.S.S.R.**

What You Will Learn

1 How to organize for international involvement.

2 Six basic strategies for international involvement.

3 How the U.S.-Canada Free Trade Agreement and Europe 1992 are altering the competitive picture for many firms in the 1990s.

4 The potential political risks associated with operations in host countries.

5 Political strategies used by organizations and governments facing international competition.

6 How cultural differences affect the management of international organizations.

7 **Skill Development:** How to diagnose and cope with global impacts on organizations in the 1990s.

Chapter Outline

Manager's Viewpoint: Going Global

Organizing for International Involvement
Commission Agent
Export Manager
Export Department
Insight: Life Support Products, Inc.
International Division
International Corporation
Multinational Corporation
Insight: ICI's Global Empire

Strategies for Achieving International Involvement
Exporting Strategy
Licensing Strategy
Franchising Strategy
Alliance Strategy
Insight: The TI-Hitachi Alliance
Multidomestic Strategy
Insight: Honda's Localization of Products
Global Strategy
Insight: Citicorp's World Without Borders

Competitive Forces
U.S.-Canada Free Trade Agreement
Europe 1992
Global Link: Raychem in Europe

Political-Legal Forces
Assessing Political Risk
Insight: GM's Political Risk Index
Political Mechanisms

Cultural Forces
View of Social Change
Time Orientation
Language
Value Systems
The Nenko System
Insight: Nagoya Sogo Bank

Experiencing Management
Skill-Building Exercise: Cultural Traits and Preferences
Manager's Memo
In the News
Management Case:
Transcontinental Industries (Malaysia) Ltd.

Going Global

From New York to Nagoya, business leaders are entranced by visions of running a global business. They think that going global is crucial to success—both their own and that of their businesses. But there are a couple of hitches: Top-level managers aren't quite sure how to go about establishing global operations, and they disagree about the precise benefits of going global. These are some of the findings that emerged from an extensive survey of chief executive officers in the United States, Europe, and Japan and other Pacific Rim nations.

Nearly 50 percent of the CEOs surveyed said that expanding abroad is a very important part of their plans to increase revenue and profit in the next five years. Some 30 percent said that globalization will be a vital means of lowering their costs or upgrading their technology. And many CEOs figure that more foreign exposure will make them smarter, even if they aren't quite sure how. "Globalization means different things to different industries," observes Seth Master, a senior associate at Booz-Allen, a consulting firm. "Everyone sees it as a winning proposition." In brief, *globalization* means looking at the whole world as the organization's market.

But plenty of pitfalls lie ahead in the race toward globalization. Although CEOs are eager to expand abroad, they acknowledge that foreign competitors will keep making inroads into their home markets. Thus they need to be more diligent in competing on the home front and not spread themselves too thin in the rush to expand abroad. Protectionist trade barriers are also a worry. Major investments in global expansion could be put at risk if countries feel threatened and therefore impose limits on what foreign investors can produce or sell within their borders.

On the surface there's much agreement about the merits of running a business globally. "I find it essential to know what's happening around the world, just to keep abreast of the opportunities," says Lester A. Hudson, Jr., president and CEO of Dan River Corporation, a textile concern. In one twelve-month period Hudson traveled to both Europe and Australia on business. That's pretty typical—68 percent of the CEOs surveyed said that they travel overseas on business at least twice a year.

Growth into overseas markets will be brisk but not overwhelming, if CEO's crystal balls are working properly. By the year 1996 CEOs expect about 26 percent of their revenue to come from outside their home region, compared with a shade less than 20 percent in 1990. Thus, as much as managers of organizations love to talk about becoming global, most organizations aren't there yet. They remain largely local in practice, with offices and major operations at home and only a few operations overseas. Of course, there are notable exceptions, even among small firms. In 1990 Bauer Aerospace, Inc., a small company in Farmington, Connecticut, sold 60 percent of its $10 million in business in aircraft-engine test equipment with European and Pacific Rim countries.[1]

Powerful global forces are increasingly responsible for shaping the opportunities and threats facing many organizations around the world. Among these driving forces are (1) Eastern Europe's disavowal of governmental planning and control of the economy, (2) reunification of Germany, (3) Europe 1992, which serves to reduce barriers to free competition and trade among its member nations, (4) fundamental redirections in the Soviet Union, (5) intense and growing competition from firms headquartered in the Pacific Rim countries, and (6) an acceleration in the opening of markets among Canada, the United States, and Mexico.[2] Organizations engaged in globalization are clearly experiencing a turbulent environment. As you will recall from Chapter 3, a turbulent environment is characterized by both extreme complexity and high rates of change. We fully expect this turbulence to prevail throughout the 1990s.

Chances are the company you will work for and your job will be affected by global forces. Employees of many major organizations, from secretaries to presidents, are already keenly aware of the importance of these forces to their companies and jobs. Some of these global organizations are IBM, Royal Dutch/Shell, General Electric, Exxon, Toyota Motors, AT&T, Merck, Hitachi, Coca-Cola, British Petroleum, General Motors, Procter & Gamble, Du Pont, Nippon Steel, Siemens, Nestlé, Ford Motor, PepsiCo, Boeing, Kodak, Sony, Citicorp, Chase Manhattan, BankAmerica, Prudential, Aetna, Merrill Lynch, and Dean Witter.[3]

Throughout this book we present global perspectives on one or more of the issues discussed in each chapter. We've already done so for Chapters 1 through 3. This chapter broadens the focus of Chapter 3 to the wider, international environment of management. In the process, we'll return to the competitive, political-legal, and cultural forces discussed in Chapter 3—this time from an international perspective.

ORGANIZING FOR INTERNATIONAL INVOLVEMENT

Although the impact of global forces is being felt more and more in the general environment, the relative importance of these forces varies widely among specific industries and firms, according to their level of direct involvement in international business. An ice cream manufacturer, such as Blue Bell Ice Cream in Brenham, Texas, has little, if any, direct international involvement; a huge bank like Citicorp, on the other hand, is truly global in its outlook and operations. Figure 4.1 shows the relative degree of complexity (vertical axis) facing managers as a result of their level of involvement in international business (horizontal axis). It also shows how a firm might organize internationally over time, starting with hiring a commission agent to represent the company in international transactions. The process can eventually lead to a firm's becoming a full-fledged multinational (global) corporation.

Competitive forces facing the firm, as well as its chosen objectives, will influence the organizational pattern it follows. Let's briefly explore the six ways of organizing for international business—from the simplest to the most complex. Chapters 10 and 11 will address the issues of organizing and structuring firms in greater detail.

Commission Agent

commission agent A broker (an individual or a firm) who represents businesses in foreign transactions in return for a negotiated percentage of each transaction's value.

A firm's first step toward internationalization might be to retain one or more commission agents in response to an inquiry from a potential foreign customer or to a perceived opportunity to sell its products abroad. A **commission agent** is a broker (a person or firm) who represents businesses in foreign transactions in return for a negotiated percentage of each transaction's value (a commission). An agent will usually carry a catalog of a firm's products and attempt to sell them to customers abroad and is likely to represent other firms as well. Using commission agents is the simplest way of organizing for international involvement. There may be no need to create new positions or departments in the organization—a top or middle manager may simply be assigned the added responsibility of working with the agent(s).

FIGURE 4.1

Organizing for International Involvement

As an organization becomes more involved in international operations, the degree of its organizational complexity normally increases.

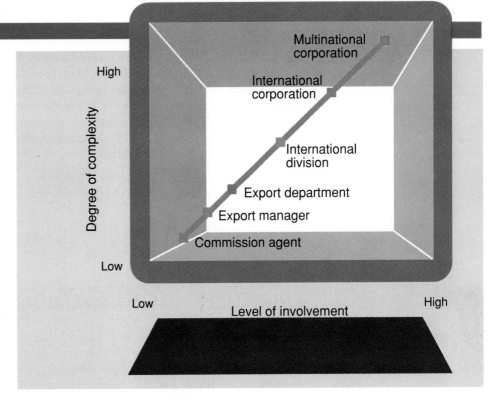

Export Manager

export manager Manager who actively searches out foreign markets for a firm's goods and services, representing only the one firm and working with a small staff.

As its exports increase, a firm may hire an export manager to take over from the commission agent. Much like a commission agent, an **export manager** actively searches out foreign markets for the firm's goods and services.[4] Unlike the commission agent, the export manager represents only his or her firm's goods and services. The export manager typically has a small staff—possibly only a secretary—and travels abroad extensively. Firms having relatively small export sales volumes are likely to limit themselves to either an export manager or a commission agent.

Part of the increased complexity of employing an export manager is that the firm must commit to a variety of ongoing costs. These costs include the export manager's base salary, benefits, office space, travel expenses, and secretarial support. Regardless of the value of the sales generated by the export manager, these costs could easily amount to $100,000 or more per year. In contrast, a commission agent receives only a percentage of the dollar value of the goods sold.

Export Department

export department The department within an organization that handles all aspects of export operations and acts as liaison between foreign customers and management.

As export activities and sales continue to expand, the export manager may have to form a full export department. This unit might consist of only a few people in addition to the export manager. An **export department** often (1) represents the interests of foreign customers to the firm's other departments and to top management, (2) meets the increasing demand for services by foreign customers, (3) makes special arrangements for customs clearance and international shippings, (4) assists foreign customers with financing of the goods they are purchasing, and (5) arranges for the collection of accounts receivable from foreign customers. An export department might also establish branches abroad to handle sales and promotional tasks.

Many small U.S. businesses could operate successfully in the international arena at one of the lower levels of involvement. However, they fall far short of their international potential:

Despite the growth of the export sector in the U.S. economy, small business has played only a small role in the foreign trade. As much as one-half of export sales from the United States historically have been made by as few as 100 firms. They can enter the smaller foreign markets that would not be profitable to a large multinational firm. Smaller firms with specialized goods and technologies should be able to respond quickly to foreign opportunities. If it is true that fewer than 20 percent of all . . . companies whose goods have an export potential are actually selling abroad at this time, it is surely also true that the vast majority of small businesses fall into the 80 percent majority that have not realized any of their export potential.[5]

Life Support Products, Inc. of Irvine, California is a good example of a small firm that successfully established an export department and used an innovative approach for entering the European market.

LIFE SUPPORT PRODUCTS, INC.

INSIGHT

Life Support Products, Inc. (LSP) is a small manufacturer of emergency-care products for the medical field. The firm, which employs seventy-eight people, decided to make the most of the exporting opportunity Europe 1992 promised to offer—whatever the risk. "From a growth standpoint, we couldn't afford *not* to risk it," says Robert Hovee, president of LSP. "Europe has 100 million more people than we have here in the United States. That's simply too large a market to ignore. We discovered the biggest hurdle would be distributing our products throughout Europe. As a small company, setting up our own distribution network was cost-prohibitive."

"At a trade show in Hamburg, Germany, we were approached by engineers from a German company called Drager," recalls Hovee. "They were interested in distributing our medical emergency products, which, unlike theirs, are designed for use in the field and in the emergency room—before the patient reaches surgery. Drager's products, designed for use in the operating theater, are more sophisticated and expensive."

One thing led to another. In November 1987, LSP signed a five-year, $25 million contract with Drager for a line of seventeen products, to be sold in Europe under both companies' names. This partnership offered LSP an attractive means of circumventing some of the worst problems inherent in exporting. "With Drager handling the distribution and marketing of our products overseas," says Hovee, "we could concentrate our efforts on preparing our products to meet the specifications of the European market."[6]

International Division

international division A division within an organization that handles not only international marketing and finance tasks, but also manufacturing operations in one or more foreign countries.

The fourth level of involvement in international business is forming an international division within the company under a general manager's direction. An **international division** handles not only marketing and finance tasks abroad, but also manufacturing operations in one or more foreign countries. These operations may range from assembly to full-scale manufacturing plants, but the point is that domestic plants no longer produce all of the company's goods.

Within a large international division, each world region (or even country) might be further broken out as a separate unit, as is suggested by the representative structure of a firm with an international division shown in Figure 4.2. Subsidiaries could be created for regions such as the Americas (Canada, Mexico, the United States, and Central and South

FIGURE 4.2

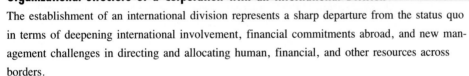

Organizational Structure of a Corporation with an International Division

The establishment of an international division represents a sharp departure from the status quo in terms of deepening international involvement, financial commitments abroad, and new management challenges in directing and allocating human, financial, and other resources across borders.

America), Europe (France, Germany, the United Kingdom, and so forth), and the Pacific Rim (Australia, Japan, Hong Kong, and so forth). The nature of the subsidiaries would depend on market size and the scope of the international division's manufacturing and service operations.[7] You will note in Figure 4.2 that domestic operations are separated from international operations. The international division represents international interests and operates as a semi-independent unit. There is usually little coordination with the domestic divisions, and what does take place occurs through the company's top management. Coleman, Briggs & Stratton, Rubbermaid, and McGraw-Hill are some large corporations that have international divisions.

Some of the factors that move an organization beyond the international division level include (1) growth in international sales and production capacity equal to 10 percent or more of that of domestic divisions, (2) diversification in product lines to serve a variety of customers, and (3) difficulties in coordinating between semiautonomous domestic divisions and the international division.

International Corporation

international corporation
A corporation with significant business interests (importing, exporting, production, marketing) that cut across national boundaries and sometimes an international division within each product group.

An **international corporation** has significant business interests that cut across national boundaries and often focuses on importing and exporting goods or services as well as

Setting the pace for the Pacific Basin, Japan was *multinational* Coca-Cola Company's top profit contributor in 1987.

multinational corporation (MNC) A corporation that views the *whole* world as its market, assessing problems and planning production and marketing strategies with that view in mind (also called global corporation or transnational corporation).

operating production and marketing units in other countries. Corporations that have diverse product lines may establish separate international divisions within each major product group. Thus, unlike the general manager of an international division, top-level managers of each product group have both domestic and international responsibilities. Procter & Gamble, Sara Lee, and H. J. Heinz are representative of large international corporations.

Multinational Corporation

A **multinational corporation (MNC)** emerges when (1) managers and other employees take a worldwide view in assessing problems and opportunities, (2) one or more subsidiaries operate in several countries, and (3) top management is willing to consider locations throughout the world for making sales, obtaining resources, and producing goods. The feature that most distinguishes a multinational corporation from an international corporation is its view of the whole world as its market. Major firms that operate as multinational corporations include IBM, Shell, Honda, General Electric, and Imperial Chemical.

A multinational corporation, sometimes called a *global corporation* or a *transnational corporation,* often competes primarily with a small number of other multinationals in each world market. Such firms view the entire world (or its major regions) as a single entity. Within this worldwide arena, one multinational pits its products or services against another's. Each company seeks to respond to local market needs while maintaining efficiency in its worldwide system.[8] One expert has identified 136 industries whose organizations will have to be multinationals with worldwide systems. These industries produce goods and services that vary from accounting, autos, banking, consumer electronics, and entertainment to pharmaceuticals, travel services, washing machines, and zippers.[9] To be competitive, firms in these industries must manufacture, conduct research, raise capital, and buy supplies wherever the advantage lies. They must keep in touch with technology and market trends all around the world.

Figure 4.3 shows a multinational corporation with worldwide product divisions. This structure is common among multiproduct and multinational U.S. manufacturing firms. Marketing and manufacturing needs of this firm vary more from product group to product group than from one area of the world to another, each product division assumes all the necessary tasks of planning, coordinating, and allocating resources among various domestic and overseas activities. This organizational structure and its communications network

FIGURE 4.3

Multinational Corporate Structure

In a multinational corporate structure managers and other employees must see the whole world as their market and take a worldwide view in assessing their problems and opportunities.

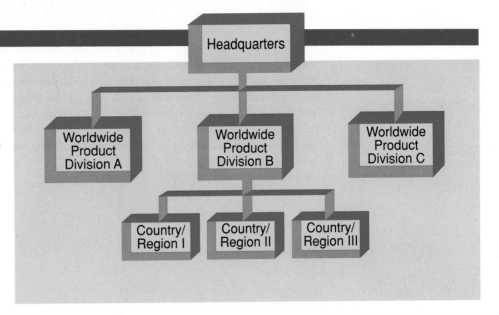

permit a smooth transfer of products or services and technologies from the home market to foreign markets within the same product group.[10]

The following Insight gives a sense of how Imperial Chemical changed to and functions as a multinational corporation.

I NSIGHT

The sun never sets on the far-flung operations of Imperial Chemical Industries (ICI). The world's thirty-eighth largest industrial corporation, ICI has sales of $21 billion a year in pharmaceuticals, film, polymers, agricultural chemicals, explosives, and other products.

In 1983 ICI began to abandon its traditional country-by-country organization and establish worldwide business units. The company concentrated its resources on its strongest units; within each, ICI focused activity in the country where business was strongest. Four of the nine units are headquartered outside Britain. Two are in Wilmington, Delaware—ICI is growing at a rate of 20 percent a year in the United States but only 2 percent to 3 percent in its original home, Great Britain. Thus a factory manager in Britain or Brazil producing advanced materials or specialty chemicals answers to a boss in Wilmington.

To avoid overlapping or duplicating research, labs were given lead roles near the most important markets. Advanced materials research went to Phoenix to be near clients in defense industries, and leather dye research went to the south of France, the heart of that market.

The necessary shifts created wrenching changes. ICI reduced its manufacturing jobs in Britain by 10,000 to 55,000; other employees were transferred or taken off pet projects. "It's a major change," says Hugh Miller, the American who heads the advanced materials and electronics group. "It's hard on people who have built national empires and now don't have such freedom. We are asking people to be less nationalistic and more concerned with what happens outside their country." The upheaval has been especially worrisome to British employees, since ICI's stronger growth rate elsewhere attracts more resources.

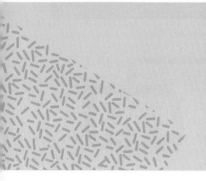

The payoff, says Miller, is better decision making. "Before, each territory would work up projects and you'd have warring factions competing in London for the same money. Now, with one person responsible for a global product line, it becomes immaterial where a project is located. Its profits will be the same. When you start operating in this manner, it takes a lot of steam out of the defense of fiefdoms." In pharmaceuticals, for example, better—and quicker—decision making has helped ICI reduce the lag time in introducing new drugs to different markets from half a dozen years to one or two. ICI hopes eventually to make such introductions simultaneous.[11]

STRATEGIES FOR ACHIEVING INTERNATIONAL INVOLVEMENT

The ways firms organize for international involvement are influenced by the numerous international strategies that can be employed.[12] This section presents a sampling of these strategies, also ranging from simple to complex, as shown in Figure 4.4. A single organization may use one or more of these strategies. Again, these strategies are only a few cases, representative of the vast range of choices available.

Exporting Strategy

The **exporting strategy** involves an organization's maintaining facilities within a home country and transferring goods and services abroad, for sale in foreign markets. An increasingly popular variation on straightforward exporting (or importing) is **countertrade,** a form of trade arrangement in which the export sale of goods and services by a producer is *linked to* an import purchase of other goods and services.[13] The most well-known example of countertrade is PepsiCo's exporting of syrup and related soft drink items to the Soviet Union in exchange for vodka.

Licensing Strategy

The **licensing strategy** involves an organization (the *licensor*) in one country making certain resources available to companies (*licensees*) in others so that they can participate in the production and sale of its goods and services abroad. This usually involves a contractual arrangement whereby the licensor provides its patents, trademarks, manufacturing expertise, or technical services to the licensee, in return for which the licensee pays a royalty on the sale of the product. Many U.S. and Canadian book publishing companies use this strategy with foreign publishers. For a royalty, the foreign publisher obtains the right to translate a book into another language and publish it or to print, market, and distribute the book in another country.

The licensor does not have to worry about making major capital investments abroad or becoming involved with the daily production, technical, marketing, or management details of the international operation. The licensee runs those operations, after importing know-how or the opportunity to legally sell a product, service, or process that is owned by the licensor.

Technological forces are playing an increasingly strong role in stimulating the use of the licensing strategy. Why? Because licensees can rapidly disseminate new technologies

exporting strategy Strategy pursued when an organization maintains facilities in its home country and transfers goods or services abroad for sale in foreign markets.

countertrade A variation on straightforward exporting (or importing) in which the export sale of goods or services is linked to the import purchase of other goods or services.

licensing strategy Strategy pursued when an organization (the licensor) makes certain resources available to another company (the licensee) in return for a fee (royalty).

FIGURE 4.4

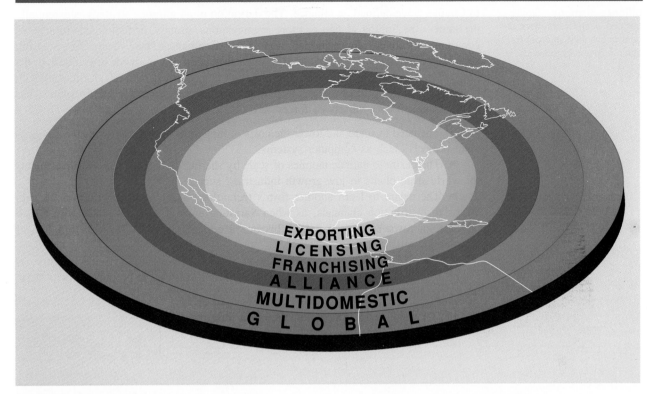

Sample Strategies for International Involvement

Organizations have many options for becoming involved internationally—from a simple strategy such as exporting to a complex global strategy that requires the support of a multinational organizational structure.

across an industry. Within the computer industry, for example, many firms are racing to license their technologies to potential users in an attempt to set industrywide standards. MIPS Computer Systems licensed its newest microprocessor designs in an attempt to head off competing designs before they captured too much of the market. MIPS signed licensing agreements with Siemens of Germany; DEC, Texas Instruments, Cypress Semiconductor, and Bipolar Integrated Technology of the United States; and Fujitou, NEC, and Kubota of Japan. For a license fee these firms can produce MIPS Computer Systems' chips and market new computers based on its designs.[14]

franchising strategy
Strategy pursued when a parent organization (the franchiser) grants another company or individual (the franchisee) the rights to use its name and produce a product or service in return for a fee.

Franchising Strategy

In a **franchising strategy,** the parent organization (*franchiser*) grants a foreign company or individual (*franchisee*) the rights to use its name and produce its product or service and provides its franchisees with a complete assortment of materials and services for a fee. There is usually active involvement by the franchiser in training and monitoring and controlling the actions of the franchisee. Kentucky Fried Chicken, Coca-Cola, and McDonald's are notable examples of global franchisers.

There are over 350 franchising companies headquartered in the United States, with more than 31,000 outlets operating in international markets. Japan has emerged as one of the largest franchising countries in the world, runner-up to the United States and Canada. Japan is the second largest market for U.S. franchisers, with a total of 7400 units, of which 72 percent represent various food categories.[15]

Alliance Strategy

alliance strategy Strategy pursued when two or more organizations unite in order to attain common objectives.

In Chapter 3 we defined an alliance. The definition of an **alliance strategy** is essentially the same—the uniting of two or more organizations, groups, or individuals to achieve common objectives. International organizational alliances take many forms, from straightforward marketing agreements to joint ownership of worldwide operations. In the past ten years U.S. and Canadian corporations have formed over 2000 alliances with European companies alone.[16] The formation of alliances, especially joint ventures, has been stimulated by a variety of forces:

▶ The need to share and lower the costs of high-risk, technology-intensive development projects, such as computer systems.

▶ The desire to gain economies of scale by sharing the large fixed-cost investments for world-scale plants in low-growth industries, such as steel and appliances.

▶ The desire to learn another firm's technology and special processes or to gain access to distribution channels, as when Samsung entered a joint venture with GE to produce microwave ovens and later became a competitor with GE in its full line of household appliances.

▶ The desire to influence the evolution of competitive activity in the industry, as when Corning Glass and Ciba-Geigy established joint ventures to produce medical diagnostic equipment.[17]

Let's consider one strategic alliance in a little more detail.

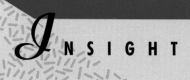

THE TI-HITACHI ALLIANCE

INSIGHT

''Oh damn! Now TI, too?'' That was the reaction of Clyde V. Prestowitz, Jr., to the announcement that Texas Instruments, Inc., and Japanese rival Hitachi Ltd. have paired up to design their version of a superchip that will be the workhorse computer-memory device for the mid-1990s.

Prestowitz, who once spearheaded the U.S. Commerce Department's semiconductor trade talks with Japan, was stunned that TI would be party to such a precedent-shattering arrangement. This was the first time that top-tier chip makers in Japan and the United States agreed to cooperate on developing a future-generation chip.

TI is collaborating with Hitachi on the design and production of a 16-megabit DRAM (dynamic random access memory), a chip that will store 16 million bits of data. That's sixteen times as much as the latest commercial DRAMs and four times the capacity of the 4-megabit prototype chips now being selectively distributed by Hitachi and a handful of other Japanese suppliers. One 16-megabit DRAM will hold 2 million characters, or nearly 500,000 words. DRAMs are the industry's main ''technology driver''—the proving grounds for new design and manufacturing techniques that then infuse into other markets, such as microprocessors.

By linking up, TI and Hitachi hedge their bets, spread the risk, and help ensure that both will end up with a viable 16-megabit chip. As a result, says Prestowitz, ''this may be a good way for two companies to share the burden of what is obviously a big swallow. So I'm prepared to accept that this deal may not be such a bad one.''[18]

multidomestic strategy Strategy pursued when a firm adjusts its products and practices to individual countries or regions, treating each uniquely.

Multidomestic Strategy

A **multidomestic strategy** involves the firm in global operations for which it adjusts its products and practices to individual countries or regions (for example, Pacific Rim versus

Europe versus the Americas). A number of successful companies have followed a multidomestic strategy: Honeywell in controls, Alcoa in aluminum, and General Foods in foods, among others. These companies treat the world as just so many separate parts and deal with each part individually. In other words, the company pursues strategies that are tailored to each of its foreign markets and views competitive challenges independently, from market to market.

Under a multidomestic strategy, management stresses the uniqueness of each region or nation. Each overseas subsidiary is somewhat independent. Each is a profit center and contributes earnings and growth in line with its market opportunity. The world headquarters coordinates financial controls and broad marketing (including product line) policies worldwide. Some research and development and production may be handled at that home office, but specific marketing and transportation operations are delegated to managers in each region or nation.[19]

In the following Insight, Hideo Sugiura, retired chairperson of Honda Motor Company, discusses how Honda attempts to localize its products.

I NSIGHT Since its modest beginning in 1948, Honda has grown into a corporation with $25 billion in sales, largely because of its successful international activities. More than 60 percent of our total sales take place outside of Japan; our products are marketed in well over one hundred countries. Moreover, we manufacture products at seventy-seven plants in forty countries outside Japan, and our cumulative total investments abroad have surpassed $1 billion, not counting over $2 billion reinvested locally by our overseas subsidiaries.

Honda is often described as an international enterprise. But in promoting internationalization, we place the utmost importance on *localization*—adapting our activities to those practiced in the countries where we operate. *Localization of products* means developing, manufacturing, and marketing the products best suited to the actual and potential needs of the customers *and* to the social and economic conditions of the marketplace. While it is true that a good product knows no national boundaries, there are subtle differences, from country to country and from region to region, in the ways a product is used and what customers expect of it. If a corporation believes that simply because a product has succeeded in a certain market, it will sell well throughout the world, it is most likely destined for large and expensive errors or even total failure.

Take our motorcycles as an example. North Americans use motorcycles primarily for leisure and sports; a racer looks for high horsepower output and speed. Southeast Asians, on the other hand, use motorcycles as a basic means of transportation, so they want ease of maintenance, at low cost. In Australia, shepherds use motorcycles to drive sheep; they look for low-speed torque, rather than high speed or ease of maintenance. So, while we do use a common basic technology, we develop different types of motorcycles for different regions. Such differences apply not only to cars and motorcycles, but to most industrial products as well. Corporations must be capable of accurately grasping such differences and producing appropriately targeted products.

To localize products, corporations must invest in research and development of both products and production efficiency. Honda earmarks 5 percent of the parent company's unconsolidated gross annual sales for R&D of products and production techniques, regardless of fluctuation in profits. In addition, we have established R&D centers in North and South America, Western Europe, and Southeast Asia. Japanese and local engineers work together to understand local market conditions and to develop the products best suited to each market.[20]

Global Strategy

global strategy A complex strategy for achieving international involvement by operating with worldwide consistency and standardization via highly independent international subsidiaries.

A **global strategy** stresses operating with worldwide consistency and standardization and low relative cost. Under global strategies, subsidiaries in various countries are highly interdependent in terms of objectives, practices, and operations. As much as possible, top managers focus on mutual coordination and support of the firm's worldwide activities. For example, Black and Decker has a subsidiary in one country manufacture part of a product line, such as power drills, and exchange components with subsidiaries in other countries to complete the product. Profit targets vary for each subsidiary, depending on the impact a subsidiary's operations have on the effectiveness of the global system.[21]

An increasing number of U.S. multinational corporations use global strategies. Several of them—along with their principal competitors—are Caterpillar and Komatsu in large construction equipment; Timex, Seiko, and Citizen in watches; and Texas Instruments, Intel, Mitsubishi, Hitachi, and Motorola in semiconductors. The following Insight highlights Citicorp's use of state-of-the-art information technologies to implement its global strategy.

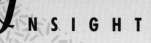

CITICORP'S WORLD WITHOUT BORDERS

INSIGHT Global companies with high-tech links can quickly mobilize resources around the world to help a client. Until a couple of years ago a potential borrower approaching a Citicorp office in Australia or Hong Kong could get the services of only that one office. The borrower might even visit several Citicorp locations to get competing offers. Today, as part of a single deal, the bank can seek out for a customer the best rates and terms offered by its offices anywhere in the world. It might draw funds from outposts in several countries, in different currencies, involving several tax jurisdictions. Such deals take a lot of time, but they are becoming more common as Citicorp's clients internationalize.

The bank began opening branches around the world in 1902 but only recently began to link them in a global business. Its strength in one market is used to gain advantage in another. Michael Callen, who runs Citicorp's investment banking worldwide, says that the technology to operate globally didn't exist at the beginning of the decade. For instance, Citicorp's investment banks in ninety countries could quote only their own exchange rates. Now they can give a client the best rate in any one of the ninety. Citicorp is testing automatic tellers that can serve clients anywhere in the world.

Part of Citicorp's global thrust comes from the sheer growth in volume of international business: The world's daily trade in currencies is over $400 billion, and the trading rooms in New York, London, and Tokyo run twenty-four hours a day. But a new way of thinking is even more important. Citicorp officers are required to work through international teams to assemble deals. To make sure its bankers help one another, the company has adopted a system of cross evaluations. A manager in New York who is supposed to work with a colleague in

Tokyo gets rated by the person in Tokyo and vice versa. Managers' bonuses are based partly on how well they collaborate.

Citicorp is not without problems. Like so many financial institutions, it's struggling to overcome losses from bad real estate and LDC (less developed countries) loans. In 1991 Citicorp cut its work force from 92,000 to 84,000 employees and trimmed its annual expenses by $800 million.[22]

A variety of ingredients must mesh in an effective global strategy. Seven of the basic ingredients are as follows:

1. The firm must be a significant competitor in the world's most important regional markets—North America, Europe, and Asia.

2. New goods and services must be developed for the whole world.

3. Profit targets should be based on product lines—such as Black and Decker's line of hand-held power drills—rather than countries or regions of the world.

4. Decisions about products, capital, research, and production must be based on global (worldwide) considerations.

5. Narrow-minded attitudes—such as "this isn't how we operate here" must be overcome. Some ways to change attitudes include training employees to think internationally, sending them to foreign countries for first hand exposure, and giving them the latest information technology.

6. Foreign managers must be promoted into senior ranks.

7. The company needs to take advantage of advanced technologies to improve information flow and communications across national boundaries, between organizational levels, and so forth.[23]

Yamaichi Securities' *global strategy* obviously must be based on worldwide trading considerations. The fourth largest securities-trading company in Japan, Yamaichi operates 24 hours a day on the international securities market.

COMPETITIVE FORCES

The United States, Canada, and other nations are bound together by worldwide competitive forces. One yardstick of the growing interdependence between international business and each nation's economy is the ratio of imports and exports (measured in dollars) to gross national product (GNP). In 1973 this ratio was about 6 percent of GNP for the United States. It has risen to over 18 percent of GNP and is expected to continue to rise. Many other countries, including Canada, Japan, Germany, and France, have even higher ratios. In addition, about 70 percent of U.S. manufactured goods must compete directly with goods manufactured abroad. More than half the nation's supplies of twenty-four important raw materials, from petroleum to cobalt, come from foreign sources. A final yardstick is the value of foreign-owned businesses and real estate in a country. Let's consider just one country—the United States. As of 1991 the value of foreign-owned businesses and real estate in the United States totaled $411 billion. The biggest foreign investors in the United States come from Great Britain ($121 billion), Japan ($75 billion), the Netherlands ($63 billion), Canada ($32 billion), Germany ($28 billion), Switzerland ($20 billion), and France ($19 billion).[24]

In recent years the number of U.S. and Canadian industries facing intense global competition has risen dramatically. Global competitive forces seem to be almost everywhere, varying for different industries and countries. For U.S. and Canadian firms two sets of forces recently emerged from the U.S.-Canada Free Trade Agreement and Europe 1992. We'll provide broad outlines of the competitive forces created by these developments, the impacts of which are certain to be felt by employees and their firms throughout the 1990s.

U.S.-Canada Free Trade Agreement[25]

Canada is the largest trading partner of the United States. Japan ranks second and Mexico third. In 1990 U.S. imports from Canada totaled approximately $86 billion, which represents 16 percent of all U.S. imports. Seventy-three percent of Canada's exports go to the United States. Canada's imports from the United States totaled approximately $75 billion in 1990, which represents 65 percent of all Canadian imports. Twenty-four percent of all U.S. exports go to Canada.[26] These strong economic ties were a key factor in the development of the U.S.-Canada Free Trade Agreement (FTA). This agreement, given final approval by the Canadian Parliament in December 1988, is being implemented in phases between 1989 and 1998.

The FTA does not eliminate all trade problems between the United States and Canada, but it does provide a framework through which these problems can be managed. The less restricted trade resulting from the agreement increases the competitive forces on firms in both countries—with the intent of achieving greater efficiency through increased competition. As with all trade agreements between countries, the FTA is a political document that attempts to resolve problems or develop compromises with respect to many competing economic and cultural interests. As such, it contains loopholes and exceptions that will be tested over the decades to come. The provisions of this act will no doubt be either received with open arms or met with resistance, depending on their effect on a particular firm or industry.

One key provision is the elimination of tariffs (a form of tax) on goods and services traded between the two countries. However, about 70 percent of U.S.-Canadian trade already was free of duty before the pact was signed. The average U.S. tariff on the 30 percent of Canadian goods subject to tariffs fell to 3 percent in 1989, from 4 percent before the agreement took effect. The average Canadian tariff went down to 9.4 percent from 9.7 percent of the value of U.S. goods being exported to Canada. One of the hundreds of side-effects of the tariff reductions was that Whirlpool Corporation's Canadian subsidiary stopped making washing machines after the pact was signed and moved that operation to

Ohio. Whirlpool then shifted the production of household trash compactors, kitchen ranges, and compact dryers to Canada.

Furthermore, the FTA will remove current limits placed on U.S. banks in Canada in the areas of growth, capital, and market share. Specifically, U.S. banks will be exempt from the 16 percent ceiling on domestic assets of all foreign banks in Canada, as well as from the individual capital limits used to implement the ceiling. The FTA also provides the United States with more secure access to Canadian energy supplies to meet long-term U.S. energy needs. This access to Canadian resources is important to reduce U.S. dependence on OPEC oil. The Canadians have agreed that they will not discriminate against U.S. consumers in the pricing of their energy resources, ensuring that U.S. consumers will not be cut off suddenly in the event of shortages. The agreement also supports uniform methods for testing and certifying technical standards, as in the area of air pollution. And finally, under the FTA both countries reserve the right to impose or reimpose import restrictions on a particular grain (specifically wheat, oats, barley, rye, corn, or sorghum) if imports increase significantly as a result of a substantial change in either country's support programs for that grain.[27]

Europe 1992[28]

The European Community (EC) currently has twelve members: Belgium, Denmark, France, Germany, Greece, Ireland, Italy, Luxembourg, the Netherlands, Portugal, Spain, and the United Kingdom. The European countries of Austria, Finland, Iceland, Norway, Sweden and Switzerland have applied for EC membership. They have been grouped into the European Free Trade Association (EFTA) for more than twenty-five years. The poten-

Europe 1992

tial role of Eastern European countries (such as Poland, Hungary, and Czechoslovakia, which intend to apply in 1995) and non-European countries (such as the United States, Canada, and Turkey) in the EC remains to be determined.[29] Turkey has already applied for membership.

The objective of Europe 1992 is to create a single market through the removal of trade barriers and the establishing of free movement of goods, people, services, and capital. The changes will go beyond economic interests to encompass social changes as well. Educational degrees, for example, will be affected. The EC Council of Ministers submitted a directive that will recognize diplomas of higher education across national boundaries. This will make it easier for professionals to work in different countries. It is clear, then, that the EC is more than an economic community: It is a state of mind, and a political force. At the same time, it should lead to less government interference in economic activities.

The basic thrust of the 1992 program is to complete the internal market established as a European objective by the Treaty of Rome over thirty years ago. As laid out in the EC's 1985 ''white paper,'' this involves the elimination of four major types of barriers:

1. *Physical barriers* at each country's borders, which prevent the free flow of goods and persons.

2. *Technical barriers,* which prevent goods produced or traded in one member nation from being sold in others.

3. *Fiscal barriers,* such as red tape and the different national tax systems, which hinder cross-border trade.

4. *Financial barriers,* which prevent the free movement of capital.

The European Commission is the EC's executive body and sole initiator of legislation. By early 1991 it had agreed on more than half of the 300 regulations that are needed to fully integrate the EC countries. As you might expect, the toughest issues have been saved for last and are not likely to have been resolved by 1992. One of the toughest issues is trying to agree on a common immigration policy for all member nations. Some member nations are concerned that they'll be flooded with immigrants as the result of an open door policy.[30]

The long-term effects of the EC regulations are likely to be (1) to increase market opportunities, (2) to escalate competition within the EC, and (3) to boost competition from companies outside the EC. The abolition of transnational trade restrictions and the relaxation of border controls will have a considerable impact on U.S. and Canadian companies doing business in Europe. Moreover, strong European companies will become formidable competitors in the North American market.

Opportunities Europe 1992 should boost productivity and cut costs by enabling companies to establish large, technologically advanced plants from which goods can be shipped directly to all EC countries. This step in turn will create opportunities by generating demand for EC-wide marketing. Marketing may evolve in Europe as it developed in the United States; that is, it may lean toward national and regional marketing rather than state-by-state marketing. The free movement of products, people, and services across national borders and the reduction or elimination of restrictive regulations should aid marketers in operating in a pan-European manner.

One example of opportunity is found in the area of fast-delivery service. As the U.S. market for overnight and same-day delivery of documents and small packages becomes saturated, firms in the delivery business seek opportunities in Europe. Although the route between Europe and the United States is already heavily served by Federal Express, the real opportunity for this company may be within the European Community—despite the intense competition it faces there.[31] United Parcel Service (UPS), for example, already plays a major role in Europe. UPS will be greatly aided by the free movement of goods. Even if national barriers do not completely fall, fewer customs restrictions will expand business activities across borders.

Threats There is considerable concern, however, that the supposedly free market of Europe 1992 will be anything but free to outsiders. A few of the threats include the following:

▶ Political pressure is being exerted by the EC Commission on U.S. and Japanese firms to conduct more research and production in Europe or face the risk of increased tariffs and other barriers.

▶ Restrictions may be placed on non-EC banks and security firms unless foreign countries, such as the United States, Canada, and Japan, grant reciprocal rights. These restrictions could range from limiting the right to acquire banks in EC countries to special taxes on foreign banks operating in EC countries.

▶ Attempts are being made to favor local suppliers in telecommunications equipment and to keep European monopolies in telephone and data transmission services.

▶ Similar restrictions favoring EC suppliers are being advocated for consumer electronics, the media, public works, textiles, and footwear.

▶ Subsidies (government support) and quotas in each EC member country may continue in agriculture, fisheries, textiles, and steel. These industries are particularly sensitive to political pressures because of well-organized interest groups.

Choice of Strategy There are a variety of strategies available for U.S. and Canadian enterprises. One is the exportation of goods and services to the European Community. In general, North American firms have had only limited success in this area. The most successful strategy has been setting up subsidiaries or branches in one or more EC countries. The establishment of subsidiaries is demonstrated by well-established companies such as Opel (subsidiary of General Motors in Germany), Ford Motor Company, and IBM. Some companies are consolidating their existing positions in Europe. Sara Lee has bought a coffee and tea firm in the Netherlands and a women's stockings company in France. Other North American firms are finding new ways to enter the EC market. Whirlpool, one of the largest U.S. manufacturers of appliances, formed a joint venture with the Dutch electronics firm N. V. Phillips. They will make major appliances under the Phillips name for sale in the EC.

Whether new on the scene or already established, many outside-EC firms are trying to consolidate their European bases. The new European environment, with its 320 million rather affluent people, provides a variety of opportunities for North American firms. This chapter's Global Link feature shows how Raychem Corporation is preparing to address new European challenges.

We close this section with a thought-provoking quote from Michael Porter, author of *The Competitive Advantage of Nations:*

> A nation's competitiveness depends on the capacity of its industry to innovate and upgrade. Companies gain advantage against the world's best competitors because of pressure and challenge. They benefit from having strong domestic rivals, aggressive home-based suppliers, and demanding local customers.
>
> In a world of increasingly global competition, nations have become more, not less, important. As the basis of competition has shifted more and more to the creation and assimilation of knowledge, the role of the nation has grown. Competitive advantage is created and sustained through a highly localized process. Differences in national values, culture, economic structures, institutions, and histories all contribute to competitive success. There are striking differences in the patterns of competitiveness in every country; no nation can or will be competitive in every or even most industries. Ultimately, nations succeed in particular industries because their home environment is the most forward-looking, dynamic, and challenging.[32]

GLOBAL *Link*

RAYCHEM IN EUROPE

William E. Mitchell, senior vice-president, notes that Raychem Corporation has over $1 billion in annual sales. About 62 percent of its business operations (and half of its 11,000 employees) are outside the United States, with more than 40 percent in Europe. Raychem supplies products as diverse as aerospace wire and cable, advanced interconnections systems, heating systems, power cable accessories, telephone splice closures, heat-shrinkable tubing and molded shapes, and fiber-optic systems. Mitchell offers a few perspectives of Raychem's top management:

First, we believe that Europe in 1992 is going to be a complicated place to do business. Hundreds of years of history won't and can't be changed overnight, or even in a few years. Additionally, change will be very different depending on the industry under discussion. Changes in the aerospace industry will be different from changes in telecommunications, and so on.

Second, the changes will take longer than expected. The great progress made since the passage of the Single European Act will almost inevitably slow down as the many details of the more than 300 pieces of enabling legislation begin to be worked out. Companies must be prepared for many ups and downs. Whatever happens won't be what we expect to happen. The key will be to remain flexible.

Third, the dynamics—social, political, economic—are too complex for simple scenarios. Nonetheless, Europe 1992 is going to happen (even if not by 1992), and it's essential to participate in what is one of the great economic events of the twentieth century.

To deal with the uncertainties ahead, Raychem has put together a European study group—with the emphasis on European. The group, staffed almost entirely by Europeans, has formed a council to assess the impact of 1992. What will happen to markets? What will happen to pricing? What will happen to logistics? What will be our ability to move people around? How can we do career development? Where should we manufacture?

Top management of Raychem is committed to our future in Europe. We spend a lot of time there, hold regular management meetings and board of directors meetings there—we believe in showing the flag.

Source: Adapted from W. E. Mitchell, "Europe 1992: Raychem in Response," *Business Forum*, Fall 1989, 42–45.

POLITICAL-LEGAL FORCES

political risk The probability that political events or actions will negatively affect the long-term profitability of an investment.

International competitive forces facing major industries have obviously become increasingly turbulent and significant during the past twenty years. Organizations also function within a web of political and legal forces, and the political forces acting on a firm engaged in international business represents risks. Recall from Chapter 3 that managers may use one or more of five political strategies—negotiation, lobbying, alliance, representation, and socialization—to manage and reduce political risk.[33] **Political risk** is the probability that political events and actions will negatively affect the long-term profitability of an investment.[34] An issue of increasing concern to all multinational corporations is the political risk associated with investing in foreign countries.

Assessing Political Risk

As suggested in Figure 4.5, grouping factors into four major categories—domestic instability, foreign conflict, political climate, and economic climate—may help management assess the seriousness of the political risk associated with conducting business in a given country.[35]

Domestic Instability Domestic instability is the amount of subversion, revolution, assassinations, guerrilla warfare, and government crisis found in a country. Such events will have a negative impact on international business in a country. For example, after the 1979 revolution in Iran, the government forced multinational corporations to leave and confiscated their properties.

Foreign Conflict Foreign conflict is the degree of hostility a nation shows toward others. Such hostility can range from the expulsion of diplomats to outright war.

FIGURE 4.5

Categories for Assessing Political Risk

The political risk of conducting business in a particular country is difficult to determine. One approach is to assess these four categories of social, economic, and political factors.

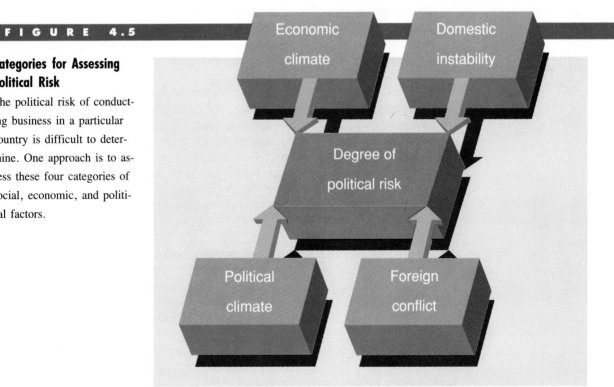

Construction on Hydro-Quebec, the world's most massive hydroelectric complex, has been stalled amid a barrage of political and environmental opposition. In Spring 1991, the utility found itself in a stormy *political climate,* because of secret contracts with 13 international firms. Canadian consumers protested that this would force them to bear the cost of a subsidy to foreign firms.

The invasion of Kuwait by Iraq is one of the more dramatic examples in recent years. In August 1990 President George Bush determined that the actions of the government of Iraq were an unusual and extraordinary threat to the national security and foreign policy of the United States. Under authority granted by the U.S. Export Administration Act of 1979, the government imposed a total ban on trade with Iraq, which directly affected many firms.

Political Climate Political climate is the likelihood of a government's swing to the far left or far right politically. Managers may evaluate the size of the Communist Party, the number of Socialist seats in the legislature, the role of the military in the political process, and the amount of control exercised by right-wing extremist groups. For instance, experts have characterized the political climate in the Philippines as one of high-risk turmoil.[36] Three factions are competing for power: a dissident right-wing military faction, the Aquino faction, and the Communist faction. These warring groups have created major concerns and risks for international corporations operating in the Philippines.

Sometimes political climate isn't so dramatic. The Japanese, for instance, are well aware that the political climate in the United States, especially, as expressed in public opinion polls, is growing increasingly negative toward their interests. In one poll, 61 percent of the respondents thought the United States should restrict Japanese imports, 63 percent thought Japanese investment in the United States should be discouraged, and 65 percent thought the Japanese unfairly restrict sales of U.S. goods in Japan.[37] Pat Choate, an outspoken critic of Japan's policies, comments on how he thinks Japan is trying to influence the U.S. political climate:

> Imagine a foreign country running an ongoing political campaign in the United States, as though it were a third major political party. Imagine it spending more than $100 million each year to hire 1000 Washington, D.C. lobbyists, super-lawyers, former high-ranking officials, public relations specialists, political advisers—even former presidents. Imagine it spending another $300 million each year to build a nationwide grass-roots political network to influence public opinion. Imagine that its $400 million per year political campaign sought to advance its economic interests, influence U.S. trade policy, and win market share in the United States for its target industries. None of this is imaginary; none of it is illegal. The country that is actually undertaking this political campaign is Japan.[38]

Economic Climate The economic climate reflects market and financial controls on investment, as well as support services and capabilities. Variables in this category are government regulatory and economic control policies (wages, prices, imports, exports), government ability to manage its own economic affairs (inflation, debt level), and government provision of support services and capabilities (roads, airports, electricity, water, sewage disposal, banking services, schools, hospitals). For example, growing U.S trade and budget deficits have been accompanied by pressures to increase protection of U.S. industry from foreign competition, such as that from Japan.[39]

As you can imagine, multinational corporations must cope with many wide-ranging political issues. Based on a five-year forecast (1987–1992), 24 percent of the eighty-five countries studied ranked high or very high in political risk; this figure is down significantly from the 63 percent classified as high risk or very high risk in the 1983–1988 five-year forecast.[40] High risk was defined as a probability of 25 percent or more that turmoil will adversely affect international business in a country. Countries ranked high in political risk include Bolivia, Chile, El Salvador, Haiti, Colombia, Honduras, the Philippines, South Africa, Nicaragua, Egypt, Iran, Iraq, and Sri Lanka. Some low-risk countries include Austria, Canada, Denmark, Germany, the United Kingdom, Japan, and Switzerland.

The following Insight describes how General Motors forecasts political risk.

I N S I G H T   The centerpiece of the General Motors (GM) political assessment system is the Political Risk Index—an annual comparison of the political environment for U.S. automakers in sixty-four countries around the world. For GM, nine variables are critical to measuring the level of political risk in any country: Three are macro political factors; two measure the policy-making process; and four reflect key regulatory issues. Each factor is assigned a weight indicative of its relative importance to GM's business overseas; the total of the weights is 100. The variables are defined (and weighted) as follows:

Macro Political Factors

1. *Leadership* (15 points): The degree to which a regime is favorably disposed toward foreign investment, including the auto industry, and has political institutions and processes that are adaptable and reasonably reliable.

2. *Social cohesion* (10 points): The degree to which a society is reasonably free of ideological, religious, class, regional, tribal, and/or ethnic conflicts.

3. *External involvement* (10 points): The degree to which the country is free of involvement with outside powers, movements, organizations, and/or institutions.

Policy Factors

4. *Development* (10 points): The capability of national policy makers and administrative processes to facilitate the necessary structural changes in the economy in the long run, as it moves from one stage of development to another, and the expected impact of those changes on foreign investors in the automotive industry.

5. *Economic management* (10 points): The capability of policy makers and administrative processes to minimize the adverse effects of cyclical fluctuations.

Regulatory Factors

6. *Finance* (10 points): The degree to which regulations restricting financial aspects of an investment, such as taking out of profits, foreign exchange, taxes, or price and credit controls, are likely to have an adverse impact.

7. *Energy* (10 points): The degree to which a motor vehicle operation will not be unduly affected by energy policies concerning availability, security of supply, control of demand, or fuel consumption.

8. *Labor* (10 points): The degree to which a motor vehicle investment will not be adversely affected by policies toward labor, such as regulations of unemployment, unionization, bargaining, or arbitration.

9. *Automotive* (15 points): The degree to which the overall management of an investment by a foreign automotive producer will not be seriously distorted by local content requirements, import restrictions, export incentives, domestication of management or ownership, functional spin-off requirements, non-auto transportation requirements, or restrictions on the ownership of cars and trucks.

Policy and regulatory factors together represent 65 percent of the total weighting, and the macro political factors account for 35 percent. This reflects the specific risks faced by the auto industry. The factors and their relative importance would differ for companies within other industries, such as Exxon in the oil industry or Citicorp in the banking industry.[41]

Political Mechanisms

Governments and businesses employ a variety of political strategies, as discussed in Chapter 3, to cope with political forces. In this section we go beyond these strategies to examine two major categories of international political mechanisms: (1) protectionism and (2) bribery and extortion. We aren't suggesting that bribery and extortion take place only in international transactions nor are we recommending their use. We simply want to give you an appreciation for international political mechanisms as they are.

protectionism Various international political mechanisms designed to help firms avoid (or reduce) potential (or actual) competitive or political threats to an industry—for example, tariffs, quotas, subsidies, cartels.

tariff A government tax on goods or services entering a country.

quota A restriction on the quantity of a country's imports or exports, usually intended to guarantee domestic manufacturers a certain percentage of the domestic market.

subsidy A direct or indirect payment by the government to its country's firms that makes selling or investing abroad cheaper and thus more profitable.

cartel An alliance formed among producers engaged in the same type of business in order to limit or eliminate competition.

Protectionism **Protectionism** includes various mechanisms designed to help an industry avoid (or reduce) potential (or actual) competitive or political threats from abroad. Four of the key protectionism mechanisms are tariffs, quotas, subsidies, and cartels.

A **tariff** is a government tax on goods or services entering a country. A tariff serves primarily to raise the price of imported goods or services. As a result, domestic goods and services gain a relative price advantage. The U.S. Rice Millers' Association claims that if even 10 percent of the Japanese rice market were opened to imports through a lowering of tariffs, the resulting lower prices would save the Japanese consumer $6 billion annually, and the United States would gain a $300 million share of the market.[42]

A **quota** is a restriction on the quantity of a country's imports (or sometimes exports). Import quotas are generally intended to guarantee domestic manufacturers access to a certain percentage of the domestic market. For example, U.S. sugar import quotas have existed for over fifty years. The intent is to preserve about half the domestic sugar market for U.S. sugar producers. Domestic sugar cane and sugar beet growers are guaranteed about 21.5 cents a pound, compared with an average of 14 cents a pound on world markets in 1990. It's estimated that U.S. consumers pay $3 billion per year in extra food costs because of sugar quotas.[43] Some experts suggest that if protectionism is politically unavoidable, then tariffs are preferable to quotas. Quotas fix the numbers of imports entering a country and thus freeze markets. Domestic producers are under less pressure to become more productive and efficient. Quotas are a hidden tax on consumers, whereas tariffs are a more obvious one.[44]

A **subsidy** is a direct or indirect payment by a government to its country's firms to make selling or investing abroad cheaper for them—and thus more profitable. For example, the Overseas Private Investment Corporation (OPIC) is a self-sustaining agency of the U.S. government that helps qualified U.S. investors establish commercial projects in developing countries. The agency has programs that offer preinvestment assistance and financing, and it also insures eligible projects against losses from political risks, including government seizure of assets, nonconvertibility of local currency into U.S. dollars, and damage caused by war, revolution, insurrection, or strife.[45]

A **cartel** is an alliance of producers engaged in the same type of business, formed to limit or eliminate competition.[46] Whereas tariffs, subsidies, and quotas are implemented through government regulations, cartels are negotiated agreements between firms or governments, as in the case of OPEC (Organization of Petroleum Exporting Countries). A primary objective of any cartel is to protect its members' revenues and profits by controlling prices and output. International cartels currently exist in oil, copper, aluminum, natural rubber, and other raw products. The best-known cartel is OPEC, which was formed in 1960. As evidenced by the recent history of the oil industry and OPEC, cartels often have a roller-coaster life. In recent years OPEC hasn't been very effective in controlling oil production by member countries.[47] Members can't agree on prices or quantities to be produced. U.S. firms are forbidden by law to form or directly participate in cartels because their purpose is at odds with preserving free enterprise and individual rights based on private property.[48]

Protectionism has strong advocates and opponents. Generally it works against consumers' interests by raising prices. Advocates claim that it protects home-country industries and jobs against unfair competition from countries with subsistence wages and special subsidies. Therefore, whether companies, business associations, and employee groups favor or oppose protectionism depends on how a particular measure is interpreted to serve their own interests.[49]

bribe An improper payment made to obtain a special favor (not illegal in some countries).

extortion The obtaining of payment in response to some kind of threat.

Bribery and Extortion A **bribe** is an improper payment (not always illegal in some countries) made to induce the recipient to do something for the payer. By offering a bribe, the payer hopes to obtain a special favor in exchange for something of value (money, a trip, a car, or the like). **Extortion** is a payment made to ensure that the recipient doesn't harm the payer in some way. The purpose of extortion is to obtain something of value by threatening harm to the payer.[50] A situation illustrating extortion is one in which a company's product sits idle on the dock of a foreign port until a customs official's demand for a $10,000 payment is met.

The practices of bribery and extortion take place throughout the world. These practices appear to occur more frequently in Algeria, Iraq, Saudi Arabia, Bolivia, Kenya, Indonesia, Mexico, and Nigeria, among others. Such countries may culturally define some forms of bribery and extortion as acceptable, as an appropriate and expected form of gift giving.[51]

The Foreign Corrupt Practices Act of 1977 makes it a crime for U.S. corporations to offer or make payments to officials of foreign governments or companies for the purpose of obtaining or retaining business. The act established specific record-keeping requirements for publicly held corporations, making it difficult for managers to conceal political payments prohibited by the act. Violators—both corporations and individuals—face stiff penalties. A company may be fined up to $1 million. A manager who directly participates in or has knowledge of any violations of the act faces up to five years in prison and/or $10,000 in fines.[52] Furthermore, the act prohibits corporations from paying any fines imposed on their directors, managers, employees, or agents.

grease payment A small payment used to get lower-level government employees to speed up required paperwork (allowed under the U.S. Foreign Corrupt Practices Act of 1977).

However, the act doesn't prohibit grease payments to employees of foreign governments whose duties are primarily ministerial or clerical. **Grease payments** are small payments—almost gratuities—used to get lower-level government employees to speed up required paperwork. Such payments are sometimes required to persuade employees to perform their normal duties.[53] Prohibiting grease payments would put U.S. firms at an extreme competitive disadvantage when conducting business abroad. Such a prohibition would also be very difficult to enforce.

CULTURAL FORCES

The cultural forces described in Chapter 3 underlie the day-to-day competitive and political forces operating within and among nations. Four important aspects of a culture that have direct implications for international management are its view of social change, time orientation, language, and value system.

View of Social Change

Cultures' different views of social change can have a significant impact on an organization's plans for international change and development. Many non-Western cultures, such as those of India, Saudi Arabia, and China, see change as a slow and natural progression. For these cultures change is part of the evolution of human beings and the universe, guided by a Supreme Being, and the attitude toward it tends to be passive or reactive. In contrast, Western cultures tend to take a more proactive approach to change. They assume that people can shape and control changes in order to achieve their own objectives and destinies. Therefore, Western managers assigned to non-Western countries often run into difficulty when trying to introduce innovations too rapidly. In cultures that hold a passive/reactive view, proposals for change must often go hand in hand with painstaking concern for their effect on interpersonal relationships.[54] Individuals in nations such as Japan, France, and Greece that are characterized by high uncertainty avoidance (see Chapter 3) are also likely to resist or react cautiously to social change. Managers plunged into these cultures have to recognize this viewpoint, plan for it, and manage change accordingly.

Time Orientation

Many people in the United States and Canada think of time as an extremely scarce commodity. Americans often say ''time is money'' or ''time is the enemy.'' Several popular books on time show an almost frenetic concern with how managers should plan their days. The need to establish and stick to tight deadlines for accomplishing tasks is a basic tenet of this style of management.

Some cultures, however, view time as an unlimited and unending resource. For example, Hindus believe that time doesn't begin at birth or end at death. The Hindu belief in reincarnation gives life a nontemporal, everlasting dimension. Because of such attitudes, employees, customers, and suppliers in some cultures are quite casual about keeping appointments and meeting deadlines—an indifference that can be highly frustrating to the many Canadian and U.S. managers who have to deal with them.

Traditionally, the Mexican attitude toward time could best be summed up in the word *mañana,* meaning ''not today''—but not necessarily tomorrow either! A manager in Mexico might have said, ''Yes, your shipment will be ready on Tuesday.'' You would arrive on Tuesday to pick it up but find it wasn't ready. No one was upset or embarrassed; they would politely explain that the paperwork hadn't been processed yet or offer some similar explanation. Time commitments were considered desirable objectives but not binding promises. This attitude toward time is beginning to change among modern Mexican professionals. As lifestyles become more complex and pressures for greater productivity increase, people in Mexico are beginning to feel more concern for punctuality, and time commitments are more frequently met.[55]

Language

Language serves to bind as well as to separate cultures. Fluency in another language can give an international manager a competitive edge in understanding and gaining the acceptance of people from the host culture. However, the ability to speak a language correctly isn't enough: A manager must also be able to recognize the nuances of phrases, sayings, and nonverbal gestures.

The story is told of several U.S. executives who were trying to negotiate with their Japanese counterparts. The American head negotiator made a proposal. The Japanese head negotiator was silent. His silence meant that he was considering the offer. The American, however, took his silence to mean that the offer wasn't good enough. So the American raised the offer! Again the Japanese considered in silence, and again the silence prompted the American negotiator to raise the offer. Finally the American reached his limit, and an agreement was struck. The Japanese head negotiator had obtained several concessions simply because the American negotiator has misread the meaning of his silence.[56]

Value Systems

In Chapter 3 we discussed differences in value systems. As part of that discussion we described four value dimensions: power distance, uncertainty avoidance, individualism, and masculinity. Differences in values among countries naturally affect how managers function in the international context. Because of continuing interest in the competitive challenge of Japanese firms, we will look at differences in value dimensions between the United States and Japan as an example and develop the management implications of these differences.[57]

U.S. and Japanese Societies Of the fifty countries studied by Hofstede (see Chapter 3), Japan and the United States ranked among the lowest in power distance (rankings of 21 and 16, respectively). In contrast, Japan had a very high uncertainty avoidance ranking of 46, whereas the United States had a relatively low ranking of 11. Although the U.S. ranking of 36 fell on the masculinity end of the masculinity-femininity continuum, it wasn't nearly as high as Japan's ranking of 50; in Japan, women are still not accepted in management circles.[58] Japan and the United States also differed significantly in terms of individualism versus collectivism. The United States had the highest individualism score, with a ranking of 50; Japan's score and ranking of 28 reflected its preference for collectivism. This difference between the two countries is important enough to warrant a bit more time on that topic here.

Collectivism means that people identify strongly with the groups to which they belong—from the family unit to the society as a whole. It emphasizes group objectives and dependence on others. Groups are not thought of as collections of individuals. Rather, the group exists first and absorbs the individual into it. Consequently the individual is governed by the norms (rules) of each group.

The Japanese form of collectivism leads to group cohesion. The short-term sacrifice of the individual's wants for the benefit of the group is commonly accepted. As a result, Japan's high levels of achievement are group-oriented. Furthermore, because Japan's value system is less diverse than that of the United States, severe conflicts caused by underlying differences in values occur less frequently.

In contrast, achievement in the United States is relatively individualistic.[59] James Hodgson, former U.S. ambassador to Japan, explains the basic differences between U.S. and Japanese societies:

> American society is first and foremost underpinned by that venerable Judeo-Christian objective of individual justice. The Japanese, however, spurn individual justice as a priority goal. Instead, they seek something in many ways the opposite; they seek *group harmony*. We American justice-seekers speak proudly of our *rights*. The harmony-minded Japanese stress not rights but *relations*. They reject our emphasis on individual rights as being divisive and disruptive.
>
> Americans make our national policy decisions and settle our many differences largely through adversary proceedings—we compete, we sue, and we vote. In Japan "adversarism" is *out*. Consensus is *in*, and it has been for centuries. The Japanese do not consider 51 percent a "majority," at least not a workable majority. The distinction that emerges from all this may be capsulized simply. In American life, the individual strives to *stand out*. The Japanese citizen, however, seeks to *fit in*. And fit in he does—into his family, his schools, his company, his union, his nation. Japan is a nation where the parts fit.[60]

U.S. and Japanese Organizations The fundamental societal differences that we've been discussing are reflected in some very basic differences between U.S. and Japanese organizations.[61] Does this mean that U.S. managers cannot transfer to their organization *any* of the ideas that have worked so well in Japan? Not at all. In fact, several Japanese management practices—such as the use of team management—have been successfully adapted to U.S. operations.[62]

However, keep in mind that, in identifying differences between the two nations' organizations and management practices, we are painting with a broad brush. Moreover, the differences in values and philosophies among U.S. firms and managers are much greater than the differences among Japanese firms and managers.

Table 4.1 characterizes and compares U.S. and Japanese organizations based on six dimensions that are strongly influenced by the contrasting values of the two nations. The theme of individualism in the United States versus collectivism in Japan is readily apparent. For many Japanese the company isn't just a place to work; it is also a sharing and caring group, which treats the employee like a family member.

Characteristics of Many U.S. and Japanese Organizations

Dimension	Many (not all) Major U.S. Organizations	Many (not all) Major Japanese Organizations
Employment	Short term, on average, but varies widely; unstable and insecure	Long term (lifetime in larger organizations); relatively secure and stable
Salary and promotion	Merit pay based on individual contribution; rapid promotion	Heavy emphasis on seniority early in career; shifts to merit pay later in career; slow promotion
Attitude toward work	Individual responsibilities	Collective responsibilities, group loyalty, duty-oriented
Decision making	Individual-oriented; relative top-down emphasis	Group- and consensus-oriented; bottom-up emphasis
Relationship with employees	Depersonalized; emphasis on formal contracts; employee resents organizational interference into his or her personal life	Personalized; employee treated as a family member; paternalism; employee expects organization to show concern for personal affairs
Competition	Relatively free and open among individuals	Very low among individuals within groups; very high among groups, such as among organizations

Source: Adapted from W. G. Ouchi and A. M. Jaeger, ''Type Z Organization: Stability in the Midst of Mobility.'' *Academy of Management Review,* 1978, 3:305–314. Used with permission.

Japanese employees are often proud of their company's success and frequently identify with their firm—an employee becomes Mr. Yamada of Sony, Mr. Tanaka of Toyota, Ms. Ogawa of Honda, and so on.[63]

This sense of closeness, of being part of a sharing and caring group, appears to be limited to fellow Japanese. U.S. managers working for Japanese subsidiaries within the United States often express feelings of being left out of the inner circle of Japanese managers. Although U.S. blue-collar workers in Japanese-owned subsidiaries enjoy a relatively high level of participation in decision making, their managerial counterparts often aren't participating in real policy making. The sense of isolation for U.S. managers is increased when they can't speak Japanese. Typically, American managers go home to their families after work, while their Japanese colleagues socialize. On weekends the Japanese managers play golf, discuss business, and informally hash out decisions. By Monday morning every manager is aware of the decisions—except the Americans. One American who served as chief counsel to a major Japanese trading company comments: ''The most difficult part of working for the Japanese is that you will always be working *with* the organization. You will never be *of* the organization because you are not Japanese.''[64]

The Nenko System

Nenko system The pattern of organizational characteristics that form the basis for managerial practices found in most large-scale Japanese organizations.

Japanese organizational characteristics form a general pattern known as the **Nenko system,** which provides the basis for managerial practices used in many large-scale Japanese organizations, such as Sony and Honda. These characteristics are summarized in the third column of Table 4.1. The Nenko system is a natural outgrowth of Japan's culture and economy.[65] Therefore, managers cannot blindly transfer it to organizations in other cultures. Companies in the United States and Canada, with their relatively strong emphasis on individualism, have found it difficult to apply all of its principles.[66]

Employment Security The Nenko system stresses lifelong employment with a particular firm. After completing formal education, the individual joins an organization with the expectation of remaining there until retirement, normally at age 55 years of age. Of course, the obligation is mutual. The employer isn't supposed to fire or lay off an employee, except in extreme circumstances. In recent years this pattern of mutual lifelong commitment has loosened. Some employers have successfully hired highly skilled employees away from other organizations. And a 1990 survey of Japanese managers revealed that 39 percent of respondents between the ages of 20 and 39 were thinking of changing jobs. The number of executive search firms in Tokyo increased from 50 to more than 250 between 1985 and 1990. In brief, loyalty is no longer absolute among some younger Japanese professionals and managers.[67] Large employers are also hiring a higher percentage of temporary employees, especially women and retirees. These employees are laid off when profit-and-loss conditions dictate.

Emphasis on Seniority Compensation and opportunities for promotion are based heavily on seniority. Many employers believe that job knowledge and skills increase with seniority. Thus lower-level managers are often paid on the basis of seniority. After managers reach about 45 years of age, however, the organization places more weight on performance than seniority in determining their salary increases.

The possible implications of this emphasis on seniority were noted by Akio Morita, chairman of the board and CEO of the Sony Corporation since 1976:

> Fortunately Japan has a lifetime employment system, which encourages the long-range view even among lower and middle management levels. For example, a member of our company may be stationed in some far-off land, struggling to learn in a country with entirely different customs and characteristics. But he realizes that with the knowledge he has gained in five years or so, he might become chief of the department in our head office that deals with this area, and that in ten years he may become director in charge of our international operations, and later have the chance of becoming a top executive of our company. He, therefore, is keenly interested in how strong the company will be in five or ten years from now, at the same time that he gives his attention to the business at hand. He is thus not only working constantly to achieve today's objectives but also paying close attention to what should be accumulated over the years ahead.[68]

Group Loyalty The Nenko system encourages group loyalty and shared obligations. Employees tend to think of themselves in terms of the organizations to which they belong, which results in their feeling a strong sense of duty and allegiance to the group. For employees with sufficient seniority, performance standards are heavily weighted toward criteria such as flexibility, group support, and loyalty. In addition, long-term commitments by managers and employees to their organizations encourage long-term training and development of employees.

Group Decision Making Managers make extensive use of group decision-making practices that lead to group consensus. However, the aim of consensus is to define the questions that need to be raised, rather than to decide what should be done. This process is much more time-consuming than letting one person make a decision and then informing the rest of the group. However, implementation of a decision tends to be quicker because employees are more familiar with the reasons for doing something and have bought into the merits of doing it.

In Japanese organizations ideas often flow up from the bottom, rather than just down from the top. Management is willing to consult with any employee who will be influenced by a major decision. Usually the parties involved reach a consensus before implementing any decision. This consensus occurs despite a strong seniority system, so younger employees are not cut out of the decision-making process. This bottom-up form of decision making is known as the **Ringi system.** Although the system is bottom-up, control is not decentralized; the superior retains the right to reject the collective recommendations of subordinates. In fact, the Ringi system is based on the centralization of decision-making authority by higher management.

The Ringi system has been criticized on the grounds that it encourages higher management to make too many decisions on a fragmented case-by-case basis. This occurs because proposals tend to move up the organization hierarchy from diverse and uncoordinated groups. Consequently, many believe, this system is better suited to short-term operational decisions than to long-term strategic decisions and plans. Others view the slow pace of the Ringi system as inappropriate for strategic planning. The system is especially inefficient for Japanese multinational corporations operating in complex, dynamic environments. For major types of strategic decisions, top managers of more and more Japanese multinational corporations have been modifying, and even abandoning, the slow, bottom-up Ringi system.[69]

The Nagoya Sogo Bank of Nagoyashi, Japan is a good example of a Japanese firm that practices the Nenko system.

Ringi system A bottom-up form of decision making used in many Japanese organizations; involves reaching a consensus among all parties affected by a decision.

I NSIGHT Nagoya Sogo Bank employs a variety of formal and informal means of communicating. Some of them ease communication among all employees, and others promote contact among managers, branch employees, or division staff. Regardless of the means—branch management meeting, party, newsletter, or companywide athletic event—the overall purpose is the same: to convey management intentions to employees and in turn to collect information about their views. Although the costs of communicating are significant, Katsumaro Kato, president of Nagoya Sogo, says the investment is reasonable considering what the program accomplishes.

To ensure cooperation Nagoya Sogo's management encourages participation. Employees participate in management in a variety of ways. They participate indirectly in round-table conferences with managers through their labor union representatives, who make employees' opinions and desires known. Final decisions are left to management, however. Union leaders also help draw up management plans. This approach "contributes to a common understanding of the management climate of the bank," Kato says. Employees participate directly by submitting suggestions or by taking part in group decision-making activities or any of a variety of other programs.

From time to time changing corporate conditions bring about labor-management problems. When they occur, Kato says, it is "necessary for labor and management to work together . . . exchanging opinions honestly with a full understanding of the realities of the situation." The solid relationship between labor and management at Nagoya Sogo provides the framework for resolving problems. An important consideration when working toward resolution, Kato adds, is "to prevent any damage to mutual trust."[70]

Cracks in the Landscape   There are some exceptions to the Nenko system and other traditional patterns in Japanese organizations and society. Highly capable and assertive individuals do leave their organizations and start businesses of their own or join smaller organizations. Firms started by such individualistic entrepreneurs include Honda, Sony, and Matsushita. Small-scale Japanese enterprises (300 or fewer employees) cannot afford to offer fringe benefits as extensive as those of giant corporations, and these smaller firms offer less job security because they are less secure in their markets.

There is evidence that some young Japanese workers are not as devoted as the preceding generation to long hours of hard work. As *Fortune* magazine recently commented: "The world's champion workaholics are starting to loosen up and play more. Japan's consumers are enjoying more choices than ever before, from imported cars to U.S.-made cockroach killers. Many young Japanese are starting to realize that some aspects of Western lifestyle are preferable to their own."[71] Some young workers have accepted the concept of "flexible individualism"—not the rugged American variety but a simple desire for self-expression in their work, lifestyle, and possessions.[72]

Child rearing and other household duties, once relegated completely to the woman, are sometimes shared by husband and wife. Materialism is leading some families to have two wage earners. Some women are continuing their education through college and are entering the workplace.[73] These trends in Japan appear to be a result of its increasingly global economic participation, which is modifying its once homogeneous culture.

CHAPTER SUMMARY

1.   There are six levels of organizing for international involvement.

   ▶ A company hires commission agents to represent it in international transactions.

   ▶ As the amount of trade grows, the company hires its own export manager.

   ▶ The company expands to a full-fledged export department.

   ▶ An international division adds manufacturing to the marketing and finance tasks already being handled abroad.

   ▶ An international corporation operates production and marketing subsidiaries, sometimes by product group, in various countries.

   ▶ A multinational corporation has managers and other employees who take a global view, operates subsidiaries around the world, and is willing to consider the establishment of new operations throughout the world.

2.   There are six basic international strategies that can be pursued by a firm.

   ▶ An exporting strategy is the transfer of goods and services abroad, for sale in foreign countries.

   ▶ A licensing strategy involves an organization's making certain resources available to companies in another country, under well-defined contractual terms.

- A franchising strategy provides foreign franchises with a complete array of materials and services.

- An alliance strategy refers to uniting two or more organizations to achieve common objectives.

- A multidomestic strategy involves adjusting products and practices to the requirements of individual regions or countries. Overall strategy is centralized, but marketing, transportation, and some production operations are decentralized to subsidiaries in host countries.

- A global strategy involves operating subsidiaries competitively in a number of countries, while maintaining product consistency, standardization, and low relative cost.

3. A variety of competitive global forces are affecting the management of an increasing number of organizations. Two such forces are the U.S.–Canada Free Trade Agreement and Europe 1992.

- The U.S.–Canada Free Trade Agreement (FTA) is increasing competitive pressures through the elimination of many tariffs, reduction of a number of nontariff barriers, stimulation of free flows of capital, and the like.

- Europe 1992 will accelerate competitive pressures by moving toward a single market among the twelve member nations. The removal of various trade barriers and the encouragement of much freer movement of goods, people, services, and capital has already influenced many companies.

4. Managers may assess political risk by monitoring four categories of factors:

- Domestic instability, or the amount of unrest in a country.

- Foreign conflict, or the degree of hostility that one country shows toward others.

- Political climate, or the likelihood that a government's orientation will shift abruptly—to either the right or the left.

- Economic climate, or the amount of control placed on investment and the supporting services and facilities provided to investors.

5. Governments and private organizations employ various political mechanisms to cope with international competitive forces. These mechanisms include tariffs, quotas, subsidies, cartels, and bribery and extortion.

6. Four of the cultural factors that directly influence businesses involved in international operations are view of social change, time orientation, language, and value system.

- In non-Western cultures that view social change as a natural process, the attitude toward change is passive or reactive. In Western cultures that view social change as a means to achieve objectives, the attitude toward change is more proactive.

- Time can be viewed either as a scarce resource to be used to the fullest or as an unlimited resource to be treated casually.

- Language, both verbal and nonverbal, can aid or frustrate business transactions. Fluency in another language gives a real competitive edge.

- Fundamentally different value systems are reflected in the different management styles of Japanese and U.S. organizations.

QUESTIONS FOR DISCUSSION AND APPLICATION

1. What factors are likely to be important to a corporation in choosing between an international and a multinational form of organization?

2. Is it possible for a single organization to make use of all six strategies for international involvement? Explain.

3. **From Where You Sit:** Based on the U.S.–Canada Free Trade Agreement, how do you think U.S. and Canadian manufacturers of high-tech products and services (computers, software, telecommunications equipment, and so forth) will benefit? Why?

4. Do you think the long-term objectives of Europe 1992 will be realized? What might some obstacles be?

5. **From Where You Sit:** Ask a top manager in a company in your community what impact Europe 1992 is having on the firm.

6. **From Where You Sit:** In the past ten years Honda Motor Company and Toyota have greatly expanded their manufacturing operations in the United States, making decisions involving hundreds of millions of dollars in investments. What political risks should they have evaluated in making these decisions? Consider the political risks of making the investments as well as the political risks of not making them.

7. What limitations are there in General Motors' Political Risk Index?

8. Should protectionism mechanisms be encouraged in the United States or Canada? Why?

9. Should managers in the United States and Canada try to adopt more of Japanese organizations' characteristics identified in Table 4.1? Explain.

10. **From Where You Sit:** Would you like to work under the Nenko system? Why or why not?

11. **From Where You Sit:** Assume you are the CEO of a small manufacturer with fifty employees and you want to develop internationally. What factors should you consider in organizing for international involvement? What factors should you consider in assessing various strategies for international involvement?

Cultural Traits and Preferences

Ten pairs of statements are presented below. Pick the statement in each pair that best represents your personal traits and preferences. There are no correct choices; choose the alternative that best represents who you are (not necessarily who you would like to become).

1. a. ☐ Family has priority.
   b. ☐ Family is usually second to work or school.

2. a. ☐ I have a fatalistic outlook.
   b. ☐ I have a master-of-own-life outlook.

3. a. ☐ I am sensitive to differences of opinion.
   b. ☐ Sensitivity is a weakness.

4. a. ☐ Title and position are more important than money.
   b. ☐ Money is a main status indicator and is a reward for achievement.

5. a. ☐ I work to live.
   b. ☐ I live to work.

6. a. ☐ Deadlines and commitments are flexible.
   b. ☐ Deadlines and commitments are firm.

7. a. ☐ Promotions should be based more heavily on loyalty to superior.
   b. ☐ Promotions should be based more heavily on performance.

8. a. ☐ Truth is a relative concept.
   b. ☐ Truth is an absolute value.

9. a. ☐ I shun confrontation.
   b. ☐ I put up a tough business front.

10. a. ☐ Money is for enjoying life.
    b. ☐ Money is an end in itself.

Interpretation

Count the numbers of a and b responses. The a responses are considered to be typical of Mexican society and managers, and the b responses are considered to be typical of U.S. society and managers. Of course, these are broad patterns of cultural traits and preferences, which do not represent all individuals in Mexico or the United States.

Question. Based on your self-description, what challenges would you expect to face in negotiating with typical Mexican managers or U.S. managers? Explain.

TO: Program Participants

FROM: Lou Grabowsky, Partner — Change of Retail Industry Practice: Southwest Region of Arthur Andersen & Co.

Subject: Conference on Globalization of the Retail Marketplace

I look forward to working with each of you during our upcoming conference. I would like to share some ideas to trigger your thinking about the globalization of the retail marketplace. By the mid-1990s successful retail organizations will need to be structured for nimbleness in order to respond appropriately and quickly to changes in the market. And there are few retail markets that aren't changing. America is aging, and the "silver streakers" are changing the way we do business. Consumers have less time to shop, yet they want better, more personalized service. Information moves so quickly that fashion trends that once took months to travel from Paris to New York to Dallas now fly halfway around the world overnight.

Technology, especially point-of-sale scanners and inventory control systems, gives us daily updates on what our customers are buying, or even what types of customers are buying what kinds of merchandise. Quick-response techniques enable nimble managers to combine on-line sales data with other electronic data (inventories, labor hours, utility costs) to make decisions in a timely fashion — such as keeping inventories on a par with demand and eliminating the need to conduct after-the-fact meetings to determine what went wrong.

Managers need nimble minds that can adapt and change. Too often, managers commit mental incest — they fall in love with their own ideas. A failure to spot changes that make old ideas worthless can be the management equivalent of putting on blinders. This almost always results in markdowns, unsold merchandise, or even business failure.

Growth and success in the 1990s requires a real, top-down commitment to changing old ways of thinking. Today's retailer is doing business in a world of incredible but wonderfully challenging changes. And the first thing that must change is the way we think. There's no time like today to start thinking about the world as a whole. Start now to identify your company's niche in the international marketplace, and challenge aggressively any thinking that limits your opportunities for growth. Yes, the future is uncertain. But, as we're learning, if you can't predict it, maybe you should create it.

Again, I look forward to our upcoming conference, where we'll share many ideas on the management implications of the gobalization of the retail marketplace.

Assume you are to be one of the program participants. What ideas would you offer?

Coke Reassigns Aggressive Head of French Unit

BY E.S. BROWNING
AND MICHAEL J. MCCARTHY

The aggressive head of Coca-Cola Co.'s French operation has been reassigned to the company's Atlanta headquarters just 18 months after being sent to conquer the French soft-drink market.

Coca-Cola confirmed that the Paris chief, William Hoffman, would be given a new position at its European headquarters office in Atlanta. Coke also said it will bring in a new chief manager for France, an American currently based in Brussels, as well as another new manager from Brussels, who is Belgian. Coke declined to give further details as the changes won't officially be announced until today.

In terms of volume, Coke appears to be doing well in France. Measured by case sales, which reflect the retail selling environment, Coke said its volume rose 22% in 1990, while the rest of the industry increased 12%. Per-capita consumption of Coca-Cola beverages rose to 48 eight-ounce servings from 29 in 1989.

But Coke won't break out financial specifics for the French operation or even confirm if it's profitable. "The company is very satisfied with the development of that bottling business," a spokesman said.

Coke officials acknowledged that Mr. Hoffman's hard-driving style had occasionally shocked French restaurant owners. At one point, cafes in Bordeaux boycotted Coke to protest the rapid installation of curbside vending machines, which they consider unfair competition. Coke had to promise to withdraw the machines.

Mr. Hoffman's emphasis on American-style sales gimmicks, such as huge promotional displays, also annoyed some French supermarket owners. So did his repeated insistence that they should stop worrying so much about profit margin and instead focus, like U.S. store managers, on volume. Some businessmen complained that he was too much of a "steamroller."

"Some of his ideas may have been a bit too innovative," said one Coke official, "but they also got the business going."

Coke officials in Paris said Mr. Hoffman wasn't available for comment. They said that he had intended to remain in France two years, and that a departure after 18 months wasn't really premature. His leaving didn't reflect dissatisfaction with his work, they said. His new job would be "a higher post," added one official.

1. What did the Coca-Cola manager do wrong in terms of cultural norms? What could he have done differently?
2. If you were a manager about to join your company's office in Europe, how would you prepare to do business there?
3. What does the article tell you about Coca-Cola's international structure? Could the same problems occur with the manager who is being brought in from Brussels?
4. What values did William Hoffman exhibit, and how do they contrast with the value rankings for France in Figure 3.2?

TRANSCONTINENTAL INDUSTRIES (MALAYSIA) LTD.

Peter Wilkins puffed on his Dunhill (London) pipe while hunched at his desk in the plush managing director's office on the eighth floor of TIML's building in Penang. The midnight breeze out of the Malacca Straits cooled the sweat on his face and mixed waterfront smells with the rich aroma of Player's tobacco coming out of his pipe. He was writing to his daughter Pat in reply to her last letter, which lay open before him.

Pat, I wonder if you can grasp my problem in the Zia Mahomed business, as you sit reading social anthropology in Penn State's graduate school. By the way, you ought to be careful about the growing crop of Americanisms that's threatening to corrupt your formerly very impeccable Oxford University style!

In the Zia Mahomed problem, I'm dealing not just with one man but with a whole culture. My own Americanization (Stanford MBA) didn't prepare me for what's on my head now. I had a much easier time in Burma as a district official of the British Government. There I had no need to try and train any Burmese to assist me in my administration. I merely told the village headmen what I wanted done, and they took it from there among the locals. Jolly good system, too. The only headaches I had in Burma were from malaria and all that. But here in Penang I'm managing director of the Malaysian operations of a

company that's committed to indigenizing its middle executive positions all over Asia. I have to find and train Malays of the right caliber and potential for these jobs.

Zia showed great ability as an inventory clerk when he joined us in 1969. He was sent to the Honolulu corporate office in 1976 for six months' management training and did splendidly there. So well, in fact, that both the bossmen and I picked him to join four other Malays as the first Malay managers in TIML.

What we forgot was that all five of them are Muslims. There's been a rising tide of Islamic favor in Malaysia since the Communist threat was contained, due to the feeling of the local mullahs that a revival of true Koranic devotion among all Muslim Malays was the only true protection against the Communists in Southeast Asia. This has led to roadblocks to a pure Malayanization program here. Of course, the top people in Honolulu are all Americans with one fixed idea about how to make managers—the American way, whether it be the Harvard Business School method or the long-range, intensive in-company management development program.

I've got Zia's confidential file here. The last notation on it is by the corporate VP for personnel. It reads: ''Not promotable until he accepts and undergoes further training in marketing strategy, effective business communication, data processing, and quantitative decision making.'' If Zia doesn't get promoted—and he's had every reason to think he will—he could resign and create trouble among all the Malay personnel in Penang. I think his problem is that he's too conscientious a Muslim to be a thorough company executive.

Wilkins remembered a book entitled *Islam in the Modern National State* in which the author noted that the mullahs of Malaysia were trained at the Al-Azhar in Cairo or Mecca and took a typical Sunni hard line on how and how far Islamic nations should pursue the modernization of their societies. Wilkins turned thoughtfully back to his letter.

In one of my earlier conversations with him after his home office management training, Zia raised a question that he said one of his mullahs had put to him: ''Can a man absorb additional modern skills and techniques without endangering his commitment to Islam?'' My answer then was short and quick: ''Look here, Zia, TIML is in the business of building the economy of your country. We're going to do it as quickly as we can with the genius of men like yourself. Is the prosperity of your people to be governed by

some old-fashioned religious leaders?'' We have gone back and forth on this issue with no results.

My first instinct was to give Zia a kind of ultimatum: either he would submit to further training in the four areas top management had pointed out, or he would be fired or suspended. Honolulu tended to see it my way. But it has come to me that TIML is actually in business by favor of the Malaysian government, and the mullahs have tremendous influence over the majority of the ministers. Firing Zia would bring TIML into disrepute with the government, and we could lose our right to continue marketing and manufacturing here. And see what Khomeini has done to Iran. I can't let TIML give any cause for that kind of disaster in Malaysia.

I've also got to remember that TIML is competing with other foreign companies and a host of Chinese and Malay businesses, which, being native, don't pose any threat to Islamic consciousness. But TIML is an American company and fairly new. If I fired Zia, these native companies could stir up trouble for us with the mullahs and with the government. TIML is a threat to them as it is, with its larger size and financial resources. I don't want to make them a gift of a weapon with which to ruin us.

Stopping his letter writing to refill his pipe, Wilkins drew the Zia Mahomed file to him and took out his draft memorandum to Honolulu:

FROM: Peter Wilkins, Managing Director, TIML, Penang
TO: Honolulu (Attention: VP Personnel)

Options for Handling Zia Mahomed's Case

1. Dismiss any Malaysian employee, managerial or otherwise, who consistently refuses to accept training commitments designed to raise his or her competence and promotability, regardless of the reasons for such refusal.
2. Incorporate cultural factors (specifically those unique to the Islamic faith) into job descriptions for managers and workers.
3. Increase incentives for undertaking training programs, for example:
   (a) family allowances for trainees at each level,
   (b) accelerated promotion for successful completion of training courses,
   (c) training bonuses.

Zia Mahomed will be interviewed within the next ten days and asked to help in achieving the second of the three options listed. His retention in the company could become more likely when he sees his new role as a facilitator for TIML's management policies. Your agreement to the recommendations in options 2 and 3 and the preceding paragraph is requested.

1. Discuss the three options proposed by Wilkins in the context of (a) the political risk factors discussed in this chapter, (b) TIML's competitive position with respect to indigenous businesses, and (c) possible recruitment of Malaysian managers from among Malays studying abroad.

2. What value dimensions from Hofstede's framework (presented in Chapter 3) are suggested in this case?

Chapter 5

ETHICS AND SOCIAL RESPONSIBILITY IN MANAGEMENT

An ethical dilemma

What You Will Learn

1 How societal, legal, organizational, and individual factors influence ethical behavior and decisions.

2 The standards and principles of three ethical approaches: utilitarian, moral rights, and justice.

3 How traditional, stakeholder, and affirmative social responsibility concepts are related to the three ethical approaches.

4 **Skill Development:** How to apply ethical approaches and social responsibility concepts to various managerial decision-making situations.

" Is Pat's main responsibility to her

friend? "

An Ethical Dilemma

Lynne Doran Cote works as a customer representative for the Tacoma, Washington office of a small computer consulting firm. The detailed client information that she uses to design her computer systems is often confidential. Lynne is aware of the sensitive nature of this privileged information and its enormous potential value to competitors. Her company constantly emphasizes the need for trust between its employees and clients.

When Doran Cote found out some months ago that an old college friend, Scott James, had been hired to fill a similar position in the company, she welcomed him. But she was puzzled—she knew that he had been convicted of a felony narcotics violation and had served a prison sentence. After talking more with James and her co-workers, Doran Cote came to realize that the Tacoma office managers knew nothing of his record. Although Lynne and Scott haven't actually discussed his past, both of them know that he wouldn't have been placed in such a sensitive job if he had reported his history truthfully. Doran Cote knows that if the information were made public, James could lose his job. Depending on the circumstances of the disclosure, the company could also be embarrassed and its reputation severely damaged.

Lynne still hasn't divulged her knowledge of Scott's past. She's been troubled by the question of her responsibilities to her employer, to her co-workers, and to the company's clients. There's some danger that a client or future client could accidentally become aware of James's prison record. Would it be ethical for her to reveal his history to her employer in the hope of protecting the company and her co-workers from the consequences of a future disclosure? Or is her main responsibility to her friend?[1]

Lynne Doran Cote's dilemma is only one example of the ethical challenges most of us face from time to time. Managers are confronted with such situations almost daily. Consider a few questions about employees' day-to-day actions that have ethical implications: Does the employee hide his or her true feelings from others? Does the employee deal with others equally? Does the employee carry through on promises? Does the employee focus mainly on looking out for himself or herself? Does the employee think that the only thing that counts is the end result, not how you get there? Does the employee usually try to retaliate—directly or indirectly—if harmed by others? Does the employee agree with the statement ''There's no point in being honest if honesty doesn't pay''? The challenge for all employees in addressing these and other questions is to apply a consistent set of decision-making criteria to ethical problems that may involve other employees, customers, the community, or the environment.

The ethical issues facing managers and other employees have grown in significance in recent years, fueled by public concern about the effects of internal decisions on groups outside the organization. In addition to absolute standards of right or wrong, economic rivalry has also pushed businesses to address issues of social and moral conduct. Some individuals still think that businesses and their managers cannot be highly ethical and earn a profit at the same time. We disagree with this simplistic attitude. In a world of increasing local and global competition it has become apparent that being significantly out of step with society's expectations can be costly. For example, in 1990 Volvo ran a TV and magazine ad that showed a six-ton truck, called Bear Foot, driving over a row of cars. It flattened all of them except the Volvo. In November 1990 Volvo withdrew the ad, admitting that steel posts had been welded to the Volvo's chassis. Without the posts the Volvo would have been crushed by Bear Foot, like the other cars in the ad. Although Volvo withdrew the ad, it was too late. It had already created the conditions for distrust of its other ads touting the superior safety of Volvos.[2]

This chapter focuses on the complex ethical and social responsibilities facing today's managers. We begin by outlining four types of factors—societal, legal, organizational, and individual—that both influence and define ethical and unethical behavior and decisions. The potential conflicts inherent in managerial ethics will become even more evident when we review three ethical approaches managers can take: utilitarian, moral rights, and justice. Finally, the last section of the chapter covers the broad concept of the social responsibility of organizations.

THE MANY FACES OF ETHICAL BEHAVIOR

ethics A set of rules that define right and wrong conduct and that help individuals distinguish between fact and belief, decide how issues are defined, and decide what moral principles apply to the situation.

moral principles The impartial general rules of behavior that are of great importance to a society and, along with the values they represent, are fundamental to ethics.

In the most basic sense, **ethics** is a set of rules that define right and wrong conduct. These ethical rules state when behavior is approved and when it is considered unacceptable and wrong.[3] In a broader sense, ethics also includes the processes of (1) making distinctions between questions of fact and belief, (2) deciding how issues are defined, and (3) deciding what moral principles apply to a situation. **Moral principles** prescribe general rules of behavior that are intended to be impartial. They are of great importance to a society and cannot be established or changed by the decisions of powerful individuals alone; nor are they established as ''true'' solely by appeals to consensus or tradition.[4] Moral principles and the values they represent are fundamental to ethics. As you will learn in this chapter, some moral principles concerning managerial behavior are widely shared; others are not.

What is considered ethical behavior may depend on the factors that influence and define ethical behaviors. Figure 5.1 identifies four such determining factors. The ethical

Core Factors that Define and Influence Ethical Behavior

When attempting to evaluate ethical behavior in any situation within an organization, four interrelated perspectives—societal definitions, legal interpretation, organizational views, and the individual's stage of moral development—must be considered.

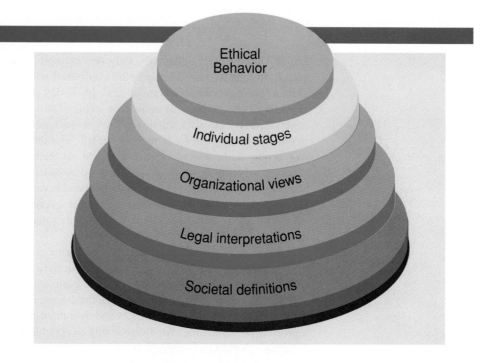

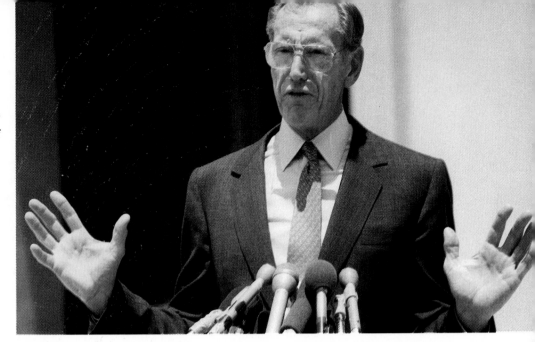

During the S&L crisis, the *societal definition* of what is ethical was put to the test. Here, Charles Keating talks to the press after the final day of arguments in the government's motion to dimiss his suit that Lincoln Savings and Loan was wrongly taken over by regulators.

implications of any single behavior or decision can rarely be understood by looking at a single factor, such as the legal interpretation of what is right or wrong. There is definitely a need for a systems viewpoint to evaluate ethical behaviors and decisions within a wider context. In this section each of the factors shown in Figure 5.1 is described somewhat independently of the others. The following sections then present a more realistic interplay of societal, legal, organizational, and individual factors in ethical or unethical behavior.

Societal Definitions

A large part of any definition of what is considered ethical comes from the society in which the behavior occurs. A variety of public opinion surveys have confirmed a disenchantment with the level of ethical behavior in general and with management practices in particular. To what extent do you agree or disagree with the following results from several surveys of U.S. adults, conducted between 1987 and 1989?

▶ 58 percent rated the ethical standards of business executives as only fair or poor.
▶ 90 percent thought white-collar crime was common or somewhat common.
▶ 76 percent saw the lack of ethics in businesspeople as contributing to crumbling moral standards.
▶ 54 percent thought that people are less honest today than they were ten years ago.
▶ High percentages of respondents thought businesses would do the following things in order to obtain greater profits: harm the environment (47 percent), endanger public health (38 percent), sell unsafe products (37 percent), and put workers' health and safety at risk (42 percent).[5]

In contrast to these relatively negative survey results, a comprehensive survey of managers revealed that 80 percent thought that their organizations were "guided by highly ethical standards."[6] (Though it's important to note that lower-level managers responding to the survey were more likely than top managers to say that their organizations were *not* guided by highly ethical standards.) And, in a recent study of honesty and trustworthiness in business, one anonymous entrepreneur attributed his longevity to his reputation for trustworthiness:

The most important reason for our success is the quality of my [product] line. But we wouldn't have survived without my integrity because our lines weren't always very successful. There are parabola curves in all businesses, and people still supported me, even though we had a low, because they believed in me.[7]

There is no research that enables us to conclude that the *perception* of business ethics is a reflection of the *reality* of business ethics or that business ethics have improved or declined over the past ten years. Regardless of the reality, though, survey results suggest that the general public perceives serious problems in the state of business ethics, whereas managers of organizations tend to see such problems as the exceptions that grab headline attention. This means that there are increased pressures on managers to make decisions characterized by societal expectations of stricter standards of ethical behavior. Managers work in more of a fishbowl than ever before, exposed by the press, with their decisions and actions judged publicly by different interest groups.[8] Auto manufacturers are judged by Ralph Nader and other consumer advocates as unethical for not doing everything possible to improve the safety of autos, such as immediately installing air bags in all cars. The manufacturers counter that they are not being unethical; rather, customers don't want to pay the cost of this additional safety, which manufacturers claim is marginal if safety belts are used. Shareholders want management to move cautiously so that the price of cars isn't driven up so much that the demand for new cars drops off, leading to lower profits and dividends.

In this chapter we will present examples of how changing societal definitions of ethical behavior eventually result in new legal requirements, as well as voluntary changes in behavior by organizations and their managers.

Legal Interpretations

law A value or standard of society that is enforceable through the courts.

What a society interprets as ethical or unethical frequently ends up being expressed through court decisions and the passage of laws within that society. **Laws** are simply society's values and standards that are enforceable in the courts.[9] Of course, the idea of operating according to the law is often inadequate as a basis for ethical management decisions and behavior. The legality of actions and decisions doesn't necessarily make them ethical. At one time, for example, it was legal for U.S. managers to discriminate against women and minorities in hiring and promotions. As our society came to recognize these practices as unethical, laws were passed in an attempt to stop them.

It's easy enough for managers to deal with behavior that is clearly both unethical and illegal, such as the theft of money. In this type of situation societal values and standards of behavior are clearly understood and reinforced by the law. But what about behavior that the courts interpret as legal and that society comes to see as unethical? The classic legal concept of *caveat emptor*—"let the buyer beware"—used to be the defense for a variety of shady business practices. During the 1950s and 1960s an increasingly aware U.S. public began to challenge the ethics of such a position. Shifting societal attitudes and values concerning *appropriate* behavior by businesses led to a flood of U.S. consumer legislation during the late 1960s and the early 1970s, which substantially diminished the concept of *caveat emptor*. As another example, into the 1960s it was common practice for banks, loan companies, and other lenders to fail to express the effective annual rates of interest charged on consumer loans. The public eventually realized that this behavior was unethical and socially irresponsible, and today federal law requires a clear statement of the true annual rate of interest on all loan agreements.

Even without specific legislation defining behavior as legal, the courts may rule on what constitutes ethical behavior and decisions by managers. Consider the case of employment-at-will. Employment-at-will is a traditional common law concept holding that employers are free to discharge employees for any reason at any time, and that employees are free to quit their jobs for any reason at any time.[10] Many employees, especially those in managerial positions, have been dismissed without explanation (at will) by their employers. Some of the court decisions described in the following Insight have undermined employment-at-will.

INSIGHT

Over the past twenty-five years courts have modified the freewheeling notion that employees can be fired for any reason. Employers have been held liable, for example, for firing employees who refused to lie before a legislative hearing, who blew the whistle about illegal conduct by their employers, or who filed workers' compensation claims. One way to sum up these cases is to say that employees can now recover damages from an employer if they are fired for reasons that undermine an important public policy.

But then the line between what is ethical and what is unethical becomes fuzzier. One court has decided that it does *not* violate an important public policy to fire an employee for reporting to the public (rather than company managers) that his or her superior is taking bribes. Another court has decided that it does *not* violate an important public policy to fire an employee who refused to reduce staffing in a hospital's intensive care unit on the grounds that it would endanger patients' lives. On the other hand, a court has decided that firing an employee for refusing to date her foreman *does* violate "the best interest of the economic system or the public good."

According to one study, as many as 1 million employees are fired in the United States each year. More than 150,000 of them would not have lost their jobs had the law stated that they could be fired only for good cause.[11]

Organizational Views

The organization itself can determine whether behavior within its walls is ethical or unethical.[12] The most fundamental organizational influence is top-level managers' commitment to ethical conduct. They may communicate this commitment through directives (memos), policy statements, speeches, publications, and, most importantly, actions.

Organizations take different approaches to establish principles of organizational conduct. The approach that is most common and is growing in popularity is setting forth expectations for the whole organization in written documents, which may include a code of ethics. The areas covered in codes and standards vary from one industry to another. Even if managers or professionals work for an organization that doesn't have a code of ethics, the professional association in their area of specialty probably has one. For example, management faculty who belong to the Academy of Management are guided by its code of ethical conduct. Figure 5.2 is a short excerpt from that code.

Codes and standards are important for communicating clear expectations. But organizations have found that even more is needed. A vigorous implementation process is also essential. Some of the mechanisms that may be a part of this process are

▶ Management involvement and oversight down the line.

▶ Attention to values and ethics in day-to-day recruiting, hiring, and promotion decisions. (For instance, don't distort the real job expectations when recruiting an employee.)

▶ Emphasis on corporate ethics in training and development programs. (Let it be known that all employees will have an equal opportunity for training and development.)

▶ Alternative ways for employees to report questionable ethics of peers and superiors. (Let it be known and demonstrate that whistleblowers will not be punished for reporting ethical misconduct directly to superiors, the human resources department, or some other entity outside of the direct chain of command.)

▶ Auditing and enforcement procedures, including disciplinary and dismissal procedures.

Excerpts from the Academy of Management Code of Ethical Conduct

Our professional goals are to enhance the learning of students, colleagues and others and to improve the effectiveness of organizations through our teaching, research and practice of management. We have five major responsibilities: to our students . . . ; to managerial knowledge; to the Academy of Management and the larger professional environment . . . ; to both managers and the practice of management . . . ; to all people with whom we live and work in the world community . . .

Student Relationships

In our roles as educators, the central principles that underlie appropriate student-educator relationships are professionalism, respect, fairness and concern.

Maintenance of objectivity and fairness: It is the duty of Academy members who are educators to treat students equitably. *Fair treatment* of students requires explaining and adhering to academic requirements and standards. Any subsequent change in these requirements or standards, either of the institution or in an individual course, should appropriately recognize the impact on students. *Impartiality, objectivity and fairness* are required in all dealings with students. Examinations should be carefully prepared and written work graded in an impartial manner. Educators should scrupulously avoid entering any overly personal relationship or accepting any gift or favor which might influence, or appear to influence, an objective evaluation of a student's work. *Appropriate evaluation* of student performance requires test design, assignments and testing conditions which minimize the possibility of academic misconduct. It is the educator's responsibility to pursue appropriate disciplinary action.

Source: "The Academy of Management Code of Ethical Conduct," *Academy of Management Journal,* 1990, *33*:901–908.

Chemical Bank has a code of ethics that sets forth explicit standards of behavior and decision making in five major sections: honesty, candor, and observance of laws; conflicts of interest; confidentiality; securities, investment and trading; and dealing with the assets of the corporation.

Some of the procedures employed by Chemical Bank to maintain these standards and the employees' reactions to them are described in the following Insight.

MAINTAINING ETHICAL STANDARDS AT CHEMICAL BANK

*I*NSIGHT To monitor and enforce its ethical standards, Chemical Bank relies principally on the chain of normal reporting relationships and its own audit process. Employees with questions about proper conduct or suspicions of misconduct are encouraged to turn first to their manager. If the manager is part of the problem, they can go to their manager's superior. If necessary, they can also go to the secretary of the corporation or to another officer at corporate headquarters.

The bank has a program, run by its human resources department, known as Intercom. Since there is no union at the bank, Intercom mainly serves to provide a grievance procedure. A small percentage of the reports to Intercom are related to ethics. Employees can report suspicions of racial discrimination to an EEO (Equal Employment Opportunities) ombudsman. Suppliers can report allegations of wrongdoing by Chemical Bank's buyers to the purchasing department.

The bank's fraud prevention and investigation department looks into charges of serious impropriety. Although employees generally agree that investigations are thorough and that accused persons are treated fairly, most think that Chemical Bank is a strict disciplinarian. It has been willing to fire employees for violations of its code of ethics, even when they are important in terms of their contribution to profitability. All interviewees in a recent bank survey agreed that the last two chairmen have set excellent examples by stressing that ethics should not be sacrificed to profits and then demonstrating consistency between their words and their deeds.[13]

The nature of an organization's culture, leadership, reward systems, and practices can work for or against ethical conduct.[14] Two researchers have developed a questionnaire to assist managers in evaluating the extent to which employees perceive organizational factors as working for (or against) ethical behavior and decisions. Sample questions from that questionnaire are shown in Figure 5.3. Respond to these sample questions with

FIGURE 5.3

Ethical Climate Questionnaire

This is a sample of the questions used within a company.

We would like to ask you some questions about the general climate in your company. Please answer the following in terms of how it really is in your company, not how you would prefer it to be. Please be as candid as possible; remember, all your responses will remain strictly anonymous.

Please indicate whether you agree or disagree with each of the following statements about your company. Please use the scale below and write the number which best represents your answer in the space next to each item.

To what extent are the following statements true about your company?

Completely False	Mostly False	Somewhat False	Somewhat True	Mostly True	Completely True
0	1	2	3	4	5

_____ 1. In this company, people are expected to follow their own personal and moral beliefs.

_____ 2. People are expected to do anything to further the company's interests.

_____ 3. In this company, people look out for each other's good.

_____ 4. It is very important here to follow strictly the company's rules and procedures.

_____ 5. In this company, people protect their own interests above other considerations.

_____ 6. The first consideration is whether a decision violates any law.

_____ 7. Everyone is expected to stick by company rules and procedures.

_____ 8. The most efficient way is always the right way in this company.

_____ 9. Our major consideration is what is best for everyone in the company.

_____ 10. In this company, the law or ethical code of the profession is the major consideration.

_____ 11. It is expected at this company that employees will always do what is right for the customer and the public.

Source: Ethical Climate Questionnaire. Copyright © 1986. B. Victor (University of North Carolina at Chapel Hill) and J. B. Cullen (University of Rhode Island).

respect to an organization in which you have been employed. Based on your responses, how would you characterize the ethical climate of that organization?

Individual Stages

Despite prevailing societal, legal, and organizational interpretations of what is ethical, we all have our own values and sense of what is right and wrong. Since some individuals on the job may be less predisposed to ethical behavior and decisions, managers of both large and small organizations need to pay close attention to values and ethics in recruiting, hiring, and promotion.

Lawrence Kohlberg (1927–1987) is probably the best-known scholar in the field of the psychology of ethical behavior and decision making. Kohlberg's model of moral development is useful for exploring questions about how individual members of an organization regard ethical dilemmas, including how they determine what is right or wrong in a particular situation.[15] Kohlberg held that people develop morally, much as they do physically, from early childhood to adulthood. As they do, their ethical criteria and patterns of moral reasoning go through six stages. Figure 5.4 shows these stages of moral development ranging from the lowest (obedience-and-punishment orientation) to the highest (universal ethical principles). (We use somewhat simpler labels for some of these stages than those used by Kohlberg.) Kohlberg did not assume that all individuals progress through all stages. For example, an adult criminal could be stuck in the first stage.

At the obedience-and-punishment stage the individual (presumably a young child) does the right thing mainly to avoid punishment or to obtain approval.[16] He or she has little awareness of the needs of others; only the immediate consequences of an action determine its goodness or badness. An employee stuck at this stage might think the only reason not to steal money from an employer is the certainty of getting caught and then fired or even arrested. Obviously, managers would not want to employ such individuals.

At the instrumental stage the individual (presumably an older child) becomes aware that others also have needs and begins to defer to them to get what he or she wants. Right behavior is now that which satisfies one's self-interest. Right is what is judged to be fair from the perspective of the individual—an ''equal'' exchange, a deal. An employee at this stage might be willing to take fewer than the allotted number of paid sick days only if paid extra to reduce absences.

At the interpersonal stage appropriate behavior is that which pleases, helps, or is approved by friends or family. Right behavior exhibits conformity to conventional expectations, often of the majority. At this stage being seen as a ''good person'' with basically good motives, is important. An employee at this stage might focus on the importance of being a loyal follower who is always friendly and who avoids or smooths conflict.

At the law-and-order stage ethical behavior is not determined only by reference to friends, family, co-workers, or others whose opinion the individual might value. Right behavior consists of doing one's duty, showing respect for authority, and maintaining the social order for its own sake. Loyalty to the nation and its laws is paramount. The person sees other people as individuals and also as parts of the larger social system that gives them their roles and obligations. An employee at this stage may rigidly adhere to organizational rules and regulations and legitimate orders from superiors. He or she is likely to resist or criticize the efforts of co-workers or superiors to bend or break the rules—for example, by taking paid sick days when they are not actually ill.

At the social contract stage the individual is aware that people hold a variety of conflicting personal views that go beyond the letter of the law. A person at this stage understands that, although rules and laws may be agreed on and for the most part must be impersonally followed, they can be changed if necessary. Some absolute values, such as life and liberty, are held regardless of different individuals' values or even majority opinion. ''The greatest good for the greatest number'' is the characteristic ethical norm at this stage.[17]

At the universal principles stage appropriate conduct is determined by one's conscience, based on universal ethical principles. These principles are founded in justice, the

FIGURE 5.4

Kohlberg's Stages of Moral Development

The six stages of moral development range from the very basic obedience-and-punishment stage through stages that involve increasingly complex levels of ethical and moral reasoning and behaviors. Each stage represents a pattern of personally held values with respect to issues that involve moral and ethical questions.

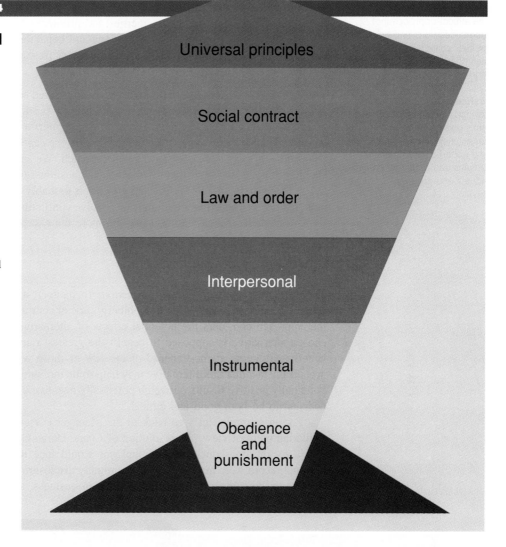

public welfare, the equality of human rights, and respect for the dignity of individual human beings. When formal rules or laws are at odds with these principles, the individual at this stage is likely to act in accordance with the principles.

Just as it's difficult to determine any individual's stage of moral development, it's a complicated matter to discover the ethics motivating managers' and other employees' behavior and decisions. To begin with, one must consider the impact of the societal, legal, organizational, and individual factors we have been discussing.[18] In the following section we'll enrich our discussion of ethics by considering several ethical approaches to decision making and behavior that apply to all four of these factors.

ETHICAL APPROACHES

utilitarian approach The ethical approach that judges the effect of decisions and behavior on others, with the objective of providing the greatest good for the greatest number of people.

We may interpret what is ethical by comparing personal and managerial decision making and behavior with each of three major ethical approaches.[19] These ethical approaches are briefly defined as follows:

The **utilitarian approach** judges the effect of decisions and behavior on others, with the primary objective of providing the greatest good for the greatest number of people.

moral rights approach
The ethical approach that judges decisions and behavior by their consistency with fundamental human rights and privileges.

justice approach The ethical approach that judges decisions and behavior by their consistency with an equitable and impartial distribution of benefits and costs among individuals and groups.

The **moral rights approach** judges decisions and behavior by their consistency with fundamental personal and group liberties and privileges.

The **justice approach** judges decisions and behavior by their consistency with an equitable, fair, and impartial distribution of benefits (rewards) and costs among individuals and groups.

Each approach provides a different but somewhat related set of principles or standards for judging the right or wrong of managerial decisions. As suggested by Figure 5.5, all three ethical approaches can, at times, reinforce and support a particular pattern of decisions and behavior; at other times decisions and behavior can be defined as ethical from the perspective of only one particular ethical approach. We suggest that all three approaches should be applied to issues that involve ethical questions. In general, a proposed course of action that is supported by all three approaches is probably the ideal solution. However, in complex decision-making situations that involve conflicting individual interests, the ability to find such an ideal solution may be more the exception than the rule.

Utilitarian Approach

The utilitarian approach focuses on *actions* (behavior), not on the *motives* for such actions.[20] It is most consistent with Kohlberg's social contract stage. A manager guided by this approach considers the potential effects of alternative actions on all involved. The chosen alternative is supposed to benefit the greatest number of people, although such benefit may come at the expense of the few or those with little power. The manager accepts the fact that this alternative may help some individuals but harm others. As long as potentially positive results outweigh potentially negative ones, the manager considers the decision to be both good and ethical.

For an example, let's go back to the Manager's Viewpoint feature. From a purely utilitarian point of view, the resolution of Lynne Doran Cote's situation would be determined by the consequences her employer would face if the details of Scott James's criminal record were made public. An untimely disclosure of James's past could result in damage to the company's reputation, a loss of business, and, eventually, other employ-

---

FIGURE 5.5

Ethical Approaches to Decision Making

Each of the ethical approaches is independent of, yet partially overlaps with, the other approaches. The ideal outcome from an ethical perspective occurs when a behavior or decision is supported by the ethical standards of all three ethical approaches.

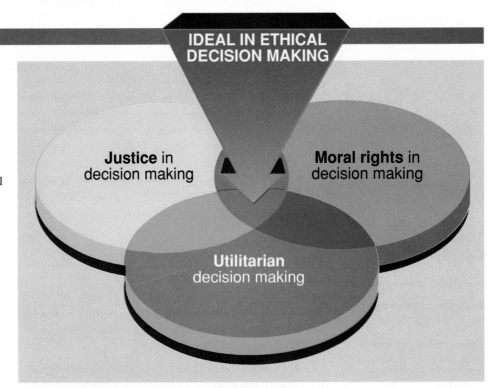

ees' losing their jobs. Thus, following the utilitarian approach, it is Lynne's obligation to tell her employer what she knows and minimize the potential negative consequences for many individuals.

Merit pay is a system that awards different employees substantially different rates of pay based on their performance. The ethical aspect of this system is justified under the utilitarian approach: Those who perform best should receive the greatest reward. However, in an economy based on a free market, the successful competitive actions of one firm (that is, the one who performs best) may cause other firms to suffer financial loss or bankruptcy. This result is also ethically justified under the utilitarian approach by the belief that, of the recognized economic systems, free enterprise offers consumers the highest-quality goods and services at the lowest prices. Thus a free-market economy provides the greatest good for the greatest number. The utilitarian approach would view bankruptcy and loss of jobs as necessary consequences of market competition.

Ethical Standards The utilitarian approach prescribes ethical standards for managers in the areas of organizational objectives, efficiency, and conflict of interest.[21]

Organizational objectives. Managers should attempt to satisfy the needs of customers, suppliers, lenders, employees, and shareholders. Providing the greatest good for the greatest number in a competitive market system means focusing on maximizing profits. Achieving high profits is thought to result in the highest-quality goods and the lowest prices for consumers. Profits are seen as the reward for satisfying consumers. If profits get too high, new competitors will enter the market, thereby increasing the supply of high-quality goods and keeping prices low.

Efficiency. Managers should try to attain organizational objectives as efficiently as possible. Efficiency is achieved by minimizing both inputs (labor, land, capital) and external costs to society (air and water pollution, use of nonrenewable resources).

Conflicts of interest. Managers should not have personal interests that conflict with the organization's achievement of its objectives. A purchasing agent having a significant financial interest in one of the firm's major suppliers faces a potential conflict of interest. The purchasing agent may be motivated to purchase from that supplier, even when the price or quality is not the best available.

The Global Link reveals how Confucian ethics differ from the utilitarian approach.

act utilitarianism The branch of the utilitarian ethical approach that emphasizes the result of providing the greatest good for the greatest number (in other words, the end justifies the means).

rule utilitarianism The branch of the utilitarian ethical approach that relies primarily on the following of predefined rules or standards in order to obtain the greatest good for the greatest number.

Act and Rule Utilitarianism The utilitarian approach has two major branches. **Act utilitarianism** emphasizes the consequences of providing the greatest good for the greatest number. In essence, the end justifies the means. **Rule utilitarianism** relies primarily on following predefined rules or standards in order to obtain the greatest good for the greatest number.

Managers often have difficulty anticipating *all* the consequences of their decisions and behavior, as required under act utilitarianism. However, a manager can usually tell whether he or she is following a rule, as required under rule utilitarianism—a distinction that may be helpful in ambiguous situations.[22] For example, under act utilitarianism a manager might agree to pay a bribe because it is necessary in order to get a job done that benefits the whole organization. Under rule utilitarianism any idea of bribery would be rejected because it is against the rules of the organization.

The utilitarian approach is consistent with the strong U.S. values of individualism, acceptance of uncertainty, and masculinity, as defined in Chapter 3. These values support the ethicalness of profit maximization, self-interest, rewards based on abilities and achievements, sacrifice and hard work, and competition.[23] Over the past twenty-five years, however, utilitarian ethics have been increasingly challenged and tempered by the moral rights and justice approaches.

GLOBAL Link

CONFUCIAN ETHICS

Confucian ethics define morality in terms of duties in certain specific relationships (father-child, master-servant, and so on). In Confucian ethics there is no sense of general charity. One has a certain duty to help people but only those with whom one has a particular relationship. On the other hand, loyalty to one's lord or master, a strong Japanese tradition dating back to feudal days, is supposed to be unconditional, overriding other loyalties and duties. The subject should gladly give his or her life for the lord.

The value placed on loyalty has survived into modern times, but the feudal lord has been replaced for many workers by the corporation. It provides all the necessities of life and guidelines for acceptable behavior. Loyalty to one's employer takes precedence over other duties—even to one's family and (in extreme cases) to the law. This orientation helps to explain several corporate and national scandals that have caused considerable turmoil in Japan and the United States.

One such affair was the Lockheed payoff scandal, which brought down the administration of Prime Minister Tanaka. In this case several employees of All Nippon Airways were found guilty of illegally taking bribes from Lockheed officials. Although they received criminal penalties, they were welcomed back to the corporation with open arms and even honored by their co-workers. Another case is the sale of banned military technology to the Soviet Union by employees of a Toshiba Corporation subsidiary. Although highly inconsistent with national interests and the international obligations of Japan, this sale was undertaken by the managers to benefit the firm.

Japanese managers responsible for these and other situations are viewed by many in Japan as having been simply misguided in reconciling their conflicting responsibilities. Of course, their actions were criticized by some groups outside the Japanese corporations. But the corporations would consider these managers' sense of duty in attempting to further corporate interests at considerable personal risk honorable.

Source: Developed from R. E. Wokutch, ''Corporate Social Responsibility Japanese Style,'' *Academy of Management Executive,* May 1990, 56–74. *See also* J. P. Alston, ''Wa, Guanxi, and Inhwa: Management Principles in Japan, China, and Korea,'' *Business Horizons,* March–April 1989, 26–31.

Moral Rights Approach

The moral rights approach to ethics holds that managerial decisions should be consistent with fundamental rights and privileges (such as those of life, freedom, health, privacy, and property), as set forth in the Bill of Rights and the United Nations' Declaration of Human Rights, for instance.[24] This approach is consistent with Kohlberg's universal principles stage of moral development. According to the moral rights approach managerial decisions and behaviors should preserve the six moral rights identified and explained briefly in the following subsections.[25] A number of U.S. and Canadian laws enacted over the past twenty-five years require managers to consider these rights in their decision making.

Life and Safety Employees, customers, and the general public have the right *not* to have their lives and safety unknowingly and unnecessarily endangered. This moral right in large part justifies the U.S. Occupational Safety and Health Act (OSHA) of 1970, which sets forth for organizations many requirements designed to increase the safety and healthfulness of work environments. For example, there are now restrictions on the use of asbestos, lead-based paint, and various chemicals in the workplace.

Truthfulness Employees, customers, and the general public have the right *not* to be intentionally deceived on matters about which they should be informed. For example, in 1987 the U.S. Transportation Department began requiring airlines to provide information on how closely actual flight arrivals and departures matched the posted schedules. At one airport an airline showed eleven flights scheduled to depart within a one-minute period—a physical impossibility given the number of runways, and an obvious misrepresentation.[26]

Privacy Citizens have the right to control access to and use of personal information by government agencies, employers, and others. This moral right was the basis for the U.S. Privacy Act of 1974. The act restricts the use of certain kinds of information by the federal government and limits those to whom this information can be released. This act allows individuals to (1) find out what personal information the government has collected, recorded, maintained, and used, (2) review relevant records and have inaccuracies corrected, (3) prevent certain uses of such records by the federal government, and (4) bring suit for damages against those who intentionally violate their rights, as specified in the act. A more recent act designed to protect privacy is the 1988 Video Privacy Protection Act, which forbids retailers from disclosing video rental records without the customer's consent or a court order. For example, a customer who rents exercise videos need not worry about getting on mailing lists for exercise equipment catalogues, fitness magazines, and the like. With the enormous amounts of data on individuals now stored in computers, there is increased concern about the potential for invasions of privacy.[27]

Freedom of Conscience Individuals have the right to refrain from carrying out orders that violate their moral or religious beliefs. An Oregon court ruled in favor of a woman who had been fired because she insisted on serving as a juror. Her boss had ordered her not to serve, knowing that she could get out of jury duty because of her young children.[28] The woman felt, however, that she had a moral obligation as a citizen to accept jury duty.

Free Speech Employees and others have the right to criticize the ethics or legality of their employers' actions. This right holds only if the criticisms are conscientious and truthful and do not violate the rights of others within or outside the organization. Virtually all federal legislation passed in the 1970s concerning occupational safety, pollution, and health contained provisions designed to protect employees who report violations of laws by their employers.[29] Employees reporting such information are often referred to as **whistleblowers.** Michigan passed a Whistleblowers' Protection Act. This act came about because of the actions of a chemical company, which sold farmers animal feed accidentally contaminated with a fire retardant. The company compounded its error by issuing a gag order forbidding employees to report this information to government investigators.

whistleblower An employee who reports to an outside authority violations of laws by his or her employer.

Private Property The legal and value systems of the United States, Canada, Great Britain, Germany, and other democratic societies uphold the individual's right to private property. This right allows people to acquire, use, and dispose of shelter and have life's basic necessities. John Locke (1632–1704), a British philosopher, believed that man by nature has rights to life, political equality, and property. The extension of that belief is that the state should not interfere with these rights; because of man's partial and biased nature, however, the state needs to protect them.[30] Thomas Jefferson and other founding fathers of the United States were influenced by Locke's view of private property:

> The great and chief end . . . of men uniting into commonwealths, and putting themselves under government, is the preservation of their property: to which in the state of Nature there are many things wanting.[31]

During the past twenty-five years the moral rights approach has served as justification for numerous laws and court rulings that limit, define, and redirect the rights of individuals in the use of their private property. The enactment of zoning codes by many municipalities, which restrict the types of structures that the owner can place on a piece of property, is one example.

The following Insight illustrates how the utilitarian and moral rights approaches would put different interpretations on the disclosure of information that could be classified as private.

ARGIE BIRD'S DECISION

*I*NSIGHT   Argie Bird accepted a job with a young, vigorous microcomputer manufacturer engaged in intense competition to become the first company, at that time, to market a software package that used the English language. The software's advantage lay in the fact that the average customer could easily use it. Bird's former employer was rumored to be the leader in the field of English-language software.

Bird's new employer led her to believe that she had been hired because of her management potential. But the first morning of her third week on the new job, Argie received the following note from the company president: "Please meet me tomorrow morning at my office at 8:15 for the purpose of discussing the developments your former employer has made in microcomputer software." If you were Bird, would you give your new employer the information? What are the reasons for your choice? Jot down your responses before reading further.

A sample of managers responded to this ethical problem. The most frequent responses, along with the ethical approach each illustrates, were as follows:

▶ 20 percent of the managers stated that it was "unethical for the employer to mislead Bird when she was hired" (moral rights).

▶ 14 percent said that it was "unethical for Argie to provide this information and unethical for the employer to ask" (rule utilitarianism).

▶ 15 percent thought the "decision to give information should be based on whether Argie had signed a security agreement with the previous employer" (rule utilitarianism).

▶ 13 percent leaned toward a decision to "provide some but not all information" (act utilitarianism).

▶ 23 percent leaned toward giving the information because "loyalty is to the new employer and it is necessary to keep her job" (act utilitarianism).

▶ 15 percent gave a variety of other responses.

The survey results suggest that according to both rule utilitarianism and the moral rights approach, Bird should refuse to reveal the information. On the other hand, the responses reflecting act utilitarianism indicate either some hedging ("provide some but not all information") or a clear tendency to give the information.[32]

Justice Approach

The justice approach evaluates managerial decisions and behavior on how equitably they distribute benefits and costs among individuals and groups.[33] It too is consistent with Kohlberg's universal principles stage. The concepts of fairness, equity, and impartiality are supported by three implementing principles: the distributive justice principle, the fairness principle, and the natural duty principle.

distributive justice principle The ethical principle that says that individuals should not be treated differently on the basis of arbitrary characteristics (such as gender or race).

Distributive Justice Principle The **distributive justice principle** requires that managers not treat individuals differently on the basis of arbitrarily defined characteristics. For example, Title VII of the U.S. Civil Rights Act of 1964 forbids employers from considering personal characteristics such as race, gender, religion, or national origin in decisions to recruit, hire, promote, or fire employees.

The distributive justice principle holds that (1) individuals who are similar in relevant respects should be treated similarly, and (2) individuals who differ in relevant respects should be treated differently in proportion to the differences between them. On this basis the U.S. Equal Pay Act of 1963 made it illegal to pay different wages to women and men when their jobs require equal skill, effort, and responsibility and are performed under similar working conditions. The act does allow wage differentials if these are based on a seniority system, a merit system, a system that measures earnings by production quantity or quality, or other nonbiasing factors such as market demand.[34]

fairness principle The ethical principle that requires employees to support the rules of the organization when they are just and the employees have voluntarily accepted benefits provided by the organization.

Fairness Principle The **fairness principle** requires employees to support the rules of the organization when two conditions are met: (1) the organization is just (or fair), and (2) the employees have voluntarily accepted benefits provided by the organization or have taken advantage of opportunities offered in order to further their own interests.[35] Employees are then expected to follow the organization's rules, even though those rules might restrict their individual choices. Rules requiring employees to be present and on time would be defined as fair because excessive absenteeism and tardiness can negatively affect fellow workers and the organization as a whole.

Both a firm and its employees have obligations (responsibilities) under the fairness principle. These mutual obligations should satisfy the following criteria:

1. *They should be a result of voluntary acts.* Employees cannot be forced to work for a particular firm, and employers cannot arbitrarily be forced to hire a particular person.

2. *They should be spelled out in clearly stated rules.* These rules should specify what both the employee and the organization are required to do.

3. *They are owed between individuals who are cooperating for mutual benefit.* The employees and managers share a common interest in the survival of the organization.[36]

Some aspects of the fairness principle are illustrated by a New York Court of Appeals ruling. The court decided that Wallace L. Wiener, fired after eight years of doing promotional work, was entitled to sue McGraw-Hill Book Company for unjust dismissal. His claim was that the company handbook on personnel policies protected him against dismissal for other than ''just and sufficient cause.'' The court ruled that the handbook provision constituted a contract between the employer and employee and that Weiner had a right to have his case tried in court—it did *not* rule on the merits of Weiner's case. In terms of the fairness principle, the court implied that the handbook on personnel policies (rules) represented the various mutual obligations between McGraw-Hill and its employees.[37]

natural duty principle The ethical principle that requires that decisions and behavior be based on certain universal obligations (not to injure another, for example).

Natural Duty Principle The **natural duty principle** requires that managers base decisions on a variety of universal obligations: (1) the duty to help others who are in need or in jeopardy, provided that the help can be given without excessive personal risk or loss, (2) the duty not to harm or injure another, (3) the duty not to cause unnecessary suffering, and (4) the duty to support and comply with just institutions. With respect to the last obligation, judges tend to frown on employee dismissals that are inconsistent with the purpose and ideals of the legal system. That is, judges view the legal system as a just institution. For example, in one landmark case the courts supported a Teamster's claim that he was fired for refusing to lie in court about certain activities of the union and a trucking firm.[38]

In this discussion of the justice approach we have highlighted only some major principles for ethical behavior and decision making. We have not examined the numerous problems that managers face in attempting to apply the justice approach in conjunction with the utilitarian and moral rights approaches when making a single decision. The following Insight illustrates the application of both the justice and the utilitarian approach.

*I*NSIGHT Master Millers Company has developed a special milling process that yields a wheat flour that produces a lighter and more uniformly textured loaf of bread than conventionally milled flour does. Unfortunately, the process gives off more dust than the existing emissions control equipment can deal with and still maintain emissions within legal limits. New emissions control equipment won't be available for at least two years. If top management waits that long to introduce the new process, however, competitors are likely to gain significant market penetration.

Gareth Woodman, the general manager, wants to use the new process during the third shift, which runs from 10 P.M. to 6 A.M. By using the process at night, the plant will be releasing the excess pollution in the dark, and it will go undetected. By the time market demand becomes great enough to utilize a second shift, the new emissions control equipment should be available. If you had to make this decision as a member of the company's top management, would you approve Woodman's request? What are the reasons for your choice? Jot down your response before reading further.

The same sample of managers who responded to the ethical dilemma in the preceding Insight responded to this one. The most frequent responses, along with the ethical approach each illustrates, were as follows:

▶ 16 percent of the managers would not use the new process, on the basis of a "concern for the environment" (justice approach).

▶ 24 percent were opposed because "it would be illegal" (rule utilitarianism).

▶ 15 percent thought that there was "too great a risk of getting caught, and the resulting negative consequences would be too great" (act utilitarianism).

▶ 18 percent felt "the pollution would not really hurt the environment" (act utilitarianism), and 5 percent saw "large potential gains with low risk" (act utilitarianism).

▶ 8 percent leaned toward doing it because "it's not their fault; equipment would be installed if available" (act utilitarianism).

▶ 14 percent of the managers gave a variety of other responses.

About 55 percent of the managers who responded expressed an unwillingness to approve Woodman's request; 15 percent of those based their decision on an act utilitarianism rationale. About 31 percent of the managers leaned toward approving the request; oddly enough, their responses also represented forms of act utilitarianism.[39]

Two noteworthy conclusions can be reached based on the managers' responses to the ethical dilemmas described in this Insight and the earlier one. First, utilitarianism—both rule and act—was the dominant ethical approach identified. Managers who justified their decisions on the basis of act utilitarianism ("the end justifies the means") almost consistently favored taking a potentially *unethical* course of action. Second, the managers who justified their decisions on the grounds of justice and moral rights were clearly a minority. Many of the conflicts between managers and consumer groups, employee groups, and government agencies may be a result of the tendency of managers to use act or rule utilitarianism as their ethical guide. In contrast, nonmanagement groups may tend to rely more on the justice and moral rights approaches to justify their positions.

Comparing Ethical Approaches

Each of the three ethical approaches—utilitarian, moral rights, and justice—has strengths and weaknesses, which are summarized in Table 5.1. Utilitarian views are most compatible with the objectives of efficiency, productivity, and profit maximization, all strong cultural values in the United States. The reason managers of many organizations overwhelmingly value this ethical approach should be obvious. The moral rights and justice approaches emphasize individual rights and the need to distribute benefits and burdens among individuals fairly. If managers relied exclusively on the moral rights and justice approaches, they probably would be less innovative, less receptive to technological change, less willing to take risks, and less efficient. These approaches place greater

TABLE 5.1

Strengths and Weaknesses of Three Ethical Approaches to Managerial Decisions and Behavior

Ethical Approach	Strengths	Weaknesses
Utilitarian The greatest good for the greatest number	1. Encourages efficiency and productivity 2. Consistent with profit maximization; is easiest for managers to understand 3. Encourages looking beyond the individual to assess impact of decisions on all who might be affected	1. Virtually impossible to quantify all important variables 2. Can result in biased allocations of resources, particularly when some who are affected lack representation, or voice 3. Can result in ignoring rights of some who are affected, to achieve utilitarian outcomes
Moral Rights Individual's rights to be protected	1. Protects the individual from injury; consistent with rights to freedom and privacy 2. Consistent with accepted standards of social behavior, independent of outcomes	1. Can imply individualistic selfish behavior that, if misinterpreted, may result in anarchy 2. Can foster personal liberties that may create obstacles to productivity and efficiency
Justice Fair distribution of benefits and burdens	1. Attempts to allocate resources and costs fairly 2. Is the democratic approach 3. Protects the interests of those affected who may be underrepresented or lack power	1. Can encourage a sense of entitlement that reduces risk, innovation, and productivity 2. Can result in reducing rights of some in order to accommodate rules of justice

Source: Adapted, by permission of the publisher, from "Organizational Statesmanship and Dirty Politics: Ethical Guidelines for the Organizational Politician," by M. Velasquez, D. V. Moberg, and G. E. Cavanagh, from *Organizational Dynamics,* Autumn 1983. Copyright © 1983 American Management Association, New York. All rights reserved.

weight on employee welfare than on organizational efficiency. At times, for instance, organizational efficiency may require the dismissal, layoff, or early retirement of employees.

As noted previously, managers who attempt to reach the *ideal* in making ethical decisions face many difficulties.[40] But when used in combination to the greatest extent possible, these three approaches increase the probability that managers will make decisions and engage in behaviors that are ethical—and will be judged so by others. Decisions and behaviors will not always be absolutely ethical or absolutely unethical. Many decisions fall into a gray area, especially those that are complex, involve many groups and individuals, and are controversial. The natural tensions created for managers by business ethics have been summed up this way:

> Rest assured that business ethics exists. But, like all ethics, it is under fire. Because it exists in the sphere of aspiration, where one's reach exceeds one's grasp, it is condemned to play the role of the critic. It lives in the gap between what is and what ought to be. To create awareness of this breach is to create discomfort.[41]

CONCEPTS OF SOCIAL RESPONSIBILITY

Struggles over various concepts of the social responsibility of organizations reflect the conflicts created by the three ethical approaches we have just discussed. Managers have no single, agreed-on concept of social responsibility to guide them. With the diverse values and ethical approaches operating around the world this lack of agreement isn't

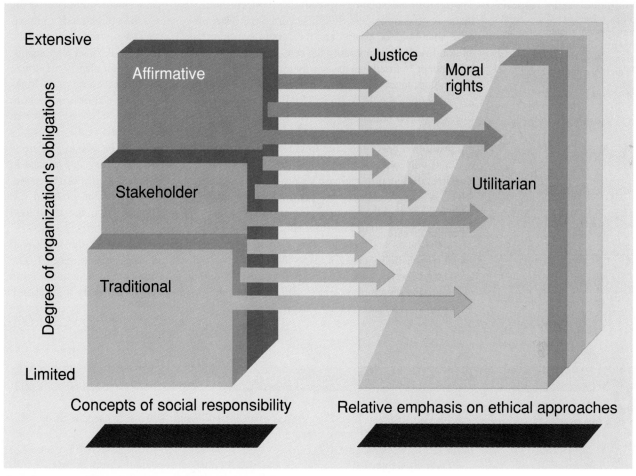

Social Responsibility Concepts and Ethical Approaches

The horizontal arrows illustrate how each concept of social responsibility is based on a different mix of the three ethical approaches. The different size boxes on the left-hand side make the point that organizational obligations (other than obeying the law and maximizing shareholder returns) are relatively limited under the traditional concept but become quite extensive under the affirmative concept.

surprising. Three commonly accepted views of social responsibility are the traditional, stakeholder, and affirmative views. Each of these concepts involves a different relative emphasis on the utilitarian, moral rights, and justice approaches. As you can see in Figure 5.6, the traditional social responsibility concept is based primarily on the utilitarian ethical approach. In contrast, the affirmative social responsibility concept draws heavily on the justice and moral rights approaches. The arrows cutting across the figure indicate the relative emphasis of each concept on each of the ethical approaches. As Figure 5.6 also indicates, the degree of an organization's obligations is relatively limited under the traditional social responsibility concept. Obligations broaden under the stakeholder concept and become substantial under the affirmative concept.

Within the United States and Canada the traditional concept emerged in the 1880s (as large corporations developed). The stakeholder concept emerged in the 1930s; (as large government developed and the ravages of the Depression were being fought). The affirmative concept emerged in the 1960s (as social unrest and societal dissatisfaction with business increased). The key features of each of these concepts are addressed in the following sections.

Traditional Social Responsibility Concept

traditional social responsibility concept The idea that management should serve the interests of shareholders, that is, maximize shareholders' profits and long-term interests.

The **traditional social responsibility** concept holds that management should serve the interests of shareholders. In other words, the overriding managerial obligation is to maximize shareholders' profits and their long-term interests. Nobel Prize–winning economist Milton Friedman is probably the best-known advocate of the traditional social responsibility concept.[42] Friedman asserts that using resources in ways that do not clearly maximize shareholder interests amounts to spending the owners' money without their consent. Managerial actions should be limited by their companies' economic needs. Profit is the bottom line. Managers should not risk profitability by involving their firms in social tasks that aren't legally required of them. This viewpoint holds that government—not business—is the institution best suited for solving social problems. According to Friedman, "there is one and only one social responsibility of business—to use its resources and engage in activities designed to increase its profits so long as it stays within the rules of the game, which is to say, engages in open and free competition without deception or fraud."[43] Although it is highly valued among many managers and shareholders, the traditional concept receives somewhat less support among the general public.

Individuals and groups often challenge management's rights under the traditional social responsibility concept, especially the rights to discipline and fire employees.[44] The account of Terry Adams and Sohio in the following Insight is one extreme example. Sohio was applying the employment-at-will principle and the principle of authority to discharge employees for unsatisfactory performance.

TERRY ADAMS AND SOHIO

*J*NSIGHT

Terry Adams, a San Francisco–based manager for Sohio Petroleum, met with her boss, who suggested improvements for handling her word-processing staff. Adams promised to work on it.

Over the course of the next six months Adams got repeated warnings, both oral and written, that she was falling short. When a final thirty-day warning came, Adams took three weeks of paid "stress leave." In her absence, superiors, including executives in Sohio's human resources department, reviewed her work. Their conclusions were most damaging to Adams. They concluded she had a habit of making "the-dog-ate-my-homework" excuses about lapses in performing even the most routine duties, such as renewing purchase orders with critical suppliers. Adams was fired.

Adams sued, alleging, among other things, wrongful discharge. In court more evidence damaging to Adams came out. For example, she had falsified the resumé that had originally helped her win the job. Nevertheless, Sohio offered to settle. Adams refused. Six years after the firing, the company won. Won? The court costs exceeded $200,000, not counting thousands of hours of management time consumed in preparing the defense. Said a company lawyer: "It was a hollow victory." Sohio does feel, however, that it was necessary to follow through on the case to ensure that employees don't conclude that poor performance is rewarded. Sohio management also thinks their strong stance on this case will help make others who may be dismissed for poor performance "think twice" before filing a lawsuit.[45]

Stakeholder Social Responsibility Concept

The **stakeholder social responsibility concept** holds that managers have obligations to identifiable groups that are affected by or can affect achievement of an organization's

Under the *stakeholder concept of social responsibility*, it was in Exxon's best interests to contribute to the cleanup of sites affected by the Valdez oil spill, such as this beach on Naked Island.

stakeholder social responsibility concept The idea that managers have obligations to identifiable groups that are affected by or can affect achievement of an organization's goals (such as important customers, shareholders, employees).

stakeholder Anyone having potential or real power to influence an organization's decisions or actions (for example, a shareholder, important customer, or union member).

objectives.[46] As suggested in Figure 5.6, the scope of obligations is greater than with traditional social responsibility. **Stakeholders** are groups having potential or real power to influence the organization's decisions and actions. Stakeholders commonly include shareholders, important customers, competitors, government agencies, unions, employees, debt holders (banks, pension funds), trade associations, important suppliers, and consumer groups.

Under the stakeholder concept the management of a firm deciding to close down a manufacturing plant should inform the employees and the community well in advance of the sixty days required by law and should spend corporate resources to reduce both the short-term and long-term adverse impacts on these stakeholders. The vast majority of managers who accept the stakeholder concept would probably endorse Peter Drucker's interpretation of a firm's obligation:

> The first "social responsibility" of business is to make enough profit to cover the costs of the future. If this "social responsibility" is not met, no other "social responsibility" can be met. Decaying businesses in a decaying economy are unlikely to be good neighbors, good employers, or "socially responsible" in any way. When the demand for capital grows rapidly, surplus business revenues available for non-economic purposes, especially for "philanthropy," cannot possibly go up. They are almost certain to shrink.[47]

Managers cite three major reasons for embracing the stakeholder social responsibility concept: (1) enlightened self-interest, (2) sound investment, and (3) interference avoidance.[48] Under the rationale of enlightened self-interest, social responsibility can be used to justify numerous managerial decisions and actions. This rationale includes the general idea that a better society creates a better environment for business.[49] Under the rationale of sound investment, social responsibility is seen as having a positive effect on a company's net worth. Socially responsible firms claim that their stocks sell at higher prices than those of less socially responsible firms. Higher stock prices, in turn, reduce the cost (interest rate) of capital and increase earnings. As you might expect, this view is highly controversial.[50] Under the rationale of interference avoidance, management aims to minimize control of company decisions by powerful stakeholders, such as government agencies and pressure groups. Industry self-regulation is often justified on the basis of interference avoidance.[51]

We suspect that the stakeholder concept is the concept most widely supported by the general public and many managers. It seems likely that through the 1990s more and more organizations will apply the stakeholder concept proactively when considering complex issues and alternative courses of action. McDonald's decision to provide nutritional data, described in the following Insight, represents the stakeholder social responsibility concept in action.

*I*NSIGHT

McDonald's, apparently feeling the heat of critics who contend that customers forsake nutrition for speed in fast food, began posting charts with information about its ingredients in 1990. The three-by-three-foot posters summarize nutritional data that had been available in 56-page booklets in the company's restaurants for more than two years. Food tray liners also display information appropriate for the time of day. For example, the contents of the breakfast Egg McMuffin show up on tray liners used in the morning; those of the Big Mac appear later in the day.

"A lot of special-interest groups are anxious for us to tell all. We've been trying, but they never seem to be satisfied," Edward Rensi, president of McDonald's USA, said in an interview. "So we thought we'd take an extra step and put the information on [posters] so they can walk up and read it."

Rensi denied that McDonald's, the world's largest restaurant company, was reacting to recent harsh criticism of its menu. In April 1990 Phil Sokolof, a Nebraska businessman-turned-cholesterol-fighter, accused the chain in full-page newspaper ads of contributing to what he termed "the poisoning of America." Sokolof was critical of the cholesterol and fat content of the food at McDonald's and other unidentified fast-food chains.

McDonald's attacked the ad as "reckless and misleading." Soon thereafter, however, its milkshakes were reformulated with a lower fat content. And the use of beef tallow high in saturated fat to cook french fries has been phased out.[52]

Affirmative Social Responsibility Concept

affirmative social responsibility concept The idea that the organization should be the initiator of actions that benefit the environment, the stakeholders, and the general public.

The **affirmative social responsibility concept** holds that managers are obligated to (1) avoid problems by anticipating changes in their environment, rather than simply reacting to them, (2) blend the organization's objectives seamlessly with those of stakeholders and the general public, and (3) take concrete, proactive steps to promote the mutual interests of the organization, its various stakeholders, and the general public.[53] This concept, as noted earlier, draws heavily from the justice and moral rights ethical approaches. If it had been operating under affirmative social responsibility, McDonald's would have initiated changes in cooking ingredients and posted nutritional information long before external pressures forced it to make changes or face the possibility of lawsuits, new legislation, and the loss of business. It might even have marketed healthier menu items and launched a campaign to convince customers to eat its nutritionally sound foods.

Obligations Affirmative social responsibility is the most difficult, complex, and expensive concept for organizations to implement. This concept includes the core obligations of the stakeholders concept, all of which suggest the need for ongoing communication among managers, stakeholders, and the general public. There are five categories of obligations and corresponding examples of expected managerial behaviors.[54]

1. *Search for legitimacy.* Managers must consider and accept broader criteria for measuring the organization's performance and social role than those required by law and the marketplace. Anita Roddick is the founder and CEO of the Body Shop, which has grown from one outlet in Brighton, England in 1976 to 500 Body Shops in the United Kingdom and the United States as well as thirty-five other countries. These shops sell only skin-, body-, and hair-care products that are biodegradable and environmentally safe. The firm is heavily into recycling, and it pays employees while they donate half a day a week to a social cause of their choice. Roddick comments: "The purpose of business isn't just to generate profits, to create an ever-larger empire. It's to have the power to affect social change, to help make the world a better place."[55]

The Body Shop's Anita Roddick (here, with staff) is a walking example of *affirmative social responsibility*. Says Roddick, "There are so many people who are kind on the outside but who commit corporate crime under the guise of profits. I could never eliminate the values that are central in my life. The business simply reflects my style of living."

2. *Ethical norms.* Managers must take definite stands on issues of public concern; they must advocate ethical norms for all in the organization, the industry, and business in general. These ethical norms are advocated even when they seem detrimental to the immediate economic interest of the organization or are contrary to prevailing ethical norms. Roddick, of the Body Shop, makes it a point not to use styrofoam and other chlorofluorocarbon-based packing materials, and she eschews the use of animal-derived products and wood from tropical rain forests. The company contributes hundreds of thousands of dollars a year to environmental causes, ranging from Greenpeace to Friends of the Earth. In 1990 the Body Shop gave financial support to a group that is cleaning up orphanages in Romania.

3. *Operating strategy.* Managers must maintain or improve the current standards of the physical and social environment; they must compensate victims of pollution and other organization-related hazards, even in the absence of clearly established legal grounds. Managers must evaluate possible negative effects of the organization's plans on other stakeholders, then attempt to eliminate or substantially reduce such negative effects prior to the plans' implementation. Again, at Body Shop, products are packaged in simple plastic containers designed for refill. Purchases go into paper sacks bearing a variety of environmental messages.

4. *Response to social pressures.* Managers must accept responsibility for solving current problems. They must be willing to discuss activities with outside groups and make information freely available to them and be receptive to formal and informal inputs from outside groups in decision making.

5. *Legislative and political activities.* Managers must show a willingness to work with outside groups for enactment of, for example, environmental protection laws. They must promote honesty and openness in government and in their own organization's lobbying activities. Coping with South Africa's policy of apartheid has been a real test for managers of multinational corporations. Apartheid is the formal policy of strict racial segregation and political, social, and economic discrimination against blacks followed in the Republic of South Africa. Black workers in South Africa want U.S. and other corporations to follow the affirmative social responsibility concept and demonstrate their opposition to apartheid. An increasing number of U.S. multinational corporations—including GM, IBM, Honeywell, Coca-Cola, and Procter & Gamble—have decided to divest and leave the country rather than fight both the South African government and the pressure groups in the United States that are demanding divestment.[56]

Hewlett-Packard is one U.S. corporation that strives to follow a number of the demanding ethical obligations of affirmative social responsibility.

INSIGHT

Hewlett-Packard (HP) employees are expected to follow the values of honesty and integrity in their relationships with people both external to and within the company. HP shows no tolerance for dishonesty in its employees' dealings. Its expectations are detailed in a booklet entitled "Standards of Business Conduct," which spells out the ethical standards the company expects employees to follow.

"Standards of Business Conduct" discusses specific employee obligations: to HP, to customers, to competitors, and to suppliers. Among the obligations to HP are those dealing with the avoidance of conflicts of interest; the refusal of significant gifts or any payments from HP customers, suppliers, or competitors; the confidential handling of proprietary and inside information; and the reporting and avoidance of payments or gifts to government officials or foreign sales agents. Obligations to customers include bans on resale price maintenance, exclusive dealing, price discrimination, and other unfair methods of competition. Obligations to competitors include the avoidance of price fixing, industrial espionage, and negative comments about competitors and their products. Among the obligations to suppliers are keeping confidential information secret and providing equal consideration to all suppliers.

General managers are required to be familiar with the standards in the booklet and to ensure that all of their employees are informed of them. They are, however, given considerable freedom to develop their own information programs.[57]

social audit An attempt by an organization to identify, measure, evaluate, report on, and monitor the effects it is having on its stakeholders and society as a whole, which are not covered in its financial reports.

Social Audit An organization run under the stakeholder or affirmative social responsibility concept may undertake a social audit. A **social audit** is an attempt to identify, measure, evaluate, report on, and monitor the effects the organization is having on its stakeholders and society as a whole—information not covered in traditional financial reports.[58] A social audit, in contrast to a financial audit, focuses on social actions rather than fiscal accountability. A social audit is an important measurement of achievement under the affirmative social responsibility concept. Conducting such an audit is typically viewed as an optional activity under the stakeholder concept. A few of the firms that undertake social audits include Atlantic Richfield Company (ARCO), Bank of America, General Motors, IBM, and Hewlett-Packard. Table 5.2 presents one possible outline for an organization's social audit and report. Objective narrative statements are recommended when quantitative measurements are unavailable. The social audit should provide a reasonable profile of an organization's performance in environmental, cultural, and economic areas without having to put a dollar sign on every activity and achievement. Although there will always be measurement problems, an organization can develop a reasonable profile and assessment of its level of social responsibility.

Some large organizations report their social responsibility accomplishments in their annual reports. These reports are distributed to stakeholders—especially stockholders, in the case of business firms. However, a number of critics have suggested that relatively few of these corporate reports rate very high in terms of the desired criteria and in terms of the expectations raised by academic research. They claim that much of what is reported is selective, and some of it is self-serving.

Although there are no hard facts, it would appear that the affirmative social responsibility concept is not widely accepted or practiced by most business organizations in the United States or Canada. There seem to be strong societal pressures for adoption of the stakeholder social responsibility concept but no widespread pressure for the affirmative concept. In fact, with increasing pressures from domestic and international competition, business organizations will probably experience diminishing expectations that they apply the affirmative concept's broader set of organizational obligations to their

Outline for Social Audit and Report

Part	Contents
1. Social expectations and response	A statement of what is expected for each program area (consumer affairs, employee relations, physical environment, local community development) The organization's reasoning as to why it has undertaken certain activities and not undertaken others
2. Social objectives and priorities	What the organization will try to accomplish What priority it places on the programs and activities it will undertake
3. Objectives in each program area	The organization's specific objective for each prioritized activity and program (in quantitative terms when possible) Description of how it is striving to reach each objective (for instance, by making available ten qualified employees for a total of 400 hours of community service)
4. Resources committed	The costs—direct and indirect—assumed by the organization in each program area
5. Accomplishments and/or progress	The extent to which each objective has been achieved (when feasible, in quantitative terms)

Source: Developed from F. Luthans, R. M. Hodgetts, and K. R. Thompson, *Social Issues in Business: Strategic and Public Policy Perspectives,* 6th ed. (New York: Macmillan, 1990), 595–613; L. L. Carson and G. A. Steiner, *Measuring Business Social Performance: The Corporate Social Audit* (New York: Committee for Economic Development, 1974), 61.

actions and decisions. Further, there seems to be no reason to expect this situation to change in the 1990s. Do you agree with this conclusion? Regardless of your response, one thing is certain: All significant managerial decisions and behavior contain within them ethical and social responsibility concepts and issues that need to be addressed, just as the potential impact of a price increase on customer demand would be.

CHAPTER SUMMARY

1. The ethics of any single behavior or decision can rarely be understood by looking at a single factor. The potential influences of four factors must be considered:

   ▶ The societal factor includes shared values and how they affect individuals' and groups' standards for acceptable behavior over time.

   ▶ The legal factor includes the enactment of new laws and interpretation of current laws that serve to define behavior that is considered ethical.

   ▶ The organizational factor includes actions and decisions beyond those mandated by the law that demonstrate the ethical standards of the organization.

   ▶ The individual factor includes behavior and values that reflect a person's stage of moral development—obedience-and-punishment, instrumental, interpersonal, law-and-order, social contract, or universal principles.

2. Managers commonly rely on one or some combination of three ethical approaches to decision making and behavior:

   ▶ The utilitarian approach focuses on actions rather than motives and has two branches: act utilitarianism and rule utilitarianism.

   ▶ The moral rights approach upholds the six fundamental rights to life and safety, truthfulness, privacy, freedom of conscience, free speech, and private property.

   ▶ The justice approach advocates impartial, equitable distribution of benefits and costs among individuals and groups, according to three principles: distributive justice, fairness, and natural duty.

3. The diverse values and ethical approaches prevalent in the United States and Canada have given rise to three different concepts of social responsibility:

► The traditional concept is based primarily on the utilitarian ethical approach. Management simply seeks to maximize profits, and the focus of the organization's social responsibilities is narrow.

► The stakeholder concept broadens the focus by reflecting to some extent the moral rights and justice ethical approaches; management has obligations to groups that are affected by the organization.

► The affirmative concept draws heavily on the moral rights and justice approaches. It obligates the organization to the broadest focus of social responsibility: utilizing organizational resources to help meet society's needs.

QUESTIONS FOR DISCUSSION AND APPLICATION

1. What does it mean to judge a decision from an ethical as opposed to a legal perspective?

2. Is it possible to improve the ethical climate of an organization? How might you do this?

3. What percentage of the adult population (18 years old and older) do you guess is at each of Kohlberg's stages of moral development? What is the basis for your estimates? Where are you?

4. **From Where You Sit:** Do you prefer the utilitarian or the moral rights approach as a guide for decisions and behavior? Explain. What personal decisions and actions within the past three months can you point to that illustrate your personal preference?

5. **From Where You Sit:** Would you be willing to engage in whistleblowing? What personal and organizational factors would you consider in reaching this conclusion?

6. Assume that you have 100 points to allocate among the utilitarian, moral rights, and justice approaches. How would you allocate those points to convey the relative emphasis managers today probably place on each approach? Explain.

7. **From Where You Sit:** Get a copy of your college booklet on rules and regulations for students. Identify one example of each of the ethical approaches, if possible.

8. What arguments can be presented in support of Peter Drucker's statement that the first ''social responsibility'' of business is to make enough profit to cover the costs of the future? What arguments can be presented in opposition to that statement?

9. Which of the social responsibility concepts—traditional, stakeholder, and affirmative—do you favor for organizations? Justify your choice.

10. **From Where You Sit:** Several years ago *Time* magazine expressed this bottom-line view of the U.S. ethical climate: ''Large sections of the nation's ethical roofing have been sagging badly, from the White House to churches, schools, industries, medical centers, law firms and stock brokerages—pressing down on the institutions and enterprises that make up the body and blood of America.''[59] Based on this chapter, what case can you present in support of and in opposition to this view? Do you personally agree or disagree with this view? Explain.

Do You Approve?

Scenario 1

The U.S. Patent Office recently issued a patent to Tiger Automotive for a device that has been proven to increase the average car's gas mileage by 45 percent. Given that Tiger is protected from direct competition by this patent, it has decided to price the new product at $45 to auto parts dealers. The device costs less than $1 to produce and distribute.

1. How would you rate this action on the following five-point scale?

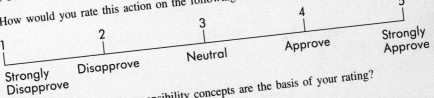

2. What ethical and social responsibility concepts are the basis of your rating?

Scenario 2

A friend of yours is the president of a company in a highly competitive industry. Your friend learns that a competitor has made an important scientific discovery that will give the competitor an advantage and will substantially reduce (but not eliminate) the profits of your friend's company for about a year. Your friend learns that there is a possibility of hiring one of this competitor's employees who knows the details of the discovery and proceeds to do so.

1. How would you rate this action on the following five-point scale?

1	2	3	4	5
Strongly Disapprove	Disapprove	Neutral	Approve	Strongly Approve

2. What ethical and social responsibility concepts are the basis of your rating?

Scenario 3

Jack Ward works in product development for an auto parts contractor. Last summer Ward's firm won a big contract to manufacture transaxles for use in a new line of front-wheel-drive cars to be introduced by a major auto manufacturer in the near future. Winning the contract was very important to the firm. In fact, just before getting the contract the firm had scheduled half its employees, including Ward, for an indefinite layoff.

Final testing of the assemblies ended last Friday, and the first shipments are scheduled to be made in three weeks. While examining the test reports, Ward discovers that the transaxle tended to fail when loaded to more than 20 percent over rated capacity and subjected to strong torsion forces. Such a condition could occur with a heavily loaded car braking hard for a curve while going down a mountain road. The consequences would be disastrous. The manufacturer's specifications call for the transaxle to carry 30 percent more than its rated capacity without failing. Ward shows the test results to his supervisor and the company president, who both indicate that they are aware of the problem but have decided to ignore the report. Chances of transaxle failure are low, and there isn't enough time to redesign the assembly. If the company doesn't deliver the assemblies on time, it will lose the contract. Ward decides not to show the test results to the auto manufacturer.

1. How would you rate this action on the following five-point scale?

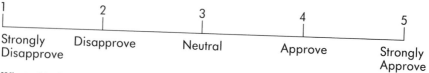

| 1 | 2 | 3 | 4 | 5 |
| Strongly Disapprove | Disapprove | Neutral | Approve | Strongly Approve |

2. What ethical and social responsibility concepts serve as the basis of your rating?

Interpretations

Scenario 1

Strongly disapprove or disapprove: reflects the justice ethical approach and affirmative social responsibility concept.

Strongly approve or approve: reflects the utilitarian ethical approach and traditional social responsibility concept.

Neutral: reflects no preference.

Scenario 2

Strongly disapprove or disapprove: reflects the moral rights ethical approach and stakeholder or affirmative social responsibility concept.

Strongly approve or approve: reflects the utilitarian ethical approach (especially act utilitarianism) and the traditional social responsibility concept.

Neutral: reflects no preference.

Scenario 3

Strongly disapprove or disapprove: could reflect the utilitarian, moral rights, or justice ethical approaches; could reflect the traditional social responsibility concept and most certainly the stakeholder or affirmative concept.

Strongly approve or approve: might reflect rule utilitarianism (Ward has no responsibility beyond telling his supervisor or the president) or act utilitarianism (the risk of death or injury is too low to hold up the sale) along with a minimal form of the traditional social responsibility concept.

Neutral: reflects no preference.

CONFIDENTIAL

To: Susan Sneed, Sales Director

From: Wayne Snider, Western District Sales Manager

Subject: Kickbacks

It has come to my attention that one of our sales reps, George Geoffrey, has been paying kickbacks to some of our largest customers for their continued business with Micrometer Electronics. At this point, George does not know that I am aware of this. I have first-hand knowledge that it is true.

I've done a thorough analysis of the situation. As I see it, if we stop the kickbacks, we stand an 80% chance of losing approximately 30% of the business from this region. (I've always wondered how George maintained such phenomenal sales!) I am well aware that we have had declining sales during the past two quarters and that pressure is being put on you to increase sales. For that reason, I'm coming to you for help in deciding what to do. I'll take whatever action you feel is appropriate.

Rest assured that I will follow your instructions and will maintain confidentiality as required. Please let me know immediately of your decision.

Question: Assume you are Susan Sneed. Write a memo to Wayne explaining your decision. Justify it using concepts you have learned from this chapter.

Cost Control May Harm Dialysis Patients

By Ron Winslow

Efforts to control costs in the nation's $3.7 billion kidney disease treatment program may be putting the lives of thousands of patients in jeopardy.

A new study says that patients whose blood-cleansing dialysis treatments average less than 3½ hours per session are up to twice as likely to die as those whose treatments are longer. More than 20,000 U.S. dialysis patients may be getting insufficient treatment, the study indicates. Meanwhile, an earlier study shows that the average length of treatments has fallen since 1983, when Medicare began trimming payments for its kidney-disease program.

"Something very fundamental is wrong," says Philip J. Held, director of renal research at the Urban Institute, a think tank in Washington, D.C., and the principal author of both reports. "It appears that a very large percentage of patients [is] being undertreated and the consequences are quite serious. We are talking about people dying."

The latest study appears in today's Journal of the American Medical Association, and it is likely to spur changes in treatment of many patients with kidney failure. The findings also raise troubling questions about the impact of cost-cutting efforts on the quality of medical care.

"Economic decisions can and do entail clinical compromises, and patients will bear the cost," say Edward E. Berger and Edmund G. Lowrie in an editorial accompanying Mr. Held's report in the medical journal. Dr. Lowrie is president and Mr. Berger vice president, government relations, of National Medical Care Inc., Waltham, Mass., the nation's largest owner of dialysis-treatment centers.

Officials at the federal Health Care Finance Administration didn't have immediate comment. The Medicare program for the elderly, administered by HCFA, pays about two-thirds of the nation's bills for treatment of kidney failure under a special program that covers patients regardless of age. In 1988, it paid $3.7 billion for 147,000 people; 110,000 were on dialysis while the others had kidney-transplant operations. . . .

In their editorial, Mr. Berger and Dr. Lowrie say that reimbursement from Medicare has dropped 44% in constant dollars since 1983, to the equivalent of $77 per treatment last year from $138 seven years earlier. In response, many centers embraced shorter treatment times, they write, to help reduce labor costs and spread capital and other fixed costs over a larger number of patients. Dr. Hakim also says payments to physicians have been frozen at about $150 per patient per month since 1981.

Nevertheless, the editorial argues, the "adverse clinical outcomes" resulting from shorter dialysis require that nephrologists "reexamine their principles for prescribing treatment."

Length of dialysis in the U.S. is shorter—and death rates are higher—than in some other countries, says Alan R. Hull, clinical professor of medicine at Southwestern Medical School in Dallas. He says U.S. patients undergo about 10 hours of dialysis a week—a figure lower than Mr. Held's study—while German patients receive 12 hours and Japanese 14. Patients fare better in those two countries than in the U.S., where the five-year survival rate for dialysis patients is 47%. In France, where treatment times reach 18 hours a week, the survival rate is 87%, Dr. Hull says. . . .

The current study is based on an analysis of 600 dialysis patients randomly selected from 36 treatment centers around the U.S. in 1984 and 1985 and tracked for three years. The researchers found that 20% of patients had treatment time under 3½ hours while 74% had "conventional" times of between 3½ hours and 4½ hours. The remaining 6% were treated for longer than 4¼ hours. . . .

At treatment centers where patients received short dialysis, median reimbursement fell $5.33 per treatment between 1982 and 1983, 25% more than the $4 drop at centers where patients received conventional treatment. The linkage between lower reimbursement and higher mortality "isn't clear-cut," Mr. Held says, "but it certainly is suggestive." Mr. Held and colleagues published a previous study linking short treatments to lower reimbursement in the American Journal of Kidney Diseases last May.

1. State the ethical issue that managers of dialysis centers face in this situation. Is the issue the same as that confronting Medicare officials?

2. What does the quote from Berger and Lowrie tell you about their concept of social responsibility? Can you justify their position?

3. Assume you are the manager of a dialysis center and you were just told by your headquarters to shorten dialysis times as a cost-cutting measure. You know that your company is in financial trouble and may not survive unless something is done. What would you do? How would you reach your decision?

REX JORDAN

Every summer since I was fourteen I worked for my father's construction company as a laborer, but when I returned home from college two summers ago, Dad told me I would be working in the office. I was elated! At that time the company was still building single-family homes primarily, and I spent those four months doing a variety of things—ordering materials, doing materials-takeoffs from blueprints, coordinating with the subcontractors and our own construction supervisor in the field, etc. Over the years the company had established relationships with a number of solid, reputable subcontractors who knew us well and provided us, for the most part, with reliable, quality work. Their fees in most cases were reasonable, and all we had to do was check periodically to be sure they were competitive.

When I came home from college last spring, however, I knew things had changed. The growth of the local economy had slowed considerably in the past year and a half. Our company hadn't started any new residential projects since I'd left the fall before. Several small commercial jobs had kept the company busy that winter, but the outlook for spring and summer was only fair, at best. In view of this, my father had taken on the construction of an eighty-room motel and restaurant on the other side of the state—a five-hour drive from our home town. This project was attractive not only because we needed the work right then, but also because it gave us an opportunity for majority ownership of the motel and restaurant after it was completed.

I was given the assignment of soliciting, receiving, and awarding subcontractors' bids for nearly every phase of construction, from excavation to sheetrocking to painting. I knew it was going to be a big job and a real challenge. Dad instructed me to call on him or others in the office for help whenever I needed it. The office staff had been cut over the winter. I knew that others would be very busy most of the time, and I would have to handle most of the bidding on my own. I was given a list of subcontractors in the new area.

I was, of course, not familiar with any of them. Most had not been contacted, but, as I found out, the majority were well aware of our upcoming construction project and were anxious to bid. The city was not a large one—in fact, smaller than ours—and was being affected by a slowdown similar to the one affecting our area. Competition was keen among the different subcontractors in the area, who were hungry for work.

Rather than having a public opening of sealed bids, we decided to just inform the subcontractors that bids would be accepted until 5:00 P.M. on a certain day. They would be told the outcome as soon as possible. We asked for written proposals, but permission was given to phone in the dollar amount of the bid (for the purpose of meeting the deadline). Of course, there had to be written confirmation within twenty-four hours. Blueprints of the project had been made available in a number of public places. Thus all of the interested subcontractors could have an opportunity to go over them.

As the bids started coming in, I was dismayed to find that most were well above the projected figures on which we had based our financing. This was a new area, and I had never met any of the contractors personally, so I was not nearly as sure as I would have been in our home area whether the bids were reasonable.

Some of the contractors attempted to take advantage of my naivety. Not long before the deadline, a plumbing contractor called me with a bid that was the lowest I had received. This plumber had been very helpful and friendly in our phone conversations during the previous two weeks, particularly after he had discovered that I was a college student and that I was relatively new to my job. "How many more plumbing bids do you hope to get, Rex?" he asked. Here my innocence showed up. I told him that his was the last I expected to receive for the plumbing contract. "Oh! Well how does mine stack up against the others?" he immediately asked. This time I hesitated. I realized what he was trying to do. I couldn't say anything to give him the idea that he was the low bidder. If I did, he could call back the next day and try to raise his bid a little, saying he had made a mistake. Realizing the awkwardness of my position, I simply told him that I couldn't give him that information until after the bids were opened. He backed off immediately. I was glad that I had made it past that one without really blowing it! Prior to the deadline I received several more calls from contractors. They wanted me to tell them how many bids I had received for their part of the job and how they looked in comparison to the other bidders. Having been almost burned once, though, I didn't give out any information. I simply said that we would notify them when the contracts were let.

As the deadline got nearer, one of my chief concerns was the electrical bid. I'd received five proposals, which ordinarily would have been plenty. However, all of them were far above the figure we had projected for that phase of the project. My dad had gone over all the bids we'd received. He was quite disappointed. "I sure hope we get one or two more bids for the electrical," he said. "I'm just afraid that our estimates were too low."

At about 4:00 the afternoon before the deadline another electrical contractor called in with a bid. I got excited when he told me his figure. It was not only below all the others by a wide margin, but it was well below our original projected figure. This particular electrician had called a number of times before with questions about the electrical layout. He'd mentioned having some difficulty putting his bid together and commented that he had never done a large commercial job like this before. He'd also said he felt competent to do the job and really needed work right now. "Am I in the ballpark with the other bids?" he wanted to know. "I sure would like to get this job."

What could I say? I recalled my dad mentioning in the morning that he now felt an electrician may not make any profit if he did the job at our original projected figure. We really needed to get the costs down any way we could. We had financing for only so much, and the rest would have to come out of our pockets. It would be so easy to just tell this electrical contractor that he was the low bidder, and send him a contract to sign. We didn't plan to make the other figures public anyway. He would probably never know how much lower he was than the others. But it seemed obvious that he had made a mistake on his figures. I wondered if we really wanted anyone to lose his shirt on this job.

1. What do you think Rex Jordan did? Why?
2. If you were in Rex Jordan's position, what would *you* do?
3. What ethical and social responsibility concepts serve as the basis of your chosen action?

Part Three

DECISION

MAKING

AND

PLANNING

VCR & Biotechnology

When it comes to creating new technology, there's really nothing like good old American know-how. But U.S. companies have demonstrated that they are rarely able to take new technology to the marketplace. Why? Putting new technology to practical use requires a long-term strategy of investment in developing and marketing new products, and many short-sighted U.S. investors are unwilling to wait. As a result of their short-sighted planning, American companies are often reduced to selling new technologies to Japanese firms, only to watch them later sell products based on this U.S. creative genius.

Take electronic products, such as the VCR, an American invention. U.S. companies didn't have the patience or the capital to make VCRs for the consumer market, and the VCR technology was sold to Japan. Today, billions of dollars worth of VCRs are sold in the United States, almost exclusively by Japanese firms that took the time to develop a VCR market, as well as to invest capital in manufacturing plants. The VCR made Japanese companies rich and created thousands of jobs for Japanese workers, at a time when manufacturing jobs were declining in the U.S.

Given this recent history, one would think that the United States would have learned the importance of long-term thinking. To the contrary, it's currently in danger of losing its advantage in the next new industry: biotechnology.

How are Japanese companies learning the secrets of biotechnology? Not simply by doing research, but, once again, by investing in U.S. know-how. The Japanese firm Mitsubishi Petrochemical, for instance, has purchased 20 percent of the U.S. biotech company Digene, a firm that has recently developed a new way to diagnose cervical cancer.

"In Japan it's very difficult to find creative research," says Dr. Norioshi Tamara, a Mitsubishi executive. It is easier, Tamara says, to invest in existing technology than to invent it. "Digene," he notes, "has already established creative technology in its own labs."

What Mitsubishi probably wants to do is learn Digene's technological secrets—which they have a right to do since they own part of the company—and eventually take that technology back to Japan where they can create products based on the new science. Even though the two firms have a noncompete clause for cancer test kits, Mitsubishi may eventually end up selling products in direct competition with Digene, based on Digene's research. Why then, do U.S. companies like Digene allow investment by the Japanese? The answer, sadly enough, is that, in many cases, U.S. companies can't raise money at home and have no choice but to rely on the long-term-thinking Japanese for capital.

Here, many biotech companies must sell stock on Wall Street or rely on venture capital firms to raise money. But both of these sources are usually looking to make money quickly, and it takes time to develop biotech products. Moreover, Wall Street is so finicky that a company's stock can rise and fall based on trends that have little to do with company performance. In Japan, companies can rely on banks that are willing to lend money over a long period of time.

Bob Files, CEO of Cetus, a biotech firm that has developed a drug used for treating cancer, notes that "it is not in our interest" to show Japanese companies the secrets of biotechnology. But he acknowledges that few biotech companies, especially small start-ups, can raise the kind of money Cetus spends: $4 million a month. Ironically, Files notes, when Cetus was raising $500 million through the sale of stock, enough to assure long-term growth, some people accused the company of behaving more like a bank than a company inventing things with a new science.

A company that employs a long-term strategy should eventually see it pay off. How can long-term strategy help our society? What are some of the dangers of short-term thinking?

Chapter 6

Bob and Elaine Smith

What You Will Learn

1 Four preconditions for meaningful decision making.

2 Basic classes of organizational decisions and the differences among them.

3 How conditions of certainty, risk, and uncertainty affect individual decision making.

4 The nature of objectives and their role in decision making.

5 The decision-making elements of the rational model, bounded rationality model, and political model.

6 Why ethics are important to decision making.

7 **Skill Development:** Learn the basic issues and procedures involved in a wide variety of organizational decision-making situations.

Motel Bandits

Tom Shaffer, the manager of a local Holiday Inn, heard a news story that's every motel manager's nightmare come true: A violent criminal gang, dubbed by the media "the Motel Bandits," was working its way through his metropolitan area. The thieves' mode of operation involved assaulting and robbing motel guests as they entered or left their rooms.

The local sheriff soon contacted Shaffer to ask if he had made any special arrangements for security. The sheriff even offered to work as a security guard when off-duty, a security measure that the local motel had used in the past. Shaffer wasn't authorized to make this decision alone and phoned his supervisor, Barbara Abelson. After reviewing his request, Abelson had the following concerns:

▶ *Cost* This particular motel had been operating for the past year at a point where its revenues just covered its costs (in other words, at break-even). Any additional expenditures would push the motel into a loss. Twenty-four-hour security, even with the employment of the off-duty sheriff, was estimated to cost $400 a day. Shaffer and Abelson discussed fencing the property, but that would cost $5,500—an idea clearly out of the question as far as Abelson was concerned, given the motel's financial straits.

▶ *Public perception* Holiday Inns had been promoting a family image. Abelson was concerned about making the motel look and feel like an armed camp.

▶ *Corporate policy* Abelson was familiar with Holiday Inns' loss prevention manual, which encourages additional security when a risk is perceived. However, no one in the organization had really emphasized this policy. What her supervisor had really emphasized was meeting quarterly budget projections.

The bottom line from Abelson's viewpoint was that no one at Holiday Inns had ever been promoted for making a motel safer—just for making it more profitable. She decided to take the risk and instructed Shaffer not to provide any extra security measures. She feared the career risk of an operating loss, created by the additional costs of providing security, more than she feared the security risk. She thought that additional security probably wouldn't stop the bandits anyway.[1]

Before reading further, do you agree with Abelson's decision?

The following evening Bob and Elaine Smith checked into Shaffer's Holiday Inn. As they entered their room, two armed men forced their way in and beat, bound, and gagged Bob. The men pushed Elaine down and demanded her money and jewelry. When she told them that her wedding ring wouldn't come off, one of the men put a gun to her head and threatened to "blow her brains out." She finally removed the ring and gave it to them. They then bound, beat, and gagged her before fleeing. The Smiths brought suit against Holiday Inns. The jury returned verdicts in their favor. They found that the criminal acts were reasonably foreseeable by the managers of Holiday Inns. The defendants, including Holiday Inns, were found negligent in not providing adequate security. The jury concluded that this negligence caused Bob and Elaine's injuries and awarded Elaine $400,000 and Bob $100,000 in compensatory damages. An appellate court upheld the awards.[2]

Every day, usually under less dramatic conditions, managers and other employees use decision processes like Barbara Abelson's—processes containing the same basic elements. They define the problem (such as the risk of robbery), gather information (asking Shaffer about the robbers' mode of operation), identify and assess the alternatives (hire guards, fence the motel, do both, or do nothing), and decide what to do. In this case the decision was to do nothing other than to encourage employees to "keep their eyes out" for individuals on the motel property who didn't appear to be motel guests. Of course, few managers are faced with outcomes as extreme as those that resulted from Abelson's decision. But all managers face a wide range of situations that require decision making. In this chapter we present the fundamentals of **decision making,** which at its core includes both defining problems and choosing a course of action from the alternatives generated. We will show how managers (in fact, all organizational employees) can systematically approach various decision situations, based on the type of problem to be solved, the possible solutions available, and the degree of risk involved.

decision making The process of defining problems and choosing a course of action from the alternatives generated.

It is useful to remind you of two of the central themes in this book. First, successful management occurs when decision making, planning, organizing, leading, and controlling all work well together. Second, issues of ethics and social responsibility are embedded in all of these processes and functions. You saw this in Figure 1.6, part of which is presented as Figure 6.1. As the figure suggests, decision-making processes are molded by ethical and social responsibility issues; in turn, fundamental decision-making processes, which are discussed in this chapter, are used to carry out the four basic managerial functions. Sometimes the functions are implemented with the assistance of decision aids (Chapter 7) that can be adapted to a variety of decision situations within the four managerial functions. Accordingly, we first discuss decision making here in Part 3 because all planning processes and issues (Chapters 8 and 9) involve decision making. But keep in mind that decision making does not involve just the planning function.

PRECONDITIONS FOR DECISION MAKING

The fundamentals of managerial decision making come into play whenever individuals are planning, organizing, leading, or controlling. Four preconditions need to exist for a complete decision-making process to occur. Individuals are likely to engage in full-blown decision processes if they can answer yes to each of the following four questions.[3]

1. *Is there a gap (or a difference) between the present situation and desired ends or objectives?* At first this gap may be experienced as only a vague sense of dissatisfaction— vague, but still worth paying attention. The gap may be immediately obvious, or multiple gaps may eventually surface, as in the Manager's Viewpoint case. The situation in that case was increased risk created by the violent criminal gang and the desired objectives were initially customer safety, profitability, and maintaining the Holiday Inn image (one gap). However, Barbara Abelson soon saw another gap being created—that between her current situation and her desired career progress, which she thought would be adversely affected by a strong response (security guards, fence).

2. *Is the decision maker aware of the significance of the gap?* Abelson seemed to be aware of the potential significance of the gap. In the final analysis, though, she rationalized that additional security would not be effective in stopping the bandits if they did strike.

3. *Is the decision maker motivated to act on the gap?* Abelson was *not* motivated to act on the gap between the normal risk for customer safety and the increased risk created by the violent gang. She apparently thought that action on this gap would only serve to create new gaps, including those involving profit objectives and her personal career objectives.

FIGURE 6.1

The Place of Decision Making in Dynamic Management

Elements of ethics and social responsibility are embedded in all decision-making processes and issues. Also, the four managerial functions are implemented through a wide variety of decision-making processes and situations. (Numbers in parentheses identify the chapters in which each topic is presented.)

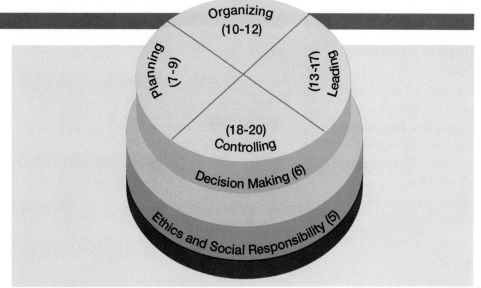

4. *Does the decision maker have the resources (ability, money) to act on the gap?* Abelson had the resources to act on the gap of increased safety risk. She wasn't motivated to do so, however, because of the risks to profitability and her career progression.

Barbara Abelson implicitly answered yes to questions 1, 2, and 4 but answered no to question 3. Because of misplaced emphasis on career concerns, she wasn't motivated to act on the key gap in the case—increased risk to customer safety.

Most individuals have to assess these four preconditions in a variety of situations daily. They often make these assessments so fast that they may not be consciously aware of making them. The relative ease or difficulty of addressing these four preconditions will vary with the class of organizational decision being made. We discuss three major classes of organizational decisions in the following section.

ELEMENTS OF ORGANIZATIONAL DECISIONS

Organizational employees (including managers) must make decisions in a variety of situations, and no single decision-making method will cover all of them. To begin with, employees need to accurately define the problem at hand. They must then evaluate alternative solutions and, finally, make a decision. Figure 6.2 shows how different combinations of types of problems (vertical axis) and types of solutions (horizontal axis) result in three major classes of organizational decisions: routine, adaptive, and innovative.

Types of Problems

The vertical axis in Figure 6.2 indicates a general classification of problems that employees deal with, ranging from the known and well-defined to the unusual and ambiguous. The bank teller with an out-of-balance cash drawer at the end of the day faces a known and well-defined problem. On the other hand, the problem of women and minorities not moving faster into management positions is complex and ambiguous: some people maintain that it is caused by overt as well as hidden forms of discrimination, and others believe that women and minorities just need more time in the management pipeline and that discrimination no longer has anything to do with the problem.[4]

Classes of Organizational Decisions

Organizational decisions fall into three classes: routine, adaptive, and innovative. Each class of decision is determined by a combination of the type of problem involved and the type of solutions considered.

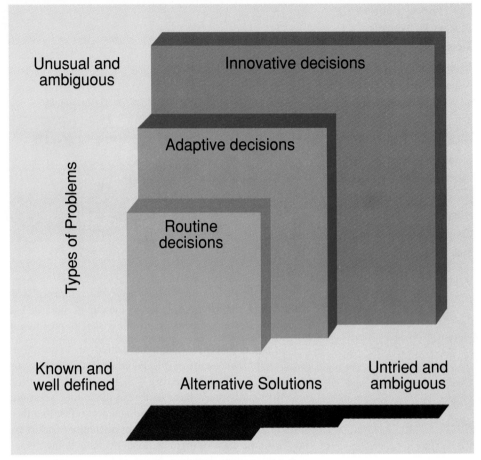

Source: Adapted from W. R. Boulton, *Business Policy: The Art of Strategic Management* (New York: Macmillan, 1984), 1987.

Types of Solutions

The horizontal axis in Figure 6.2 classifies the solutions available to managers for dealing with various types of problems. These solutions also range from the known and well-defined to the untried and ambiguous. The bank teller with an out-of-balance cash drawer follows a specific, well-defined procedure—check all deposit slips against deposit receipts and cash tickets and recount all the cash. In contrast, researchers at one of Hewlett-Packard's labs several years ago were kicking around the concept of vaporization in a coffee percolator. They thought the same concept could be applied the problem of developing better printers. Management freed the engineers to work on the project without really knowing if it would lead anywhere. HP has now sold over 1 million printers incorporating the new thermal printing technology this team created.[5]

Classes of Organizational Decisions

We can classify organizational decisions as routine, adaptive, or innovative. The key to each classification lies in the type of problem faced and the type of solution used.[6]

Routine Decisions **Routine decisions** are standardized choices made in response to relatively well-defined and known problems and solutions. Employees often find a solution to their problems in established rules or standard operating

routine decision A standardized choice made in response to a relatively well-defined and known problem and solution.

procedures (to be discussed in more depth in Chapter 7) or, increasingly, in computer software. Cleaning buildings, processing payroll vouchers, preparing customers' orders, and making travel arrangements are a few examples of tasks requiring routine decisions.

However, employees need to guard against the tendency to make routine decisions when the problem really calls for an adaptive or innovative decision. At a meeting a manager says, "Let's spend more on ads. When we did that in 1991, sales jumped." Simply increasing the frequency of ads or the amount spent on them is a routine decision. But this form of routine thinking can be faulty logic. The implication is that, because sales increased after an increase in advertising expenditures, the ad increases caused sales to rise. In fact, the sales may have gone up for any number of reasons, including blind luck. The case for increased advertising requires firmer proof, and the causes of lagging sales require deeper analysis. At a minimum, the need for adaptive decision making exists.

adaptive decision A choice made in response to a combination of moderately unusual and only partially known problems and alternative solutions.

Adaptive Decisions **Adaptive decisions** are choices made in response to a combination of moderately unusual and only partially known problems and alternative solutions. Adaptive decisions often involve gradually modifying past routine decisions and practices. As suggested in the following Insight, adaptive decisions can have enormous consequences for a firm's profitability.

ADAPTIVE DECISIONS AT H. J. HEINZ

I N S I G H T

Heinz managers have learned to stand conventional cost-cutting logic on its head to get both better quality and lower costs. They discovered that, paradoxically, (1) adding workers can boost overall cost-effectiveness, and (2) slowing down a production line can cut costs. With these and other measures, it is estimated that Heinz may save at least $250 million a year by the mid-1990s. Heinz's experience with its StarKist plants is an example.

Trying to be a low-cost producer, Heinz had cut the work force by 5 percent at its StarKist tuna canning factories in Puerto Rico and Samoa. With tough competition from low-wage rivals in Thailand, keeping a lid on labor costs seemed to make sense. But the fish cleaners were so overworked that they were leaving literally tons of meat on the bone every day. Mr. Connolly, who heads Heinz's total quality management effort, said: "We discovered that we had to add people, not subtract them. In the past we just wouldn't have done that." So managers slowed down the StarKist production lines, hired 400 hourly workers and 15 supervisors, and retrained the entire work force. They installed four more lines to take some of the load off each worker and to expand volume. All told, StarKist increased labor costs by $5 million, but cut out $15 million in wastage. Net saving: $10 million annually.[7]

The StarKist managers made several adaptive decisions because the types of problems they faced were somewhere between being known and well-defined and being unusual and ambiguous. The alternative solutions were also between being known and well-defined and being untried and ambiguous. The point of this Insight is that managers may initially misjudge the problem (high labor costs) and misidentify the solution (cut the work force). The ability to diagnose a problem and find its solution in moderately or entirely new ways is often crucial. Managers, employee teams, and professionals (human-resource specialists, engineers, financial analysts, editors, computer system analysts, accountants, and so on) are thus frequently involved in making adaptive decisions.

continuous improvement
The overall effect of a large number of small, incremental improvements resulting from streams of adaptive decisions made over time.

Continuous improvement occurs when streams of adaptive decisions are made over time in an organization, resulting in a large number of small, incremental improvements year after year. Adaptation somewhat resembles the wheel in a hamster cage—a ladder wrapped into a cylinder, with no beginning and no end. Each turn of the wheel improves an existing product (or service) and/or its production methods. Year after year the organization's goods or services keep getting better, more reliable, and less expensive. John P. McTague, research vice-president at Ford Motor Company, asserts: "The accumulation of a large number of small improvements is the surest path, in most industries, to increasing your competitive advantage."[8] Highly innovative companies like Rubbermaid, which often introduces more than a hundred new products annually, make numerous adaptive decisions each year. For example, in product development Rubbermaid makes extensive use of focus groups (small groups of customers that meet face to face). No customer gripe is too small to consider. When focus group participants complained of puddles in their dish drainers, Rubbermaid responded with a drain tray made a bit higher in back to help water flow into the sink.[9] This change involved adaptive decision making.

innovative decision A choice that is based on the discovery, identification, and diagnosis of an unusual and ambiguous problem and the development of unique or creative solutions.

Innovative Decisions **Innovative decisions** are those that are based on the discovery, identification, and diagnosis of unusual and ambiguous problems and the development of unique or creative alternative solutions. Innovative decisions normally represent a sharp break with the past. Therefore, to be effectively innovative, individuals must be especially careful in defining the problem and creating solutions.

Innovative decisions frequently involve a series of small, interrelated decisions made over a period of months, or possibly even years. Leading-edge innovations often take years to develop and involve numerous professional specialists and teams. It is estimated, for instance, that IBM will spend $435 million to develop the next generation of chip-making methods, which will use x-rays instead of light to "print" circuit patterns on silicon.[10] The people and teams involved at various times during the decision-making process may include groups in the organization's task environment. General Electric often develops products in conjunction with its industrial customers. Collaborating with BMW, GE's plastics unit created the first auto body panels made with thermoplastics for the carmaker's Z1 two-seater.[11]

An important fact to keep in mind is that innovative decisions don't normally happen in a logical, orderly sequence. They may be made before problems are fully understood. Earlier actions can thus affect current decisions. Over the past twenty years, Hanover Insurance has gone from the bottom of the property and liability industry to a position among the top 25 percent in the United States. It is viewed as a major innovator in this sector of the insurance industry. William O'Brien, the CEO of Hanover, shared a few of his thoughts on innovation as anything but a logical, orderly sequence:

Petaks Caterers of New York City made an *innovative* customer service decision when they installed a fax machine to handle takeout orders.

> We had to get beyond mechanical, linear thinking. The essence of our jobs as managers is to deal with "divergent" problems—problems that have no simple answer. "Convergent" problems—problems that have a "right" answer—should be solved locally. Yet we are deeply conditioned to see the world in terms of convergent problems. Most managers try to force-fit simplistic solutions and undermine the potential for learning when divergent problems arise. Since everyone handles the linear issues fairly well, companies that learn how to handle divergent issues will have a great advantage.
>
> The next basic stage in our progression was coming to understand inquiry and advocacy. We learned that real openness is rooted in people's ability to continually inquire into their own thinking. This requires exposing yourself to being wrong—not something that most managers are rewarded for. But learning is very difficult if you cannot look for errors or incompleteness in your own ideas.[12]

Innovation will never be a logical, orderly process. Defining unusual and ambiguous problems will remain an evolutionary process, affected by many points of view, vested interests, and bits and pieces of information that become available at different times.

Pressures from interest groups will ebb and flow, which requires shifting attention from one unusual and ambiguous problem to another and changing definitions to involve or exclude various individuals. Sometimes the real problem doesn't materialize until well into the decision-making process, even after some action has been taken.[13]

Effective employees recognize the need to make innovative decisions to keep their organizations competitive. The following Insight reports just a few of the innovative decisions made by Frieda Caplan, the founder and CEO of Frieda's Finest, since she started her specialty wholesale vegetable business in 1962.

INSIGHT

Frieda Caplan describes her company as a "market expander" and says that "innovation excites me." Relying on intuition, simple marketing tools, and her own willingness to keep an open mind, Caplan has taken shoppers and grocers for a thirty-year walk on the wild side. Hers was the first small company to brand label all its fruit and vegetables—and in bright purple.

Caplan virtually invents vegetables. One example is dwarf acorn squash. In 1983 a distributor called to say his supply of acorn squash had come in too small, only baseball size. Caplan knew that consumers had gone wild for other so-called baby vegetables. Why not baby squash? She asked for samples and found them delicious. The grower's irrigation system, she learned, had failed at a specific point in the growing cycle. She convinced other farmers to simulate those growing conditions. Her company recently sold over 4,000 cases of the dwarf squash. "To be a successful marketer of any kind, you have to be totally open to weird new concepts," Caplan says.

Frieda's Finest now sells more than 300 items: jicama, cherimoya, passion fruit, purple potatoes, elephant garlic, tamarindos, tamarillos, cilantro, sapote, babaco, chayote squash, and burpless cucumbers. No one at Frieda's goes out looking for strange produce: "People think we travel all over the place," Caplan says. "We don't. Everybody brings us things."

When Caplan thinks something's going to be a hit, she says, "I feel it in my elbow." The company is small and nimble, the process of introducing new items refreshingly direct—marketing done at treetop level. Go by the gut, then let it fly. It leaves the company perpetually in a test-marketing phase. "Test marketing and regular marketing are the same thing at Frieda's," Caplan admits.

Consider the company's April 1988 introduction of the coquito, the tiny, coconutlike fruit of the chilean palm. A grower sent samples, hoping Frieda's Finest would like them and order more. "We just put them in the kitchen on the shelf," Caplan recalls. "We waited to see what people's reactions would be." The staff fell in love with them. A produce buyer wanted to place an order as soon as he heard about them. Frieda's started promoting them to food editors and produce buyers. "Now, we can't get enough of them."

Frieda Caplan's cardinal rule: "Always have an open door; always listen to what anyone has to offer."[14]

As this Insight suggests, innovative decisions are often made on the basis of incomplete and rapidly changing information. The conditions of the task environment facing Frieda Caplan and her associates have been unusual and ambiguous—in contrast to the conditions that faced Barbara Abelson at Holiday Inns. The following section explores the various conditions found in decision-making environments.

Managers and other employees make decisions based on the amount and accuracy of information available to them. Decisions involve future action and results, which cannot always be foreseen. Decisions also involve differing levels of risk or uncertainty. Routine decisions are most often made under conditions of near certainty, or low risk. Adaptive decisions are usually accompanied by moderate levels of uncertainty and risk. Innovative decisions generally involve high levels of uncertainty and risk. Not all of Frieda Caplan's marketing decisions have paid off. This isn't surprising, since they are made under conditions of risk and uncertainty. Some products have been out-and-out failures: Her fruit-flavored fortune cookies bombed, as did colored walnuts. Produce buyers refused to see either item as anything but a seasonal novelty.[15]

State of Nature

state of nature The conditions, situations, and events that individuals cannot control but that may in the future influence the outcomes of their decisions.

The **state of nature** consists of those conditions, situations, and events that individuals cannot control but that may in the future influence the outcomes of their decisions.[16] Our discussion of general and global environmental forces in Chapters 3 and 4 introduced various aspects of the state of nature confronting employees of organizations. These forces can range from new technologies or the entrance of new competitors into a market to new laws or political turmoil. Besides attempting to identify these forces, key employees must estimate their potential impact on the organization. In early 1990 there were few, if any, individuals in the world who recognized the possibility, let alone the probability, of Iraq's invading Kuwait and the enormous consequences of that action. The effects of the state of nature always occur in the future, anywhere from a split second to many years ahead. Individuals may be hard pressed to identify, much less predict, what those influences will be, especially when the time horizon is in years. More often than not individuals have to make adaptive or innovative decisions based on limited information available at one point in time. Therefore the amount and accuracy of information and individuals' conceptual skills (see Chapter 1) are crucial to sound decision making.

We can classify the state of nature according to three conditions: certainty, risk, and uncertainty. Figure 6.3 shows these as regions on a continuum. When individuals can identify the state of nature and its potential impact with great confidence, they make decisions under the condition of certainty. As information about the state of nature dwin-

---

FIGURE 6.3

State of Nature and Classes of Decisions

Most important organizational decision making takes place under the condition of risk. Decisions can range from low risk (routine decisions) to moderate risk (adaptive decisions) to high risk (innovative decisions).

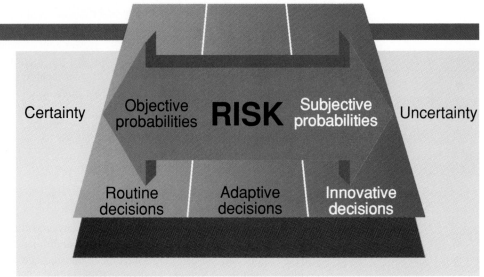

In 1970, Harry Quadracci, president of Quad/Graphics, *risked* a second mortgage on the *probability* that magazines would soon use only the color established by his own printing company. His gamble paid off. Quad/Graphics is now the country's largest privately held printer of magazines, catalogs, and freestanding inserts.

dles and becomes ambiguous, the condition of risk enters into decision making. Individuals must begin to base their decisions on either objective (clear) probability or subjective probability (best guesses or hunches). The condition of uncertainty occurs when individuals have little or no information about the state of nature. Under this condition they have no way of making even a best guess about the likely state of nature.

Certainty

certainty The condition that exists when individuals are fully informed about a problem, the alternative solutions are obvious, and the possible outcomes of each solution are known.

Certainty is the condition under which individuals are fully informed about a problem, alternative solutions are obvious, and the possible results of each solution are known. Under certainty individuals can control, or at least anticipate, events and their outcomes. In terms of Figure 6.2 certainty means that both the problem and the alternative solutions are known and well-defined. Once an individual identifies alternative solutions and their expected results, making the decision is relatively easy. The individual simply chooses the solution with the best potential outcome. For example, a purchasing agent for a printer is expected to order standard-grade paper from the supplier who offers the lowest price and the best service. Of course, the decision-making process isn't usually that simple. A problem may have may possible solutions, and calculating the expected outcomes for all of them might be extremely time-consuming and expensive.

Decision making under conditions of certainty is rare for top and middle managers. Such straightforward decisions are usually delegated. Many day-to-day decisions of first-line managers are made under conditions of near certainty. For example, a first-line manager may ask some production employees to work overtime. The manager can determine the cost of the overtime with certainty. The manager can anticipate with near certainty the number of additional units that will be produced. Thus the cost of the extra units can be figured with near certainty before the overtime is scheduled.

Risk

risk The condition that exists when individuals can define the problem, specify the probability of certain occurrences, identify alternative solutions, and state the probability that each solution will lead to desired results.

Risk is the condition under which individual can define the problem, specify the probability of certain occurrences, identify alternative solutions, and state the probability that each solution will lead to desired results.[17] In terms of Figure 6.2, risk generally means that the problem and the alternative solutions fall somewhere between the extremes of being known and well-defined and being unusual and ambiguous.

probability The percentage of times a specific outcome would occur if a particular decision were made a large number of times.

Probability is the percentage of times that a specific outcome would occur if an individual were to make a particular decision a large number of times. The most commonly used example of probability is that of tossing a coin: With enough tosses of the coin, heads will show up 50 percent of the time and tails the other 50 percent. Consider another example from business. United Parcel Service (UPS) received government approval in 1990 to initiate a new route between the United States and Japan. The state of nature faced by UPS before the decision was approval or no approval (go–no go) by the U.S. and Japanese governments. UPS managers, based on the current circumstances and past decisions of the U.S. and Japanese governmental agencies, could assign probabilities to the two possibilities.

The amount and quality of information available to an individual about the relevant state of nature can vary widely—as can the individual's estimates of risk. The type, amount, and reliability of information influence the level of risk and whether the individual estimates the probability of an outcome as objective or subjective probability (see Figure 6.3).

objective probability The likelihood that a specific outcome will occur, based on hard facts and figures.

Objective Probability **Objective probability** is the likelihood that a specific outcome will occur, based on hard facts and figures. Individuals can sometimes determine the likely outcome for a given event by examining past records. For example, although life insurance companies cannot determine the year in which each policyholder will die, they can calculate objective probabilities that specific numbers of policyholders, in various age categories, will die in a particular year. These objective probabilities are based on the expectation that past death rates will be repeated in the future.

Changes in the state of nature can alter expectations and practices and thus shift the basis for judging the likelihood of an outcome from objective probability to subjective probability. In 1990 the Clean Air Act was passed in the United States. The act contains major provisions to reduce acid rain, smog and airborne particles, and emissions of toxic chemicals. But because the outcomes are unknown, all of the cost figures of this legislation are said to represent little more than educated guesses. Ben Cooper, director of governmental affairs for the Printing Industries of America, commented: ''The biggest problem our members have with the coming clean air rules is that they don't know what to do.''[18]

subjective probability The likelihood that a specific outcome will occur, based on an individual's personal judgment and beliefs.

Subjective Probability **Subjective probability** is the likelihood that a specific outcome will occur, based on personal judgment and beliefs. Such judgments vary among individuals, depending on their intuition, previous experience with similar situations, expertise, and personality traits (such as preference for risk taking or risk avoidance). For instance, a theater owner thinking about changing the price of popcorn uses subjective probabilities in trying to determine the effect of a 10 percent price increase on the average amount of popcorn sold per customer. She might estimate that there is a 30 percent chance of sales dropping 5 percent, a 10 percent chance of sales dropping 10 percent, and a 50 percent chance that sales will stay the same. Not knowing for sure what will happen to popcorn sales, the owner must decide, based on her intuition and previous experience, whether to increase the price at the risk of losing volume.

Recall Barbara Abelson's analysis of probabilities in the Manager's Viewpoint feature. She assigned a very low subjective probability to motel customers' being attacked and a high subjective probability to security expenditures' cutting deeply into profits and hurting her career.

Uncertainty

uncertainty The condition that exists when an individual cannot clearly define the problem, identify alternative solutions, or assign probabilities to outcomes.

Uncertainty is the condition under which an individual doesn't have the necessary information to assign probabilities to the outcomes of alternative solutions. In fact, he or she may not even be able to define the problem, much less identify alternative solutions and possible outcomes.[19] In terms of Figure 6.2, uncertainty means that the problem and the alternative solutions are both ambiguous and highly unusual.

Dealing with uncertainty is an important facet of the jobs of many managers and various professionals, such as research and development engineers, market researchers, and planners.[20] Organizations face uncertainty when they enter new markets or launch significantly different products or services requiring the use of novel technologies. Uncertainty is present even when organizations do considerable research and planning before committing resources to production. "The impossibility of total prediction is clearly illustrated by the principle that if we had tomorrow's newspaper today, a good deal of [the events reported] would not happen."[21] Yet at times individuals must make decisions under the condition of uncertainty. They may base these decisions solely on their intuition and a belief that they will lead to desirable results.[22]

The Global Link feature tells how Philips N.V. of the Netherlands has positioned itself to deal with uncertainties created by Europe 1992 and other global uncertainties (see Chapter 4).

OBJECTIVES AND DECISION MAKING

Decision making under risk and uncertainty in organizations is directly coupled with objectives in one of two ways: (1) Decision processes are triggered by a search for better ways to achieve established objectives, or (2) decision processes are triggered by an effort to discover new objectives, revise current objectives, or drop objectives. The Global Link on Philips N.V. of the Netherlands revealed a variety of objectives in spreading a sense of urgency for change. This section explores the coupling of objectives and decision making. Of course, the four core managerial functions—planning, organizing, leading, and controlling—would be merely random activities if they were not based on objectives.

Objectives are crucial in giving employees, managers, and whole organizations a sense of order, direction, and meaning. Setting objectives is especially important in adaptive and innovative decision making. For example, the planning process, which focuses heavily on facilitating organizational adaptation and innovation, is vitally concerned with identifying possible new objectives, revising objectives, and setting forth ways to better accomplish present objectives.

What Objectives Are

objective A specific result or outcome to be attained; indicates the direction in which decisions and actions should be aimed.

Objectives are basically results to be attained. They indicate the direction in which decisions and actions should be aimed. Clear objectives also specify the quality or quantity of the desired results. In the Manager's Viewpoint, Barbara Adelson considered three basic objectives: safety of motel customers, profitability of the motel, and her career progress. Many objectives guide our behavior without our giving them much thought. For example, we automatically go through the motions of driving, such as observing the speed limit, looking around us, using seat belts, and so on, with the objective of getting to and from work or school safely. Sometimes individuals deliberately choose to modify or change objectives, which often involves a full-blown decision-making process.

Objectives are also called goals, ends, purposes, standards, deadlines, targets, and quotas.[23] Whatever they are called, objectives specify results and outcomes that someone believes to be desirable and worth achieving. The objective chosen, however, doesn't always ensure an organization's or person's well-being. Many savings and loan institutions as well as commercial banks established a high-growth objective during the 1980s. To achieve this growth it became necessary to make high-risk loans and engage in other questionable practices. The high-growth objective of "bigger is better" had devastating consequences, including the savings and loan crisis and the loss of many jobs.

GLOBAL Link

PHILIPS N.V. FACES EUROPE 1992

Philips N.V., of the Netherlands, is Europe's largest electronics company, with reported annual revenues of over $25 billion. It's second in the world behind Matsushita of Japan in sales of consumer electronics. Philips used Europe 1992 to help spread a sense of urgency for change throughout its huge organization.

Philips's managers viewed Europe 1992 as not just a European but a global challenge. The company's European moves were designed to improve its global market positions for major new products, such as high-definition television (HDTV), which is expected to have a $50 billion market by the year 2000. The company also prepared for the greater competition and uncertainty created by a barrier-free Europe through lowering operating costs and instituting other savings.

The ambitious plans of chairman Cornelis Van Der Klugt include a program that involves closing as many as 50 of Philips' 180 European factories and cutting as many as 20,000 employees from the work force of 310,000. The firm is spending $250 million a year to encourage employees to take early retirement. The objective is to cut overall company costs by $500 million annually.

Will these and other decisions improve the long-term success of Philips? No one really knows. Only time will tell.

Sources: Developed from T. F. Gross, ''Lesson from Philips,'' *Management Review*, September 1989, 29; and J. Kapstein, ''A Would-Be World-Beater Takes a Beating,'' *Business Week*, July 16, 1990, 40–41.

Objectives can cover the long run (years) or the short run (hours, days, or months). Long-range, or general, organizational objectives such as survival, growth, and profitability often remain stable. However, the development of specific, short-range objectives for departments and projects requires constant managerial attention. Specific production, human resource, marketing, and financing objectives usually change from year to year or even quarter to quarter. This kind of change can be dramatic when new leadership comes to an organization stuck in bureaucratic, routine ways of doing things. For example, Mike Walsh joined the Union Pacific Railroad as its CEO in 1986. He found many fiefdoms, little objective setting, and scant attention to customers. One step he took toward improvement was to have managers and teams of employees set specific performance objectives for their areas of responsibility. A few of the results by 1990: Locomotive availability (the percentage of the fleet that isn't up on the racks for repair) improved from 86 percent to 93 percent, in effect adding about 175 locomotives. Billing accuracy rose from 87 percent to 93 percent, with an eventual target of 97 percent. New procedures to identify danger spots on the tracks in hot weather and detect cracks in wheels cut derailment expenses by 15 percent, or $12 million a year.[24]

Benefits of Setting Objectives

Setting objectives can yield several benefits. These benefits are the same whether the objectives apply to an entire organization, a specific department or division, a work group, or an individual employee. First, objectives serve to focus individual and organizational decisions and efforts. They provide a set of stated expectations that everyone in the organization can understand and work to achieve. Second, objectives obviously aid the planning process. After diagnosing problems and the competition, managers usually establish objectives as a part of their planning efforts. Third, objectives motivate people and stimulate better performance. Clear objectives often raise productivity and improve the quality of work.[25] Fourth, objectives assist in performance evaluation and control. According to an old saying, "If you don't know where you're going, you'll never know when you get there."

Employees in organizations aren't the only people who can benefit from setting objectives in terms of evaluation and control. For example, your objective may be to get a B in this course. Let's say that you get a D on the first exam. This feedback would serve as a powerful incentive to assess your efforts so far and to work to avoid the same result on the next exam. In doing this type of assessment you act in a self-controlling way to get back on the road toward achieving your objective.

Operational and General Objectives

operational objective
Objective that states in quantitative terms what is to be achieved, for whom, and within what time period.

general objective
Objective that provides broad direction for managerial decision making in qualitative terms.

Operational objectives state in quantitative terms what is to be achieved, for whom, and within what time period. A simple operational objective is "to reduce my weight by twenty pounds within three months." It specifies what, in quantitative terms (lose twenty pounds), for whom (me), and a measurable time period (three months). **General objectives** provide broad direction for managerial decision making in qualitative terms. One of the general objectives of the Smithsonian Library in Washington, D.C. is to serve as an educational resource for the people of the United States as well as the rest of the world.

The following Insight spotlights Merck & Co., Inc., a leading pharmaceutical company, and includes examples of its general, long-range organizational objectives. These objectives provide a strong sense of vision and constant guidance for daily and annual decision-making efforts throughout the company.

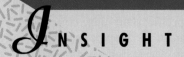

Merck & Co., Inc. is a multinational corporation engaged primarily in the business of discovering, developing, producing, and marketing products and services to maintain and restore health. (That is Merck's basic mission, or statement of purpose.) Merck's industry-leading drugs include Pepcid (for ulcers), Mevacor (for high cholesterol), and Vasotec (for high blood pressure).

Merck is composed of highly interdependent divisions and subsidiaries. Each has a specific charter and access to the resources it needs to achieve overall corporate objectives. The company's seven general objectives are:

1. To be the premier ethical pharmaceutical company.
2. To expand wherever successful operations are possible.
3. To become an increasingly important factor in the biomedical sciences.
4. To have patients understand that Merck will always put their interests first.
5. To maintain an atmosphere that encourages excellence and job satisfaction.
6. To keep the company's financial position strong.
7. To enhance stock value through earnings growth.

R. Roy Vagelos, Merck's CEO, commented on several of these objectives:

> Merck will continue to build its growth on the discovery, development, and marketing of products and services based on superior technological innovation in biology, chemistry, and engineering. As the scientific community adds dramatically to basic biochemical knowledge, the pharmaceutical industry stands on the threshold of numerous discoveries that could result in major products. The very special thing we have is the ability to spot early those areas that might lead to breakthroughs, by being very good at the scientific side—biology and chemistry—while also being able to recognize the medical importance of what we discover.[26]

From 1987 through 1991 Merck & Co. was ranked number one in *Fortune*'s annual list of the most admired U.S. corporations. The eight key characteristics evaluated by *Fortune* are (1) quality of management, (2) quality of products or services, (3) innovativeness, (4) long-term investment value, (5) financial soundness, (6) ability to attract, develop, and keep talented people, (7) community and environmental responsibility, and (8) wise use of corporate assets.[27] As you can see, some of these characteristics could have been used in developing Merck's general objectives.

Hierarchy of Objectives

hierarchy of objectives
The formal linking of objectives between and across organizational levels in order to achieve the objectives of the organization as a whole.

Management usually tries to *link* objectives—from one organization level to another and across departments at one level. This is no easy task and can be the source of many conflicts. A **hierarchy of objectives** represents the formal linking of objectives between and across organizational levels so that meeting the objectives of the lowest-level units allows objectives at the next higher organizational level to be reached, and so on, until the objectives of the organization as a whole are achieved.

Figure 6.4 presents a simple hierarchy of objectives for an organization with five levels. All of the objectives shown in the figure are operational objectives. Note that objectives for the lower-level organizational units become more detailed, narrower in scope, and easier to measure. The arrows pointing in both directions are to indicate that setting and reaching objectives involves the back-and-forth flow of decisions between organizational levels. Top management should not unilaterally set objectives and impose them on the rest of the organization.

A Simplified Hierarchy of Objectives

This simplified hierarchy of objectives suggests that objectives at the various organizational levels should be linked and mutually supportive. The two-way arrows represent the mutual decision making that must take place between levels. Not shown is the necessary interaction between individuals at the same level.

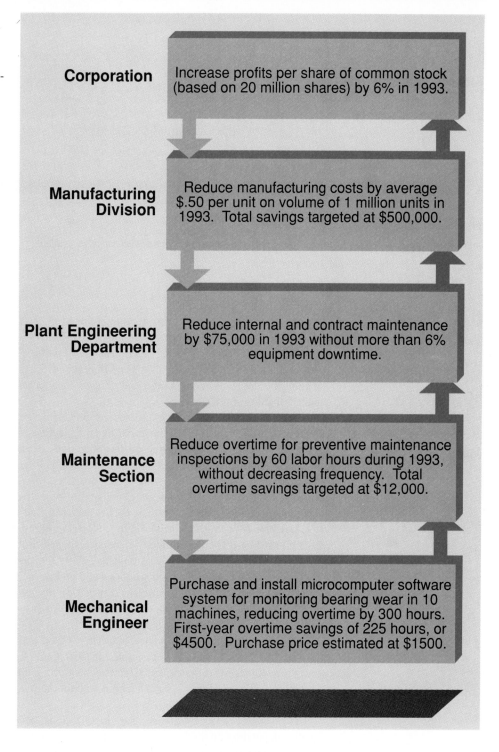

Corporation
Increase profits per share of common stock (based on 20 million shares) by 6% in 1993.

Manufacturing Division
Reduce manufacturing costs by average $.50 per unit on volume of 1 million units in 1993. Total savings targeted at $500,000.

Plant Engineering Department
Reduce internal and contract maintenance by $75,000 in 1993 without more than 6% equipment downtime.

Maintenance Section
Reduce overtime for preventive maintenance inspections by 60 labor hours during 1993, without decreasing frequency. Total overtime savings targeted at $12,000.

Mechanical Engineer
Purchase and install microcomputer software system for monitoring bearing wear in 10 machines, reducing overtime by 300 hours. First-year overtime savings of 225 hours, or $4500. Purchase price estimated at $1500.

We deliberately kept Figure 6.4 simple by *not* including all the performance objectives found at each organization level or the interaction between departments at the same level (such as production and marketing). Also, the figure doesn't reflect the influence of various stakeholders—unions, shareholders, and the government, for instance—in setting objectives.

FIGURE 6.5

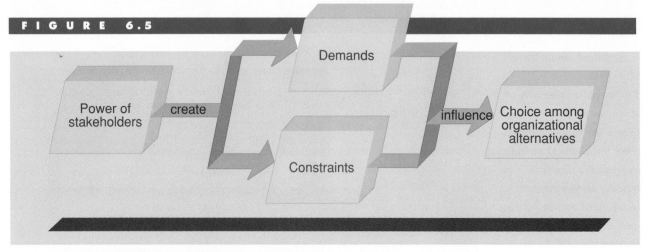

Stakeholders and Choice among Alternatives

Stakeholders create demands and constraints, which in turn influence the alternatives available to managers who must choose and set objectives.

The Role of Stakeholders

Objectives are not set in a vacuum. As mentioned in earlier chapters, a variety of stakeholders (customers, stockholders, suppliers, government agencies) have an impact on an organization and its employees. This impact is felt in the decision-making process used to choose or revise objectives. As suggested in Figure 6.5, stakeholders play a crucial role in shaping the demands, constraints, and choices of alternatives that managers face when setting objectives.[28]

Demands are the desires expressed by powerful stakeholders that an organization make certain decisions and achieve particular objectives.[29] Even stakeholders within an organization do not always agree on the objectives of their departments, divisions, or overall organization or the means for achieving them. When William Norris was the CEO of Control Data Corporation, some board members disagreed with him over the high priority given to affirmative social responsibility objectives and the corporate resources devoted to achieving them.[30] When profits declined, the board, with the support of the stockholders, encouraged Norris to retire. Norris's retirement was quickly followed by a reduction in the resources allotted to social responsibility objectives.

Constraints limit the types of objectives set, the decisions made, and the actions taken. Two important constraints are laws and ethics. A manager facing declining sales could not legally obtain a government contract by giving the contracting officer a kickback. Likewise, it is unethical for a salesperson to promise customers a product that cannot be delivered at the quoted price.

Choices are objectives, decision alternatives, and actions that organizations are free to select, but don't have to. For example, in 1990 Aetna Life & Casualty stopped writing new auto policies in six states, and Cigna began pulling out of the home and auto business altogether.[31] These companies made choices about the markets (states) and services to be dropped.

The relative level of choice that organizations have in setting objectives varies greatly, depending on the level of stakeholder power. Organizations can have high choice in setting objectives when external stakeholder power is not overwhelming. This is the situation at Rubbermaid and Merck, among others. They are leading competitors in their markets and have sufficient human, technological, and financial resources to be both proactive and reactive with respect to their stakeholders (customers, stockholders, suppliers, government agencies, and so on). Some organizations, facing powerful external stakeholder demands and constraints, have low choice in setting objectives. Texas Utility, a company that generates electricity from nuclear energy, seems to fall in this category. Government bodies and pressure groups have made strong demands and place strict con-

The choices for managers at this Texas nuclear power plant are limited or restricted by *stakeholder* requirements.

straints (governmental regulations) on where these utilities can build nuclear power plants, how they must be constructed, how they are to be operated, how nuclear wastes must be disposed of, and so on.

DECISION-MAKING MODELS

We've discussed the preconditions to and circumstances surrounding most real decision making. In this last section we present three decision-making models—rational, bounded rationality, and political—crafted by management theorists to describe various decision-making processes. As you will see, organizational objectives are common to all these models.

The Rational Model

rational model The decision-making model that consists of a series of steps managers or teams should follow to increase the likelihood that their decisions will be logical and well-founded.

The **rational model** consists of the series of steps that individuals or teams should follow to increase the likelihood that their decisions will be logical and well-founded. A rational decision permits the maximum achievement of an objective within the limitations to which the decision is subject. This definition addresses the rationality of means (how to best achieve an objective) and not of ends (that is, objectives). For example, the objective of many public utility companies is to generate electricity at the lowest possible cost. One way to achieve this objective is to minimize the cost of the fuel used to power the generators. Some power plants are designed with the capability to switch from one type of fuel to another. The plant manager and his or her team members can choose among natural gas, oil, or coal, depending on their relative costs. If the cost of natural gas skyrockets relative to those of oil and coal, the rational decision would be to shift to oil or coal. To continue to use natural gas under those circumstances would be an irrational decision.

Figure 6.6 shows the rational decision-making model as a seven-step process. It begins with defining and diagnosing the problem and moves through the succeeding steps to following up and controlling. When making routine decisions, individuals can follow these steps easily. In addition, individuals are more likely to utilize this process in situations involving conditions of near certainty or low risk when they can assign objective probabilities to outcomes. Of course, individuals often make routine decisions under

FIGURE 6.6

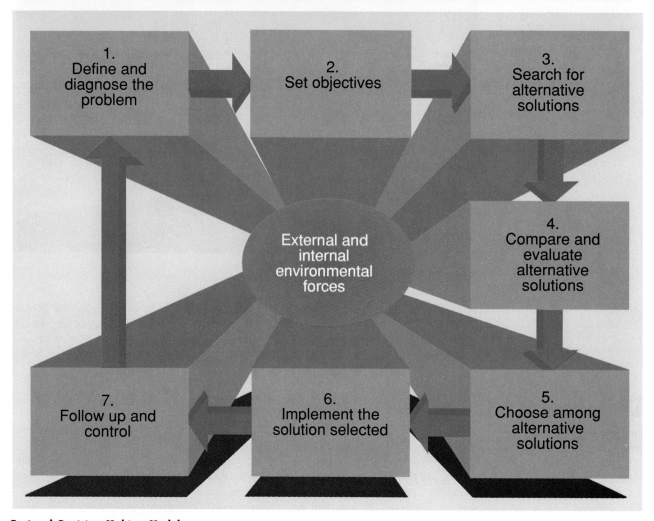

Rational Decision-Making Model

The rational decision-making model sets forth a step-by-step process that individuals and teams should follow to increase the likelihood of logical, well-founded decisions.

conditions that approximate certainty without using all the steps in the model. For example, if a particular problem tends to recur, decisions (solutions) would be written as standard operating procedures or rules. Similarly, individuals or teams rarely follow the steps in Figure 6.6 in rigid sequence when making adaptive or innovative decisions.[32]

Step 1: Define and diagnose the problem If managers or teams are unaware of the true problems and their possible causes, no effective decision making can occur.[33] Problem definition and diagnosis involves three conceptual skills: noticing, interpreting, and incorporating. Noticing means that individuals or teams monitor numerous external and internal environmental forces and decide which ones are contributing to the problem or problems. Interpreting means that individuals or teams assess the forces they have noticed and determine which are causing the real problem and are not just symptoms of it. Finally, incorporating means that individuals or teams relate their interpretations to the current or desired objectives (step 2) of the department or organization.[34] If noticing, interpreting, and incorporating are done incorrectly when diagnosing a problem, the individual or team is likely to choose a poor solution.

Let's consider two examples of the need for sound problem definition and diagnosis. Taking aspirin for headaches may do the trick in the short run, but headaches are most often a symptom, not the problem. The problem underlying the symptom could be physiological (such as eyestrain) or psychological (stress). Also, problems are sometimes incorrectly defined in terms of proposed solutions. For example, the members of a marketing department may assert that "the problem is that our department is understaffed." Acting on this definition of the problem, department members focus on the obvious objective of obtaining funds for new positions. The more basic problem may relate to selling strategies' becoming ineffective as a result of competitors' actions.

Fundamental to problem definition and diagnosis is asking lots of probing questions. Stop for a moment. How would you define the word *question*? Our use of the word goes beyond the dictionary definition: an act or instance of asking. We like the multiple, coupled meanings expressed by two creativity experts:

> A question is an invitation to creativity.
> A question is an unsettled and unsettling issue.
> A question is a beginning of adventure.
> A question is a disguised answer.
> A question pokes and prods that which has not yet been poked and prodded.
> A question is a point of departure.
> A question has no end and no beginning.[35]

By asking a variety of *who, what, when, where, how,* and *why* questions, individuals and teams will improve the odds of effective problem definition and diagnosis.

Step 2: Set objectives Once individuals or teams have defined a problem, they can set specific objectives for eliminating it. For example, let's say that top management has defined excessive manufacturing costs as a problem. This is really a symptom of the problem, however. The real problem could be defective supplies (inputs) getting into the production process, or production workers' inadequate quality control–inspection skills, or any of a number of other possibilities. Management can convert the seeming problem into a hierarchy of objectives for everyone, from the division level down to the mechanical engineer. The objectives spell out the desired results: what is to be achieved and by what date. As shown in Figure 6.4, the objective of the engineering department, for instance, might be to reduce internal and contract maintenance by $75,000 in 1993, with no more than 6 percent equipment downtime.

Under the condition of uncertainty, setting precise objectives can be very difficult. Individuals or teams may have to identify alternative objectives, compare and evaluate these objectives, and choose among them. For example, a business career might be your overall objective, but you could be uncertain about which specific path to follow. Should you become an accountant or a sales representative or choose one of many other occupations that can lead to a satisfying career in business? In order to arrive at an answer, you'll have to consider several alternative paths for achieving your general objectives.

Step 3: Search for alternative solutions Individuals or teams must look for alternative ways to achieve an objective.[36] This step might involve seeking additional information, thinking creatively, consulting experts, undertaking research, and similar actions. However, when there seem to be no feasible solutions for reaching an objective, there may be a need to modify it. For example, some people set impossible objectives for themselves and then try harder and harder to achieve them. The solution selected might be to work longer and longer hours, literally seven days a week. The ultimate result may be high stress and dissatisfaction that eventually force these individuals to reexamine their objectives and decide which are really important.

Alternative solutions to product development problems are tested by the experts at Fischer-Price's on-site nursery school. In 1968, the company began the in-house program in its research and development building, to obtain feedback on new toy designs.

Step 4: Compare and evaluate alternative solutions Once individuals or teams have identified alternative solutions, they must compare and evaluate these alternatives. This step emphasizes expected results, including the relative cost of each alternative.[37] In Chapter 7 we present several aids for rationally comparing and evaluating alternative solutions.

Step 5: Choose among alternative solutions Decision making is commonly associated with having made a final choice. Choosing a solution is, however, really only one step in the rational decision-making process.[38] Many managers complain that when recent college graduates receive a project assignment, they tend to present and discuss only one solution. Instead of comparing and evaluating several alternatives, a manager can only accept or reject the choice being presented. Choosing among alternative solutions might appear to be straightforward. Unfortunately, though, this step may prove difficult when the problem is complex and ambiguous and involves high degrees of risk or uncertainty.[39] Consider what happened to General Electric (GE) when it rushed to embrace the wrong solution.

GE'S REFRIGERATOR BLUNDER

*I*NSIGHT

In response to profit declines and cost pressures in its refrigerator division triggered by new international competition, General Electric (GE) introduced a new refrigerator model in 1986 that used a revolutionary type of compressor (the pump that creates cold air). Roger Schipke, the refrigerator division's former chief, states: ''The project was your worst nightmare come true. I don't even want to think about it anymore.'' As of 1991, GE has voluntarily replaced 1.1 million defective compressors and has taken pretax losses of over $500 million. Obviously the new, lower-cost compressor was the wrong solution to what GE saw as its problem.

The story of what happened is a complicated one. In brief, mistakes were committed at practically every organizational level. In designing the compressor, engineers made some flawed assumptions (for example, ''Rotary technology is effective in air conditioners; therefore it can be effective in refrigerators'') and then

failed to ask the right questions (such as "What will be the long-term effect of the much higher level of heat created by the rotary compressor as compared with that of the traditional compressor?"). Managers, anxious to cut costs, pushed the engineers to accelerate "life testing" of the compressor, curtailed field testing, and rushed into production.

Ultimately the disaster could be traced to poor corporate communication. Several low-level salaried employees at GE—the technicians who did the actual preproduction testing—say they suspected that the compressor might be defective and told their superiors. But senior executives, six levels removed, heard only good news.

Dietrich Huttenlocher, a former technical trouble-shooter at GE who was part of the research team that investigated the failure, comments: "GE learned a hard lesson: Don't cut corners on the testing."[40]

Step 6: Implement the solution selected A well-chosen solution isn't always successful. A technically correct decision has to be accepted and supported by those responsible for implementing it if it is to be an effective one. If the selected solution cannot be implemented for some reason, another one should be considered. The importance of participation in making a decision by those charged with implementing it is explored in detail in Chapters 14 and 16.

Step 7: Follow up and control Implementing the preferred solution won't automatically achieve the desired objective. Individuals or teams must control implementation activities and follow up by evaluating results. If implementation isn't producing satisfactory results, there is a need to take corrective action. Environmental forces affecting decisions change continually. Thus follow-up and control may indicate a need to redefine the problem or review the original objectives. Feedback from this step could even suggest the need to start over, and repeat the entire decision-making process. That is what GE did in responding to the feedback on defective compressors. In brief, GE redesigned the compressor and, of course, changed its testing procedures. The new compressor was introduced in the fall of 1990.

You might think of the rational model as an ideal, nudging individuals or teams closer to rationality in making decisions. At best, though, human decision making only approximates this ideal. When dealing with some types of problems, individuals don't even attempt to follow the rational model's seven steps.[41] The bounded rationality and political models are based on observations of actual decision processes in organizations. Such observations suggested that the rational model is modified or even ignored in practice, especially when it comes to adaptive and innovative decisions.[42]

The Bounded Rationality Model

The bounded rationality model was first introduced by Herbert Simon, a management scholar, in the mid-1950s. It contributed significantly to the Swedish Academy of Sciences' decision to award him the 1978 Nobel Prize in economics for his "pioneering research into the decision-making process within economic organizations."

bounded rationality model
The decision-making model that emphasizes the limitations of the individual's rationality.

The **bounded rationality model** is particularly useful because it emphasizes the limitations of the individual's rationality and thus provides a better picture of the day-to-day decision process often used by individuals. It partially explains why different individuals may make different decisions when they have exactly the same information. The bounded rationality model reflects the individual's tendencies (1) to select less than the best objective or alternative solution (that is, to satisfice), (2) to engage in a limited search for alternative solutions, and (3) to have inadequate information and control over external and internal environmental forces influencing the outcomes of decisions.[43]

satisficing The practice of selecting an acceptable (that is, easier to identify, less controversial, or otherwise safer) objective or alternative solution.

Satisficing Satisficing is the practice of selecting an acceptable objective or alternative solution. In this case acceptable might mean easier to identify and achieve, less controversial, or otherwise safer than the best available objective or alternative. For example, profit objectives are often quantified—a 12 percent rate of return on investment or a 6 percent increase in profits. Such objectives may not be the maximum attainable. They may, in fact, represent little more than top management's subjective judgment of reasonable goals, that is, ones that are challenging but not too difficult to achieve.[44]

In an interview almost thirty-five years after introducing the bounded rationality model, Herbert Simon described satisficing for a management audience:

> Satisficing is intended to be used in contrast to the classical economist's idea that in making decisions in business or anywhere in real life, you somehow pick, or somebody gives you, a set of alternatives from which you select the best one—maximize. The satisficing idea is that first of all, you don't have the alternatives, you've got to go out and scratch for them—and that you have mighty shaky ways of evaluating them when you do find them. So you look for alternatives until you get one from which, in terms of your experience and in terms of what you have reason to expect, you will get a reasonable result.
>
> But satisficing doesn't necessarily mean that managers have to be satisfied with what alternative pops up first in their minds or in their computers and let it go at that. The level of satisficing can be raised—by personal determination, setting higher individual or organizational standards, and by use of an increasing range of sophisticated management science and computer-based decision-making and problem-solving techniques.
>
> As time goes on, you obtain more information about what's feasible and what you can aim at. Not only do you get more information, but in many, if not most, companies there are procedures for setting targets, including procedures for trying to raise individuals' aspiration levels [objectives]. This is a major responsibility of top management.[45]

Limited Search Individuals usually make a limited search for possible objectives or alternative solutions to a problem, considering the options only until they find one that seems adequate. For example, when trying to choose the "best" job, college graduates cannot evaluate every available job in their field. They might hit retirement age before obtaining all the information.

Even the rational decision-making model recognizes that identifying and assessing alternative solutions costs time, energy, and money. In the bounded rationality model, individuals stop searching for alternatives as soon as they hit on an acceptable one.

Inadequate or Misinterpreted Information Bounded rationality means that individuals frequently have inadequate information about problems and that the state of nature, which cannot be controlled by individuals, will influence the results of their decisions.[46] For example, management might decide to purchase automatic stamping machines to make disc brakes for automobiles. By reducing labor costs, the machines could pay for themselves within two years. But management might fail to anticipate either union resistance or declining automobile sales. In those cases the machines could not be used effectively, and their pay-out time could more than double.

The bounded rationality model provides meaningful insights into the limitations on individual decision making. However, this model does not tell the whole story. There are a number of information-processing biases to which individuals often fall prey when they engage in decision making. Five of these are as follows:

1. *Availability bias* If a person can easily recall specific instances of an event, he or she may overestimate how frequently the event occurs. Individuals who have been in serious automobile accidents often overestimate the frequency of such accidents.

2. *Selective perception bias* What people expect to see often biases what they *do* see. People seek information that's consistent with their own views and downplay information that conflicts with their preconceptions. An example might be parents who are unwilling to acknowledge that their child received a failing grade because of poor performance and lack of effort rather than poor instruction or instructor bias.

3. *Concrete information bias* Vivid, direct experience usually dominates abstract information; a single personal experience can outweigh statistical evidence. An initial bad on-the-job experience may lead a worker to conclude that most managers can't be trusted and are simply out to exploit their subordinates.

4. *Law of small numbers bias* Small samples may be deemed representative of a larger population (a few cases ''prove the rule''), even when they aren't. A number of Arab-Americans experienced hostility from some non-Arabs after the invasion of Kuwait by Iraqi forces. Apparently these individuals incorrectly attributed the unsavory characteristics of Saddam Hussein (sample of one) to Arab-Americans in general.

5. *Gambler's fallacy bias* Seeing an unexpected number of similar chance events can lead to the conviction that an event not seen will occur. For example, after observing nine successive reds turn up in roulette, one might incorrectly believe that chances for a black on the next spin are greater than 50/50.[47]

The Political Model

political model The model that describes the decision-making process in terms of the particular interests and objectives of powerful stakeholders.

power The ability to influence or control individual, departmental, divisional, or organizational decisions and outcomes.

The **political model** describes the decision-making process in terms of the particular interests and objectives of powerful stakeholders. Before describing this model, however, we need to define power. **Power** is the ability to influence or control individual, departmental, divisional, or organizational decisions and outcomes.[48] To have power is to be able to influence or control (1) the definition of the problem, (2) the choice of the objective, (3) the consideration of alternative solutions, (4) the selection of the alternative to be implemented, and, ultimately, (5) the actions and success of the organization. Let's look at these elements from the viewpoint of the political model.

Problem Definition In the political model, internal and external stakeholders try to define problems for their own advantage. The U.S. Surgeon General's Office and the American Cancer Society have defined cigarette smoking as a major health hazard. The U.S. tobacco industry has consistently argued that tobacco products do not represent a significant health problem and have lobbied against restrictive legislation and regulations. Cigarettes have not been taken off the market, but an agreement was reached many years ago that tobacco companies would put health warnings on each cigarette package and discontinue advertising cigarettes on television. In this situation, problem definition was subject to negotiation between stakeholders.

Choice of Objectives The political model recognizes the likelihood of conflicting objectives among the stakeholders. The choice of objectives will be strongly influenced by the relative power of stakeholders. Often no clear ''winner'' will emerge, but if power is concentrated in one stakeholder, the organization's major objectives will likely reflect that stakeholder's objectives. When H. Ross Perot was CEO and principal owner of EDS (a computer services firm), the company reflected his personal power and objectives. After selling EDS to General Motors, Perot lost much of that power. His inability to sufficiently influence the board's decisions and objectives led Perot to sell his stock in GM for a reported $750 million and to step down from its board of directors.

On the other hand, a balance of power among several stakeholders leads to extensive negotiation and compromise in the decision-making process. It's then characterized by the push and pull of the stakeholders who have both power and conflicting objectives.[49] A balance of power may lead to compromise, as in most union-management bargaining, or end in stalemate, as in the case of the tobacco companies and the U.S. Surgeon General's office.

Search for Alternative Solutions Some objectives are likely to represent a win-lose situation: My gain is your loss, and your gain is my loss. Stakeholders will therefore often distort and selectively withhold information in order to further their own interests. Such actions can severely limit management's ability to make innovative decisions, which, by definition, require utilizing all relevant information as well as exploring a full range of alternative solutions.[50]

Stakeholders within the organization often view information as a major source of power and use it accordingly. The rational decision-making model calls for managers or teams to present all relevant information openly. Employees operating under the political model, however, would view such free disclosure as naive and as making it more difficult for them to achieve their own objectives. Information is often (1) piecemeal and based on informal communication ("Did you know that . . . ?"), (2) subjective rather than based on hard facts ("Those computer printouts don't really matter around here"); and (3) defined by what the powerful stakeholders consider important ("What does the boss think?" or "How will our customers respond?").[51]

The following Insight relates some experiences of a commissioner of education in Minnesota. (The commissioner of education is the chief executive officer of Minnesota's department of education.) These experiences reflect the political model of decision making in action.

As the governor's political appointee, Minnesota's commissioner of education had been given the mandate to promote excellence in education. She defined that charge to include making fundamental statewide changes in the educational system, an objective she identified by the slogan "Restructuring Education." Restructuring in this case meant redefining the roles of teachers, students, parents, and administrators. More decision-making authority would be delegated to parents, teachers, and students at each school than had been in the past. Fewer orders would be given by the state legislature and district education offices.

The commissioner spent much of her first year in office trying to sell external stakeholders on her plan. Despite considerable effort to build working relationships with those stakeholders (or perhaps because of it), the commissioner's efforts to make changes met with growing resistance. Her reorganization of the department, its first overhaul in more than a decade, led to complaints from those within it (internal stakeholders) and other vested groups that the commissioner was moving too fast. Challenges to her restructuring efforts mounted among the traditional educational establishment. During the budget review process, the finance department blocked her changes, calling them too costly in a period of fiscal restraint. Legislators were preparing their own initiatives for educational innovation, which they intended to introduce in the next legislative session.

The commissioner stopped and took stock of the situation. With the help of consultants she identified two broad coalitions that were forming around her restructuring plan: one that supported her program and one that favored the slow, step-by-step improvement approach. Members of the traditional educational establishment—most school board members, superintendents, principals, teachers, and their representative organizations—were in the latter group. They saw restructuring as a threat to their control over students and to their decision-making power. They preferred to press for increased funding and supported making incremental improvements without changing the educational system's basic structure. Those likely to support some form of educational restructuring were a collection of business

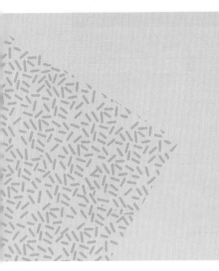

leaders, citizen groups and their advocates, academics, taxpayers, the governor, reform-minded educators, and legislators.

After much deliberation, the commissioner developed a "bridging strategy." This strategy involved bringing together the various factions so that a coherent policy of educational change could be implemented. This was accomplished primarily through the use of many decision-making teams that included individuals from the diverse interest groups.

There were times when the bridging strategy appeared doomed to failure. The advocates of restructuring criticized the commissioner for moving too slowly and siding too often with the traditional educational establishment. The opponents of restructuring criticized her for moving too quickly and being too closely aligned with the agents of change. The fact that each group accused the commissioner of siding with the other is perhaps the best testament to her fairness and evenhandedness and to the success of her bridging strategy.[52]

Through proactive and ethical management of the political model the commissioner was able to persuade diverse groups with conflicting objectives to place greater emphasis on common, higher-order objectives (students' educational needs). Once they did this, stakeholders, through participation and consensus, gradually developed viable solutions to the educational system's problems.

THE IMPORTANCE OF ETHICS IN DECISION MAKING

In Chapter 5 we addressed three ethical approaches that are worth reviewing here:

▶ The utilitarian approach judges the effect of decisions and behaviors on others, with the primary objective of providing the greatest good for the greatest number of people.

▶ The moral rights approach judges decisions and behaviors by their consistency with fundamental personal liberties.

▶ The justice approach judges decisions and behaviors by their consistency with an equitable, fair, and impartial distribution of benefits (rewards) and costs among individuals and groups.

The ethical approach followed can influence how problems are defined, the types of alternative solutions considered acceptable, and the setting of objectives. In the Manager's Viewpoint feature, Barbara Abelson applied the utilitarian approach to decision making. If she had used the moral rights approach, she would have felt a stronger obligation to protect the safety and property of the motel's customers. (The $500,000 award to Bob and Elaine Smith indicates that the jury and several judges who heard the case thought the moral rights approach should have been given greater weight in this situation.) In contrast, Minnesota's commissioner of education appeared to draw on all three ethical approaches: She wanted the greatest good for the greatest number of students (utilitarian approach); she recognized the rights of all stakeholders to participate in the decision-making process (moral rights approach); and she dealt impartially with all the stakeholder groups (justice approach).

Table 6.1 is a basic checklist for evaluating the ethics of a decision. It draws attention to some of the more common sources of unethical decisions. A check in the yes column may suggest that the proposed decision needs to be modified or discarded. Obviously, however, the checklist doesn't yield pat conclusions about the ethics of tough decisions.

Checklist for Identifying Ethical Decisions

	Yes	No
1. Does my decision treat me as an exception to a standard that I would expect others to follow?	_____	_____
2. Would I offend customers by telling them of this decision?	_____	_____
3. Would I offend qualified job applicants by telling them of this decision?	_____	_____
4. Is my decision biased in anyone's favor?	_____	_____
5. Will I have to pull rank (use coercion) to implement this decision?	_____	_____
6. Would I prefer to avoid the consequences of this decision?	_____	_____
7. Did I avoid any of the above questions by telling myself that I could get away with it?	_____	_____

Source: Adapted from M. R. Hyman, R. Skipper, and R. Tansey, ''Ethical Codes Are Not Enough,'' *Business Horizons,* March-April 1990, 17.

In this chapter we have set forth some fundamentals of organizational decision making. In Chapter 7 we will build on these fundamentals by presenting aids for making routine, adaptive, and innovative decisions.

CHAPTER SUMMARY

1. Four preconditions required for decision making to occur are (1) the existence of a gap between the current situation and desired objectives, (2) awareness of the significance of the gap, (3) motivation to close the gap, and (4) access to the resources needed to act effectively.

2. Combinations of various types of problems and alternative solutions yield three major classes of decisions: (1) routine, (2) adaptive, and (3) innovative.

3. The three classes of decisions involve varying degrees of risk which form a continuum from certainty to uncertainty. The greater the manager's or team's certainty about a situation and future events, the lower the level of risk. The state of nature consists of those conditions, situations, and events over which the individual or team has no control but which may influence the outcomes of decisions.

4. Objectives indicate the direction that decisions and actions should take and the quality or quantity of the results desired. Four benefits derived from setting objectives are (1) focusing decisions and efforts, (2) aiding the planning process, (3) motivating people and stimulating performance, and (4) assisting performance evaluation and control. The formal linkage within an organization of lower-level and higher-level objectives is a hierarchy of objectives.

5. The rational model of decision making states that individuals or teams ideally should follow a sequence of steps when making decisions: (1) define and diagnose the problem, (2) set objectives, (3) seek alternative solutions, (4) compare and evaluate alternative solutions, (5) choose among alternative solutions, (6) implement the solution selected, and (7) follow up and control the results.

6. The three core elements of the bounded rationality model are (1) satisficing, (2) limited search, and (3) inadequate or misinterpreted information. This model recognizes the practical limitations on individuals' decision making.

7. The political model emphasizes the role of powerful stakeholders in decision making. In particular, political clout tends to influence decision making in terms of identifying problems, setting objectives, generating alternative solutions, and even choosing which solution to implement.

8. Ethical concepts and issues are embedded in every step and aspect of decision making.

QUESTIONS FOR DISCUSSION AND APPLICATION

1. What are the preconditions for meaningful decision making?

2. Give an example of an adaptive decision. Why do you classify it as an adaptive decision?

3. Give an example of an innovative decision. Why do you classify it as an innovative decision?

4. **From Where You Sit:** It is said that people have a tendency to be solution-minded, rather than problem-oriented. What example of this tendency can you identify from your personal experience?

5. **From Where You Sit:** What are some problems you have encountered involving conditions of certainty, risk, or uncertainty? How did you respond? (The Skill Development Exercise may help with your answer.)

6. **From Where You Sit:** What does your hierarchy of objectives look like? Begin with passing this course as your most specific objective.

7. Why can individuals, whose rationality is limited according to the bounded rationality model, be expected to make reasonably rational decisions at times?

8. **From Where You Sit:** Have you ever observed the political model of decision making in action? Explain.

9. What elements of the decision-making process are affected by ethical concepts and issues? Give an example of how an ethical concept or issue could affect each of the elements identified.

Decision Making in the Daily Life of Managers

Instructions:

For each incident below, indicate your degree of approval of each course of action by assigning any number of points from 0 to 100. Total points assigned for all six alternatives *must* equal 100.

1. You are the manager of a small group of workers. Unfortunately, your philosophy and the company's philosophy conflict, and your influence with upper management is limited. Your group is dissatisfied with company policy.

   Would you ask employees:

   a. _____ To fall in line in almost all cases.

   b. _____ To make up their own minds.

   c. _____ To follow the majority decision of all members.

   d. _____ To follow your position on issues.

   e. _____ To communicate their concern to management.

   f. _____ Not to fall in line in almost all cases.

2. A group of employees under you develops an improved tool capable of increasing productivity by 50 percent. Actual productivity increases 10 percent, and quality improves as well. The group withholds information about the tool from the methods engineer.

   Would you:

   a. _____ Tell the methods engineer in almost all cases.

   b. _____ Attempt to convince the employees to divulge the information.

   c. _____ Be satisfied with the 10 percent increase.

   d. _____ Speak to each worker individually to assess the situation.

   e. _____ Ask the workers to increase their output.

   f. _____ Not tell the methods engineer in almost all cases.

3. You are a manager in the production department of your firm. The firm has stringent regulations against the consumption of alcohol on business premises. One hot afternoon you find an "old timer" drinking a bottle of beer.

   Would you:

   a. _____ Report the person in almost all cases.

   b. _____ Reprimand the person and give a warning.

   c. _____ Ask for an explanation of this behavior.

   d. _____ Lay off the person as allowed in the union contract.

   e. _____ Overlook the incident after making certain that the person sees you.

   f. _____ Not report the person in almost all cases.

...d out that a shipper has been "working a deal" with the majority of your best
...people, whereby they all gain financially at the expense of the organization. The
...ounts are not large, but the practice is widespread. You are the sales manager.

Would you:

a. _____ Fire all the guilty parties in almost all cases.

b. _____ Fire the shipper and keep the salespeople.

c. _____ Call a meeting to tell them you know what they are doing but not fire anyone.

d. _____ Overlook the situation, assuming it to be a "bonus."

e. _____ Try to catch them in the act.

f. _____ Not fire all guilty parties in almost all cases.

5. Due to rapid expansion of your organization, your "open door" policy is taking up a disproportionate amount of time.

Would you:

a. _____ "Close the door" in almost all cases.

b. _____ Try to have your secretary screen employees before they reach you.

c. _____ Institute a formal communication system, such as a company newsletter.

d. _____ Work after hours so as to maintain your close relationship with employees.

e. _____ Set up an appointment book.

f. _____ Not close the door in almost all cases.

6. A new production process will increase profits by an estimated 10 percent. It will also
significantly pollute a large river running through a nearby town. Government regulations
do not affect your firm.

Would you:

a. _____ Introduce the process in almost all cases.

b. _____ Introduce the process only if profits are lower than usual.

c. _____ Introduce the process only if your competitor does.

d. _____ Not introduce the process unless pressured by upper management.

e. _____ Not introduce the process if residents of the town complain.

f. _____ Not introduce the process in almost all cases.

7. A friend is having difficulty at work with subordinates. Informally you have heard it said
that your friend is too autocratic and disorganized. The friend has asked you for your
opinion of why problems exist.

Would you:

a. _____ Tell your friend what you have heard in almost all cases.

b. _____ Tell your friend that he/she is too autocratic but not discuss organizational ability.

c. _____ Tell your friend that he/she is disorganized but not discuss his/her autocratic
behavior.

d. _____ Tell your friend that what he/she does at work is his/her own business.

e. _____ Ask your friend what he/she thinks the problem is.

f. _____ Not tell your friend what you have heard in almost all cases.

8. As manager of a radio station, you are faced with a dilemma. Your program manager works a twelve-hour day, but the popularity of the station is declining, and it is losing money. The program manager has worked for your organization for five years.

Would you:

a. _____ Fire the program manager in almost all cases.

b. _____ Replace the person and give him/her another job.

c. _____ Take over some of the program manager's duties yourself.

d. _____ Ask the person to look for another job but continue to employ him/her.

e. _____ Try to determine the person's weaknesses so that you can help.

f. _____ Not fire the program manager.

9. Your best salesperson has difficulty relating to peers. The position of sales manager is open, and this salesperson has told you that he/she plans to leave if not promoted.

Would you:

a. _____ Give the person the job in almost all cases.

b. _____ Tell the person that he/she needs more management training.

c. _____ Tell the person that you hate to lose a great salesperson to gain a questionable sales manager.

d. _____ Ask the person what qualities he/she has to do a good job.

e. _____ Tell the person to prove he/she can get along with others first.

f. _____ Not give the person the job in almost all cases.

10. A bright young scientist joined your research team in the past few months. The scientist has come to you with a letter from a competing firm offering a job with a 25 percent salary increase.

Would you:

a. _____ Offer an equal salary in almost all cases.

b. _____ Ask why he/she is showing you the letter.

c. _____ Try to sell the advantages of your firm.

d. _____ Tell the scientist that he/she can make as much at your firm after a time.

e. _____ Tell the person that loyalty should count for something.

f. _____ Not offer to increase salary.

Scoring. Transfer your raw scores from the questionnaire to the S columns in the following grid. Using the conversion table below the grid, convert each raw score in each S column to an AS score, and enter the converted score in the AS column. Total the AS columns vertically. Then total all the AS sums horizontally. Divide the total by 10 (the number of incidents). Round up if the result contains a decimal part of .5 or more. Note whether your score falls within the low, medium, or high range.

	1		2		3		4		5		6		7		8		9		10	
	S	AS	S	AS	S	AS	S	AS	S	AS	S	AS	S	AS	S	AS	S	AS	S	AS
a																				
b																				
c																				
d																				
e																				
f																				
Totals		+		+		+		+		+		+		+		+		+		

Sum of totals ____ ÷ 10 = ____ Total Score

Conversion Table

S	0	1–3	4–6	7–11	12–20	21–30	31–40	41–60	61–80	81–90	91–100
AS	1	7	13	19	26	30	32	29	21	7	0

Range	Low	Medium	High
Total Score	0 – 75	76 – 95	96 – 156

Interpretation. *Low scores.* Scores of 0–75 indicate a self-reported intolerance for ambiguity. Despite complex or contradictory cues, you say you are able to make clear-cut, unambiguous decisions. Those with this style often appear to be able to "cut through the smoke" and recommend a clear-cut course of action when others are unwilling to move. One of the disadvantages of this style is that you may appear to be precipitous and perhaps even bullheaded.

Medium scores. Scores of 75–95 indicate a self-reported moderate tolerance for ambiguity. When the cues in a situation are complex or contradictory, you try to sort them out and narrow the alternatives so that you have identified feasible courses of action. One of the advantages of this style is that you may be seen as a sensitive, understanding person who can see many sides of a problem. One of the disadvantages of this style is that you may be seen as opportunistic or self-serving.

High scores. Scores of 96–156 indicate a self-reported high tolerance for ambiguity. You will find it easy to postpone a decision when the cues for decision making are ambiguous or not clear-cut. One of the advantages of this style is that you may often appear wise and unwilling to rush into complex or novel situations. One of the disadvantages of this style is that you may appear "wishy-washy" and indecisive, surrendering your power to others.

1. How congruent is your score with your self-perception of your tolerance for ambiguity? You can also check this perception with friends and family.

2. How congruent is your score with the level of tolerance for ambiguity required for your desired level of management?

TO: All Vice-Presidents
FROM: Donald McDonald, President
SUBJECT: Decision Making at Zap Computers

I've just read an interesting case study on Zap Computers. As you might know from general business articles on Zap Computers, it is able to implement in two or three months decisions that often drag on for a year or more at our firm and many others. I've selected some key portions from this case study to share with you.

Zap executives claim to "measure everything." They review bookings, scrap, inventory, cash flow, and engineering milestones on a weekly and sometimes daily basis. The monthly review is more comprehensive, emphasizing ratios, such as revenue per employee, and margins. The executives maintain fixed targets for margins and key expense categories. These targets themselves are not so unusual—what is striking is the number of people who can recite them. Zap executives attend three regularly scheduled operations meetings each week. One is a staff meeting to cover general topics, another is to cover products, and the third is to review engineering schedules. The tone at each is emotional, intense, and vocal.

The Zap top management team plays an important role in gathering real-time data. The VP of Finance is responsible for the financial model of the firm, which is run at least weekly. The model itself allows Zap executives to translate possible decisions into operating results. The finance group also provides updated operational data, usually daily.

Other executives are also essential to the real-time information network at Zap. The VP of Marketing is charged with tracking competitors' moves as they occur. This means constant phone calls and frequent travel. The VP of R&D also works the phone, to maintain a complex web of university and business contacts. Zap executives favor electronic mail or face-to-face meetings. As they described it, "We E-mail constantly." They are frequently in and out of each other's offices. On the other hand, Zap executives avoid time-delayed media such as memos. They are seen as too slow and too dated. Overall, dedication to real-time information gives Zap executives an extraodinary grasp of the details of their business.

Within the next weeks, please give me a memo on your views of Zap's decision-making process. I will put your views together in a consolidated report. This report should be used as a "thought starter," for consideration and discussion of our own decision process.

Question: Assume you are one of the vice-presidents. How would you respond to this memo?

NWA Weighs Sale of Routes, Merger Option

By Asra Q. Nomani

Northwest Airlines Chairman Alfred Checchi broached the idea of merging with a stronger airline or selling the carrier's lucrative Pacific routes in talks last week with the airline pilots' union, according to union officials.

Mr. Checchi mentioned the options amid deepening losses by Northwest and its closely held parent, NWA Inc., which is hamstrung by huge debt payments from a $3.65 billion buy-out that Mr. Checchi led in August 1989.

On Friday, the carrier reported a fourth-quarter loss of $121 million as compared to a $116 million net profit for the year-ago period. The carrier was hurt by high fuel costs.

The Air Line Pilots Association said Mr. Checchi discussed a possible merger with AMR Corp.'s American Airlines or Delta Air Lines as a possible solution to the company's troubles. As another solution, it said, Mr. Checchi explored the idea of selling the Pacific routes as a step toward retrenching the carrier as a solely domestic airline.

It isn't clear how seriously Mr. Checchi is mulling a merger or a Pacific route sale. He could be using the specter of the moves to pressure unions to accept proposed wage cuts. The pilots' union said Mr. Checchi indicated he favors pay cuts over the other options. Yet, consideration of a merger or route sale is considered a sign of the carrier's financial troubles.

"To even broach the subject is unusual," said Andy Murphy, a pilots' union official for Northwest who attended the meeting in which the alternatives were discussed. "It was surprising to hear the options broached. They didn't paint a rosy picture."

Mr. Checchi's comments about a possible merger or a Pacific route sale came early last week when he and John Dasburg, the airline's president and chief executive officer, met with the pilots' union. The union disclosed discussions of the options in a three-page letter it released Friday to its members.

A Northwest spokeswoman wouldn't comment on the specific points raised at the meeting, except to say: "We're ruling nothing out." She added, "Our discussions with the pilots are private, and we don't intend to discuss them publicly."

In its letter, the union called a Pacific route sale "totally unacceptable." Although Northwest recently cut about 15% of its service there because of a reduction in traffic since the start of the Persian Gulf war, those routes have long been a source of consistent profits for the airline. They have had double-digit traffic growth, while domestic traffic has grown in single digits.

Mr. Murphy, the union official, said the Northwest executives didn't indicate whether they were talking to American, Delta or any possible buyers of the Pacific routes.

Friday, company officials continued talking to pilots' union officials about wage cuts. The union said the company is seeking an immediate one-year 10% pay cut, and another 10% one-year cut in costs with a renegotiation of work rules and benefits. In October, the company had unsuccessfully tried to convince its unions to accept a six-month 10% wage cut.

Northwest executives face a predicament. Even though Northwest is probably strong enough to survive the consolidation wave sweeping through the industry, it might end up the weakest behind American, Delta and UAL Corp.'s United Airlines.

For the year, Northwest Airlines said it had a loss of $10 million versus a $355 million net profit for the earlier year. The airline said NWA Inc. had a 1990 net loss of $302 million. It said the year-earlier numbers weren't released. Further details of Northwest's results become publicly available on March 30. Although NWA is closely held, Northwest has to report its financial results to the Department of Transportation.

1. Does Checchi seem to be making a routine, adaptive, or innovative decision here? Explain why.

2. Which is the least risky path he can take? the riskiest?

3. Imagine that you are on Checchi's staff. What information should you have ready for him so he can make an informed decision in this situation?

FACIT AB COMPANY

Facit AB Company became large and profitable making and selling business machines and office furnishings. Although Facit made many products, its top managers believed that the key product line was mechanical calculators and that products such as typewriters, desks, and computers were peripheral. In fact, top management declined to authorize the production of computers and electronic calculators designed by one of the company's subsidiaries. Facit concentrated on improving the quality and lowering the costs of mechanical calculators, thus facilitating their production and sale. Technological change was seen as slow, incremental, and controllable. In the mid-1960s Facit borrowed large sums of money and built new plants that enabled it to make better mechanical calculators at lower costs than any other company in the world. Between 1962 and 1980 employment rose 70 percent, and sales and profits more than doubled. By 1980 Facit employed 14,000 people who worked in factories in twenty cities in five countries and in sales offices in fifteen countries.

Engineers within Facit concentrated on technologies clearly related to mechanical calculators. Facit personnel understood these technologies well. Top, middle, and lower-level managers agreed on how a mechanical-calculator factory should look and operate, what mechanical-calculator customers wanted, what the key to success was, and what was unimportant or silly. Procedures were pared to essentials, bottlenecks were eliminated, and no resources were wasted gathering irrelevant information or analyzing tangential issues. Costs were low, service fast, glitches rare, understanding high, and expertise great.

Finally, one long-time customer canceled a large order for voting machines after Facit failed repeatedly to produce machines of adequate capability. Some lower-level managers and engineers were acutely aware of the electronic revolution in the world at large, but this awareness did not penetrate to top management. The advent of electronic calculators took Facit's top managers by surprise. Relying on the company's information-gathering procedures, top management surmised that Facit's customers would switch to electronics very slowly because they liked mechanical calculators. Facit had no system for gathering information from people who were buying electronic calculators.

Actual demand for mechanical calculators dropped fast. Facit went through two years of loss, turmoil, and contraction. Top management's contraction strategy aimed at preserving the mechanical-calculator factories by closing the typewriter and office-furnishings factories. But, with bankruptcy looming, the board of directors finally sold Facit to a larger firm.

Facit's top managers had viewed the company as a harmonious system that evolved slowly by conforming to plans. They had believed that their industry was focusing on price competition instead of technologically stable products. For many years their central challenge had been competitive threat. Although they did interpret electronic calculators as a new aspect of competitive threat, this marginal revision left the central challenge basically the same. Thus they thought it could be met through the familiar planned evolution. Two years of plant closings, managerial transfers, and financial losses convinced top managers that planned evolution no longer met the challenge of competitive threat, that the company was designed to change slowly and could not change quickly, that a harmonious system for producing mechanical calculators could never produce electronic calculators, and that the competitive threat was an unmeetable challenge.

After Facit was sold, the new top managers did not even see the competitive threat. They discovered that demand for typewriters was at least three times and demand for office furnishings at least two times the company's production capacities. Sales personnel had been turning down orders because the company could not fill them. In fact, Facit faced weak competition in the typewriter and office-furnishings markets. Moreover, a subsidiary had designed electronic calculators and computers. In less than a year the company had turned around and had added a line of electronic products.

1. What difficulties in problem identification are illustrated by this case?
2. How did problem definition and diagnosis influence the choice of objectives by the old management and by the new management?

Chapter 7

DECISION-MAKING AIDS

Zita and Tom

What You Will Learn

1 The benefits and limitations of normative decision making.

2 Three aids for making routine decisions: rules and standard operating procedures and artificial intelligence.

3 Two aids for making adaptive decisions: breakeven analysis and the payoff matrix.

4 Two aids for making innovative decisions: the decision tree and Osborn's creativity model.

5 Skill Development: How to apply the appropriate type of decision-making aid to a given problem.

No Easy Choices

By the time coffee arrived, Zita and Tom were deep in an after-dinner discussion about managerial decision making. Zita, manager of the small-parts division of a manufacturing company, had taken a management science course. Tom, human resource director of the same company, hadn't.

"I tell you," Zita argued, "chances are you *can't* make a decision without having your emotions color it. Answer this for me. You've got two options: (A) a 100 percent chance to win $3000; and (B) an 80 percent chance to win $4000. Which one would you take?"

Tom thought for a few seconds and chose alternative A, the guaranteed $3000.

"That's my point exactly!" Zita exclaimed. "B actually has a *higher* potential payoff, or 'expected value,' according to probability theory."

As Zita explained it, the expected value is the possible gain multiplied by the probability of obtaining it. Thus the expected value of alternative A is $3000 ($3000 × 1.0 probability) versus $3200 for alternative B ($4000 × 0.8 probability).

Zita pointed out to Tom that, as many stock market analysts have concluded, most people are concerned about the 20 percent chance of no gain with alternative B. In general, people seek certainty and low risk while avoiding uncertainty and high risk. That's why more people invest in relatively stable industries and large companies—Johnson & Johnson, Coca-Cola, Procter & Gamble, and so on—than in high-risk startup businesses.

But are choices really that simple? Consider which of the following alternatives *you* would choose:

(A) A 100 percent chance to lose $3000

(B) An 80 percent chance to lose $4000 with a 20 percent chance to lose nothing

You'd probably choose alternative B. Yet alternative A has a more favorable expected value ($3000 × 1.0 probability = $3000 loss) than does alternative B ($4000 × 0.8 probability = $3200 loss). Most people select alternative B because it offers a 20 percent chance of losing nothing, even though it is riskier.

Why? Because people worry more about loss than about risk. The fear of loss leads many people to take bad risks. Aversion to loss is a powerful human emotion. So powerful, in fact, that managers, investors, and the rest of us often prefer an alternative other than the one with the highest expected value.[1]

The Manager's Viewpoint illustrates both the potential limitations and the benefits of quantifying decision making, that is, of using numbers to aid in making choices. One of the potential limitations is that a course of action that the numbers say is rational may not seem so rational to the decision maker. We can account for this apparent inconsistency in at least two ways. First, most decision-making aids consider only the conscious, intellectual thought processes of the decision maker. When actually selecting a course of action, however, the individual may be so influenced by the powerful *emotions* aroused by conditions of risk and uncertainty that he or she ignores the numbers. The fear of loss is one such emotion. Second, many decision-making aids simply don't take into account other important factors such as political forces. The most logical decision might not be proposed if the individual thinks his or her superior won't accept it.

On the other hand, the benefits of formalizing decision making as a set of variables that can be weighed allows the individual to compare alternatives objectively. Variables are presented in the same numerical terms or units. (In business, the most common numerical terms are dollars and cents.)

This chapter will help you develop some decision-making skills that managers and employees need on a daily basis. We discuss six decision-making aids that prescribe logical, step-by-step procedures for assessing new projects and allocating such resources as money, equipment, and personnel. Although each of these aids has certain limitations, they are useful for analyzing various problems and making some types of decisions.[2] We selected these six aids because they are widely used and typical of a whole range of *general* decision-making aids that employees and managers can use to help them analyze various problems. These problems can affect virtually any department of any organization—accounting, data processing, finance, marketing, human resources, production, and many others.

NORMATIVE DECISION MAKING

normative decision making Any prescribed step-by-step process individuals may use to help them make decisions.

Before describing the specific decision-making aids, we'll put them in a framework. **Normative decision making** is any prescribed step-by-step process individuals may use to help them make decisions.[3] The rational model described in Chapter 6 (see Figure 6.7) is an example of normative decision making. Recall that that model includes seven prescribed steps: (1) define and diagnose the problem, (2) set objectives, (3) search for alternative solutions, (4) compare and evaluate alternative solutions, (5) choose among alternative solutions, (6) implement the alternative selected, and (7) follow up and control the results. The bounded rationality and political models also presented in Chapter 6 are descriptive models (representations of how individuals actually make decisions) rather than normative models (prescriptions for how individuals ought to make decisions).

Normative decision making is commonly based on the following assumptions:

▶ The objectives can be stated and agreed on by the decision makers involved.
▶ The nature of the problem can be defined and agreed on by the decision makers involved.
▶ Some information about the problem is available.
▶ The state of nature affecting the problem ranges from certainty to uncertainty.[4]

As you'll see in this chapter, normative decision-making aids offer the following potential benefits:

▶ Hidden assumptions and their implications are more likely to be brought out into the open and clarified. Most step-by-step decision-making processes require that assumptions be identified and alternatives be assessed.
▶ The reasoning underlying a decision may be communicated to others more effectively. Laying out all the assumptions, alternatives, and probabilities makes the basis for a decision easier to see.
▶ Judgment can be improved. Defining the true nature of problems, collecting relevant information, and quantifying data where possible enhance the likelihood of making the best choice.
▶ Decision makers may become more aware of powerful emotional forces, such as the fear of loss, when choosing among alternatives.[5] This was demonstrated in the Manager's Viewpoint.

▶ Common biases affecting individual or team decision making can be reduced. In Chapter 6 we noted five of the more common types of bias: availability bias, selective perception bias, concrete information bias, law of small numbers bias, and gambler's fallacy bias.[6]

Recall that Chapter 6 set forth three classes of organizational decisions: routine, adaptive, and innovative (see Figure 6.2 for a summary). In this chapter two techniques are presented for every class of decision. First we discuss using rules or standard operating procedures and using artificial intelligence. These techniques are especially applicable to routine decisions. We then present two aids for assisting individuals in making adaptive decisions: breakeven analysis, and the payoff matrix. And finally we review the fundamentals of decision trees and Osborn's creativity model, both of which are especially useful in helping to make some kinds of innovative decisions.

ROUTINE DECISION MAKING

Routine decisions, as you'll recall from Chapter 6, are those relatively well-defined and known choices made in response to relatively well-defined and known problems. Several aids are available to assist in routine decision making. Rules and standard operating procedures provide solutions to a wide range of such problems. Although it seems fairly innovative, artificial intelligence, to date, has most often been used as an aid in making routine decisions.[7]

Rules and Standard Operating Procedures (SOPs)

rule The specification of a course of action that must be followed in dealing with a particular routine problem.

standard operating procedure (SOP) A series of rules that must be followed in a particular sequence when dealing with a certain type of routine problem.

Rules and standard operating procedures (SOPs) specify actions or steps to be taken to prevent or correct (eliminate) a particular well-defined problem. Rules and SOPs are fundamental to most organizations. A **rule** specifies a course of action that must be followed in dealing with a particular routine problem and thus establishes uniformity in routine decision making. A **standard operating procedure (SOP)** is a series of rules that employees must follow in a particular sequence when dealing with a certain type of routine problem. In other words, SOPs prescribe not only how employees should make certain decisions but also what their decisions should be.[8]

Organizational rules and SOPs affect all employees in their daily work. For example, most organizations have comprehensive rules and SOPs for employee travel. They outline in detail (1) the types of travel that are eligible for reimbursement, (2) the procedures for obtaining permission to travel, (3) the categories of and limitations on expenses (such as rooms and meals) that may be reimbursed, and (4) the procedures for requesting travel reimbursement. For example, employees of Texas A&M University, a large state-supported school with 41,000 students, must follow numerous rules and SOPs in order to be reimbursed for travel expenses. The travel rules and SOPs appearing in the *Policy and Procedure Manual* have a classification number (c.14) and an issue date (September 1, 1989). The full set of travel rules and SOPs fills nineteen pages of single-spaced text. They are presented under seven major categories, each of which has many subcategories. The manual also provides administrators with rules and SOPs for handling the thousands of other routine decisions made daily throughout the university in areas such as retention and disposition of public records, safeguarding classified information, carpeting and draping of university offices, student records, outside employment and consulting, and refuse collection.

Texas A&M University isn't unique in having extensive rules and SOPs. Eastman Kodak, Sears, and Bank of America are among the thousands of organizations that have numerous rules and SOPs to guide employees in making routine decisions. The larger and more bureaucratic an organization is, the more extensive are its rules and SOPs.

Siemens Corporate Research pursues research in machine learning, focusing on self-orienting machines like this mobile intelligent machine. Equipped with sensors and *artificial intelligence*, it self-navigates and orients itself to a changing environment.

artificial intelligence (AI) The ability of a properly programmed computer system to perform functions normally associated with human intelligence, such as comprehending spoken language, making judgments, and learning.

expert system A computer program that stores, retrieves, and manipulates data, diagnoses problems, and makes limited decisions, based on detailed information about a specific problem.

Artificial Intelligence

Artificial intelligence (AI) is the ability of a properly programmed computer system to perform functions normally associated with human intelligence, such as comprehending spoken language, making judgments, and even learning.[9] In recent years, computer software representing the first steps toward AI has been developed. Most business applications of AI occur through what's called an expert system.

Expert Systems An **expert system** is a computer program that stores, retrieves, and manipulates data, diagnoses problems, and makes limited decisions based on detailed information about a specific problem.[10] It helps users find solutions by posing a series of questions about a specific situation and then offering solutions based on the information it has received.

An expert system has the following basic characteristics:

▶ It is programmed to use factual knowledge, if-then rules, and specific procedures to solve certain complex problems. If-then rules are logical steps for progressing toward a solution.

▶ It is based on the thought processes used by effective managers or specialists when they search among possible alternatives for a ''good enough'' solution.

▶ It provides programmed explanations, so the user can follow the assumptions, line of reasoning, and process leading to the recommended alternative.[11]

Digital Equipment Corporation (DEC) uses an expert system—Expert Configurator (XCON)—that has more than 2500 rules. XCON helps DEC adapt its computer system designs to a customer's specifications. It determines whether all the necessary components have been included and then draws a set of diagrams showing the proper relationships among the components. Prior to development of XCON, errors by human checkers had been costing DEC a minimum of $10 million per year. Most of these errors have now been eliminated.[12]

A fairly new expert system, dubbed MOC, for Manufacturing Operations Consultant, keeps tabs on DEC's strategic position. For example, MOC takes only fifteen minutes to lay out how a sudden shift in demand will affect production, inventories, and gross margins and to advise which factories need adjusted production plans. MOC now covers DEC's top eighty products, but the program is being expanded to include materials and parts orders. The system also enables managers and specialists to play what-if games. ''It shows us how decisions at the strategic level will play out on the shop floor,'' notes Dennis O'Connor, head of DEC's AI technology center. ''If you have an early indication of new trends, you can adjust quickly.''[13] MOC is at the cutting edge of AI and represents an application of the expert systems approach to adaptive decision making.

DEC is only one of an increasing number of organizations making use of expert systems. Some of these organizations are Xerox, Northrop Corp., Boeing, Ford, Lockheed, VISA, and ARCO.

Assessment of AI   Evaluations of AI range from claims that it is on the verge of transforming the way managers and others make decisions (that is, machines will make them) to extreme skepticism. One skeptic is Hubert Dreyfus, outspoken professor of philosophy at the University of California at Berkeley. In his view, true intelligence cannot be separated from the person who has it. ''A digital computer is not a human being,'' he says. ''It has no body, no emotions, no needs. It hasn't been socialized by growing up in a community, to make it behave intelligently. I'm not saying computers *can't* be intelligent. But digital computers programmed with facts and rules about our human world can't be intelligent. So AI as we know it won't work.''[14]

Beau Sheil, director of artificial intelligence at the Price Waterhouse technology center provides a more positive view:

> Our limited ability to capture knowledge in machine-usable form sharply constrains the kind of AI applications it is currently practical to build to those that focus on rather narrow domains of knowledge. As a result, these specialized systems will tend to find their natural use as assistants to human specialists, since the tasks these systems can carry out are unlikely to be of much use to someone who knows little about their field. In particular, at no time soon will we see any automated secretaries, general-purpose household robots, or mechanical practitioners in law or medicine. We must look first to simpler, more specialized tasks.[15]

The bottom line at this time is that AI can help most with routine decisions. However, as demonstrated by MOC at DEC, it can be an aid in making more adaptive decisions as well. With further advances in computer technology, AI may one day help managers make innovative decisions.

ADAPTIVE DECISION MAKING

Adaptive decisions, also discussed in Chapter 6, involve a combination of moderately ambiguous problems and alternative solutions. Breakeven analysis and the payoff matrix are two particularly helpful aids that individuals may use to diagnose problems and make adaptive decisions. There are a variety of software packages for personal computers (PCs) that make it relatively easy to use these aids. Of course, there are numerous other aids that are useful for making adaptive decisions. (Chapter 9 reviews seven aids that are particularly helpful in making adaptive and innovative decisions during the planning process.)

Breakeven Analysis

breakeven analysis   A decision-making aid that looks at the various relationships between levels of sales (revenues) and costs in order to determine the point where total sales equal total costs.

Breakeven analysis looks at the various relationships between levels of sales (revenues) and levels of costs in order to determine the point where total sales equal total costs. It shows basic relationships among units produced (output), sales revenue, costs, and profits for a firm or a product line. This aid can be useful in projecting profits, controlling expenses, determining prices, and, most important, in helping to choose among alternatives. The numbers used in the analysis can be developed from historical data or from the decision maker's estimates. A breakeven analysis based on historical data, for example, might be used to make year-by-year comparisons of product line profits. This aid helps decision makers probe moderately ambiguous problems, such as why total sales are below

FIGURE 7.1

Monthly Breakeven Analysis

The vertical axis represents thousands of dollars of sales or costs per month, and the horizontal axis represents thousands of units produced per month. The firm's monthly breakeven point occurs at 80,000 units of production, where both total costs and total revenues equal $70,000.

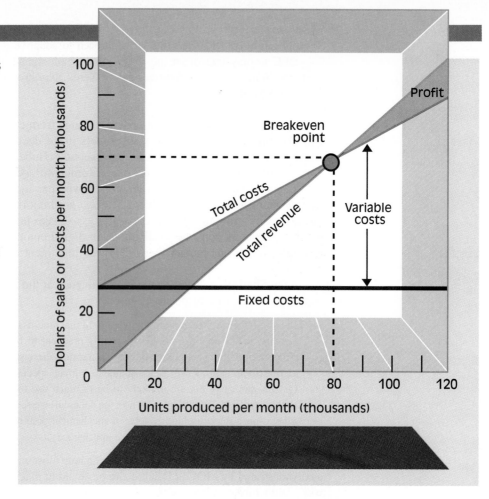

total costs, and stimulates the need to search for new alternatives. It can help answer questions such as these: At what point should a particular good or service be discontinued? How much will the company lose or gain with each combination of sales, costs, and units of goods or services produced? What will happen if fixed costs rise 8 percent and sales don't change?

Variables and Relationships Seven variables are used in breakeven analysis:

▶ **Fixed costs:** costs that remain constant over a specific period of time, regardless of the number of units produced (for example, insurance premiums, real estate taxes, administrative expenses, and interest).

▶ **Variable costs:** costs that tend to vary with changes in the number of units produced but not necessarily in proportion to each additional unit of output (for example, direct labor, electricity, raw materials, packaging, and transportation)

▶ **Total costs:** the sum of all fixed and variable costs.

▶ **Total revenue:** total dollars received from sales.

▶ **Profit:** excess of total revenue over total costs.

▶ **Loss:** excess of total costs over total revenue.

▶ **Breakeven point:** the point at which total costs equal total revenue.

Figure 7.1 illustrates the relationships among these variables for a hypothetical firm. Monthly costs (fixed and variable costs) and monthly revenues are plotted versus monthly units produced in order to determine profit, loss, and the breakeven point. When monthly production and sales go above that point, the firm sells more than it spends and makes a profit; below that point, costs exceed sales, and the firm suffers a monthly loss.

Valley Nissan in Dublin, California, holds year-end clearances to minimize losses due to a gap between *decision makers' estimates* and year-end revenues.

Assessment Although employees often use breakeven analysis when making adaptive decisions, it has several potential limitations. First, the assumption that expected profits depend only on various levels of units sold may be misleading. Profits are also influenced by changes in the price or quality of competing products, improvements in production processes, and increases in marketing effectiveness. Second, general economic conditions may cause the relationships among the variables to shift. For example, a surge in general business activity might rapidly drive up the cost of certain raw materials (a variable cost). Third, it can be difficult to accurately quantify all the variables.

An individual can partially overcome these limitations by doing several breakeven analyses, basing each one on different assumptions and estimates.[16] However, the individual may still need to consider factors other than the seven variables used in breakeven analysis. We'll discuss some of these other factors in connection with the payoff matrix and the decision tree.

payoff matrix A decision-making aid in the form of a table (matrix) identifying possible states of nature, probabilities, and outcomes (payoffs) associated with the alternative strategies being considered.

The Payoff Matrix

A **payoff matrix** is a table of figures or symbols used to identify the possible states of nature, probabilities, and outcomes (payoffs) associated with alternative strategies.[17] Table 7.1 shows a payoff matrix. The payoff matrix is based on the assumption that the

TABLE 7.1

Payoff Matrix _____

Strategy (Alternative)	Possible State of Nature				
	N_1	N_2	N_3	. . .	N_m
	Probability that each state of nature will occur				
	P_1	P_2	P_3	. . .	P_m
	Outcome of Strategy				
S_1	O_{11}	O_{12}	O_{13}	. . .	O_{1m}
S_2	O_{21}	O_{22}	O_{23}	. . .	O_{2m}
S_3	O_{31}	O_{32}	O_{33}	. . .	O_{3m}
.	.	.	.		.
.	.	.	.		.
.	.	.	.		.
S_n	O_{n1}	O_{n2}	O_{n3}	. . .	O_{nm}

decision makers are able to identify desired objectives and specify alternative strategies. Employees can use the payoff matrix to help make a variety of adaptive decisions, such as whether to open a new branch store, whether to increase (or decrease) the price of a product, and whether to rent or buy an office building.

Variables and Relationships   The payoff matrix includes four variables:

▶ *Strategies:* feasible alternatives that have been identified. In Table 7.1 they are S_1, S_2, S_3 . . . , S_n.

▶ *States of nature:* anticipated conditions (certainty, risk, uncertainty) that are relevant to the decision. In Table 7.1 they are N_1, N_2, N_3, . . . , N_m.

▶ *Probability:* the likelihood that each state of nature will occur. In Table 7.1 the probabilities are P_1, P_2, P_3, . . . , P_m. The sum of all the probabilities in the payoff matrix must equal 1.0. It is assumed (expected) that at least one of the specified states of nature will occur. A matrix with four states of nature could have probabilities of 0.1, 0.2, 0.2, and 0.5 (which sum to 1.0) for those states of nature. Because it embodies so many possible strategies to which probabilities can be assigned, the payoff matrix of Table 7.1 indicates that the decision is being made under the condition of risk. If the condition were one of certainty, the payoff matrix would show only one state of nature. Under a condition of uncertainty, a payoff matrix would not be very useful, because there would be no data on which to base probabilities.

▶ *Outcome:* the expected payoff (a profit or a loss) for each combination of a strategy and a state of nature. In Table 7.1 the outcomes are O_{11} through O_{nm}. For example, O_{11} in Table 7.1 is the outcome if the first strategy (S_1) is chosen *and* the first state of nature (N_1) occurs.

conditional value (CV)
The outcome (payoff) for the combination of a particular state of nature and a specific strategy.

expected value (EV)   The weighted-average outcome for each strategy in a payoff matrix.

Each outcome on a payoff matrix is called a **conditional value (CV),** because its value is based on a particular state of nature and a specific strategy.

Expected Values   The payoff matrix is useful only when the decision maker can assign probabilities to states of nature. In order to work toward a decision when the matrix consists of two or more states of nature, the expected value for each strategy must be calculated. The **expected value (EV)** is the weighted-average outcome for each strategy. That is, the expected value is the sum of the conditional values after each has been multiplied by its probability. For example, we can present each of the expected values for the payoff matrix in Table 7.1 as follows:

$$EV_1 = P_1 O_{11} + P_2 O_{12} + P_3 O_{13} + . . . + P_m O_{1m}$$
$$EV_2 = P_1 O_{21} + P_2 O_{22} + P_3 O_{23} + . . . + P_m O_{2m}$$
$$EV_3 = P_1 O_{31} + P_3 O_{32} + P_3 O_{33} + . . . + P_m O_{3m}$$
$$.$$
$$.$$
$$.$$
$$EV_n = P_1 O_{n1} + P_3 O_{n2} + P_3 O_{n3} + . . . + P_m O_{nm}$$

In the following Insight the payoff matrix is applied to a specific decision situation.

THE PRESIDENT'S DECISION

$\mathcal{I}$ **N S I G H T**   A university president is trying to decide how many seats to add to the football stadium. The available information and the assumptions being made are as follows:

▶ Most of the games during the past two years have been sold out. If more seats had been available, additional tickets could have been sold for those games.

▶ The president and administrative staff believe that the football team will be good, if not excellent, during the next three years. The squad has a large number of sophomores and juniors, and an excellent group of freshmen has been recruited.

▶ A modular seating system has been chosen because of its low cost, excellent quality, and ease of installation. The system comes in units of 4000 seats.

▶ Moderate increases (4 percent per year) are anticipated in the current student enrollment of 30,000 and the local town population of 100,000. The town is thirty miles from a major metropolitan area.

The president and staff have decided to consider four alternative strategies. They have also developed subjective probabilities for four levels of additional seating demand (states of nature).

Seating Demand	Probability of This Level of Demand
4,000	0.50
8,000	0.30
12,000	0.15
16,000	0.05
	1.00

The president and staff have assumed that there is a 50 percent probability that 4000 added seats will be sold out but only a 5 percent probability that 16,000 added seats will be sold out.

The conditional values *(CV)* in this case show what would happen if each state of nature (seating demand) and strategy (seat expansion) were to occur. A conditional value can be determined for each combination of a strategy and a state of nature using the following equation:

$$CV = (R \times Q_d) - (C \times Q_c),$$

where CV = conditional value, R = revenue per seat, Q_d = quantity of seats demanded, C = total costs per seat, and Q_c = quantity of seats constructed.

For the 4000-seat strategy, the cost of each seat will be $30 per year over the payback period. The maximum potential revenue per season will be $80 per seat. Thus, if 4000 seats were demanded (O_d) and 4000 seats were constructed (O_c),

$$CV = (\$80 \times 4000) - (\$30 \times 4000)$$
$$= \$320,000 - \$120,000$$
$$= \$200,000 \text{ (profit)}$$

The conditional values (outcomes) for the four strategies under each of the four states of nature are shown in Table 7.2. Note, however, that the probabilities associated with different seating demands (states of nature) have not yet been considered.

From the information in Table 7.2 and the probabilities listed earlier, the president and staff can develop the expected values. The first step in calculating the expected values is to multiply each conditional value by the probability of occurrence assigned to each state of nature. For example, the expected value for constructing 4000 stadium seats and having a demand of 4000 seats is

$$EV = CV \times P$$
$$= \$200,000 \times 0.50$$
$$= \$100,000$$

Table 7.3 shows the expected values for each probability of demand.

TABLE 7.2

Conditional Values for Stadium-Expansion Decision (in thousands of dollars)

Seats Constructed (Strategies)	Seating Demand (States of Nature)			
	4,000	8,000	12,000	16,000
4,000	$200	$200	$200	$200
8,000	80	400	400	400
12,000	−40	280	600	600
16,000	−160	160	480	800

TABLE 7.3

Expected Values for Stadium-Expansion Decision (in thousands of dollars)

	Seating Demand				
	4,000	8,000	12,000	16,000	
Seats Constructed (Strategies)	Probability of Demand				Total Expected Value
	0.50	0.30	0.15	0.05	
4,000	$100	$ 60	$ 30	$ 10	$200
8,000	40	120	60	20	240
12,000	−20	84	90	30	184
16,000	−80	48	72	40	120

The next step is to obtain the *total* expected value for each strategy by adding the expected values for all possible outcomes. For 4000 seats, the total expected value is

$$\$100,000 + \$60,000 + \$30,000 + \$10,000 = \$200,000$$

The total expected value for each strategy is given in the last column of Table 7.3. For example, the total expected value for constructing 8000 seats is $240,000. Based on the information available and the assumptions made, the optimum strategy is to construct 8000 additional seats.

Three of the four decision-making aids we've presented so far (excluding rules and standard operating procedures) require individual judgments. These judgments pertain to setting objectives, defining problems, making assumptions, and assigning probabilities. These aids are therefore of little help with innovative decision making, in which there is so much unknown territory. In the following section we examine two aids that are typical of those used in various high-risk, innovative decision-making situations.

INNOVATIVE DECISION MAKING

Recall from Chapter 6 that innovative decisions are choices that involve a combination of discovering and diagnosing unfamiliar and ambiguous problems and developing unique and creative alternative solutions to them. The two aids we present next can help employees think as systematically as possible about objectives, problems, and alternatives when making innovative decisions.

The Decision Tree

decision tree A decision-making aid that breaks a problem down into a sequence of logically ordered smaller problems and identifies relationships among present choices, states of nature, and future choices.

The **decision tree** permits decision makers to break a problem into a sequence of logically ordered smaller problems. By combining the solutions to these smaller problems, the decision maker can arrive at a solution to the larger problem. A decision tree is generally more useful than a payoff matrix when analysis of a problem requires considering a sequence of strategies, each dependent on preceding ones. A decision tree identifies relationships among present choices, states of nature, and future choices.

Some experts claim that ''decision-tree analysis is the most widely used form of decision analysis. Decision makers have used it in making business decisions in uncertain [and risky] conditions since the late 1950s.''[18] Decision tree analysis has been applied successfully to complex problems having significant financial implications, in areas such as marketing and pricing, plant expansion, the introduction of new products, and the purchase of another firm. In short, this aid is an effective tool for helping decision makers to assess strategies, risks, objectives, and monetary gains.[19] As with breakeven analysis and the payoff matrix, there are many PC-compatible software packages that implement decision tree analysis. Many organizations use decision tree analysis for a wide variety of problems. For example, Rubbermaid uses the technique when introducing new products, Quaker Oats when acquiring new companies, Eli Lilly when developing new drugs, Kraft Foods when planning special price and coupon promotions, Bell South when pricing telephone services, and AMOCO when exploring for oil.

Variables and Relationships Numerous calculations and branches may be involved in a decision tree. The critical elements in constructing a tree are the assumptions and probabilities from which the payoffs are estimated. There are four basic variables in decision tree analysis:

▶ The *skeleton* of the decision tree, which shows graphically the strategies, possible outcomes from each strategy, and states of nature identified.
▶ The *probabilities* of the various outcomes.
▶ The *conditional values* (or *costs*) associated with the outcomes.
▶ The *expected values* associated with the payoffs or costs.

(See the discussion of the payoff matrix for the definitions of the last three terms.)

The skeleton of the tree is made up of *nodes* (usually represented by circles, squares, and rectangles) and lines that connect the nodes. Each node may represent a decision point (course of action to be taken) event point (an outcome from a decision), or the probability of a state of nature. Each event point is linked to a subsequent decision. This process permits decision makers to consider every reasonable alternative and follow it to its conclusion.

The following Insight discusses possible marketing strategies for Brite and White, a new chewing gum. The alternatives proposed by the marketing team provide a simplified example of the use of a decision tree and outline the steps involved in developing such a tree for other situations.

TORONTO SWEETS—THE BRITE AND WHITE DECISION

I N S I G H T

Toronto Sweets, a manufacturer of various candies and chewing gums, is considering the introduction of a new chewing gum, tentatively called Brite and White. This chewing gum is expected to appeal to people's health consciousness because

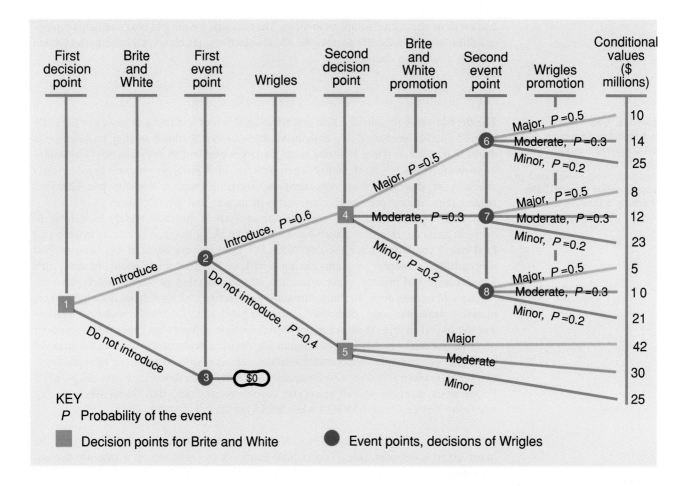

First decision point | Brite and White | First event point | Wrigles | Second decision point | Brite and White promotion | Second event point | Wrigles promotion | Conditional values ($ millions)

Major, P=0.5 — 10
Moderate, P=0.3 — 14
Minor, P=0.2 — 25

Major, P=0.5 — 8
Moderate, P=0.3 — 12
Minor, P=0.2 — 23

Major, P=0.5 — 5
Moderate, P=0.3 — 10
Minor, P=0.2 — 21

Major — 42
Moderate — 30
Minor — 25

Major, P=0.5
Moderate, P=0.3
Minor, P=0.2

Introduce, P=0.6

Introduce

Do not introduce, P=0.4

Do not introduce

$0

KEY

P Probability of the event

■ Decision points for Brite and White   ● Event points, decisions of Wrigles

of three ingredients: a sugar substitute, fluoride, and a special antiplaque substance. If introduced, the gum will be promoted as an after-meal oral freshener that is both healthy and tasty. The developmental cost for Brite and White is estimated to be $10 million. This figure includes costs for new equipment, marketing research, new personnel, employee training, and so forth. The profit from Brite and White will depend primarily on three factors: (1) whether Wrigles, Toronto Sweets' chief competitor, introduces a similar product, (2) the type of promotional campaign launched for Brite and White, and (3) the type of competitive campaign used by Wrigles.

Three types of promotional campaigns are being considered: (1) a major campaign costing $5 million, (2) a moderate campaign costing $2 million, and (3) a minor campaign costing $1 million. Tom Kaplan, the CEO of Toronto Sweets, has asked Rose Durand, vice-president of marketing, to recommend whether or not to introduce the product and, if it is to be introduced, which promotional campaign to adopt. After considerable thought and many meetings with her key marketing personnel, Durand constructed the decision tree shown in the figure.

The first decision point, node 1, presents Toronto Sweets' two basic alternatives: introduce Brite and White or do not introduce it. If Toronto Sweets doesn't introduce the new product, the payoff is obviously $0 (see event point 3). If Toronto Sweets does introduce the new product Durand and her marketing team have concluded that Wrigles has two possible reactions: introduce a similar chewing gum or do not introduce a similar chewing gum. She and her team have assigned a subjective probability of 60 percent (0.6) to Wrigles' introducing a competing gum and a subjective probability of 40 percent (0.4) to Wrigles' not introducing a gum. (These probabilities are shown after event node 2 as $P = 0.6$ and $P = 0.4$.) The second decision point involves the three alternative promotional strategies for Brite and White: major, moderate, and minor. Durand and her marketing team have concluded that if Wrigles doesn't introduce a similar chewing gum, promotional effort on behalf of Brite and White at decision node 5 will not bring any reaction from Wrigles. If Wrigles does introduce a similar chewing gum, it will challenge the promotional campaign selected for Brite and White at decision node 4 with a major, moderate, or minor campaign of its own. Durand and her team think that if Wrigles offers a competing product and Toronto Sweets launches Brite and White with a major promotion, the probabilities of Wrigles' responses are 0.5 for a major promotion, 0.3 for a moderate promotion, and 0.2 for a minor promotion.

If Wrigles matches a major Brite and White promotion with a major promotion of its own, the conditional value (profit) for Toronto Sweets is estimated to be $10 million. Conditional value in this case means the outcome, based on the best estimate by Durand and her team members, prior to adjusting for the probability of a major promotion by Wrigles. The $10 million amount appears at the upper right-hand corner of the figure. For a major promotion by Toronto Sweets and a moderate promotion by Wrigles, the conditional value will be $14 million. Obviously, a moderate or minor promotion by Wrigles is expected to have much less impact on potential sales and profits for Brite and White. Other combinations of promotional campaigns, subjective probabilities, and conditional values appear at the ends of the various branches.

The best way to analyze the sequence of decisions for Brite and White is to work backward from the end of each right-hand branch. By working backward you can determine that the two best promotional alternatives for Brite and White are to (1) launch a major promotion, if Wrigles doesn't introduce a similar product, and (2) to launch a moderate promotion, if Wrigles introduces a similar product. The following analysis of these alternatives is presented in two stages, to correspond with the sequence of decisions.

Stage one: The initial expected gross profit with a moderate promotion for Brite and White to compete with Wrigles is

$$(\$8 \text{ million} \times 0.5) + (\$12 \text{ million} \times 0.3) + (\$23 \text{ million} \times 0.2)$$
$$= \$12.2 \text{ million} - \$2 \text{ million promotional costs}$$
$$= \$10.2 \text{ million}.$$

The initial expected gross profit with a major promotional effort for Brite and White and no competing product by Wrigles is much simpler to calculate. It is the conditional value of $42 million less $5 million in promotional costs, or $37 million.

Stage two: The expected value for introducing Brite and White is the sum of the initial expected gross profit if Wrigles *does* introduce a similar product ($10.2 million) multiplied by its probability (0.6), plus the initial expected gross profit if Wrigles *doesn't* introduce a similar product ($37 million) multiplied by its probability (0.4), less the development costs ($10 million). Thus the expected value is

$$(\$10.2 \text{ million} \times 0.6) + (\$37 \text{ million} \times 0.4) - \$10 \text{ million} = \$10.92 \text{ million}$$

Rose Durand recommended to Tom Kaplan that Brite and White be introduced. She further recommended a moderate promotional campaign if Wrigles introduces a competitive product and a major promotional campaign if Wrigles doesn't.

Assessment The preceding Insight demonstrates the usefulness of the decision tree in assessing alternatives that involve a sequence of interrelated decisions. Of course, the subjective probabilities assigned were judgments by Rose Durand and her marketing staff. Changing those probabilities could lead to substantially different outcomes. The account also contains several simplifying assumptions. For example, it was assumed that the initial alternatives were to spend or not to spend $10 million to develop Brite and White chewing gum. In reality, the decision makers would probably develop decision trees based on alternative strategies for investing the $10 million. Such strategies might include launching other types of products, building a new plant, or buying out a supplier.

The Creative Process and Climate

Before discussing another technique for innovative decision making, we need to look at a few fundamentals of the creative process and climate.[20] These fundamentals are important, no matter which aid is used to spur creativity.

creativity The ability to visualize, foresee, generate, and implement new ideas.

Creativity is the ability to visualize, foresee, generate, and implement new ideas. Creative thinking increases the quality of solutions to organizational problems, helps stimulate innovation, revitalizes motivation and commitment by challenging personal skills, and serves as a catalyst to effective team performance. It's fair to say that in organizations of the 1990s creativity is no longer optional—it's necessary for success.

There are five interconnected elements in the creative process that you can apply yourself:

1. *Preparation.* A thorough investigation must be made to ensure that all parts of a problem are understood fully. During this stage, you observe, search for, and collect an inventory of facts and ideas.

2. *Concentration.* Personal or organizational energies and resources are focused on solving the problem, and a commitment is made to find and implement a solution.

3. *Incubation.* There is an internalization and subconscious ordering of gathered information. This stage may involve a significant struggle—a subconscious conflict between what is currently accepted as reality and what may be possible. You must relax, sometimes distancing yourself from the problem, and allowing your subconscious to search for possible solutions. A successful incubation stage can lead to a harvesting of fresh ideas and new ways of thinking about a problem. Ray Bradbury, the science fiction writer, once said that he often had flashes about good material during the half-awake state before real sleep. Often he forced himself completely awake to make notes on these ideas. You can coach yourself to receive dream images by telling your subconscious "Give me a dream about [the problem you're working on]. Wake me as soon as the dream is over." (With practice, you'll be able to dream and wake like this.) As soon as you're awake, *don't* open your eyes but *do* review your dream. Then open your eyes and, using the pad and pencil you have left by your bedside, quickly write down the main elements of the dream.[21]

4. *Illumination (or the Eureka connection).* This is the moment of discovery, the instant of recognition, as when Archimedes climbed into his bath and observed the water overflowing the tub. Your mind connects a problem with a solution through an observation or occurrence. Ray, the research lab director in a chemical firm, demonstrates the illumination stage in these words:

> Somebody came to me recently with the problem of making silicon nitride powders. We can make silicon nitride fibers, but could we make very fine powders? We came up with some solutions that we thought could do it, but neither of us was satisfied with them.
>
> About a month later an idea popped into my head which I think solves the entire thing.[22]

5. *Verification.* Finally, the solution or idea must be tested. As its creator, you seek corroboration and acceptance of the new approach.

Hartmut Esslinger shows off a shower head by frogdesign, his wildly *innovative* product design firm. Frogdesign has given a completely bold, new look to products as diverse as the NeXT computer, Louis Vuitton luggage, and dentist's chairs.

This process applies to various types of creativity. One is *novelty,* or an original approach to a problem. Novelty involves seeing a possibility before anyone else does, as the first frozen yogurt companies did. A second type of creativity is *synthesis,* or the combining of existing ideas from various sources into a new whole. A number of organizations have expanded their markets by synthesizing new services to offer in order to complement existing product lines. Finally, *extension* involves expanding an idea to another application. Fast food restaurants' success with the drive-through concept was extended to banking as well as to other service industries.

In the musical *Fiddler on the Roof* a beautiful song entitled ''Tradition'' tells about the virtues of having strong cultural traditions. Many benefits to families, organizations, and society are derived from tradition-based holidays, rituals, and ceremonies. But ''we've always done it this way'' is a major reason why creativity can't even get a toehold in some organizations. In Chapter 2 we discussed bureaucratic management, an organizational system that relies on rigid rules and procedures, a set and strict hierarchy, and a narrow division of labor, and in which employees are expected to perform only prescribed duties. Naturally, this type of organizational climate is alien and hostile to creative thinking.

A creative climate can be encouraged through less bureaucratic management and positive leadership. In brief, a creative climate consists of the following attributes:

▶ Trust, so that people can try and fail without prejudice.

▶ An effective system of internal and external communication, so that the organization and its members are fully aware of needs and objectives.

▶ A variety of personality types within the organization and on its teams.

▶ A process that ensures the survival and ultimately the reward of potentially useful ideas.

▶ A merit system that is based, at least in part, on the generation and implementation of innovative ideas.

▶ Flexibility in organizational structure and financial and accounting systems, so that new approaches can survive.

This chapter's Global Link feature presents comments by Makoto Kikuchi, director of Sony Corporation's research center, on the Japanese creative climate and process. Kikuchi takes issue with the all too common stereotype that Japan's rapid development is based on imitation rather than creativity and innovation.

The Skill-Building Exercise at the end of this chapter provides a way for you to assess your own barriers to creative thought and innovative action. Part 4 of this book contains many ideas for developing a creative climate, but for now we simply emphasize that the effectiveness of Osborn's creativity model and other such aids will be influenced by the type of work environment into which they are introduced.

GLOBAL *Link*

JAPANESE CREATIVITY

Foreign commentators have long held that Japan's technological development is a result of imitation, not creative thinking. This notion is based on an exceedingly narrow definition of creativity.

I believe that ideas derived from outside "hints" can be creative. One historian has suggested that the creativity of the Japanese lies in their ability to make the most of outside stimuli. I agree, and I believe this helps explain why the mature phase of the electronics products life cycle, which lends itself more to elaboration and refinement rather than to brand-new concepts, has helped give Japan a competitive edge in technological development.

The following scenario frequently occurs. An American researcher presents some abstract concept for a new mechanism or process at a scientific symposium. Within six months or a year the researcher finds that a Japanese paper has been published, analyzing each facet of the idea in detail using a working model, while neither the American nor his or her colleagues has made any progress with it.

Rather than saying that the Japanese are good imitators, it might be more accurate to say that they excel at putting two and two together. Surely this is a form of creativity also. Perhaps it is collective, rather than individual, creativity that the Japanese excel in. Something at work in the society at large keeps moving us in the right direction. In the West, a handful of highly talented individuals shoulder the burden of progress. They find it hard to believe that Japan has advanced as a result of all its people pulling together.

Although we Japanese are also attracted to Western-style creativity in science and technology, it is tied to much broader cultural values. Thus in order to adopt Western-style creativity wholesale, we would first have to adopt Western-style individualism. And to do that, we might have to give up the very qualities that enabled us to overtake the United States in 64-kilobit RAM VLSIs, for example. As a side effect, our subways might become sinister places, unsafe at night. We might turn into a litigious society, resorting to legal confrontation to settle every minor dispute.

We Japanese should give serious thought to our goals, social as well as economic, and consider whether it is in our interests to abandon what has served us so well thus far. It may be that the world today could do with more, not less, of the kind of creativity that has made Japan the technological giant it is today.

Source: Excerpted from M. Kikuchi, "The Case for Japanese Creativity," *IHJ Bulletin: A Quarterly Publication of the International House of Japan,* Summer 1984, 1–2. *See also* S. M. Tatsuno, *Created in Japan: From Imitators to World-Class Innovators* (New York: Harper Business, 1990).

Osborn's Creativity Model

Osborn's creativity model
A three-phase problem-solving process that involves finding facts, ideas, and solutions and helps overcome blockages to creativity and innovation.

Osborn's creativity model is a three-phase problem-solving process that involves finding facts, ideas, and solutions. This model is designed to help overcome blockages to creativity and innovation, which may occur for a variety of reasons. Managers use the model to make innovative group decisions built on cooperation and freewheeling thinking.[23] It can be used with all kinds of groups—for example, a manager and subordinates or a team of employees. Sufficient time and freedom must be allowed for the model to work well. Some degree of external pressure and self-generated tension can spur creativity, but too much pressure or pressure from the wrong sources (such as an order from top management to determine within ten days why quality has deteriorated) will often undermine creativity.[24]

The five decision-making aids discussed so far tend to focus on step-by-step analysis. In contrast, Osborn's creativity model stimulates novel ideas and curiosity. It encourages decision makers to find new ways of identifying and considering problems and generating solutions.[25] The model has three phases: fact finding, idea finding, and solution finding.

Fact-Finding Phase Fact finding involves defining the problem and gathering and analyzing important data. Although the Osborn creativity model provides some fact-finding procedures, they aren't nearly as well developed as the idea-finding procedures.[26] One way to improve fact finding is to begin with a broad view of the problem and then proceed to define subproblems. This phase requires a distinction between a symptom of a problem and an actual problem. For example, a manager claims that negative employee attitudes constitute a problem. A deeper investigation might suggest that negative employee attitudes are only symptoms. The real problem may be a lack of information from superiors.

Idea-Finding Phase Idea finding involves generating tentative ideas and possible leads and then developing the most likely of these ideas by modifying and combining them and adding others, if necessary. Osborn maintains that a person can generate more good ideas by following two principles. First, defer judgment: An individual can think up almost twice as many good ideas in a single length of time if he or she defers judgment on any idea until after creating a list of possible leads to a solution. Second, quantity breeds quality: The more ideas an individual thinks up, the more likely she or he is to arrive at the potentially best leads to a solution.[27]

brainstorming An unrestrained flow of ideas within a group, with all critical judgments suspended, in order to come up with possible solutions to a problem.

To encourage uninhibited thinking and thus generate ideas, Osborn developed seventy-five questions to use when brainstorming a problem. **Brainstorming** is an unrestrained flow of ideas within a group, while all critical judgments are suspended. The group leader must use some judgment about which of the seventy-five questions are most appropriate to the problem. The group leader is not expected to use all of them in one session. The following are examples of the types of questions that could be used in a brainstorming session:

How can this issue, idea, or thing be put to other use?
How can it be modified?
How can it be substituted for something else, or can something else be substituted for part of it?
How could it be reversed?
How could it be combined with other things?[28]

A brainstorming session should follow four basic rules:

1. *Criticism is ruled out.* Participants must withhold critical judgment of ideas until later.
2. *Freewheeling is welcomed.* The wilder the idea, the better; it's easier to tame down an idea than to think up new ones.
3. *Quantity is wanted.* The greater the number of ideas, the greater the likelihood that some are useful.

Millions of dollars of cost savings and major quality improvements are being realized through the creative problem-solving efforts of Harris Corporation's PEOPLE teams, in *brainstorming sessions* like this one.

4. *Combination and improvement are sought.* In addition to contributing ideas of their own, participants should suggest how ideas of others can be turned into better ideas, or how two or more ideas can be joined into still another idea.[29]

These rules are intended to separate judgment and creative imagination. The two are incompatible and relate to different steps in the decision-making process.[30] The leader of one brainstorming group put it this way: "If you try to get hot and cold water out of the same faucet at the same time, you will get only lukewarm water. And if you try to criticize and create at the same time, you [won't do either very well]. So let's stick solely to *ideas*—let's cut out *all* criticism during this session."[31]

A brainstorming session should have from five to twelve participants in order to foster a diversity of ideas, yet maintain in each member a sense of identification and involvement with the group. The session should normally run not less than twenty minutes or more than an hour. Brainstorming could consist of several idea-generating sessions. For example, subsequent sessions could address each of the ideas previously identified. Guidelines for leading a brainstorming session are presented in Table 7.4.

TABLE 7.4

Guidelines for Leading a Brainstorming Session

Basic Leadership Role

▶ Make a brief statement of the four basic rules.
▶ State the time limit for the session.
▶ Read the problem and/or related question to be discussed and ask, "What are your ideas?"
▶ When an idea is given, summarize it, using the speaker's words as far as possible. Have the idea recorded by a participant or an audiotape machine. Follow your summary with the single word "Next."
▶ Say little else. Whenever the leader participates as a brainstormer, group productivity usually falls.

Handling Problems

▶ When someone talks too long, wait until he or she takes a breath (everyone must stop to inhale sometime), break into the monologue, summarize what was said for the recorder, then point to another participant and say "Next."
▶ When someone becomes judgmental or starts to argue, stop him or her. Say, for example, "That will cost you one coffee or soda for each member of the group."
▶ When the discussion stops, relax and let the silence continue. Say nothing. The pause should be broken by the group and *not* the leader. This period of silence is called the "mental pause" because it is a change in thinking. All the obvious ideas are exhausted; the participants are now forced to rely on their creativity to produce new ideas.
▶ When someone states a problem rather than an idea, repeat the problem, raise your hand with five fingers extended, and say, "Let's have five ideas on this problem." You may get only one or you may get ten, but you're back in the business of creative thinking.

Source: Adapted from A. F. Osborn, *Applied Imagination,* 3rd rev. ed. New York: Charles Scribner's Sons, 1963, pp. 166–196.

Solution-Finding Phase Solution finding involves identifying and evaluating tentative courses of action as well as deciding how to implement the chosen course of action. The solution-finding phase relies on judgment, analysis, and criticism. A variety of decision-making aids—such as those presented earlier in this chapter—can be used.[32] To initiate this phase, the leader might ask the group to identify from one to five of the most important ideas generated. Each participant would be asked to jot down these ideas and evaluate them on a five-point scale. An extremely important idea would get five points; a not-so-important idea would get one. The highest combined scores indicate the actions or ideas to be investigated further.

Assessment A basic assumption of the Osborn creativity model is that most people have the potential for greater creativity and innovation in decision making than they use. General Motors, IBM, and U.S. Steel, as well as nonbusiness organizations, including the U.S. Air Force and Army have used this model.[33]

Osborn's creativity model has been widely modified. The following Insight, a review of a software program for individual brainstorming, is but one example of such modification. In this case, two modifications are involved: (1) the focus is on individual versus group brainstorming; and (2) a personal computer is used to aid idea finding.

MindLink, a PC-compatible software program, asks you to do no less than throw away a good deal of your normal pattern of thinking. You are to consider how seemingly unrelated things—the crossing of an elephant with an oil well, the headline of today's newspaper and a credit card, a trip to the shopping mall and playing tennis, or the feeling that a poem gives you and driving a car—might ultimately lead you to the solution to your problem. MindLink challenges you to make the leap from traditional thought patterns into irrelevant, absurd, or even contradictory thoughts. The developers believe this increases your chances of coming up with truly novel, or breakthrough, ideas. Sometimes you have to forget a problem to solve it.

The three main sections of MindLink are called "Idea Generation," "Guided Problem Solving," and "General Problem Solving." All sections use so-called idea triggers to force divergent thinking. In all, there are more than forty idea triggers in the program. For example, one idea trigger uses poems to stimulate ideas. Any one of more than thirty poems could appear at a given time. Another trigger invites you to put yourself into someone else's situation—from Mahatma Gandhi's to an investment banker's to a traffic cop's.

After each seemingly unrelated-to-the-problem trigger exercise the program asks you to imagine how the imagery, wishes, thoughts, or ideas generated could be used to help solve your particular problem. The best ideas then progress through a disciplined "building" process until, finally, you end up with an action plan for the ideas you'd like to pursue.[34]

The Osborn model or any other aid intended to stimulate creativity cannot guarantee innovative outcomes. However, the appropriate use of such aids usually increases the likelihood of creative and innovative decisions.[35]

1. Normative decision-making aids provide step-by-step procedures for helping individuals make rational decisions. Although they reveal hidden assumptions, clarify underlying reasoning processes, improve judgments, increase awareness of emotional responses, and reduce judgmental biases, they are limited by the impossibility of eliminating all emotional and attitudinal biases, of foreseeing all future events, and of acquiring complete data.

2. Two aids for finding routine solutions to known and well-defined problems are (1) rules or standard operating procedures (SOPs), which prescribe specific ways of solving organizational problems and making managerial decisions; and (2) artificial intelligence (AI), which is a computer system that is programmed to manipulate data and make limited judgments based on information that users enter.

3. Two aids used in making adaptive decisions are (1) breakeven analysis, which shows graphically the relationships between levels of sales (revenues) and levels of costs and identifies the breakeven point; and (2) the payoff matrix, a table that helps decision makers mathematically evaluate alternative solutions once objectives have been set and alternative strategies specified.

4. The decision tree and Osborn's creativity model help decision makers solve unstructured and ambiguous problems, which often call for creative, unique decisions made under conditions of relatively high risk or uncertainty. The decision tree breaks each large problem into a series of logically ordered alternative strategies and possible outcomes, which are then assigned probabilities and costs. Osborn's creativity model is designed to reduce blocks to creativity and innovation through group brainstorming.

QUESTIONS FOR DISCUSSION AND APPLICATION

1. **From Where You Sit:** As an employee, why should you be interested in normative decision-making aids?

2. Identify differences between rules and SOPs and artificial intelligence.

3. How might AI be used in adaptive decision making?

4. **From Where You Sit:** Describe one way in which you have been personally affected by an application of AI.

5. What are the similarities between breakeven analysis and the payoff matrix?

6. When can the decision tree be used more effectively than the payoff matrix?

7. How might different individual opinions influence decision tree outcomes?

8. **From Where You Sit:** Develop a decision tree to help answer the question "Should I go to college?" with respect to a future event, such as choosing a company to work for.

9. **From Where You Sit:** Evaluate the degree to which an organization you have worked for has a creative climate.

10. **From Where You Sit:** Describe a situation you have been in within the past six months where Osborn's creativity model would have been useful. Why would it have been useful?

Personal Barriers to Creative Thought and Innovative Action

Instructions:

For each of the statements in this inventory, refer to the following scale and decide which number corresponds to your level of agreement with the statement. Write that number in the blank to the left of the statement.

Strongly Agree	Agree	Agree Somewhat	Disagree Somewhat	Disagree	Strongly Disagree
1	2	3	4	5	6

1. I evaluate criticism to determine how it can be useful to me.

2. When solving problems, I attempt to apply new concepts or methods.

3. I can shift gears or change emphasis in the abstract.

4. I get enthusiastic about problems outside my specialized area of concentration.

5. I always give a problem my best effort, even if it seems trivial or fails to arouse enthusiasm.

6. I set aside periods of time without interruptions.

7. It is not difficult for me to have my ideas criticized.

8. In the past, I have taken calculated risks and I would do so again.

9. I dream, daydream, and fantasize easily.

10. I know how to simplify and organize my observations.

11. Occasionally, I try a so-called unworkable answer and hope that it will prove to be workable.

12. I can and do consistently guard my personal periods of privacy.

13. I feel at ease with colleagues even when my ideas or plans meet with public criticism or rejection.

14. I frequently read opinions contrary to my own to learn what the opposition is thinking.

15. I translate symbols into concrete ideas or action steps.

16. I seek many ideas because I enjoy having alternative possibilities.

17. In the idea-formulation stage of a project, I withhold critical judgment.

18. I determine whether an imposed limitation is reasonable or unreasonable.

19. I would modify an idea, plan, or design, even if doing so would meet with opposition.

20. I feel comfortable in expressing my ideas even if they are in the minority.

21. I enjoy participating in nonverbal, symbolic, or visual activities.

22. I feel the excitement and challenge of finding a solution to problems.

23. I keep a file of discarded ideas.

24. I make reasonable demands for good physical facilities and surroundings.

25. I would feel no serious loss of status or prestige if management publicly rejected my plan.

26. I frequently question the policies, objectives, values, or ideas of an organization.

27. I deliberately exercise my visual and symbolic skills in order to strengthen them.

28. I can accept my thinking when it seems illogical.

29. I seldom reject ambiguous ideas that are not directly related to the problem.

30. I distinguish between the trivial and the important physical distractions.

31. I feel uncomfortable making waves for a worthwhile idea if it threatens the inner harmony of the group.

32. I am willing to present a truly original approach even if there is a chance it could fail.

33. I can recognize the times when symbolism or visualization would work best for me.

34. I try to make an uninteresting problem stimulating.

35. I consciously attempt to use new approaches toward routine tasks.

36. In the past, I have determined when to leave an undesirable environment and when to stay and change the environment (including self-growth).

Scoring Sheet

Instructions:

Transfer your inventory responses to the blanks provided below. Then add the numbers in each column, and record the totals.

	A	B	C	D	E	F
	1. ____	2. ____	3. ____	4. ____	5. ____	6. ____
	7. ____	8. ____	9. ____	10. ____	11. ____	12. ____
	13. ____	14. ____	15. ____	16. ____	17. ____	18. ____
	19. ____	20. ____	21. ____	22. ____	23. ____	24. ____
	25. ____	26. ____	27. ____	28. ____	29. ____	30. ____
	31. ____	32. ____	33. ____	34. ____	35. ____	36. ____
Column Totals	____	____	____	____	____	____

Profile Sheet

Instructions:

Plot the scores from your scoring sheet onto the following graph. The vertical axis, which represents your numbered scores, ranges from 6 to 36. The horizontal axis, which represents the columns on your scoring sheet, ranges from A to F. The key at the bottom of this page identifies the barriers in each column. Connect the points you have plotted with a line. The high points represent your barriers.

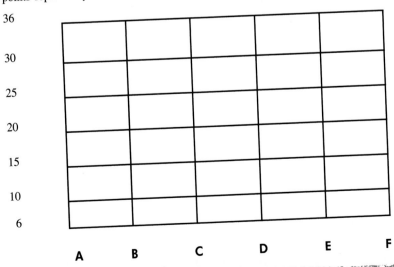

Key to Barriers

A = Barriers related to self-confidence and risk taking

B = Barriers related to need for conformity

C = Barriers related to use of the abstract

D = Barriers related to use of systematic analysis

E = Barriers related to task achievement

F = Barriers related to physical environment

TO: Robert Gage, Director of Human Resources
FROM: Mike Mobley, President
SUBJECT: Individual Creativity

While on vacation, Bob, I had a chance to do some reading on creativity. As we've discussed, we are under increasing pressure to be innovative and creative as an organization. Individual creativity in our employees (including managers) will play a central role in our ability to create marketing opportunities and respond swiftly to competitor threats. Based on my reading, I listed key attributes of creative people:

1. *Creative people are spontaneous.* They don't need a script to lead their lives. They take direction from each day's events and from the work they do. Creative people love to respond to events, rather than perform to someone else's standards.

2. *Creative people are independent.* They're able to work alone, be alone, and stand alone in their convictions and desires—often against great odds and despite objections from others.

3. *Creative people are enthusiastic, idealistic, and responsive.* They believe that enthusiasm makes all else possible. Some people consider them hyperactive.

4. *Creative people are bold.* They act with the confident, charge-ahead single-mindedness of people who have important work to do and know what that work is, even if others don't. They're free with their opinions because they like to test ideas and see if someone will challenge them.

5. *Creative people see things where others don't.* Creative people put things together, on a canvas or in a stew pot. They may put 2 and 2 together and come up with 22 instead of 4.

6. *Creative people push beyond, around, or through the wall.* Every problem is an opportunity; every obstacle is a challenge. A creative person looks at a challenge in much the same way a mountain climber looks at a mountain.

As I reread my list, I have to wonder about the blocks to individual creativity we may have established. Our formal procedures might be hampering creativity. Within the next week or so, I would like a memo from you sharing your thoughts on: (1) whether we have established blocks to individual creativity, (2) how we might reduce or remove those blocks, and (3) the risks in doing so. I'm not looking for a thoroughly researched response. What I really want is your gut reaction.

Question: Assume you are Robert Gage, and formulate a response to the president's memo. Base your response on the creative climate of an organization you have worked for.

Apple's Sculley Looks for a Breakthrough

BY G. PASCAL ZACHARY

John Sculley, chief executive officer of Apple Computer Inc., is giving up some authority over the company's new-product efforts to spend more time on a few potential "breakthrough" projects he thinks will push the Cupertino, Calif., company into vast new markets.

"The things we're interested in go beyond the definition of personal computing as we know it today," Mr. Sculley says.

Mr. Sculley first disclosed his plans to reorganize Apple's research and development activities in a meeting last week with about 50 of his senior managers. Details are still to be worked out, but he stressed that he retains his title of chief technical officer and would continue to have the last word "on product decisions and our technical relations with other companies."

However, Mr. Sculley has handed off day-to-day responsibility for most of Apple's existing product lines to Michael Spindler, the company's chief operating officer. The shift is a boost for Mr. Spindler, a native of Germany who is widely credited with instilling a fresh sense of vigor at Apple, the world's second-largest supplier of personal computers.

Since Mr. Spindler was promoted from his post as European chief a year ago, Apple has introduced a spate of new products at aggressive prices in a bid to increase its slumping share of the personal-computer market. The tactic appears to have worked so well that even though Apple has a large backlog for its newest computers, Info-Corp., one market researcher, finds that the company's market share has made "a phenomenal comeback."

With Apple's traditional computer business on an upswing, Mr. Sculley now wants to push the company into new areas. People who know him well say he is driven by an impulse to push Apple into a sharply different product category that ulti-mately would equal or surpass in importance the company's Macintosh computer, considered a stunning breakthrough when it was first released in the mid-1980s.

Mr. Sculley, who has no formal training in engineering and first made his reputation as a marketeer at Pepsi, has long wanted to put to rest the charge that he has flourished as Apple's chief executive simply by skillfully managing the legacy of Mr. Jobs, who left the company almost six years ago. Thirteen months ago, Mr. Sculley took complete charge of Apple's product activities and has since impressed some industry watchers. "Though he's really not a nerd, he is a good product strategist," says Stewart Alsop, editor of PC Letter, a newsletter.

At the moment, Mr. Sculley's best bet to gain credit for a breakthrough product of his own may lie with Apple's unannounced effort to build a notebook-sized computer that recognizes handwriting. The project, code-named "Newton," may appeal to consumers who would rather write than type and who prefer an "electronic notebook" to a conventional computer. "Newton" is critical to Apple's future because a number of rivals, including International Business Machines Co., are hard at work on similar gadgets.

Apple, however, may seek to distinguish itself from the pack by incorporating wireless communication in its electronic notebooks. Mr. Sculley says he is a fan of an emerging class of machines called personal communicators, which some envision as a combination cellular phone and pocket computer.

Another project close to Mr. Sculley's heart centers on a proposed product that, if released, would represent Apple's first foray into the field of consumer electronics. This "living room" system combines a compact-disk player and a stripped-down Macintosh (minus disk drives, a keyboard and a monitor).

1. John Sculley has his own definite ideas about where Apple should be headed. How do you think this will affect the corporate decision-making process at Apple?

2. Would a decision tree be useful in helping to decide whether to introduce a new product, such as the Newton computer? Would any other aids be useful?

3. What role might Osborn's creativity model play in decision making at a computer company? Where might it be appropriate or inappropriate?

INTERVIEWER EFFECTIVENESS AT PATRIOT COMPUTER

Part A

You work for Patriot Computer, a company that manufactures computer chips. Because work in a clean room involves great detail, you know that only 15 percent of the applicants for a clean-room technician's job can perform it successfully; the remaining 85 percent, for a variety of reasons, cannot. It's important to have good performers on the job, so you hired a highly skilled interviewer to assess job applicants. Based on a study you conducted, you know that Melissa, your interviewer, is accurate in her assessments of both job success and failure 80 percent of the time. A job candidate has just been interviewed by Melissa. She recommends hiring the individual, commenting, "This person is sure to work out for us."

Questions

1. What is the probability that Melissa's judgment is correct and the applicant will be a good performer?
2. Explain how you arrived at your answer.

Part B

You decide that one way to improve your hiring procedure is to have two interviewers assess the potential of each applicant. You hire George away from a recruitment agency. Well trained, but not yet completely familiar with the specific needs of your company, George is able to correctly assess employees only 60 percent of the time. Like Melissa, he is as accurate at predicting who will be successful as who will fail.

Melissa is on vacation for several days. You still have jobs to fill, so you ask George to interview an applicant. After talking with the applicant, George emphatically states the applicant should not be hired. You're somewhat concerned about making a decision based solely on his judgment (after all, he's accurate only 60 percent of the time).

Questions

3. What do you think is the probability that the employee will be a poor performer as George suggests and thus should not be hired?
4. Explain how you arrived at your answer.

Part C

Melissa is now back on the job. She's still correct in her assessments 80 percent of the time; George's accuracy rate is still 60 percent. As you already know, 85 percent of all applicants do not have the ability to perform the technical work, but 15 percent do. A new candidate comes into the human resources office. After interviews, Melissa and George make their recommendations. George says that the person definitely should not be hired. Melissa disagrees, saying she believes the woman will be a good performer.

Questions

5. What is the probability that George is right, and the person will be a poor performer?
6. What is the probability that the applicant will be a good performer, as Melissa suggests?
7. Explain how you arrived at your answer.

Chapter 8

STRATEGIC PLANNING AND MANAGEMENT

Lee Iacocca

What You Will Learn

1 The differences between strategic planning and tactical planning.

2 The benefits and characteristics of effective planning.

3 How stage of diversification is likely to affect the planning process.

4 The key issues of planning and strategy at the corporate level, the business level, and the functional level.

5 Eight core tasks in the strategic planning process.

6 How the product life cycle model and the generic strategies model can assist in the generation of new strategies and the evaluation of current business-level strategies.

7 **Skill Development:** How to develop a business-level plan.

Chapter Outline

Manager's Viewpoint
Lee Iacocca—A Vision for the Auto Industry

Basics of Planning
Strategic Planning
Tactical Planning
Benefits of Planning
Planning Effectively

Levels of Strategy and Planning
Global Link: Strategic Planning in Brazil
Stages of Diversification
Levels of Strategy within Large Organizations
Insight: GM's Technology Strategy

The Strategic Planning Process
Task 1: Develop Mission and Objectives
Insight: Ford's Mission and Objectives
Task 2: Diagnose Threats and Opportunities
Insight: Suppliers Speak Out
Task 3: Assess Strengths and Weaknesses
Insight: Stempel on GM's Weaknesses
Task 4: Generate Alternative Strategies
Task 5: Develop Strategic Plan
Insight: GM's Strategic Plan
Task 6: Develop Tactical Plans
Task 7: Control and Assess Results
Task 8: Repeat Planning Process

Models of Business-Level Strategy
Product Life Cycle Model
Generic Strategies Model

Ethics and Strategic Planning
Insight: Akers on Competitiveness and Ethics

Experiencing Management
Skill-Building Exercise: Marzilli's Fine Italian Foods

Manager's Memo

In the News

Management Case
Singing the Small Business Blues at Sharpco

Lee Iacocca—A Vision for the Auto Industry

It would be hard to find a more outspoken business leader than Lee Iacocca, head of Chrysler Corporation. And Chrysler is generally considered the financially weakest North American auto firm currently trying to rise to the challenge of global competition. What does Iacocca have in mind to meet this challenge? This undaunted CEO has a vision—not only for Chrysler but for the auto industry throughout all of North America. What kind of strategy will it take for North American–based firms (Chrysler and its competitors, Ford and General Motors) to compete in a global industry through the 1990s? Here's what Iacocca thinks:

There's a feeling that anyone associated not just with cars but with American industry as a whole is some kind of dope who should either get out or see the inevitable: the Far East is going to overpower us on everything from microchips to aircraft. Our job is to change that perception through good products and marketing. We have to get to car buyers and tell them, "Look, we're in the ball game. Our factories are good. Our quality is better than ever." You've got to keep the quality up, be a low-cost producer, and have good stuff. From 1980 to 1985 the products we were shipping weren't as good as they should have been. I'm not saying we were shipping crap, but little by little we began to lose our position.

The competition is vicious out there for all of our lines (Chrysler, Dodge, Jeep, Eagle Premier, New Yorker, Laser, Plymouth, and so on). Look at our Eagle Premier. Giugiaro of Italy styled it, and France's Renault did a heck of a job engineering it. We're selling 50,000 a year now through the new Eagle dealer group. I imagine we'll double that when Dodge dealers get a version of it. It's a first-class car.

When you look at car lineups today, U.S. versus foreign, we're not in a bad position on cost, price, fuel economy, styling, or features. What worries me more than any single thing I've seen is that Nummi (Chrysler competitor, General Motors' joint venture with Toyota) builds two identical cars in their U.S. plant. One is sold as a Japanese car, the other as an American car. Americans buy the Japanese brand. Both cars have the same engineering, same design, same workers, same everything, and when they come down the line, the American brand gets crossed off the order form. U.S. products, and cars in particular, are better than they're given credit for. I'm not crying about it; it's my job to convince people.

I think we'll be doing more joint ventures with American companies in the future. Look at GM and us getting together, as we are about to do, to make truck transmissions and four-wheel-drive equipment. It is historic, in my opinion. If GM can ask Toyota to be its partner at Nummi, why can't GM and Chrysler build a small car together? If we want to be a full-line car and truck producer, we'll need a partner. Will we do more with Fiat than sell Alfa Romeos this year? I don't know. We have a deal going with Hyundai of Korea, which will be a big player. We have a twenty-year association with Mitsubishi. However, Japan has been totally insensitive to the economic problems America is now facing. I endorse the UAW (United Auto Workers) proposal to cap Japanese auto makers' total share of the U.S. market (to under 30 percent), including the Plymouth Laser and other vehicles that are built in American factories such as the one Chrysler shares with Mitsubishi.[1]

Iacocca's strategic thinking reveals how he believes Chrysler can deal with the interplay of global competitive forces in the auto industry. For the "Big Three" (Chrysler, Ford and GM) to be effective global competitors, they need new or improved strategies related to, most importantly, perceived customer satisfaction, as well as marketing, quality of products, and control of production costs. Chrysler's mission remains being a full-line car and truck producer. To pursue this mission, Chrysler, according to Iacocca, is likely to make increasing use of joint ventures (one type of alliance strategy) with both domestic (GM) and foreign (Fiat, Hyundai, and Mitsubishi) firms.[2]

Throughout this chapter we'll use the auto industry and auto firms to illustrate many of the concepts and issues of planning and strategic management. We do this for three reasons. First, the auto industry is on the front lines of today's global competition. Second, planning and strategic management are tightly coupled with the changing forces in the task and general environments, which were the focus of Chapters 3 and 4. Most people can readily identify the environmental forces in action in the auto industry. Third, as customers, most people have experienced the results—either good or bad—of the planning and strategic management of specific auto firms.

In the first part of this chapter we'll discuss the nature, role, and scope of planning and introduce you to three levels of strategy and planning. This will set the stage for a summary of the basic steps in the process of strategic planning. Since you'll probably be primarily involved with tactical planning in your first job, you may be wondering why you need to study the process of strategic planning. An appreciation of this domain, however, should help you identify with the overall thrust of the organization and develop tactical plans that will feed into overall objectives, strategies, and plans. Also, with the increasing emphasis on participation by employees at all levels, you may well be called on to contribute your thoughts and analysis to the development of strategic plans.

Basics of Planning

planning The formal process of (1) choosing an organizational mission and overall objectives for both the short run and the long run, (2) devising divisional, departmental, and even individual objectives based on organizational objectives, (3) choosing strategies and tactics to achieve those objectives, and (4) deciding on the allocation of resources.

Planning is often considered the most basic managerial function. When done properly, planning establishes the rationale and sets the direction for the organizing, leading, and controlling functions. In Chapter 1 we stated that planning means defining goals and objectives for future performance and deciding on ways to reach them. Now we need a more comprehensive definition. **Planning** is the formal process of (1) choosing an organizational mission and overall objectives for both the short run and long run, (2) devising divisional, departmental, and even individual objectives based on organizational objectives, (3) choosing strategies and tactics to achieve those objectives, and (4) deciding on the allocation of resources (people, money, equipment, facilities, and so on) to the various objectives, strategies, and tactics. Iacocca's comments reflect some of the key elements in this definition of planning. He restated Chrysler's mission of continuing as a full-line car and truck producer and noted the overall objectives of higher quality, lower-cost production, better marketing, and increased customer satisfaction. One strategy that he mentioned specifically was increased use of joint ventures.

Strategic Planning

There are many types of planning, but we divide them, for now, into two basic categories: strategic planning and tactical planning. **Strategic planning** is the process of deciding on

strategic planning The process of deciding on and analyzing the organization's mission, overall objectives, general strategies, and major resource allocations.

and analyzing the organization's mission, overall objectives, general strategies, and major resource allocations. In developing strategic plans, managers and others take an organizationwide approach. The overall purpose of strategic planning and management is to deal effectively with environmental opportunities and threats in terms of the organization's strengths and weaknesses.[3] The major elements in strategic planning are mission, objectives, strategies, and resource allocation.

mission The organization's reason for existing; the identification of what business it's in.

Mission The organization's **mission** is its reason for existing. A statement of mission answers the basic question ''What business are we in?'' It thus describes the organization in terms of the goods or services it supplies, the markets it is currently pursuing or plans to pursue in the future, and the client needs it aims to satisfy. When Lee Iacocca became chairman and CEO of Chrysler in 1979, he and the other top managers had to decide on Chrysler's future mission. Many experts thought Chrysler should get out of the automobile business as soon as possible and reorganize through bankruptcy proceedings, but Iacocca and his management team reaffirmed the company's mission to be a full-line manufacturer of passenger cars and trucks. Shortly after turning Chrysler around in 1981, however, Iacocca began to diversify into the aerospace and defense business. He now says trying to diversify was his big sin, because it siphoned management attention and money from the crucial task of producing new vehicles. Chrysler has since sold most of these businesses. Says Iacocca: ''If we went astray—you know people do go astray now and then in many areas—man, we got focused in a hurry.''[4]

An organization's stated mission, objectives, and strategies have meaning only if they stimulate all organization members to think and act strategically—not just once a year but every day. William Lawrence, executive vice-president for planning, technology, and government affairs at TRW, pinpoints *focus* as one of the key words for the 1990s: ''*Focus* means figuring out, and building on, what the company does best. It means identifying the evolving needs of your customers, then developing the key skills—often called the core competencies—critical to serving them. It means setting a clear, realistic mission and then working tirelessly to make sure everyone—from the chairman to the middle manager to the hourly employee—understands it.'' Such self-assessment led Cleveland-based TRW, once a loosely knit agglomeration of eighty businesses, to shed nearly half its units and grab early leadership in the burgeoning market for automotive air bags.[5]

Objectives As you will recall from our discussion of objectives in Chapter 6, an organization's objectives are the results to be achieved. When possible, objectives should state both the *quality* and the *quantity* of results, as well as the date for achieving them. One of Chrysler's strategic objectives in 1990 was to reduce manufacturing and other costs by $2.5 billion. Another was to replace virtually every one of its models with newly designed cars between 1993 and 1996.[6]

strategy Major course of action that an organization plans to take in order to achieve its objectives.

Strategies **Strategies** are major courses of action that an organization plans to take in order to achieve its objectives. For example, one of Chrysler's strategies in order to introduce a new line of cars is the development of a new LH car platform, or underbody, by 1993. It will replace the 1980 K-car platform. The new platform will accommodate front-, rear-, and all-wheel-drive configurations, if all goes according to plan.[7]

Resource Allocation When an organization allocates resources, it distributes money, personnel, plants and equipment, land, and other resources among alternative uses. As part of the strategic planning process, resource allocation generally means the allocation of money to various uses.[8] For example, Chrysler has budgeted $15 billion for product development between 1990 and 1995.[9]

Tactical Planning

Tactical planning is the process of making detailed, short-term decisions concerning what to do, who will do it, and how to do it. Middle and first-line managers as well as other employees are often involved in tactical planning. The process generally includes the following tasks:

▶ Developing annual budgets for each department, division, and project
▶ Choosing specific means of implementing organizational strategies
▶ Deciding on courses of action for improving current operations

Departmental managers and employees can use tactical plans to anticipate the actions of other departments or outside suppliers. For instance, Chrysler and certain tire companies develop joint monthly and quarterly tactical plans for the delivery of specific quantities and types of tires to Chrysler's assembly plants.

Table 8.1 summarizes the characteristics of strategic and tactical planning. Despite their different characteristics, strategic and tactical planning are closely linked in a well-designed planning system. The essence of the need for planning is neatly captured in the following business proverbs:

▶ Any organization that doesn't plan for its future isn't likely to have one.
▶ The most effective way to cope with change is to help create it.
▶ When you don't know where you're going, any road will get you there.

Benefits of Planning

Organizations survive only if they can simultaneously manage change, maintain a degree of stability, minimize confusion, and establish a sense of direction.[10] Organizations that effectively accomplish this feat are more likely to progress and grow. As the rate of change and degree of complexity in the business world increase, managers and other employees must find better ways to anticipate and respond to change.

Three of the primary benefits of planning are (1) the identification of future opportunities, (2) anticipation and avoidance of future problems, and (3) the development of courses of action (strategies and tactics).[11] If these primary planning benefits are realized, the organization has a better chance of achieving general objectives. These include adapting and innovating in order to create desirable change, improving the effectiveness of employees and managers, and maintaining organizational stability. The achievement of general objectives should lead the organization to its ultimate objectives—long-term growth, profitability, and survival. Both strategic and tactical planning are concerned with developing courses of action, improving the effectiveness of employees and managers, and ensuring profits.[12]

TABLE 8.1

Characteristics of Strategic and Tactical Planning

Dimension	Strategic Planning	Tactical Planning
Types of decisions involved	Adaptive and innovative	Routine and adaptive
Condition under which decision making occurs	Risk (subjective probabilities) and uncertainty	Certainty and risk (objective probabilities)
Where plans are primarily developed	Middle to top management	Employees, up to middle management
Time horizon	Long term (usually two years or more)	Short term (usually one year or less)
Intended purpose	Assuring long-term survival and growth	Means of implementing strategic plans

Planning allowed entrepreneurs Dan and Stan Gallery to *identify a future opportunity* when they switched from the hot dog vending business to vending the vehicle itself: pushcarts. Gallerys' Carts of Colorado now dominates the pushcart market.

Planning Effectively

Planning only works well when managers and employees keep in mind that plans are the means—not the ends.[13] Managers sometimes approach planning from one of two extremes that are ineffective because they fail to use plans as means. One of these extremes is the extinction-by-instinct approach: Managers and employees are so concerned with solving immediate problems and making quick decisions that they neglect to plan strategically or tactically. Firms in simple, stable environments (producing baked goods or canned foods, for instance) may use this approach for years without loss in profitability. However, firms in complex and changing environments (producing, say, autos or computers) are likely to fail or to show little growth if they use this approach.[14] The other extreme is the paralysis-by-analysis approach: Managers and others get so bogged down in planning every detail and for every eventuality that they neglect making the really important decisions.[15]

Let's consider several factors that characterize effective strategic planning.

Stimulating Entrepreneurship Effective strategic planning is likely to stimulate entrepreneurship. To see what that means, refer to Chapter 1, where the entrepreneur role was defined as designing and starting a new project or enterprise. Entrepreneurs have the drive and ability to create new ventures, new businesses, and major changes. In the process they focus energy and intellect on initiating, doing, and achieving—that is, on building an organization.[16] Similarly, effective strategic planning stimulates new ideas and encourages doing the right things (as opposed to just doing things right). In some organizations, though, strategic planning has achieved just the opposite by becoming overly bureaucratic (such as by having lots of planning forms that must be filled in properly) and absurdly quantitative (such as by requiring dollars-and-cents justification for everything).

Tactical planning is generally narrow in focus. It is normally more routine and adaptive, rather than highly innovative. Its thrusts include defining immediate problems, number crunching, and short-term objectives.[17] Effective strategic planning, on the other hand, encourages flexibility rather than rigidity. It often supports innovative alternatives to rules and standard operating procedures.

Managing Risk and Uncertainty Effective strategic planning helps reduce risk and uncertainty, or it improves the understanding of the risks and uncertainties associated with decisions. Unfortunately, even the most effective planning can't eliminate risk and uncertainty. As one planning manager noted, ''No amount of sophistication is going to dismiss the fact that all our knowledge is about the past and

Through *effective strategic planning*, Browning-Ferris Industries (BFI) expanded into collecting recyclables curbside. By the beginning of 1990, BFI was recycling for over 900,000 North American households.

all of our decisions are about the future."[18] We might add, of course, that all of our actions are in the present.

Managers can reduce the risks and uncertainties associated with decision making through contingency planning. **Contingency planning** involves identifying alternative future possibilities and then developing an action plan for each of them. For example, a number of North American firms have developed contingency plans for the possibility that OPEC nations sharply reduce the flow of oil. A plan calling for a shift from oil to natural gas when the price of oil climbs to $35 per barrel is an example of such a contingency plan. Although the price of oil shot up in 1990, the increase wasn't due to the actions of OPEC. The Iraqi invasion of Kuwait, a totally unforeseen possibility, was the source of the problem. Yet the contingency plans that had been in place in anticipation of adverse actions by OPEC were helpful in coping with the rapid rise of oil prices.

Planning for *all* possible contingencies isn't feasible. Managers and others would soon find themselves in the paralysis-by-analysis situation if they tried. Contingency planning should normally be limited to anticipating and responding to the following kinds of events:

▶ Events that cannot be foreseen with any degree of precision, such as a possible reduction in the flow of oil by OPEC members.

▶ Events that are beyond the direct control of the organization, such as moves by the Federal Reserve to raise the interest rate.

▶ Events that have major positive or negative impacts on the organization. For example, each year the heads of General Electric's thirteen businesses develop five one-page "charts," memos that summarize possible opportunities and obstacles in their industries over the next twenty-four months. When Hungary opened its doors to foreign ownership in state-run companies, GE needed just sixty days to cut a deal for 50 percent of Tungsram, the country's leading lighting company. Tungsram had been on GE's charts for years.[19]

▶ Events that are based on major assumptions that may not be valid, such as the assumption that the U.S. government will not establish additional major barriers to the import of foreign-made automobiles.[20]

Identifying Assumptions To assume is to take for granted or to accept something as a fact. In the planning sense, an **assumption** is an underlying belief about a given issue, problem, or the future.[21] Individuals always make assumptions during the strategic planning process. The statement "the price of oil will be $35 per barrel in 1995" is an assumption. In Chapter 9 we present two planning aids designed to assist individuals in the identification and evaluation of assumptions.

contingency planning The process of identifying alternative future possibilities and then developing an action plan for each of them.

assumption A prediction that an important future event, over which an organization has little or no control, will or will not occur.

Our discussion so far of the benefits and effectiveness of strategic planning and management has assumed such activities are conducted in a Western-style, industrialized society. This chapter's Global Link feature reports the experiences of a professor who worked in Brazil and presented seminars on strategic planning and management to Brazilian students and executives. As you can see, the strategic concepts in this chapter aren't necessarily applicable throughout the world.

LEVELS OF STRATEGY AND PLANNING

The nature of strategic planning varies from organization to organization, depending on the organization's complexity, or stage of diversification, and on the level within the organization at which the planning is done.

Stages of Diversification

diversification Characteristic that reflects the number of different goods and/or services a company produces and the number of different markets it serves.

Diversification refers to the number of different goods and/or services a company produces and the number of different markets it serves.[22] The degree of diversification classes firms in four basic stages: a single business, a dominant business, related businesses, and unrelated businesses.[23] As Figure 8.1 indicates, the different form, or stage, of diversification of a firm affects the scope of the firm's planning process. A firm that

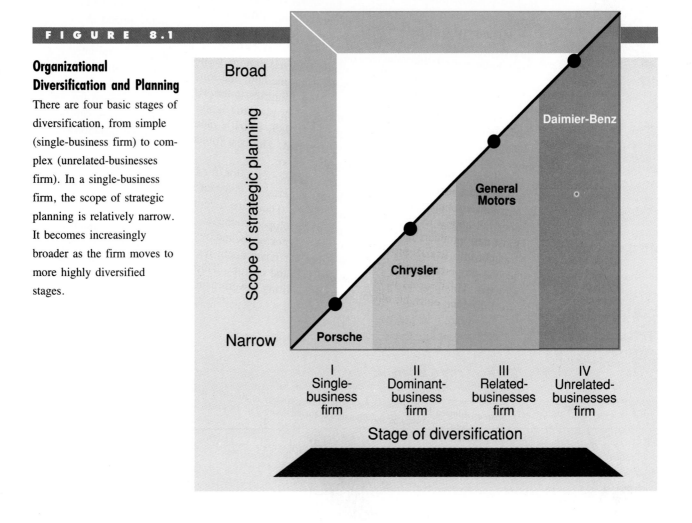

FIGURE 8.1

Organizational Diversification and Planning

There are four basic stages of diversification, from simple (single-business firm) to complex (unrelated-businesses firm). In a single-business firm, the scope of strategic planning is relatively narrow. It becomes increasingly broader as the firm moves to more highly diversified stages.

Scope of strategic planning

Broad

Narrow

Daimier-Benz

General Motors

Chrysler

Porsche

| I | II | III | IV |
| Single-business firm | Dominant-business firm | Related-businesses firm | Unrelated-businesses firm |

Stage of diversification

GLOBAL Link

STRATEGIC PLANNING IN BRAZIL

I began to question colleagues and managers about the applicability of popular American and Western European strategic models in Brazil. A number of criticisms arose, some of them vague, some of them quite pointed. Some of the criticisms were (1) "Why talk about 'cost' strategies when prices are set by the Ministry of Finance?" (2) "In our business, you don't need to know strategy, you have to know how to dance," and (3) "Our strategy here is to obey the orders and whims of headquarters."

Most contemporary strategic planning makes assumptions about the business environment that do not hold true in many developing countries. These countries require strategic responses quite different from those that are appropriate in advanced economies. Contemporary strategic models don't work in Brazil for this reason.

To begin with, in Brazil most prices are determined by government decree. The state establishes prices through "industry councils" composed of representatives from industry and government. This requires competitors to band together to negotiate the highest possible prices. Thus profit margins are a function not of competition between firms, as in free-market economics, but of negotiation with the government. Price is a key component of traditional strategic thinking. Price controls destroy pricing strategies based on supply and demand, because products are almost invariably priced at the highest permissible rate.

Business strategists in Western industrialized nations assume that the general environment is sufficiently predictable to make medium-and long-range plans reliable. But the general environment in developing countries is frequently so volatile that speculative maneuvering rather than consistent planning is the dominant approach to business. For example, between 1985 and 1989, Brazil's monthly inflation rates varied from −2 percent to more than 30 percent. The best forecasts of annual inflation usually miss their mark by 50 percent or more.

Product innovation is a major performance criterion for many businesses in industrialized countries. Although change is certainly constant in Brazil, innovation does not appear to play such a critical role. There are several reasons for this. First, most new products have their origin in developed countries. Before a new product is brought into Brazil, provisions for the transfer of technology and payment for intellectual property must be made. Second, the government regulates every step of this process. This process is very bureaucratic and corrupt. Third, some new technologies are forbidden outright; others languish awaiting government approval.

Source: Adapted from R. E. Nelson, "Is There Strategy in Brazil?" *Business Horizons,* July-August 1990, 15–23. Copyright 1990, by the Foundation for the School of Business at Indiana University. Reprinted by permission.

produces different types of goods or services for unrelated markets often must have a broad-based planning system. A firm involved in a single product or service line needs a less elaborate planning system. In other words, the complexity and scope of a firm's strategic planning depend partly on its stage of diversification.

A **single-business firm** provides a limited number of goods or services to one segment of a particular market. For example, Porsche provides a limited line of high-performance sports and touring cars to a narrow segment of the auto market.

A **dominant-business firm** serves various segments of a particular market. For example, Chrysler Corporation has diversified into different segments of the car and truck market. In 1987 Chrysler acquired American Motors Corporation (AMC). A key motivation for the acquisition was the desire to enter the rapidly growing market for four-wheel-drive vehicles through AMC's very successful Jeep line.[24]

A **related-businesses firm** provides a variety of similar goods and/or services. Its divisions generally compete in the same markets, use similar technologies, and share common distribution channels. At one time GM would have been considered a dominant-business firm. However, it acquired Electronic Data Systems and Hughes Aircraft Company in the 1980s, because these firms possessed technological capabilities that were crucial to GM's other divisions. Through its auto and truck loans and insurance, GM thought it could readily attract customers for other forms of loans and insurance, so General Motors Acceptance Corporation moved into mortgage banking and General Motors Insurance Corporation moved into life and homeowners' insurance coverage. Because of these actions, GM is now classified as a related-businesses firm.[25]

An **unrelated-businesses firm** provides diverse goods and services to many different markets. Often referred to as a conglomerate, such a firm usually consists of a number of distinct strategic business units. A **strategic business unit (SBU)** is a division or subsidiary of a firm that serves a distinct product-market segment. It has a well-defined set of customers and/or covers a specific geographic area. An SBU is usually evaluated on the basis of its own income statement and balance sheet. Strategic business units are also used by large dominant-business firms (Chrysler) or related-businesses firms (GM).[26]

The top managers and teams within each SBU are responsible for developing the strategic plan for their unit. This strategic plan is normally submitted to corporate headquarters for review. Top management at headquarters is heavily involved in determining which firms the organization might acquire or divest itself of. It also decides where to reduce, maintain, or increase the firm's capital investment commitments.

SBU's are used by such unrelated-businesses firms as Litton, U.S. Industries, Fuqua, IT&T, and Daimler-Benz. During the past ten years many North American firms have backed away from the highest stage of diversification by selling off unrelated or loosely related businesses.[27] Ford sold its Ford Aerospace Corporation to the Loral Corporation in 1990. However, many major foreign firms have been moving into the unrelated-businesses stage of diversification. For example, Daimler-Benz, the German firm best known as the manufacturer of the Mercedes-Benz, has acquired MTU (a manufacturer of aircraft engines and diesel motors for tanks and ships), Dornier (which makes commuter planes, rocket and satellite parts, and medical equipment) and AEG (which makes computers, household appliances, automation equipment, public transportation systems, and broadcasting equipment).[28]

Levels of Strategy within Large Organizations

Large-scale, diversified organizations often develop strategies and plans at three levels: the corporate level, the business level, and the functional level. Figure 8.2 shows these levels in Ford Motor Company. We will define these strategy levels and illustrate them using Ford and other firms.

Corporate Level **Corporate-level strategy** guides the activities of organizations that have more than one line of business. Diversification is a key issue in corporate-level strategy and planning. Top management devises a corporate strategy

corporate-level strategy
Any strategy that guides the activities of an organization having more than one line of business.

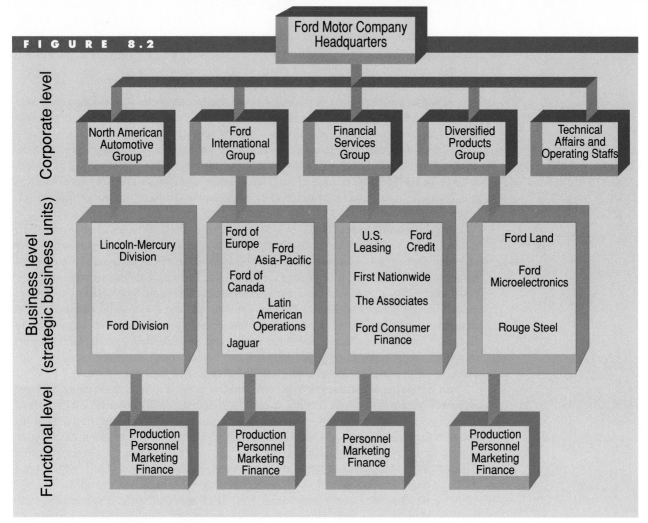

FIGURE 8.2

Corporate level

Business level (strategic business units)

Functional level

Ford Motor Company Headquarters

North American Automotive Group

Ford International Group

Financial Services Group

Diversified Products Group

Technical Affairs and Operating Staffs

Lincoln-Mercury Division

Ford Division

Ford of Europe   Ford Asia-Pacific
Ford of Canada
Latin American Operations
Jaguar

U.S. Leasing   Ford Credit
First Nationwide
The Associates
Ford Consumer Finance

Ford Land
Ford Microelectronics
Rouge Steel

Production Personnel Marketing Finance

Production Personnel Marketing Finance

Personnel Marketing Finance

Production Personnel Marketing Finance

Ford Motor Company's Strategy Levels

The three levels of strategy—corporate level, business level, and functional level—are illustrated with Ford. For simplicity, we show only some of the company's business-level units and functional areas and have grouped Ford headquarters and Ford's five sectors (North American Automotive Group, Ford International Group, and so on) at the corporate level.

Source: Developed from Ford Motor Company 1990 Annual Report.

to determine the role of each separate business within the overall organization. Strategies focus on the kinds of businesses the firm wants to engage in, ways to acquire or get rid of businesses, allocation of resources among the businesses, and ways to manage the businesses.[29] At Ford, the office of the chief executive (which includes four executives), the board of directors, and the heads of the company's five sectors are closely involved with corporate-level strategy.

To provide a better understanding of corporate-level strategy, we'll look at five specific corporate-level growth strategies: forward integration, backward integration, horizontal integration, concentric diversification, and conglomerate diversification.

Forward integration occurs when a company enters the businesses of its customers. This strategy moves the company closer to the ultimate consumer. If Ford decided to acquire some of its 10,500 franchised dealerships and/or open company-owned dealerships, Ford would be engaging in forward integration.

Backward integration occurs when a company enters the businesses of its suppliers. This strategy is implemented by acquiring suppliers or by creating new businesses that provide the same goods or services as suppliers. For example, in 1990 Cie

forward integration
Growth strategy that involves a company's entering the businesses of its customers.

backward integration
Growth strategy that involves a company's entering the businesses of its suppliers.

de Saint-Gobain, a French glass manufacturer, acquired NORTON, a manufacturer of abrasives, many of which are used in glass making. Many years ago Ford established a subsidiary, the Rouge Steel Company, to supply some of the steel Ford needed to manufacture cars and trucks.

Joint ventures can be used as an alternative means to traditional forms of backward, forward, and horizontal integration. Ford established a joint venture with Mazda to develop the 1991 Ford Escort and Mercury Tracer. Mazda engineered the new cars, and Ford was responsible for exterior and interior design.[30] Firms in the automobile industry have formed numerous joint ventures—it's one of Chrysler's key corporate-level strategies. A firm often uses joint ventures within its own industry or in other industries when it has only some of the required capabilities, as in the case of the Mazda-Ford joint venture.[31]

horizontal integration
Growth strategy that involves a company's acquiring of a competitor.

Horizontal integration occurs when a company acquires a competitor. In the United States, antitrust and other laws place limits on such acquisitions to ensure a degree of competition. Chrysler's purchase of AMC and Ford's purchase of Jaguar are examples of horizontal integration in the auto industry. Another example of horizontal integration is McCaw Cellular Communications' 1990 acquisition of a majority interest in its rival, LIN Broadcasting, for $3.8 billion. An example of both backward *and* horizontal integration is Ford's acquisition of 25 percent of Mazda Motor Corporation—since their joint venture, Ford and Mazda both compete and cooperate with each other.

concentric diversification
Growth strategy that involves a company's acquiring or starting a business related to it in terms of technology, markets, or products (sometimes called *related diversification*).

Concentric diversification, sometimes called *related diversification,* occurs when a firm acquires or starts a business related to it in terms of technology, markets, or products (goods or services). Generally, a related-businesses firm acquires another company or starts a new venture. There must be some common thread linking the two firms, such as a common set of customers, similar technology, overlapping distribution channels, compatible managerial skills, or similar goods or services.[32] For example, Ford Motor Credit Company was the second largest finance company in the world and had 9200 employees and 274 offices. When Ford acquired Meritor Credit Corporation in 1989, this more than doubled Ford's home-equity loan base and provided entry into the manufactured-home financing field. Meritor and Ford Credit's consumer-loan operations were then combined to create Ford Consumer Finance Company.[33] The common thread in this concentric diversification was providing consumer credit needs.

Another example is Intel's mission to become the premier building block supplier to the computer industry. Although Intel intends to keep concentrating on microprocessors (such as its successful 386 chips and new line of 486 chips, the brains of the IBM personal computer and many others), it has begun, on a small scale, to make personal computers that are sold by customers (including AT&T and Unisys) under their own names. Explaining this strategy, Intel's CEO, Andrew Grove, says, "I have to invest in capabilities. Should there be a shift in the marketplace by our customers to increasingly buy finished or semifinished systems, I want to be able to respond to it."[34]

Conglomerate diversification is a corporate-level growth strategy that adds unrelated goods or services to a firm's product line. Generally one company acquires another company or starts a venture in a totally new field. Firms operating in the unrelated-businesses stage of diversification most often use this strategy. As noted previously, Daimler-Benz has engaged to some degree in conglomerate diversification. It was reorganized in 1989 as a holding company with overall managerial responsibility for three divisions: Mercedes-Benz, AEG (microelectronics, systems technology, and so forth), and Deutsche Aerospace. A research and technology division was also established within the headquarters of the holding company. This division is involved in developing new fields of activity, especially those based on high technologies.[35] Another example of conglomerate diversification is Matsushita Electric Industrial's acquisition of MCA, a U.S. entertainment company, for $6.3 billion in 1990.

conglomerate diversification Growth strategy that involves a company's adding unrelated goods or services to its product line.

A business-level strategy by using laser welding technology.

business-level strategy
Strategy that guides the operations of a single business, outlining how it will compete.

functional-level strategy
Strategy that consists of guidelines for managing a firm's functional areas.

Business Level Once top management agrees on the corporate-level strategy (or strategies) and plans, they can turn their attention to the business-level strategy and plans. **Business-level strategy** guides the operations of a single business and answers the question "How do we compete?" A single-business firm or an SBU provides a particular line of goods or services to a specific industry or market segment. Its top managers are involved with planning for (1) how the firm can maintain a competitive edge, (2) how each key functional department (production, human resources, marketing, finance) can contribute to the firm's overall effectiveness, and (3) how resources should be allocated among the functions.[36]

One of Honda's objectives in the late 1980s was to expand its automobile manufacturing facilities in order to overcome production capacity constraints. The business-level strategy for meeting this objective included (1) installation of a new production line at its Suzuka plant in Japan in 1989; (2) beginning construction of a new plant in Japan during 1990, (3) completion during 1990 of a second U.S. plant, in East Liberty, Ohio, with an annual capacity of 150,000 cars, and (4) construction of an engine plant in the United Kingdom, with a capacity of 70,000 engines a year.[37] Business-level strategy and planning is examined in depth in the last two sections of this chapter.

Functional Level **Functional-level strategy** consists of guidelines for managing a firm's functional areas, such as manufacturing, marketing, human resources, finance, engineering, and research and development. Each functional strategy and plan should be designed to contribute to the business-level strategies and plans. Functional-level strategies often involve a combination of tactical and strategic planning (refer to Table 8.1).

Functional-level, business-level, and corporate-level strategies may be so tightly linked that there are no clear dividing lines between them. General Motors' technology strategy for its line of automobiles is a prime example.

GM'S TECHNOLOGY STRATEGY

INSIGHT

The number of high-tech features in GM vehicles continues to increase, contributing to better overall vehicle performance and quality. At the same time, technology is a powerful tool for improving manufacturing processes and operational efficiency. Through the Technical Staffs Group, as well as Electronic Data Systems (EDS), GM Hughes Electronics (GMHE), and Group Lotus, GM has established a significant technological edge.

Technological features available today from GM have been designed to improve the safety, comfort, and convenience of vehicles. Remote keyless entry systems make it possible for an owner to unlock the car doors or trunk lid from up to thirty feet away. Heads-up displays allow drivers to view vehicle speed and signal indicator data without having to look away from the road. High-performance multivalve engines are improving fuel economy and vehicle responsiveness.

EDS, one of GM's divisions, is a leader in providing technology-based solutions for the management and movement of data, voice, and image information. It's working with GM on a variety of automation projects—from vehicle assembly to warehousing. One such project is the C4 program, a computer-aided engineering, design, and manufacturing system that will shorten production lead times and reduce production costs. When C4 is fully implemented by 1993, a new vehicle concept will become a computer image early in its design phase. The computer system will then be used to design the vehicle's individual parts and create the tooling that will eventually make those parts. EDS is also working on other projects, including validation of electronic control systems, computer simulations, development of holographic rear-window stoplights and radar collision-warning systems, and factory automation.[38]

THE STRATEGIC PLANNING PROCESS

We have presented the key concepts and issues of planning and strategic management. In this section we expand on some of these concepts and issues and present them as a process of strategic planning. This process will focus on business-level planning, with some consideration of functional-level planning. Considerably more attention is given to functional-level issues and planning in Chapter 9.

The primary purpose of formulating business-level strategies is to establish superior value in the eyes of customers and/or to achieve lower costs. Thus the primary reference points for such strategies are customers, competitors, suppliers, and other stakeholders.[39] We can break the process of strategic planning at the business level into a sequence of eight core tasks. These core tasks are summarized in Figure 8.3. Keep in mind, however, that managers and others involved in business-level strategic planning may jump back and forth between tasks, or even skip tasks, as they develop strategic plans. A proposed strategy may be abandoned if it can't be implemented for some reason that wasn't apparent at first. In addition, the bounded rationality and political decision-making models discussed in Chapter 6 often influence how the planning process unfolds, as well as which issues are considered.

Task 1: Develop Mission and Objectives

The organizational mission and objectives are developed by answering the following questions: Who are we? What do we want to become? What are our guiding objectives? These general objectives provide broad direction for decision making and may not change from year to year. It is also important to note that they are not developed in isolation. As suggested by the two-way arrows in Figure 8.3, the mission and objectives are developed through diagnosis of environmental threats and opportunities (task 2) *and* assessment of the organization's strengths and weaknesses (task 3).

Excerpts from Ford's statement of mission and general objectives for the 1990s are provided in the following Insight. Note that these excerpts contain Ford's diagnosis of the competitive environment in the automobile industry, as well as a brief assessment of its strengths and weaknesses.

FORD'S MISSION AND OBJECTIVES

*I*NSIGHT We will build on Ford's proven capabilities as we take on the challenges of the new decade. We have the people, the experience, the financial resources, the organizational structure, the dealer networks, and the supply base. We have improved our quality, invested in new products and technology, modernized or built new plants, increased efficiency, and made acquisitions.

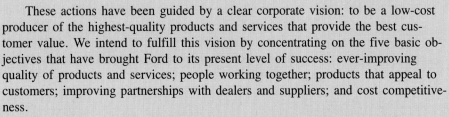

These actions have been guided by a clear corporate vision: to be a low-cost producer of the highest-quality products and services that provide the best customer value. We intend to fulfill this vision by concentrating on the five basic objectives that have brought Ford to its present level of success: ever-improving quality of products and services; people working together; products that appeal to customers; improving partnerships with dealers and suppliers; and cost competitiveness.

The talent and energy of thousands of employees are devoted to quality at Ford. We know how important quality is to our customers and consider it our most important priority. In the United States Ford has held quality leadership among domestically designed and built cars and trucks for nine years. Our aim is to build on that achievement and to become best-in-class among all competitors worldwide. One of the principles used in this effort is the concept of continuous improvement. This means constantly challenging ourselves to make our products and services better so buyers increasingly choose Ford cars and trucks over the competition.[40]

Task 2: Diagnose Threats and Opportunities

In Chapters 3 and 4 we presented a variety of important environmental forces, both domestic and global, that can affect an organization. These forces can represent significant threats or opportunities for an organization. Its strategic planning must take these threats and opportunities into account.

Political forces and stakeholders within and outside the organization play a key role in determining the organization's current mission and objectives as well as possible changes in them.[41] Of course, managers of an organization will negotiate with powerful stakeholders (banks, government, major customers, suppliers) in an attempt to limit such stakeholders' influence over the organization.

The forces that exert the strongest influence on an organization's strategic planning process are the industry and market competitive forces.[42] Michael Porter has suggested a framework for diagnosing the forces that drive the industry and market competition confronting a firm at any particular time.[43] This framework, shown in Figure 8.4, includes five forces. The combined strength of these forces determines the long-run profit potential in an industry. In turn, this affects each individual firm's overall profit potential, growth prospects, and even likelihood of survival. Effective strategic planning will include a careful diagnosis of these forces. A number of specific variables affect the strength of each force. A review of all of them is beyond the scope of this book. We will simply describe each force and highlight a couple of its variables. It might be helpful to refer to Chapter 3 for more complete descriptions of these forces.

Rivalry among Existing Firms The rivalry among existing firms in an industry varies with top management's view of threats or opportunities, strategies that firms pursue, and competitors' reactions to those strategies. These strategies and reactions include price increases or decreases, advertising campaigns, introduction of new goods or services, and changes in customer service.

Two variables affecting the strength of rivalry with an industry are the number of firms and the rate of industry growth. These variables have been central to the increased intensity of competition among auto makers. The auto industry—the world's biggest industry—is global in scope. It has become more diverse and complex since 1970. Some 175 auto makers throughout the world produce more than 45 million cars, trucks and buses annually. Twenty years ago General Motors, Ford, and Chrysler worried primarily about each other as major rivals in the United States and Canada. Today, though they continue to worry about each other, they also have to

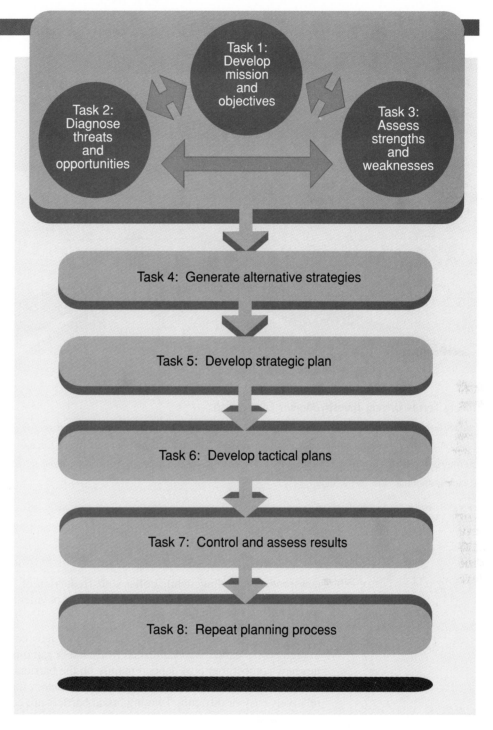

Strategic Planning Process

The strategic planning process is presented as a sequence of eight core tasks. The focus is on business-level planning rather than corporate-level or functional-level planning. The arrows indicate the primary sequence of planning tasks. In practice, the sequence is neither purely systematic nor one-way, as the two-way arrows suggest.

Task 1: Develop mission and objectives

Task 2: Diagnose threats and opportunities

Task 3: Assess strengths and weaknesses

Task 4: Generate alternative strategies

Task 5: Develop strategic plan

Task 6: Develop tactical plans

Task 7: Control and assess results

Task 8: Repeat planning process

worry about Toyota, Volkswagen, Nissan, Volvo, Peugeot, Honda, Renault, Fiat, Mazda, Mitsubishi, Suzuki, Fuji (Subaru), Daihatsu, Daimler-Benz (Mercedes-Benz), Isuzu, Rover Group, and BMW, among others. No longer can the auto industry be characterized as an *oligopoly,* that is, a market dominated by a few firms. The slow growth rate of the auto industry has also intensified competition. Most experts believe that demand will grow no more than 2 percent per year through 1995. Coupled with this, production capacity is expected to exceed demand by 4 million units in the United States and Canada by 1994.[44] These trends will contribute to intense price, quality, and service competition among automakers for years to come. In fact, competition had already become so intense that GM found it necessary to cut its dividend by 47 percent in early 1991 and institute a sweeping cost-reduction program that hit

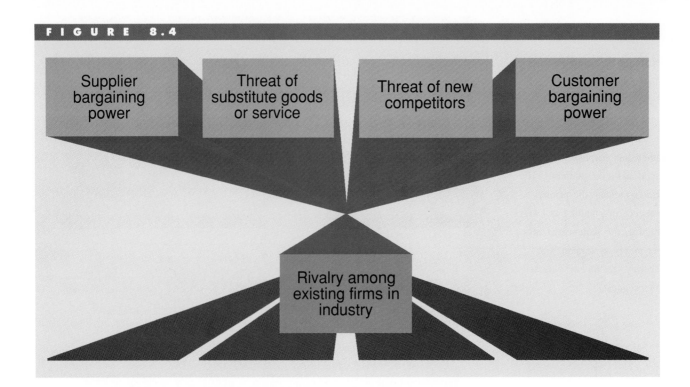

Primary Forces Driving Industry/Market Competition

Competition within an industry reflects the industry's underlying economic structure and is based on the five core competitive forces in this figure. The combined strength of these forces determines the long-run profit potential in the industry, which, in turn, influences the prospects of each individual firm in the industry.

Source: Based on Michael E. Porter, *Competitive Strategy: Techniques for Analyzing Industries and Competitors,* (New York: Free Press, 1980), p. 4.

new-product spending, white collar staff (reduction of 15,000 employees by 1993), and parts suppliers (reduction of $2 billion in payments to parts suppliers by 1993 through price rollbacks).[45]

Threat of New Competitors   The entry of new competitors is often a response to high profits earned by established firms and/or rapid industry growth. The difficulties new competitors face depend mainly on the barriers to entry and the reactions of established competitors. Barriers to entry are factors that make entering an industry relatively easy or difficult. Two important barriers are economies of scale and capital requirements.

For many years the economies of scale associated with high-volume production and the enormous capital requirements of the auto industry served as significant barriers to entry, effectively limiting competition for North American automakers. New auto manufacturing technologies (such as robotics) and an explosion in competition from foreign automakers have lowered these barriers.[46] In 1991 Japanese automakers had eleven plants in Canada and the United States—producing 2.2 million cars. One forecast suggested that Japanese manufacturers could take up to 50 percent of the American car market by 2000, significantly higher than the 26 percent they held in 1990.[47]

Customer Bargaining Power   The bargaining power of customers depends on their relative ability to play one firm off against another in order to force down prices, obtain higher quality, or buy more goods or services for the same price. For example, can GM press for lower prices and better quality from suppliers because it is a large-volume customer. The bargaining power of customers is likely to be high in the following situations:

▶ A small number of customers purchase relatively large volumes from the seller.
▶ Customers purchase standard and undifferentiated goods or services.
▶ Customers can easily switch from one seller to another.[48]

The bargaining power of auto industry customers was relatively low until the mid-1970s. It has increased substantially since that time because more competitors have gained entry to the auto industry. Customers can choose from vastly increased numbers of makes and models, dealers, and financing plans. During the last several years many automakers and dealers have introduced special financing and rebate programs and have extended the length of coverage of their warranties. These strategies were chosen to attract and retain customers.

Supplier Bargaining Power The bargaining power of suppliers increases when they can raise prices or reduce the quality of their goods and services with little fear of customer reaction. The situations that tend to make suppliers more powerful are similar to those that make customers more powerful. The bargaining power of suppliers is likely to be high in the following situations:

▶ A small number of suppliers sell to a large number of buyers in an industry.
▶ Suppliers do not have to worry about substitute goods or services that their customers can readily buy.
▶ Suppliers' goods or services are differentiated.[49]

The bargaining power of suppliers relative to automakers is weak. The following Insight contains excerpts from a *Ward's Auto World* study of relationships between suppliers and the Big Three and provides a sense of this power imbalance.

---

*I*NSIGHT

There is disillusionment among auto suppliers over the ideals of closer relationships, long-term contracts, early supplier involvement in product programs, and a greater commitment based on mutual trust. These lofty aims of the new relationships [between the Big Three automakers and their suppliers] are summed up in this observation by a supplier at a Supplier Council meeting scheduled by the Chevrolet-Pontiac-Canada Group of General Motors Corp.: "I wonder, 'What has happened? What went wrong?' For three years we've had good schedules, business has been good, and yet why all the griping? Are we a bunch of greedy, narrow-minded folks? Why is morale so low?"

What has happened, he goes on, is that since 1986, within the relationships, suppliers have encountered roadblocks to working more closely with automakers, including organizational changes that stymie contacts with engineers and purchasing people.

He and other suppliers underscore the belief among suppliers "that an inequity of sacrifice exists." Automakers are profiting at suppliers' expense. A source at a Japanese partmaker that sells to the Big Three states: "The finance boys are in total control [at GM]. It's a money grab, and they are foaming at the mouth. They've got a lot, but they want more."

"Granted, this industry was fat and needed cost controls," says a high-ranking official of a U.S. supplier, "but with inflation running 3 percent to 5 percent a year, you eventually run out of places to cut, and then you have no guts to put money back into [plant and research and development] investments.'' Adds the president of a small independent supplier: ''The question is, Will quality survive these [cost] pressure games?''[50]

Threat of Substitute Goods or Services The seriousness of the threat of substitute goods or services depends on the ability and willingness of customers to change their buying habits. Substitutes limit the price that firms in a particular industry can charge for their goods and services without risking a loss in sales. Currently autos have no direct substitutes. Indirect substitutes, however, have been sources of competitive pressure. When car prices rise substantially, some customers defer buying new cars by simply keeping their old cars longer, or they purchase used cars instead of new cars. Other customers substitute lower-priced cars for higher-priced cars when faced with ''sticker shock.''

Task 3: Assess Strengths and Weaknesses

Assessing internal strengths and weaknesses enables managers to identify their organization's core competencies. This assessment covers the organization's relative competitive position, human resource skills, technological capabilities, financial resources, and managerial depth and the values and backgrounds of its key employees.

At least three tests can be applied to identify core competencies in a company. First, a core competency should provide potential access to a wide variety of markets. Honda's core competency in engines and power trains enables it to make not only cars, but also snowmobiles, jet skis, gasoline-powered lawn mowers, and motor scooters. Second, a core competency should make a major contribution to customers' perceived benefits from the good or service. Clearly, Honda's engine expertise fills this requirement. This is also why Honda has made such a large dollar commitment to Formula One auto racing. Third, a core competency should be difficult for competitors to copy. Honda's commitment to designing and manufacturing quality engines and power trains has given it the ability to make top-notch products. Chrysler, on the other hand, is becoming increasingly dependent on Mitsubishi and Hyundai for engines because it views engines and power trains as just one more part of a car.

Most individuals find it easier to assess strengths than to assess weaknesses. Weaknesses are often interpreted as the fault of management and employees. Some managers and employees perceive statements of organizational weaknesses as personal threats to their position, influence, and self-esteem. But weaknesses are not self-correcting and are likely to become worse if not dealt with as part of strategic planning. The failures of high-fashion retailers Bloomingdale's and Sakowitz are only two of many examples of what happens when key employees are unable or unwilling to acknowledge weaknesses until they are too large to correct. These retailers did not revise their purchasing, pricing, and credit policies in response to actions by their competitors and changing customer preferences.

Table 8.2 shows a basic framework for diagnosing business-level or functional-level strengths and weaknesses. It shows only some of the categories to be evaluated. This framework is best suited to a single-business firm or an SBU. In many companies key employees are required to develop statements of opportunities, threats, strengths, and weaknesses for the entire organization. The specific issues identified by plant managers will be different from those raised by top managers. Plant managers will focus on manufacturing opportunities, threats, strengths, and weaknesses, whereas chief executives must assess current and potential competitors, governmental changes and regulations, societal trends, and the like. All of the issues raised are put together in a working strategic plan.

TABLE 8.2

Framework for Diagnosing Strengths and Weaknesses

Instructions: Evaluate each category item on the basis of the following scale.

A = Superior to or better than anyone else. Beyond present need (top 10%).
B = Better than average. Good performance. No problems.
C = Average. Acceptable. Equal to competition. Not good, not bad.
D = Problems here. Not as good as it should be. Deteriorating. Must be improved.
F = Real cause for concern. Situation bad. Crisis. Must take action to improve.

Category	Item	Scale				
		A	B	C	D	F
Finance	Availability of loans	——	——	——	——	——
	Debt-equity ratio	——	——	——	——	——
	Inventory turnover	——	——	——	——	——
	Profit margin	——	——	——	——	——
	Other	——	——	——	——	——
Production	Labor productivity	——	——	——	——	——
	Plant/store location	——	——	——	——	——
	Degree of obsolescence	——	——	——	——	——
	Quality control	——	——	——	——	——
	Other	——	——	——	——	——
Organization and administration	Ratio of staff to line managers	——	——	——	——	——
	Quality of staff	——	——	——	——	——
	Quality of middle managers	——	——	——	——	——
	Communications	——	——	——	——	——
	Other	——	——	——	——	——
Marketing	Share of market	——	——	——	——	——
	Product/service reputation	——	——	——	——	——
	Advertising efficiency/effectiveness	——	——	——	——	——
	Consumer complaints	——	——	——	——	——
	Other	——	——	——	——	——
Technology	Product/service	——	——	——	——	——
	Research and development capabilities	——	——	——	——	——
	Other	——	——	——	——	——

Source: Adapted from *Long-Range Planning for Your Business,* M. L. Kastens, pp. 52–53. Copyright ©
1976 by AMACOM, a division of American Management Association, New York. All rights reserved.

Robert Stempel became chairman of the board and CEO of General Motors in 1990.
In the following Insight he reports on various weaknesses in GM, particularly in its
management and organization.

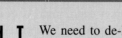

STEMPEL ON GM'S WEAKNESSES

We need to de-layer the organization and restructure to eliminate redundancies. In
our plants, we've had seven layers from the plant floor to the manager. In some
plants, we are now down to four. We're looking at our staff operations to see if
they are duplicating our operating activities. Blending them will take out some
people. In our engine plants, we're looking at bringing the engineering staff functions in with the manufacturing personnel. If it is better in the human resources
area to have a centralized function serving five or six plants as opposed to each
plant having its own, then we will probably centralize that.

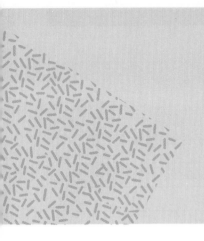

After we converted to front-wheel drive in our small-car lines, lo and behold, we wound up with fourteen or fifteen different kinds of drive shafts, a half-dozen rear suspensions, and so on. Now it's time to say, "Okay, among that array of components, which ones are best for what we're trying to do?" Drive shafts on one particular car line will come down from over a dozen to two. That's where we can get economies of scale.

I think every domestic maker has seen a generation of people who don't even know what a Chevrolet, Ford, or Plymouth is. They know very well what a Honda, Toyota, or Nissan is. These people are the ones to whom we simply have to say, "Hey, we've got some good cars of interest to you, too." But we've got to build a car that's equal to or better than [Japan's] in features, shape, size, and appearance.[51]

Task 4: Generate Alternative Strategies

After assessing a firm's opportunities, threats, strengths, and weaknesses, managers and other involved employees can turn to generating alternative strategies for the organization.[52] These strategies, in turn, must be evaluated in terms of environmental forces and the organization's strengths and weaknesses.[53]

To avoid too much complexity we will consider generating and evaluating alternative strategies for only an SBU or a single-business firm. Companies such as IT&T, Daimler-Benz, Ford, and GM encompass a number of strategic business units, some of which are related and some of which are unrelated. The task of generating and evaluating alternative strategies for such firms is very complex.

During our earlier discussion of organization levels of strategy we looked at five corporate-level growth strategies. Here we'll highlight the three growth strategies most common to business-level strategy and planning.[54]

market penetration strategy A business-level strategy that seeks growth in current markets with current goods or services.

A **market penetration strategy** involves seeking growth in current markets with current goods or services. A firm might increase market share by increasing the rate of purchase of the product (for example, getting customers to buy new cars more often), attracting competitors' customers (getting Ford truck owners to buy Chevrolet trucks), or buying a competitor (Ford bought Jaguar). Market penetration may also be achieved by increasing the total size of the market through converting nonusers into current users (providing a financing package that enables college seniors to buy new cars).

market development strategy A business-level growth strategy that seeks new markets for current products.

The **market development strategy** involves seeking new markets for current products. Three of the principal ways to accomplish this are finding new geographic markets (Chrysler formed a partnership with Steyr, an Austrian manufacturer, to build minivans for Europe starting in 1991), finding new target markets (VCRs started with educational and commercial target markets and moved into the home entertainment market with great success), and finding new uses (vans were adapted from service-type vehicles to spacious and luxurious people movers).

product development strategy A business-level growth strategy that seeks to develop new or improved goods or services for current markets.

A **product development strategy** involves developing new or improved goods or services for current markets. Four approaches can be taken to developing improved products: improve features (introduce CD players in cars), improve quality in terms of reliability, speed, efficiency, or durability (increase gasoline mileage), enhance aesthetic appeal (1991 Buicks and Oldsmobiles were sleeker in appearance than the 1990 models), or add models (the four-door version of the Honda Civic).

Task 5: Develop Strategic Plan

After generating alternative strategies, management must develop a strategic plan. This plan should specify the actions to be taken in order to achieve organizational objectives. The strategic plan also addresses how the required technological, marketing, financial and human resources will be obtained, how manufacturing and research and development will be conducted, and how organization and management capabilities will be utilized. To address GM's weaknesses, threats, opportunities, and strengths, a twenty-six-point strategic plan was developed in 1990. The following Insight provides a glimpse of a few elements of this plan.

*I*NSIGHT

General Motors has chosen a number of strategies to better manage its business, simplify its product lineup, improve productivity, reduce costs, and produce vehicles that meet the highest standards of quality and value.

GM has implemented demand-driven manufacturing techniques to reduce production times, lower operating costs, and reduce inventory, as well as increase product quality and improve flexibility to respond to market changes. One such technique is assembly-line job sequencing, introduced at all North American assembly locations. This method allows better control of the order in which jobs flow down an assembly line. Labor and equipment are thus used more efficiently. There is also a better match between what is produced and the products customers want.

With the help of EDS (Electronic Data Systems), GM has developed a sophisticated "just-in-time" inventory management system. This system communicates planned material requirements to suppliers and authorizes material shipments only as required. The result—better inventory management and lower costs.

The new engine division was merged with GM's transmission subsidiary. This combined group can more closely coordinate the designs of new engines and transmissions so that these components mesh together better.

To improve component quality, GM is involving suppliers earlier in the product design process. In addition, to deliver consistent quality, GM is concentrating on longer-term relationships with fewer suppliers. The average number of suppliers to a GM assembly plant today is about 425, versus 800 in 1986.

On the global scene, GM is moving rapidly into Eastern Europe. For example, Opel (a GM European subsidiary) plans to build engines in Hungary, with a local partner, for export to Western European assembly plants. The engines will be swapped for fully assembled Opels to be sold in Hungary. GM plans a similar move in Czechoslovakia.[55]

Task 6: Develop Tactical Plans

The purpose of tactical plans is to help implement strategic plans. As indicated in Figure 8.3, middle and first-line managers and employee teams normally develop their tactical plans from the organization's strategic plan. Our discussion of management by objectives in Chapter 9 explores how managers, teams, and individual employees throughout the organization develop tactical plans.

Task 7: Control and Assess Results

Strategic and tactical planning must be accompanied by controls to ensure implementation of the plans and evaluation of their results. Chapter 18 is devoted to managerial control. If the plans haven't produced the desired results, managers and teams should consider changing the controls, mission, objectives, or strategies, or the plans themselves. Earlier in this chapter we noted how the lack of planning can lead to extinction by instinct and how poor planning can lead to paralysis by analysis. A thorough assessment of the results of planning will reveal whether either of these approaches was followed.

Task 8: Repeat Planning Process

The forces that affect organizations are constantly changing. Sometimes these changes are gradual and foreseeable. At other times they are abrupt and unpredictable. Whatever the nature of the change, managers and other employees must be ready to adapt or innovate by repeating the planning process. Planning needs to be viewed as an ongoing process. Remember, planning is always a *means,* never an *end* in itself.

MODELS OF BUSINESS-LEVEL STRATEGY

In this final section we present two models of business-level strategy: the product life cycle model and the generic strategies model. Each of these provides a different means for generating and evaluating alternative strategies (task 4 in Figure 8.3). In combination, these models can be powerful aids to managers and other employees in the business-level planning and management process.

Product Life Cycle Model

product life cycle model
A model of business-level strategy that emphasizes planning according to the life cycle phase of the firm's goods or services.

The **product life cycle model** specifies the market phases that many goods and services go through during their lifetime and stresses strategic plans based on these phases. Figure 8.5 shows one popular version of a product life cycle, with five phases: introduction, growth, maturity, decline, and termination. The vertical axis shows whether market demand (sales volume) for the product (or service) is increasing, stable, or decreasing. The horizontal axis shows time. For fad products, such as Teenage Mutant Ninja Turtles, the time span for all five phases might be a couple of years or less. In contrast, automobiles have been on the market for more than seventy-five years. This industry now appears to be in the maturity phase. (As noted earlier, market demand for autos is expected to increase by no more than 2 percent per year through 1995.) Not all products move through each stage, however.

Although strategic planning for each good or service is influenced by its life cycle phase, management can sometimes intervene in the cycle, shifting a mature or declining product or service into a new growth stage. For example, several years ago Japanese manufacturers, unlike U.S. manufacturers who accepted that motorcycles and radios were in the maturity stage, developed new markets (re-entered a growth stage) for motor scooters, all-terrain vehicles (ATVs), and Walkman radios.[56]

According to this model, emphasis on strategies and functional areas (such as marketing, production, R&D, and finance) needs to change for different phases of the product life cycle.[57] During the introduction and growth phases, the dominant strategic concerns are with product development (R&D), finding new customers (marketing), and financing start-up, expansion, and marketing costs. Risk and the possibility of failure are great in these two initial phases.

During a product's maturity stage a dominant strategic concern is the need to reduce per-unit production costs. Cost-cutting measures such as shutting down obsolete plants, laying off employees, and automating may be utilized. Chrysler and other automakers have used such means, with varying degrees of success, to cut their per-unit costs. Another dominant strategic concern during the maturity phase is to maintain, or even in-

FIGURE 8.5

Product Life Cycle Model

This traditional product life cycle model suggests there are five basic stages in the evolution of a successful good or service. The total sales volume (market demand) increases rapidly through the growth stage, remains relatively stable during the maturity stage, and eventually declines.

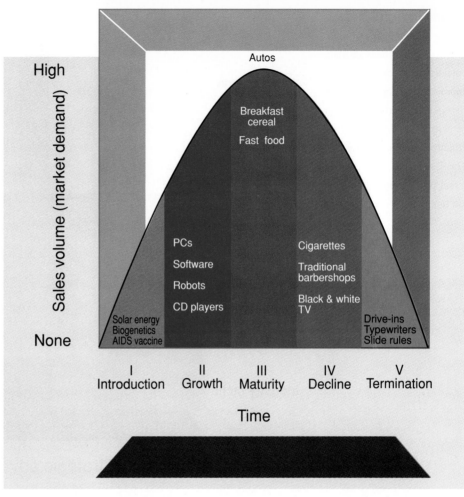

Source: Adapted from S. Michael, ''Guidelines for Contingency Approach to Planning,'' *Long Range Planning,* 1979, 12(6):63. Reprinted with permission from *Long Range Planning.* Copyright © 1979, Pergamon Press, Ltd.

crease, market share at the expense of competitors. Because of the relatively slow growth rate in a mature market, significant growth must come at the expense of competitors' sales or through buying out competitors. Many experts claim that all of Japan's eleven car and truck companies can't survive. Paul Fraker, one auto expert, concluded: ''It's clear that Japan simply has too many auto companies. By the end of the decade, competition will thin the ranks of Japanese automakers to four or five groups.''[58] Fuji, Daihatsu, and Suzuki are expected to be among the first acquired by other organizations.

During the decline phase of a product's (or service's) life cycle, there continues to be a strong strategic emphasis on efficiency (reduced costs per unit). This effort is often associated with reducing capital investment, rather than holding it steady as in the maturity phase. Product or service options and variations are often standardized and their number reduced. Efforts are also made to improve marketing efficiency. Mergers or acquisitions among competing firms accelerate during the decline phase.

In the termination phase there are sharp reductions in availability and possibly the total elimination of a good or service. Most drive-in theaters throughout North America have closed down during the past decade. The primary reason for the closing of many of these theaters is home VCR technology along with its channel of distribution: the video store.

Generic Strategies Model

Michael Porter suggests in this model that there are three potentially successful strategic approaches to coping with the five industry and market competitive forces and competing effectively in an industry. These strategies apply to different combinations of strategic target and strategic advantage.

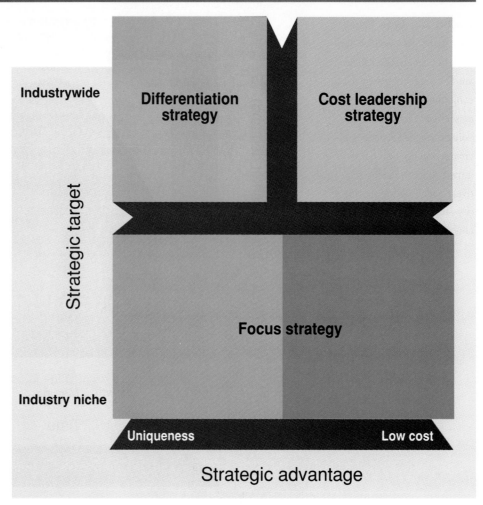

Source: Adapted from M.E. Porter, *Competitive Strategy: Techniques for Analyzing Industries and Competitors* (New York: Free Press, 1980), p. 39. Adapted with permission of The Free Press, a Division of Macmillan, Inc. Copyright © 1980 by The Free Press.

Generic Strategies Model

generic strategies model
A framework of three basic business-level strategies that can be applied to a variety of organizations in diverse industries.

niche A narrowly defined market segment that many competitors may overlook, ignore, or have difficulty serving.

The **generic strategies model** consists of a framework of three basic business-level strategies that can be applied to a variety of organizations in diverse industries.[59] This model is called ''generic'' because all kinds of organizations can use it, whether they are manufacturing, service, or not-for-profit organizations. Figure 8.6 shows the parts of this model. The strategic target dimension (vertical axis) indicates how widely the good or service is intended to compete: throughout the industry or within a particular industry niche. A **niche** is a narrowly defined market segment that many competitors may overlook, ignore, or have difficulty serving, such as a specific geographical area (the South or the West Coast) or a specialized group of customers (teenagers, physicians, or retirees).[60] The strategic advantage dimension (horizontal axis) indicates the basis on which the good or service is intended to compete: uniqueness as perceived by the customer or low cost to the customer. The various combinations of these two variables—strategic target and strategic advantage—suggest three different generic strategies: differentiation strategy, cost leadership strategy, and focus strategy.

differentiation strategy
The business-level strategy that emphasizes competing with all other firms in an industry by offering a product that customers perceive to be unique.

Differentiation Strategy The **differentiation strategy** emphasizes competing with all other firms in the industry by offering a good or service that customers perceive to be unique. This strategy is dominant in the auto industry. Organizations attempt to create unique value (benefits) by influencing customer perceptions and/or providing real differences. A variety of offerings are associated with the differentiation strategy, including innovative product design (BMW), high quality (Ford's theme "Quality is Job 1"), unique brand image (Mercedes-Benz), technological leadership (Honda's four-wheel steering), customer service leadership (GM's Mr. Goodwrench), an extensive dealer network, and product warranty (Mazda's bumper-to-bumper warranty). One of the shortcomings of the differentiation strategy depends on the relative ease with which offerings can be copied or imitated. As soon as most or all competitors imitate the offering (such as a bumper-to-bumper car warranty), it is no longer effective as a means of differentiation.

cost leadership strategy
The business-level strategy that emphasizes competing with all other firms in an industry by providing a good or service at a price as low as or lower than theirs.

Cost Leadership Strategy The **cost leadership strategy** emphasizes competing with all other firms in the industry by providing a good or service at a price as low as or lower than other firms' prices. This strategy attempts to maximize efficiency and minimize costs. Autos produced and marketed primarily under the cost leadership strategy include the Hyundai, Ford Escort, Subaru Justy, Nissan Sentra, Mazda 323, Suzuki Alto G-Type, Toyota Tercel EZ, Daihatsu Mira, Chevrolet Sprint, and Honda Civic. A variety of strategic actions are associated with a cost leadership strategy, such as constructing plants that yield high economies of scale, constantly striving to control overhead and production costs to reduce per-unit costs, minimizing R&D, service, sales force, advertising, and similar costs, or avoiding customers whose demands would result in high selling or service costs. High volume and/or rapid growth are often needed for profitability. For example, the new Ford Escort, designed for global sales, is assembled in twelve locations worldwide with an annual capacity of 900,000 units.[61]

focus strategy The business-level strategy that emphasizes competing in a specific industry niche by offering either a unique product or a low-cost product.

Focus Strategy The **focus strategy** emphasizes competing in a specific industry niche by offering either a unique product or a low-cost product. Organizations attempt to create a unique product image by catering to the specific demands of the selected niche, ignoring other potential customers. The strategic actions associated with the focus strategy are adaptations of the actions associated with the differentiation and cost leadership strategies, but they're applied to a specific market niche. Autos produced and marketed using primarily the focus strategy with a differentiation emphasis include Acura Legend LS, Porsche, Lexus LS500, Rolls-Royce, Infiniti 45, BMW 735i, Mercedes-Benz 420 SEL, Cadillac Allente, Lincoln Mark II, Jaguar XJ6, Ferrari, and Maserati. Only a small percent of American car buyers can afford these cars since their sticker prices range from about $40,000 on up.[62] Oshkosh Truck, in contrast, follows a cost leadership strategy to a specific market niche in the production of heavy duty military vehicles.

Smaller firms with limited resources will most often choose one of the two versions of the focus strategy, that is, a cost leadership version or a differentiation version, applied within a specific niche. Larger firms with substantial resources and a wider product line will most often employ various combinations of these three generic strategies.[63] For example, Ford's Lincoln-Mercury Division products range from low-cost autos (the basic Topaz) to autos with unique characteristics for special industry niches (Lincoln Continental and Lincoln Town Car). Table 8.3 summarizes the key features of the generic strategies model and gives further examples of organizations that have successfully used them.

Overview of Generic Strategies Model

Business-level Strategy	Key Features	Examples
Differentiation Strategy	Premium quality Brand image Technological leadership Customer service	Hyatt Hotels—travel accommodations Coleman—camping equipment Mary Kay—cosmetics Rolex—watches
Cost Leadership Strategy	Tight production cost and overhead control Efficient scale of facilities Efficient service, sales-force, and advertising Competitive pricing	Briggs and Stratton—small engines Southwest Airlines—travel Du Pont—chemicals Walmart—retailing
Focus Strategy	Careful identification of target market (niche) Cost leadership emphasis or differentiation emphasis Constant review of industry niche customer demands	AFG Industries—specialized glass for microwave ovens, shower enclosures, and patio table tops Oshkosh Truck—heavy-duty military vehicles Nieman Marcus—elite retailing

ETHICS AND STRATEGIC PLANNING

At this point we want to return briefly to the theme of Chapter 5. Managerial and employee decisions, including those involved in strategic planning, need to be evaluated from an ethical and social responsibility perspective.[64] John Akers, chairman of the board of IBM, has spoken of the relationship between competitiveness and ethics. Some of his thoughts are presented in the following Insight.

AKERS ON COMPETITIVENESS AND ETHICS

INSIGHT

Ethics and competitiveness are inseparable. We compete as a society. No society anywhere will compete very long or successfully with people stabbing each other in the back; with people trying to steal from each other; with everything requiring notarized confirmation because you can't trust the other fellow; with every little squabble ending in litigation; and with government writing reams of regulatory legislation, tying business hand and foot to keep it honest.

First, we should fortify the practical ethical buttresses that help all of us—from childhood on—and understand and do exactly what is required of us. The simplest and most powerful buttress is the role model: parents and others who by example set us straight on good and evil, right and wrong.

Second, the time has come to take a hard look at ethical teaching in our schools—and I don't just mean schools of business. An enormous amount of work needs to be done to help young people think clearly about complex ethical issues.

My third suggestion is this: let's keep our sense of order straight. Let's put first things first. We have all heard shortsighted businesspeople attribute a quotation to Vince Lombardi: ''Winning is not the most important thing; it's the only thing.'' That's a good quotation for firing up a team, but as a business philosophy it is sheer nonsense. There is another, much better Lombardi quotation. He once said he expected his players to have three kinds of loyalty: to God, to their families, and to the Green Bay Packers, ''in that order.'' He knew that some things count more than others. Business men and women can be unabashedly proud of their companies. But the good of an entire society transcends that of any single corporation. The moral order of the world transcends any single nation-state. And one cannot be a good business leader—or a good doctor or lawyer or engineer—without understanding the place of business in the greater scheme of things.[65]

CHAPTER SUMMARY

1. Through strategic planning, managers and other employees take a broad, long-range view of their organization's mission, objectives, courses of action, and allocation of resources. Tactical planning focuses on short-term decisions and actions that serve to implement the strategic plan.

2. Three benefits of planning are (1) identifying future opportunities, (2) anticipating future problems, and (3) developing appropriate strategies and tactics. Effective planning stimulates entrepreneurship, helps employees deal with risk and uncertainty, and facilitates the identification of assumptions.

3. Diversification involves four stages: (1) the single-business firm, (2) the dominant-business firm, (3) the related-businesses firm, and (4) the unrelated-businesses firm. At each stage the range of the organization's goods, services, and markets determines the scope and complexity of its strategic planning.

4. Organizations may need to develop strategies and plans at three levels: (1) corporate level, (2) the business level, and (3) the functional level.

   ▶ Corporate-level strategic planning guides the activities of various businesses (or product lines) within a parent organization. Five corporate-level growth strategies are forward integration, backward integration, horizontal integration, concentric diversification, and conglomerate diversification.

   ▶ Business-level strategic planning directs the operations and performance of a single organization or a strategic business unit (SBU) that provides a particular line of goods or services.

   ▶ Functional-level strategic planning creates guidelines and tactics for managing each functional area and specifies how each will contribute to the organization's business-level strategies and objectives.

5. The strategic planning process can be broken down into eight interrelated tasks: (1) develop the mission and objectives, (2) diagnose threats and opportunities, (3) assess strengths and weaknesses, (4) generate alternative strategies (market penetration strategy, market development strategy, or product development strategy), (5) develop a strategic plan, (6) develop tactical plans, (7) control and assess the results of both strategic and tactical plans, and (8) repeat the planning process.

6. Two business-level strategy models were reviewed. The product life cycle model emphasizes planning according to the market phases that many goods and services go through—introduction, growth, maturity, decline, and termination. The generic strategies model provides a framework of three basic business-level strategies (differentiation, cost leadership, and focus) applicable to a variety of organizations in diverse industries.

1. **From Where You Sit:** What do you think were the organizational objectives of the high school you attended? What seemed to be its strategy?

2. What are the key differences between strategic planning and tactical planning?

3. Identify a firm that is in the single-business stage of diversification. Where does this firm's good or service seem to fall in the product life cycle model? What are the key implications of this for the firm?

4. What are the primary differences between corporate-level, business-level, and functional-level strategies?

5. **From Where You Sit:** What are the primary forces driving industry and market competition for Wendy's as a corporation and the local Wendy's in your community?

6. How have the primary forces driving industry and market competition affected companies in the airline industry?

7. **From Where You Sit:** Which types of environmental threats and opportunities should the college in which you are enrolled monitor and diagnose? Which three are most important? Why?

8. **From Where You Sit:** What are the major strengths and weaknesses of the supermarket store you shop at most frequently? What are the two greatest weaknesses and two greatest strengths?

9. **From Where You Sit:** What strategies might be considered for overcoming or reducing the weaknesses identified in Question 8?

10. To compete effectively in the 1990s, do you think firms should select one of the generic strategies—differentiation, cost leadership, or focus—and stick with it? Explain.

11. **From Where You Sit:** Identify a retailing firm in your community that follows a cost leadership strategy and one that follows a differentiation strategy. Identify all of the ways in which these two firms are different and similar. Are their respective strategies successful? Why?

Marzilli's Fine Italian Foods

Introduction. This exercise can be undertaken by you alone, the class as a whole, or groups of five to eight class members. Study the description of this situation, then answer the two questions about it, following the guidelines for strategic thinking that are given.

The Situation. Marzilli's Fine Italian Foods is a grocery store founded in 1935 by Gino Marzilli and his wife, Maria. Gino and Maria were immigrants. In its early years the business provided Italian specialty grocery items to the residents of an Italian immigrant neighborhood in the center-city area. Gino's family ran a grocery store in Milan, Italy, and his own store had much of the flavor of Milan.

Over the years the business has been quite successful. In 1952 Gino and Maria bought a large building not far from the original store. The building was remodeled and provided them with a much larger store area plus an apartment to live in. In 1960 they began producing homemade pasta and a series of high-quality sauces to be used with Italian foods. The recipes were developed by Maria, and the products, sold exclusively at the store, have continued to be quite popular.

Gino and Maria retired to Florida in 1972, turning the business over to their only child, Jim Marzilli. Jim has been involved in the business all of his life. He's married, but his wife has not been involved in the business. They and their four children live in a southern suburb of the city.

Although the business remained very successful in the 1980s, recently the sales revenues have shown a steady decline. Jim attributes this decline to several factors. Most important is the fact that most of the old Italian population has moved from the center-city area to the suburbs. These people are dispersed in five or six southwestern suburbs that are a forty- to sixty-minute drive from the old neighborhood. Thus many of the store "regulars" shop infrequently at Marzilli's, although the store is crowded on Fridays and Saturdays, particularly before holidays and feast days. A related factor is that the center-city neighborhood where the store is located is *now* populated by young professionals. Although some of them patronize the store, they purchase only a limited number of items, such as bread and certain sauces. Jim feels that this is because their knowledge of Italian cuisine is limited, although many seem to be interested in Italian cooking.

Over the past year the business has been barely at the breakeven point, and Jim feels it is time to do something about the situation. He would like the store to be the busy meeting place for Italians that it was in the 1950s but realizes that times have changed. He is 52 years old and does not want to retire or sell the business. Three of his four children now live out of town and are not interested in the business, but his youngest son Dom has expressed some interest. Dom lives in an apartment above the store and works downtown for a market research firm. His wife June is a teacher and has helped in the store during rush times. Although June is not Italian, Jim says that she is almost as great an Italian cook as he and his mother. Dom and June have no children.

At this point, Jim sees two basic options:

1. *Maintain the same line of products, but cut back on the number of employees and store hours.* He now has six employees and thinks he could get along with four. And since much of the business comes from old customers who come on Fridays and Saturdays, Jim feels that he could maintain the same level of sales by being open only Tuesday through Saturday.

   The cutback of employees and shorter hours will cut costs; if sales remain at about the same level, Jim thinks the business will be profitable in the coming years.

2. *Start adding "American" foods to attract more of the current neighborhood residents.* Marzilli's would thus become a neighborhood grocery store rather than an Italian specialty food store. Jim would retain some Italian foods to serve his old customers, but the store would gradually evolve into a neighborhood grocery store. There are no grocery stores within a four- or five-block radius, and Jim feels that he could pick up a lot of neighborhood trade.

Questions

1. What planning process can you recommend that would allow Jim Marzilli to make a wise decision about the future of the business?

2. Which of the two options would you recommend to Jim?

Guidelines for Strategic Thinking

1. Keep loose; open up your thinking; keep an open mind.

2. Remember that planning is a means, not an end; don't confuse *how* you accomplish your objectives with *what* your objectives are.

3. Ask questions that you may not have had the time to ask previously.

4. Focus on opportunities, not on resources.

5. Identify your assumptions. Concentrate on the "restrictive assumptions"—those that you assume cannot be changed—and change them.

6. Generate as many ideas as you can—the more the better. There is no such thing as a stupid idea. Some may prove better than others for the current situation, but you will not know which ideas are superior unless you express all that occur to you.

TO: Abby Keck, President, Biz-Mart Consulting
FROM: Benton Richards, President, Feed Seed Supply
SUBJECT: Business Concepts

I enjoyed meeting with you, Abby, to discuss the various business concepts I'm deciding on for my small firm. When we met, I may have sounded confused, but I think I now have a clearer sense of these concepts, and I've summarized them here:

Production Orientation. The key to business success is producing quality goods and services at a reasonable cost. Such products do not have to be promoted—they will sell themselves. If possible, our goods and services should be standardized to keep costs down.

Sales Orientation. The key to business success lies in persuading potential customers to buy goods and services, through advertising, personal selling, and/or other means. Potential customers must be informed and convinced of the benefits of our goods and services.

Marketing Orientation. The key to business success is directing all company activities and personnel efforts toward satisfying customers, while providing satisfactory profits to the firm. We should find out what benefits customers want and then provide these benefits in our goods and services.

Societal Orientation. The key to business success lies in satisfying the important stakeholders of the company. These stakeholders include customers, employees, stockholders, governmental agencies, suppliers, and the public at large. All of their interests should be considered when making decisions.

Your comments on these concepts and the criteria for judging them that you suggested will definitely help me chart a clearer course for my company. However, during our meeting you said that "these concepts may not be mutually exclusive." If this is true, how can these different orientations be brought together?

I look forward to receiving your thoughts on this subject. After I've studied your reply, I'll be in touch to set up our next meeting.

Question: Assume you are Abby Keck. How would you reply, based on the concepts presented in this chapter?

Governors Group to Urge 200 Firms To Cut Waste by Using Less Packaging

By Frank Edward Allen

The Coalition of Northeastern Governors will issue today a broad challenge to the nation's 200 largest makers of consumer packaging, urging them to reduce substantially the volumes of solid waste their products generate.

The strategy could provide an important test of the effectiveness of voluntary efforts to curtail solid waste. Despite heightened consumer awareness, America's waste stream continues to grow at a rapid rate, and packaging now accounts for more than 30% of it. This year, about a dozen states are expected to consider legislation that would impose packaging standards on consumer-goods makers.

Scott Paper Co., Procter & Gamble Co. and Campbell Soup Co. said they have agreed to accept the coalition's challenge and already have developed plans for compliance. In addition, officials of the nine-state group said they expect several other major corporations, including Sears, Roebuck & Co., Digital Equipment Corp. and Du Pont Co., to accept the challenge promptly.

"We're asking them to follow our preferred packaging guidelines, and we have every reason to believe they will," said Anne Stubbs, executive director of the coalition's policy research center in Washington.

The guidelines call for specific efforts to reduce waste at the source, but don't prescribe volume or percentage goals or suggest target dates. They do, however, suggest a hierarchy of preferences for distributing consumer goods: no packaging; minimal packaging; returnable, reusable or refillable packaging; recycled content and recyclable packaging.

Critics of the coalition's voluntary approach, including several environmental groups that stopped participating in the project last fall, said they think the plan is inadequate.

All 200 companies will receive written invitations to accept the coalition's challenge. In addition, they will receive manuals that describe, step by step, how to implement waste-reduction plans and how to involve suppliers and customers. Those handbooks will be supplemented with a series of workshops, scheduled to begin in about six weeks.

"We think a lot of companies still aren't getting the message," said Tom Rattray, P&G's associate director of packaging development. He said he is pleased that the coalition decided to "do something simple, like tell them."

Philip E. Lippincott, Scott Paper's chairman and chief executive, said that merely challenging companies to adopt the guidelines isn't enough. "We must give companies the tools they need" to become part of the reduction effort "as quickly as possible," he said.

At Scott, meeting the new goals will require help from suppliers. Frank Consoli, the company's manager of packaging, said he intends to write individual letters to 50 of Scott's major suppliers of packaging materials, urging them to join in the reduction efforts.

As an example of what's possible, he described how Scott and its suppliers developed lighter packaging for bathroom tissue used in airports, hospitals and office buildings. The result is a jumbo roll that replaces 12 individually wrapped, thousand-sheet rolls. The new product eliminates 11 rolled cardboard cores, allows for a much smaller shipping carton and reduces overall weight by 35%. . . .

But Maine Gov. John R. McKernan Jr., who helped develop the plan, defended the voluntary approach. "We decided this way is better than trying to pass legislation," he said. "By creating the right conditions with these big companies, many of them being headquartered in our region, we have a chance to bring change to the whole packaging industry."

In response to the governors' challenge, Scott Paper said it will reduce packaging waste by 10%, or 32.8 million pounds, by 1995, using 1990 as the base year. Scott, the largest maker of sanitary tissue products in the U.S., also pledged to increase the average amount of recycled content in its paperboard cartons to at least 75% by 1992.

Similarly, Procter & Gamble said it will expand such recent waste-reduction programs as those that have eliminated outer cartons for Head & Shoulders shampoo and Crest for Kids toothpaste. P&G also said it will extend efforts to recycle plastic in film packaging, bottles and other containers. . . .

Stephen J. Conway, Scott's senior vice president for environmental affairs, said the 32.8 million pounds of waste the company intends to eliminate by 1995 is equivalent to the trash generated by 5,500 American families in one year.

Mr. Conway said he thinks more companies are likely to make stronger efforts at waste reduction if they are encouraged rather than threatened. "When you tell people in industry that they have to do something, they get a hump in their back," he said. "But when you ask them to help, they want to pitch in."

1. Imagine that you work for a small computer software manufacturer and that you have been asked to help devise a functional-level strategic plan for reducing packaging. What does your plan involve?

2. What new corporate strategies might be needed at a company intent on changing its packaging policy?

3. Might other companies be affected by changes in one company's environmental strategy? What about suppliers?

SINGING THE SMALL BUSINESS BLUES AT SHARPCO

"There seems to be a conspiracy out there to keep me from making money and to increase my stress level," said James Sharplin. Sharplin is sole owner of Sharpco, Inc., a small company that manufactures steel items for heavy equipment and rebuilds heavy tracks and related components for crawler tractors, or "dozers."

Sharplin went on to explain the elements of the "conspiracy." "The workers," he said, "try to get as much pay as they can for doing as little as possible. Customers want us to repair their equipment for less than our cost. Then they bring it back a year later, expecting warranty work. Half of the customers try to pay a little late—and if I don't hound them, they'll pay a lot late, or not at all. Suppliers try to give us inferior merchandise at premium prices—everything from paint that doesn't cover to steel that has flaws.

"And government! I'd swear half of my time is spent filling out forms, worrying about incomes taxes, trying to keep a worker I fired for stealing from collecting unemployment compensation, meeting with the fire marshal to explain why we don't have a fire extinguisher on every column—it just goes on and on. Sometimes I think even the equipment is involved in the conspiracy. Yesterday I was just getting ready to load a rush job on a customer's truck and the crane broke down. Mom and Dad used to say, 'If it's not one thing, its another.' I've become convinced that it's five or six others."

After getting all of that out of his system, Sharplin remarked that things were really much better than he had ever expected. Only fourteen years before that he had left an eight-to-five job with a local Caterpillar dealer to start his own business. Like many small firms, Sharpco was started "on a shoestring." With the help of two brothers Sharplin built a small metal building and opened up shop with just a set of tools and two welding machines.

At first Sharplin and his crew of two did repair work for local equipment owners and steel fabrication for a few construction firms. The company was profitable, though, and over the years Sharplin bought more machinery, hired more workers, and expanded the building several times. By 1990 sales were consistently exceeding $1 million a year. Profits after Sharplin's $50,000 salary were averaging $70,000 a year.

In 1991 Sharplin was able to move the business into a new 30,000-square-foot facility on the interstate highway. The new plant had been built from the ground up, according to Sharplin's specifications. "It seems almost like a dream," he said. "I'm still hemmed in by the conspiracy I was talking about, but I really am my own boss. And now I have a place of business that I can really be proud of. In fact, there's not a tractor dealer in town, and certainly not a welding shop, that has a place as nice as this one."

Sharplin mentioned a number of other advantages of having his own business. Two of his nephews work at Sharpco. He had been able to help one of his brothers out of a bind by lending him a few thousand dollars. His nine-year-old daughter often comes to the office and spends the whole day with her father. Sharpco has a company-paid medical plan. There is a copy machine, all kinds of tools and equipment, and even a computer available for Sharplin's personal use.

Summing up, Sharplin said, "I reckon I work a lot more hours than if I worked for someone else, but I say what those hours are. I think people respect me more than they would if I worked for somebody else. If I had stayed with the Caterpillar dealer, I'd be lucky to be making $30,000 a year by now. Here I am, practically a millionaire in just fourteen years, with a plant that will last me until I retire—if I ever decide to do that." James settled into his leather upholstered chair behind the Chippendale desk he had bought for his new office. "I don't suppose I really have much reason to gripe."

1. What business-level and functional-level issues are facing James Sharplin and Sharpco?
2. Is there evidence that Sharplin has engaged in strategic planning? Explain.
3. What are Sharpco's strategies? Are they likely to be effective over the long run? Explain.
4. Evaluate Sharpco's situation with respect to the primary forces that typically drive industry market competition (see Figure 8.4). Make assumptions as needed.
5. Is James Sharplin a strategic manager? Explain.

Chapter 9

PLANNING AIDS AND

IMPLEMENTATION

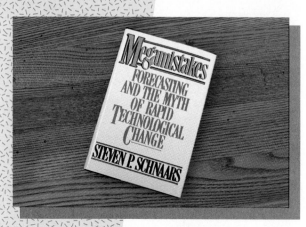

Megamistakes

What You Will Learn

1 The essentials of three forecasting aids: scenarios, the Delphi technique, and simulations.

2 How to use two aids designed to surface and challenge assumptions: dialectical inquiry and devil's advocacy.

3 The phases of management by objectives.

4 How the program evaluation and review technique (PERT) is applied in project management.

5 **Skill Development:** How to apply specific planning aids all the way through to implementation.

Chapter Outline

Manager's Viewpoint
Technological Megamistakes

Forecasting Aids
Scenarios
Global Link: Pan-Pacific Scenario
The Delphi Technique
Simulations
Insight: The St. Ignatius Hotel Reservations Simulation
Assessment of Forecasting

Surfacing Assumptions
Dialectical Inquiry Method
Insight: New Product Decision
Devil's Advocacy Method

Management by Objectives
Philosophy and Management Style
Setting Up and Linking of Objectives
Insight: Management by Objectives at Cypress Semiconductor
Participation
Action Planning
Implementation and Control
Insight: Mike Gantz's Plight
Performance Reviews
Insight: Boehringer Mannheim's Performance Review System
Assessment of Management by Objectives

Project Management
Program Evaluation and Review Technique (PERT)
Insight: Using PERT in House Construction
Ethics in Project Management

Experiencing Management
Skill-Building Exercise: Job Objectives Questionnaire

Manager's Memo

In the News

Management Case
Metropol of Canada

Technological Megamistakes

The main "reason technological forecasts have failed is that the people who made them have been seduced by technological wonder. A passionate focus on technology for its own sake spells disaster." In the words of Steven Schnaars, author of *Megamistakes: Forecasting and the Myth of Rapid Technological Change,* managers' forecasts of the future are too often "derailed by the lure of technological gadgetry." Consider a few of the examples and lessons offered by Schnaars.

Pick up the phone and see the person you are talking to on a small TV-like screen built into the phone console. By 1985, AT&T was convinced, there would be 3 million of these gadgets generating $5 billion in revenues for the company. Picturephones were an intriguing technological development. But AT&T got so carried away by the technology it forgot how people really use telephones. The company overlooked the obvious fact that customers wouldn't rush out to increase the cost of their phone service by a factor of ten. Contrary to company hype, talking to people by Picturephone isn't at all like meeting them in person. Worse, Picturephone terminals would have cost $1,500, and the monthly service fee would have been $100. The lesson: a focus on technology for its own sake spells disaster.

Another example is home banking, once a vision of the future promoted by such outfits as Chase Manhattan and Chemical. Though more than 20 million households now have personal computers, only about 100,000 people have bothered to sign up for any of the forty-one different bank-at-home services. After five years in the business, Chemical Bank discontinued its home banking with approximately 25,000 subscribers. Home banking turned out to be another technology in search of a market. "What are the benefits? Do you really want to go home from a hard day's work and shuffle your money between accounts?" asks Schnaars. Few people have banking needs so complicated that they need a computer to juggle them, even though the cost is only $10 to $12 a month plus phone charges. "It was technological wonder. It wasn't even forecast-based. It was just that everybody in the industry was doing it, and they were afraid to be left out," concludes Schnaars.

Another common blunder, according to Schnaars, is betting on a new product whose success depends on blindly extrapolating current trends into the future. He points to the 1960s, when proponents of the Supersonic Transport (SST) justified mass production of their Mach 1 bird by pointing to the trend from slow prop planes to fast jets and assuming that the SST was the inevitable next stage. So what if costs for this airplane were also increasing at supersonic speeds. So what if no one bothered to find out how many people would pay three times the fare to fly the Atlantic in about half the time. The Concorde eventually cost $4 billion, ten times original estimates. The market, on the other hand, has turned out to be pretty modest. Only sixteen Concordes were ever built, and today only fourteen are still flying.

Focus on fundamentals, Schnaars advises. Who and where are the customers? How large is the market? Does the technology offer a real, added benefit? "Be especially suspicious of forecasts based on accelerating trends in growth," he says. "In the past they have led to the largest errors."[1]

Now that you have learned the basics of planning outlined in Chapter 8, it's time to add some specialized skills to your planning toolkit. One such skill is forecasting. The Manager's Viewpoint feature warns of the dangers of simpleminded thinking when acting on or making plans based on forecasts. Managers need to avoid getting swept away with the technological wonder of sophisticated forecasting methodologies. "There is absolutely no evidence that complicated mathematical models provide more accurate forecasts than simpler models that incorporate intuitively pleasing rules of thumb," claims Schnaars.[2]

One recent study identified forty-nine planning aids and techniques and reviewed thirty of them.[3] Our objectives in this chapter are much more modest. We hope to give you at least a few "intuitively pleasing rules of thumb." Our approach is chronological, moving from the earliest planning phases (forecasting what might come to pass), to the assumptions and objectives embedded in forecasts and plans, to the end of the process—implementation—when plans must be made realities. The first section covers the basics and limitations of forecasting, as well as the essentials of three frequently used forecasting aids. Because planning is always based on someone's assumptions, the next section comments on two aids for surfacing and challenging those assumptions. Next we present the phases of management by objectives, an effective approach to not only developing but also carrying out, or implementing, plans. Implementation is also the theme of the last section of the chapter, where we discuss project management as a process for implementing specific plans and strategies.

FORECASTING AIDS

forecasting Predicting, projecting, or estimating future events or conditions in an organization's environment.

Forecasting involves predicting, projecting, or estimating future events or conditions in an organization's environment. An important part of any planning process, forecasting is, by definition, concerned with "reading the tea leaves," or foreseeing events or conditions that are likely to be outside the firm's direct control. Firms such as PepsiCo, Hilton Hotels, and Liz Claiborne develop forecasts covering areas such as markets, technology, customer attitudes, political trends, and international conditions.

extrapolation The projection of some tendency from the past or present into the future.

Most forecasting is based on some form of extrapolation. **Extrapolation** is the projection of some tendency from the past or present into the future.[4] The simplest, and at times most misleading, form of extrapolation is the linear, or straight-line, projection of a past trend into the future.[5] In 1974, for instance, most U.S. electric utilities made plans to double their generating capacity by the mid-1980s, based on forecasts of a 7 percent annual growth in demand. It is important to make forecasts in this industry because electric utilities have to begin building new generating plants five to ten years before they'll actually be needed. But during the period from 1975 to 1985 the demand for electricity actually grew at only a 2 percent annual rate. Despite the postponement or cancellation of many projects in the works, the excess generating capacity eventually meant higher customer rates and lower profits for many electric utilities.

Even though forecasting is uncertain, it's still necessary. Managers have to make use of whatever help is available to them. Three forecasting aids—scenarios, the Delphi technique, and simulations—are examples of the ones commonly used in strategic planning. As suggested in Figure 9.1, elements of scenarios, the Delphi technique, and simulations overlap; the three aids are not mutually exclusive.[6] All of them focus on gaining clarity and understanding of their possible futures.

Scenarios

scenario A written description of a possible future that is used as a forecasting aid.

A **scenario** is a written description of a possible future. *Scenario* became a popular business term in 1967, with the publication of Herman Kahn and Anthony Weiner's book, *The Year 2000*. **Multiple scenarios** are simply written descriptions of several alternative

**Three Interrelated
Forecasting Aids**

As suggested by the overlapping circles, these popular
forecasting aids have some
elements in common.

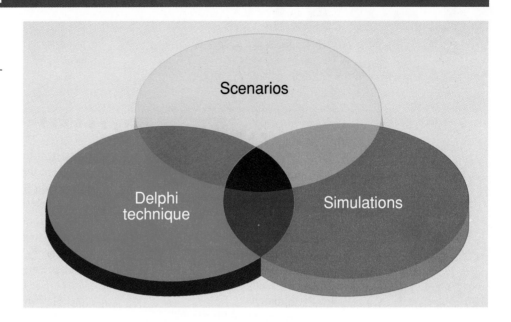

multiple scenarios Written
descriptions of several alternative futures.

futures. Planners use scenarios to address questions such as these: What future environment might exist for the organization? How might some potential (hypothetical) situation
come about? What alternative strategies might exist for preventing, diverting, encouraging, or dealing with these futures?[7] Thus scenarios are intended to serve four broad
purposes:

▶ Provide a wide range of possibilities against which to evaluate strategies.
▶ Provide a broader vision of alternative events.
▶ Assist in the identification of events that warrant the development of contingency
plans.
▶ Assist individuals in seeing broad patterns, generalizations, and interrelationships.

Scenarios are quite useful in forcing those involved in planning to evaluate preliminary plans against future possibilities.[8] Royal Dutch/Shell, which has been doing scenario planning for twenty years, currently has two twenty-year scenarios in place. The
first, called "Sustainable World," predicts increased concern about global warming
trends and an expanded emphasis on conservation, recycling, and emissions controls. The
second scenario, entitled "Mercantilist World," postulates an increase in protectionism, a
slump in world growth, and a de-emphasis of environmentalism. Shell management realizes that these two scenarios don't include everything that might happen in the future, and
that neither will be a perfect predictor. Group planning coordinator Peter Hadfield points
out: "They're there to condition the organization to think."[9]

Hadfield also believes that scenario planning has helped Shell be better prepared than
its competitors for external shocks. In the early 1980s, for example, while most forecasters were predicting a steadily increasing price for crude oil, Shell, in one of its scenarios,
had considered the possibility that the price would slide to $15 a barrel. As a hedge against
such an eventuality, the company began looking into cost-saving exploration technologies. When the slump hit, Shell was able to sustain a higher level of drilling activity than
many of its competitors.

This chapter's Global Link feature describes one possible scenario for the business
environment in the twenty-first century—a world trade bloc. The Pan-Pacific scenario,
one of four scenarios developed by Duk-Choong Kim of Sogang University in South
Korea, is viewed by him as the most likely one. Do you agree?

GLOBAL Link

PAN-PACIFIC SCENARIO

The argument that the center of global economic activity is shifting—or has already shifted—from the Atlantic and the United States and Europe to the Pacific and Asia (with or without North America) is not new. The general notion that the Asian countries bordering on the Pacific Ocean have the strongest economies has been accepted by many experts.

The Pan-Pacific scenario represents a trading bloc that includes Australia, Canada, China, the Asian nations (South Korea, Singapore, Hong Kong, etc.), Japan, New Zealand, the United States, and perhaps Mexico and some other Central and South American nations.

This scenario is based on the following assumptions: (1) The activity of the recent past will continue and accelerate in the Asia-Pacific area. (2) U.S. military forces will leave Asia. (3) Japan's military strength will increase. (4) The international environment of the late 1990s and early twenty-first century will be characterized by peaceful coexistence rather than wars.

The advantage of the Pan-Pacific scenario is that such a grouping would tend to force the European family—under the European Community—to reduce its natural tendency for protectionism in favor of actively engaging in open competition for world markets. A bloc including the United States, Japan, and China could not be ignored or casually alienated.

One strength of this scenario is that it includes the democratic societies of the United States and Canada. This grouping comes closer than other scenarios to including values and institutions that may represent the spirit of the times of the Pacific era. The market system has demonstrated that it is more capable than any other of maintaining global prosperity and satisfying the basic needs of people. This is in contrast with the failures of centrally planned systems in China, the U.S.S.R., Eastern Europe, North Korea, and elsewhere.

Source: Adapted from Duk-Choong Kim, ''World of Warring Trade Blocs?'' In *Pan-Pacific Business Association Newsletter*, February 1990, 1–5.

The Delphi Technique

The **Delphi technique,** named after an ancient Greek oracle, is a forecasting aid based on a consensus of a panel of experts.[10] The experts refine their opinions, step-by-step, until consensus is reached. Because the technique relies on opinions, it obviously isn't foolproof. But the consensus arrived at tends to be much more accurate than a single expert's opinion.[11] The method was developed at the Rand Corporation in the early 1950s to obtain expert opinions on how many Soviet atomic bombs would be required to do a specific amount of damage to the United States. The Delphi technique is now recognized as an important aid to strategic planning.

Basic Steps The Delphi technique involves three basic steps:

1. *A questionnaire is sent to a group of experts.*   These experts remain unknown to one another. The questionnaire requests numerical estimates of specific technological or market possibilities. It also asks for expected dates and an assignment of probabilities to each of these possibilities.

2. *A summary of the first round is prepared.*   This report may show the average, median, and quartile ranges of responses. The report, along with a revised questionnaire, is sent to the experts who completed the first questionnaire. In the second round they are asked in the second questionnaire to revise their earlier estimates, if appropriate, or to justify their original opinions.

3. *A summary of the second round is prepared.*   This report often shows that a consensus is developing. The experts are now asked in a third questionnaire to indicate whether they support this emerging consensus and the explanations that accompany it. To avoid blind agreement, they are encouraged to find reasons for *not* joining the consensus.[12]

Three rounds are generally recommended. Although more rounds could be used, the experts often begin dropping out after the third round because of other time commitments. The number of participating experts has ranged from only a few to 140. The actual sample size will depend on the objectives desired. A range of fifteen to twenty is recommended for a fairly narrow issue. With increasing sample size, there will be a corresponding increase in the amount of coordination required, as well as costs incurred.[13]

Delphi Questionnaires The heart of the Delphi technique is, of course, the series of questionnaires. The first questionnaire may include broadly worded questions. In later rounds the questions become more specific, because they are built on responses to the preceding questionnaires.

Figure 9.2 shows a Delphi questionnaire developed for student and classroom use. The questionnaire is concerned with possible developments in typical American business firms over the next twenty years. You might want to take a few minutes now to answer the questions.

TRW, a major advanced-technology firm, began using the Delphi technique in 1960 to forecast developments in such diverse fields as space, transportation, and housing. Goodyear Tire and Rubber Company now uses the method to plan tire research and other company activities through the year 2000. In recent years the Delphi technique has been effectively applied to help identify and solve problems and set objectives and priorities in areas as diverse as environmental consequences of business strategies, urban redevelopment, energy conservation, pollution control, and housing.[14]

Simulations

A **simulation** is a method, or a representation of a real system. The model usually describes the behavior of the real system (or some aspect of it) in quantitative and/or qualitative terms. A simulation may show how a number of variables (such as profit, market

**Delphi Questionnaire:
Future Developments in
North American Businesses**

The following 10 questions
are concerned with future
possible developments in the
typical North American business firm within the next
twenty years or so. In addition to giving your answer to
each question, you are also
being asked to rank the questions from 1 to 10. The ranking 1 means you feel that you
have the best chance of making an accurate projection for
this question relative to the
others. The ranking 10 means
you regard that answer as
least probable. Please rank all
questions such that every
number from 1 to 10 is used
exactly once. "Never" is also
an acceptable answer.

Rank (1–10)	Questions	Year
_____	1. In what year will women serve as presidents of at least five of the *Fortune* 500?	_____
_____	2. In what year will most boards of directors of publicly held corporations contain members who represent primarily the consumer rather than the stockholders?	_____
_____	3. In what year will managers regularly be paid for working a 35-hour week?	_____
_____	4. By what year will business have effectively reduced its pollution of the environment to a nondangerous level?	_____
_____	5. In what year will top management in half of the hundred largest manufacturing firms rely on computerized systems as their primary tool for planning?	_____
_____	6. By what year will the use of mind-stimulating drugs be employed by 10% of top-level managers as an aid in determining corporate policy alternatives?	_____
_____	7. In what year will energy prices make operations unfeasible for most North American industrial corporations?	_____
_____	8. By what year will an MBA degree be a minimum requirement for entry into the management training programs of most corporations?	_____
_____	9. In what year will prime interest rates make it totally prohibitive for corporations to expand their plant capacities?	_____
_____	10. In what year will most corporations' financial statements reflect a significant level of accounting for social costs and assets (for example, pollution, welfare, and human resources)?	_____

Source: Dr. Harvey Nussbaum, School of Business Administration. Wayne State University, Detroit. Reprinted by permission.

share, and level of quality) change depending on changes in other variables (such as inflation rate, competitors' price changes, and unemployment rate).

Computers are often employed in creating simulations. For example, Abbot Laboratories, a major diversified health care company, uses SIMPLAN, a general software modeling language that can be learned easily by people who have no prior computer programming experience. SIMPLAN creates a computerized simulation of the relationships among marketing, production, and finance at Abbot. The marketing model consists of a simulated pricing segment driven by simulated market demand. The production model converts the sales volumes called for by the marketing model into raw material and inventory requirements. The results from these models drive the financial model. The end result of the total process is a set of reports that contain sales projections, materials and labor requirements, and projected income statements for alternative scenarios.[15]

Simulations are often used to forecast the effects of environmental changes and internal management decisions on an organization or any of its departments or strategic business units. The objective of simulations is to reproduce or test reality without actually experiencing it. Most simulations are intended to let management ask numerous "what if" questions.[16] For example, "What profits can we anticipate next year if inflation is 8 percent and we continue current pricing policies?" or "What profits can we expect next year if inflation is 12 percent and we open two new plants?" In order to answer such questions analysts often develop complex equations and use computers to perform many of the step-by-step computations required. Such models can be used to simulate virtually any area of concern—such as profits, sales, and earnings per share—in need of a fore-cast.[17]

Typical Questions and Variables   A simulation can help planners deal with three common strategic questions:

1. What general effects will a changed economy have on the firm if its key strategies remain unchanged?

2. What will be the specific effects on the firm if a particular strategy is selected in anticipation of certain changes in the economy (such as an increase in interest rates to 13 percent)?

3. Are there particular combinations of strategies that will enable the firm to take advantage of changes in the economy?

Types of environmental variables used in a simulation might include inflation rate, short-term interest rate, tax rate, and unemployment level. Strategies used in a simulation could affect price, sales, dividends, cash flow, depreciation, or production capacity. The performance measure used to present the outcome of a simulation model might be an income statement, a financial ratio (such as debt-to-equity ratio, return on equity, or earnings per share), or a balance sheet (assets and liabilities).

Manufacturing processes have often been the subject of computer simulations.[18] In the past, simulations of manufacturing systems were performed mainly by mathematical experts. These experts believed in the results of their simulations, but managers and teams often didn't because the results were presented in the form of hard-to-interpret computer printouts. Simulation of manufacturing systems now utilizes a new technology—computer graphics. Using graphic displays, the simulation evolves step by step on the screen for all to see. This technique appears to be giving many managers more confidence in simulation results.[19]

Hotel managers have traditionally accepted the notion that a full house is hard to attain. Even the language of the front desk reflects the uncertainty of the reservations system in its use of such terms as ''expected arrivals'' and ''expected departures.'' When rooms are tight, reservations managers gamble on these expectations, using history and instinct to ''guesstimate'' how many reservations will be no-shows, how many scheduled departures will stay beyond their indicated check-out date, and how many unexpected guests (walk-ins) will arrive seeking accommodations. Simulation allows each reservation activity to be studied as a separate event. The reservations system can be divided into individual components, such as booking, canceling, no-shows, and walk-ins, each of which can be predicted using a different probability distribution. The following Insight looks at one such simulation.

THE ST. IGNATIUS HOTEL RESERVATIONS SIMULATION

*I*NSIGHT   The reservations manager of the St. Ignatius Hotel, a 371-room luxury property in a large Southeastern city, wanted to improve the hotel's reservations policies using simulation. From Sunday through Thursday the hotel's major market was corporate business. Like many urban luxury hotels, the St. Ignatius used leisure-oriented packages to fill rooms on weekend nights. The hotel was very sensitive to costs associated with overbooking because it had an unusually high percentage of repeat customers. The reservations manager's goal was to maximize profit.

The hotel's average rate was $125 per occupied room. All fixed costs—labor, amortization, and consumables—were estimated at $50 per room. Management requested that a reasonably large "penalty" for refusing a confirmed reservation be built into the simulation model, since the hotel relied so heavily on repeat business. Without such a penalty, the model would overbook in anticipation of cancellations and no-shows, with no regard for the intangible costs of turning away a regular guest who had a reservation. In essence, incorporating a penalty in the model assigned a dollars-and-cents cost to the bad will, bad publicity, and loss of repeat business that could result from refusing a confirmed reservation. Managers in the reservations and front office areas agreed that the penalty should be determined by multiplying the number of rooms overbooked by the power of 1.5 and multiplying the result by $200.

The specific steps of the simulation were as follows:

(1) Initialize the model by setting the previous day's occupancy level.

(2) Repeat the simulation for a specified number of days forward (the St. Ignatius model used thirty days). Given the previous day's occupancy, the model generated anticipated departures, early departures, and stay-overs.

(3) Generate anticipated arrivals, cancellations on the day of arrival, and no-shows.

(4) If rooms are available, generate the expected number of walk-ins.

(5) From the above data, obtain an expected occupancy, based on the interactions of the various components of the reservation system. The model used this value as the previous day's occupancy in the next iteration.

(6) Calculate profit or loss.

Since the model extended over time, the result of each day's simulation was carried forward to project the occupancy on subsequent dates. As more data were received, the simulation could be run again with the changed components.

It became clear from running the simulation that the St. Ignatius management's "no overbooking" policy was too conservative. The hotel could maintain a no-walk policy (that is, accept all reservations and walk-ins) and still increase profits by $101 per day, or $36,865 per year.[20]

Assessment of Forecasting

Because the future is rarely the same as the past, basing forecasts entirely on historical data is rather like steering a ship by watching its wake. Insight, judgment, and skill are needed to construct reliable forecasting models. Even though forecasting has grown increasingly reliable, disenchantment with it has also grown, perhaps because of overreliance on forecasters' abilities and their forecasts. Several years ago, Robert Lohr, an executive at Bethlehem Steel, blamed his firm's $768 million operating losses partly on "the investments we made because we believed in the boom that an economist promised us." A major metal-mining concern, AMAX, dug itself an $879 million hole by accepting forecasts of continuing inflation. Those projections led the company to assume that prices for its copper, molybdenum, and other metals would keep rising. Instead, prices fell 50 percent.[21]

Although tremendous progress has been made in developing forecasting techniques over the past twenty-five years, the future remains as unknown as ever. Even the most sophisticated forecasting techniques cannot reflect sudden, unanticipated changes. In fact, over the past twenty-five years, environmental complexity and change may well have outpaced improvements in forecasting techniques.[22] The totally unanticipated Gulf War, with its many consequences for businesses and other institutions, is a dramatic reminder of this point.

Simulations can be used to train employees. Here, interactive videodisck technology uses a touch-sensitive screen to upgrade technical skills at Bethlehem Steel.

Surfacing Assumptions

As we've seen, all planning techniques have limitations and pitfalls. An obvious one is that a plan can never be better than the assumptions on which it is based. The assumptions described in the Manager's Viewpoint feature about demand for picturephones and home banking in the 1980s were clearly invalid. And the plans that resulted proved disastrous.

The dialectical inquiry method and devil's advocacy method are two useful aids that assist managers in identifying and evaluating assumptions that may underlie plans, strategies, and practices. The assumptions surfaced and challenged aren't necessarily flawed or invalid, but that could be the case. For example, this process is likely to expose any political (hidden) agendas to manipulate outcomes for personal gain.

Dialectical Inquiry Method

dialectical inquiry method
A process for systematically examining strategic planning issues from two or more opposing points of view in order to analyze the underlying assumptions.

The **dialectical inquiry method** is a process for systematically examining strategic planning issues from two or more opposing points of view.[23] It's especially useful with problems that require innovative solutions.[24] This method is most effective in situations that have one or more of the following characteristics:

▶ Individuals can't agree on a process for developing a plan and strategies.
▶ Individuals don't know or can't agree on a clear definition of objectives, the factors under their control, or the factors beyond their control.
▶ Individuals must deal with two or more stakeholders (such as shareholders, suppliers, customers, employees, and government agencies) with vested and potentially conflicting interests.
▶ Individuals face states of nature that involve a condition of high risk or uncertainty.[25]

The dialectical inquiry method consists of four phases: identification phase, dialectical phase, consolidation phase, and strategy creation phase. Generally a group of from twelve to thirty people participate in the process. During part of each phase all the participants meet as a single group. Most of the activities, however, are undertaken by teams of three to five people. Each team member has a different area of responsibility, which might reflect product line, organization function (such as marketing, finance, production, or personnel), type of customers served, and so on.[26]

Identification Phase The identification phase is intended to reveal the participants' hidden or informal assumptions. An assumption is an underlying belief about a given issue, problem, or the future. The members of an electric utility who believe that their firm is a monopoly and in the business of providing electricity are likely to view problems and generate strategies quite differently from the employees at the same utility who believe that the firm has many competitors and is in the energy business.

The following sequence of tasks should get participants to reveal their assumptions:

1. State the proposed (or current) plan or strategy for dealing with the problem.
2. Identify any information that supports the plan, the strategy, or the definition of the problem.
3. Identify the underlying assumptions on which the plan or strategy or definition is based.

A *detailed* list of the underlying assumptions should be developed in order to ensure that nothing is being left out. This list should also include organizational and stakeholder objectives.[27]

Dialectical Phase The purpose of the dialectical phase is to identify opposing strategies and potential solutions. If necessary, the problem may also be redefined during this phase. The following sequence of tasks should be undertaken:

1. Engage in assumption negation; that is, challenge with an opposing assumption each assumption on which the strategy or plan was based.
2. Drop from consideration any opposing assumption that is unlikely.
3. Search for data to support the remaining opposing assumptions. These assumptions can serve as a basis for developing one or more entirely new strategies or plans.

The dialectical phase ends when the participants conclude that they can't identify any more plausible opposing assumptions and strategies.

Consolidation Phase The consolidation phase focuses on bringing together the diverse sets of assumptions generated in the first and second phases. A consolidated set of acceptable assumptions won't always emerge from this phase. If power is balanced among the participating stakeholders, the result could be a standoff. Or, the most powerful decision makers might impose their will. However, the following sequence of tasks can eventually lead to agreement:

1. If various stakeholders are participating in the process, form teams representing the major stakeholder groups.
2. Each stakeholder group ranks the sets of assumptions on two criteria: the relative importance of each assumption to their group, and the relative certainty of each assumption.
3. Each stakeholder group discusses the assumptions considered important but uncertain.
4. Each group is asked to modify its assumptions to the extent possible in order to arrive at a consensus.

Eventually, agreement on a set of assumptions (usually a set of compromise assumptions) can be achieved. The need to compromise on assumptions and the need to make decisions based on a new set of assumptions, which are likely to be quite different from these developed in the first place, makes this the most difficult phase.

Strategy Creation Phase When an acceptable set of assumptions has been developed, the strategy creation phase proceeds in a step-by-step manner, similar to the rational decision-making model. Decision-making techniques such as the payoff matrix or decision tree can be quite useful in this phase of the process.

The following Insight illustrates the use of the dialectical inquiry method in deciding whether to release a new product.

𝓘 N S I G H T

Managers of a division of a large corporation were thinking about releasing a new product. They focused on two questions: Should the new product be released? And, if so, what should the strategy for its release be?

Eighteen key people, including the CEO and company vice-presidents, were assembled for a three-day planning session. During the first meeting, the group was asked to name the major issues they assumed needed resolution. The group mentioned some sixty issues initially and finally agreed on fifteen key issues. Working teams were formed, based on individually preferred solutions to those fifteen issues.

Each team created a list of stakeholders, stated its assumptions, and rated the issues. Each team then produced a graph illustrating the degrees of importance and certainty it assigned each assumed issue. Meeting in a general session, the teams presented their results and debated their points of view. During intensive discussion, some issues were discarded because the group assigned and assumed low degrees of importance and/or high degrees of certainty to them. The group finally assigned priorities to only three key issues:

1. What should be the price of the product?
2. Should it be marketed directly or through dealers?
3. Will adequate funds for expansion be available from banks or a new stock issue?

Each of the teams spent nine months investigating these three issues. The group discussed and debated the results of these investigations in another planning session. The managers decided to release the new product, to market it directly, and to price it at $4000. Funds were obtained, production began, and the product had some success.

Using the dialectical inquiry method, the managers determined and evaluated the critical issues. They then identified, collected, and used relevant information. As a result, they based their decision and strategy on solid information, rather than guesswork.[28]

Assessment of Dialectical Inquiry There have been few well-designed studies of the effectiveness of the dialectical inquiry method. Although the method appears promising, its automatic use in many organizations is premature. It is designed to promote healthy conflict among participants in order to sharpen alternative points of view. But if the individuals involved are already engaged in power struggles and distrust each other, the dialectical inquiry method may well be ineffective. In this type of situation, it could deepen rather than resolve conflict. Like any planning aid, the dialectical inquiry method should not be applied across the board. This method is most likely to be effective in those situations involving a high degree of uncertainty and basic agreement on the organization's mission.[29]

Devil's Advocacy Method

devil's advocacy method
The process by which one person or team critiques a preferred plan or strategy in order to surface and challenge its assumptions.

In the **devil's advocacy method** one person within a decision-making group (the devil's advocate) is appointed to critique a preferred plan or strategy. The process is much simpler than that of the dialectical inquiry approach. The purpose, however, is the same—to stimulate constructive controversy as a means of surfacing and challenging assumptions.[30]

The devil's advocate acts like a good trial lawyer, presenting arguments against the majority position as convincingly as possible. He or she tries to punch holes in the assumptions underlying the plan, ferret out its internal inconsistencies, and reveal problems that may lead to its failure. Rather than have one person play the role of devil's advocate, another option is to form a team to play that role. The individual or team should remain sensitive to unpopular views and present the most reasonable case possible for alternative viewpoints and plans.

The Gould Company uses a version of this approach in evaluating companies to acquire. Each company it considers is analyzed by two teams, a green team and a red team. The green team argues for acquisition; the red team argues against it. The divergent results of their analyses are then presented to top management as input for a final decision.[31] In this application, there is no effort to have the two teams meet and resolve their differing perspectives. A third team—top management—does that.

The assessment of the dialectical inquiry method applies, for the most part, to the devil's advocacy method. Both approaches have been used effectively to improve planning and decision making. However, both can backfire if power struggles and distrust dominate relations among the participants.

MANAGEMENT BY OBJECTIVES

management by objectives (MBO) A philosophy of and approach to management that guides the planning process by helping managers integrate strategic and tactical plans.

Management by objectives (MBO) is both a philosophy of and an approach to management.[32] As a planning aid, it helps managers and teams integrate strategic and tactical planning.[33] More specifically, management by objectives provides a means for translating key organizational objectives and strategies into tactical plans and actions.

Philosophy and Management Style

Management by objectives reflects a positive philosophy about people and a participative management style. It has the following attributes:

▶ Mutual problem solving between individuals and teams at different organizational levels.
▶ Trusting and open communication.
▶ Emphasis on win-win relationships, in which both sides gain through cooperation.
▶ Rewards and promotions directly based on job-related and team-related performance and achievement.
▶ Minimal use of political games, fear, or force.
▶ A positive, proactive, and challenging organizational culture.

Unfortunately, many companies have implemented the procedural aspects of management by objectives in a top-down fashion and ignored its philosophical foundation. In such cases, management by objectives has acquired a bad reputation, unjustifiably because it wasn't implemented as intended.

There are five major purposes for employing the MBO approach:

1. To emphasize that there is *no single objective* for the organization, its departments, and teams, or its individual employees.

2. To stress that setting objectives and making tradeoffs among them *involves risk and uncertainty*.

3. To clarify objectives and their relative *priority*.

4. To enhance the *relationships* among organizational objectives, departmental objectives, team objectives, and individual job objectives.

5. To *focus* organizational resources and employees' energies and expenditures of time.

Setting Up and Linking of Objectives

Figure 9.3 outlines the basic MBO process. It consists of seven interconnected phases.[34] The distinguishing feature of management by objectives is the setting up and linking of objectives for the entire organization, its divisions and SBUs, departments, teams, and as many individual jobs as possible.[35] These objectives specify the quality and quantity of results expected within a certain period of time. Phases 1–3 of the MBO process should provide clear answers to two basic questions: "Why are we here?" and "If this is why we're here, what should we accomplish?" These phases will include managers, teams, and individual employees at different organizational levels.

Organizational Mission In phase 1 the organization's mission and broad objectives are set, usually by top management and the board of directors. They state what the organization is and what it is trying to become. This phase corresponds to the organizational mission and objectives task in strategic planning discussed in Chapter 8. Organizational objectives are often broad, general statements that change little, if at all, from one year to the next. You may recall from Chapter 8 that Chrysler's mission is to be a full-time manufacturer of passenger cars.

Strategic Objectives In phase 2 managers and teams develop more specific strategic objectives. These objectives are often more quantitative than general objectives and specify a time period for accomplishment. For example, a strategic objective might be increasing profits by 20 percent within three years. Strategic objectives are likely to be revised over time. You may recall from Chapter 8 that one of Chrysler's strategic objectives in 1990 was to replace virtually every one of its models between 1993 and 1996 with newly designed cars.

Departmental, Team, and Job Objectives In phase 3 middle to first-line managers develop tactical objectives for departments and teams. These support the strategic objectives. For example, one objective of the production department might be to reduce electrical consumption by 10 percent over the next twelve months.

Figure 9.4 illustrates in detail the relationship between an organization's strategic objectives (left-hand side) and the tactical objectives (right-hand side) of selected functional departments such as marketing, production, and personnel. These specific tactical objectives are a step toward implementing the strategic objectives and are consistent with the hierarchy-of-objectives concept presented in Chapter 6.

Also in phase 3 first-line managers and employees develop individual job objectives. For example, a machine operator's objective might be to reduce waste and

FIGURE 9.3

The Basic MBO Process

Management by objectives is an approach that integrates strategic planning and tactical planning. Moreover, it serves as a means for translating tactical plans into day-to-day decisions and actions. As with any process, the effectiveness is highly influenced by the organization's underlying philosophy and management style. As suggested by the arrows, effort must be two-way in order to achieve long-term effectiveness.

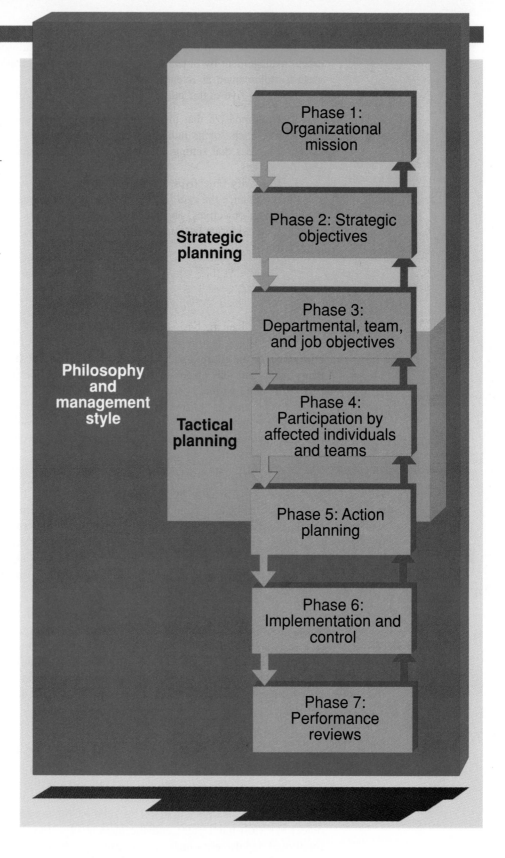

spoilage from 6 percent to 5 percent within the next six months. Those objectives that can only be achieved through team effort (which is frequently the case with product or service quality) can be established by the team as a whole. Many organizations don't set objectives for individuals who perform highly routine jobs, such as assembly-line

FIGURE 9.4

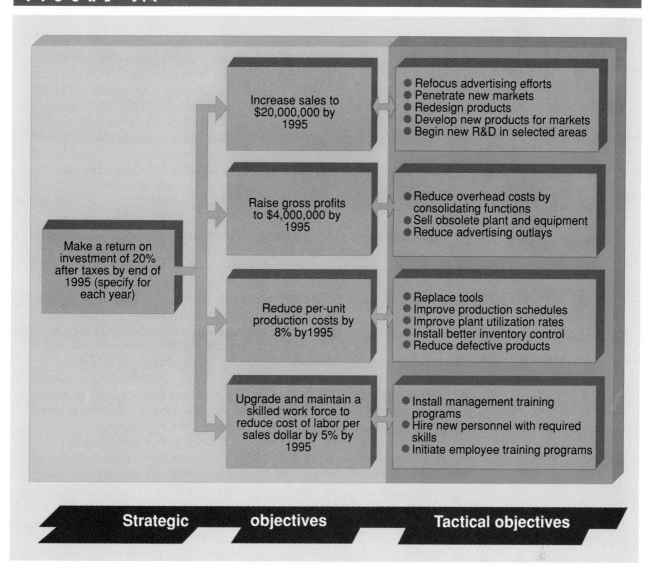

Strategic objectives   **Tactical objectives**

Linking Strategic and Tactical Objectives

For MBO to be effective, organization members must spend considerable time and thought linking up strategic objectives and tactical objectives. Effective linking requires mutual problem solving within teams and among individuals, both across departments and between organizational levels. The exclusive use of top-down, one-way objective setting rarely works.

Source: Adapted from G. A. Steiner, *Strategic Planning* (New York: Free Press, 1979), 167–170.

work. In these kinds of jobs, individual employees may have little choice or control over how their work is performed or the pace at which they work. Their production rates depend on the speed of the line and how well the assemblers preceding them have done their jobs.

The following account of Cypress Semiconductor Corporation, a chipmaker in California's Silicon Valley, describes an enthusiastic application of managing by objectives. As you read this Insight, think about how you would evaluate Cypress's use of the basic MBO process, shown in Figure 9.3.

INSIGHT

Among the pictures, plaques, and other objects lining the wall behind T. J. Rodger's desk, one sign in scribbled script stands out: "Be Realistic—Demand the Impossible." It's a joke—but not really. Rodgers is president and CEO of Cypress Semiconductor Corporation, the hot Silicon Valley chipmaker he started in 1983; his drive and passion for details are already legendary.

As proof, Cypress managers and employees need look no further than the intricate, computerized MBO system Rodgers expects them to master—what he calls "turbo MBO." It's a system that painstakingly sets thousands of objectives for all of Cypress's 1400 employees every single week and then relentlessly monitors how well those objectives are being met. In any given week, 6000 objectives in the data base come due.

Cypress uses the system to keep track of the seemingly countless tasks involved in manufacturing a semiconductor. Attention to detail is vital at a company that produces 160 complex, state-of-the-art chips. "A semiconductor is a very unforgiving entity," Rodgers explains. "If it takes 1000 tasks to make one and you do 999 right but then you forget one or do one wrong, the semiconductor won't work. Our system forces management to stick its nose in a big book every single week and find out what is going on. We can't afford surprises."

Every Monday morning begins the same way. Project leaders, who may or may not be managers, sit down with the members of their project team and map out all jobs for the week. This task can be as simple as ordering a file cabinet or as complex as making crucial last-minute changes in the circuitry of a new chip. The teams also outline how the tasks will be done. Some employees might go to three project meetings a week and agree to accomplish specific objectives at each one. All the new objectives for the week are put into the computer.

On Tuesday mornings all forty managers sit down at their computers and review the objectives set on Monday for all the employees they supervise. They fine-tune their priorities, making sure that no one is overburdened with work and that key projects are moving ahead fastest, and update the computerized information.

Rodgers meets with his seven vice presidents each Wednesday afternoon. The executives first review the status of all the managers' objectives. Any manager who is behind on more than 35 percent of his or her objectives is "spotlighted," and the appropriate vice president is asked to explain. (If a delinquency persists, the vice president must sit down with the manager and remedy the problems.) Next, all the vice presidents are scrutinized. Any who are behind on more than 20 percent of their objectives are spotlighted. (Rodgers keeps track of their progress and takes corrective action as necessary.) The rest of the meeting focuses on the status of objectives for critical projects. Says Rodgers: "We're constantly whipping out our printouts and asking, 'Where do things stand?'" By the end of the meeting computerized objectives have been fine-tuned yet again.[36]

Goals and Criteria for Setting Objectives Objectives provide standards against which effectiveness can be evaluated, or measured. For example, a sales manager's specific objectives for the year might be to increase sales by 5 percent, maintain private-label sales at 7 percent of total sales, and hold advertising expenses at last year's level. All of these provide clear quantitative standards against which performance can be measured. The sales manager's more general objectives for the year might be to develop a quota system for all salespeople, prepare and recommend an incentive compensation system for area managers, and shift the advertising emphasis from wholesalers to consumers. Although not as quantitative as the specific objectives, these are also clear standards to which results can be compared.

Setting objectives includes identifying specific areas of team or job responsibility and standards of performance.[37] When setting objectives, participants should consider the following advice:

▶ Objectives should be specific enough to have significance for the department, team, and employee. A poor objective would be ''to maximize the welfare of the firm and of society.'' A better one would be ''to achieve an 8 percent sales increase for 1993, while maintaining the gross profit margin of 40 percent on all sales.''

▶ Objectives should normally be broad enough to keep the employee or team from having to concentrate on dozens of day-to-day objectives.

▶ Decision making should not get so embroiled in political power struggles and conflicts that efforts to set clear objectives become futile. For example, using the dialectical inquiry method in a power struggle setting may actually inflame conflicts.

Participation

As suggested by phase 4 of Figure 9.3, management by objectives requires broad participation by individuals and teams in the setting of objectives. When objectives are established and implemented exclusively from the top down, management by objectives exists in name only. In such a situation lower-level individuals and teams come to view the management by objectives process as a system of measurement and control, rather than one of planning and motivation.[38] If top management uses management by objectives only to pressure individuals or departments to perform better, they can expect failure or only limited success.

Of course, some objectives have to come from the top.[39] For example, the U.S. Environmental Protection Agency has required that companies achieve environmental objectives within a specified period of time or pay stiff fines. Consequently, top management may require that managers and employees set objectives relating to environmental hazards within their departments.

When a superior and subordinate are setting objectives, they will ideally agree on the objectives the subordinate will attempt to achieve in a specific period of time, the general actions (tactics) to be taken by the subordinate to accomplish the objectives, and how progress toward the objectives will be measured and the specific dates for such measurements.[40] Even if they can't agree on all of these aspects, the process of setting objectives normally leads to higher performance than if no objectives are set.[41]

Action Planning

In phase 5 of the basic MBO process managers and teams develop action plans for accomplishing the desired objectives. For example, a strategic objective of the vice president of marketing might be to increase sales volume by 10 percent within twelve months. To achieve this objective, the vice president might develop the following tactical action plan with his or her subordinates:

1. Release new product Z, developed to supplement the product line, within six months.

2. Evaluate the feasibility of a price reduction to stimulate demand for products X and Y within three months.

3. Increase the specific sales volume targets of sales personnel in Los Angeles, Dallas, and New York by 10 percent.

4. Increase the on-time delivery for products X and Y by 5 percent within four months.[42]

The extent to which employees are involved in developing an action plan varies. Developing a departmental action plan might involve discussion by a team consisting of the departmental manager and most employees.[43] On the other hand, an action plan to achieve an individual's job objectives might be developed by the individual and submitted to his or her superior for review and comment.

Implementation and Control

Phase 6 of the MBO process involves translating tactical plans into day-to-day actions that will lead to the attainment of the stated objectives. Management by objectives allows individuals and teams freedom in performing their tasks. Managers should be available to coach and counsel subordinates, as needed, to help them reach objectives but should not control their every activity. Teams and individuals must be trusted to work effectively toward agreed-on objectives. At the same time they must feel free to discuss problems with their superiors or others who can help them. The Insight detailing the MBO system at Cypress Semiconductor illustrated an effective implementation and control phase; the following Insight illustrates the need to go beyond the mere setting of objectives with subordinates in order to be effective.

INSIGHT

Mike Gantz knew he was in trouble. After only two years as vice president of marketing and sales at Acme Products, his boss had just suggested that he resign. Actually, Gantz had seen it coming. Prior to coming to Acme, Gantz had earned an excellent reputation as the best division sales manager in a large, diversified industrial firm. He credited much of his success to a highly participative management style. In implementing management by objectives, for example, he had actively involved his subordinates in setting objectives and granted them considerable latitude in meeting those objectives. This approach produced a highly motivated and productive team of subordinates.

Gantz had been recruited to work the same magic at Acme Products, one of his former division's competitors. The results of his considerable efforts had been very disappointing. After two years of his leadership, Acme lost almost as much market share as top management had expected Gantz to gain. Customer dissatisfaction was at an all-time high, and turnover of salespeople had nearly tripled. As far as Acme Products was concerned, Gantz was a disaster and had to go!

Most of the managers reporting to Gantz at Acme did not have the abilities or initiative of his previous subordinates. Acme did not have the well-developed personnel, financial, and marketing systems that Gantz had grown accustomed to in his previous job. And Acme's corporate culture was very different as well. Extensive participation and trust had been the norm at Gantz's previous firm, but his new subordinates were used to being told exactly what to do and then followed closely to make sure they were actually doing it right.

How could a manager with a proven record fail so badly? Gantz's problem probably came about in large measure from his failure to diagnose the situation and recognize the difference in the capabilities and expectations of his new subordinates. He should have chosen MBO practices appropriate to this new and different situation and emphasized being a supportive resource and coach, providing more directive and decisive leadership.[44]

Performance Reviews

The last phase in the MBO process calls for systematic reviews to measure progress, identify and resolve problems, and revise (drop or add) objectives. If these performance

After objectives have been agreed upon, they become the basis for the *performance appraisal* process. Ideally, performance appraisal is mutual problem-solving between manager and employee.

reviews are conducted properly, managers, teams, and individual employees can learn significant lessons from the immediate past and apply those lessons to future decisions and actions.[45]

Objectives that have been agreed on form the basis of the review process. Management by objectives emphasizes that individual subordinates and teams must review their own performance and actively participate in evaluating it. Ideally, performance appraisal is mutual problem solving by the manager and team or subordinate: The manager encourages the subordinate to identify obstacles or problems that affected the achievement of his or her objectives and to suggest ways to improve performance. Thus performance reviews provide feedback to individual employees or teams, letting them know how well they are achieving agreed-on objectives. Knowledge of results is essential to improved performance. This MBO method of evaluation is considerably different from subjective evaluation of subordinates' personality traits and personal characteristics in terms such as *conscientious, enthusiastic,* and *creative.*[46]

Unfortunately, however, the review process isn't always so simple. For example, two objectives of a furniture salesperson may be an 8 percent sales increase and a 40 percent average markup on goods sold during the next year. Sales figures tell the salesperson how well he or she is doing in meeting these objectives, but factors beyond the salesperson's control can influence results. These factors might include the general state of the economy, store location and hours, advertising campaigns, and credit availability.

Similarly, performance in many managerial jobs can't be easily measured. Homer Wilson, vice-president of operations at Hoechst Celanese Chemical Company, has said that one of his objectives is to build morale and develop people's careers. This type of general objective must be evaluated on the basis of judgment. The manager must decide whether the objective was achieved before he or she can ask why it was—or wasn't.[47]

The MBO process calls on superiors to shift from being just judgmental and critical to being helpful and willing to engage in mutual problem solving. Some managers interpret this type of performance evaluation and the whole MBO process as ''soft.'' Quite the contrary! People have been demoted, dismissed, and otherwise held fully accountable under this system; however, the bases for such actions are less subjective. With management by objectives, managers should be able to make demotions or dismissal decisions more easily when corrective actions have failed.[48] Moreover, the MBO process is intended to minimize the need for formal disciplinary action.

The following Insight focuses on the performance review aspects of the MBO system used at Boehringer Mannheim Corporation, an Indianapolis-headquartered health care company with approximately 2500 employees. The firm produces medical diagnostic equipment, implant devices, orthopedic implant devices, and pharmaceuticals.

INSIGHT

To emphasize that management by objectives wouldn't be a one-shot program, efforts were made at Boehringer Mannheim to build in follow-up and follow-through. Shortly after attending training sessions, each employee met with a consultant for individualized counseling on objective setting. Conducted with complete confidentiality, these sessions gave each person help in grappling with the task of setting objectives for his or her job.

A basic ground rule was that everyone's objectives would be reviewed formally by a superior at quarterly intervals. The review would note whether an employee was on target, below target, or above target for each objective. It would also point out when an individual's objectives might need modification because of changing, uncontrollable external factors. The individual is assured that four times a year he or she will have the opportunity to meet with the boss, review progress toward objectives, and receive help if needed.

Performance appraisal and reward systems were modified to make them consistent with and supportive of the program. The annual performance review process was redesigned to focus on improving future performance, not merely on recording the past.

Each person was responsible for meeting the basic requirements of his or her regular job. In addition, the individual and superior identified a few achievement areas that were most critical to the organization's objectives. "Stretch" was built into an objective in each of these areas. For example, a production manager had the traditional targets of filling production quotas, meeting delivery schedules, achieving quality levels, controlling costs, and so forth. She also, however, set stretch objectives to help engineering cut the time required to get a new product on line; implement a new, computerized order-tracking system; and devise a materials-handling system that reduces costs below mandated levels. A cash incentive bonus was tied to attaining stretch objectives. Special recognition awards were also created, to provide financial rewards to those who weren't eligible for a bonus. Employees quickly realized they were not only being paid for their regular job but also being given an opportunity to earn additional rewards, directly related to individual stretch.[49]

Assessment of MBO

Research findings on the effectiveness of MBO systems are mixed. Management by objectives is often difficult to evaluate because neither the philosophy nor the phases outlined in Figure 9.3 are fully implemented. However, two contrasting views of management by objectives have emerged:

▶ The MBO programs most likely to be successful are characterized by (1) emphasis on setting objectives, (2) frequent communication and feedback between subordinates, teams, and managers regarding progress toward objectives, stumbling blocks, or the need to revise objectives, and (3) opportunities for individual subordinates and teams to participate in setting their objectives.[50]

▶ When management by objectives is used as a top-down club to control people, it is likely to be ineffective. If the values of those in the organization are strongly antagonistic to its philosophy and expected management style, then it is probably doomed to failure.

Managers who have a good grasp of the purpose and philosophy of management by objectives should be able to reduce paperwork and the amount of time spent supervising nitty-gritty, day-to-day tasks. However, some managers focus on MBO procedures without adequately understanding or accepting the MBO philosophy. These managers are so impressed with the logical, rational flow of the process that they continue developing it in great detail. The resulting avalanche of paperwork leads to information overload and clogged decision-making channels.[51] Such frustrating situations occur all too frequently. Management by objectives is not a cure-all for solving management problems, but its potential benefits justify serious consideration.

PROJECT MANAGEMENT

project A one-time activity with a well-defined set of desired results.

project management The processes, techniques, and concepts used to run a project and achieve its objectives.

A **project** is a one-time activity with a well-defined set of desired results. Other characteristics of a project include a clear start and finish, a time frame for completion, uniqueness, an involvement of a number of people on an ad-hoc basis, a limited set of resources (people, money, and time), and sequencing of activities and phases. **Project management** refers to the processes, techniques, and concepts used to run a project and achieve its objectives. The essentials of project management can be applied to projects as simple as developing a thirty-page business plan in an entrepreneurship course or as complex as constructing a sixty-story office tower.[52]

Program Evaluation and Review Technique (PERT)

One of the useful aids in project management is the **program evaluation and review technique (PERT).** It is a special technique that shows diagrammatically the sequence of activities and events required to reach an overall project objective. In its first major application, in 1958, PERT was used in the U.S. Navy's ballistic missile program, more popularly known as the Polaris missile program. The Navy's prime contractor cited PERT as a major reason for completing the program two years ahead of the original schedule. Several government agencies now require companies with which they have contracts to use PERT. This technique is normally used for one-of-a-kind projects (such as Disney World and Epcot Center), projects that involve a new production process (such as a robotic auto plant), or those that require interlocking processes (such as tract housing). Project managers use PERT to analyze and specify in detail what is to be done, when it is to be done, and the likelihood of achieving the objective on time. As commonly used in practice, PERT consists of four major elements: (1) a network, (2) a critical path, (3) resource allocations, and (4) cost and time considerations.[53]

program evaluation and review technique (PERT) A project management aid that shows diagrammatically the sequence of activities and events required to reach an overall project objective.

Network A **PERT network** is a diagram showing the sequence and relationships of the activities and events needed to complete a whole project. As shown in Figure 9.5, events (the boxes) are points where decisions are made or activities are completed. Activities (the arrows) are the physical or mental tasks performed in order to move from one event to another. The network is the foundation of the PERT approach. To build one, the project team must identify key project activities, determine their sequence, decide who will be responsible for each activity, and calculate the amount of time needed to accomplish each. The network diagram identifies the relationship among the sequence of events and the activities. For example, the arrows in Figure 9.5 show that event 3 cannot occur until activities A, B, and C have been accomplished. A PERT network makes it visually obvious that the different managers or teams responsible for the various activities must coordinate their work.

PERT network The diagram showing the sequence and relationships of the activities and events needed to complete a project.

Critical Path Every project follows paths, or sequences of events and activities. A complex project like the construction of Disney World and Epcot Center consists of thousands of activities and hundreds of paths. Work goes on concurrently along each separate path. Of course, with such huge projects it's common to have a master PERT

FIGURE 9.5

Basic PERT Network

The critical path is shown by the wide-band arrows. It is the sequence of activities with the longest elapsed time, the one that determines the length of the entire project. To cut project time, the project team needs to focus on the critical path.

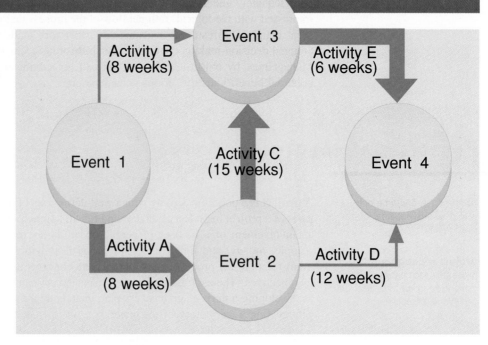

critical path The path through a PERT network with the longest elapsed time, which determines the length of the entire project.

network and individual PERT networks for each facility. The **critical path** is the path with the longest elapsed time, the one that determines the length of the entire project. Therefore, to shorten the time for project completion, the project team must give the most attention to activities along the critical path.

The bold arrows in Figure 9.5 identify the critical path, which requires a total elapsed time of twenty-nine weeks. This time equals the sum of the number of weeks scheduled for completing activities between events 1 and 2, events 2 and 3, and events 3 and 4. Any delay in activity completion along the critical path will cause a delay in project completion.

Resource Allocation In order to undertake the necessary activities, project teams require a variety of resources. Resource availability greatly influences the length of time between events and the costs associated with each activity. Project leaders must estimate types and amounts of required materials, equipment, facilities, and human resources as accurately as possible. For example, the first major activity in constructing a house is excavating and pouring footings. A contractor might estimate that a house without a basement will require one backhoe, one backhoe operator, and three laborers for four days, as well as sand for fill, wood for concrete forms, steel reinforcing rods, and concrete.

Cost and Time Of value to management is PERT's ability to help reduce cost and time. The project team prepares cost estimates for each activity (task), such as excavating and pouring footings for a house. Similarly, time estimates are made for each activity. For example, Figure 9.5 shows that activity A *should* take eight weeks.

Four time estimates are often made for each activity.[54] The *most likely time* is the estimated time required to complete an activity, taking into consideration normal problems and interruptions. The *optimistic time* is the estimated time required to complete an activity if virtually no problems occur, if everything goes right. The *pessimistic time* is the estimated time required to complete an activity if unusual problems and interruptions occur. Given Murphy's law, the assumption is that major problems will arise, although even the pessimistic estimate doesn't normally take into account rare, catastrophic events, such as fires, tornadoes, floods, and war. The

Part of the *PERT network* for new projects at Walt Disney World is the construction of models like this planned shopping, dining, and entertainment center near the Disney Yacht and Beach Club hotels.

expected time represents a weighted average of the most likely, optimistic, and pessimistic time estimates.

By developing alternative time estimates, the project team can anticipate and react quickly to problems or opportunities. If an activity is running behind schedule, it might be advantageous to have people work overtime or hire additional people; if an activity is ahead of schedule, the project leader might speed up delivery of supplies needed for later activities. But if a PERT network has not been made, it might not be obvious to project leaders that further action is required.

After a project is underway, PERT becomes a control mechanism. Using PERT's reporting procedures, a project team can monitor differences between actual and planned times and costs for each activity.

The following Insight describes an application of PERT to the construction of a modest single-story house with no basement.

I NSIGHT

In planning the construction of a house, the contractor has to determine (1) the major activities to be performed, (2) the time required for each activity, (3) the sequence in which the activities must be completed, and (4) the manpower needed for each activity. Table 9.1 shows a contractor's estimates. The list of nineteen major activities is presented roughly in the sequence required for project completion. Each activity could be broken down further if the contractor wanted more detail. The total expected time is shown in regular working days; that is, it doesn't include weekends and legal holidays.

A PERT network based on Table 9.1 is shown in the figure. This network contains the major job activities (A,B,C, . . . , S), the sequence of those activities, and the expected number of days between the beginning of one job activity and the next. The circles designate events. Circle E1 represents the project beginning, circle E2 represents completion of excavation and footings, and so on to circle E16, which represents project completion.

The wide arrows in the figure indicate the critical path. The critical path totals 49 working days.

FIGURE 9.6

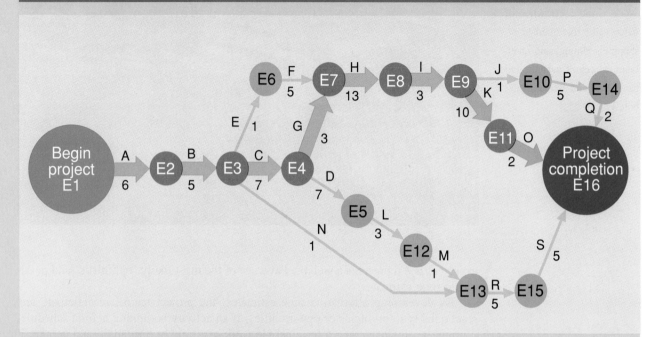

Simplified PERT Diagram for Constructing a House

$$A(6) + B(5) + C(7) + G(3) + H(13) + I(3) + K(10) + O(2) = 49 \text{ days}$$

Thus it will take about 10 weeks, or $2\frac{1}{2}$ months, including weekends and holidays, to complete the house. If the contractor wants to reduce overall construction time, he or she must reduce the amount of time required for activities along the critical path.

Assessment of PERT Most useful when projects are complex and require tight coordination, PERT helps reduce project time and costs under the following conditions:

▶ The project consists of a well-defined collection of job activities.

▶ The job activities may be started and stopped independently of one another. Continuous-flow processes, such as oil refining, where jobs or operations follow each other in a strict time sequence day after day, don't lend themselves to the use of PERT.

▶ The job activities are ordered; that is, they must be performed in a particular sequence or often in multiple simultaneous sequences that create complex networks. For instance, the foundation of a house must be laid before the walls are erected.[55]

As with other decision and planning aids, there are a number of PC-compatible and mainframe software systems for PERT and other project management aids. For example, Open Plan, provided by Welcom Software Technology, enables the user to handle projects with up to 100,000 activities. (Of course, this software version is too large to be run on a PC.) Open Plan creates easy-to-read graphics and can provide up to 256 calendar schedules per project. There are a variety of other features—such as cost scheduling and control—with Open Plan and similar project management software systems.

Ethics in Project Management

Like so many professional areas, project management has been concerned with ethical behaviors and decisions in recent years. Much of this attention has been directed through

TABLE 9.1

PERT Activities and Times for Constructing a House

Job Activity	Description of Activity	Immediate Preceding Activity	Expected Work Time (Days)	Expected Slack Time (Days)	Total Expected Time (Days)	Labor Needed
A	Excavate, pour footings	—	4	2	6	1 backhoe operator, 2 laborers
B	Pour concrete foundation	A	2	3	5	1 carpenter, 2 laborers
C	Erect frame and roof	B	4	3	7	5 carpenters, 5 laborers
D	Lay brickwork	C	6	1	7	3 masons, 2 laborers
E	Install drains	B	1	0	1	2 plumbers, 1 laborer
F	Install plumbing	E	3	2	5	2 plumbers, 1 laborer
G	Install wiring	C	2	1	3	3 electricians
H	Fasten plaster and plasterboard	F, G	10	3	13	2 laborers, 1 finisher
I	Lay finished flooring	H	3	0	3	2 carpenters
J	Install kitchen equipment	I	1	0	1	2 carpenters
K	Finish carpentry	I	7	3	10	2 carpenters
L	Finish roofing and flashing	D	2	1	3	4 roofers
M	Fasten gutters and downspouts	L	1	0	1	2 laborers
N	Lay storm drains	B	1	0	1	1 backhoe operator, 4 laborers
O	Sand and varnish floors	K	2	0	2	1 painter
P	Paint	J	3	2	5	2 painters
Q	Finish electrical work	P	2	0	2	2 electricians
R	Finish grading	M, N	2	3	5	3 laborers
S	Pour walks; landscape	R	5	0	5	1 landscape gardener, 2 laborers

Source: J. D. Wiest and F. K. Levy, *A Management Guide to PERT/CPM,* © 1969, pp. 16–20. Adapted by permission of Prentice-Hall, Inc., Englewood Cliffs, N.J.

the Project Management Institute, a nonprofit professional organization dedicated to advancing the state of the art in project management. It publishes *Project Management Journal* and the *PM Network*. In addition, the association champions a code of ethics for the project management profession. The following is an excerpt from it.

Project management professionals shall, in their work:

Provide the necessary project leadership to promote maximum productivity while striving to minimize costs.

Apply state-of-the-art project management tools and techniques to ensure that quality, cost, and time objectives, as set forth in the project plan, are met.

Treat fairly all project team members, colleagues, and co-workers, regardless of race, religion, sex, age, or national origin.

Protect project team members from physical and mental harm.

Seek, accept, and offer honest criticism of work and properly credit the contribution of others.

Assist project team members, colleagues, and co-workers in their professional development.[56]

These ethical codes are relevant to team leaders of any type of project, including student group projects.

1. Forecasting, an important early part of planning, is the process of estimating future events or conditions in an organization's environment. Three important forecasting aids are scenarios, the Delphi technique, and simulations. Scenarios are written descriptions of possible futures. The Delphi technique uses a process of consensus building among experts to arrive at estimates of future events and conditions. Simulations are models of real systems that permit the testing of alternatives, often on a computer.

2. The dialectical inquiry method and the devil's advocacy method are useful aids for surfacing and challenging assumptions. The dialectical inquiry method is a team process that involves systematically examining issues from opposing points of view. The devil's advocacy method involves a critique of a preferred plan or strategy by one person or team.

3. Management by objectives (MBO) is both a philosophy of and an approach to management. It guides and implements the planning process via seven basic phases: (1) organizational mission, (2) strategic objectives, (3) departmental, team, and job objectives, (4) participation by affected teams and individuals, (5) action planning, (6) implementation and control; and (7) performance reviews.

4. Project management refers to the processes, techniques, and concepts used to run a project and achieve its objectives. One useful project management aid is the program evaluation and review technique (PERT). PERT has four major elements: (1) network, (2) critical path, (3) resource allocation, and (4) cost and time estimates.

1. It's September 1998, and the Joneses have settled down for an evening at the tube. Joe Jones aims his remote control zapper at a 3-by-5 screen across the room and taps in a three-digit code to call up the fifth rerun of his all-time favorite flick, *Rambo XIII*. The family doesn't drive to a videocassette rental store for a movie anymore, and the number of such outlets is shrinking. Of course, there is network TV for free, but nothing much there grabs the Joneses tonight. It's time for a rerun of Rambo. Or almost anything else on film the Joneses can think of. It's all there— thousands of shows—ready to be punched up by computer. Welcome to the impending age of fiber-optic TV. Welcome to the fast-developing wonders of electronic switching systems. Watch out, investors in cable systems. Be alert, those of you who use TV for marketing purposes. Technology is about to change your worlds.[57]

   Do you agree with this forecast? Why? What argument(s) can be offered in support of this scenario? In opposition?

2. Reread the Global Link feature describing the Pan-Pacific scenario. Develop a scenario based on assumptions opposing those stated for this scenario.

3. What are some of the benefits of multiple scenarios?

4. What are some dangers of the consensus-building process? How does the Delphi technique avoid them?

5. What are the similarities and differences between the Delphi technique and simulations? Explain.

6. **From Where You Sit:** Identify a team situation you have been in within the past year that might have benefited from the use of the devil's advocacy method or the dialectical inquiry method. How would you have implemented either of these methods?

7. **From Where You Sit:** What would you like or dislike about Cypress's MBO system if you worked there?

8. **From Where You Sit:** How might the MBO process have made a difference in your last job? Which phases would you likely have been involved in?

9. **From Where You Sit:** For two projects you have been engaged in within the past six months, list the characteristics that made the activity a project.

10. **From Where You Sit:** Use the program evaluation and review technique (PERT) to develop an action plan for your successful completion of the next academic year.

EXPERIENCING MANAGEMENT

SKILL-BUILDING EXERCISE

Job Objectives Questionnaire

Each of us has certain objectives that are part of our work. Sometimes these objectives are spelled out in detail; at other times the objectives are simply intuitively "understood." The following statements refer to your job and to the objectives that are associated with your job. Read each statement and then write next to it the number from the scale below that best describes how true you feel the statement to be. (If you prefer, you can think about a job you've had in the past.) You may want to use a separate sheet of paper to record your responses.

				Scale			
−3	−2	−1		0	1	2	3
Definitely Not True	Not True	Somewhat Not True		Uncertain	Somewhat True	True	Definitely True

1. Management encourages employees to define job objectives.

2. If I achieve my objectives, I receive adequate recognition from my superior.

3. My objectives are clearly stated with respect to the results expected.

4. I have the support I need to accomplish my objectives.

5. Achieving my objectives increases my chances for promotion.

6. My superior doesn't dictate my job objectives to me.

7. I don't need more feedback on whether or not I'm achieving my objectives.

8. My superior will "get on my back" if I fail to achieve my objectives.

9. My job objectives are very challenging.

10. Management wants to know whether or not I set objectives for my job.

11. My superior will compliment me if I achieve my job objectives.

12. My objectives are very clear.

13. I have the necessary authority to accomplish my objectives.

14. Achievement of objectives is rewarded with higher pay here.

15. My superior encourages me to establish my own objectives.

16. I'm kept informed of my progress toward my objectives.

17. My superior will reprimand me if I'm not making progress toward my objectives.

18. Achieving my objectives requires my full interest and effort.

19. Management makes it clear that defining job objectives is favorably regarded.

20. My superior gives me more recognition when I achieve my objectives.

21. My objectives are very concrete.

22. I have sufficient resources to achieve my objectives.

23. My pay is more likely to be increased if I achieve my objectives.

24. My superior has less influence than I do in setting my objectives.

25. I have good knowledge of whether I'm achieving my objectives.

26. If I fail to meet my objectives, my superior will reprimand me.

27. Attaining my objectives requires all my skill and know how.

Job Objectives Scoring Key. You score your responses to the Job Objectives Questionnaire as follows: For each of the nine "scales" (A through I), compute a total score by summing the answers to the appropriate questions. Be sure to *subtract* minus scores.

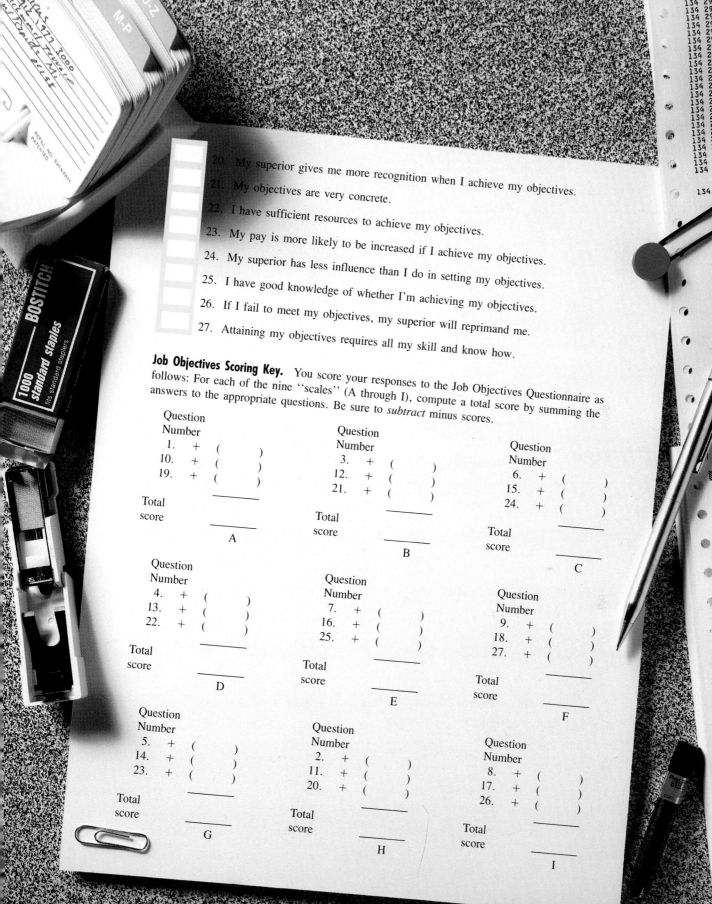

Question Number	
1.	+ ( )
10.	+ ( )
19.	+ ( )

Total score ___

A

Question Number	
3.	+ ( )
12.	+ ( )
21.	+ ( )

Total score ___

B

Question Number	
6.	+ ( )
15.	+ ( )
24.	+ ( )

Total score ___

C

Question Number	
4.	+ ( )
13.	+ ( )
22.	+ ( )

Total score ___

D

Question Number	
7.	+ ( )
16.	+ ( )
25.	+ ( )

Total score ___

E

Question Number	
9.	+ ( )
18.	+ ( )
27.	+ ( )

Total score ___

F

Question Number	
5.	+ ( )
14.	+ ( )
23.	+ ( )

Total score ___

G

Question Number	
2.	+ ( )
11.	+ ( )
20.	+ ( )

Total score ___

H

Question Number	
8.	+ ( )
17.	+ ( )
26.	+ ( )

Total score ___

I

On the following graphs circle the total score for each scale. The higher the score, the more effective the organization is in applying that particular concept of management by objectives.

A	Management emphasis on objectives	−9	−7	−5	−3	−1		1	3	5	7	9
B	Clarity of objectives	−9	−7	−5	−3	−1		1	3	5	7	9
C	Participation in setting objectives	−9	−7	−5	−3	−1		1	3	5	7	9
D	Control over resources	−9	−7	−5	−3	−1		1	3	5	7	9
E	Knowledge of results	−9	−7	−5	−3	−1		1	3	5	7	9
F	Challenge of objectives	−9	−7	−5	−3	−1		1	3	5	7	9
G	Contingent material reward	−9	−7	−5	−3	−1		1	3	5	7	9
H	Contingent personal reward	−9	−7	−5	−3	−1		1	3	5	7	9
I	Contingent personal punishment	−9	−7	−5	−3	−1		1	3	5	7	9

TO: Mary Youngblood
FROM: Clint Slocum, President
SUBJECT: Managing cultural diversity

According to several recent demographic studies, changes in the economy will be matched by changes in the work force and the jobs it will perform. These studies forecast major demographic shifts in five areas by the year 2000.

1. The population and work force will grow more slowly than at any time since the 1930s. Population growth, which was climbing at almost 1.9 percent per year in the 1950s, will slump to only 0.7 percent per year by 2000; the labor force, which exploded by 2.9 percent per year in the 1970s, will be expanding by only 1 percent annually in the 1990s.

2. The average age of the population and the work force will rise, and the pool of young workers entering the labor market will shrink. As the baby boom ages and the baby bust enters the work force, the average age of the work force will climb from 36 today to 39 by the year 2000. The number of young workers aged 16 to 24 will drop by almost 2 million, or 8 percent.

3. More women will enter the work force. Almost two-thirds of the new entrants into the work force between now and the year 2000 will be women, and 61 percent of all women of working age are expected to have jobs by 2000.

4. Minorities will be a larger share of new entrants into the labor force. Non-whites will make up 29 percent of the new entrants, between now and 2000, twice their current share.

5. Immigrants will represent the largest share of the increase in the population and the work force since the First World War. Even with the new immigration law, it is projected that approximately 600,000 legal and illegal immigrants will enter the United States annually throughout the balance of the century. Two-thirds or more of the immigrants of working age are likely to join the labor force.

These demographic shifts mean that the new workers entering the work force between now and 2000 will be much different from current employees. Let's assume these forecasts are true. What do you see as the major implications of these changes for most organizations in the year 2000? I'd like you to put your response in a memo to be passed out at one of our upcoming executive meetings. I'm hoping it will trigger a companywide questioning of our assumptions and practices in relation to these demographic shifts.

Question: Assume you are Mary Youngblood, devil's advocate. Compose a memo that identifies five major implications of these demographic shifts for the management of any organization—not just your own firm.

Life-Cycle Analysis Measures Greenness, But Results May Not Be Black and White

BY DAVID STIPP

Good grief, it always does look greener on the other side.

Last June, a study by environmental consultant Franklin Associates Ltd. indicated polystyrene "foam" containers were getting a bad rap—paper alternatives, it seemed, eat more energy, pollute more and create more trash by weight than foam ones do.

But environmentalists countered that the foam resists biodegrading and makes more trash by volume than paper does. Heeding them, McDonald's Corp. in November said it would phase out foam.

But then this month, the journal Science published a study by a Canadian chemistry professor suggesting foam cups are better for the environment than paper ones.

So which side really is greener?

The best hope to answer that is "life-cycle analysis"—the toting up of every environmental risk associated with making, using and disposing of products. In principle, it's the ultimate measuring stick to set the record straight on the nitty-gritty environmental choices consumers face. In practice, it's becoming spin controllers' favorite joystick.

"It's unfortunate that life-cycle analysis has been picked up by ad and marketing people," says Bruce Vigon, an expert on the analyses at Battelle, a research institute in Columbus, Ohio. Formerly, corporate technical types did most such studies for internal use, aiming to cut manufacturing waste and to do the right thing environmentally, he says. Now that green is in, marketers are seizing the life-cycle initiative—and often playing down, distorting or quietly sending to landfills findings that undercut their pitches.

Consider the foam fracas. After McDonald's said it would phase out foam packages, polystyrene proponents counterattacked by wheeling out the Franklin study, which was sponsored by the Council for Solid Waste Solutions, a plastics industry group. On newspaper editorial pages, they lambasted McDonald's move, citing the study to support assertions that the company had adopted a misguided policy to get green zealots off its back.

That's rubbish, counters Richard Denison, a senior scientist at the Environmental Defense Fund, a Washington, D.C., group that is helping McDonald's shape environmental policies. He notes that Franklin's study used paperboard packages but that McDonald's is switching to a plastic-paper sandwich wrap that is "much thinner and lighter."

Indeed, a McDonald's spokesman says that in a recent unpublished study it sponsored, Franklin compared foam containers with the wrap McDonald's is switching to and found that the latter really does have lower environmental costs in most respects than the foam alternative. (The study by the Canadian chemist was about relatively thick paper cups and thus doesn't bear directly on McDonald's packaging switch.)

Cooking the books in life-cycle analyses is especially easy because no one knows just how to measure and compare all the environmental risks associated with products. Often data on pollutants emitted in manufacturing aren't available. Even when the data are known, the associated risks may not be. And the field is fraught with controversial accounting practices. . . .

Given all the quandaries, some experts contend that it's futile to try to sort products into good and bad categories with life-cycle analyses. "The public wants simple answers, but it's not going to get them," maintains Robert Hunt, a researcher at Franklin Associates, Prairie Village, Kan. His company compiles data but leaves drawing conclusions to others.

Environmentalist Barry Commoner slams the life-cycle fad from another angle: Using the studies to recommend products "puts a badge of legitimacy on existing levels of pollution," he contends. Whether or not a study shows paper cups are better than plastic ones, he says, it reinforces the idea that throwaway cups are environmentally sound.

Still, many environmentalists want to sponsor more life-cycle analyses to counter the ones funded by industry—which has had something of a monopoly on the data and deep pockets needed to conduct the studies and publicize them.

Fearing that a kind of life-cycle arms race between foes in environmental disputes is going to undermine their field, experts on the subject are moving to lay down the law. In a project funded by the U.S. government, Battelle's Mr. Vigon is spearheading a report, due this summer, on how to do life-cycle analysis right.

Among other things, the emerging standards may include a broadening of the meaning of life-cycle analysis, says Mary Ann Curran, an Environmental Protection Agency official helping to develop the standards. Traditional analyses are essentially "inventories" of pollutants and other environmental costs, she explains. The new idea is to begin with such inventories and then go on to analyze products' overall environmental "impact" and specify ways to lessen the harm that's done.

This broad, forward-looking approach may counter the objection that the analyses enshrine the status quo. But it will also bring to the fore the problem of finding a basis to compare diverse kinds of environmental fallout—which the traditional inventory approach sidesteps.

Simplifying rules of thumb will probably be needed to crack this "apples-vs.-oranges" nut. For instance, when alternative products use about the same amount of similar raw materials, the amount of recycled ingredients each contains might determine which is better, suggests the Environmental Defense Fund's Mr. Denison.

Sometimes a single environmental cost or benefit will clearly overwhelm other factors, making detailed, apples-oranges comparisons unnecessary, he adds. Example: The large electricity savings offered by compact fluorescent light bulbs, which cut pollution from power generation, are thought to greatly outweigh their main environmental drawback—the fact that they contain small amounts of toxic mercury.

Still, solving the apples-oranges problems is likely to require "consensus building" on environmental priorities as much as technical ingenuity, says Battelle's Mr. Vigon. The EPA recently started brokering a consensus by issuing a landmark study ranking risks posed by various environmental problems. But the level of agreement needed to make life-cycle analyses credible to all the sides in environmental debates won't be achieved anytime soon.

1. How does life-style analysis fit in with forecasting? What are the strengths and weaknesses of this type of analysis?

2. Would scenarios, decision trees, or simulations be useful to McDonald's in deciding whether paper or foam containers are better? Which methods do you think would be most effective?

3. Assume that you work for a company that sells frozen foods and have been asked to evaluate the company's options concerning packaging. What would you do if faced with conflicting reports from the plastics industry and from environmentalists?

METROPOL OF CANADA

Vandalism, theft, and terrorism are bad news. Bad news, that is, for everyone except those in the security business, which is a growth industry. The market for security guards and security hardware is worth about $800 million in Canada, with 60,000 people earning a living as guards or investigators. The third-largest security company, with an estimated 7 percent of the national Canadian market, is Winnipeg's Metropol Base-Fort Security Group. In the past few years Metropol has expanded rapidly and earned a reputation for high quality—a rarity in the security business.

As spring arrives in Winnipeg, Metropol President Pat Haney is worried about the company's future. Competition, especially from large multinationals such as Pinkerton's, Inc., is increasing, which may reduce already low profit margins. Haney is also concerned that Metropol's services aren't sufficiently diversified: Security guards account for fully 90 percent of the company's revenues. Haney needs to make some key decisions about the company's future, including how to distinguish Metropol's services from those of its competitors.

Metropol was founded in 1952 by George Whitbread, a former Royal Canadian Mounted Police officer. In 1975 Whitbread sold it to former Manitoba premier Duff Roblin. Haney came aboard in 1976 to run the Winnipeg operation, which at the time accounted for 80 percent of Metropol's business. In the late 1970s and early 1980s Metropol expanded into Saskatchewan and Alberta. In 1984 it took over the leading Alberta security firm, Base-Fort Security Group, Inc. Of Metropol's $30 million in sales in 1991, 70 percent were in western Canada. The company has offices in all four western provinces as well as in the Northwest Territories, Quebec, and Newfoundland.

Anyone can enter the security business simply by opening an office. Start-up costs are low, and neither the company nor its employees requires any accreditation. Thus Metropol has hundreds of competitors, ranging in size from a couple of ex-cops operating out of a basement to big multinationals. Vendors of security hardware—such as alarms, fences, locks, safes, electronic surveillance devices (ESDs), and monitoring equipment—also compete with providers of guards.

Most customers don't understand the difference in services provided by various companies. As a result, business often goes to the cheapest competitors. Customers have the upper hand and don't hesitate to switch if they think they've found a better deal. Government agencies and firms that place a low priority on security usually choose the lowest bidder. Moreover, customers find it a simple matter to bring the security function in-house if they see a chance to cut costs. Most security companies earn average pretax profits of only 4 percent on gross sales. Thus there is little room for price cutting.

Although the primary basis of competition is price, Haney believes it's possible to succeed by offering superior service. "We have attempted to provide greater value to our customers than our competitors," he says. For example, Metropol has a 24-hour dispatch service at a cost of $100,000 a year. Many of the other firms use answering services. Haney says some customers, who at first say price is their only consideration, find they like the extra service and are willing to pay for it. Metropol also gives its guards special training in reacting to such emergencies as bomb threats, hostage taking, and fires.

Despite offering a high level of service, Metropol manages to keep costs as low as its competitors', partly because its size allows economies of scale when buying such items as uniforms. Cost control is a key to success in a low-margin business. Metropol therefore analyzes every expense activity for every job, looking for deviations from budget.

Of Metropol's 2000 employees, 1900 are security guards and the remainder are administrative personnel. Like other security firms, Metropol experiences an annual turnover of about 100 percent, probably because pay is low and the work is usually boring. Haney's favorite clients are those who are concerned about the high turnover and are willing to pay extra to ensure that guards assigned to them earn more than the minimum wage.

Haney is considering five possibilities for the future: (1) continuing the company's current course, (2) expanding geographically, (3) expanding the range of products and services, (4) diversifying into other service areas, and (5) serving the home-security market.

If he decides to follow the current course, Haney would try to make Metropol the fastest-growing security guard company in western Canada, with the highest profits, the lowest employee turnover rate, and the most satisfied customers. This strategy would require a formal marketing program, even tighter cost control, and better employee motivation.

Geographic expansion would involve an attempt to make Metropol a national Canadian company. Following this strategy, Haney's first priority would be to establish the company in the Toronto area, because that's where most national companies make their decisions about security. Southern Ontario itself offers substantial business. Metropol could buy a local firm, merge with another

company, or bid on contracts and open an office once one was obtained.

Expanding the company's line of security products and services would enable Metropol to satisfy customers who dislike having to contract with different firms for guards, fences, locks, and emergency security devices. Haney is investigating a deal with a large distributor of security hardware. The distributor would provide Metropol with brand equipment and train Metropol's staff in its use. Metropol could then package hardware and guards in whatever mix its clients wanted.

Diversifying into other service areas might mean expanding into nursing, secretarial, and janitorial services. This strategy would capitalize on the company's existing procedures and expertise in hiring people for contract jobs. An example of this strategy is provided by Drake International, Inc., which started in Winnipeg as a supplier of temporary secretaries. Drake became an international success by expanding operations to provide temporary staff in such fields as health care, engineering, and security. However, Metropol had previously tried unsuccessfully to diversify into the commercial cleaning business.

The final possibility is expanding into the home-security market as a supplier of such products as alarm systems, locks, mobile checks, and house sitting. Haney is exploring an opportunity to become a franchiser of home alarm systems to small retailers. Metropol could pass along volume discounts to its dealers who would also get the benefit of cooperative advertising. Metropol would set up the central monitoring system.

1. Develop the outline of an MBO system for Metropol, based on its current product and service line.

2. What are the implicit assumptions for each of the five strategies being considered by Haney?

3. Evaluate each of the strategies. Which strategy should Haney adopt? Explain.

Part Four

ORGANIZING

Au Bon Pain

Instead of selling burgers or fried chicken, the fast food chain Au Bon Pain serves croissants filled with everything from ham to chocolate, not to mention coffee, salads, and sandwiches. This unusual concept has proven quite successful—even though the stores sell ''yuppie food,'' their customers come from a wide variety of backgrounds. And every year since its founding, company earnings have increased.

But even a good concept couldn't prevent Au Bon Pain from having the same problems that plague all fast food restaurants. When company president, Ron Shaich, visited his stores, he was often appalled by what he saw: dirty bathrooms and long lines, symptoms of poor customer service. At times, Shaich actually found himself cleaning up a bathroom or serving customers.

"What it forced us into was a top-down type of organization," Shaich recalled, In other words, the company had to force standards of quality on its restaurant managers from above, as is the case with so many companies in the U.S.

But forcing quality standards on managers didn't solve the problem at Au Bon Pain. Managers in turn imposed the standards on their staffs. But, without incentives for workers to perform better, the only notable result was the usual increased employee turnover. In the fast food business, quick customer service means shorter lines, which ultimately results in more customers. (After all, who wants to spend ten minutes in line just to grab a croissant and a cup of coffee on the way to work?) But with unmotivated employees serving food, the quality and speed of service suffered.

The conclusion? Top-down management, Shaich said, was no more effective than sticking one's fingers in the dike.

If imposing quality from the top down wouldn't improve service, what would? The company considered paying store crews higher salaries but feared this would only start a salary war with other fast food chains, without assuring that Au Bon Pain would attract the best workers. Management felt that basing pay on performance was the key to solving the problem, but how should it be implemented? The company found the solution by instilling a "storekeeper mentality" in managers. How? By making managers into business partners.

As business partners, managers shared a store's profits about 50/50 with the company. A partner/manager could now earn up to $100,000 if he or she ran a profitable operation; under the old system, a manager earned about $30,000 a year. But along with the chance to earn more money came an increase in responsibility. In order to make an operation more efficient, partner/managers had to find ways to cut costs and increase profits. One partner/manager discovered that, simply by compacting the trash, the store saved $700 a month in disposal costs. Partner/managers also looked for ways to reduce the amount of leftover food and tried harder to improve the quality of service.

Acting like a storekeeper, a partner/manager was allowed to determine how much to pay staff. Under the old system, managers could raise someone's pay only ten cents an hour; now, a valuable employee could be given a dollar-an-hour based on productivity. As one manager put it, "Employees respond to the fact that they're working for *me,*" rather than for a corporation.

The only problem left was eliminating poor partner/managers. Au Bon Pain hired mystery shoppers to visit every store at least once a week. Shoppers graded each store to see if company standards were being met. If a partner/manager couldn't run a store efficiently, he or she was subject to dismissal. It was, Shaich said, somewhat Darwinian: The managers who could figure out how to run an efficient store could do very well, but those who couldn't fell "right off the map."

Would this type of decentralized authority and responsibility work in other kinds of companies? Is there something about the world of fast food that makes this form of organizational reform successful? Something about the service sector of the economy?

Chapter 10

FUNDAMENTALS

OF ORGANIZING

Aircraft assembly

What You Will Learn

1 Four basic elements of organizational structure and how they're shown in an organization chart.

2 Four types of departmentalization and the advantages and disadvantages of each.

3 Three principles of coordination and the tension between coordination and departmentalization.

4 The relationships among authority, responsibility, accountability, and delegation.

5 Factors that affect managerial decisions to centralize or decentralize decision making.

6 Differences between line and staff authority.

7 **Skill Development:** How to "read," interpret, and evaluate any organization's structure.

Chapter Outline

Manager's Viewpoint
Shakeup at McDonnell Douglas

Organizational Structure
Basic Elements of Organizational Structure
The Organization Chart

Departmentalization
Functional Departmentalization
Insight: The Pep Boys: Manny, Moe, and Jack
Place Departmentalization
Insight: American Airlines
Product or Service Departmentalization
Insight: Harris Corporation
Matrix Departmentalization
Insight: Piper Aircraft
Selecting an Organizational Structure

Coordination
Unity of Command Principle
Scalar Principle
Span of Management Principle
Global Link: Corporate Networks
Coordination versus Departmentalization

Authority
Responsibility
Accountability
Delegation of Authority
Centralization and Decentralization of Authority
Line Authority and Staff Authority

Experiencing Management
Skill-Building Exercise: Centralization or Decentralization: What's Your Choice?

Manager's Memo

In the News

Management Case
Organizing for Renewal

"This new structure puts those who work on the same plane on the same team."

Shakeup at McDonnell Douglas

When one of its DC-10s ended up strewn across an Iowa cornfield, it was only one of a series of jolts for McDonnell Douglas. Four crashes over a span of fifteen years, military budget cuts, production bottlenecks, and a shaky organizational structure were all spelling financial losses for the $15-billion-a-year aerospace manufacturer. And no one knew what group in the organization was to blame for these losses.

With a corporate goal of producing high-quality products at lower costs, McDonnell Douglas has been an organization in which manufacturing departments, until recently, called most of the shots. With manufacturing in deep trouble, though, it became sales and marketing's call. According to CEO John McDonnell, cost overruns in the company's airline production business had to be stopped. Thanks to a worldwide increase in air travel, the backlog of airplane orders was at an all-time high. Outside suppliers couldn't keep pace with the increased orders, and the company couldn't build enough parts of its own. To further aggravate cost-overrun and production-slowdown problems, the company had many inexperienced workers who needed costly training if product quality was to be maintained. The company sometimes incurred expensive and time-consuming repair work as a result of workers' inexperience.

Top management rethought how the airplane division manufactured planes and changed the organization's structure to make that division more competitive. A Total Quality Management System was introduced. This meant that the old *functional* structure, in which an engineer's work was spread thin over several different types of planes, was scrapped and replaced by a new, *product* structure that allows a group of people to focus on a single type of plane. This new structure improves communication by putting those who work on the same plane on the same team. Moreover, each team is now solely responsible for its own work, which put an end to the finger pointing and frustration caused by engineers' and managers' lack of authority and accountability.

But reorganizations are rarely bloodless for the managerial ranks. In the process of restructuring for its Total Quality Management System, McDonnell Douglas cut or drastically changed more than 5000 managerial and supervisory jobs. People could apply for 2800 newly created jobs. The other 2200 managers were assigned as technicians, to work in design offices and on production lines.[1]

Charging top managers with increasing the productivity of their organizations has given great importance to their role as resource allocators. Total quality production programs and downsizing require that managers adjust their organization's structure to be more flexible in the 1990s. Managers have often been too far removed from the day-to-day operations of their organization to structure it properly. It may take a dramatic turn of events, such as that faced by McDonnell Douglas, for such managers to get a real grasp on organizational problems.

In this chapter we focus on organizational structure, the formal system that enables managers to divide up work, coordinate tasks, and delegate authority and responsibility in order to achieve organizational objectives most efficiently. First we'll examine elements of an organization's structure and various types of departmentalization that allow managers to determine who performs which activities. Then, after discussing how managers divide up work and coordinate tasks, we'll look at lines of authority that affect the flow of real decisions in an organization.

ORGANIZATIONAL STRUCTURE

organizational structure
A formal system of working relationships that both separates tasks (clarifies who should do what) and integrates tasks (tells people how they should work together).

Organizational structure is a formal system of working relationships that both separates and integrates tasks. Separation of duties makes it clear who should do what. Integration of duties tells people how they should work together. Organizational structure helps employees work together effectively by (1) assigning human and other resources to tasks, (2) clarifying employees' responsibilities and how they should mesh using job descriptions, organization charts, and lines of authority, (3) letting employees know what is expected of them through rules, operating procedures, and performance standards, and (4) devising procedures for collecting and evaluating information that will help managers make decisions and solve problems.

Basic Elements of Organizational Structure

specialization The process of identifying particular tasks and assigning them to individuals or teams who have been trained to do them.

For our purposes, let's view organizational structure as including four basic elements: specialization, standardization, coordination, and authority.[2]

Specialization is the process of identifying particular tasks and assigning them to individuals or work groups who have been trained to do them. At McDonnell Douglas teams of engineers work on only one type of plane. Middle managers are responsible for directing the work of several related groups, such as production, flight operations, and energy policy. Functional managers usually supervise one particular function, such as marketing, accounting, or quality control. First-line managers might be in charge of a specific area of work, such as printing, medical records, or data processing. As you can see, one can specialize in any of a number of different jobs. Later in this chapter we'll see how the principle of specialization is applied through different forms of departmentalization.

standardization The process of developing an organization's procedures in such a way that employees perform their jobs in a uniform and consistent manner.

Standardization defines an organization's procedures in such a way that employees perform their jobs in a uniform and consistent manner. This may strike you as mechanical, but if jobs weren't standardized, an organization couldn't achieve its goals. Just walk into any McDonald's, Wendy's or Burger King—every person has a job with well-defined standards. These include how long a customer may be kept waiting for service and the length of time food stays on the warming trays. Standards permit managers to measure an employee's performance against some criteria. From the very start, job descriptions and application forms standardize the selection of employees. On-the-job training programs develop standardized skills and reinforce values important to the organization's success. Managers use written procedures, job descriptions, instructions, rules, and regulations to standardize their subordinates' jobs.

coordination The formal and informal procedures that integrate the activities performed by separate groups in an organization.

Coordination is the formal and informal procedures that integrate the activities performed by separate groups in an organization. In bureaucratic organizations, such as the IRS, rules are enough to link such activities. In less structured organizations, such as Tandem Computers, coordination requires managerial sensitivity to companywide problems, willingness to share responsibility, and effective interpersonal communication. Later in this chapter we'll look at some specific principles of coordination.

authority The right to decide and act.

Authority is basically the right to decide and act. Various organizations distribute authority differently. In a centralized organization, such as Tandy Corporation, top managers make decisions and then communicate them to lower-level managers. In a decentralized organization, such as Hewlett-Packard, some decision-making authority is given to lower-level managers. Firms often combine the two approaches by centralizing certain functions, such as accounting and purchasing, and decentralizing others, such as production and human resources. We'll spend time later in this chapter discussing authority.

The Organization Chart

One way to visualize the interrelationships of these four basic elements is to create an **organization chart.** The organization chart is a diagram showing the reporting relationships of functions, departments, and individual positions within an organization. Figure 10.1 is the organization chart for J. C. Penney Company. The chart could be expanded to show even greater detail by including the titles of departmental managers and identifying work groups within the departments according to the specific tasks they perform. For example, ''Regions'' on the right-hand side of the chart might include all stores and their staffs from Boston to Dallas.

In general, an organization chart provides four major pieces of information about an organization's structure:

1. *Tasks.* The chart shows the range of different tasks within the organization. For instance, Penney's tasks range from insurance to specialty retailing.

2. *Subdivisions.* Each box represents a subdivision of the organization that is responsible for a portion of the work. For example, the president of J. C. Penney Stores and Catalog is responsible for all merchandise and speciality retailing.

3. *Levels of management.* The chart shows the management hierarchy; from the chairman of the board down to the various divisional managers. All those directly subordinate to the same individual usually appear at the same management level and are directly connected to that individual.

4. *Lines of authority.* Vertical lines connecting the boxes on the chart show which positions have authority over others. At J. C. Penney the organization's treasurer reports to (that is, derives authority from) the finance manager, who in turn reports to the vice chairman for finance, who reports to the chairman of the board.

Managers have debated the advantages and disadvantages of organization charts for years.[3] One advantage is that such a chart shows employees how the pieces of the entire organization fit together, including how their own specialized tasks relate to the whole. Thus everyone knows who reports to whom and where to go with a particular problem. The chart also helps managers detect gaps in authority or duplication of tasks in the organization.

A major disadvantage of the organization chart is that it's just a piece of paper; it simply can't show everything about an organization's structure. For example, it can't show who has the most clout or where the vital informal channels of communication lie. In addition, employees may incorrectly read status and power into their jobs, based on the proximity of their boxes to the chairman of the board's box. These disadvantages can be overcome only if the chart is used for its intended purpose—to reveal the basic, formal structure of the entire organization.

DEPARTMENTALIZATION

In the preceding section we outlined the four basic elements of organizational structure. Specialization means that managers subdivide work and assign it to individuals and work units (called task forces, divisions, teams, or departments). Standardization means that managers create procedures to improve the consistency of their departments' performance.

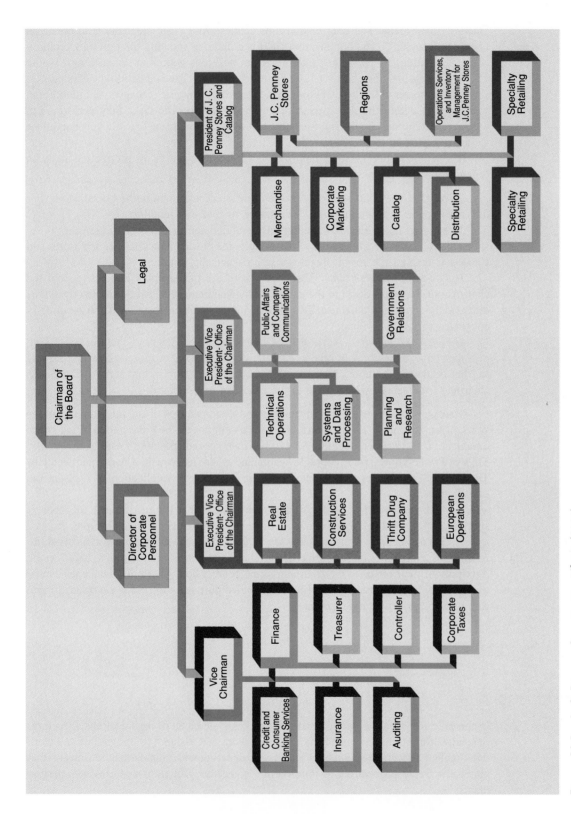

Figure 10.1 J. C. Penney Organization Chart (1990)

The company's upper-level management positions are shown here by boxes containing titles. Lines lead to the departments (functions) reporting to each manager. Note that each division is color-coded differently. Lighter shades of each color indicate those reporting to the division head or to other bosses in the division.
(*Source:* Adapted with permission from chart provided by Don Christenson, J. C. Penney Insurance Company, Dallas.)

departmentalization
Subdividing work and assigning it to specialized groups within an organization.

Subdividing work and assigning it to specialized groups within an organization is called **departmentalization.** Management can use any of four basic types of departmentalization: by function, by place (or location), by product or service, and by a matrix. Division of work is the first step in departmentalization, but *how* management groups people and jobs depends on the goals it views as most significant. At McDonnell Douglas, changing the basis of departmentalization from functional to product was essential to achieving the Total Quality Management System.

The key to effective departmentalization lies in organizing people and activities in such a way that decisions easily flow throughout the organization. Large, complex organizations, such as Borden, American Express, and Levi Strauss, actually use different forms of departmentalization at various organizational levels to facilitate this flow. Levi Strauss, for instance, has eight product divisions, including Jeanswear, Womenswear, and Menswear, that reflect the product structure. Each product division is then broken down into functional departments, such as accounting, production, and marketing, that support the division's products.

In describing the advantages and disadvantages of each type of departmentalization, we will emphasize specialization and standardization—which departmentalization addresses directly. We'll only touch on the other two elements of organization, coordination and authority, but will discuss them in more detail later in the chapter.

Functional Departmentalization

functional departmentalization Type of departmentalization that groups employees according to their areas of expertise and the resources they draw on to perform a common set of tasks.

Recall that functions are tasks that an organization carries out, such as production, marketing, and finance. **Functional departmentalization** groups employees according to their areas of expertise and the resources they draw on to perform a common set of tasks. Functional grouping is the most widely used and accepted in practice.[4]

Functions vary widely, depending on the nature of the organization. For example, hospitals do not have product development departments, but they do have admitting and nursing departments. Churches do not have production departments, but they do have religious education departments. Delta Airlines has operations, traffic, and finance departments. Toys ''R'' Us and other large retail chains have general merchandising, physical distribution, and support services departments (such as legal, human resources, and accounting).

The following Insight looks briefly at the Pep Boys organization, an excellent example of functional departmentalization. At Pep Boys four basic functional areas are very clearly defined, as is the line of authority within each.

THE PEP BOYS: MANNY, MOE, AND JACK

*I*NSIGHT

Pep Boys was a single store in Philadelphia in 1921. Since then it has grown to include more than 243 stores in eleven states. Pep Boys provides customers with convenient stores at which to shop for all their automotive needs. The company is primarily organized by function, as shown in the figure on the next page. Specialists in the various functional areas—finance, merchandising, store operations, and administration—perform different tasks. Each of these contributes to providing service to customers. For example, specialists in the store operations departments handled all issues surrounding the expansion and operation of stores when Pep Boys recently entered four new states and replaced outmoded stores in others.

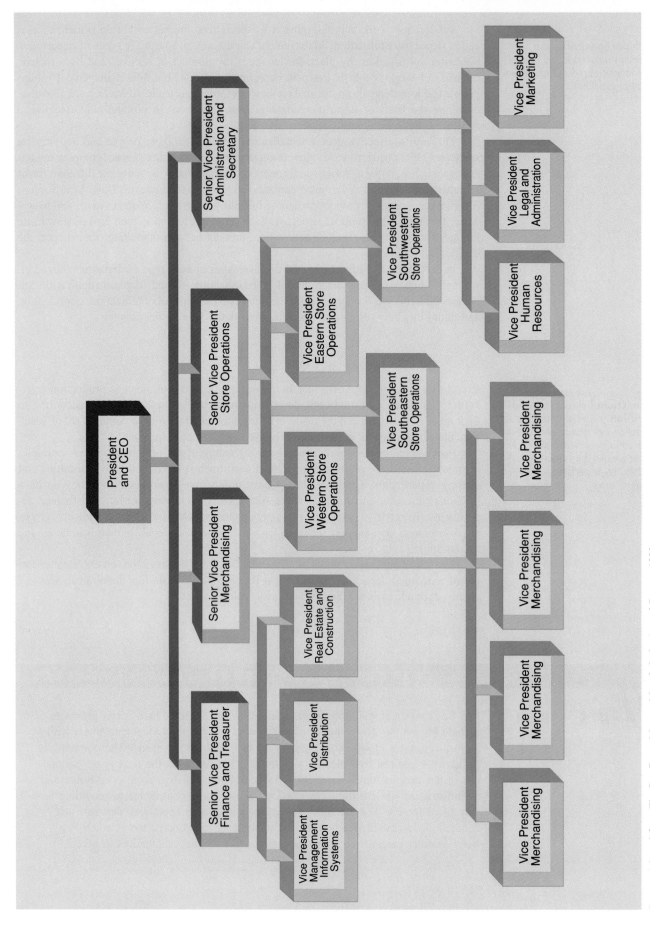

Source: Adapted from The Pep Boys: Manny, Moe & Jack, *Annual Report,* 1990.

TABLE 10.1

Advantages and Disadvantages of Functional Departmentalization

Advantages

1. Promotes skill specialization.
2. Reduces duplication of resources and coordination problems within functional area.
3. Enhances career development and training within department.
4. Allows superiors and subordinates to share common expertise.
5. Promotes high-quality technical problem solving.
6. Centralizes decision making.

Disadvantages

1. Emphasizes routine tasks.
2. Reduces communication between departments.
3. May create conflict over product priorities.
4. Can make scheduling difficult across departments.
5. Focuses on departmental as opposed to organizational issues.
6. Develops managers who are experts in narrow fields.

Source: Adapted from J. McCann and J. R. Galbraith, ''Interdepartmental Relations,'' in P. C. Nystrom and W. H. Starbuck (eds.), *Handbook of Organizational Design,* vol. 2 (New York: Oxford University Press, 1981), 61.

As Table 10.1 indicates, grouping tasks and employees by function can be both efficient and economical. It is efficient, particularly for small organizations, because it centralizes authority and decision making at the top.[5] For example, the Warner Corporation, a $16 million plumbing company in Washington, D.C., provides only plumbing services. *All* functions, such as accounting, dispatching, truck maintenance, and human resources, focus on delivering quality plumbing services to customers. The president, Tom Warner, has the authority to make decisions that bind the whole company to a course of action. Larger firms often assign responsibility for several departments to one senior manager. This was done by Pep Boys in the administration functional area.

Departmentalization by function is economical because it results in a simple structure, appropriate for organizations that sell a narrow range of goods or services almost exclusively within one market area. Management creates one department for each major task to be performed, such as engineering, sales, or research and development. This structure holds down administrative expenses because everyone in a department shares training, experience, and resources across all products. Job satisfaction increases, as workers improve their skills by interacting with others in their functional area. Employees see clearly defined career paths laid out in their own departments. The result? The company can more easily hire and promote personnel who have high-quality problem-solving skills in each area of specialization.

The disadvantages of functional departmentalization become obvious when an organization has diversified products or markets. For instance, J. C. Penney offers a variety of services and a variety of products, ranging from life insurance to men's clothing. Making decisions quickly becomes difficult when managers have to work their way through layers of higher management for approvals. In addition, when there's friction between departments, managers have to spend time resolving the problems. For example, a sales representative may lose a good account because he or she has to wait for the sales manager to get the production manager to make a scheduling decision. As John McDonnell learned at McDonnell Douglas, it is difficult to pinpoint accountability and performance levels of managers in separate functions. Which department was the culprit responsible for declining profits: production, sales, or personnel?

Another disadvantage is that top management may have a hard time coordinating the activities of employees from different departments. Functional departmentalization also tends to deemphasize the objectives of the entire firm. Employees may focus on departmental objectives, such as meeting their own budgets and schedules, and miss the big picture. Since functional managers worry about their own areas of expertise, they may

Place departmentalization of the Postal Service at Austin, TX.

have difficulty seeing other managers' points of view. Employees develop a loyalty to their own department, which may, in turn, put up walls between departments instead of encouraging employees to identify and coordinate with their counterparts in other functional areas.

Place Departmentalization

Place departmentalization is commonly used by organizations with operations in many different locations. Management groups all functions for a geographic territory at one location under one manager, rather than dividing functions among different managers or grouping all tasks in one central office. Many large companies that have set up regional and district offices use place departmentalization. Similarly, many federal agencies, such as the IRS, the Federal Reserve Board, and the U.S. Postal Service, use place departmentalization to provide nationwide services. And multinational firms often use place departmentalization to address cultural and legal differences in various countries, as well as the lack of uniformity among geographic markets.[6] Part of American Airlines' operations offers a good example of place departmentalization.

place departmentalization
Type of departmentalization that groups all functions for a geographic area (place) under one manager.

The advantages of place departmentalization, highlighted in Table 10.2, are primarily those of efficiency. If each unit is relatively small and in direct contact with its market, it can adapt more readily to client or environmental demands. For production, place departmentalization might mean locating near raw materials or suppliers. Potential gains include lower costs for materials, lower freight rates, and perhaps lower labor costs. For marketing, locating near clients might mean better response and service to them. Salespeople could spend more time selling and less time traveling. Being closer to the customers could also help sales managers pinpoint the marketing tactics most likely to succeed in a particular region.

Table 10.2 also shows some disadvantages of place departmentalization. Organizing by location clearly increases problems of control and coordination by top management, which is often far away. In order to be sure of uniformity and coordination, organizations such as Blockbuster Video, Southland (7-Eleven stores), the U.S. Postal Service, State Farm Insurance, and Sheraton Hotels make extensive use of rules that apply in all locations. If regional units are allowed to become significantly different from one another, top management may have difficulty imposing uniform rules and schedules. Also, employees

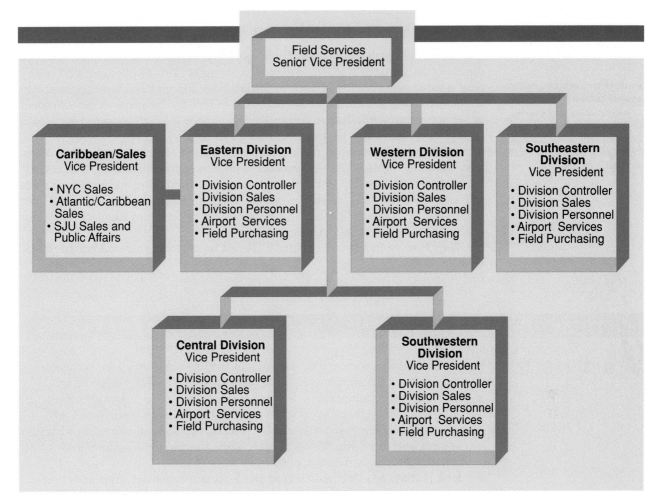

Source: Al Casey, retired CEO, American Airlines. Reprinted by permission.

may emphasize their own units' objectives and needs more than the whole organization's, or they may focus only on problems that occur within their territory and feel little concern for problems elsewhere. Finally, because most of the functional departments must be duplicated at each location, the cost to the entire organization is increased. For example, personnel at the various IRS locations are all performing the same functional jobs.

TABLE 10.2

Advantages and Disadvantages of Place Departmentalization

Advantages

1. Equipment used for products is all in one place, saving time and costs.
2. Managers develop expertise in solving problems unique to one location.
3. Managers know customers' problems.
4. Method is suited to multinational organizations.

Disadvantages

1. All functions—accounting, purchasing, manufacturing—are duplicated at each location.
2. May cause conflicts between each location's objectives and corporate objectives.
3. May require extensive rules and regulations to coordinate and ensure uniformity of quality among locations.
4. Doesn't foster employee knowledge of problems at other locations.

Source: Adapted from J. McCann and J. R. Galbraith, "Interdepartmental Relations," in P. C. Nystrom and W. H. Starbuck (eds.), *Handbook of Organizational Design,* vol. 2 (New York: Oxford University Press, 1981), 61.

Product or Service Departmentalization

product or service departmentalization Type of departmentalization that divides the organization into self-contained units, each capable of designing and producing its own goods or services.

You can see by now that as an organization grows, the weaknesses of functional and place departmentalization begin to overshadow their strengths. This fact becomes particularly clear when the organization expands its product lines and attracts diverse customers. In response, top management often turns to product or service departmentalization. **Product or service departmentalization** divides the organization into self-contained units, each capable of designing and producing its own goods or services.[7]

This form of departmentalization is frequently used by organizations that have operations around the world. Large multiproduct companies such as Matsushita, Quaker Oats, Arthur Anderson, CitiCorp, McDonnell Douglas, and Harris Corporation also take this approach. Each of these companies started with functional departmentalization, but growth and an increasing inability to serve the needs of particular customers made that structure unworkable or uneconomical.

The following Insight looks briefly at Harris Corporation's product departmentalization.

HARRIS CORPORATION

I NSIGHT

Harris Corporation is a worldwide company focused on four major core businesses: electronic systems, semiconductors, communications, and Lanier Worldwide Inc., an office equipment manufacturer. It uses advanced technology to provide innovative, cost-efficient, high-quality solutions to the problems of commercial and governmental customers throughout the world. It has annual sales of more than $3 billion and employs more than 35,000 people. Harris Corporation's organizational structure is shown in the figure opposite.

John Hartley, president and CEO of Harris, believes that this structure is especially appropriate in highly competitive environments, because each business faces unique opportunities and challenges. Lanier Worldwide, Inc. is a division that markets, sells, and services a sophisticated line of office equipment, including photocopiers, fax machines, laser printers, dictating equipment, and telephone systems. The Semiconductor Division manufactures standard and custom-designed integrated circuits that are used in laptop portable computers. These two businesses sell to different customers, who have unique demands for product quality, service, and delivery.[8]

The advantages and disadvantages of product or service departmentalization are shown in Table 10.3. One advantage is increased specialization, which allows managers and workers to concentrate on their particular product line or service. Another is that management can more accurately pinpoint costs, profits, problems, and successes within each line of business. Furthermore, each business can develop its own distinctive competence, or strategic advantage (see Chapter 8). For example, a distinctive competence for Lanier Worldwide is low-cost manufacturing of fax units, and for Harris's Electronic Systems Division it's research and development. Finally, because their attention is more focused, managers are more likely to remain sensitive to changes in consumer demand and to adapt their products or services quickly to meet those changes.

One major disadvantage of product or service departmentalization is inefficient use of resources. For instance, functions are duplicated for each product line or service (that is, each business). And products or services with seasonal highs and lows may result in high personnel costs. For example, Jostens has high demand for high-school yearbooks in the spring but low demand in the summer, so fewer workers are needed then. The company is therefore faced with the choice of transferring employees to other product lines or laying them off. Either way, personnel costs can be unusually high.

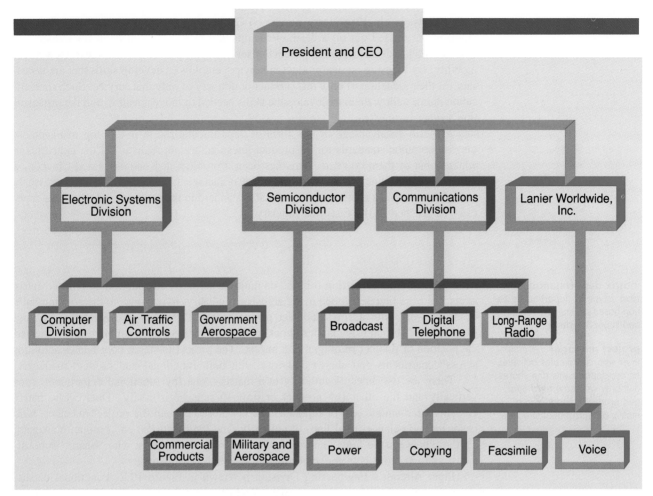

President and CEO

Electronic Systems Division

Semiconductor Division

Communications Division

Lanier Worldwide, Inc.

Computer Division

Air Traffic Controls

Government Aerospace

Broadcast

Digital Telephone

Long-Range Radio

Commercial Products

Military and Aerospace

Power

Copying

Facsimile

Voice

Source: Adapted from Harris Corporation, *Annual Report,* 1990.

A second disadvantage of this type of departmentalization is the difficulty of coordinating across divisions. Employees tend to focus on their product or service, rather than on the broader objectives of the company. This situation often creates unhealthy competition within the organization for scarce resources. For example, at Harris Corporation, managers from different product lines might disagree over the allocation of capital funds

TABLE 10.3

Advantages and Disadvantages of Product or Service Departmentalization

Advantages

1. Suited to fast changes in a product or service.
2. Allows greater product or service visibility.
3. Fosters a concern for customer demand.
4. Clearly defines responsibilities.
5. Develops managers who can think across functional lines.

Disadvantages

1. May not use skills and resources effectively.
2. Doesn't foster coordination of activities across product or service lines.
3. Fosters politics in resource allocation.
4. Restricts problem solving to a single product or service.
5. Limits career mobility for personnel outside their product or service line.

Source: Adapted from J. McCann and J. R. Galbraith, "Interdepartmental Relations," in P. C. Nystrom and W. H. Starbuck (eds.), *Handbook of Organizational Design,* vol. 2 (New York: Oxford University Press, 1981), 61.

among divisions. In 1988 Harris purchased GE's solid-state plant for its Semiconductor Division but missed out on a desirable acquisition of a document plant for Lanier.

Yet another disadvantage of product or service departmentalization is restricted career mobility. By focusing on one product or service, employees develop skills that are necessary for the production of only that product or delivery of only that service. Such specialization doesn't allow them to develop the skills needed to move ahead within the organization's other businesses.

A fourth disadvantage of this form of departmentalization is that top management may set common standards for *all* product lines that are not realistic for the industries in which some of them compete. This has been a problem at Kentucky Fried Chicken, a fast-food product line within PepsiCo. PepsiCo managers have put tremendous pressures on K.F.C. to attain a profitability level that is standard in the beverage industry but simply can't be reached in the fast-food industry.

Matrix Departmentalization

matrix departmentalization Type of departmentalization based on multiple authority and support systems.

project manager A manager who coordinates activities across departments and shares authority with both functional and product managers in a matrix organizational structure.

Matrix departmentalization is based on multiple authority and support systems.[9] Matrix structures were first developed in the aerospace industry, in response to the government's desire to work with a single contact person in each company. To meet this demand Boeing, LTV, General Dynamics, Lockheed, and Piper Aircraft, among others, created the position of **project manager** in a matrix. The project manager coordinates activities across departments and shares authority with both functional and product managers.

There are two lines of authority in a matrix—one (by functional department) runs vertically and the other (by product or project) runs horizontally. Thus every matrix contains three unique sets of relationships: (1) those between the project manager, who heads up and balances dual lines of authority, and the functional and product managers; (2) those between the functional managers and product managers, who ''share'' subordinates; and (3) those between subordinates and their dual managers.

Piper Aircraft's Engineering Division is shown in Figure 10.2. Functional departments are represented by the columns, product teams by the rows. The term *matrix organization* was coined to describe such a matrixlike crossing of functional and product structures.

Matrix departmentalization tries to capture the advantages of the functional and product forms while minimizing their disadvantages. It helps break down barriers by allowing employees from different functional departments to pool their skills in solving a common problem, and it increases the organization's abilities to use human and financial resources wisely and to adapt to changing business conditions.

Few organizations can switch suddenly from functional or product or service departmentalization to a fully functioning matrix form. Matrix departmentalization requires flexibility and cooperation at all levels of the organization. An effective matrix structure depends on open, direct lines of communication. Furthermore, both managers and subordinates may need to learn new skills, such as how to resolve interdepartmental conflicts and how to run meetings effectively. Because the matrix form of organization is so complicated, organizations should use it only under the following conditions:

▶ Strong competition requires the organization to provide multiple, innovative, state-of-the-art products. Under such pressure, managers must give equal consideration to coordinating the production of various goods or services and the technical expertise needed to develop them. It took 3M teams nearly six years to perfect Post-it Note Pads. The teams had to coordinate the efforts of marketing, research, and production personnel.

▶ Managers must process large amounts of information because of rapid market and technological changes. Combining product or service coordination with technical expertise can ease companywide communication of important information. At Procter & Gamble, ''multifunctional project teams'' are formed to champion new products. Each team has the authority and responsibility for a specific product, such as Ultra Pampers.

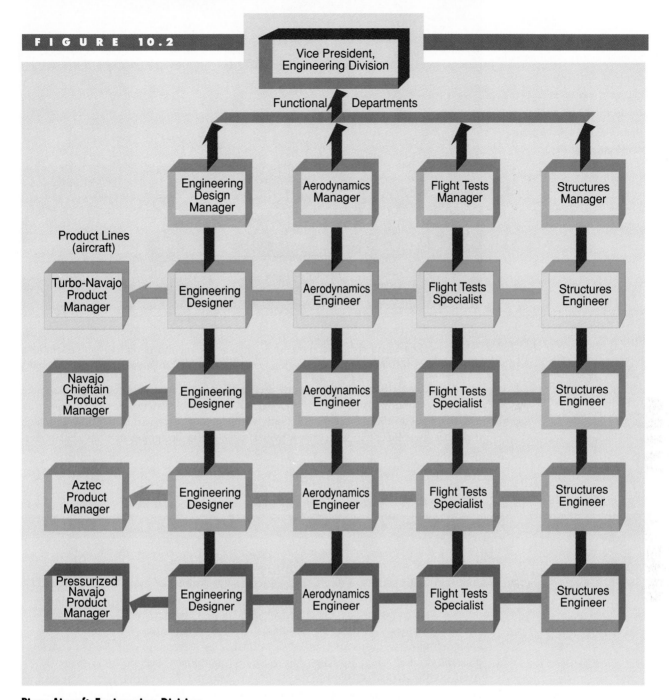

FIGURE 10.2

Vice President, Engineering Division

Functional Departments

Engineering Design Manager | Aerodynamics Manager | Flight Tests Manager | Structures Manager

Product Lines (aircraft)

Turbo-Navajo Product Manager — Engineering Designer | Aerodynamics Engineer | Flight Tests Specialist | Structures Engineer

Navajo Chieftain Product Manager — Engineering Designer | Aerodynamics Engineer | Flight Tests Specialist | Structures Engineer

Aztec Product Manager — Engineering Designer | Aerodynamics Engineer | Flight Tests Specialist | Structures Engineer

Pressurized Navajo Product Manager — Engineering Designer | Aerodynamics Engineer | Flight Tests Specialist | Structures Engineer

Piper Aircraft Engineering Division

The arrows indicate the direction of reporting relationships in the matrix. For instance, an engineering designer, aerodynamics engineer, flight tests specialist, and structures engineer all report to both the Turbo-Navajo project manager and the managers of their respective functional departments.

(*Source:* W. F. Joyce, ''Matrix Organization: A Social Experiment,'' *Academy of Management Journal,* 1986, *29*: 536–561.)

▶ The organization needs to use its resources efficiently but is unable to assign separate facilities for each product or service. Instead, it must have the ability to shift personnel from one area to another, according to the needs of various product or service lines. Allied Corporation created teams to investigate the market potential for commercial

More companies are striving to make *matrix departmentalization* as effective as possible. One way to do so is to conduct in-house training sessions like this one on team development at Ford.

chemicals. Specialists from different areas, such as chemicals, marketing, and operations, were used at different times to develop commercially viable suggestions.

Matrix departmentalization is now used in many organizations, such as banks, management consulting firms, advertising agencies, and school systems. Some companies use a matrix at all levels, and others use it only within certain divisions. The following Insight describes how Piper Aircraft uses a matrix structure in designing new and customized products.

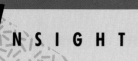

INSIGHT

At Piper Aircraft, the engineering division is responsible for designing and testing both new and modified aircraft. Only after design prototypes have been flown and certified by the Federal Aviation Administration (FAA) does Piper's production division take responsibility for quantity production of the new models.

Designing aircraft requires considerable technical expertise. Therefore the engineering division forms specialized departments to concentrate on different components, such as wing, fuselage, tail assembly, and power and electrical systems. Although the overall design process is fragmented, the departments become interdependent as construction of the prototype progresses. The wing must fit the fuselage, the power system must deliver thrust to propel the aircraft at the desired speed and weight, and the electrical systems have to provide sufficient control to maneuver the aircraft.

Figure 10.2 shows how Piper's engineering division uses matrix departmentalization in this design process. Appointed to develop each new aircraft model, a project manager is responsible for the overall scope of the project, for ensuring that personnel from the various departments perform their jobs correctly and on schedule. Functional department managers provide technical support to employees from their group who have been temporarily assigned to a project manager. Thus the role of the project manager is to assemble a group of employees from various departments into a team that assumes responsibility for the success or failure of the new aircraft. The project manager has the authority to overrule any of the functional managers—even on technical matters—but uses that right sparingly.[10]

TABLE 10.4

Advantages and Disadvantages of Matrix Departmentalization

Advantages

1. Gives flexibility to managers in assigning people to projects.
2. Encourages interdepartmental cooperation.
3. Develops project managers' interpersonal, informational, and decisional roles.
4. Involves and challenges employees.
5. Makes specialized knowledge available to all projects.

Disadvantages

1. Is costly to implement.
2. Requires good interpersonal skills.
3. May reward political skill as opposed to managerial skills.
4. Increases frustration levels for employees who receive orders from two bosses.
5. May lead to more discussion than action.

Source: Adapted from J. McCann and J. R. Galbraith, "Interdepartmental Relations," in P. C. Nystrom and W. H. Starbuck (eds.), *Handbook of Organizational Design,* vol. 2 (New York: Oxford University Press, 1981), 61.

Table 10.4 shows several advantages and disadvantages of matrix departmentalization. Among the advantages is that project managers can tap specialized skills from different areas and thereby solve complex problems with maximum efficiency. In addition, all key personnel associated with a project work together as a team under one project manager. This arrangement lessens the coordination problems associated with departmentalization by function or product. The project manager can also gain valuable experience in three managerial roles—interpersonal, informational, and decisional. Finally, team members are exposed to and can draw on the diverse backgrounds of other members, which encourages innovation, improves the quality of solutions, and eases their implementation.

Matrix departmentalization has several disadvantages, though. One is the conflict that sometimes arises between employees' loyalty to their department and to their project team. Often department heads view team members as part of their functional units and want them to work on departmental matters. Office politics sometimes create stress and strain for employees. Employees must still earn promotions within their functional departments. Such dual loyalties and responsibilities erode the effectiveness of the project teams.

Another disadvantage is that a member of a project team needs finely tuned interpersonal skills to communicate effectively with specialists from other departments. Finally, team morale can be adversely affected by personnel shifts, when one project ends and a new one begins. Some team members no longer have jobs in the new project and must return to their functional areas to await new assignments. Fear of not having meaningful work or of being laid off at the end of a project may lead to job dissatisfaction.

Selecting an Organizational Structure

No particular type of departmentalization—functional, place, product or service, or matrix—is best. Managers must select the organizational structure that matches the firm's specific conditions. Table 10.5 lists characteristics that could help a manager decide which structure is best for a given situation.

Alphagraphics, a quick-printing firm and other small organizations that have standard products and diverse customers would probably find functional departmentalization to be most appropriate. Procter & Gamble and other organizations with large and diverse product lines would find product departmentalization most useful. Merck and other organizations in the pharmaceutical business with a number of complex technologies would probably find matrix departmentalization appropriate. Delta Airlines and other organizations

TABLE 10.5

Organizational Characteristics and Type of Departmentalization

Organizational Characteristic	Type of Departmentalization Favored
Small size	Functional
Global or national scope	Place
Depends on highly competitive state-of-the-art technology	Matrix
Critical to use scarce resources appropriately	Matrix
Customer base is:	
Changing	Matrix
Diverse	Product or service
Stable	Functional
Makes use of specialized equipment	Product or service
Requires skill specialization	Functional
High transportation costs for raw materials	Place

that operate across a wide range of national and international regions might benefit from place departmentalization. Clearly, the choice depends on the situation. It is even possible for one organization to use all four types of departmentalization. Sears, for example, uses all four effectively to coordinate the activities of its different companies, such as Allstate Insurance and Dean Witter and Reynolds.

COORDINATION

Departmentalization divides the organization's work and allows for specialization and standardization of activities. However, in order to achieve organizational objectives, managers also need to coordinate people, projects, and tasks. Coordination is the process of integrating all the parts of the whole to achieve common objectives. Without coordination, people's efforts are likely to end in delay, frustration, and waste. Coordination is one of the basic elements of organizational structure for precisely that reason.

Many managers believe that good people can make any organizational structure work. Although this may be overstating the case, people who can work well together to get things done are an extremely valuable asset. A good analogy is football, where teamwork is of the essence. During practice sessions NFL coaches try to transform many individual players into one smoothly functioning team. Players learn their tasks in this cooperative effort and how each part relates to every other part as well as to the whole. Coordination is required as the players execute their functions, particularly when they are called on to innovate or adjust to the unexpected in a game situation. Similarly, managers have to encourage employees to subordinate their individual interests to the organization's broader goals.

In this section we present three basic principles of coordination: the unity of command principle, the scalar principle, and the span of management principle. These are valuable additions to your toolkit of management skills.

unity of command principle The basic principle of organizational coordination that states that an employee should have only one boss.

Unity of Command Principle

The **unity of command principle** states that an employee should have only one boss. Every employee needs to know who is giving the orders and to whom he or she reports.

Managers must minimize any confusion over who makes decisions and who implements them, because uncertainty in this area can lead to serious productivity and morale problems. Matrix departmentalization intentionally violates this principle, however, in order to gain flexibility.

Scalar Principle

scalar principle The basic principle of organizational coordination that states that a clear and unbroken chain of command should link every person in the organization with someone a level higher, to the top of the organization chart.

The **scalar principle** states that a clear and unbroken chain of command should link every person in the organization with someone a level higher, all the way to the top of the organization chart. Tasks should be delegated clearly, with no overlapping or splitting of assignments. This principle is illustrated in Figure 10.3, which shows part of the organizational structure of American Express Company's Travel Related Services Group (division). At American Express, the manager of the Optima Gold card reports to the Vice President, Consumer Credit Card Group, USA. That Vice President in turn reports to the Executive Vice President of Travel Related Services, who reports to the CEO.

If it were followed faithfully the scalar principle would require that job-related communications between employees in different departments at the same level (such as the Africa manager and the tours manager in Figure 10.3) always be approved by their respective superiors. Obviously, strict adherence to this principle would waste time and money—and be extremely frustrating. In practice, informal relationships across departmental lines spring up to facilitate problem solving and communication within the organization.

As American and foreign corporations scramble for position in the global marketplace, they are discovering that the unity of command and scalar principles they have followed for decades may no longer be effective. New challenges are creating problems, and solving them is taking nothing less than a whole new way of thinking about how a modern corporation should be run. This chapter's Global Link feature shows how some multinational companies are bypassing the unity of command and scalar principles when they create networked organizations.

Span of Management Principle

span of management principle The basic principle of organizational coordination that says that the number of people reporting directly to any one manager must be limited.

The **span of management principle** states that the number of people reporting directly to any one manager must be limited because one manager can't effectively supervise a large number of subordinates. Span of management is a concept as old as organizations. In fact, it began with Roman military commanders' belief that narrow spans of management were effective in combat situations.[11] The traditional viewpoint of management (Chapter 2) holds that the number of subordinates reporting to any one manager should range between four and twelve.

For the most part successful organizations in the 1990s will have flat structures. Many companies—Gillette, Firestone, and Pacific Bell, among others—have already flattened by cutting the layers of management between the CEO and first-line supervisors. This means that the span of management has broadened, with a much larger number of people reporting to each manager. For example, when Victor Kiam bought Remington Razors, there were only 480 employees. He ran the business with six senior executives in key functional areas, such as production, sales, and engineering. Less than ten years later Remington has more than 2000 employees and 80 senior managers with clearly defined authority and responsibilities. Since he cannot directly oversee eighty people, Kiam has delegated decision making to those managers. Each of them has clear goals and is assigned problems that can be broken down into manageable parts.[12]

There is no ''correct'' number of subordinates that a manager can supervise effectively. According to the National Conference Board, four key factors determine the best span of management for a given situation:

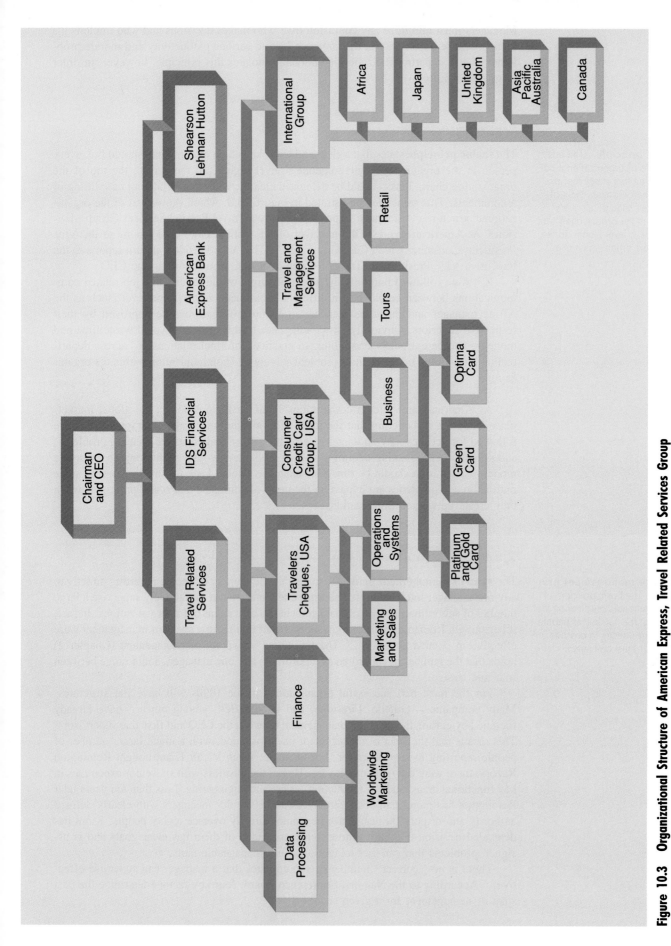

Figure 10.3 Organizational Structure of American Express, Travel Related Services Group

Application of the scalar principle at American Express means that the manager of the Optima Card Group reports to the vice president, Consumer Credit Card Group, USA. That vice president in turn reports to the executive vice president of Travel Related Services, who reports to the CEO. (*Source:* American Express Company, *1989 Annual Report.*)

GLOBAL Link

CORPORATE NETWORKS

Foreign expansion of corporations is creating bigger and sometimes more bureaucratic organizations. At the same time, though, companies must be more flexible than ever to compete successfully around the world. Responding quickly to fast-changing technology and the diverse demands of regional markets requires product innovation and differentiation on an unprecedented scale. Competition forces management to put in place stringent cost cutting measures and other efficiencies.

Figuring out how to be both big *and* responsive to change has been a continuing headache for Ciba-Geigy, AT&T, Rockwell International, and other companies pursuing a global strategy. How, for example, can top management bring growing ranks of foreign managers into the creative decision-making process? And how can it make sure that all managers are kept informed of all developments that affect them?

The answers to these and other questions have begun to come together in a new concept of management organization. Informally dubbed the *corporate network*, this concept holds that a large or multinational corporation should be managed not through a vertical chain of command but as a vast network of employees who are linked together by an extensive communications system and united by a clearly articulated corporate vision. Broadly speaking, a networked organization is one in which all employees in all parts of the world create, produce, and sell the company's products. At GE, Jack Welch uses networks in which technology, information, managers, and management practices flow freely from one division to another. When inspectors at the aircraft engineering division check the integrity of metal parts, for example, they use x-ray technology developed by the medical systems division.

The corporate network is perceived as the antidote to the rigidity of functional departmentalization. As more and more managers now recognize, innovation is by nature informal and spontaneous. This means that marketing managers in Japan and Spain, say, must be part of the process when a product or service for their markets is being developed in California and manufactured in Ohio. If they want to discuss customer complaints about product quality, they don't call headquarters, they call the quality-control manager in Ohio. This is a clear violation of the scalar principle.

Pursued on a companywide scale, these lateral working relationships push more of the strategic planning and decision making down to the middle layers of management. Top management's job, then, is to put in place the mechanisms that promote the necessary interactions—not to control them but to create conditions under which they'll flourish. In short, the corporate network is not so much a new organizational structure as it is a departure from the whole idea of structure, in which management control is replaced by coordination.

Sources: Adapted from F. V. Guterl, ''Goodbye, Old Matrix,'' *Business Month*, February 1989, 32–38; and J. Barker, D. Tjosvold, and J. R. Andrews, ''Conflict Approaches of Effective and Ineffective Project Managers: A Field Study in a Matrix Organization,'' *Journal of Management Studies*, 1988, 25: 167–168; B. Dumaine, ''What the Leaders of Tomorrow See,'' *Fortune*, July 3, 1989, 48–62.

1. *The competence of both the manager and the employees.* If employees are new to a task, they obviously take up more of a manager's time than knowledgeable employees do. New employees work best under closer supervision.

2. *The similarity or dissimilarity of tasks being supervised.* At Remington, there is a wide span of management, because all managers can focus on one product, the electric razor. The more numerous and dissimilar the products, the narrower the span.

3. *The incidence of new problems in the manager's department.* The manager must know enough about the operations of his or her department to understand precisely the problems that subordinates are likely to face. If the manager knows these, then a span can increase.

4. *The extent of clear operating standards and rules.* At McDonald's there are extensive rules to govern the behavior of employees. Under conditions like this a manager's span may be wide because rules do a lot of the controlling.

Coordination versus Departmentalization

In any organization there is a tension between coordination and departmentalization. Figure 10.4 illustrates the extent of this tension under the four types of departmentalization.

Situation A represents the case where the forces for coordination are stronger than those for departmentalization. For example, Pep Boys has kept pace with the changing needs of car owners by stocking a large assortment of automotive tires, parts, and accessories for domestic and imported cars and trucks. To provide speedy, efficient service to customers, coordination of departmental activities must be smooth and flawless. When a problem arises, top managers must be able to quickly coordinate the actions of various functional departments—such as merchandising, marketing, and distribution—to find a solution. Under such conditions, functional departmentalization provides the necessary degree of coordination.

When forces for coordination and departmentalization are equal, as in situation B in Figure 10.4, a matrix form of departmentalization works best. The matrix structure addresses the conflict between, say, the product manager's need to satisfy clients and the functional department's need to provide technical help. Employees move from product to product, depending on which tasks must be completed next. Keith Glegg, manager of the Electronics Division of Canadian Marconi Company, used a matrix structure to effectively manage growth. Each of the division's products contained a major radar system with a unique design and customer specifications. The different products shared manufacturing facilities and functional departments. His idea was to identify each of the radar products with an identifiable task group headed by a project manager. The project manager was responsible for everything associated with that product. The functional managers assigned employees in their departments to the different projects. Upon completion of a project, employees would return to their home functional department.

When forces for departmentalization are stronger than those for coordination—shown as situation C—top managers are likely to use place or product or service departmentalization. Managers decide what is appropriate for only their product or service, and they decide without having to consider the impact of their decisions on other product lines. Each product manager at Harris Corporation faces different problems requiring different solutions. Since each product line is unique, there is little need for or advantage in coordinating activities between lines. Some coordination, however, might take place across products (or services) by having managers of each line use similar reporting forms or techniques for financial, accounting, or purchasing information so that comparable data are collected at the corporate level.

FIGURE 10.4

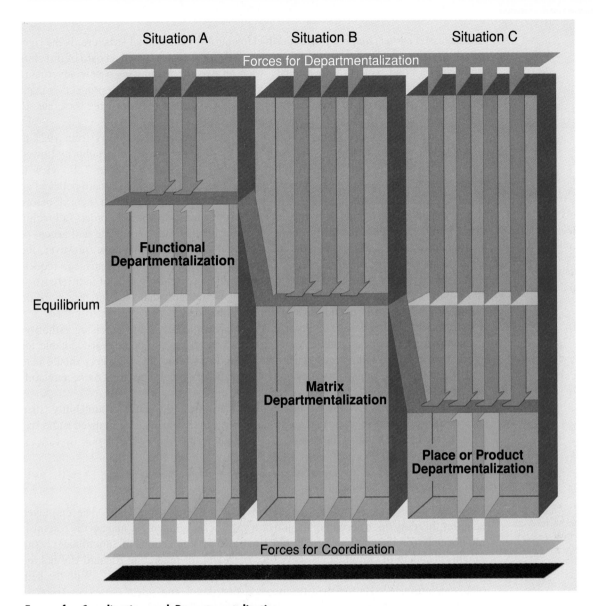

Forces for Coordination and Departmentalization

Tensions between the forces for coordination and those for departmentalization can be of different relative strengths and call for different forms of departmentalization.

For multinational companies, such as GE, American Express, and IBM, the use of several types of departmentalization and methods of coordination is most likely. In such organizations there is no single best way to balance the tension between coordination and departmentalization. Figure 10.3 shows that American Express is organized into four product/service groups, or divisions. The Travel Related Services Group is further departmentalized by function and place. The methods of coordination vary for each product line, depending on the circumstances facing that division. In some functional departments, the scalar principle will be implemented effectively, along with narrow spans of management. In departments that reflect place departmentalization, violation of the scalar principle is common, and wide spans of management are effective.

As discussed earlier, *authority,* the fourth element of organizational structure, is the right to act or make a decision.[13] Authority is exercised, for instance, when a board of directors authorizes a bond issue to raise capital, when an executive approves a new advertising campaign, when a sales manager signs a contract with a client, when a production manager promotes a worker to first-line manager, and when a supervisor fires someone. In short, authority is the glue of organizational structure.

Chester Barnard, president of New Jersey Bell Telephone Company from 1927 to 1948, held a somewhat different view of authority.[14] He maintained that authority flowed from the bottom up, rather than from the top down. As noted in Chapter 2, his view is known as the *acceptance theory of authority.* This doesn't mean that Barnard believed an employee should analyze and judge every decision made by an immediate superior before either accepting or rejecting it. Rather, he thought that most decisions or orders fall within the subordinate's **zone of indifference,** which means that the subordinate will accept or obey them without question. If a decision or order falls outside that zone, however, the subordinate will question whether to accept or reject it. For example, a manager's request that a secretary take dictation probably falls within the secretary's zone of indifference— it's a part of the job description. But the manager's request that the secretary work on Saturday probably falls outside that zone, and the secretary may decide to refuse.

Authority implies responsibility and accountability. That is, by exercising authority, managers accept the responsibility for acting and are willing to be held accountable for success or failure. Furthermore, when delegating tasks to others, managers should take care to match the responsibility they confer with authority and then insist on accountability for results.

In the following sections we briefly review responsibility and accountability, then move on to explore delegation and questions of centralized versus decentralized authority. Finally, we examine the roles of line and staff authority.

zone of indifference The intangible area within which fall the decisions or orders a subordinate will accept without question.

Responsibility

Responsibility is an employee's obligation to perform assigned tasks. The employee acquires this duty upon accepting the job or a specific assignment. A manager is responsible not only for carrying out certain tasks but also for the actions of subordinates. Ann Flavin, president of Optigraphics, gave vice president for marketing Richard Harmel the responsibility for marketing a new product—a baseball card, Sportflics™. With the help of his subordinates, Harmel had to choose a distributor and select the stores (such as Wal-Mart and 7-Eleven) that would carry the cards, decide what price to charge, and guess what moves competitors (such as Topps) would make to avoid losing sales. Responsibility demands that Harmel take these tasks seriously and that Flavin provide him with the tools (advertising money, displays at trade shows, personnel) to accomplish the marketing program's objectives. Flavin reviews Harmel's progress on a quarterly basis to make sure his plan is working and to help him reach his goals.

responsibility An employee's obligation to perform assigned tasks.

Accountability

Accountability is the expectation that each employee will accept credit or blame for results achieved in performing assigned tasks. Management also expects employees to report the results of their work. This feedback enables management to determine whether effective decisions are being made and whether tasks are being performed properly. A manager cannot check everything an employee does, so the manager establishes guidelines within which work must be done. The employee is accountable for performance within these limits. Thus, unlike authority, accountability *always* flows from the bottom

accountability The expectation that each employee will accept credit or blame for results achieved in performing assigned tasks.

up. The news assistant is accountable to the senior reporter, the senior reporter is accountable to the editor, the editor is accountable to the publisher of the newspaper, and so forth.

Accountability is the point at which authority and responsibility meet. For example, the state grants you the authority to drive an automobile and gives you responsibility for obeying traffic laws. You are then held accountable for your behavior while driving a car. At Optigraphics, Flavin gave Harmel authority consistent with the responsibility for marketing a new product. She therefore had the right to hold him accountable for the results. When either authority or responsibility are lacking, managers cannot judge a subordinate's accomplishments fairly. And when managers are reluctant to hold subordinates accountable for their tasks, subordinates can easily pass the buck for nonperformance.

Delegation of Authority

delegation of authority
The process by which managers assign the right to act and make decisions in certain areas to subordinates.

Delegation of authority is the process by which managers assign the right to act and make decisions in certain areas to subordinates. In other words, the manager assigns a task to a subordinate along with adequate authority to carry it out effectively. Delegation starts when the structure of the organization is being established and tasks are divided. It continues as new tasks are added during day-to-day operations. Delegation of authority occurs when a company president assigns to an executive assistant the task of preparing a formal statement for presentation to a congressional committee, or when the head of a computer department instructs a programmer to debug a new management reporting system. In each case a manager gives decision-making powers to a subordinate. The basic components of the delegation process are determining expected results, assigning tasks and the authority to accomplish them, and holding others accountable for results achieved.[15] It is not practical to separate these components.

Improving Delegation   There are six principles that are useful for improving delegation of authority:

1. *Establish objectives and standards.*   Subordinates should participate in developing the objectives they will be expected to meet. They should also agree to the standards that will be used to measure their performance.

2. *Define authority and responsibility.*   Subordinates should clearly understand the work delegated to them, recognize the scope of their authority, and accept their accountability for results.

3. *Involve subordinates.*   The challenge of the work itself won't always encourage subordinates to accept and perform delegated tasks well. Managers can motivate subordinates by involving them in decision making, by keeping them informed, and by helping them improve their skills and abilities.

4. *Require completed work.*   Managers should require that subordinates carry a task through to completion. The manager's job is to provide guidance, help, and information—not to finish the job.

5. *Provide training.*   Delegation can be only as effective as the ability of people to perform the work and make the necessary decisions. Managers should continually appraise delegated responsibilities and provide training aimed at building on strengths and overcoming deficiencies.

6. *Establish adequate controls.*   Managers should provide timely, accurate reports that enable subordinates to compare their performance to agreed-on standards and to correct their deficiencies.[16]

Barriers to Delegation   Managers often fail to delegate authority because of psychological and organizational barriers.[17] The biggest psychological barrier to delegation is fear. A manager may be afraid that if subordinates don't do the job properly, the manager's own reputation will suffer. "I can do it better myself." "My subordinates are not capable enough." "It takes too much time to explain what I want done." All of these are reasons managers give for not delegating authority. Failing to delegate can be justified only if subordinates are untrained or poorly motivated. However, it is the manager's responsibility to overcome such deficiencies. Managers may also be reluctant to delegate because they fear that subordinates will do the work their own way, do it too well, and outshine the boss!

Among the organizational barriers that may block delegation is a failure to clearly define authority and responsibility. If managers themselves don't know what is expected or what to do, they can't clearly delegate authority to others. The Challenger space shuttle disaster in January 1986 has been blamed on the combined failure of NASA and Morton Thiokol (NASA's principal contractor for booster rockets) to clearly define authority and responsibility. A presidential commission found that NASA engineers had sufficient information about the O-rings prior to the flight to cancel it, but this information didn't reach the people with authority to do so. NASA managers failed to properly delegate decision-making authority and responsibility to those people (the engineers) who knew the crew would be in serious danger. Failure to delegate in this case cost lives and demoralized NASA employees.

Overcoming Barriers to Delegation Effective delegation requires that managers give their subordinates real freedom to accomplish assigned tasks. Managers must accept that there are several ways to deal with a situation—their own way isn't necessarily the one their subordinates will choose. Of course, subordinates will make errors, but they should be allowed to develop their own solutions to problems and to learn from their mistakes. This is very difficult for many managers to accept, but unless they do, they won't delegate effectively. They will be so busy with minor tasks or with checking on subordinates that they will fail to complete their own important assignments. Managers must keep in mind that the advantages of delegation justify giving subordinates freedom of action, even at the risk of allowing mistakes to occur.

Barriers to delegation can also be overcome through improved communication between managers and subordinates. Managers who make it a point to learn the strengths, weaknesses, and preferences of their subordinates can more effectively decide which tasks can be delegated to whom. Such knowledge will give them greater confidence in their delegation decisions. In addition, subordinates who are encouraged to use their abilities and who feel that their managers will back them up will, in turn, become more eager to accept responsibility.

Centralization and Decentralization of Authority

centralization of authority A management approach that is characterized by authority concentrated at the top of an organization or department.

decentralization of authority A management approach characterized by a high degree of delegated authority throughout an organization or department.

Centralization and decentralization of authority are basic, overall management philosophies of delegation, of where decisions are to be made.[18] **Centralization of authority** is characterized by authority concentrated at the top of an organization or department. **Decentralization of authority** is characterized by a high degree of delegated authority throughout an organization or department. Decentralization is an approach that requires managers to decide what and when to delegate, to carefully select and train personnel, and to formulate adequate controls.

Neither centralization nor decentralization is absolute. No one manager makes all the decisions, even in a centralized setting. And total delegation would end the need for middle and first-line managers. Thus there are only degrees of centralization and decentralization. In most organizations some tasks are relatively centralized (for example, payroll systems, purchasing, and personnel policies), and others are relatively decentralized (marketing and production for instance). At General Mills, which manufactures food products such as Cheerios, Gold Medal flour, and Betty Crocker cake mixes and operates Red Lobster and Olive Garden restaurants, each vice president has the authority to delegate production and marketing decisions to subordinates. According to CEO Bruce Atwater, delegating these decisions is necessary to stay in tune with customer tastes, be innovative, and stay ahead of the competition. On the other hand, General Mills centralizes purchasing decisions, so it can use its vast buying power to get all managers a ''good'' price from suppliers.

3M Corporation's offices, which have an open, unstructured design, reflect its *decentralized corporate culture*.

corporate culture The norms, values, and practices that characterize a particular organization.

Factors Affecting Centralization and Decentralization Several factors can affect management's decision to centralize or decentralize decision-making responsibilities. Let's briefly consider six of these factors.

1. *Costliness of decisions.* Cost is perhaps the most important factor in determining the extent of centralization. As a general rule, the more costly the decision is to the organization, the more likely it is that top management will make it. For instance, the General Mills decision to sell off Izod apparel, Parker Toys, and Eddie Bauer retail outlets was made by CEO Atwater and his staff. Decision costs may be measured in dollars or in intangibles such as the company's reputation in the community, social responsibilities, or employee morale.

2. *Uniformity of policy.* Managers who value consistency favor centralization of authority. These managers may want to assure customers that everyone is treated equally in terms of quality, price, credit, delivery, and service. At Pep Boys, a nationwide tire sales promotion requires that all 243 stores charge the same price. Uniform policies have definite advantages for cost accounting, production, and financial departments. And they enable managers to compare the relative efficiencies of various departments. In organizations with unions, such as General Motors and American Airlines, uniform policy also aids the administration of labor agreements regarding wages, promotions, fringe benefits, and other personnel matters.

3. *Corporate culture.* A firm's culture will play a large part in determining whether authority will be centralized. **Corporate culture** refers to the norms, values, and practices characterizing the organization.[19] Caring about its employees and serving its customers are the dominant values in J. C. Penney's corporate culture. Management actions have reinforced these values ever since founder James Cash Penney laid down the seven guiding principles, called the ''Penney Idea.'' For instance, one store manager was warned by a top manager for making too much profit—it was unfair to customers. Customers can return merchandise with no questions asked. Everyone within the company is treated as an individual. Employees are encouraged to participate in decisions that will impact them, and layoffs are avoided at all costs. Long-term employee loyalty is especially valued. Decision making at Penney's is decentralized in the retail area for merchandising but centralized in finance areas.

PepsiCo has a very different corporate culture, reflecting its desire to overtake Coke's share of the soft drink market. Managers compete fiercely against one another to gain market share, to squeeze more profit out of their product line, and to work harder. Employees who don't succeed are fired. Even the company picnic is characterized by intensely competitive games, which teams strive to win at all costs.[20] Everyone knows the corporate culture and either thrives on the creative tension it creates or leaves. At PepsiCo each brand manager is responsible for his or her decisions. Decentralizing so that decisions are made by those closest to the customers clearly establishes accountability.

4. *Availability of managers.* Many organizations work hard to ensure an adequate supply of competent managers, an absolute necessity for decentralization. These organizations believe that practical experience is the best training for developing managerial potential. They are therefore willing to permit managers to make mistakes involving small costs.

5. *Control mechanisms.* Even the most avid proponents of decentralization, such as DuPont, GE, Marriott, and Sears, insist on controls to determine whether actual events are meeting expectations.[21] Each hotel in the Marriott chain collects certain key data, such as number of beds occupied, employee turnover, number of meals served, and the average amount guests spend on food and beverages. Analysis of the data helps the manager control important aspects of the motel's operation and compare it against the performance of others in the chain. If a motel's operations are not within certain guidelines, then management can take some decision-making responsibility away from it.

6. *Environmental influences.* External factors, such as unions, federal and state regulatory agencies, and tax policies, affect the degree of centralization within a firm. Governmental policy on the employment of minorities, for example, makes it hard for a

company to decentralize hiring authority. And a local manager can't establish hours and wages that violate government limits on number of hours worked and the minimum wage. Unions with long-term contracts also exert a centralizing influence on many organizations. When they bargain on behalf of the employees of an entire organization, such as Ford, Delta Airlines, or the National Football League, management can't risk the decentralization of labor negotiations. But when small local or regional unions represent employees in various departments, top management may delegate the authority to negotiate the terms of labor contracts to departmental managers.

Advantages of Decentralization   Used successfully, decentralization has several advantages. First, it frees top managers to develop organizational plans and strategies. Lower-level managers handle routine, day-to-day decisions. Second, it develops lower-level managers' conceptual skills. According to Jack Welch, president of GE, decentralization prepares managers for positions requiring greater judgment and increased responsibility.[22] Third, because subordinates are often closer to the action than higher-level managers, they may have a better grasp of all the facts. This knowledge may enable them to make better, faster decisions. Valuable time can be lost when a subordinate must check everything with his or her boss. Fourth, decentralization fosters a healthy, achievement-oriented atmosphere among managers.

Line Authority and Staff Authority

line authority   The authority to direct and control immediate subordinates who perform activities essential to achieving organizational objectives.

staff authority   The authority to direct and control subordinates who support line activities through advice, recommendations, research, technical expertise.

In a typical organization **line authority** belongs to managers who have formal authority to direct and control immediate subordinates who perform activities essential to achieving organizational objectives. Line authority thus flows through the primary chain of command, according to the scalar principle. On the other hand, those with **staff authority** direct and control subordinates who support line activities through advice, recommendations, research, and technical expertise. Staff managers and employees support line functions with specialized services and information.

Line functions are closely tied to organizational objectives and methods of production. These functions differ from one type of organization to another. For example, Figure 10.5 shows an abridged version of the Toys "R" Us organization chart. In this case line departments are those that perform tasks that directly support the organization's goals, such as marketing, store merchandising, and physical distribution. Staff departments are those that provide specialized skills in support of the line departments, including finance and administration, real estate, and management information systems. The line departments follow the line of authority from the office of CEO down to the vice presidents for divisional merchandising. All staff departments exist at the corporate level, to support the line managers.

In organizations that provide services rather than produce goods the distinction between line and staff isn't quite the same. For example, in a hospital, although healing is a key organizational goal, it is the technical *staff* (physicians) who treat patients and *line* managers who are the administrators dealing with hospital maintenance and finance. Similarly, in a university, although education is the key goal, the professional *staff* (faculty) do the job of educating and performing research, and *line* managers (deans, registrars) perform support and auxiliary functions. In both cases many of the line functions resemble staff functions in goods-producing businesses.

Location of Staff Departments   The location of staff departments within an organization is usually determined by the differences between generalized and specialized functions. If staff services are used extensively throughout the organization, departments may need to be located relatively high up in the hierarchy, so that managers can make decisions in the best interests of the whole company. Most large organizations centralize general staff functions at the top. In Toys "R" Us, for instance, the corporate staff consists of offices that handle finance and administration,

FIGURE 10.5

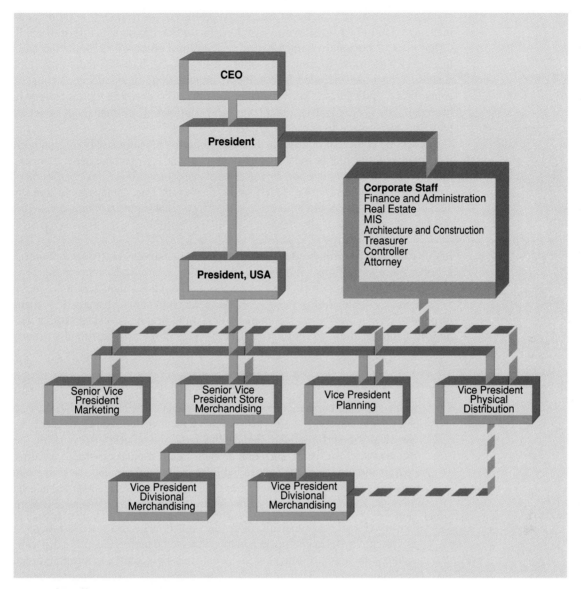

Line and Staff Structure at Toys "R" Us

Line authority flows through the primary chain of command, shown as red lines. Staff, or indirect, authority is shown by the blue lines.

(*Source:* Abridged from Toys "R" Us *Annual Report,* 1989.)

real estate, management information systems, treasury functions, and corporate legal staff. The vice presidents who manage these staff functions are usually in corporate policy-making positions. The vice president for real estate at Toys "R" Us is responsible for developing companywide store location sites.

If a staff department provides necessary services to a specific line function, it should be located near that function both physically and in terms of managerial authority. A staff specialist who performs some support functions that a line manager would otherwise have to perform usually reports directly to that line manager.

Line and Staff Conflicts Because of differences in their roles, line and staff managers don't always see eye-to-eye. One factor that aggravates line-staff conflict is differences in personal characteristics.[23] A group composed of both line and staff managers was asked to rank personality traits on the basis of their importance to success. The traits included forcefulness, imagination, independence, cooperation, adaptability, and caution. Staff managers felt that to succeed in their jobs they had to be imaginative, cooperative, adaptable, and cautious. Line managers believed that they had to be forceful and independent.

A second source of conflict is that staff departments are usually located higher in the organizational hierarchy than line departments. Top management often calls on them to analyze data and report on the effectiveness of various line departments. Thus they gain informal authority, much to the dismay of line managers. In this kind of situation line managers often perceive staff efforts as attempts to check on and control their activities.

In this chapter we highlighted the basic ways that managers can structure their organizations. As organizations get more involved in global activities and perhaps downsize to improve their competitive position in the marketplace, managers must inevitably rethink their organization's design. In the next chapter we discuss how managers respond to changes in the environment by designing organizations appropriately, how they use information systems and different technologies to accomplish this goal.

CHAPTER SUMMARY

1. There are four basic elements of organizational structure: Specialization is the process of identifying tasks and assigning them to individuals or teams trained specifically to perform them. Standardization is the process of developing the procedures by which the organization promotes uniform and consistent performance. Coordination involves the formal and informal procedures that integrate tasks performed by separate groups. Authority is the right to make decisions and take action. An organization chart can depict the interrelationships among these four elements.

2. Four types of departmentalization are: functional departmentalization, which groups employees according to common tasks to be performed; place departmentalization, which groups functions and employees by geographic location; product or service departmentalization, which groups employees in self-contained units, each responsible for its own product or service; and matrix departmentalization, which gathers project teams from various functional and product departments, each under the authority of a project manager.

3. Managers can use three principles in coordinating employee activities: The unity of command principle states that each employee should report to only one boss. The scalar principle states that a clear, unbroken chain of command should link every person in the organization with his or her superior. The span of management principle states that the number of subordinates who report directly to a particular manager should be limited.

4. Authority is the right to make decisions and take action. Responsibility is the obligation to perform assigned tasks. Accountability is the expectation that each employee will accept credit or blame for results of his or her performance. Delegation is the managerial assignment of authority to subordinates.

5. Six factors affect managers' decisions to centralize or decentralize authority: (1) costliness of decisions, (2) uniformity of policy, (3) corporate culture, (4) availability of good managers, (5) control mechanisms, and (6) environmental influences.

6. Line authority flows through the primary chain of command, according to the scalar principle, and is held by those managers whose activities are essential to achieving organizational objectives. Staff authority is held by managers whose offices support line activities via provision of specialized services and information.

1. What problems is Pep Boys likely to face because of the way it is organized?

2. When is product departmentalization preferable to functional departmentalization?

3. What problems is Harris Corporation likely to face because of the way it is organized?

4. What problems can arise in a matrix structure?

5. What conditions should be present before an organization adopts a matrix structure? Could a matrix structure be used in your business school? Explain how.

6. What problems might arise in a company that uses several forms of departmentalization?

7. What concepts are important in establishing corporate networks? What principles of coordination are violated?

8. Why do some subordinates fail to accept the authority delegated to them?

9. How can an organization strive to make authority equal to responsibility?

10. **From Where You Sit:** When might a failure to accept delegated authority *not* be a failure but a contribution?

11. Why do some managers find it difficult to delegate decision-making powers to subordinates?

12. What factors suggest that an organization is relatively decentralized?

13. Is J. C. Penney centralized or decentralized? Explain.

14. Why might organizations appear more centralized to middle and first-line managers than to top managers?

15. **From Where You Sit:** Would you prefer to work in a centralized or decentralized company? Why? (The Skill Development Exercise that follows may help you answer this question.)

16. Could an organization survive without staff managers? What limitations might this put on line managers?

17. **From Where You Sit:** If you were applying for a job on the corporate staff of Toys "R" Us, what concerns would you have?

Centralization or Decentralization: What's Your Choice?

People differ in their organizational and work-setting preferences. Debates on how the organization should be run consume untold hours around the water cooler. Such debates very often involve specific personalities and policies, but they also tend to reflect the general biases or preferences of the individuals involved. The inventory below is designed to help you survey your own preferences. There are no right or wrong answers. Instead, the inventory is designed to stimulate your thoughts about working in a centralized or decentralized organization.

Instructions

Your preferences are to be expressed by circling one of the following responses for each statement:

SA—Strongly Agree
A—Agree Somewhat
U—Undecided
D—Disagree Somewhat
SD—Strongly Disagree

Your first reaction to each statement is probably the best. Spending too much time debating your feelings with yourself will only leave you undecided.

I prefer to work in an organization where

1. Goals are defined by those in higher-level positions.

2. Methods and procedures for achieving goals are specified for me.   SA A U D SD

3. Top management makes important decisions.   SA A U D SD

4. My loyalty counts as much as my ability to do the job.   SA A U D SD

5. Clear lines of authority and responsibility are established.   SA A U D SD

6. Top management is decisive and firm.   SA A U D SD

7. My career is pretty well planned out for me.   SA A U D SD

8. I can specialize.   SA A U D SD

9. My length of service is almost as important as my level of performance.   SA A U D SD

10. Management is able to provide the information I need to do my job well.   SA A U D SD

11. A chain of command is well established.

12. Rules and procedures are adhered to equally by everyone.

13. People accept the authority of the leader's position.   SA A U D SD

14. People are loyal to their boss.   SA A U D SD

15. People do as they have been instructed.   SA A U D SD

16. People clear things with their boss before going over his or her head.   SA A U D SD

SA A U D SD

SA A U D SD

Scoring

Each question attempts to assess your preference for either a centralized or a decentralized organization. The more you agree with each statement, the more you prefer decision making to be centralized. By assigning a 5 to each SA response, a 4 to each A response, and so on down to a 1 for each SD response, you can score the strength of your preferences.

Interpretation

Total Score	Preference Type
76–80	You strongly prefer centralized decision making.
65–75	You're an organization person—you'll follow the rules.
48–64	You're undecided.
32–47	You're prone to working in a decentralized organization.
Less than 32	You strongly prefer decentralized decision making.

To: High School Staff
From: Wanda Boyd, Superintendent
Re: Implementation of New Computer System

As you know, our school district has been regarded as one of the most innovative in the state. We decentralized decision making five years ago to give teachers the freedom and flexibility to try new ideas. This encouraged many of you to adopt the latest teaching techniques in your classes. Administrators and guidance counselors told me that many of you became highly motivated, and our morale surveys indicated that many of you were very satisfied with our school system.

The failure of the bond issue last year has changed things. The district is running at a deficit. Salaries and costs for innovative teaching materials have simply outstripped our revenues. It is obvious that the taxpayers do not want tax increases.

You also know that I have hired a staff expert in administrative controls. Her first job will be to install a computer system that will give my office control over all expenditures. Many decisions that in the past were decentralized will now be centralized. Rules and procedures will be put in place to make sure that any new educational program's costs will be in line with its budget. Approval of new programs will be contingent on cost efficiency, and innovations will be adopted only if they have districtwide appeal. I hope that you will give our new staff member your very best cooperation in these trying times.

Question: Assume that you have been elected by your fellow teachers to write a response to the superintendent's memo. What would you write?

Revamp at Olivetti Has Yet to Add Up

By Richard L. Hudson
and Guy Collins

IVREA, Italy—In 1988, one of Italy's best-known computer executives, Vittorio Cassoni, took the helm at Ing. C. Olivetti & Co. with grand plans to revive the ailing computer maker. He promised nothing less than "the launch of a new Olivetti."

Nearly three years later, the company's shareholders can be forgiven if they're pining for the old Olivetti.

Since Mr. Cassoni's appointment as managing director, the company's stock price has slid to one-fifth its 1986 peak. Though Mr. Cassoni says he expects profit to increase this year, next month Olivetti will report dismal 1990 results—its fourth consecutive annual profit drop, a plunge of more than 40% to about $100 million. Revenue stagnated in 1990 at 9.04 trillion lire ($7.71 billion).

A corporate reorganization ordered by Mr. Cassoni and Olivetti's globe-trotting chairman, Carlo De Benedetti, caused so much turmoil inside the company that order growth temporarily slowed to 3.2%. Orders have since rebounded.

Some chronic problems, such as customer complaints about service and quality, linger on. One client, Finnish bank Okobank, says Olivetti still hasn't corrected a problem with its 650 automated teller machines. The machines sometimes freeze up in winter, accidentally confiscating depositors' bank cards. "They know about the problem and I trust them [to fix it], but those machines have to work," says Velimatti Myndtinen, Okobank's director of information technology.

Mr. Cassoni's inability so far to restore Olivetti's former glory illustrates a maxim in the tough world of selling computers: What goes down seldom comes up. . . .

But in an interview at Olivetti headquarters here near Turin, Mr. Cassoni insists a recovery is already under way. A barrage of new products—including a line of minicomputers to be unveiled this week at the annual European computer fair—can recover market share. One impediment last year, a weak dollar that hurt Olivetti's foreign sales, probably won't be around this year, he says; after adjusting for currency, revenue grew 3% last year. . . .

The force of Mr. Cassoni's will became clear early. With a mandate from Mr. De Benedetti to clean house, he scrapped Olivetti's centralized structure and broke the company into three main divisions each focusing on a different market: the mass market, professional computer systems buyers and the computer-service market. He ordered a crash program to make Olivetti a bigger force in computers using standardized components. He introduced his managers to a U.S. business institution, the working breakfast. He ordered more memorandums and meetings.

"If you are selling [meeting-room] flip charts, we are the best customer in the world," jokes one Cassoni lieutenant, Elserino Piol.

But there were two main problems. One was Mr. Cassoni's misfortune in having begun the reorganization in January 1989, just as the European computer market shifted into low gear.

The second problem was internal chaos caused by the reorganization. Several former Olivetti officials—all of whom asked not to be named—said turf battles erupted between the two biggest Olivetti divisions, the mass-market Olivetti Office unit and the professional Olivetti Systems & Networks unit. Stephen Pinning, managing director of Fastnet Systems PLC, a London dealer for Systems & Networks, says Fastnet was astounded 15 months ago to find itself bidding against an Olivetti Office dealer for a British government contract.

The worst fighting appeared to end after the resignations last year of two division chiefs. "Forget the first 18 months" of the reorganization, says Mr. Piol. The main point is, he says, that Olivetti has emerged with "a better winning attitude."

Some big Olivetti customers agree. Brian Bath, manager of equipment services at Barclays Bank PLC, praises the way Olivetti is servicing the banking company's computer-related equipment, assigning more than 200 employees to the task under a multiyear contract.

But that isn't the Olivetti many other, especially smaller, customers know and still complain about. "The Olivetti product is certainly good, but not the technical backup," says Luigi Dioli, computer purchasing manager for Milan's Sacred Heart University, whose administration has 250 to 300 personal computers.

1. Describe Olivetti's new departmentalization structure in terms of what you have learned in this chapter.

2. What factors do you think influenced Cassoni in changing Olivetti's organizational structure?

3. Do you think turf battles are a necessary aspect of reorganization? How might they be prevented?

ORGANIZING FOR RENEWAL

In today's business environment the only constant is change. There are organizations that somehow effectively manage change, continuously adapting their bureaucracies, strategies, systems, products, and cultures to survive the shocks and to prosper under the same forces that destroy their competition. They move from strength to strength, adjusting to crises that have led others in their industry to fail. They are masters of *renewal*.

A formidable barrier to change and renewal is the organizational split. The most obvious split is that between labor and management. Then there's the classic line-and-staff split. Marketing versus manufacturing. The New York office versus Chicago. One division versus another (or versus the rest of the company). The German (or French or European) operation versus the domestic operation. The common ingredient in splits is a communication breakdown. Trust disappears—or never gets established. Organizational gridlock is the result.

Sometimes the split is evident as open warfare. Other times it's more subtle. When it masquerades as consensus, it can be even more destructive. Its symptoms in that case include excessive politeness, excruciatingly correct behavior, and formal "agreements" that each department promptly goes about trying to undermine in private.

Barriers have to be removed, or at least dramatically lowered, in order for renewal to happen. That was the starting point for the phenomenal turnaround in the fortunes of GE's Appliance Park in Louisville, Kentucky. The man who led it, senior vice president and group executive Roger Schipke, recalls, "In the early 1970s we had thirteen corporate VPs in major appliances, and they all had different agendas. We were paralyzed. No one could make a decision."

Schipke sat down and designed an organization that would foster teamwork and strike a balance between short- and long-range thinking. "I blew up the [separate] functions and created four major operating units. Two divisions—production, and sales and service—are 'now' organizations. The other two—technology and marketing—are 'future' groups. One problem was that 99.9 percent of the people here were so focused on making income for the quarter that they had no concern for [what would happen] two years down the road. I wanted each pair [of divisions] to get involved with the other—to talk to each other. Linkages between them are crucial." Schipke comments that swimming against the organizational tide is one of the hardest things he's had to do. "People seem to want a narrow, functional self-concept. I'm trying to create a one-team business perspective."

To a certain point, the ability to identify strongly with something small is good. Highly departmentalized companies like Hewlett-Packard, Johnson & Johnson, and 3M have been unusually innovative over the years. They renew by being small and big at the same time. But too much identification with the small unit has problems of its own. It creates too strong a sense of "us." "They" becomes not just outsiders, but the rest of the company. The benefit of being a part of a large organization is lost.

Even though importance is placed on teamwork by many organizations in the 1990s, Morgan Guaranty Bank's president, Robert V. Lindsay, says that research revealed a clear customer need "for a close relationship between our [securities] traders and the people who produce [deals] for their clients." He created a single division, which combined trading and capital market activities under one department. This department grouped together managers who had tended to argue for their spread (their share of the profit margin) against the clients' needs. The reorganization accomplished two things, according to Lindsay. First, it eliminated the issue of who gets credit for the spread, and second, it formed the basis for better chemistry and closer relationships between the two groups.

John F. Ruffle, Morgan's vice-chairman, says that the top management team could see

strong political camps forming and attitudes hardening between operations (the administrative activities) and the line units. "We had to decentralize. We eliminated the operations division, and we placed a number of its components into the business units. We also made [the operations] people feel a part of the business, partly to get more of us oriented toward the client as our master."

1. What basis of departmentalization lends itself best to change and renewal? Why?
2. Why would a matrix form of departmentalization work at GE?
3. What basis of departmentalization is Morgan Guaranty using? Why?

Chapter 11

ORGANIZATION DESIGN

Debbi Fields

What You Will Learn

1 How different environments influence organizational structure.

2 The differences between mechanistic and organic organizational structures.

3 The effects of technology on the design of manufacturing and service organizations.

4 How environment and technology combine to determine the amount of information an organization must process.

5 Two strategies organizations can use to increase their ability to process information and two others they can use to reduce their need to process information.

6 Four stages of evolution through which most organizations pass.

7 **Skill Development:** How to choose the organization design that best fits a firm at a particular time.

"Her fear of delegating became a

liability."

Growing an Organization with Debbi Fields

Creating something new, given the old ways of doing it, is an art. A textbook example of a successful entrepreneur, Debbi Fields began baking cookies the old way—from scratch—as a teenager. Later, the fact that her husband Randy's clients always liked her cookies convinced her that she could create something new by going into the cookie business. The couple borrowed $50,000 and opened their first store in 1977 in Palo Alto, California. Fields sold $50 worth of cookies the first day. Now, with more than 370 Mrs. Fields Cookies stores worldwide, over 8000 employees, and sales exceeding $135 million, Fields understands that designing an effective organization is an art.

Fields's first lesson in organization design came from her early difficulty delegating authority. Since she has no formal business school training, she attributes her success to learning by trial and error. When the organization grew beyond the size she and her husband could handle, her fear of delegating became a liability. This fear arose from her caring too much for employees and seeking to spare them from failure and lost self-esteem. But eventually Fields was forced to delegate authority, because that was the only way the business could grow.

Once she got past the fear of delegating, though, there was no stopping her. She decided to relocate her business to Park City, Utah. In order to expand her organization, Fields decided to open stores around the country. That way she knew her cookies would always be fresh and she could cater to the interests of local customers. She chose to maintain a small staff at the new corporate headquarters in Park City to assist store managers in their accounting, selling, human resource, and production tasks. Debbi and Randy Fields believe that keeping their corporate support staff small will encourage store managers to solve problems on their own rather than relying on other people to solve them. Besides, those who work close to the "action" are able to make informed decisions better than those removed from it. In the sales division the regional manager is in charge of six district managers, each of whom manages four stores. But each regional manager also runs a store, so that he or she will better understand the problems facing managers in that region.

To retain all the strengths of smallness and maintain effective communication channels from headquarters to the stores, Fields made some more decisions about organization design. At headquarters, for instance, financial responsibility for store management is the job of the store controllers, each of whom manages the finances of twenty-five to eighty-five stores. They review daily computer reports that summarize sales—overall and by product—for each store. Within twenty-four hours, Debbi or Randy Fields personally reviews these figures.[1]

One of the key ingredients in managing any business is the arrangement of various organizational functions and tasks. Debbi and Randy Fields have chosen functional departmentalization to organize their staff at headquarters and place departmentalization for the individual stores. In Chapter 10 we identified functional and place departmentalization as two of four basic ways to structure an organization. We also discussed the kinds of decisions managers make when choosing among these four types of departmentalization: What are the best ways to coordinate functions and departments? Should management centralize or decentralize decision making? How broad should the span of management be? What decisions should be delegated to store managers and what others should be made at headquarters? How much authority should staff people have? According to Debbi Fields, these weren't easy questions to answer.

In this chapter we'll explore how the basic building blocks you learned about in Chapter 10 can be put together to create an overall design for an organization. We'll also begin to examine the types of information systems that are needed to support the design of the organization. Finally, we touch on the concept of organization life cycle and its impact on organization design.

WHAT IS ORGANIZATION DESIGN?

organization design The process of determining the structure and authority relationships for an entire organization.

Organization design is the process of determining the structure and authority relationships for an entire organization.[2] Organization design is a means of implementing the strategies and plans that embody the organization's goals (see Chapter 8). When we talk about organization design, then, we are talking about managers' decisions concerning the organization's very nature, shape, and features.

To some extent managers and employees make design decisions all the time—not just during major upheavals, such as expansions or reorganizations. For example, American Cyanamid, a manufacturer of industrial and agricultural chemicals, forms matrix teams to develop new industrial products, fertilizers, and herbicides. Xerox has used special teams to create desk-top publishing software and an innovative integrated office system. In any organization, every time a new department is formed, new methods of coordination are tried, or a task is assigned to a different department, the organization design is being tested or tinkered with. This isn't necessarily a bad thing. In fact, you can think of design features as tools with which managers work, just as sailboat captains use the sails, rigging, and rudder as tools to steer their boats. Captains frequently ''fine-tune'' their boats, even when sailing a relatively steady course. The effective manager is also constantly fine-tuning his or her organization design in light of changes in the environment or technology.

There are few hard and fast rules for designing an organization. Every firm's organization design is the result of many decisions and historical circumstances. The practice of matching organization design to the strategy of the firm is not new. In his landmark study of seventy large organizations, Alfred Chandler found that organization design follows strategy.[3] The choice of organization design makes a difference because not all forms of design support a particular strategy equally well. This structure-follows-strategy theory is based on the idea that, like a plan, an organization's design should be a means to an end, not an end in itself.

Organization design is no more than the sum of managerial decisions for implementing a strategy and, ultimately, achieving the organization's objectives. Thus the design of the organization acts both as a ''harness,'' helping people pull together in the performance of their diverse tasks, and as a means of coordinating the various tasks in ways that promote the attainment of the firm's goals.

Figure 11.1 shows the key factors that affect an organization's design. All four of these are discussed in depth in the following sections.

FIGURE 11.1

Factors in Organization Design

Four factors in particular—environment, technology, information processing, and life cycle stage—influence the design of an organization. Each factor plays a different role in determining the design, depending on the situation.

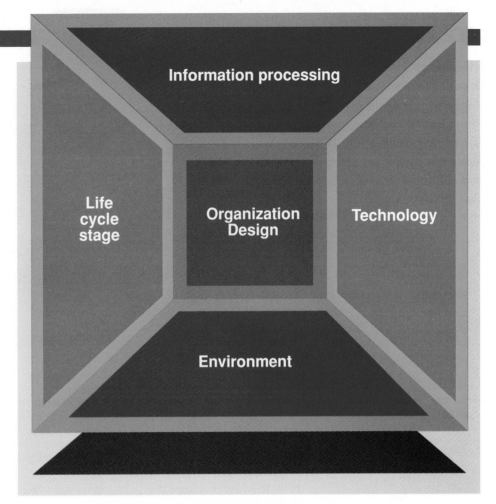

ENVIRONMENT AND ORGANIZATION DESIGN

In a sense, everything outside the organization is its external environment (Figure 11.2). In Chapters 3, 4, and 5 we discussed many of the forces that shape the environment within which an organization operates. In this section we concentrate on how environmental stability or change influences an organization's design—that is, shapes its departments, coordination mechanisms, and control systems.

An organization that provides goods or services in an environment with slow technological innovation and relatively few competitors has problems that are different from those of an organization in a growing, changing, competitive market.[4] The first environment is stable; the second, changing and uncertain. You learned in Chapters 3 and 6 that the relative stability of an organization's environment has major implications for its internal structure. The competitive forces—customers, competitors, suppliers, new entrants, and substitute goods and services—dictate the type and amount of information managers need in order to make decisions. Most firms, however, operate in both stable and changing environments. As a result, some departments may undergo little structural change, while others may change considerably.

Environmental Forces That Shape Organization Design

Various forces in the organization's external environment have an impact on its design. Some forces, such as competition and technology, will affect the design more than others.

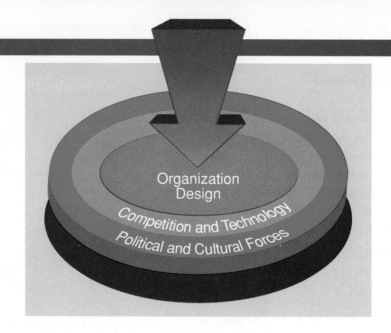

Organization
Design

Competition and Technology

Political and Cultural Forces

Stable Environment

stable environment An organizational environment characterized by little change in products, technology, competitive forces, markets, or political forces.

A **stable environment** is characterized by little change, and what change does occur has minimal impact on the organization's internal operations.[5] A stable environment has several features:

▶ Products that haven't changed much in recent years.
▶ Little technological innovation.
▶ A fixed set of competitors, customers, and other stakeholders.
▶ Consistent government policies.

In a stable environment, top management can keep track of what is going on. For example, companies in the brewing, ice cream, fast food, glass container, farm equipment, and industrial tools industries operate in relatively stable environments. Although they may make slight changes in their products, these changes can be incorporated easily into the existing manufacturing processes.

Changes in the quantity of the product produced and sold, rather than the quality of the product, are likely to occur in a stable environment. Such changes usually have little impact on the organization's structure. Since the product itself doesn't change significantly from year to year, production managers don't have to alter whole manufacturing processes. Firms in highly stable environments are likely to develop extensive distribution systems and to invest heavily in capital equipment. These firms adapt to fluctuations in demand by changing the size of their work force, not by changing their product or their production methods. For example, the production of beer requires a large capital investment and an extensive distribution system (local distributors, trucks, warehouses). If demand shifts, production systems change slowly, because the final product is still beer. If beer sales should drop off, a large brewery such as Anheuser-Busch, Miller, or Coors would probably lay off personnel rather than switch to making breakfast cereal. Changes in production methods and equipment would cost too much to justify entry into new product lines.

A stable environment means a relatively high level of sales predictability. Firms operating in this type of environment can base planning and sales efforts on the information provided by common business indicators.[6] For instance, the U.S. Department of Commerce prepares annual output projections for various industries based on changes that occurred during the preceding ten years. Firms operating in stable environments use these indexes to forecast market changes and sales trends.

In the *stable environment* of soap manufacturing, Dial bar soap remains the nation's leading deodorant bar. Consumers continue to prefer the gold bar over others. Its manufacturing process changes very little from year to year.

The following Insight focuses on McDonald's, an example of a firm operating in the relatively stable fast food environment.

𝒥 N S I G H T

McDonald's operates in a relatively stable environment; for instance, fast food technology has remained fairly constant over the past decade or so. Despite the stability of the environment, the fast food industry is fiercely competitive. Two of McDonald's chief competitors, Burger King and Wendy's, are continually upping the ante. Nevertheless, McDonald's has grown to become the largest fast food restaurant chain in the world, with more than 11,000 restaurants. It opens a restaurant somewhere in the world every seventeen hours and is the largest commercial owner of real estate in the United States. How does McDonald's make it work?

To begin with, new McDonald's managers must attend an intensive ten-day training program at Hamburger University, the company's management training center in Elk Grove, Illinois. McDonald's even brought over the employees who would be responsible for operating the Soviet Union's first McDonald's, in Moscow's Pushkin Square. The curriculum includes hands-on experience in a McDonald's restaurant, as well as intensive classroom study. Subjects range from day-to-day restaurant management to more general courses in business management, accounting, marketing, personnel management, and community relations.

Trainees learn quickly that at McDonald's standards are important in maintaining effectiveness. Analysts have broken down every job into its smallest steps and then automated the whole process. For example, the videotape introducing new employees to French fries starts with boxes of frozen fries rolling off a delivery truck. Employees are instructed to stack them in the freezer six boxes high, leaving one inch between stacks and two inches between stacks and freezer wall. The process of cooking and bagging the fries consists of nineteen steps. McDonald's has standardized other products and work activities as well. The basic hamburger patty must be a machine-cut, 1.6-ounce chunk of pure beef—no lungs, hearts, cereal, soybean, or other fillers—with no more than 19 percent fat content. Hamburger buns must have 13.3 percent sugar in them. French fries are kept under the light for only seven minutes. A flashing light cues the cook at the exact moment the hamburger patties have to be flipped. Specially designed scoops determine the

precise number of fries in each pouch. McDonald's demands a certain quality in its product and service. Although the standardization of work reduces freedom of employees, it provides uniformity and consistency of products for consumers.

McDonald's management has also developed coordination mechanisms that include a detailed organizational structure and the provision by corporate staff of operating, public relations, and advertising services to restaurant managers. In addition, area field consultants regularly visit all restaurants to ensure that each franchise conforms to McDonald's rules and regulations. McDonald's operating manual is a 385-page book covering the most minute details of running a restaurant. In foreign countries, however, McDonald's operators need some decision-making leeway. For example, shortly after U.S. planes bombed Libya in 1986, a mob gathered in front of a McDonald's in Barcelona, Spain to protest. The company manual didn't have instructions on how to handle the situation, so the owner simply "shut down the store and got the hell out of there." That night the restaurant was firebombed.

Finally, McDonald's has a stable and consistent promotional strategy embodied in the person of Ronald McDonald, who despite his international celebrity remains the same funloving clown that Ray Kroc introduced in 1963. A company survey indicated that 96 percent of all American children can identify Ronald McDonald, who is second only to Santa Claus in recognition level.[7]

Changing Environment

changing environment An organizational environment that is unpredictable because of frequent shifts in products, technology, competitive forces, markets, or political forces.

A **changing environment** is unpredictable because of frequent shifts in products, technology, competitors, markets, or political forces.[8] This type of environment has certain characteristics:

▶ Products and services that are continuously changing or evolving.

▶ Major technological innovations that make production processes or equipment obsolete.

▶ Ever-changing sets and/or actions of competitors, customers, or other stakeholders.

▶ Unpredictable governmental actions that reflect the current level of political clout wielded by various interest groups for consumer protection, product safety, pollution control, and civil rights.

Firms operating in a changing environment usually experience *constant* pressure to adapt to meet new customer preferences and demands. These companies often alter their products and services in order to do so. Organizations in the telecommunications, computer hardware and software, electronics, and fashion industries operate in changing environments.

When a technology is changing, organizations dependent on it must be able to respond quickly, generating new ideas that can affect either the product itself or the way it is manufactured. In the electronics industry, breakthroughs in integrated circuits and miniaturization significantly affected the nature of other products. For example, the introduction of electronic digital watches produced a revolution in the market dominated for centuries by Swiss-made watches. Swiss firms had always stressed the craftsmanship that went into each hand-wound timepiece. However, they were unable to compete with this technological innovation. As a result, many Swiss watch manufacturers suffered declining sales and revenue.

Technological advances have also transformed the personal computer, motorcycle, microwave, and computer communications industries. Computer communications used to be simple. A company simply leased a few phone lines from AT&T and bought some modems from a supply house. It then began sending data between its home office and its branches. If service failed, the company just called the modem supplier or AT&T. Today data communications is a whole new world. There are many more service and equipment providers, including local phone companies, satellite suppliers, microwave vendors, and local-area networking companies. And corporate computer networks are far more complex, often containing analog and digital links of all types, as well as intermixed voice, data, and video traffic. Network management systems, which allow trained personnel to monitor performance, identify problems, and take remedial action, now make up a computer communications market worth some $195 million. This market should soon be worth $300 million. Products designed to assist network management range from simple, self-diagnostic features packaged within each system to full-blown command centers that provide a single point of control over the entire operation. Different products monitor different parameters and offer varying capabilities to take corrective action.

The following Insight takes a brief look at how the Tennessee Valley Authority (TVA) has been restructured to cope with its changing environment.

WILL TVA'S LIGHTS GO OUT?

INSIGHT

In 1988, Marvin Runyon quit his job running Nissan's U.S. manufacturing operations to head up the Tennessee Valley Authority (TVA), At that time TVA's lights were beginning to flicker. Its rates had been rising so rapidly they threatened the organization's long-term competitiveness. Some of its best customers, such as the cities of Memphis and Oak Ridge, Tennessee, were looking at other suppliers for their electrical power.

What brought TVA to its knees was its nuclear power program. This was the biggest and most ill-executed nuclear power program in the United States. Of the seventeen nuclear power units proposed by TVA in the 1960s, eleven were scrapped after spending nearly $11 billion, and the others produced only 19 percent of the system's electrical power. These were all shut down in 1985 because of a change in the public's opinion about the safety in generating nuclear power. After the accident at Three-Mile Island outside of Harrisburg, Pennsylvania in the spring of 1979, citizen groups started protesting the use of nuclear power. Clearly, the environment had changed, and the TVA was caught in the middle. To pay off these power plants, TVA's rates had increased an average of 10.2 percent a year since 1980. In comparison, the industry average was 7.3 percent. By 1987 the TVA was pricing itself out of business.

Runyon had to redesign the TVA to save $300 million each year for the following three years. How did he do it? First, he eliminated five levels of middle managers. This not only reduced the number of employees at TVA, cutting employment costs by over 30 percent, but also enabled Runyon to assign clearer limits to authority and responsibility for each manager, depending on the job. Second, Runyon redesigned the organization to reflect its strategy. That is, businesses that were not directly related to making electricity, such as fertilizer plants, were sold off.[9]

Matching Structure to Environment

Firms operating effectively in stable environments tend to choose organizational structures that differ from those chosen by firms operating in changing environments. Researchers Tom Burns and Gene Stalker labeled these contrasting structures mechanistic and organic, respectively.[10] Table 11.1 highlights the differences between the two.

TABLE   11.1

Differences between Mechanistic and Organic Structures

Mechanistic	Organic
▶ Tasks are highly specialized.	▶ Tasks tend to be interdependent.
▶ Tasks tend to remain rigidly defined unless changed by top management.	▶ Tasks are continually adjusted and re-defined through interaction.
▶ Specific roles (rights, obligations, and technical methods) are prescribed for each employee.	▶ Generalized roles (responsibility for task accomplishment beyond specific role definition) are accepted.
▶ Structure of control, authority, and communication is hierarchical.	▶ Structure of control, authority, and communication is a network.
▶ Communication is primarily vertical, between superior and subordinate.	▶ Communication is both vertical and horizontal, depending on where needed information resides.
▶ Communications primarily take the form of instructions and decisions issued by superiors and of information and request for decisions supplied by subordinates.	▶ Communications primarily take the form of information and advice among all levels.

Source: Adapted from T. Burns and G. M. Stalker, *The Management of Innovation.* London: Tavistock, 1961, pp. 119-122.

mechanistic structure
Organizational structure in which activities are broken down into specialized tasks and decision making is centralized at the top.

A **mechanistic structure** is one in which management breaks activities down into separate, specialized tasks. Tasks, authority, responsibility, and accountability for both managers and subordinates are defined by level in the organization. Firms using this structure resemble the bureaucratic organizations discussed in Chapter 2. Decision making is centralized at the top. Top management decides what is important and how to share this information with others. Their objective is to train employees to work efficiently. When one employee leaves, another can slip into the empty spot—like interchangeable machine parts. Thus the mechanistic structure seems best suited to firms operating in stable environments, such as the IRS, Taco Bell, UPS, and Coors. In such environments, where employees tend to perform the same tasks over and over, job specialization and standardization are particularly appropriate. Figure 11.3, block A, shows the match between an organization's stable environment and mechanistic structure.

An **organic structure** places less emphasis on giving and taking orders and more on encouraging managers and subordinates to work together in teams and to communicate

In a *mechanistic structure,* jobs are made as efficient as possible. This St. Louis auto assembly plant initiated the use of a mechanical arm to help employees like Scott Merrick (left) and Luvell Anderson lift and install Ford Aerostar seats.

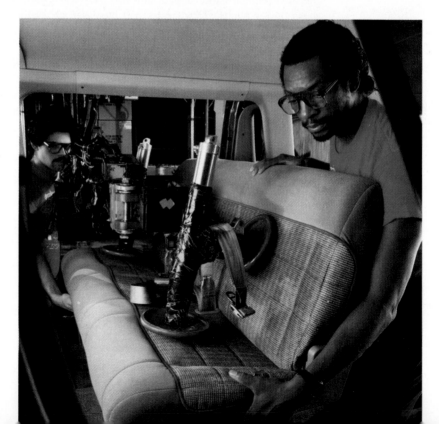

FIGURE 11.3

Matches and Mismatches of Structure and Environment

The ideal matches are of a mechanistic structure and a stable environment and of an organic structure and a changing environment.

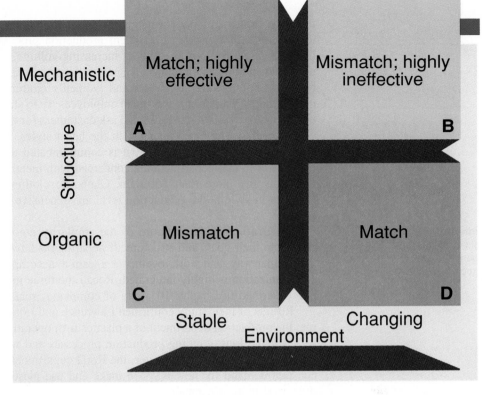

openly with each other. In fact, employees are encouraged to communicate with anyone who might help them solve a problem. Decision making is decentralized. Authority, responsibility, and accountability flow to employees with the expertise required to solve problems. An organic organizational structure is well suited to a changing environment. In Figure 11.3, block D shows this relationship. Steve Jobs structured NeXT Computers along organic lines so that it could move swiftly into new markets. Positions must be constantly redefined to cope with the organization's ever-changing needs. Employees must be skilled at solving a variety of problems.

organic structure Organizational structure that stresses teamwork, open communications, and decentralized decision making.

Differentiation and Integration The findings of Burns and Stalker were supported and extended by Paul Lawrence and Jay Lorsch, who examined the organization designs of three departments—production, research and development (R&D), and marketing—in ten different companies. They found that departments in companies operating in stable environments, such as can manufacturing companies, were designed differently than the same departments in companies operating in unstable environments, such as plastics manufacturing firms. They also found that all three departments in the same company would not be affected to the same extent by the firm's environment. That is, employees in R&D departments in the can companies viewed their environment as more unstable than employees in production departments in the same companies did.

The key to organization design for a manager was to structure the department to match the challenges posed by its external environment. Production departments in both stable and unstable environments were structured more mechanistically than R&D departments were. Departments designed to fit their environments were more effective than those that had been misdesigned. To capture the character of design differences between departments, Lawrence and Lorsch used the terms *differentiation* and *integration*.[11]

differentiation The measure of the difference that exists among departments with respect to structure, tasks, and managerial orientation.

Differentiation is the measure of the differences among various departments with respect to their structure, tasks, and managerial orientation. If departmental managers have different goals and structure their departments differently, an organization can be classified as highly differentiated. For example, a production manager might be concerned about reducing costs, meeting daily production quotas, and following rules that ensure an efficient production process. In contrast, a marketing manager might be concerned about increasing volume, introducing innovative products, and making last-minute changes to satisfy an important customer. Liz Claiborne, a manufacturer of men's and women's clothing, is a highly differentiated organization. Marketing department employees try to stay abreast of the latest fashion trends. They attend trade shows and ask customers for their design preferences. Their goal is to have the line in sync with the latest styles. However, once a decision is made to produce a certain item, it is communicated to the production department. Employees in that department are concerned with meeting production quotas in order to supply the more than 3500 Liz Claiborne clothing outlets around the world. Changes in style at the production level are expensive and must be avoided if at all possible.

integration The measure of similarity among various departments with respect to their goals and structure.

Integration is the measure of the similarity among various departments with respect to their goals and structure. If departments have similar goals, are organized in a similar way, and work together as a team to accomplish organizational objectives, an organization is highly integrated. Recall the three important principles of integration described in Chapter 10: unity of command, scalar, and span of management.

Results of their study confirmed Lawrence and Lorsch's expectations. For example, the production department of a plastics firm operating in a changing environment would retain long-standing production processes and would be organized along formal, mechanistic lines. However, the R&D department in the same firm would face constant demand for new ways to make and use plastic and, as a result, would be organized more organically.

Research thus supports the importance of designing an organization's structure to fit its environment. It also emphasizes the importance of integration. Successful firms use a variety of integrative tools depending on the situation. In stable environments, following the chain of command is most effective. In unstable environments, the use of task forces greatly improves coordination among departments. The presence of mechanistic structure in certain departments and organic structure in others doesn't necessarily reduce the firm's overall effectiveness.

The following Global Link explores how Black & Decker has restructured itself to go global in a changing environment. It uses different types of differentiation and integration to achieve its goals. As we've said in Chapter 4, a *global corporation* looks at the whole world as one market. It manufactures, conducts research, raises capital, and buys supplies wherever it can do the best job. It keeps in touch with technology and market trends around the world. National boundaries and regulations tend to be irrelevant. Corporate headquarters might be anywhere.

TECHNOLOGY

In Chapter 2 we noted that technology is a major contingency variable that affects the design of an organization.[12] In general, technology is the process that transforms information and raw materials into finished products. Most people associate it only with the machinery used in manufacturing plants, but technology exerts a broad influence on our everyday lives. Our schools, banks, hospitals, governments, and stores all use technology heavily. Therefore we can analyze the impact of technology within a variety of settings. Its importance in the design of an organization cannot be overstated.

Technological Interdependence

A firm's technology has a significant impact on its organizational structure and design. Different types of technologies generate various types of internal interdependence. **Technological interdependence** is the degree of coordination required between individuals

GLOBAL Link

By 1990, Black & Decker (B&D), manufacturer of power tools for home and professional users, had manufacturing plants in 10 countries and sold its products in nearly
100. Design centers, manufacturing plants, and marketing programs were focusing on
making and selling products to a worldwide market. But it wasn't always that way.

In 1981, earnings had begun to slip, and a worldwide recession caused a significant downturn in the power-tools segment of B&D's business, its bread and butter.
B&D's problems were partly a result of its own strategy. By 1982, B&D operated
twenty-five manufacturing plants in thirteen countries on six continents. It had three
operating groups as well as the headquarters in Maryland. Each group had its own
staff, which led to duplication and overstaffing. In addition, individual B&D companies, such as B&D of West Germany, operated autonomously in each of the more
than fifty countries where B&D sells and services products. The company's philosophy had been to let each country adapt products and product lines to fit the unique
characteristics of each market. The Italian firm produced power tools for Italians, the
British subsidiary made power tools for Britons, and so on.

As a result, countries did not communicate well with each other. Successful
products in one country often took years to introduce in others. For example, the
highly successful Dustbuster, introduced in the United States in the late 1970s, was
not introduced in Australia until 1983. When efforts were made to introduce B&D
home products into European markets, the European managers refused to comply.
They felt that home appliances and products were uniquely American and would not
do well outside of the United States.

In order to meet the tailor-made specifications of different markets, design centers were not being used efficiently. At one point, eight design centers around the
world had produced 260 different motors, even though it was determined that the
firm needed fewer than 10 different models. Plant capacity utilization was quite low,
employment levels were high, and output per employee was unacceptable.

As B&D moved into the mid-1980s, management realized that something had to
be done. One area in which the Japanese had not made significant inroads was
housewares and small appliances. So B&D acquired the small appliances division of
General Electric in 1984 in order to give it more shelf space in housewares and also
a large enough line of products to provide economies of scale in manufacturing.

To gain some efficiencies from being a global corporation, starting in 1987,
B&D tried to match staffing requirements with sales and limited the number of motors it was going to use around the world. Standardizing motors has allowed B&D to
develop a global product strategy. Such a strategy allows B&D to change features for
local market tastes, but retain its essential features. Presently, B&D organizes its
business around product lines. Product lines, such as automotive, have common distribution channels, technologies, customers, competitors, or geographic markets.
Product line managers have responsibility for all functions, such as manufacturing,
advertising, and sales, within their product line.

Sources: Adapted from S. Flack, "All Leverage Is Not Created Equally," *Forbes,* March 19, 1990, 39–40;
S. Paloney, "Team Approach Cuts Costs," *HR Magazine,* November 1990, 61–62; G. T. DiCamillo,
"Winning Turnaround Strategies at Black & Decker," *Journal of Business Strategy,* March/April 1988,
30–33; J. D. Daniels and L. H. Radebaugh, *International Business,* 5th ed. (Reading, Mass. Addison-
Wesley, 1989), 449–450.

FIGURE 11.4

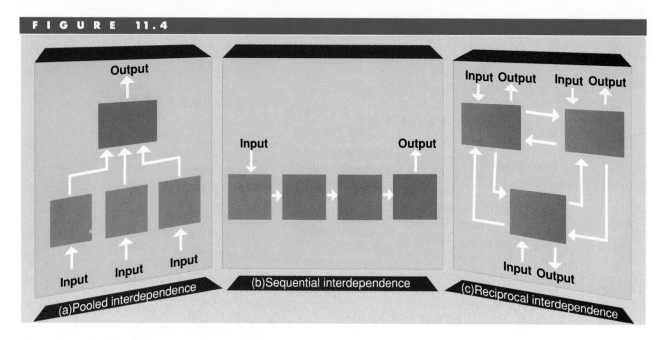

Three Types of Technological Interdependence

Coordination methods vary by type of interdependence. (a) In pooled interdependence, coordination is achieved by rules and procedures. (b) In sequential interdependence, it is achieved by plans and schedules. (c) In reciprocal interdependence, it is achieved by employees' talking among themselves and adjusting their plans as situations change.

technological interdependence The degree of coordination required between individuals and departments to transform information and raw materials into finished products.

pooled interdependence The type of technological interdependence in which there is little sharing of information or resources among individuals and/or departments.

sequential interdependence The type of technological interdependence in which the flow of information and resources between individuals and/or departments is serialized.

reciprocal interdependence The type of technological interdependence in which all individuals and departments are encouraged to work together and to share information and resources in order to complete a task.

and departments to transform information and raw materials into finished products. There are three types of technological interdependence: pooled, sequential, and reciprocal.[13] Figure 11.4 shows how these different types of interdependence coordinate the efforts of employees in order to achieve desired results.

Pooled interdependence, illustrated in part (a) of the figure, involves little sharing of information or resources among individuals within a department or among departments. Although the various departments contribute to overall organizational efforts, they work on their own specialized tasks. For example, in commercial banks the separate savings, loan, and real estate departments work independently of one another. NCNB Bank achieves coordination by requiring each department to meet certain standards and follow certain rules. These rules are consistent for all of its banks in various states and apply to all routine situations, such as check cashing and making deposits. There should be few exceptions.

Sequential interdependence, illustrated in part (b) of Figure 11.4, serializes the flow of information and resources between individuals within the same department or between departments. That is, the output from department A becomes the input to department B, the output from department B becomes the input to department C, and so on. A typical example of sequential interdependence is an automobile assembly line. To ensure coordination between its departments (or work stations), managers must carefully schedule when parts arrive and leave each department.

Reciprocal interdependence, illustrated in part (c) of the Figure 11.4, encourages every individual and department to work with every other individual and department; information and resources flow back and forth until the task is completed. For example, hospitals use resources from several departments—such as x-ray, nursing, surgery, and physical therapy—to restore a patient's health. Each specialist and department supplies some of the resources needed to assist the patient. Doctors and professionals from each specialized area meet to discuss the patient's recovery. The method of coordination is mutual adjustment, achieved through group meetings.

Management's job is the most difficult in the case of reciprocal interdependence. Designing an organization to handle this type of interdependence is very challenging. The structure of the organization must allow for frequent communication among departments. Planning is required, but, because plans can't anticipate or solve all problems, managers must rely on face-to-face communication to make the needed adjustments.

Most managers choose either a matrix or a network form of organization (see Chapter 10) to handle the problems that might arise with reciprocal interdependence. Galoob Toys developed a network structure to cope with such problems. The marketer of Micro Machines, Galoob Toys depends on independent inventors and entertainment companies to dream up most of its products and outside specialists to do most of the design and engineering work. Once a design/engineering decision is made, it goes back to the inventor for final approval. Galoob farms out manufacturing and packaging to a dozen or more contractors in Hong Kong. When the toys arrive in the United States, they are distributed nationwide by commissioned manufacturers' representatives, and Commercial Credit Corporation is employed to collect money from them. Robert and David Galoob, the owners, spend most of their time making all the parts of their company fit together. Phones, fax machines, and telexes are in constant use as schedules are revised and adjusted to accommodate design modifications, shortages of raw materials, customer order changes, and so forth.

Service Technologies

Technological interdependence is fairly obvious in a manufacturing firm's assembly line. But what is technology's role in the design of service organizations? Service organizations are clearly significant. They are employing more people in the United States than manufacturing organizations are: The service sector accounts for 71 percent of the nation's employment and more than 68 percent of its gross national product. Service organizations have grown so rapidly in number and size that they account for nearly 90 percent of all new, nonfarm jobs created in the United States since 1953.[14] Some service organizations are quite large: Bank of America Corporation has more than 90,000 employees; Sears, more than 520,000; and Marriott more than 225,000.

What differentiates service organizations from manufacturing organizations? Service organizations have two distinguishing characteristics:

Intangibility. The output of a service firm is intangible. It cannot be stored. The output is used immediately or lost forever. It's impossible to hold seats on a plane or train in inventory. If these seats aren't sold prior to departure, the revenue is lost forever. Manufactured goods, such as cars, TVs, and computers, can be stored and sold at some later time.

Closeness of the customer. There is direct customer contact in the production of most services. The employees of a travel agency are, in a very real sense, simultaneously producing and selling a service to the clients. Service employees dispense output directly to the customers, but production employees in manufacturing firms are separated from the customers.

These two features have an important implication for managers: The simultaneous production and consumption of services means that quality control cannot be achieved by the inspect-and-reject method traditionally used in manufacturing plants. Instead, quality control must occur at the point of service delivery. The service provider is responsible for ensuring quality of service during each interaction with the client.

routine service technology
Technology used by an organization that operates in a relatively stable environment and services customers who are relatively sure about their needs.

Types of Service Technologies There are two basic types of service technologies: routine and nonroutine. **Routine service technologies** are used by organizations operating in environments that are relatively stable and servicing customers who are

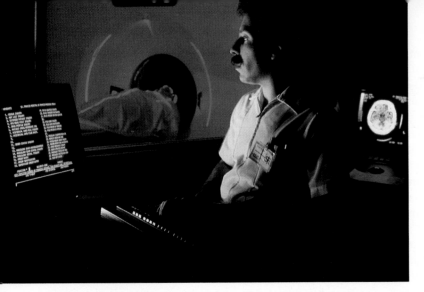

Nonroutine service technology (left) at Long Island's St. Francis Hospital, where a radiology management system reports on patient information and scheduling. *Routine service technology* (right): take-out order entry at Pizza Hut.

nonroutine service technology Technology used by an organization that operates in a complex and changing environment and services customers or clients who are unaware of their needs or imprecise about their problems.

relatively sure about their needs. Organizations such as retail stores, fast food restaurants, banks, travel agencies, gas stations, and bookstores employ routine service technologies to serve their customers. These organizations aren't so much involved with producing the service as with dispensing it. The information being exchanged is simple, and the tasks standardized. The demand on the service provider is fairly precise, and thus employees interact with customers for only short periods of time. For example, consider the interaction between a bank teller and a customer who wants to make a deposit—it has all these qualities.

Nonroutine service technologies are used by organizations that operate in complex and changing environments. Complexity arises because clients are generally unaware of their needs or imprecise about their problems and don't know how to go about solving them. New problems are encountered every day by managers, and variety is high[15] Consequently there is demand for creativity and novelty as the service provider strives to develop techniques that are appropriate to the situation at hand. The types of service firms using nonroutine technologies include legal, accounting, brokerage, marketing/advertising, medical, and architectural firms. The focus is on meetings between the service provider and the client and the tasks/skills needed by the service provider to solve the client's problem. Each meeting between the client and the organization lasts a relatively long time. The outcome depends on the client's willingness to provide the manager with information he or she needs to solve the client's problem.

Organization Design and Service Technology Selected organization design features (specialization, standardization, coordination, authority) and their relationships with the two types of service technologies are shown in Table 11.2. Firms using nonroutine service technologies tend to be organic. They are organized more informally, and decision making is decentralized. Because problems facing such a firm are unique, reciprocal interdependence among employees is common. Firms employing routine service technologies, however, can be designed along more mechanistic lines. Specialization is low and standards common, because customers' needs are known. Decision making is centralized with top management. Pooled technological interdependence, which stresses routine tasks and standardization, ensures the effectiveness of the firm.

An example of an organization design that matches a service technology is found at Holiday Corporation, the world's largest hospitality company, with revenues exceeding $1.6 billion. It operates Holiday Inns, Embassy Suites, Hampton Inns, Homewood Suites, and Harrah's casinos. Together, these represent more than 1800 hotels with 358,000 rooms and some 250,000 employees, worldwide.

TABLE 11.2

Matching Design Features with Service Technologies

Organization Design Features	Type of Service Technologies	
	Routine	*Nonroutine*
Needs of client	Known	Unknown
Structural characteristics		
Specialization	Low	High
Standardization of activities	High	Low
Span of management	Wide	Moderate
Authority	Centralized	Decentralized
Organizational structure	Mechanistic	Organic
Environment	Stable	Changing
Technological interdependence	Pooled and/or sequential	Reciprocal
Examples	Banks, retail stores, fast food chains, hotels and motels	Legal firms, brokerage houses, marketing and advertising firms, accounting firms

Source: Adapted from P. K. Mills, *Managing Service Industries* (Cambridge, Mass.: Ballinger, 1986), 19–52.

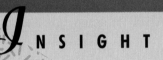

STAYING AT HOLIDAY INN

At every Holiday Inn, things are run by the numbers. Top management, located in Memphis, Tennessee, makes no apologies for using a highly centralized form of decision making that limits the choices made by the managers at the various properties. These choices include what recipes cooks have available to them, the type of liquor to be stocked in the lounges, and the number of employees needed to run the hotel smoothly. The cleaning staff performs its forty tasks according to a numbered list to ensure that all rooms are cleaned by 3:00 P.M. This list includes all tasks, from dusting the tops of pictures and vacuuming the room to checking the TV to make sure it works and keeping the telephone books in good condition. All these tasks are planned to take no more than twenty-four minutes per room.

According to Michael Rose, president and CEO of Holiday Corporation, the system must work reliably all the time to ensure that Holiday will be able to deliver a quality product—exceptional service. Deviations from the rules are not allowed without written permission. Holiday Corporation uses a routine service technology to ensure that its guests are treated the same way every visit.[16]

INFORMATION-PROCESSING STRATEGIES

Part of technology's impact is that it determines the pattern of problems and information needs within an organization.[17] Information is important because nearly every activity in an organization involves information processing. Managers spend nearly 80 percent of their time actively exchanging information as they, along with other employees, attend meetings, talk on the telephone, receive reports, read computer printouts, and so on. Information thus helps hold the organization together.

The purpose of this section is to describe how information processing affects the design of an organization. The design of an organization's information-processing system is *contingent* on the stability of its environment and its technology.[18] The basic effect of rapid changes, or instability, in an organization's environment and technology is to create uncertainty (recall the discussion in Chapters 6 and 7). With respect to organization design, *uncertainty* refers to the gap between the amount of information required to perform a task and the amount of information that the organization already possesses.[19]

Uncertainty limits managers' ability to plan for the effects of change. Three factors contribute to the degree of uncertainty: (1) the diversity of the organization's outputs, (2) the number of different technical specialists on a project, and (3) the level of difficulty in achieving objectives. The greater the diversity of high-quality products and the number of different technical specialists, the greater the number of factors a manager must assess prior to making a decision. Although the organizational structure should provide for the information on which employees and managers can base decisions, sometimes managers may not be able to obtain all the information they need to achieve organizational objectives. To solve this problem, they can turn to one of two general approaches: (1) increase the organization's ability to process information, or (2) reduce the need to process information. These two general approaches and specific strategies for implementing them are shown in Table 11.3.

Increasing the Ability to Process Information

Managers can increase their organization's ability to process information by creating vertical information systems or lateral relations.[20] Both strategies enable the organization to better manage the information it needs to process. These strategies are especially useful when the people or departments involved are either sequentially or reciprocally interdependent.

Vertical Information Systems A **vertical information system** is an information-processing strategy managers can use to send information efficiently up and down the levels of the organization. With such a system the organization can constantly update rapidly changing information, giving managers the right information at the right time for planning and coordinating. By bringing information up to top management, vertical information systems tend to support centralized decision making.

vertical information system An information-processing strategy managers can use to send information efficiently up and down the levels of an organization.

The types of businesses that have effectively invested in vertical information systems include Ticketmaster outlets, airline reservation departments, off-track betting parlors, and supermarkets. Most of these information systems are computerized. For example, many supermarkets now use optical scanners at their checkout counters. As purchases pass over the eye of the scanner, the cost, item type, and related data are read directly from the universal product code (UPC) into a computer. When the store manager wants to know how a special coupon affected a product's sales volume, the

---

TABLE 11.3

Information-Processing Strategies

General Approach	Strategy
Increase the organization's ability to process information	1. Create vertical information systems 2. Create lateral relations
Reduce the organization's need to process information	1. Create slack resources 2. Create self-contained tasks or departments.

Source: Adapted from J. R. Galbraith, *Designing Complex Organizations* (Reading, Mass.: Addison-Wesley, 1973), 15. Reprinted with permission.

computer readily provides the information. The manager can also determine the percentage of sales from each department (produce, meat, dairy, and so on). Finally, these systems process information faster than manual keying and reduce checkers' errors.

This chapter's Manager's Viewpoint feature looked at the organization design of Mrs. Fields Cookies. Mrs. Fields can also be used to illustrate the relationship between information processing and design for organizations that use a routine service technology. The following Insight details how Debbi and Randy Fields use vertical information systems to effectively manage their stores.

HÍ-TECH COOKS AT MRS. FIELDS

I N S I G H T

The objective of being able to run each store essentially as she ran the original Palo Alto store guides the implementation of vertical information systems at Debbi Fields's company. Her goal was to put as much decision making and intelligence into the store-level PCs as was necessary to free each manager to do the thing the company does best—sell cookies.

Daily communication between headquarters staff, regional managers, and store managers is supported by two computer-based systems. PhoneMail answers the phone and takes, stores, replays, and transfers messages. This system puts Fields's voice into every store and enables her to communicate ideas and concerns promptly. FormMail electronically sends and stores typed messages that can be read at the convenience of the receiver. Fields answers all requests within forty-eight hours.

A program called Daily Planner plays an important role in the way store managers plan and replan each day's activities. Each store manager enters daily sales projections (based on sales a year earlier, adjusted by the store's growth factor) into the store's PC, together with additional information requested by the program, such as the day of the week, whether it is a school day, and the weather. Suppose it is a Tuesday, a school day. The computer goes back to the store's hour-by-hour, product-by-product performance on school-day Tuesdays. Based on that information, the Daily Planner tells the manager what will have to be done today, hour-by-hour, product-by-product, to meet the sales quota. It tells the manager how many customers will be needed each hour and how much should be sold. It also tells her or him how many batches of cookie dough need to be mixed and when to mix them to meet the demand and to minimize leftovers. As the day progresses, electronic cash registers automatically feed data into the company's computer in Park City, Utah. If sales are down, this central computer then tells the manager to try several promotional tactics—such as giving away free cookies—to lure more people into the stores.

Computer systems also play an informational role in the hiring process at Mrs. Fields. The system evaluates the probability that an applicant will make a successful employee by reviewing, in light of the company's past experience, the applicant's answers to a series of questions presented on a video display terminal. The people who match profile are honest and punctual and have good people skills, good work experience, and good sales ability. The system also places new hires on the payroll and reminds individual store managers when a performance appraisal is due.[21]

Several themes run through the use of vertical information systems at Mrs. Fields. First, programs automate routine tasks—such as data gathering, analysis, and retrieval—and permit store employees to devote more time to selling. Second, store managers can use program output to help make better decisions.

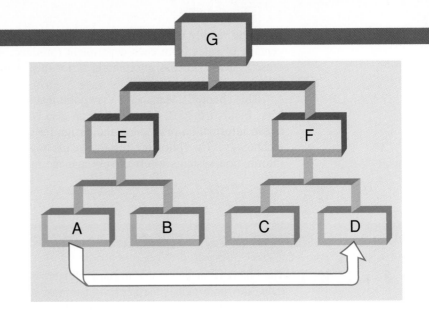

Lateral Relations

With lateral relations, if a problem in department A affects the operation of department D, the managers of the two departments can work together to find a solution, rather than refer the problem up through the hierarchy to managers E and G.

lateral relations An information-processing strategy by which decision making is put in the hands of those with access to the information needed to make the decision.

Lateral Relations **Lateral relations** is an information-processing strategy that cuts through the chain of command and increases coordination among functional departments by pushing decision making down to where the relevant information exists. In contrast to vertical information systems, which centralize decisions by bringing information up to top managers, lateral relations tend to decentralize decisions. There are two methods of implementing this strategy: (1) establishing direct contact between employees or departments or (2) creating a new position to integrate information.

The simplest form of lateral relations is to allow direct contact between two employees or departments that share a common problem, in order to facilitate joint decision making. Figure 11.5 illustrates lateral relations. If department A is falling behind in its production of parts needed by department D, the manager of A could contact the manager of D directly, instead of referring the problem up through managers E and G and back down through manager F. If the managers of A and D can arrive at a mutually satisfying solution, the number of problems flowing up the hierarchy is reduced. This process also increases the number of managers actively dealing with environmental change. Top managers can devote their attention to problems that cannot be solved by lower-level managers.

The second alternative is to create a new position within the organization, the integrator, to process information. An **integrator** facilitates communication between departments, bypassing formal lines of communication within the hierarchy. Matrix managers and expediters are examples of employees who facilitate communication between departments. They gather information from two or more departments and increase the flow of timely communication within the organization.

integrator An employee or manager who facilitates communication between departments, bypassing formal lines of communication within the hierarchy.

Kodak manufactures many products—including film, photocopiers, cameras, photographic paper—and sells them around the world. A product manager was given authority and responsibility for each line, and each line had functional managers who were responsible for technical decisions relating to their functions. Kodak's customers, however, wanted Kodak to add tailor-made products for separate markets, have only one Kodak representative (instead of separate product-line salespeople) call on them, and also maintain its costs. This led Kodak to establish the position of integrator. The integrator's job was to coordinate the needs of each customer with the technical product expertise of various Kodak employees.

Reducing the Need to Process Information

Managers can reduce the need to process information by either reducing the number of exceptions (problems) that occur or reducing the number of factors to be considered when exceptions do occur. Two strategies used to implement this approach are slack resources and self-containment.

slack resources Extra resources, such as materials, money or time, that an organization stockpiles in order to be prepared to respond to environmental changes.

Slack Resources **Slack resources** are extra resources, that is, materials and other resources that organizations stockpile in order to be prepared to respond to environmental changes. Slack resources can reduce the need to process information by reducing the number of problems likely to arise. One form of slack resources is an organization's ability to lengthen production and delivery schedules or increase lead times. When an organization overestimates the length of time needed to complete a project, it creates slack—extra time—in the schedule that can be used for dealing with unexpected difficulties. The student who writes a term paper well in advance of the due date builds slack into his or her schedule—extra time that can be used for editing and typing.

One effect of slack resources is to reduce departmental interdependence. For example, if a manufacturing firm maintains extra inventory to meet unexpected sales demand, less communication is needed among the purchasing, production, and sales departments. However, if purchasing keeps only a minimal amount of inventory on hand (no slack), the three departments must coordinate activities very closely to avoid creating an unmanageable backorder situation.

Creating slack resources also has negative cost and customer relations implications, however. Increasing manufacturing lead time generates inventories that cost money to store. This money is tied up, when it could be used for other purposes. Moreover, extending time horizons for planning, budgeting, and scheduling may lead to lower performance expectations. Customers may not be able to live with extended schedules because of their own plans or commitments.[22]

Self-Contained Tasks or Departments The second strategy for reducing the need to process information is to assign *all* activities concerning a specific product, project, or geographic region to one group. This effectively reduces the number of factors to be dealt with when exceptions, or problems, arise. The self-contained strategy involves choosing product or place rather than functional departmentalization. Recall from Chapter 10 that Harris Corporation and American Express pursued product departmentalization because they were having problems with their functional organization. In a product-organized firm—for example, Procter & Gamble, General Foods, or PepsiCo—each product group has its own resources for the functional areas of accounting, marketing, manufacturing, personnel, and finance.

Organization along product lines enables a company to achieve flexibility and adaptability. It also reduces the amount of information a manager needs to process in two ways.[23] First, product departmentalization reduces the number of products and consumers each group deals with; that is, managers deal with limited product and customer demand. And within the organization, managers have little need to share information concerning manufacturing costs, delivery schedules, distribution channels, and the like with managers in other groups. One manager's concerns aren't relevant to another. Second, specialization across product lines is reduced. In functional departmentalization, an accountant must know something about all of the organization's products; with a product-based structure, an accountant needs to know about only one product line. Thus uncertainty is reduced because all necessary information will pertain to only a limited set of product problems.

Implications for Global Organizations

The evolution of global organizations has been characterized by a growing need to balance several conflicting objectives: meeting requirements for economic survival, adjusting to demands from host countries, and integrating company operations throughout the world.[24] Some companies have extensive manufacturing operations in several countries and must integrate their manufacturing process through effective information processing. Each plant produces only part of the product line or carries out only part of the process, depending on the local cost and availability of resources (labor, energy, raw materials, and skills). This approach also achieves economies of scale.

Experiences at Black & Decker, discussed in the Global Link, imply a strong role for information-processing systems. Before its redesign, each territory manager would propose different projects. They would be competing for financing from headquarters for similar products produced in different territories, such as Australia, Canada, and India. Now, with one person responsible for a global product line, in what country the product is manufactured is immaterial. The product manager's profits will be the same. Some companies, such as Westinghouse, ITT, and GTE, forgo the potential benefits of integration and give much more leeway to their subsidiaries. Each subsidiary is free to pursue its own strategy in reaching its corporate objectives. For instance, in a country where national culture plays an important role, the subsidiary would pursue a national strategy, with all manufacturing carried out within the host country. In some industries, such as telecommunications and microelectronics, R & D activities are also carried out by employees from the host country.

American Express has 33.3 million cardholders, of whom 9.3 million are not U.S. citizens.[25] This company has designed extensive vertical information systems that allow it to process data from anywhere in the world, twenty-four hours a day. American Express also uses self-contained units to produce its advertising. The trick is to design a global advertising strategy and then create ads that appeal to cardholders in individual countries. Its worldwide agency, Ogilvy & Mather, tailors ads for each country. In Japan, for example, the ''Membership has its privileges'' ad is translated into ''Peace of mind only for members.'' A typical ad shows a young couple visiting the drift ice in the north—a remote and exclusive place that appeals to the crowded Japanese—and rejoicing that their American Express card allows them to stay two days longer.

ORGANIZATIONAL LIFE CYCLE

organizational life cycle
A sequence of major stages of development (usually birth, youth, midlife, and maturity) through which any organization evolves.

So far in this chapter we have explored the relationships among an organization's environment, its technology, and its need to process information. Each of these affects managers' decisions about organization design. In this section we turn to a related topic—organizational growth. Like people, organizations are born, grow older, and eventually die. Organization designs follow a predictable pattern through the stages of this life cycle. An **organizational life cycle** is a sequence of major stages of development through which any organization evolves. Although every organization passes through the life cycle at its own pace, there are usually four stages: birth, youth, midlife, and maturity.[26] These stages are sequential and follow a natural progression. Each stage presents managers with unique opportunities and organizational design problems. Table 11.4 shows how the range of design issues facing managers evolves as their organization passes through each stage.

Birth Stage

birth stage The first stage of the organizational life cycle, in which the organization is created.

In the **birth stage** the organization is created. The focus is on providing the product or service and surviving in a changing marketplace. The organization's size, typically measured by the number of employees, is small, and its operations are informal and nonbureaucratic. The founders are engaged in all of the firm's activities, from production to

Organization Design Features at Various Life Cycle Stages

Design Feature	Life Cycle Stage			
	Birth	*Youth*	*Midlife*	*Maturity*
Size	Small	Medium	Large	Very large
Environment	Changing	Less changing	Somewhat stable	Stable
Structure	Organic	Less organic	Somewhat mechanistic	Mechanistic
▶ Differentiation	Low	Moderate	High	Very high
▶ Integration	High	Moderate	Some use of integrators	High
Technological interdependence	Reciprocal	Pooled and sequential	Sequential	Sequential and pooled
Information-processing strategies	Lateral relations	Lateral relations and slack resources	Vertical information systems	Self-contained departments

Source: Adapted from R. E. Quinn and K. S. Cameron, ''Organizational Life Cycles and Some Shifting Criteria of Effectiveness: Some Preliminary Evidence,'' *Management Science,* 1983, *29:* 33–51; L. E. Greiner, ''Evolutions and Revolutions as Organizations Grow,'' *Harvard Business Review,* July–August 1972, 37–46.

marketing. Employees work long hours to help the organization survive. There are few rules and procedures to coordinate people: Employees form informal task forces and simply do whatever is necessary to get the work done.

I Can't Believe It's Yogurt entered the birth stage when it was founded in 1978 by Bill and Julie Brice, while they were students at Southern Methodist University.[27] They pooled the $10,000 that their parents had set aside for college tuition in order to open their first store because they believed that customers wanted a tasty, low-calorie, low-fat dessert. (They both graduated two years later, using their own money.)

Youth Stage

youth stage The second stage of the organizational life cycle, in which the organization competes successfully and is formalizing its design.

In the **youth stage** the organization is a successful competitor in the marketplace, and, because the organization has survived and knows how to compete in its industry, its environment is less uncertain. It has more employees, and a division of labor is emerging. Functional departments are formed, and their managers are given the authority and responsibility to make decisions in their fields of expertise. This structure now requires that departments pool their resources and process tasks in some sequence.

I Can't Believe It's Yogurt was in the youth stage when it started franchising stores in 1983. At that time most people still associated yogurt with hippies and health food fanatics. The Brices were still making most of the decisions, and they worked closely with franchise managers to make sure that their efforts were successful. The Brices still ran the company, on an informal basis.

Midlife Stage

midlife stage The third stage of the organizational life cycle, in which the organization has become large, successful, and bureaucratic.

By the **midlife stage** the organization has succeeded and grown quite large. It looks more like a bureaucracy, with rules, procedures, and job descriptions for employees. To further its growth, a professional staff (accountants, lawyers, human resource personnel, and so on) is hired to evaluate and coordinate the activities of employees. Top managers delegate decision making to subordinates and invest money in vertical information systems to keep them abreast of what's going on.

I Can't Believe It's Yogurt was moving toward the midlife stage in 1983 and is now well into it. It has more than 175 stores operating in twenty-three states, ninety full-time and sixty part-time employees at headquarters, and sales of over $22 million. It has developed a formal package for people who are deciding whether or not to buy an I Can't Believe It's Yogurt franchise. The package includes a step-by-step description of what the Brices expect from their franchise owners. A manual detailing the recommended procedures for location selection, architectural design, construction, equipment ordering, and inventory purchasing is also available. All new managers must attend a ten-day training program at Yogurt U in Dallas, Texas. The school's curriculum includes store operations, human resource management, customer service, security, and purchasing, among other topics. An operational specialist is assigned to a small group of stores to help managers continuously improve their operations.

Maturity Stage

maturity stage The final stage of the organizational life cycle, in which the organization is large and mechanistic and operating in a stable environment.

In the **maturity stage** the organization is large and mechanistic and operates in a stable environment, where competitors are well known. It has numerous functional departments, each with its own area of expertise, to handle the problems of running the business. If the organization has grown too large for a functional basis of departmentalization, different product divisions are formed. Rules, procedures, and budgets are used by top managers as means to integrate and coordinate employee activities across multiple products and/or different geographical locations.

At this point in the life cycle some organizations begin to decline. To offset this tendency and regain some innovation and flexibility, the organization may be broken down into smaller units. In recent years Sears, Roebuck has handled the threat of decline by laying off employees and getting out of unprofitable businesses. It has set up separate business units to run its car rental (Budget), insurance (Allstate), brokerage (Dean Witter Reynolds), and financial (Discover Card) operations. Organizations that fail to revitalize themselves may level off as mature organizations or even go into a steady decline.

FITTING AN ORGANIZATION WITH A DESIGN

To conclude, let's look at how the key factors we've discussed in this chapter affect the design of some of the organizations highlighted in the Manager's Viewpoints, Global Links, and Insights in this and Chapter 10. We've said that an organization's design should reflect its environment, technology, information needs, and life cycle stage. No single design is going to be appropriate for an organization all of the time. Rather, managers choose a design that fits the organization's needs at a given time, and as these needs change, so must the design. An organization design is a blueprint to help an organization achieve its objectives; it's not an end in itself.

In any organization, some activities and skills are always more critical to success than others. For instance, at Mrs. Fields Cookies, an organization in the midlife stage of its life cycle, tight control is essential. The organization is trying to provide its customers with a high-quality product in a very competitive, but somewhat stable, market. Debbi and Randy Fields chose a routine service technology and a vertical information system to achieve this objective. This choice of design enables Fields and her headquarters staff to keep in constant daily contact with store managers and closely monitor each store's profitability.

Pep Boys, McDonald's, and Holiday Inns are all in the mature stage of their organizational life cycles. The environment is stable, and competitors are well-known and established. Customers can shop around to find the best price and quality. These organizations have also chosen to fit their design around a routine service technology. This service technology is appropriate because many of the jobs performed by employees are routine, such as controlling inventory and processing customers' orders. A mechanistic structure fits the needs of their technology and the conditions of their environments.

Grouping and Coordinating Activities

We have indicated that managers can put in place one of four types of departmentalization, or a mixture of these, to achieve their organization's goals. A functional form of departmentalization is appropriate when the organization is in either its birth or its youth stage. For example, the Brices used this form at I Can't Believe It's Yogurt during the organization's youth stage. Information was easily processed within each function. The Brices coordinated the various decisions made by the functional managers. Pooled interdependence supports functional departmentalization. However, a functional form of departmentalization doesn't always result in an effective organization. McDonnell Douglas, for example, had to drop this form and change to product departmentalization to regain its effectiveness.

The matrix form of departmentalization, employed in Piper Aircraft's engineering department, may be appropriate when the entire organization is very large and mature and operates in a fairly stable environment. Piper chose to implement this structure in its engineering department in an attempt to maintain that department's creativity and innovation. Reciprocal interdependence serves members of a matrix best because it promotes the integration of both functional and product managers' activities. The stage of the project becomes the basis for the choice of technology and the assignment of employees: In the engineering design stage, as we've discussed, Piper uses reciprocal interdependence with a matrix; in the manufacturing stage it uses sequential technological interdependence to coordinate employees who are functionally assigned.

When key activities can be grouped around individual products, a product form of departmentalization is appropriate. This form is usually chosen by managers whose organization is operating in a stable market and is in the mature stage of its evolution. At Harris Corporation and Black & Decker, for instance, there is little need to process information between product lines. Each product line is self-contained, with its own engineers, accountants, manufacturing processes, marketing campaigns, and other functional areas. Top managers rely on pooled interdependence to coordinate activities among divisions.

If the organization operates across several geographical areas, each with its own special needs, then place departmentalization is often appropriate. I Can't Believe It's Yogurt and American Airlines use this form effectively. At I Can't Believe It's Yogurt, now in its midlife stage, the Brices don't believe that there is a need to process information quickly among their stores. Therefore, they have chosen to use self-contained units (the individual stores) for their information-processing strategy. American Airlines uses vertical information systems extensively to simultaneously transmit information to all managers concerning changes in flight schedules, weather, and so on. Top managers at both I Can't Believe It's Yogurt and American Airlines have chosen a routine service technology to deliver goods and services to customers. This type of service technology relies extensively on rules and standard procedures to coordinate the behavior of employees.

Determining the Authority Structure

Determining how much authority and freedom to make decisions employees should have is part and parcel of choosing a design. In the case of Mrs. Fields Cookies, most key decisions are made by top management. To ensure that top managers have the needed information, Debbi and Randy Fields have implemented vertical information systems, which enable them to efficiently transmit information down the chain of command. A mechanistic structure supports the centralization of decision making.

In a matrix structure, decisions should be delegated to those managers closest to the scene of the action. The crucial administrative skill is selecting managers to head up each project and delegating enough authority to them to carry out the necessary tasks. At Piper Aircraft decision making is delegated to each project manager in the matrix. An organic, as opposed to a mechanistic, structure supports the project manager's role in this matrix. To increase this manager's ability to process information, matrix structures rely on lateral relations, which allow product and functional managers to coordinate their tasks. Reciprocal interdependence characterizes the relationships among managers.

CHAPTER SUMMARY

1. Organizations operate in either relatively stable or changing environments. A stable environment is characterized by few product or service changes, little technological innovation, a fixed set of competitors and customers, and consistent government policies. A changing environment is characterized by continuous product and service changes, major technological innovation, an ever-changing set of competitors and customers, unpredictable government policies, and rapid changes in individual values and expectations.

2. Firms operating in stable and changing environments tend to choose mechanistic and organic organizational structures, respectively. In a mechanistic structure management concentrates on specialization, standardization, and centralized authority. The organization tends to be highly differentiated. In an organic structure management concentrates on teamwork, communication, constant job redefinition, and decentralized authority. The organization tends to be well integrated.

3. Three types of technological interdependence affect organizational structure: pooled, sequential, and reciprocal. Pooled interdependence requires little sharing of information and other resources by departments and individuals working on specialized tasks. Sequential interdependence serializes the flow of information and other resources between individuals and departments to accomplish tasks. Reciprocal interdependence encourages the flow of information and other resources back and forth between individuals and departments to accomplish tasks.

4. Service organizations differ from manufacturing organizations in that their products are intangible and they are close to their customer. There are two types of service technologies: routine and nonroutine. Routine service organizations adopt mechanistic structures, whereas nonroutine service organizations adopt organic structures.

5. Environment and technology together will determine the amount of information that a firm needs to process. In a stable environment, technological interdependence is likely to be pooled or sequential. There is relatively little need to share information internally or to process greatly varying amounts of externally generated information. In a changing environment, technological interdependence more often is reciprocal, with great need for sharing information internally and also for processing large amounts of externally generated information.

6. In order to manage uncertainty, with respect to organization design, firms can either increase their ability to process information, by creating vertical information systems or lateral relations, or reduce their need to process information, by utilizing slack resources or forming self-contained tasks or departments.

7. Organizations grow and evolve over time. As they pass through four life cycle stages—birth, youth, midlife, and maturity—they will choose different organizational designs.

1. What are the main features of stable and changing environments?

2. How can members of an organization tell whether it is in a stable environment?

3. How does McDonald's environment affect the way it is designed?

4. What are the differences between a mechanistic and an organic structure? How would you classify McDonald's structure?

5. What is the relationship between differentiation and integration? Between environmental stability and change?

6. What are the strengths and limitations associated with the organization design of a global corporation, such as Black & Decker?

7. Give some examples of pooled, sequential, and reciprocal technological interdependence.

8. What problems do you think the use of multiple forms of technological interdependence might create for managers?

9. **From Where You Sit:** What type of service technology does your college use? What are the implications of this?

10. **From Where You Sit:** Visit your local bank. Can you identify how its service technology affects your behavior as a customer?

11. Discuss how the interaction of the environment and technology influences selection of the most effective information-processing strategy.

12. How could an organization be designed in order to increase its ability to process information?

13. How could an organization be designed in order to reduce its need to process information?

14. What information-processing strategies and aids are used at Mrs. Fields Cookies? How do they affect a store manager's ability to make decisions?

15. How does an organization's life cycle stage affect its managers' choice of organization design?

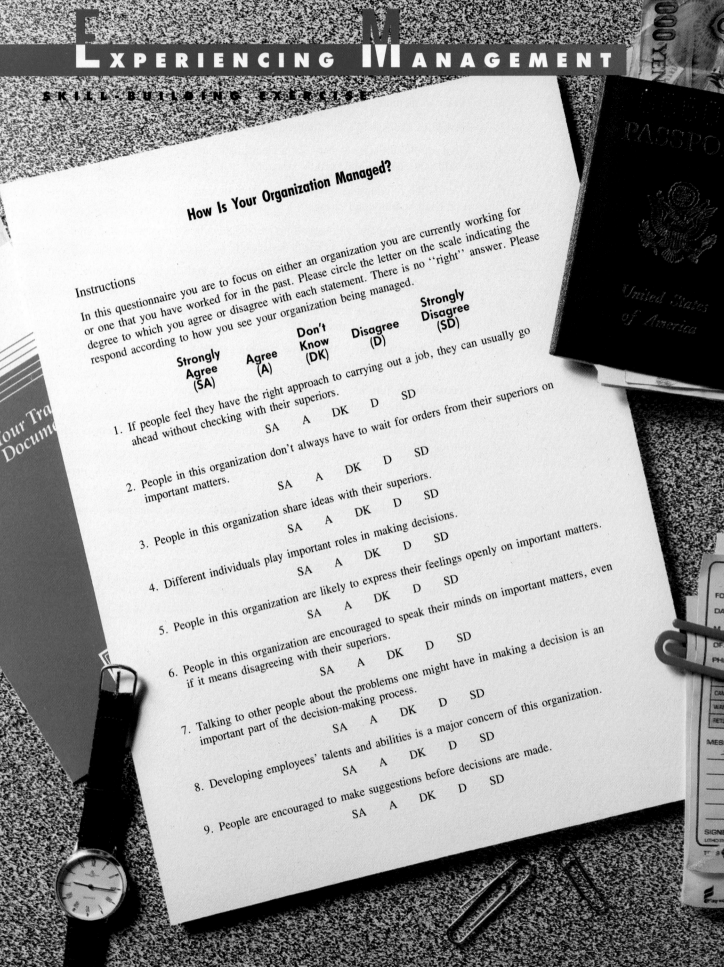

EXPERIENCING MANAGEMENT

SKILL-BUILDING EXERCISE

How Is Your Organization Managed?

Instructions

In this questionnaire you are to focus on either an organization you are currently working for or one that you have worked for in the past. Please circle the letter on the scale indicating the degree to which you agree or disagree with each statement. There is no ''right'' answer. Please respond according to how you see your organization being managed.

Strongly Agree (SA)	Agree (A)	Don't Know (DK)	Disagree (D)	Strongly Disagree (SD)

1. If people feel they have the right approach to carrying out a job, they can usually go ahead without checking with their superiors.

   SA   A   DK   D   SD

2. People in this organization don't always have to wait for orders from their superiors on important matters.

   SA   A   DK   D   SD

3. People in this organization share ideas with their superiors.

   SA   A   DK   D   SD

4. Different individuals play important roles in making decisions.

   SA   A   DK   D   SD

5. People in this organization are likely to express their feelings openly on important matters.

   SA   A   DK   D   SD

6. People in this organization are encouraged to speak their minds on important matters, even if it means disagreeing with their superiors.

   SA   A   DK   D   SD

7. Talking to other people about the problems one might have in making a decision is an important part of the decision-making process.

   SA   A   DK   D   SD

8. Developing employees' talents and abilities is a major concern of this organization.

   SA   A   DK   D   SD

9. People are encouraged to make suggestions before decisions are made.

   SA   A   DK   D   SD

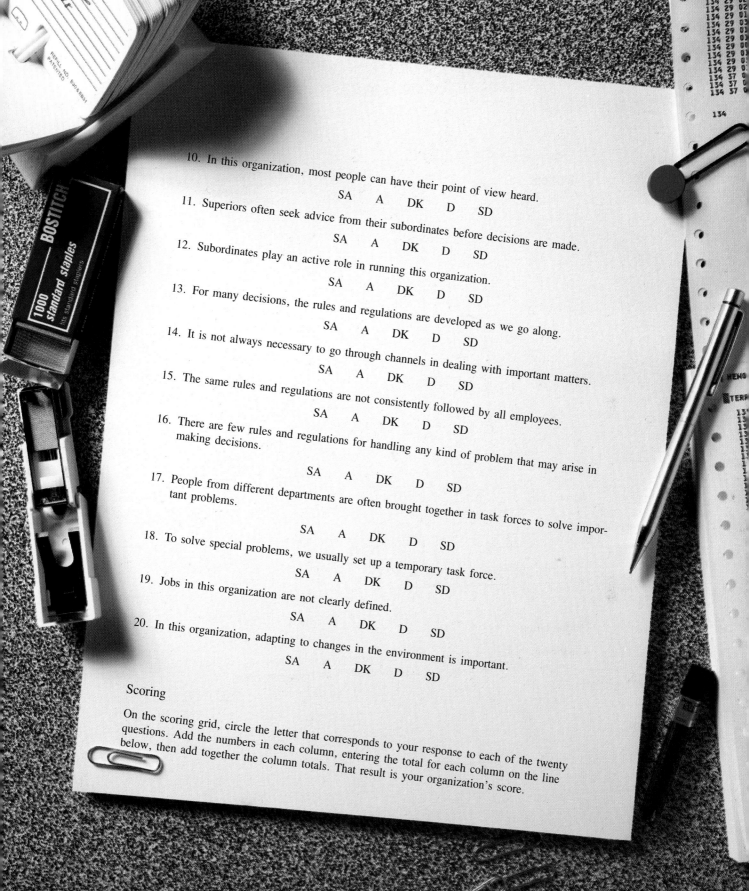

10. In this organization, most people can have their point of view heard.

SA   A   DK   D   SD

11. Superiors often seek advice from their subordinates before decisions are made.

SA   A   DK   D   SD

12. Subordinates play an active role in running this organization.

SA   A   DK   D   SD

13. For many decisions, the rules and regulations are developed as we go along.

SA   A   DK   D   SD

14. It is not always necessary to go through channels in dealing with important matters.

SA   A   DK   D   SD

15. The same rules and regulations are not consistently followed by all employees.

SA   A   DK   D   SD

16. There are few rules and regulations for handling any kind of problem that may arise in making decisions.

SA   A   DK   D   SD

17. People from different departments are often brought together in task forces to solve important problems.

SA   A   DK   D   SD

18. To solve special problems, we usually set up a temporary task force.

SA   A   DK   D   SD

19. Jobs in this organization are not clearly defined.

SA   A   DK   D   SD

20. In this organization, adapting to changes in the environment is important.

SA   A   DK   D   SD

Scoring

On the scoring grid, circle the letter that corresponds to your response to each of the twenty questions. Add the numbers in each column, entering the total for each column on the line below, then add together the column totals. That result is your organization's score.

QUESTIONS	Strongly Agree	Agree	Don't Know	Disagree	Strongly Disagree
1.	5	4	3	2	1
2.	5	4	3	2	1
3.	5	4	3	2	1
4.	5	4	3	2	1
5.	5	4	3	2	1
6.	5	4	3	2	1
7.	5	4	3	2	1
8.	5	4	3	2	1
9.	5	4	3	2	1
10.	5	4	3	2	1
11.	5	4	3	2	1
12.	5	4	3	2	1
13.	5	4	3	2	1
14.	5	4	3	2	1
15.	5	4	3	2	1
16.	5	4	3	2	1
17.	5	4	3	2	1
18.	5	4	3	2	1
19.	5	4	3	2	1
20.	5	4	3	2	1

Score ____ ____ ____ ____ ____   Total Score ____

100–80	79–40	39–20
Highly Organic	Mixed	Highly Mechanistic

Interpretation

A high score indicates a highly organic and participatively managed organization. A low score is associated with a mechanistic or bureaucratically managed organization.

To: Terry Hartshorn, CEO, Pacificare Health Systems, Inc.
From: Faye Rice, V.P., Marketing
Re: Industry trends in health care

Health care costs in the United States today run about $650 billion a year. According to government figures, health care costs for employers more than doubled between 1980 and 1988: Organizations now spend more than $3000 per employee for medical benefits each year.

Membership in HMOs (health maintenance organizations) grew by more than 20% annually during the 1980s, but in 1990 it grew by only 5%. In 1980 there were approximately 662 HMOs operating in the Unites States, but there are fewer than 575 today. This number is expected to continue to drop as weaker plans fold or merge with stronger ones.

Along with the projected industry consolidation, we are likely to see increasingly tighter state legislation regulating HMOs. This means that surviving HMOs will have to be larger and financially stronger. New entries into our industry are likely to be fewer.

What problems and opportunities do these trends pose for us? First, since 1986 we have offered our members comprehensive health care services for a fixed monthly payment. The payment generally remains the same regardless of the frequency, extent, or nature of health services actually provided. We have been known to custom-tailor our products and services for clients, but it appears that we can't charge extra for our extra care. Perhaps we need to rethink that policy, or to routinize our service technology in many areas, to reduce our costs.

Second, many employers are reducing the number of HMO options offered to their employees, to help cut their overall cost of health care. They are looking for HMOs that have demonstrated their ability to hold costs down while maintaining customer satisfaction. We presently have separate operations based in four western states. It might mean that we'll have to rethink our place-based organizational structure in order to save dollars and get more efficient.

Third, a competitor in Washington just opened a residential Secure Horizons program for senior citizens in retirement communities. Perhaps we should enter that market. But I wonder if our current organization design would support a move like that.

Please let me have your thoughts on an organization design for Pacificare that would address the issues I've outlined here.

Question: Assume that you are Terry Hartshorn. Draft a response to Faye Rice containing your ideas about an appropriate design for an organization operating in such a changing environment.

In Clash Between Art and Efficiency, Did Steinway Pianos Lose?

BY JUDITH VALENTE

NEW YORK—Few musical instruments have received higher praise than the pianos crafted by Steinway & Sons. Franz Liszt once called the Steinway piano "a glorious masterpiece." Another 19th-century composer, Gioacchino Rossini, said its sound was "great as thunder, sweet as the fluting of a nightingale."

Steinway is famous for the sound created by its rich, hand-molded woods and the unique engineering features that date back more than a century: the layout of the strings, the diaphragmatic soundboard, the accelerated action that gives a quick response when the keys are pressed.

But lately, some people in music circles have been wondering what's going on at Steinway. In recent years, some of the 138-year-old company's most experienced workers have left the piano maker, claiming an erosion of quality. Some customers also have complained that their brand new $28,000 pianos have cracked soundboards, the large wooden pieces that sit under the strings and amplify the sounds. . . .

"Pure hokum," responds John Birmingham, one of the owners of the company, to charges that quality has slipped. In fact, he says, the company has spent millions to improve its pianos.

It's certainly true that Steinway's customers are a particularly demanding lot. But even so, given Steinway's status in the musical world, just the perception of a decline in quality strikes a sour note heard round the world. Steinway's cachet has allowed it to charge premium prices: up to $10,000 for upright pianos and as much as $62,000 for special-order concert grands.

The disharmony began when CBS Inc. bought the company from the Steinway family in 1972. Repeated management changes under CBS took their toll. Dealers sometimes complained that pianos were badly tuned, their finishes sloppy. In 1978, CBS tapped a longtime piano-industry executive to provide a steadying hand, and Steinway began turning around.

But complaints have intensified again since 1985, when John and Robert Birmingham took the company over in a $53.5 million leveraged buy-out. The brothers, who inherited a fortune from the family heating oil business in Waltham, Mass., had no experience in the music industry. John owned a company making plastic windows for envelopes, while Robert was a former ad executive and a partner in a catalog business selling products with bear themes. . . .

The Birminghams say they found the factory lagging behind the times. He says there wasn't even a computer-controlled system of tracking parts and inventory. The operation was too "reliant on a few craftsmen," he says.

From a textbook standpoint, they made the right moves. They hired managers with extensive experience in manufacturing to streamline operations. They invested $8 million in equipment such as a new machine that makes the piano's felt hammers and other small parts more consistent.

They built a computer data base from old engineering drawings and specifications that had been kept around for years in dusty loose-leaf binders and in notebooks foremen carried in their back pockets. Their research engineers even hooked up parts of the late Vladimir Horowitz's concert grand to a computer to try to unlock the mysteries of its fine sound.

Their hope was to make the company more efficient and to achieve more consistency in the quality of the final product. Yet the more scientific Steinway became, the more some in the music business began to wonder whether the instruments were losing their personality. They say the new approach ignored what's most important: the human touch that's been Steinway's hallmark ever since Heinrich Engelhard Steinweg (later Steinway) built his first piano in the kitchen of his German home. "Steinways are a work of art; if they weren't, we wouldn't be playing them," says classical pianist Jose Feghali. . . .

The controversy comes at a poor time because the industry is hurting. Shipments to dealers have fallen three years in a row. Steinway also faces mounting competition from Japanese and Korean manufacturers, whose mass-produced pianos sell for half as much. . . .

Much of the furor within Steinway began with the exodus of several executives with extensive experience in piano-making. The Birminghams forced out the head of the Queens factory, Joseph Pramberger, whose family had worked there for three generations. They brought in Daniel Koenig, an engineer who had spent 21 years at General Electric Co. working on steam turbines and motors. . . . [He filled key posts] with executives from the manufacturing business. Steinway's new president had been with John Birmingham's plastics factory. The new vice president for operations came from a furnace induction business. Longtime foremen were reshuffled. "The music industry is made up largely of people enamored of music and the instruments they make, but they don't necessarily have great management skills," John Birmingham says. "We thought it was important to have people in there with good solid business experience." He adds: "There's a romance on the part of people in this industry who think they're the only ones who can do anything."

Shortly after taking the job, Mr. Koenig warned in an internal memo that the traditional "guild hall" system in which apprentice and journeymen craftsmen toiled under older workers until they reached master craftsman level was no longer viable because of changes in the work force. Steinway, he said, needed to stop depending on "a core of old-time foremen," and should move into "a document-driven and controlled manufacturing operation as quickly as possible."

1. Is the piano manufacturing industry's external environment stable or changing? Support your position.
2. Was the introduction of technology appropriate in an industry like Steinway's?
3. Is Steinway similar to a service agency in any way? Is music tangible or intangible?

WOOLWORTH'S—GETTING BACK ON TRACK

When F. W. Woolworth opened his first store in Lancaster, Pennsylvania more than a century ago, his vision was to define a store not by the nature of its wares, but by their price. His stores carried just about anything, as long as it didn't cost more than a dime. Woolworth's was present in almost everyone's childhood. It was a sprawling, popcorn-scented, rummage-sale kind of place where children could buy birthday gifts for their parents and still have change left over for candy.

In early 1982 Woolworth's faced its greatest challenge—survival. Profits from its stores were very small in 1980 and had turned into a significant loss in 1981. That loss continued into 1982. Woolworth's had to borrow $900 million at a time when its stock was at its lowest level since 1962, the U.S. economy was in a recession, and interest rates were high.

That was the situation when, in 1982, Woolworth's undertook and completed one of the most successful corporate redesigns in retail history. The two major features of the redesigning effort were the discontinuance of the $2 billion Woolco business in the United States by closing down, over an eighteen-month period of time, 372 stores; and the sale, for just under $280 million, of Woolworth's 52.6 percent equity interest in Woolworth's, Great Britain. This action resulted in increased financial resources for new and more profitable businesses.

Since 1982 the structure of Woolworth's has changed markedly. The general merchandise business has achieved increases in revenues and profits each year since 1984, and all indications are that this will steadily continue.

However, Woolworth's specialty operations—such as Woolworth Express, Kinney Shoes, and Kids Mart—have accounted for 50 percent or more of its profits since 1985. Of the more than 3600 stores opened between 1983 and 1989, 95 percent of them were specialty stores. Woolworth's now has over 1840 Foot Locker stores carrying men's, women's, and children's athletic footwear.

Woolworth's also has strengthened its global operations by starting product lines in Canada and Australia. Some of its most profitable specialty stores started in Canada, including Lady Foot Locker, Sportelle, Northern Reflections, Randy River, and Raglans. For just under $70 million, Woolworth's acquired 280 Mathers specialty stores in Australia. This purchase tripled the size of Woolworth's operations in Australia, put it into new product and geographical markets, and provided opportunities for considerable economies of scale in buying, marketing, and operating.

How has Woolworth's succeeded while other merchandisers, such as Montgomery Ward, Target, and Kmart, have experienced troubles in growing? First, each line of business has its own functional departments, such as legal, accounting, taxation, human resources, finance, and auditing. Each product line has virtually complete authority over and responsibility for buying, merchandising, advertising, distribution, store operations, and store location functions. Product line managers are also responsible for development of new specialty store formats and are urged to be creative, entrepreneurial, and venturesome. Top managers at Woolworth's believe that product managers know their own operational, merchandising, and organizational strengths and weaknesses better than top management does because they are closer to the customer. Top managers provide product managers with realistic performance targets and they jointly set financial objectives for the product line.

In addition, management information systems help each product manager run his or her operation efficiently. Computerized inventory systems let buyers at each product headquarters check each day on the sales of any item at any store in its chain. The computer deducts each sale from inventory and automatically reorders when inventory is running low. The Express Stores are drugstores that don't carry prescription drugs—just health and beauty aids for the most part. The Express stores use bar codes instead of price stickers, enabling Woolworth's to use laser scanner–equipped cash registers that cut the normal checkout time in half and get customers out of the store more quickly.

1. What kind of environment is Woolworth's operating in, and how has this affected the structure of the company?

2. What kind of service technology does Woolworth's use?

3. What impact does Woolworth's environment have on its information-processing strategies?

4. How has Woolworth survived the mature stage in its organizational life cycle?

Chapter 12

Human Resource

Management

Diamond-Star assembly line

What You Will Learn

1 Key components of the staffing process.

2 The tools and techniques for planning human resource needs.

3 The critical sources of recruitment.

4 Stages in the selection, hiring, and orientation of personnel.

5 Features of compensation and benefit plans.

6 Several methods of appraising performance, and problems arising from the subjective nature of the process.

7 How training and development programs can improve employees' performance.

8 **Skill Development:** How to plan for and fulfill an organization's human resource needs—from recruitment through training and development.

Selecting Employees at Diamond-Star Motors

An anxious group of job applicants sits watching a video about Diamond-Star Motors Corporation. They are on the first leg of their journey through Diamond-Star's employee selection process. The company spokesperson tells them that, if they are chosen, they will have the opportunity to learn several jobs. They will also be encouraged to suggest ideas—or, in the company's lingo, *Kaizen*—that will improve the whole plant's efficiency.

When it opened its doors, Diamond-Star, the Normal, Illinois–based joint venture of Chrysler and Mitsubishi, received more than 50,000 job applications. It ended up hiring only 300. The selection process lasts three grueling days and follows a basic belief that high quality results not so much from individual performance as from each individual's impact on their team. On the first day of testing, applicants are asked to perform tasks in a simulated factory assembly line. This gives them a taste of what they will be doing and lets the company weed out those who simply can't do the job. The simulation is preceded by written tests and a medical examination that includes a drug test. Only after passing all these tests do applicants see plant managers for interviews.

This selection process is also followed when employees are up for promotion. Workers identified as having leadership potential are evaluated in an assessment center for possible placement as group leaders on factory work teams. The assessment center evaluates employees on their ability not only to master new skills quickly, but also to then teach them to others.[1]

The human resource function doesn't operate in a vacuum, somewhere inside an organization. Many of the aspects of the organization's external environment and of its design influence the scope of the human resources activities it performs. For example, in Chapter 8 we showed how the strategy of the firm affects its use of key resources, including human ones. In Chapters 10 and 11 we described how structure and technology can influence the design of an organization.

Let's look at some examples. La Quinta Inns is an organization with more than 275 motels in the southwestern part of the United States that cater to the traveling salesperson. La Quinta has chosen a low-cost strategy to compete in the motel industry. It is organized along functional lines and uses a mechanistic structure to deliver a routine service. To maintain its low-cost advantage, it needs to reduce employee turnover. Through its human resource management program, La Quinta has found that one sure-fire way to cut turnover is to hire only husband-and-wife teams to run motels. Each team receives extensive hands-on training in all activities (maintenance, reservations, housekeeping, billing) before being assigned to a motel. The emphasis of the entire human resource management program is on keeping costs down. Marriott operates in the same industry but is organized along product lines—resort, business, and budget motels. Managers are trained to perform their functions within a product line. Marriott motels aren't staffed with husband-and-wife teams but with people who want a career in the organization. A person's selection is based on broad criteria, such as initiative, mobility, and good interpersonal rela-

human resource management The process of analyzing and managing an organization's human resource needs to ensure satisfaction of its strategic objectives.

tions. Superb service is a key strategic weapon for Marriott, so it recruits new employees who have that service orientation.

Human resource management is the process of analyzing and managing an organization's human resource needs to ensure satisfaction of its strategic objectives.[2] The process requires first setting staffing objectives and then comparing current personnel to those objectives. Only then can the organization effectively consider strategies to move it in the desired direction.

In this chapter we look at some ways organizations are tackling vital human resource management functions. We first examine the staffing process as a whole—from planning and recruiting to selection and orientation. Then we examine compensation and benefits management and how these functions can help an organization attract the right people. Next we focus on the performance appraisal process, exploring why it is necessary and how various organizations use it. Finally, we look at how organizations can help their people grow further, through training and development.

The staffing process

staffing The process by which organizations satisfy their human resource needs by forecasting future needs, recruiting and selecting candidates, and orienting new employees.

Staffing is the process by which organizations satisfy their human resource needs. They forecast future needs, recruit and select candidates to meet these needs, and then orient new employees to their jobs and to the organization.[3] Staffing is one of the ways in which an organization may try to control and direct the actions of its employees. Some organizations deliberately seek to attract, hire, and retain certain types of people—resulting in the image of a stereotypical employee. For example, at PepsiCo the corporate motto is "We take eagles and teach them to fly in formation." The eagles are managers. Each manager gets to act like an entrepreneur—taking risks, issuing few memos, and working sixty-hour weeks. However, once the team makes a decision, all managers follow. Obviously, only aggressive overachievers survive at PepsiCo.[4] At LTV, where most of the work is defense-related, the preference is to hire people with military experience. Hiring employees with similar beliefs, values, and attitudes is one way an organization can work toward its objectives.

But staffing and hiring aren't the same thing. The staffing process encompasses a much broader range of activities than simply hiring people. It also includes easing employees' entrance into an organization, as well as their movement through (promotion, job rotation, transfer) and out of (termination, retirement) it.

Figure 12.1 highlights the following components of the staffing process:

▶ *Planning* Before hiring anyone, the organization needs to forecast its human resource requirements. By doing so, a firm can determine the number of employees to hire and the types of skills they will need. Moreover, management will be able to determine when it will need these employees.

▶ *Recruitment* The organization should then develop a pool of job candidates from which to select qualified employees. Candidates are recruited by, for example, running ads, contacting employment agencies, and visiting college campuses.

▶ *Selection and hiring* After recruiting candidates for available positions, the organization selects and hires those people who are most likely to perform well on the job. These decisions can be difficult. Diamond-Star Motors' assessment centers are an example of an excellent, well-developed selection system.

▶ *Orientation* Once employees are hired, they must be oriented to their jobs and the organization in general. Effective orientation programs familiarize new employees

The Staffing Process

The staffing process involves not only hiring new employees, but also working with employees currently in the organization.

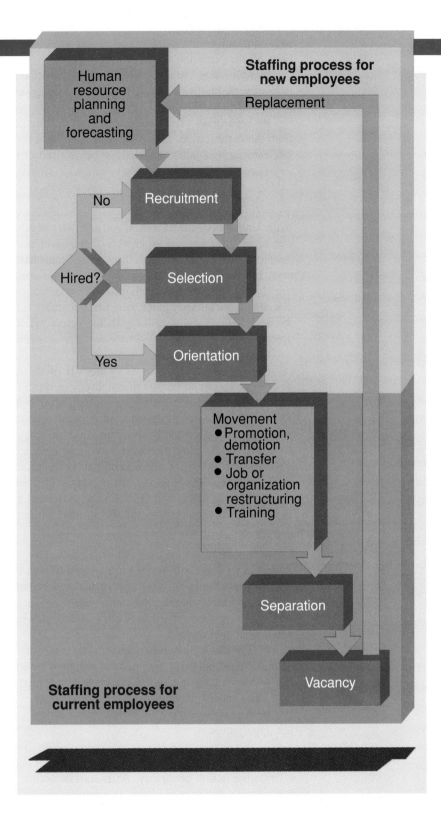

with company policies, safety codes, and work expectations. They also include explanations of compensation and employee benefits.

▶ *Movement* After completing the orientation process, an employee remains a participant in the staffing process. Promotions, demotions, transfers, restructuring, and training are all part of staffing.

▶ *Separation* The final stage in the staffing process is separation of the employee from the organization. Separation can occur as a result of the employee's finding a new job, retiring, becoming disabled, or being fired or outplaced.

Regulatory Influences

In the United States and Canada, and a number of other countries, people have determined that equal opportunity in all aspects of employment is a worthy and just goal. As a result the regulatory environment in the United States has a major impact on the staffing process. Executive orders, laws, and court rulings specify required, acceptable, and unacceptable human resource activities. These affect not only recruitment, selection, and placement, but also pay plans, benefits, penalties, and terminations. Let's briefly consider the major equal employment legislation before examining the components of the staffing process in more detail.[5]

Antidiscrimination Laws Title VII of the Civil Rights Act of 1964 prohibits discrimination in all phases of employment on the basis of race, color, religion, sex, or national origin (except where such a factor is a valid occupational qualification). There are other laws designed to protect job applicants and employees from discriminatory treatment on the basis of age (age 40 and over), handicap, or veteran status. Categories of employees covered by these laws are legally called **protected groups.** These requirements for nondiscriminatory treatment apply to private as well as public organizations. Compliance with the laws is monitored by the Equal Employment Opportunity Commission (EEOC) and enforced by the Justice Department.

The legal requirements of the antidiscrimination laws are broad. Among other things, they provide that:

▶ An employer may not fail or refuse to hire, discharge, or otherwise discriminate against any person with respect to pay, conditions, or privileges of employment because of race, color, religion, sex, age, or national origin.

▶ An employer may not limit, segregate, or classify employees in any way that would deprive them of employment opportunities because of race, color, age, religion, sex, or national origin.

▶ The EEOC may bring action in federal district court if it is unsuccessful in eliminating alleged unlawful employment practices by means of persuasion.

▶ Organizations can only use employment tests that are directly related to a specific job. Tests should be validated for each company.

▶ An employer may not include any discriminatory statements in advertisements for job opportunities.

Affirmative Action Programs The EEOC can ask certain employers to set up affirmative action programs. **Affirmative action programs** are intended to ensure that a firm's hiring procedures guarantee equal employment opportunity, as specified by the law.[6] These programs require the organization first to perform a utilization analysis comparing the present work force to the relevant labor market. The relevant labor market includes both geographic and skill components. For national organizations—for example, Avon, Aetna Life Insurance, and Kodak—the relevant labor market for managers would be all candidates who live in the United States and possess managerial knowledge and skills. In these same companies the relevant labor market for secretaries would be candidates who live in the local area and have appropriate secretarial skills.

protected group A category of people who are specifically covered by federal antidiscrimination laws on hiring and employment.

affirmative action program A legally mandated program intended to ensure that a firm's hiring procedures guarantee equal employment opportunity as specified by the law.

Iva Wilson, president of Philips Display Components, is one of the few *women in top management* at a high-tech company.

work-force analysis A listing of all of a firm's job titles and salary rates and a breakdown by sex and ethnic/racial background of the total number of people holding each job title.

availability analysis A study that determines whether minorities' and women's representation in an organization is proportionate to their numbers in the relevant labor market.

The organization is also required to conduct a work-force analysis. A **work-force analysis** lists all job titles and salary rates in the organization, reports the total number of people holding each job title, and breaks down these numbers by sex and by ethnic/racial background. A related availability analysis is then conducted. An **availability analysis** is a study that determines whether minorities' and women's representation in the organization is proportionate to their numbers in the relevant labor market. If there are discrepancies between the makeup of a company's current work force and that of its relevant labor market, the company must design specific programs with timetables and objectives to correct them.

Work-Force Trends

According to the Bureau of Labor Statistics, annual work-force growth in the United States will slow dramatically, from 2 percent a year for the period 1976 through 1988 to 1.2 percent from 1991 to 2000. That's because the baby boomers are aging, and fewer people are entering the work force. Between 1991 and 2000 only 32 percent of new employees will be white males. Women will make up 48.6 percent of the work force, and minorities will hold 24 percent of all new jobs.[7]

Work-force developments projected for the 1990s are rooted in the demographics of today's work force. In some areas of the world—for instance, Pakistan, Indonesia, Brazil, and Spain—women have not been absorbed in large numbers and represent a huge untapped resource. In other countries—for instance, the United States, Britain, Sweden, Thailand, and Canada—women represent a significant percentage of the work force. Although looming labor shortages have been forecasted for many industrialized nations, the world's work force is growing fast. From 1985 to 2000, the work force is expected to grow by some 600 million people, or about 27 percent (that compares with 36-percent growth between 1970 and 1985). The growth will take place unevenly. The vast majority of new workers will join the work forces in developing countries, such as Mexico, Pakistan, India, and the Philippines. In countries like Mexico and Pakistan, the work force will grow at about 3 percent a year. In contrast, growth rates in the United States, Canada, and Spain will be closer to 1 percent a year, Japan's work force will grow just 0.5 percent a year, and Germany's work force (including the Eastern sector) will actually decline.

As we mentioned in our discussion of demographics in Chapter 3, the watchword for recruiting this new work force mix is ''managing diversity.'' Companies such as Corning, Hewlett-Packard, and Procter & Gamble are putting diversity into management titles. For example, King-Ming Young is designated the Project Manager for Managing Diversity, at Hewlett-Packard. According to Young, who deals with a U.S. work force that is 19 percent minority and 40 percent female, the goal of the program is to work on improving understanding between men and women and between African-Americans and whites.[8] Companies in general are training workers to be more tolerant of language and cultural differences, to identify and reject any racial and sexual prejudices, and to better accommodate the handicapped.

Affirmative action programs that aim to correct the past exclusion of women and minorities have made some impact. According to the EEOC, the percentage of managers who are women has grown from 17 percent in 1978 to 27 percent, and the percentage from minorities has gone from 7 percent to 9.5 percent. However, less than 4 percent of managerial women sit on the boards of directors of U.S. organizations, only one African-American manager heads a Fortune 1000 company, and African-American women still hold less than 2 percent of management jobs.[9]

Implications for Managers In the recruitment process, the human resources department normally has the responsibility for assuring compliance with laws requiring equal employment opportunity and affirmative action. These laws, however, affect all managers, because they determine the pool of applicants from which the managers can choose and the procedures that managers must follow after a person has been placed. Managers in the human resources department must educate and train others in their organization with respect to these laws and their implications. Remember, even job titles can be sexist or discriminatory. For example, the job titles "salesman" and "foreman" are outdated; salesperson and supervisor are usually used instead.

Human resource planning

The first stage of the staffing process, **human resource planning,** involves forecasting the organization's human resource needs and planning the steps to be taken to meet them. It consists of developing and implementing plans and programs that ensure that the right number and type of individuals are available at the right time and place to fulfill organizational needs.[10] Human resource planning is thus directly tied to strategic planning (see Chapter 8). We mentioned how La Quinta's low-cost strategy in the motel industry requires them to retain employees and how they meet that requirement—by hiring couples. La Quinta's human resource planning system helps top management identify those plans and programs that will attract couples to join the motel chain.

Determining an organization's human resource needs is the foundation of human resource planning. We'll look in more detail at some of the tools and techniques used for planning and forecasting these needs: skills inventories, job analyses, replacement charts, and expert forecasts.

Skills Inventory   A **skills inventory** is a detailed file maintained for each employee that lists his or her level of education, training, experience, length of service, current job title and salary, performance history, and personal demographics such as age, gender, race, and marital status. Many organizations use computerized human resource information systems for storage and easy retrieval of such vital job-related information. IBM, for example, maintains files on more than 100,000 employees. These files can help an organization's top managers spot human resource gaps when making plans for diversification or global expansion. For example, Daiwa Securities planned to open a new office in Rome. Human resource managers forecasted the need for Italian-speaking college graduates with five years of financial experience to staff the office. By searching through its computerized human resource file, Daiwa's managers discovered that no currently employed personnel meet these requirements. In order to commence operations in Rome, Daiwa had to recruit and train such personnel.

Job Analysis   A **job analysis** is a breakdown of the tasks for a specific job and the personal characteristics determined to be necessary for their successful performance. A thorough job analysis has two parts: a description and a specification. A **job description** is a detailed outline of a position's essential tasks and responsibilities. A **job specification** is a listing of the personal characteristics, skills, and experience a worker needs to carry out those tasks and assume those responsibilities. Figure 12.2 reproduces part of a job description and part of a job specification for a sales associate position at Zale Corporation.

The job specification helps the human resource administrator and department manager identify the right candidate for the job. Job descriptions are used more often to develop sound and fair compensation and performance appraisal systems. However, job descriptions also allow recruiters to give potential candidates realistic descriptions of vacant positions.

human resource planning
Forecasting a firm's human resource needs and planning the steps to be taken to meet them.

skills inventory   A detailed file maintained for each employee that lists his or her level of education, training, experience, length of service, current job title and salary, performance history, and personal demographics.

job analysis   A breakdown of the tasks and responsibilities of a specific job and the personal characteristics, skills, and experience necessary for their successful performance.

job description   A detailed outline of a position's essential tasks and responsibilities.

job specification   A listing of the personal characteristics, skills, and experience a worker needs to carry out a job's tasks and assume its responsibilities.

Job Description and Job Specification Statement

A sales associate position description from Zales that includes both a job description and a job specification.

JOB TITLE

Sales Associate

Job Description

Primarily responsible for selling merchandise to customers who enter the store. Additional responsibilities include certain merchandising and house-keeping duties. Examples of duties required include:

- Handles repairs, including providing estimates, maintaining repair records, sending merchandise to repair shop, following up on overdue repairs.

- Straightens and cleans display and understock merchandise, cases, and windows; sets up merchandise displays; and otherwise maintains store appearance.

- Asks questions of customer to determine what he or she is looking for in terms of merchandise type, style, cost, etc.

- Makes suggestions on how to mix methods of payment in financing a purchase.

- Attempts to close a sale several times.

Job Specification

Personal characteristics important to success include:

- Previous sales experience.

- Maturity.

- Well-groomed and neat appearance.

- Aggressive and persistent demeanor.

- High school education.

replacement chart A diagram showing each position in an organization's management hierarchy, with the name of each incumbent and the names of candidates eligible to replace him or her.

Replacement Chart A **replacement chart** is a diagram showing each position in the organization's management hierarchy, with the name of each incumbent and the names of candidates eligible to replace him or her. These charts, which are usually confidential, provide a simple means of forecasting management needs and internal availability.

Figure 12.3 is a sample replacement chart covering four management positions. It gives the position titles, the name of each position's incumbent, the names of likely candidates for each position, their years of tenure in the department, and their promotional potential. Replacement charts are usually developed with this much detail only for top-level managers. Holders of lower-level positions may not be considered suitable replacements for upper-level incumbents. Gaps in a firm's replacement chart—positions for which there are no suitable replacements—point to the need for enhanced management development or, perhaps, outside recruiting. Jack Welch, CEO of General Electric, says that one of his assessment practices is to have each vice president name a potential replacement. If a vice president can't name a successor, he or she hasn't spent enough time grooming subordinates for advancement.

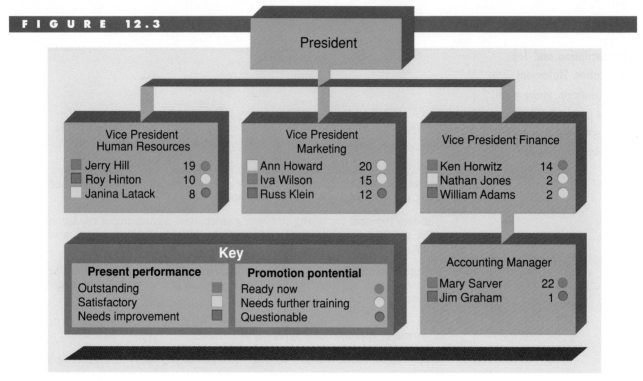

FIGURE 12.3

President

Vice President
Human Resources

■ Jerry Hill	19	●
■ Roy Hinton	10	○
□ Janina Latack	8	○

Vice President
Marketing

□ Ann Howard	20	○
■ Iva Wilson	15	○
■ Russ Klein	12	●

Vice President Finance

■ Ken Horwitz	14	●
□ Nathan Jones	2	○
■ William Adams	2	○

Key

Present performance		Promotion pontential	
Outstanding	■	Ready now	●
Satisfactory	□	Needs further training	○
Needs improvement	■	Questionable	○

Accounting Manager

■ Mary Sarver	22	●
■ Jim Graham	1	○

Management Replacement Chart

Note that there is only one suitable replacement currently available for the manager of accounting position.

Expert Forecasts A variety of expert forecasting methods—some simple, some complex—can be used to determine an organization's demand for human resources. The forecasting method used depends on the pertinent time frame, the type, size, and strategy of the organization, and the accuracy of the information available. More than 60 percent of all major firms employ some sort of expert forecasting. One popular method is the three-step Delphi technique, discussed with respect to strategic planning in Chapter 9.[11] As applied to staffing, the Delphi technique makes use of eight to ten experts who take turns presenting forecasts and assumptions to the others, who then revise their own forecasts, in order to reach a consensus. The experts' predictions are based on underlying assumptions, such as the company's expected rate of growth and the area's future unemployment rate. Managers have found the Delphi technique useful in making one-year predictions and in generating human resource forecasts for areas in which the human resource manager has limited knowledge.

Experts are predicting great changes in global organizations' human resource practices after the economic union of the European Community in 1992. This chapter's Global Link feature focuses on some of the effects forecasters see.

RECRUITMENT

recruitment The process of searching, both inside and outside an organization, for employees to fill vacant positions.

When there aren't enough candidates immediately available to meet the demand that human resource planning predicts, the organization must attract people to fill its jobs. **Recruitment** is the process of searching, both inside and outside the organization, for

GOING GLOBAL WITH HR PRACTICES

A major force behind today's push to "go global" is the changes that are taking place in Europe. As we discussed in Chapter 4, twelve separate countries will be unified into a single European Community (EC) in 1992. This unification is being designed to set up common markets for goods, services, capital, and labor.

Although the EC won't remove all international differences, major changes in human resource practices will result. For example, the EC is planning legislation that will affect how and where organizations locate and how they manage, develop, and compensate their employees. This legislation will erase the major differences in employment practices that had existed from country to country. In Belgium, for instance, companies planning layoffs must give employees three months' notice for every five years of service, but Greek organizations have no such requirement. Workers in Luxembourg get a minimum of twenty-five working days a year as a vacation, but organizations in the United Kingdom have no national mandate to guide their vacation policies. Eventually every worker in the EC will have the right to ongoing training. A system based on credits allotted annually and accumulated throughout an individual's working life will be created. Standardized curricula and courses at vocational schools will mean that workers will be qualified for jobs throughout the EC.

Finally, there is the rise of the "Euro-executive." Who is this person? A Euro-executive is one who speaks English plus one or two European languages. Nationality is less important than flexibility, ability to adapt, and appreciation of cultural differences. Ideally such an executive will have worked in a number of different capacities and locations. Mobility, initiative, creativity, team building, and independence are all musts. The abilities to initiate change and to get results are critical.

Source: Adapted from R. Sedel, "Europe 1992: H.R. Implications of the European Unification," *Personnel,* 10/89, pp. 19–24.

employees to fill vacant positions.[12] Recruitment should also be concerned with identifying potential employees' needs. In this way recruitment not only attracts individuals to the organization, but also increases the chances of retaining them once they're hired.

At Motorola, the recruiting department's performance is measured by how well its recruits do on the job. Are they well qualified for the job, or do they need a lot of remedial training? Have they been hired at the right salary, or do they leave within six months for a higher-paying job at another company?

The following Insight takes a look at how Burger King has tried to recruit people into its organization.

RECRUITING FOR BURGER KING

INSIGHT

Burger King has been very innovative when it comes to recruiting workers. At least seven approaches have been used:

Agencies for the handicapped The Florida region is experiencing great success with its "Be Capable" program. More than 100 handicapped young people, hired through various local agencies, are working in Burger King stores there.

Senior citizens This growing population is being reached by posting available positions at senior citizens' centers. Burger King hopes that these older employees will have a positive influence on the younger ones and feels they represent a wealth of experience that can greatly benefit the fast food industry.

Theater commercials Recruiting commercials are being aired before the main feature in movie theaters in Detroit and San Francisco.

"Ask me . . ." campaign Using employees as recruiters is a proven winner. "Ask me about working for Burger King" buttons, t-shirts, posters, and so forth are successful gimmicks in the Florida region.

Crew referral Burger King offers cash incentives to employees for recruiting. Different regions handle this in different ways. In areas where young people are exceptionally hard to recruit, cash is awarded simply for bringing in an applicant; in others, only for a new hire.

Providing transportation When a store can't hire from its local community—maybe because it's in an affluent neighborhood where the kids don't work or in a nonresidential area where there aren't any kids—Burger King is providing transportation or bus fare to entice recruits from out of the area.

TV show Burger King is working with an advertising agency to develop a fourteen-minute television program that will promote the idea of learning through work. It will not focus on Burger King, but rather on the fast food industry and many advantages its offers to young people.[13]

Factors Affecting Recruiting

In order to develop an effective recruiting program, a human resource plan must first be developed. A well-developed human resource plan determines the types of jobs the organization will need to fill in the future, and a thorough job analysis pinpoints the knowledge, skills, and abilities qualified applicants will need to possess.

In addition to the human resource planning activities we've discussed, the organization must consider its external environment in developing a recruiting program. Three external factors affect the recruiting process: government regulations, labor unions, and the labor market.

Government Regulations As we noted earlier, an organization's recruiting policies and practices are significantly influenced by the regulatory environment. The EEOC requires employers to maintain records on the number of openings in various job groups and the number of applicants for them (broken down by race/ethnicity, gender, and other characteristics). Because of an affirmative action program, an organization's work force may be expected to reflect the composition of the relevant labor market. Thus, if a community is 60 percent white, 30 percent black, and 10 percent other racial/ethnic backgrounds, the organization's work force should parallel those percentages. When, in the EEOC's opinion, a company underemploys members of a designated minority, the agency may require the company to engage in special recruiting efforts.

union shop A company whose agreement with labor stipulates that all employees covered by the contract must be union members or join the union within sixty to ninety days of being hired.

Labor Unions About three-fifths of the states permit a union shop provision in management-labor contracts. A **union shop** is a company whose agreement with labor stipulates that all employees covered by the contract must be union members or join the union within sixty to ninety days of being hired.[14] This practice prevents a company from diluting union influence by hiring only workers who are against unions. The UAW, for example, has made union security a key issue in its negotiations with GM, Ford, and Chrysler. (In states with right-to-work laws, however, employees cannot be forced to join a union.)

Labor Market The labor market itself greatly influences recruiting efforts. If the local supply of qualified workers in a job category exceeds local demand, wages will be depressed and recruitment will be relatively easy. On the other hand, when the local supply of qualified workers is limited, recruiting efforts intensify. For example, in late 1987 the unemployment rate in Sarasota, Florida was only about four percent. Lechmere, Inc., a discount retail chain owned by Dayton Hudson, was about to open a store there, with workers in short supply. Like most retailers, Lechmere usually relied on hiring a lot of part-timers—typically teenagers and homemakers—a practice that gave the company lots of flexibility. But with few available interested workers, Lechmere had to devise new recruitment incentives. The company offered its Sarasota workers raises based on the number of jobs they learned to perform. Cashiers were encouraged to sell records, tapes, and sporting goods and even to operate forklifts in the warehouse. The pay incentives, along with the prospect of a more varied and interesting day, proved successful enticements to people to come work for the organization.[15]

Sources of Recruitment

Faced with the cost of recruiting, organizations try to identify and attract qualified employees who will stay with them. Typically, a department manager submits a personnel requisition to the human resources department. The requisition details the job title, salary range, department in which the opening exists, and so on. Most importantly, the requisition usually contains a job specification outlining the qualifications required to perform the job.

Using such requisitions, a recruiter searches for candidates, either inside or outside the organization. Table 12.1 lists several of the more common recruitment sources. Some sources, such as unsolicited applications, are relatively inexpensive. Others, such as executive search firms, can be quite expensive. Which source a recruiter turns to is usually determined by the type of job to be filled. For example, a position at Ernst & Young or Arthur Andersen specifying an undergraduate accounting degree will be more readily filled through on-campus recruiting efforts or an ad in a professional journal than through a classified ad in the Sunday paper.

Usual Sources for Recruitment of Job Candidates

Source	Comment
Educational institutions	High schools can be an excellent source for office, clerical, and secretarial employees. And trade and vocational schools provide many machinists, mechanics, paraprofessionals, and so on. Colleges and universities provide most management trainees and professionals.
Public employment services	Many states and the federal government provide employment services at no charge. Such services list primarily the unemployed and to a less extent those seeking a job change. The military also provides some placement assistance for veterans.
Private employment services	These services differ according to who pays for them. Search consultants, or ''headhunters,'' are paid by the organization and tend to focus on upper-level professionals and managers. Employment agencies, on the other hand, collect their fees from job seekers.
Unsolicited applications	Many jobs are filled by walk-ins or write-in candidates. Walk-ins tend to seek lower-level jobs, but many professionals mail in unsolicited resumés.
Employee referrals	One of the best and most consistently used sources of new employees is referral of candidates by current employees. However, reliance on employee referrals may perpetuate past discrimination, if the work force is homogeneous. A predominantly white male work force may refer mostly white males, thereby inviting an EEOC investigation.
Advertisements	Newspapers carry many help-wanted ads, particularly in their Sunday editions. Available professional positions that require specialized backgrounds are advertised in many professional journals.

Selection and hiring

The next step in the staffing process is actually filling the vacant position. Table 12.2 lists seven information sources available to managers making selection decisions. In-depth interviewing, testing, and using assessment centers may take considerably more time and money than the other methods. Diamond-Star Motors, for instance, spends about $13,000 per employee in the selection process. The following sections describe some methods human resource managers use to select from a pool of recruited candidates.

Sources of Information That Aid Selection Decisions

▶ Resumés
▶ Reference checks
▶ Job applications
▶ Realistic job previews
▶ Interviews
▶ Tests
▶ Assessment centers

Resumés

A well-written resumé is clear, concise, and easy to read and understand. The sample resumé in Figure 12.4 contains six key categories of information: (1) personal data (name,

JENNIFER A. BOUGHRUM
3100 University Blvd.
Dallas, Texas 75205
(214) 691-2736

CAREER OBJECTIVE
To obtain an entry-level position in a real estate department
in a global financial institution.

EDUCATION
        Southern Methodist University   Dallas, Texas
        Bachelor of Business Administration (dual major) May 1990
            Finance and Real Estate and Urban Land Economics
            Cumulative G.P.A.   3.43/4.0
        University of Valencia   Valencia, Spain, summer 1989
        Foreign Exchange Student   Barranquilla, Colombia, summer 1985

WORK EXPERIENCE
        Intern, Janet Kafka and Associates, International Marketing
            and Public Relations Firm
            Dallas, TX, 1989 to 1990.
            Provides Marketing Representation, Consultation, and
            Promotional Services to International Clients in
            selected industries.
        Foreman, College Pro Painters, U.S., Ltd.
            Darien, CT summmer 1987, 1988.
            Budget Maintenance and Customer and Employee Relations.
        Sales Representative, Lettitia Lewis Women's Clothing
            Boutique, New Canaan, CT 1985, 1986.
            Retail Sales, Inventory Control, and Coordination of
            additional stores.

HONORS AND EXTRACURRICULAR ACTIVITIES
        Financial Management Association National Honor Society
        Sigma Delta Pi, Spanish Honorary Society
        Order of Omega, Greek Honorary Society
        Southern Methodist University, Campus Guide
        Women's Symposium, Topics Discussion Leader Chairperson
        Alpha Kappa Psi, Business Fraternity
        Delta Delta Delta Sorority

REFERENCES
        Dr. John Peavey   Dr. John W. Slocum, Jr.
        Cox School of Business   Cox School of Business
        SMU   SMU
        Dallas, TX 75275-0333   Dallas, TX 75275-0333
        (214) 692-3148   (214) 692-3157

Sample Resumé

Source: Used with permission of Jennifer A. Boughrum.

address, and telephone number), (2) career objectives, (3) education (including GPA, degrees, and major fields of study), (4) work experience, highlighting special skills and responsibilities, (5) honors and activities, and (6) references, with their addresses and telephone numbers.

Of course, as a college graduate, you will probably be preparing a resumé of your own. Remember, managers don't have the time to read long, involved resumés, so limit yours to one or two pages. The *How To Pack Your Career Parachute* supplement to this textbook offers some useful tips on resumé preparation.

Reference Checks

Because resumés can easily be falsified, managers should request references and conduct reference checks. Many human resource managers have educational qualifications, including schools attended, degrees, dates, and major areas of study, checked routinely. An applicant's work experience is more difficult to check, however, because employers are often reluctant to provide evaluations of former employees. Their concern stems from cases in which reference givers have been successfully sued by former employees who were given bad references. In fact, by law, organizations are required to provide only the job title and dates of employment.

Job Applications

Most organizations require candidates to fill out a job application. In many cases this application serves the same purpose as a resumé. Employers can also use it to gather information for EEOC reports. A common misconception is that questioning applicants about their race, age, marital status, and national origin is illegal. In reality, employers are sometimes required by the government to ask such questions. During the recruitment phase, for instance, an organization may need to record demographic data in order to analyze and defend its recruitment techniques. It *is* against the law, however, to use this kind of information in a discriminatory way. To guard against charges of discrimination, organizations usually request that such information be given only on a voluntary basis. Table 12.3 lists subjects that would fall into that category. EEOC calls questions that may raise suspicions of discrimination ''problem questions'' in its affirmative action literature.

Realistic Job Previews

realistic job preview A screening technique that clearly shows candidates' tasks, or requirements.

A screening technique that is gaining in popularity is the realistic job preview.[16] A **realistic job preview** clearly shows candidates a job's tasks, or requirements, thus pointing out its good and bad aspects. In many cases this technique has reduced the turnover rate among those hired. Apparently, applicants who would probably become dissatisfied with the job and soon quit remove themselves from the running based on the preview. American Airlines has one of the airline industry's best realistic job previews. Potential flight

TABLE 12.3		
Potentially Sensitive Job Application Questions	**Subject of Question**	**Possible Type of Selection Bias**
	Height or weight	May indicate sexual bias.
	Eye or hair color	May indicate racial bias.
	Birthplace	May indicate national-origin bias.
	Marital status	May be used to discriminate against women planning to have children.
	Birth date	May be used to discriminate on the basis of age.
	Child-care plans	May be used to discriminate against women.

attendants are shown a variety of tasks that they will be required to learn and perform, such as safety procedures and service techniques. In a full-size cabin mockup, at the Dallas/Fort Worth Learning Center, they get a realistic look at the job.

Interviews

In making a final selection decision, most human resource managers rely on a combination of interviews and tests. Although commonly used, interviews are relatively poor predictors of on-the-job performance. Most people can remain alert and pleasant for a thirty-minute interview, but their behavior during the session will probably not be an accurate indication of how well they'll perform or relate to co-workers. Furthermore, research indicates that interviewers tend to decide about a person early in the interview. They spend the rest of the time seeking information to support their decision.[17]

Interviewers are likely to make three types of errors in judgment: (1) A **contrast error** occurs when an interviewee is rated as particularly good or bad, based on a comparison with the preceding interviewee. (2) A **similarity error** occurs when the interviewer forms a bias in favor of candidates who look or act like the interviewer. (3) The **halo effect** occurs when the interviewer judges the candidate's overall potential on the basis of a single characteristic (such as how well the candidate dresses or talks or where she or he attended college), allowing it to overshadow the candidate's other characteristics.

To overcome some potential interview problems, Digital Equipment, Motorola, Boeing, Chaparral Steel, and Johnsonville Foods, among others, are using a panel interview. In a **panel interview** several current employees simultaneously interview one applicant. Because all employees hear the same responses to the questions, panel interviews produce more balanced evaluations than interviews conducted by one person. On the other hand, panel interviews are expensive, because many people are involved. But Boeing, for one, judges the extra costs worthwhile, because the applicant and the panel members get a chance to assess how well they might work together.

Despite its potential drawbacks, an interview does serve useful purposes. The communication allows interviewer and applicant to learn what each has to offer the other. In addition, although it may not necessarily determine whether someone will perform well, an interview may indicate how well an applicant will fit in with other members of the work group. Finally, human nature is such that most people simply won't hire someone they haven't met. Table 12.4 lists some dos and don'ts of interviewing that should enable you to conduct useful interviews.

---

contrast error Interviewer error that occurs when an interviewee's rating is based on a comparison with the preceding interviewee.

similarity error Interviewer error caused by a bias in favor of candidates that look or act like the interviewer.

halo effect Interviewer error that occurs when the interviewer judges a candidate's overall potential on the basis of a single characteristic, allowing it to overshadow other characteristics.

panel interview A job interview conducted by a group of the organization's current employees.

T A B L E   12.4

Dos and Don'ts of Interviewing

Do	Don't
1. Read the job description prior to the interview.	1. Interrupt the candidate or be sarcastic, "cute," or otherwise rude. The applicant deserves respect.
2. Structure the interview based on the job analysis. Make sure that questions are job-related and prepared ahead of time.	2. Let first impressions control you. Reserve judgment until the end of the interview.
3. Compare the interviewee's personal characteristics with the requirements of the job, not with those of previous interviewees.	3. Talk too much. Let the applicant do most of the talking. Try to guide the discussion, not lead it.
4. Take notes and write down what the interviewee says. Let him or her know ahead of time that you will be taking notes.	4. Overemphasize negative information about the candidate. Remember, everyone has strengths and weaknesses.
5. Leave time between interviews to review your notes and make a judgment about the candidate.	

When you first enter the business world, however, you will probably *be* interviewed before you're in a position to conduct interviews. Typically, college graduates go through three types of interviews: on-campus, plant or office, and final selection. (To learn how to prepare successfully for these interviews, see the *How To Pack Your Career Parachute* supplement to this textbook.) The following Insight spotlights the characteristics that many interviewers look for in prospective employees. The employer can learn much from resumés, but interviewers look for and listen to how candidates express themselves.

Tests

cognitive ability test A written test that measures general intelligence, verbal ability, numerical ability, reasoning ability, and so forth.

In addition to interviews, many organizations use tests to screen and select candidates. Tests may be oral, written, or performance-based. In fact, an interview can be considered a form of oral test. A common type of written test, the **cognitive ability test,** measures general intelligence, verbal ability, numerical ability, reasoning ability, and so on. Such tests have proved relatively successful in predicting which applicants are qualified for certain jobs. Another type of test commonly used in industry is the performance test. **Performance tests** require job candidates to perform simulated job tasks. Two examples would be a typing test for secretarial candidates and a code-writing test for computer programmers.

performance test A test that requires job candidates to perform simulated job tasks.

Personality Tests Unlike cognitive ability and performance tests, personality tests have no right or wrong answers. **Personality** refers to the unique blend of characteristics that define an individual. Although most managers believe that personality plays an important role in job success or failure, personality tests generally aren't considered very useful for employee selection. One reason is that there are many such tests, each of them designed to measure one aspect of a person's personal-

personality The unique blend of characteristics that define an individual.

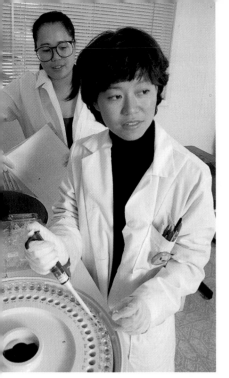

PharmChem in Menlo Park, California, *drug-tests* urine samples.

reliability The measure of the degree to which a test provides consistent scores.

validity The measure of the degree to which a test measures what it's supposed to measure.

assessment center A human resource selection tool that simulates job situations in order to assess potential employees' performance.

ity. For example, the Minnesota Multiphasic Personality Inventory (MMPI) is designed to test maladjustment. Ten personality traits—such as depression, hysteria, and social introversion—are measured. It's appropriate as a selection device for high-stress jobs—police officer, nuclear power plant employee, air traffic controller—but it's not an appropriate selection tool for nonstressful jobs. Only under stress do these unproductive personality traits surface and affect a worker's performance.[19] A second reason why personality tests aren't considered effective has to do with the relevance of personality to the work itself. For instance, in highly structured job situations, such as in a toll booth or on an assembly line, where workers' behavior is highly controlled by rules and guidelines, an individual's personality is unlikely to have an effect on performance.

Drug Testing One of the most controversial recent issues for managers has been drug testing.[20] American laboratories process more than 20 million drug tests a year, about half of them for organizations. It has been estimated that drug abuse costs U.S. industry more than $100 billion annually in turnover, absenteeism, and shoddy workmanship. Organizations will spend more than $300 million on urine tests that may not even be accurate. IBM, Kodak, AT&T, 3M, and Westinghouse, among others, require all job applicants to provide urine specimens. At IBM, if applicants fail the test, they are given a second chance if they come up with solid medical evidence that they are drug-free. If they don't, they can reapply after six months.

Most controversial of all, however, is random drug testing of *all* employees—not just job applicants. Some companies, such as Southern Pacific Transportation Company, indicate that the injury rate has fallen 60 percent since they started random testing. After six years with a drug program, Commonwealth Edison reports a 25 to 30 percent reduction in absenteeism and a reduced rate of increase in medical costs. Although random testing may be a strong deterrent to drug use, a major question is the possible violation of employees' civil rights.[21]

Validity and Reliability All tests should be judged on two basic criteria: reliability and validity.[22] **Reliability** measures the degree to which a test provides consistent scores. For example, if you stepped on a bathroom scale and it read 150 pounds and a minute later you reweighed yourself and it read 140 pounds, the scale would not be too reliable. **Validity** is a measure of the degree to which a test measures what it's supposed to measure. For example, a valid test to measure an electrical engineer's knowledge would not contain questions about financial statements or the history of the creative arts.

Unless a test is both reliable and valid, the organization using it won't receive a good return on its investment and may face legal action. Using invalid and/or unreliable tests to discriminate against a minority group is indefensible. Any test that is not job-related but serves to reject a disproportionate number of a protected class (African-Americans, veterans, people between the ages of 40 and 70) is discriminatory.

Assessment Centers

An **assessment center** is a human resource selection tool that simulates job situations in order to assess potential employees' performance. One situational test common to assessment centers is the in-basket exercise. Job candidates receive a stack of letters, notes, memos, telephone messages, faxes, and so forth and are usually told to imagine that they have been promoted to a new position. They are given an hour to deal with these communications in an appropriate manner. In most cases they will have the opportunity to explain or discuss their decisions in a follow-up interview with a counselor.[23] This book's end-of-chapter Manager's Memos are versions of in-basket exercises. A more realistic version is The Complete Manager, the computer simulation that accompanies this textbook.

Another common activity used by assessment centers is the leaderless group discussion. Participants are given a problem requiring a group decision. The way candidates handle themselves in this situation helps reveal their leadership qualities and interpersonal skills. The overall evaluation is used to predict whether a candidate is likely to succeed in the position being filled.

Assessment centers are used not only to predict managerial potential, but also to develop managers' interpersonal skills. Large organizations, such as Xerox, AT&T, and Diamond-Star Motors, among others, use a number of assessors working with a small group of candidates (no more than twenty) over a period of several days to probe each candidate's managerial abilities.

Like the more traditional tests, assessment centers are subject to standards of validity and reliability. Although there are some limitations to the use of assessment centers— such as their costliness and uncertainty as to whether the person will actually perform as well under "real" conditions—they have been proven successful in selecting qualified managers for many organizations.[24]

ORIENTATION

orientation A formal or informal program that introduces new employees to their job responsibilities, their co-workers, and company policies.

Once the selection and hiring process is complete, the employee enters orientation. **Orientation** is either a formal or an informal program that introduces new employees to their job responsibilities, their co-workers, and the company's policies. It typically lasts one to two days. Employees often simply sign employment agreements and are told where and when to report to work. Then orientation is left to co-workers or the new employee's supervisor and may involve little more than telling the new employee where to park, when and how they get paid, and where the restrooms are.

Effective orientation programs serve two purposes. First, they inform new employees about benefits, company procedures, and other routine matters. Second, and more important, these programs socially orient new employees, by fine-tuning their job-related expectations, identifying reporting relationships, and setting a tone for their work.

The following Insight may give you a heightened perspective on what an effective orientation program does. Note the things that are stressed by John Fulkerson, human resource director for Pepsi-Cola International, during a formal orientation program with new employees.

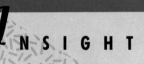

PEPSI'S EXPECTATIONS

At Pepsi we did our own three-year study of a hundred successful and a hundred less successful managers. We have found the top three qualities of successful managers to be:

1. The ability to handle business complexities.
2. The ability to lead and manage people.
3. Drive and results orientation.

All these qualities support our company's results orientation, which lies at the heart of our company's business strategy. We operate on the principle of telling people what to expect, showing them how to develop, and helping them reach these goals. We realize that with 1200 international employees selling 40 billion

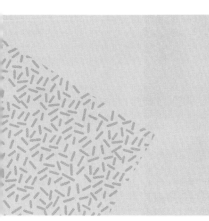

eight-ounce servings of Pepsi annually in 145 different countries, there is no one answer. People must quickly learn that there are a hundred ways to do anything.

During orientation we focus on clear communication of expected results and risk taking, with no punishment for making mistakes. Communications are critical. It is important for a manager in Spain to know, for example, when to check with New York to see what Australia is doing in a particular circumstance. Successful managers talk with others, and this lessens their chances of making a mistake.

We want employees who aren't defensive and who don't complain about the way things are. If you are defensive and complain, you will be viewed as immature and won't last long around here. We like communication open and above board. If there's a problem, let's solve it quickly.[25]

After reading the Insight about Pepsi, you should be able to see four benefits of a formal orientation program.

1. It promotes development of realistic job expectations. Even experienced workers must gain a fundamental understanding of their new organization and ''how things really work,'' because every organization has unique norms, networks of co-workers, and ways of getting things done. The information provided at Pepsi's orientation programs reduces new employees' anxieties about what's expected and corrects their expectations before they formally start their job.

2. Properly oriented employees can get up to speed quickly, because they know which behaviors are valued and which are not.

3. Formal orientation programs reduce the time and effort required by managers to train new employees. In addition, if an organization institutes a formal orientation program, instead of asking busy managers to orient new employees—a task that many busy managers assign to an assistant or a secretary—it ensures systematic coverage of key points.

4. An effective orientation program reduces employee turnover. Properly oriented new employees are eased into their jobs and therefore, feeling more comfortable, are more apt to stay than employees thrust hurriedly into their new jobs with little orientation.

COMPENSATION AND BENEFITS

compensation The wages or salaries, stock options, bonuses, and other monetary items paid to employees in exchange for their labor.

When an employee signs an employment contract with an organization, a compensation figure is included. **Compensation** is the wages or salaries, stock options, bonuses, and other monetary items paid to employees in exchange for their labor. The purpose of any compensation system is to reward employees equitably and to serve as a means to attract potential new employees and retain good employees.

Organizations often utilize wage and salary surveys to determine compensation rates. These surveys compare compensation paid nationwide for jobs in the same industry, as well as that paid in the relevant labor market. For example, a financial analyst earning a salary of $27,546 at NCNB in Dallas could be expected to earn a higher salary at Citicorp in New York City, because the cost of living is higher in New York City.

benefits Pensions, health and life insurance, vacations, sick leave, child care, and similar nonmonetary remuneration for employees.

Benefits are pensions, health and life insurance, vacations, sick leave, child and elder care, and similar nonmonetary remuneration for employees. Benefits are often referred to as ''indirect'' compensation, because they don't vary directly in proportion to an employee's compensation. The cost of benefits varies between 36 and 42 percent of an employee's total compensation.

Day-care entrepreneurs Linda Mason and Roger Brown both provide a needed *benefit* and give their own staff of 50 steady on-the-job training.

Why do organizations use benefits programs? They believe that benefits help attract good employees, increase employee morale, reduce turnover, and make wise use of compensation dollars.

One of the major problems facing employees is that of child and elder care. The "graying" of America is forcing more and more employers to focus on ways to assist employees who are caring for elderly relatives. The following Insight highlights how some companies are trying to help employees cope with both child and elder care.

INSIGHT

As more and more families rely on the salaries of both husband and wife to make ends meet, providing child or elder care is becoming a major issue. When AT&T settled negotiations with its major unions in 1989, a key clause in the agreement was a comprehensive family-care package that included $5 million allocated for a study exploring ways to provide community-based child care. Johnson & Johnson is building its first on-site day-care center in New Jersey. The building, designed by I. M. Pei, will accommodate 200 children and include an isolation ward for sick youngsters. Dayton-Hudson is spending $8 million to help train home-care providers so its employees can hire qualified, responsible babysitters. The company expects to train 8000 home-care providers over a three-year period. IBM has committed $25 million to child-care and elder-care programs. These companies know that by providing these fringe benefits to their workers, absenteeism and job turnover can be reduced.

As early as 1981 Champion International in Stamford, Connecticut saw that the problem of caring for aging relatives affected both productivity and profitability. It began offering help through its employee assistance program. The program pays half the cost of elder care and allows employees three visits with a licensed psychiatrist or psychologist to obtain help in dealing with problems associated with caring for elderly relatives.[26]

PERFORMANCE APPRAISALS

Once employees begin working, managers are responsible for providing them with feedback about their performance. Human resource planning and the staffing process establish the framework for new hires, and performance appraisals establish specific criteria for determining promotions and salary changes once employees are on board.

When you become a manager, one of your chief responsibilities will be to rate your employees' performance. Your opinions and judgments will determine who is promoted, demoted, transferred, and dismissed, and the size of the raise each employee receives. You will have to explain your ratings to your subordinates, who may—in fact, probably will—disagree with you on at least some counts. Performance appraisal may seem a formidable task, but it doesn't have to be.

performance appraisal
The process of systematically evaluating each employee's job-related strengths and weaknesses and determining ways to improve his or her performance.

Performance appraisal is the process of systematically evaluating each employee's job-related strengths and weaknesses, as well as determining ways to improve her or his performance.[27] This function is essential if the organization is to reward fairly the efforts of good performers, redirect the efforts of struggling performers, and know when to let go of inadequate performers. However, few organizations have been able to develop and implement effective performance appraisal systems. As a result, performance appraisal continues to be a challenging human resource management issue.

Before considering some particular uses and methods of performance appraisal, let's look at some of the characteristics of an effective performance appraisal system. In general, an effective performance appraisal system is one that is designed to help employees reach their potential and increase their productivity. The system can accomplish this overall goal in three specific ways:

1. By providing clear feedback to employees on how well they are doing. With clear, accurate feedback, employees can decide how to improve performance and what constitutes adequate and acceptable behavior. Thus managers should share performance appraisals with employees rather than keeping them secret.

2. By providing a structure for personal growth and development, through examining potential as well as actual work behavior. Effective managers realize that it is their responsibility to see that both the individual and the company benefit from improved performance.

3. By allowing managers to base short- and long-range administrative decisions about pay increases, promotions, and transfers on performance. In such a case employees will continue to engage in behaviors that benefit the company.

A good example of an effective performance appraisal system is that used by Brooklyn Union Gas Company.[28] There are three major parts to this system. First, as in an MBO plan (see Chapter 9), each employee and his or her supervisor develop a list of five or six key job responsibilities and use it to identify specific performance goals. In order for this process to work effectively, supervisors must have good communication and goal-setting skills. Second, a two-day training program, designed by the company's human resources department, covers the critical skills that supervisors and managers need to master. Finally, to keep goals up to date and specific, performance appraisals are held every six months.

Uses of Performance Appraisals

Performance appraisals are invaluable aids for making many human resource management decisions, as Brooklyn Union Gas has found out. A particularly important use is helping managers distinguish between good and poor performers. Let's discuss some important ways that managers use performance appraisal information.

merit pay plan A compensation plan designed to pay people according to their job performance.

outplacement activities A series of services offered to terminated employees to minimize the length of their period of unemployment.

leniency A common, often intentional, rating error that occurs when a manager rates all employees in a group higher than they deserve, for any of a number of reasons.

Reward Decisions Most organizations try to motivate employees by basing pay, bonuses, and other financial rewards on performance.[29] **Merit pay plans** are designed to pay people according to their job performance. Most managers are compensated according to merit pay plans, because there are no hard data on which to judge their performance. That is, managers don't sell quotas of life insurance policies or write computer programs or the like—they coordinate the efforts and activities of the employees who do. B. F. Goodrich, Timex, and Westinghouse, on the other hand, use quarterly performance bonuses to motivate managers. These organizations have found that a lump-sum payment of $5000 is more striking than a merit increase of $100 a week. A major problem with both merit pay plans and performance bonuses is how to accurately measure an employee's performance, a topic that we cover in the next section of this chapter.

Personnel Movement Performance appraisal information also helps managers decide on personnel movement. Who should receive a promotion? Who should be transferred, demoted, or terminated? Like many major organizations, the McDonnell Douglas Corporation started a job rotation program to develop future general managers. Based on their performance appraisals, highly rated managers are offered a three-year rotation outside of their division and functional area. After completion of the program, they should have a breadth of experience that will enable them to perform the duties of general managers.[30]

Outplacement activities are offered to employees who have been terminated. **Outplacement activities** are a series of services designed to minimize the length of terminated employees' period of unemployment. After defusing the ousted employee's anger, the outplacement counselor offers a range of services ranging from help with writing resumés and videotaped rehearsals for job interviews to the provision of office, secretarial, and research facilities. Outplacement firms, such as Drake Beam and Morris or King Chapman Broussard & Gallagher, are not in the business of finding the displaced person a job, but of teaching him or her how to find one.[31]

Feedback on Performance A primary purpose of any performance appraisal system is motivating employees to improve job performance. Performance evaluations provide employees with feedback about their specific strengths and weaknesses, as well as guidelines for how to build on the strengths and counteract the weaknesses.

Training Needs Identifying areas of poor performance allows the manager to suggest training programs to improve certain skills. Training programs may range from classes to teach specific activities—such as operating a forklift—to those designed to develop proficiency in a management skill—such as communicating.

Problems with Performance Appraisals

Subjectivity Most people who have given or received a performance appraisal would agree that a major problem is the subjective nature of the process. Let's briefly examine four errors managers commonly make when giving performance appraisals.[32]

1. *Rater characteristics* Characteristics of the rater exert a subtle and often indirect influence on performance appraisals. Younger and less experienced managers, who may have received low evaluations themselves, tend to rate others more strictly than older, more experienced managers do. The personality traits of the rater also affect the process. It should be useful for you to know that managers who have high self-esteem, low anxiety, good social skills, and emotional stability give more accurate performance appraisals than managers with the opposite personality traits.[33]

2. *Leniency* **Leniency,** a common—and often intentional—rating error, occurs when a manager rates all employees in a group higher than they deserve. This may be

Out-of-work executives can research new jobs from the New York offices of *outplacement firm* Right Associates.

done for any of a number of unprofessional reasons, such as avoiding conflict, giving employees a morale boost, creating a good record for the group, or making oneself look good. Leniency is particularly likely to occur when there are no organizational norms against high ratings and when rewards are not tied to performance appraisals. When rewards *are* tied to appraisals, there is a natural limit to the number of extraordinarily high ratings the organization can afford or a manager can give.

3. *Halo effect* As in interviewing, the **halo effect** occurs in rating when the rater allows his or her knowledge of an employee's performance on one dimension to color the rating on all other dimensions. In some cases an equal rating on all dimensions does not reflect an error in judgment—an employee may actually perform at the same level in all areas. However, most people do some things better than others, so their ratings should vary from one performance dimension to another.

4. *Central tendency* **Central tendency** is a rating error that occurs when a manager gives an average rating to all employees, even when their performance varies. Managers with broad spans of management and little opportunity to observe behavior are likely to play it safe by rating most of their subordinates in the middle of the scale rather than high or low.

central tendency A rating error that occurs when a manager rates all employees as average, even when their performance varies.

Political Issues Any realistic discussion of performance appraisals must recognize that organizations are political places. In other words, office politics often play a role in deciding who gets what raise, promotion, or demotion. One survey of managers asked why politics play an important role in the performance appraisal process.[34] The results showed that the role was due to several factors:

▶ Managers have to interact daily with their subordinates and want to avoid conflict.
▶ The formal appraisal process results in a permanent written document.
▶ The formal appraisal can have considerable impact on the subordinate's career and advancement.
▶ Performance appraisal evaluations are usually tied to money.

One vice president summarized it this way:

As a manager, I will use the review process to do what is best for my people and the division. . . . I've got a lot of leeway—call it discretion—to use this process in that manner. . . . I've used it to get my people better raises in lean years, to kick a person in the pants if he/she really needed it, to pick up a person [who was] down or even to tell [someone] that [he/she was] no longer welcome here. It is a tool that the manager should use to help him to do what it takes to get the job done. I believe most of us here . . . operate this way regarding appraisals. . . . Accurately describing an employee's performance is really not as important as generating ratings that keep things cooking.

Managers suggested several reasons why politics are so prevalent and why accuracy isn't their primary concern in giving performance appraisals. One manager offered the following comments:

The mere fact that you have to write out your assessment and create a permanent record will cause people not to be as honest or as accurate as they should be. . . . We soften the language because our ratings go in the person's file downstairs [in the human resources department] and it will follow [him or her] around [for a] whole career.

The money issue was often cited as a major cause of intentional distortions in ratings. Although the logic of tying pay to performance ratings is sound, this linkage increases the likelihood that ratings will be politically biased. Managers are guilty of using performance appraisals as an opportunity to elevate their employees to compensation levels that have little, if any, relationship to the employees' performance. A director of research and development candidly described the rater's problem:

Since the pay raise my people get is tied to the ratings I give them, there is a strong incentive to inflate ratings at times to maximize their pay increases to help keep them happy and motivated, especially in lean years when the budget for raises is low. . . . Conversely, you can also send a very strong message to a nonperformer that low ratings will hit [him/her] in the wallet. . . . There is no doubt that a lot of us manipulate ratings at times to deal with the money issue.

Although managers only occasionally admitted to using it themselves, the up-and-out rating process was almost universally discussed—as something *other* managers do. One plant manager remarked:

I've seen it happen, especially when you get a young person in here who thinks [he/she is] only going to be here a short while before [being] promoted. People like that become a real pain. . . . If you want to get rid of them quick, a year and a half of good ratings should do it. . . . A lot of people inflate ratings of people they can't stand, or [people] who think they are God's gift to the department, just to get rid of them.

Methods of Performance Appraisal

The problems that we've discussed exemplify how difficult it is for managers to evaluate subordinates' performance objectively. Most attempts to solve these problems have focused on devising new methods of appraising performance. As a result, many different types of rating formats and evaluation techniques exist. Unfortunately, none appears to be significantly better than the others. Here we'll focus on two general types of methods: ranking methods and graphic rating methods.

ranking method A performance appraisal method that compares employees doing the same or similar work.

Ranking **Ranking methods** are methods of appraising performance that compare employees doing the same or similar work. In simple ranking, the rater simply lists employees from best to worst.[35] A variation of this method, alternation ranking, requires the rater to select the best employee, then the worst, the second best, the second worst, and so on.

Ranking methods are easy to use. They also reduce the effects of leniency, because the rater can't give everyone a high evaluation. Rankings are especially useful for making defensible promotion decisions or reducing the size of the work force. The manager can simply select names from the top down on the ranking list until all promotion vacancies are filled—or from the bottom up until all necessary reductions are made.

Ranking methods have disadvantages, though, which limit their usefulness for certain appraisal purposes. Because rankings tend to be based on overall performance, they aren't very useful in providing specific feedback. To know that she or he is ranked fourth out of ten people, for example, doesn't tell an employee what she or he needs to do to become the top-ranked employee, or even the second. Furthermore, rankings indicate that one person is performing better than another, but not by how much or in what ways. Thus ranking methods are of limited use in making pay decisions. To determine equitable pay raises, managers need to know something about the degree of difference among those evaluated. Another disadvantage of ranking methods is that raters must be familiar with the performance of all employees being ranked, which effectively limits the number of employees that can be evaluated by each rater.

graphic rating method A method of performance appraisal that evaluates employees on a series of performance dimensions along a five- or seven-point scale.

Graphic Rating **Graphic rating methods** of performance appraisal evaluate employees on a series of performance dimensions, usually along a five- or seven-point scale.[36] Such scales are the most widely used form of performance evaluation. A typical rating scale may be from 1 to 5, with 1 representing poor performance and 5 representing outstanding performance. Figure 12.5 illustrates four common rating

FIGURE 12.5

Samples of Rating Scale Formats

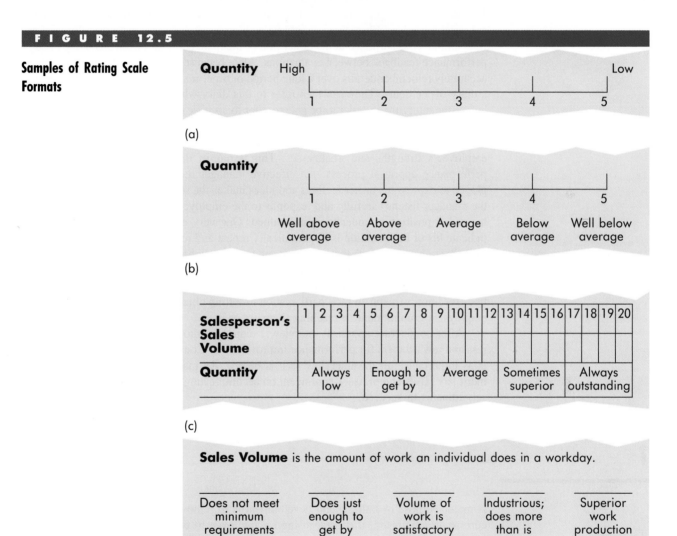

(a)

(b)

(c)

(d)

Example (d) is the preferred format because it specifies exactly what ''quantity of work'' means at each point on the scale. Example (a) may pose a problem for raters, because each rater will interpret differently what a 1 or a 5 means. Example (b) assumes that what is average for one person is also average for another. And example (c) has too many points on the scale.

Source: Adapted from R. S. Schuler and V. L. Huber, *Personnel and Human Resource Management,* 4th ed. (St. Paul, Minn.: West Publishing, 1990), 203.

scales that could be used to evaluate a salesperson's sales volume. The more clearly and specifically the scales and the performance dimensions are defined, the better. For example, it's always a good idea to state precisely what is meant by quantity, as in part (d).[37]

Performance Appraisal Interviews

Performance appraisal is not a single act or a particular form used to evaluate job behavior. After the manager uses one of the forms to evaluate his or her employees, the manager must communicate his or her performance appraisal judgments to the employee. This is usually carried out in the performance appraisal interview.

Most experts agree that several activities should occur before, during, and after the appraisal interview. First, there should be no big surprises during an appraisal interview. If an employee is surprised at his or her rating, the manager hasn't been providing enough performance feedback between evaluations. Also, because it's difficult for most people to accurately remember details over a long period of time, managers should consider keeping a diary of incidents. They can then refer to this diary when writing the review and just before the interview in order to be able to refer to specific events. Of course, the manager should first have discussed these incidents with the employee soon after they happened.

During the interview manager and employee should exchange information about the employee's strengths and weaknesses. This is one of the most important steps in the performance appraisal process. An effective manager recognizes that allowing an employee to express his or her feelings and ideas makes the session more worthwhile. When the manager listens carefully and responds to the employee, the employee is assured that his or her position is understood and valued. One very effective way for a manager to indicate his or her attention is to periodically repeat and reinforce what the employee has said. It is also important that the manager focus on job-related performance and avoid discussing facets of personality, such as habits and mannerisms, that don't affect job performance. Finally, it is important that manager and employee mutually agree on objectives for improvement. In fact, participation in setting objectives is one way to increase an employee's commitment to reaching them.

After conducting appraisal interviews, managers should follow subordinates' progress and reward them for performance improvements. Communicating about performance is as important after the interview as it is before. By making valued rewards—such as merit pay raises and praise—contingent on accomplishing objectives, managers motivate subordinates to succeed.

TRAINING AND DEVELOPMENT

A major purpose of training and development is to remove the performance limitations, current or anticipated, that are causing an employee to perform at less than the desired level. An organization may save money by recruiting trained individuals, but many organizations have found that training and development programs are preferable to hiring experienced employees. EDS, for example, has found that hiring ''green'' recruits is better than hiring experienced workers from other organizations because it doesn't have to *retrain* the new employees to do things its way. Because training and development are so important and costly, organizations want them carried out as effectively as possible.

training Improving an employee's skills to the point where he or she can do the current job.

Training for the Job

Training refers to improving an employee's skills to the point where he or she can do the current job. The training methods usually used by organizations are shown in Table 12.5.

TABLE 12.5

Training and Development Methods

Method	Advantage(s)	Disadvantage(s)
Job rotation	Provides exposure to many jobs; real learning experience	Doesn't convey full sense of responsibility; time on each job is too short
Programmed instruction	Provides individualized learning and feedback	Time-consuming to develop; cost-effective only for large groups
Videotape	Conveys consistent information to all employees	Doesn't provide for individual feedback
Simulation	Creates lifelike situations to teach interpersonal and conceptual skills	Can't always duplicate real situations; costly to design and run
Role playing	Gives insights into others' jobs; focuses on interpersonal skills	Can't create real situations
Interactive video	Self-paced learning with computer feedback	Costly to develop and requires staff to implement

Source: Adapted from R. S. Schuler and V. L. Huber, *Personnel and Human Resource Management,* 4th ed. (St. Paul, Minn.: West Publishing, 1990), 380.

Training is particularly important to organizations that provide a standardized service to their customers, such as the Walt Disney Company. One of the reasons for Disney's success is the training that employees receive at Disney University. The following Insight gives you a look at how Disney employees are trained there to provide extraordinary, and consistent, customer service.

MAKING DREAMS COME TRUE AT DISNEY

*I*NSIGHT Walt Disney said that it takes people to make a dream come true. To make sure that customers' dreams come true, he founded Disney University in Anaheim, California in 1955.

According to Bill Ross, manager for human resource training at Disney U., employees attending Disney U. learn how to play their roles—such as Mickey Mouse and Snow White—and play them well. Disney U. trainers use audio-visual programs, role playing, and other training methods to teach employees proper Disney behaviors. Trainees are shown examples of both good and bad guest relations, and copies of guest complaints are circulated to all trainees so they can be taught which behaviors to avoid. Training focuses on helping employees understand what customers expect to see and what Disney wants its guests to experience. For example, to create a warm, intimate atmosphere, employees greet all guests at Disney hotels personally and call them by their first names. Training in guest courtesy is required for all new Disney employees. Telephone operators learn how to "Put a Smile in Their Voice." Finally, all new employees experience the park as guests before starting to work. This gives them first-hand experience in being a guest and helps them appreciate how a guest feels about standing in line for a long time or being served quickly and in a friendly way in a restaurant.[38]

Many organizations are spending considerable sums of money on remedial training programs for employees. There are about 25 million adults in the United States who are unable to read, write, or do simple arithmetic. Therefore, organizations such as McGraw-Hill, Monsanto, and Scott Paper, among others, have training programs designed to help employees write letters to customers, read warning labels on chemical containers, or understand machine operating symbols.[39] These organizations believe that if employees can become proficient in these basic skills, they can perform a wider variety of jobs and better deal with new technologies.

Development Programs

development program
Program designed to improve employee's conceptual and human relations skills in preparation for future jobs.

Development programs seek to improve an employee's conceptual and human relation skills in preparation for future jobs. Given the increasingly complex demands placed on managers, many organizations invest a great deal of time and money in development programs. It is estimated that U.S. organizations spend more than $60 billion each year on training and development.[40] Before sending an employee to a development program, a needs analysis is done to identify his or her particular problems. The needs that are usually examined include the abilities to set goals and objectives for others, negotiate interpersonal conflicts, and conduct performance appraisal reviews.

On-the-Job Programs

On-the-job development programs are tailored to fit the individual's specific needs. IBM, for example, requires all of its managers to attend at least forty hours of management development programs each year. Many employees go to IBM's development center at Armonk, New York for these programs. Such programs are geared to helping managers gain insight into how their organization operates and upgrade their specific managerial practices for future jobs at IBM.

Off-the-Job Programs

Off-the-job development programs remove employees from the stress and daily routines of their jobs, enabling them to focus more fully on the learning experience. Employees from a variety of organizations attend such programs. Participants learn not only from the instructor, but also from their peers.

Some organizations send selected employees to university-sponsored management development programs. Penn State, Duke, Northwestern, Dartmouth, Harvard, and Stanford, among others, offer such programs, which run from two to sixteen weeks in length. Many managers who attend such programs are slated for either a promotion or an assignment in a different division or department. The organization wants to broaden these managers' perspective and prepare them for general (as opposed to functional) management positions.

The Center for Creative Leadership was established as a nonprofit organization in 1970, to encourage and develop creative leadership and management practices.[41] It accomplishes this goal through research and management development programs. In one of the most popular programs, Looking Glass, participants engage in an organizational simulation. Looking Glass re-creates ''a day in the life'' of the top twenty managers of a mid-sized glass manufacturing organization. In running this corporation for eight hours, students face more than a hundred diverse managerial problems, ranging from whether or not to purchase a new plant to environmental pollution problems to filling a vacant plant manager position. Participants see how their management style affects others' motivation and commitment and discover how an organization's design can promote as well as hinder effective problem solving.

One of the greatest challenges to off-the-job development programs takes place when the employee returns to his or her job: If the organization does not encourage and reinforce the behaviors that the employee has newly mastered, he or she will become discouraged and will give them up. An employee who has gone through an on-the-job development program can easily call or see fellow co-workers who went through the same program and ask them for advice. The employee who's just completed an off-the-job program, on the other hand, probably has no co-workers to turn to. The support and encouragement of co-workers are critical if the employee is to retain newly learned behaviors.

1. The staffing process normally includes six phases: (1) planning and forecasting human resource needs, (2) recruitment, (3) selection, (4) orientation, (5) movement, and (6) separation.

2. Four tools and techniques used to plan and forecast human resource needs are (1) a skills inventory, (2) job analysis, (3) a replacement chart, and (4) expert forecasts.

3. The organization recruits candidates both internally and externally. Candidates are located through internal skills inventories and external means, such as newspaper ads, employment agencies, colleges and technical schools, and word of mouth. Recruitment is influenced by three external factors: government controls, labor unions, and the labor market. Recruiters must keep in mind the constraints on recruiting policies and practices imposed by federal and state laws and court decisions concerning protected groups.

4. The selection and hiring process may involve review of applications and resumés, reference checks, tests, realistic job previews, or personal interviews.

5. New employees can be oriented formally or informally to their jobs and the organization. Formal orientation is carried out by the human resources department and supervisors and informs new employees what's expected of them in terms of job performance and work-related behaviors. Informal orientation is carried out on the job by co-workers and supervisors and deals mainly with work-group norms.

6. Compensation and benefits are used to attract and retain productive employees. Compensation refers to monetary rewards, and benefits are indirect compensation, such as pensions, insurance plans, and paid vacation. Benefits also include such employee programs as child and elder care, maternity leaves, and drug rehabilitation.

7. Four important uses of performance appraisals are (1) to make reward decisions (raises, bonuses, and other rewards), (2) to make personnel movement decisions (promotions, demotions, transfers, outplacements), (3) to give subordinates constructive feedback on their performance over a specified time, and (4) to identify training and development needs. Two performance appraisal methods are ranking and rating scales. Performance appraisals are affected by the rater's subjectivity and by office politics.

8. Training programs seek to maintain and improve current job performance. Development programs seek to teach behaviors that employees will need in the future. Both training and development can be conducted on the job or off the job.

1. Discuss the steps in the staffing process.

2. **From Where You Sit:** How do you feel about a company's hiring only certain types of people? What drawbacks might this sort of policy have?

3. How does the federal government ensure equal employment opportunity? What does this regulation mean for employers? How does it affect staffing and performance appraisals?

4. In what ways have equal employment opportunity and affirmative action affected recruitment?

5. Identify the various sources for recruitment. Which are likely to be most effective for filling secretarial jobs, positions in skilled trades, and professional and managerial posts?

6. What sources of information do managers use to help them make selection decisions?

7. Describe the various types of tests used for selection. Which are likely to be most effective? Which are likely to be most controversial? Why?

8. Why are some organizations putting in day-care centers or providing child- and/or elder-care services for employees?

9. Discuss the various methods of appraising performance. Which is likely to be easiest for managers to use?

10. Why might a manager deliberately distort a performance appraisal?

11. **From Where You Sit:** A manager once said: "Let's just say that there are a lot of factors that tug at you and play on your mind that cause you to soften the ratings you give. It may not have a great impact all the time, but when you know a 5 will create problems and a 6 will not, many managers give a 6." Why do you think managers inflate appraisals?

12. **From Where You Sit:** Arrange for an interview with the manager of the human resources department of a local organization. Ask this manager to describe the performance appraisal system used in the organization. What strengths and limitations do you see in the system?

13. Teachers often contend that students should not evaluate their teaching performance. Administrators support the position that student evaluations should be used. What performance appraisal errors are students most likely to commit in this situation? How can these be minimized?

14. What are the advantages of on-the-job training and development programs? Do these offset the need for off-the-job programs?

What Questions Can You Ask During an Employment Interview?

John Richards is the recruitment manager for the human resources department of a county government. Recently John has become aware of a problem concerning the employment interview questions asked by members of his staff and the staffs of other departments. He has received complaints from job candidates that some departments focus their interviews on previous work experience, and others concentrate on the likelihood that the candidate will ''fit in'' on the job. Consequently, in an effort to standardize the interviewing process, John has prepared the following list of ten questions that each interviewer should ask every candidate.

Instructions

Read each of the ten questions. Place a check mark in the appropriate column to indicate whether the question is legal or illegal (and therefore should not be asked).

LEGAL   ILLEGAL

1. How old are you?

2. Have you ever been arrested?

3. Do any of your relatives work for this organization?

4. Do you have children, and if you do, what kind of child-care arrangements do you have?

5. Do you have any handicaps?

6. Are you married?

7. Where were you born?

8. What organizations do you belong to?

9. Do you get along well with other men/women?

10. What languages can you speak and/or write fluently?

Answers

The following evaluations provide clarification rather than strict legal interpretations. Employment laws are constantly changing.

1. *How old are you?*

   This question is legal but inadvisable. An applicant's date of birth or age can be asked, but it is essential to tell the applicant that federal and state laws prohibit age discrimination. It is a good idea to avoid focusing on age, unless an occupation requires extraordinary physical ability or training and a valid age-related rule is in effect.

2. *Have you ever been arrested?*

This question is illegal unless an inquiry about arrests is justified by the specific nature of the business—for instance, law enforcement or handling controlled substances. Questions about arrests are generally considered suspect since they may tend to disqualify minority groups. Convictions should be the basis for rejection of an applicant only if their number, their nature, or how recent they are renders the applicant unsuitable. In that case the question(s) should be specific—for example, Have you ever been convicted for theft? Have you been convicted within the past year on drug-related charges?

3. *Do any of your relatives work for this organization?*

This question is legal if the intent is to discover nepotism.

4. *Do you have children, and if you do, what kind of child-care arrangements do you have?*

Both parts of this question are illegal; they should not be asked in any form because the answers would not be job-related. In addition, they might imply sex discrimination.

5. *Do you have any handicaps?*

This question is illegal as phrased here. An applicant does not have to divulge handicaps or health conditions that do not relate reasonably to his or her fitness to perform the job.

6. *Are you married?*

This question is legal, but may be discriminatory. Marriage has nothing directly to do with job performance.

7. *Where were you born?*

This question is legal, but it might indicate discrimination on the basis of national origin.

8. *What organizations do you belong to?*

As stated, this question is legal; it is permissible to ask about organizational membership in a general sense. It is illegal to ask about membership in a specific organization when the name of that organization would indicate the race, color, creed, sex, marital status, religion, or national origin ancestry of its members.

9. *Do you get along well with other men/women?*

This question is illegal; it seems to perpetuate sexism.

10. *What languages can you speak and/or write fluently?*

Although this question is legal, it might be perceived as a roundabout way of determining an individual's national origin. It is not permissible to ask how any given language was learned.

To: Store Managers
From: George Berger, Vice-President, Human Resources
Re: Employee selection

The success of Tandy is based on the profitability of our retail stores. As you know, 75 percent of all our compensation is directly tied to store profitability. With more than 80 percent of Tandy's work force in direct sales, it is important that we select the best-qualified personnel and then enhance their sales through training.

During the past year I've traveled around the country and interviewed more than 167 of you. Using the questions that I asked during the interviews, I've developed a computerized program for you to administer as a final step in the employee selection process. I think that the program will help you to determine a person's aptitude for qualifying customers, making sales presentations, closing sales, and providing after-sales service. This isn't a test that a person can flunk, but you might find it useful in making selection decisions. For instance, if you hire a salesperson who the program shows isn't particularly strong in closing sales, you'll know in advance that a training program for that person should focus on closing sales skills.

Question: Assume that you are a store manager who received this memo from Berger. Write him a memo outlining your views on using this computerized program in the selection process.

Managers Are Sent to 'Charm Schools' To Polish Up Their Interpersonal Skills

By Dana Milbank

On the grounds of Arthur Andersen & Co.'s headquarters outside Chicago, a senior executive jumps off a flagpole and onto a trapeze. Colleagues pass a bucket of water between two nearby trees. Others try to scale a wall.

This is no company circus; the antics are part of a program at the accounting firm to teach employees interpersonal skills. Jumping from the pole teaches confidence; passing the bucket and scaling the wall teaches teamwork. The firm also trains its employees in skills such as running meetings and listening to others.

Arthur Andersen is one of many companies placing new emphasis on "people skills" for their managers and executives. In the past, even ornery managers could succeed by just knowing the business. But increasingly, managers with "people conflicts" are being sent to school to learn how to relate better to others.

"Pure technical knowledge is only going to get you to a point," says Lawrence A. Weinbach, Arthur Andersen's chief executive. "Beyond that, interpersonal skills become critical."

The training doesn't always work, of course. Randall P. White, director of the Center for Creative Leadership's Executive Development Program, estimates that although 10% or 15% of the participants in his programs are highly receptive and change dramatically, an equal amount are hopeless. Some sit in the back of the room and tell counselors they were "forced" to attend and that they have no problems. When confronted with poor reviews, one manager claimed he was a good manager but all his workers were stupid.

For many, the courses are only marginally useful. "It wasn't anything with bands playing and choirs singing," says David Spector, a security manager for Digital Equipment Corp.

Consultants and psychologists who administer the courses admit they can't change a manager's personality, but they think they can change behavior. Clients typically are strongly motivated, if only out of self-interest: Taking the course may give them an edge for a promotion. For some, the alternative could be losing a promotion or even a job.

The training ranges from daylong preventive courses for new employees to intensive, one-on-one counseling for hardened corporate ogres at a cost to a company of $25,000.

The Center for Creative Leadership, Greensboro, N.C., estimates that half of all managers and 30% of all senior managers have some type of difficulty with people. But discovering such a weakness in a so-called charm school can be humbling.

Consider Richard S. Herlich. When he was promoted to director of marketing for an American Cyanamid Co. division, he saw himself as an enlightened manager. He delegated responsibility, encouraging subordinates to set their own deadlines. "I thought I had the perfect style," he says.

But then he attended the center's week-long Leadership Development Program. In surveys that his peers, subordinates and superiors answered for the course, he found he was too trusting, aloof and a poor communicator. The diagnosis was confirmed in role-playing games with feedback from the other participants. "I was devastated," Mr. Herlich says.

When he went back to work, he held a meeting to discuss his problems with his 15 subordinates, who said his aloofness was intimidating. So he became more involved in their work and learned to set deadlines; projects that had taken six or seven months were done in three.

Bethlehem Steel Corp. plant manager Robert Siddall had just the opposite problem. An aggressive and sometimes abrasive leader, he got into damaging clashes with the labor union head, and many of his 170 workers came to view him as dictatorial. Mr. Siddall had been to behavioral schools before without success, but when his boss asked him to go to the Leadership Development Program, he knew he had to take it seriously or abandon his hopes of advancement.

Each member of his small group in the program had been rated by bosses, peers and subordinates. And participants secretly rated each other. Mr. Siddall learned through these reviews that his style was too structured and domineering. "I'm very strong technically," he says, but "I really didn't fit in well on an interactive basis." Instructors taught Mr. Siddall to act like a "coach" and to try to listen and respect other points of view.

He says he gets along with the union leader now. His performance ratings have improved and his workers now refer to the "old Bob" and the "new Bob." "If I start screaming and yelling, they say, 'old Bob, old Bob,'" he says. "We have a lot more fun together." He also believes he's back on track for a promotion.

Some managers are put off by courses with names such as "reflective listening," "cooperative problem solving" and "conflict resolution." Yet graduates have learned to create better work environments. . . .

Other learn how to confront problems head on and not be overly sympathetic.

1. What evaluation techniques would be most useful in finding candidates for an executive charm school? Should someone be forced to attend?

2. Assume you head the human resource department of a small manufacturing company. How would you tell the company vice president that she needs to polish her interpersonal skills?

3. You have been directed to devise a performance-appraisal system that is free of organizational politics. What would you do?

PHYSICIAN SALES & SERVICE, INC.

What do you do if you can't hire experienced people to work for your company? Perhaps you can't pay them what they want—or they won't budge for other reasons. At first glance, this would seem to be a problem for most young companies. But some don't see it that way. Instead, they choose to grow their own.

One such company is Physician Sales & Service, Inc. (PSS), a $31 million business headquartered in Jacksonville, Florida. PSS has discovered that young, inexperienced people can be a tremendous asset in a growing business. Of its 258 employees, for instance, fewer than 40 percent had worked for another company. The availability of young employees—and their eagerness to learn and grow—has enabled the company to open fourteen offices throughout the Southeast. "As the company grows," says CEO Patrick Kelly, "the goal is to have about 80 percent of our sales and marketing people home-grown."

The decision to hire young people and teach them what they need to know can be intimidating. For one thing, it's a commitment of limited time and money. But it can pay off in many ways. Many of the early PSS hires, in fact, have moved into management positions. "One of the great advantages of hiring young people," Kelly notes, "is that we can introduce them to our way of doing business. We don't have to change a lot of bad habits."

Back in April 1983, when Kelly and Bill Riddell, executive vice president for sales and marketing, started the company with two other partners (who have since left), they didn't think they had much choice about where to get people. Having worked in sales for another medical supply company, they realized that top performers who already knew the business would be too expensive to

hire. The challenge, then, was to find a way to teach inexperienced employees the ropes quickly and economically—and to provide them with a sense of purpose along the way. Fortunately, Kelly had given this a good deal of thought at his old company. So by the time PSS opened its doors, it had come up with an interesting approach.

New hires aspiring to sales jobs were required to work a normal forty-hour week doing all the routine jobs—unloading, stocking, delivering, and so on. Far from being an end in itself, unloading boxes, they were told, was a great way to learn about the range of products the company handled. And making deliveries? It acquainted them with doctors' offices and how they worked. Kelly and Riddell went out of their way to let employees know that they wouldn't be doing these things forever. The result, says Riddell, was that "the enthusiasm level was incredible." With young trainees doing a portion of the grunt work, PSS found that is needed fewer full-time permanent employees in warehouse and customer service jobs.

The daytime regimen, however, was only part of what went into growing experienced employees. On nights and weekends, for example, sales trainees were required to learn about the vendors they'd be representing, the vendors' products, and medical terminology. To assist in this learning process, Kelly collected relevant material in two thick binders. Aspiring salespeople had weekly assignments—and took weekly tests. They were also expected to participate in evening role-playing exercises, in which they "sold" products to managers and peers.

Riddell and Kelly estimate that about 20 percent of newly hired college graduates are asked to leave within two months. Usually, says Riddell, they don't like the pressure of weekly assignments and the lack of free time.

"Differing people have different goals in life," he comments. "Our feeling is that the demands we make during the early months aren't a whole lot different from the work they'll do later on. So it's better to know this early."

Growing your own employees may require less up-front investment than raiding your competitors. But free it's not. Riddell figures that PSS invests anywhere from $20,000 to $25,000 in an aspiring salesperson during his or her first eighteen to twenty-four months. That figure includes the salary earned during the initial months and the support received during the subsequent year, when the salesperson is still a cash drain on the business until he or she is on full commission. But it doesn't reflect all that PSS gets in return: highly motivated employees driving delivery vans and learning how to sell.

1. What do you think are the best sources of new employees for PSS? Why?
2. Could PSS be successful with its recruiting and hiring practices if it wasn't a growing company? Why or why not?
3. Describe the orientation program you would put new employees through if you were a manager at PSS.
4. What method of performance appraisal might work best at PSS?

Chapter 13

Motivation in Organizations

Avis employee ownership

What You Will Learn

1 The importance of motivation to managers, employees, and organizations.

2 How individuals' needs, as defined by Maslow's hierarchy of needs, motivate them to perform their jobs.

3 How certain characteristics of the work situation affect job satisfaction and performance.

4 The basic assumptions and concepts underlying the expectancy approach to motivation.

5 What makes rewards equitable and inequitable.

6 How managers can use rewards and punishments to influence employees in organizations.

7 **Skill Development:** Awareness of what motivates you, so that you can motivate yourself *and* help motivate your subordinates.

"We feel close contact with management."

Roberta Beckelman
Avis

Why Avis People Try Harder

It's been a long time since Avis was the also-ran of the rental car business. Its cherry-red booths in airport terminals draw 30 percent of air travelers who rent cars. Its shuttle buses, which carry customers from rental counter to car, are late only 4 percent of the time. And customers complain about the service 40 percent less often than they did in 1987. In fact, when Pittsburgh-based Westinghouse named Avis its primary rental car agency, every Avis employee in Pittsburgh signed a letter to the company's travel managers, pledging to provide the best possible service.

What's been happening at the "We Try Harder" company? In 1987 Avis's 12,500 employees bought the company. Avis's employee stock ownership plan, or ESOP, has proven particularly effective: Self-ownership has sparked employees' motivation to give customers the extra service that has made such a difference for Avis.

Another secret behind Avis's success is involving *all* employees, not just managers, in organizational decisions. There are monthly participation group meetings that discuss everything from billing to car cleaning. If district managers want to upgrade the carpeting in their offices, employees are asked for their opinions on the suggestion before the final decision is made. Avis's top managers have found that letting employees participate in decisions about their own jobs has made the company more profitable than ever. For instance, one employee suggested that the Avis sales force promote its own credit card rather than the American Express card. Making that move reduced the number of transaction fees paid to American Express as well as concession fees Avis pays to American Express and to the airport for every paid (cash) rental. This improved profits by $40,000 a year. All employees and managers share equally in the profits. "We feel close contact with management," says Roberta Beckelman, a telecommunications specialist at Avis's Worldwide Reservation Center in Tulsa. That's quite a change. In the past, people felt management didn't really listen to their ideas. Now *employees* are suggesting ways to tighten up performance standards.[1]

Some, but certainly not all, of employees' performance is related to managers' efforts. In the 1990s, employees, along with their managers, are striving to improve their performance. At Hearing Technology, Inc., President Tom Huber uses, with great success, a team approach to employee motivation. At weekly meetings (held at 7:30 A.M. to avoid distractions) employees are encouraged to talk about problems. For instance, sales and marketing employees discussed customer feedback with employees in production. Now, after some production changes, the firm is able to fill a customer's order within four days instead of eight. The focus is on solving problems, not on placing blame. All employees have a major say in who gets hired, how salaries are increased, and how jobs are structured. Employees are learning how to work together to solve problems and are highly satisfied with their jobs.[2]

motivation Any influence that elicits, channels, or sustains people's behavior.

Motivation is any influence that elicits, channels, or sustains people's behavior. This chapter is about motivated performance, like that at Avis. As a manager, you'll be responsible for helping employees perform their jobs effectively and efficiently. But you can't fulfill this responsibility until you understand what motivates both them and you. In this chapter we'll introduce you to various factors that initiate and sustain employee behaviors. We'll also explore the ways managers and employee teams can use rewards to enhance everyone's performance.

FACTORS AFFECTING MOTIVATION

To provide a very basic understanding of motivation, we'll focus for a moment on three of the many factors that influence motivation: individual differences, job characteristics, and organizational practices.[3] Figure 13.1 graphically displays the interaction among these three factors, or sets of variables. In order to develop an effective motivation program, managers must consider how the interaction among these factors affects employee performance on the job. Remember, though, that some factors that affect an employee's job performance may be outside of a manager's control. For instance, worrying about a sick child in the day-care center or about the need to help parents financially or about a recent divorce is bound to affect an employee's performance.

individual differences
Personal needs, values, attitudes, and interests that people bring to their jobs.

Individual Differences

Every person is unique. **Individual differences** are those personal needs, values, attitudes, and interests that people bring to their jobs. Because these characteristics vary from person to person, so will what motivates people. One employee may be motivated by money and hold out for a job paying a high salary. Another may be motivated by security and accept a lower paying job that involves few risks of unemployment.[4] Still another may thrive on challenges and seek a position that stretches her or his abilities to the limit. An overseas assignment can give an employee just such a chance to tackle something new. Learning to handle the challenges of such a job gives an employee an advantage in today's increasingly global organizations. At DuPont, for example, where almost half of

FIGURE 13.1

Interaction of Motivational Variables

Individual differences are those unique characteristics each person brings to his or her job. Job characteristics are what make some jobs challenging and interesting and others dull and routine. Organizational practices refer to the systems that are used by the organization to motivate, retain, and control employees.

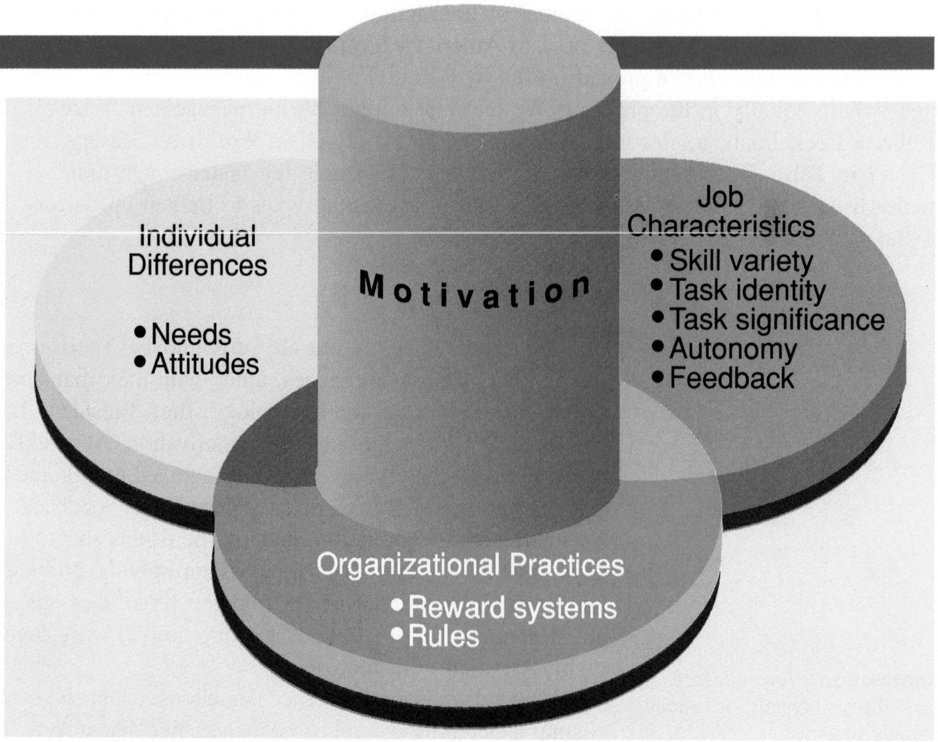

Individual Differences
• Needs
• Attitudes

Motivation

Job Characteristics
• Skill variety
• Task identity
• Task significance
• Autonomy
• Feedback

Organizational Practices
• Reward systems
• Rules

sales are foreign, an overseas assignment is becoming essential for promotion to top management. In Chapters 1 and 12 we highlighted the changing demographics of the workplace and discussed how organizations have designed plans to attract, motivate, and retain the new diversity of workers.

Job Characteristics

job characteristics The dimensions of a job that determine its limitations and challenges.

Job characteristics are the dimensions of the job that determine its limitations and challenges. These characteristics include the variety of skills required, the degree to which the employee can do the entire task from start to finish (task identity), the significance attributed to the job, autonomy, and the type and extent of performance feedback that the employee receives. Different jobs may rate high on some characteristics and low on others. For example, the job of airport shuttle bus driver at Avis requires performing a repetitive task and would rate low on autonomy, skill variety, and significance but high on task identity. The driver also gets feedback (complaints or thanks) from customers. In contrast, the job of bus mechanic rates high on skill variety and task identity. As Avis and other organizations have found, an employee who derives satisfaction from the job and its particular characteristics will be more motivated to perform well than one who doesn't.

Organizational Practices

organizational practices The rules, personnel policies, managerial practices, and reward systems of an organization.

Organizational practices are the rules, personnel policies, managerial practices, and reward systems of an organization. Policies defining fringe benefits (such as paid vacations, insurance, child/elder care, and so forth) and rewards (such as bonuses and/or commissions) can attract new employees and convince older employees to remain with a company. Rewards can motivate employees, but if they are to do so effectively, they must be administered fairly and based on performance. Corning, Inc., for example, installed a bonus program for everyone from "secretaries to chairman." These annual bonuses are based on success in hitting company targets for profitability. In 1988 the bonus payout was 7.5 percent of salary; in 1989 it was 8.7 percent. But if corporate results go down, so too do employees' bonus checks. "We just aren't going to keep paying people the same amount of money if the company isn't performing," says Paul Regan, a senior vice president.[5]

Interaction of Factors

As Figure 13.1 shows, the three factors we've described interact to influence an employee's motivation. Essentially this interaction involves (1) the personal qualities the employee brings to the workplace, (2) the activities the employee performs in the work situation, and (3) the organizational systems that affect the employee in the workplace.

In working with employees on motivation, managers need to consider all three factors. Managers must understand, for instance, that the way they apply certain rules and rewards can either motivate or demotivate subordinates. The following Insight takes a look at how Tom Monaghan, president and CEO of Domino's Pizza, motivates his employees using these three factors.

DELIVERING MOTIVATION AT DOMINO'S

I N S I G H T   Why would anyone want to deliver pizza for a living? According to Tom Monaghan, president and CEO of Domino's Pizza, people work for challenge, for the rewards of their efforts, and for a sense of belonging. Even working at a some-

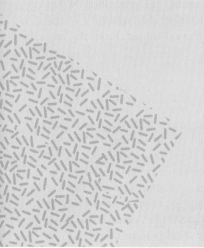

what routine and standardized job like pizza delivery, it's possible for people to feel part of a group, a family, with the sense of belonging that families create. Ninety-eight percent of Domino's franchise owners started out as delivery people, then moved up to store managers. They are proud to be members of the Domino's family.

In addition, everyone at Domino's has a chance to try out his or her ideas, each of which will succeed or fail on its own merits. New products, such as a breakfast pizza with ham and bacon and a low-calorie pizza, reflect employees' creativity and innovation.

Monaghan knows that people are also motivated by rewards. In addition to generous performance incentives—such as free trips to the Indy 500 and BMWs for top managers—Domino's headquarters provides other perks, such as a fitness center, a recreation lake, jogging and ski trails, and a sports medicine center, available to all employees.[6]

content approach The category of theories of motivation that assumes employees are motivated by the desire to fulfill inner needs.

There are three well-known categories of theoretical approaches to understanding motivation. First is what has been called the **content approach.** These theories answer a "what" question, such as "What factors motivate people?" or "What needs do people seek to satisfy at work?" The answers to these questions assume that individuals have inner needs that they are motivated to reduce or fulfill at work. For example, someone who has a strong need to belong may be more highly motivated to join an organization than to start an at-home business. An employee with a strong need for self-esteem might be motivated to produce high-quality products, because producing quality satisfies such a need. Abraham Maslow's hierarchy of needs and Frederick Herzberg's two-factor model are content theories that we'll examine here.

process approach The category of theories of motivation that assumes employees choose certain behaviors in order to meet their personal goals.

The secondary category of theories is the **process approach.** These theories are so labeled because they emphasize the "how" and "why" of people's choosing certain behaviors to meet their personal goals. For example, individuals may see a strong possibility of receiving some desired reward—such as a promotion or a salary increase—if they perform in a certain way, such as by working hard. In other words, the prospect of the reward motivates them to work hard. Two of the most useful process theories are the expectancy model and the equity model.

reinforcement theory Behavior theory of motivation that holds that behavior is a function of its consequences (rewards or punishments).

The third approach, **reinforcement theory,** deals with how the outcomes of past actions influence future actions. It's based on the belief that behavior that results in rewarding outcomes (pay raises, promotions, or praise) is likely to be repeated. Behavior that results in punishing outcomes (demotions, pay cuts, or reprimands) is less likely to be repeated. People behave as they do because they have learned through experience that certain behaviors are associated with certain kinds of outcomes.

CONTENT THEORIES

need A strong feeling of deficiency in a particular aspect of a person's life that creates an uncomfortable tension, which the person attempts to reduce.

As we've said, content theories hold that motivation springs from a desire to satisfy a need. A **need** is a strong feeling of deficiency in some aspect of a person's life. This sense of deficiency creates an uncomfortable tension, which the individual strives to reduce, usually by taking some action to satisfy the need. Some people are driven by a need to succeed; others by the need to be well liked, to gain power and/or wealth, or to feel secure in their jobs. If an individual succeeds in reducing the sense of deficiency, the intensity of the motivating force is also reduced.

FIGURE 13.2

Maslow's Hierarchy of Needs

There are five categories of needs in Maslow's hierarchy: physiological, security, affiliation, esteem, and self-actualization. As a need becomes satisfied, it no longer motivates a person. Only unsatisfied needs can motivate.

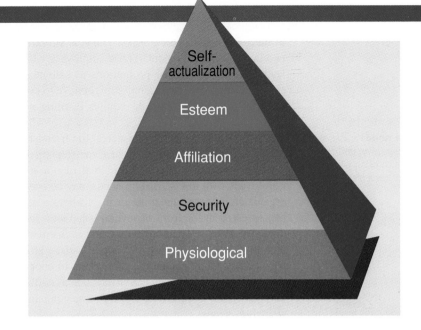

hierarchy of needs
Maslow's content model of motivation that suggests people have a complex set of needs arranged on five levels, which they attempt to meet, from the bottom (most basic) up.

Maslow's Hierarchy of Needs

The most widely used model for studying motivation within organizations is Abraham Maslow's **hierarchy of needs model.**[7] Maslow, a psychologist, suggested that people have a complex set of needs. Maslow's model contains five categories of needs, which he arranged in order of importance (see Figure 13.2): physiological (at the base), security, affiliation, esteem, and self-actualization (at the top).

Four basic assumptions underlie Maslow's hierarchy of needs:

1. A satisfied need is not a motivator. Once a need is satisfied, another emerges to take its place. Thus people are always striving to satisfy some need.

2. The needs network for most people is very complex. That is, a number of different needs affect a person's behavior at any one time.

3. In general, lower-level needs must be satisfied before higher-level needs become strong enough to stimulate behavior.

4. There are many more ways to satisfy higher-level needs than there are to satisfy lower-level needs.

physiological needs The most basic human needs—for food, clothing, shelter—which occupy the lowest level in Maslow's hierarchy.

Physiological needs are those for food, clothing, and shelter. As the most basic human needs, they occupy the lowest level in Maslow's hierarchy. People try to satisfy physiological needs before all others. For example, the primary motivation of a very hungry person is obtaining food rather than, say, recognition of achievements.

security needs The fairly basic human needs for safety, stability, and absence of pain, threat, and illness, which occupy the second level of Maslow's hierarchy.

Security needs include the needs for safety and stability, as well as for absence of pain, threat, and illness. As with physiological needs, people deprived of the means to satisfy security needs become preoccupied with obtaining them. Many workers express their security needs as a desire for a stable job with medical, unemployment, and retirement benefits.

People motivated by the fear of losing their job, a motivator highly evident in the early 1990s, usually aren't terribly innovative. As we indicated in Chapter 1, the thinning of middle-management ranks nationwide has been profound. United States companies have eliminated nearly one of four middle-management jobs since 1980. In an era of layoffs and downsizing, job security becomes a powerful motivator. Lack of job security stifles innovation and risk taking while prompting caution. As the U.S. economy slips in and out of recession, more and more employees are becoming concerned about losing their jobs. Because of continued belt tightening, raises and bonuses are being squeezed, and employees are having to accept interdepartmental transfers just to remain employed. In the face of defense cutbacks, Hughes Aircraft eliminated more than 14,000 jobs and two layers of management. Those employees who survived were encouraged to consider lateral moves instead of promotions to safeguard their job security with Hughes. An electrical engineer, for example, might have to switch to a quality control job just to have a secure job. Such a switch requires learning new skills, which can be frightening to employees.[8]

affiliation needs The needs for friendship, love, and belonging, which occupy the third level of Maslow's hierarchy.

    Affiliation needs are the needs for friendship, love, and belonging. This level in Maslow's hierarchy represents a clear step up from the truly basic physiological and security needs. Employees with high affiliation needs enjoy working closely with others. Employees with low affiliation needs may be content to work on solitary tasks. When an organization doesn't meet her or his affiliation needs, an employee's dissatisfaction may be expressed in the form of several behaviors, including frequent absenteeism, low productivity, stress-related behaviors, and even emotional breakdown. Managers who recognize that subordinates are striving to satisfy affiliation needs should act in supportive ways. They might encourage co-workers to cooperate more closely and to participate in company-organized social activities, such as softball teams and picnics. Domino's recreation center is a good example of how one company is attempting to satisfy its employees' affiliation needs.

esteem needs The needs for self-respect, personal achievement, and recognition from others, which occupy the fourth level of Maslow's hierarchy.

    Esteem needs are needs for self-respect, a sense of personal achievement, and recognition from others. In order to satisfy these needs, people seek opportunities for achievement, promotion, prestige, and status—for recognition of their competence and worth. Managers who perceive that employees are motivated by esteem needs emphasize the hard work and finely honed skills required for success. They may publicly reward achievement with published performance lists, bonuses, praise, lapel pins, and articles in the company paper. These and other forms of recognition help to build employee pride. When the need for esteem is dominant, managers can promote job satisfaction and high-quality performance by providing opportunities for exciting, challenging work and recognition of accomplishment.

self-actualization needs Needs related to personal growth, self-fulfillment, and the realization of one's full potential, which occupy the highest level of Maslow's hierarchy.

    Self-actualization needs are related to personal growth, self-fulfillment, and the realization of one's full potential. A self-actualized person accepts both his or her own self as well as others. Traits commonly exhibited include initiative, spontaneity, and problem-solving ability. Managers who recognize this level of motivation in employees can help them discover the growth opportunities inherent in their jobs. For example, managers motivate by involving employees in the decision-making process, restructuring their jobs, or offering them special assignments that call for special skills. At Merck, scientists can

At GM's Saturn plant, *affiliation* and *esteem needs* are clearly being met. Factory employees are organized into teams of about ten members, who share decisions on everything from being co-workers to buying equipment for the plant.

John Allegretti (center) found his *self-actualization needs* met when Hyatt Corporation executives Don DePorter (left) and Tom Pritzker (right) supported his developing and running a spinoff waste-consulting company.

attend law school and become patent attorneys; at Hewlett-Packard, a technical ladder has been set up so scientists can earn salary advances without taking on management tasks.

Application by Managers Maslow never claimed, by the way, that his hierarchy was a fixed, rigid order that applied to all people. He believed that people are motivated to satisfy those needs that are foremost at specific times in their lives. The strength of a specific need depends on the extent to which it and all lower-level needs have been satisfied. Thus Maslow's model predicts a dynamic, step-by-step process in which a continuously evolving set of needs motivates behavior. Physiological needs are the most basic and must be satisfied first. Self-actualization needs are fulfilled last and least often.

Research supports Maslow's view that, until basic needs are satisfied, people will not be concerned with higher-level needs.[9] However, there is little evidence to support the view that people must meet their needs in the sequence defined by Maslow's hierarchy (Figure 13.2). For example, it has not been proven that all people must satisfy social needs (aspects of Maslow's affiliation and esteem needs) before moving on to satisfy self-actualization needs. Some people pay little attention to social needs as long as they are free to do what they do best, whether that be playing chess, working out, or solving computer-programming problems.

Research shows, in fact, that managers should assume a two-part hierarchy with physiological and security needs at the bottom and affiliation, esteem, and self-actualization needs at the top. Unless an organization helps employees satisfy the two lower-level needs, addressing the three higher-level needs won't influence on-the-job behavior. Moreover, if an employee's lower-level needs appear to become threatened, they will take on even greater importance. British Airways laid off 22,000 employees in 1983 because it was losing money, and those who remained were concerned that they would also be let go. Flights were delayed and customer service slipped, because employees were sitting around talking and worrying about losing their jobs. It was only when the airline clearly indicated that there would be no further layoffs that employees began searching for ways to improve customer service and operational efficiency. Managers and employees shared ideas on improving baggage handling and ticket taking. Today British Airways is highly profitable and has one of the best reputations in the world for service.[10]

The implication of a two-part hierarchy is that once basic needs are satisfied, no single other need is likely to emerge as the best candidate for motivating subordinates. Managers will have to address more than one need simultaneously. Therefore, managers must continually reevaluate *what* motivates their subordinates and *how* to motivate them. To better understand this aspect of the needs hierarchy, go back and reread the Manager's Viewpoint Feature on Avis. What needs are motivating those employees?

For years, many workers in Soviet bloc countries had their lower-level needs met because of governmental policies. They had little chance of satisfying their higher-level needs, however, because of the autocratic style of the ministries governing their industries. As a result, these workers did what they were told and nothing more. Although they often produced shoddy goods, customers had no choice but to purchase them, so the quality really didn't matter. Now that these countries are entering the world market, however, their managers and employees will have to be motivated to produce high-quality goods at competitive prices.

Trying to understand what motivates another person is never easy. And when a manager is working with subordinates from another culture, the task becomes even more difficult. In recent years, experts have written many books on how to motivate people from different cultures. These books have raised questions about the usefulness of American management practices abroad. This chapter's Global Link Feature clearly illustrates this problem by examining the differences in need importance among managers in six countries.

ARE NEEDS SIMILAR IN DIFFERENT COUNTRIES?

Some experts believe that as the world becomes more industrialized, employees' needs are likely to become more similar. Others believe that patterns of management and employee behavior are largely culture-bound. A behavioral scientist from Britain surveyed managers from various countries concerning how important and how satisfied each of Maslow's needs was for them. The results of this study are summarized in the table (1 indicates the most importance and satisfaction, and 5, the least).

Need Importance

	Physiological	Security	Affiliation	Esteem	Self-actualization
Germany	2	5	4	3	1
France	3	4	5	2	1
United States	4	3	5	2	1
Japan	4	3	5	2	1
India	1	5	4	3	2
Malawi	1	4	5		2

Need Satisfaction

	Physiological	Security	Affiliation	Esteem	Self-actualization
Germany	3	1	2	4	5
France	2	3	1	4	5
United States	1	2	3	4	5
Japan	1	5	3	2	4
India	3	3	2	5	5
Malawi		2	1		4

In most industrialized countries, self-actualization needs were the most important, followed by esteem. It's striking that for managers in India and Malawi, two less developed countries, the most important needs were physiological.

How satisfied needs were also varied by country. U.S. managers closely followed Maslow's needs hierarchy; managers in Malawi deviated considerably.

These data indicate that we can't assume that all managers have the same needs or even that cultural differences are important sources of motivation. For example, the political reality of Malawi appears to explain why its managers rate physiological needs high. As with many African nations, power in Malawi is centralized at the top, with the country's president involved in many decisions that affect employees in organizations. A change in political power can result in the loss of one's job and means of satisfying physiological needs. On the other hand, Malawian managers rated affiliation needs as the most highly satisfied. This may reflect the culture, which has the communal nature of most African societies. Social interaction is central to the life of the individual, even in the business community.

FIGURE 13.3

Dissatisfaction

Satisfaction

Traditional View

No satisfaction

Motivators

Satisfaction

Herzberg's View

Dissatisfaction

Hygienes

No dissatisfaction

Views of Job Satisfaction

Herzberg called factors associated with good feelings motivator factors and those associated with dissatisfaction, hygiene factors.

Herzberg's Two-Factor Model

Maslow's theory focused on the individual, but the second content theory looks at the content of jobs and their tasks. This theory was first developed because routine assembly-line jobs were shown to reduce employee motivation and contribute to job dissatisfaction. One of the keys to Avis's success has been to redesign jobs so workers perform meaningful and responsible work.

Frederick Herzberg was among the first behavioral scientists to look at motivating employees from a different angle.[11] Herzberg's initial major study examined the relationship between job satisfaction and productivity for 200 accountants and engineers. In carrying out their research, Herzberg and his associates asked participants to describe job experiences that produced good and bad feelings about their jobs. Herzberg found that although the presence of a particular job characteristic, such as responsibility, might increase job satisfaction, lack of that same characteristic didn't necessarily produce dissatisfaction. Conversely, if lack of a characteristic, such as job security, produced dissatisfaction, it didn't follow that high job security caused satisfaction. As shown in Figure 13.3, managers traditionally believed that satisfaction and dissatisfaction were at opposite ends of a single continuum, and employees were in various stages along it. Herzberg and his associates stated that there are really two continuums: one ranging from no satisfaction to satisfaction and the other ranging from dissatisfaction to no dissatisfaction.

Herzberg's results led him to conclude that two separate and distinct kinds of experiences produced job satisfaction and job dissatisfaction. Thus the model based on his research has been called the **two-factor model.** Those factors associated with positive feelings about the job Herzberg labeled motivator factors. Those associated with feelings of dissatisfaction were labeled hygiene factors. Table 13.1 lists the motivator and hygiene factors.

Motivator factors are those that are intrinsic (internal) to the job, including the challenge of the work itself, responsibility, recognition, achievement, and advancement

two-factor model Herzberg's theory of motivation, which states that distinct kinds of experiences produce job satisfaction (motivator factors) and job dissatisfaction (hygiene factors).

motivator factors The instrinsic factors of a job that, when present, should create high levels of motivation: challenge of the work, responsibility, recognition, achievement, and advancement and growth.

TABLE 13.1

Examples of Motivator and Hygiene Factors

Motivator Factors	Hygiene Factors
Sources of Job Satisfaction	*Sources of Job Dissatisfaction*
▶ Challenge of the work itself	▶ Working conditions
▶ Responsibility	▶ Company policies
▶ Recognition	▶ Supervision
▶ Achievement	▶ Co-workers
▶ Advancement and growth	▶ Salary, status, and job security

hygiene factors The extrinsic factors of a job that, when positive in nature, maintain a reasonable level of job motivation but do not necessarily increase it: working conditions, company policies, supervision, co-workers, and salary and job security.

and growth. These factors determine whether a job is exciting and rewarding. When all five of them are present, they should create high levels of motivation and spur employees to superior performance—*if* there are no dissatisfiers.

Dissatisfiers are found among the hygiene factors. **Hygiene factors** are those that are extrinsic (external) to the job, including working conditions, company policies, supervision, co-workers, and salary, status, and job security. These five factors determine the context in which work is performed. Is the cafeteria air-conditioned? Are rules fair? Does the company provide free parking? Let's assume that the cafeteria is air-conditioned and that employees receive various fringe benefits. Will they be more highly motivated to perform than if those factors were not present? According to Herzberg, the answer is no! Herzberg suggested that although positive external factors are needed to maintain a reasonable level of job satisfaction, their presence does not necessarily increase the level of job satisfaction.

The managerial implications of the two-factor model are significant. For many years firms that require workers to perform routine, assembly-line tasks have been plagued with personnel problems such as high turnover, absenteeism, grievances, and low productivity. These firms generally rely on hygiene factors alone to motivate employees. According to Herzberg and others, however, because hygiene factors do not improve performance, management should instead focus on motivator factors to solve this problem.

Detractors criticize the two-factor model because of flaws in its research methodology and the fact that it doesn't consider differences in individuals' needs.[12] However, many managers accept the two-factor model for several reasons. First, it's easy to understand; managers can easily identify motivator and hygiene factors. Second, the actions required to improve employee performance are straightforward: Give employees challenging jobs and allow them to make suggestions on ways to improve their jobs; focus on the job itself and not on the physical work environment. At PepsiCo, 60 percent of management moves regularly among Frito-Lay, KFC, and overseas assignments. Each new assignment challenges the manager to learn a new business and a new functional area (such as marketing, quality control, or human resources). Third, improved performance does not depend on significant increases in financial outlay, such as higher salaries and added fringe benefits. It depends on increases in motivator factors, such as responsibility and performance recognition.

The Hackman-Oldham Job-Enrichment Model

job-enrichment model An extension of the two-factor model for motivation that emphasizes ways to change specific job characteristics in order to satisfy more of employees' higher-level needs.

Job-enrichment models extend Herzberg's work by focusing on how managers can change specific job characteristics in order to motivate employees and promote job satisfaction. The common theme of these models is helping workers satisfy more of their higher-level needs. The most popular and extensively tested job-enrichment model is that developed by J. Richard Hackman and Greg Oldham.[13]

FIGURE 13.4

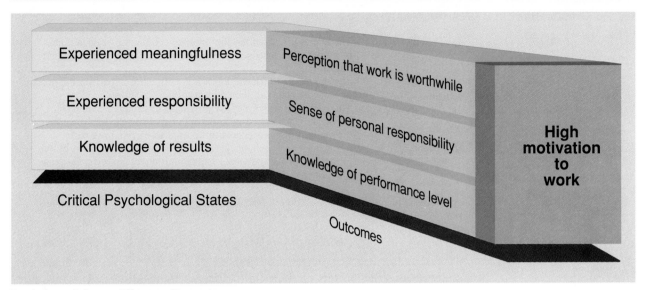

Psychological States Affecting Motivation

If an employee's job is meaningful, allows the employee to feel a sense of ownership, and lets the employee know how well he or she is doing, it is highly motivating.

Source: J. R. Hackman and G. R. Oldham, *Work Redesign* (Reading, Mass.: Addison-Wesley, 1980), 73. Reprinted with permission.

experienced meaningfulness The psychological state that's a measure of the degree to which employees perceive their work as valuable and worthwhile.

experienced responsibility The psychological state that's a measure of the extent to which employees feel personally responsible for the quality of their work.

knowledge of results The psychological state that's a measure of the extent to which employees receive feedback about how well they are performing.

Critical Psychological States As shown in Figure 13.4, the Hackman-Oldham model indicates that three critical psychological states affect motivation in the workplace. When any of these psychological states is low, employee motivation is low.

1. **Experienced meaningfulness** is the degree to which employees perceive their work as valuable and worthwhile. For example, if you believe that packing rubber bands in a box or making change at a toll booth is a trivial task, then you will not be highly motivated to perform it. You would feel the same way even if you had sole responsibility for performing the job and received feedback on how well you were doing.

2. **Experienced responsibility** is the extent to which employees feel personally responsible for the quality of their work. If you believe your job performance is entirely determined by rules, you will have less reason to feel accountable for your actions. The opposite is true when you have to make decisions about your behavior.

3. **Knowledge of results** is the extent to which employees receive feedback about how well they are doing the job. If you're given no information about the outcome of your efforts, you won't care much about the quality of your performance.

We can illustrate the concepts represented by these psychological states with an analogy to the game of golf. The player hits the ball and sees where it goes. He or she is provided with immediate feedback in the form of the score on each hole, which tells the golfer how well he or she is playing against a standard (par). Personal responsibility for performance is high—even though golfers may make excuses for poor performance. Experienced meaningfulness can also be high when the golfer sees her or his efforts translated at once into a score that can be compared to par and to the scores of partners. Because all three psychological states are usually high among regular players, motivation is usually high. In fact, some golfers exhibit motivated behavior states rarely seen at work: getting up before dawn, playing in rain and snow, feeling despair or joy (depending on how the round went), and even violence (breaking a club after a muffed shot).

Key Job Characteristics

▶ Skill Variety	The degree to which the job involves a variety of different work activities or requires the use of a number of skills and talents.
▶ Task Identity	The degree to which the job requires completing an identifiable piece of work, that is, doing a job with a visible beginning and outcome.
▶ Task Significance	The degree to which the job has a substantial impact on the goals or work of others in the company.
▶ Autonomy	The degree to which the job provides substantial freedom, independence, and discretion to the individual in scheduling work and determining the procedures to be used in carrying out tasks.
▶ Feedback	The degree to which carrying out work activities required by the job results in the individual's obtaining direct and clear information about his or her performance.

Source: Adapted from J. R. Hackman and G. R. Oldham, *Work Redesign* (Reading, Mass.: Addison-Wesley, 1980), 78–80. Reprinted with permission.

Influence of Job Characteristics   Table 13.2 lists the five key job characteristics described earlier in this chapter: skill variety, task identity, task significance, autonomy, and feedback. These characteristics influence the three critical psychological states. As Figure 13.5 shows, skill variety, task identity, and task significance all contribute to the experienced meaningfulness of work. Jobs lacking these characteristics seem trivial and worthless. To offset feelings of meaninglessness, workers sometimes play mental games. For example, parking lot attendants and traffic officers admit to occasionally playing license-plate poker in their heads. Autonomy fosters feelings of personal responsibility. When jobs provide autonomy, employees will view performance as directly related to their own efforts and decisions. When autonomy isn't possible, as in much staff work, the manager has an increased responsibility to give employees adequate feedback. Feedback provides employees with knowledge of the results of their efforts.

growth-need strength   The extent to which a person desires a job that provides personal challenges, sense of accomplishment, and learning (personal growth).

Growth-Need Strength   The last feature of the Hackman-Oldham model is **growth-need strength,** that is, the extent to which an individual desires a job that provides personal challenges, a sense of accomplishment, and learning. As we indicated earlier, some employees want jobs that satisfy only their lower-level needs, and others want jobs that will satisfy their higher-level needs. Individuals with strong needs for challenge, growth, and creativity are likely to respond positively to job-enrichment programs. If an individual's growth needs are weak, however, attempts at job enrichment may only increase stress and job dissatisfaction.

Different individuals bring different needs to the job, so employees will respond to the same job in different ways. What may be a good job for one person will be bad for someone else. The job-enrichment model demonstrates this concept by showing that the strength of a person's need for growth defines the relationship of job characteristics to performance and/or satisfaction. The following Insight describes how Volvo used job enrichment to improve productivity.

THE DEATH OF THE ASSEMBLY LINE

*I*NSIGHT   Since 1990, Volvo has been producing its 740 model without an assembly line. Instead, the plant forms teams of seven to ten hourly workers who assemble four cars per shift. The plant is divided into areas where teams work. The teams largely manage themselves, handling scheduling, quality control, hiring, and other

duties normally handled by first-level managers. Since members are trained to handle all assembly jobs, they work an average of three hours before repeating a task. This eliminates the classic problems associated with work cycles of one or two minutes, where the mind-numbing routine leads to boredom, inattention, poor quality, and high absenteeism. More than 80 percent of the team's work at Volvo can be done from a comfortable work position that limits bending and stretching. Volvo gives each worker sixteen weeks' training before he or she is allowed to join a work team. On-the-job training lasts an additional sixteen months. There are only two levels of management.

Why did Volvo change its system? According to Roger Holtback, president of the Volvo Car Corporation, "We didn't do this because we are nice guys." The problem is that Sweden's highly educated and well-trained work force doesn't like to work in factories. And more pay doesn't motivate Swedish employees to come to work. With unemployment less than 2 percent, there is no lack of jobs. Assembly-line plants in Sweden experience more than 20 percent absenteeism and more than 33 percent of its workers quit within a year. Absenteeism at this Volvo plant is less than 8 percent.[14]

Application by Managers The Hackman-Oldham job-enrichment model suggests that managers must first study their subordinates' jobs to identify core job

---

FIGURE 13.5

Hackman-Oldham Job-Enrichment Model

Jobs that permit employees to make decisions, receive feedback on how well they are doing, and use their skills lead to high critical psychological states, which in turn lead to high motivation and job satisfaction and high performance levels.

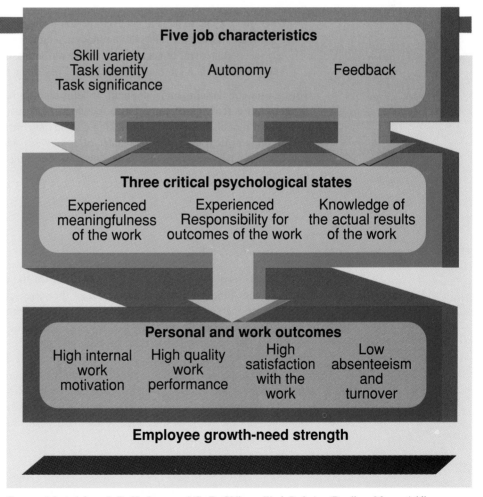

Source: Adapted from J. R. Hackman and G. R. Oldham, *Work Redesign* (Reading, Mass.: Addison-Wesley, 1980), 83. Reprinted with permission.

characteristics that can be changed.[15] For example, an effort to increase the skill variety of a job could overload an employee who is already working on numerous complex tasks. By also understanding their subordinates' personal needs for growth and achievement, managers can make realistic decisions about redesigning jobs to improve employee performance and job satisfaction. For those employees who do not want to grow on the job, enrichment programs have been found to be frustrating and dissatisfying. This point is illustrated in a 1976 study in which auto workers from Detroit worked in Sweden as engine assemblers in a SAAB plant. These jobs allowed them a great deal of freedom and responsibility with respect to performing their jobs. After one month, however, 75 percent of the Americans reported that they preferred their traditional assembly-line jobs. As one worker said, "If I've got to bust my a____ to have a meaningful job, forget it; I'd rather be monotonous."[16] Clearly, enriched jobs are not for everyone.

There has been resistance to job-enrichment programs by some union members and managers. To quote one AFL-CIO leader, "If you want to enrich the job, enrich the paycheck . . . that's the kind of job enrichment unions believe in." And managers have found it difficult to assess the results of job enrichment in dollars and cents. For example, what is the cost of a poor decision or a redundant inspection? Will these costs be lowered by introducing a job-enrichment program? Without answers to such questions, managers often have a difficult time determining whether a job-enrichment program will pay off.

Although there are some cases in which employees don't want their jobs enriched, Jack Hoffman, a manager at General Electric, best summarizes how most managers and employees feel:

> What we're trying to do is to get every person feeling important about his or her job, whether they sweep the floor, drive screws in a unit, interact with customers, coordinate in a certain area, or are an individual contributor. What we know is that people want more out of a job than a pay check. They want a feeling of input.[17]

This is what job enrichment is all about. It helps identify how jobs can be designed to give workers those feelings of importance to which Hoffman refers. In particular, the job-enrichment model specifies that enriching certain elements of jobs is effective in improving the three critical psychological states of employees, thus enhancing their work effectiveness. In Chapter 16 we examine how job enrichment concepts can be applied to self-managed teams.

PROCESS MODELS

Our discussion of motivation so far has focused on the different needs that employees bring to their jobs and how characteristics of the job itself can influence their behavior. However, neither Maslow's nor Herzberg's model adequately explains why people behave in so many different ways as they seek to fulfill their needs and achieve their objectives. To learn why, we need to explore employees' motivational process. Therefore, in this section we introduce two process models of motivation: expectancy and equity. The expectancy model suggests that motivation, performance, and job satisfaction all depend on the belief that effort expended on certain activities will lead to desired results. The equity model emphasizes that people are motivated to seek equality with other employees in the rewards they receive for their performance.

Expectancy Model

The process of satisfying needs requires making decisions. These decisions often involve choosing between highly desirable alternatives. For example, a manager is offered a promotion requiring relocation to a distant city. Before accepting, the manager must decide whether the increase in salary and status is worth uprooting the family. Similarly, a production worker may wonder if a promotion to supervisor will cut her or him off from friends on the production line. And a college graduate may have to decide whether to accept a job at Canon, Fujitsu, or Rockwell International. Basic to the expectancy model is the belief that people are capable of deciding what they want and then estimating the chances of achieving their objectives. The expectancy model tries to account for the differences in human behavior by tracing each step in the motivation process—from the initial decision to make an effort to the ultimate reward.

Vroom's Expectancy Theory The most widely accepted approach to explaining how people make such decisions is Victor Vroom's **expectancy theory,** which argues that people choose among alternative behaviors according to their expectation that a particular behavior will lead to one or more desired outcomes (such as pay, recognition, or new challenges).[18] Expectancy theory further predicts that an employee will be motivated to improve performance if the employee knows that he or she is capable of the desired behavior, believes that satisfactory performance will result in the desired outcome, and places a high value on that outcome. Vroom's expectancy theory rests on three basic assumptions:

1. *Forces at work in the individual and in the job situation combine to motivate and determine behavior.* As Maslow stated, people seek to satisfy different needs. Forces in the job situation influence how they go about doing so.

2. *People make conscious decisions about their own behavior.* For example, an individual decides whether to accept a job with the organization, come to work or call in sick, put in overtime, strive for a promotion, and so forth.

3. *Selecting a course of action depends on the expectation that a certain behavior will lead to a desired outcome.* In essence, individuals tend to behave in ways that they believe will help them achieve their objectives (such as a promotion or job security) and avoid behaving in ways that will lead to undesirable consequences (such as a demotion or criticism).

Figure 13.6 illustrates the relationships among the key concepts of expectancy theory. Let's consider each concept in more detail.

Before acting, the individual must assess the chance that expending the required effort will enable him or her to achieve the desired behavior. **Expectancy** is the belief that effort will lead to first-order outcomes. A **first-order outcome** is any work-related behavior—such as satisfactory performance, creativity, reliability, or habitual tardiness—that is the direct result of the effort an employee expends on a job. **Instrumentality** is the perceived link between first-order outcomes and the attainment of second-order outcomes. The individual must believe that certain work-related behaviors will lead to desired outcomes. This link is typically expressed as a probability. If you achieve an A in this course, you expect your grade to increase the likelihood of your receiving approval from your parents, graduating from college, and getting a better job—your desired second-order outcomes. A **second-order outcome** is the result, good or bad—such as a raise, promotion, demotion, acceptance by co-workers, or job security—brought about by a first-order outcome.

For example, at Johnsonville Foods, Inc., in Sheboygan, Wisconsin, employees rate themselves and fellow employees on seventeen performance dimensions that fall into three categories: quality and quantity of work, teamwork, and personal development. All final scores, with names deleted, are then passed to a profit-sharing group that carves out five categories of performance: superior, better-than-average, average, below-average, and poor. Employees expect that if they work hard they'll be rated as superior performers by their fellow employees. This superior rating means a larger share of the profit-sharing money that is paid to employees on a quarterly basis by the company.[19]

Valence is the value or weight that an individual attaches to a first- or second-order outcome. Thus the valences of various outcomes can motivate behavior and influence

FIGURE 13.6

Key Concepts of Expectancy Theory

People exert effort to produce work-related behaviors and receive the desired outcomes.

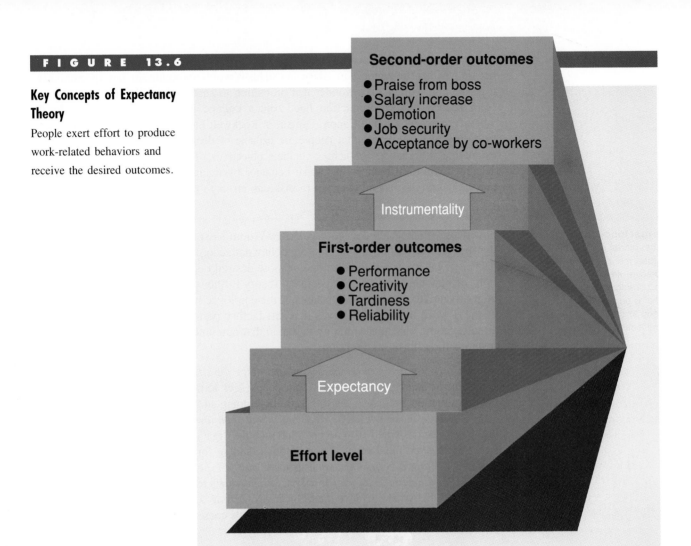

decisions. Since valences are subjective, the same outcome may have a high valence for one person and a low valence for another. For example, a promotion to the higher-paying position of art director would appeal more to an individual who values (places a high valence on) financial gain and increased responsibility than to an individual who values creativity and independence as a staff artist.

The valence of a first-order outcome, such as performance, depends on the valences assigned to second-order outcomes and on the instrumentalities between outcomes. Let's continue with the Johnsonville Foods example. Getting a superior performance rating from fellow workers will mean a lot to someone who values money. If, however, the person receiving a superior performance rating then receives the ''cold shoulder'' from fellow workers, he or she might reevaluate whether such performance and the money it brought are worth being given the silent treatment by co-workers.

Motivation is therefore determined by individual beliefs about the relationship between effort and behaviors and the expectation that certain behaviors (first-order outcomes) will produce the desired results (second-order outcomes). Simply put, the theory holds that people do what they can once they have decided that they want to do it.

Porter-Lawler expectancy model The process model of motivation that states job satisfaction is the result rather than the cause of performance.

Porter-Lawler Expectancy Model Lyman Porter and Edward Lawler have extended the basic expectancy theory. The **Porter-Lawler expectancy model** states that satisfaction is the result rather than a cause of performance.[20] Different levels of performance lead to different rewards. The rewards, in turn, produce different levels of job satisfaction. Figure 13.7 shows the complete Porter-Lawler expectancy model,

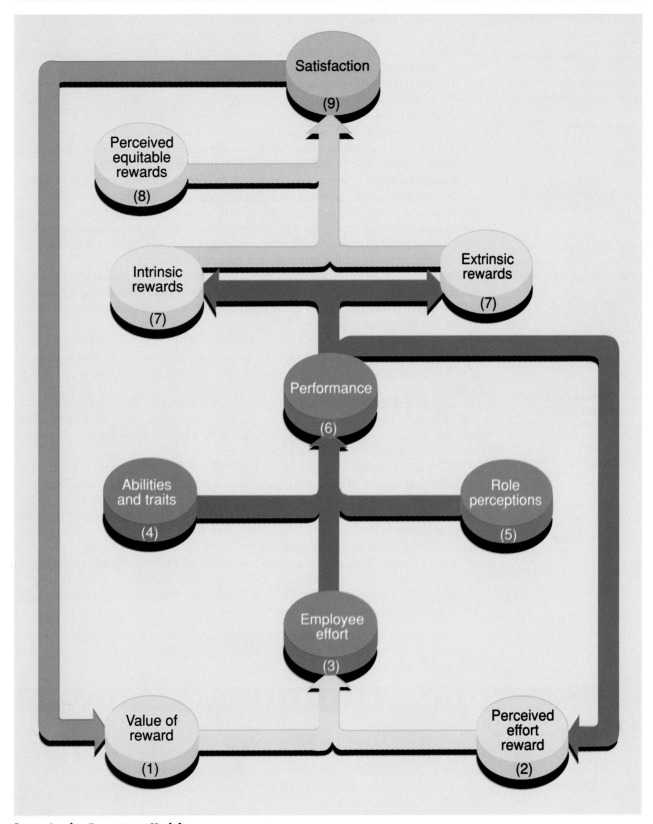

Porter-Lawler Expectancy Model

The Porter-Lawler expectancy model attempts to account for individual differences and organizational practices in the motivational process.

Source: From L. W. Porter and E. E. Lawler, III, *Managerial Attitudes and Performance* (Homewood, Ill.: Irwin, 1968), 165. Used with permission.

value of reward The importance that a person places on benefits to be obtained from a job.

perceived effort reward The individual's perception of the amount of effort on which certain rewards depend.

employee effort The amount of energy—physical and/or mental—exerted to perform a job task.

ability An individual's mastery of the skills required to do a job.

trait Individual personality characteristic that can affect a person's job performance.

role perception The employee's belief that certain tasks should be performed—certain roles should be played—in order to perform a job successfully.

performance The level of the individual's work achievement that comes only after effort has been exerted.

which draws together personal, job, and organizational characteristics in explaining the motivational process.

The **value of reward** is the importance that a person places on benefits to be obtained from a job, such as friendship of co-workers, promotion, a good salary, or a feeling of accomplishment. Some workers might prize the friendship of co-workers; others might value money more highly.

The **perceived effort reward** is a person's perception of the amount of expended effort on which certain rewards depend. Suppose a manager wants to transfer from the Southwest territory to the Northwest. He or she might feel that chances of getting the transfer have little to do with performance level but rather depend on factors other than performance—such as luck, "pull," or the state of the economy. Under such conditions the manager would perceive a low effort-reward possibility.

Employee effort is the amount of energy exerted to perform a job task. In other words, how hard is the employee trying? In baseball, a shortstop's attempt to throw the runner out at first base is an example of effort. Whether the effort results in an out is a measure of performance. Effort refers solely to the energy expended—not to how successful it is. The amount of effort applied depends on the interaction between the value of the reward and the effort-reward probability.

Of course, effort doesn't lead directly to performance; it is mediated by individual abilities and role perceptions. **Ability** refers to an individual's mastery of the skills required to do a job, such as conceptual, technical, and communication skills. **Traits** are individual personality characteristics—such as the strength of various needs—that can affect a person's job performance. Thus abilities and traits are relatively independent of the work situation. Although employees can learn new skills by practicing on the job, they generally acquire basic abilities and traits before beginning work.

Role perception is the employee's belief that certain tasks should be performed—that is, certain roles played—if he or she is to carry out a job successfully. Role perceptions determine how employees define their jobs and the types of efforts they believe are essential to effective performance.

All of the five preceding factors affect performance. **Performance** is the level of the individual's work achievement that comes only after effort has been exerted. It depends not only on the amount of effort exerted, but also on the individual's ability and role perception. An employee may exert a great amount of effort, but if he or she has little ability or has inaccurately assessed what it takes to succeed in the organization, resulting performance may be low.

Let's consider how a manager can use these six factors to improve employee productivity and job satisfaction. The following Insight highlights how John Davis, vice president of marketing and training at Re:Member Data, successfully used them. The particular ones he applied are indicated in brackets.

*I*NSIGHT Re:Member Data Company sells data-processing systems to credit unions. Once a sale is made, employees convert the customer's database to the new system and teach the customer's employees how to run the system. Prior to John Davis's arrival, systems design employees would learn about new customers when orders landed on their desks. They never knew which customers were being courted, what the salespeople were promising them, or how many jobs would arrive next week or next month. All this ignorance was costly. Once, a salesperson promised a customer that the system could easily handle the customer's needs—only to find out later that the customer had some 120 different forms, each one requiring programming. Instead of taking a month, the job took several months and resulted in poor customer relations.

What did Davis do? First, he developed a detailed cost-accounting system. Under the system, each employee keeps a record of the time spent on each job, materials costs, travel, and so on. Now employees realize how much effort is required to complete each job [employee effort]. Second, a computer tracks each employee's time, daily sales, salary costs, and expenses. Each employee is provided with a monthly printout showing how much the company made or lost on each job [perceived effort reward]. Now, for similar jobs employees know what the projected rewards will be [value of reward]. Third, employees have learned to do their jobs more efficiently because they understand exactly what is required of them. Employees can now decide whether or not a trip to the customer's plant is really needed [role perception].

What's the result? Profits are up [performance]. Since all employees now also participate in a profit-sharing system, they're learning skills in areas such as customer relations that will help save the company money [abilities and traits]. By saving the company money, the employees' profit-sharing pool increases.[21]

reward A job outcome that an employee desires.

extrinsic reward Reward supplied by the organization, such as pleasant working conditions, fair salary, or job security.

instrinsic reward Reward derived by the individual from a job, such as self-recognition, performance, or personal growth.

perceived equitable reward The amount of reward employees believe they should receive relative to what other employees receive.

satisfaction An attitude determined by the difference between the rewards employees receive and those they believe they should have received—the smaller the difference, the greater the satisfaction.

Rewards are job outcomes that employees desire. Figure 13.7 identifies two basic types of rewards: extrinsic and intrinsic. **Extrinsic rewards** are those given by the organization, such as fair supervision, pleasant working conditions, a good salary, status, job security, and fringe benefits—what Herzberg called hygiene factors. **Intrinsic rewards** are personally satisfying outcomes, such as achievement, self-recognition, performance, responsibility, and personal growth—basically Herzberg's motivator factors. In the Porter-Lawler model both intrinsic and extrinsic rewards are desirable. As Avis, Volvo, Johnsonville Foods, and other companies have discovered, intrinsic rewards are much more likely to produce higher job satisfaction than are extrinsic rewards. Employees at Re:Member Data receive extrinsic rewards such as bonus checks and intrinsic rewards in the form of, for example, a sense of esteem and expanded job knowledge.

Perceived equitable reward is the amount of reward that employees believe they should receive relative to what other employees receive. For example, a middle manager might expect a certain salary, a merit bonus, a personal secretary, a private office with windows, a reserved parking place, a car, country club privileges, challenging job assignments, and recognition. Such expectations are based on the employee's perceptions of job requirements, job demands, and the contributions he or she makes in relation to others in the company. In essence, perceived equitable reward reflects the level of reward that the individual feels he or she deserves for high performance in a particular job.

Satisfaction is an attitude determined by the difference between the rewards employees receive and the rewards they believe they *should have* received.[22] The smaller the difference, the greater the employee's satisfaction. People often compare the rewards they receive with the rewards that others receive. If an employee believes that the comparison shows unfair treatment, the result is his or her dissatisfaction.

In some unionized organizations, all union employees receive the same across-the-board pay increase, regardless of performance. That is, the clerk with the highest level of performance receives the same percentage increase as the lowest-performing clerk. High-performing employees are generally dissatisfied with such arrangements, because their actual rewards fall below a fair level based on their performance. A similar situation faces most public school teachers. Generally, raises are based on the amount of time spent in the system and number of credits earned beyond a bachelor's degree, rather than on performance in the classroom.

Satisfaction is important for several reasons. First, research shows that the relationship between satisfaction and job performance is not so much "satisfaction leads to performance" as "performance leads to satisfaction." Second, satisfaction is related to absenteeism, tardiness, turnover, and commitment. The more satisfied employees are, the less likely they are to be absent or late or to leave the company. Satisfaction influences people's perceptions about their work environment. Satisfied employees focus on the positive, not the negative, aspects of their work. They are therefore more likely to make a commitment to the organization than are dissatisfied employees.

Application by Managers   The Porter-Lawler expectancy model presents several specific steps that managers can take to motivate employees:[23]

1. *Determine the rewards that each employee values.*   To be motivators, rewards must be based on each employee's values. Managers can determine which rewards their subordinates want simply by asking them or by observing their behaviors.

2. *Clearly identify the desired level of performance.*   Since we've noted that performance leads to satisfaction, managers must clearly express what it takes to perform well and to be rewarded. It is desirable that managers and subordinates agree on the types and levels of performance expected. That is the case at Johnsonville Foods, for example.

3. *Make sure that performance levels are attainable.*   If employees believe that management has set unattainable performance levels, their motivation will be low.

4. *Link rewards and performance.*   To maintain or increase motivation, managers must clearly link rewards and performance. At Intel Corporation and W. L. Gore & Associates, among thousands of other organizations, raises are tied strictly to performance. If top performers take home more than seasoned employees who have simply logged more hours, it's because the system is rewarding performance, not seniority.

5. *Make sure that rewards are adequate.*   Major rewards act as big motivators. At the Hyatt Regency Hotel in Chicago, employees who dream up new businesses that the Hyatt uses are permitted to run them. John Allegritti, for example, designed a new waste disposal system for the hotel. That business did so well that Hyatt management let him set up a new waste-disposal consulting company called International RecycleCo Inc. Besides serving many Hyatts, this company had more than twenty-four clients in eight states in 1990.[24]

The expectancy model also has limitations that managers must recognize. One of the major limitations, as you may have noticed, is its complexity.[25] Do people really consider how expectancies, instrumentalities, and outcomes interact every time they make decisions? How accurately can employees assess certain work outcomes as attainable and others as not? Do managers analyze motivation situations by using the model? Although these questions don't always have positive answers, the expectancy model does lead managers to concentrate on how their behaviors affect those of their subordinates and on ways they can improve the performance of their subordinates.

Equity Model

equity model   A process model of motivation that is concerned with individuals' beliefs about how fairly they're treated compared with their peers.

The **equity model** is concerned with individuals' beliefs about how fairly they're treated compared with their peers. One of the manager's most difficult tasks is to assure equity in rewarding performance. In Chapter 12 we discussed how important the performance appraisal system is in maintaining workers' motivation to reach the organization's goals. An effective performance appraisal system is equitable. That is, employees believe in the fairness of the distribution of the rewards. Employees of Lincoln Electric, a manufacturer of industrial electrical meters in Cleveland, Ohio, work under a payment plan that has produced spectacular productivity since 1934. Employees receive a set payment for each acceptable piece they produce. In addition, each worker receives a year-end bonus, based on an annual merit rating of his or her dependability, ideas, quality of work, and output. Employee bonuses average 97.6 percent of their regular earnings. The company has not lost any money for fifty-four years and has not laid off any employees in the last forty-three years. Employees are up to three times more productive than their counterparts at

Tommy LaSorda, Dodgers manager, on *rewards:* "People say, God, you mean to tell me you've got a guy making a million and a half dollars and you got to motivate him? I say, absolutely."

outcome A reward obtained from work, such as a promotion, a challenging assignment, and friendly co-workers.

input According to the equity model of motivation, what an employee gives to a job—such as time, effort, education—in order to obtain a desired outcome.

TRW, McDonnell Douglas, and Motorola, because they believe the system is fair and equitable.[26]

The primary research on the equity model was done by J. S. Adams.[27] He stated that individuals mentally form ratios to compare their outcomes and inputs with those of similar others to determine whether they have been treated fairly. **Outcomes** from work include both intrinsic and extrinsic rewards, such as promotions, challenging assignments, pay, and friendly co-workers. **Inputs** are what the employee gives to the job, such as time, effort, education, and commitment to the organization. The possible results of the comparison process are summarized in Table 13.3. For the sake of comprehension, we've provided a simple dollars-per-hour example to illustrate how the ratios work. In reality, of course, the ratios can be quite complex, involving factors not nearly as precisely comparable as those shown in the table.

TABLE 13.3

The Equity Model of Motivation: Comparing Hourly Wages

	Ratio Comparison	Perception
Equity	$$\frac{\$50}{5 \text{ hrs. work}} = \frac{\$100}{10 \text{ hrs. work}} = \$10/\text{hr.}$$ $$\frac{\text{Outcomes (self)}}{\text{Inputs (self)}} = \frac{\text{Outcomes (other)}}{\text{Inputs (other)}}$$	"We're being treated equally."
Inequity	$$\left[\frac{\$50}{5 \text{ hrs. work}} = \$10/\text{hr.}\right] < \left[\frac{\$100}{5 \text{ hrs. work}} = \$20/\text{hr.}\right]$$ $$\frac{\text{Outcomes (self)}}{\text{Inputs (self)}} < \frac{\text{Outcomes (other)}}{\text{Inputs (other)}}$$	"I'm getting less than I deserve for my efforts."
Inequity	$$\left[\frac{\$50}{5 \text{ hrs. work}} = \$10/\text{hr.}\right] > \left[\frac{\$25}{5 \text{ hrs. work}} = \$5/\text{hr.}\right]$$ $$\frac{\text{Outcomes (self)}}{\text{Inputs (self)}} > \frac{\text{Outcomes (other)}}{\text{Inputs (other)}}$$	"I'm getting more than I deserve."

In general, as a result of such a comparison the employee will feel equitably rewarded, under-rewarded, or over-rewarded. If employees feel that inequities exist, they will choose one of six alternatives in an effort to reduce the inequity:

1. Increase their inputs to justify higher rewards—when they feel that they are over-rewarded in comparison with others.

2. Decrease their inputs to compensate for lower rewards when they feel under-rewarded.

3. Change the compensation they receive through legal or other actions, such as leaving work early, stealing the company's supplies, and so on.

4. Modify their comparisons by choosing another person to compare themselves against.

5. Distort reality by rationalizing that the inequities are justified.

6. Leave the situation (quit the job) if the inequities cannot be resolved.

Inequities can arise out of many situations, but they usually occur with respect to promotions, salary increases, perks, and other human resource management actions. Before Union Carbide moved its corporate offices from New York City to Danbury, Connecticut, it had one of the most class-conscious office environments in America. Every management rank had a different kind of ashtray, a different kind of water pitcher, a different office design, and a different style of furniture. When somebody moved up, Carbide had to change all the trappings in that person's office. When Carbide moved to Danbury, it asked employees what features they wanted in the new building. As it turned out, no one wanted Mark Cross wastebaskets or marble-top tables—everyone wanted the same furniture. There is no executive dining room, no executive parking, and all executive offices are the same size. Carbide has noticed that both performance and satisfaction have increased since the move.[28]

Merit pay often causes feelings of inequity. Although it is supposed to be based on performance, merit pay is a source of bitter disputes among employees. Many companies put aside a set number of dollars for merit increases or allocate only a set number of merit increases to be given companywide. Thus if an organization has a lot of deserving employees, but its funds are limited, a lot of employees will feel that their performance (inputs) has not been recognized.

Remember that it doesn't matter what the *manager* feels is equitable.[29] Equity and fair treatment are in the minds of the employees. Since people have different needs and desires and want different experiences at work, equity is difficult to establish. Even if an organization gave all employees the same rewards, some people would still believe that they were being treated inequitably.

The following Insight, which focuses on a CEO's compensation versus the firm's performance, shows that inequity is found even among the ranks of corporate leadership.

WHO ARE THE MOST OVERPAID AND UNDERPAID CEOS?

INSIGHT Ask CEOs how much they should be paid and most say that they should be paid according to their organization's performance. *Fortune* conducted a study of CEO compensation in its top 500 companies. Researchers produced a performance score for each company and collected data on what the CEO of each company was paid. A computer model ranked the company's performance and the pay of its CEO to determine whether the compensation the executive received was in line with the firm's performance. According to these data the most underpaid CEO was Sam Walton of Wal-Mart: He should have been paid $1,954,000 but was actually paid only $325,000. Another underpaid CEO was John Akers of IBM, who was paid

$1,957,000 when he should have been paid $3,879,000. On the other hand, among the most overpaid executives were Martin Davis of Gulf and Western (computer model's equitable pay of $1,796,000 versus actual pay of $6,339,000) and Paul Fireman of Reebok (computer model's equitable pay of $4,040,000 versus actual pay of $11,439,000).

What do these data mean? According to Peter Drucker, a famous management consultant, poorly performing firms usually have wide salary gaps between management levels. Overpayment leads to a lack of teamwork, a lack of trust between managers and employees, and a lack of employee commitment and loyalty to the organization.[30]

REINFORCEMENT THEORY

Throughout this chapter we have implied that rewards and punishments are important in motivating people. Another approach to motivation, called behavior modification, focuses on the wise use of rewards and punishments to encourage or inhibit behavior. This approach has its foundations in the work of B. F. Skinner.[31] Stated very simply, **reinforcement theory** suggests that behavior is a function of its consequences (rewards or punishments). Behavior that gets rewarded is likely to be repeated; behavior that is ''punished'' is likely to be avoided. If you receive a reward (such as a bonus, a compliment, or a promotion) for superior performance, you are likely to continue performing at a high level in anticipation of future rewards. However, if the consequences of a particular behavior are unpleasant (management's disapproval or a demotion in rank), you will tend to modify the behavior.

Figure 13.8 shows the basic reinforcement process. A person's response (behavior) to a stimulus (situation) results in specific consequences (rewards and punishments), which in turn shape future behavior. For example, suppose you work in a high-tech firm. You come to a monthly staff meeting with a proposed style sheet for all diagrams created for user manuals, much like the existing style sheets for text. If your manager praises your initiative and creativity, you will probably be motivated to come up with other innovations. However, if your manager gives you a disapproving look and says that the firm is perfectly happy with the existing conditions, your behavior isn't rewarded. You will probably conclude that new ideas lead to negative consequences, that the best way to earn a positive reward is to just follow orders. The point is, a manager who wishes to change a behavior must also change the specific consequences of that behavior. Behavior modification relies on three basic principles: (1) measurable behavior, (2) types of reinforcement, and (3) schedules of reinforcement.[32]

Measurable Behavior

measurable behavior
Work-related behavior that can be quantified (number of units produced, percentage of defective units, and such).

gain-sharing program An incentive program under which all employees of a department get a bonus when the department exceeds a predetermined, measurable goal.

Measurable behavior is behavior that can be expressed in terms of quantity—number of units produced, percentage of defective units, number of meals served, number of students taught, and the like. Thoughts and feelings are not considered. Many companies, such as Firestone and Carrier, have instituted gain-sharing programs as incentives. In **gain-sharing programs,** *all* departmental employees get a bonus when a department beats predetermined performance targets, such as high productivity or courteous customer service. For such a program to be successful, performance targets must be measurable. The advantages to companies include better coordination and teamwork among employees, expanded employee knowledge about the business and focus on objectives, and

FIGURE 13.8

Reinforcement Process

The way in which a person responds to a given stimulus determines the consequence experienced and thus shapes his or her future behavior.

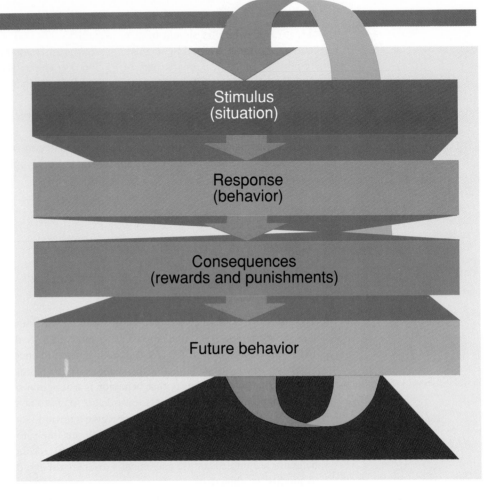

Stimulus
(situation)

Response
(behavior)

Consequences
(rewards and punishments)

Future behavior

Winning team from Preston Trucking, where ''Preston people . . . make the difference.''

improved employee work habits. The major disadvantage is that performance targets focus only on measurable objectives. Thus employees often ignore important objectives—such as interdepartmental cooperation, quality, and the training of new employees—that can't be measured as easily. Only behaviors that can be observed and measured are relevant to behavior modification.

Types of Reinforcement

Table 13.4 lists four types of reinforcement that can modify behavior: positive reinforcement, avoidance, punishment, and extinction. The first two types, positive reinforcement and avoidance, strengthen or maintain desired behaviors. The second two, punishment and extinction, can be used to reduce or stop undesired behaviors.

Positive reinforcement offers rewards to increase the likelihood that a desired behavior will be repeated. Anything that encourages an individual to repeat a desired behavior can be classified as a positive reinforcer. Some common positive reinforcers used by organizations include praise, recognition of accomplishment, promotion, and salary increases. Many of us regard these reinforcers as desirable.

Preston Trucking, a Maryland-based carrier, uses surveys and other bottom-up communication tools to positively reinforce workers' behaviors. An employee suggestion program brought in 4412 money-making ideas in one year. The average payment by the company (reinforcer) was $300. Hyatt Hotels' top managers wanted to learn firsthand what was rewarding about work in their hotels. All top managers spent one day changing

TABLE 13.4

Reinforcement Effects

Reinforcement Type	Stimulus	Response	Consequence or Reward
Positive reinforcement			
Application increases the likelihood that a desired behavior will be repeated.	Promotion will result from continued excellent performance.	Continued excellent performance	Promotion, salary increase, pat on the back
Avoidance			
Likelihood of desired behavior is increased by knowledge of consequence.	Reprimands will result from tardy behavior.	Punctuality	No reprimand
Punishment			
Application decreases the likelihood that an undesired behavior will be repeated.	Employee is reprimanded (suspended) for tardiness.	Cessation of tardiness	No further reprimands (suspensions)
Extinction			
Removal of any reinforcement to eliminate an undesired behavior.	Employee's constant gossiping is ignored.	Eventual let-up in gossip	Increased attention of co-workers and management

Source: From MANAGEMENT AND PERFORMANCE by Andrew D. Szilagyi. Copyright © 1984 by Scott, Foresman and Company. Reprinted by permission of HarperCollins Publishers.

positive reinforcement A technique that offers rewards to increase the likelihood that a desired behavior will be repeated.

avoidance An attempt to avoid unpleasant consequences by maintaining desired behaviors.

punishment A technique that attempts to discourage undesirable behavior by the application of negative consequences whenever it does occur.

extinction A technique that is actually an absence of any reinforcement, either positive or negative, following an incidence of undesired behavior.

sheets, pouring coffee, running elevators, and the like. President Darryl Hartley-Leonard worked as a doorman at the Hyatt in Chicago alongside the regular door captain. He refused to take tips at first, but fellow doormen quickly set him straight. In the end, aside from a sore back, Hartley-Leonard got positive reinforcement when his fellow doormen praised his work! Herb Kelleher, CEO of Southwest Airlines, works at least one day every three months as either a ticket agent, flight attendant, or baggage handler, to keep in touch with what rewards people really want from their jobs.[33]

Avoidance is the maintenance of desired behavior in order to escape or avoid the known unpleasant consequences. Some students come to class on time in order to avoid a reprimand from the instructor. Similarly, most employees learn not to abuse coffee breaks and lunch hours if this behavior incurs the disapproval of supervisors. In both cases people are acting to avoid the unpleasant results that are likely to follow undesired behavior. Unlike the other three, the avoidance technique is applied by the employee, not by the manager (organization).

Instead of encouraging desired behavior, managers can also try to discourage undesired behavior. **Punishment** is the application of negative consequences whenever undesired behavior occurs. The purpose of punishment is to decrease the likelihood that the individual will repeat the undesired behavior. For example, a manager may discipline an employee who comes to work late, neglects to clean up the work area, or turns out too many defective parts. The disciplinary action might take the form of a verbal reprimand, a monetary fine, a demotion, or, if the employee persists, a suspension—all with the intention of discouraging the behavior.

Extinction is the absence of any reinforcement, either positive or negative, following an incidence of undesired behavior. The theory is that if undesirable behavior is simply

TABLE 13.5

Schedules of Reinforcement

Type	Description	Example
Fixed interval	Reinforcement given at a fixed time, regardless of behavior.	Weekly, biweekly, or monthly paycheck
Variable interval	Reinforcement given at variable times, regardless of behavior.	Praise/criticism during random inspections
Fixed ratio	Reinforcement given after a fixed number of behaviors, regardless of time.	Sales commissions; pay for piece-rate work
Variable ratio	Reinforcement given after a variable number of behaviors, regardless of time.	Promotions

ignored, it will eventually cease. For example, the pedestrian who ignores the heckling of disruptive adolescents by walking past them, rather than arguing with them, is trying to stop the undesired behavior (heckling) through extinction.

Schedules of Reinforcement

The effectiveness of the reinforcement process in motivating employees depends not only on the type of reinforcement, but also on the frequency with which reinforcement is provided. Table 13.5 lists the four most commonly used schedules of reinforcement: fixed interval, variable interval, fixed ratio, and variable ratio. Depending on the circumstances, some will be more effective than others.

fixed interval schedule
Reinforcement schedule that provides reinforcement at fixed time intervals such as weekly or twice monthly.

The **fixed interval schedule** provides reinforcement at fixed time intervals—for example, a weekly, twice-monthly, or monthly paycheck. This type of reinforcement schedule provides the least immediate incentive for performing well. Employees know that they will be paid for a minimal level of desired behavior during that time interval.

variable interval schedule
Reinforcement schedule that provides reinforcement at irregular intervals of time.

A **variable interval schedule** provides reinforcement at irregular intervals of time. Inspection crews work on this type of schedule. If employees don't know when their manager is going to drop in, they will maintain a reasonably high level of desired behavior.

fixed ratio schedule
Reinforcement schedule that provides reinforcement after a fixed number of desired behaviors has occurred.

A **fixed ratio schedule** provides reinforcement after a fixed number of desired behaviors has occurred. Salespeople on commissions and workers on piece-rate systems operate under this type of schedule. Motivation is usually high as employees approach the point at which reinforcement is next due.

variable ratio schedule
Reinforcement schedule that provides reinforcement after a varying number of desired behaviors occurs during an unspecified amount of time.

A **variable ratio schedule** provides reinforcement after a varying number of desired behaviors occurs, regardless of the time elapsed. This is the most powerful type of reinforcement schedule for maintaining desired behaviors. Except for promotions, it is also the most difficult for managers to use effectively. Employees paid under this schedule wouldn't know when to expect the reinforcement (paycheck). They would have difficulty paying bills on time or planning a trip, because paychecks of various size would arrive at different times during the year. A manager who praises a salesperson after getting the third, fifth, tenth, and seventeenth orders is using a variable ratio schedule by varying the number of desired behaviors needed for reinforcement. (State lotteries and gambling casinos use this reinforcement system to keep people betting and playing the slot machines.)

In the following Insight about one of Union National Bank's incentive programs you should be able to identify the three basic principles of the reinforcement model: measurable behaviors, types of reinforcement, and schedules of reinforcement.

Union National Bank is a gleaming glass and white marble building in Little Rock, Arkansas. The bank has seventy-five individualized incentive programs for 70 percent of its 485 employees, from entry level clerks to senior vice presidents. In one year it paid $1 million in incentives. Spurred by several principles of reinforcement, employee productivity has increased 200–300 percent. Furthermore, the average net profit per employee has been $11,000 per year, compared with about half that amount at other Little Rock banks.

Because it operates in a competitive environment, Union National wanted to get maximum productivity out of a minimum number of employees. To accomplish that objective, it started by analyzing the behavior of clerks in the proof department. These employees encode a machine-readable number on the bottom of checks to prepare them for processing by computer. Accuracy and speed are essential. Uncoded checks cannot be credited to the bank's account and thus represent lost interest.

Before beginning the program, the bank made two promises: (1) no one will lose her or his job as a result of increased productivity, and (2) no one will make less money. For five weeks analysts collected data showing the number of checks each clerk processed each hour. During this period the average production was 1065 checks per hour. This was in line with the industry average of 900–1100 checks per hour. After management posted a weekly graph and praised high performers, production increased to 2100 checks per hour. When management later stopped posting the graph and praising employees, performance dropped to previous levels.

At that time top management decided to change the program slightly. In addition to reinstating the graph, it paid proof clerks a bonus on their daily output. This bonus was figured each day but paid at normal payroll times. In three months production had increased to 2800 checks per hour, the maximum rate for which incentive money was paid. Any production above this rate did not increase a clerk's pay. Management then raised the maximum to 3000 checks per hour, and production soon increased to this new level. Currently there is no maximum, and performance averages 3500 checks per hour, more than three times the rate before the program.

Turnover in the proof department was once a major problem for the bank. Before the incentive program, turnover was 110 percent; now it is close to 0 percent. Absenteeism fell from 4.24 percent to 2.23 percent. Overtime went from 475 hours a year to 13 hours, and savings from processing checks faster is about $100,000 a year.[34]

In designing its incentive program, Union National Bank applied five principles of reinforcement:[35]

1. *Positive reinforcement.* The bank uses two types of positive reinforcement—incentive bonuses and praise. Earning incentive bonuses and receiving praise from management provide strong extrinsic rewards.

2. *Immediacy.* To get maximum productivity, reinforcement must be immediate. The proof clerks' bonus earnings are figured on a daily basis and paid semimonthly.

3. *Contingency.* Rewards (positive reinforcement) should be contingent on performance level. The bank pays incentive bonuses only for specific, predefined work outputs. During a peak work period a proof clerk will earn more than during a slack period, and a highly productive clerk will earn more than an average one.

TABLE 13.6

Six Guidelines for Using Reinforcement Theory

Guideline	Comment
▶ Don't reward all individuals equally.	To be effective reinforcers, rewards should be based on performance. Rewarding everyone equally in effect reinforces poor or average performance and ignores high performance.
▶ Failure to respond can also modify behavior.	Managers influence their subordinates by what they do not do as well as by what they do. For example, failing to praise deserving subordinates may cause them to perform poorly the next time.
▶ Tell individuals what they can do to receive reinforcement.	Setting performance standards lets individuals know what they should do to be rewarded; they can then adjust their work patterns to get these rewards.
▶ Tell individuals what they are doing wrong.	If managers withhold rewards from subordinates without indicating why they are not being rewarded, the subordinates may be confused about what behaviors the manager finds undesirable. The subordinates may also feel that they are being manipulated.
▶ Don't punish in front of others.	Reprimanding subordinates might sometimes be a useful way of eliminating an undesirable behavior. Public reprimand, however, humiliates subordinates and may cause all the members of the work group to resent the manager.
▶ Be fair.	The consequences of a behavior should be appropriate for the behavior. Subordinates should be given the rewards they deserve. Failure to reward subordinates properly or overrewarding undeserving subordinates reduces the reinforcing effect of rewards.

Source: Adapted from W. Clay Hamner, ''Reinforcement Theory and Contingency Management in Organizational Settings.'' In Henry L. Tosi and W. Clay Hamner (eds.), *Organizational Behavior and Management: A Contingency Approach,* rev. ed. (New York: Wiley, 1977), 93–112.

4. *Individualization*. The bank's program is designed to reward individual performance. Thus low performers do not adversely affect high performers.

5. *Measure output, not process*. Reinforcement programs should focus on how much employees produce, not how they do it. The bank's incentive bonuses are based on specific, finished outputs.

Application by Managers W. Clay Hamner suggests six guidelines for managers to follow when using the reinforcement model. Table 13.6 lists these guidelines as well as comments on each one. A number of firms that use these guidelines—including Emery Air Freight, Michigan Bell, Standard Oil, General Electric, and Procter & Gamble—have reported encouraging results. According to their accounts, use of reinforcement principles results in major improvements in efficiency, cost savings, attendance, and productivity.

Although the reinforcement model has many positive features, managers should be aware of several problems.[36] First, the model may oversimplify behavior. It does not recognize individual characteristics, such as needs and values. Second, there may be too much emphasis on manipulating and controlling subordinates. Finally, with its heavy emphasis on external rewards, the model tends to ignore the fact that an increasing number of employees are motivated by the job itself.

CHAPTER SUMMARY

1. Motivation is any influence that causes, channels, or sustains employee behavior. Properly motivated, employees will perform efficiently and effectively. Without motivation, employees will find reasons to stay away from work and perform poorly when at work.

Three key variables affecting motivation are individual differences, job characteristics, and organizational practices.

Three general approaches to motivation are content approaches, which try to determine what needs people want to satisfy at work; process approaches, which emphasize how and why people choose certain behaviors and goals; and reinforcement approaches, which stress how past behaviors can influence future actions.

2. Maslow's hierarchy of needs is a content model of motivation. It identifies five categories of individual needs: physiological, security, affiliation, esteem, and self-actualization. People are motivated to satisfy these needs, according to their importance at specific times in their lives.

3. Herzberg's two-factor model is a content model, which states that factors in the work situation strongly influence performance. Motivator factors—including the challenge of the work itself, responsibility, recognition, achievement, and advancement and growth—are intrinsic to the job and can create high levels of motivation and satisfaction. Hygiene factors—such as reasonable working conditions, company policies, and benefits—are extrinsic to the job and relate to feelings of dissatisfaction with the job. These factors can hurt employee performance if not present but don't necessarily increase it when present.

   The job-enrichment model states that three critical psychological states—experienced meaningfulness, experienced responsibility, and knowledge of results—lead to high motivation and job satisfaction. Job characteristics—skill variety, task identity and significance, autonomy, and feedback—influence the critical psychological states differently.

   Employees will respond to job challenges differently. Those with high growth needs will seek jobs that meet their higher-level needs; those with low growth needs will focus on meeting their lower-level needs. Thus individuals with high growth needs are more likely to respond positively to job-enrichment programs than individuals with low growth needs.

4. The expectancy model is a process approach to motivation that states that people make conscious decisions about their own behavior and select a course of action because they expect a certain behavior to lead to a desired outcome.

   The Porter-Lawler expectancy model explains the motivational process in terms of value of reward, perceived effort reward, effort, abilities and traits, role perceptions, performance, rewards, perceived equitable reward, and satisfaction.

5. The equity model, also a process model of motivation, is based on the assumption that people want to be treated equitably. An equitable situation is one in which people with similar inputs experience similar outcomes. When inequities exist, people aren't satisfied, performance drops, and they then choose from among six action steps to reduce their inequity.

6. The reinforcement model suggests that behavior is a function of rewards and punishments. There are four types of reinforcement: Positive reinforcement offers rewards to encourage a desired behavior; avoidance attempts to avoid unpleasant consequences by maintaining a desired behavior; punishment applies negative consequences to discourage repetition of an undesired behavior; and extinction applies no reinforcement following (ignores) an undesired behavior. Managers can provide reinforcement at fixed or variable time intervals or according to fixed or variable ratio schedules.

QUESTIONS FOR DISCUSSION AND APPLICATION

1. **From Where You Sit:** Think about a job that you have held. How did the organization attempt to motivate you to achieve maximum performance?

2. **From Where You Sit:** If you realize that lower-level needs in Maslow's hierarchy are motivating you, what implications does that have for your behavior on the job?

3. Using Maslow's hierarchy, analyze the Avis program. What needs did this company satisfy?

4. What are the managerial implications of Herzberg's two-factor model?

5. Evaluate this statement: "A satisfied worker is a productive worker." Under what conditions will this be true or false?

6. What concepts did Volvo use to motivate its workers? Why can't other companies use the same principles?

7. **From Where You Sit:** Visit a local fast-food restaurant. How could you apply the job-enrichment model to motivating employees in this setting?

8. What does the Porter-Lawler expectancy model say that managers should do to improve employees' performance?

9. **From Where You Sit:** How can you use the equity model to determine your level of satisfaction with your grade in this course?

10. What reinforcement principles were used by Union National Bank to improve productivity?

11. **From Where You Sit:** How might your instructor motivate you if he or she decided to use the reinforcement model?

12. **From Where You Sit:** Why is it so difficult to motivate others? When is it difficult (or easy) to motivate yourself?

13. What are the similarities among content, process, reinforcement models of motivation? What are some major differences?

Work Motivation Questionnaire

This questionnaire is designed to assess the kinds of needs that are important to you. There are no right or wrong answers. The best response to any item is simply the one that best reflects your feelings—either as you have experienced them or as you anticipate you would experience them—in a work situation. Respond to the twenty statements by indicating the degree to which each is true for you. Using the following key, circle the letter that best indicates how true and accurate the statement is.

C = Completely true
M = Mostly true and accurate   S = Slightly true and accurate
P = Partly true and accurate   N = Not true and accurate

1. I believe that the real rewards for working are good pay, working conditions, and the like.

   C M P S N

2. This most important thing to me in evaluating a job is whether it gives me job security and employee benefits.

   C M P S N

3. I would not want a job in which I had no co-workers to talk with and share work stories.

   C M P S N

4. I want a job that allows rapid advancement based on my own achievements.

   C M P S N

5. Searching for what will make me happy is most important in my life.

   C M P S N

6. Working conditions (office space, equipment, and basic physical necessities) are important to me.

   C M P S N

7. I would not want a job if the equipment was poor or I was without adequate protection against layoffs.

   C M P S N

8. Whether the people were compatible would affect my decision about whether or not to take a promotion.

   C M P S N

9. A job should offer tangible rewards and recognition for one's performance.

   C M P S N

10. I want a job that is challenging and stimulating and has meaningful activities.

   C M P S N

11. If I took a job in which there were strong pressures to rush and little time for lunch, coffee breaks, and the like, my motivation would suffer.

   C M P S N

12. My motivation would suffer if my fellow employees were cold or held grudges toward me.

   C M P S N

13. Being a valued member of the team and enjoying the social aspects of work are important to me.

   C M P S N

14. I'm likely to work hardest in a situation where there are tangible rewards and recognition for one's performance.

   C M P S N

15. Going as far as I can, using my skills and capabilities, and exploring new ideas are what really drive me.   C M P S N

16. An important factor for me is that my job pays well enough to satisfy the needs of my family and me.   C M P S N

17. Fringe benefits, such as hospitalization insurance, retirement plans, and dental programs, are important to me.   C M P S N

18. I would likely work hardest in a job where a group of employees discuss and plan their work as a team.   C M P S N

19. My accomplishments give me an important sense of self-respect.   C M P S N

20. I would work the hardest in a job where I could see the returns of my work from the standpoint of personal interest and growth.   C M P S N

Scoring

Directions

In the table below, circle the number that corresponds to the letter you circled for each of the twenty statements.

1 C = 5 M = 4 P = 3 S = 2 N = 1	**2** C = 5 M = 4 P = 3 S = 2 N = 1	**3** C = 5 M = 4 P = 3 S = 2 N = 1	**4** C = 5 M = 4 P = 3 S = 2 N = 1	**5** C = 5 M = 4 P = 3 S = 2 N = 1
6 C = 5 M = 4 P = 3 S = 2 N = 1	**7** C = 5 M = 4 P = 3 S = 2 N = 1	**8** C = 5 M = 4 P = 3 S = 2 N = 1	**9** C = 5 M = 4 P = 3 S = 2 N = 1	**10** C = 5 M = 4 P = 3 S = 2 N = 1
11 C = 5 M = 4 P = 3 S = 2 N = 1	**12** C = 5 M = 4 P = 3 S = 2 N = 1	**13** C = 5 M = 4 P = 3 S = 2 N = 1	**14** C = 5 M = 4 P = 3 S = 2 N = 1	**15** C = 5 M = 4 P = 3 S = 2 N = 1
16 C = 5 M = 4 P = 3 S = 2 N = 1	**17** C = 5 M = 4 P = 3 S = 2 N = 1	**18** C = 5 M = 4 P = 3 S = 2 N = 1	**19** C = 5 M = 4 P = 3 S = 2 N = 1	**20** C = 5 M = 4 P = 3 S = 2 N = 1

Totals
Need
Motives

Basic creature comfort	Safety	Social or affiliation	Self-esteem	Self-actualization
___	___	___	___	___

Interpretation

For each of the five need motives, there is a minimum of 4 and a maximum of 20 points. Scores of 18 or more are quite high and suggest that the motives measured by that scale are very important to you. Scores from 13 to 17 suggest that the motives measured are moderately important to you. Scores from 9 to 12 suggest that the motives are not especially important to you. Scores below 9 are quite low and suggest that the motives measured are not at all important to you.

To: Joy Tsaras, Vice-President, Manufacturing
From: Bill Detwiler, Manager
        New Product Division
Re: Morale and turnover problem

We have been talking about ways to improve morale around here for more than a year, but nothing has happened. Good people are leaving. Just the other day, Cathy Cook, who was responsible for vendor relations, quit. At times she would work from 7:30 in the morning to 11:30 at night. People told her to slow down, but she said her job was so demanding she couldn't. Finally, her boyfriend got sick of the long hours and took off. Bonnie Stedt told me just the other day that she was working 12-hour days, Saturday mornings, and Sunday evenings. Although she doesn't expect others in her department to work that hard, few people even stop her to say "thanks" for her extra effort. According to our internal survey, almost 80% of our managers believe that they have to push themselves and their workers in order to compete more effectively internationally. In the same survey, 47% of our employees say that they want more responsibility.

Based on these and a lot of other comments, I recommend that we share a few ideas with our managers. First, we aren't all Lee Iacoccas, who can inspire workers to joyous and extraordinary effort by the sheer force of our personalities. We must therefore reward high-performing employees differently from lower-performing ones. Second, if we have to restructure, let's ask employees' ideas on how to go about it. I believe that people will work hard if they have a choice. Third, don't let work turn into an endurance contest. It's okay for people not to work on weekends.

Please let me know your thoughts on these three ideas.

Question: Assume that you are Joy Tsaras. What are some motivational problems that Bill Detwiler's memo have highlighted for you? Write a response to it.

Cutting Payrolls Without Axing Any Employees

BY UDAYAN GUPTA

Chopping employee costs is fast emerging as the major priority for many small businesses. But some are discovering that subtler measures—including moves to increase productivity—are healthier for a company than mere ax-wielding.

When her travel-agency business slowed late last year, Lois Eida thought she might have to lay off three of her five employees. But she discovered a way to scrape by—at least for now. She got New York state to subsidize her payroll through a so-called shared-work program. Under terms of the program, the employees work fewer hours—but the state will make up the difference in their take-home pay for as long as 20 weeks.

"I didn't have to lay off my employees," Ms. Eida says. "And I still get to have them until the business turns around." At least, she hopes for a turnaround before the benefits run out.

Managing employee costs has become one of the most important recession-busting strategies for small businesses. But many small firms say they can't simply slash payrolls the way big companies often do. After all, small companies tend not to have a lot of extra personnel to begin with, and each employee may play a crucial operating role. At Ms. Eida's New York travel agency, Lois Lane Travel, "we need the continuity of service that long-time employees provide," the entrepreneur adds.

Such strategies as the shared-work program, which currently is in place in more than a dozen states, are helping both employers and states cut costs, says Margaret Eighmey, a spokeswoman for New York state's labor department. . . .

Typically, small firms can qualify for shared-work programs if they can show their sales have dropped and they may have to lay off employees.

When business slowed down at Bardy's Diamond Center, a jewelry retailer in Greensboro, N.C., the company decided to seek help from Oechsli Institute, a Greensboro consulting firm, to make its sales personnel more productive.

Even though sales-per-employee at Bardy's had dropped, "we didn't want to let our salesmen go," says Terry Kahn, a Bardy's vice president. "We felt we couldn't rehire them when we really needed them." Like many other small-business

owners, Mr. Kahn thinks the recession will be short-lived—and thus doesn't warrant such drastic measures as layoffs.

As an alternative, Oechsli six months ago created a "buddy system," pairing up employees. Pair members became accountable to the other for their performance; Oechsli says that helped Bardy's because employees working in pairs set more-realistic goals and missed fewer days of work. (Employees are more willing to be prodded by peers than by supervisors, Oechsli says.) As a result, Bardy's sales have picked up, and it is performing better than most other jewelers in the area, which are reporting double-digit declines in sales, Mr. Kahn says. . . .

Other companies are trying to hold the line on employee costs by "renting" professionals instead of hiring them full-time. Small companies all want flexibility to match payroll size with the volume of business they do, says John Thompson, chief executive officer of Interim Management Corp., a New York concern that specializes in recruiting and placing professionals for short-term assignments. Many small firms are trying to stay flexible by hiring professionals for the short term, he says.

When a small New York apparel company, in the midst of a sales slump, wanted to reorganize its business, it hired a temporary general manager, Mr. Thompson says. To put its house in order, the company needed someone from the outside who was familiar with cost-control methods in other manufacturing businesses, he explains. Within seven months, the executive had established new reporting methods, reduced costs—and departed. The apparel company, which Mr. Thompson didn't identify, thus managed to get a full-time professional for the short term without investing the large sums of money each permanent hire requires. Mr. Thompson says the company "had to pay out less in benefits, and there also was less tumult."

Small businesses are discovering it is better to pull back and conserve resources now than to risk losing everything, says Abraham Getzler, a New York management consultant. "They know that every dollar they save will help them survive," he says. "They can more than get it back when the economy turns up."

1. What effect might a mandatory shared-work program have on employee motivation?
2. Discuss the Oechsli Institute's "buddy system" in terms of Maslow's hierarchy.
3. Assume you are a branch office manager and have just been told by your main office to reduce payroll costs. Formulate a program that would keep employees motivated and enable you to cut your payroll at the same time.

MOTIVATIONAL SECRETS OF TOMMY LASORDA

Tommy Lasorda, manager of the Los Angeles Dodgers, has been called "the master motivator." He has been named the National League's Manager of the Year twice, and over the past decade has led the Dodgers to two world championships. *Fortune's* Associate Editor Brian Dumaine recently interviewed Lasorda. Here are his tips on motivating people.

First, I want my players to know that I appreciate what they do for me. I want them to know that I depend on them. A good leader is someone who's in front, but not so far ahead that he can't hear their footsteps.

Second, you have to talk to them. I take them out and work with them. I believe in hugging or patting my players on the back when they do something well. Just because they're making millions of dollars, doesn't mean that they're motivated. Everybody needs to be motivated.

Third, when I come into this clubhouse, if I'm dejected and depressed and my players see me that way, what's the attitude and the atmosphere of the clubhouse going to be? If I walk in full of enthusiasm, self-confidence, and proud to be putting that uniform on, that's contagious.

Fourth, you gotta get players believing in themselves and having fun. People have to enjoy themselves.

Fifth, I can remember once when a player wanted to talk to me about his lack of playing. If I told him that it's because you don't do this or that, what have I done for him? Now tomorrow I've got to put the same guy in the lineup which I just told can't do this or that. So, I don't tell him he can't do this or that. I just tell him that right now, I'm playing what I think are the best nine guys on this team.

Sixth, even when a guy fails, I try to give him a mental picture that he's going to get a base hit the next time at bat. I try to put positive pictures in the minds of my players.

Seventh, loyalty is very important. Loyalty means that you give in return what is given to you. Good leaders should know everyone's name and ask if there is anything that they can do to make their subordinates' life easier. That's how you get loyalty and good performance.

1. Using Maslow's hierarchy of needs, analyze Lasorda's motivational system.
2. How does Lasorda use the equity model to motivate his players?
3. What roles do the principles of reinforcement play in Lasorda's motivational style?
4. If you could, would you like to play for this type of manager? Why?

Chapter 14

THE DYNAMICS OF

LEADERSHIP

Max DePree

What You Will Learn

1   Five core skills of effective leaders.

2   Where leaders get power and how they use it effectively.

3   The traits successful leaders theoretically possess.

4   Three behavioral models of leadership.

5   Four contingency models of leadership and the situational factors that influence a leader's effectiveness.

6   Who transformational leaders are and how they motivate others.

7   **Skill Development:** How to fit the right leadership style to a given situation.

The Art of Leadership at Herman Miller Company

A young woman who works on the assembly line shows up in the president's office—mad. Not only does she get in to see the president, but he sits there and listens to what she has to say. She complains that two workers were unjustly fired and says she thinks the president should know about it and rehire them.

At most American companies this employee wouldn't have gotten past the security guards, let alone into the office of the president. But at Herman Miller, an $800 million office furniture manufacturer, this is standard practice. Herman Miller ranks ninth in *Fortune's* survey of America's most admired organizations and sixth in terms of management excellence by those who know the industry.

At the heart of Herman Miller's management is a system of fairness, trust, and cooperation between managers and workers. For example, in the event of a hostile takeover by a corporate raider, all workers who lost their jobs would receive checks similar to the ''golden parachutes'' of top management. And when employees are hired, managers often focus more on their character and ability to get along with others than on what they have done in prior jobs.

All employees are organized into work teams. The team leader evaluates team members every six months. The work team also evaluates its leader. In fact, work teams *elect* their leaders, who also discuss production shifts and grievances with supervisors when needed. And if workers don't like what they hear from their supervisor, they can go directly up to the next management level.

Top management at Herman Miller takes great pains to avoid authoritarian leadership practices and other habits that could erode team feelings of trust and cooperation. Max DePree, the company's chairman, has even written a book, *Leadership Is an Art,* in which he warns leaders to watch out for poor management practices—such as not taking the time to go to retirement parties or becoming more concerned with status symbols than with people. Does such an effort mean poor profits? Not at all.[1]

leadership The ability to influence, motivate, and direct others in order to attain desired objectives.

Leading is different from managing. Managing focuses on bringing order and consistency to the organization. This includes planning, organizing, staffing, budgeting, controlling, and setting quality goals. **Leadership** is the ability to influence, motivate, and direct others in order to attain desired objectives.[2] According to management consultant David Fearon, ''leadership isn't just a single act, but a flow of many acts of leading and following.'' Effective leaders work with subordinates and co-workers to create visions and strategies as means to achieve the organization's goals.

And being an effective leader doesn't always mean being a manager. At Herman Miller, Federal Express, General Mills, and many other companies, teams of workers select their own leaders, and it's these team leaders (not managers) who take on the leadership roles. Federal Express has been particularly successful in using teams to help it increase its productivity. FedEx organized its 1000 clerical employees into teams of five to ten and gave each team the training and authority to manage themselves. Each team elected its own team leader. With the help of these teams, the company cut services glitches, such as incorrect bills and lost packages, by more than 13 percent. In one year the teams' ideas saved the company more than $2 million.[3]

In this chapter we begin by examining the basics of leadership, including the skills, motivations, and behaviors that underlie effective leadership. Then we introduce three types of models—based on traits, behaviors, and situations—to help you predict which leadership style will be most effective in a given situation. We conclude the chapter with a look at a new type of leader for the 1990s—the transformational leader.

Dynamics of leadership

The bare-bones basics of leadership include a leader, a follower or followers, and a specific situation. Leadership occurs only when someone *influences* others to act. Over the long run, a leader can't simply threaten or coerce people into complying. The exchange between leader and team must satisfy both parties. This is one of the reasons why Herman Miller has been so successful. By electing their leader, group members *voluntarily* agree to accept that person's direction. They will permit the leader to make decisions that affect them in specific situations.

Quite a bit can be learned about the conditions for successful leadership from the experiences of Herman Miller, Federal Express, and other organizations. First, a mutual trust must be established between followers and leaders. Giving employees more freedom to act autonomously and make decisions is a necessary first step. Second, leaders must do their homework. Others will follow a lot more willingly if they are confident that the leader knows at least as much as they do. John Sculley found this out when he came to Apple Computer from PepsiCo in 1983. Apple employees were at first suspicious of Sculley because of his lack of technical background. It was only after he learned the business that others gained confidence in his decisions. Third, effective leaders encourage others to take risks. If a project fails, the person's career shouldn't be derailed. According to Frederick Smith, founder of Federal Express, "fear of failure must never be a reason not to try something different."[4]

Core Leadership Skills

Now we can turn our attention to some of the core leadership skills that effective leaders have learned from their experiences. These skills are emphasized throughout the text in the Experiencing Management sections and in the Complete Manager computer simulation game.

Leaders come from many different backgrounds. And successful organizations don't always wait for leaders to come along. They tend to seek out people with potential leadership skills and expose them to experiences designed to develop that potential. If

MBA students at the University of Chicago participate in an Outward Bound program that builds *leadership and teamwork* by requiring the support of fellow students.

FIGURE 14.1

Core Leadership Skills

Empowerment, intuition, self-understanding, vision, and value congruence are the five core leadership skills that most effective leaders possess.

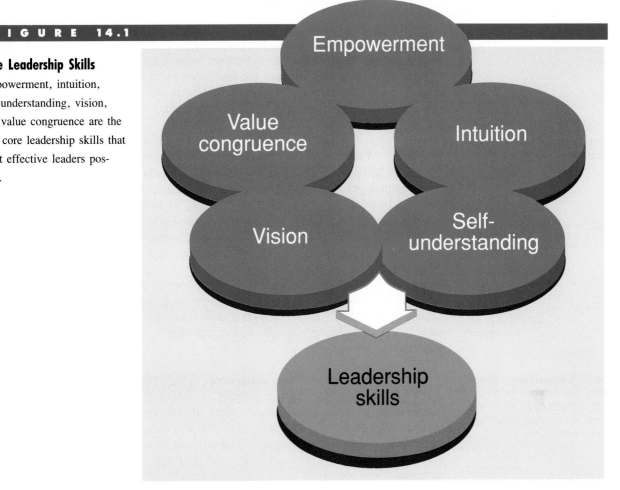

you're aware of the basic skills organizations look for in leaders, you can start developing them in this course. Figure 14.1 shows five core skills possessed by effective leaders: (1) empowerment, (2) intuition, (3) self-understanding, (4) vision, and (5) value congruence.[5] In Chapter 1 we suggested that conceptual, interpersonal, technical, and communication skills were essential for managing. These skills, however, aren't sufficient for effective leadership. They simply provide the foundation for a leader's core skills.

Empowerment **Empowerment** occurs when a leader shares influence and control with followers. In doing so, the leader involves team members in deciding how to achieve the organization's goals, thus giving them a sense of commitment and self-control. Empowerment satisfies basic human needs for achievement, a sense of belonging, and self-esteem and enables team members to live up to their potential. When employees have these positive feelings about their work, the work itself becomes stimulating and interesting, and the leader has done a good job.

Intuition The abilities to scan a situation, anticipate changes, take risks, and build trust are all facets of **intuition.** Good leaders have an intuitive feel for changes that will occur around them. They move quickly in serving new customers, they find new competitive advantages, and they exploit company strengths. When he founded Wal-Mart, Sam Walton followed his intuition that the United States needed a low-cost retailer with a great distribution system.

Self-understanding **Self-understanding** is the ability to recognize one's strengths and compensate for one's weaknesses. Corporations that have done a good job at developing leaders—such as Johnson & Johnson, 3M, Hewlett-Packard, and

empowerment Being able to share influence and control with followers.

intuition The abilities to scan a situation, anticipate changes, take risks, and build trust.

self-understanding Being able to recognize one's strengths and compensate for one's weaknesses.

General Electric—put an emphasis on creating challenging opportunities for young management employees. These opportunities give the employees chances to stretch and develop the skills they need to become better leaders. According to James Burke at Johnson & Johnson, "leaders are developed by challenges." Leaders at General Electric receive peer performance appraisals that provide feedback in areas such as delegating decisions and setting clear priorities. This feedback becomes the basis for increasing self-understanding.

vision Being able to imagine a different and better situation and ways to achieve it.

Vision **Vision** is the ability to imagine a different and better situation and ways to achieve it. Jan Carlzon, CEO of Scandinavian Airline Systems (SAS), has vision. He imagined—envisioned—SAS as the best airline in the world for the frequent business traveler. Since employees are likely to make a strong commitment to a vision when they are actively involved in realizing it, Carlzon invited all employees to suggest improvements that would help SAS achieve his vision.

Having vision doesn't always mean imagining a new, original goal. Vision is often evident in a simple, realistic corporate strategy that serves the interests of important groups, such as customers, employees, and stockholders. Ray Kroc, founder of McDonald's, incorporated vision in his company motto, "quality, service, cleanliness & value." He repeated this motto to employees for the rest of his life. Its success lies in its being a simple vision, one that employees can identify with and implement.

value congruence Being able to understand the organization's guiding principles and employees' values and reconcile the two.

Value Congruence **Value congruence** is the ability to understand the organization's guiding principles and employees' values and reconcile the two. Copeland Corporation, an Ohio-based manufacturer of refrigerator and air-conditioner compressors, was on the verge of being shut down by disagreements between employees and management. The organization's beliefs and its employees' values were out of sync. Top management was autocratic, and the employees wanted to make decisions as teams. Only after both union and management groups jointly decided on an approach to turn the company around was the company saved. Shop-floor quality teams composed of supervisors, technicians, and union members now make decisions that reflect both management and employee concerns.

All five leadership skills shown in Figure 14.1 are evident in this chapter's Global Link feature. We have put the skills in brackets to highlight them.

Motivations to Lead

No one can be forced to assume a leadership position against his or her will. Those who don't want to become leaders usually don't. Employees often turn down promotions because they simply aren't motivated to become leaders in the job situation, although they may take leadership roles in other arenas—clubs, or local politics. Others view a leadership role at work as a challenge and opportunity and thus seek it out. What motivates people to lead?

Extrinsic Rewards Leadership can provide substantial extrinsic rewards, particularly in the form of salary, bonuses, and stock options.[6] As we mentioned in Chapter 13, many companies, including Lincoln Electric, have introduced gain-sharing plans in which employees are paid bonuses if their departments reach certain performance targets. Team leaders in these companies are usually paid more than team members in recognition of their skills in planning, organizing, scheduling, and resolving conflicts. At Chicago Title Company, for instance, a salesperson makes around $28,000 a year, and this person's immediate supervisor earns around $60,000 a year. A general rule of thumb is that CEOs earn about 85 times as much as entry level employees.

GLOBAL Link

BRITISH CEOs AS EFFECTIVE LEADERS

Charles J. Cox and Cary L. Cooper of the University of Manchester conducted interviews with forty-five chief executives of major British companies. Each company had over a thousand employees and a successful financial record. The purpose of the study was to learn more about the leadership skills of successful British managers. Like so many similar studies, this one found a great range of skills among the executives interviewed. Nevertheless, Cox and Cooper found that successful British leaders share several characteristics and skills, including the following:

▶ *Achievement and ambition.* These leaders are all ambitious people, showing a high need to achieve and strong determination. They have a positive approach to life and a high level of self-confidence; they believe that they're in charge of their own lives. [self-understanding]

▶ *Ability to learn from adversity.* Most of the CEOs interviewed have experienced setbacks and problems during their careers. They've taken advantage of these as opportunities for learning and development. [self-understanding]

▶ *High dedication to the job.* All of the CEOs work very long hours (60–70 a week). They regard their job as the most important element of their lives. [self-understanding]

▶ *Sound analytical and problem-solving skills.* These CEOs demonstrate the abilities to analyze a problem and to find an effective solution. These skills involve having clear objectives, the energy and commitment to achieve them, and the willingness to take calculated risks. This process is both creative and rational. [intuition]

▶ *High level of people skills.* All of these top managers achieve their organizational objectives through other people. They operate in an open and consultative style. When necessary, however, they can be forceful. [empowerment]

▶ *High level of innovation.* When making changes, these leaders are not constrained by the existing system. They challenge established procedures and assumptions. Thus they produce something new rather than a modification of what currently exists. [vision]

Source: Adapted from C. J. Cox and G. L. Cooper, ''The Making of the British CEO: Childhood, Work Experience, Personality and Management Style,'' *Academy of Management Executive,* 1989, 3:241–247. For a study of American CEOs, see D. L. Kurtz, L. E. Boone, and C. P. Fleenor, *CEO: Who Gets to the Top in America* (East Lansing, Mich.: Michigan State University Press, 1989); C. J. Russell, ''Selecting Top Corporate Leaders: An Example of Biographical Information,'' *Journal of Management,* 1990, 16:73–86.

Intrinsic Rewards Leadership is often sought even when it carries no monetary rewards. For example, the softball team captain, United Way chairperson, church leader, and PTA president willingly occupy these leadership positions even though they receive no pay. Why? Because they can satisfy some of their esteem and self-actualization needs through leadership roles.

Followers also help leaders to satisfy some of these needs. The leader receives rewards from the group, just as group members receive rewards from the leader. Intrinsic rewards of leadership include the knowledge that leaders can affect the lives of others as well as their own lives. To remain in a leadership position, the leader must help group members gain satisfactions that are otherwise beyond their reach.

Bases of Power

power The ability to make things happen the way one wants them to happen.

The motivation to lead and the core leadership skills won't necessarily produce a leader. **Power,** the ability to make things happen the way one wants them to happen, is central to leadership. An effective leader must have power and know how to use it wisely. The bases of a leader's power tell us a great deal about why others follow him or her. One of the most useful frameworks for understanding the power of leaders was developed by John French and Bertram Raven. They identified five types of power: legitimate, reward, coercive, referent, and expert.[7]

legitimate power Type of power based on a leader's formal position in the organization's hierarchy.

Legitimate Power Power based on the leader's formal position in the organization's hierarchy is **legitimate power.** In deciding on new directions for the Fort Worth Museum of Science and History, Director Don Otto has greater legitimate power than the museum's curator of science. In allocating funds for capital expenditures, scheduling overtime, and setting inventory levels, the curator of science has more legitimate power than a science instructor reporting to her.

reward power A type of power based on a leader's ability to reward followers.

Reward Power **Reward power** is power that stems from a leader's ability to reward followers. In other words, employees follow their supervisor's requests in the belief that their behavior will be rewarded. The supervisor may be able to reward them through more favorable job assignments, preferred vacation schedules, promotions, and/or pay increases.

coercive power A type of power based on followers' fear of punishment by the leader.

Coercive Power The ability of the leader to obtain compliance through fear of punishment is **coercive power.** Punishment may take the form of official reprimands, less desirable work assignments, pay cuts, demotions, suspensions, or termination. A manager who says ''I want these appliances shipped by June 15th or heads will roll'' is using coercion. Coercive power may be less effective than, say, reward power for the same reasons that punishment isn't a good motivator (see Chapter 13). Some workers respond to coercion by falsifying performance reports, stealing company property, and similar negative behavior, rather than by improving their performance.

referent power A type of power based on followers' personal identification with the leader.

Referent Power A power based on followers' personal identification with the leader is **referent power.** The followers are likely to have a personal liking and admiration for the leader and a desire to be like her or him. Referent power is usually possessed by leaders with admirable personal characteristics, charisma, or excellent reputations.

expert power A type of power based on a leader's specialized knowledge.

Expert Power **Expert power** is power based on a leader's specialized knowledge. This is a key source of power for managers in the 1990s. Drew Lewis, chairman of Union Pacific, has built his career on financial expertise. In the 1970s he helped rescue a group of Eastern railroads by forming Conrail. As chairman of Warner Communications, he renegotiated major cable contracts, greatly reducing the company's huge financial losses. Then he restructured and streamlined Union Pacific, a big railroad with diverse other business holdings. Expert power can be narrow in scope, however, since a leader's expertise is often limited to specific areas. For instance, Steven Jobs, co-founder of Apple Computer, was a computer genius, but he lacked the necessary organizational skills to run Apple when it became large and successful.

Leaders will use all five types of power at different times. Effectiveness as a leader comes from knowing which type or combination to use in each situation.

Role of Team Members

Power also comes, as we have implied, from team members' willingness to follow the leader's direction and the leader's ability to satisfy team members' needs.

Access to resources, information, and key decision makers gives some leaders an edge in influencing events and passing on information and rewards to subordinates. Such leaders are said to have clout.[8] **Clout** is someone's pull or political influence within an organization. These are some common examples of what clout can do:

clout   Pull or political influence within an organization.

▶ Get a good job for a talented employee
▶ Obtain approval for expenditures beyond the budget
▶ Get above-average salary increases for subordinates
▶ Gain easy access to top people in the company
▶ Find out early about important decisions and policy shifts

Power is most easily gained when a leader's job includes freedom to make decisions, results in recognition (visibility and notice), and is relevant (central to major organizational problems and issues). Bella Goren, manager of domestic yield at American Airlines, is a leader with clout. She has gotten her subordinates better-than-average raises and has been assigned to important task forces that report to a senior vice president. Her department is responsible for finding ways to increase the number of passengers on each flight, a key success factor closely watched by Bob Crandall, American's president. Power is also strengthened through being plugged into peer networks. These networks provide information faster than formal systems of communication.

The leader's use of different types of power or clout can lead to one of three types of behavior in team members: commitment, compliance, or resistance.[9] Committed subordinates are enthusiastic about carrying out their manager's expectations and make a maximum effort to do so. On the other hand, subordinates who merely comply with their leader's requests will do only what has to be done—usually without much enthusiasm. In most cases, resistance by subordinates will be expressed as pretending to respond to their manager's requests or even intentionally delaying or sabotaging plans. As Table 14.1 shows, expert and referent power tend to result in subordinate commitment; legitimate and reward power tend to result in compliance; coercive power tends to result in resistance.

TABLE 14.1

Types of Leader Power and Resulting Behavior of Subordinates

Power Type	Commitment	Compliance	Resistance
Legitimate	Possible	Likely	Possible
Reward	Possible	Likely	Possible
Coercive	Unlikely	Possible	Likely
Referent	Likely	Possible	Possible
Expert	Likely	Possible	Possible

Source: Adapted from G. A. Yukl, *Leadership in Organizations,* 2nd ed. (Englewood Cliffs, N.J.: Prentice-Hall, 1989), 44.

Highly motivated subordinates usually perform tasks better than unmotivated ones. The motivation generated by expert and referent power usually leads to high levels of performance. Effective leaders are thus likely to rely on expert, referent, and reward power. They use legitimate and coercive sources of power only minimally. Legitimate power is effective when a leader simply requires that an employee perform a task that is within the employee's capabilities and job description. In some situations coercive power may be effective in getting subordinates to comply with rules, as indicated in Chapter 13. In general, however, when leaders threaten or punish, they get back a lot of anger from others.

Power is changing within organizations because the structure of organizations is changing. Peter Drucker, author of *The New Realities,* predicts that employees in the so-called knowledge-based organizations (such as AT&T, MCI, IBM, NEC, and Xerox) will not put up with just being told what to do.[10] Managers in these organizations have found that real power comes from inspiring commitment.

Delegating decision making to those who are positioned to make things happen gets team members committed. One organization that has taken this new view of power to heart is Johnsonville Foods. This relatively small, but rapidly growing specialty foods and sausage maker in Sheboygan, Wisconsin was discussed in Chapter 13. The following Insight provides clues on how that organization's management uses power to get employees committed.

EMPOWERING EMPLOYEES AT JOHNSONVILLE FOODS

I NSIGHT Ralph Stayer, CEO of Johnsonville Foods, sees his job as resembling that of an orchestra conductor. He has to get his employees working in harmony, committed to the organization's objectives.

As part of Stayer's effort to empower employees, Johnsonville has no human resources department. Instead, it has its Personnel Development and Lifelong Learning Development. Employees meet with counselors who help them develop their personal goals, such as putting a child through college or learning sign language so they can communicate with deaf employees more effectively. And each employee receives a small allowance to spend on a personal growth project.

Business-wise, if a team wants a new machine, members work out the finances for the new equipment and present them to management. This process is in line with Stayer's desire for objectives to be set as far down in the organization as possible. When a customer demands special service, every sales representative has the power to offer it. This allows top management's time to be devoted to choosing which goals to fund for the overall good of the company.[11]

Approaches to Understanding Leadership

For years researchers in the behavioral sciences have tried to discern why some people are successful leaders and others aren't. If there were a simple answer, all leaders would be successful. Because there *isn't* a simple answer, there are libraries full of books and articles on the topic. The following sections look at three basic theoretical approaches to leadership: traits models, which focus on the personal characteristics of leaders; behavioral models, which concentrate on leaders' behaviors; and contingency models, which examine the relationship between the situation and a leader's behavior. Each model uses a different set of factors to describe and predict what styles of leadership are most effective.

Johnsonville Foods CEO Ralph Stayer (second from left) *empowers* shop-floor employees by getting them to help forge corporate strategy.

TRAITS MODELS

traits models Theories of leadership based on the assumption that certain physical, social, and personal characteristics are inherent in leaders.

Many early studies of leadership were directed at identifying personal traits of leaders. **Traits models** are based on the assumption that certain physical, social, and personal characteristics are inherent in leaders. According to this view, the presence or absence of these characteristics distinguishes leaders from nonleaders. These are some of the key traits commonly identified with leaders:

Physical: young to middle-aged, energetic, striking appearance, tall, slender
Social background: educated at the right schools, socially prominent or upwardly mobile
Personality: adaptable, aggressive, emotionally stable, dominant, self-confident
Social characteristics: charming, tactful, popular, cooperative
Task-related characteristics: driven to excel, acceptant of responsibility, full of initiative, results-oriented

There is some common-sense support for the notion that effective leaders have certain interests, interpersonal skills, and personality traits.[12] However, traits models generally aren't very helpful in understanding leadership. Research hasn't proved that traits consistently separate potential leaders from nonleaders. This doesn't mean that certain traits have nothing to do with effective leadership. It simply means that traits must be evaluated in relation to other factors, such as the situation and team members' needs.

Limitations

The major limitations of traits models are that they focus so much on physical and personality characteristics. Physical characteristics do not correlate with successful leadership; they are only related to *perceived* leadership ability. Physical characteristics may be helpful in the physical performance of some jobs (such as in the police or the military), but effective leadership rarely depends on a person's height, strength, or weight.

Although some personality traits have been linked to effective leadership, results aren't consistent. For example, personality traits found to relate to a sales manager's effectiveness include gregariousness, risk taking, impulsiveness, exhibitionism, and egocentrism. On the other hand, these traits are not commonly found among successful coaches of sports teams. Their personality traits usually include self-assertion, self-assurance, a strong need for power, and a low need for security. And there are successful sales managers and coaches who have personality profiles completely different from those mentioned.[13]

Organizational Implications

Despite these limitations, traits models shouldn't be dismissed too hastily. For one thing, leadership may depend heavily on social characteristics. Leaders are likely to have a high level of social skills: including communication, problem solving, and negotiation. That is, they are socially assertive but in a positive way. They tend to have more energy than others and are a little smarter, but not outright geniuses. (Geniuses often have a difficult time communicating with the rest of us.) Although none of these traits is absolutely necessary, each can help individuals perform in leadership roles.

BEHAVIORAL MODELS

behavioral models
Theories of leadership that focus on differences in the actions (behaviors) of effective and ineffective leaders.

Once it was determined that leaders do not have a uniform set of personal traits, researchers turned their attention to trying to isolate the behaviors characteristic of effective leaders. **Behavioral models** of leadership focus on differences in the actions of effective and ineffective leaders. In other words, they look at what effective and less effective leaders actually do: how they delegate tasks to subordinates, where and when they communicate to others, how they perform their roles, and so on. Unlike traits, behaviors can be seen and learned. If behaviors can be learned, then individuals can be trained to lead more effectively.

Theory X and Theory Y

Assumptions and beliefs about team members and how to motivate them often influence a leader's behavior. Table 14.2 lists two contrasting sets of assumptions held by leaders about their team members. These sets of assumptions are called Theory X and Theory Y.[14]

Theory X A set of negative assumptions about team members that leads to a directive leadership style.

Managers who believe that team members are motivated mainly by money, are lazy and uncooperative, and have poor work habits will treat them accordingly. Such managers tend to use a directive leadership style: They tell people what to do. They lead by telling their subordinates what's expected of them, instructing them how to perform their job, insisting that they meet certain standards, and making sure that everyone knows who's boss. Douglas McGregor, author of *The Human Side of the Enterprise,* labeled this leadership style **Theory X.**

On the other hand, leaders who believe that their people are hard-working and cooperative and have positive work habits will treat them accordingly. Such leaders use a

TABLE 14.2

Comparison of Theory X and Theory Y Assumptions

Assumptions of Theory X		*Assumptions of Theory Y*
▶ The typical employee dislikes work and will avoid it if possible. ▶ Employees want direction whenever possible. ▶ Managers must coerce employees (threaten them with punishment) to get them to work.	**versus**	▶ People like to work. ▶ Employees who are committed to the company's objectives will exercise self-direction and self-control. ▶ Employees learn to accept and even seek responsibility at work.

Theory Y A set of positive assumptions about team members that leads to a participative leadership style.

participative leadership style: They act by consulting their subordinates, requesting their opinions, and encouraging them to take part in planning and decision making. According to McGregor, these leaders practice **Theory Y.** By and large, it's clear that employees prefer Theory Y because of the opportunities to get involved in the decision-making process that these leaders afford them.

Since 1980 *Fortune* magazine has conducted a poll to determine who are America's toughest bosses. The "toughest" boss is defined as the leader who is demanding, unrelenting, stubborn, impatient, and generally hard to please. An effective tough boss pushes team members to their limits, but an ineffective tough boss pushes them for minor results. People often find that when they get fired by such a leader, it comes as a relief. The following Insight looks at two of the bosses who made one of these *Fortune* lists: Hugh McColl, chairman of North Carolina National Bank (NCNB) Corporation, and Robert Crandall, chairman of American Airlines. Both of these effective leaders practice Theory X more than Theory Y.

I N S I G H T

According to those who know Chairman Hugh McColl, there's no place for individuals at North Carolina National Bank (NCNB). It's a team-driven bank—the key word being *driven*. McColl expects Herculean efforts from his people all the time. There's no golf in the middle of the day with clients or coasting to retirement. He believes that if managers are not leading, they should be fired. McColl looks for people who are able to conform to the bank's ways of doing things. He's often seen walking the halls and breathing down subordinates' necks. He never seems to rest, and he expects others to move just as fast as he does. Subordinates at the bank see McColl as leading with aggressiveness and perfection. He causes tension and expects subordinates to manage under it.

The chairman of American Airlines, Robert Crandall, is a bear for detail. A former subordinate once said that Crandall has a fear that someone will ask him a question he can't answer. So he endlessly probes, challenges, and questions subordinates. Everything is either black or white. Crandall is famous for his budget reviews. Although American averages more than 2500 flights a day, he's been known to sit down with managers who oversee a few cities that handle only several flights a day and go through their financial budgets, line by line. His willingness to look at the tiniest details plus his extensive knowledge put great pressure on his top managers to treat their subordinates similarly. Crandall often totally dominates meetings—which may be eight hours long, without a break—with a mixture of energy, swearing, and bluff.[15]

Ohio State and University of Michigan Models

Researchers at Ohio State University took another approach to studying leadership styles. They asked employees to describe the behaviors of their supervisors. Based on the responses, the researchers identified two leadership styles: considerate and initiating-structure.[16]

considerate leadership style Leadership style identified by the Ohio State model and characterized by concern for employees' well-being, status, and comfort.

A **considerate leadership style** is characterized by concern for employees' well-being, status, and comfort. A considerate leader seeks to create a friendly and pleasant working climate. Such a leader assumes that subordinates want to do their best and that his or her job is to make it easier for them to do theirs. A considerate leader seeks acceptance by treating subordinates with respect and dignity and tends to downplay the use of both legitimate power and coercive power. Max DePree practices this style at Herman Miller.

Robert Crandall, CEO of American Airlines, uses the *initiating-structure leadership style*.

initiating-structure leadership style Leadership style identified by the Ohio State model and characterized by active planning, organizing, controlling, and coordinating of subordinates' activities.

production-centered leadership style Leadership style identified by the University of Michigan model and characterized by setting standards, organizing and paying close attention to employees' work, and interest in results.

employee-centered leadership style Leadership style identified by the University of Michigan model and characterized by encouraging employees to participate in decision making and making sure they are satisfied with their work.

managerial grid model A behavioral model of leadership that identifies five leadership styles that combine differing proportions of concern for production and concern for people.

Typical behaviors of a considerate leader include:

▶ Expressing appreciation when employees do a good job
▶ Not demanding more than employees can achieve
▶ Helping employees with their personal problems
▶ Being friendly and accessible
▶ Rewarding employees for jobs well done

It should come as no surprise that the considerate leadership style is usually readily accepted by subordinates. Advocates contend that this style of leadership generates good will and leads to high job satisfaction on the part of team members. Other positive outcomes include closer cooperation between leaders and subordinates, increased motivation of subordinates, more productive work groups, and low turnover and grievance rates.

The **initiating-structure leadership style** is characterized by active planning, organizing, controlling, and coordinating of subordinates' activities. In addition to accepting the assumptions of Theory X, both Hugh McColl and Robert Crandall use this style of leadership. Typical behaviors of an initiating-structure leader include:

▶ Assigning employees to particular tasks
▶ Establishing standards of job performance
▶ Informing employees of job requirements
▶ Scheduling work to be done by team members
▶ Encouraging the use of uniform procedures

As you might expect, leaders who were rated high in initiating structure had higher employee grievance and turnover rates and lower employee satisfaction than leaders rated high in consideration did. Current research suggests that effective leaders exhibit both considerate and initiating-structure behaviors. Employees' reactions to initiating-structure leaders depended on whether they also believed that the leaders were considerate. If so, their behavior was viewed as effective. If these leaders were believed inconsiderate, however, subordinates viewed their behavior as "watching over employees' shoulders."[17]

Similar studies of leadership behavior were undertaken by researchers at the University of Michigan. They classified leaders' behaviors as either production-centered or employee-centered. Leaders who follow a **production-centered leadership style** set standards, organize and pay close attention to employees' work, and are very interested in results. Those who have an **employee-centered leadership style** encourage employees to participate in making decisions and make sure they are satisfied with their work. This type of leader's primary concern is with the welfare of team members. The researchers found that employee-centered leaders were more likely to be in charge of high-performing teams than were production-centered managers. More effective leaders were those who had supportive relationships with their team members and encouraged them to set and achieve their own high-performance objectives.[18]

Managerial Grid Model

The **managerial grid model,** developed by Blake and Mouton, identifies five styles that combine differing proportions of concern for production (similar to initiating-structure and production-centered styles) and concern for people (similar to consideration and employee-centered styles).[19] These styles are plotted on a grid in Figure 14.2 and summarized in the following paragraphs.

At the lower left-hand corner of the grid, point (1,1), is the *impoverished style,* characterized by low concern for both people and production. The primary objective of managers having this style is to stay out of trouble. They pass orders along to employees, go with the flow, and make sure that they can't be held accountable for mistakes. They exert the minimum effort required to get the work done and avoid being fired or demoted.

At the upper left-hand corner, point (1,9), is the *country club style,* identified with high concern for people and low concern for production. Managers who use this style try

The Managerial Grid Model

The vertical scale measures concern for people, and the horizontal scale measures concern for production. The points on the grid are plotted according to the amount of each factor a style embodies. Point (1,1), for example, indicates low concern for both factors.

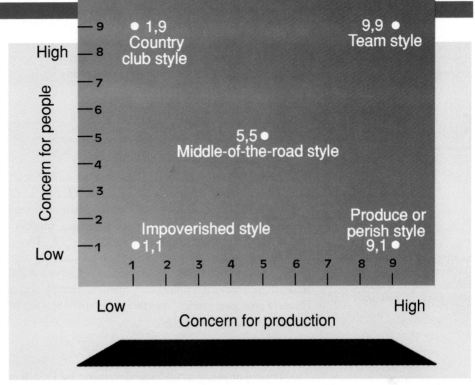

to create a secure and comfortable family atmosphere and trust that their people will respond productively. Thoughtful attention to the need for satisfying relationships leads to a friendly, if not necessarily productive, atmosphere and work tempo.

High concern for production and low concern for people are reflected at point (9,1) in the lower right-hand corner. This is the *produce-or-perish style.* Leaders following this style don't consider team members' personal needs to be relevant to achieving the organization's objectives. They use their legitimate and coercive powers to pressure subordinates to meet production quotas. They believe that operational efficiency results from arranging the work so that employees merely have to follow orders.

In the middle of the grid, point (5,5) indicates the *middle-of-the-road style.* Middle-of-the-road leaders seek a balance between workers' needs and the organization's productivity objectives. Adequate performance is obtained by maintaining employee morale at a level sufficient to get the work done.

In the upper right-hand corner, at point (9,9), is the *team style,* which shows high levels of concern for people and production. Leaders who favor this style attempt to establish cohesive work groups and foster feelings of commitment among workers. High rates of both production and job satisfaction should result. By introducing a "common stake" in the organization's purposes, the leader builds relationships of trust and respect. Max DePree of Herman Miller and Ralph Stayer of Johnsonville Foods have both used the team style effectively in their organizations.

Organizational Implications

Behavioral models have played an important role in developing the theory of leadership. They changed the focus away from who leaders are (traits) toward what leaders do (behaviors). However, leadership behaviors that are appropriate in one situation aren't necessarily appropriate in another. Steven Jobs's considerate leadership style effectively motivated skilled and creative people when Apple first started. But when Compaq, Tandy,

IBM, and others began to compete strongly with Apple, the company needed a leader who had a more initiating-structure style (production-centered). Jobs was replaced by John Sculley, who had the initiating-structure leadership style that was in line with the demands of a highly competitive marketplace. It remains to be seen whether Jobs's style will prove effective at NeXT, his new computer company.

CONTINGENCY MODELS

contingency models
Theories of leadership that hold that the situation is critical in determining the best leadership style.

Because the behavioral models failed to find sets of actions by leaders that were consistently appropriate to all situations, other models of leadership had to be devised. The next step in the evolution of knowledge about leadership was the creation of contingency or situational models. According to **contingency models** of leadership, the situation is critical in determining the best leadership style. The situational factors these models consider are shown in Figure 14.3. Each contingency model looks at only a few of these. In the following sections we examine the four most influential contingency models of leadership: Fiedler's contingency model, Hersey and Blanchard's situational model, House's path-goal model, and the leader-participation model.

Fiedler's Contingency Model

The first contingency model was developed by Fred Fiedler and his associates.[20] **Fiedler's contingency model** suggests that successful leadership depends on matching the

FIGURE 14.3

Situational Factors Influencing a Leader's Effectiveness

There are many situational factors that affect leadership. Each contingency model looks at only a few of these at a time.

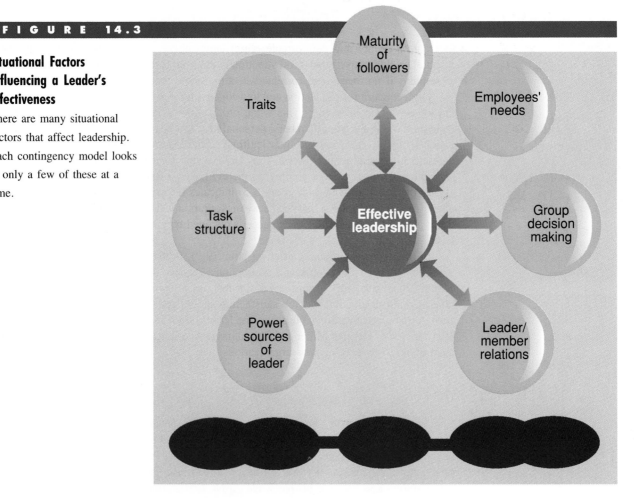

Fiedler's contingency model A leadership model that suggests successful leadership depends on matching the situation and the leader's style.

least preferred co-worker (LPC) According to Fiedler's contingency model, the employee with whom a leader can work least well.

relationship-oriented leader A leader concerned about employees' feelings and welfare.

task-oriented leader A leader concerned with getting the job done.

leader-member relations The extent to which a leader is accepted by the group.

task structure The degree to which the job is routine.

leader position power The extent to which a leader has legitimate, coercive, and reward power.

leader's style to the situation's demands. Each leadership style is most effective when it is used in the right situation. According to this model, the manager has to understand his or her own leadership style, diagnose the particular situation, and then achieve a good match between style and situation by either changing the situation to match his or her style or giving the leader role to someone on the team whose style does match the situation.

Leadership Styles What differentiates this model from others is the method of characterizing a leader's style. A leader's style in this model is considered a trait, and thus is difficult to change. To determine his or her style, the leader is asked to describe his or her **least preferred co-worker (LPC),** that is, the employee with whom he or she can work least well. A high-LPC leader describes the least preferred co-worker in a favorable light. He or she perceives that strong and positive emotional ties with others are important to being an effective leader. Such a person is called a **relationship-oriented leader** and is similar to a leader with a considerate or an employee-centered style. A leader who describes the least preferred co-worker in an unfavorable light is a low-LPC leader. A low-LPC manager, or **task-oriented leader** structures the job for team members and closely watches their behaviors. Called a **task-oriented leader** (similar to initiating-structure and production-centered leaders), this person is not very concerned with the human relations aspect of the job but simply wants to get the job done, not really caring how team members feel about her or his leadership style.

Situational Variables Fiedler identified three variables in the work situation that help determine which leadership style will be effective: leader-member relations, task structure, and the leader's position power. **Leader-member relations** determines the extent to which the leader is accepted by the group. This is the most important determinant of a leader's effectiveness. A leader who gets along well with team members and whose expertise and ability to get things done are respected may not have to rely much on formal authority. However, a leader who is disliked, isn't trusted, and appears to lack clout in the organization has to rely on legitimate and coercive power to get others to perform their tasks.

Task structure is the degree to which the job is routine. A simple and routine job is likely to have clearly defined performance standards (such as making a pizza in 12 minutes) and detailed instructions on how to do the work. When giving directions, the leader can refer to the standard operating procedures. A complex and nonroutine job, in contrast, presents a leader and subordinates with many alternatives for getting it done; there are no clear guidelines that can be consistently applied to the job. Under these conditions the leader has to play a major role in guiding and directing team members.

Leader position power is the extent to which a leader has legitimate, coercive, and reward power. Having strong position power simplifies a leader's ability to influence subordinates. Low position power makes the leader's task difficult because he or she has to rely on personal, as opposed to organizational, sources of influence.

Figure 14.4 illustrates Fiedler's contingency model of leadership. The three basic situational variables are shown on the far left. The eight numbered columns represent possible combinations of the three variables and are arranged from the most favorable situation (1) to the least favorable situation (8) for the leader. The leadership style best suited to each combination of variables is indicated in the bottom row of boxes.

Obviously, the more pleasant the leader-member relations, the more structured the task, and the stronger the leader's position power, the more favorable the situation is for the leader. Thus a leader will have the most control and influence in situations fitting in column 1. A leader will have somewhat less control and influence in situations in column 2: The leader is accepted and the tasks are structured, but he or she has little position power. In column 8 a leader's control and influence are very limited: She or he is not accepted by team members and has little position power, and the tasks are unstructured.

FIGURE 14.4

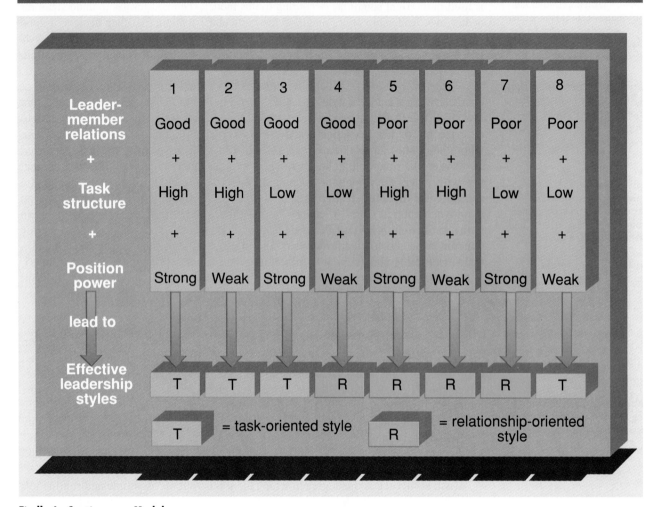

Fiedler's Contingency Model

The left-hand side of the figure shows how the basic contingency variables "add up" to determine whether a task-oriented or a relationship-oriented style is appropriate.

Effective Leadership Styles As suggested in Figure 14.4, task-oriented leaders perform most effectively in the most favorable situations (columns 1, 2, and 3) and in the least favorable situation (column 8). In the most favorable situations the leader is well respected, has freedom to reward and punish subordinates, and subordinates' activities are clear and specific (as in payroll, data entry, and maintenance). In the least favorable situation (column 8), tasks are unstructured, group support is lacking, and leader's position power is low. The unpopular president of a school PTA or Red Cross fund-raising drive is an example. In such a case, the only hope for achieving *any* results appears to be task-oriented leadership.

Relationship-oriented leaders, on the other hand, are generally most effective in moderately favorable situations. These are situations in which tasks are structured but the leader is disliked, or vice versa. Regardless of the situation, the leader must depend on the team's willingness and creativity in order to accomplish the tasks. Beth Londo, a manager at the Burgundy Group, is well liked by her team members. She had to put together a proposal for a series of management training programs for Allstate Insurance Company. Allstate sketched out a rough idea of what they wanted and asked Beth and her team to submit a proposal. The team members needed to decide on the content of the program, a schedule of training activities, and methods of evaluation. Because the task is unstructured and Beth is well liked by her team members, a relationship-oriented leadership style is effective.

Limitations Fiedler's model, like any other, has its limitations.[21] First, the situational variables are complex and difficult to assess. Measurement of actual leader-member relations, task structure, and position power must necessarily be subjective. Second, the model pays little attention to the characteristics of team members. Whether they are highly skilled professionals or unskilled laborers could make a major difference to the appropriate leadership style. Third, the model assumes that the leader has the skills (see Figure 14.1) to competently direct the team's efforts. But if the leader lacks these core leadership skills, others aren't likely to respect the leader or trust his or her judgment, negating the situational variables. Finally, the logic underlying the LPC scale is open to question. Fiedler asserts that LPC measures a fixed trait and that a leader cannot easily change his or her leadership style to fit a situation. When a leader's style and the situation do not match, he argues, the situation, *not* the leader, should be changed to fit the leader's style. This is often not practical. For example, many jobs at Texas Instruments are performed by engineers and scientists. Given the scope of these jobs, it would be difficult to restructure them to fit a leader's style.

Organizational Implications Both relationship-oriented and task-oriented leaders perform well in some but not all situations. For example, an outstanding team leader who is promoted to quality control manager may fail because his or her task-oriented leadership style doesn't match the demands of the new situation. As tasks become more complex and nonroutine, different leadership styles must be used to motivate others and direct their work.

Even though it remains controversial, Fiedler's contingency model is an interesting approach to understanding leadership and one that many managers find appealing. Its greatest contribution may be its redirection of research in the field, rather than provision of any firm answers. Researchers started to more closely examine the situation before attempting to find the leadership style that is most appropriate. Fiedler pointed out that we cannot accurately label a manager as good or poor. Rather, we must think of the leader who performs well in one situation but not in others. Leadership effectiveness depends more on situational variables than on leadership style. Top management might attempt to change a leader's style when it might be easier to make the situation more favorable or to shift the leader to a situation that better matches her or his style.[22]

Hersey and Blanchard's situational leadership model Contingency model that suggests that the levels of directive and supportive behaviors of leaders will vary based on the level of maturity of the employee or team.

directive behavior One-way communication from leader to followers.

supportive behavior Two-way communication between leader and followers.

maturity Subordinate's ability to set high but attainable goals and accept responsibility for reaching them.

Hersey and Blanchard's Situational Leadership Model

Hersey and Blanchard's situational leadership model suggests that the levels of directive (similar to initiating-structure and production-centered) and supportive (similar to considerate and employee-centered) behaviors of leaders will vary based on the level of maturity of the employee or team.[23]

Directive behavior occurs when a leader engages in one-way communication—spelling out followers' duties and telling them what to do and where, when, and how to do it. Directive leaders structure, control, and supervise team members. **Supportive behavior** occurs when a leader engages in two-way communication—listening, providing encouragement, and involving followers in decision making. **Maturity** is defined in this context as a subordinate's ability to set high but attainable goals and willingness to accept responsibility for reaching them. It's related to the task and not to a person's age. People have varying degrees of maturity, depending on the specific task they are trying to accomplish. This model prescribes different combinations of directive and supportive leader behaviors for different levels of subordinates' maturity. In contrast to Fiedler, who believes that a leader's style is relatively rigid, Hersey and Blanchard emphasize a leader's flexibility to adapt to changing situations.[24]

Hersey and Blanchard's Situational Leadership Model

A leader's most effective style is influenced by the maturity of team members. With immature team members, a directive style of leadership is effective; with highly mature team members, a delegating style is most effective.

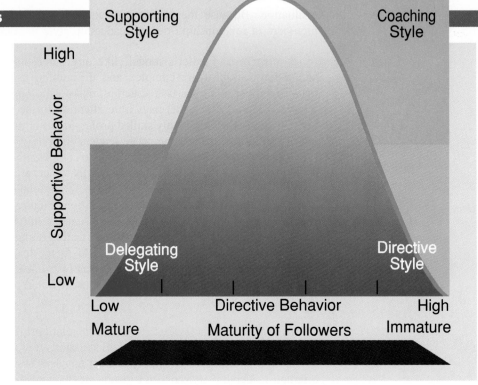

Source: Paul Hersey and Kenneth Blanchard, *Management of Organizational Behavior: Utilizing Human Resources,* 5e, © 1988, p. 188p. Adapted by permission of Prentice-Hall, Englewood Cliffs, New Jersey.

directive style   A leadership style characterized by the giving of clear instructions and specific direction to immature employees.

coaching style   A leadership style characterized by expanding two-way communication and helping maturing employees build confidence and motivation.

supporting style   A leadership style characterized by active two-way communication and support of mature employees' efforts to use their skills.

delegating style   A hands-off leadership style characterized by giving responsibilities for carrying out plans and making task decisions to the highly mature employees.

Figure 14.5 portrays the relationship between Hersey and Blanchard's leadership styles and levels of follower maturity. The curve running through the four leadership quadrants indicates the level of directive and/or supportive behavior characterizing each style. The maturity level of the individual or team being supervised ranges from mature to immature.

A leader with a **directive style** (lower right-hand quadrant) provides clear instructions and specific direction. When an employee first enters the organization, directive leadership is most appropriate. Newcomers are usually committed, enthusiastic, and energetic. They are anxious to get started and learn. Since commitment is high, a lot of support from the leader isn't needed *or* appropriate.

As employees learn their tasks, a directive style is still important, because they aren't yet ready to assume total responsibility for getting the job done. But a leader needs to begin showing supportive behavior in order to build employees' confidence and maintain a high level of enthusiasm. This style, called the **coaching style,** encourages two-way communication and helps build confidence and motivation on the part of the employee, although the leader still has responsibility and controls decision making.

Once team members feel confident performing their tasks, the leader no longer needs to be directive. However, the leader does need to open up communication through active listening and to support subordinates' efforts to use the skills they have already learned. This is called the **supporting style,** because the leader and the team share decision making and no longer need or expect a directive relationship.

The **delegating style** is appropriate for a leader whose employees are highly mature with respect to a particular task, that is, both competent and motivated to take full responsibility. Even though the leader may still identify problems, the responsibility for carrying out plans is given to experienced followers. They are permitted to run the show and decide how, when, and where the task is to be done.

The following Insight focuses on leadership practices at Chaparral Steel of Midlothian, Texas, one of the most efficient steel mills in the world. The leaders there practice a delegating style of leadership, which is very effective.

During a tour a visiting manager asked a Chaparral manager, "How do you schedule coffee breaks in the plant?"

"The workers decide when they want a cup of coffee," came the reply.

"Yes, but who tells them when it's okay to leave the machines?" the visitor asked.

The Chaparral manager just shrugged his shoulders.

All new employees of Chaparral Steel take a course entitled "The Chaparral Process." This course tells them what happens to a piece of steel as it moves through the mill. It also covers company accounting, finance, marketing, and sales. Once trained, employees understand how their job relates to the welfare of the entire organization. Monthly financial statements, including a chart that tracks profits, are posted in the mill.

Several years ago a team leader and several employees went to Asia, Europe, and South America to evaluate new steel mills. When the team returned, they discussed advantages and disadvantages of various mills with other employees and with top management. The choices were narrowed down to a few, and the team took off again to evaluate the final ones before making a recommendation. Top management and the team chose a new mill. The team ordered it and even oversaw its installation. Other companies may spend more than two years studying and finally installing a machine, Chaparral employees completed the entire project in one year.

Chaparral does not hand employees automatic pay raises. It uses a pay-for-skills system that bases any increases on what the employee has learned, not on seniority. If an employee, for example, learns how to run a new piece of equipment, he or she might get a 5 percent raise. There remains considerable debate among employees and managers over the merits of this system.[25]

The Hersey and Blanchard situational leadership model has generated a lot of interest. The idea that leaders should be flexible with respect to the leadership style they choose is appealing to many managers. The leader must constantly monitor the maturity level of subordinates in order to determine what combination of directive and supportive behaviors is most appropriate. An inexperienced (immature) employee may perform at as high a level as an experienced employee if directed and closely supervised by a manager. If the leader's style is appropriate, it should also help employees increase their level of maturity. Thus as a leader helps a team evolve toward a highly mature level, her or his leadership style needs to evolve as well. At Chaparral Steel highly mature teams perform under a delegating style of leadership, the highest performance level achievable.

There are, however, some drawbacks to the Hersey and Blanchard model.[26] First, can leaders actually choose a leadership style when faced with a new situation? The answer to this question has important implications for management selection, placement, and promotion. At Chaparral a person might not be promoted unless he or she has a flexible leadership style. Some people can read situations better and adapt their style more effectively than others. Although leaders at Chaparral Steel have adapted effectively, what are the costs of training leaders to be flexible? Do these costs exceed the benefits? Second, the model ignores many factors—such as personality traits and the power base of the leader—that could influence a leader's choice of style. Third, a team may be composed of employees at differing levels of maturity. Under this condition, what is the best style? Large teams may make a generalized leadership choice almost impossible. Finally, the model does not distinguish among types of tasks and among the reasons for low maturity. That is, are tasks routine or varied? simple or complex? Does immaturity reflect a lack of motivation or a lack of ability, or some combination or both?

House's path-goal model
A contingency model of leader-ship that states that effective leaders clarify the paths, or means, by which employees can attain both high job satisfaction and high performance.

House's Path-Goal Model

Another contingency model was developed by Robert House.[27] **House's path-goal model** states that effective leaders, by clearly specifying the task, reducing roadblocks to task achievement, and increasing opportunities for task-related satisfaction, clarify the paths, or means, by which employees can attain both high job satisfaction and high performance. The leader's function is to motivate team members and help them reach their highly valued, job-related objectives. The specific style of leader behavior should be determined by two contingency variables: employee characteristics and task characteristics. A version of the path-goal model is shown in Figure 14.6.

Like the other two contingency models, the path-goal model does not provide a formula for the best way to lead. Instead it stresses that the effective leader should select the style most appropriate to a particular situation and the needs of team members. The model identifies four styles of leadership:

Achievement-oriented leadership is the style of the leader who sets challenging goals, expects followers to perform at their highest level, and shows confidence that they will meet this expectation.

Directive leadership is the style of the leader who lets followers know what's expected of them and tells them how to perform their tasks. This style is similar to the initiating-structure and production-centered styles.

Participative leadership is the style of the leader who consults with followers and asks for their input and suggestions before making a decision.

Supportive leadership is the style of the leader who is friendly and approachable and shows concern for followers' psychological well-being. This style is much like the considerate and employee-centered styles.

FIGURE 14.6

House's Path-Goal Model

The choice of leadership style depends on the characteristics of team members and the task.

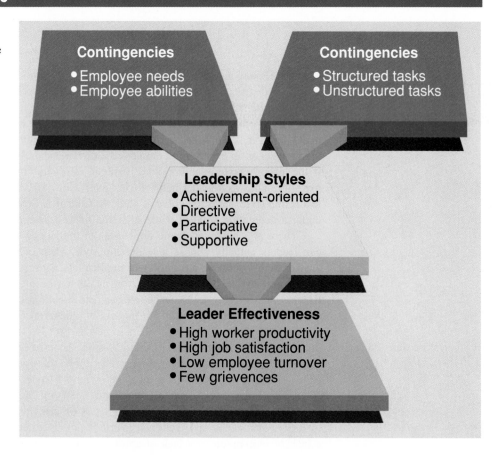

Leadership at W. L. Gore is a *participative* process, in which the traditional chain of command has been replaced by a "lattice" system. Any employee can take an idea to any manager. A machine operator can talk directly with plant leaders.

Employee Characteristics House's first contingency variable is employee characteristics. The model states that employees will accept a particular leadership style if they perceive it as an immediate source of job satisfaction or as necessary for future job satisfaction. For example, if employees have high needs for self-esteem and affiliation, they may readily accept supportive leadership. On the other hand, employees who have high needs for autonomy, responsibility, and achievement are more likely to accept and be motivated by achievement-oriented leadership. Beth Pritchard, who heads Johnson's Wax Insect Control Division, set a radical course when she took over. She changed formulas of successful products, revamped packaging, and assigned a team member to each region of the United States to focus on the needs of customers there. She accomplished her objectives by using an achievement-oriented leadership style—her team members could handle responsibility and make decisions without constantly seeking her advice.

Task Characteristics The other contingency variable of the path-goal model is task characteristics. When tasks are routine and simple, employees will regard directions as unnecessary. Under this condition, directive leadership may increase performance by preventing "goofing off," but it may also decrease job satisfaction. Participative or supportive leadership is likely to increase satisfaction with the leader and with company policies, even though the tasks are unsatisfying. On the other hand, when tasks are nonroutine and complex, directive or achievement-oriented leadership is more appropriate than supportive leadership. Team members in this kind of situation appreciate the leader who clarifies the paths to their objectives. When Stanley Gault took over as CEO of Rubbermaid in 1980, that producer of household items was in financial trouble. Gault immediately told his team members and others that he was aiming for a 15 percent average annual growth in sales and a billion dollars in sales by 1990. He clarified how the organization would achieve these goals—by selling off unprofitable divisions and introducing more than a thousand new products in the 1980s. He says that as a leader you must define objectives and strategies and show others what you expect from them.

Organizational Implications Teams performing routine and simple tasks have reported higher job satisfaction when leaders provided supportive rather than directive leadership.[28] Teams performing nonroutine and complex tasks have reported higher productivity when their leader provided directive leadership, but they haven't necessarily reported higher job satisfaction. Like Fiedler's and Hersey and Blanchard's models, House's model indicates that participative leadership styles are not always effective. A participatory style is needed most when employees' acceptance of the decision is important, when the leader doesn't have some of the information needed to make a decision, and when the problem is unstructured. Directive or task-oriented leadership seems to work better when employees don't share the manager's and/or organization's objectives, when the production schedule is critically short, and when employees are receptive to top-down decisions.

Leader-Participation Model

leader-participation model
A contingency model of leadership that provides a set of rules to determine the amount and form of participative decision making that should be encouraged in different situations.

One of the more recent contributions to the contingency approach is the leader-participation model proposed by Victor Vroom and Philip Yetton and revised by Arthur Jago in 1988. The **leader-participation model** provides a set of rules to determine the amount and form of participative decision making that should be encouraged in different situations.[29] Recognizing that a task can be structured or unstructured, these researchers suggest that the leader should adjust her or his behavior to reflect the team's task structure. This is a normative model—it provides a sequence of rules that the researchers believe a leader should follow in determining the form and amount of team member participation in decision making.

Decision-Making Styles According to the Leader-Participation Model

Decision Style	Definition
AI	Leader makes the decision alone.
AII	Leader asks for information from team members but makes the decision alone. Team members may or may not be informed as to what the situation is.
CI	Leader shares the situation with each team member and asks for information and evaluation. Team members do not meet as a team, and the leader alone makes the decision.
CII	Leader and team members meet as a team to discuss the situation, but the leader makes the decision.
GII	Leader and team members meet as a team to discuss the situation, and the team makes the decision.

A = autocratic; C = consultative; G = group

Source: V. H. Vroom and P. W. Yetton, *Leadership and Decision-making* (Pittsburgh, Pa.: University of Pittsburgh Press, 1973). Reprinted by permission of the University of Pittsburgh Press.

The model states that decision effectiveness is gauged by both decision quality (the quality of the decision made by the team) and decision acceptance (the degree to which team members are committed to the decision the team has made). To arrive at the best decision, a leader needs to analyze the situation and then choose one of five decision-making styles. These are summarized in Table 14.3. There are two autocratic styles (AI and AII), two consultative styles (CI and CII), and one group style (GII). The leader must analyze the situation in order to determine the most effective style of leadership, or how much participation to use. The leader's analysis is guided by eight contingency questions, which must be answered in this order:

QR *Quality requirement:* How important is the technical quality of this decision?

CR *Commitment requirement:* How important is team member commitment to the decision?

LI *Leader information:* Do I have sufficient information to make a high-quality decision?

ST *Problem structure:* Is the problem well structured?

CP *Commitment probability:* If I were to make the decision by myself, is it reasonably certain that my team members would be committed to the decision?

GC *Goal congruence:* Do team members share the organizational goals to be reached by solving this problem?

CO *Subordinate conflict:* Is conflict among team members over preferred solutions likely?

SI *Subordinate information:* Do team members have sufficient information to make a high-quality decision?

The leader-participation model, incorporating the eight contingency questions and the five leadership styles, is diagrammed in Figure 14.7. To use this model, the leader starts on the left side and asks the first question, "How important is the technical quality of this decision?" The answer, high or low, determines the path to the second situation, where the leader asks "How important is team member commitment to the decision?" Once the leader answers that question, either high or low, he or she goes to the next question, continuing in this fashion until the eighth question is asked and an appropriate leadership style is determined. The leadership style will lead to a high-quality decision that will be accepted by team members.

The following Insight will help you understand how to use the leader-participation model. Based on information provided in the feature, you'll choose the appropriate leadership style.

FIGURE 14.7

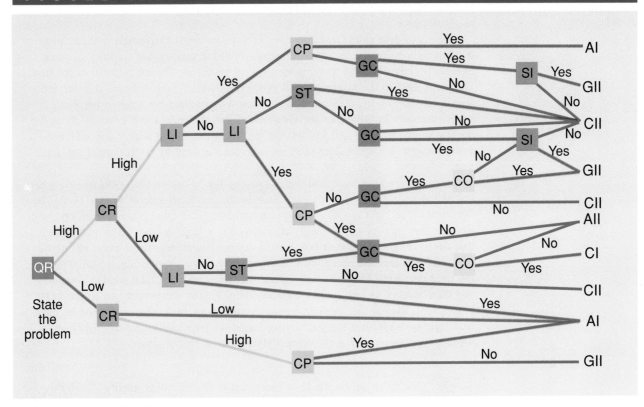

Leader-Participation Model

The leader must analyze the situation by answering eight contingency questions in order to choose the appropriate style of leadership.

Source: V. H. Vroom and A. G. Jago, *The New Leadership* (Englewood Cliffs, N.J.: Prentice-Hall, 1988). Used by permission of the authors.

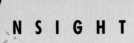

INSIGHT Angelita Guajardo is vice president for operations at Telex Aerospace, a large aerospace company in Tulsa, Oklahoma. The company has been under competitive pressure to reduce its costs and increase its efficiency. Several months ago the manufacturing manager requested funds for new machines. Guajardo gave her permission to buy and install them, but much to her surprise, productivity has *not* increased, and employee turnover *has* increased.

She believes that nothing is wrong with the machines and that they were installed properly. Other companies in Tulsa have similar machines and haven't reported declines in productivity. Representatives of the company in Dallas that manufactured the machines have checked their installation and told Guajardo that the machines were properly installed and should operate "just fine."

She suspects that changes in the ways people are required to work might be the problem. This view is not, however, widely shared by the other vice presidents, the manufacturing manager, and her first-line managers. Those managers indicate that production has declined because of poor training, lack of adequate financial incentives to increase production, time needed to train new employees to replace those who left the firm, and low morale. Clearly these are issues that affect the operation of the entire plant and over which Guajardo and the others might disagree.

The president calls Guajardo into her office. She is displeased with the production figures for the last three months—both the quality and quantity of work have fallen off since the new machines were installed. She expresses concern that Guajardo "get to the bottom of this problem quickly" and indicates that the problem is Guajardo's to solve but that she would appreciate knowing of her plans within the next four days or so. Guajardo shares the president's concern about the decline in productivity and knows that the manufacturing manager and her first-line managers are upset. Her problem is to decide what to do to correct the situation.

If you were Guajardo, and were applying the leader-participation model, what leadership style would you choose? Start at the left-hand side of Figure 14.7. The first box to the right is QR (quality requirement). You must make a decision about whether the importance of quality requirements is high or low. After you make that decision, go to the next box, or CR (commitment required). Once again you must make a decision about the importance of having subordinates committed to the final decision. After you have made that decision, you face another decision and then another. As you make each decision, follow the proper line to the next box. Eventually, at the far right-hand side of Figure 14.7, you will arrive at the best style of leadership for you to use, based on your eight answers. To check whether you've arrived at the correct style, review this analysis:

		Answers
QR	*Quality requirement:* How important is the technical quality of the decision?	Highly important
CR	*Commitment requirement:* How important is team member commitment to the decision?	Highly important
LI	*Leader information:* Do you have sufficient information to make a high-quality decision?	Probably not
ST	*Problem structure:* Is the problem well structured?	No
CP	*Commitment probability:* If you were to make the decision by yourself, is it reasonably certain that your team members would be committed to the decision?	Probably not
CG	*Goal congruence:* Do team members share the organizational goals to be attained in solving this problem?	Yes
CO	*Subordinate conflict:* Is conflict among team members over preferred solutions likely?	Yes
SI	*Subordinate information:* Do team members have sufficient information to make a high-quality decision?	Yes

The answer is GII. Most leaders choose the GII leader-participation style in this type of situation.

The leader-participation model provides an excellent guide for determining the type and degree of team member participation to incorporate in decision making. It confirms the findings of other research—that leaders use participation when the quality of the decision is important, when it's important that team members accept decision and unlikely that they'll do so unless they're allowed to have some say in it, and when team members can be trusted to strive for team, as opposed to individual, goals.[30]

This model also stresses that the situation—not the leaders themselves—should be given leaders' and researchers' attention. Along with Hersey and Blanchard's and House's models, the leader-participation model states that the leader can adopt different

TABLE 14.4

A Comparison of Four Contingency Models

	Fiedler's Contingency Model	Hersey and Blanchard's Situational Model	House's Path-Goal Model	Leader-Participation Model
Key situational variables	Task structure Leader-member relations Leader position power	Level of followers' maturity	Task characteristics Employee characteristics	Eight diagnostic questions concerning time, quality, and acceptance
Leadership styles	Task-oriented Relationship-oriented	Directive Supportive Coaching Delegating	Achievement Directive Participative Supportive	Autocratic I and II Consultative I and II Group II
Implications	Leader's style is matched to situation, or situation is changed to fit leader's style. High or low control situations favor task-oriented leader. Moderate control situations favor relationship-oriented leader.	Effective leaders choose a style to match the maturity level of their followers.	If tasks are routine and simple, supportive or participative leadership is best for team members who want their social needs satisfied. If tasks are nonroutine and complex, directive or achievement-oriented leadership is best for team members who want to self-actualize on the job.	Effective leaders analyze the situation by answering the eight contingency questions, then choose among the five styles, depending on the answers.

styles of leadership to meet the demands of different situations. But, before choosing a leadership style, the leader must assess the situation. Not all leaders, however, can behave in ways suggested by the model. Although they may know how they *should* behave, they may lack the core leadership skills to tailor their behavior to meet the specific situation.

Comparing Contingency Models

Effective employees can also be effective leaders. Leaders need to be able to direct and motivate others to achieve both high productivity and job satisfaction. Although this sounds simple, the four contingency models offer somewhat different advice about choosing an effective leadership style. Table 14.4 compares the elements of the four models.

The following Insight lets you apply (and compare) these approaches in choosing a leadership style for a group project, a situation you may be familiar with.

CHOOSING A LEADERSHIP STYLE

I N S I G H T Laura Cardinal, a professor at Southern Methodist University, teaches a course in business policy. Every year she divides the class into several teams, consisting of from four to six students with different responsibilities for marketing research, finance, production, human resources, accounting, and customer services. Three teams are responsible for developing detailed business plans for each client, either a local or a national organization. At the end of the semester, managers from the organizations attend class and listen to the three analyses of their firms. They critique the presentations and then choose the best plan. The presentation and ultimate choice heavily influence each student's grade for the course.

Suppose you're elected to lead one of the student teams preparing a business plan for Murata Business Machines, a company that makes fax machines and other telecommunications equipment. Your objective is to beat the other two Murata teams and have your plan adopted. What leadership style should you choose?

Fiedler's contingency model According to Fiedler's contingency model, your effectiveness depends on the match between the situation and your particular leadership style. The three situational variables to be considered are leader-member relations, task structure, and position power. You and your team members probably have good leader-member relations. You were chosen because others in the team perceived you to be trustworthy and easy to work with. Your team's task is relatively unstructured. You have no formal power to make team members work on their assignments. Under these conditions, what style of leadership does the Fiedler model recommend? Look at Figure 14.4 and find the column for contingency variable ratings of good, low, and weak, respectively. This model says that a relationship-oriented leadership style is likely to work best in this situation.

Hersey and Blanchard's situational leadership model According to Hersey and Blanchard's model you must assess the maturity level of those on your team in order to determine the appropriate leadership style to use. If members of your team have set low goals and appear unwilling to take responsibility for the project (immaturity), then a directive style of leadership is most likely to lead to high performance. If you want to improve the maturity level of your group members so that they will assume more responsibility, your best bet is to reduce your directive behavior a little by giving members opportunities to assume increased responsibility for their part of the team's project. If improved performance follows, then increase your supportive behaviors until you've adopted a coaching, or even supporting, style. On the other hand, if team members show a willingness to take their responsibilities seriously and have the knowledge to perform the necessary tasks, it may be quite appropriate for you to provide little direction and help. A delegating style is then required.

House's path-goal model According to House's path-goal model, a leader's major function is to provide a path via which team members can increase their job satisfaction and productivity. This is done by clarifying the nature of the task, increasing the opportunities for job satisfaction, and helping members complete the task. The task is somewhat unstructured, but the team needs to perform well so that it will win the competition and each member will receive a high grade. Under these conditions, which style of leadership does House's model recommend? A direct leadership style, because it will enable you to give specific directions about what is supposed to be done when, where, by whom, and at what level of performance. If you can clarify the ways to complete the task for team members and guide them in doing their tasks, your team should achieve its objective.

Leader-participation model According to the leader-participation model, your assessment of the situation is the key. Using the eight contingency questions (see Figure 14.7) will help you choose a leadership style that produces the highest-quality decisions and team members' commitment. This is how you answer the questions:

QR Quality requirement: How important is the technical quality of this decision? High	**CR** Commitment requirement: How important is team members' commitment to the decision? High

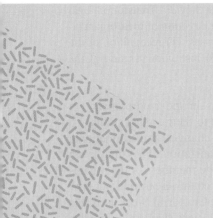

LI Leader information: Do you have sufficient information to make a high-quality decision? No	**CG** Goal congruence: Do team members share the organizational goals to be attained in solving this problem? Yes
ST Problem structure: Is the problem well structured? No	**CO** Subordinate conflict: Is conflict among team members over preferred solutions likely? Yes
CP Commitment probability: If you were to make the decision by yourself, is it reasonably certain that your team members would be committed to your decision? No	**SI** Subordinate information: Do team members have sufficient information to make a high-quality decision? Yes

Based on these answers, which leadership style would work best? Follow the paths in Figure 14.7 to the correct answer. The paths point to a GII style of leadership. You should meet with team members to generate and evaluate alternatives and help them reach a consensus on what is the best solution.

TRANSFORMATIONAL LEADERSHIP

The leadership models we have examined clearly don't agree on how leaders should influence followers. Early models focused on personality traits, and most of the later ones look at leader behaviors as determined by contingency or situational factors. In the past few years, many U.S. organizations have realized that they will have to make major changes in the ways they do things in order to survive. A new look at trait theories has resulted. And many now feel that the type of leadership that is needed by top managers for tomorrow's organizations is what has been labeled *transformational*.[31]

Motivating Teams

transformational leadership A style of leadership that provides extraordinary motivation to employees by appealing to their higher ideals and moral values and inspiring them to think about problems in new ways.

Transformational leadership is, quite simply, leading by motivating. Transformational leaders provide extraordinary motivation by appealing to team members' higher ideals and moral values and inspiring them to think about problems in new ways. In terms of Maslow's needs hierarchy (see Chapter 13), transformational leaders tap the higher-order needs of others. Followers of these leaders feel trust, admiration, loyalty, and respect for the leader and are motivated to do more than they thought they could, or *would*, do.[32] A leader can motivate followers by making them more aware of the importance and value of their task and making them place their own self-interest behind that of their team or the organization.

Special Attributes of Transformational Leaders

What attributes do these leaders possess?[33] In a rebirth of interest in a form of trait theory, researchers have noted that successful transformational leaders have the following traits: they see themselves as change agents, are wise risk takers, believe in people and are sensitive to their needs, are able to clearly communicate their vision, and trust their intuition. These attributes are consistent with the core skills of effective leaders discussed earlier.

But transformational leaders go beyond these skills in what they *do*. Transformational leaders engage in several behaviors that help them change the direction of their organizations. These behaviors are viewed as a sequence of three phases: (1) recognition of the need for major change, (2) creation of a new vision, and (3) institutionalization of the change.

Recognizing the Need for Change When changes in the environment are slow, many top managers fail to recognize them as threats to their organizations. To make members of an organization aware of environmental changes, transformational leaders often challenge current assumptions about the organization. They may even have subordinates write dissenting opinions. They encourage members of the organization to visit other organizations, including those in other countries, to find out how they operate and deal with problems. Top management at Chaparral Steel used this technique very successfully when preparing to purchase a new steel mill. Finally, transformational leaders encourage people to measure the organization's performance against their competitors', not just against last year's performance.

The Manager's Memo in Chapter 1 cited the Malcolm Baldridge National Quality Award as the standard of excellence in U.S. businesses. The winner is producing goods or services that are the equal of any in the world and whose quality continues to improve. So far, Motorola, the nuclear fuel division of Westinghouse, Milliken and Company, Xerox Business Systems, Cadillac, and Globe Metallurgical have won this award. When Xerox's David Kearns declared quality improvement to be the company's driving principle in 1983, he encouraged his top management to start measuring Xerox's quality against that of others in the industry. Under Kearns's guidance, Xerox management looked for the best competing products and manufacturing methods in the world to serve as benchmarks, and then set out to better them. They quickly found out that Xerox's copiers had only a 90 percent chance of working and its suppliers' parts were only 92 percent error free. After having closely monitored its competitors' standards, Xerox now exceeds those standards and produces copiers that work 99.97 percent of the time; suppliers are supplying Xerox with quality parts 99.70 percent of the time.[34]

Creating a New Vision In contrast to the visions that lead entrepreneurs—such as Paul Fireman at Reebok, Joseph Canion at Compaq Computer, or Philip Knight at Nike—to found new organizations, successful visions in large organizations are rarely the product of a single person's creative spirit. A vision evolves over a period of time, after many people, who will have to implement the vision, participate in decisions that shape it.

The following Insight discusses how Lou Gerstner, former president of American Express's Travel Related Services Group, created and implemented a new vision for that division.

LOU GERSTNER'S VISION FOR AMERICAN EXPRESS

*I*NSIGHT When Lou Gerstner became president of the Travel Related Services Group at American Express in 1979, he had to overcome 130 years of history. To compete successfully against Visa and MasterCard, American Express had to develop a new market niche. Gerstner's vision was to focus on the global marketplace of the affluent customer. To implement this vision, he brought together people running the organization and questioned all principles by which they used to conduct business. He challenged two beliefs: that the division should only have the green card and that the product had limited potential for growth and innovation.

During the next decade, he changed the division's way of doing business. He developed an entrepreneurial culture by rewarding people who took calculated risks. He clearly communicated to all employees both his vision and their role in creating an exciting place to work. He started a program called ''Great Performers'' to recognize and reward truly exceptional customer service managers, an important factor in the division's success. Today American Express offers Gold and Platinum cards, as well as a revolving credit card known as Optima. The division offers a wide variety of travel-related products such as insurance, luggage, traveler's checks, and personal items. It offers its corporate clients a system to monitor and control travel expenses. As a result of these innovations, the division's income has risen more than 500 percent in the past ten years.[35]

Institutionalizing the Change In order to successfully implement major organizational changes, the transformational leader must work with a group of people who become committed to the vision. He or she must also be able to rely on the support of key managers in the organization. Involving others in the vision helps develop their commitment to it. In some cases the leader may even have to make personnel changes, replacing some people in key positions with others who possess the skills and commitment necessary to implement changes successfully.

CHAPTER SUMMARY

1. The dynamics of leadership include leaders, team members, and specific situations. A leader influences followers to act. When followers accept the leader's way of doing things, they expect the leader to reward them in some significant way.

2. Leaders have several important types of power, five of which are legitimate, reward, coercive, referent, and expert.

3. Traits models of leadership were early attempts to determine the personal characteristics that make a leader successful. Groups of characteristics include physical, background, personality, social, and task-related.

4. Behavioral models of leadership provide a way of identifying effective leaders by their actions. Three important behavioral models are Theory X and Theory Y, which represent two quite different ways that leaders view their subordinates and thus manage them; the Ohio State and University of Michigan models, which identify two leadership styles; considerate and initiating structure (Ohio State), or two leader behaviors, production-centered and employee-centered (University of Michigan); and the managerial grid model, which identifies various combinations of concern for people and for production.

5. The four most influential contingency leadership models are Fiedler's contingency model, which suggests that successful leadership depends on matching the demands of the situation to the leadership style; Hersey and Blanchard's situational leadership model, which states that leaders must adapt their leadership style to the maturity level of their followers; House's path-goal model, which holds that effective leaders clarify the paths, or means, by which team members can attain both high job satisfaction and high performance; and the leader-participation model, which states that leaders can choose one of five leadership-decision styles, depending on the situations facing the leader and team.

6. Transformational leadership involves inspiring, and thereby motivating, individuals to reach their highest goals.

1. How do the bases of a leader's power influence followers' behaviors?

2. Describe the basic elements in the Ohio State and University of Michigan leadership models. How can these concepts help you to become a more effective leader?

3. *Fortune* magazine ran a cover story entitled "The Seven Keys to Business Leadership" in its October 1988 issue. The seven keys were (1) trust your subordinates, (2) develop a vision, (3) keep your cool, (4) encourage risk, (5) be an expert, (6) invite dissent, and (7) simplify. Of these, which one(s) do Robert Crandall and Max DePree exhibit, based on their actions as reported in this chapter?

4. Describe Fiedler's three situational variables and his contingency approach to leadership.

5. **From Where You Sit:** Evaluate this statement: "Leaders are born, not developed."

6. Explain how Hersey and Blanchard's situational leadership model relates the maturity of followers to different leader behaviors.

7. **From Where You Sit:** How could you apply Hersey and Blanchard's situational model on the job?

8. **From Where You Sit:** What managerial implications does House's path-goal model hold for you?

9. In what ways are the four contingency models of leadership similar and dissimilar?

10. **From Where You Sit:** Pick a student leader at your school. What style of leadership does that person use? When is that style most and least effective? Why?

11. **From Where You Sit:** How would you know whether a transformational leader is present in your class? What behaviors and skills might she or he show to others?

12. **From Where You Sit:** The statement "Good management controls complexity; effective leadership produces useful change" is insightful. What have you learned from this chapter that will help you evaluate this statement?

13. **From Where You Sit:** Peter Drucker, noted management consultant, said, "Whenever anything is being accomplished it is being done by a monomaniac with a mission." In light of what you have learned about leadership, evaluate that statement.

What's Your Leadership Style?

The following questions analyze your leadership style according to the Ohio State model. Read each item carefully. Think about how you usually behave when you are the leader. Then, using the following key, circle the letter that most closely describes your style. Circle only one choice per question.

A = Always   **O = Often**   **?=Sometimes**   **S = Seldom**   **N = Never**

1. I take time to explain how a job should be carried out.

2. I explain the part that co-workers are to play in the group.   A O ? S N

3. I make clear the rules and procedures for others to follow in detail.   A O ? S N

4. I organize my own work activities.   A O ? S N

5. I let people know how well they are doing.   A O ? S N

6. I let people know what is expected of them.   A O ? S N

7. I encourage the use of uniform procedures to get things accomplished.   A O ? S N

8. I make my attitudes clear to others.   A O ? S N

9. I assign others to particular tasks.   A O ? S N

10. I make sure that others understand their part in the group.   A O ? S N

11. I schedule the work that I want others to do.   A O ? S N

12. I ask that others follow standard rules and regulations.   A O ? S N

13. I make working on the job more pleasant.   A O ? S N

14. I go out of my way to be helpful to others.   A O ? S N

15. I respect others' feelings and opinions.   A O ? S N

16. I am thoughtful and considerate of others.   A O ? S N

17. I maintain a friendly atmosphere in the group.   A O ? S N

18. I do little things to make it pleasant for others to be a member of my group.   A O ? S N

19. I treat others as equals.   A O ? S N

20. I give others advance notice of change and explain how it will affect them.   A O ? S N

21. I look out for others' personal welfare.   A O ? S N

22. I am approachable and friendly toward others.   A O ? S N

Scoring Form

The boxes below are numbered to correspond to the questionnaire items. In each box, circle the number next to the letter of the response alternative you picked. Add up the numbers you circled in each of the columns.

Column 1

1	2
A = 5 O = 4 ? = 3 S = 2 N = 1	A = 5 O = 4 ? = 3 S = 2 N = 1
3 A = 5 O = 4 ? = 3 S = 2 N = 1	**4** A = 5 O = 4 ? = 3 S = 2 N = 1
5 A = 5 O = 4 ? = 3 S = 2 N = 1	**6** A = 5 O = 4 ? = 3 S = 2 N = 1
7 A = 5 O = 4 ? = 3 S = 2 N = 1	**8** A = 5 O = 4 ? = 3 S = 2 N = 1
9 A = 5 O = 4 ? = 3 S = 2 N = 1	**10** A = 5 O = 4 ? = 3 S = 2 N = 1
11 A = 5 O = 4 ? = 3 S = 2 N = 1	**12** A = 5 O = 4 ? = 3 S = 2 N = 1

Total Column 1 = ____

Column 2

13	14
A = 5 O = 4 ? = 3 S = 2 N = 1	A = 5 O = 4 ? = 3 S = 2 N = 1
15 A = 5 O = 4 ? = 3 S = 2 N = 1	**16** A = 5 O = 4 ? = 3 S = 2 N = 1
17 A = 5 O = 4 ? = 3 S = 2 N = 1	**18** A = 5 O = 4 ? = 3 S = 2 N = 1
19 A = 5 O = 4 ? = 3 S = 2 N = 1	**20** A = 5 O = 4 ? = 3 S = 2 N = 1
21 A = 5 O = 4 ? = 3 S = 2 N = 1	**22** A = 5 O = 4 ? = 3 S = 2 N = 1

Total Column 2 = ____

Interpretation

The questions scored in Column 1 reflect an initiating-structure leadership style. A score of greater than 47 would indicate that you describe your leadership style as high on initiating structure. You plan, organize, direct, and control the work of others.

The questions scored in Column 2 reflect a considerate style. A total score of greater than 40 indicates that you are a considerate leader. A considerate leader is one who is concerned with the comfort, well-being, and contributions of others.

In general, managers rated high on initiating structure and moderate on consideration tended to be in charge of higher-producing groups than those whose leadership styles are the reverse.

To: First-Line Supervisors
From: Career Development Department
Re: What is leadership?

Over the past twenty years the Forum Corportion has conducted extensive ongoing research into specific practices that distinguish high-performing leaders from others. During the 1980s Forum identified three trends that it believes affected leadership: (1) change of organizational structures to flatter, leaner ones; (2) a new, more diversified work force with rising expectations, less organizational loyalty, and less reverence to authority; and (3) the quality movement. Long before quality and customer satisfaction became buzzwords in U.S. organizations, the Japanese had concluded that innovation, the power of teams to make decisions, and the ability to motivate employees throughout the ranks of the organization must exist in order for the organization to be successful.

Here are some of the Forum's key findings on leadership:

1. Without leaderhip, organizations falter in times of rapid change.

2. As it becomes more customer-focused, an organization becomes more dependent on the existence of personal initiative and leadership skills at all levels.

3. Positions and titles bear no relation to leadership effectiveness. Leaders are placed throughout the organization.

4. Leadership involves more teamwork than individualism. Building relations across teams in organizations is more important than fostering a daring, isolated high achiever.

5. Leaders inspire others to take on the tasks of leadership.

6. Leadership isn't style, it's actions.

Question: Write a memo indicating how these findings will probably affect you in your first management job. Indicate how your own leadership style measures against those six findings.

Old Flamboyance Is Out as Louis Gerstner Remakes RJR Nabisco

BY GEORGE ANDERS

IRVING, Texas—Among the casual shoppers in Aisle 3 of the Tom Thumb supermarket one recent Thursday morning, Louis V. Gerstner Jr. stands out. He is wearing a suit. He is accompanied by a young executive with a clipboard. And he is thinking of spending, say, $200 million.

Mr. Gerstner, chief executive officer of RJR Nabisco Holdings Inc., is scouting for small, food-company acquisition candidates. Bread, cakes, cereals, spices and a dozen other categories all draw a look.

When Mr. Gerstner is intrigued by what he sees on the shelf, he lingers a moment to engage his strategy chief, Stephen Wilson, in rapid-fire dialogue about profit margins and market share. When Mr. Gerstner is unimpressed, he walks on, forcing Mr. Wilson to abandon all talk of that acquisition idea, flip ahead in his notes and start afresh.

This is the new RJR: A no-nonsense, impatient company where top-level strategy meetings are sometimes held on the linoleum aisles of supermarkets. Bureaucracy, flamboyant spending and intra-company rivals are out. Teamwork, urgency and a Japanese-style fixation on quality are in.

RJR Nabisco might not be quite as much fun or as innovative as a few years ago, when it had far more debt and the freewheeling F. Ross Johnson ran the show. He was willing to spend billions on new plant technology and a smokeless cigarette that flamed out. And in legendary style, Mr. Johnson put sports celebrities on the payroll for big bucks and little work and built up a fleet of 11 corporate jets known as the RJR Air Force.

But competitors, analysts and customers all say that today's RJR is a lot more efficient. Propelling all these changes is the 49-year-old Mr. Gerstner, a one-time McKinsey & Co. management consultant and the former president of American Express Co. Selected in early 1989 to run RJR Nabisco by its major shareholder, the buy-out firm of Kohlberg Kravis Roberts & Co., Mr. Gerstner instantly got broad authority. "We're financial people," says KKR partner Henry Kravis. "Lou makes the long-run operating decisions." . . .

Mr. Gerstner's style—a mixture of charm and cajoling, broad strategic thoughts and sudden intrusions into the nitty-gritty of business—holds lessons for almost any new manager.

But after two years at RJR, he can't claim to be a hero yet. The company's biggest money-maker, the Winston cigarette, has been losing market share for years. And RJR's debt burden doesn't allow it to make the kind of big acquisitions in the food business being made by its major rival, Philip Morris Inc. What's more, the company's free-spending bureaucratic culture has been so ingrained that Mr. Gerstner won't be rid of it anytime soon. Reshaping RJR, he told managers in a closed-door briefing last fall, "is like crossing the Sahara. It just goes on and on and on."

When Mr. Gerstner took over RJR in March 1989, its executive suite was desolate. A host of top managers had quit in the wake of the failed bid for the company by Mr. Johnson, who lost out to KKR. Since then, Mr. Gerstner has filled these slots with his kind of people, bringing in a general counsel from American Express and a chief administrative officer from H.J. Heinz, and hiring as his head of tobacco operations a former RJR hand who had left during the mid-1980s for a post at Citicorp. Gone are the pranks and profanity that caused the company's old Atlanta executive offices to be known as the Fraternity. People now start work at 8 a.m., show an occasional sparkle of dry wit, and otherwise favor such a serious, collegial tone that executives now suggest that headquarters be known as the Seminary.

In two stages in 1989 and 1990, Mr. Gerstner moved RJR's headquarters out of Atlanta to four floors of unremarkable rented space in a midtown Manhattan bank building. Small signs of penny-pinching can be found. Paneling is mahogany where visitors might notice, stained hardwood where they won't. Busy hallways are linked with cheap industrial green carpeting. Walls are covered with rayon.

Gone are the elaborate printed reports operating divisions once sent to headquarters, such as one immense briefing ensemble that Mr. Gerstner derisively calls "the rainbow." It came in red, green and blue binders, telling the CEO everything that had happened the previous month. "If I'm doing my job, I'm talking to division managers all the time," Mr. Gerstner says. "I know what's in the book weeks before all the numbers are typed in."

Such headquarters triumphs are small stuff, though, in the overall sweep of RJR. Even after some buyout-related divestitures, the company's sales exceed $13 billion a year, and its vast work force sprawls throughout the U.S., Latin America, Canada and Western Europe. Drawing on his McKinsey training, Mr. Gerstner spent much of his first year learning RJR Nabisco's business from the bottom up. He logged 250,000 miles visiting bakeries from Chicago to Beijing, attending salesmen's conferences and eating dinner with low-level managers.

Starting early last year, Mr. Gerstner pulled back and tried to develop a broad strategy for the company. The R.J. Reynolds tobacco business was hugely profitable but losing market share. The food company was a financial success, but showed more in-fighting and complacency than Mr. Gerstner wanted.

In speech after speech, Mr. Gerstner aired his strategic thoughts to groups of employees: Cut bureaucracy. Act with a sense of urgency. Emphasize quality and teamwork. He printed up pale gray cards with eight such points and mailed them to all 64,000 employees. Partly because of the boss's personality and partly because of RJR's debt load, the Gerstner agenda, at least for now, include no big risks, no big innovations: It centers on running the current operations to maximum efficiency.

The full program isn't clicking yet. In Winston-Salem, N.C., for example, domestic tobacco chief James Johnston says he is "disappointed" at progress so far in changing his unit's corporate culture. Mr. Johnston, the 44-year-old Gerstner hire from Citicorp who once ran Reynolds's Japanese operations, says he is eager to stir up creative problem-solving among all his employees. But he says many employees still seem comfortable awaiting directives from their boss, answering with a snappy "Yes, sir," and then going off to do a task whether they believe in it or not. . . .

Mr. Gerstner has stepped carefully with Nabisco. He began a recent Dallas speech to Nabisco sales managers by saying: "I'll go anywhere to be with salesmen." He praised the cookie operation as "a tower of strength" and added: "When I joined the company, I heard within 20 minutes that you guys were really good. It's true."

Yet once he wins people's trust, Mr. Gerstner begins goading, prodding. When Dallas sales manager Wayne Yowell proudly mentioned that Nabisco's local market share had risen 1.7 percentage points in the past year, to 49.7%, Mr. Gerstner quickly asked if that figure will top 50% this year. "That's our goal," Mr. Yowell said, slightly taken aback. "But it gets harder once you get near 50%."

"No it doesn't," Mr. Gerstner calmly replied. "It gets easier. Think how little the next guy has."

1. How is Louis Gerstner's leadership style changing RJR Nabisco? What appear to be his strongest core skills?

2. Discuss Gerstner's leadership style in terms of Theory X and Theory Y.

3. Imagine you are a manager working for Gerstner at RJR Nabisco. What type of leadership style might you have to assume to be effective in such an environment?

MICHAEL EISNER AT DISNEY

Michael Eisner, the chief executive officer (CEO) of the Walt Disney Company, had a significant business problem on his hands. One of Disney's largest competitors, MCA, had announced that it was developing a major tourist attraction—a new theme park similar to the Universal Studios movie attraction in Los Angeles. What could Eisner do? How could he compete with this new entry into the theme park market? He knew that if he didn't move quickly, the Disney Company would lose valuable market share in the tourist industry and suffer a substantial loss of revenues. If he delayed or put the wrong competitive program in place, people who would have gone to Disney World in Orlando would visit MCA's new park instead.

Eisner understood that this is the sort of business crisis that tests the systems a leader already has in place. Very often a challenge in the market comes up too fast for an organization to develop a new way of doing things, and the crisis forces managers to face a tough question: Will they be able to implement a competitive program in an organized and effective way? If not, they will wind up scrambling for ideas once the crisis is forced on them and will miss the "response window."

In dealing with the MCA challenge, Eisner's team called on the same systems they use normally to deal with every major business decision. First they turned the project over to Disney's Imagineering, a think-tank plus carpentry shop, which developed design and engineering requirements for a park that could compete directly with MCA's new one. Then a six-person strategic planning team reviewed the plan to be sure that the economics made sense. Finally Eisner and his staff reviewed the financial and technical analysis and made a decision.

The idea that came out of that creative development process was the Disney-MGM theme park. It was built at Disney World in Orlando, further solidifying Disney's prominence in the tourist industry, and the Disney team beat MCA to market by a full year.

Why has the Disney Company remained unique and continued to grow, even after its founder's death? Eisner believes that creative ideas provide the fuel needed for growth and that the pursuit of new ideas is the key to success. He believes he must give his employees free rein if he hopes to foster a spirit of innovation within a financially sound corporation. Fresh new TV spinoffs of longtime Disney favorites—including "DuckTales," "TaleSpin," and "Chip 'n Dale's Rescue Rangers,"—have resulted from this freewheeling spirit.

Eisner and his team believe that there are six fundamental leadership activities that will keep the Disney magic alive *and* financially healthy through the 1990s.

1. *Foster creativity.* By encouraging innovation a company can grow and succeed. When Disney designed its chain of retail stores, it laid them out in a way new to retailing, so that a three-year-old can have fun in them. There are tiers of stuffed Disney characters for toddlers to play with, cartoons running nonstop on large-screen TVs throughout the store, and cheerful sales clerks. The whole atmosphere is geared toward renewing that warm and fuzzy feeling people associate with Disney.

2. *Exploit the most globally profitable niches.* By the time Eisner arrived on the scene, Disney World at Orlando was already

on its way to becoming the most popular vacation destination in the United States. Disney's five Orlando hotels are among the country's most profitable. When EuroDisneyland begins operating in France in 1992, with another six hotels, Disney will have over 20,000 rooms worldwide.

3. *Stay ahead technologically*. In addition to developing and patenting its own 3-D camera, Disney has found unique applications for lasers and fiber optics.

4. *Control costs*. Disney studios can produce a film for $14.5 million, compared with the industry average of $18 million. The studio usually keeps costs down by avoiding the most expensive stars and focusing instead on creating the best scripts.

5. *Be financially creative*. Tokyo Disneyland is the only company theme park that Disney doesn't own and operate outright. It licenses the operation to a Japanese company and collects royalties.

6. *Add a touch of distinction*. Eisner wants Disney's buildings to be architecturally appropriate to the setting. Orlando's hotels thus sport dolphins and Florida colors of terra cotta and green.

1. What leadership skills has Eisner shown at Disney?
2. Is he a transformational leader?
3. Choose a contingency model presented in this chapter and analyze Eisner's leadership style. Why has it been effective?

Chapter 15

ORGANIZATIONAL

COMMUNICATION

Closing a plant

What You Will Learn

1 The six elements in the communication process.

2 Three important types of nonverbal messages.

3 Organizational channels of communication.

4 Barriers to communication and ways to overcome them.

5 Guidelines for effective communication.

6 **Skill Development:** How to communicate effectively and persuasively within an organization.

Chapter Outline

Manager's Viewpoint
When AT&T Closed a Plant

The Communication Process
Sender (Encoder)
Receiver (Decoder)
Message
Insight: How Is Your Office Designed?
Insight: The Thought That Counts in Asia
Channels
Insight: E-Mail at Westinghouse
Feedback
Perception

Barriers to Effective Communication
Organizational Barriers
Individual Barriers
Overcoming Barriers
Global Link: Lost in the Translation

Guidelines for Effective Communication

Experiencing Management
Skill-Building Exercise: Communication Skills
Survey

Manager's Memo

In the News

Management Case
Hartsmoth Company

"Communicate, communicate, communicate."

Roger Bullock
AT&T

When AT&T Closed a Plant

When Ken Raschke walked outside the plant that night, he thought he might get shot. Ken, the manufacturing manager for AT&T's Winston-Salem, North Carolina, plant, had just broken the news at a meeting with 3750 employees that the plant was being closed down.

The following months became a living nightmare for employees and their families. Rumors about other jobs, uncertainty about finding another job, and the stress of lost income all took their toll. Families broke up. Drug and alcohol abuse became common, and stress-related health problems increased.

Realizing that it had a responsibility to its 3750 employees, AT&T set about developing a communication system designed to help them make decisions about their future. First off, AT&T offered jobs at other AT&T plants to all employees with over 15 years of service, and it made immediate retirement available to employees with at least 30 years of service. For employees who wanted neither to relocate nor to retire, free training was provided. Psychological counseling was made available free of charge to all employees.

After the news broke, Roger Bullock, manager of human resources at the plant, advised managers to "Communicate, communicate, communicate. Tell what you know, don't withhold information from anybody, give them information that projects the future as far as you reasonably can."

To communicate with employees as effectively as possible, AT&T

1. Established an Employee Assistance Center in the company cafeteria, where any employee could seek information when the plant was open.

2. Sent employees numerous memos jointly signed by the union and management so that employees would receive one "official" word.

3. Answered all questions in writing and distributed the answers to all employees.

4. Published newsletters regularly, color-coding questions and answers for quick recognition.

5. Held job fairs at which prospective employers inside and outside of AT&T interviewed people.[1]

As is often the effect of a traumatic event, this plant closing brought management and employees closer. Because AT&T addressed its employees' needs through open communication, it experienced no declines in production, quality, or service in the months during which the plant was closing down.

Whether in a school district, bank, transportation system, or manufacturing plant, there is always a need for effective communication. Communication is to an organization as the bloodstream is to a person. Just as a person can develop hardening of the arteries, which impairs physical efficiency, an organization can develop ineffective communication channels, which impair its productive efficiency. And just as heart bypass surgery may be necessary to save a person's life, an organization may have to revamp its communication system in order to survive.

Communication affects how people in an organization relate to each other. Without *effective* communication, managers can accomplish very little. Recall that in Chapter 1 we

Management Roles in Communication

The central role communication plays in the three managerial roles identified by Mintzberg: interpersonal, informational, and decisional.

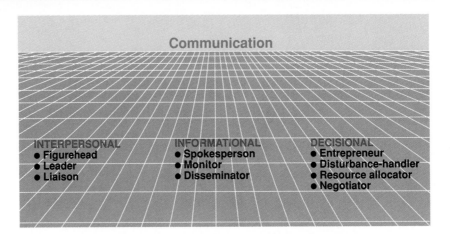

Communication

INTERPERSONAL
● Figurehead
● Leader
● Liaison

INFORMATIONAL
● Spokesperson
● Monitor
● Disseminator

DECISIONAL
● Entrepreneur
● Disturbance-handler
● Resource allocator
● Negotiator

discussed the work of Henry Mintzberg,[2] who described the manager's job in terms of three categories of roles. Communication plays a vital part in each, as is apparent in Figure 15.1.

In their interpersonal roles, managers act as figureheads and leaders of their organizations. Top managers spend about 45 percent of their ''contact'' time with peers, about 45 percent with people outside their company, and only about 10 percent with superiors.

Roger Bullock played the informational role in the process of closing the AT&T plant. He exchanged information about anything that involved the closing with employees, peers, subordinates, and others. In addition, he provided information about the plant's closing to suppliers, local and state government officials, and union leaders.

In their ''decisional'' (decision-making) roles, managers decide whether to undertake new projects, how to handle disturbances, and distribute resources. Although some managerial decisions may be reached in private, many are based on information that others provide.

In Chapter 1 we also pointed out that communication may be verbal or nonverbal and may take many forms, including face-to-face interactions, phone calls, faxes, electronic mail, notes posted on bulletin boards, letters, memos, reports, and oral presentations. In this chapter, we will examine how communication takes place, identify some barriers to communication, and explore ways of improving communication in organizations.

THE COMMUNICATION PROCESS

communication The transfer of information and understandings from one person to another via meaningful symbols.

Communication is the transfer of information and understandings from one person to another via meaningful symbols. It is a way of exchanging and sharing ideas, attitudes, values, opinions, and facts. Significantly, communication is a process that requires both a sender, who begins the process, and a receiver, who completes the communication link.[3]

Within the organization, managers use the communication process to carry out their four functions (planning, organizing, leading, and controlling) and to play their three roles (interpersonal, informational, and decisional). A manager must have access to relevant information in order to make sound decisions. However, until the manager effectively communicates these decisions to others, they cannot be carried out. For example, American Airlines posted a sign on the employees' bulletin board that read, ''NO SMOKING HERE.'' American Airlines managers thought they had communicated a message not to

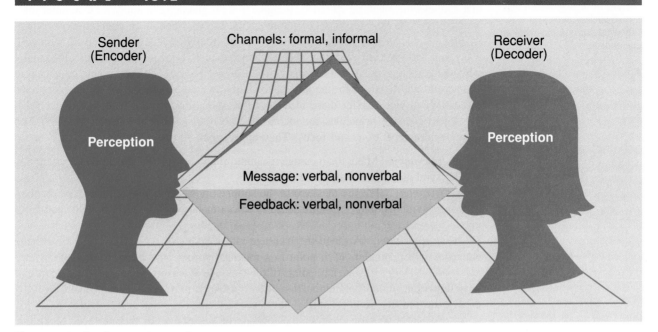

Sender
(Encoder)

Channels: formal, informal

Receiver
(Decoder)

Perception

Perception

Message: verbal, nonverbal

Feedback: verbal, nonverbal

Elements in the Communication Process

The basic elements in the communication process include sender, receiver, channel, message, and feedback.

Source: Adapted from R. C. Huseman. J. M. Lahiff, and J. M. Penrose, Jr., *Business Communication: Strategies and Skills,* 3rd ed., 1988, p. 38, The Dryden Press. Copyright © 1988 by CBS College Publishing. Reprinted by permission of Holt, Rinehart & Winston, Inc.

smoke in that area. However, the sign was only the start of the communication process. Until employees actually read and understood the "NO SMOKING HERE" sign, communication had not taken place.

A large portion of managers' time is spent communicating with other people. Few managers spend most of their time alone at their desks thinking. Managers typically spend 60 percent of their working day communicating with superiors, peers, and subordinates; writing memos, letters, and reports; and talking to others on the phone. In doing so, they are engaged in the communication process, which involves six basic elements:

1 Sender (encoder)
2 Receiver (decoder)
3 Message
4 Channels
5 Feedback
6 Perception

Figure 15.2 shows how these elements interact during the communication process. Managers and employees who are concerned with improving their communication skills need to be aware of these elements and of how they contribute to successful communication. We will discuss the roles of the sender and the receiver first, because they are the actors in the process. We will then move on to the remaining four elements.

Sender (Encoder)

sender The source of information and initiator of the communication process.

The **sender** is the source of information and the initiator of the communication process. The sender tries to choose the type of message and the channel that will be most effective. The sender then encodes the message.

encoding *Translating thoughts or feelings into a medium—whether written or oral—that conveys the meaning intended.*

Encoding translates thoughts or feelings into a medium—whether written or oral—that conveys the meaning intended. Imagine you are planning to apply for a summer job. You will get the best response by phoning first to see whether an opening exists, then writing a letter, and then phoning again to confirm that your letter was received. You will want your letter to convey certain ideas and impressions. For example, you should explain why you are interested in that company. You also need to provide background information about your qualifications for the job and explain how you believe the job will further your career. When you transfer these ideas to paper, you are encoding your message.

There are five principles for increasing encoding accuracy: relevancy, simplicity, organization, repetition, and focus. They apply to all forms of communication.

1 Relevancy. Make the message meaningful and significant, carefully selecting the words, symbols, or gestures to be used.

2 Simplicity. Put the message in the simplest possible terms, reducing the number of words, symbols, and/or gestures used to communicate the intended thoughts and feelings.

3 Organization. Arrange the message into a series of points in order to facilitate understanding. Complete each point in a message before proceeding to the next.

4 Repetition. Restate key points of the message at least twice. Repetition is particularly important in oral communication, wherein words may not be clearly heard or fully understood the first time.

5 Focus. Focus on the essential aspects, or key points, of the message. Make the message clear, and avoid unnecessary detail. In oral communication, emphasize significant points by changing your tone of voice, pausing, gesturing, or using appropriate facial expressions. In written communication, underline key sentences, phrases, or words.

Receiver (Decoder)

receiver *The person who receives and decodes (or interprets) the sender's message.*

decoding *Translating encoded messages into a form that is meaningful to the receiver.*

listening *Paying attention to a message, as distinguished from merely hearing it.*

The **receiver** is the person who receives and decodes (or interprets) the sender's message. **Decoding** translates messages into a form that has meaning to the receiver. The person who receives your letter about a summer job reacts to it first on the basis of whether there are any jobs open. If there aren't, the receiver probably won't pay much attention to it. If there are jobs to be filled, the receiver will probably compare what you wrote about yourself with the type of person the organization wants to hire.

One of the major requirements of the receiver is the ability to listen. **Listening** involves hearing, *and paying attention to,* the message. Of the 75 percent or more of their time that managers spend in communicating, about half is spent listening to others. Becoming a better listener is an important way for managers to improve their communication skills. Studies have shown that most people can recall immediately only about 50 percent of what someone tells them. Two months later, they can recall only 25 percent.[4] That's why managers often use several media, such as newsletters, E-mail, and the telephone. For example, after the 1987 merger of the Burroughs and Sperry corporations to form Unisys Corporation, managers had to inform more than 90,000 employees about the organizational changes and how these changes would affect their jobs. To accomplish this feat, they explained the changes in a 32-page report, written in simple language. They also invited employees to become part of ''focus groups'' to resolve problems associated with the changes. And in 1988, Unisys managers followed up these practices with letters, employee newsletters, and weekly public reports on changes.

Several guidelines for effective listening are presented in Table 15.1.

Message

message *That body of verbal (oral and written) symbols and nonverbal cues that represents the information the sender wants to convey to the receiver.*

The **message** contains the verbal (oral and written)[5] symbols and nonverbal cues that represent the information the sender wants to convey to the receiver. Like a coin, a

Guidelines for Effective Listening

▶ Stop talking! You can't listen if you're talking.
▶ Show a talker that you want to listen. Paraphrase what's been said to show that you understand.
▶ Remove distractions.
▶ Try to see the other person's point of view.
▶ Go easy on argument and criticism, which put people on the defensive and may make them "clam up" or become angry.
▶ Before each person leaves, confirm what has been said.

message has two sides, and the message sent and the message received aren't necessarily the same. Why? First, encoding and decoding of the message may vary because of differences between the sender's and the receiver's backgrounds and viewpoints. Second, the sender may be sending more than one message. When you prepared your resumé for the summer job inquiry, did you type it or write it out in longhand? Was it neat or sloppy? If it was sloppy and contained misspelled words, this in itself sends a clear message to the receiver: The job really isn't important to you; you don't care enough about it to take the trouble to be neat.

Managers (just like everyone else) use three types of messages: nonverbal, verbal, and written. Although the use of nonverbal messages is extremely important, many managers do not recognize this fact. Accordingly, we will discuss nonverbal messages at greater length than the other two types.

nonverbal messages
Messages transmitted through facial expressions, movements, body position, and physical contact rather than by means of words.

Nonverbal Messages   All messages not spoken or written constitute **nonverbal messages.** Nonverbal communication is very powerful.[6] It relies on facial expressions, body movement, gestures, and physical contact. When people communicate in person, as much as 60 percent of the content of the message is transmitted through facial expressions and body movement.

Suppose you are sitting in class, bored. It's one of those days when you really wish you'd forgotten to set the alarm. For something to do, you glance around the room—and at the other end of your row an attractive student of the opposite sex is staring at you.

You look away. The other looks away quickly. You glance back. The other glances back. You smile faintly. You incline your head toward the professor and roll your eyes. The other smiles wider and nods once. You glance toward the door. The other looks at you, then at the clock, then at the door.

The open, brightly colored design of Apple Computer's Learning Center sends a *nonverbal message* about its function as a basic training center for new employees.

(Photo: Sharon Risedorph/Courtesy of STUDIOS Architecture)

Without saying a word, you've set up a meeting place, a time, and an opening conversation with another student. These nonverbal messages have resulted in effective communication.

When talking with someone, managers can effectively reinforce or supplement their words by means of nonverbal messages. Let's look at three of the many kinds of nonverbal messages that managers should be aware of and should use effectively: our use of space, our personal appearance, and our body language.

proxemics The study of the way people use physical space to convey messages about themselves.

1 Space. How close we are to the other person, where we sit or stand, and how we arrange our office can have a real impact on communication.[7] The term **proxemics** refers to the ways in which we use physical space to convey a message about ourselves. Think of how you would feel if you walked into class midway through the term and someone was sitting in "your seat." You'd probably feel angry because your space, or territory, had been invaded. Space and the use of space have communicative importance. (To test how important your territory is to you, complete the quiz shown in Figure 15.3.)[8]

Status or power also is often communicated through spatial arrangements in corporate offices in North America. Top managers have larger offices, windows with better views, plusher carpeting, and higher-quality furnishings than middle managers. Meriting a personal secretary, the seating arrangement at meetings, a chauffeured limousine, use of a private dining room, and the ability to summon employees for discussion—all send messages via the use of space. The following account illustrates how managers use space, when designing corporate headquarters, to convey messages to employees and customers about their organization.

HOW IS YOUR OFFICE DESIGNED?

*I*NSIGHT There are various elements of office design that influence attitudes, behaviors, and (through symbolic messages) impressions. Senior managers at Home Box Office (HBO) chose not to move into the top floor of the company's new office building but instead moved into the middle floor. This location sent employees the message that titles were not valued and that senior managers really wanted employees to drop by to talk informally.

The placement of chairs has also been found to affect communication. People seated face-to-face are more likely to argue than people seated at right angles. Placing chairs directly next to one another often inhibits communication among those seated, and placing chairs back-to-back results (not surprisingly) in no communication at all. When Chembank redecorated its corporate boardroom, changing the design from one in which the board members directly faced senior management to one in which everybody shared a U-shaped table, greater participation resulted.

Finally, office decor has been found to send out strong messages. Plants and flowers convey warmth and friendliness. Certificates, trophies, and plaques suggest that the organization values good performance. Flags, logos, seals, and pictures of the organization's leaders communicate that the organization values structure.[9]

2 Personal appearance. Most of us have heard it said that "Clothes make the person." Style consultants for major corporations believe that the way a person dresses definitely communicates something to others. According to most managers, employees should ask themselves, "Is the way I'm dressed going to hurt or help my business?" Like it or not, people still judge you partly on the basis of how you look. If you are dressed appropriately, management sees you as better organized than people who dress inappropriately.[10]

How Territorial Are You?

Instructions: Circle one number to answer each question as follows: 1 = strongly agree, 2 = agree, 3 = not sure, 4 = disagree, and 5 = strongly disagree.

1. If I arrive at my apartment (room) and find my roommate sitting in my chair, I am annoyed if he or she doesn't at least offer to get up immediately.

    1   2   3   4   5

2. I do not like anyone to remove anything from my desk without asking me first.

    1   2   3   4   5

3. If a stranger puts a hand on my shoulder when talking to me, I feel uncomfortable.

    1   2   3   4   5

4. If my suit jacket is lying on the back of a chair and another student comes in and chooses to sit in that chair, I feel that he or she should ask to move my jacket or choose another chair.

    1   2   3   4   5

5. If I enter a classroom and "reserve" a chair with a notebook, I am annoyed or offended upon my return to find my book moved and someone sitting in "my seat."

    1   2   3   4   5

6. If a person who is not a close friend of mine gets within a foot from my face to talk to me, I will back off or uncomfortably stand my ground.

    1   2   3   4   5

7. I do not like strangers walking into my room (apartment).

    1   2   3   4   5

8. If I lived in an apartment, I would not want the landlord to enter it for any reason without my permission.

    1   2   3   4   5

9. I do not like my friends or family borrowing my clothes without asking me first.

    1   2   3   4   5

10. If I notice someone staring at me in a restaurant, I become annoyed or uncomfortable.

    1   2   3   4   5

Add the numbers that you circle for all 10 statements. Then compare your total with the following definitions.

10-25 points: *High territorial.* Your instincts for staking out and protecting what you consider yours are high. You believe strongly in your territorial rights.

26-39 points: *Ambiguous about territory.* You may act territorial in some circumstances but not in others. You are somewhat unsure about how you feel about the use of space.

40-50 points: *Not territorial.* You disagree with the entire concept of territoriality. You dislike possessiveness, protectiveness, and jealousy. The concept of private ownership is not central to your philosophy of life.

---

3 Body language.   The body and its movement—particularly those of the face and eyes, which are very expressive—tell other people a lot. Up to 55 percent of the content of a message is communicated by facial expression and body posture; another 38 percent is based on inflection and the tone of the speech. The words themselves account for only 7 percent of the content of the message.

The ability to interpret facial expressions is an important part of communication. Eye contact is a direct and powerful way of communicating nonverbally. In the United States, social rules suggest that in most situations, brief eye contact is appropriate. We often interpret prolonged eye contact as either a threat or a sign of romantic interest, depending on the context.[11]

Posture also communicates meaning by signaling one's degree of self-confidence or interest in what is being discussed. The more interested you are, the more likely you are to lean toward the person who is talking. On the other hand, leaning away may communicate a lack of interest. A good poker player watches the eyes of the other players as new cards are dealt. Pupil dilation often betrays whether the card(s) just dealt improved the player's hand. Similarly, tension and anxiety typically show in a person's legs and feet. People are often able to hide their tension from the waist up but may give themselves away by crossing their legs tightly and tapping their feet.

The following Insight focuses on how nonverbal messages can help or hinder you in communicating with Asian managers. Note especially how some practices that North Americans believe to be acceptable can lead to communication problems.

Verbal Messages Managers communicate verbally (orally and in writing) more often than in any other way. Oral communication takes place face-to-face and over the telephone. Many managers prefer face-to-face communication, because nonverbal messages are an important part of it. To get their meaning across on the telephone, they must choose their words and tone of voice more carefully.

Effective verbal communication requires the sender to (1) encode the message in words (and nonverbal cues) that will convey it accurately to the receiver, (2) convey the message in a well-organized manner, and (3) try to eliminate distractions in the situation.[13]

Written Messages Managers usually prefer oral to written messages, because oral communication is quicker and the sender and receiver can interact. However, businesses use many forms of written messages (such as reports, memoranda, letters, and newsletters). These media are most appropriate when information has to be distributed to many people at scattered locations and when it is necessary to keep a record of what was sent. The following are some guidelines for good written messages:

▶ The message should be drafted with the receiver clearly in mind.

▶ The contents of the message should be well thought out ahead of time.

▶ The message should be as brief as possible, without extraneous words and ideas. Important messages should be prepared in draft form first and then polished.

▶ If the message has to be long, include a brief summary on the first page. This summary should clarify the main points and contain page references that the reader can use to locate details on each item.

▶ The message should be carefully organized. State the most important point first, then the next most important point, and so on. This way, even if the receiver reads only the first few points, the essentials of the message will get across.

▶ Make the subject clear by giving the message a title.

▶ Make the message more readable by using simple words and short, clear sentences.

Channels

channel The path a message follows from sender to receiver.

information richness The information-carrying capacity of a channel of communication.

The **channel** is the path a message follows in going from the sender to the receiver. **Information richness** pertains to the information-carrying capacity of the channel.[14] Not all channels can carry the same richness of information. Some channels are highly informative for both senders and receivers; others provide little information. As shown in Figure 15.4, face-to-face is the richest channel because it conveys several information cues simultaneously, including oral communication and nonverbal cues. Face-to-face also provides immediate feedback so that understanding can be checked and misinterpretations corrected. The telephone is somewhat less rich than face-to-face. Immediate feedback is possible, but visual cues are lacking. Written communications are less rich, because feedback is slow and only information that is written down is received. Numbers tend to be used to describe simple data, such as absenteeism, turnover, checkbook balances, number of grievances, and the like. Channels low in richness are considered *lean,* because they are effective mainly for sending specific data and facts. For sending routine cost figures to employees in the production department, Bill Houchin of DSC Technologies uses a simple budget report—a lean channel. On the other hand, Patrick Foley, president of Hyatt Hotels, regularly schedules meetings with employees at Hyatt to obtain information on employee morale and to communicate future expansion strategies. He chooses a *rich* channel to send this information.

A relatively new *channel of communication*—the sometimes infamous 900 number—is being used by Pratt & Whitney engineers to handle customers' technical questions.

Information Richness of Channels

Different channels have the capacity to carry more or less information.

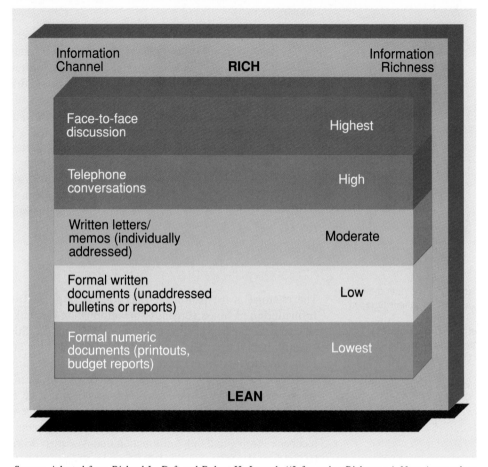

Source: Adapted from Richard L. Daft and Robert H. Lengel, ''Information Richness: A New Approach to Managerial Behavior and Organization Design,'' in Barry M. Staw and Larry L. Cummings, eds., *Research in Organizational Behavior,* vol. 6 (Greenwich, CT: JAI Press, 1984), 191–233.

In addition to selecting a specific channel, the manager must choose among four *types* of channels to communicate with employees. These are downward, upward, and horizontal channels and the grapevine.

Downward Channels   Managers use **downward channels** to send messages to employees or customers. For instance, the American Airlines reservation center in Fort Worth receives more than 160,000 calls a day. To communicate effectively with its 2700 employees in this center, American managers use downward channels to communicate to employees

downward channel   A channel of communication that managers use to send messages to employees or customers.

▶ How to handle special fares
▶ Job descriptions detailing duties and responsibilities
▶ Policies and procedures explaining what is expected of employees, and the organization's rules, and employee benefits
▶ Feedback about an individual's job performance
▶ News of activities and events that management believes it is important for employees to participate in (charitable organizations, blood drives, and the like)

Downward communication is probably the most frequently used channel in organizations. George Pratt, President of InteCom, Inc., devotes nearly 50 percent of his time to communicating with employees through meetings, policy directives, and memos and to explaining InteCom's objectives, strategic plans, and activities. It may also be the most misused, because some managers give little thought to allowing employees to respond. In fact, the fundamental problem with downward communication is that too often it is one-way: It's a lean channel that doesn't encourage feedback from those who receive it. To correct this problem, managers should urge employees to use upward channels.

upward channel A channel of communication by which subordinates send information to superiors.

Upward Channels Some managers do not see the value of encouraging employees to participate formally in setting objectives, planning, and formulating policies. The result is failure to provide **upward channels.** These are the channels by which subordinates send information to superiors. Such channels are the only formal means that employees have for communicating with higher-level managers in the organization. When you complete an evaluation survey at the end of a course, rating the course, book, and instructor, you are using an upward channel of communication.

Managers should encourage upward communication. It provides feedback on how well employees understand the messages they have received, and it enables employees to voice their opinions and ideas. For upward communication to be effective, it must be allowed to occur freely. If effective, upward communication can provide an emotional release and, at the same time, give employees a chance to participate, the feeling they are being listened to, and a sense of personal worth.

However, managers should also be aware of problems that can plague upward communication.[15] First, few employees want their superiors to learn anything negative about them, so they usually screen out bad news. Most try to impress their superiors by emphasizing their contributions to the company. Some may even try to make themselves look better by putting others down. Second, an employee's personal anxieties, aspirations, and attitudes almost always color what he or she says. How many of you would tell your instructor that this course is terrible (even if it were)? Few would, for fear that the instructor would hold their candor against them and "reward" it with a low grade. Finally, the employee may be competing for the manager's job and thus be willing to stand by and let the manager stumble. Politics is a way of life in most corporations.

horizontal channel A channel that managers use when communicating across departmental lines.

Horizontal Channels Managers use **horizontal channels** when communicating across departmental lines. Horizontal channels may be either formal or informal, depending on whether they follow the formal organizational structure. They frequently connect people on the same level in the company. Messages communicated horizontally are usually related to coordinating activities, sharing information, and solving problems. Horizontal channels are extremely important in today's hi-tech organizations. At Fidelity Investments Southwest in Irving, Texas, each of the 106 employees sits in a cubicle 5 feet square. These employees handle about 12,000 consumer service calls a day. The employees are organized in teams, including a team manager. That structure facilitates communication to and from all employees. Though employees may have to move around to be part of a customer service team, belonging to a team helps members to communicate freely with each other.

grapevine The organization's informal communication system.

Informal Channels We have concentrated on formal channels of communication so far, but we do not underestimate the importance of informal channels of communication. Although we know less about them, we know that the grapevine is one source of information for managers. The **grapevine** is the organization's informal communication system.[16] The term comes from a Civil War practice of hanging telegraph lines loosely from tree to tree, like a grapevine. The grapevine functions to ease communication problems between managers and/or employees. The path that messages follow along the grapevine is based on social interaction. American Airlines has recognized the importance of this channel to the extent of maintaining a "grapevine file" in the computer's on-line systems. This file enables employees to ask managers and other employees questions, offer compliments and criticism, and verify rumors.

E-mail (left) and *voice mail*—information technologies that are changing the face of organizational communication.

Managers and employees also spend considerable time meeting with peers and others outside the organization. They attend the meetings of professional associations, trade shows, and other gatherings. As a result they develop various close, informal associations and working relationships with talented and useful people both inside and outside the organization. Managers use these networks to help each other, trading favors and calling on each other's resources for career advancement or other types of support. For example, a recent survey of 1005 organizations conducted by *Fortune* found that 86 percent of these organizations have reduced their managerial ranks during the past five years. Fierce international competition and heavy corporate debt loads have forced organizations to cut their work forces. Managerial downsizing has outplaced a number of middle- and top-level employees. Drake Beam and Morin, the nation's largest outplacement firm, has found that most outplaced employees find their next job through contacts with friends and others whom they met in the course of doing their jobs. The business schools at Stanford, Northwestern, and other universities have also started outplacement services for their alumni who need counseling. These networks help outplaced managers find new jobs.[17]

The Impact of Technology New information technologies are rapidly changing the methods of communication available to managers and employees—and thus the channels of communication. Telephone answering machines (voice mail), fax machines, teleconferencing, closed-circuit television systems, computerized report preparation, and videotaping are examples of communication methods developed during the past 25 years.

At Bank of America, Boeing, Memorex, Digital Equipment, Westinghouse, Manufacturer's Hanover Trust, and Cummins Engine Company, managers and other employees are using an even more advanced method of communicating with each other. **Electronic mail (E-mail)** uses computer text-editing to send written information quickly, inexpensively, and efficiently.[18] Messages are sent, in seconds, at the sender's convenience. They are read at the receiver's convenience. Senders and receivers usually process their own electronic mail. They don't have to give messages to, or receive messages from, secretaries or telephone operators. Messages appear on (and disappear from) video screens with no hard copies left behind, unless a hard copy is specifically desired.

electronic mail (E-mail)
Channel of communication by which written information is sent via computer text-editing.

Electronic mail has become popular with managers for several reasons. First, a manager doesn't have to wait "maybe a week" for a response, because information can usually be sent, returned, and recalled in a matter of moments. Second, E-mail is relatively inexpensive, because it can "piggyback" on computers and other equipment that many companies already have in place. Third, it increases productivity by eliminating the need for the paper-handling steps required in traditional interoffice or intercompany communication systems. On the other hand, one disadvantage has been observed in companies that use E-mail extensively. Employees who might never confront a co-worker face to face are less hesitant to explode at others via E-mail—a phenomenon called *flaming*.

The following account describes the benefits of using electronic mail at Westinghouse—without flaming.

E-MAIL AT WESTINGHOUSE

I N S I G H T

Westinghouse Electric Company began using electronic mail in 1980. Today some 6000 PCs connect 10,700 Westinghouse employees, along with 1000 customers. The system covers the United States and parties in 37 foreign countries.

To illustrate how E-mail works, consider the options available to President Paul E. Lego for communicating with a manager in Tokyo. He can use traditional mail. It may take weeks to get a reply. He can send a message via a telex center. To do so, he must dictate a letter containing the message, and this letter has to be retyped at the telex center. It may then take up to 8 hours for the telex message to arrive in Tokyo. (The same procedure, in the opposite direction, must be followed for Lego to receive a reply.) Lego can, of course, call Tokyo. Given that 5:00 P.M. in Pittsburgh is equivalent to 6:00 A.M. in Tokyo, however, timing as well as cost make the telephone a less-than-optimal messaging system. E-mail enables Lego to send a message before leaving work in the evening and to have an answer waiting on his computer when he arrives for work the next morning. More important, E-mail is 90 percent less expensive than overseas calls and letters and 75 percent less costly than telex.

Lego estimates that electronic mail and other automated office techniques, such as teleconferencing, have had a positive effect on profits at Westinghouse. Up to one-third of the company's 6 percent annual increases in the productivity of white-collar workers since the early 1980s has been attributed to these technological advances.[19]

Feedback

feedback The receiver's response to the sender's message.

Because effective communication must be two-way, the receiver should provide feedback to the sender. **Feedback** is the receiver's response to the sender's message. Providing feedback is the best way to show that a message has been received and to indicate whether it has been understood. Managers should not assume that everything they say or write will be understood exactly as intended. If they don't encourage feedback, they are likely to misjudge how much their subordinates understand. Thus they will be less effective than managers who encourage feedback.

Whenever a message is sent, the actions of the sender affect the reactions of the receiver. The reactions of the receiver, in turn, affect the later actions of the sender. If the sender receives no response, either the message was never received or the receiver chose not to respond. In either case, the sender is alerted to the need to find out why the receiver did not respond. When a sender receives rewarding feedback, he or she continues to produce the same kind of message. When feedback is *not* rewarding, the sender eventually changes the type of message.

Receiver reactions also tell the sender how well objectives or tasks are being accomplished. However, in this case the receiver exerts control over the sender by the kind of feedback she or he provides. Thus the sender must rely on the receiver for accurate and complete information. Such feedback assures the sender that things are going as planned or brings to light problems that have to be solved.

Procter & Gamble, 3M, IBM, and other companies have set up guidelines to help ensure that feedback in their organizations is effective. In general, these guidelines state that feedback should have the following characteristics:[20]

1 It should be helpful. If the receiver of the message provides feedback that adds to the sender's information, the feedback is more likely to be helpful.

2 It should be descriptive rather than evaluative. If the receiver responds to the message in a descriptive manner, the feedback is more likely to be effective. If the receiver is evaluative (or judgmental), the feedback is likely to be ineffective or even to cause a breakdown in communication.

3 It should be specific rather than general. The receiver should respond specifically to points raised and questions asked in the message. If the receiver responds in generalities, the feedback may indicate evasion or lack of understanding.

4 It should be well timed. The reception—and thus the effectiveness—of feedback is affected by the context in which it occurs. Giving feedback to a person during half-time of a football game or at a cocktail party is different from giving the same person feedback in the office.

5 It should not overwhelm. Verbal communication depends heavily on memory. Accordingly, when large amounts of information are involved, verbal feedback is less effective than written feedback. People tend to "tune in and out" of conversations. They may fail to grasp what the speaker is saying if the message is too long and complex.

Perception

perception The meaning ascribed to a message.

Perception is the meaning ascribed to a message by either sender or receiver (see Figure 15.1). Our perceptions are influenced by the objects we see, by the ways we organize these objects in our memory, and by the meanings we attach to them. The ability to perceive varies from person to person. Some people, having entered a room only once, can later describe it in detail, whereas others can barely remember anything about it. Thus the mental ability to notice and remember differences is important. How we interpret what we perceive is affected by our past. A clenched fist raised in the air by an employee on strike and walking the picket line could be interpreted as an angry threat against the organization *or* as an expression of union solidarity and accomplishment. The attitude we bring to a situation colors our perception of it. You can acknowledge that rejection of your application to graduate school reflects your having partied too much as an undergraduate, or you can blame that biased admissions officer.

selective perception The process of screening out information that one wishes or needs to avoid.

Many problems in communication can be traced to two problems of perception: selective perception and stereotyping. **Selective perception** is the process of screening out information that we aren't comfortable with or don't want to be bothered with. Many of us "tune out" TV commercials, and we have all been accused of listening only to what we want to hear. Both are examples of selective perception. In organizations, employees often do the same thing. Manufacturing employees pay close attention to manufacturing problems, whereas financial employees pay close attention to the bottom line. These employees filter out information that deals with other areas of the organization and focus on information that is directly relevant to their own jobs. In the *Preview Case,* most of the AT&T employees focused on what was happening in their plant and ignored other information, such as the general state of the economy, unemployment rates in other cities, and the like.

stereotyping *Making assumptions about an individual solely on the basis of her or his belonging to a particular gender, race, age group, or the like.*

Stereotyping is the process of making assumptions about individuals on the basis of their belonging to a certain gender, race, age group, or the like. Stereotyping in this manner distorts reality, because it assumes that all people of any one gender, race, or age have similar characteristics, which simply isn't true. Many organizations, such as Corning Glass Works and Arthur Andersen, have instituted classes to teach employees about managing a diverse work force and to demonstrate how stereotyping can lead to inefficiency and turnover. Karen Kallow conducts sessions for Arthur Andersen employees on gender issues. She points out that successful women are often stereotyped as having to (1) take more risks and be consistently more outstanding than men; (2) be tough, but not macho; (3) be ambitious but not to expect equal treatment; and (4) take responsibility but follow the advice of others. These stereotypes place unrealistic expectations on women, even though mounting evidence suggests that when careers are matched, women are remarkably similar to men in their characteristics, abilities, and motives.[21]

In brief, then, our ability to encode and decode is based on our ability to perceive the message and situation accurately. Thus this ability may vary widely. The type of message we send, the channel of communication we use, and our ability to respond all depend on our perceptions.

BARRIERS TO EFFECTIVE COMMUNICATION

One of the first steps in communicating more successfully is to identify barriers to the process. These barriers hinder the sending and receiving of messages by distorting, or sometimes even completely blocking, intended meanings. We've divided these impediments into organizational and individual barriers, although there is obviously some overlapping. We list these barriers in Table 15.2.

Organizational Barriers

Channels of communication, both formal and informal, are largely determined by organizational structure. The degree of specialization present in the organization may also affect clear communication.

Structure Whenever one person holds a higher position than another, communication problems are likely to occur. The more levels in the organization, and the farther the receiver is from the sender, the harder it is to communicate a message effectively.

Figure 15.5 illustrates the loss of understanding as messages are sent through downward channels. To help reduce this problem, top managers increasingly are

TABLE 15.2

Barriers to Communication

Organizational
Structure of the organization
Specialization of task functions by members
Different objectives
Status relationships among members

Individual
Conflicting assumptions
Semantics
Emotions
Communication skills

Levels of Understanding

Given 100 percent understanding at the top-management level, by the time a message has passed through another five levels, only 20 percent of the original message may be understood.

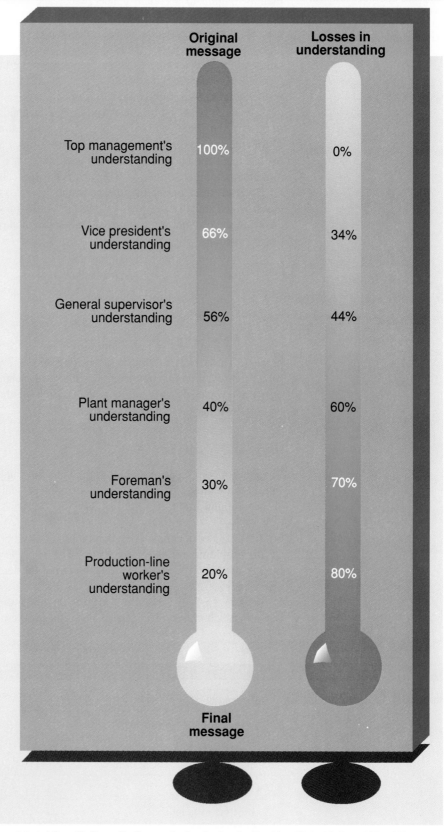

	Original message	Losses in understanding
Top management's understanding	100%	0%
Vice president's understanding	66%	34%
General supervisor's understanding	56%	44%
Plant manager's understanding	40%	60%
Foreman's understanding	30%	70%
Production-line worker's understanding	20%	80%

Final message

Source: Adapted from E. Scannell, *Communication for Leadership,* New York: McGraw-Hill, 1970, p. 5. Reproduced with permission.

The *status* message conveyed by the intimidating office of a law firm executive could serve as a *barrier to communication*.

using video tapes that deliver the same message to all employees at various locations. In doing so, these managers use both verbal and nonverbal messages and cut out intervening receivers/senders in order to increase the probability that their original message will be received intact. Exxon's management used video tapes to announce the decision to relocate the company's corporate headquarters from New York City to Irving, Texas. The video tapes also stressed the reasons for the relocation and the need for employee cooperation during the move.

Specialization As knowledge becomes more specialized, professionals in many fields develop their own jargon, or shorthand, to simplify communication among themselves. However, this often makes communication with people in other fields difficult. For example, a tax accountant and a marketing research manager might have difficulty communicating successfully. Moreover, in an attempt to make themselves indispensable, some people intentionally use the language of specialization to obscure what is going on. Employees often use their specialized language when trying to give others ''snow jobs.'' Most of us have resorted to snow jobs on occasion to protect ourselves and our egos. A plumber recently wrote to HUD, a government agency, to find out whether it was safe to use hydrochloric acid to unclog drains. A bureaucrat wrote, ''The efficacy of hydrochloric acid is indisputable, but corrosive acid is incompatible with metallic permanence.'' The plumber wrote back saying he agreed and was using it. A fax message from the bureaucrat arrived immediately at the plumber's store. It read, ''Don't use hydrochloric acid. It eats the hell out of pipes.'' Then the plumber understood.

Different Objectives When AT&T decided to close its plant in Winston-Salem, different objectives surfaced. AT&T chose to close this plant because it was the smallest plant. The company assumed that the work and employees from the smallest plant could more easily be absorbed by its larger plants than vice versa. However, closing the plant was unjustified in many workers' eyes. Some took a substantial cut in pay, in addition to losing company-paid fringe benefits, just to stay in the area while their children finished school or to be close to friends and relatives.

status Social rank in a group.

Status Relationships **Status** is a person's social rank in a group. Some typical symbols of status, such as roomy offices and special privileges, were discussed earlier in this chapter. These symbols are usually visible, external things that attach to a person or job and serve as evidence of social rank. They emerge most clearly when we compare different levels of management. Each higher level usually has the authority to give itself additional perquisites (perks).

Status may be a significant barrier to effective communication because (1) it is often used to insulate managers from things they don't want to hear, and (2) it influences the amount and kinds of information that subordinates channel upward.

Individual Barriers

The Center for Creative Leadership at Greensboro, North Carolina, estimates that half of all managers and 30 percent of top managers have some difficulty in communicating with others. The center has found that often managers are aloof and are poor communicators. Through an intense training session at the center, managers can learn how to improve their communication skills. The center's staff works with managers who think that their messages are clear and effective when, in fact, they aren't. These managers' words, phrases, and references may be clear to some employees, puzzling to others, and obscure to still others. This kind of problem can be caused by conflicting assumptions, by semantics, by emotions, and/or by lack of effective communication skills.[22]

Conflicting Assumptions The sender assumes that the receiver will interpret the message as the sender intends. But a key work or phrase may mean one thing to the sender and something else to the receiver. For example, a sales representative phoned in a special order, asking that it be shipped "as soon as possible." Five days later, the sales rep got a call from the irate customer wanting to know when the order would be delivered. Upon checking with the shipping department, the sales rep found that the order was being shipped that day. "I thought I told you to ship it as soon as possible," shouted the rep. "That's just what we're doing," yelled the shipping manager. To the salesperson, "as soon as possible" meant *now*. To the shipping department, which often received that kind of order from sales reps, it meant something totally different.

semantics The study of the way words are used and the meanings they convey.

Semantics The study of the way words are used and the meanings they convey is called **semantics.** Misinterpretation of word meanings can play a major role in communication failure. Most words in the dictionary have several meanings; some common words have as many as 18. One example of a common word with many meanings is *charge:*

Please charge the battery.
Charge it.
You are charged with running a red light.
The charge for this service is $25.00.
Let's charge ahead on this new plan.

When two people attribute different meanings to the same words but don't realize it, a barrier exists. Faculty members who say, "This is an easy test," can mislead students who don't know the faculty member's definition of *easy*.

emotion A subjective reaction, or feeling.

Emotions An **emotion** is a subjective reaction, a feeling. Remembering experiences, we recall not only events but also the feelings that accompanied them. Thus when we communicate, we convey emotions as well as facts and opinions. The sender's feelings influence her or his encoding of the message and may or may not be apparent to the receiver. If they are clear, then both the sender's and the receiver's feelings affect decoding of the message and the nature of the response.

Communication Skills The ability to communicate varies from person to person. Some differences in communication skills result from culture, education, and training, whereas others stem from basic personality characteristics. For instance, Japanese businesspeople speak little, compared to Americans, because they prefer to wait and listen. The higher their managerial position, the more they listen. Hiroyoshi Takanaka, general manager of Honda Motors' China Division, says Japanese have a saying: "He who speaks first at a meeting is a dumb ass."[23]

Articulate, persuasive, and confident people communicate more effectively than those who are less so. Some people are naturally better listeners than others—or train themselves to be. Anxious people may be too preoccupied with personal problems or

Overcoming Barriers to Communication

Regulate the flow of information.
Encourage feedback.
Simplify the language used in the message.
Listen actively.
Restrain negative emotions.
Use nonverbal cues.
Use the grapevine.

with what they are going to say next to pay close attention to what other people are saying. People under considerable stress may also be unable to listen properly.

Communication effectiveness is also influenced by the timing of messages. Managers who relay important instructions to employees on the Friday afternoon before a Monday holiday show poor timing. The employees' attention has already shifted from work to their plans for the long weekend. In contrast, the department manager who asks for new funds after the company has achieved its financial objectives for the year shows good timing. Under these circumstances, the department manager's superior is likely to listen to the request.

Overcoming Barriers

The good news is that you *can* overcome barriers to effective communication. You must first be aware that they exist and can cause serious organizational problems. Then you must be willing to invest the effort and time necessary to overcome the barriers. Several ways of overcoming barriers to communication are presented in Table 15.3.

Regulate the Flow of Information Managers who receive too much information suffer from information overload. They should set up a system that identifies priority messages for immediate attention. One way of doing this is to instruct subordinates to bring the manager information only when significant deviations from objectives and plans occur (this is known as exceptions reporting). When everything is going as planned, the manager doesn't need a report. In addition, messages should be condensed. Procter & Gamble recommends that all messages be limited to a page or less. Key assumptions usually get lost in 10-page proposals, and loose logic may be camouflaged. Not so on a single page.

Encourage Feedback Managers and others should follow up to determine whether important messages have been understood. Feedback lets the manager know whether the employee understands the message accurately. Feedback doesn't have to be verbal; in fact, actions often speak louder than words. The sales manager who describes desired changes in the monthly sales planning report receives feedback from the report itself when it is turned in. If it contains the proper changes, the manager knows the message was received and understood. Similarly, when you talk to a group of people, look for nonverbal feedback that will tell you whether you are getting through to them.

Simplify the Language of the Message Because language can be a barrier, managers and others should choose words that subordinates will understand. Sentences should be concise, and managers should avoid jargon that people will not understand or that may mislead. In general, understanding is improved by simplifying the language used—consistently, of course, with the nature of the intended audience.

Listen Actively Employees need to become good listeners as well as good message senders. Recently, several organizations have developed training programs to improve employee listening. For example, at an LTV Middle Management Program taught in Grand Prairie, Texas, the content includes awareness training in "active listening" to what others have to say, reducing "noise" to improve communication, and developing better communication skills through role playing and team presentations.[24]

Restrain Negative Emotions   Like everyone else, managers convey emotions when communicating, but negative emotions can distort the content of the message. When a manager is emotionally upset, he or she is more likely than at other times to phrase the message poorly. And when a subordinate is emotionally upset, he or she is more likely to misinterpret the message. The simplest answer in such a situation is to call a halt until the people involved can restrain their emotion—that is, until they can be descriptive, for the most part, instead of evaluative.

Use Nonverbal Cues   Managers and other employees should use nonverbal cues to emphasize points and express feelings. Recall the methods of nonverbal communication that we have already discussed. Managers and others also need to make sure that their actions reinforce their words so that they don't send mixed messages.

Use the Grapevine   Because managers couldn't get rid of the grapevine in an organization even if they tried, they should use it to send information rapidly, test reactions before announcing a final decision, and obtain valuable feedback. Too, the grapevine frequently carries destructive rumors, reducing employee morale and organizational effectiveness. Managers who are "plugged into" the grapevine can partially counteract this negative effect by making sure that relevant, accurate, meaningful, and timely information gets to employees. In the *Complete Manager* computer simulation that accompanies this text, you can use the grapevine to learn about opportunities and problems that arise in running your organization.

As hard as managers try to communicate their messages to others effectively, they often fail. Communicating with managers in foreign countries poses even more problems for managers, because mistakes in translation can lead to some embarrassing blunders (see the accompanying Global Link).

GUIDELINES FOR EFFECTIVE COMMUNICATION

To be effective communicators, managers must understand not merely the concepts presented in Figure 15.1 but also the guidelines for effective communication. These guidelines, as presented throughout the chapter, are summarized in Table 15.4. We have expressed them in terms of the American Management Association's eight guidelines that managers can use to improve their communication.[25]

TABLE 15.4

Guidelines for Effective Communication

Clarify your ideas before communicating.
Examine the true purpose of the communication.
Consider the setting in which the communication will take place.
Consult with others, when appropriate, in planning communications.
Be mindful of the nonverbal messages you send.
Take the opportunity to convey something of help to the receiver.
Follow up the communication.
Be sure your actions support your communication.

GLOBAL Link

LOST IN THE TRANSLATION

Translation errors cause many blunders in international business. In fact, the largest number of blunders in advertising promotions is caused by faulty translation. These blunders fall into three categories: carelessness, multiple meanings, and idioms.

Carelessness Consider the experience that Otis Engineering Corporation had when it participated in an exhibition held in Moscow. Initially, the company's representatives couldn't understand why its display was laughed at and scorned. Much to their embarrassment, they discovered that a translator had labeled their product as "equipment for orgasms" rather than "completed equipment."

An American auto manufacturer advertised its battery as "highly rated." Unfortunately, when the company introduced its car in Venezuela, the translation described the battery as "highly overrated."

Multiple Meanings Translated messages can also convey more than one meaning. Consider the trials and tribulations of Parker Pen Company. In ads destined for Latin America, Parker wanted to use the word *bola* to describe its ballpoint pen. However, the firm discovered that the word has various meanings in different Latin American countries. In some, *bola* conveys the intended meaning of "ball," but in another, it means "revolution." It is used as an obscenity in yet another country and means "lie" in still another. Fortunately, the company recognized this problem before forging ahead. However, a few years later, Parker decided to use its slogan "Avoid embarrassment—use Parker Pens" in Latin America. The slogan was intended to show that Parker pocket pens wouldn't leak when put in a shirt pocket. But anticipated sales never materialized. Why? The Spanish word for "embarrassment" is also used to indicate pregnancy, so the Parker Pen Company was unknowingly promoting its pens as contraceptives!

Idioms Everyone in the United States has probably heard the advertisement for Pepsi-Cola "Come alive with Pepsi." When the ad campaign was introduced in Germany, the company was forced to revise the ad because it discovered that its translation of "come alive" into German conveyed "come out of the grave."

An American company advertised its product to a Spanish audience by claiming that anyone who did not wear its brand of hosiery just "wouldn't have a leg to stand on." But when the copy was translated, it actually stated that the person "would have only one leg."

According to management consultant Peggy Golden, companies should routinely have translated messages translated back to the original language to ensure the integrity of the message.

Source: Adapted from J. Lieblich, "If You Want a Big New Market," *Fortune*, November 21, 1988, 181–188; D. Ricks and V. J. Mahajan, "Blunders in International Marketing: Fact or Fiction," *Long Range Planning*, 1984, *17*(1):78–82.

Clarify your ideas before communicating. Analyze the problem to clarify it in your mind before sending a message. Communication often is ineffective because the message is inadequately planned. Part of good message planning is considering the goals and attitudes of those who will receive the message.

Examine the true purpose of the communication. Before you send a message, ask yourself what you really want to accomplish with it. Decide whether you want to obtain information, convey a decision, or persuade someone to take action.

Consider the setting in which the communication will take place. You convey meanings and intent by more than words alone. Trying to communicate with a person in another location is more difficult than doing so face-to-face.

Consult with others, when appropriate, in planning communications. Encourage the participation of those who will be affected by the message. They can often provide a viewpoint that you might not have considered.

Be mindful of the nonverbal messages you send. Tone of voice, facial expression, eye contact, personal appearance, and physical surroundings all influence the communication process. The receiver considers both the words and the nonverbal cues that make up your message.

Take the opportunity to convey something helpful to the receiver. Considering the other person's interests and needs often presents opportunities to the sender. You can make your message clearer by imagining yourself in the other's position. Effective communicators really try to see the message from the listener's point of view.

Follow up the communication. Your best efforts at communication can be wasted unless you succeed in getting your message across. You should follow up and ask for feedback to find out whether you succeeded. You cannot assume that the receiver understands; feedback in some form is necessary.

Be sure your actions support your communication. The most effective communication is not in what you say but in what you do. Actions speak louder than words.

CHAPTER SUMMARY

1. The six elements of the communication process are the sender (encoder), the receiver (decoder), the message, channels, feedback, and perception.

2. Of the many possible forms of nonverbal messages, managers should be particularly aware of, and should be able to use effectively, space, physical appearance, and body language.

3. The channels of communication are both formal and informal. Formal channels include downward, upward, and horizontal channels. Managers most frequently use downward channels to send messages through the various levels of the organization. Upward channels allow employee participation in decision making, and they provide feedback to management. Horizontal channels are used between peers in different departments and are especially important in matrix organizations. Informal channels are often as important as formal channels of communication. They constitute the *grapevine,* which exists in every organization. Managers can never eliminate the grapevine and thus should learn to utilize it to send messages and receive feedback.

4. Barriers to communication hinder the sending and receiving of messages by distorting or even blocking intended meanings. Barriers can be either organizational or individual. Organizational barriers can result from the structure of the organization itself, from the jargon that often grows up around high specialized tasks, from various departments having different objectives, and from the insulating effects of differences in status. Individual barriers can result from conflicting assumptions on the part of the sender and receiver, from misinterpretation of the meanings of words, from the inappropriate expression of emotion, and from deficits in the overall ability of the individual to communicate.

5. Guidelines for effective communication include clarifying your ideas, examining your true purpose, considering the setting, consulting with others, being mindful of nonverbal messages, taking the opportunity to convey something helpful to the receiver, following up, and being sure your actions support your communication.

QUESTIONS FOR DISCUSSION AND APPLICATION

1. Discuss the three most common types of nonverbal communication.

2. **From Where You Sit:** Visit the president's office at a local bank. What nonverbal messages does the office convey? How did these messages affect your communication with the president?

3. An old song title goes, "Your lips tell me no, no, but there's yes, yes in your eyes." Describe another communication situation that illustrates inconsistency between verbal and nonverbal messages.

4. What were the methods that AT&T managers used to communicate with employees? Were these messages effective?

5. How is electronic mail affecting corporate communications?

6. What are the major barriers to communication and how can managers overcome them?

7. Why do communication difficulties arise in organizations?

8. The world is a busy and confusing place, and people are constantly bombarded by multiple messages. How do people simplify these messages in order to handle the confusion?

9. **From Where You Sit:** Discuss some problems that U.S. managers may encounter when doing business overseas.

10. **From Where You Sit:** Allan Weisberg, at Johnson & Johnson Hospital Services, says an effective communicator practices the seven "C's":

    ▶ Care about what you do.
    ▶ Have the confidence to know what you know by doing your homework.
    ▶ Concentrate on your ideas and how you can best present them to your audience.
    ▶ Be comfortable.
    ▶ Be in control.
    ▶ Be conversational.
    ▶ Be concise.

How well do you practice these seven "C's"?

Communication Skills Survey

The purpose of this exercise is to help you gain insights into your own communication skills. Think back to a work or other organizational experience you have had, and respond to each statement by circling the response that best fits your attitude and behavior. Remember, there are no right or wrong answers.

Statement	Strongly Agree	Slightly Agree	Not Sure	Slightly Disagree	Strongly Disagree
	5	4	3	2	1
1. When responding, I try to use specific details or examples.	5	4	3	4	5
2. I tend to talk more than others.	1	2	3	2	1
3. If the other person seems not to understand me, I try to speak more slowly and more distinctly.	5	4	3	4	5
4. I tend to forget that some words have many meanings.	1	2	3	4	5
5. When I give feedback, I respond to the facts and keep the feelings out of it.	1	2	3	4	5
6. I am not embarrassed by periods of silence when I'm talking to someone.	5	4	3	2	1
7. I concentrate hard to avoid distracting nonverbal cues.	5	4	3	4	5
8. Listening and hearing are the same things.	1	2	3	2	1
9. I make sure the person wants feedback before I give it.	5	4	3	2	1
10. I avoid saying "Good," "Go on," etc. while the other person is speaking.	5	4	3	2	1
11. I try to delay giving feedback so I can have more time to think it through.	1	2	3	4	5
12. I enjoy using slang and quaint local expressions.	1	2	3	2	1
13. My feedback focuses on how the other person can use my ideas.	5	4	3	4	5
14. Body language is important for speakers, not listeners.	1	2	3	4	5

Your Tra
Docume

15. I use technical jargon only when talking to experts.

    5   4   3   2   1

16. When someone is wrong, I make sure she or he knows it.

    1   2   3   4   5

17. I try to express my ideas in general, overall terms.

    1   2   3   4   5

18. When I'm listening, I try not to be evaluative.

    5   4   3   2   1

Communication Skills Survey Scoring Sheet

Transfer your numeric responses from the survey onto this scoring sheet and sum the categories and total. For instance, your Feedback Skill score is the sum of your responses to statements 1, 5, 9, 11, 13, and 16.

Feedback Skill	Listening Skill	Articulation Skill
1 _____	2 _____	3 _____
5 _____	6 _____	4 _____
9 _____	8 _____	7 _____
11 _____	10 _____	12 _____
13 _____	14 _____	15 _____
16 _____	18 _____	17 _____
Subtotals _____		
Total _____		

Place an X on each of the three continuums to mark your subtotals.

Feedback Skills (High) |————+————+————+————+————+————| (Low)

Listening Skills (High) |————+————+————+————+————+————| (Low)

Articulation Skills (High) |————+————+————+————+————+————| (Low)

         30   25   20   15   10   5   0

Place an X on the Communication Skills Continuum below to mark your total score.

(High) |————+————+————+————+————+————+————+————+————| (Low)

    90   80   70   60   50   40   30   20   10   0

Communication Skills Continuum

To: Juan Martinez, Vice-President, Marketing
From: Chuck Anderson, Manager, Customer Services
Re: Communication Problem

During the past several months, we have been receiving a lot of complaints about your credit card statements from our users. Several long-time card holders even cut up their credit cards and sent them in with their bills. We surveyed about 100 customers to determine the problem. These data told us that we have three major problems: (1) it is not clear to the card users what they owe at the end of the billing period, (2) card users can't find their total line of credit, and (3) our annual interest rate is confusing them. Several of my people have talked to people in the computer center about making the type larger or more legible and even about changing the format of our statements. But you know those people. They seem only to be interested in doing programming projects and told my people to handle the customers themselves. I personally called Hugh, the manager of the computer center, and told him about the treatment my people received. He just laughed and said he would speak to his people when he had time. In the meantime, we called the folks at Optigraphics, who make the forms we print our statements on, to see if they could make the changes we believe would satisfy our customers. They said no problem. It would just take a little reformatting on the computer to handle the new forms.

Juan, you know we are trying to maintain our family atmosphere in the store. Service is our key competitive weapon. We have not accepted Visa, Mastercard, or American Express because of the costs involved. Our customers shop at Houts because of our caring tradition. I hate to bring these problems to you, but our group needs some advice.

Question: Assume that you are Juan Martinez and have received and read this memo. You arrange a meeting with Chuck. What would you plan to do and say in this meeting?

The Multimedia Benefits Kit

By Claudia H. Deutsch

Dianne H. McGowan, an assistant vice president at Citicorp, used a worksheet to test several medical plans. "Turned out that a cheaper plan is actually better at my salary," she said.

Sharon A. Smith, a Citicorp administrative assistant, ran "what if" scenarios on a computer, and increased by 2 percentage points the amount of salary she earmarked for savings. "I never realized the impact of tax-free plans on take-home pay," she said.

Anne M. Slattery, managing director of Citicorp's retail bank, bought long-term disability insurance after reading a brochure on it. "This is the first time I've thought about benefits since I joined the bank more than 20 years ago," she said.

To Gerald M. Lieberman, Citicorp's senior human resources officer, such anecdotes represent welcome vindication for a project that has consumed much of his time—and several million of Citicorp's dollars—over the last year: blitzkrieging 56,000 employees with software, workbooks, videos, seminars, almost every teaching tool fathomable, to explain their options under Choices 91, the flexible benefits plan that goes into effect come January.

"We were determined to leave nothing to chance," Mr. Lieberman said.

Such thoroughness was crucial for Citicorp. Upwards of 1,200 companies now offer flexible, or cafeteria-style, plans that let employees take a one-from-column-A, one-from-column-B approach to benefits. But most of those companies have been tinkering with their benefits ever since tax reform legislation changed some ground rules in 1986.

Citicorp, in contrast, has not changed its benefits plan for decades, so its employees must absorb a formidable amount of data at once. Moreover, the bank has made a slew of acquisitions in recent years, each of which had its own benefits plan. That means that there was no companywide basis for comparing the new plan to old ones.

And worst of all, the change has come at a time when the bank's financial performance has been, to put it euphemistically, quite soft.

The upshot is that employees were suspicious of any new benefits plan, and morale was in danger of plunging. "I'd expected a cut in benefits for a long time, so I figured this was it," said David E. Spence, a manager of distribution planning who says he has grown to appreciate the flexible plan.

In fact, the new plan does not involve takeaways, and Citicorp's 1991 benefits tab is not likely to be lower than this year's. But Mr. Lieberman recognizes that facts pale in the face of perception. "We had to get employees to stop worrying whether we were taking anything away and worry instead about making the right choices," Mr. Lieberman said.

Citicorp's multimedia approach is one that consultants say will become de rigueur for all sorts of corporate communications, as demographic trends dictate work forces and customers with ever-more-varied cultural backgrounds.

"Citicorp was one of the first to recognize that some people learn best by reading, some by having a person explain things, some by interactive software and some by television," said Michael B. Wright, a benefits consultant at Hewitt Associates in Lincolnshire, Ill.

Indeed, since mid-July each Citicorp employee has received a printout of his or her benefits from last year, along with a computer disk and an extensive workbook that included base salary and other personal data, numbers that could be used to figure out the tax implications or out-of-pocket expenses of some benefits choices. Employees received brochures describing the different benefits. And about 1,000 human resources people, each of whom had been given special training, traveled to different Citicorp sites to meet with employees and explain benefits.

Since September there has even been a telephone hotline that is staffed 20 hours a day, six days a week, so that people in all time zones can use it from home or work. The telephone operators have access to employees' personnel data and thus can answer specific questions. And, there is a take-home video to guide the employee through the other tools.

1. Fit the introduction of the new Citicorp benefits plan into the communication process described in this chapter. Discuss the sender, the receiver, and so on.

2. Was there an implied message from management to Citicorp employees in this process? Are implied messages important?

3. If you were a Citicorp employee and disliked some aspects of the new benefits program, what communication channels would you use to convey your feelings?

HARTSMOTH COMPANY

Mary Ellerbrock, project leader for the Hartsmoth Company, had fourteen computer programmers reporting to her. These programmers were working on the development of three major information systems for Chrysler Corporation. Each of her programmers was assigned to one of three teams. Each team was responsible for one of the information systems. Ellerbrock decided that she could better control the development of the projects, and free more time for her administrative responsibilities, by assigning team leaders to each project area. The team leaders, she decided, would be called ''lead programmers.'' Before announcing her decision to all the programmers, however, she decided to discuss it privately with each of the three prospective lead programmers. She wanted to be sure that they understood the project and were willing to accept this new responsibility.

Ellerbrock called Tom Hall into the office and told him that she would like him to be the lead programmer on projects related to the billing and pricing systems. She carefully explained to Tom that this position carried the authority to direct the project-related activities of the people assigned to the project area. These people were Kim Chin, Robert Swift, Jack Bell, and Susan Proy. Ellerbrock clearly explained how project-related activities were distinguished from areas of administrative authority, which she would retain. Tom Hall accepted the new position and, as he was leaving the office, asked Ellerbrock to announce and explain the new position to the other programmers. Ellerbrock assured Tom that she would do so the next day. The following week Ellerbrock began her annual vacation.

One morning while Ellerbrock was still on vacation, Tom Hall asked Bob Swift to prepare the computer operator procedure for a system test that had to be run that night. Later that day, Tom asked Bob whether the test procedure was ready; Bob replied that it was not.

Tom asked, ''Why not, didn't you have enough time?''

''No,'' Bob replied, ''I had enough time, but where I worked before, that task was the responsibility of the project's systems analyst.''

Tom was getting upset. ''Fortunately or unfortunately, it is a programming responsibility here; I explained that to you earlier. I'm the lead programmer on this project; now why didn't you do as I asked?''

''You're the lead programmer?'' Bob seemed surprised. ''To my knowledge, we don't have a lead programmer on this project.''

1. Why was there a communication breakdown?
2. What barriers to communication do you believe affected the communication?
3. If you were Tom, what would you do?

Chapter 16

GROUPS, TEAMS, AND ORGANIZATIONAL CULTURES

TI Team

What You Will Learn

1 Some basic facts about groups and teams and how groups develop.

2 A group process model for describing and analyzing both informal groups and formal teams.

3 How to use teams effectively.

4 The essentials of quality improvement teams.

5 How organizational cultures are created and transmitted.

6 The characteristics and implications of clan and market cultures.

7 **Skill development:** How to participate effectively as both a team member and a team leader.

Texas Instruments' Hierarchy of Teams

Many American organizations are discovering an innovation that may be *the* productivity breakthrough of the 1990s. The still controversial innovation may be called a self-managed team, a cross-functional team, a high-performance team, or, to coin a phrase, a superteam. Says Texas Instruments' CEO Jerry Junkins, "No matter what your business, these teams are the wave of the future." At one of the company's chip factories in Texas, James Watson, vice president of the semiconductor group, helped create a hierarchy of teams. Like a shadow government, they work within the existing organizational hierarchy.

The steering team is at the top. It consists of the plant manager and the heads of manufacturing, finance, engineering, and human resources. The steering team sets strategy and approves large projects. Below the steering team, the factory has three types of teams: corrective action teams, quality improvement teams, and effectiveness teams. The first two are cross-functional and consist mainly of middle managers and professionals, such as engineers, human resource experts, and accountants. Corrective action teams form to tackle short-lived problems, such as a decline in productivity, and then disband. Quality improvement teams work on long-term projects, such as streamlining the manufacturing process. The corrective action and quality improvement teams guide and check the effectiveness teams. Effectiveness teams consist of professional workers and blue-collar employees who do day-to-day production work.

What's to keep this arrangement from becoming just another hierarchy? "You have to keep changing and be flexible as business conditions dictate," says Watson. He contends that one of the steering team's most important responsibilities is to show a keen interest in the teams below it. "The worst thing you can do to a team is to leave it alone in the dark. I guarantee that if you come across someone who says teams didn't work at his company, it's because management didn't take interest in them." Watson suggests that the steering team periodically review everyone's work and adds, "It doesn't have to be a big dog-and-pony show. Just walk around and ask, 'How are you doing?'"[1]

You should realize that what Texas Instruments is doing isn't unique. It is only one of many organizations of the 1990s that have recognized the necessity of getting a lot of work done with and through teams. Many other organizations—such as Boeing, Caterpillar, Digital Equipment, Ford, General Electric, and Procter & Gamble—are making increasing use of teams.[2] Teams provide a forum for making decisions, sharing information, improving functional coordination, building trust, and smoothing interpersonal relations. Whether they're called squads, project groups, committees, or task forces, teams create vital links between different individuals, functions, departments, and levels of the organization.[3] Such linking is clear in the various types of teams used at Texas Instruments.

The increasing use of teams is consistent with a growing shift from mechanistic to organic organizations in the 1990s. A mechanistic organization, as explained in Chapter 11, is one in which management breaks down activities into separate, specialized tasks.

Objectives, authority, responsibility, and accountability are rigidly defined by level and position for both managers and subordinates. In contrast, an organic organization encourages all employees to work together in teams and to communicate openly with one another. Employees are encouraged to form an association with anyone who might help solve the problems at hand. David Fearon, management consultant and professor, portrays the changing landscape for organizations in these words:

> Effective teams are the leading edge of total quality accomplishments. Americans must learn, once again, how to *be* in teams, of many types, simultaneously and to give and take. It is time to rediscover the management power of teams and other groups. *Management* is knowledge of how and why to advance an organization in its environment. Few managers can think this out alone.[4]

The great importance of teams to organizations is reflected in the large amount of time managers and others spend in team meetings. These meetings are usually not the time traps they have a reputation for being. The good news about team meetings is how varied they are in purpose, style, length, format, and even technology. They range from quick huddles in someone's office to voice mail get-togethers to multi-day planning retreats. Many top managers report spending 50 percent or more of their time in team meetings. For first-line managers and professionals, time spent in such meetings varies from 25 to 50 percent.[5] It's been estimated that 20 million team meetings take place in North American businesses every day.[6] And most experts expect the use of teams to increase in organizations, especially among nonmanagerial employees.

The general objective of this chapter is to improve your understanding of groups, especially teams, and how they can be used effectively. We'll also look at organizational cultures, since the way teams evolve, operate, and make decisions are effected by the presence of a strong organizational culture. Of course, the influence of a strong organizational culture isn't just one way. First, teams can be messengers and enforcers of cultural values, norms, and ways of operating. Teams can also be the trigger points and facilitators for bringing about changes in the organizational culture. Texas Instruments' hierarchy of teams is the center piece of its adaptation of its culture to a higher rate of market and technological changes in its environment. On the other hand, teams and informal groups can be enclaves for resistance or even opposition to efforts to create or maintain an organizational culture. The relationship between groups and teams and organizational culture will be developed in the last part of this chapter.

Basic facts about groups

group Two or more individuals who come into personal and meaningful contact on a continuing basis.

team A group organizationally empowered to participate in decision making, exercise influence over how their objectives are met, and, often, establish many of those objectives.

Most of us belong to six or more groups, some at work, some in our community, some formally organized and some informal and social in nature. A **group** is two or more individuals who come into personal and meaningful contact on a continuing basis.[7] If five strangers shoot baskets together just to pass a few spare minutes, they don't constitute a group. If five individuals play basketball together every Saturday, share a common goal of winning games, and communicate freely among themselves, they are a group and probably think of themselves as a team. However, in this book we limit the concept *team* to clusters of people who must collaborate, to some degree, to achieve common objectives, which are normally linked with departmental, divisional, or organizational objectives. We view all teams as groups, but not all groups as teams. **Teams,** for our purposes, are groups organizationally empowered—that is, delegated authority and discretion—to participate in decision making, exercise influence over how their objectives are achieved, and, often, establish many of those objectives.[8]

Types of Groups

formal group An organizational group whose purpose and tasks relate directly to the attainment of stated organizational objectives.

There are two types of groups within organizations: formal and informal. A **formal group** is one whose purpose and tasks relate directly to the attainment of stated organizational objectives. Formal groups are generally used to pass along and share information, train people, gain commitment, and help make decisions.[9] Formal groups are often an official part of the organization's structure. They are its departments, sections, task forces, teams, project groups, quality circles, committees, and board of directors. Some formal groups, for example, the steering team at Texas Instruments, exist over an extended time. Other formal groups have a shorter life, like Texas Instruments' corrective action teams.

Managers and some other professionals (such as planners, market researchers, and quality control specialists) have a long history of team involvement within organizations. In recent years, though, there has been a push to empower nonmanagerial employees to undertake various management tasks—often in collaboration with managers. This development is exemplified by Texas Instruments' hierarchy of teams. The three major classes of worker-management teams are problem-solving teams, special-purpose teams, and self-managing teams. A **problem-solving team** may consist of five to twenty-one hourly and salaried employees, often volunteers, from different areas of a department. Such a team may meet one or two hours a week, or as needed, to discuss ways to improve quality, productivity (efficiency), and the work environment. The authority of a problem-solving team to implement its ideas may range from none to limited. Although these teams can improve quality and reduce costs, they don't fundamentally reorganize work or change the role of managers. A team of clerks at Federal Express spotted and eventually recommended the solution to a billing problem that was costing the company $2 million a year. The use of problem-solving teams began to grow in North America in the late 1970s.[10]

problem-solving team A formal group of hourly and salaried employees, often volunteers, who meet to discuss ways to improve quality, productivity, and the work environment.

special-purpose team A formal group of employees from various departments or even two organizational levels that is empowered with responsibility to handle any of a number of possible special situations.

A **special-purpose team** may consist of five to thirty employees, often from various departments and sometimes two organizational levels. The tasks of such a team include designing and introducing work reforms and new technology, meeting with customers and suppliers to improve inputs or outputs, linking separate functions (marketing, finance, manufacturing, and human resources) to increase product or service innovations, and/or improving links among tactical and strategic decisions and plans. These teams usually operate with a much greater degree of empowerment than problem-solving teams. They emerged during the early 1980s and are spreading rapidly, even into unionized companies. For example, Blue Cross & Blue Shield of Connecticut formed dozens of customer action teams to serve specific markets. Each close-knit team combines a variety of professional skills: ''The claims processors literally sit right next to the customer service person,'' says Executive Vice President Bud Torello. The teams that service

A very special *formal group* at John Deere is its apprentice training team, in which shop-floor foremen and operators help trainees develop skills but also instill a sense of the John Deere culture.

school systems around the state, for example, have to be prepared for an onslaught of telephone calls each afternoon at about three, when school teachers turn their attention to things like medical claims. Torello notes, ''By segmenting your organization and giving each of these teams the freedom to succeed, you get people thinking about what's really important.''[11]

self-managing team A formal group of employees who work together on a daily basis to produce an entire good (or major identifiable component) or service and perform a variety of managerial tasks connected with their jobs.

A **self-managing team** normally consists of five to fifteen employees who work together on a daily basis to produce an entire good (or major identifiable component) or service. These teams perform a variety of managerial tasks, including scheduling work and vacations, rotating job tasks and assignments among members, ordering materials, deciding on team leadership (which can rotate among members), and setting tactical objectives. They are empowered to control how they perform their jobs. Each member often learns the multiple skills required by all of the jobs and tasks that have to be performed by the team. The use of these teams fundamentally changes how work is organized. The impact is usually enormous. Self-managing teams have raised productivity 30 percent or more and increased quality substantially. One or more managerial levels are typically eliminated with the introduction of these teams, thereby creating a flatter organization. Self-managed teams began to spread rapidly in the late 1980s and appear to be the wave of the future.

For example, Johnsonville Foods, which we've discussed in earlier chapters, uses self-managing teams that hire and fire members, buy equipment, write budgets, and so on. Ralph Stayer, CEO and owner, comments: ''Everyone looks at what we're doing and says, ' . . . that's kind of flaky, that's kind of goody-goody, warm and fuzzy.' It isn't a soft or crazy deal. I'm a real hard-nosed pragmatic guy. . . . Teach people to do for themselves; this way you get a far better performance.''[12]

informal group A group that develops because of the shared day-to-day activities, interactions, and sentiments of its members and for the purpose of meeting their own needs.

The second major category of groups is **informal groups.** These develop because of the shared day-to-day activities, interactions, and sentiments of people for the purpose of meeting their own needs—they may support, oppose, or be neutral toward organizational objectives.[13] A social group is one of the most common types of informal groups, within or outside of organizations.

The formal organizational structure often greatly influences the development of informal groups. It does so through such things as the physical layout of the work space, the creation of departments, and the type of technology used.[14] For example, moving some people from one building to another is likely to disrupt the membership of informal groups—the distance between the members may make it difficult for them to continue to communicate face to face. Or a new manager might tell subordinates to ''shape up or ship out,'' compelling them to form an informal group united against the manager.[15]

Group Development

There are many different ways to describe how groups develop. It's always risky to generalize about the development of a group without knowing something about its members, tasks and objectives, size, formal or informal leadership, physical surroundings, and so on.[16] However, within those limitations, new groups often pass through several basic stages. We'll briefly consider each of them.[17]

Forming stage In the process of forming, the group's task behavior is an attempt to become oriented to its goals and procedures. The amount of information available and the manner in which it is presented are critical to group development. Testing and resolving interdependencies between members are the major relationship behaviors. Understanding leadership roles and getting acquainted with other group members facilitate development.

Storming stage Conflict begins to emerge, signaling the second stage of group development. The storming process involves resistance or emotional responses to task demands and interpersonal hostility in relationships. Group members may engage in behaviors that challenge the leaders, or they may isolate themselves from group interaction. If conflict is permitted to exceed controllable limits, anxiety and tension permeate the group. If conflict is suppressed and not permitted to occur, resentment and bitterness result. This can lead to apathy or abandonment. Although conflict resolution is often the goal of groups during the storming stage, conflict management is generally what is achieved. In fact, conflict management is a more appropriate goal because it is desirable to maintain conflict at a manageable level in order to encourage the continued growth and development of the group.

Norming stage Norming is characterized by cooperation. The dominant task-related themes are communication and expression of opinions. Sharing of information and influence promotes cooperation and synergistic outcomes. Cohesion is the relationship theme. A blend of harmony and openness is created by the work effort, which increases morale and team-building efforts. Group unity develops, and shared responsibilities increase, typically leading to decision making by consensus and democratic leadership styles.

Performing stage Some groups never become effective performers, regardless of how long they exist. Members should come to trust and accept each other in the performing stage. To accomplish tasks, diversity of viewpoints, rather than blind conformity, is supported and encouraged. Members are willing to take risks such as presenting "wild" ideas without fear of being put down by the group. Careful listening and giving feedback to others take place. The listening and feedback focus on the group's tasks and objectives, rather than on personal characteristics of other members. There is a sense of clear and shared objectives. Leadership within the group is more flexible and often shifts among members in terms of who is most capable of solving a particular problem. In terms of relationship behaviors, the group accepts the reality of differences and disagreements and works on them cooperatively and enthusiastically. The group tries to reach consensus on important issues and avoids internal politics. Let's expand a little on the description of the performing stage by considering the characteristics that determine team effectiveness. An effective team normally has the following characteristics:

- ▶ Members know why the team exists.
- ▶ Members have adopted procedures for making decisions.
- ▶ Members have achieved trust and openness among themselves.
- ▶ Members have learned to receive help from and give help to one another.
- ▶ Members have achieved a sense of freedom to be themselves, while feeling a sense of belongingness with others.
- ▶ Members have learned to accept and deal with conflict within the team.
- ▶ Members have learned to improve their own functioning.[18]

The degree to which one or more of these characteristics is absent determines the extent to which the team is likely to be ineffective. In later sections of this chapter we'll present suggestions for increasing teams' effectiveness.

Adjourning stage The adjourning stage involves termination of task behaviors and disengagement from relationships. Conclusion of the group is not always planned. A planned group conclusion usually involves recognition for participation and achievement as well as an opportunity for members to say personal goodbyes. Adjournment of the group should be accomplished within a set time frame and have a recognizable ending point.[19]

One of the most useful ways to describe and analyze groups in some detail is the Homans systems model, developed by George Homans in the late 1940s.[20] This model is useful because it provides some reasons why people act as they do within groups and teams, gives individuals a means for diagnosing group and team processes, considers contingency factors likely to affect group and team processes and outputs, and suggests how groups and teams are likely to develop and change over time. The Homans systems model consists of two major, interrelated parts: the internal system and the external system.

Internal System

internal system The part of Homans systems model that includes the activities, interactions, sentiments, and norms that group members develop over time.

The **internal system** includes the activities (tasks), interactions, sentiments, and norms that group members develop over time. As shown in Figure 16.1, these variables are interrelated: A change in one may result in a change in the others. If individuals continue to meet in a common situation, they develop an esprit de corps, a pattern of activities, interactions, and sentiments that goes beyond what's required to do the job. These conditions lead to an internal system of social structure and norms. Thus a group should be thought of as a system, not simply the sum of individual members' behaviors. The way members interact substantially influences their effectiveness as a group. Freedom to develop the group's internal system leads directly to fulfillment of members' needs to belong, achieve satisfaction, and commit themselves to the task. It also helps create and

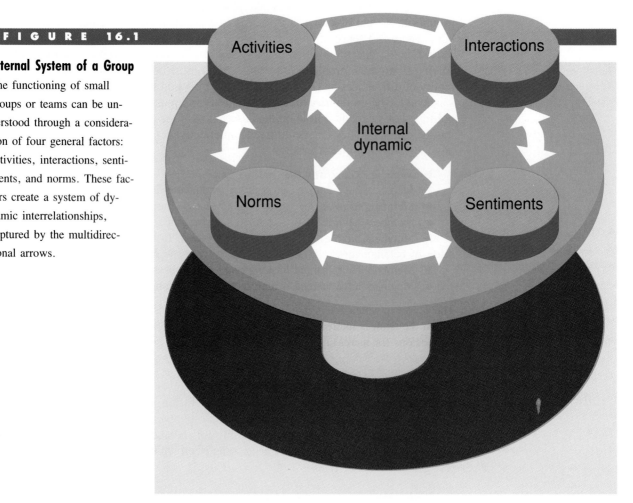

FIGURE 16.1

Internal System of a Group

The functioning of small groups or teams can be understood through a consideration of four general factors: activities, interactions, sentiments, and norms. These factors create a system of dynamic interrelationships, captured by the multidirectional arrows.

maintain group morale, which is one of the reasons for the many successes with self-managing teams.

Activities Activities include many types of task behaviors: analyzing problems, evaluating alternatives, making decisions, operating a machine, writing a memo, and so on. In an organizational team, task-related activities usually take up most of the employees' time. For professionals and managers, task activities rather than social behaviors are likely to be of primary interest.

Interactions Interactions are communications between two or more people. The type and amount of interaction can be identified by answering these questions:

With whom do the members communicate?
How often do they communicate with one another?
How long do they communicate?
Who starts the communication?

Interactions occur with both task-oriented behaviors and relationship-oriented behaviors.[21] Recall from the Manager's Viewpoint feature that there are four types of formal task-related teams at Texas Instruments: steering team, corrective action teams, quality improvement teams, and effectiveness teams. The interactions of these teams are likely to be dominated by task-related behaviors. For the teams to be effective, however, important relationship behaviors must also be present: warmth, praise, and acceptance of others; encouragement of participation by all members; and resolution of team conflicts and tensions.[22] These ideas are consistent with the performing stage of group development. Management often has a strong influence over the interaction patterns of formal groups such as teams, task forces, committees, departments, and so forth. This is not the case with informal groups, such as employees who lunch together on a regular basis.

Sentiments Sentiments include day-to-day emotions such as anger, happiness, and sadness, as well as deeper feelings such as trust, distrust, openness, and closeness. Sentiments reflect the emotional climate of a group. The four sentiments most likely to influence team effectiveness and productivity are trust, openness, freedom, and coordination. The more these sentiments are present, the more likely it is that the work team will be effective and productive.[23]

Figure 16.2 reproduces a brief questionnaire used for diagnosing trust, openness, freedom, and coordination in a team. Take a couple of minutes and complete this questionnaire for one of your teams or informal groups. Circle the appropriate score for each statement, then score the questionnaire as follows:

Trust: Add the point values circled for statements 1–5.
Openness: Add the point values circled for statements 6–10.
Freedom: Add the point values circled for statements 11–15.
Coordination: Add the point values circled for statements 16–20.
Grand total: Add the four totals (possible range is 0–60).

The higher the scores, the more effective and productive the team is likely to be. A score of 5 or less for one of the variables may suggest that a lack of that sentiment is blocking team effectiveness and should be worked on. A grand total of 20 or less suggests severe team problems.

A high score for trust might indicate that you trust the team and see the team climate as trusting and as a good environment for yourself and the other members. On the other hand, a low score for trust might indicate that you distrust the team and see the team as a threatening and defensive environment. It has been suggested that the building of trust within and between teams is a critical need in today's organizations.[24]

A high score for openness suggests that you see the team as open and spontaneous and the members as willing to share their feelings. A low score suggests that you view team members as fearful, cautious, and unwilling to express their feelings and opinions.

Team Sentiments Questionnaire

Circle the number that corresponds to your degree of agreement with each statement: SD = strongly disagree; D = disagree; A = agree; SA = strongly agree.

Statements	SD	D	A	SA
Trust				
1. Members of this team trust each other very much.	0	1	2	3
2. People are playing roles in this team and not being themselves.	3	2	1	0
3. Some members are afraid of the team.	3	2	1	0
4. The team treats each person in the group as an important member.	0	1	2	3
5. Members seem to care very much for each other as individuals.	0	1	2	3
Openness				
6. Members of this team are not really interested in what others have to say.	3	2	1	0
7. Members of this team tell it like it is.	0	1	2	3
8. Members often express feelings and opinions outside of the team that differ from those they express inside.	3	2	1	0
9. Members of the team are afraid to be open and honest with each other.	3	2	1	0
10. We don't keep secrets here.	0	1	2	3
Freedom				
11. Members do what they ought to do in this team out of a personal sense of responsibility to the team.	0	1	2	3
12. This team puts excessive pressure on each member to work toward team goals.	3	2	1	0
13. When decisions are being made, members readily express their thoughts.	0	1	2	3
14. The team spends a lot of energy trying to get members to do things they don't really want to do.	3	2	1	0
15. Members of the team are growing and changing all the time.	0	1	2	3
Coordination				
16. Everyone on this team does his or her own thing with little thought for others.	3	2	1	0
17. People work together as members of a well-oiled team.	0	1	2	3
18. We need a lot of controls here to keep the team on track.	3	2	1	0
19. There is little destructive competition within this team.	0	1	2	3
20. You really need to have some power if you want to get anything done within this team.	3	2	1	0

Source: Adapted from J. R. Gibb, ''TORI Group Self-Diagnosis Scale,'' in J. W. Pfeiffer and J. E. Jones (eds.), *The 1977 Annual Handbook for Group Facilitators* (San Diego, Calif.: University Associates, 1977). Used with permission.

A high score for freedom suggests that the team allows individual choice and encourages you to direct your energies toward your desired objectives. A low score for freedom might indicate that you see the team creating great pressures on members to conform, to do things they don't want to do, and to work toward team objectives, regardless of the significance of those objectives.

A high score for coordination might mean that you see the team as a smoothly functioning unit, working effectively and cooperatively. A low score may indicate that you see the group as unable to work well as a team, missing significant ingredients needed to function effectively.

The greater the degree to which the four sentiments are present, the higher the expected level of group cohesiveness. **Cohesiveness** refers to the strength of members' desire to remain in the group or team and their commitment to it. Cohesiveness cannot be dictated by top management. It is a reflection of the members' sentiments toward one another and the team as a whole. A cohesive group can work for or against organizational objectives.[25] For example, a cohesive group with negative sentiments toward higher man-

cohesiveness The group trait that indicates the strength of the members' desire to remain in the group and their commitment to it.

agement and the organization may promote standards that limit the productivity of individual members. In contrast, a cohesive group with positive sentiments toward organizational objectives may support and reinforce high quality and productivity among individual members.

norm An informal rule of behavior that is widely shared and enforced by members of a group.

Norms Norms are the informal rules of behavior that are widely shared and enforced by members of a group. They set standards for members' behaviors under specific circumstances. Norms of work teams may define how much members should do, what they wear, where they eat, what kinds of jokes are acceptable, how members should feel about the organization, and how they deal with their manager.

A group norm exists when three criteria have been met.[26] First, there is a standard of appropriate behavior for group members. For example, members of a work team may feel they should do a certain amount of work. Second, members must generally agree on the standard. This doesn't mean that all group members need to agree fully, but if most members have widely varying opinions about how much work is enough, for example, the team does not have a productivity norm. Third, the members must be aware that the group supports the particular standard through a system of rewards and punishments—rewards for compliance and punishments for violations. For example, a team member who produces more integrated circuit boards per day than the group norm may get the silent treatment until he or she complies with that norm.[27]

Figure 16.3 indicates that most norms develop as the result of one or more of four factors.[28] Superiors or co-workers may make an *explicit statement* with respect to

FIGURE   16.3

Development of Group Norms

The norms of a specific group or team are often based on a combination of the four factors shown in this figure. Changing the norms of a group or team requires diagnosing the role of each of these factors.

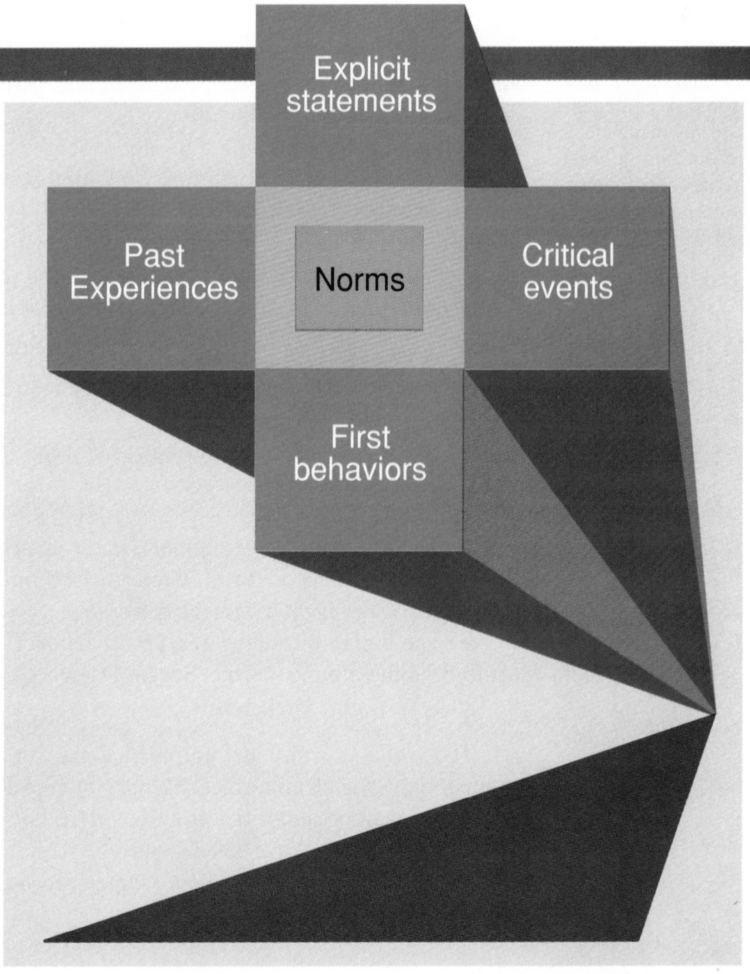

Explicit statements

Past Experiences

Norms

Critical events

First behaviors

Source: Adapted from D. C. Feldman, ''The Development and Enforcement of Group Norms,'' *Academy of Management Review,* 1984, 9:50–52.

rules to enable the team to meet its objectives. For example, management might explicitly prohibit smoking (except in designated areas) at a petroleum refinery for safety reasons. If team leaders and members accept and help enforce this prohibition, it becomes a team norm as well as a formal rule of the organization. *Critical events* in a group's history may lead to the development of norms. Group members may view a whistle blower with scorn, thus establishing a norm for what may and may not be communicated to outsiders. The *first behaviors* in new groups or teams may emerge as norms, setting future expectations and standards. For example, the seating arrangement at a group's first meeting may lead to norms dictating where each team member is to sit. Seating arrangements also influence who talks to whom. The carryover of norms from *past experiences* also influences the formation of norms in a new situation. Students and professors do not have to create new norms about acceptable classroom behavior as they go from class to class; they simply carry them over.

The ability of a group to enforce its norms depends on the importance of the rewards and punishments to its members and the probability that they will be applied to individual members.[29] Individuals who value the rewards and recognize the punishments might still violate the group's norms if they believe they can get away with it. This is especially true if other rewards far outweigh the punishments for violating the group's norms. Take, for example, a salesperson at Michelson's Shoes whose informal work group will punish her (by not talking to her) for bringing in more orders than the group's norm. If the additional income she can earn is considerable and/or if acceptance by the group isn't important, she will likely break this performance norm.

group social structure
The pattern of interactions and relationships in a group, determined primarily by members' contributions to achieving the group's objectives, acceptance of the group norms, and personal characteristics.

Group Social Structure **Group social structure** is the pattern of interactions and relationships in a group, determined primarily by members' contributions to achieving the group's objectives, acceptance of the group's norms, and personal characteristics.[30] Analyzing a group's social structure requires evaluating the group's leader, communication patterns, and member status (differential ranking). Figure 16.4 illustrates a group social structure. Juanita is the group leader, Dick is the deviant, four of the individuals are solid group members of equal status, and Rao is a marginal member, but not a trouble-making deviant. The following observations of group dynamics help analyze this group's social structure:

▶ A member of higher status more often initiates interaction with a person of lower status than vice versa. Juanita would initiate interaction with Daewoo or Susan more often than they would with her.

▶ The higher a member's status, the wider is his or her range of interaction. Juanita would tend to interact with everyone else in the group, but Dick would tend to interact with no one.

▶ The group leader's sentiments carry greater weight than do those of the followers. Juanita's expressions of trust, openness, freedom, and coordination would influence the group more than Dick's deviant behavior.

▶ The higher the status of a group member, the nearer the member's activities will conform to the group's norms. Susan, Daewoo, Gillian, and Sam will probably conform; Rao may conform; Dick won't.

The social structure and norms of some work teams have traditionally discriminated against women and minorities. Gender or racial stereotyping by some teams still may prevent women or minorities from having a fair chance to demonstrate their abilities.[31] Some organizations have taken concrete steps to make their management teams more diverse. A few examples of how women are moving onto management teams are presented in the following Insight.

FIGURE 16.4

A Group Social Structure

Many groups and teams develop a social structure that differentiates the members in terms of their relative rankings and contributions to objectives. Those who contribute most often receive the highest status. In self-managing teams, leadership usually rotates among the members. In such situations, there is likely to be a flat (little hierarchy) and democratic social structure.

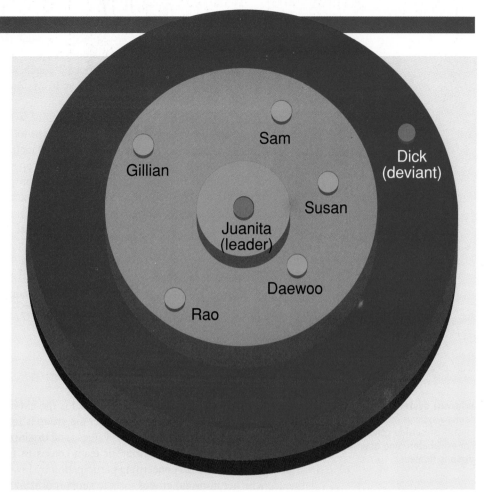

WOMEN IN MANAGEMENT TEAMS

I NSIGHT   Women have long complained that their input is often ignored, particularly in a team situation. During a leadership conference at Du Pont, Marcia Coleman, a laboratory director, confronted a male colleague, Vice President Anthony J. Cardinal. "Did you notice what happened in the meeting whenever a woman offered a thought?" asked Coleman. Cardinal replied that he hadn't. "Pay attention tomorrow," she suggested. The next day Cardinal noticed that whenever a woman brought up an idea, the conversation swept past her. "I had never appreciated the problem before. I started to get an inkling of what women go through every day," Cardinal said.

Like a growing number of companies, Du Pont is training male managers to help them identify and overcome the ways they subconsciously still treat women unfairly. "Men have to understand that their behavior can exclude women in a variety of ways," says Elsie Y. Cross, a Philadelphia-based consultant who conducts training on race and gender bias for Johnson & Johnson, Exxon, and others.

Honeywell managers were intrigued by an employee survey in which women cited personal relationships as the key element in upward mobility. Men said relationships were least important. To get women into the management loop, Honeywell is trying to influence the way workplace relationships are established. The company started forming teams of promising young women and minorities and more experienced executives. The experienced "coaches" give advice on career strategies and corporate politics. At Corning and 3M, managers are trying a one-on-one mentoring approach.

During a gender-awareness workshop at Corning, women executives complained that their male colleagues never invited them to lunch. The women felt they were missing out on useful gossip. That could include news of someone being transferred, which would mean that a job had opened up. Or it could be a comment about the boss's being interested in a new product category. Tidbits like these are often the root of one element of success—the one that executives usually call being in the right place at the right time. For the male executives at Corning, realizing that they were cutting the women out was just the first step. Now coed executive groups can be seen frequenting Corning's favorite lunch haunts. "Men didn't intend to be exclusionary, they just were," says Susan B. King, president of Corning's Steuben Glass division and the company's highest-ranking woman. "There was a level of discomfort for them when women showed up because Corning had always had a white, male-dominated culture."[32]

External System

external system The part of Homans systems model that consists of outside conditions that exist before and after the group is formed.

The second part of the Homans systems model is the **external system,** which consists of outside conditions that exist before and after the group is formed, including management's values, the technology used, members' values, and organizational structure. These conditions will continue even if the group or team ceases to function.

Management's values concerning participation by lower-level employees are likely to influence whether informal groups form to support organizational objectives or undermine them. A rigid assembly-line technology is likely to thwart the development of informal groups and thus increase employees' feelings of isolation and job dissatisfaction. People who value collectivism strongly, as the Japanese do, are very comfortable working in teams. In contrast, it is somewhat more of a challenge to form work teams among people who strongly value individualism. However, when such individuals are empowered through self-managed teams, they gain more control and influence over their work. This result is consistent with their valuing of individualism—and thus increases their satisfaction. Organizational structure has a direct influence on the formation and functioning of formal and informal groups. For example, Texas Instruments has formed many types of teams in the process of loosening up its previously rigid hierarchical organizational structure.

Figure 16.5 indicates that the external system influences the development of the internal system. Changes in the group's external system can generate massive changes in its internal system. After all, the external system may even impose the conditions of the group's or team's survival. For instance, a reduction in the work force could create havoc for established informal or formal groups by removing many of their members. The internal system, in turn, directly affects quality, productivity, member satisfaction, and absenteeism and turnover.[33] Positive team sentiments, such as a strong sense of coordination, are likely to help reduce absenteeism and turnover. Sentiments of trust and openness, as well as achievement-based norms, are likely to help achieve higher levels of quality and productivity. These effects eventually provide feedback to both the internal and external systems, which may result in action to modify the internal system. For example, low productivity might motivate management to talk to the team about what's needed to increase it.

FIGURE 16.5

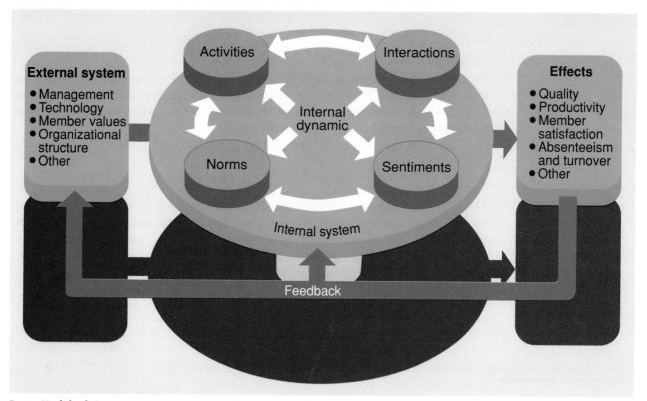

Basic Model of Group Process

This model demonstrates that groups and teams have effects in a variety of areas. These effects, in turn, provide feedback to both the internal and external systems. In addition, the elements of the external system influence the development of the group's or team's internal system.

Organizational Implications

The primary implications of the Homans systems model for teams and managers are in the areas of individual and team empowerment, internal and external systems diagnosis, and constructive norms.

Teams may make more of an effort to achieve organizational objectives if members are empowered (allowed some freedom and responsibility) to do their jobs. Conversely, if their freedom and responsibility are sharply restricted, team members may well reduce their level of commitment, continuing to perform satisfactorily but with little enthusiasm for improving quality and productivity. Pat McNulty, who manages an innovative General Mills cereal plant in Georgia with self-managed teams, observes: "Nobody knows the job as well as those doing it. If you empower those people to make the decisions, they make good ones." The payoff? Reduced costs, better quality, greater efficiency. McNulty expects productivity to be 30 to 40 percent higher than that of traditional cereal plants. "You feel like you're going to your own business, not like you're going to do something for somebody else," comments General Mills worker Rhonda Lunsford.[34]

Managers and leaders can understand and anticipate team actions only by diagnosing the group's internal and external systems. The Homans systems model provides guidance in making these diagnoses. The relationships among sentiments, interactions, activities, norms, and social structure are useful in suggesting the patterns of behavior to be expected in teams. For example, a manager or team leader who issues orders that are inconsistent with team norms (such as ones radically changing productivity standards) may well face a team united in demanding a change in the orders. Or a manager trying to change or eliminate established communication patterns may face consequences ranging from complaints to increased absenteeism and turnover.

Managers and team leaders can provide more effective guidance by encouraging the establishment of team norms that support the external system's organizational objectives. Where there is mutual interdependence among employees (such as on a project team), the use of team rewards rather than just individual rewards is often effective. These rewards could be in the form of praise and recognition of the team as a whole or even a compensation system based, in part, on team effectiveness.

Consider how Aetna Life has reacted to many of these implications. Aetna Life reorganized its home office operations, forming self-managed teams of clerks, technical writers, underwriters, and financial analysts to handle customer requests and complaints. To facilitate teamwork, Aetna is using a new line of "team" furniture designed by Steelcase. The furniture establishes small areas that Steelcase calls neighborhoods. A central work area with a table lets teams meet when they need to, and nearby desks provide privacy. Says William Watson, an Aetna senior vice president, "I can't tell you how great it is. Everyone sits together, and the person responsible for accounting knows who prepares the bills and who puts the policy information in the computers to pay the claims. You don't need to run around the building to get something done."[35]

USING TEAMS EFFECTIVELY

This section begins with a general discussion of team decision making, then moves on to cover three factors—task type, team size, and team leader role—that help to shape team decision making and outputs.

Team Decision Making

There is considerable controversy over when team decision making is appropriate. Some individuals think that it's a waste of time and should only be used when the politics of the situation demand it. Others believe that team decision making is often superior to individual decision making and should be used whenever possible.[36] Of course, the use of any form of team decision making has potential advantages *and* disadvantages.[37] As suggested in Figure 16.6, however, the advantages often outweigh the disadvantages.

This McDonnell Douglas underwater troubleshooting team has to make *team decisions* in planning a project before going underwater.

FIGURE 16.6

Advantages and Disadvantages of Team Decision Making

There are a variety of potential advantages and disadvantages to team decision making. In general, the advantages outweigh the disadvantages, especially in mature and effective teams.

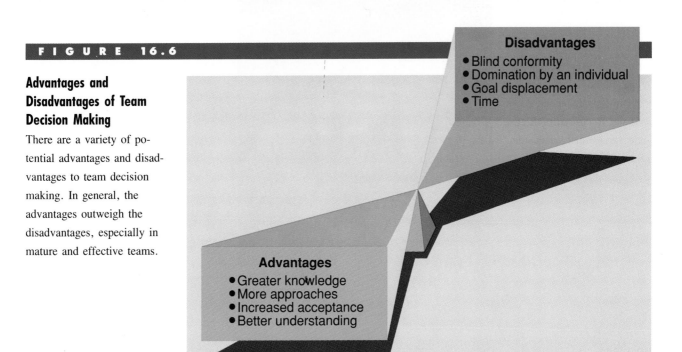

Disadvantages
- Blind conformity
- Domination by an individual
- Goal displacement
- Time

Advantages
- Greater knowledge
- More approaches
- Increased acceptance
- Better understanding

Advantages There are four potential advantages to team decision making: greater knowledge, a diversity of approaches, increased acceptance, and better understanding.

A team's information and knowledge should be and usually are greater than those of any one member. If the group's members have various skills and sources of information about the task, each might be able to fill gaps in the knowledge of others. For example, when Ford Motor Company decided to produce the Taurus model, it formed a project team. The team members were from various departments, including marketing, engineering, production, accounting, personnel, and legal. The team's purpose was to solve the problems of designing, making, and marketing Taurus.

Individuals tend to develop tunnel vision, regarding only their part of the problem as important. When individuals on a team share a problem, their discussion can stimulate the search for a variety of approaches. By challenging one another's thinking, team members may arrive at a decision that recognizes all viewpoints and reaches a consensus or a workable compromise.[38]

A person who is given a chance to influence a team's decisions may be more committed to the decision and accept more responsibility for making it work than someone who is just told what to do. A high-quality solution handed down by a superior may not be carried out as effectively as a lower-quality solution developed by or with the team. Thus effectiveness relates not only to the quality of the solution, but also to the team's power to resist or implement it.[39]

Someone who solves a problem alone usually has the additional task of persuading others to implement the solution. As a result, further problems are often caused by subordinates' or co-workers' inadequate understanding of the solution. If those who must implement a decision have helped to make it, communication failure isn't so likely—they already know how and why the decision was made.

Disadvantages The potential advantages of team decision making are not guaranteed. In addition, there are four potential disadvantages: blind conformity, domination by an individual, goal displacement, and wasting of time.

Social pressures to maintain friendships and avoid disagreements can lead to blind conformity, in which group members unquestioningly accept a decision. This is

Teams like this one at IBM's Business Recovery Services in Tampa, Florida, work together to provide technical assistance to customers using a new service that safeguards against disasters.

groupthink An agreement-at-any-cost mentality that results in ineffective team decision making and poor solutions.

especially a problem when a solution is based more on personal feelings than on facts and analysis. Moreover, team acceptance of a decision isn't necessarily related to the quality of that decision. When decision-making teams are cohesive and conform blindly, a condition called groupthink might develop. **Groupthink** is an agreement-at-any-cost mentality that results in an ineffective team decision-making process and poor solutions. If a team does not have the final say, a superior or other team can always reject or modify the team's decision or encourage its members to go back and analyze the decision-making processes.[40] Recall Texas Instruments' hierarchy of teams. The corrective action teams and quality improvement teams guide and check the effectiveness teams.

Team effectiveness can be reduced if one individual such as the team leader, dominates the discussion by talking too much or being closed to other points of view. Some team leaders try to control the team and provide the major input to decisions—these are not the actions of good problem solvers. Team leaders need to be aware of their potential for dominating the team and the negative effects this can have. Even the brightest team members can't upgrade team decisions if they are not permitted—much less encouraged—to contribute.

One major goal of team decision making is to solve a problem effectively. Team members need to consider possible causes of the problem and various alternative solutions to it. Some members, though, may become so enthusiastic about and involved in winning support for one alternative that they lose sight of the goal—to find the best solution. This goal displacement can lower the quality of the decision. When it occurs, the team should go back to the beginning, generate new alternatives, and avoid evaluating them for the time being. If evaluation is clouded by a lack of facts—or controversy over the facts—the group session can be stopped until the facts can be supplemented and clarified.[41]

Time costs money, so a waste of time becomes a disadvantage if a decision made by a group could have been made just as effectively by an individual working alone. If the cost of a middle manager's time is assumed to be $40 per hour, a two-hour meeting attended by ten middle managers costs the organization $800. The results may well be worth this cost, but not if nine of those managers could have better spent their time on other tasks.

The following Insight demonstrates how some of the advantages of team decision making may be achieved while several potential disadvantages are minimized. AT&T Credit Corporation is a subsidiary of the American Telephone & Telegraph Company headquartered in Morristown, New Jersey. It provides financing for customers who lease equipment from AT&T and other companies.

𝒥 **N S I G H T**

Thomas Wajnert was made president of AT&T Credit (ATTC) when it was formed. Wajnert decided to hire his own employees and give them "ownership and accountability." His first concern was to increase efficiency, not to provide more rewarding jobs, but in the end he did both.

In 1986 ATTC set up eleven teams consisting of ten to fifteen newly hired workers in a high-volume division serving small businesses. The three major lease-processing functions were combined in each team. No longer were calls from customers shunted from department to department. The company also divided its national staff of field agents into seven regions and assigned two or three teams to handle business from each region. That way the same teams always worked with the same field agents, establishing personal relationships with them and their customers. Above all, team members took responsibility for solving customers' problems. ATTC's new slogan was "Whoever gets the call owns the problem."

The teams largely manage themselves. Members make most decisions on how to deal with customers, schedule their own time off, reassign work when people are absent, and interview prospective new employees. The only supervisors are seven regional managers who advise the team members rather than give orders. These self-managing teams process up to 800 lease applications a day, compared to 400 under the old system. And instead of taking several days to give a final yes or no, the teams do it within 24 to 48 hours. As a result, ATTC is growing at a 40 to 50 percent compound annual rate, Wajnert says.

The teams also have economic incentives for providing good service. A bonus plan tied to each team's costs and profits can produce extra cash. The employees, most of whom are young college graduates, can add $1,500 a year to their average salaries and pay raises as they learn new skills. "It's a phenomenal learning opportunity," says twenty-four-year-old team member Michael LoCastro.[42]

Task Type

One of the most important factors to consider in determining whether an individual or team approach to decision making should be used is the type of task involved.[43] This point was developed in the discussion of the leader-participation model in Chapter 14. Refer to Table 14.3 and Figure 14.7 to review the situational attributes and diagnostic questions that help to determine when team decision making is appropriate. In brief, some form of team process is desirable when one or more of the following conditions exists:

▶ Various bits of information must be brought together to produce a good solution, for example, when attempting to develop a new product, improve quality, or increase productivity.

▶ Skills and knowledge need to be pooled to deal with unstructured and complex tasks, such as deciding how to reduce per unit costs during the coming year.

▶ Different ideas about the best means for dealing with a problem or task need to be resolved.

▶ Team acceptance of the chosen solution is crucial to effective implementation.

Because employees at all levels are faced with these conditions more and more often, the use of problem-solving teams, special-purpose teams, and self-managing teams is rapidly spreading.

Team Size

As team size increases, a number of changes in the decision-making process occur. The optimal team size seems to be from five to twelve members. Members of larger teams have difficulty in directly communicating (interacting) with each other. In general, as team size increases, the following effects are likely to be observed:

▶ Demands on leader time and attention are greater, and the leader is more psychologically distant from the other members. This becomes much more of a problem in self-managing teams, where multiple individuals can take on leader roles.

▶ The team's tolerance of direction from the leader is greater, and the team's decision making becomes more centralized.

▶ The team atmosphere is less friendly, the actions are less personal, more subteams (cliques) form within the team, and, in general, the members are less satisfied.

▶ The team's rules and procedures become more formalized.[44]

These findings suggest that team performance can be influenced by controlling team size. For innovative decision making the ideal team size is between three and nine members.[45] If a team has more than nine members, subteams might be formed. The purpose of subteams is to encourage all team members to share ideas when analyzing task-related problems, information, and alternative solutions. The full team can then meet to discuss subteam (task force) assessments and recommendations. In some instances, different subteams work on the same set of problems and then share and discuss their conclusions with the entire team. The leader of a large team needs to be aware of the possibility that subteams, or cliques, may form on their own, each with its own leader and agenda. Although more resources are available in large teams, these resources can create a backlash that hurts overall team effectiveness if each unofficial subteam lobbies strongly for its own position.

Very large groups usually follow highly formal procedures, such as Robert's rules of order, to maintain order and keep the group focused on the agenda. Large team meetings may be efficient when the primary purpose is to state, interpret, or reinforce new policies, procedures, or plans. Coupled with an adequate opportunity for questions and answers, a large team meeting may satisfy the objective of informing the membership. Voting is the method often used to reach agreement in large groups. Unfortunately, voting alone doesn't reveal the intensity of members' feelings, either positive or negative, or generate acceptable alternatives.

A leader's behavior in small team sessions should be quite different from that in large team sessions. With small teams, a considerate style of team leadership is most effective. With large teams, a more directive, task-oriented style may be necessary.

Leader Role

Team leaders should not reject or promote ideas because of their own personal views. They must be receptive to member contributions, and not judge them. Good team leaders summarize information, stimulate discussion, create awareness of problems, and detect when the team is ready to resolve differences and agree to a unified solution.[46] In terms of the leader-participation model presented in Chapter 14, this behavior would represent the GII, or group, decision style. You may recall that member participation is extremely high with this style. The group (team) style of decision making may seem strange to some individuals, because it certainly isn't consistent with the popular conception of leadership. The management of disagreement, of time, and of change are three important aspects of the leadership role in teams.

Management of Disagreement A skillful team leader can create an atmosphere for disagreement that stimulates innovative solutions while minimizing the risk of bad feelings. Disagreement can be managed if the leader is receptive to differences within the team, delays the reaching of decisions, and separates idea generation from idea evaluation. This last technique makes it less likely that an alternative solution will be identified with one individual rather than the team.

Management of Time To manage time effectively a team leader must strike a proper balance between permissiveness and control. Rushing through a team session can prevent full discussion of the problem and lead to negative feelings, as well as a possibly faulty solution. On the other hand, unless the leader keeps the discussion moving, members will become bored and inattentive. Unfortunately, some leaders feel it necessary to push for an early solution because of time constraints. Such a move ends discussion before the team has had a chance to work effectively.

Management of Change When there are disagreements within a team, some members have to change their opinions in order for the team to reach a consensus. If members offering the best alternatives are persuaded by other team members to abandon their argument, the outcome suffers. The leader can protect individuals holding a minority view by discouraging other team members from expressing hostility toward them. The leader can also give individuals with a minority view the chance to influence the majority. Team leaders do this by keeping the minority view before the team, encouraging discussion of that view, and clarifying any misunderstanding.

QUALITY IMPROVEMENT TEAMS

quality improvement team
A group of employees who meet regularly to find ways to achieve both quality in fact and quality in perception.

Throughout this chapter we have identified and illustrated many types of teams being used in organizations, including those with quality as a focus. Given the critical role of quality issues in global competition, we want to say a bit more about such teams. Chapter 20 discusses the specifics of quality management and control. A **quality improvement team** consists of employees who meet regularly to find ways to achieve quality in fact (meeting standards and then raising and beating those standards) and quality in perception (meeting or exceeding customers' expectations nearly 100 percent of the time).[47] Quality improvement teams should cover the whole organization and involve all levels of employees, not just nonmanagerial personnel.

Quality improvement teams are the next generation of quality circles, first discussed in Chapter 1. Quality circles are still dominant in most organizations with quality improvement programs. A **quality circle** is a group of employees from the same work area, or performing similar tasks, who voluntarily meet on a regular basis to identify, analyze, and propose solutions to problems in the workplace.[48] Meetings usually lasting an hour or so are held once every week or two during or after regular working hours. Members are usually given overtime pay if the quality circle meets after work. Members normally receive eight or more hours of formal training in decision making and team processes, which they are expected to apply in their quality circles.

quality circle A group of employees from the same work area, or performing similar tasks, who voluntarily meet on a regular basis to identify, analyze, and propose solutions to problems in the workplace.

Quality circles and quality improvement teams usually deal with such issues as product and service quality, working conditions, productivity, safety, tools and equipment, work methods and procedures, reporting requirements, communication, control mechanisms, and job structures. Quality circles normally do *not* gripe or discuss issues such as wages and salaries, personality clashes, hiring or firing, disciplinary actions, or major resource allocations. Quality circles, unlike most quality improvement teams, do not have the authority to implement their proposed solutions, which are normally presented to management for further consideration, approval, or rejection.

Guidelines for Effectiveness

The general guidelines for the effectiveness of any team also apply to both quality circles and quality improvement teams. Some especially important guidelines, though, are as follows:

▶ The circle or team should have the authority to call on experts in the organization to help it solve problems. Moreover, it needs the full support of the organization.

▶ Members should agree to set objectives for the coming year within three months of circle or team establishment and to revise these objectives for each succeeding year.

▶ Members should agree to contribute their leadership skills and other abilities to the circle's or team's efforts.

▶ Decisions should be made by consensus, and enough time should be allowed to discuss all the issues thoroughly.

▶ All conflicts arising among members or with those outside the circle or team should be discussed openly.[49]

Phases of Development

Interest in and use of quality circles have grown enormously. One indicator of this growth is membership in the International Association of Quality Circles. In 1978, it had 100 members; today the association has more than 7000 members.[50]

Quality circles often go through four phases when introduced into an organization.[51] During the first phase, results are very positive. A small number of circles are formed, members are highly motivated and creative, and management is enthusiastic. In the second phase, utilization of quality circles becomes widespread. An implicit assumption is that the greater the number of circles, the more the improvements. In the third phase, the organization takes one of two paths. Along the first path, more attention is given to the effective use of quality circles. Management emphasizes quality of proposals rather than number of quality circles. Following this path may bring management to the conclusion that the quality circle tasks and team processes should be fully integrated into the organization's structure in the fourth phase. Thus if the quality circles are discontinued, it isn't because they were a failure. Rather, it's because all employees and managers, not just volunteers, are engaged in team decision making and addressing the types of issues once considered the province of quality circles. In this situation a form of team management, including quality improvement teams, is introduced into the organization. The process of team building and management is discussed in Chapter 21.

The other path during the third phase is followed when management is disillusioned with quality circles. Reasons for backlash against quality circles include (1) resistance of first-line and middle managers, who feel threatened, (2) participation in decision making by nonmanagers isn't consistent with the broader organizational culture, (3) too many of the ideas generated by the quality circles are not implemented, without explanation, and circle members become cynical, (4) the extra costs exceed the benefits, and (5) too many quality circle members are unskilled or unmotivated.[52] Following this path to the fourth phase, management may simply phase out the quality circle program.[53]

Quality circles are often one part of a quality improvement program. This is the case at Florida Power & Light, which won the Deming Prize in 1989. The Deming prize is a prestigious award for quality control presented annually by the Union of Japanese Scientists and Engineers. Florida Power & Light was the first non-Japanese company to win this prize. The role of quality circles in achieving this recognition is noted in the following Insight.

*I*NSIGHT As Florida Power & Light (FP&L) prepared to enter the 1980s, it became obvious to company management that a major change was needed within the organization. A search was undertaken to find a management system that could help the company cope with its rapidly changing business environment. The management system adopted is known as QIP—the quality improvement process. It is based on a process that the Japanese call TQC—total quality control. After observing first-hand some of the impressive results achieved by the Japanese, FP&L executives decided to establish an American program based on the same principles.

Although quality improvement teams were introduced in FP&L as early as 1981, it wasn't until 1985 that a total quality control process began to be implemented companywide. In addition to quality improvement (QI) teams, QIP includes a planning process called policy deployment and a control process called quality in daily work.

The quality improvement (QI) teams, or quality circles as they are often known, provide a bottom-to-top communications system that gives every employee an opportunity to share in the improvement process. There are more than 1800 teams at FP&L.

The second element of QIP is a corporatewide planning process in which targeted goals are communicated from the top to the bottom of the organization. Policy deployment is essentially the company's corporate road map to customer satisfaction. It is the driving force of QIP and focuses all of the company's resources on a few high-priority goals. Concentrating on what customers consider most important to them, top management selects goals to be achieved in five to seven years. As these objectives filter down through the organization, short-term plans spanning one to two years are developed at lower levels.

The third element of QIP is known as QIDW (quality in daily work) and focuses on *how* things are done. It is especially effective in areas where the same tasks are done over and over. Employees use tools such as flow charts to illustrate the steps of their work process and control charts to measure and monitor the process. The QI teams often became involved in this element as well.[54]

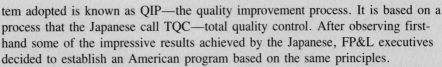

ORGANIZATIONAL CULTURES

The building-blocks of group norms, activities, sentiments, and social structure carry over to the concept of organizational culture. For example, just as groups can't exist without shared norms, neither can an organizational culture exist without norms that are shared by most employees and sentiments, such as core values, that are common to most groups and teams.

We've talked about different types of organizations—mechanistic, bureaucratic, organic, and so on. Differences in organizations can extend to their very personalities and identities. **Organizational culture** is an organization's personality—the way of thinking and doing things in it—which is shared by most or all of its members and which must be learned by new members if they are to survive and progress in the organization. This definition highlights three important characteristics of organizational culture: It's learned; it's shared, and it's transmitted.[55] Thus organizational culture is very much like the culture you may have learned about in a sociology or history class.

Organizational culture doesn't just happen. It's cultivated by management, learned by employees, and passed on to new employees. Also, it can change (though not easily) over time. Where a well-developed organizational culture exists, there is much less distinction between formal and informal norms, activities, sentiments, and interactions. Of course, this doesn't mean that a well-developed culture can simply be described in a new employee's handbook—although that *is* done by organizations such as Hewlett-Packard and IBM—or even that employees can fully explain it to an interviewee. Many times some or all of an organization's culture may be unstated, and members may even be unaware of the culture in the sense of not consciously verbalizing it.[56]

organizational culture
The organization's personality, the way of thinking and doing things in it, which is shared by most of its members and which must be learned by new members if they are to survive and progress.

We focus here on organizations having strong organizational cultures. Not all organizations have a single strong culture. In fact, some organizations have several strong, differing subcultures. If those groups don't trust and cooperate with one another, subculture differences may lead to political power struggles and gamesmanship, which can hinder organizational effectiveness.[57] A strong organizational culture can prevent the formation of subcultures that work against one another.[58] Even in an effective organization with a strong organizational culture, subcultures with some unique characteristics usually exist. For example, IBM's marketing subculture has strong norms about proper dress—in the legendary blue suits and white shirts—which its tieless R&D subculture doesn't share.

Entire books have been written about how organizational culture is created and transmitted. The most common elements that combine to characterize an organizational culture are core values, socialization and norms, rituals, and legends. You should also keep in mind that top management plays a pivotal role in determining the type of organizational culture created and transmitted.[59]

Core Values

core value A value that is central to an organization's culture and is likely to reflect a work-related value of the society, or part of the society, in which the organization operates.

The **core values** of organizational culture are likely to reflect the work-related values of the society, or part of the society, in which it operates. This relationship is especially true in those societies having relatively uniform and shared work-related values. In Chapter 3 we discussed Hofstede's four work-related societal value dimensions: power distance, uncertainty avoidance, individualism, and masculinity. In the following sections we'll relate them to organizational cultures.[60]

Power Distance Recall that power distance is the extent to which individuals accept the unequal distribution of power. In organizations in societies ranked medium to high in power distance, such as Siemens in Germany, communication and decision making flow generally from the top to the bottom of the organization. An autocratic management style is one of Siemens's core values and is widely accepted within the company. In low to moderate power distance societies, such as those of the United States and Canada, organizational cultures are more likely to recognize that employees have basic rights and to support subordinates' participation in decision making. In addition, control systems in such organizations are based on trust in subordinates' ability to complete their tasks.

Uncertainty Avoidance Uncertainty avoidance is the extent to which individuals feel threatened by ambiguous and risky situations and try to avoid or reduce them. In high uncertainty avoidance (that is, low risk-taking) societies, such as France and Mexico, organizations are likely to be less entrepreneurial, to rely extensively on written rules and rigid and formal structures, and to emphasize employment stability. These characteristics are also reflected in the core values of Germany's Siemens and Volkswagen. The United States and Canada tend to be low on uncertainty avoidance (that is, high on acceptance of risk). Apple Computer, PepsiCo, and Merck are among the firms that reflect especially low uncertainty avoidance in their organizational cultures.

Empowerment means creating conditions that encourage risk taking—which is inherent to adaptive and innovative decision making—by individuals and teams at many organizational levels. For example, Nordstrom has long been heralded as one of the champions of customer service. Its successful efforts to hire, motivate, and keep some of the best salespeople in the retail industry have given it a national reputation. Not only do Nordstrom salespeople coddle the customer, but Norstrom buyers walk the salesfloor, listening to customers and acting on their likes and dislikes. Buyers make localized, as opposed to centralized, merchandising decisions. They use their own judgment, exercising creativity to match merchandise to customers' ever-changing needs and desires. Nordstrom's top five directors use decentralized reporting relationships with store managers and buyers to stay one step ahead of fashion trends. Thus the company responds quickly to customers' changing tastes and can better anticipate heavy demand, indecision, or confusion over certain fashions.[61]

Individualism Individualism reflects the importance of the individual. Organizations in societies such as those of the United States and Canada, which are high on this dimension, tend to emphasize personal initiative and achievement, reward performance, and encourage competition. In contrast, organizations in societies such as Japan's, which is high on the collectivism dimension, tend to emphasize group achievement and cooperation within the organization, but competition between organizations (for example, between Japanese and American products). Organizational cultures like those at IBM, Black & Decker, Merrill Lynch, and PepsiCo reflect different blends of the characteristics of individualism.

Masculinity Masculinity refers to the notion that men should be assertive and women nurturant. This dimension measures the extent to which individuals tend to endorse objectives emphasizing assertiveness and self-interest (such as earnings and career advancement) rather than those emphasizing helpfulness and mutual interests (such as cooperation and friendliness). In general, U.S. and Canadian firms tend to have relatively moderate masculinity characteristics. Sweden's Volvo Company, on the other hand, has an organizational culture that emphasizes nurturing characteristics that mirror Sweden's ''femininity'' attributes (nurturing, people orientation).

The following account describes the core values of IBM in concrete terms. IBM continues to orient new employees, both formally and informally, in ''the IBM way.''

THE IBM WAY

*I*NSIGHT Thomas J. Watson, Sr., articulated values and a code of behavior for IBM when he founded the company in 1914. Anyone who worked for him thereafter knew exactly what IBM was all about. These values were reaffirmed by his son, Thomas Watson, Jr., in 1956, when he became IBM's second CEO. They are uncomplicated and can be easily understood by everyone from the CEO's office to the mailroom.

1. The individual must be respected.
2. The customer is the final arbiter. IBM is dedicated to achieving total customer satisfaction.
3. Excellence and superior performance must be executed across our enterprise.
4. We are committed to leadership in the markets we choose to serve.

These values remain at the heart of the company's operations today. They are so revered and encompassing that they directly influence every organizational action and policy. The company drives home its core values at meetings, in internal publications and memos, at company gatherings, and in private conversations. Management demonstrates by personal deeds and actions what these values mean.

Since IBM's earliest days, an ongoing campaign has stressed that *each individual makes a difference*. The company tries to create a small-business atmosphere, keeping branch offices small—with about one manager to every twelve employees. Superior performance is rewarded by recognition, promotions, and money. There are no automatic raises, that is, no cost-of-living increases. Each

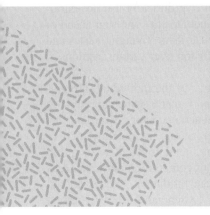

person is paid on the basis of what he or she produces, not on seniority. Those who do exceptionally well are paid accordingly.

You might notice a host of little things at IBM headquarters in Armonk, New York that support the IBM way. For instance, there are no titles on doors or desks, no executive bathrooms, no reserved parking spaces, and no executive dining room. All in all, it's a very democratic environment, where everyone is treated with equal respect. Even IBM's equal opportunity policy and affirmative action programs go far beyond government guidelines: The company's minority population equals or exceeds the percentage in the U.S. population. Actions, tactics, strategies, implementation, inspection, measurement, recognition, and commitment—those are what's important. Not just words.[62]

This chapter's Global Link feature provides an interesting contrast to IBM's organizational culture. It presents the work-related values of the University of Brunei and their implications for change. The university is a new and rapidly developing organization with about 160 employees. It's located in the small but extremely oil-rich nation of Brunei, which lies at the geographical hub of Southeast Asia. Brunei has strong ties with Malaysia in terms of language, religion (Islam), and ethnic orientation. It has a population of a quarter million and one of the highest per capita domestic incomes in the world.

organizational socialization The systematic process by which an organization brings new members into its culture.

Through *organizatonal socialization*, new employees learn the norms of a particular culture. A particularly hard-working culture might require that business be done in a "power breakfast."

Socialization and Norms

Organizational socialization is the systematic process by which an organization brings new members into its culture.[63] Through socialization, individuals learn the ropes and are introduced to the norms of the organization. Strong organizational cultures generally have well-developed methods for selecting the right types of employees and, once selected, for molding them. Molding, in terms of the proper organizational norms, sentiments, activities, interactions, and practices, takes place in various ways.[64] The most powerful way is through consistent role modeling, teaching, coaching, and enforcement by team members and managers—starting at the top and spreading throughout the organization.

One of IBM's socialization mechanisms for enforcing the value of respect for the individual is the penalty box. Often a person sent to the penalty box has committed an offence against IBM's culture; harsh handling of a subordinate, questionable actions against a competitor, and distortion of a report are but a few examples. Most penalty box assignments involve a lateral move to a less desirable location. For example, a branch manager in Chicago might be moved to an out-of-the-way staff position at headquarters in Armonk, New York. To an outsider, penalty box assignments look like normal assignments, but insiders know what's really happened. Penalty boxes provide a place for people to continue working while they contemplate the mistakes they've made and the hard feelings they've created are gradually forgotten. This mechanism is one of many things IBM does to lend credence to employees' beliefs that the firm won't act to end a career without good cause. Even managers with outstanding track records make serious mistakes. Don Estridge, maverick pioneer of IBM's successful personal computer line and later head of that division, broke out of a penalty box.[65]

The socialization that takes place in an organization—explicitly and formally or implicitly and informally—is supported by organizationwide norms.[66] Table 16.1 presents examples of positive and negative organizationwide norms. A few of the organizations that adhere to all of the positive norms listed are IBM, Compaq, 3M, Johnson Wax, America West Airlines, and Microsoft Corporation.

UNIVERSITY OF BRUNEI'S ORGANIZATIONAL CULTURE

Brunei's social culture and the University of Brunei's organizational culture are characterized by high power distance. This tendency is reflected in the day-to-day life at the university: Employees and administrators prefer close supervision, employees are afraid to disagree with their superiors, there is a low level of trust, decision making is highly centralized, there are many levels in the hierarchy, and the proportion of administrative to nonadministrative personnel is high. In fact, centralization is carried to extraordinary lengths. For example, all university staff, whose offices are dispersed across the campus, have to obtain their supplies from a central supply point with one door and one officer-in-charge. The officer frequently locks the door because this is the only way he can keep at bay the endless stream of "customers" converging on him from all corners of the university. This considerable waste of high-level human resources seems to the university a necessary cost to safeguard the principle of tight centralization. Any kind of criticism—even constructive—is frowned upon, no matter who offers it.

Strong uncertainty avoidance is also apparent in the university. There appears to be emotional resistance to change, little risk taking, a preference for a clear organizational structure that must be respected at all costs, a preference for clearly laid out rules and regulations that should never be broken, and a strong feeling that conflict in organizations is undesirable and to be avoided whenever possible. Unwillingness to reverse a decision despite convincing evidence of its failure to accomplish what was intended is an example of uncertainty avoidance. This may be a defense against a loss of face.

The organizational culture is also characterized as one of low individualism (high collectivism). The manifestations of this orientation include policies and practices based on loyalty and a sense of duty, promotion based on seniority, little concern with modern management ideas, and policies and practices that vary according to personal relationships between particular individuals. Certain rules and regulations—such as those pertaining to leave, housing, travel, equipment purchases, and so on—are routinely broken for friends and relations. In less than harmonious personal relationships, the apparent flexibility about these rules quickly changes to a rigid application of them.

Finally, the university culture seems to be best characterized by a medium level of masculinity. There are few women in the more-qualified, better-paying jobs, and those who are tend to be very assertive. There was only one woman holding a senior administrative position in the late 1980s, and her manner was assertive and uncompromising—in short, masculine.

Source: Adapted from P. Blunt, "Cultural Consequences for Organization. Change in a Southeast Asia State: Brunei," *Academy of Management Executive,* 1988, 2:235–240.

Examples of Organizationwide Norms

Positive Norms	Negative Norms
1. Be open, honest.	1. Maintain secrecy, stonewalling, "play your cards close to the chest."
2. Be cost-effective.	2. "Spend it or burn it."
3. Develop and be a mentor to subordinates.	3. "Watch out for number one."
4. Take responsibility.	4. Avoid responsibility, pass the buck.
5. Maintain loyalty to the organization.	5. "Bad-mouth" the organization.
6. Promote "all for one and one for all."	6. Achieve your objectives at the expense of others.

Source: Adapted from E. Jansen and M. A. Von Glinow, "Ethical Ambivalence and Organizational Rewards," *Academy of Management Review,* 1975, *10*:817. Used with permission.

Fortune magazine noted the importance of socialization:

> Many of the great American companies that thrive from one generation to the next—IBM, Procter & Gamble, Morgan Guaranty Trust—are organizations that have perfected their processes of socialization. Virtually none talk explicitly about socialization; they may not even be conscious of precisely what they are doing. Moreover, when one examines any particular aspect of their policy toward people—how they recruit or train or compensate—little stands out as unusual. But when the pieces are assembled, what emerges is an awesome internal consistency that powerfully shapes behavior.[67]

Rituals

ritual A relatively elaborate and planned set of dramatic expressions carried out through a special event.

A **ritual** is a relatively elaborate and planned set of dramatic expressions carried out through a special event.[68] Commencement at a university or college is a ritual. The commencement program is the event, and the dramatic expressions include the procession of faculty and honored guests, the procession of graduates, the invocation, the statement of welcome, the speech by a special guest, and the awarding of diplomas.

Performance-driven organizational cultures use a variety of rituals of enhancement. They serve to publicly recognize individuals and teams for outstanding achievement, motivate other individuals and teams toward similar achievements, spread good news about the teams and organization, and emphasize the mutual nature of organizational, team, and employee objectives.[69] Two of the rites of enhancement used in IBM's marketing divisions are the Hundred Percent Club and the Golden Circle. Each year IBM marketing representatives who achieve their annual objectives become members of the Hundred Percent Club. Membership in the club is publicized throughout the company. Marketing representatives are expected to gain membership at least once every three years; failure to make it for three consecutive years probably means the marketing representative won't get a chance the fourth year. The top 10 percent of the Hundred Percent Club members are elevated to the Golden Circle. Their achievements are acknowledged throughout the organization. They are invited to an all-expenses-paid convention in a place such as Bermuda or Hawaii and are given full VIP treatment.[70]

Legends

legend A well-known story about some significant person or event, based on historical fact but embellished with fictional details.

A **legend** is a well-known story about some significant person or event, based on historical fact but embellished with fictional details.[71] Legends are passed on by organizational "storytellers," who help maintain cohesion and guidelines for employees to follow. These legends may even relate much of what it takes to get ahead in the organization. The story in the following Insight is one that Tom Watson, Jr., often told. The Legend of the Wild Ducks stated and reinforced the need for both individualism and team play at IBM.

INSIGHT

There was once a nature lover who liked watching the wild ducks fly south in vast flocks each October. Out of compassion he started putting feed for them at a nearby pond. After a while some of the ducks no longer bothered to fly south; they wintered at the pond on what he fed them. In time they flew less and less. After three or four years they grew so fat and lazy that they found it difficult to fly at all. Thomas Watson, Jr. found this story in the writings of the Danish philosopher Soren Kierkegaard, and he always ended it with the point that you can make wild ducks tame, but you can never make tame ducks wild again. Watson would further add that ''the duck who is tamed will never go anywhere anymore. We are convinced that business needs its wild ducks. And in IBM we try not to tame them.''

Watson told this story again and again to impress on people the value of deviance and the tolerance for ''outlaw heroes'' in a company well-known for its conformity and standardized ways. It's reported, however, that an employee once told Watson that ''even wild ducks fly in formation.'' This rejoinder immediately became part of the wild ducks story, precisely because it makes another important point about IBM's culture: ''We're all flying in the same direction.''[72]

Types of Organizational Cultures

Many frameworks have been developed for describing different types of organizational cultures. With only a few exceptions, these frameworks are extensions of two basic types: organizational clan culture and market culture. In brief, a **clan culture** is based on extensive socialization and widely shared values and norms. A **market culture** is based on impersonal relationships that are established via negotiated terms of exchange.[73]

Figure 16.7 presents a questionnaire that compares the clan culture to the market culture. The attributes at the end of each continuum in the figure are typical of their respective cultures. Each five-point continuum suggests that an organization's culture can be characterized more or less by the attributes that anchor the ends of the continuum. You should place an X at the point on each continuum that you think best-represents the organizational culture of an organization in which you have been deeply involved.

Clan Culture With a clan culture the organization's employees are almost a fraternal group. Everyone recognizes an obligation beyond the simple exchange of labor for salary. It's understood that required contributions to the organization (such as hours worked per week) may exceed any contractual agreements. The individual's long-term commitment to the organization (loyalty) is exchanged for the organization's long-term commitment to the individual (security). This relationship is based on mutual interests. Hewlett-Packard, IBM, Johnson & Johnson, Merck, J. C. Penney, and Brooklyn Union Gas, for instance, have clan cultures.

The clan culture accomplishes unity through a long and thorough socialization process. Members progress through the ranks by pursuing traditional career paths in the organization. Long-time clan members serve as mentors and role models for newer members. It is through these relationships that the values and norms of the organization are maintained over successive generations of employees. The clan is aware of its unique history and often documents its origins and celebrates its traditions in various ceremonies. Statements of its credo, or publicly held values, are reinforced. Members and teams have a shared image of the organization's style and manner of conduct. John Sculley, who turned around Apple Computer, united the badly divided company through his emphasis on becoming ''One Apple.'' Apple had become two working companies by 1986, when Steven Jobs, one of its founders, and Sculley began to disagree following the market failure of the Macintosh XL.[74]

clan culture A type of organizational culture based on extensive socialization and widely shared values and norms.

market culture A type of organizational culture based on impersonal relationships that are established via negotiated terms of exchange.

FIGURE 16.7

Organizational Cultures Questionnaire

Instructions: For each of the following items, place an x on the one of the five positions along the continuum that best corresponds to your organization's position with respect to the statements at each end of the continuum.

Clan Culture	Relationship between individual and organization	Market Culture
Fraternal relationship		Contractual relationship
Mutual long-term commitment		Mutual short-term commitment
Rests on mutual interests, a shared fate		Rests on self-interest, utilitarianism
Sense of tradition, history, company style		Place to work, make money
Hierarchy influences relationships		Terms of exchange influence relationships

	Relationships among organizational members	
Pride in membership		Independence from peers
Sense of interdependence, identification with peers		Limited interaction
Pressure from peers to conform to norms		Little pressure from peers to conform to norms
Stresses team rather than just individual initiative, ownership		Stresses individual initiative, ownership

	Process of socialization	
Thorough, deep socialization		Little socialization
Superiors are mentors, role models, agents of socialization		Superiors are distant, are negotiators, resource allocators
Many rich norms govern a wide range of behaviors		Few norms governing behaviors

	Work-related core values	
Low to moderate power distance		High power distance
High to moderate uncertainty avoidance		Low to moderate uncertainty avoidance
Mixture of individualism/ collectivism		High individualism
Mixture of masculinity/ femininity		High masculinity

Source: Primarily developed from J. Kerr and J. W. Slocum, Jr., "Managing Corporate Culture through Reward Systems," *Academy of Management Executive,* 1987, *1*:98–108.

In a clan culture members share a sense of pride in membership. The socialization process results in a strong sense of identification among members and a strong sense of interdependence. The up-through-the-ranks career pattern results in an extensive network of colleagues whose paths have crossed and who have shared similar experiences. Communication, coordination, and integration are facilitated by shared goals, perceptions, and behavioral tendencies. A clan culture generates feelings of personal ownership of a division, product, or ideas. In addition, pressure to conform to important norms is considerable. The very richness of the culture creates an environment in which few areas are left totally free from normative pressures. Depending on the types of norms, the culture may or may not generate risk-taking behavior or innovation.

Our earlier discussion of IBM suggests that it would fall along the far left to the middle of the continua in Figure 16.7. Herman Miller, Inc., the fast-growing office furniture maker, provides another example of the clan culture in action.

INSIGHT

Max DePree, chairman of Herman Miller, and his forebears have built a thriving enterprise, in large part because of sturdy bridges between management and employees. All hands are dedicated to fine design and insist on top quality, but they also know where profits come from. DePree's father D. J., who founded the company in Zeeland, Michigan in 1923, set the tone with profit-sharing and employee-incentive programs long before they were fashionable.

At the heart of Herman Miller's management system are what Max DePree calls covenantal relationships between top management and all employees. He defines the company's central mission as "attempting to share values, ideals, goals, respect for each person, the process of our work together." In contrast, he says, many companies settle for contractual relationships, which he says "deal only with precedent and status."

When top managers at Herman Miller are hiring key employees, they focus more on character and the ability to get along with people than on traditional resumé milestones. The senior vice president for research was once a high school football coach. A marketing senior vice president is a former dean of the agriculture school at Michigan State. DePree recruited Michele Hunt, a young black woman from the state's Department of Corrections, where she was training to become a prison warden. Now in charge of human resources and employee relations, she may be the only U.S. executive to hold the title Vice President for People.

Everyone at Herman Miller knows the limits of the company's team style. Diane Bunse, a shift manager, describes the decision-making process as "participative, not permissive." DePree explains that Herman Miller is not a democracy: "Having a say does not mean having a vote." So managers have to be both firm in decision making and sympathetic in explaining their decisions. Says Edward Simon, Jr., president and chief operating officer: "To be successful here, you have to know how to dance."

In his book, *Leadership Is an Art,* DePree presents the warning signs of a company in decline. Among them are "dark tension" among key managers, a decrease of participation rituals such as retirement and holiday parties, people failing to tell or to understand historic company anecdotes (what he calls tribal stories), the issuing of an excessive number of manuals, and a general loss of grace and civility.[75]

Market Culture With a market culture the relationship between individual and organization is contractual. Obligations of each party are agreed on in advance. The individual is responsible for some level of performance, and the organization promises a specified level of rewards in return. Increased levels of performance are exchanged for increased rewards, as outlined in a negotiated schedule. Neither party recognizes the right of the other to demand more than was originally specified. The organization does not promise (or imply) security; the individual does not promise (or imply) loyalty. The contract, renewed annually if each party adequately performs its obligations, is utilitarian, since each party uses the other as a means of furthering its own goals. Rather than promoting a feeling of membership in a social system, the market culture encourages a strong sense of independence and individuality that encourages everyone to pursue his or her own interests. Organizations such as Warner Communications, ITT, and General Electric have market cultures.

The market culture doesn't exert a great deal of normative pressure on the organization's members. Members do not share a common set of expectations regarding management style or philosophy. There is little pressure from peers to conform to specific behavior or attitudes. Much of superiors' interactions with subordinates consist of negotiating performance-reward agreements and/or evaluating requests for resource allocations. A superior's influence on subordinate's rewards is limited. Superiors are not very effective as role models or mentors, and the absence of long-term commitment by both parties weakens the socialization process.

Relations among co-workers are distant. There are few economic incentives for cooperating with peers. Managers do not interact frequently with their counterparts in other divisions, nor do they develop an extensive network of colleagues within the company. Vertical career paths result in little understanding of or identification with the problems of other divisions.

The market culture isn't designed to generate loyalty, cooperation, or a sense of belonging to a social system. Members don't feel constrained by norms, values, or allegiance to an accepted way of acting and thinking. But the market culture does generate personal initiative, a strong sense of ownership and responsibility for operations and decisions, and an entrepreneurial approach to management. The individual is free to pursue objectives with a minimum of organizational constraints.

PepsiCo appears to be another organization that leans toward a market culture, as suggested in the following Insight. However, you will note some elements consistent with a clan culture.

PEPSICO'S MARKET CULTURE

*I*NSIGHT Wayne Calloway, CEO of PepsiCo, is described by his colleagues as "tough as nails." Calloway runs a boot camp for managers that makes Parris Island look like Coney Island. He sets back-breaking standards and raises them methodically each year. Those who can't cut it wash out. To prove him- or herself, each manager gets to act like an entrepreneur—risk taking is expected, memos scarce, meetings few, and second-guessing rare. Sixty-hour weeks are typical, and managers often work Saturdays and Sundays. But teamwork counts too. If the team says move to Patagonia, you move. Although only aggressive achievers survive at PepsiCo, those who do seem to love it. Perched in Calloway's office in Purchase, New York is a bronze eagle, a gift from his managers. It bears the inscription "We're proud to fly in your formation."

To the winners go the spoils—first-class air travel, fully loaded company cars, stock options, and bonuses that in good years can hit 90 percent of salary for top managers. Promotions come fast—every two to three years is standard. Corporate politics will always exist, but PepsiCo strives to get as close as an organization of this size can to a meritocracy. In the words of former chairman Donald Kendall, "PepsiCo is the ultimate capitalistic engine."

At the heart of PepsiCo's organizational culture is management evaluation, designed to weed out the weak and nurture the strong. The annual performance review requires a boss to sit down with each of his or her managers at least once a year and discuss performance. The focus is on what the manager actually did this year to make a big difference in the business, not whether she's a nice person or he wears the right clothes. Did she meet the sales target? Did he develop a suc-

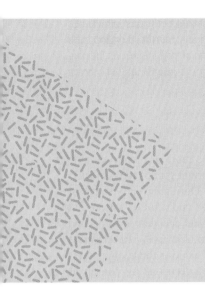

cessful new taco chip or soda commercial. Says Michael Jordan, the hard-driving CEO of Frito-Lay, ''Nothing is ever good enough.'' If the manager met the goals, fine. The boss then typically ups the standards for next year.

But pity the manager who isn't getting results. First the boss will try to find out why and help to fix it, but after a year or two of missing the mark, the loser's a goner. Brenda Barnes, a fast-rising, thirty-five-year old vice president at Pepsi-Cola with 700 people under her control, sums it up best when she says, ''We'll never be nor should we be a warm and cuddly environment.'' There is a merciful side to all this: People tend to get weeded out early in their careers rather than later, when it's much harder to find another job.

Such a harsh system has costs. One manager who wasn't considered PepsiCo material found himself walking around the hallways with his face twitching. When the inevitable day of reckoning arrived, he asked his reviewer *why* he hadn't made it. Looking him straight in the eye, his executioner replied, ''You're not enough of a b———.''[76]

Implications for Managers and Teams

Managers and teams constantly face the need to determine which attributes of organizational culture should be preserved and which should be modified.[77] In Chapter 21 we'll consider a variety of issues involved in changing organizations to make them more innovative and creative. Here we'll discuss briefly only a few of the things that managers and teams can do to maintain or change organizational culture:[78]

▶ Set the example.
▶ State and reinforce values.
▶ Socialize.
▶ Don't underestimate the power of values, socialization, rituals, and legends.

Top management cannot delegate responsibility for creating and transmitting organizational culture. The strongest influences on culture formation are top management's day-to-day activities, interactions, sentiments, and norms, as perceived throughout the organization.

In order to maintain or change organizational culture, managers and teams usually have to explicitly communicate and reinforce values, norms, and sentiments that are important to the organization.[79] These can be clearly communicated through promotions, pay raises, appointments to key committees, and other visible rewards.

Managers and teams should be aware that they can influence the way employees think, feel, and act within the organization.[80] In the United States, with its emphasis on individualism, socialization in firms such as Mary Kay Cosmetics, American Airlines, and Ford Motor Company attempts to blend individuality with group and organizational concerns. These organizations attempt to create a sense of unity without uniformity or blind conformity. Many organizations encourage entrepreneurship at lower organizational levels, going so far as to create strategic business units (SBUs), whose heads are encouraged to act like entrepreneurs.

Managers and teams shouldn't underestimate the power of values, socialization, rituals, and legends in maintaining or changing organizational culture.[81] The culture changes required as a result of AT&T's breakup have been dramatic.[82] Many employees expressed feelings of anger and sorrow. One employee summarized the intense personal loss in these words: ''It was like waking up in familiar surroundings [your home], but your family and all that you held dear were missing.''[83] Such is the potential power of a strong organizational culture.

A subtle bias of our presentation has been to emphasize the positive aspects of a strong organizational culture. A strong organizational culture could also have negative aspects, with norms and practices such as ''only white, Anglo-Saxon Protestants

(WASPs) are promoted beyond first-line manager.'' Moreover, strong cultures sometimes block recognition of the need for change, such as the need to actively recruit, develop, and promote women and minorities on their merits. Top managers in organizations having strong cultures, with their pervasive systems of socialization, must guard against ''brain washing'' employees and suppressing individuality.[84]

CHAPTER SUMMARY

1. An informal group is two or more people who meet on a more or less continuing basis for some purpose or to engage in some activity. Formal groups have specific purposes and tasks that relate to a set of stated objectives. During the early stages of group development, members usually are rather tentative and a lot of sorting out occurs. Later, at least in effective teams, bonds of trust and acceptance form, and members gain a clearer vision of the team's purpose and objectives. An effective team focuses on its objectives and the tasks required to achieve those objectives, allows each member to participate fully, and arrives at decisions by consensus whenever possible.

2. The Homans systems model contains two parts: the internal system and the external system. The internal system includes the activities, interactions, sentiments, and norms that the group members develop over a period of time. These factors are interrelated and eventually determine the group's social structure. The external system affects the internal system and consists of management's values, technology, member values, and organizational structure. These outside conditions exist before and after the group is formed.

3. Advantages of team decision making include greater knowledge, a diversity of approaches, increased acceptance, and better understanding than may be attainable from individual decision making. Disadvantages include blind conformity, domination by an individual, goal displacement, and wasting of time. Three important factors that affect team decision making are (1) task type, (2) group size, and (3) leader role.

4. Quality improvement teams utilize the group process to allow employees to discuss, analyze, and propose or even implement solutions to problems that affect their work or product quality.

5. Organizational culture is the organizationwide personality, the way of thinking and doing things, that is shared by most or all members of the organization. Organizational culture is created and transmitted in many different ways. Among the most important are through core values, socialization and norms, rituals, and legends.

6. There are many types of organizational cultures; two are the clan culture and market culture. A clan culture is based on extensive socialization and widely shared values and norms among organizational members. A market culture is based on impersonal relationships that are established through negotiated terms of exchange.

QUESTIONS FOR DISCUSSION AND APPLICATION

1. **From Where You Sit:** List all of the groups of which you are currently a member and classify them by type.

2. What are the stages of group development? Which stage is most critical?

3. **From Where You Sit:** Select one team to which you have belonged, and, on the basis of your personal experience, identify its desirable or undesirable effects on behavior. Use the Homans systems model to develop your response.

4. Describe the social structure of the team identified in Question 3.

5. Jane described her work as " . . . friendly, just great. All the people get along together, and we bowl and play softball after work." However, quality and production records show that Jane's group is one of least productive in the plant. Why might this be?

6. **From Where You Sit:** How well did your last superior help you meet the emotional problems often experienced when entering a new group? What steps did he or she take or fail to take to reduce those problems?

7. Besides advantages of team decision making identified in the text, give two other potential advantages.

8. What are the similarities and differences between a group and an organizational culture?

9. **From Where You Sit:** Based on the core values presented in the chapter, how would you describe the culture of an organization in which you have been involved? Do these values work for or against achieving the objectives of the organization?

10. **From Where You Sit:** Would you like to work in an organization with a strong organizational culture? Why or why not?

11. Do you think top management should try to explicitly shape and change the culture of an organization? Why or why not?

Team Development Scale

Instructions

Think of a team of which you are currently a member. For each question, circle the number above the answer that is most descriptive of this team.

1. To what extent do I feel a real part of the team?

5	4	3	2	1
Completely a part all the time	A part most of the time	On the edge— sometimes in, sometimes out	Generally outside, except for one or two short periods	On the outside, not really a part of the team

2. How safe is it on this team to be at ease, relaxed, and myself?

5	4	3	2	1
I'm perfectly safe being myself; mistakes aren't held against me.	I feel most people would accept me if I were completely myself, but there are some I'm not sure about.	Generally, I have to be careful what I say or do on this team.	I'm quite fearful about being completely myself on this team.	I would be a fool to be myself on this team.

3. To what extent do I feel ''under wraps,'' that is, have private thoughts, unspoken reservations, or unexpressed feelings and opinions that I have not felt comfortable bringing out in the open?

1	2	3	4	5
Almost completely under wraps	Under wraps many times	Slightly more free and expressive than under wraps	Quite free and expressive much of the time	Almost completely free and expressive

4. How effective are we as a team in extracting and using the ideas, opinions, and information of all team members when making decisions?

1	2	3	4	5
We don't encourage everyone to share ideas, opinions, and information with the team when making decisions.	Only the ideas, opinions, and information of a few members are really known and used when making decisions.	Sometimes we hear the views of most members before making decisions, and sometimes we disregard most members.	A few are hesitant about sharing their opinions, but we generally have good participation in decision making.	Everyone feels his or her ideas, opinions, and information are given a fair hearing before decisions are made.

5. To what extent are the goals the team is working toward understood, and to what extent do they have meaning for me?

1	2	3	4	5
I feel extremely good about our team's goals.	I feel fairly good, but some things are not too clear or meaningful.	A few things we are doing are clear and meaningful.	Many of the goals are not clear or meaningful to me.	I do not understand or feel involved in the goals of the team.

6. How well does my team work at its tasks?

5	4	3	2	1
Coasts, loafs, makes no progress	Makes a little progress; most members loaf	Progress is slow; spurts of effective work	Average or above in progress and pace of work	Works well and achieves definite progress

7. Who largely influences our planning and the way we operate as a team?

5	4	3	2	1
One or two team members	A clique	Shifts from one person or clique to another	Most of the members, but some are left out	All members of the team

8. What is the level of responsibility for work in our team?

5	4	3	2	1
Each person assumes personal responsibility for getting work done.	A majority of the members assume responsibility for getting work done.	About half assume responsibility, about half do not.	Only a few assume responsibility for getting work done.	Nobody (except perhaps one) assumes responsibility for getting work done.

9. How are differences or conflicts handled in our team?

1	2	3	4	5
Differences or conflicts are denied, suppressed, or avoided at all cost.	Differences or conflicts are recognized but remain largely unresolved.	Differences or conflicts are recognized, and a few members make attempts to work them through.	Differences and conflicts are recognized, and our team makes some attempts to deal with them.	Differences and conflicts are recognized, and the team usually works them through satisfactorily.

10. How do people relate to our team leader, chairman, or "boss"?

1	2	3	4	5
Our leader dominates the team; people are often fearful or passive.	Our leader tends to control the team, but people generally agree with our leader's direction.	There is some give and take between our leader and the team members.	Team members relate easily to our leader and usually are able to influence leader decisions.	Team members respect our leader, but we work together as a unified team with no one dominant.

Interpretation

Add the point values circled for all statements to arrive at a total team development score. Scores of 40 to 50 suggest an effective team. Scores of 10 to 30 suggest a very ineffective to marginally functioning team. Scores of 31 to 39 suggest an average team.

TO: Richard Friedman, Director
                  Real Estate Center
FROM: Jill Etter, Senior Editor
SUBJECT: Team Ineffectiveness

Thank you for the invitation to provide my views on the team effectiveness of the publications section within the Real Estate Center. As you know, I have been very frustrated over the publications section's all-too-frequent tendency to miss publication deadlines, make errors in publications, and demonstrate a lack of innovation. You have stated repeatedly that the publications section needs to work as a team, and with only nine members, this shouldn't be a problem.

You asked me to tell you what I think about the "team" I am supposedly a member of. You probably won't like to hear what I have to say, but you told me that my views would be held in confidence, so I'll be totally honest with you.

1. My manager rarely tolerates leadership efforts by other team members.
2. Some team members, three in particular, are unable to handle the current requirements of their work.
3. Too many individuals do not seem willing to put themselves out for the team.
4. There is too much emphasis placed on conformity.
5. We often fail to finish things satisfactorily.
6. We have meetings, but don't understand their purpose.
7. Little time is spent on reviewing what the section does, how it works, and how to improve it.
8. Only a few members suggest new ideas; when suggestions are made, there is no follow-through on them.

If I sound frustrated, I am! I can't take much more of the publications section. You and others outside the section tell me that I'm doing a great job. I very much appreciate the feedback, but it's just not enough. I look forward to hearing from you.

Question: Assume you are Richard Friedman. Write a memo in response to Jill Etter's.

'Green' Executives Find Their Mission Isn't a Natural Part of Corporate Culture

BY JOANN S. LUBLIN

After a yearlong investigation, the Environmental Protection Agency fined Walt Disney Co. $550,000 last summer for the illegal dumping of hazardous cleaning solvents used at Disneyland in California.

Disney might have avoided the fine if it had appointed a vice president of environmental policy sooner, suggests Kym Murphy, who moved into the new post last April. "I like to think we would have been doing our homework more thoroughly," says Mr. Murphy, a former marine biologist who reports to Disney's president.

In the past year or so, about two dozen service and consumer-goods companies—including S.C. Johnson & Son Inc., the Kraft General Foods unit of Philip Morris Cos., and Colgate-Palmolive Co.—have named environmental-policy officers, trying to befriend the Earth and to cash in on the "green" marketing boom. In some companies, the new senior executives are directing wholesale shifts in marketing strategies and increased spending to improve the environment. But often they face a struggle getting the time, authority and money to achieve their objectives.

An environmental-policy officer must "be able to change the direction of a company from the top," plus "be someone who has the ear of the CEO," says Ralph Cavanagh, energy program director for the Natural Resources Defense Council in San Francisco. Where executives lack this clout, he says, "these positions are being created for window-dressing purposes."

Environmental affairs have long been a priority in heavy industry, where producers of chemicals, oil, paper and steel have relied mainly on technical experts to bring heavy pollution under control at production plants.

Now, attention is shifting to the consumer sector, where environmental-policy executives often bring a background in product development, marketing or law. They are typically charged with curbing the environmental impact of product design, development, manufacturing, packaging and marketing—whether or not they get the power to implement their mandates. The officials also may give environmental-awareness training to the work force and promote their stocks to portfolio managers; polls show the environment has become the No. 1 concern of "socially responsible" investors. . . .

Mr. Murphy, for example, does a lot more than worry about EPA rules—though he concedes that Disney's fine last year accelerated "the timing of certain things," such as a companywide environmental-impact audit. He already has created separate environmental-affairs departments at Disney's six major business units, including its theme parks, resorts and movie studios.

The Disney executive also has written a corporate environmental-policy statement, expanded a small recycling program throughout the company and begun both a staff newsletter and "Environmentality," an employee-incentive program featuring Disney character Jiminy Cricket. Staffers receive a coffee mug for pledging environmental good deeds, such as making two-sided copies and using carpools. Mr. Murphy says he may offer substantial cash awards for the best "green" ideas from employees. In his spare time, he's lobbying Disney President Frank Wells to produce a TV series or special on the environment.

But reforming an entire organization is a tall order, and environmental-affairs executives face a variety of obstacles. Target Stores, a discount retail chain owned by Dayton Hudson Corp., hired marketing executive Ann Aronson last fall as its first environmental-program manager. She is expanding a companywide environmental task force to include higher-level officials. But her job, supervised by a vice president, holds limited power.

For instance, she can't dump suppliers who fail to meet packaging guidelines being drafted by her task force for the use of recycled paper and non-polluting inks. "I'm not in the buying division," Ms. Aronson says.

Some companies make their environmental assignments a part-time duty. Glenda Goehrs, environmental-affairs vice president at GSD&M, an Austin, Texas, advertising agency, spent a year—and nearly $100,000 on recycling and employee-education efforts—before the agency relieved her in late January of her second role, chasing new clients. The environmental duties were "taking all my time, evenings and weekends," Ms. Goehrs says. . . .

Even environmental officers with a full-time commitment and their chief executive's ear some-times find their new roles frustrating, largely because bureaucracies resist change. Ben & Jerry's Homemade Inc., a premium ice-cream maker based in Waterbury, Vt., promotes itself as socially responsible. Yet some of its 325 employees balked when Gail Mayville installed two recycling receptacles at every desk for sorting paper as part of her corporate recycling initiative.

"People were asking: 'Why are we doing this?'" says Ms. Mayville, Ben & Jerry's environmental-program developer since December 1989. "For years and years, people just tossed their paper into the basket without having to think what kind of weight or color it was." She overcame their resistance through fliers, bulletin-board signs and individual training.

1. Can an environmental officer make lasting changes in corporate culture, or must the changes always come from top management? Explain.

2. Employees at socially responsible Ben & Jerry's Homemade, Inc., balked at reforms. Why? How far can management go in forcing employees to conform to changes in corporate culture?

3. Imagine that you've just been named environmental director of a small manufacturing company. How would you go about making environmental concern part of your company's corporate structure?

CONSOLIDATED LIFE

This case is based on a real situation. The names of the insurance company and individuals have been changed to protect their identity.

Part I

It all started so positively. Three days after graduating with his degree in business administration, Mike Wilson started work in the policy issue department of a prestigious insurance company, Consolidated Life. The work of the department was mostly clerical and did not require a high degree of technical knowledge.

Rick Belkner was the division's vice president, "the man in charge" at the time. Belkner was an actuary by training, a technical professional whose leadership style was *laissez-faire*. He was described in the division as "the mirror of whomever was the strongest personality around him." It was also common knowledge that Belkner made $60,000 a year and spent a lot of time doing crossword puzzles.

Mike Wilson was hired as a management trainee and promised a supervisory assignment within a year. Because of a management reorganization, however, it was only six weeks before he was placed in charge of an eight-person unit. The reorganization was intended to streamline workflow, upgrade and combine the clerical jobs, and make greater use of the computer system. Many of the clerical staff felt threatened.

Management realized that a flexible supervisory style was necessary to pull off the reorganization without considerable turnover, so they gave supervisors a free hand to run their units as they saw fit. Wilson used this freedom to implement group meetings and training classes in his unit. By promising raises, working long hours, participating in mundane tasks, and using a flexible management style, he was able to increase productivity, reduce errors, and minimize lost time. The dramatic improvement of his unit earned Wilson the reputation of a "superstar," despite being viewed by upper management as unorthodox. They tolerated his loose, people-oriented management style because of his excellent results.

A Chance for Advancement. After a year Wilson received an offer from a different division of Consolidated Life to manage a marketing office. The pay was excellent, and it offered an opportunity to turn around an office in disarray. The reorganization in his present division was almost complete, and most of his friends in management had moved on to other jobs. He decided to accept the offer. During his exit interview he was assured of a position if he ever wanted to return.

The new job was satisfying for a short time, but it soon became apparent to Wilson that it didn't have the long-term potential he had been promised. After bringing in a new staff, computerizing the office, and auditing the books, he began looking for a position that would both challenge him and give him the autonomy he needed to be successful.

Eventually, word got back to his former vice president, Rick Belkner, that Wilson was looking for another job. Belkner offered Wilson a position at the same pay he was now receiving and with control over a fourteen-person unit in his old division. After considering other options, Wilson decided to return to his old division, feeling that he would be able to progress steadily over the next several years.

Enter Jack Greely. Upon his return to the policy issue department, Wilson became aware of several changes that had been made during the six months he had been away. The most important change was the hiring of a new divisional senior vice president, Jack Greely, who had been given total authority to run the division. Greely's reputation was "tough but fair." It was necessary for people in his division to do things his way and "get the work out." Belkner now reported to Greely.

Wilson also found himself reporting to one of his former peers, Kathy Miller, who had been promoted to manager during the reorganization. Wilson had always "hit it off" with Miller and foresaw no problems in working with her.

After a week Wilson realized the full extent of the changes that had been made. Gone was the loose, casual atmosphere that had marked his first tour in the division. Now stricter, task-oriented management was practiced. Morale of the supervisory staff had decreased to an alarmingly low level. As a result, the quality of work being done was poor. Jack Greely was the major topic of conversation in and around the division. People joked that MBO now meant "management by oppression."

Wilson's Idea: A Supervisors' Forum. Wilson felt that a change in management style was necessary in order to improve a frustrating situation. He requested permission from Belkner to form a supervisors' forum for all the managers at Wilson's level in the division. He explained that the purpose would be to enhance the existing management-training program. The forum would include weekly meetings, guest speakers, and discussions of topics relevant to the division and the industry. Wilson thought that the forum would show Greely that he was serious about both his job and improving morale in the division. Belkner okayed the initial meeting.

At the meeting ten of Mike's peers in the company eagerly took the opportunity to "brainstorm" it. The group drafted a memo to Belkner (with a copy to Greely), outlining proposals for further training opportunities and exchanges of information among departments. The group felt that the memo accurately and diplomatically stated their dissatisfaction with the current situation. Nonetheless, they pondered the likely results of their actions and what else they could have done.

Part II

An emergency management meeting was called by Belkner at Greely's request to address the "union" being formed by the supervisors. Four general managers, Belkner, and Greely attended the meeting. During the meeting it was suggested that the forum be disbanded to "put them in their place." Belkner, on the other hand, felt that if "guided" in the proper direction, the forum would die from lack of interest. His stance was adopted, but it was common knowledge that Greely was strongly opposed to the forum and wanted its organizers dealt with. It was clear to everyone that Wilson was a marked man.

Wilson had always been a friendly and open supervisor. The major reason his units had been successful was the attention he paid to each individual and how they interacted with the group. He had a reputation for fairness, was seen as an excellent judge of personnel for new positions, and was noted for his ability to turn around employees who had been in trouble. He motivated people through a dynamic, personable style and was known for his general lack of regard for the rules. He treated rules as obstacles to management and usually used his own judgment in deciding what was important. His office had a sign reading, "Any fool can manage by the rules. It takes an uncommon man to manage without any." It was an approach that flew in the face of company policy, but it had been overlooked in the past because of his results. Because of Wilson's actions with the supervisors' forum, though, he was now regarded as a thorn in management's side, not a superstar, and his oddball style only made things worse. Now, faced with rumors that he was on the way out, Wilson sat down to appraise the situation.

Part III

Wilson decided on the following course of action:

1. Keep the forum alive but moderate its tone, so it doesn't step on Greely's toes.

2. Don't panic. Simply outwork and outsmart the rest of the division by retraining and remotivating personnel.

3. Evoke praise from vendors and customers through excellent service and direct that praise to Greely.

Impressive Results. The results after eight months were impressive. Wilson's unit improved processing speed by 60 percent and lowered errors by 75 percent. His staff became the most highly trained in the division. He had copies of several letters to Greely that praised the unit's excellent service. In addition, the supervisors' forum had attained grudging credibility, although its scope of activity was restricted. Wilson had even begun submitting reports on time as a concession to management.

Wilson was confident that the results would speak for themselves. One month before his scheduled promotion and one month after receiving a merit raise in recognition of his exceptional work record, Miller called him into her office. She informed him that after long and careful consideration the decision had been made to deny him his promotion because of his lack of attention to detail. Wilson was stunned and said so. But before he said anything else, he asked to see Belkner and Greely the next day.

The Showdown. Sitting face to face with Belkner and Greely, Wilson asked whether they agreed with Miller's appraisal. They both said they did. When asked if any other supervisor surpassed his ability and results, each stated that Wilson was one of the best, if not *the* best they had. Then why, he asked, would they deny him a promotion when others of less ability were approved. The answer came from Greely: "We just don't like you. We don't like your management style. You're an oddball. We can't run a division with ten supervisors all doing different things. We need people who conform to our style and methods so we can measure their results objectively. There's no room for subjective interpretation. It's our feeling that if you really put your mind to it, you can be an excellent manager. It's just that now you create trouble and rock the boat. We don't need that. It doesn't matter if you're the best now, sooner or later as you go up the ladder, you will be forced to pay more attention to administrative duties, and you won't handle them well. If we correct your bad habits now, we think you can go far."

Wilson was shocked. He turned to Belkner and demanded, "You mean it doesn't matter what my results are? All that matters is how I do things?" Belkner leaned back in his chair and said in a casual tone, "In so many words, yes."

Wilson left the office knowing that his career at Consolidated was over and immediately started looking for a new job.

1. Does Consolidated Life appear to have a strong organizational culture? Explain your response by referring to the ways that organizational cultures are created and transmitted.

2. How would you characterize the core values at Consolidated Life? Was there agreement or disagreement over one or more of these values? Explain. Use Figure 16.7 to guide your analysis.

3. Based on Homans systems model (see Figure 16.5), how would you explain what happened with the supervisors' forum? (The supervisors' forum should be considered as the internal system.)

4. Did task type, team size, and leader role discussed in relation to groups play a particularly important role in the supervisors' forum? Explain.

Chapter 17

CONFLICT AND STRESS

MANAGEMENT

Liz Aberdale (left)

What You Will Learn

1 Different views of conflict.

2 The effects of four types of role conflict and the impact of role ambiguity.

3 A contingency model of conflict management.

4 The influence of different interpersonal conflict-management styles on an individual's effectiveness.

5 How negotiation can aid conflict resolution or reduction.

6 The sources and effects of work-related distress and the major approaches to managing it.

7 **Skill Development:** How to diagnose and manage conflict and stress for the best possible outcomes.

Valuing Differences at Digital

Digital Equipment Corporation's top management concluded that the usual equal employment opportunity (EEO) and affirmative action programs for creating a diverse work force weren't going to be enough. Top management wanted to move beyond EEO and affirmative action programs to the kind of environment where all employees could realize their potential. Digital decided that meant an environment where individual differences weren't just tolerated but were valued— even celebrated. In the past, these programs focused on bringing women and members of minority groups into positions typically occupied by white males. When these individuals didn't fit the stereotypic white male behavioral profile, it was often assumed that there was something wrong with them, rather than with the stereotype.

The resulting program and philosophy, called Valuing Differences, has two components. First, through what Digital calls core groups, the company helps people get in touch with the stereotypes and false assumptions they may harbor. These voluntary groups of 8 to 10 people work with company-trained facilitators whose job is to encourage discussion and development and, in the company's words, "to keep people safe" as they struggle with their prejudices. Digital also runs a voluntary two-day training program called "Understanding the Dynamics of Diversity," which thousands of Digital employees have now participated in.

Second, the company has named a number of senior managers to various internal Cultural Boards of Directors and internal Valuing Differences Boards of Directors. These boards promote openness to individual differences, encourage younger managers committed to the goal of diversity, and sponsor frequent celebrations of racial, gender, and ethnic differences, such as Hispanic Heritage Week and Black History Month.

In addition to the Valuing Differences program, the company preserved its EEO and affirmative action functions. Valuing Differences focuses on personal and group development, EEO on legal issues, and affirmative action on systemic change. According to Alan Zimmerle, head of the Valuing Differences program, EEO and Valuing Differences are like two circles that touch but don't overlap. The first represents the legal need for diversity, the second Digital's desire for diversity. Affirmative action is a third circle that overlaps the other two and holds them together via policies and procedures.

Together, these three circles can transform legal and social pressures into the competitive advantages of a more effective work force, higher morale, and the reputation of being a better place to work.[1]

Groups, teams, and organizational cultures don't always run smoothly. In fact, they *can't* if they are to be adaptive, innovative, and creative. Diversity among employees can be one of many sources of *conflict* and intense *stress* for individuals and groups in organizations. Digital is a leader in taking positive steps to help employees reduce stereotypes and prejudices about others. Barbara Walker, one of the leaders in Digital's Valuing Differences program, notes: "The best way for people to work effectively with each other is to recognize and celebrate, not deny, each other's differences. Stereotypes, they learned, grew out of ignorance; thus learning about their differences is the surest way to eliminate stereotypes.''[2] Other organizations (such as Avon, Corning, Procter & Gamble, Xerox, and IBM) have also initiated programs to emphasize the need to value and respect differences among employees. As we will see in this chapter, diversity is only one of the many potential sources of intense conflict and stress for employees. We will also see that neither stress nor conflict is necessarily harmful, though both must be understood and ''managed.''

The first section of this chapter considers the nature of conflict management and introduces three basic viewpoints on conflict. The next section focuses on individual conflict and role ambiguity in terms of role expectations, role episodes, and types of role conflict. The third section presents a contingency model of conflict that will help you diagnose the conflict situations you will face. There follows an examination of five different interpersonal conflict-management styles that various individuals can use effectively. This section includes a discussion of how negotiations can aid in conflict reduction or resolution among individuals, teams, and organizations. The final section zeroes in on one possible outcome of intense conflict—stress—and how to manage it. This chapter is directly relevant to *all* employees in their day-to-day work, not only to those in managerial roles.

INTRODUCTION TO CONFLICT

conflict Opposition arising from disagreements due to incompatible objectives, thoughts, or emotions within or among individuals, teams, departments, or organizations.

goal conflict Conflict that arises because desired objectives and preferred outcomes differ.

cognitive conflict Conflict that arises because ideas or thoughts are perceived as incompatible.

affective conflict Conflict that arises because people's feelings or emotions are incompatible.

conflict management Interventions designed to reduce (or, in some cases, to increase) conflict.

Conflict is common within and between organizations—especially in the nineties, which are witnessing increased empowerment of individuals and teams at all organizational levels and the need to adapt and innovate rapidly as a result of intense global competition. **Conflict** is opposition arising from disagreements due to incompatible objectives, thoughts, or emotions within or among individuals, teams, departments, or organizations.[3] This definition recognizes three basic types of conflict.

▶ **Goal conflict** is a situation in which desired objectives and preferred outcomes appear to be incompatible within or among individuals, teams, departments, or organizations.

▶ **Cognitive conflict** is a situation in which ideas or thoughts are perceived as incompatible.

▶ **Affective conflict** is a situation in which feelings or emotions are incompatible; that is, people become angry with one another.

Digital's Valuing Differences program is intended to deal with these three types of conflicts. (1) Some *goal conflicts* existed at Digital because of the perception that the employment and promotion of minorities and women would reduce career opportunities for others (especially white males). (2) *Cognitive conflicts* were represented by the stereotypes and false assumptions some individuals and groups embraced. (3) *Affective conflicts* were expressed through negative feelings and communications among some individuals who differed in gender, race, ethnicity, or other dimension. Digital's Valuing Differences program is a strong intervention designed to reduce goal, cognitive, and affective conflicts springing from gender, racial, ethnic, and other types of individual and group differences. **Conflict management** consists of interventions designed to reduce excessive conflict or, in some cases, to increase insufficient conflict.

The approaches that individuals and organizations can use to manage conflict vary widely, and we'll discuss several of them in this chapter. The approach an individual chooses is likely to be influenced by her or his fundamental view of conflict—negative, positive, or balanced.

At a few exceptional corporations that *value differences,* women don't just survive— they thrive. Director Hooper (right) was promoted from staff ranks to head Baxter Travenol's Canadian division.

Negative View

To many, the word *conflict* suggests negative situations: war, destruction, aggression, violence, and hostility. The traditional view of management (see Chapter 2) typically included the idea that conflict was undesirable. Conflict, it was felt, could be reduced or eliminated through careful selection of people, training, detailed job descriptions, elaborate rules, and incentive systems. These prescriptions are still useful for reducing and preventing some undesirable conflicts.

Conflict within organizations can be especially destructive when management openly or tacitly expects interdependent individuals or groups to compete with one another. In such situations, one person's or one team's success is achieved at the expense of the other individual or group.[4] Employees involved in frequent, intense conflicts of this sort may experience high levels of stress and may respond by withdrawing from the situation. Their discomfort may be expressed psychologically (apathy and indifference) or physically (tardiness, absenteeism, and high turnover). In more extreme cases, they may react with aggressive and hostile behavior, such as stealing or damaging property.

Intense conflicts often lead to biased perceptions and gross distortions of reality. This can cause people to make decisions that increase conflict rather than reduce or resolve it. In the heat of such situations, we often concentrate so hard on making our own point that we ignore the other person's needs and point of view. Winning becomes more important than coming up with a mutually beneficial solution. Thus negative emotions can interfere with efforts to reach a fair resolution of the issues at the root of the conflict.

Employees at all levels may also dislike conflict because they feel it interferes with productivity and efficiency. In sum, many employees believe that conflict disrupts organizational routines and is therefore undesirable.

Positive View

In some ways, the job of managers and teams is to make sure that there is perpetual constructive conflict. Employees and teams that adopt this more positive attitude toward conflict may view conflict situations as exciting, intriguing, and challenging. Conflict may result in better choices if it does not take place in a setting where people try to score points and beat one another. Instead, conflict can stimulate a search for the reasons behind different viewpoints and for effective ways to resolve them. The positive approach may thus lead to creativity, innovation, and change. By providing employees with more information about their organization's operations, conflict can show where corrective actions are needed. Those who adopt this positive attitude, then, view conflict as a necessary condition for achieving individual and organizational objectives.[5]

The dialectical inquiry method and the devil's advocacy method, discussed in Chapter 9, are based on a positive view of conflict.[6] They represent interventions designed to stimulate conflict or allow it to "surface" in a controlled manner. The dialectical inquiry method is a process for examining strategic issues completely and systematically from two or more opposing points of view. The devil's advocacy method involves setting up a conflict: appointing a person within a decision-making team to critique a preferred plan or strategy.

Balanced View

Our attitude toward conflict is *relative* rather than absolute. To us, organizational conflict is inevitable and may at times be desirable. It is possible to prevent many conflicts, but some need to be met and managed instead. Conflicts that often must be managed include those among co-workers, superiors and subordinates, teams, departments, and the organization and external groups (such as major customers, suppliers, unions, and government agencies). Most effective employees have a balanced view of conflict. Through proper management of conflict, it is frequently possible to minimize its negative effects and maximize its positive effects.

ROLE CONFLICT AND AMBIGUITY

role conflict Conflict resulting from a person's being subjected to strong and inconsistent pressures or expectations.

role A group of related tasks and behaviors.

role set The collection of roles occupied by other individuals that are directly related to the role of the person in question.

role ambiguity Confusion created by inadequate or unclear information or by uncertainty about the consequences of one's behavior.

Most conflict that individuals experience is some form of role conflict or role ambiguity. **Role conflict,** at the most basic level, may occur when a person is subjected to strong and *inconsistent* pressures or expectations.[7] A **role** is a group of related tasks and behaviors that an individual is expected to carry out. Roles abound within organizations (superior, subordinate, peer) and outside of organizations (husband or wife, father or mother, woman or man). The role of student involves tasks and activities such as reading books, attending classes, writing papers, taking tests, and participating in student groups.

An individual's **role set** is a collection of roles that are directly related to that individual. For example, a press foreman in a plant that produces trim parts for automobiles has a role set consisting of 19 other people and their roles: general foreman, superintendent, sheet-metal foreman, inspector, shipping-room foreman, and 14 press operators.[8] All the people acting in these roles influence and are influenced by the press-foreman role. A role set for a student may include instructors, friends, family, employer, and boyfriend or girlfriend or spouse.

Individuals may experience difficulties with their role set beyond that created by role conflict. For some individuals, the tensions and anxieties created by role ambiguity may be much more serious than potential role conflicts. **Role ambiguity** includes job-related experiences under one or more of the following conditions: (1) inadequate information about one's expected performance objectives, (2) unclear or confusing information about expected on-the-job behaviors, and (3) uncertainty about the consequences (such as a pay raise, promotion, or dismissal) of certain on-the-job behaviors.[9] As we'll demonstrate later in the chapter, role ambiguity is a common source of intense stress for some individuals.

Role Expectations

role expectations Views held by others about what an individual should or should not do.

Role expectations are the views held by others about what an individual should or should not do. When role expectations are cloudy, the individual may experience role ambiguity. The members of a role set are influenced by their own actions and by those of the other members. They may be rewarded or punished on the basis of someone else's behavior. Someone else may have to perform a task before they can perform their own.[10]

For a quarterback to complete a pass, for example, the line must block and the receiver must hold on to the ball. In turn, the quarterback's performance influences the actions of members of the offensive team. They develop expectations about what the quarterback should and should not do. Members of the role set (*role senders*) communicate expectations to the individual (*focal person*) whose role is the focus of the set at that particular time.

Role senders may also exert pressure on the focal person to meet their expectations. This is called **role pressure.** An instructor who tells students that they must have an average of 90 or higher to earn an A is an example of a role sender creating role pressure. The sender exerts pressure through one or more types of power (reward, expertise, referent, coercive, or legitimate).[11] If two individuals in conflict can reward each other in meaningful ways, they will probably be strongly motivated to seek a win–win resolution.

So far, we have identified the role sender and the focal person as different people. Actually, one person can—and often does—play both roles. A person's *inner voice* provides do's and don't's for each role that person plays. The pressures that these internal role expectations exert can be just as great as, or even greater than, pressures from external ones. For example, your perception of your role as an ideal student might conflict with your awareness of your actual student role. Let's assume that your ideal student role is that of studying to be an artist. However, because of parental pressure, your actual role involves studying to be an accountant. The conditions that breed role conflict and stress are present. When too large a gap exists between the role expectations, the resulting conflict can lead to severe stress.

role pressure Attempts on the part of role senders to induce the focal person to meet their expectations.

role episode Role senders' attempts to influence the behavior of the focal person and the responses of that focal person, which in turn influence the future expectations of the role senders.

Role-Episode Model

A **role episode** includes (1) attempts by one or more role senders to influence the behavior of a focal person and (2) the responses of the focal person, which in turn, influence the role sender's *future* expectations of the focal person. Figure 17.1 provides a model of a role episode. The manager's expectations are translated into pressures that are communicated to an employee. Under some circumstances, an employee may exhibit strong emotional responses (yelling back), physical responses (rising blood pressure), and cognitive responses (refusing to comply).

The subordinate's *emotional response* is his or her feelings about the pressures—positively motivated, angry, frustrated, happy, or whatever. The *cognitive response* is his or her thoughts about the pressures. These feelings and thoughts influence the way the employee responds to the manager. The response provides feedback to the manager—feedback that influences the manager's future expectations of the employee. A manager may handle an employee who responds to pressure with hostility differently from the way she handles an employee who responds with passive acceptance. If an employee responds to pressure by exhibiting signs of high stress, the manager can react in several ways—easing up, reassigning the employee, trying to help the employee deal with the pressures, or even dismissing the employee.

Types of Role Conflict

Earlier we stated that *role conflict* may occur when a person is subject to strong and inconsistent pressures or expectations. In other words, when the individual responds to one set of pressures, it becomes more difficult to respond successfully to the other(s). The severity of the role conflict depends largely on the reward power and coercive power exerted by the role senders and on the focal person's desire to meet expectations.[12] The pressure that results when two managers in a matrix organization pressure an employee at the same time to complete different projects immediately may create severe role conflict. Such conflicts often lead to stress within both the focal person and one or more role senders.

FIGURE 17.1

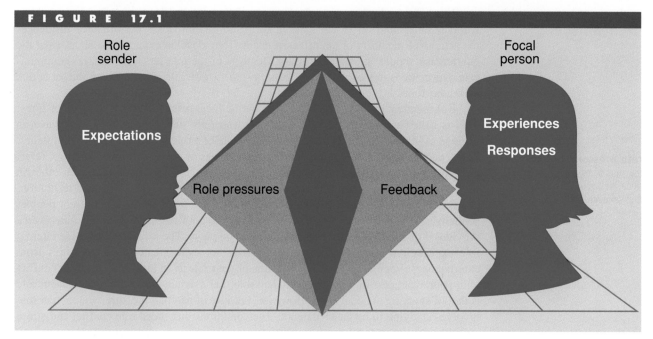

Role sender

Expectations

Role pressures

Focal person

Experiences

Responses

Feedback

Role Episode Model

A course syllabus sets forth expectations, including the basis for grades. This creates role pressure, which you can experience in a variety of ways—motivation inspired by interest and challenge, fear and anxiety that this course is going to be impossible, and so on. If you are motivated by interest and the challenge, you may respond by studying hard, participating in class discussions, and so on. These responses provide feedback to the instructor that you are on target with expectations.

Now let's look at the four basic types of role conflict: intrasender role conflict, intersender role conflict, interrole conflict, and person–role conflict.

intrasender role conflict
Conflict caused by receiving mixed messages from a single role sender.

Intrasender Role Conflict **Intrasender role conflict** may be caused by receiving a mixed message of do's and don't's from a single role sender. A manager might instruct an employee to complete a particular task today and then, a short time later, assign still another task to be completed the same day. If each task requires a full day to complete, intrasender conflict and stress result. Another example is that of one spouse who pressures the other to spend less on food—and then complains about the quality of meals. Or an instructor might assign a paper to be completed and turned in during the same week in which that same instructor is giving a major exam.

intersender role conflict
Conflict that results when pressures from one role sender are incompatible with those from another role sender.

Intersender Role Conflict **Intersender role conflict** may occur when pressures from one role sender are incompatible with those from one or more other role senders. For example, managers and team members who must meet the expectations of multiple stakeholders with conflicting demands (stockholders, customers, government agencies, unions, and so on) often experience intersender role conflict and stress.[13] A study of directors of federally supported manpower agencies indicates that they experienced conflicting pressures from three powerful stakeholder groups: their own staffs, local community leaders, and state and regional administrators responsible for providing program funds and evaluating results. Support from all three stakeholder groups was needed to operate an effective manpower program.[14]

Intersender role conflict may also be experienced by a conscientious employee who is part of a work team that has lower production norms than those of manage-

interrole conflict Conflict that occurs when role pressures associated with membership in one group conflict with those associated with membership in another.

ment. Conflict occurs because the employee values friendly relations with fellow employees but also wants to be a high performer.

Interrole Conflict **Interrole conflict** may occur when role pressures associated with membership in one team or organization conflict with those stemming from membership in others. Pressure to work overtime or take work home may conflict with pressure to devote more attention to family matters. When this type of conflict becomes intense, individuals may cope with severe stress by withdrawing from one of the roles. In an extreme example, a spouse might change jobs or even get a divorce.

Reports of interrole conflicts are increasing for both men and women who are parents and also want successful fast-track careers.[15] Interrole conflicts and stress for women who are attempting to blend their work, spousal, and parenting roles can be especially difficult.[16] The need to rely on others and to learn through constructive feedback how to manage these conflicts is addressed the section on stress management.

person–role conflict Conflict that results from differences between the pressures exerted by one's role(s) and his or her needs, attitudes, values, or abilities.

Person–Role Conflict **Person–role conflict** may occur when differences arise between the pressures exerted by the focal person's role(s) and his or her own needs, attitudes, values, or abilities. As implied in the Manager's Viewpoint on valuing differences at Digital, confronting stereotypes is an important source of person–role conflict. Barbara Walker, the manager charged with promoting international diversity at Digital: "As they began to talk openly and frankly with each other, they learned that despite the pain and vulnerability that came with acknowledging their own racism, they were even greater victims when they denied it."[17] Stereotypes are resistant to modification because they serve to (1) reduce internal conflicts and inner insecurities, (2) maintain basic values about an individual's role in society, and (3) provide a convenient way to maintain "inner" order and interpret others' behaviors.[18] Stereotypes serve these purposes by classifying individuals into groups according to simplistic criteria (gender, age, race, religion, national origin, occupation, or the like) and then assigning a common set of abilities, traits, and behaviors to all individuals within that group.

Some white males who work for members of minority groups or women may initially experience person–role conflict. The following comments by black managers illustrate this problem.

WHEN THE BOSS IS BLACK

*I*NSIGHT As a vice president at Rockwell International in Anaheim, Calif., Earl S. Washington oversees a mostly white work force of 1500. "I find myself under the magnifying glass every day, proving that I understand how to run this business," he says. "All bosses are second-guessed," explains Xerox vice president Gilbert H. Scott, who heads a staff of 800 in the Southwest and California, 75 percent of whom are white. "If you're a black boss, you're probably second-guessed more." But sometimes patience wears thin. If faced with a white employee who could not accept working under a black superior, says Rockwell International's Washington, he would help the recalcitrant employee find new work—at another company. "I'm not going to tolerate it," he says.

Collier W. St. Clair, a vice president for the Equitable Financial Services Co., was a district sales manager. One of his responsibilities was hiring, but many white applicants balked when they saw that their boss would be black. "A lot of

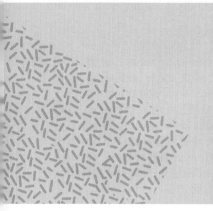

them didn't come back for a second interview," he says. "I finally started asking people if they would have any problem working with me."

Many black managers say their biggest problem is learning not to bristle at every challenge to their authority. The armed forces pioneered the elevation of blacks to supervisory ranks after President Harry Truman ordered desegregation in 1948. In 1987 Brigadier General Fred Augustus Gorden became the first black officer to serve as commandant of cadets at West Point. While he was walking across the campus one day, a white cadet failed to give the requisite salute. Gorden paused. Still no salute. He could have severely disciplined the cadet, but he chose simply to talk with him instead. "I've learned to pick and choose my battles," he explains.[19]

No single pattern is used by all individuals to manage role conflicts. The individual's personality and the types of interpersonal relationships among the role senders enormously influence the approach that is adopted. Let's now consider a balanced view of conflict through what is known as the contingency model of conflict. This model will help you understand the organizational situations in which role conflicts and role ambiguity are likely to be most problematic. It also outlines the situations in which particular interpersonal conflict-management styles are most likely to be effective.

CONTINGENCY MODEL OF CONFLICT

distributive variable In the contingency model of conflict, the degree to which the goals of those in conflict are perceived as incompatible.

integrative variable In the contingency model of conflict, the degree to which the goals of those in conflict are perceived as compatible.

win–lose conflict situation In the contingency model of conflict, the situation that exists when the parties have many more conflicting goals than shared goals; that is, when one person's gain is another's loss.

politics The maneuvering that employees engage in when seeking selfish goals that are opposed to the goals of others in the organization.

The contingency model of conflict helps teams, managers, and other employees diagnose the conflict situations they will face. The model suggests that different conflict-management approaches are appropriate for different types of situations. This model is constructed from two contingency variables—the distributive and the integrative—that serve to identify four basic conflict situations.[20]

The **distributive variable** refers to the degree to which one or more objectives (goals) of the individuals or teams in conflict are perceived as incompatible. This variable is shown as the distributive continuum in Figure 17.2. In a highly distributive relationship, one person's (or one group's) gain is another's loss. For example, most team sports are played until one team wins and the other loses. The **integrative variable** refers to the degree to which one or more of the objectives (goals) of the individuals or teams are perceived as compatible. This variable is shown as the integrative continuum in Figure 17.2. In a highly integrative relationship, one person or team can gain only as another person or team gains. For example, doubles partners in tennis have a vested interest in one another's playing well. Cooperation and support between them increases the probability of their winning more matches. By cross-classifying the distributive and integrative variables, we can construct the four-cell contingency model of conflict. It is shown in Figure 17.2.

Win–Lose Conflict Situation

A **win–lose conflict situation** occurs when there is a high-distributive and low-integrative relationship (cell 1 of Figure 17.2). One person's gain is another's loss. Typically, a win–lose situation occurs when there is a direct conflict in objectives. Organizations normally try to minimize internal win–lose situations because of their negative effects on performance and employee attitudes. Internal win–lose situations are closely associated with workplace **politics**—the maneuvering employees engage in when they are seeking

FIGURE 17.2

Contingency Model of Conflict

Each conflict situation is determined by the way the individuals or teams diagnose and interpret the distributive and integrative contingency variables. This grid shows the extremes of four conflict situations. Conflict situations can be characterized at any place on the grid, including the middle point.

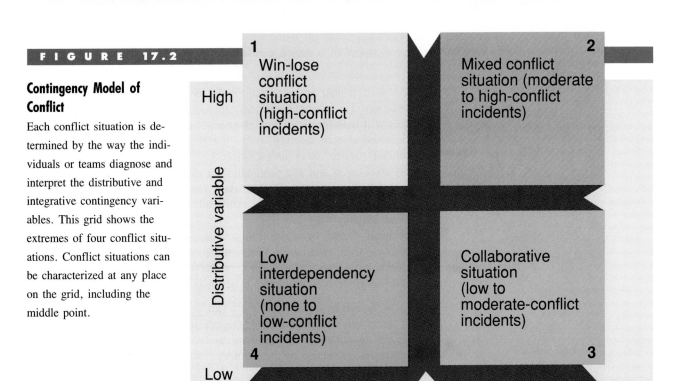

selfish goals that are opposed to the goals of others in the organization. In win–lose situations, the frequency and intensity of conflict incidents and politics are quite high.

One particularly intense form of politics occurs in family-run businesses. Louisville's celebrated Bingham family feuded so long and fiercely that Barry Bingham, Sr., the owner of the *Courier-Journal* and the *Louisville Times,* chose to sell the newspapers to Gannett in 1986 rather than leave them to his feuding children to tear apart.

Consider another example: Leonard S. Shoen started U-Haul International, the Phoenix-based car and truck rental business. He began transferring stock to his children while they were still young. The trouble was that the Shoen children kept coming—eight sons and five daughters from three different mothers. Shoen parceled out the shares as the children arrived and ultimately gave away 95 percent of the company. U-Haul grew into Amerco, with revenues of about $1 billion. In 1986 two of Shoen's sons, Edward and Mark, seized control. The senior Shoen found himself voted out of the business, and soon thereafter his eldest son, Sam, who had been running the company, quit. The family has since split into two camps. Edward and Mark are running the show; Leonard and Sam are suing to regain control of the company. The battle has grown violent, stockholder meetings degenerating into slugfests. In one outlandish incident, Michael Shoen was reportedly beaten up by Edward and Mark. Michael's photograph, complete with bruises, was splashed across the business section of the *Arizona Republic* newspaper. Says Leonard Shoen, ''I created a monster.''[21]

mixed conflict situation In the contingency model of conflict, the situation that exists when there are many shared goals and many conflicting goals.

Mixed Conflict Situation

A **mixed conflict situation** occurs when the relationship is both high-distributive and high-integrative (cell 2 in Figure 17.2). Union–management relationships often are mixed conflict situations. Distributive issues usually concern the relative allocation of rewards and the relative priority assigned to objectives. For example, management focuses on increased profits, whereas the union's emphasis is on pay increases, fringe benefits, job security, and the like.

The integrative aspect of a mixed conflict situation often includes the following features:

▶ The individuals, teams, or organizations decide jointly on the terms that will govern their interaction. For example, the management and union representatives may agree on when they will hold meetings, how their meetings will be conducted, and what issues will be discussed at each meeting.

▶ The individuals, teams, or organizations recognize that they can obtain rewards from their mutual association and that termination or deterioration in their relationship will result in losses. A long-drawn-out strike damages both the organization and the union: The organization experiences losses in profitability, and union members sacrifice their paychecks and possibly their jobs.

▶ The individuals, teams, or organizations believe that they will *increase* the rewards to each other via their association. For example, union–management cooperation and mutual problem solving may lead to gains in productivity. Through higher productivity, it is possible to improve both employee benefits and profit levels.

Relationships in the mixed situation are more varied and seemingly inconsistent than those in the other three cells of Figure 17.2. Managers, teams, and individuals can move mixed-situation issues toward either the win–lose cell or the collaborative cell. The direction of this movement is influenced by the attitudes, communication patterns, and decision processes established between the teams or individuals.[22] Later in the chapter, we'll discuss how the direction of this movement is determined.

Collaborative Situation

collaborative situation In the contingency model of conflict, the situation that exists when the parties have many more shared goals than conflicting goals.

A **collaborative situation** occurs when a high-integrative and low-distributive relationship exists (cell 3 in Figure 17.2). The actions of one individual, team, or organization have desirable effects on the other. Because the objectives are compatible and often mutually reinforcing, attainment of objectives by one party enhances the attainment of objectives by the other. Conflicts are not so intense or so long-lasting as in the win–lose and mixed conflict situations. However, conflicts still occur because of interpersonal difficulties, coordination, requirements, and debates over the most effective *means* of reaching the common objectives.[23]

Kansas City, Missouri-based Barton Nelson, Inc. is a case in point. Founder B. J. Nelson and his wife Mary run this family firm with nine of their ten children. Boasting $20 million a year in sales, this firm has a niche in the $1-billion-a-year self-adhesive note market. The family says votes aren't counted because nearly all decisions are reached by consensus. For example, brothers Dwight, Charles, and Barton, III, became convinced of the need to reorganize production along product lines, but brother Gregory, who heads that division, demurred. So all of them talked about it for six months until Gregory changed his mind. Similarly, says Charles, who is in charge of sales, "Some of us wanted to move the business to Colorado about five years ago. We had the votes to do it, but it would have made a couple of people unhappy. So we didn't." That, says sister Kathy Goscha, who heads personnel and purchasing, is the result of being part of a big family. "You really learn cooperation and negotiation," she says.[24]

It's not unusual, however, for individuals or teams to make an *incorrect* diagnosis and misinterpret a collaborative situation as a win–lose or mixed situation.[25] The Shoen family feud in the management of U-Haul is a dramatic example.

low-interdependency situation In the contingency model of conflict, the situation that exists when the parties interact little and have few shared or conflicting goals.

Low-Interdependency Situation

A **low-interdependency situation** occurs when the relationship is both low-distributive and low-integrative (cell 4 in Figure 17.2). In this situation, conflict is nonexistent or at a minimum. Individuals or groups simply have no reason to get together. The manager of the local Kroger's supermarket seldom discusses local business problems with the manager of a Kroger's in another state.

The following Insight compares the relationships between the sales and production departments in two districts of the same organization. The two districts are similar in technology, economic and market conditions, structure of the departments, and basic tasks. Coordination between the two departments is primarily an *ad hoc* arrangement in both of the districts. The districts produce a wide variety of metal windows, doors, and sashes for industrial and building customers.

INSIGHT

The primary areas of coordination between production and sales are acceptance of new orders, production scheduling, and quality control. These tasks are important, because items are usually produced only on request from customers. The size of the orders can vary from several dozen to several thousand items. These factors create the potential for both collaboration and conflict between the production and sales departments.

The Elgin district is characterized as a win–lose situation, the Bowie district as a collaborative situation. The following differences emerge.

Variable Examined	Elgin District	Bowie District
Goals and orientation toward decision making	Each department emphasizes the requirements of its own particular task.	Each department stresses common objectives whenever possible and in other cases tries to balance goals.
Information handling	Each department (1) minimizes the other's problems or tends to ignore them and (2) minimizes or distorts the information communicated.	Each department tries to (1) understand the other's problems and give consideration to them and (2) provide the other with full, timely, and accurate information relevant to joint decisions.
Freedom of movement	Each department tries to gain maximum freedom for itself and to limit the freedom for the other through the following actions: (1) circumventing formal procedures, (2) emphasizing formal rules, (3) trying to fix the future performance of the other department, (4) using pressure tactics, such as hierarchical appeals, (5) blaming the	Each department tries to increase its freedom to attain objectives through the following actions: (1) accepting informal procedures that boost task achievement, (2) down-playing the differences between production and sales, (3) encouraging open interaction patterns; (4) searching for solutions rather than using pressure tactics, (5) focus-

Variable Examined	Elgin District	Bowie District
	other for past failures in performance.	ing on the diagnosis and correction of rules rather than on placing blame.
Attitudes	Each department harbors negative-feelings toward the other. Desires to threaten, vent hostilities, and retaliate are common.	Each department adopts trusting and positive attitudes toward the other.

Several factors enhance collaboration at Bowie and increase win–lose conflicts at Elgin. First, with better relations and help from the home office, Bowie is able to produce more items for inventory. This reduces the peak-load pressures on the production department that often spur conflicts between sales and production. Second, Bowie's equipment and physical plant are better. Third, there is a greater status gap in terms of age, education, and experience between sales and production managers at Elgin than at Bowie. Finally, managerial styles at Elgin differ more than those at Bowie. For example, Elgin's sales manager has an aggressive personal style, and the production manager lacks human and conceptual skills. This is not the case at Bowie. These differences may be important factors in explaining how the managers' relationships developed as collaborative or competitive.[26]

One of the most important implications of this Insight is that individuals, through their actions and attitudes, can move a department or team toward a different situation. In this Insight, we started with the assumption that the relationship between sales and production is basically a mixed conflict situation. Through their actions and attitudes, the individuals at Elgin moved from a mixed to a win–lose situation and those at Bowie from a mixed to a collaborative situation.

The contingency model is a useful framework for *diagnosing* the nature of the conflict between two or more individuals, teams, or organizations. Further, the model suggests that different conflict-management approaches are appropriate for different conflict situations. For example, a win–lose conflict may be dealt with partially by some form of third-party intervention in the person of the individuals' superior or an arbitrator. On the other hand, to reduce the development of negative attitudes and stereotypes, a mixed-conflict situation should be dealt with through improved problem-solving approaches. In the following discussion of interpersonal conflict-management styles, these options are presented in detail.

CONFLICT-MANAGEMENT STYLES

interpersonal conflict
Disagreements over objectives, policies, rules, or decisions and incompatible behaviors that create anger, distrust, fear, resentment, or rejection.

Interpersonal conflict is broadly defined as (1) disagreements or incompatible interests over objectives, policies, rules, and decisions and (2) incompatible behaviors that create anger, distrust, fear, rejection, or resentment.[27] All of us—not just managers—cope with interpersonal conflict through one or a combination of five interpersonal conflict-management styles: avoidance, smoothing, forcing, compromise, and collaboration.[28]

Figure 17.3 provides a useful model for understanding and contrasting these five conflict-management styles. The vertical axis indicates the degree to which the person is *assertive* in attempting to satisfy his or her own concerns. The horizontal axis indicates the

Model of Interpersonal Conflict-Management Styles

Each of us—not just managers—uses one or more of five interpersonal conflict-management styles. A person's style or styles is influenced by the interaction of two key variables: the desire to satisfy concerns of others and the desire to satisfy one's own concerns.

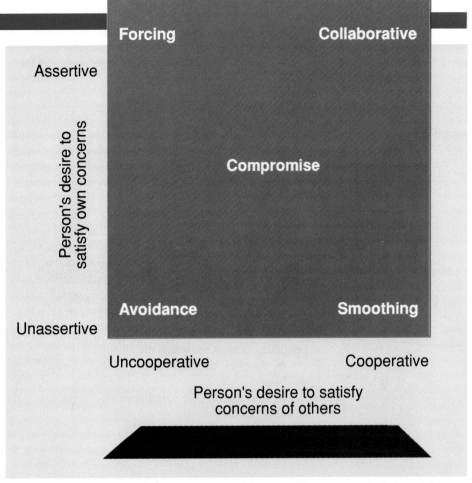

Source: Adapted from K.W. Thomas, ''Conflict and Conflict Management,'' in M.D. Dunnette (ed.), *Handbook of Industrial and Organizational Psychology* (Chicago: Rand McNally, 1976), 900. Used with permission.

degree to which the person is *cooperative* in attempting to satisfy the concerns of others. The five interpersonal conflict-management styles represent the different combinations of assertiveness and cooperativeness one might use in a conflict situation.[29]

Avoidance Style

The **avoidance style** is the tendency to withdraw from conflict situations or to remain neutral. Employees who are unavailable for conferences, delay answering ''problem'' memos, or refuse to get involved in conflicts are using an avoidance style. Avoidance-prone individuals tend to act simply as a communication link, relaying messages between superiors, peers, or subordinates. When asked to take a position on controversial issues, these individuals might say, ''I haven't had time to study the problem fully,'' ''I need more facts before making a judgment,'' or ''Perhaps the best way is to proceed as you think best.''

When unresolved conflicts affect the achievement of objectives, the avoidance style leads to negative results for the organization. However, under certain circumstances, the avoidance style is desirable. It is appropriate, for example, when

▶ The issue is minor or of only passing importance, so it is not worth the individual's time or energy to confront the conflict.

▶ There isn't enough information to the individual to deal with the conflict effectively at that time.

avoidance style The tendency to withdraw from conflict or remain neutral.

► The individual's power is so low compared to the other person's that there is little chance of bringing about change (disagreement with, say, a major new strategy already approved by top management is generally futile).

► Others can more effectively resolve the conflict.

Smoothing Style

smoothing style The tendency to minimize or suppress differences and to emphasize common interests.

The **smoothing style** is the tendency to address conflict situations by minimizing or suppressing real or perceived differences, while emphasizing common interests. The smoothing-prone individual might reason, ''If it makes others happy, I won't challenge their views'' or ''I don't want to say anything that might hurt the feelings of others when discussing problems'' or ''We shouldn't risk our friendship, so let's not worry too much about the problem; things will work out.'' Individuals who adopt the smoothing style act as though the conflict will go away in time. They appeal for cooperation. These individuals try to reduce tensions and stress by offering reassurance and support. This style shows concern about the emotional aspects of conflict, but it exhibits little interest in working on the roots of the conflict. The smoothing style simply encourages individuals to cover up or gloss over their feelings. Therefore, it is generally ineffective when used as a dominant style. The smoothing style may, however, be effective on a short-term basis when

► The individuals are locked in a potentially explosive emotional conflict, and smoothing is used to defuse the situation.

► Keeping harmony and avoiding disruption are especially important in the short run.

► The conflicts are based primarily on the personalities of the individuals and can't be easily resolved.[30]

Forcing Style

forcing style The tendency to use power to make others agree with one's position.

The **forcing style** is the tendency to use power to dominate another person and require the other person to agree with your position. The forcing style produces outcomes that are satisfactory to only one of the parties. Forcing-prone managers may use such phrases as ''If you don't like the way things are run, get out'' and ''If you can't learn to cooperate, I'm sure others can be hired who will.'' When someone disagrees with them, they try to cut her or him off to secure their position.

Forcing-prone individuals assume that conflicts involve win–lose situations.[31] When dealing with conflicts between subordinates or departments, forcing managers may threaten or actually use demotion, dismissal, negative performance evaluation, and other punishments in order to win. When conflicts occur between peers, an employee who exhibits the forcing style might try to get his or her way by appealing to their superior. This represents an attempt to use the superior to force the decision on the opposing individual. Especially for those subjected to it, the forcing style is likely to be associated with high levels of personal stress.

The following Insight reveals Bill Heatton's frustrations over several conflicts and his own inner conflicts over finding the best style for resolving them. He is uncomfortable relying on the forcing style but doesn't seem to understand that other options are available to him.

BILL HEATTON'S DILEMMA

I NSIGHT

Bill Heatton is the director of research at a \$250-million division of a large West Coast company. The division manufactures exotic telecommunications components and has many technical advancements to its credit. During the past several years, however, the division's performance has been spotty at best. Multimillion-dollar losses occurred in some years, despite efforts to make the division more profitable. Several large contracts have resulted in major financial setbacks. In each case, the various departments in the division all blamed other departments for the problems. Listen to Bill's frustration as he talks about his efforts to influence Ted (the marketing director) and Roland (the program manager who reports to Ted).

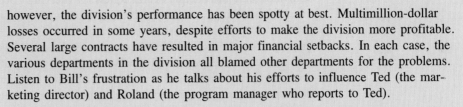

> Another program is about to come through. Roland is a nice guy, but he knows nothing and never will. He was responsible for our last big loss, and now he's in charge of this one. I've tried to convince Ted, his boss, to get Roland off the program, but I get nowhere. Although Ted doesn't argue that Roland is capable, he doesn't act to find someone else. Instead, he comes to me with worries about my area.
>
> I decided to respond by changing my staffing plan, assigning to Roland's program the people he and Ted wanted. I had to override my staff's best judgment about who should be assigned. Yet I'm not getting needed progress reports from Roland, and he's never available for planning. I get little argument from him, but there's no action to correct the problem. That's bad because I'm responding but not getting any response.
>
> There's no way to resolve this. If they disagree, that's it. I could go to a tit-for-tat strategy, saying that if they don't do what I want, we'll get even with them next time. But I don't know how to do that without hurting the organization, which would feel worse than not getting even!
>
> Ted, Roland's boss, is so much better than his predecessor that I hate to ask that he be removed. We could go together to our boss, the general manager, but I'm very reluctant to do that. You've failed in an organization if you have to go to your boss. I have to try hard because I'd look bad if I had to throw it in his lap.
>
> Meanwhile, I'm being forceful, but I'm afraid it's in a destructive way. I don't want to wait until the program has failed to be told it was all my fault.[32]

Bill is clearly angry and frustrated, and this leads him to behave in ways he doesn't feel good about. Like other managers who want very much to influence an uncooperative co-worker whom they cannot control, Bill has begun to think of these managers as the enemy. Bill's anger is narrowing his sense of what is possible. He thinks about revenge but is too dedicated to the organization to actually harm it. He is genuinely stuck.[33] As we shall see, Bill would benefit from the compromise and collaborative styles discussed in the next two sections.

Overreliance on forcing saps the other person's work motivation because his or her interests haven't been considered. Relevant information and other possible alternatives are usually ignored. However, there are some organizational situations in which the forcing style may be necessary, such as when:

▶ Emergencies require quick action.

▶ Unpopular courses of action (such as cost cutting and the dismissal of employees for unsatisfactory performance) must be taken in the name of long-term organizational effectiveness and survival.

▶ The person needs to take action for self-protection and stop others from taking advantage of him or her.[34]

compromise style The tendency to effect agreement by sacrificing some of one's own interests.

Compromise Style

The **compromise style** reflects the tendency of individuals to sacrifice some of their interests by making concessions to reach an agreement. The attitude of compromise-prone individuals might be expressed as follows: "I let other people win something if they let me win something" or "I try to hit on a fair combination of gains and losses for both of us" or "I try to find a position between theirs and mine." Compromise is shown in the middle of Figure 17.3. This position indicates that it achieves a balance between assertive and unassertive behaviors and a balance between cooperative and uncooperative behaviors. However, some research suggests that many individuals (including managers) see the compromise style as a very strong form of cooperation in which the person is trying to satisfy the concerns of others.[35]

The compromise style is likely to be appropriate when:

▶ Agreement enables each party to be better off, or at least not worse off, than if no agreement had been reached.

▶ It simply isn't possible to achieve a total win–win agreement.

▶ Conflicting objectives or opposing interests block agreement on one party's proposal.

When it is used too early in conflict situations, the compromise style may create several problems. First, individuals may be encouraging compromise on the stated issues rather than on the real ones. Second, it's easier to accept an initial compromise position as presented than to search for alternatives that are more acceptable to all the parties. For example, few employment issues have been as divisive or emotionally charged as the rights of smokers and of nonsmokers in the workplace. On the one hand, many smokers believe that their right to smoke at work is a basic freedom; they view a ban or curb on smoking at work as the employer's (or, in some cases, the state's) denial of their independence and freedom of choice. Many nonsmokers, on the other hand, believe their right to enjoy a clean and safe environment is violated by co-workers who smoke at work and by employers who fail to prohibit, or at least regulate, smoking in the workplace.

The most effective policies on smoking appear to be based on compromises that are reached after a thorough discussion of the issue and of possible solutions. The effective policies tend to be acceptable to the vast majority of the employees on both sides of the issue. A policy that bans smoking entirely will anger and threaten the smokers, though it is likely to delight nonsmokers; thus such a policy may increase tension between the two groups. By contrast, a policy that allows smoking in designated, nonwork areas is likely to satisfy both groups, thus easing the resentment between them. Some policies allow smokers to take a certain number of smoking breaks each day in designated areas. Such a policy should permit the company's nonsmokers to take an equal number of breaks each day; otherwise, they may feel they are being treated unfairly—even discriminated against. Of course, a number of state and local laws set the boundaries for smoking policies developed by organizations.[36]

Finally, compromise may be inappropriate to all or part of the situation. There may be a better way of resolving the conflict, such as through the collaborative style.

Collaborative Style

collaborative style The tendency to identify the causes of conflict, share information, and seek a mutually beneficial solution.

The hallmark of the **collaborative style** is willingness to identify the underlying causes of conflict, to share information openly, and to search for mutually beneficial solutions. Marjory Williams, the founder and chief executive officer of SHE, Inc./Laura Caspori Ltd. (an affiliated women's clothing retail chain), has this to say about the relative efficacy of the forcing and the collaborative styles:

I believe that negotiating is *not* a game. It's a business relationship in action. Nothing can kill a negotiation more quickly and more completely than a me-against-you or "gotcha" approach. While the "gotcha" approach may work once, it's hardly likely to produce a successful, ongoing business relationship. Over time, both partners have to win. Otherwise, the loser will drop out. Most businesspeople respond favorably to an approach that results in mutually beneficial solutions. There's a catch, though. "Mutually beneficial" means not only that both parties benefit from the deal, but that they also *perceive* that they are benefiting.[37]

Collaboration-prone individuals might describe their approach by saying, "I try to deal with all concerns—theirs and mine," "I try to get all viewpoints and issues out in the open," or "If we don't agree at first, we should spend some time thinking about why and then look for the best alternative that we can agree on." With the collaborative style, conflicts are recognized openly and evaluated by all concerned. Sharing, examining, and assessing the reasons for the conflict should lead to development of an alternative that effectively resolves the conflict and is acceptable to all parties.[38] The Barton Nelson, Inc. case is a prime illustration of collaborative styles in action. Recall too the Insight on the Elgin and Bowie Districts. The people in the Bowie District made extensive use of the collaborative style. And recall the Manager's Viewpoint on valuing differences at Digital. The success of this program has depended on the participants' use of the collaborative style.

The collaborative style of conflict management is especially appropriate when

▶ The parties involved have one or more common objectives and disagree mainly over the best *means* to achieve them.

▶ A consensus should lead to the best overall solution to the conflict.

▶ There is a need to make high-quality decisions on the basis of expert judgments and the best information available.

Guidelines for Use Among the many guidelines for using the collaborative style, we offer five important ones.

1 Ask for and give feedback on the major points.

2 Consider compromise only *after* analyzing the real problems and generating alternative solutions. Remember that the other person's view of reality—though different—may be just as valid as yours.

3 Never assume that you know what the other person is thinking; check out your assumptions in plain language.

4 Never label (*coward, neurotic, child*) the other person.

5 Forget the past and stick with the here and now. What either of you did last year or last month or yesterday morning is not so important as what you are doing and feeling now.[39]

The guidelines for effective communication presented in Chapter 15 reinforce and supplement these guidelines for practicing the collaborative style. (See especially Table 15.1 and Table 15.4.) All such guidelines are easy to state but difficult to practice spontaneously and naturally. Effective collaboration requires more than opening up to others; it also demands opening up to oneself and gaining self-insight.

The collaborative style has great potential for the effective management of conflict, but those involved must be ready and willing to use the guidelines. And although collaboration is often regarded as the best overall style, each style, as we have noted, may be useful in specific situations.[40]

Barriers to Use If collaboration is so effective, you might ask, why isn't it used more frequently? Certain barriers to using the collaborative style exist.

1 Time limitations often constrain the direct sharing of feelings about issues involved in a conflict.

2 Group norms may support the view that employees shouldn't express negative feelings toward others.

3 Traditional and out-of-date role expectations include the assumption that managers should command and firmly control subordinates. This top-down organizational norm sometimes makes it difficult for managers to use the collaborative approach, even when it is their preferred style.

The use of collaboration is influenced by the type of organizational culture and the prevalent leadership style. Supportive and participative managers use the collaborative style more than autocratic managers do. The collaborative style is more natural in open and supportive organizational cultures than in those that are closed and autocratic.

Negotiation and Conflict Styles

negotiation A process by which individuals or groups with both common and conflicting goals present and discuss proposals for reaching an agreement.

Negotiation is a process by which individuals or groups with both common and conflicting objectives present and discuss proposals for reaching an agreement.[41] Negotiation isn't limited to the bargaining table in organizational disputes. Each of us engages in negotiations. Children and parents negotiate over allowances, chores, and hours. Spouses negotiate over how money is to be spent, who is to perform what household duties, and so on. The negotiation process is particularly important in the mixed conflict and win–lose conflict situations discussed earlier in the chapter (see Figure 17.2). At times, the negotiation process is seen as each party relying on the forcing style and invoking the compromise style only as a last resort. In fact, collaboration is a core ingredient in successful negotiations. Consider the view of Leonard Greenhalgh, who teaches a course on negotiation at Dartmouth's business school.

> North American managers have an old-fashioned notion of what competition is all about. When they think of competition, they think in adversary terms: You dump a supplier if you can find one with a cheaper product. You abandon the customer if you can find a more profitable one.
>
> But now we're dealing in a global market, where other managers are in collaborative business cultures. American managers don't have a really fine sense of what collaboration is all about. You can't have an adversary, me-first mentality and get a complicated production program or an R&D joint venture to work. Managers must learn to evolve from a contractually oriented business culture where, if it's not in the contract, they do whatever they want. What's missing is good will, trust, and a genuine concern for the other person's welfare. Managers need to do business based on relationships.[42]

It is not rare for various combinations of all five conflict-management styles to be used in the negotiating process. This is especially true when the negotiations involve several important and complex issues, as in union–management negotiations and customer–supplier negotiations. The key to successful negotiation is the combination of styles that dominate the process.[43] If the collaborative and compromise styles dominate negotiations, the parties usually experience positive and effective outcomes. Some use of the smoothing style is also likely in effective negotiations. It is relatively painless to use the smoothing style as a gesture of ''good will'' by giving ground on issues that are of considerable importance to the other party, but not to you.[44]

In contrast, less effective negotiations are often dominated by the forcing and compromise styles, with the avoidance style also in evidence. When neither party has the power to force its preferred solutions on the other, the compromise style may be used as a backup. The avoidance style may appear when the parties avoid addressing issues for which they feel no solution is possible. In effect, such issues are simply ''tabled'' for possible consideration at another time. These contrasting patterns of conflict-management styles tend to appear in a wide variety of negotiating relationships: between co-workers, managers and subordinates, customers and suppliers, departments, organizations, and even countries.[45]

Before deciding what conflict style(s) to use, you should diagnose the conflict situation that has created a need for negotiations. Answering the following questions will help you focus on the issues and their underlying causes rather than on the personalities involved.

1 What is it you want or need? Are you sure?
2 What do you think the other person or group wants or needs? Are you sure?
3 Do you and the other party differ over facts? objectives? methods? roles?
4 What could you lose if the conflict continues or escalates?

5 What common objectives do you and the other person or group have in this matter?

6 If you decide to collaborate to help resolve this conflict, what are the first steps you might take?[46]

The Global Link that follows is based on the views of North Americans who have engaged in repeated business negotiations in the Federal Republic of Germany. It reveals the dominant negotiating style of Germans. Understanding this style should help you engage in effective negotiations with German managers if the need arises—and it should help you appreciate how such styles can vary across cultures.

Ethical Dilemmas

Ethical dilemmas are present in many conflict situations. As we noted in Chapter 5, the resolution of ethical dilemmas is influenced by the stage of moral development of the individuals engaged in the conflict (see Figure 5.2) and by the ethical approach they take (utilitarian, moral-rights, or justice). One obvious ethical dilemma that arises in negotiations is how much information should be shared with the other party.[47] Consider this situation:

> You are a real estate broker in the Lakes region. Times have been tough during the recession, but you now have a prospect for a shorefront home. If you close the sale, you will earn a $10,000 commission. The property has no boat dock, but you have overheard the prospective buyers (husband and wife) discussing where they would have a new dock built. The couple has not talked to you about the dock, but you know having it is important to them. You also know that on this particular lake, it is almost impossible to get the state licensing authority's approval to build a new dock. No new permits have been issued for two years.[48]

Would you discuss the dock problem with your clients?

The real estate broker is faced with interrole and person–role conflict. Revealing the dock problem is the ethical action; not revealing it would be an economically motivated compromise of ethics. This incident also suggests the ethical problem of focusing exclusively on one's own interests, with no concern for the interests of others, when negotiating and making decisions.[49]

WORK-RELATED STRESS

stress The individual's emotional, physical, and cognitive response to excessive demands.

nonspecific response An emotional, physical, and/or cognitive response that the one who experiences it cannot control.

Individuals subjected to extreme conflicts, to ambiguity, or to the ineffective conflict-management styles of others may experience high levels of work-related stress. Those who experience multiple and severe conflict incidents are the ones most likely to experience intense stress. For example, the forcing style (especially when used repeatedly by one's boss) is a possible source of work-related stress. Before expanding on the sources of stress, we need to define several terms.

Stress consists of the individual's response—emotional, physical, and cognitive—to any situation that places excessive demands on that person. Stress often creates a **nonspecific response,** which means that certain emotional, physical, and cognitive responses occur automatically. That is, we don't consciously control them.[50] Heat (a physical stressor) produces sweating; cold (another physical stressor) produces shivering; and fear (an emotion) may produce a fight-or-flight response. Hans Selye, often regarded as the father of stress management, notes, however, that stress is not something to be avoided: "Complete freedom from stress is death."[51]

What did Selye mean? There are two major types of stress. All conflict and ambiguity aren't negative, nor is all stress bad. **Eustress** is pleasant or constructive stress (such as

GLOBAL Link

NEGOTIATING STYLE OF GERMAN MANAGERS

The vast majority of German managers have experience in more than one firm, though most tend to become specialists within one industry. German managers are more like American managers than are most other Europeans (except perhaps the Dutch). But although German managers have a greater entrepreneurial spirit than other Europeans, they still tend to be more risk-averse than their American counterparts. This cautious and conservative behavior makes them more willing to seek compromise than to assume the risk of confrontation or controversy.

Because of the structure of most German firms, Germans are slow to reach decisions. Decisions are made by committee. Most German firms require two or more signatures on everything. Many negotiations are conducted with technical people, not businesspeople, and people with technical backgrounds tend to be deliberate and extremely cautious. Thus American negotiators must be well versed in all technical aspects of the items under discussion.

German negotiators frequently suffer from an extreme case of the "not invented here" syndrome; that is, they tend not to be receptive to technical suggestions. They are especially sensitive to unfavorable comparisons with the French and the British.

Most Germans are people of their word. A handshake is as good as a written contract. Although German negotiators always have an objective in mind, they may be vague in letting the Americans know what it is. But once the objective is out in the open, negotiations proceed quickly. The Germans *do* respond to logic and thoroughness. They are quite concerned with the precision of the written word. They are also very conscious of "face." It is well to avoid open disagreements with managers when staff people are present.

Good negotiators must be sensitive to emotionally charged issues. These would include, for example, Germany's technical excellence and any proposed solution that would require changes in the level of employment. Negotiators should be polite to all of the many staff people, but they should focus on the one or two key players. The Germans do not play at negotiating; they are serious and honest.

Breaks in the negotiations may be required to allow the German team to gain approval of some proposal. But before such a break, an agreement must be reached on the duration of the break and the topic to be discussed immediately after it. Otherwise, negotiations may become drawn out.

A short working lunch is an effective means of getting a German manager's attention, because such a lunch is not consistent with the routine heavy noon meal. The period just after lunch is a good time to introduce important issues. Friday afternoons are also extremely productive times: Germans typically want to clear things up before leaving for the weekend.

_____

Source: Adapted from D.N. Burt, "The Nuances of Negotiating Overseas," *Journal of Purchasing and Materials Management,* Winter 1989: 56–62.

eustress Pleasant or constructive stress.

distress Unpleasant, detrimental, or disease-producing stress.

stressor Any situation that places special demands on the individual.

the positive emotions one experiences upon being congratulated for doing a good job, creating a novel solution, or negotiating a good agreement). **Distress,** on the other hand, is unpleasant, detrimental, or disease-producing stress. Most of the literature dealing with stress focuses on distress, as we do in this chapter. Thus our use of the term *stress* refers primarily to *distress.* A **stressor** is any situation that places special demands on the individual. The individual may experience these demands consciously or unconsciously.[52]

Sources of Distress

There are many potential sources of distress in the workplace.[53] All the types and sources of conflict and role ambiguity discussed earlier in this chapter are potential sources of distress. Figure 17.4 identifies three common categories of work-related stressors: conditions that exist in the physical environment, role conflict, and role ambiguity.

Use Figure 17.4 to assess your level of work-related stress in your present job or one you had in the past. The scoring directions for the completed questionnaire are also included in this table: Scores in each of the three categories can range from 3 to 15. Any

---

FIGURE 17.4

Stress-Assessment Questionnaire

Instructions: Listed below are various kinds of problems that may—or may not—arise in your work. Indicate to what extent you find each of them to be a problem or concern.

Factor	Responses				
This Factor Is a Problem	**Never**	**Seldom**	**Sometimes**	**Usually**	**Always**
Physical Environment					
1. Feeling you are too hot or too cold	1	2	3	4	5
2. Thinking there is a good chance of being seriously injured on the job	1	2	3	4	5
3. Thinking there is a real possibility of getting some disease from this job	1	2	3	4	5
Role Conflict					
4. Feeling you must do things you personally feel to be unethical	1	2	3	4	5
5. Having a boss who keeps assigning different tasks and allowing too little time to complete them	1	2	3	4	5
6. Receiving too many incompatible pressures from too many people	1	2	3	4	5
Role Ambiguity					
7. Not knowing what the people you work with expect you to accomplish	1	2	3	4	5
8. Being unclear about how you are to perform the tasks in your job	1	2	3	4	5
9. Not knowing how your manager evaluates your performance	1	2	3	4	5

▌ *Add the three numbers you circled in each of the three categories and enter the totals in the blanks.*
Physical environment (items 1–3)   _____

Role conflict (items 4–6)   _____

Role ambiguity (items 7–9)   _____

▌ **Total** (add the three scores)   _____

score of 10 or more suggests a problem that deserves your attention. The overall score can range from 9 to 45. A total score of 27 or more suggests a more-than-desirable amount of stress in two or three categories. Such distress could be a reason for low job satisfaction, a desire to quit the job, or high absenteeism.

Effects of Distress

Distress is associated with a variety of potentially negative effects.[54] These effects fall into one or more of five categories.

▶ *Subjective effects:* Anxiety, aggression, apathy, boredom, depression, fatigue, frustration, guilt and shame, irritability and bad temper, moodiness, low self-esteem, threat and tension, nervousness, and loneliness.

▶ *Behavioral effects:* Accident-proneness, illegal drug use, emotional outbursts, excessive eating or loss of appetite, excessive drinking and smoking, excitability, impulsive behavior, impaired speech, nervous laughter, restlessness, trembling, and excessive sleeping (or the inability to sleep).

▶ *Cognitive effects:* Inability to make decisions or to concentrate, frequent forgetfulness, hypersensitivity to criticism, mental blocks, and denial.

▶ *Physiological effects:* Increased blood and urine catecholamines and corticosteroids, increased blood glucose levels, increased heart rate and blood pressure, dryness of the mouth, sweating, dilation of the pupils, difficulty in breathing, hot and cold spells, lump in the throat, numbness and tingling in parts of the limbs, hives, and indigestion.

▶ *Organizational effects:* Absenteeism, poor union–management relations, low productivity, high accident rates, high turnover rates, work of inferior quality, antagonism at work, and job dissatisfaction.[55]

These effects aren't mutually exclusive; that is, a person experiencing distress may show more than one adverse effect. An individual does not typically experience effects in all these categories, or all the specific effects within a given category, at the same time. Everyone experiences some negative effects of distress at times, but a severe problem is unlikely to arise unless distress is intense and frequent.

Some people who experience a high level of distress over an extended period suffer from burnout. **Burnout** is a psychological process, brought about by continuous work distress, that results in emotional exhaustion, depersonalization (such as a sense of being and acting alone in the world), and decreased accomplishments.[56] Some people experi-

burnout Emotional exhaustion, depersonalization, and decreased accomplishment brought about by continuous work distress.

Burnout is an occupational hazard for certain highly stressed professionals, such as bond traders.

ence burnout in response to intense work stressors.[57] Burnout and severe distress don't just happen. They involve a complex interplay of personal, job, work-setting, and organizational culture characteristics.[58] Individuals who do succumb to burnout seem to progress through three stages:

1 Puzzlement, confusion, and the appearance of frustration
2 Intense frustration and anger
3 Apathy, withdrawal, and despair[59]

The effects of distress and burnout have received widespread attention in recent years from the general public, business and health organizations, researchers, and the news media. Numerous suggestions have been advanced for managing stress and avoiding burnout. The following Insight conveys burnout as a surprisingly large number of entrepreneurs experience it. This account contrasts sharply with the popular conception of all entrepreneurs as heroes in total control of their lives.

Everett Jewell didn't know it at the time, but he was a victim. "I'm tired," Jewell told his attorney at 3:30 one spring afternoon. "I'm going home." Stretched out in his recliner chair, the president of Jewell Building Systems, Inc., fell asleep in seconds, woke after midnight, and staggered to bed. He opened his eyes at 10:00 the next morning. Then he fell back asleep until dinner time. He remained sluggish and unable to concentrate, week after week, for another three months.

There's no clinical name for it—no exotic virus to dignify the condition. Jewell was simply burned out. It was only after he suffered all those months that he began to understand that the underlying cause of his ailment was his management style.

More than half the 1139 small-business owners surveyed by Geneva Corporation, a California-based mergers-and-acquisitions company, pointed toward burnout or boredom when asked why they were thinking of selling the business. "They said it in different ways, but that's what it boiled down to," says David Hoods, president of Geneva Marketing Services, Inc.

Of course, burnout isn't unique to company founders, but the story of their condition may well be. Tired of "working for somebody else," many founders long to control their own lives. Ironically, some become more enslaved by their own companies than they ever were by any boss. Some entrepreneurs resemble spiders caught in their own web.

The web that holds them isn't the company. It's often their own style of management. Starting a company involves bearing up under extraordinary pressure and working long hours. Many founders fail to share the pressure (and the hours) with others as the company grows. They fail to delegate any of their authority. They often feel guilty about spending any time away from their companies. Doing everything, and doing it year after year, exacts a terrible toll.[60]

Stress (distress) management can be broken down into various actions.[61] Let's consider several such actions—both individual and organizational—for preventing and reducing distress.

Individual Distress Management

Awareness of the causes of distress and understanding of the responses (emotional, physical, and cognitive) to stressors are fundamental to individual distress management. There are many actions that individuals can take to eliminate or manage their own distress.

▶ *Clarify your values.* It's important to run not on the fast track, but on *your* track.

▶ *Improve your "self-talks."* We all talk to ourselves, and many of our self-talks are needlessly negative: "I'm going to fail this test." "There's no way I can get out of this mess." Discipline yourself not to overreact emotionally. Why be enraged when simple irritation will get your message across?

▶ *Learn how to relax.* All you need is a quiet room. Get comfortable. Then close your eyes, breathe rhythmically (preferably from your abdomen), and blot out distractions for 10 to 15 minutes. Do this twice a day.

▶ *Exercise regularly.* Try to exercise at least 3 times a week for 20 minutes at 75 percent of your maximum predicted heart rate. Make sure your doctor approves, and start gradually.

▶ *Get the leisure you need.* The best way to avoid burnout is to allow yourself proper leisure to renew your commitment to work and recharge your batteries. If you're a workaholic, consider that you owe it to yourself to take time off. Otherwise, you will jeopardize your chances of keeping on top of a rough job over the long haul.

▶ *Adopt dietary goals.* Maintain normal weight. Remember to eat a *real* breakfast.

▶ *Avoid "chemical haze."* One definition of distress is loss of control; the need to acquire control through artificial means accounts for some uses of nicotine, alcohol, and drugs.[62]

In addition, two substantial *inner* actions are implied in several of the positive actions noted above. You can manage stress better by resolving to *change what you can change* and *resolving not to live passively with what you can't change.*

Changes in Behaviors and Attitudes Experiences associated with some stressors are more directly attributable to one's personal attitudes and characteristics than to the stressors in the situation. In other words, the same incident may be stressful for one person but not for another. Distress is often in the eye of the perceiver. Accordingly, we should be able to manage distress to some extent by modifying our attitudes and behaviors. For example, we can learn to make more use of the collaboration and compromise styles of conflict management and less use of the forcing and avoidance styles. In this way we may be able to reduce the number of conflict incidents and resolve more effectively those that act as intense stressors. We need to set reasonable objectives, evaluate priorities carefully, allow more time for each task, improve time management, and simply reduce the total number of tasks. These actions may enable us to go a long way toward avoiding and reducing distress.

This advice is especially important for the individual who exhibits Type A behavior. The **Type A** *behavior pattern* is that of a "person who is aggressively involved in a chronic, incessant struggle to achieve more and more in less time, and if required to do so, against the opposing efforts of other things or other persons."[63] In contrast, the **Type B** *behavior pattern* is that of a person who is often contemplative, nonaggressive, realistic in objectives pursued, and not hypercritical of self or others. Type A and Type B behavior patterns have been contrasted as follows:

> The Type A individual is extremely competitive, constantly tending to challenge others—in sports, at work, and even in casual discussions. Type A people characteristically overreact and generally are hypercritical—both of themselves (to themselves) and of others (more openly). They might fume at something a Type B person would brush off as inconsequential.
>
> Type A's are said to have a great sense of urgency concerning time. They tend to thrive on deadlines and create them if none exist. Similarly, they establish difficult goals if none are set for them, and are quick to become impatient when goals and deadlines are not achieved. In contrast, Type B's are more contemplative. They take the time to ponder alternatives and usually feel there is plenty of time.[64]

The type A and B patterns represent extreme profiles. Many individuals fall between these extremes.[65]

Type A behavior pattern
Chronic, aggressive struggle to achieve more in less time, in opposition to the efforts of others if necessary.

Type B behavior pattern
Contemplative, nonaggressive pursuit of realistic objectives.

Withdrawal The simplest way of coping with distress is probably withdrawal (flight) from the stressors. This may involve being absent, changing jobs, or even changing careers. Under certain circumstances, withdrawal may be an appropriate and healthy form of coping. Consider someone who works for a highly autocratic manager who constantly makes unrealistic demands and uses primarily the forcing style of conflict management. One perfectly realistic coping strategy would be to transfer to another department or look for a job with another organization. Of course, withdrawal can also be an unhealthy means of attempting to escape having to deal with reality.

Organizational Distress Management

Organizations, teams, and managers are often able to take positive actions to reduce the intensity and number of stressors on employees or increase their ability to cope with them.[66]

Setting Objectives Adopting a participative means of setting objectives (such as MBO) should help to reduce and resolve role conflicts and uncertainties. These factors are often major sources of distress and burnout. Clearly, delegating authority and encouraging employees to participate in decisions that affect their day-to-day work lives are also likely to help control stress levels.

Emotional Support *Emotional support* is the empathy, caring, love, and trust displayed by others toward an individual.[67] Emotional and other forms of support in the workplace can be provided by superiors, co-workers, and subordinates. Emotional support appears to help individuals cope with stressors.[68] Organizational cultures that convey a sense of caring provide strong emotional support, helping employees to cope successfully with performance expectations and pressures. The use of collaborative, smoothing, and compromise conflict-management styles often creates a perception of caring, empathy, and trust. This builds mutual emotional support within the organization.

Special Programs Counseling and ''wellness'' programs, physical fitness facilities, leadership training, group decision making, structural and job redesign, flextime, and career development activities represent some of the other steps that organizations can take to prevent and reduce the distress experienced by employees.[69]

The working environment at Hewlett-Packard supports *wellness* in its campuslike settings, with plenty of open spaces for eating and recreation.

flextime Practice of allowing employees to vary their arrival and departure times to suit their needs.

wellness program Program instituted by an organization to promote the physical and psychological health of employees.

Flextime allows employees, within certain limits, to vary their arrival and departure times to suit individual needs and desires. For example, flextime might enable a parent to be at home when the children arrive from school, thus eliminating stress inflicted by worrying about what they might be doing while unattended.

Wellness programs are designed to promote employees' physical and psychological health. Such programs are part of a growing preventive approach whereby employees reduce their susceptibility to illness and ease the effects of stressors by changing the way they live. Wellness programs usually include courses in stress management, weight reduction, giving up smoking, exercise (aerobics), and the like. Do wellness programs work? Consider the experience of Johnson & Johnson.

JOHNSON & JOHNSON'S WELLNESS PROGRAM

𝒥NSIGHT

Johnson & Johnson (J&J) has spent more than a century selling health-care products to consumers—to make money. And has spent 11 years selling healthful living to its own employees—to save money.

Cost containment has been a major goal of J&J's wellness program since day one—and that objective has been met. The company says that in 1989 the program saved $378 per employee by lowering absenteeism and slowing the rise in the company's health-care expenses. The annual cost of the program, which offers checkups and encourages healthful eating and exercise habits, is $200 per employee.

J&J is one of only a handful of companies that have made comprehensive examinations of the costs and benefits of their wellness programs. Its study took three years and involved 8000 employees. Wellness was tested just as the company would experiment with a new drug, by comparing a test group and a control group. The company tracked the medical costs and productivity of 5000 workers at three subsidiaries where top managers were willing to give the wellness program a try. The control group consisted of other departments that didn't have such a program. During the first year, the wellness program cost more than it saved. In the second year, it broke even. And in the third year, it saved enough money to pay back the losses incurred during the first year.

The wellness program was such a success that J&J began marketing it to other companies. So far, Johnson & Johnson Health Management, Inc. is providing varying levels of service to about 60 companies that employ a total of more than 850,000.

"The way you change the health of the whole population is to get the whole population to make small changes in a lot of areas," says Curtis S. Wilbur, a Johnson & Johnson executive who helped write a study on the wellness program.

The wellness program at J&J is called Live for Life. It is voluntary. Live for Life tries to persuade employees to act: to exercise, to watch their diets and lose weight, to quit smoking, and/or to do whatever else might be called for. Signs in hallways and brochures sent to employees promote various aspects of the program, and workers win prizes for participating. Employees are asked to stop in for follow-up health-risks profiles. Live for Life now is available to all 35,000 J&J employees in the United States. At headquarters in New Brunswick, New Jersey, nearly two-thirds of the workers participate to some degree. The average employee, for instance, exercises in the gym nearly twice a week.[70]

1. Conflict can be both positive (stimulating) and negative (destructive).

   ▶ Conflict can stimulate a search for the reasons behind differences in approach and for innovative solutions to problems.

   ▶ Conflict can be destructive when interdependent employees or teams have to compete against each other.

   ▶ Most effective employees and managers have a balanced view of conflict. They attempt to manage positive conflict to make it work creatively, and they try to eliminate negative conflict.

2. Four types of role conflict are intrasender, intersender, interrole, and person–role conflict.

   ▶ Intrasender role conflict may occur when the role sender conveys mixed messages.

   ▶ Intersender role conflict may occur when pressures from more than one role sender are incompatible.

   ▶ Interrole conflict may occur when pressures associated with one role (such as employee) collide with those of another (such as parent).

   ▶ Person–role conflict may occur when the focal person's role(s) is at variance with his or her personal needs, attitudes, values, or abilities.

   ▶ Role ambiguity can also be a source of conflict and intense stress.

3. The contingency model of conflict helps managers diagnose the basic conflict situations they face.

   ▶ A win–lose conflict situation occurs when objectives are diametrically opposed—one person's gain is another's loss.

   ▶ A mixed conflict situation exists when the parties have both competing and mutual interests.

   ▶ A collaborative situation exists when the objectives of the parties are compatible and often mutually reinforcing (a win–win situation).

   ▶ In a low-interdependency situation, the parties have little reason for interacting and thus no occasion to experience conflicts.

4. There are five basic interpersonal conflict-management styles: the avoidance, smoothing, forcing, compromise, and collaborative styles. Conflict resolution often depends on negotiation. Successful negotiation depends on using the mix of the conflict-management styles that is appropriate to the situation.

5. Three of the most common sources of job-related distress are conditions that exist in the physical environment, role conflict, and role ambiguity.

6. The effects of distress may be subjective, behavioral, cognitive, physiological, and/or organizational.

7. Several individual and organizational approaches can be taken to avoid or reduce distress.

   ▶ Individual actions include clarifying values, improving self-talks, learning how to relax, exercising regularly, taking enough time for leisure pursuits, following the proper diet, and avoiding ''chemical haze.'' Of course, these actions often flow from fundamental choices, such as resolving to change behaviors and attitudes or even to withdraw from the situation.

▶ Organizational actions include participatory objective setting and decision making, promotion of an organizational culture that conveys a sense of caring and emotional support, and sponsorship of wellness programs.

1. Why is conflict inevitable in organizations?

2. **From Where You Sit:** Drawing on your own experiences, give examples of intrasender, intersender, interrole, and person–role conflicts.

3. What is role ambiguity? How is role ambiguity important to an understanding of conflict and personal distress within organizations?

4. What are the key elements of the contingency model of conflict?

5. **From Where You Sit:** To what extent do you tend to use each of the five interpersonal conflict-management styles? (If you'd like to learn more about these styles, complete the Skill Building Exercise that follows.)

6. **From Where You Sit:** Think of a current or past relationship with someone who had much more power than you. How would you describe that person's relative use of the five interpersonal conflict-management styles? How would you evaluate that person's conflict-management effectiveness?

7. What do you think are the key differences between the negotiating style of German managers (as described in the Global Link) and that of individuals in your home country?

8. **From Where You Sit:** Do you see yourself as exhibiting more of a Type A or a Type B behavior pattern? What is your basis for this self-characterization? Do you think that individuals who know you well would agree with it?

9. **From Where You Sit:** What are the major stressors in your life at the present time? Do some of these stressors create a sense of eustress and others a sense of distress? Explain.

10. **From Where You Sit:** What do you usually do to manage distress? Is this approach effective? Explain.

Conflict-Management Style Incidents

Instructions

Your task is to rank the five alternative courses of action in each of the following four incidents. Rank the alternatives from the most desirable or appropriate way of dealing with the conflict to the least desirable. Rank the most desirable as 1, the next most desirable as 2, and so on, with the least desirable as 5. Enter your rank in the space next to each item. Next, identify the conflict style being used with each of the possible courses of action (forcing, smoothing, avoidance, compromise, or collaboration).

Incident One

Pete is lead operator of a production molding machine. Recently, he has noticed that one of the men from another machine has been coming over to his machine and talking to one of his men (not on break time). The efficiency of Peter's operator seems to be falling off, and his inattention has resulted in some rejects. Pete thinks he detects some resentment among the rest of the crew. If you were Peter, you would:

_____ a. Talk to your man and tell him to limit his conversations during on-the-job time.

_____ b. Ask the foreman to tell the lead operator of the other machine to keep his operators in line.

_____ c. Confront both men the next time you see them together (as well as the other lead operator, if necessary), find out what they are up to, and tell them what you expect of your operators.

_____ d. Say nothing now; it would be silly to make something big out of something so insignificant.

_____ e. Try to put the rest of the crew at ease; it is important that they all work well together.

Incident Two

Sally is the senior quality-control (Q-C) inspector and has been appointed group leader of the Q-C people on her crew. On separate occasions, two of her people have come to her with different suggestions for reporting test results to the machine operators. Paul wants to send the test results to the foreman and then to the machine operators, because the foreman is the person ultimately responsible for production output. Jim thinks the results should go directly to the lead operator on the machine in question, because the lead operator must take corrective action as soon as possible. Both ideas seem good, and Sally can find no ironclad procedures in the department on how to route the reports. If you were Sally, you would:

_____ a. Decide who is right and ask the other person to go along with the decision (perhaps establish it as a written procedure).

_____ b. Wait and see; the best solution will become apparent.

_____ c. Tell both Paul and Jim not to get uptight about their disagreement; it isn't that important.

_____ d. Get Paul and Jim together and question both of them closely.

_____ e. Send the report to the foreman, with a copy to the lead operator (even though it might mean a little more copy work for Q-C).

Incident Three

Ralph is a module leader; his module consists of four very complex and expensive machines and five crew members. The work is exacting, and inattention or improper procedures could cause a costly mistake or serious injury. Ralph suspects that one of his men is taking drugs on the job, or at least showing up for work under the influence of drugs. Ralph feels that he has some strong indications but knows that he doesn't have a "case." If you were Ralph you would:

—— a. Confront the man outright; tell him what you suspect and why and that you are concerned for him and for the safety of the rest of the crew.

—— b. Ask that the suspected offender keep his habit off the job; what he does on the job *is* part of your business.

—— c. Not confront the individual right now; it might either "turn him off" or drive him underground.

—— d. Give the man the "facts of life"; tell him drug use is illegal and unsafe and that if he gets caught, you will do everything you can to see that he is fired.

—— e. Keep a close eye on the man to see that he is not endangering others.

Incident Four

Gene is a foreman of a production crew. From time to time in the past, the product development section has tapped the production crews for operators to augment their own operator personnel to run test products on special machines. This has put very little strain on the production crews, because the demands have been small, temporary, and infrequent. Lately, however, there seems to have been an almost constant demand for four production operators. The rest of the production crew must fill in for them, usually by working harder and taking shorter breaks. If you were Gene, you would:

—— a. Let it go for now; the "crisis" will probably be over soon.

—— b. Try to smooth things over with your own crew and with the development foreman; we all have jobs to do and cannot afford conflict.

—— c. Let development have two of the four operators requested.

—— d. Go to the development supervisor—or the supervisor's foreman—and talk about how these demands for additional operators could be met without placing production in a bind.

—— e. Go to the supervisor of production (Gene's boss) and get him or her to "call off" the development people.

Assessment

Incident One: a. compromise; b. forcing; c. collaboration; d. avoidance; and e. smoothing.

Incident Two: a. forcing; b. avoidance; c. smoothing; d. collaboration; and e. compromise.

Incident Three: a. collaboration; b. compromise; c. avoidance; d. forcing; and e. smoothing.

Incident Four: a. avoidance; b. smoothing; c. compromise; d. collaboration; and e. forcing.

To: Gail Brooks, Vice-President, Human Resources
From: Susan Adair, President
Subject: Work/Family Balance

As we discussed at our recent planning retreat, work/family balance is fast becoming the career issue of the decade. The depth of managerial and personal concern about this issue in general was crystalized in an article I just read by Felice Schwartz in the <u>Harvard Business Review</u> (January–February 1989: 65–76). Two major points in this article have drawn powerful reactions from a variety of sources: (1) The cost of employing women is greater than that of employing men (because of turnover related to maternity). (2) To reduce this cost, organizations should provide more flexible employment arrangements for women who want to combine career and family.

On the second point, Schwartz identified two groups of working women: (1) *Career-primary women* put career first and are willing to make sacrifices in their personal lives, such as foregoing children, to reach the top. (2) *Career-and family-women* are willing to trade some career growth and compensation for freedom from the constant pressure to work long hours.

This article has generated a tremendous amount of interest—and no small degree of controversy. Though Schwartz is a long-time feminist and supporter of advancement for women, she has been roundly criticized by other feminist leaders on several grounds:

1. For giving (male) executives a ready excuse for denying women promotions.
2. For "sacrificing" the promotion opportunities of the majority of women (those who want balance) on the altar of those who are willing to give up everything else for the career.
3. For presenting only two tracks.
4. For not acknowledging a woman's option to shift gears and increase or decrease her work involvement at different points in her career.
5. For appearing to place all the responsibility for family care on the mother's shoulders.

This whole area seems to contribute to many types of severe conflict and stress. Again, as we discussed at our retreat, we need to establish an organizational strategy for avoiding and reducing such conflict and stress.

Question: Assume you are Gail Brooks. Write a response to Susan Adair.

Fear and Stress in the Office Take Toll

By Thomas F. O'Boyle

On the Richter scale of anxiety, three people recently suffered earthquakes:

An advertising salesman treated by Bruce Yaffe, a New York internist, screamed so loudly when he argued with his boss that he punctured a lung. Another patient, an office receptionist, had such severe stress-induced vomiting that she eventually had to quit her job. And a third, a Wall Street broker treated by physician Larry Lerner for hypertension, was so certain his death was imminent that he refused to take his children to the park for fear they would be abandoned when he died.

Though extreme examples, the intense stress these patients feel is shared by many nowadays. Human resource managers, as well as doctors, psychologists and pollsters, agree that workplace stress is way up. Layoffs—and the pervasive fear of dismissal—are jangling nerves. Even survivors aren't secure; many must work longer hours amid more belt tightening. Moreover, workplace stress is often compounded by troubles at home: tighter personal finances, for instance, or marital tensions.

"Stress is here. You can feel it rise right up off the page in the newspapers we read," says Clinton G. Weiman, corporate medical director at Citicorp in Manhattan. "People feel the crunch, and eventually it gets reflected in the health care system.". . .

Doctors say that while some stress is healthy, too much can cause chronic headaches, chest and neck pains, sleeping disorders, depression, indigestion, diarrhea, ulcers, swollen glands, fever and fatigue. In the workplace, excessive stress has been tied to lower productivity, increased accidents, higher absenteeism and alcohol and drug abuse. . . .

For many, stress is simply the by product of working in a more competitive world. Karen Richards, a 37-year-old vice president who supervises bond trading and underwriting at a bank in eastern Pennsylvania, has to sell twice as many municipal bonds as she did five years ago to maintain the same profit.

Her employer, First Eastern Bank Corp. of Wilkes-Barre, Pa., is the last large bank in eastern Pennsylvania that hasn't been acquired by a bigger rival yet. She figures she would lose her job if the bank were bought out. Meanwhile, her schedule is so full there's little free time for stress alleviating activities, such as exercise.

Balancing the demands of personal and professional lives adds to the anxiety felt by many. For one chief executive, business is slumping, forcing the layoff of many trusted employees at the Northeast engineering concern he founded, including his best friend. His mistress is threatening to reveal their affair to his wife. And his teenage son recently announced that he thinks he's homosexual.

Then there's Ken Dubuque, a self-described workaholic and senior vice president at Mellon Bank in Pittsburgh. Head of the bank's strategic planning and corporate development functions, Mr. Dubuque says he loves his job and doesn't find it particularly stressful.

But the demands are great. He works 70 hours a week, staying at least one night a week until midnight, and typically devotes several hours to his job on weekends. "I can never complete this job," he says, "If you're neat and tidy, you'll go nuts."

Most stressful, he says, is how his schedule affects his personal life. His four-year-old daughter sees him only on weekends. His wife wants "adult attention" when he comes home, most nights after 8 p.m., and "I'm dead."

It's a tough balancing act, and Mr. Dubuque, whose workaholic father recently suffered a stroke from which he's still partially blind, confesses that "sometimes I wonder whether it's worth it."

That's a question occurring to many executives and professionals. "I'm having more and more clients say, 'I want to get out of here. This is just too much.' They want to buy a ranch in Montana and move away from all the pressure," says Dee Soder, a New York psychologist whose Endymion Co. provides stress-management counseling.

To combat anxiety attacks, employers have embraced a myriad of therapies. Chase Manhattan Corp., where the payroll will soon be pared 12%, this week initiated a program of lunch-time support groups, led by professional therapists, for employees feeling stress.

Citicorp has also made extensive use of lunch-time stress counselors. One, Dr. Art Ulene of NBC's "Today" show, recently advised employees "to change the way you think about some of the things that drive you crazy" as one method for lowering stress. Standing in line at the supermarket, which Dr. Ulene once found intolerable, can be less annoying if it's viewed as an opportunity to meet interesting people, he told the audience amid laughter.

Linda Schoenthaler, a financial planning consultant and senior partner at Circle Consulting Group in New York, treats colleagues to matinee outings on Broadway while her firm sponsors brownie tasting bakeoffs.

Meanwhile, at Hoffmann-La Roche Inc., the Nutley, N.J.-based subsidiary of the Swiss pharmaceutical concern, employees receive after-hours instruction in a variety of stress management methods. They include meditation, breathing exercises and a technique called "dot stopping." A form of biofeedback, the technique teaches employees to control their stress by recalling a wonderful moment and focusing on the feelings and sensations they had then.

1. List the job-related stressors discussed in this article and compare them with those presented in this chapter.

2. If you were Ken Dubuque's manager, how would you help him overcome stress?

3. Speculate about Dubuque's management style. What effects might it have on you if you worked for him?

HALLOWE'EN "BLUE FLU"

On October 31 at 10 P.M., a sudden wave of illness hit the uniformed members of the Summit County Police Department. Several superior officers, sergeants, and lieutenants checked out ill at the same time throughout the six precincts. While this exodus was going on, the personnel assigned to the midnight-to-8-A.M. tour of duty started calling in sick for the tour and unable to report for their assigned duties. A case of the "blue flu" was hitting the department on one of the busiest nights of the year. A number of individuals, apparently dissatisfied with what they viewed as "stalling tactics" by an impartial arbitrator, decided to stage a walkout in order to pressure the arbitrator into reaching a favorable decision quickly.

Upon learning of this action, the board members of the Superior Officers Association hurriedly convened a special meeting to decide what to do. All of the people who had called in sick were members of the Superior Officers Association. The first objective of the board was to confine the walkout to the ranks of superior officers and not involve members of the Patrolmen's Benevolent Association. The board felt that this approach would minimize the ill effects on the public. The board also began contacting all members of the Superior Officers Association and asking them to return to work. In addition, steps were taken to ensure that some supervisors were on duty throughout the walkout.

In the meantime, the commissioner responded immediately to the walkout by stating that any officer calling off duty on October 31 would be suspended. This suspension order was applicable to any superior officer calling in sick for any tour. It even included those officers who had been ill or suffered injuries prior to October 31. All detective superiors were to report for duty in uniform to be available as substitutes.

The commissioner had been assured by the Superior Officers Association that there would be enough superior officers working to continue the operation of the department. However, the commissioner was apparently afraid that patrolmen would walk out in sympathy. Thus he maintained a firm stance, setting up teams of detectives and detective superiors who were to follow up his suspension order by picking up all police equipment previously issued to the suspended officers. The pickup of equipment began at 11 P.M., and the 18 officers who had called in sick or gone off duty at 10 P.M. were the first to have their police equipment picked up.

Trouble began almost immediately. Officers with many years on the job had to explain to their spouses what had happened and why their equipment was being picked up. The Superior Officers Association was soon hearing about threats of divorce and separation. In order to prevent violence and to alleviate the anxiety being caused by the picking up of equipment, the Association attempted to negotiate with the commissioner. At first the commissioner was reluctant to talk, but finally he agreed to make some changes.

Although the commissioner continued to believe his original stand was correct, he agreed to allow any police officer who had been suspended to report back to duty upon submission of an acceptable doctor's note. He further agreed to collect only the shield and identification card of the members participating in the walkout. This information was conveyed personally and by telephone to all the participating members. Arrangements were made for the department police surgeons to examine the members. And those members who claimed they could not afford to see a doctor were authorized to submit the bills to the Superior Officers Association.

By November 2, all 130 officers believed to have participated in the action either had returned to duty or were accounted for. Official charges were then brought against the 130 members of the Superior Officers Association who had participated either willingly or "by accident." The cases of all members suspended were turned over to the deputy commissioner for review and trial. Of the 130 cases reviewed, 68 were formally charged, including the 18 members who had gone off duty "ill" on October 31. This group had aroused the intense anger of the commissioner.

When the formal charges were drawn up, each member had to appear at an open hearing conducted in an auditorium and plea guilty or innocent. Those who pleaded guilty were immediately fined a day's pay for each day absent. The 18 "instigators," however, were not allowed to plead guilty at this hearing but were ordered to appear for trial on February 18. It was rumored that this group would face not only a fine but also dismissal from the force.

Negotiations between the commissioner and the Association continued up to the day of the trials. With the department back to normal, and seeing that he had accomplished his objective, the commissioner allowed the 18 officers (all men) to plead guilty to the charge of misconduct and be fined 5 days' pay. In addition, each was to have included in his file a letter indicating the part he played in the action and a note stating that he was on probation for a year. Any type of disciplinary charges brought against him during this period would result in immediate dismissal from the department.

Throughout the "blue flu," the county executive, Albert Scott, said nothing. However, he kept in close contact with the commissioner. Scott, by law, had the right to invoke the sanctions of the state's "no strike law" against the union. Instead, he chose to leave the matter in the hands of the commissioner. Under the provisions of the law, the county executive could have fined each person participating in the action 2 days' pay for each day lost. He could also have levied on the Superior Officers Association a fine so large it would have "broken" the treasury. However, the county executive was satisfied with the commissioner's actions and refrained from taking any action himself.

All members of the force soon learned that the arbitrator's decision had been made earlier and had actually been submitted on the day of the walkout! The action had had no effect on the arbitrator's decision. As a result, the "blue flu" incident came to be referred to as the Hallowe'en fiasco. In their bids for re-election to office, the top members of the Superior Officers Association went down to resounding defeat.

Memories linger on. Although no families split up as a result of the activities launched following the walkout, spouses continue to bring it up. Working relationships are strained. The animosity that developed the night the detectives picked up the equipment is still festering four years later.

1. What types of conflicts occurred here?
2. How would you characterize this situation in terms of the contingency model of conflict?
3. What types of distress are apparent?
4. What are the causes of the conflicts?
5. Identify the conflict-management style in evidence. Were they effective?
6. Can this situation be improved? Explain.

Part Six

CONTROLLING

Lessons from Japan

EMERGENCY RETURN

As recently as the 1950s, fully automatic manufacturing was a science fiction dream. Today that fantasy is reality, as fully automated systems replace human beings throughout industry. In fact, automated systems, which require humans only to design and maintain them, are now considered a necessity. They're cheaper, turn out more consistent products, and allow the United States, Japan, and Europe, for example, to compete with nations that can rely on huge, inexpensive labor pools.

Since the same kinds of automatic machines can be bought by the United States, Japan, and Europe, the country that operates them the most efficiently will lead the world in manufacturing. The machines have to be up and running almost constantly in order to achieve maximum productivity, and as the Japanese have demonstrated, the best way to keep these machines running is to have skilled, motivated workers operating them.

One comparison between U.S. and Japanese approaches to the same automatic machine clearly shows the advantage of having a skilled, motivated work force. The machine, which assembles automobile engine heads, is a complicated piece of equipment longer than a football field. Occasionally, as one would expect of anything that huge, something goes wrong and the machine has to be shut down. In Japan, where the machine was run by skilled engineers, it was down only 10 percent of the time. In a U.S. factory, where the same machine was operated by unskilled workers, it had 50 percent down time. Down time translated into a loss of about $500 a minute.

Instead of training its existing work force or hiring skilled labor, the U.S. factory, in an attempt to improve productivity, installed a computer to run the machine and fully automate the system. The computer, by design, automatically shut down the machine if a problem occurred. In addition, the computer could diagnose the problem and tell the operators how to get things moving again. With the computer serving as the brain of the machine, only three workers were needed to oversee it. The result: there was some improvement in productivity, but the machine was still up and running only two-thirds as often as the one in Japan, the one run by human beings.

Why would the U.S. version—a computerized, "idiot-proof" system—be less effective than the system in Japan run by engineers? Because the U.S. workers weren't motivated or trained sufficiently to keep the machine up and running. In the Japanese firm, any down time is treated like a crisis; in the U.S. firm, no one seemed to care.

"If you idiot-proof the world, you get a world full of idiots," notes Steven Cohen, an expert on manufacturing. "If you organize production on the assumption that your workforce consists of fools, they're going to behave like fools." It's cheaper, he adds, to use computers in combination with human skills, not as a substitute for them. The conclusion: New machines, no matter how sophisticated, will be only as effective as the workers who run them.

Another example of the successful use of skilled labor in Japanese manufacturing is the Seiko watch factory. There, the production workers are engineers and designers who not only assemble watches, but also create new designs for them at the rate of three a day. In the United States, the very idea of a production worker designing a new product seems far-fetched.

The effectiveness of Japanese manufacturers can be traced directly to a management philosophy that emphasizes hiring skilled people or training unskilled workers. In fact, one of the most productive automobile plants in the States is managed by Toyota, in a joint venture with General Motors. At the California plant, managers tend to treat workers with respect—not like they're a bunch of fools—and give them the training they need. The result is a motivated, productive work force.

Why might there be an advantage to having highly trained engineers running automated systems? Why might such a skilled work force be more motivated to ensure quality than an unskilled one?

Chapter 18

CONTROLLING

Wal-Mart employee

What You Will Learn

1 Four basic elements of control.

2 The effectiveness of various methods of organizational control.

3 Six steps of the corrective control model.

4 Five categories of managerial controls.

5 Three controversial control methods.

6 **Skill Development:** How to assess and improve control methods at any level in an organization.

All Marts Are Not Equal

Since taking over as CEO in 1987, Joseph Antonini of Kmart has been trying to patch up the discount chain's financial picture. He has refurbished old stores, introduced classier goods, and recruited sports and Hollywood stars to do TV spots. To keep Kmart's core customers, he cut prices on 8,000 items.

Wal-Mart, however, is fast outstripping Kmart in profits and sales. Wal-Mart's profits per square foot were around $5 in 1978 and rose to $20 by 1990. Over the same period, Kmart's went from around $5 to just under $8. For 1991, Kmart's sales were near $32 billion and Wal-Mart's just topped $32.6 billion, and Wal-Mart's sales increases have been greater.

What's Kmart's problem? According to many, it's lack of an effective control system. There are still too many sloppy Kmart stores. Merchandise isn't displayed consistently from store to store. Bad distribution means that stores often run out of merchandise while it just sits there in a warehouse. These and other administrative problems have raised Kmart's selling expenses to 23 cents on the dollar compared to 16 cents at Wal-Mart.

At Wal-Mart, computer technology allows headquarters staff and store employees to talk to one another on video monitors via satellite. Electronic point-of-sale cash registers also enable managers to keep an up-to-the-minute account of all store inventory. Over 30,000 products are tracked by a centralized computer inventory management system from the time an order is placed with a vendor, to delivery to a distribution center and then a store, through customer check-out. Kmart has started to install a computer system similar to Wal-Mart's.

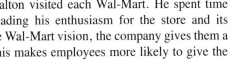

Another problem is that Antonini doesn't like to receive bad news. There are few people who dare to tell him things are going wrong. The Kmart corporate culture favors telling the chairman what he wants to hear. Not so at Wal-Mart. Sam Walton, CEO of Wal-Mart, started a tradition that has resulted in effective controls. At Wal-Mart, all associates (employees) are encouraged to offer suggestions whenever they see a better way of doing something. All associates at Wal-Mart's general offices in Bentonville, Arkansas are invited to a 7:30 A.M. Saturday morning breakfast meeting to discuss issues. These meetings have engendered a family feeling and a set of group norms. Control comes not from browbeating, but from getting associates to learn and appreciate the Wal-Mart way of doing business.[1]

The Manager's Viewpoint illustrates the importance of the controlling process, one of the basic managerial functions. This process is vital to the survival and effectiveness of individuals, groups, departments, organizations, and society. At Wal-Mart, employees are urged to exercise self-control and to make suggestions on how to improve the organization. For example, until recently, Sam Walton visited each Wal-Mart. He spent time with associates, listening to them and spreading his enthusiasm for the store and its customers. To get associates committed to the Wal-Mart vision, the company gives them a share in the profits. Walton found out that this makes employees more likely to give the

Basic Managerial Functions

Controlling is one of the basic functions of successful management.

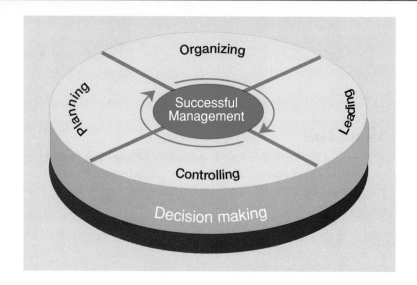

kind of effort that is takes to outperform the competition. They control themselves rather than relying on others.

In Chapter 1 we stated the central theme of this book: Successful management occurs when leading, planning, organizing, decision making, and controlling all come together. Figure 18.1 is a further reminder of this core theme (it was part of Figure 1.6, Management as a Dynamic Process).

In this chapter we focus on issues, processes, strategies, and methods of organizational control. We first identify and describe the basic elements: types, sources, and patterns of control. Next, we present guidelines for assessing the effectiveness of organizational controls, followed by a description of a six-step corrective control model. Then we review five categories of managerial controls, including specific methods within each category. Finally, we look at computer monitoring, drug testing, and undercover security agents—three controversial practices some organizations are using to control employees.

BASIC ELEMENTS OF CONTROL

control   The methods and mechanisms used to ensure that behaviors and performance conform to an organization's objectives, plans, and standards.

For our purposes, **control** refers to the methods and mechanisms used to ensure that behaviors and performance conform to an organization's objectives, plans, and standards. To most people the word *control* has a negative connotation of restraining, forcing, delimiting, watching, or manipulating. Du Pont uses hidden, long-distance cameras to monitor its loading docks around the clock. General Electric uses tiny, fish-eye lenses behind pinholes in walls and ceilings to watch employees suspected of crimes.[2] Most American employees resent such practices because of their deeply held values of individualism and democracy. Methods of managerial control are thus often the focus of controversy and power struggles within organizations.[3]

In the 1990s, however, control isn't something managers do *to* employees, but rather *with* them. It's useful and necessary for everyone on the team. For example, effective control has been one of the keys to Wal-Mart's rising sales and profits over the past decade, because it has enabled them to plan more accurately. We can illustrate this point best, perhaps, by showing how control interacts with planning:

▶ Planning is the formal process of making decisions about objectives, strategies, tactics, and resource allocation. Controls are measures that help ensure that behaviors and results are consistent with those plans, objectives, and standards. Thus planning and controlling go hand in hand.

▶ Planning prescribes *desired* behaviors and results. Controls help maintain or redirect *actual* behaviors and results.

▶ Managers and teams cannot effectively plan without accurate and timely information. Control processes are the means by which they obtain much of this essential information.

▶ Managers and teams cannot effectively control without plans to indicate the purposes to be served by the control process. Thus planning and control complement and support each other.

Preventive and Corrective Controls

There are two types of organizational controls, preventive and corrective. **Preventive controls** are intended to reduce errors and thereby minimize the need for corrective action. Safeway Stores in Oakland, California has dashboard computers in its 800 trucks. These computers record driving speed, oil pressure, engine RPMs, and when and how long the truck is stopped. Safeway uses these data to hold down maintenance and fuel costs. Drivers are rewarded for good driving behavior. Similarly, air traffic controllers prevent crashes by ensuring that airline personnel follow well-defined standards, rules, and procedures during takeoffs and landings.

Rules and regulations, standards, human resource recruitment and selection procedures, and training and development programs function primarily as preventive controls. They all direct and limit the behaviors of employees and managers. The assumption is that, if employees comply with these restrictions, the organizaion is likely to achieve its objectives. Again, control mechanisms are needed to make sure that rules and regulations are being followed and are working.

Corrective controls are intended to change unwanted behaviors and make performance conform to established standards or rules. Safeway's computer-based dispatching program uses corrective controls. When a district sales manager discovers that a store is running out of a special, he or she can instruct a driver to change routes and make an emergency delivery there. An air traffic controller engages in corrective control by instructing a pilot to change altitude and direction to avoid another plane.

Sources of Control

There are four primary sources of control in most organizations: stakeholders, the organization itself, groups, and individuals.[4] These are shown in Table 18.1, which gives examples of preventive and corrective controls related to the four sources of control.

preventive controls
Organizational controls intended to reduce errors and thereby minimize the need for corrective action.

corrective controls
Organizational controls intended to change unwanted behaviors and make performance conform to established standards or rules.

T A B L E   18.1

Examples of Different Sources and Types of Control

| | Type of Control | |
Source of Control	*Preventive*	*Corrective*
Stakeholders	Maintaining quotas for hiring people in protected classes	Changing recruitment policies to attract qualified personnel
Organization	Using budgets to guide expenditures	Disciplining an employee for violating a "No Smoking" safety regulation in a hazardous area
Group	Advising a new employee about the group's norm in relation to expected level of output	Harassing and socially isolating a worker who doesn't conform to the group norms
Individual	Deciding to skip lunch because you are running behind schedule in completing a project	Revising a report you have written because you are dissatisifed with it

stakeholder control
Control over an organization exerted by outsiders, such as stockholders, customers, or government agencies.

organizational control
Control over a company stemming from its formal strategies and mechanisms for pursuing its objectives.

group control The norms and values that group members share and maintain through rewards and punishments.

individual self-control
Control mechanisms operating consciously and unconsciously within each person.

Stakeholder control refers to pressure from outside sources, such as customers, governmental agencies, stockholders, or banks, on organizations to change their behaviors. Coca-Cola, for example, was boycotted several years ago by the followers of the Reverend Jesse Jackson over a disagreement about opportunities for African-Americans within Coca-Cola. The organization had followed the letter of the law for employment practices and had committed millions of dollars to the development of distributorships owned by African-Americans. Embarrassed by the negative publicity, whether justified or not, Coca-Cola's top managers responded by focusing even greater attention on hiring, promotion, and support for minority employees and entrepreneurs.

Organizational control refers to a company's formal strategies and mechanisms for pursuing its objectives. Examples include rules, standards, budgets, and audits. **Group control** refers to the norms and values that group members share and maintain through rewards and punishments. Punishments, such as giving a member the silent treatment, were described in Chapter 16. **Individual self-control** consists of control mechanisms operating consciously and unconsciously within each person.

Standards of professionalism are becoming an increasingly important mechanism for individual self-control. Becoming a professional involves acquiring detailed knowledge, specialized skills, and specific attitudes and ways of behaving. The entire process may take years of study and socialization. Certified public accountants, lawyers, business school graduates, and physicians, among others, are expected to engage in individual self-control based on the standards of their professions.

Patterns of Control

Stakeholder, organizational, group, and individual controls form patterns that differ widely from one organization to another.[5] As we suggested in Chapter 16, strong organizational cultures usually produce mutually supportive and reinforcing organizational, group, and individual controls. At Kmart, unfortunately, this has had a negative impact on profitability and sales. On the other hand, controls from the different sources may operate at odds with each other. When this happens, internal conflict or apathy can result.

In our discussions of motivation, leadership, and groups, we have focused on some managerial practices used to achieve greater compatibility among organizational, group, and individual controls. Actual control patterns in organizations are often influenced by give and take among managers, groups, and individuals. The following Insight is an account of such give and take.

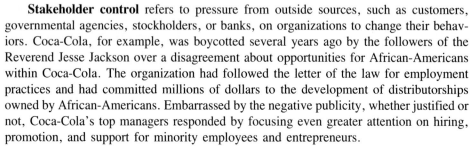

BUREAUCRACY AT WORK

I N S I G H T A personnel officer was transferred to a certain government installation, where a controller had been working for years. The new personnel officer had a higher Civil Service rating than the controller. Previously, whenever the controller wanted to move someone, change a job description, or hire somebody, he would send a request to the personnel office to justify the changes, and the changes would be approved. Soon after the new personnel officer arrived, the controller submitted a request for a new position. The personnel officer sent the controller's request back, indicating that there was no justification for the position. The personnel officer's control system consisted of a manual that specified a fixed number of people to do the various jobs in the controller's office. According to the manual, the controller couldn't justify the new position.

The personnel officer was in the habit of signing and submitting a time card weekly and not clocking in daily, as required by the rules. The controller, appar-

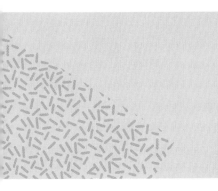

ently angered by the personnel officer's refusal to approve the new position, told him to clock in every day. The personnel officer hadn't punched a time clock in fifteen years. He complained to the installation's manager, who pointed out the regulations required all employees to punch in daily. The personnel officer complied. About a month later, the controller resubmitted the request for the new position. The personnel officer approved it. The personnel officer did not continue to punch in daily after approving the request. Everybody was happy. The personnel officer and the controller achieved their objectives by implicitly agreeing to subvert the formal organizational control system, not by complying with it.[6]

Managers and teams cannot achieve an effective pattern of control by focusing only on formal organizational controls. Individual and group controls can exert strong influences on employees' behavior. However, formal controls can directly affect the establishment and range of employee behaviors. Thus, in setting up such controls, managers need to keep clearly in mind the purposes intended.[7]

The Global Link illustrates stakeholder control exerted by a foreign government and limiting a global corporation's effectiveness. This feature highlights only one company's experiences, but many multinational corporations have faced similar bureaucratic obstacles.

EFFECTIVENESS OF ORGANIZATIONAL CONTROLS

One way of evaluating the effectiveness of formal organizational controls is by comparing their costs and benefits. Such a cost-benefit analysis addresses three basic questions:

1. For what desired behaviors and results should organizational controls be developed?

2. What are the costs and benefits of the organizational controls required to achieve the desired behaviors and results?

3. What are the costs and benefits of utilizing alternative organizational controls to obtain the desired behaviors and results?

The effectiveness of organizational controls is the difference between their costs and the improvement in behaviors and results.

Starting in January 1990, Motorola began screening all employees for traces of illegal drugs. The costs of this effort were projected to exceed $1.5 million the first year and $1 million annually thereafter. The cost of in-house rehabilitation programs ranges anywhere from $4,000 to $10,000 per month per employee enrolled. Is it worth it? According to Motorola, ridding itself of illegal drug addicts may save it $190 million annually. This amount was arrived at by figuring lost productivity and absenteeism due to drug-related employee problems.[8]

Cost-Benefit Model

Figure 18.2 shows a cost-benefit model for gauging the effectiveness of an organization's control system. The horizontal axis indicates the amount of organizational control, ranging from low to high. The vertical axis indicates the costs and benefits of control, ranging from zero to high. For simplicity, the cost-of-control curve is shown as a direct function of the amount of organizational control.

Managers have to consider tradeoffs when choosing the amount of organizational control to use. With too little control, costs exceed benefits and the organizational controls

GLOBAL L'ink

SO YOU WANT TO BUILD JEEPS CHEAP IN CHINA?

In 1983 top managers from American Motors Corporation (AMC) were given the red carpet treatment as they filed into the Great Hall of the People in Beijing. After four years of on-again off-again negotiations, AMC and the Chinese government had agreed to jointly produce Jeeps. AMC and Beijing Automative Works formed a new venture called Beijing-Jeep Company (BJC), of which the Chinese owned 69 percent. The People's Republic hoped to attract outside investors and obtain the assembly-line technology it needed to catch up with the West. AMC anticipated nothing less than enormous sales. In fact, the *Detroit Free Press* hailed the agreement as "one of the shrewdest industrial strokes of the decade."

After the venture started, the two sides clashed over the nature of the new jeep and the method by which it would be made. AMC wanted it to look like its Cherokee; Chinese officials wanted it to look like a military jeep. AMC said that it could not make that type of jeep from its existing product and developing a military design would cost over $1 billion. Neither side had the money.

During a trial run in 1985, the first Cherokee had to be pushed off the line at BJC. Workers had forgotten to tighten the clutch. Once the bugs were worked out, AMC's vice president bullishly predicted that the new company would sell 40,000 a year.

In the fall of 1985, the government of the People's Republic imposed severe foreign exchange restrictions. BJC needed hard currency to import Cherokee parts kits. It couldn't exchange its local earnings for dollars because the domestic currency was not convertible. The Chinese government balked at granting import licenses until the kits were paid for.

By the winter of 1986, BJC was broke. To keep going, it borrowed over $1 million from the employees' health and welfare fund. American managers at BJC had never heard of this fund before. They were surprised to learn that the difference between the $40,000 salaries of top Chinese managers and their less than-$200-a-month take-home pay went into the fund.

BJC did not deliver the promised Cherokees to the Chinese government in 1986 because the foreign exchange problem had not been resolved. Moreover, BJC faced $3.1 million in debts for capital projects.

The ultimate irony for AMC (now a part of the Chrysler Corporation) was that it expected to reap huge profits by selling superior products to the Chinese with its modern technology. Instead, it was forced to sell military-style jeeps to the Chinese. As of late 1986, only 24,500 jeeps had been produced, of which less than 2,000 were Cherokees.

In 1989 Chrysler found that BJC was not distributing the proceeds from its sales to Chrysler. BJC was forced to shut down its production line because the customs bureau in Tianjin suddenly announced a major tariff increase on parts kits. Then on June 3, 1989, when Chinese troops drove into Beijing to quash student demonstrations in Tiananmen Square, Chrysler urged its managers to leave China.

Adapted from J. Mann, *Buying a Jeep*, N.Y.: Simon & Schuster, 1989.

FIGURE 18.2

Cost-Benefit Model of Organizational Control

This cost-benefit model shows how the amount of control can result in either a profit or a loss.

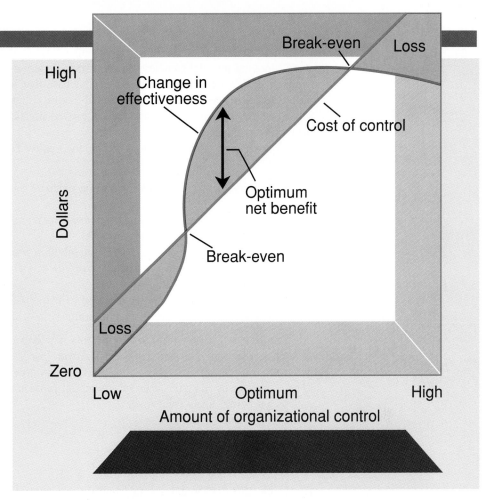

are ineffective. As the amount of organizational control increases, effectiveness also increases—up to a point. Beyond a certain point, further increases in the amount of control result in decreased effectiveness. For example, an organization might benefit from reducing the average managerial span of control from twenty-one to sixteen employees. However, to further reduce it to eight employees would require doubling the number of managers. The costs of the increased control (managers' salaries) might far outweigh the expected benefits. Such a move might also make workers feel overmanaged and under too much surveillance. This, in turn, could lead to dissatisfaction, high absenteeism, and increased turnover.

Figure 18.2 shows two break-even points. They indicate where the amount of organizational control moves from a loss to a net benefit and then returns to a loss. The optimal amount of control is difficult to calculate. Effective managers probably come closer to achieving it than ineffective managers do.

The following Insight provides an example of the costs and benefits associated with implementing new organizational controls.

SNIFFING OUT BAD RISKS AT TRAVELERS

*I*NSIGHT   Several years ago, Travelers Mortgage Services began to worry about problems in its loan-granting process. With all the stories in the press about suspect lending policies of savings and loan associations, Travelers became concerned about its instances of bad loans.

With the support of senior management, a new quality control department started looking into deficiencies in processing, underwriting, appraisals, and settlements. It had to develop a computerized database that included the borrower's name, address, zip code, employer, Social Security number, telephone number, seller's name, and so forth. The database proved invaluable for detecting fraud by loan applicants.

Working with the finance department, the quality control department was able to:

▶ Identify high-risk characteristics and evaluate monthly loans for those criteria.

▶ Trace agents' activities to show overall weaknesses in loan origination and underwriting.

▶ Monitor and evaluate the overall distribution and composition of loans.

▶ Spot appraisers who consistently overrate properties and help them improve their performance.

▶ Examine loans by employment type to help spot potential problems with loans made to borrowers who work on commission or are self-employed.

The cost to Travelers of establishing this new department, hiring additional personnel, and designing new computer software programs was more than $500,000. Was it worth it? According to Travelers, yes. It saved the company millions of dollars by allowing it to spot potential problems that had previously gone undetected before loans were made.[9]

Criteria for Effective Controls

Designing effective organizational controls and control systems isn't simple, because many issues must be considered.[10] However, organizational controls or control systems are likely to be effective if they are linked to desired results, objective, complete, timely, and acceptable. These criteria refine and make more specific the ideas presented in the cost-benefit model.

As suggested by the assessment method in Table 18.2, a control may more or less satisfy each of these criteria. The table also implies that a particular control or control system should be designed and evaluated in terms of all five criteria. The total score from such an assessment can range from a low of 5 to a high of 25. The higher the total score, the greater the likelihood that the control or control system is effective. Organizational controls that fail to reasonably satisfy the five criteria may actually do more harm than good. Let's consider each of the criteria in more depth.

TABLE 18.2

Method for Assessing the Effectiveness of Organizational Controls

	Evaluation				
Criteria	Definitely Not	Unlikely	Can't Tell	Probably	Definitely
1. The control or control system is linked to desired results.	1	2	3	4	5
2. It is objective.	1	2	3	4	5
3. It is complete.	1	2	3	4	5
4. It is timely.	1	2	3	4	5
5. It is acceptable.	1	2	3	4	5

Linkage to Desired Results Controls should help an organization to achieve desired results, such as standardizing performance, protecting the organization's assets, and/or maintaining the quality of products or services. Travelers changed its control system to reduce the instances of bad loans.

Objectivity The objectivity of organizational controls is the degree to which they are impartial and cannot be manipulated by employees for personal gain. In the United States, the Financial Accounting Standards Board (FASB) and several government agencies devote a great deal of effort to developing principles and practices to ensure that financial statements more objectively and accurately reflect reality.

A new accounting control system for sales was designed at J. Walter Thompson to be more objective and less easily manipulated. Herbert Eames, Jr., the executive vice president for finance, said: "The primary difference is that we now have one general ledger system and one chart of accounts. We don't have a multitude of charts, accounts and systems. As a result, it's easier for the auditors to go through one account process and one set of audit materials."

Completeness Completeness is the degree to which the control or control system encompasses all the desired behaviors and results. A purchasing manager evaluated solely on the basis of costs per order may allow quality to slip. A computer salesperson evaluated only on the basis of sales volume may ignore after-sales service. Thus, there is a need to balance quantitative (measurable) controls with more qualitative (subjective) controls.

Timeliness Timeliness is the degree to which the control or control system provides information when it is needed most. Timeliness is measured in terms of seconds for evaluating the safe movement of trains and planes or in terms of months for evaluating the performance of middle managers. Computer-based technology has played a major role in increasing the timeliness of information. The computer system at Wal-Mart gives store managers daily data on each department's sales, as well as profitability for the entire store.

Acceptability When organizational controls are widely resisted or ignored, managers should try to find out why. It may be that the controls should be dropped or modified, that they should be backed up with rewards for compliance and punishments for noncompliance, or that they aren't linked to desired results. Recall the controller and personnel officer in the chapter's first Insight feature. Both of them found the outcome of formal organizational controls unacceptable, choosing instead to satisfy their needs for greater individual self-control.

CORRECTIVE CONTROL MODEL

corrective control model
A six-step process that allows managers to detect and correct deviations from an organization's objectives, plans, and standards.

The **corrective control model** allows managers to detect and correct deviations from an organization's established objectives, plans, and standards. This process relies heavily on feedback and reaction. As shown in Figure 18.3, the corrective control model has six steps: (1) define the subsystem (an individual, a department, or a process), (2) identify the characteristics to be measured, (3) set standards, (4) collect information, (5) make comparisons, and (6) diagnose problems and make corrections. Let's look at each of these in greater detail.[11]

FIGURE 18.3

Corrective Control Model

The corrective control model has six steps that managers and employees should follow.

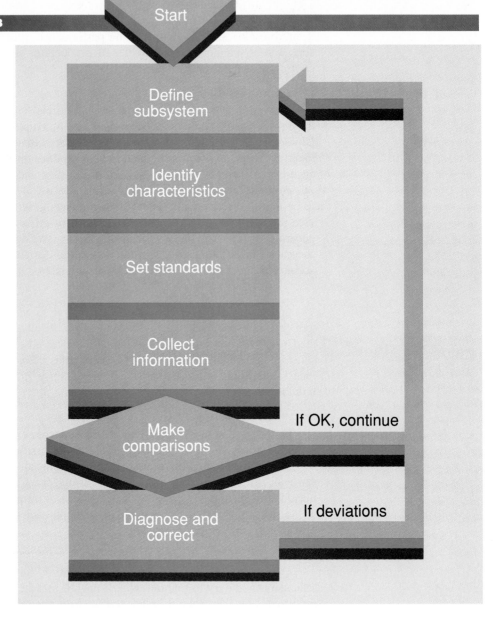

Start

Define subsystem

Identify characteristics

Set standards

Collect information

Make comparisons

If OK, continue

Diagnose and correct

If deviations

Defining the Subsystem

A formal control subsystem might be created and maintained with and by an employee, a department, or an entire organization. The controls could focus on specific inputs, production processes, or outputs. Input controls often limit the amount by which raw materials used in the production process can vary from organization standards.[12] For example, elaborate controls (including inspections and laboratory testing) are used in breweries to guarantee that the water and grains used to make beer meet predetermined standards. Such controls ensure that the right quantity and quality of inputs enter the production process.

Many formal controls are applied during the production process. For Coors, Miller, and other brewers, these include timing the cooking of the brew, monitoring temperature in the vats, sampling and laboratory testing of the brew at each stage of the process, and visual inspection of the beer prior to final packing. Finally, output controls are also used. For brewers, these range from specifying the levels of distributor inventories to monitoring consumer attitudes toward the beer and related services.

Corrective control of a product: Wendy Abraham runs an in-water test of a MerCruiser motor at the Marine Power Division's Stillwater, Oklahoma, plant.

Identifying the Key Characteristics

The types of information to be obtained about a department must be identified. Establishing a formal corrective control requires early determination of the characteristics that can be measured, the costs and benefits of obtaining information about each characteristic, and whether variations in each characteristic affect the department's performance.

After identifying the key characteristics, managers must selectively choose the ones to be measured. The **principle of selectivity,** also known as Pareto's law, states that a small number of characteristics always account for a large number of effects. In brewing beer, for example, three characteristics that greatly influence the final product's quality are water quality, temperature, and length of brewing time. The control aspect of a management-by-objectives (MBO) system (discussed in Chapter 9) is based on the principle of selectivity. The direct control of objectives makes possible the control of the few, but vital, characteristics that can account for major variations in results.

principle of selectivity
The idea that a small number of characteristics always account for a large number of effects (also known as Pareto's law).

Setting Standards

standards Criteria against which qualitative and quantitative characteristics are evaluated.

Managers should set standards for each characteristic measured. **Standards** are criteria against which qualitative and quantitative characteristics are evaluated. Standards are often interrelated. A considerable amount of departmental coordination is usually required in setting standards. Tuttle, Neidhart & Seyman, Inc., a global human resources consulting firm, has the objective of providing the highest-quality services for its clients. It has strict standards for screening job applicants. According to John Semyan, a managing director, these include five years of work experience, excellent diagnostic abilities, ability to communicate effectively with diverse clients, ability to provide answers that clients will accept and implement, knowledge, and several essential attitudes, such as high ethical standards, empathy and trust, self-motivation, energy, and mobility.[13]

Increasingly, managers are developing control systems based on performance standards (performance objectives). There are many possible types of performance standards. The following are examples from five different functional areas:

▶ *Inventory:* Monthly finished goods inventory should be maintained at the sales level forecasted for the following two-month period.

▶ *Accounts receivable:* Monthly accounts receivable should be no more than the dollar value of the previous $1\frac{1}{2}$ months' sales.

▶ *Sales productivity:* The dollar value of sales per salesperson should be $1,000 greater than the comparable month for the previous year and $12,000 greater annually.

▶ *Employee turnover:* The turnover of field sales personnel should be no more than 2 per 100 salespersons per month and no more than 20 per 100 salespersons annually.

▶ *Production waste:* Waste should amount to no more than $50 per month per full-time production worker and no more than $600 per year per full-time production worker.

Collecting Information

Information on each of the standards can be collected by people or by automatic means. Examples of the latter are the devices used at Disney World to count the number of people who use each ride or the turnstiles at libraries, which count the number of people who enter.

If information is collected by the individual or group whose performance is to be controlled, its validity must be checked. Employees and managers have an incentive to distort or conceal information if negative results will be used to criticize or punish them. Moreover, when formal controls emphasize punishment, strong group controls (see Chapter 16 for a list of these) often emerge to distort the information that is reported to management. This type of response obscures the pinpointing of responsibility.

Top managers may create special departments, as Travelers Mortgage did, or rely on regular departments to collect information by monitoring or auditing certain activities. The human resources department at Dr Pepper/7-UP collects data from the U. S. Labor Bureau and the company's competitors in order to determine, for example, whether starting salaries for various jobs are sufficient and affirmative action guidelines are being followed. Similarly, a controller's department will collect and analyze information to make sure income and expenditures are recorded in line with established accounting standards.

Making Comparisons

In order to make comparisons, managers must find out whether there is a difference between what *is* happening and what *should be* happening. They must compare information about actual results with performance standards. Making these comparisons allows employees and managers to concentrate on controlling deviations or exceptions. Overcontrolling becomes less likely and the manager can use his or her time more effectively. If there is no apparent difference between what is and what should be happening, the individual or department normally continues to function without any change.

Diagnosing and Correcting Problems

Diagnosis involves assessing the types, amounts, and causes of deviations from standards. Action is needed to eliminate those deviations. The fact that a characteristic can be controlled, however, doesn't necessarily mean that is should be controlled. At times, the problem may be one of undercontrol because the timeliness of information and the linkage of corrective controls to desired results are inadequate. Computer-based management information systems (discussed in Chapter 19) often assist in overcoming corrective control inadequacies.[14]

McDonald's maintains an effective control system at its more than 11,000 outlets. It uses many of the steps of the corrective control model.

QUALITY CONTROL AT MCDONALD'S

INSIGHT

Sales at the average McDonald's restaurant grew by 15 percent over a two-year period in the late 1980s. Burger King's sales for the same period grew by less than 1 percent. Why?

One of the reasons is McDonald's quality control. David Giarla is a quality control inspector for McDonald's, responsible for fifteen restaurants in the southern Connecticut area. Most managers and employees know him. But they can't

always be sure when he'll show up. The expectation of a visit keeps them on their toes.

When Giarla walks into a restaurant, he orders a regular meal. He sits down and inspects the food. This day he doesn't like the Big Breakfast biscuit. He reports to the manager that the biscuit is too small; it ought to be puffier and rounder. The hash browns are great, and Giarla tells that to the teenager tending the deep fryer. He sees a problem with an ice cream cone a woman is eating. McDonald's cones are supposed to piled three inches high, not six. He discusses that with the manager and counterperson.

After finishing his meal, he walks into the kitchen. He checks the dates stamped on the hamburger bun wrappers, a box of sliced cucumbers, cheese, and a bag of milk-shake mix. These are all fine. He checks the temperatures on the grill and fryers and looks at the fingernails of some employees. No problems in these areas.

Before he leaves the store, he spends time with the manager discussing the biscuit issue. He believes that the dough has been kneaded too much. He recommends that the biscuit maker review a McDonald's videotape, kept at every franchise, which contains instructions for making biscuits and other items.[15]

Managerial Controls

Corrective control methods can be thought of as tools that help managers assess how well their departments are doing. In fact, throughout the book, we have been discussing various facets of control. For example, in Chapter 8, you learned how a firm's strategy helps focus (control) employees' behavior. Wal-Mart, for example, is a low-cost retailer compared to J. C. Penney. Therefore, the control systems Wal-Mart uses focus on maintaining a low-cost strategy. In Chapter 12, we discussed human resource management. Performance appraisal systems help managers appraise the behaviors of employees and compare these against a standard. Deviations are noted and corrective control procedures are used to correct any problems.

In this section we'll explore five categories of managerial controls that are applicable to different situations and provide examples of specific methods within each category. The five categories of managerial controls, shown in Figure 18.4, are bureaucratic, organic, market, financial, and machine.

Effective managerial control normally requires a combination of appropriate methods from two or more of the five categories. Control methods within the categories have the potential for complementing one another *or* working against one another. Thus management should select and assess control methods in relation to one another.

Bureaucratic versus Organic Controls

bureaucratic controls
Methods of managerial control that are formal, rigid, and structured.

organic controls Methods of managerial control that are flexible and rely on self-management abilities of groups and individuals.

Bureaucratic controls include extensive rules and procedures, top-down authority, tightly written job descriptions, and other formal methods for preventing and correcting deviations from desired behaviors and results.[16] Bureaucratic controls are part of bureaucratic (mechanistic) management, covered in Chapters 2 and 11. In contrast, **organic controls** include flexible authority, looser job descriptions, individual self-controls, and other methods for preventing and correcting deviations from desired behaviors and results. Organic management was also explained in Chapter 11.

Organic controls are very consistent with a clan culture, described in Chapter 16. The power of group controls and individual self-controls is often referred to as a clan control

Principal Categories of Managerial Controls

Achieving managerial control can be done using some combination of five categories of control methods, depending on the situation.

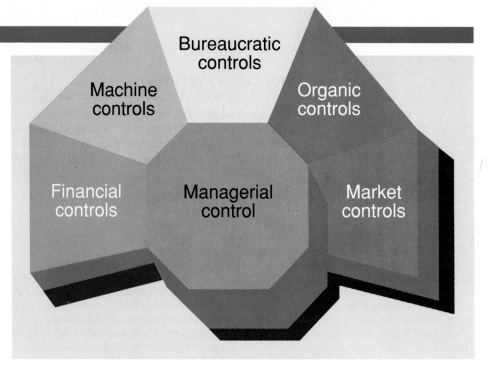

strategy. A clan is simply a group united by common interests (objectives) and characteristics. In Chapters 14 and 16, you learned how groups of employees can manage themselves with little direction from a supervisor.[17] These self-managed teams use many organic controls as shown in the following Insight.

*I*NSIGHT

In the early 1980s life on the shop floor at A. O. Smith, a Milwaukee automobile parts manufacturer, was dull. Union stewards argued with management over work rules. Workers repeated the same task, either welding or riveting parts to truck frames, every 20 seconds. Absenteeism was running as high as 20 percent on some days. No one paid much attention to quality. Wages were based on piece-work pay. Workers were encouraged to get them out the door, junk or not. Ford Motor Company was rejecting 20 percent of the door frames because they didn't fit. Something had to happen, or the company would go bankrupt.

Top management decided to involve employees and formed several quality circles. The union strongly opposed these circles, but the company pressed ahead. As quality got better, the union's opposition lessened. It became clear that improving quality and cutting costs were the only ways the company was going to survive.

Now there are teams of five to seven workers who rotate from job to job. The members of the team select team leaders who assume managerial duties, such as scheduling production and overtime, ordering maintenance work, and monitoring quality control. All members of the team are involved in building a quality product. With team members taking over duties and controls from first-line supervisors, the company has been able to reduce the number of those managers. In 1980 the ratio of first-line supervisors to workers was 1 to 10. Today it is 1 to 34. The company is training the remaining managers to put aside bureaucratic methods of control and adopt more organic methods.[18]

Characteristics of Bureaucratic and Organic Control Methods

Bureaucratic Control Methods	Organic Control Methods
Use of detailed rules and procedures whenever possible	Use of detailed rules and procedures only when necessary
Top-down authority, with emphasis on positional power	Flexible authority, with emphasis on expert power and networks of control
Activity-based job descriptions that prescribe day-to-day behaviors	Results-based job descriptions that emphasize objectives to be achieved
Emphasis on extrinsic rewards (wages, pensions, status symbols) for controlling performance	Emphasis on both extrinsic and intrinsic rewards (meaningful work) for controlling performance
Distrust of team controls, based on an assumption that team objectives conflict with organizational objectives	Harnessing of group controls, based on an assumption that group objectives and norms assist in achieving organizational objectives
Organizational culture not recognized as a source of control	Organizational culture seen as a way of integrating organizational, group, and individual objectives for greater overall control

Table 18.3 contrasts bureaucratic and organic controls to help you understand the differences between these two types of control methods. For example, the table says that detailed rules and procedures are used whenever possible as a bureaucratic control method. The Insight feature on McDonald's illustrates the effective use of bureaucratic controls. In contrast, detailed rules and procedures are used only when necessary as an organic control method. Keep in mind, however, that an organization or a department does not have to be either totally bureaucratic or totally organic in its control methods. Safety rules to protect life and property should be uniform and highly detailed under both the bureaucratic and organic methods of control.

Keep in mind, too, that large organizations consist of a number of departments, which can differ widely in their emphasis on bureaucratic or organic controls. Mechanistic characteristics in certain departments and organic characteristics in others don't necessarily reduce a firm's overall effectiveness. For example, if the production department faces a relatively stable environment and the marketing department faces a changing one, managers of the two departments are likely to choose different ways to divide and coordinate the work. The production manager will probably choose a mechanistic structure, and the marketing manager will probably choose a more organic structure. All organizations utilize some combination of bureaucratic and organic control methods, normally in conjunction with one or more of the other categories shown in Figure 18.4: market, financial, and machine.

Market Controls

market control The use of price competition to evaluate the output and productivity of an organization.

Market control occurs when price competition is used to evaluate the output and productivity of an organization. The idea of market control started in economics. A dollar value is an effective standard of comparison because managers can compare prices and profits to evaluate the efficiency of their organization. Market controls support a market culture, as discussed in Chapter 16. You might find it useful to scan Figure 16.7 (page 562) to refresh your knowledge of such a culture.

In order to be effective, market controls must generally satisfy the following requirements:

▶ Competition must be present for efficient pricing.

▶ Costs of the resources used in producing the outputs can be measured monetarily.

▶ The value of the outputs can be clearly defined and monetarily priced.

▶ Competitively based prices can be set for these outputs.

Two methods that may satisfy these requirements for effective market controls are profit-sharing plans and customer monitoring.

Profit-Sharing Plans **Profit-sharing plans** provide employees with supplemental income based on the profitability of an entire organization or a selected subunit.[19] The subunit may be a strategic business unit, a division, a store in a chain, and so on. Profit-sharing plans generally have four objectives:

▶ To increase employee identification with the organization's profit objectives, allowing greater reliance on individual self-control and group controls.

▶ To achieve a more flexible wage structure, reflecting the company's actual economic position and maintaining control over labor costs.

▶ To attract and retain workers more readily, improving control of selection and lowering turnover costs.

▶ To establish a more equitable reward system, helping to develop an organizational culture that recognizes achievement and performance.

Many factors influence whether the objectives of a profit-sharing plan can be achieved.[20] First, employees must believe that the plan is based on a reasonable, accurate, and equitable formula. The formula, in turn, must be based on valid and consistently reported financial and operating information. Employees must trust top management to report profits honestly. Second, employees must believe that their efforts and achievements contribute to profitability. Third, employees must believe that the size of profit-based incentives will increase proportionally as profitability increases. These factors are also crucial in determining the effectiveness of gain-sharing plans. Gain-sharing plans pass on the benefits of increased productivity, cost reductions, and improved quality through regular cash bonuses to employees.

Lincoln Electric Company is a good example of a company that has effectively combined profit sharing and gain sharing. The following Insight presents the major parts of Lincoln Electric's plan.

Part of the process of *market controls* is *customer monitoring* by means of questionnaires like this one used by Hilton Hotels.

profit-sharing plan A program that provides employees with supplemental income based on the profitability of an entire organization or a selected subunit.

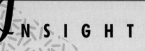

PROFIT SHARING AT LINCOLN ELECTRIC

INSIGHT

Lincoln Electric Company is the world's largest manufacturer of welding machines and electrodes, enjoying more than 40 percent of the U. S. market for arc-welding equipment and supplies. It employs 3600 workers in two factories near Cleveland and approximately 600 in three factories abroad. In addition, the company maintains a 200-person field sales force.

An open-door policy is practiced throughout the company. Employees are encouraged to take problems to the person most capable of resolving them. Perhaps because of the quality and enthusiasm of the Lincoln work force, close supervision is almost nonexistent. A typical production manager, for example, supervises as many as 100 employees. Obviously, this span of control doesn't allow close monitoring of subordinates.

Each manager formally evaluates his or her subordinates twice a year using performance review cards. Marks on the cards are converted to numerical scores, which have to average 100 for each evaluating manager. Individual scores nor-

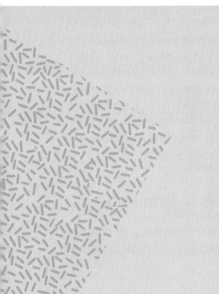

mally range from 80 to 110. Any score over 110 requires a special letter of justification to top management. Managers discuss individual performance ratings with the employees concerned.

Basic wage levels for jobs at Lincoln are determined by a wage survey of similar jobs in the Cleveland area. These rates are adjusted quarterly to conform with changes in the Cleveland Area Consumer Price Index. Most of the base wage rates are translated into piece rates. Practically all production workers and many others, such as forklift drivers, are paid by piece rate. Once established, piece rates are only changed if a substantive change in the way a job is done results from a source other than the worker doing the job.

In December of each year, a portion of annual profits is distributed to employees as bonuses. Since 1934 these bonuses have averaged about the same as an employee's annual wages and somewhat more than after-tax profits. Individual profit-sharing bonuses are exactly proportional to performance ratings. For example, a person with a score of 110 would receive 110 percent of the standard profit-sharing bonus as applied to his or her regular earnings. Exceptional worker performance at Lincoln is a matter of record. The typical Lincoln employee earns about twice as much as other factory workers in the Cleveland area. Yet the labor cost per sales dollar at Lincoln is well below industry averages. Worker turnover at Lincoln is practically nonexistent except for retirements.[21]

customer monitoring Systematic efforts by an organization to obtain feedback from customers concerning the quality of goods and services.

Customer Monitoring **Customer monitoring** consists of systematic efforts to obtain feedback from customers concerning the quality of goods and services. Such monitoring is done in order to prevent problems or learn of their existence. Customer monitoring is being used increasingly in corrective control, in an attempt to assess or measure customers' perceptions. Based on this assessment, management may make corrections within the organization before business is lost because of customers' dissatisfaction.

Customer monitoring is often used in service-oriented organizations.[22] Hotels and restaurants may ask customers to judge the quality of their service by completing a "Customer Satisfaction Card." After the purchase of their service or product, many firms follow up with telephone interviews or mail questionnaires to obtain information from customers. A unique method of obtaining feedback from customers and the public in general is used by Chemical Waste Management, Inc., the largest hauler of toxic wastes in the United States. The company's phone number is painted prominently on each truck, and the local manager's name and home address are displayed at each storage facility. These displays are intended to improve the company's control over its employees' compliance with laws and operating standards.

Financial Controls

financial controls Methods of managerial control that are intended to prevent the misallocation of financial resources and provide timely financial information.

Financial controls include a wide range of methods, techniques and procedures that are intended to prevent the misallocation of financial resources and provide timely financial information so that corrective action can be taken if needed. The monitoring aspect of financial controls is performed by external auditors (certified public accounting firms, such as Arthur Andersen, Price Waterhouse, and Coopers & Lybrand) and/or internal auditing departments (such as accounting, controller, and treasury). The primary responsibility of external auditors is to the shareholders. The auditors' role is to assure stockholders that the firm's financial statements present its true financial position and are in conformity with generally accepted accounting principles.

Because there are so many methods, techniques, and procedures for financial control, we'll focus on two of the more essential: comparative financial analysis and budgeting.

comparative financial analysis An evaluation of a firm's financial condition for two or more time periods or in comparison to similar firms.

ratio analysis A method of financial comparison that involves selecting two significant figures, expressing their relationship as a proportion or fraction, and comparing its value for two time periods or with ratios of similar organizations.

Comparative Financial Analysis A **comparative financial analysis** evaluates a firm's financial condition for two or more time periods. When data are available from similar firms, they are used in making comparisons. Industry trade associations often collect information from their members and publish it in summary form. Publicly owned firms publish income statements, balance sheets, and other financial statements. These sources are often used by managers and outsiders to assess changes in the firm's financial indicators and compare its financial health with that of other firms in the same industry. Companies that have multiple production plants (such as GM, Ford, Exxon, and IBM), retail outlets (such as Kmart, Wal-Mart, Sears, J. C. Penney, and Foley's), restaurants (such as McDonald's, Wendy's, Red Lobster, and Bennigan's), hotels (such as Hilton, Holiday Inns, and Hyatt) compare the financial records of all units for control purposes.

The most common method of comparison is ratio analysis. **Ratio analysis** involves selecting two significant figures, expressing their relationship as a proportion or fraction, and comparing its value for two periods of time or with ratios of similar organizations.[23] There are many kinds of ratios. The most common types used by organizations are profitability, liquidity, activity, and leverage; these are listed in Table 18.4.

Return on investment (ROI) is generally seen as the most important profitability ratio because it indicates how efficiently the organization is using its resources. If the value of this ratio is greater than one, it means that the organization is using its resources effectively. The current ratio indicates an organization's ability to pay bills on time. A current ratio should be well above 1:1, and if a firm has a ratio of 2:1, it might be financially sound. If an organization has a low current ratio, it might mean that it has unnecessary inventory, a lot of cash sitting idle, or heavy accounts receivable that are difficult to collect. Inventory turnover refers to how many times during a year the organization's inventory changes. A value less than 1 indicates that the organization is selling or producing goods that aren't in high demand by customers. Debt ratio is computed to assess an organization's ability to meet its long-term financial commitments. A value of .40 would indicate that this organization has 40 cents in liabilities for every dollar of its assets. The higher this ratio, the poorer credit risk the organization is perceived to be by financial institutions.

Financial ratios have little value unless you know how to interpret them. For example, an ROI of 10 percent doesn't mean much unless you compare it to some other organizations in the same industry. An organization with an ROI of 5 percent in an

TABLE 18.4

Examples of Financial Ratios

Type	Example	Calculation	Interpretation
Profitability	Return on investment (ROI)	$\dfrac{\text{Profit after taxes}}{\text{Total assets}}$	Productivity of assets
Liquidity	Current ratio	$\dfrac{\text{Current assets}}{\text{Current liabilities}}$	Short-term solvency
Activity	Inventory turnover	$\dfrac{\text{Sales}}{\text{Inventory}}$	Efficiency of inventory management
Leverage	Debt ratio	$\dfrac{\text{Total debt}}{\text{Total assets}}$	How a company finances itself

industry where the average ROI is 11 percent might be performing poorly. In the retail industry, the average inventory turnover is 2.9. J. C. Penney's inventory turnover is 2.5, which indicates that it needs to manage its inventories more effectively.[24] It can do this by offering "specials" to stimulate customer demand, lowering prices, or not carrying items that move slowly.

budgeting The process of categorizing proposed expenditures and linking them to objectives.

Budgeting **Budgeting** is the process of categorizing proposed expenditures and linking them to objectives. Budgets usually express the dollar costs of various tasks or resources. For example, production budgets may be based on hours of labor per unit produced, machine downtime per thousand hours of running time, wage rates, and similar information. The major budget categories usually include labor, materials and supplies, and facilities (property, buildings, and equipment).

Budgeting has three primary objectives: (1) to assist managers in planning their work more effectively, (2) to assist in resource allocation, and (3) to assist in controlling and monitoring resource utilization during the budget period. When managers assign dollar costs to the resources needed, they sometimes realize that proposed tasks aren't worth the cost. Managers can then modify or abandon them.

When budgeting for completely new tasks, managers usually have to estimate dollar costs. Budgeting for established tasks is easier because historical cost data are available. In either case, those who prepare budgets must exercise judgment, whether using historical data or forecasts of changing conditions and costs. Budgets are often developed for a year and then broken down by month. Managers are thus able to track their progress in meeting the budget as the year unfolds—and to take corrective action when necessary.

The control aspect of budgeting may be either corrective or preventive. When budgeting is used as a corrective control, the emphasis is on identifying deviations from the budget. Deviations alert managers to the need to identify and correct their causes or to change the budget itself.

The power of a budget, especially when used as a preventive control, depends on whether managers and employees view it as an informal contract to which they have agreed. One study asked first-line managers about their companies' budgets. The question was "Do you feel that budgets or standards are frequently a club held over the head of the manager to force better performance?" Twenty percent of the 204 respondents replied yes and sixty-eight percent answered no.[25] Most managers who must live by budgets accept their use by top management as a control mechanism. Some managers, however, view budgets with fear and hostility. This usually occurs when an organization enforces budget controls with threats or punishment.

There is no single classification system for budgets. Specific individuals, sections, projects, teams, committees, departments, divisions, or strategic business units may be assigned budgets within which they are expected to operate. The following are the most common types of budgets used in business:

▶ *Sales budget*—a forecast of expected revenues, generally stated by product line on a monthly basis and revised at least annually.

▶ *Materials budget*—expected purchases, generally stated by specific categories, which may vary from month to month because of seasonal variations and inventory levels.

▶ *Labor budget*—expected staffing, generally stated by number of individuals and dollars for each job category.

▶ *Capital budget*—targeted spending for major tangible assets (new or renovated headquarters building, new factory, or major equipment), often requires a time horizon beyond one year.

▶ *Research and development budget*—targeted spending for the refinement or development of products or services, materials, and processes.

▶ *Cash budget*—expected flow of monetary receipts and expenditures (cash flow), generally developed at least once a year for each month of the year.

The types of budgets and budget categories used are strongly influenced by top management's philosophy and the organizational structure. An organization designed by function usually has a budget for each functional department (marketing, production, finance, human resources, and so on). On the other hand, an organization with a product structure usually has a budget for each product line. American Brands has a product structure (Swingline Staples, Jergens Lotion, Sunshine Saltines, Regal China, and others) and uses product-line budgeting.

Although several types of budget processes can be used for planning and control purposes, we'll discuss only one of them here. **Zero-base budgeting (ZBB)** is a method of justifying activities and programs in terms of efficiency and organizational priorities, based on looking at the activities and programs as if they were entirely new.[26] This is different from basing budgets on past experience or costs. The objective of ZBB is to assist managers in allocating or reallocating resources to their most cost-effective uses. Since the U.S. Department of Agriculture (USDA) developed this method in the early 1960s, it has also been used by other government agencies and many firms, such as Texas Instruments, Eastern Airlines, Owens-Illinois, and New York Telephone.

Zero-base budgeting weaves together the planning and control processes. As a planning technique, it helps managers achieve strategic objectives in response to proven needs and perceived threats, risks, or opportunities. As a control technique, it forces managers to examine their functions and operations thoroughly.

Zero-base budgeting is essentially a bottom-up process that includes two major parts. The first is a decision package—a description of what is needed in order to accomplish each major objective. Decision packages generally include the following:

> ▶ Objective to be achieved
> ▶ Description of tasks
> ▶ Alternative ways of achieving the objective
> ▶ Consequences of not performing the tasks
> ▶ Advantages of retaining the tasks
> ▶ Personnel, equipment, space, and other resources required during the current budget year
> ▶ Resources needed for the tasks during the next budget period

The second major part of ZBB involves ranking the decision packages. Managers may use a formal cost-benefit analysis or a subjective evaluation to do the ranking. Sometimes key managers rank on a scale from ''essential'' to ''would be nice to have.''

Zero-base budgeting is consistent with management by objectives. In fact, it serves as a particularly useful tool within the action-planning and objective-setting steps of an MBO system. The departments that can make the best use of ZBB are legal, traffic, public relations, advertising, production control, human resources, credit, and financial management. All of these provide service, advice, control, or information to other departments. Managers of departments such as production or marketing, for which profit-related objectives can be established, may find that other budgeting techniques are better.

Machine Controls

Machine controls are methods that use instruments or devices to prevent and correct deviations from desired results. The use of machines in business has gone through several major stages of development.[27] Machines initially increased productivity by giving workers better physical control over certain tasks. Eventually the interaction of workers and machines created a mutual control system. A new threshold was reached with automation. **Automation** refers to the use of devices and processes that are self-regulating and operate independently of people within a defined range of conditions. Automation usually involves linking machines with other machines to perform tasks.

Machine control of other machines, as with computer-operated robots, for example, co-opts part of the managerial control function. That is, machines can now participate in

---

zero-based budget (ZBB) A method of justifying activities and programs in terms of efficiency and organizational priorities, based on looking at the activities and programs as if they were entirely new.

machine controls Methods of managerial control that use instruments or devices to prevent or correct deviations from desired results.

automation The use of devices and processes that are self-regulating and operate independently of people within a defined range of conditions.

Machine controls at work at Bethlehem Steel's Burns Harbor rolling mill. The new computer-controlled system sets the speed of the strip passing through the mill, adjusts the tension of the rolls, and monitors sequencing.

the control process with managers. For example, computers in oil refineries monitor and make automatic adjustments in the refining processes. These adjustments are based on data collected by the computers during all refining stages. The impact of such automatic machine control on management has been reported in a number of studies. One researcher found that the introduction of an advanced automated system in one large factory reduced the number of middle management jobs by 34 percent.

There has been a steady shift toward machine controls in production operations. This trend is discussed in Chapter 20. The shift began with machines being given control of some production tasks, such as using automatic sensors instead of visual inspection in steel production. With the advent of assembly-line, mass-production technology, machines supplemented rules and regulations as a means of directly controlling production workers. In continuous-process or robotic operations, machines control machines.

Advanced machine control is widespread in the automobile industry. In its brake plant at Saginaw, Michigan, Chevrolet installed an automated system that controls four cranes, records inventory, directs five miles of conveyors, and diagnoses tool problems for the maintenance staff. Chrysler's computer-controlled system in its Syracuse, New York plant expands or contracts a boring tool to adjust for the temperature and tool wear. The system feeds the exact diameters of finished pistons to the machines tooling the cylinder blocks so they can adjust their bits.

ETHICAL ISSUES CONCERNING CONTROL

Some methods of control, particularly those that are aimed directly at the behavior of individuals, pose ethical dilemmas for managers and employees. To illustrate this problem, we'll consider three controversial control methods: computer monitoring, drug testing, and undercover security agents.

computer monitoring The use of special software to collect highly detailed quantitative information on employees' performance for management.

Computer Monitoring

Computer monitoring refers to the use of special software to collect highly detailed quantitative information on employees' performance for management. An estimated 7 million U.S. workers are currently being monitored electronically, often without their knowledge.[28] Employees who work at computer terminals in data-processing service bureaus, insurance companies, airlines, telemarketing firms, and telephone companies are those most often monitored in this way. Information collected by computers may include the number of key strokes, number of customers served, length of time required to serve each customer, minutes away from the computer terminal, number of corrections and changes made, and so on.

This method of control is causing growing concern among unions, civil libertarians, and legislators because it violates employees' right to privacy. The tension associated with computer monitoring is demonstrated in the following Insight. Pacific Southwest Airlines monitors service representatives as part of its system of preventive and corrective control.

INSIGHT

Pacific Southwest Airlines monitors both the telephone and computer use of its service representatives. William Hastings, the firm's director of corporate communications, said, "Our customer complaints have gone down since we've instituted monitoring. Productivity has improved markedly, although we don't use productivity records to discipline employees. We instituted electronic monitoring to take the subjectivity out of supervisory monitoring of workers."

Toni Watson, a reservations clerk at Pacific Southwest Airlines in San Diego, thinks monitoring is counterproductive. "My numbers may have improved since monitoring began, but I'm certainly not a better worker," Watson said. "I get customers on and off as fast as I can. Sometimes I take time with people, especially elderly customers, who are confused by the wacko fare structures. But then I know I have to make up the time with others or accumulate demerits and face discipline."

Mary Williams, a former reservations taker, said, "The monitoring stripped my job of its dignity. One night I got a serviceman whose sister was killed in an auto accident. He had to get to upstate New York, but he kept breaking down in tears. I took 15 minutes with him. My supervisor told me I was costing the airline money."[29]

Drug Testing

President Reagan's 1987 Commission on Organized Crime recommended that all U.S. companies test employees for drug use.[30] The commission was reacting to the increased use of illegal drugs within all segments of American society, the reluctance of employers to report known or suspected drug use by former employees for fear of a lawsuit, and employer liability for negligent hiring. In addition, the Drug-free Workplace Act of 1988 requires all federal government contractors and fund recipients to certify that they will maintain a drug-testing program. The requirements of the act do not, however, include mandatory implementation of a drug-testing program. Instead, the primary focus is on employee awareness and drug rehabilitation.

Earlier in this chapter we briefly described how Motorola is combating its drug problems in its plants. It is estimated that illegal drugs are costing U.S. organizations as much as $100 billion a year. Drug abuse leads to increased absenteeism, shoddy products, workplace accidents, and skyrocketing insurance claims. Health care costs and accident rates are more than 10 percent higher for abusers. According to a recent survey of 1,000 organizations, 48 percent of them test for drugs prior to employment, up from 21 percent just several years ago. This survey found that most of the nation's top 1,000 organizations' drug-testing programs fall into two areas: pre-employment testing and testing of current employees.

Pre-employment Testing Private sector employers may require any job applicant to submit to a drug-screening test, unless limited by state law. Most drug use is tested by examining body fluids, although hair analysis, video-based testing of eye-hand coordination, and pupillary reaction tests have been used. Employers can state a preference to hire only qualified candidates. Since drug use may negatively affect job performance, these organizations can choose to hire only applicants who pass a drug-screening test. IBM, Kodak, and others use a plan with the following elements:

▶ *Notification.* Applicants are notified of the screening on the physical exam questionnaire to minimize claims of invasion of privacy.

▶ *No rescheduling of test.* Candidates are not allowed to postpone the test after appearing at the doctor's office and realizing that drug testing is part of the physical exam.

▶ *Test validity.* In the event of a positive test, the test is repeated using the same sample in order to ensure validity. Samples are usually kept in the doctor's office for 180 days in case of a lawsuit.

▶ *Confidentiality.* Confidentiality is maintained by recording positive test results only on the doctor's records. Only the applicant is made aware of the test results.

Testing Current Employees The testing of current employees raises further issues. Employers who test employees usually follow one of these policies:

1. *Random testing.* All employees tested at random. Those selected are tested at predetermined dates. Trucking companies report that drugs were found in nearly a third of all tractor-trailer drivers involved in accidents. Many trucking companies now perform random drug tests on their drivers.

2. *Testing based on probable cause.* An employee is tested only if his or her behavior causes a reasonable suspicion on the part of supervisors. Signs that abuse is probable include possession of drug paraphernalia, suspicious behavior, and drastic mood or personality shifts.

3. *Testing after an accident.* All employees involved are tested after any accident or major incident on the job.

Some organizations have established elaborate policies and procedures to control drug and alcohol abuse among their current employees. General Dynamics, for instance, spells out its program in a ten page document. It requires managers to give employees, in writing, information on employee assistance programs, the effects of alcohol and drug abuse on co-workers and others, and how General Dynamics will conduct its tests. Capital Cities/ABC, a media conglomerate, also has an extensive program, including educational assistance, employee counseling, the use of various drug tests, drug-sniffing dogs, and undercover operations, if needed.

Undercover Security Agents

Employee theft is the unauthorized taking, control, or transfer of an organization's money and/or property by an employee. It costs organizations more than $40 billion annually in the United States alone.[31] A rule of thumb says that any company loses 1–2 percent of its sales to employee theft. Employee theft includes pilferage (repeated stealing of small amounts), kickbacks, securities theft and fraud, embezzlement (taking assets entrusted to one's care), arson, burglary, vandalism (malicious destruction of assets), shoplifting, insurance fraud, check fraud, and credit card fraud. Although the news media have played up the role of outsiders in computer-related crime, most of it is committed by employees.

The primary reason for the growth of internal security staffs and security firms, such as Pinkerton, Brink's, Burns, and Guardsmark, is management's need to bring the increasing rate of employee theft under control.[32] These security firms provide companies with undercover security agents, often in response to just a feeling that theft is taking place. Companies that sell their trash have used such agents posing as trash collectors because they suspect collusion between employees and trash collectors. Some retail department stores use undercover agents to check that salespeople are ringing up sales and not acting in collusion with ''customers'' in theft. A Pinkerton undercover agent went to work as a production employee at a manufacturing company. The agent discovered that continual inventory shrinkage of 1 percent per year was due to widespread pilfering. Group norms had developed among employees in support of small amounts of stealing at this plant.

entrapment Luring an individual into committing a compromising or illegal act.

Undercover security seems to be tolerated and generally accepted—both legally and socially—as long as there is no hint of entrapment. **Entrapment** is luring an individual into committing a compromising or illegal act.

1. Four basic elements of managerial control are (1) the type of control, (2) the source of control, (3) the pattern of control, and (4) the purpose of control. Preventive controls, such as rules, standards, and training programs, are designed to reduce the number and severity of errors requiring corrective action. In contrast, corrective controls are designed to bring incorrect behaviors in line with established standards. There are four sources of organizational control: stakeholders, the organization itself, groups, and individuals. Patterns of the different kinds of control vary from mutually reinforcing to independently operating to conflicting.

2. The effectiveness of formal organizational controls is measured in terms of costs and benefits. The cost-benefit model highlights the tradeoffs that occur as management increases or decreases control. At some point, increasing controls ceases to be effective. The effectiveness of specific controls is evaluated according to whether they are linked to desired results, objective, complete, timely, and acceptable.

3. The corrective control model consists of six interconnected steps: (1) define the subsystem, (2) identify the characteristics to be measured, (3) set standards, (4) collect information, (5) make comparisons, (6) diagnose and correct any problems.

4. Categories of managerial controls include: (1) bureaucratic, (2) organic, (3) market, (4) financial, and (5) machine. Effective managerial control usually requires using several methods from two or more of these categories.

5. Ethical dilemmas concerning control methods surround the use of computer monitoring, drug testing, and undercover security agents.

1. How are planning and control linked?

2. **From Where You Sit:** Why do so many people resent being controlled?

3. **From Where You Sit:** Visit a local fast-food restaurant. What types of preventive and corrective controls can you identify?

4. What are some control problems of self-managed teams?

5. What are the characteristics of effective control systems?

6. **From Where You Sit:** How would you apply the six steps in the corrective control model to your college career?

7. Using the corrective control model, what suggestions would you make to Joseph Antonini, CEO of Kmart?

8. A *Business Week* editor paid a fee to a credit bureau, got a password, and used his own PC to call up the personal file for Vice President Dan Quayle. The editor found out Quayle's credit card information, the size of his mortgage, and the fact that he shops more at Sears than at Brooks Brothers. Given the ready access to such information, what steps should organizations take to protect the individuals' rights to privacy?

9. Some managers believe that they should control the lives of their subordinates. Others believe that the fewer controls, the better. Evaluate each statement in light of your knowledge of control.

10. **From Where You Sit:** What are signs of drug abuse on your campus? Do you think your college should initiate controls for abuse on campus? What are the ethical problems involved?

Controlling Ethical Behavior

The following questionnaire lists behaviors that you and others might engage in on the job. For each item, circle the number that best indicates the frequency with which you would engage in the behavior. Put an X over the number you think best describes how others you know behave. Finally, put a check mark beside the behavior if you believe that management should design a system to control that behavior.

Behavior	Most of the time	Often	About half the time	Seldom	Never
1. Blaming an innocent person or a computer for errors	5	4	3	2	1
2. Passing on information that was told in confidence	5	4	3	2	1
3. Falsifying time/quality reports	5	4	3	2	1
4. Claiming credit for someone else's work	5	4	3	2	1
5. Padding an expense account by more than 5 percent	5	4	3	2	1
6. Using company supplies (pencils, pens, telephones) for personal use	5	4	3	2	1
7. Accepting favors in exchange for preferential treatment	5	4	3	2	1
8. Giving favors in exchange for preferential treatment	5	4	3	2	1
9. Asking a subordinate or friend to violate company rules	5	4	3	2	1
10. Calling in sick to take a day off	5	4	3	2	1
11. Concealing one's errors	5	4	3	2	1
12. Taking longer than necessary to do a job	5	4	3	2	1
13. Doing personal business on company time	5	4	3	2	1
14. Taking extra personal time (lunch hour, leaving early, doctor's appointments) without checking with supervisor	5	4	3	2	1

15. Seeing a violation of company policy and not reporting it	5	4	3	2	1
16. Overlooking boss's mistakes to prove loyalty to him/her	5	4	3	2	1
17. Asking a secretary to lie about one's whereabouts	5	4	3	2	1
18. Telling co-workers that one is going somewhere but actually going somewhere else	5	4	3	2	1

1. Do your co-workers seem to engage in these behaviors more often than you do?

2. Which behaviors occur most frequently?

3. What are the differences between the most and least frequently occurring behaviors?

4. What are the most important items that should be controlled? Why? What do these reveal about your own preference for control?

5. How should management go about establishing programs for controlling them?

To: Pedro Silva, Vice-President, Operations
From: Carlos Morales, Manager, Corporate Real Estate
Re: Control Systems

As we begin to expand our hotel chain from Venezuela and Aruba to other countries, such as Jamaica and St. Thomas, we need to establish a formal control system for all of our hotels. I propose the following:

<u>Strategic controls</u>. A high occupancy rate (percentage of rooms rented) is critical. Our cost structure indicates that we need to maintain a 72 percent occupancy rate. As you know, large companies such as Merck, Amoco, Bristol-Myers Squibb, and Texaco start looking for convention hotels two years in advance. Therefore, a check of projected occupancy rates two years ahead would clearly spot periods of time in each hotel where low occupancy is likely. The sales and marketing department could then start working with smaller organizations in an attempt to attract them into these slower times.

<u>Tactical controls</u>. These controls, covering six months down to a few weeks, focus on tailoring services and expenses to fit the forecasted occupancy rate. Personnel levels for various departments, such as catering and housekeeping, should be set, and detailed monthly budgets prepared.

<u>Operational controls</u>. Daily control based on short-term results can use all of our financial ratios. Most ratios deal with labor inputs or expenses per guest-day. Maid costs, laundry costs, coffee shop income—all on a guest-day basis—are some examples. We could track these ratios for each month and compare them over time, between hotels in our chain, and possibly with competitors' values.

Question: Assume that you are Silva and have received this memo. From your knowledge of managerial controls, write Morales a memo outlining the positive and negative features of his plan.

Campbell Chef Cooks Up Winning Menu

BY ALIX M. FREEDMAN

David W. Johnson, known for his turnaround of Gerber Products Co., swept into Campbell Soup Co. at the company's most perilous moment. On his arrival last January, part of the controlling Dorrance clan was pushing for the company's sale, fed up with its tepid financial performance.

How to cook up a quick fix? With a back-to-basics recipe that has transformed Campbell from a company that pursued revenue growth no matter what the cost into a down-sized outfit that is run strictly for the bottom line.

In short order, Mr. Johnson has overturned the company's paternalistic culture, pared back new products and squeezed extra pennies out of old trademarks, especially those famed red-and-white soup cans. Now Wall Street is convinced that the perennial laggard is poised to be the food industry's next highflier.

"Campbell is a tremendous turnaround story," says Nomi Ghez, an analyst at Goldman Sachs & Co. She predicts Campbell will grow an average of 25% annually in the next two years, the highest rate for any food concern and almost double the average 14% rate projected for its rivals. . . .

"We're ticking and clicking," boasts Mr. Johnson. "The most important difference in this organization," he adds, "is that I have people focused on delivering excellence in terms of measured results." . . .

For now, Mr. Johnson has concocted a marketing plan that departs sharply from the expansion-minded strategy of his more visionary predecessor, R. Gordon McGovern. Mr. McGovern's smash hits, such as Prego spaghetti sauce and Le Menu frozen dinners, were few. Most brainstorms—from Oriental TV dinners to Star Wars cookies—frittered away management's time and huge sums of money.

Mr. Johnson is bent on wringing as high a return as possible from Campbell's tried-and-true brands: Pepperidge Farm, Swanson, Le Menu, V-8. New-product rollouts, which have been dwindling steadily, are scrutinized for their payback potential. Reflecting the focus on core brands, Campbell will trim last year's $1.2 billion in marketing and advertising costs by 5% this fiscal year.

"This isn't an attempt to reduce marketing efforts," emphasizes Herb Baum, president of Campbell North America. "Our marketing budget as a percent of net sales is among the highest in the industry." . . .

To encourage more accountability at Campbell, its new chief executive has reshaped bonuses. For the first time, at least 20% of management bonuses are tied to company financial performance. To keep managers focused on the competition, Mr. Johnson has set up bulletin boards that display the ranking of 16 food companies based on growth in per-share earnings. Formerly at the bottom, Campbell is now near the top.

Vestiges of the paternalism of Jack Dorrance's era have vanished. Employees are no longer allowed to wander into the company health club during work hours—exercise must be done at lunch or before or after the workday. While Mr. Johnson had to back down from his unpopular effort to prohibit coffee breaks in the cafeteria, employees got the message. Now they don't linger very long.

But Campbell's "top spoon"—Mr. Johnson's immodest moniker for himself—still hasn't tackled a big challenge: how to compete with international giants Nestle S.A. and Philip Morris overseas, without acquisitions that would dilute the Dorrance family's control.

"Campbell is a large company, and it will be much more profitable. But it is difficult to see where the company will generate the size and resources to move out of its present confines," says a spokesman for the Dorrance family dissident group, which holds a 17.4% block of stock.

Mr. Johnson has restored some harmony among the Dorrance kinfolk, and in the past year no serious suitors for Campbell have surfaced. But the profit rebound has, if anything, encouraged the family dissidents' hopes for selling the company. They figure a better performer will bring an even better price. Says the dissident spokesman: "We're in a win-win situation."

1. Using the criteria discussed in this chapter, assess the effectiveness of David Johnson's managerial controls.

2. Consider Johnson's policy changes and attempted changes concerning coffee breaks and use of the company health club. What did the company gain by his actions? What were the tradeoffs?

WHAT HAPPENS WHEN THE CEO COOKS THE BOOKS?

The letter G has broken away from the huge sign above Regina Company in Rahway, New Jersey. A tattered flag hangs over the building where vacuum cleaners used to be made. By early 1990 all the workers were gone. Donald Sheelen took over as president of this company in 1984 and transformed it into a marketing powerhouse. By 1988, he had more than tripled sales and profits. What happened?

Sheelen led Regina to a leveraged buyout from General Signal Corporation in 1984. During the next seventeen months he introduced several new products and took the company public. The Homespa, which used a vacuum motor to blow bubbles in water and create, for less than $100, the effect of a whirlpool, became a major success. He also created the Housekeeper in an attempt to compete in the market for upright vacuum cleaners.

Wall Street investors, eager to find hot growth-potential stocks for their investors, began to notice the company. Several Wall Street brokerage firms, such as Shearson Lehman Hutton Inc., told potential investors that the company's stock could appreciate by 50 percent in a year. Investors liked Sheelen's no-frills approach to business. He often showed up at meetings with rumpled suits and his shirttails untucked. He had a vision of replacing Hoover as the leading maker of vacuum cleaners. At the entrance to his office he placed a Hoover doormat so that his people could walk over Regina's rival. By June 1988 the price of Regina's stock reached a high of $27.50 a share, up from $5.25 in 1985. Sheelen's compensation was well over $570,000.

Trouble was brewing, however. When his secretary tried one of the first Housekeeper vacuums, the handle fell off and the belt slipped off the motor. "There were so many things wrong with it," recalls his secretary, "but he didn't want to hear it. He said, we'll fix it on the next go-round." Sheelen was so anxious to keep the company's image improving on Wall Street that he had skipped proper testing. Products returns swamped the company. More than 40,000 Housekeeper vacuums were returned in three months. This represented about 15 percent of its sales. Desperate, Sheelen ordered Regina's financial officer not to record the returned products. The financial officer objected, but then obeyed by having his staff alter the company's computer systems. The returns, meanwhile, kept piling up. The problem became so severe that the company had to rent another building to store the defective products.

Sheelen also told the financial officer to come up with sales of about $180 million and per-share earnings of $1.20. By recording a sale when Regina received an order, rather than when it shipped the goods, accountants were able to put an extra $6 million worth of sales on the books. By understating expenses for repairing the returned vacuum cleaners, they squeezed an additional $3 million in profits. Sheelen and the financial officer also rigged the company's computer system to generate about 200 fake invoices worth $5.4 million for the final days of 1988. When Sheelen and his secretary met Wall Street analysts, he showed the superiority of a Housekeeper over a Hoover by sprinkling corn flakes on the carpet and vacuuming them up. The impressed analysts didn't know that the Regina model was rigged by engineers to have greater suction and could not be purchased in the stores. These behaviors enabled Sheelen to fool the investors one more time.

Things came to a head during a board of directors meeting in September 1988. Conversations at previous board meetings had focused mainly on product and marketing plans. Sheelen told his board members that he would get them the numbers. After three board meetings without any specific numbers, the members demanded to see the financial statements or they would resign. An outside audit of the books revealed that the company would post substantially lower sales because of a slowdown in orders and excessive product returns. Sheelen assigned most of the blame to computer snafus and a computer virus. The news sent Regina stock from $17 to $7 in one day. A week later, Sheelen made a full confession to the U. S. attorney and pleaded guilty to mail and security fraud. He was sentenced to serve a prison term.

1. Who is at fault here?

2. What types of control should have been used in the company to prevent these abuses?

3. How could the corrective control model have helped outside investors understand the problems at Regina?

4. Do you think that organizations should rely on self-control procedures set by managers. Why?

5. How would you have handled this situation if you were the financial officer of Regina?

Chapter 19

INFORMATION MANAGEMENT

TECHNOLOGIES *

Jerry Junkins

What You Will Learn:

1 The effects of information technology on individuals and organizations.

2 What information technology is and what its capabilities are.

3 The important stages in the development of any computer-based information system.

4 The main factors to be considered in developing an effective information system.

5 How to cope with resistance to technology.

6. Skill Development: How to make information technology a core element of both the control and planning functions.

*This chapter contributed by Lori C. Dowell, Texas A&M University

Chapter Outline

Manager's Viewpoint
Texas Instruments' Networked Information Technologies

The Value of Information
Data and Information
Information as a Resource

Capabilities of Information Technologies
Insight: Rockwell International's Executive Information System
Communication Systems
Global Link: Electronic Integration of World Financial Markets
Decision Support Systems
Expert Systems
Executive Support Systems

Creating an Information System
Determining Information Needs
Identifying System Constraints
Setting Objectives
Design Stages
Insight: Netherlands Gas
Implementing an Effective Information System
Incorrect Assumptions That Undermine System Effectiveness

Coping with Technological Innovation
Insight: Technology Integration at Du Pont
Resistance to Information Technology
Overcoming Resistance

Ethical Dilemmas of Information Technology Use

Experiencing Management
Skill-Building Exercise: Are Microcomputers Productive?

Manager's Memo

In the News

Management Case
Frito-Lay—In the Chips

Texas Instruments' Networked Information Technologies

Nearly 38,000 computer terminals, or one for every two employees, tie Texas Instruments' private telecommunications network together. This network ranks as one of the most sophisticated in the world. Satellites, desktop computers, 1,250 minicomputers, and 40 mainframe computers at twenty sites link activities ranging from ordering parts to designing chips to manufacturing chips to quality control to distribution.

This computer-based information network is the key to Texas Instruments' ability to manage its 77,000 employees in offices and plants in forty countries. It unifies and reinforces the company's team-oriented culture and provides the means for worldwide quality control and coordination. Quality control and coordination are critical to the company in its high-stakes battle with Japanese and European competitors for market share in the semiconductor business.

Communicating the Texas Instruments' approach to a vast array of managers and employees who have different needs, operate in different cultures, and work in different time zones "is a tough part of the management process," says Jerry Junkins, president and CEO. "That is still the biggest problem we have," he adds. Mainframe computers alone handle about 5 million requests daily for information through regional hubs in Singapore, Bedford (England), Dallas, and Miho (Japan). Each overseas request for information is beamed from a company-owned earth station via leased satellite to the company's headquarters in Dallas. The information in turn is beamed back to the hubs and then sent from each hub to sites in each region.

Texas Instruments' most innovative and strategic use of information technology may be its design automation centers. Fifteen advanced software-development and semiconductor-design facilities are located in strategic markets and linked by satellite to large mainframe computers around the world. This network of design centers allows the company to use the same design procedures and tools in all parts of the world. The design network made it possible for Acorn, a British computer company, to make last-minute, highly technical changes in its Acorn Master Series Computer.

Not all TI communications appear on a computer screen. The "blue book" on quality controls for specific customers' products can be found on the desks of TI professionals worldwide. This is one way to communicate the objective of uniformly high quality to all employees of the company. "The real trick (to obtaining quality) is not country by country," said George Graham, a vice president of corporation staff in Dallas who manages quality for TI. "The real issue is how to integrate everything people are trying to do, how we tie it together."[1]

Texas Instruments is only one of many organizations using information technologies at all levels and all locations to network (tie together) a whole organization. And networking based on information technologies is not limited to giant organizations. It is estimated that U.S. companies hooked up 3.8 million personal computers in small office networks in 1990—an increase of 48 percent over 1989. For many organizations, networks have become fundamental to the ability to produce and deliver goods and services—their very nervous systems.[2]

In 1958, in the *Harvard Business Review*, Harold J. Leavitt and Thomas L. Whisler forecasted what organizations of the future would look like. Here are their predictions for the 1980s:

▶ *The role and scope of middle managers will change.* Many of the existing middle management jobs will become more structured and move downward in status and compensation. The number of middle managers will decrease, creating a flatter organization. Those middle management positions that remain will be more technical and specialized. New mid-level positions with titles such as analyst will be created.

▶ *Top management will take on more of the innovating, planning, and creating.* The rate of obsolescence and change will quicken, and top management will have to continually focus on the horizon.

▶ *Large organizations will recentralize.* New information technologies will give top managers more information. This will extend top management's control over the critical decisions of subordinates. Top executives choose to decentralize only because they are unable to keep up with the changing size and complexity of their organizations. Given the chance, however, they will use information technology to take more control and recentralize.[3]

No one can deny the tremendous impact the information technology revolution is having on today's organizations. **Information technologies (ITs)** help individuals or organizations assemble, store, transmit, process, and retrieve data or information. The new generation of managers and employees are naturally more knowledgeable than their counterparts of a few decades ago about the uses and benefits of technological advancements. Managers at Texas Instruments and many other companies view information technology as a strategic asset that they can use to maintain an edge in the fiercely competitive world market. Advancements in telecommunications and networking allow employees to exchange information more freely than ever. Computer systems are also being developed that can think intelligently, learn, and make recommendations to decision makers through applications of artificial intelligence, mainly expert systems.[4]

Leavitt and Whisler's predictions were strongly criticized through the 1960s, 1970s, and early 1980s. But now, in the 1990s, they don't seem so farfetched. In particular, organizations are, indeed, undergoing structural changes because of new information technologies.[5] Information technologies are making it possible to reduce the information "float" in organizations. That is, in the past many decision processes took longer than they needed to because information and decisions had to pass through numerous organizational layers before anything actually happened. Today's information technologies make it possible to eliminate several of those layers. Managers whose main function was to serve as assemblers and relayers of information are no longer needed. Organizations can reduce the number of first-line and middle-level managers. Information technologies streamline many of the communication, coordination, and control functions that first-line and middle managers traditionally performed. These managers have been freed from some routine tasks and can take on more responsibility.

Organizations of the 1990s also require many more specialists. These specialists are concentrated in the first-line ranks and play a critical role in ensuring the successful integration of information systems. For example, at Southern California Edison Company, since a large number of middle management positions have been eliminated, many first-line managers occupy new information specialist positions.[6] The skills of such specialists allow them to deliver the appropriate technology and provide sufficient and relevant knowledge for using the information system in an efficient and effective manner.[7]

These changes in the overall shape of an organization's structure and in the composition of its work force lead to decentralization of operational decisions, but greater centralization of strategic decisions, as was predicted by Leavitt and Whistler in 1958. Decentralization results in delegation of more operational decision-making power and authority to first-line employees. In some ways, organizations of the 1990s will resemble professional firms, such as CPA firms, law firms, and group medical practices. The most successful of such firms attract and retain employees by providing an environment that is intellectually engaging. In these organizations there are few jobs that consist solely of overseeing the work of others. Many employees take on management roles for short periods of time by serving as leader of a team or task force. Employees' jobs change all the time, depending on the project being worked on.

To harness a resource as valuable as information technology, an approach is needed that is organizationwide and as dynamic as the technologies themselves. In this chapter we examine several issues involving the effective use of information technology. First, we briefly discuss the value of information. Next, we look at what information technologies can do. Then we examine the creation of computer-based information systems, including how to determine an organization's information needs and the constraints that affect a system design. Finally, we note how organizations cope with technological information.

THE VALUE OF INFORMATION

Today's organizations store and process vast amounts of data, which managers and other employees must turn into useful information. In turn, this information enables them to perform their jobs better. Although the terms *data* and *information* are often used interchangeably, we make a distinction between them in order to understand the value of information.

chief information officer (CIO) A top-level manager who is responsible for fulfilling an organization's information-processing needs and coordinating all of its information systems.

Effective employees control their information. They are not controlled by it. Too often users' lack of knowledge places them at the mercy of the information system department. To solve this dilemma, some organizations, including J. C. Penney, have created the position of **chief information officer (CIO).** The CIO is usually a top manager who is responsible for fulfilling the organization's information-processing needs and coordinating information systems throughout the organization.

Data and Information

data Raw facts and figures.

Data are raw facts and figures. Every organization is concerned with processing facts and figures about its operations in order to create current, accurate, and reliable information. Many decisions are based on data such as market statistics, operating costs, inventory levels, sales figures, and so forth.

Raw data are much like raw materials. They are not very useful until they are processed. The processing of raw data involves comparison, classification, analysis, and summarization to make the data useable and valuable to employees at all organizational levels. Thus the relationship of data to information is the same as that of raw materials to finished goods or services. **Information** is useful knowledge derived from data.[8]

information Useful knowledge derived from data.

Information as a Resource

Unlike many physical resources, information doesn't lend itself to an easy determination of value.[9] Information has no intrinsic value. Its value is determined by those who use it to make decisions. Employees at different levels and in various functional areas of an organization have different information needs. They want to support the specific types of decisions they are responsible for making. For example, top managers are typically interested in information on overall organizational performance and on competitors' activities. But detailed information on competitors is not likely to be useful to a production team in a plant. These employees want specific information about the availability of raw materials, their productivity, rate of defects, and so on. To a sales manager, information on raw materials has little value. Sales personnel want to know the amount and types of goods and services that can be promised for delivery at various times.

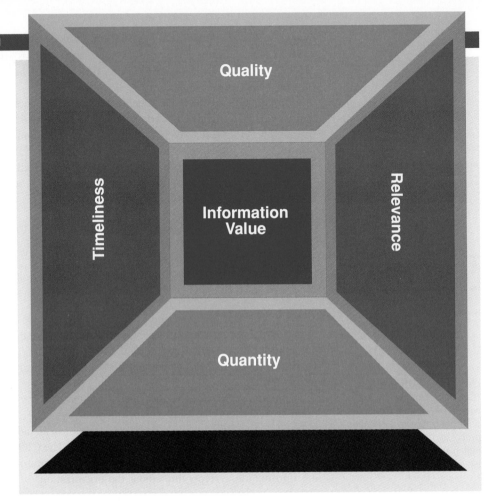

To be considered a resource, then, information must have value.[10] Figure 19.1 shows four common criteria used to assess the value of information: quality, relevance, quantity, and timeliness.

Quality The quality of information is measured by how accurately it portrays reality. The more accurate the information, the higher its quality. The degree of quality required varies according to the needs of those who will use the information. Employees responsible for production inventory control need high-quality information about the precise amounts of raw materials available and resupply schedules. Sales managers concerned with five-year sales forecasts might require lower-quality information, such as general market trends and sales projections. Such long-term forecasting probably isn't based on detailed weekly sales information, for instance.

Relevance The relevance of information depends on the extent to which it directly assists decision making. Too often managers and other employees receive information that is of little or no use and may actually slow the decision-making process by adding confusion. For example, a self-managing production team needs detailed information about inventory levels, delivery dates, and production schedules in order to make good decisions. Such information is relevant to their decision making. These team members don't need information about the organization's global strategy. The relevance of information can differ for the same person at different times. For example, in January, summer sales estimates may not be relevant to Mattel managers trying to project next December's sales. Yet, summer sales figures may be useful the following October when Mattel needs to project next summer's sales before setting production goals.

Frito-Lay salespeople use hand-held computers to print invoices in their trucks and feed sales data immediately to the company's mainframes—thus meeting the *timeliness* criterion for information.

Quantity Quantity refers to the amount of information available to employees when they need it. In the decision-making process more information is not always better.[11] In fact, too much can lead to information overload—a critical problem if the extra information isn't relevant to the decisions being made. Therefore, care must be taken to control the amount of information provided to employees. The provision of information—relevant or not—costs time and money. And information overload can cause job dissatisfaction. For example, Tony Parnigoni was a Midwestern field advertising supervisor for Procter & Gamble. He was on the road most of the time in his seven-state territory. His supervisors and others reached him mostly through an electronic voice-mail system, which he monitored all day. Afraid of missing a message, he also checked it just after waking up and just before falling asleep. At the end of a hectic year, the twenty-seven-year-old Mr. Parnigoni quit. "It's almost like the voice mail was your boss," he said. "It's who you worked for, who you were responsible to."[12] This is only one aspect of the potential dark side of the revolution in information technologies.

Timeliness Timeliness means that managers and employees must receive the information they need to make decisions before that information ceases to be useful. Top managers who make strategic organizational plans often receive production and sales information on a monthly or quarterly basis. First-line production managers, on the other hand, need daily and weekly information concerning production operations to ensure that they meet their objectives. If they received such information only quarterly or even monthly, it would not be timely.

CAPABILITIES OF INFORMATION TECHNOLOGIES

Effective organizations are always looking for ways to improve the way work is done. Information technologies offer a wide range of capabilities through computers, software applications, and telecommunications.[13] Some well-known uses of information technology in manufacturing, which we'll discuss in the next chapter, include computer-aided-design (CAD), factory floor automation, production scheduling and control, and material management information systems. Information technology has deeply penetrated the office and service environments as well. American Express uses a knowledge-based expert system to handle credit authorization decisions, provide customer service, answer general inquiries, process card applications, and provide support for business establishments.[14] The following Insight describes how Rockwell International turned to information technology to help its executives make better and faster decisions.

INSIGHT

Having spent sizable sums of money to automate the grass-roots operations of its companies, executives at Rockwell International began to look for ways to bring automation to "Mahogany Row." A good way to do so is through an executive information system (EIS), such as that adopted at Rockwell's North American Aircraft (NAA) Division in El Segundo, California. One of Rockwell's foremost reasons for adopting the EIS was to better respond to the changing climate in which it does business. As the prime contractor for the Air Force's B-1B bomber, NAA was one of the major aerospace companies being affected by the downturn in defense spending. The division saw business dwindle as the B-1B production program wound down. Consequently, NAA made major changes in its work force structure, its cost management, and even its physical facilities. The demands for relevant information to help executives manage these changes prompted the move to an EIS.

The division's executive council members, for example, found themselves spending several hours each month in a cost performance presentation. As described by Art Goudreault, vice president of materials and one of the early proponents of an EIS, the council would typically wade through pages of detailed cost and budget reports for each unit in the division. A question would surface occasionally, and a council member would be charged with coming up with a solution. Yet for every page that required action, there were numerous pages that did not. Goudreault wanted to know if there was some way to spend less time looking for problems and more time solving them. He approached Nick Corritori, director of the information systems department, and asked for help.

At about this time, a decision was made to move the executives from offices located in a centralized building to facilities located closer to their departments. The division president, John Pierro, faced the problem of how to communicate with vice presidents who were no longer down the hall. Pierro's solution was to equip each executive's office with a personal computer connected to a network with electronic mail capabilities.

Pierro and Goudreault intuitively sensed the value of the EIS and its impact on the division. Pierro saw EIS as a tool that could provide him and the vice presidents with information that would lead to better and faster decision making. The system could also be used as a feedback monitor to gauge how effectively decisions were being implemented. To accomplish these objectives, Pierro established several guidelines to be followed in developing the system. However, the bottom line was fiscal—the system was required to produce benefits that would be reflected in financial statements. The system did produce the objectives set out for it.[15]

As this Insight suggests, information technologies are more than an automating tool. They can fundamentally reshape the way an organization operates. The networking of executives through an EIS allowed Rockwell to move them out of an executive suite and put them in direct, physical contact with the units for which they are responsible. The EIS also provided significant new problem-solving capabilities.

The emerging information technologies that organizations are exploiting to achieve their objectives can be classed in four categories: communication systems, decision support systems, expert systems, and executive support systems.[16]

Communication Systems

There is a tremendous need to transmit all types of information within and between organizations. Communication systems enhance an organization's ability to be in immediate touch with all of its parts, as well as important suppliers, customers, and other external groups. **Communication systems** include teleconferencing, facsimile, local and wide area networks, electronic mail, and integrated systems. Texas Instruments and IBM, among others, make use of all of these.

Teleconferencing allows meetings to be conducted between participants in one room and those in another room via video transmission systems and television screens. **Facsimile (fax) machines** scan a sheet of paper electronically and convert the light and dark areas to electrical signals, which are transmitted over telephone lines. At the other end, a similar machine reverses the process and reproduces the original image. **Networking** is the process by which computers communicate with one another. **Local area networks (LANs)** refer to computers that are linked within a limited geographical area. **Wide area networks** refer to the linkage of computers separated by great distances. As discussed in Chapter 15, **electronic mail (E-mail)** allows users to transmit textual messages through their networked terminals or personal computers.

Integrated systems are various information systems networked in order to achieve closer links among design, production, and service activities in an organization, as well as direct information exchanges with customers and suppliers.[17] With integrated systems it's possible to have effective horizontal coordination, not only within organizations, but across them. For example, Magicorp, a small company that might be described as a service integrator, runs a slide-making shop and relies on other companies for the rest of its operations. People who use graphics software on their personal computers send data by phone to Magicorp's office in Wilmington, Ohio. Why Wilmington? Because Airborne Express has its hub there, making fast turnaround quite feasible. There's another element of networking here. Rather than do its own marketing, Magicorp relies on graphics software vendors to promote its services, for which it pays them a royalty.[18]

Integrated communication systems can link parts of an organization that are geographically dispersed, as demonstrated in the Manager's Viewpoint feature on Texas

Digital Equipment Corporation recently equipped the LEGO Group with a completely *integrated system*. Digital's production systems let them centralize operations and distribute information throughout the organization.

"Digital helps the LEGO Group fit all the pieces of our business together."

Instruments, or link an organization with suppliers, as illustrated by Magicorp. But information technologies are also the driving force behind the increasing globalization of world financial markets. Instantaneous electronic linkages are being created to join customers, financial institutions, and governments that regulate financial markets. A glimpse of these profound developments is provided in this chapter's Global Link.

Decision Support Systems

decision support system (DSS) A complex set of computer programs and equipment that allows users to analyze, manipulate, format, display, and output data in different ways.

Simply stated, a **decision support system (DSS)** is a complex set of computer programs and equipment that allows end users—usually managers and professionals—to analyze, manipulate, format, display, and output data in different ways. Such a system aids decision making because the user can pull together data from different sources and view them in ways that may differ from the original formats. The system makes it possible for the data to be printed out or to be presented in the form of charts or graphs.[19]

A DSS allows users to evaluate many alternatives quickly. Actually many of you may be familiar with DSS and not even know it. Have you used an electronic spreadsheet such as Lotus 1-2-3, Multiplan, Javelin, EXCEL, or QUATTRO? If so, you have used one form of DSS software. These electronic spreadsheets will automatically recalculate a formula when you change the value of one of the variables.

One popular software package that aids users' decision making is Interactive Financial Planning System (IFPS) developed by EXECUCOM Systems Corporation in Austin, Texas. IFPS is a powerful financial planning aid that allows users with no programming experience to develop sophisticated financial models. Once a model has been developed, IFPS lets users ask what-if questions about performance. Many organizations, including National Products, Capex, and Louisiana National Bank, use IFPS to develop financial planning models in order to monitor and control their financial resources.

Expert Systems

expert system (ES) A computer-based system that is designed to function like a human expert in solving problems within a specific area of knowledge.

An **expert system (ES)** is a computer-based system that acts in a manner similar to a human expert. These systems have problem-solving capabilities within a specific area of knowledge. Expert systems differ from decision support systems in that they actually make the decision. If requested, the system can explain its path of reasoning to the user. The expert system is an application of artificial intelligence, the ability of computers to simulate the thought processes of human beings.[20] (See Chapter 7 for a discussion of artificial intelligence and expert systems.)

Expert systems vary in terms of the complexity of both knowledge and technology. The simplest type of system has low levels of complexity in both of these areas. An example is a personal budgeting system running on a PC. The key thrust of such low-level

Damaged parts can be replaced within hours by the John Deere Parts Distribution Center's *telecommunication* computer.

GLOBAL Link

ELECTRONIC INTEGRATION OF WORLD FINANCIAL MARKETS

The same force that is causing the breakdown of localized banking and finance within the United States—technology that is cost-effective, instantaneous, and geographically unlimited—is also causing the breakdown of nation-specific banking and finance. World markets may not yet be fully integrated and some countries may still continue to shelter their financial institutions, but it is clear that this is a transient state.

As this historical process unfolds, various accommodative measures must be taken. For example, the laws and conventions surrounding finance must become increasingly homogeneous throughout the world. It will become more and more difficult for a single country, even one as large as the United States, to restrict the lines of commerce in which financial institutions may engage. It will also become more and more difficult for countries not to grant foreign-based multinational financial institutions a regulatory framework identical to that governing domestic financial institutions. It will become increasingly difficult to maintain marked dissimilarities in tax laws. In addition, it will become increasingly difficult to control the movements of populations, particularly of those people whose skills are not country-specific (such as people engaged in finance). In short, the world of finance is destined to become a true world market, perhaps uniquely so.

Electronic finance is influencing world financial affairs in two ways. There is, first, the matter of regulation. It is becoming increasingly clear that as the foreign branches of international banks come into contact with one another, certain common rules of the road must be devised. One example of this is in the area of the capital adequacy of commercial banks. In the past, each nation imposed its own capital-to-asset ratio and its own definition of capital. The 1987 Basel Agreement among the world's major central banks—which will eventually internationalize bank capital regulations—is in the process of changing this.

Monetary policy, the other area in which electronic integration is important, will develop along supranational lines. The need for a coordinated approach to macroeconomic policy among the major capitalist countries of the world is so much in the news these days that it is almost trite to mention it. Things are rapidly getting to the point where defining even a domestic money supply is impossible. With fully integrated world financial markets and complete convertibility of all the major currencies, the notion of domestic monetary policy is becoming less important. What is ultimately needed is a world monetary policy. Indeed, it is virtually impossible to conceive of a domestic monetary policy in a world dominated by electronic finance.

Adapted from D. G. Luckett, "On the Computerization of Finance," *Business Horizons*, November–December 1989, 42–46.

expert systems is to improve personal decision making and thereby increase productivity. In contrast, strategic impact expert systems involve high levels of knowledge and technological complexity. Lincoln National's Life Underwriting System is an example. The process of underwriting an individual's life insurance application requires complex medical, financial, and insurance knowledge. Lincoln National also requires that an applicant's hobbies (such as mountain climbing) and vocation (possibly requiring frequent international flying) be factored into policy evaluation and pricing. In many of these areas the information that an underwriter receives needs to be clarified and interpreted. Lincoln National's four best senior underwriters spent a good portion of their time for several years as consulting experts in the development of this expert system.[21]

Executive Support Systems

executive support system (ESS) Any information technology that integrates managers and other professionals into an organization's information flow.

Executive support systems (ESS) include electronic messaging systems, executive presentation systems, management information systems, and group decision support systems. They use technology to integrate selected managers and other professionals—not just top executives—into an organization's information flow. Users of electronic messaging systems may send messages over the phone that can be stored, annotated with comments, and distributed to many different people. Executive presentation systems utilize computer graphics to enhance presentation skills. This text's illustrations exemplify the types of graphics that a fairly sophisticated executive presentation system can produce. **Management information systems** provide managers with up-to-date financial, market, human resource, or other information about the status of the organization, its major departments or divisions, and its environment.

management information system A type of executive support system that provides managers with up-to-date financial, market, human resource, or other information about the status of the organization, its parts, or its environment.

Finally, a **group decision support system (GDSS)** is a set of software, hardware, and language components that support a team of people engaged in a decision-related meeting.[22] A GDSS aims to improve the process of group decision making by removing common communication barriers, providing techniques for structuring decision analysis, and systematically directing the pattern, timing, or content of discussion. Facilitators play a crucial role in the use of GDSS. They allow the participants to concentrate on the issues at hand rather than struggling to use the technology themselves. Computer literacy and familiarity with a keyboard are seldom found in most of today's senior executives, and this must be taken into account. Requiring the executive to use a computer may well jeopardize the decision outcome, as slow data manipulation and increasing frustration will result in disinterest and lack of support. Even computer-literate users need time to become familiar with the system. A typical GDSS room could include a series of terminals or workstations linked together through some form of networking, a large main screen visible to all and controlled by the facilitator, a photocopying whiteboard to record the options as they emerge, and a three-color video projector or large monitor.[23]

group decision support system (GDSS) A set of software, hardware, and language components that support a team of people engaged in a decision-related meeting.

CREATING AN INFORMATION SYSTEM

The implementation of new information technologies requires careful thought and planning if they are to provide the value the organization anticipates and desires. The most important decision concerning the adopting of any form of information technology is determining what information is actually needed. Far too often organizations develop information systems without any real understanding of the true need or the costs involved. An organization wouldn't undertake construction of a new manufacturing plant unless it were absolutely essential. Information technology development should be approached in the same way.

Many organizations have a strategic plan, either by design or by default. Organizations should make sure that any proposed information system will be in sync with their

J. C. Penney stores' *information needs* have inspired direct satellite broadcasts of different clothing lines to stores, thus cutting down buyers' travel time.

knowledge workers
Employees whose jobs involve the creation, processing, and/or distribution of information.

overall mission and strategy. The objectives for an information system should make sense in terms of organizational plans, financial and technical resources, market, customers, competition, and return on investment. Questions that need to be asked include these: Is the organization planning to change or add to its customer base or its goods and services? What are the current financial constraints? Do competitors use such technology? Another factor that must be considered is the information system's acceptance by knowledge workers. **Knowledge workers** are employees whose jobs involve the creation, processing, and/or distribution of information. They are the ones most interested in the information system. Knowledge workers include clerical and service staff, supervisors, middle management and professional staff, and executives. The information system should support the operational, managerial, and decision-making information needs of knowledge workers according to the objectives and strategies of the organization.[24]

Determining Information Needs

The first step in designing an information system is determining the organization's current information needs.[25] This means thoroughly auditing the types and amounts of information employees currently use in performing their jobs. Management information has implications for managerial decisions and actions. Figure 19.2 illustrates the evolution from raw data through management information to decisions. Note that knowledge of the environment progresses from disorganized data to successively more refined and sharply focused information.

Information needs generally vary by department and individual employee. Information needs also vary according to the type of decision to be made. Decisional activities occur at three levels: strategic, tactical and operational.[26] Characteristics of information

FIGURE 19.2

From Data to Decisions and Actions

The number of raw facts and figures that can be collected from the environment and within the organization are endless. The challenge is to collect the appropriate data and analyze it properly to obtain useful information. Managers and other employees use information to help make decisions and take action.

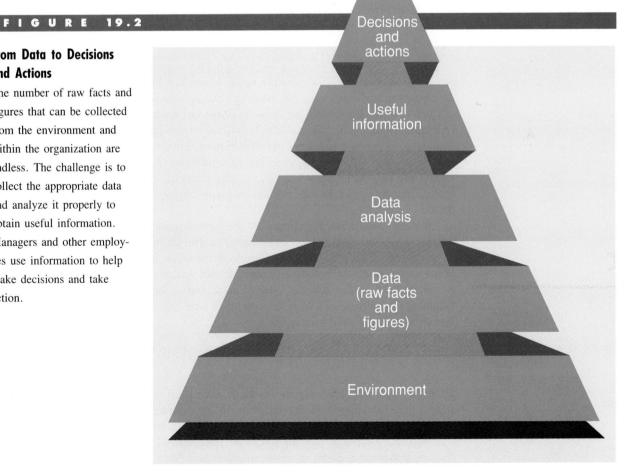

Decisions and actions

Useful information

Data analysis

Data (raw facts and figures)

Environment

Information Requirements by Decision Type

Information Characteristic	Requirement		
	At Operational Level	At Tactical Level	At Strategic Level
Source	Internal ←————————————→ External		
Scope	Narrow, well-defined ←————————→ Broad		
Aggregation level	Detailed ←————————————→ Composite		
Time horizon	Historical ←————————————→ Future-oriented		
Currency	Recent ←————————————→ Long-term		
Frequency of use	Daily, continuous ←————————→ Periodic, infrequent		
Type	Quantitative ←————————————→ Qualitative		

Source: Adapted from G. A. Gorry and M. S. Scott Morton, "A Framework for Management Information Systems," *Sloan Management Review,* Fall 1971, p. 59.

used by knowledge workers at these levels are summarized in Table 19.1. These characteristics are source, scope, aggregation level, time horizon, currency, accuracy, frequency of use, and type.[27]

As indicated in Table 19.1, strategic decisions often require information from external sources, such as financial analysts and competitors. The information must be broad in scope, composite (highly aggregated), future-oriented, and qualitative. In contrast, information needs for operational decisions are substantially different. Operational decisions require a lot of internal information (such as inventory levels) that is well-defined, detailed, reported daily or weekly, precise, and quantitative. Tactical decisions, which are of most concern to middle managers and professionals, represent the middle ground between strategic and operational decisions.

Identifying System Constraints

After the organization's information needs have been identified, the users and system developers must consider the constraints on the existing system. Constraints, mentioned in Chapter 6, are limitations that cause choices to be made. Constraints may be internally or externally imposed. External constraints vary from organization to organization and include government regulations, supplier requirements, technological progress, and customer demands. For example, government regulations require automobile manufacturers to produce cars with safety features such as seatbelts, with exhaust systems that emit limited amounts of certain chemicals, and with engines that meet fuel efficiency standards.

Internal constraints are created by the organization itself. They also vary among organizations and even among departments within an organization. Probably the most common internal constraint on the development of an information system is the cost. Management wants the best system possible, but, unfortunately, information technology is usually very costly. Another internal constraint is lack of support from employees, including top managment. Without support, or with only limited support, an information system is unlikely to be successful.

Setting Objectives

Once the organization's information needs have been established and the system constraints have been identified, the objectives for the information system should be set. They should focus on the purposes the information will serve, who it will be used by, and how it will be used. One objective for Rockwell International's EIS was that it had to have features that made it useful as an investigative tool, that is, for answering what-if ques-

FIGURE 19.3

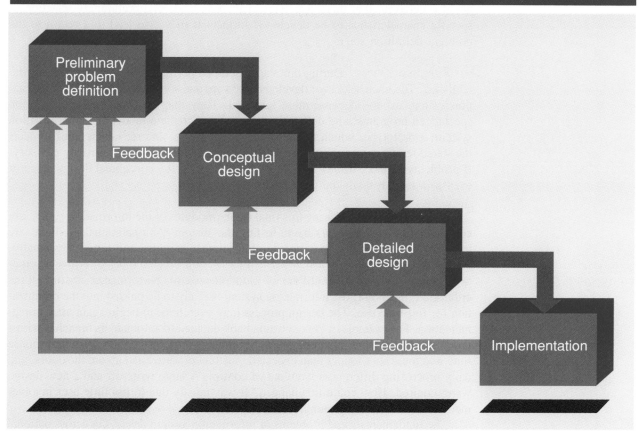

Four Stages of Information Systems Development

The four stages of information systems development form anything but a step-by-step linear progression. Note the many feedback loops between stages, including the need to redefine the problem as a result of unexpected difficulties in implementation.

tions, such as "What would happen if the company relied on more overtime to meet an increase in demand rather than adding more employees?"[28] Management should also establish detailed objectives for the system's cost and operating personnel. Setting objectives establishes the direction for developing and implementing the information system.

Design Stages

Although there are many ways to create an information system, the basic underlying design process is generally the same. Figure 19.3 shows the four stages in the design of information systems.[29] Various feedback loops show that the process is never cut and dried. In the following sections we explain what each stage involves.

Preliminary Problem Definition A task force of information users may be given the job of determining in detail the information needs, the constraints limiting the system, and the objectives.

Conceptual Design This stage should also be primarily user-led, although system development experts can act as resources. During this stage, information generated in the preliminary problem definition stage is used to develop alternative designs that meet the organization's criteria. These alternatives are evaluated in terms of how well they satisfy organizational needs and objectives. More accurate cost constraints are also determined at this stage. This evaluation leads to a preliminary selection of specific characteristics to be developed further. It may also lead to a return to the problem definition stage.

Detailed Design During this stage, detailed performance specifications are established. The team selects or develops hardware and software components. Information system experts become more involved: They map information flow, develop specialized programs, and define databases. They create a model of the information system, a prototype, which they evaluate, test, refine, and reevaluate until it meets the stated requirements. Users are still involved, but their role is primarily advisory. If problems surface, it may be necessary to return to the conceptual design stage or even to a reanalysis of the problem definition.

Implementation During this final stage, modules of the information system are connected and tested. Users begin testing the system. As operational problems are identified and corrected, one module after another is added and tested. Eventually, the entire system is assembled and tested for all conceivable types of errors. Corrections continue to be made until the information system's performance satisfies all the criteria. At this point, the information system is ready to be phased into the organization for full-time use. The design process may even have to begin again after implementation. For example, a Pennsylvania bank decided to automate its branches with a new automatic teller computer system. Six months after installation, system response time was four times longer than expected, customers were lined up out the doors, and daily processing differences were out of control. A large write-off and a new design were required. How could this happen? It was mostly due to too little user involvement from the very beginning.[30]

The fundamentals and problems of information system design cut across national boundaries. The following Insight presents a classic example of an effectively designed information system.

*I*NSIGHT

Netherlands Gas is involved in the purchase, conditioning, selling, and transporting of natural gas. Netherlands Gas supplies over half of the energy requirements of the Netherlands.

A great deal of the provision of information, especially gas transmission data and marketing data, has been automated over the years. Virtually all the main processes are supported by one or more automated information systems. The growing degree of automation created a diversity of hardware and software. This led to problems of compatibility and integration. Therefore, it was decided to prepare a plan before proceeding with the development of any new systems. A methodology of new system development was based on two premises: (1) the information system must support the strategic objectives of Netherlands Gas, and (2) information must be treated as one of the assets of the business. The methodology provides for a phased approach involving an analysis of corporate objectives, business processes, and information requirements followed by bottom-up implementation of the information system.

The objectives of the organization were established. Based on these objectives, critical success factors (CSFs) for information systems were determined. CSFs make it possible to determine the degree to which an information system is contributing to the achievement of corporate objectives. The business processes and information requirements were determined by means of interviews with first-line managers and other users. The existing information systems were also studied and evaluated. In addition, the organizational structure was examined. The aim was to determine which new information systems could be developed and put into operation. Design of the information systems then began, which led to developing plans for their implementation. The Netherlands Gas planning team was able to look back on a successful project. It was completed on time and kept within budget.[31]

Implementing an Effective Information System

Some organizations are more effective than others at implementing information technologies. Some organizations receive few benefits from their systems and incur high development and maintenance costs. Why? Here are some of the most common reasons why information systems may not be implemented successfully:

▶ *Inadequate project definition*—the inability to clearly define the expected results desired by the user

▶ *Lack of general information*—the tendency to gradually reduce the quality and quantity of information processed

▶ *Poor scheduling and allocating of resources*—ineffective selection and training of human resources, determination of work, and estimation of activity durations

▶ *Loss of control*—inability to locate, analyze and resolve potential problems before they occur.[32]

Although each information system has unique characteristics, seven factors commonly affect the implementation of effective systems. These are shown in Figure 19.4. They emerge during the initial stages of system development and continue to be important in everyday operations.

User Involvement   As noted earlier, information system users must be heavily involved in the design process. Their input gives system designers an accurate picture of current work flow within and between departments, costs, and the time it takes to perform various functions. This input may help in the identification of operational inefficiencies. Users typically know how information affects decision making, and designers often don't. For example, employees in an accounting department understand the flow of financial information and how financial reports are prepared and distributed. By working with the accounting staff, systems experts can tailor the system to these users' needs. The resulting system is more likely to be effective.

User participation during the implementation stage is critical. Users often spot problems or deficiencies in the new system. Taking part in implementation also helps users understand the reasons for the new system and prepares them for the ultimate change in job tasks.

Support of Top Management   A key factor in the implementation of effective information systems is strong, visible commitment and support from top management. Like any major organizational undertaking, information technology applications must have involvement from top managers in order to succeed. Without their support information technology is less likely to be integrated into the organization. This is why strategic information systems planning is so important. Strategic planning can help foster a positive attitude toward system development from the beginning. For example, at Phillips 66, price information from 240 motor fuel terminals, formerly available on various bits of paper, now appears on the computer screens of executives at headquarters in Bartlesville, Oklahoma. They monitor trends but let local managers set prices.[33]

FIGURE 19.4

Factors Determining the Effectiveness of Information Systems

Seven factors are vital to the effective implementation of an information system, as shown in this figure. Of the seven factors, the involvement by users through all of the stages is probably the single most important.

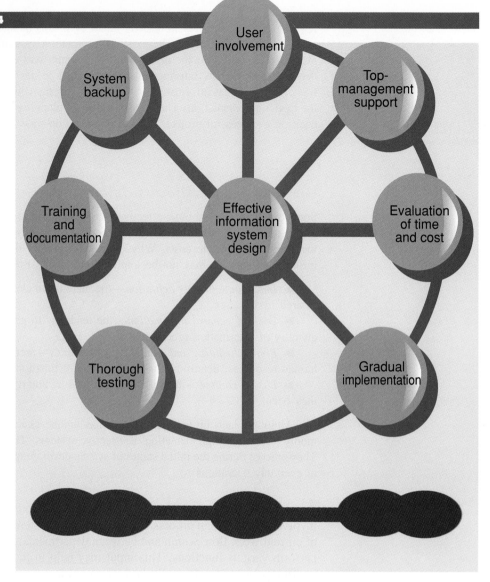

Evaluation of Time and Cost A third factor involved in implementing an effective information system is a thorough evaluation of the time and cost requirements. The design and implementation stages are often more extensive and costly than anticipated. During the initial development stages, it is difficult to predict time and cost requirements accurately. However, management should have some idea of the cost of not improving the organization's information system.

To keep the development process on schedule and within budget, systems designers must project time and costs in detail. The projected schedule should include project benchmarks and perhaps even a PERT network (see Chapter 9). This type of activity is carried out for any major construction project, such as a building, highway, or custom house. Justification of the design, installation, and projected maintenance costs helps prevent cost overruns and guides decisions.

Gradual Implementation Any major new technology should be introduced in phases. The new information system should not be turned on one day and the old system abandoned at the same time. Too many things can and will go wrong: The new system doesn't work as expected, it generates bad information, no one knows how to use it, and so on. By implementing the system gradually, problems due to design

The *Los Angeles Times* gradually *implemented* the use of Goss Colorliner presses beginning in 1989.

glitches and unforeseen events can be managed. Software problems can be resolved before employees become too dependent on the system. Technical support staff can train users to work with the new system before their jobs depend on it. Gradual implementation also give employees time to adjust, thus minimizing resistance to change.

As recently as 1984, students registered for classes at Texas A&M University by picking up computer cards for each class. Because they had to go to so many different locations around campus and wait in lines, the registration process took at least a full day. Then a new registration system was slowly phased in. At first data entry personnel entered only late registrations on terminals linked to the main computer. By 1986 the entire registration process was handled by the information system. Students now register by contacting the main computer directly. They enter class and fee information from a push-button telephone and can respond to a computer-triggered voice. The transition from computer cards to telephone registration could have created many problems and much confusion if the system had been implemented all at once.

Thorough Testing Another factor that affects the development of an effective information system is thorough testing for software and hardware problems. Testing should be performed on individual modules, on sets of modules as the system is assembled, and then on the entire system once it is operational. The testing process should anticipate probable errors, as well as actions that are unlikely to occur. The effects of incorrect commands, improper data, poor environmental conditions, and other possible problems should all be checked. The biggest problems with a new technology arise from events that are not expected to occur or could not occur—but do.

Training and Documentation The introduction of any new technology requires training of users and adequate documentation of operational procedures. An information system is of little value if no one knows how to use it properly. Too often those in charge of the information system gain power because everyone in the organization is overly dependent on them. As a result, a power struggle may develop between managers and other employees who formerly controlled the flow of information and the system development staff. Organizations can avoid this sort of interdepartmental conflict by fostering cooperation. Users don't have to know how to program computers, but they should understand the capabilities and limitations of their information system. And, systems development personnel must understand the capabilities and information needs of the users.

System Backup The last factor influencing the implementation of an information system is the presence of alternative systems for accomplishing the same tasks in case of system failure. Computer systems are notorious for developing problems at the "wrong times." If users are too dependent on an information system, they may believe the quicker the fix, the better. Quick alterations to the system, however, may overlook real problems that may lead to other problems. A backup procedure—or even access to a backup computer system—will give the organization time to track down such problems, carefully evaluate them, and correct them properly. This approach doesn't ensure a problem-free future, but it does encourage solutions that are less likely to create additional problems.

Several years ago, all communications in and out of United Airlines ticketing offices in the Seattle, Washington area went dead. Business stopped and the switchboards lit up with angry callers. Several hours later, the telephone company informed United Airlines management what had happened. The telephone company had hired a firm near Seattle to put up a sign warning people to be extra careful when digging near a certain spot because a telephone cable lay close to the surface. The subcontractor accidentally had rammed the warning sign's post through the very cable it was supposed to protect. That cable was the only one in the area that could handle United's computer reservation traffic. Soon after, the airline installed a backup network based on satellite technology.[34]

Even if all seven of these factors are addressed during the development and implementation stages, there is no guarantee that an information system will be effective. Some tasks simply don't lend themselves to computerization. Sears, Wal-Mart, Kroger, and others have improved inventory control with computerized point-of-sale cash registers. However, these information systems haven't been able to substitute for sales personnel in dealing with customers' questions and problems. Some tasks cannot be adapted to even the most carefully designed information system. A system's chances of success are greatly enhanced though if the seven key factors have been thoroughly considered.

Incorrect Assumptions That Undermine System Effectiveness

Why are newly developed information systems sometimes almost unused in organizations? Five common but incorrect assumptions often underlie the design of such systems.[35] Acting on one or more of these incorrect assumptions is enough to make an information system ineffective and too expensive. Let's take a look at each of them.

Users Aren't Receiving the Data and Information They Need It's a mistake to assume that users aren't getting the data and information they need. Although users often don't receive all of the data and information required to make the best decisions, in many cases the problem is one of too much data rather than the wrong information. Excessive or irrelevant data is troublesome because it detracts from solving the problem at hand.

Users Will Request Only the Data and Information They Need A second mistake is assuming that users need all of the data and information they request. System designers may assume that users know what and how much data and information they need in order to do their jobs. Unfortunately, this assumption ignores the fact that some users receive far more data and information than necessary. They may simply maintain that volume of incoming data and information as an indicator of their political importance in the organization. Other users may not be able to evaluate how much or what data and information they need.

More Data and Information Lead to Better Decisions Another mistake is to assume that providing users with more data and information automatically results in better decisions. This simply isn't true. Other factors affect the quality of decision making. For example, users can handle only a limited amount of data and information, no matter how accurate or relevant it is. The user facing an unusual and unfamiliar situation may actually become confused by the large amounts of available data and information. Organizational politics can also prevent users from making good decisions. The decision to launch the ill-fated space shuttle Challenger was apparently affected by political considerations. Despite available data and information on the potential hazards of launching under existing conditions, NASA decided to proceed.

Improving Data and Information Flow Improves Performance The fourth mistake is assuming that improving data and information flow among departments automatically leads to greater coordination of decision making and improved performance. The opposite is likely when departments are competing and have negative attitudes toward one another. Under this condition, each department may use the available data and information to make itself look better at the expense of other departments.

Users Don't Have to Understand the Information System to Use It The final mistake is assuming that users don't need to understand how an information system works in order to use it. In fact, users should be able to evaluate the sources of data and information in order to determine quality and relevance. In addition, users who don't understand how an information system works are less likely to trust the data and information it produces.

COPING WITH TECHNOLOGICAL INNOVATION

People are the key to any effective technological innovation. New technologies cannot fulfill their promises of increased productivity and reduced operating costs if employees are not able or willing to adapt to their new work conditions.[36] Even the best designed information system will be ineffective if users overtly or covertly resist it. On the other hand, enthusiastic support, particularly from top management, can greatly enhance a system's development and use. The following Insight reveals Du Pont's view of technology integration.

TECHNOLOGY INTEGRATION AT DU PONT

I N S I G H T Ed Mahler, Du Pont's future computer technology visionary, says that technology integration is 10 percent a technology problem and 90 percent a people problem. Mahler has been very successful in integrating knowledge systems (expert systems) technology into ongoing operations at Du Pont. He analyzed the operations and people and developed an approach to integration that met their needs. Du Pont has reported a 1200 percent return on investment in utilizing knowledge systems technology.

Mahler elaborates on his view of system integration:

People perceive personal threats in new technology, including the loss of status, a struggle to learn the new, a change in job content, and loss of employment. This perception of a negative work environment can be a powerful impediment to progress. Business leaders are increasingly looking to information systems as an "agent of change." But, in order for information systems to be effective as a "change agent," we must modify—and in some cases create—an entirely new internal culture. We must understand employee perceptions, understand our work force, stress a clear set of values and provide a positive work climate.

It is up to us to ensure that our employees perceive their work environment positively. That climate is created through providing clear direction, rewarding risk-taking, championing technology integration, encouraging informal innovation efforts, and rewarding results. Technology is not an end in itself, merely a means to an end—solving business/industry problems.[37]

Resistance to Information Technology

Like any major organizational change, the implementation of information technology may meet with resistance. In Chapter 21 we'll detail some ways that resistance to change can be reduced or overcome. In this section we highlight how this resistance is manifested when new information technologies are introduced. The resistance of some employees to automated information systems resembles the feelings of workers facing industrialization in earlier times. Some employees in both eras have feared that they would be replaced by mechanical counterparts.

Two basic factors can trigger opposition to new information technologies. First, people in general do not like to be in highly uncertain situations. Employees, including managers, may feel helpless, powerless, and out of control when they see their workplace changing rapidly as new technologies are introduced. Second, employees may have fears of displacement and feelings of incompetence regarding new technologies. They may think that the computer will replace their decision-making responsibilities and thus reduce the security of their position within the organization. Three types of resistance to information technology are especially common: avoidance, projection, and aggression.[38] Another reaction that frequently occurs involves feelings of stress and anxiety.

avoidance Withdrawal from a frustrating or uncomfortable situation.

Avoidance **Avoidance** is withdrawal from a frustrating or uncomfortable situation. This type of resistance to an information system is particularly damaging when exhibited by top management. Top managers unwilling to use the information generated by the new information system send a clear signal of its unimportance. Avoidance is often a symptom of computer anxiety. This fear of, or discomfort with, computer-based technology is disappearing as computers become a part of everyday life.

projection A psychological mechanism used to place blame for problems on someone or something else.

Projection **Projection** is a psychological mechanism used to place blame for problems on someone or something else. For example, saying "it was a computer error" is a common way of projecting responsibility for a human error onto the information system. This method of resistance is most often exhibited by operating and clerical personnel.

Aggression Aggression involves striking back at the person or object that appears to be the cause of a frustrating situation. Aggression against computer-based information technologies takes many forms: entering incomplete or inadequate data, abusing the equipment, introducing a software virus, or outright sabotage. An employee may also withhold information from a systems analyst about how the process really works.

Anxiety and Stress Implementation of a new system may cause considerable stress and anxiety because the system takes over certain information-processing functions of some jobs. First-line managers may be the most affected. They have little control over the information that top management receives. Moreover, middle managers can use information generated by an information system to evaluate the job performance of first-line managers. Of course, information technologies may also affect top and middle levels of management by making job performance deficiencies more evident.

Information technologies may cause subtle changes in employees' interpersonal relations. In addition to altering the way the organization formally collects and dis-

Mead has mastered *overcoming resistance* to change by involving veteran papermakers in the implementation of advanced electronic control systems in the company's mills.

seminates information, new information technologies may change informal information flows. Departments may be reorganized, disrupting traditional patterns of behavior and communication. Managers don't receive the same information they received in the past. Other employees have less control over the information they receive. These changes may cause significant stress and anxiety if management doesn't recognize and plan for them.[39]

Three key underlying factors can trigger reactions of stress and anxiety.[40] First, employees may feel they are less needed and less competent, even though the system is a success. This disparity results in mental confusion. Second, information generated by a computer-based system is usually much more explicit and less easily adapted for political purposes. Thus the systematic procedures of the information system may reduce the political power of some individuals and departments. Finally, the role of the employee may shift from one based on personal political power to one based on explicit information and technical competence.

Overcoming Resistance

There are no simple guidelines for eliminating problems caused by employee and managerial resistance to information technologies. These situations and problems must be handled on an individual basis. However, top management support and continual user involvement can forestall much potential or actual resistance. The following paragraphs highlight some general guidelines for neutralizing resistance to technological innovation.[41]

User Participation As stated repeatedly in this chapter, the people who will use the information system should be involved in its design and implementation. This helps reduce employees' anxiety and stress. And people who contribute to defining how their jobs will change may gain confidence in the new technology.[42]

User Orientation Everyone affected by the information technology should receive a thorough orientation in its design and operation. By conveying this information to those who use the system daily, managers can detect early signs of resistance. In addition, employees who understand how the information technology can help them perform their jobs generally adjust to it more readily.

Phased Introduction Introducing the new technology gradually, in phases, gives employees time to adjust. This helps to reduce resistance. It also allows time for handling employee displacement and retraining.

Revised Performance Guidelines Information technologies often substantially redefine jobs. New ways of measuring job performance that take into account the new ways of doing tasks may need to be developed. The revised standards must be explained clearly so that managers and other employees will know how their performance is going to be evaluated. New incentive plans and reward systems that are consistent with the changes must also be developed.

ETHICAL DILEMMAS OF INFORMATION TECHNOLOGY USE

Most of the potential ethical dilemmas associated with the use of computer-based management information technologies fit into just three general categories: rights of privacy, individualism, and depersonalization. These potential dilemmas are given life in the following situations. We'll look at some other ethical issues in the next chapter.

Kraft USA knows quite a lot about macaroni-and-cheese eaters and other customers—how old they are and how often they shop, for starters. The company's marketing and research staff can figure out whether its customers fill the grocery cart in one trip or grab a few items several times a week, whether they spend afternoons clipping coupons, how many children they have, whether they eat out or entertain friends at home, and whether they earn their living behind a desk or on the factory floor. The information on Kraft's customers comes from those scanners found at more and more supermarket checkout counters. Every time a clerk whisks a purchase over the scanner it electronically records what was bought, who makes it, the size, and the price. That data is then fortified with information derived from research into what shoppers watch on television, the type of neighborhood they live in, and the kind of supermarket they shop in.[43] Does this kind of electronic information gathering impinge on consumers' rights of privacy?

There are increasing concerns about telecommunications' blurring of traditional boundaries separating work and leisure time. Information technology can make it harder to escape work. If one has a car phone, for example, does that give the boss or subordinates the right to call any time? If the company installs a personal computer in an employee's home, is it all right for the boss to request that proposals be reviewed on a weekend? Information technology is so new that norms and customs for its use are still being developed. How can these safeguard employees' individual needs?

Some information systems take the face-to-face personal contact out of communications, with harmful effects. One result is something called flaming. Because people can tap away at a computer terminal and send messages to others without ever facing them, more people are firing off nasty comments to co-workers or bosses that they would never deliver in person. Assured of anonymity, people can send flaming notes instantly via phone line to dozens or hundreds of people in offices all over the country.[44] Is this depersonalization unavoidable?

CHAPTER SUMMARY

1. Information is useful knowledge derived from data. It is an essential resource for the management of an organization. The value of information is assessed on the basis of quality, relevance, quantity, and timeliness.

2. Information technologies are impacting most organizational areas in the form of computers, software applications, and telecommunications. Four categories of information are communication systems, decision support systems, expert systems, and executive support systems.

3. Creating an information system begins with a determination of the organization's information needs. System constraints must be identified, and objectives set. The designing of the information system involves four stages: (1) preliminary problem definition, (2) conceptual design, (3) detailed design, and (4) implementation.

4. Seven factors generally contribute to the effectiveness of an information system: user involvement, support of top management, information system's development, everyone else in the organization is more likely to recognize its importance, evaluation of time and cost, gradual implementation, thorough testing, training and documentation, and system backup.

5. Implementing a new information system may cause resistance or stress and anxiety within the organization. The resistance most often takes the form of avoidance, projection, and/or aggression. User participation, user orientation, phased introduction, and revised performance guidelines are effective ways of neutralizing resistance.

QUESTIONS FOR DISCUSSION AND APPLICATION

1. **From Where You Sit:** Find three organizational examples that support Leavitt and Whisler's predictions. What problems might these organizations be facing now, and in the future?

2. What are some contributions that new information technologies can make to organizations?

3. What is the relationship between data and information? Give two examples of a report or document that might be considered information by one person but data by another. What would have to be done to transform the report into information for the second person?

4. **From Where You Sit:** Identify three ways that your life has been affected by one or more of the types of information systems described in this chapter.

5. **From Where You Sit:** Define a decision—either personal or organizational—that you (or your superior or a friend) have recently made (or are making). What sort of information system might have helped to make a better decision?

6. What are the differences in the information needs and requirements of top, middle, and first-line managers?

7. **From Where You Sit:** Describe your college's student registration system. How would you design and implement an information system to support it or improve it? What questions would you ask? Who would you ask? What resistances might you encounter, and how would you overcome them?

8. Identify and discuss specific examples of resistance behavior that workers may demonstrate. What types of actions would cause these behaviors? How could the resistance be reduced or prevented?

9. **From Where You Sit:** Has your right to privacy and sense of individualism ever been violated by a computer-based information technology? Explain.

Are Microcomputers Productive?

After the case we have made that computers are effective, you might be surprised to come across this article in *Fortune* magazine: "The Puny Payoff from Office Computers." According to this story, U.S. businesses have spent billions of dollars on computers, but a study by an economist in the investment banking house of Morgan Stanley found that "white-collar productivity—output per worker hour—stands just about where it was in the late 1960s." Another surprising article, this time in *Computerworld*, is titled "Study Finds PCs [Personal Computers] Not Fully Utilized." Here you would read that the firm Touche Ross & Co. surveyed 526 companies and found that "small business has heartily embraced microcomputers but may not be using them effectively." What's going on?

Instructions

Do a study yourself of an office with which you are familiar that has one or more microcomputers. To determine whether or not these microcomputers are being used effectively, answer the following questions:

Do people try to teach themselves on microcomputers because the machines are so inexpensive that organizations don't want to pay consultants' fees or tuition for courses?
____ Yes ____ No

Are new users so elated at the few tasks they're able to teach themselves that they don't explore beyond the functions that they can learn without formal instruction?
____ Yes ____ No

Are computers underused? Do many personal computers sit idle much of the time?
____ Yes ____ No

Are computers used in ways that partly wipe out their efficiencies. For instance, does electronic mail produce a lot of "electronic junk mail," such as trivial messages to people who don't need to receive them? ____ Yes ____ No

Does word processing, because of the ease of revision, bring out perfectionism, such as additional drafts being made even when they aren't really necessary? ____ Yes ____ No

Are computers used for applications with low payoffs—that is, for trying to make people's present jobs more efficient rather than changing the way work is done?
____ Yes ____ No

Interpretation

If you answered yes to any of these questions, you know in precisely what ways microcomputers are *not* being used effectively.

To: June Miller, Director of Systems Development
From: Danny Strawser, Director of Personnel
Subject: Inefficiency of Retirement Benefit Counseling System

I have just had a long meeting with our retirement benefits counselor over some problems she is having. Her job is to counsel employees on their benefit packages and options. The retirement package allows employees to supplement employer contributions and to exercise limited control over how all contributions are invested (for example, in stocks or bonds).

Currently, she is manually responding to employee requests for monthly retirement income projections based on several variables (such as future contributions, income projections, and planned retirement age). Her problems are as follows: First, it often takes one full day to get salary data from the data processing department. Second, employee data are stored in many files that are not always properly updated. When conflicting data become apparent, she can't do her projections until that conflict has been resolved. Third, the computations are complex. It often takes one full day or more to create a retirement scenario for a single employee. Fourth, there are some concerns that projections are being provided to unauthorized individuals (such as former spouses or nonimmediate relatives). Finally, the complexity of the calculations (there are a lot of "if this, do that" instructions) results in frequent errors, many of which probably go undetected.

I would appreciate it if we could set up a time to discuss these problems and the possibility of developing an information system that addresses them and makes our retirement benefits counselor more effective and efficient. Please contact me as soon as possible.

Question: Assume that you are June Miller and you conclude that a new information system is called for. What actions might you take?

Data Mills Delve Deep To Find Information About U.S. Consumers

BY MICHAEL W. MILLER

NEW YORK—Nicholas Iannelli, two days old, whines softly as a nurse's aide takes him from his hospital bassinet and positions him beneath a big metal camera. "Come on, sweetheart," she whispers, then clicks the shutter.

In a flash, Nicholas is back in the nursery, and his vital statistics embark on a lifelong journey into a vast network of direct-marketing computers.

St. Vincent's Medical Center on Staten Island sends an order-card filled out by Nicholas's parents to the offices of First Foto in Red Bank, N.J. The Iannellis get snap shots. Their names, address and phone number go into the files of First Foto's owner, Hasco International Inc., whose hospital cameras shoot about 1.6 million newborns each year. The company passes along the data it collects to a Massachusetts outfit that does a brisk business sharing its lists with companies such as Kimberly-Clark Corp. and Sears, Roebuck & Co. They will fill the Iannellis' mailbox with ads for diapers and toys.

Scavenging for the personal details of people's lives is today a high-tech, billion-dollar industry. It is the invisible engine of junk mail and junk phone calls. And it has been instrumental in the erosion of personal privacy.

The industry has its tentacles in a thousand corners where personal information resides, from car registrations to mortgage records to birth announcements. It buys data from all manner of companies. Bookstores sell lists of their customers. Magazines and newspapers (including The Wall Street Journal) sell or rent their subscription lists. The industry also plucks data directly from consumers who don't always realize that they are feeding computers just by filling out questionnaires, entering contests, redeeming coupons or making a simple phone call.

"You go through life dropping little bits of data about yourself everywhere," says Evan Hendricks, editor of Privacy Times, a Washington, D.C., monthly. "Most people don't know that there are big vacuum cleaners sucking it up."

Some people are upset by what they do know of all this. Last year, the software company Lotus Development Corp. attracted national attention to the personal-data business by announcing plans to sell "Marketplace," a set of personal-computer disks containing data on about 120 million U.S. households. That news brought Lotus lots of cards, letters and phone calls it didn't want—30,000 protests in all. In January, Lotus decided the product was more trouble than it was worth and killed it.

Three committees of Congress plan hearings on the boom in personal data-gathering. A 1990 survey by one big data-gatherer, Equifax Inc., concluded that nearly 80% of Americans are distressed about threats to their privacy.

Nevertheless, fund-raisers and marketers have never been hungrier for tidbits of personal information. It is essential raw material for businesses shifting from mass-media advertising to direct-marketing via mail and phone. The strategy, which costs much more per targeted consumer, makes economic sense only when they know enough about a household to consider a personal pitch worthwhile.

And companies know a staggering amount.

Even if a baby happens to make it home from the hospital without landing in First Foto's database, the infant will still probably crawl into the files of Metromail Corp. of Lombard, Ill., one of the biggest of the information gatherers. The company promotes its "Young Family Index Plus," which lists 67,000 new births each week, about 85% of the 4.1 million babies born in the U.S. each year. Metromail baby-finders clip birth announcements, call Lamaze coaches and get names from companies that deal in baby supplies.

The quest continues as children get older. A kid who reaches the 10th grade in school will almost certainly wind up in a computer in Great Neck, N.Y., where American List Corp. stores yearbook listings and other data about virtually every high-school class. Marketers also can get lists of 100,000 buyers of novelty items advertised on Dubble Bubble gum wrappers, and 73,467 members of the Dairy Queen Birthday Club. Another ice-cream club (Farrell's) in 1983 sold a list of 18-year-olds to the Selective Service System.

Buy a house in any of 575 U.S. counties, and a Metromail agent will come into possession of public records on the sale and the mortgage. ("Be the first to know the 'second' they close," is a Metromail slogan.) Buy a car in most states and the registration information (name, address, make), finds its way to R.L. Polk & Co. of Detroit. (Among its many customers: The Wall Street Journal, which buys lists of new BMW and Mercedes-Benz owners from Polk.)

Consumers Marketing Research Inc. of South Hackensack, N.J., sells lists sorted by any of 78 ethnic and religious groups. It produced a list of Italian voters for Mario Cuomo when he ran for governor of New York, black households for the United Negro College Fund, and Japanese men for a Brooks Brothers promotion of suits in small sizes. For a maker of lederhosen, CMR prepared a list of German names with those thought to be Jewish deleted.

If anyone succumbs to too many of these pitches and files for personal bankruptcy protection, a scout for Jefferson Mailing Lists may well spot the court record. "It has turned out to be a tremendous list," says Jeff Figler, who runs the small Poway, Calif., firm and says it adds 35,000 names a month to its list. "They want to re-establish their credit, so when they buy something, they're going to be conscientious."

1. Can a company go too far in collecting data on potential customers or clients? Where would you set the limits?

2. Imagine you are starting a business selling computer supplies by mail order. What kind of data would you require, and how would you turn it into useful information?

3. What levels of management would need information about customers and their buying habits? Would different levels of management need different kinds of information? Why?

FRITO-LAY—IN THE CHIPS

Paul Davis noticed the beginnings of a disturbing trend in the weekly sales data for the Dallas division of Frito-Lay Inc., which he heads. Sales of the company's Lay's and Ruffles potato chips brands were headed down—by all comparisons. The low sales numbers showed up in red on his computer screen. With a few keystrokes, Davis was able to plunge quickly through snapshots of information that showed him the cause—a competitor was making inroads. Not only that, the competitor was doing the damage by deeply discounting its products and getting key display space in a leading grocery chain. Because salty snacks like potato chips are often an impulse buy, the location and amount of supermarket display space are critical.

Davis and his regional managers were able to react almost instantly. They pulled comparative data—from the retailer's own sales—that convinced the retailer that the deep discounts were hurting the store's bottom line. It would be more profitable for the supermarket to reallocate space in Frito-Lay's favor. The system that allowed Davis to quickly assemble a detailed presentation based on the chain's own scanner data is, in his words, "powerful." Frito-Lay's managers and planners can pinpoint sales, turnover, and space allocation for its own products and those of its competition. They can compare a retailer's return on inventory for Frito-Lay products, competitors' products, and other food categories. "We have a one-week report on new promotions," said Allen Dickason, director of systems development. "We can respond to competition's response to us."

Frito-Lay—with roughly half of the $9.6 billion U.S. market for chips—took an early lead in using scanner data, although its competitors weren't far behind. "Every one of [its] large competitors is working on something like this," said Lynda Applegate, a Harvard Business School professor who researches strategic use of information technol-

ogy. "What's different about Frito-Lay is that they are going not only faster but further than most. They are building an information infrastructure that enables them to package information and deliver it to all levels of the organization," Applegate explains.

Frito-Lay credits its new system, an initial $40 million investment, with savings of $39 million a year on returned products. More important, Frito-Lay's executives consider the system crucial to the company's new strategy of decentralization. Frito-Lay faces intense competition and a sophisticated, fragmented market. The behemoth had to learn to move quickly and in a number of directions at once.

"This is really a bag-by-bag kind of business. It's 10,000 people doing thousands of things a day," said Charles Feld, vice president of management services and the architect of Frito-Lay's new system. Bobby R. Wright is one of the 10,000. Every working day he drives a delivery truck to twelve to fourteen customers on a specified route. For more than two years, he's had something different on his truck. Right above the cartons of bean dip, salsa, and Grandma's cookies, there's a mount for a handheld computer. It's with these devices that Frito-Lay's internal information revolution began. Wright's route takes him to a number of small accounts: convenience stores, service stations and sandwich shops. At each stop he casts an experienced eye over the display shelves. He doesn't need to count. He knows how many bags of Doritos or Ruffles will fill the empty space, and he keys the number into the handheld computer. When Wright finishes the call, the computer prints out an itemized sales ticket, automatically factoring in any promotional allowances for the retailer, cutting the potential for error. At the end of the day, instead of tallying his accounts, Wright simply downloads the computer at the district warehouse to send the information into a central database. At the same time, new information can be "uploaded" into the computer. Every week, Wright's district manager can hold a "one-on-one" with him, spotting problem areas or sales potential.

Two management layers above the district managers, Paul Davis scrutinizes a larger chunk of information every week, packaged to fit his needs. Included in his executive information package is another huge chunk of data—supermarket scanner transactions purchased from Information Resources, Inc. The division manager can use this data to find out who's hurting Frito-Lay the most and how, and allocate dollars to move against that.

Frito-Lay is striving toward the next step. "Strategic advantages never last. You are always only six months to a year ahead of everyone else," explains Feld. By mid-1992, Feld and Dickason hope to have manufacturing, logistical, and marketing data integrated into the system. About 120 managers are now on line with executive information software, and that number will increase to 600 by 1992, they say. "We know people are using handheld computers out there," Dickason said. "But we don't believe they've built the systems behind [them] to sum up that information, capture it accurately, and make it work on a day-to-day basis."

1. What types of information technologies are used at Frito-Lay?
2. What was the likely effect of implementing the new system at each organizational level mentioned? Explain. Identify one form of resistance that might have arisen at each level.
3. Why is Frito-Lay's new system considered to be a strategic competitive weapon?

Chapter 20

OPERATIONS MANAGEMENT

David Kearns (left)

What You Will Learn

1 The nature and importance of the systems view of operations management.

2 The key types of operations management decisions and their role in improving productivity.

3 Three common strategies for arranging resource flow in the transformation process.

4 How innovative office, service, and manufacturing technologies have influenced operations management.

5 The key concepts and issues of total quality management and control.

6 The basic concepts and issues of inventory management and control.

7 **Skill Development:** How to continuously improve quality and productivity in response to rising customer expectations and increasing competitive pressures.

Xerox's Leadership through Quality

Xerox Corporation, which makes more than 250 types of document-processing equipment, carried away the coveted Malcolm Baldrige National Quality Award in 1989. That same year Xerox Canada Inc. won Canada's first National Quality Award. Quality is a critical factor to the success of any organization. Attaining total quality has been the top priority at Xerox, according to David T. Kearns, its CEO and chairman.

In 1983, we introduced what we call our Leadership-through-Quality process—a management system that depends heavily on employee involvement and focuses the entire company on the achievement of total quality. We changed the role of first-line management from that of traditional, dictatorial foreman to that of a supervisor functioning primarily as a coach and expediter. At the time Leadership-through-Quality was introduced, I told our employees that customer satisfaction would be our top priority and that it would change the culture of the company. We redefined quality as meeting the requirements of our customers. It may have been the most significant strategy Xerox had ever embarked on. Nearly seven years have passed, and what I said then still stands.

Our first step in implementing the Leadership-through-Quality process was to train management with their own work groups. The training, usually conducted off-site in about three-and-a-half days, was similar to what we had already been giving our manufacturing people. Emphasis was placed on identifying quality shortfalls and the problems that caused them, determining root causes, developing solutions, and implementing them. The work groups were taught interpersonal skills, a six-step problem-solving process, and a nine-step quality improvement process. To assure the commitment of management at every level, Leadership-through-Quality training began with our top-tier work group—my direct subordinates and me. It then cascaded through the organizations led by senior staff, gradually spreading worldwide to some 100,000 employees.

At the same time the training started, we intensified and formalized the analysis of our position in the marketplace. In addition to conversations with customers and periodic surveys of the marketplace, we turned to benchmarking, the process of measuring ourselves against the goods, services, and practices of our toughest competitors. For example, we benchmarked L. L. Bean for distribution procedures, Deere Company for central computer operations, Procter & Gamble for marketing, and Florida Power & Light for its own quality process. This kind of benchmarking has become the responsibility of each corporate subunit. Approximately 240 different departments and units of our company now benchmark against comparable areas in other organizations. We even scrapped a multi-million-dollar assembly line because its design isolated individual operators and made it impossible for them to talk to one another.

Our employee-involvement teams were given considerable empowerment. Nowhere is this more dramatically demonstrated than in manufacturing. Individual assemblers have the authority to stop the assembly line when problems are identified. They are fixed on the spot by the operators as a team.

There is no magic formula to a successful quality program. The key is involvement. From the top to the bottom of our management team, we have a deep and real commitment to employee involvement. We know that if we fail to maintain this commitment, Xerox won't survive in today's global market. That's a powerful incentive.[1]

operations management
The systematic direction, control, and evaluation of the entire range of processes that transform inputs into finished goods or services.

Every organization—private or public, manufacturing or service—engages in operations management. **Operations management** is the systematic direction, control, and evaluation of the entire range of processes that transform inputs into finished goods or services.[2] It used to be known as production management, but this term came to be associated primarily with manufacturing operations. The efficiency and effectiveness of operations management play a central role in determining whether an organization achieves its overall objectives.

Xerox Corporation had lost dominance in the industry it created by becoming complacent about operations management. After the introduction of the Leadership-through-Quality program in 1983, the company renewed itself literally from top to bottom. Did the renewed focus on operations management at Xerox have its intended effects? David T. Kearns reviews the results:

▶ After reducing our supplier base, we achieved a 45 percent cost reduction and substantial improvement in the quality of purchased parts—from 92 percent defect-free in 1985 to 99.5 percent defect-free in 1990.

▶ Defects in production-line parts have been reduced more than 90 percent since 1982.

▶ We reduced average manufacturing costs by 20 percent from 1982 to 1986, and they are continuing to come down. During the same period we cut the time to bring a new product to market by as much as 60 percent.

▶ Machine performance during the first thirty days following installation improved 40 percent from 1986 to 1990.[3]

In this chapter we describe the nature of operations management and its critical importance to quality and productivity in the manufacturing and service sectors of the economy. We identify nine key decisional areas of operations management and then go into some detail about four of them: positioning strategy, technology choices, quality management and control, and finally, inventory management and control.

INTRODUCTION TO OPERATIONS MANAGEMENT

We'll look at operations management from a systems view of organizations that includes four basic components: environmental factors, inputs, transformations, and outputs.

Environmental factors, which we've discussed in earlier chapters, influence operations management in various ways. Recall that such factors can be grouped into cultural, political, and market influences. Examples of these influences include group norms (cultural), legislation requiring tighter health and safety standards (political), and price competition (market).

Inputs include human resources (managers and workers), capital (equipment, facilities, and money), materials, land, energy, and information. Examples include assembly-line workers and dentists (human resources), a factory and zero-coupon bonds (capital), seed corn (materials), a farm (land), electric power (energy), and market analyses (information).

Transformations are the operations that convert inputs into outputs. Examples include turning bauxite (a raw material, or mineral) into aluminum ingots through the use of an electric furnace, salt water into fresh water through desalinization, and cavities into fillings through various dental skills (use of a drill) and materials (metal or porcelain).

Outputs are the goods, services, and waste products created through transformations. Examples include vans from Chrysler's Windsor, Ontario assembly plant, government social security checks, and waste (garbage, air pollution, water pollution).[4]

Figure 20.1 provides a systems view of the components of operations management and their interaction. The five numbered circles in the transformations box indicate that production of a good or service often requires a number of separate operations. An operation can be manufacturing a part or assembling parts manufactured elsewhere, combining fresh vegetables into a salad at a salad bar, or entering a code number and transaction information into an automated teller machine.[5]

Customers often come into direct contact with the operations management system. They even actively participate in the transformation process in self-service operations. Customers also provide essential feedback to organizations concerning satisfaction with purchased goods and services. Customer feedback—along with performance feedback, such as knowledge of the frequency of equipment breakdowns—closes the system loop. This information helps managers and other employees to decide whether to make changes in the goods and services provided, the transformation processes used, and/or the inputs utilized.

FIGURE 20.1

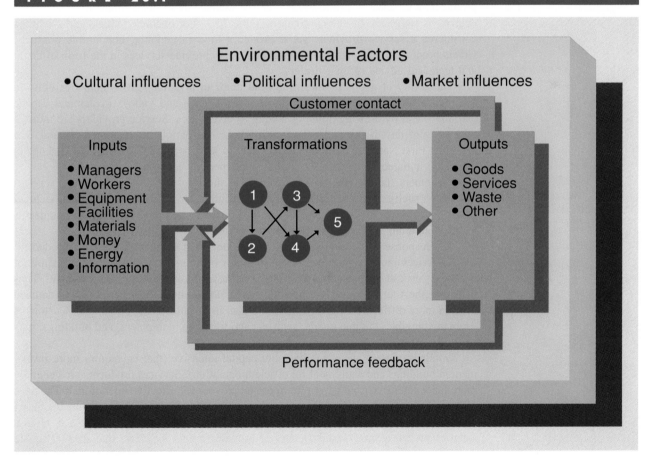

Systems View of Operations Management

Operations management, as suggested in this figure, is based on the systems view of organizations. In the past, operations management, which was then called production management, considered problems primarily from a closed systems view of the organization. (Recall from the discussion of the systems viewpoint in Chapter 2 that a system is an association of interrelated and interdependent parts.)

Source: Adapted from L. J. Krajewski and L. P. Ritzman, *Operations Management: Strategy and Analysis,* 2nd ed. (Reading, Mass.: Addison-Wesley, 1990), 3–5.

Typical Characteristics of Goods and Services Producers

Primarily Goods Producers	Continuum of Characteristics	Primarily Services Producers
	Mixed	
Tangible, durable	←————————————→	Intangible, nondurable
Output can be inventoried	←————————————→	Output cannot be inventoried
Low customer contact	←————————————→	High customer contact
Long response time	←————————————→	Short response time
Capital-intensive	←————————————→	Labor-intensive

Differences between Goods and Services Producers

Operations management, as we've said, is necessary for the production of services as well as manufactured goods. Table 20.1 summarizes five areas of difference between goods producers and services producers. Often, of course, these distinctions are a matter of degree, as suggested by the continua in Table 20.1. For example, McDonald's is often considered a service provider, yet it produces food (a tangible, nondurable product). Goods producers, such as Chrysler and Ford, also provide services in the form of credit and technical advice to their dealers.

The ability of goods producers to hold items in inventory gives them flexibility in scheduling flows in the transformation process. Peaks and valleys in demand can be partially offset by drawing down or adding to inventories. Service providers are more at the mercy of day-to-day and even hour-by-hour fluctuations in customer demand. For example, First National Bank of Chicago had to shift personnel to eliminate backups in telephone-initiated funds transfers during peak periods each day.

Customers themselves are often inputs to the transformation process for services producers, such as doctors or hairdressers. In contrast, most customers for manufactured goods have little or no direct contact with the transformation process. Customer contact is left to marketing departments, distributors, or retailers.

The response to customer demand has to be much quicker for services producers. Many services must be provided within minutes or hours of being demanded. Think of checkout lines at supermarkets or service at fast-food restaurants, for example. Thus matching short-term productive capacity (especially the number of personnel) to demand is often more difficult for service providers than in manufacturing operations. Customers for many tangible, durable goods, such as cars, furniture, computers, and buildings, may be willing to wait days, weeks, or months.

Goods producers are generally more capital-intensive (that is, require more investment in buildings and equipment for efficient operation). Services producers are generally more labor-intensive (that is, require more employees for effective operations). The need for larger plants and more and better equipment runs up the cost for many manufacturing facilities. For example, Chrysler's Windsor, Ontario assembly plant has 2.5 million square feet, but a branch bank (a service provider) might have less than 10,000 square feet.

Importance of Operations Management to Productivity

Productivity improvement is important from a national and even a global perspective.[6] The United States and Canada have experienced declining rates of productivity growth, which began in the latter part of the 1960s, and, until recently, much lower rates of productivity growth than Japan, Korea, Italy, France, Sweden, West Germany, and other

Southern Pacific Railroad conductor uses *new technology* to take freight inventory at a San Francisco station with a Grid Systems "Grid Pad."

countries. Although annual productivity improvements of 5 percent or more occurred in the metals, textiles, tire, and auto industries between 1983 and 1990, services productivity continues to lag. With several notable exceptions, it has increased by only a few tenths of a percent annually since 1979. The exceptions are deregulated services industries (railroads, airlines, and telecommunications), which had annual productivity increases of 5 percent or more between 1982 and 1990.[7]

Improving U.S. and Canadian productivity is key to maintaining and restoring their competitive positions internationally in automobiles, electronic equipment, bicycles, motorcycles, cameras, small appliances, and steel. International differences in rates of productivity growth influence exports, standards of living, and choice of jobs.[8] Thus productivity improvement is important to all of us.

Operations management can greatly improve productivity, a major concern of both goods and services producers. In particular, three applications of operations management principles have resulted in improved productivity.[9] First, investing capital in new technology and carefully managing its introduction are critical for long-term productivity growth in both the service and manufacturing sectors. Second, reducing waste, rejects, and returns through improved quality control pays off immediately in both sectors. Third, cutting work-in-progress inventories in the manufacturing sector reduces both the amount of money tied up in inventories and physical space requirements and thus increases productivity.

There are no standard measures of productivity that can be used by all organizations. The most general measure is **total-factor productivity,** which is the ratio of outputs (amount of goods and services produced) to total inputs used (quantities of labor, capital, materials, and so on).[10] This indicator of economic efficiency is normally expressed in monetary terms. **Partial productivity,** on the other hand, is the ratio of output to a single input, usually labor, capital, materials, or energy. The following are two examples of partial productivity ratios: units produced per day divided by labor hours of production employees per day and total store sales per month divided by total labor hours of sales personnel per month.[11]

These and other measures are meaningful only if the outputs produced are also sold. The assessment and improvement of productivity in service operations, such as retailing, is especially challenging. The following Insight describes one of the more dramatic examples of productivity improvement in a retailing organization through the application of new technology.

total-factor productivity
A measure of economic efficiency, the ratio of outputs to total inputs used.

partial productivity The ratio of output to a single input, usually labor, capital, materials, or energy.

INSIGHT

Seiyu Supermarkets set out to develop a model store that would significantly increase retail productivity. Their model store in a suburb of Tokyo is about 5000 square feet in size and employs many technological innovations. Management worked directly with manufacturers in designing the necessary equipment. The results may revolutionize supermarket operating procedures.

Technological innovations used in the store include a computer-driven robotic system for unloading and loading of the delivery trucks, a programmable robot that places merchandise in appropriate aisles, an automatic cold-cut dispenser (type of meat and slicing thickness, as well as weight, cost, or number of slices desired are programmed by the customer), on-line liquid crystal diode (LCD) displays of merchandise prices, and automatic audio descriptions of products and recipes in which they can be used (activated when the merchandise is picked up by shoppers).

Data provided by management show significant gains in productivity, with the potential of reducing the number of employees by 20 percent. Time allocated to materials handling and other routine management tasks has been reduced by nearly one-third. The time gained, now spent on planning and decision making, is almost three times as much as can be devoted to such functions in Seiyu's conventional stores.

The unique technologies developed for the store also serve as a profit center. Seiyu is making them available to others through licensing agreements. In addition, the level of customer service has significantly increased.[12]

Types of Decisions Involved in Operations Management

Application of operations management requires consideration of at least sixteen types of decisions. *Operations Management: Strategy and Analysis* and other operations management textbooks discuss these types of decisions in detail.[13] An effective operations management system will link the sixteen types of decisions, some of which you will recognize as strategic. Here are examples of nine of the sixteen types of operations management decisions:

1. *Product plans:* What products (goods or services) should we offer?
2. *Competitive priorities:* Should our relative emphasis be on low price, high quality, fast delivery time, or product choice?
3. *Positioning strategy:* Should we organize resources around products or processes?
4. *Location:* Should we expand on-site, add a new facility abroad, or relocate the existing facility?
5. *Technological choices:* What transformation operations should be automated to improve productivity?
6. *Quality management and control:* How can we best achieve the quality levels necessary to maintain or better our competitive position?
7. *Inventory management and control:* What are the best methods for determining and maintaining the right inventory levels?
8. *Materials management:* How should we select and evaluate suppliers?
9. *Master production scheduling:* Should we make to inventory or make to order?[14]

Space limitations won't allow us to discuss all nine of these types of decisions, so we'll concentrate on four of them: positioning strategy, technological choices, quality management and control, and inventory management and control.

POSITIONING STRATEGY

positioning strategy The method chosen by an organization for managing the resource flow in the transformation process.

Positioning strategy is the method chosen by an organization for managing the resource flow in the transformation process. Figure 20.2 provides a framework for comparing positioning strategies. The vertical axis indicates that the pattern of resource flow can range from unstable and unpredictable to continuous process (that is, stable and predictable). The horizontal axis indicates that product type and volume can range from one-of-a-kind custom products (goods or services) produced in very small volumes to standard products produced in high volumes. The three circles indicate the likely ranges of three common positioning strategies: process-focus, intermediate, and product-focus.

FIGURE 20.2

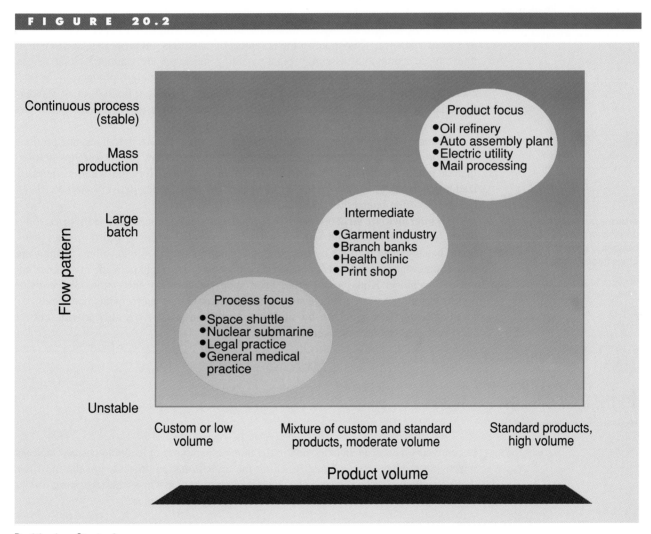

Positioning Strategies

Of the wide range of positioning strategies, the primary continuum of choices is represented by the three circles. The choice of strategy relates to product type and volume (left to right) and resource flow pattern (top to bottom). Few organizations can or do position themselves too far outside one of the circles.

Source: Adapted from R. H. Hayes and S. C. Wheelwright, "Linking Manufacturing Process and Product Life Cycles," *Harvard Business Review,* January-February 1979, 133–140.

process-focus strategy A positioning strategy that organizes the physical layout of the equipment and work force around each operation in the transformation process.

A **process-focus strategy** organizes the physical layout of the equipment and work force around each operation in the transformation process. This strategy is designed to meet the requirements of custom-made products and low-volume production. Since a wide variety of products share each resource, scheduling is crucial. Routines for different products vary, and the resource flow pattern is unstable, changing from one order to the next. Similar equipment and operations (such as painting stations, drill presses, and welding stations) are grouped in separate areas of the shop. For example, one department may perform welding operations for all products passing through the transformation process. In a general medical practice, there is usually an effort to treat each patient as unique (product) and to treat each one based on an individualized diagnosis of the symptoms (unstable flow pattern).

product-focus strategy A positioning strategy that organizes the physical layout of the equipment and work force around a few outputs.

A **product-focus strategy** organizes the physical layout of the equipment and work force around a few outputs. This strategy is designed to fit high-volume, highly automated production of a few standard products with a continuous process or mass-production resource flow pattern. Production follows a linear flow, with various operations arranged in a fixed sequence. This organization is typical of cafeterias, oil refineries, and assembly lines. In an automobile assembly plant, welding machines are stationed along several different assembly lines to perform the same operation on different products. A service example is automated teller machines (ATMs), which provide a limited set of standard financial services (the products) on a continuous basis using a well-defined (stable) process.

A process-focus strategy generally works well with customized products and products with short life cycles. Normally, less emphasis is placed on low price and quick delivery than on quality. In contrast, a product-focus strategy is better for high-volume, standardized products with long life cycles. In this case, low price, quick delivery, and consistent quality are often competitive priorities.[15]

intermediate strategy A positioning strategy somewhere between a process-focus and a product-focus strategy.

An **intermediate strategy** yields an organization of equipment and work force somewhere between that achieved with a process focus and that achieved with a product focus. Some batching can be done by merging and handling several similar orders at the same time. Some standard products or standard component parts might be made in advance and put in inventory. Kinko's and other print shops adjacent to universities and colleges appear to follow an intermediate strategy. Batches of course supplements may be run off in advance for later purchase by students. And these print shops also provide custom services based on customer orders.

TECHNOLOGICAL CHOICES

Recent years have seen an explosion in the number and types of technologies available for improving productivity and quality within the transformation process. For the most part these innovative technologies have been computer-based. Let's consider some of the developments in office, service, and manufacturing technologies.

Office Technologies

In Chapter 19 we discussed many information technologies that are revolutionizing the office environment of managers and other professionals. Personal computers are the dominant force in office automation. Today's most powerful personal computer has the capacity of a 1970s mainframe that cost $1 million. Managers in virtually all leading organizations use personal computers to communicate with each other, with subordinates, with customers and suppliers, and with larger computers. Here are some other uses of personal computers and other computer-based office technologies:

NYNEX's *cellular phone technology* is used to link the Boston Fire Department with a nationwide hazardous chemicals database.

▶ Personal computers have become the workstation of choice in many organizations for accessing public databases. And personal computers are capable of inputing to fax machines or acting as telex/TWX terminals.

▶ Pioneering users have begun to apply video imaging to their use of optical disks, graphics workstations, and new control software to merge video images with text and data.

▶ Organizations have begun to realize that voice communications systems also play an important part in office automation. In certain applications—in credit and collections, for instance—telephone signals interface with computer files.

▶ Organizations are using information technologies to exchange data and documents—everything from memos and price lists to orders and inventory status—electronically. Such interorganizational exchange tends not only to cut internal costs but to create a tighter bond between organizations and their customers.[16]

Another fairly new technology—cellular phones—is literally creating mobile offices. Cellular phone technology allows oral or electronic transmissions to be "handed off" automatically over special frequencies from one geographic area (cell) to another while the users are in their automobiles. In 1987 there were 300,000 cellular phone subscribers in North America. This leaped to about 4.5 million in 1990 and is forecast to be 27 million by 1996.[17] The following Insight reviews this mobile office revolution.

THE MOBILE OFFICE

*J*NSIGHT

More and more men and women are discovering that the office can go almost anywhere they go. The spread of cellular technology and the widening array of portable electronic equipment mean that increasing numbers of employees are no longer required to spend certain hours in an office to do their jobs.

Such technology cannot only increase responsiveness to customers but can improve operations for organizations already on the road. Some courier firms, such as Federal Express and Airborne Express, have equipped their vehicles with computers that are linked to a central office by cellular telecommunications. Drivers get assignments on their computers, print hard copies on attached printers, and go from job to job without having to return to home base. Vehicles with such equipment can be tracked wherever they are. In addition, using computers in vehicles for purposes such as inventory control can help keep costs down. Michael Meresman, editor of the periodical *The Mobile Office*, comments, "We're definitely moving away from the standard office working situation. The trend is for people

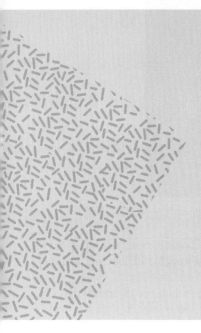

to make better use of their time and have a more flexible work situation. Mobile electronics definitely helps that.''

Since 1988, manufacturers have introduced such items as pocket telephones (some weighing less than a pound) as well as portable battery-powered computers, fax machines, printers, answering machines, copy machines, and even paper-shredding devices, all of which can be operated almost anywhere. ''People got used to receiving messages on their cellular phones,'' says Judy Pirani, an industry analyst with CAP International, a market research firm in Norwell, Massachusetts. ''The next logical step was to get documents—blueprints and so forth—on a mobile fax.''

''As cellular phones increase their penetration into small businesses, you'll see the rate of fax machines in that market increase,'' says David P. Bergevin, marketing manager for Toshiba American's Telecommunications System Division. ''In the next few years, fax machines will increase to a fairly sizable segment of the small-business market. So you try to design your product so it is easily transferable from an office to a car market.'' On the horizon, the experts see even smaller and more affordable electronic tools that inevitably will make the mobile office a practical option for many millions of people.[18]

Service Technologies

Airlines' computerized reservation systems, banks' ATMs, and credit card companies' billing and customer service systems are only three of the many consumer-oriented service technologies.[19] Three computer-based service technologies widely used within organizations are bar coding, integrated computer order systems, and open networks.

bar coding Information encoded as black bars of varying widths alternating with spaces, which can be read by an optical scanner into a computer.

Bar Coding **Bar coding** consists of black bars of varying widths alternating with spaces that can be read by an optical scanner into a computer.[20] Information contained in a bar code can include product name, lot number, manufacturing location, shelf location, and price. Bar coding has greatly increased productivity in supermarkets during the past decade. It speeds up the checkout process, reduces checkout errors, and makes inventory control more effective. Many new applications of bar coding are being developed, including some for goods producers. For example, some goods, such as appliances, are being tracked in inventories through the use of bar coding.

Integrated Computer Order Systems More and more suppliers are placing computer terminals in their customers' offices. These terminals are connected to the suppliers' computers, so customers can place orders instantly at any time. Telephoned orders and mailed hard-copy order forms are eliminated. American Hospital Supply has placed terminals in the purchasing offices of many hospitals, allowing purchasing agents to order supplies more easily and efficiently. The hospitals can keep smaller inventories of many supplies, thus reducing their inventory costs. American Hospital Supply benefits by making it more difficult for these customers to switch to other suppliers.

open network A computer-based information system that enables parts of highly dispersed service operations (including customers) to interact readily.

Open Networks An **open network** is a computer-based information system that enables parts of highly dispersed service operations (including customers) to interact readily. Such a system is best thought of as a spider web because of the intricate and structured quality of its interconnections. Open networks are being used increasingly by multinational banks, financial and professional service companies, engineering and construction enterprises, research and health care firms, and accounting and advertising organizations.[21] Some of the specific attributes of an open network are detailed in the following Insight on Arthur Andersen, a leader in applying technology to professional services.

INSIGHT

Arthur Andersen has to connect its 40,000 knowledgeable professionals with thousands of clients, each with a mix of operations around the United States and in 200 other countries. The company's cumulative experience is growing so fast that, according to executives, "Even those in the know may not have the best answer to the totality of a complex question." Consequently, individuals at Arthur Andersen can no longer rely on their personal knowledge, even of whom to call for information. The open network the company has implemented captures the history of contacts with major clients, keeps up electronically with changing requirements of the Internal Revenue Service and the Financial Accounting Standards Board, and attempts to catalogue the sources of solutions to particular problems. The firm has also developed an electronic bulletin board that allows any professional to query any other individual in the company to find useful solutions for special problems or special knowledge.

Arthur Andersen operates in a highly decentralized, real-time mode. Each local office is as independent as possible. Partners say that the firm's distinctive competency has become "empowering people to deliver better-quality, technology-based solutions to clients in a shorter time." Customers now look to Arthur Andersen to deliver computer-based solutions to systems problems in a league with EDS and IBM.[22]

Manufacturing Technologies

Of the new generation of manufacturing technologies, two of the more important ones are robots and computer-aided manufacturing (CAM).[23]

robots Reprogrammable, multifunctional manipulators that can perform repetitive tasks efficiently.

Robots **Robots** are reprogrammable, multifunctional manipulators.[24] A robot's frame is a substitute for the human arm, and its microprocessor (computer) takes the place of the human brain. Robots have been programmed to perform numerous tasks in several major areas: materials handling, welding, spray painting and other finishing, assembling, inspection and testing, materials removal, and water-jet cutting.[25]

One of the advantages of robots is flexibility. A robot can be programmed to move in various ways, depending on the job it is doing and the product it is making.[26] Of course, robots also perform repetitive tasks without tiring or complaining about poor working conditions. Robots generally cost between $20,000 and $100,000 each, but prices are dropping steadily. The payback period for an investment in a robot is usually two to three years or less.[27] An estimated 37,000 robots were being utilized in the United States in 1990, compared to an estimated 225,000 in Japan.[28]

Tactile (feel) and optical (sight) sensing systems represent one of the major areas of robot development.[29] In one Japanese factory, where Matsushita Electric makes Panasonic VCRs, a robot winds wire thinner than a human hair through a pinhole in the video head sixteen times and then solders it. There are 530 of these robots in the factory, and they wind wire twenty-four hours a day. The robots do this job five times faster and much more reliably than the 3000 Japanese homemakers who, until 1989, used microscopes to do the work on a subcontract basis in their homes. The robots can even inspect their own work![30]

In the service sector, robots have been used for years in nuclear power plants, where employees would risk exposure to radiation, and under the sea, where divers would require cumbersome and costly life-support systems. Anticipated applications of robots include assisting with the care of the handicapped and elderly, picking oranges, cleaning office buildings and hotel rooms, guarding buildings, and even helping surgeons. In fact, some brain surgeons are already using a robot that drills into the skull with great precision.[31]

computer-aided manufacturing (CAM) A wide variety of computer-based technologies used to produce goods.

Computer-Aided Manufacturing **Computer-aided manufacturing (CAM)** encompasses a wide variety of computer-based technologies used to produce goods.[32] The complete CAM process begins with **computer-aided design (CAD),** which uses special software to instruct a computer to draw specified configurations on a display screen, including dimensions and details. This reduces the time spent in the design process and makes it easier to explore alternative designs. The database resulting from CAD is used to help generate all of the instructions to guide the CAM process, including the sequential routing of components to various machines, operating instructions for each machine, provisions for testing components against specifications, reporting of the unit costs of each operation, combining design information with materials specifications, and expected waste and scrap rates that may affect procurement (purchasing) requirements.[33]

computer-aided design (CAD) The first part of a CAM process, involving special software that instructs a computer to display detailed configurations on a screen.

CAM will have an increasing impact on many activities in the manufacturing sector: process planning, production scheduling and control, machining instructions, machine performance, parts testing, assembly operations, shipping, cost accounting, personnel assignments, finished goods inventories, work in process inventories, and procurement purchasing.

CAM has become an important part of the competitive strategy of an increasing number of firms. A few of these are Xerox, Westinghouse, Texas Instruments, Hewlett-Packard, Northrop Corporation, Lockheed, and Ford.[34] The following Insight describes how NCR has used CAM to improve its competitiveness.

CAM AT NCR

INSIGHT

Like most manufacturers, NCR used to develop products in a series of steps, starting with design and engineering, progressing through letting contracts for various materials, parts, and services, and finally going to production. Each step was largely independent of the others. Changes made at any post-design stage, especially after production started, caused major traumas. Late fixes would ripple back through the various departments involved in a project, causing everything that had gone before to be reworked. That would delay the product and push its costs through the ceiling. So NCR decided to test a new method: do everything concurrently using CAM.

In Atlanta, Georgia, where NCR makes terminals for checkout counters, the company tried concurrent engineering, one type of CAM, for developing its latest machine. The work started in January 1987, and the product rolled out twenty-two months later—in half the normal time. The new terminal has 85 percent fewer parts than its predecessor and can be assembled in two minutes, or one-fourth the time. That convinced NCR. It tore down the wall that separated its design and manufacturing departments.

Now the plant's 100 engineers are located in a pool of identical cubicles. When a project starts up, the engineers play musical cubicles so that specialists involved in design, software, hardware, purchasing, manufacturing, and field sup-

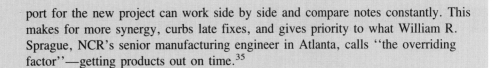

port for the new project can work side by side and compare notes constantly. This makes for more synergy, curbs late fixes, and gives priority to what William R. Sprague, NCR's senior manufacturing engineer in Atlanta, calls "the overriding factor"—getting products out on time.[35]

CAM is compatible with the product variety and flexibility associated with a process-focus strategy and the low per-unit costs associated with a product-focus strategy (see Figure 20.2). The most direct impacts of CAM are elimination of the cost versus variety tradeoff for goods producers and removal of rigid plant setups as a barrier to rapid product innovation. The demand for CAM has grown rapidly because flexibility is needed to meet ever-changing competition.[36] Competition, in turn, is based on the need to constantly improve the characteristics of goods and services in order to respond to changing customer demand. The life of many products has decreased to the point where 50 percent of sales often occur in less than three years. Shorter product life cycles mean that manufacturing plants must be designed to outlive the good they were originally designed to produce. In addition, technological advances have accelerated to the point that new goods, materials, and processes are introduced almost daily.[37] CAM and other advanced manufacturing technologies are complemented by several quality and inventory control methods, the focus of the next two parts of this chapter.[38]

The application of major technologies—office, service, or manufacturing—is a significant management challenge within a country. But the transfer of technology across national borders usually faces even greater problems, due to differing cultures, norms, laws, tax policies, and so forth. The Global Link feature reviews five of the many strategies used by organizations for a wide variety of international technology transfers.

QUALITY MANAGEMENT AND CONTROL

The Manager's Viewpoint feature at the beginning of this chapter emphasized the importance of quality management and control at Xerox. David T. Kearns, chairman and CEO, noted that quality was defined as "meeting the requirements of our customers."[39] In this section we discuss the importance of quality management to competitive strategy, the key dimensions of quality, and the meaning and process of total quality control.

Competitive Strategy and Quality

Quality management and control is increasingly seen as a strategic component of effective competition.[40] *Fortune*'s annual ranking of America's most admired corporations has always included "quality of products or services" as one of eight key dimensions of reputation. For 1991, three of the most-admired corporations on this dimension were Merck (pharmaceuticals), Rubbermaid (rubber and plastic products) and Procter & Gamble (soaps, cosmetics). Many managers and employees realize that there are several key organizational benefits to offering superior quality (as perceived by customers). These include stronger customer loyalty (more repeat purchases), less vulnerability to price wars, ability to command a higher relative price without losing customers, lower marketing costs, and lower warranty costs.

value From a competitive perspective, the relationship between quality and price.

From a competitive perspective, **value** is the relationship between quality and price. Figure 20.3 is a competitiveness value map on which an organization can determine its price versus quality position relative to competitors.[41] Recall that Xerox undertook a

GLOBAL Link

INTERNATIONAL TECHNOLOGY TRANSFERS

With a parallel introduction strategy, a firm introduces a new technology simultaneously in its home country and a foreign country. Du Pont is noted for the parallel introduction of new chemical products and manufacturing processes on a global scale. Computer chips made by Intel are usually introduced simultaneously in U.S. computers made by IBM and Japanese computers manufactured by Fujitsu.

With the delayed introduction strategy, a new technology is first introduced in the home country. Later, after experience is gained and improvements made, the technology is transferred to a foreign country. European pharmaceutical firms, such as Hoffman-LaRoche and Ciba-Geigy, and even some U.S. pharmaceutical firms, such as Vestar and Genentech, often introduce a new drug in a European country before trying to market it in the United States. This is because the United States has stricter government requirements for approval of drugs. The delayed introduction strategy has been used for interferon drugs used for cancer treatment, liposomes for drug delivery, and non-ionic contrasts for imaging techniques.

With a sequential transfer strategy, a technology is transferred to a foreign country only after the technology is completely through its life cycle in the home country. Crown Cork and Seal, for example, transferred its three-piece can manufacturing technology to less developed countries only after a more modern two-piece technology was introduced in the home country, the United States.

With the joint venture strategy, two or more firms join in a business venture that transfers a product or manufacturing process across national boundaries. Toyota and General Motors formed a joint venture to manufacture the Chevrolet Nova, which is similar to the Toyota Corolla, in California. The commercial aviation business has had several multinational joint ventures. Airbus Industrie, which manufactures and sells the A300, A310, and A320 jet aircraft, is a joint venture of Aerospatiale (France), Deutche Airbus (West Germany), British Aerospace (United Kingdom), and CASA (Spain). General Electric has separate joint ventures with SNECMA of France and Rolls Royce of the United Kingdom to produce jet engines.

With the licensing strategy, a firm in one country gives the right to use its technology to a firm in another country. For example, U.S. defense contractors have licensed firms in Japan, Europe, and Egypt to produce an F-15 aircraft or M-1 tank. Some subassemblies are usually made in the home country, and final assembly occurs in the host country. Personnel are provided to help with the technology transfer process. Bristol Laboratories has licensed pharmaceutical firms in Mexico to produce antibiotics, and Merck has done the same in India. And, in a licensing strategy with a twist, IBM and Samsung Electronics of Korea agreed to swap patents on semiconductor products through a cross-licensing agreement.

From R. T. Keller and R. R. Chintra, International Technology Transfer: Strategies for Success. *Academy of Management Executive*, May 1990, pp. 33–43. Reprinted with permission.

Competitiveness Value Map

Here relative price is shown ranging from lower to higher on the vertical axis and relative quality is shown ranging from inferior to superior on the horizontal axis. Customers perceive outstanding value, for example, when the product or service exhibits some combination of superior relative quality and lower relative price.

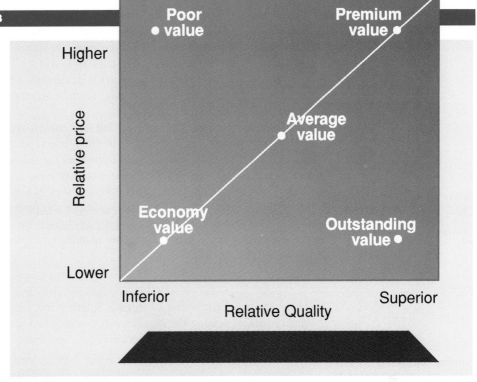

Source: Adapted from B. T. Gale and R. D. Buzzell, ''Market Perceived Quality: Key Strategic Concept,'' *Planning Review,* March/April, 1989, 10.

benchmarking The process of measuring an organization's goods, services, or practices against those of its toughest competitors.

diagnosis of its relative quality through **benchmarking,** the process of measuring an organization's goods, services, or practices against those of its toughest competitors.

As suggested in Figure 20.3, customers who perceive superior quality at a lower relative price receive outstanding value. Organizations that provide such value are likely to grow and prosper. In contrast, the provision of inferior quality at a higher relative price results in poor value to customers. This situation is likely to invite new competitors. If organizations continue to offer poor value, they will wither and die. Figure 20.3 also plots premium value (high price, superior quality), average value (average price, average quality), and economy value (low price, inferior quality). Competitive pressure in the 1990s will require organizations to provide greater relative quality at the same or lower price as competitors.[42]

Beginning in the 1980s North American automobile firms undertook a massive transformation to become competitive with foreign automobile firms that had been offering superior quality for a comparable price. A similar incentive operated at Xerox, according to David T. Kearns:

> Initially, we dismissed the Japanese by telling ourselves that they were catering to low-volume users, a market segment of only marginal interest to us. We had always been successful, and we assumed that we would continue to be successful. Then we discovered that they were cutting into our market share by selling better, more reliable copiers at prices approximating our cost for producing comparable products. We learned firsthand how far we had fallen behind when we began producing and marketing a copier in the United States that had been designed by our own Japanese affiliate, Fuji Xerox. To our amazement, the reject rate for the Fuji Xerox parts proved to be a fraction of the rate for American parts.[43]

Heightened global competition has been a major force behind management's sharpened interest in quality management and control. North American manufacturers and service providers used to focus solely on the costs of maintaining or increasing quality. Armand Feigenbaum, Chairman of General Systems (a leading quality-consulting firm) comments, ''More than 80% of the consumers we surveyed last year said that quality was more important than price. In 1978, only 30% said so.''[44] Product quality and costs are increasingly seen as inversely related. That is, the costs of improving quality are often less than the resulting savings in reworking, scrap, warranty expenses, product liability, and so forth.[45]

Total costs for quality management and control typically include expenditures for prevention (quality planning, worker training, and supplier education), appraisal (product inspection and testing), internal failures (reworking and scrap), and external failures (warranty and product liability). These categories of costs suggest that improved quality can lead to increased productivity. This attitude is widely held among Japanese manufacturers and explains much of their dedication to improving product quality and ultimately attaining the objective of zero defects. And it's an outlook that's increasingly shared by managers and employees of North American manufacturers and service providers.[46]

Meaning of Quality

There are two basic views of quality: internal and external. The internal view is that quality means meeting the organization's established specifications and standards. This view is rather limited because it ignores customers and actions by competitors. The external view is that **quality** means achieving the results that customers value and expect.[47] Organizations such as Xerox, among others, are increasingly using the external view to define quality.

quality According to the external view, achievement of the results that customers value and expect.

The total quality of goods or services can't be effectively represented as a single dimension. Nine of the most common dimensions of quality are performance, features, conformance, reliability, durability, serviceability, responsiveness, aesthetics, and reputation.[48] Table 20.2 provides a brief definition of each of these dimensions, along with examples of how it is reflected in a good (stereo amplifier) and a service (checking account). These dimensions indicate that customers' expectations and perceptions, as well as competitors' products and services, must be continuously monitored and assessed to ensure effective quality management and control. As we've mentioned, the past failures of U.S. automakers to adequately assess customer perceptions and foreign competition resulted in staggering declines in sales and market share.

Total Quality Control

total quality control An organizational strategy that makes quality a responsibility of all employees.

Total quality control is an organizational strategy that makes quality a responsibility of *all* employees. It is pursued through a variety of preventive and corrective methods that are intended to ensure customer satisfaction.[49] Total quality control includes planning and designing for quality, preventing defects, correcting defects, and continuously building increased quality into goods and services as far as is economically and competitively feasible.[50] That is, total quality control involves building in quality from product planning to design to design evaluation to preproduction to purchasing to production to sales and service. The strategy puts the top priority on quality rather than short-term profits.

traditional quality control Inspection of products during or at the end of the production process.

In contrast to total quality control, **traditional quality control** refers mainly to product inspection during or at the end of the production process. With this approach the responsibility for quality control is often assigned to a particular department, such as a quality control department or a relatively small group of inspectors and lab technicians. The focus is on corrective controls, that is, fixing mistakes after the fact rather than making the product right the first time.[51] Table 20.3 shows the major differences between traditional and total quality control. Let's now consider some of the specific things that managers can do to implement total quality control.

Deming's Recommendations W. Edwards Deming, ninety years old in 1991, is regarded as the man who taught the Japanese about quality control. He designed a

The Meaning of Quality

Dimension	Definition	Examples	
		Stereo Amplifier	*Checking Account at Bank*
Performance	Primary product or service characteristics	Signal-to-noise ratio, power	Time to process customer requests
Features	Added touches, secondary characteristics	Remote control	Automatic bill paying
Conformance	Fulfillment of specifications, documentation, or industry standards	Workmanship	Accuracy
Reliability	Consistency of performance over time	Mean time to failure	Consistency of time to process requests
Durability	Useful life	Useful life (with repair)	Keeping pace with industry standards
Serviceability	Resolution of problems and complaints	Ease of repair	Resolution of errors
Responsiveness	Person-to-person contact, including timeliness, courtesy, and professionalism	Courtesy of dealer	Courtesy of teller
Aesthetics	Sensory effects, such as sound, feel, and look	Oak-finished cabinet	Appearance of bank lobby
Reputation	Past performance and other intangibles	*Consumer Reports* ranking	Advice of friends, years in business

Source: Developed from P. E. Plesk, ''Defining Quality at the Marketing/Development Interface,'' *Quality Progress,* June 1987, 28–36; D. A. Garvin, ''Competing on the Eight Dimensions of Quality,'' *Harvard Business Review,* November–December 1987, 101–109.

four-day seminar for Japanese executives in 1950 and subsequently became almost a ''guru'' to Japanese industry. To honor his contributions, Japanese industry created the Deming Prize in 1951. This annual prize, highly esteemed in Japan, recognizes the company that has attained the highest level of quality that year.[52]

Until 1980 Deming's work received relatively little notice from top management in North American industry. Then NBC broadcast a documentary contrasting Japanese and American product quality. Deming was prominently featured on the program as the world's major authority on quality control. He was soon in demand everywhere and signed a long-term consulting contract with Ford. Deming asserts, ''We in America will have to be more protectionist or more competitive. The choice is very simple. If we are to become more competitive, then we have to begin with quality.''[53]

Deming believes that poor quality is 85 percent a management problem and 15 percent a worker problem. His recommendations for total quality control are

Traditional versus Total Quality Control

Traditional Quality Control	Total Quality Control
Screen for quality.	Plan for quality.
Quality is the responsibility of the quality control department.	Quality is everybody's responsibility.
Some mistakes are inevitable.	Strive for zero defects.
Quality means inspection.	Quality means conformance to requirements.
Scrap and reworking are the major costs of poor quality.	Scrap and reworking are only a small part of the costs of nonconformance.
Quality is a tactical issue.	Quality is a strategic issue.

deceptively simple. Here, briefly, are a few of them:

▶ Accept the doctrine that poor quality is flatly unacceptable. Defective materials, workmanship, products, and service will *not* be tolerated.

▶ Gather statistical evidence of quality *during* the process, not at the end of the process. The earlier an error is caught, the less the cost to correct it.

▶ Rely on suppliers that have historically provided quality, not on sampling inspections to determine the quality of each delivery. Instead of many suppliers, select and stay with a few sources that furnish consistently satisfactory quality.

▶ Depend on training and retraining employees to use statistical methods in their jobs, not on slogans, to improve quality.

▶ Employees should feel free to report any conditions that detract from quality.

▶ Managers should be guided by statistical methods to help people do their work better, not by production standards. Statistical techniques detect *sources* of poor quality. Teams of designers, managers, and workers can then eliminate those sources.[54]

Malcolm Baldridge National Quality Award At the end of Chapter 1 we noted that the Malcolm Baldridge National Quality Award is an annual recognition of U.S. companies that excel in quality achievement and management. The award, a gold-plated medal encased in a crystal column, was created by the U.S. Congress in August 1987. Six prizes are possible every year: two to manufacturing companies, two to service companies, and two to small businesses with fewer than 500 employees. From 1988 through 1990, only nine companies have received the Baldridge Award.

The manufacturers who have won the award include Motorola (1988), Commercial Nuclear Fuel Division of Westinghouse (1988), Milliken & Co. (1989), Xerox Business Products Division (1989), Cadillac Motor Car Division (1990), and IBM's manufacturing operation in Rochester, Minnesota (1990). Only two firms in the small businesses category have received the award: Globe Metallurgical of Cleveland (1989) and Wallace Company of Houston (1990), a distributor to firms in the energy industry. Federal Express Corporation (1990) was the first service firm to receive the Baldridge Award. No service company had won through 1989.[55]

Companies participating in the award process submit applications, including completion of an examination. This examination is reviewed by a team of U.S. quality experts, who also visit the companies. The 1990 application guidelines filled a 36-page booklet. Here is a summary of the seven examination categories for 1990 along with their maximum point values (totaling 1000 points):

1. *Leadership* (100 points): Senior management's success in creating quality values and in building those values into the way the company operates.

2. *Information and Analysis* (60 points): The effectiveness of the company's collection and analysis of information for quality improvement and planning.

3. *Strategic Quality Planning* (90 points): The effectiveness of the company's integration of customers' quality requirements into its business plans.

4. *Human Resource Utilization* (150 points): The success of the company's efforts to realize its work force's full potential for quality.

5. *Quality Assurance of Products and Services* (150 points): The effectiveness of the company's systems for assuring quality control of all its operations and for integrating quality control with continuous quality improvement.

6. *Quality Results* (150 points): The company's improvements in quality and demonstration of excellence in quality based on quantitative measures.

7. *Customer Satisfaction* (300 points): The effectiveness of the company's systems to determine customers' requirements and its demonstrated success in meeting them.[56]

Together the seven examination categories cover all the major components of an integrated, prevention-based quality system built around continuous quality improvement. Most of Deming's prescriptions are represented within these categories.

The following Insight gives a few highlights of Motorola's progress to the Baldridge

Award in 1988 and its continuous quality improvement process since then. Motorola is headquartered in Schaumburg, Illinois, thirty miles west of Chicago. It manufactures pagers (two-way radios), cellular telephone systems, computers, semiconductors, modems, automotive-electronics, and military and space electronics. It is one of the few North American firms that takes the best Japanese manufacturing methods, refines them, and uses them to make American products.[57]

In 1981 Motorola set itself a goal of reducing defects by 90 percent by 1986. Former chairman Robert Galvin, a quality fanatic, implemented the whole range of quality improvement techniques: statistical measures, training, employee involvement, emphasis on customer satisfaction, and so forth. And the goal was achieved. Motorola got good enough to export its pocket pagers to Japan. In 1987 the company set new targets: another 90 percent improvement by 1989 and yet another by 1991.

The corporate goal is to achieve a quality level by 1992 that is equivalent to what the statisticians and industrial engineers call "six sigma," which means six standard deviations from a statistical performance average. In plain English, six sigma translates into 3.4 defects per million opportunities, or production that is 99.99966 percent defect-free. Five sigma is 233 defects per million, and four sigma is 6210. Airlines achieve 6.5 sigma in safety—counting fatalities as defects—but only 3.5 to 4 sigma in baggage handling. Doctors and pharmacists achieve an accuracy of just under five sigma in writing and filing prescriptions. In 1990 Motorola was operating at about five sigma.

In applying the six sigma guideline to support services and white-collar operations, every administrative department must go through the following six steps:

1. Define the major functions or services performed.
2. Determine the internal customers and suppliers of these services.
3. Identify the customer's requirements, as well as quantitative measures to assess customer satisfaction with respect to those requirements.
4. Identify the requirements and measurement criteria that the supplier to the process must meet.
5. Flow-chart or map the process at the macro, or interdepartmental, level and at the micro, or intradepartmental, level.
6. Continuously improve the process with respect to effectiveness, quality, cycle time, and cost.

Since speed is an element of quality, Motorola now does things faster too. The company cut the time it takes to fill an order for portable radios from fifty-five days to fifteen; 1991's goal was seven days. Not even the corporate legal department is exempt. Motorola's patent lawyers used to take eighteen to thirty-six months to write and file a patent claim. That time has been cut in many cases to two months, and the six sigma goal is one day for getting the information about an invention from the engineers and filing the claim.[58]

The Total Quality Control Process

The total quality control process generally focuses on measuring inputs, transformation operations, and outputs (including customer expectations and requirements). The results of these measurements enable managers and other employees to make decisions about product or service quality at each stage (again including customer expectations and requirements).

Inputs Quality control generally begins with the inputs to production, especially the raw materials and parts used in the transformation process. Automobile assembly plants, such as Chrysler's Windsor, Ontario T-van (minivan) plant, could not function if raw materials and parts did not meet or exceed predetermined standards. Fierce foreign competition has caused all North American automakers to toughen and more vigorously enforce input standards.

Transformation Operations Quality control inspections are also made during and between successive stages of production. Work-in-process inspection can result in the reworking or rejecting of an item before the next operation is performed on it. One of the objectives of quality circles, discussed in Chapter 16, is improving the quality of transformation operations.

statistical process control
The use of statistical methods and procedures to determine whether production operations are being done correctly, to detect any deviations, and to find and eliminate their causes.

The systematic and widespread use of statistical process control is one of Deming's key recommendations. **Statistical process control** is the use of statistical methods and procedures to determine whether production operations are being done correctly, to detect any deviations, and to find and eliminate their causes.[59] Statistical process control methods have been around for decades but have only recently been widely used. They serve primarily as preventive controls.[60] Ford makes extensive use of statistical process control and, since 1984, has also offered three-day courses on this method to its suppliers. These suppliers, such as Velcro (a manufacturer of fasteners), are required to demonstrate that they have a commitment to quality improvement.[61] Obviously, improvements in suppliers' outputs improve the quality of Ford's inputs.

Outputs The most traditional and familiar form of quality control is the assessment made after completion of a product or provision of a service. With goods, quality control tests may be made before the items are shipped to customers. The amount returned by customers because of shoddy workmanship or other problems indicates the effectiveness of the quality control process. Service providers, such as barbers and hairdressers, usually involve their customers in checking the quality of outputs by asking if everything is okay. However, the satisfactory provision of a service is often more difficult to assess than the satisfactory quality of goods.

measuring by variable A total quality control method that assesses characteristics for which there are quantifiable standards (such as diameter or weight).

measuring by attribute A total quality control method that assesses characteristics as either acceptable or unacceptable.

Determining the amount or degree of the nine dimensions of quality shown in Table 20.2 is fundamental to total quality control. The more accurate the measurement, the easier it is to compare actual to desired results. Quality dimensions are generally measured either by variable or by attribute. **Measuring by variable** assesses characteristics for which there are quantifiable standards, such as length, diameter, height, weight, or temperature. **Measuring by attribute** assesses characteristics as either acceptable or unacceptable. Measuring by attribute is usually easier than measuring by variable. For example, testing TVs by turning them on as a final check results in a simple yes or no decision regarding acceptable quality. However, setting and reaching quality guidelines is usually not that simple. In the production of a new kind of bus—called the flexible bus—several years ago, the trade-off between the strength needed in the bus frame and the light weight needed to improve fuel efficiency was misjudged. Several cities that purchased this "new generation" of bus experienced numerous problems, including cracked frames.

The assessment of product quality doesn't reveal what the quality level should be. Desired levels of quality are strongly influenced by an organization's strategy and culture (as at Maytag) and by its competition (as at Ford, GM, Chrysler, Honda, and Toyota). The importance of organizational strategy and employee attitudes toward quality control cannot be overstated. Stephen Moss of the consulting firm Arthur D. Little has worked with corporations in both Japan and the United States. He made the following observation in 1980:

> The U.S. manager sets an acceptable level of quality and then sticks to it. The Japanese are constantly upgrading their goals. The American assumes a certain rate

of failure is inevitable, while the Japanese shoots for perfection and sometimes gets close.[62]

Fortunately, the marketplace worked, and the number of North American firms that have improved quality has increased substantially. A major shift from the use of traditional quality control to total quality control is part of the reason.

Response to Quality Problems

The provision of quality services and goods constantly and from the beginning is an ideal and can't always be attained. Therefore how managers and employees respond to quality problems is critical. Here are three specific prescriptions for recovering from quality problems:

▶ *Encourage customers to complain and make it easy for them to do so.* Comment cards in service delivery facilities and toll-free telephone numbers are only two of the possible alternatives here. British Airways' Video Point booths, in which disembarking passengers could videotape their concerns, made an unusually strong statement that the company wanted to know when its customers were unhappy. However, customers were reluctant to be videotaped because of concerns with their appearance after long trips. Thus this novel approach was discontinued.

▶ *Make timely, personal communications with customers a key part of the strategy.* Organizations frequently make two fatal mistakes in problem resolution: They take too long to respond to customers, and they respond impersonally. Timely, personal communication with unhappy customers offers the best chance to regain the customer's favor. North Carolina's Wachovia Bank & Trust has this "sundown rule": Employees must establish contact with a complaining customer before sunset on the day a complaint is received.

▶ *Encourage employees to respond effectively to customer problems and give them the means to do so.* Organizations must market the idea of problem resolution to employees. This involves, among other things, setting and reinforcing problem-resolution standards and giving employees the freedom to solve customer problems. It's less likely that employees will truly try to solve customer problems if doing so creates a small mountain of red tape. When American Express cardholders telephone the 800 number on their monthly statement, they talk to a highly trained customer service representative. This person has the authority to solve 85 percent of the problems on the spot and the ability to do so through the advanced information technology capabilities at American Express.[63]

INVENTORY MANAGEMENT AND CONTROL

inventory The amount and type of raw materials, parts, supplies, and unshipped finished goods an organization has on hand at a given time.

inventory control The operations management decision area concerned with setting inventory levels, obtaining feedback about changes in them, and signaling the need for action to avoid insufficient or excess inventory.

As we noted earlier, inventory management and control is one of the key decision areas in operations management. **Inventory** is the amount and type of raw materials, parts, supplies, and unshipped finished goods an organization has on hand at a given time. **Inventory control** is concerned primarily with setting maximum, optimum, and minimum levels of inventory; obtaining feedback about changes in inventory levels; and signaling the need for action to avoid going above or below the predetermined levels. Controlling the amount of inventory may have an enormous effect on a firm's capital requirements and the productivity of its capital. If a firm can cut its average inventory value from $10 million to $8 million, with everything else being equal, it can operate with $2 million less in capital or borrowed funds on which it would have to pay interest. This reduction in the amount of money tied up in inventory has the effect of increasing the productivity of the $8 million in inventory by 20 percent. Inventory management and control is of interest to both goods producers and service producers. For example, supermarkets are constantly analyzing how many items of each good they should stock and how much shelf space should be allocated to each item.

Purposes of Maintaining Inventories

Five important purposes of maintaining inventories are (1) to achieve independence of transformation operations, (2) to allow flexibility in the production schedule, (3) to safeguard against problems caused by variations in delivery of input materials, (4) to meet variations in product demand, and (5) to take advantage of economic order quantities. Let's look at the impact of each of these purposes on operations management.

Input materials and partially completed goods are often stocked at each workstation to provide some independence of operation. Thus, if the operators at one station are delayed, they will not delay those at any of the following workstations.

Inventories allow flexibility in the production schedule because a stockpile of finished goods lessens the pressure to produce a certain amount by a particular date and provides for shorter lead times. **Lead time** is the elapsed time between placing of an order and receiving the finished goods. In general, larger finished goods inventories result in shorter customer lead times. For example, some auto dealers use the availability of a large number of cars as part of their marketing strategy. They advertise that customers can get the car of their choice today.

Inventories provide a safeguard against problems caused by variations in the delivery of input materials. An operations manager cannot always count on raw materials arriving on a specific date. Possible reasons for delays include labor problems, transportation holdups, bad weather, and late shipments by suppliers. Without a backup inventory of input materials, even slight delays can shut down an entire operation.

Inventories help meet variations in market demand for the firm's outputs. A company can seldom produce or provide the number of items needed to exactly match market demand. Therefore a common practice is to maintain a safety, or buffer, inventory. This inventory can be used in meeting unanticipated market demand. For example, hospitals must maintain certain quantities of surgical supplies, blood, and medicines to be ready for possible emergencies involving treatment of many patients. Inventories may also be increased to meet seasonal changes in demand for items such as swimsuits. Retailers constantly try to forecast shifts in customer demand in setting inventory levels.

Inventories enable management to take advantage of economic order quantities. It costs money to purchase materials and to carry those materials in inventory. These costs—as well as any offsetting supplier discounts for quantity ordering—are important in determining the most economical size of an order.

Inventories may also serve other purposes, such as stabilizing employment, hedging against inflation, reducing the risk of possible future shortages, and eliminating the need for possible future overtime.[64]

Inventory Costs and Cost Tradeoffs

Inventory costs are the expenses associated with maintaining inventory, including ordering costs, carrying costs, shortage costs, and set-up costs. Managers need to consider all of these costs when making decisions about inventory levels. Let's briefly consider each type:

▶ Ordering costs are the expenses associated with placing the order and/or preparing the purchase order. These generally aren't very large.

▶ Carrying costs are the expenses of holding goods in inventory. These costs include losses due to obsolescence, insurance premiums, rent on storage facilities, depreciation, taxes, breakage, pilferage, and capital invested.

▶ Shortage costs are the losses that occur when there is no stock in inventory to fill a customer's order. The customer must either wait until the inventory is restored or cancel the order. It is difficult to determine the costs resulting from a customer's decision to cancel an order or to place future orders elsewhere.

▶ Set-up costs are the expenses of changing over to make a different product. These costs include the time required to get new input materials, make equipment changes, make

lead time The time elapsed between placing of an order and receiving the finished goods.

inventory costs The expenses associated with maintaining inventory, including ordering costs, carrying costs, shortage costs, and set-up costs.

FIGURE 20.4

Cost Tradeoffs in Determining Inventory Levels

The vertical axis measures the average annual cost associated with different reorder quantities and different carrying costs. The horizontal axis indicates reorder quantities. The total costs curve is simply the sum of ordering cost and carrying cost at each possible order quantity.

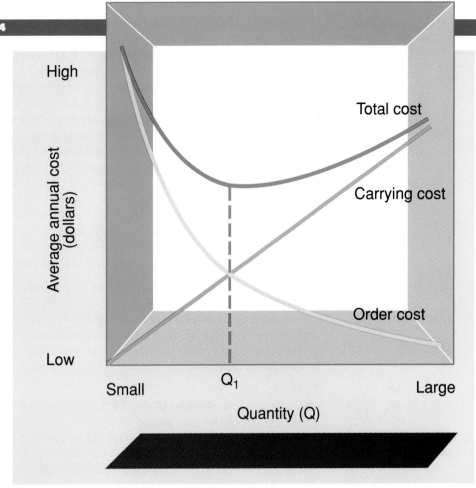

changes in the sequence of production processes, and clear out inventories of other items. They also include the costs of additional administrative time, employee training, idle time, and overtime.

Evaluating specific inventory purposes and costs is part of the control process for determining desirable inventory levels and the ideal size of orders to replenish inventories. "How much do I order?" is a practical question whose answer depends on cost tradeoffs that every inventory manager must evaluate. Figure 20.4 identifies the typical cost tradeoffs involved in determining appropriate order quantities. It suggests that as quantity ordered increases, total ordering cost decreases. However, as order quantity and average inventory level increase, the carrying cost of the inventory also increases. Why? More money and space are tied up by the inventory. The optimal order quantity is that which provides the lowest total inventory costs. This quantity, labeled Q_1 in the figure, is often called the **economic order quantity.** For more precision than Figure 20.4 can provide, more complicated inventory calculations must be made.[65]

economic order quantity
The optimal quantity to order to achieve the lowest total inventory costs.

Systems for Inventory Management and Control

Two developments that have significantly affected inventory management and control are materials resource planning and the just-in-time system. Materials resource planning appears to have the greatest application in conjunction with the process-focus and intermediate positioning strategies (see Figure 20.2). In contrast, the just-in-time system has relatively better potential as a means of tighter inventory control with a product-focus strategy.

materials resource planning II (MRP II) A computerized information system for managing dependent-demand inventories and scheduling stock replenishment orders.

Materials Resource Planning II **Materials resource planning II (MRP II)** is a computerized information system for managing dependent-demand inventories and scheduling stock replenishment orders. It initiates production of various components, releases orders, and offsets inventory reductions. The dependent demands for components, subassemblies, and raw materials (transformation process inputs) are calculated from the demand schedules of those who will use the outputs (customers) or from forecasts. Replenishment orders are time-phased relative to the date the stock is needed. For example, if a firm needs to replenish the stock of an item in week 6 to avoid a stockout and the lead time is 4 weeks, the purchase order will be issued in week 2.[66] Ideally, items arrive just before they are needed, and finished goods are produced just before they are to be shipped. Based on the assumption of uneven demand, MRP II attempts to minimize inventory investment while achieving zero stockouts, maximize operating efficiency, and improve customer service.

Materials resource planning II helps meet three basic information requirements of operations management: (1) What is needed? (2) How much is needed? (3) When is it needed? The following components are used to provide this information:

▶ A master production schedule shows which goods are to be produced, when and in what quantities.

▶ A bill of materials describes the inputs—raw materials, parts, or subassemblies—for each finished good or component to be produced.

▶ An inventory-status file shows inventory on hand and on order for each stock item by time period (day, week, or month), including information on lead time, order size, and supplier.[67]

Materials resource planning II also calculates gross and net financial requirements for inputs and outputs by time period.

To be successful this system requires precise information, as well as extensive coordination and cooperation between individuals and departments. The intent is to get all departments to work to the same schedules and priorities. For example, the failure of sales personnel to report sales precisely and on a timely basis could throw the whole system off. The major problems with the MRP II system have usually been associated with lack of communication and cooperation between individuals in different departments or organizations.[68]

just-in-time (JIT) system An inventory control system that delivers the smallest possible quantities to each stage of the transformation process at the latest possible time without affecting operations.

Automotive body parts are painted, assembled, and delivered from General Motors' Kansas City facility to a nearby GM assembly plant on a *just-in-time* basis.

The Just-In-Time (JIT) System The **just-in-time (JIT) system** delivers finished goods just in time to be sold, subassemblies just in time to be assembled into finished goods, parts just in time to go into subassemblies, and purchased materials just in time to be transformed into parts. At each stage of the transformation process, a JIT system delivers the smallest possible quantities at the latest possible time in order to eliminate as much inventory costs as possible.

Like MRP II, the JIT system affects much more than just the inventory control department. It requires fundamental changes in the relationship between a manufacturer and its suppliers. The traditional use of forcing and compromise as conflict-management styles must shift to the use of collaboration and compromise. The JIT system has major implications for quantities purchased and produced, quality expectations, and suppliers used. The implications for quantities purchased and produced include:

▶ Steady output rate by manufacturer.
▶ Frequent deliveries in small quantities by supplier to manufacturer.
▶ Long-term contracts and blanket orders with suppliers.
▶ Delivery quantities variable from delivery to delivery but fixed for overall contract term.
▶ Little or no overage or underage acceptable in deliveries.[69]

The implications of the JIT system for quality expectations include:

► Manufacturer helps suppliers to meet quality requirements.

► There are close relationships between buyer's and supplier's quality control people.

► Suppliers are urged to use a system of total quality control at each step in their production process.[70]

The implications of the JIT system for suppliers used include:

► Few suppliers, who are often nearby.

► Repeat business with the same suppliers and competitive bidding mostly limited to new parts.

► Suppliers are encouraged to extend the JIT system to their suppliers.

► Suppliers control shipping by using company-owned trucks or contract trucks, contract warehousing, and trailers for freight consolidation storage where possible, instead of common carriers.[71]

As suggested by these implications, JIT is a very demanding system for employees and managers. It requires high levels of communication, coordination, and cooperation. With the JIT system, buffer inventories, idle time, and other forms of slack are drastically reduced. Everyone must be marching in tight formation for JIT to work. Even coffee breaks must be carefully coordinated within and between work teams.[72]

As described in the following Insight, Chrysler first used the JIT system to control inventory levels at its Windsor, Ontario assembly plant for minivans (Dodge Caravan, Plymouth Voyager, and Mini-Ram vans). It has since extended the use of JIT company-wide and is considered to be one of North America's leaders in the use of this system.

THE JIT SYSTEM AT CHRYSLER'S WINDSOR PLANT

INSIGHT

Like many other new auto facilities, Chrysler's Windsor, Ontario assembly plant uses the JIT system and advanced materials control techniques. The Windsor plant applies the JIT system to subassemblies produced in the plant as well as to parts provided by suppliers. The assembly facility, containing 2.5 million square feet of space, was converted to a whole new way of automobile manufacturing in 1984. The plant was designed to have a maximum capacity of approximately seventy vehicles per hour and normally operates with two shifts per day and 3000 workers per shift.

Sheet metal parts are received almost hourly in returnable racks from nearby suppliers. Engines come from as far away as Mexico and Japan, sometimes twice a week, sometimes daily. Depending on their sizes and quantities, trim parts are received on an hourly to a weekly basis.

The fact that the whole facility is filled with production equipment leaves very little room for storage of the thousands of parts used in assembling mini-vans. It was planned that way. If you operate on a JIT system for a few high-value parts, you might as well operate that way for all parts. This is especially true when the suppliers' plants are close by. Storage must be used as a hedge against delivery problems only for items that take a long time to arrive at the plant, such as engines.

The JIT system has had a major impact on the Windsor facility, creating a whole new way of operating. Everyone is aware that the plant could come to a grinding halt if key components, such as seats, are not received on time. With a single-line, continuous flow production process and mixed styles, colors, and options, the system either works or the whole facility shuts down.[73]

1. The systems view of operations management looks at the interrelated processes by which an organization transforms resources into goods and services. Four basic components of the systems view of organizations are environmental factors, inputs (human and physical resources), transformation, and outputs (goods, services, waste products).

2. Operations management plays an important role in improving quality and productivity for both goods and services producers. Operations management requires consideration of at least sixteen types of decisions.

3. Positioning strategy involves the decisions managers make in organizing the flow of resources during the transformation process. The three most common positioning strategies are the process-focus strategy, the intermediate strategy, and the product-focus strategy.

4. There are increasing numbers of technological choices for improving quality and productivity in the transformation process, most of them computer-based. Innovative office technologies revolve around the personal computer. Three widely used service technologies are bar coding, computerized order systems, and open networks. In manufacturing, two important technologies are robots and computer-aided manufacturing.

5. Quality management and control is a strategic component of effective competition. Nine dimensions of quality are (1) performance, (2) features, (3) conformance, (4) reliability, (5) durability, (6) serviceability, (7) responsiveness, (8) aesthetics, and (9) reputation. Total quality control is a strategy that involves building in quality from product planning through sales and service. In contrast, traditional quality control refers to the inspections that take place during or at the end of the production process. The total quality control process focuses on measuring inputs, transformation operations, and outputs (including customer expectations and requirements) to determine whether goods or services are of acceptable quality.

6. Five important purposes of maintaining inventories are (1) to achieve independence of transformation operations, (2) to allow flexibility in the production schedule, (3) to safeguard against unexpected delivery problems, (4) to meet variations in demand, and (5) to take advantage of economic order quantities. When deciding how much inventory to keep on hand, managers must evaluate four types of costs: ordering, carrying, shortage, and setup. The optimal inventory level (and economic order quantity) is determined by weighing certain cost tradeoffs. Materials resource planning (MRP II) is a computerized system for managing inventories and scheduling orders. The just-in-time (JIT) system aims to deliver the smallest possible quantities at the latest possible date at all stages of the transformation process in order to minimize inventory costs.

1. Why is operations management important to employees and managers in the service sector?

2. **From Where You Sit:** Give an example of each of the following for both a services provider and a goods producer: (a) inputs, (b) transformation process, (c) outputs, and (d) feedback.

3. **From Where You Sit:** Choose a good or service that you consume and assume you are a manager of the organization that provides this good or service. What measures might you use to track changes in your firm's productivity?

4. Do the three positioning strategies apply to small organizations as well as large ones?

5. What types of problems should management anticipate because of the increasing use of robots?

6. **From Where You Sit:** Describe and evaluate an organization (public or for-profit) with which you have had one or more transactions during the past three months in terms of the nine dimensions of quality.

7. **From Where You Sit:** Some people claim that North American industries are losing their competitive edge because the quality of foreign-made goods is superior and their price is competitive. Do you agree? Why? Can you cite a special personal experience?

8. Why is the JIT system not useful for all types of transformation operations?

Assessing Total Quality

The nine dimensions of quality listed in Table 20.2 appear in the left-hand column below. Identify one or more examples of each dimension for a fast-food outlet such as McDonald's, Burger King, Dairy Queen, or Wendy's. You may want to visit the outlet you select and focus your observations in terms of these dimensions. Record the specific examples below or on a separate sheet. Also note your assessment of whether the example represents superior, average, or inferior quality.

Outlet Selected: _____

Dimension of Quality	Examples	Quality Rating (superior, average, inferior)
Performance		
Features		
Conformance		
Reliability		
Durability		
Serviceability		
Responsiveness		
Aesthetics		
Reputation		

To: Julia Rodriguez, Vice-President of Production
From: Howard Sheridan, Production Manager
Subject: Quality Control Problems

I share your frustration over the cancellation of our contract with the government of Canada because of poor quality. As you requested, I have made a study of our quality control inspection procedures. My findings are summarized as follows:

1. We make a quick visual check of raw materials when they arrive. Raw materials that should be rejected are sometimes accepted because no replacement materials are available.

2. No regular inspections are scheduled during production, although some spot checks are made during the machining process.

3. Some parts are inspected randomly, and others get 100 percent inspection. A defect tally sheet is prepared on all materials. Tools for determining defects are calibrated once a year. If parts are accepted, they proceed to inventory; if rejected, they are returned for more work or scrapped.

4. All completed assemblies get a "cold check" (without electrical connection) and defects are recorded. Typical defects include missing components and incorrect mounting of parts. Assemblies with electrical characteristics needing checking proceed to "hot check," where performance is tested over a period of time. Then the units proceed to the cleanup area, where they are inspected for fingerprints and excess dirt. A further cleanliness check is made before goods are shipped.

My feeling is that our quality problems are the fault of suppliers and inspectors. Of course, quality management and control is not an area of expertise for me, nor was I expected to concentrate on it in the past. Before you arrived four months ago, I was always encouraged to produce it and ship it as quickly as possible.

Your ideas on how we might get a better handle on our quality problems are most welcome.

Assume you are Julia Rodriguez. Write a memo in response to Howard Sheridan.

'Value Pricing' Is Hot As Shrewd Consumers Seek Low-Cost Quality

BY JOSEPH B. WHITE

ANN ARBOR, Mich.—James Magyar wasn't thinking about the recession when he recently went shopping at Micro Age Computer here. But he ended up giving the economy a tiny boost.

Mr. Magyar was planning to buy an extra computer to handle mailing lists and word processing for the nonprofit business he runs. But he found out he could buy an Apple Macintosh Classic, with the same power and most of the same features as the Macintosh SE models that he already had, for half the price of the old SE.

So he bought two computers instead of one, spending a total of $2,590. "I wanted the biggest bang for the buck, and the Classics fit that bill nicely," he says.

What's the new Macintosh Classic's secret? Simple, says Ann Arbor Apple dealer Richard Weir: "It's more for a hell of a lot less."

Offering more for a lot less—or as marketing experts put it, "value pricing"—is proving to be a crucial tactic for a wide variety of companies in these recessionary times. It could even be the spur that unlocks consumer spending, bringing the recession to a hoped-for quick end.

PepsiCo Inc.'s Taco Bell chain saw its fourth-quarter sales jump 15% in response to a "value" menu offering 59-cent tacos and 14 other items for either 79 cents or 99 cents.

Even in today's depressed car market, General Motor Corp.'s Pontiac division can't build enough of a special two-door Grand Prix that offers, for about $17,000, the racy exterior look of a model that sold for $26,000 last year. "We don't have any in stock," complains Skokie, Ill., Pontiac dealer Gary Grossinger. "They way underestimated demand for that car."

This isn't just old-fashioned price-cutting, though that is an important element. It is price cutting coupled with ingenuity that lets manufacturers maintain or even enhance quality while still earning a profit. These companies have discovered that when consumers say "value," they don't mean cheap. Instead, many Americans who came to enjoy top-quality brand-name goods during the 1980s are now demanding that manufacturers figure out how to maintain high quality, but at substantially reduced prices.

"If it's got a brand name at a low price, it's home free," says Eric Miller, editor of Research Alert, a consumer-research newsletter in Long Island City, N.Y. "If it appears cheap, it croaks."

Many companies learned from the most-recent recession that it can be dangerous to cheapen products just to cater to price-conscious buyers. GM's Cadillac division is still smarting from its 1981 decision to sell an "economy" Cadillac, the Cimarron, that was really a thinly disguised Chevrolet Cavalier.

More recently, in March 1989, Sears Roebuck & Co. launched a value pricing campaign it called "everyday low pricing." The strategy struck a chord with shoppers, and crowds flooded Sears stores. Unfortunately for Sears, shoppers found that "prices in other stores were still lower," says Kurt Barnard, publisher of a newsletter, Retail Marketing Report. The strategy backfired and Sears soon had to resort to special promotions.

So now companies from Seventh Avenue to Silicon Valley are scrambling to deliver on the value pricing promise of low-cost quality. They are remanufacturing, redesigning, repackaging and repricing products. They want their wares both to appeal to consumers and to sell for less—over the long haul, not just during sales.

The value-pricing trend is gaining impetus from the current recession, but its roots run far deeper. Even before the economy soured last fall, market researchers were detecting signs of a fundamental shift in consumer attitudes, particularly among members of the baby-boom generation now entering their 30s and 40s, the peak years for child-rearing, home-buying and other big, long-term commitments. . . .

Catering to sophisticated but bargain-conscious consumers is forcing manufacturers and service providers to rethink some fundamentals of 1980s marketing. Car makers during the 1980s tried to push consumers to buy more-expensive models in part by offering cheap cars that were dowdy-looking and ill-equipped. . . .

Toyota Motor Corp. engineers embarked on a mission to achieve what one Toyota planner calls an "epic-making costdown" when it redesigned its least expensive model, the Tercel. The result, launched last fall, is a little car with a smooth, big-car external profile, and 7% more horsepower and a quieter ride than its predecessor. The base price starts at just $6,588, but Toyota officials say the car is a money maker.

Taco Bell redesigned its restaurants, shrinking kitchen space, so that 70% of the floor space was devoted to seating, compared with 30% in the past. Many of the value menu items are new, and specifically designed for easy preparation in the new, smaller kitchens. The moves to cut costs and increase traffic have paid off: Taco Bell's operating profit soared 99% in the latest fourth quarter. Rival McDonald's Corp. is experimenting with cutting prices and advertising special "Value Meals," such as a Big Mac, a large order of fries and a medium drink, for $2.99.

At Apple, engineers decided "we couldn't have low prices if we didn't have a new design" for the Macintosh computers, says Brian Loucks, product manager for the Apple Macintosh Classic.

Selling the old Apple Macintosh SE at Mac Classic prices "wouldn't have been sustainable."

To produce the Macintosh Classic, which sells for as low as $900 Apple engineers jettisoned features of the old Macintosh SE that most customers ignored. Apple also redesigned the Macintosh's brain, or logic board. The saving from the simpler design "is measured in dollars, not cents," Mr. Loucks says.

Despite all this work, Apple still has to accept lower profit margins to sell the Classic at half the price of its predecessor model. Apple—and dealers such as Ann Arbor's Mr. Weir—are counting on volume to make up the difference. So far, it is working. Shipments of Macintosh computers jumped 50% in the quarter ended Dec. 31, and the Cupertino, Calif., company is scrambling to fill orders by expanding Macintosh Classic production capacity at factories in Ireland and Singapore.

1. Value pricing is proving to be a crucial tactic for a variety of industries. What types of industries might find it successful? For which might it fail?

2. Draw a competitiveness value map for Sears.

3. Imagine you work for a small computer company that is looking into value pricing. You have been asked to come up with a recommendation. Where would you begin your research? Trace your path to coming up with a final plan.

LONGHORN PRODUCTS

In 1974 David Ream achieved his lifelong dream of starting his own company, Long-horn Products, a machine shop located in San Antonio, Texas. After two difficult years, the firm grew steadily. Annual sales now exceed $500,000.

Longhorn Products produces a variety of small metal parts that it sells to other manu-facturers in the Southwest. About 50 percent of customer orders are for one-of-a-kind parts. The average order is for 35 pieces, and order quantities range from 1 to 500 pieces. Delivery lead times (which Ream calls ''cycle times'') vary from one to four months, de-pending on work content, materials require-ments, and capacity bottlenecks. Ream's competitive priorities are to produce a wide range of customized jobs, handle peaks and valleys in demand, and consistently meet due dates promised to customers.

One of Ream's main tasks is to decide how a job will be performed, including the manufacturing operations and materials needed. He uses two sources of information: a blueprint of the detailed design provided by the customer, and a routing sheet listing each operation to be performed, time standards for it, and materials costs.

Longhorn primarily uses general-purpose machines that provide production flexibility. Most workers are trained to operate several different machines, giving them job variety and necessitating frequent interaction among the workers, shop manager, and Ream.

Ream and the shop managers constantly look for new ways to reduce setup times (the time to change a machine over from one job to the next), improve tooling, perform an operation on a more efficient machine, make (rather than buy) a component, change rout-ing sequences, or even redesign a product.

Longhorn operates one full shift of twenty-six workers supplemented by a second shift of only six workers. Machine capacity is the main limitation. Work overloads are han-dled with overtime and increased use of ma-chines and employees on the second shift. Equipment capacity isn't well balanced. Weekly usage per machine varies from three to eighty hours, with an average of four and a half. Because of variations in product mix, Ream describes the workload at most ma-chines as ''feast-or-famine.'' However, there is enough machine flexibility to temporarily reroute jobs to other machines.

Space is cramped, and Ream is looking at relocation options. The current layout groups workers and equipment functionally: an area for drill presses, one for welding sta-tions, another for brake presses, and so on. A fair amount of shop space is needed to store in-process jobs. Materials handling paths are complex, with considerable criss-crossing from one area of the plant to another. Materi-als are moved by the machine operators them-selves.

In order to buffer operations and reduce bottlenecks, Ream quotes reasonably long delivery lead times—averaging two months—to customers. With a typical job actually tak-ing only 100 work hours for all setup and processing activities, work-in-process inven-tory is large.

Longhorn has little influence over its suppliers because of its low volumes. Vendor relationships are informal, and there are no long-term purchasing agreements. Very few purchased items are stocked in inventory, which minimizes inventory but lengthens pro-duction time. Ream is currently considering stocking some high-usage raw materials and manufactured subassemblies to cut delays. Because of their customized nature, finished goods are rarely stocked. Usually, as soon as an order is finished, it is shipped directly to the customer.

Production planning isn't formalized or projected very far into the future. Using lead-time estimates and orders already booked, Ream projects total monthly output for three months ahead. His projections influence how aggressively he bids on new jobs.

Ream uses a manual system to release and follow up on orders. When all necessary materials and tooling are available, he releases the order to the shop. The routing sheet, a record card, and the blueprint are placed in a folder and sent to the shop manager, signaling that work can begin.

Scheduling of work is complex. It demands much of the shop manager's time. He schedules work assignments only a day or two in advance. Longer schedules are of little value, because of unexpected bottlenecks, rush orders, and rework problems. Longhorn workers are responsible for the quality of their work. Only spot checks of outgoing shipments are made. Scrap and rework are sometimes a problem.

1. Which of the nine types of operations management decisions are illustrated in this case?

2. What positioning strategy is used at Longhorn Products? Is it appropriate? Why?

3. Should David Ream establish a just-in-time (JIT) system? Why?

4. Should Ream establish a materials resource planning II system? Why?

5. Does Longhorn Products practice traditional quality control or total quality control? Should any changes be made in this area?

Part Seven

MANAGEMENT IN A CHANGING WORLD

Brew-Ha-Ha

Like most entrepreneurs, Jim Koch had a dream. He always wanted to make beer like his father and grandfather before him, but he knew that brewing beer was a precarious way to make a living. In fact, Jim's father operated four different breweries, and each one of them failed.

Still Koch, who today runs the Boston Brewing Company—the brewer of Samuel Adams Lager—didn't let the dream die. Even though he went to Harvard, earned an MBA, and worked as a business strategy consultant, he kept a careful eye on the brewery business, looking for a way to enter the market.

His first step was to analyze the beer-making history of America. "Trying to start a brewery," he once noted, "is like trying to start your own oil company. You just don't do it."

Why? History showed that small, regional brewers had been slowly squeezed out of the market by the big breweries. During the 1950s and 1960s, there were hundreds of local breweries, such as Piels and Ballantine. Over time, some regional brands survived, but most small brewers were put out of business by companies like Anheuser-Busch—the company that brews Budweiser—which used big advertising budgets to mass-market their beer. In fact, by the time Koch was ready to launch his venture, Anheuser-Busch had captured nearly 40 percent of the beer market and was brewing 5,000,000 barrels of beer a month. (Koch first brewed his beer, just 2,000 barrels at a time, in a brewery he rented once a month in Pittsburgh, before moving his operation to Boston.)

Koch knew it would be foolish to try to slug it out with the giants. In order to break into the business, he would have to find a niche, a distinctive section of a larger market, with its own consumer appeal.

Koch's research also revealed that the fastest-growing segment of the beer business belonged to the imported brands, such as Becks. Imported beers were more expensive than American brands; moreover, their ads often showed handsome, wealthy young people drinking beer in luxurious settings. The price and product positioning helped persuade consumers that imported beer was better than anything brewed in America.

But, when looking at the import market, Koch saw an opening, one that could be exploited with the right product: an American beer positioned as the highest-price, highest-quality alternative to the imports.

Even the name, Samuel Adams, was important to Koch's strategy. Samuel Adams was a patriot, "who instigated and nurtured the American Revolution," Koch noted. "And he was a brewer."

To compete against the imports, Koch had to brew a high-quality beer. He chose a beer that was darker and more aromatic than the imports. In addition, his beer had more body and a distinctive bitter flavor. But was it really a better beer? The judges at the 1985 Great American Beer Festival in Denver thought so. Koch's brew won first prize, over 93 other entries, just seven weeks after he started making beer.

Still, one contest victory isn't enough to guarantee sales. So Koch's next step was twofold. Since his advertising budget was small, he challenged the imports directly, staging taste tests and promotions in Boston's pubs and inviting the press to attend. Not only did Sam Adams win local taste tests, but Koch used the events to accuse importers of selling a substandard beer that was created solely for the U.S. market. In other words, he called the importers frauds. His competition denied the charges, but in the process, the media reported Koch's statements and helped garner much-needed attention for Koch and his beer.

Has the strategy worked? So far, so good. In fact, in 1990, the company brewed 110,000 barrels of beer, and business was growing. But would Koch, like any entrepreneur, have been able to pull this off without extensive research? How important was it for Koch, or any entrepreneur, to make a distinctive product?

Chapter 21

ORGANIZATIONAL CHANGE

AND INNOVATION

3M's research lab

What You Will Learn

1 The challenges managers face as a result of changes in the work force and the world.

2 The basic steps managers should follow in achieving planned organizational change.

3 Reasons why individuals and organizations resist change and methods for overcoming such resistance.

4 Four approaches to achieving effective organizational change.

5 **Skill Development:** How to prepare for and deal with organizational change.

Chapter Outline

Manager's Viewpoint
Innovation and Change at 3M

Sources of Change
A Changing Work Force
Managerial Challenges

Planned Organizational Change and Innovation
Assess Changes in the Environment
Determining the Performance Gap
Insight: Closing the Performance Gap at Procter & Gamble
Diagnose Organizational Problems
Identify Sources of Resistance
Insight: Mike Walsh at Union Pacific
Set Objectives for the Change Effort
Search for Change Approaches
Implement the Change
Follow Up the Change

Approaches to Organizational Change and Innovation
Technology Approach
Insight: The Information Revolution at IBM
Structure Approach
Global Link: Unilever's New Structure
Task Approach
Insight: Simpler Design Leads to Big Profits at CalComp
People Approach
Insight: Team Building at Trison Properties Management

Experiencing Management
Skill-Building Exercise: How Innovative Are You?

Manager's Memo

In the News

Management Case:
Hewlett-Packard Rethinks Itself

"Workers at 3M are rewarded for

innovation."

Innovation and Change at 3M

For decades 3M has relied on a strategy of staying ahead of its competition by spinning out new products. The company makes more than 60,000 items, including Scotch tape, floppy discs, and Post-it brand notes. Products developed in just the preceding five years accounted for nearly $3.5 billion of the company's sales in 1990.

Although 3M has been successful at innovation, competitors around the globe have recently been able to develop products more cheaply and faster. In response, 3M has asked employees to streamline their operations and boost their productivity by 35 percent—in effect, to *change* the way they innovate.

In order to meet the general goals of improving productivity by 35 percent and generating 25 percent of the company's sales from new products, each division has agreed to meet specific goals. Top management didn't tell divisional managers how to achieve these, because each manager faces unique business situations. Each division and plant was asked to identify its problems and propose ways to solve them. To help divisions share ways to reach the overall goal, a manufacturing council was established.

So far, results have been encouraging. Workers at an Aberdeen, South Dakota, plant, which assembles respirator masks used by painters, decided to rethink their entire manufacturing process. It turned out that filter materials were returned to a warehouse after each step in the process to await the next step—seven round trips in all. Plant managers formed teams of factory employees to help figure out ways to untangle the flow of materials and parts through the plant. The workers arrived at a radical solution: Scrap the traditional assembly line, and organize the machinery and workers around work teams, each of whom is responsible for making the complete product. This strategy eliminates the need for trips to the warehouse. The workers' solution, along with a new inventory control program, has increased productivity by 54 percent.

Workers at 3M are rewarded for innovation. The Aberdeen workers were treated to pizza parties and received trophies and bonuses after they met their goals. To encourage cooperation, the company pegged individual bonuses to the creativity of solutions worked out by their teams.[1]

You may wonder how companies such as 3M, Merck, and Hewlett-Packard, among others, always seem to have new products on the market. Behind each of these successful companies is a well-designed strategy for planned change. Merck, for example, assigns a design team leader to each promising new drug product. The leader must shepherd the product through the entire process—from basic research to final government approval. The leader must also persuade other employees to join his or her team. This builds unity and helps researchers feel that they have something invested in a project. Merck also spends more than $21,000 per employee each year for research, compared with an industry average of $12,700. This isn't the only reason Merck is a leader in the drug industry, but it does help the company find and retain the best scientists in the world.[2]

You may also wonder why some companies that were successful at one time are no longer successful. The answer is simple: Organizations are never static. And they can't continue to be successful if they fail to change and adapt. Think of Osborne Computer, U.S. Steel, People Express, and a lot of savings & loan associations. These highly profitable companies were unable to maintain their success because they didn't adapt fast enough. For example, Osborne computers, founded in 1981, had sales of more than $100 million within eighteen months, but in September 1983 it filed for bankruptcy. Why? When Osborne started, it had a niche in the small computer market. It sold its microcomputers for hundreds of dollars less than Apple, IBM, or other manufacturers did; it had lined up Computerland, Sears, and Xerox retail stores as outlets. Osborne managers delegated authority and responsibility to make decisions to those closest to the "action" but didn't give them any guidelines. As a result, advertising budgets were overspent, inventories were improperly managed, and financial controls weren't in place. When a slump hit the microcomputer market in 1983, Osborne wasn't prepared to weather it and failed.

As we discussed in Chapters 3, 4, and 8, shifts in consumer preferences, technological breakthroughs, and demands from diverse interest groups all create powerful forces that require organizational change. Most people—whether students, employees, managers, or consultants—are involved with organizations that are changing. To be effective employees or managers, you must learn how to deal creatively with day-to-day conditions that require adaptation and cause tension and frustration. The major purpose of this chapter is to help you understand how organizations can survive, operate effectively, and innovate in a changing world.

SOURCES OF CHANGE

In his book *The Fifth Discipline* Peter Senge argues that organizations must learn.[3] That is, they must find ways to expand employees' capacity to create and to produce results if they want to succeed in the 1990s. The old bureaucratic command-and-control model won't be up to the challenges ahead:

▶ *It won't be fast enough* to match the new-product development time of foreign competitors or to spot new market opportunities.

▶ *It won't be wise enough* to deliver the high levels of service customers will increasingly demand.

▶ *It won't be smart enough* to manage a diverse work force or to motivate its smartest employees.

For an organization to learn, employees inside it have to tell one another the truth. At Honda, an organization that practices learning, information on performance, quality, consumer satisfaction, and competition gets circulated widely. Rewards are equitably distributed among all employees. There is an extraordinarily high degree of trust between managers and employees, based on a common set of values. Middle managers are responsible for creating the conditions in which learning can take place. Working in multifunctional teams (including design, production, and marketing), they must integrate top management's strategic goals with employee inputs on production problems.

Speed—fast-paced adaptation to change—has become a competitive weapon for many firms. Citibank has introduced as many as three new financial services in one week. The Limited, a women's retail fashion chain, rushes new fashions off the design board and into its 3200 stores in less than sixty days. Honda and Toyota can take a car from concept to market in three years, while U.S. automakers often need up to five.[4]

Change is an integral part of life. In the 1990s the fast pace of change and the prospect that it will come faster and faster are affecting every part of life, from personal values to technology. So many things are changing today that a kind of "temporary

Rates of Change Over the Past 100 Years

The relative rates of change experienced within six areas fundamental to our society and our lives.

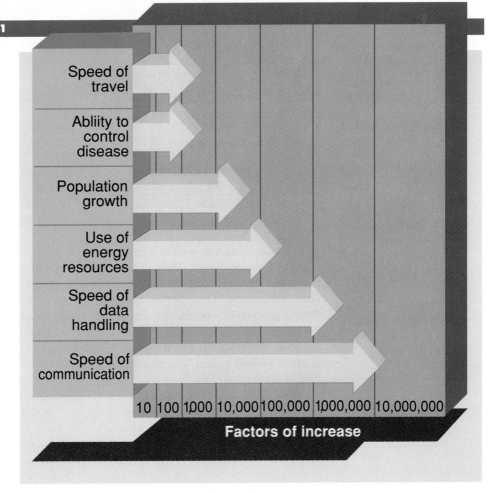

society'' is arising, characterized by relatively impermanent housing, jobs, friendships, and neighborhoods. Events move so quickly that long-term stability is threatened, and even personal values may fall victim to a ''throw-away'' lifestyle. Figure 21.1 shows relative rates of change in six areas of our society over the past century.

A Changing Work Force

In Chapters 1 and 12 we indicated some of the changes taking place in the U.S. work force. For instance, the majority of new workers are better educated than those who preceded them. Over half the young people in the United States today have some college education. By the year 2000 most jobs will require a high school education.

In the 1970s and 1980s, women held the majority of jobs as insurance adjusters and examiners, computer operators, secretaries, elementary school teachers, cashiers, nurses, and retail salespeople. Although a gap still exists between the salaries of men and women, an increasing number of women are taking advantage of educational opportunities and are entering traditionally male domains. The U.S. Department of Education reports that over 37 percent of students earning MBAs and roughly 40 percent of law students are women. More and more women are taking jobs as accountants, lawyers, bankers, and institutional investors. If current trends continue through 2000, the majority of the 15 million new entrants into the job market will be women. Women also make up 25 percent of all small business owners and are starting up businesses at a faster rate than men are. In fact, by 2000, women could own 50 percent of all small businesses. The U.S. Department of Labor estimates that women hold 40 percent of the managerial jobs in the United States.[5]

Contrary to popular opinion, workers haven't abandoned the traditional work ethic of a day's work for a day's pay. Today's workers however, want their work to provide

It's a *changing work force* today. Morgan Guaranty already fills half its management training programs in New York with foreign recruits.

personal satisfaction as well as a paycheck. They expect to be involved in decisions that affect them and their jobs. They do *not* function like automatons, mindlessly following the boss's orders, nor can they be regarded as insignificant cogs on a giant impersonal wheel. For example, at the General Motors–Toyota joint venture in California, top management divides production workers into teams, each under the direction of a team leader chosen by team members. These teams divide the work. Status differences between blue-collar and white-collar workers are minimized: Everyone eats in the same cafeteria, there are no reserved parking spaces, and executives and clerks work in the same open area, rather than in separate offices.

Table 21.1 compares goals and dreams of managers in the 1970s with those of managers in the 1990s. Some management consultants predict that the typical organization in 2000 will have half the management levels it has today. As companies flatten their structures to become more competitive, they'll be reducing the number of rungs on the managerial ladder. This will also lengthen the time between promotions—tomorrow's managers will hold each position longer. Managers will have to make lateral moves in order to learn new skills and be personally challenged. Such personal growth will make sense because future managers will be generalists who are knowledgeable in several areas, as opposed to specialists who understand only finance, production, or marketing.[6]

Implications for Managers The number of management jobs eliminated is increasing as corporate raiders such as Carl Icahn and T. Boone Pickens, Jr. emerge as powerful figures in the business world. Experts estimate that between 1990 and 2000 more than 1 million managers will lose their jobs because of mergers and efforts to streamline organizations.[7] *Downsize, dismantle,* and *leveraged buyout* (LBO) have become corporate bywords. Oxzy Chemical, Kodak, CBS, Gillette, and Goodyear, for example, have already made managerial cuts of 20 percent or more.

TABLE 21.1

Climbing the Ladder, Then and Now

For Managers in the 1970s	For Managers of the 1990s
Every job was supposed to be upward.	Lateral moves are routine and desirable.
Promotions within two years.	Jobs last longer; responsibilities evolve with no title change.
Personal feelings were secondary to corporate harmony.	It's acceptable to speak out and try to reshape things.
Success meant job security all the way to retirement.	Success means inner fulfillment and money.
Good pay was your age times $1,000.	A good pay package includes profit sharing or equity.

Source: Adapted from D. Kirkpatrick, ''Is Your Career on Track?'' *Fortune,* July 2, 1990, 39.

When Ralston-Purina and Quaker Oats competed to take over food giant Anderson-Clayton, they were after that firm's most profitable brand product—Gaines dog food. After Quaker won the battle, it kept Gaines and sold off the remaining products. Quaker then dismissed many of Anderson-Clayton's long-term employees in order to cut expenses and finance the acquisition. In a society that equates who a person is with what he or she does for a living, suddenly losing this source of identity is a shock.

Mergers, acquisitions, and stock buybacks have led some managers to reduce their commitment to their companies. In the past most managers expected to have a lifetime career in one company. Companies that fostered this practice were widely admired and considered to be well run. Today's employees have learned to be "free agents."[8] The free agent believes that any employment relationship is temporary. Thus an increasing number of employees view their organizations as places where they temporarily earn a living. Loyalty is no longer as fashionable. Few organizations value loyalty as much as they did in the past. Because of this "be ready to leave" attitude, the 1990s are likely to be characterized by short-term employment relationships. During her or his career, the average person may relocate seven or eight times, be unemployed for up to a year, and be fired at least once.

Managerial Challenges

How well managers run their organizations depends heavily on how well they create and respond to changes. GM's former chairman Roger Smith has noted that creating organizational change is comparable to an "elephant learning to dance." Let's consider four key challenges facing today's and tomorrow's managers.

First, *organizations must be designed so that they can learn.* As we discussed earlier, successful organizations learn to encourage employees to produce creative results. Ray Stata, CEO of Analog Devices, said that his biggest task is to get employees to work as a smoothly functioning team. He has found that if you can get members of a team to really work together, instead of working as individuals, they quickly realize how much they need one another to perform their jobs successfully. Employees must teach other employees how to solve problems.

Second, *managers must realize that the bases of power in organizations are changing.* In the future, employees will demand more participation in decision making than they did in the past.[9] Expertise—not just position in the management hierarchy—will be an important source of authority. Organization charts may shift with every new product or service. For example, in NASA's Skylab project, authority is based on expertise. Thus each time the project enters a new phase, the team member most qualified and knowledgeable in the field becomes the "boss." In general, traditional hierarchies are cumbersome when rapid response times and flexibility are needed. Participative management and matrix structures provide organizations with flexibility to roll with the punches.

Third, *organizations must find ways to allow individuals and teams at lower levels to develop their own ideas.* These people are called intrapreneurs. **Intrapreneurs** are employees who develop new products and new markets for their organizations.[10] According to Gifford Pinchot, who coined the term in his book *Intrapreneuring,* organizations need to find ways to combine the advantages of being small and being large. Some companies have encouraged employees to experiment, innovate, and fail—to work with almost total freedom. Project failure doesn't doom a person's career in such organizations. For example, 3M has a policy that allows engineers to spend part of their time working on their own projects. Arthur Fry, a 3M chemical engineer, used to get annoyed at how pieces of paper that marked his church hymnal always fell out when he stood up to sing. He knew that Spencer Silver, a scientist at 3M, had inadvertently discovered an adhesive that had low sticking power. Normally that would be bad, but for Fry it was good. He figured that markers made with that adhesive might stick lightly to something and then come off easily. The company allowed Fry 15 percent of his time to work on the project. Fry made samples and then sent the small yellow pads to company secretaries. They were delighted

intrapreneur An employee who develops a new product and a new market for his or her organization.

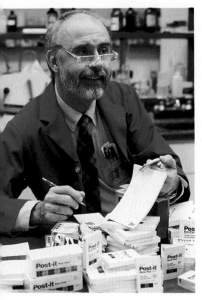

Arthur Fry, a 3M chemical engineer-cum-*entrepreneur*, was given 15 percent of his time to work on developing his invention: Post-it notes.

with the product. Thus Post-its were born. Sales of these little yellow (and pink and green and blue) note pads have increased to more than $200 million annually.

Fourth, organizations must recognize that *the global village is a reality*. Managers and their organizations live in an expansive environment of worldwide economic connections.[11] With the collapse of the Berlin Wall and the unification of the two Germanys, many companies are geared up to invest in the Eastern bloc countries—Volkswagen in East Germany, General Electric in Hungary, and McDonald's in the Soviet Union. Over the next few years, Coca-Cola will invest $140 million in East Germany to upgrade bottling and distribution systems. Just a decade ago, most companies were not engaged in the global marketplace. Today, well over half of *Fortune*'s 500 earn major portions of their sales revenues from businesses scattered all over the world.

With globalization moving full speed ahead, many U.S. and European multinationals are buying their way into new markets through mergers, acquisitions, and strategic alliances. In Chapter 4 we indicated that strategic alliances marry one party's manufacturing skills or product to another's distribution.[12] These alliances are often quicker and cheaper than expanding a business overseas. A recent strategic alliance was formed between General Electric and Samsung. The microwave oven, invented in the United States more than forty years ago, became the best-selling kitchen appliance in the world. Odds are that if you buy one, it will have been made by Samsung, a firm based in South Korea. Samsung makes more than 80,000 microwave ovens a week and sells them around the world under the General Electric label. General Electric has the marketing know-how to sell microwaves, and Samsung has the manufacturing technology to produce them at a low cost.[13] Similarly, a joint venture between Ford and Mazda was established to make the 1991 Ford Escort. Under this arrangement Mazda engineered the car, Ford designed it, and then Ford and its U.S. suppliers built 80 percent of the cars sold in the United States.

PLANNED ORGANIZATIONAL CHANGE AND INNOVATION

Organizational change has two interrelated objectives: fitting the organization to its environment, and changing the behavior of employees. In managing change, managers can follow the eight steps shown in Fig. 21.2, although change programs don't always proceed in the order given. These steps constitute the basic components of planned organizational change, however, no matter what sequence they're taken in. The following sections consider each step separately.

Assess Changes in the Environment

An organization's external environment is constantly changing, but the degree and rate of that change are the important factors. The environmental elements most responsible for change are competition, technology, politics, culture, and the work force (refer to Chapters 3, 4, 5, 8, and 12). One of management's primary functions is to monitor these elements and the changes they bring so the organization can operate effectively.

The degree and rate of change determines whether a company's external environment is relatively stable or relatively unstable. Relatively stable environments can be found in the brewing, insurance, and commercial banking industries. Within each of these industries the products, customers, suppliers, methods of distribution, and prices are similar. Companies try to differentiate their products and advertise extensively to create demand. Ford and Chrysler generally compete for the same car buyers, charge similar prices, negotiate with the same international labor union, and face similar distribution problems. Insurance premiums charged by large insurance companies—such as State Farm, All-

FIGURE 21.2

Planned Organizational Change

Organizational change starts with an accurate assessment of changes in the environment and extends through following up on what has happened after the change has been completed. Once the process is complete, the change may trigger new problems that need to be addressed.

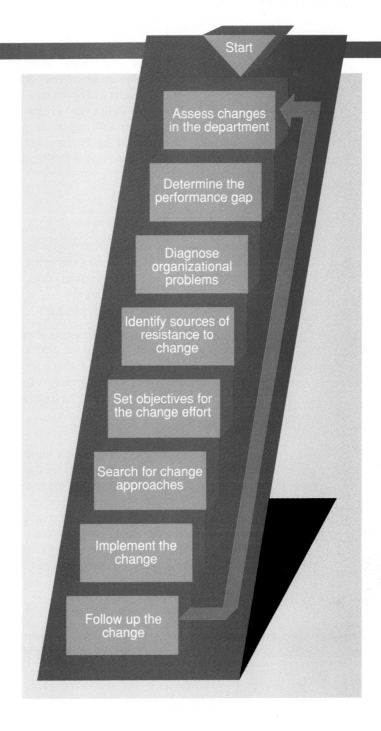

Start

Assess changes in the department

Determine the performance gap

Diagnose organizational problems

Identify sources of resistance to change

Set objectives for the change effort

Search for change approaches

Implement the change

Follow up the change

state, Prudential, Travelers, and Hartford—are similar. They differentiate their products via the services that each provides to policyholders. On the other hand, companies that choose to operate multiple businesses and sell unrelated products face greater instability with respect to their external environment. Firms that have adopted this strategy include W. R. Grace, ITT, Gulf & Western, and Alco Standard. W. R. Grace is a diversified, worldwide corporation that has 550 separate companies, operates plants in 47 states and 43 countries, employs more than 49,000 people, and has annual sales of more than $6.1 billion. The 550 different companies are organized into three broad product lines: specialty chemicals, general business, and natural resources. Each business represents different challenges to W. R. Grace's management in terms of government regulation, competition, customers, and the value of the dollar. Top management constantly buys and sells businesses in order to meet the demands of its corporate strategy.[14]

As we've stressed before (see Chapters 19 and 20), most industries have undergone—and are still undergoing—tremendous technological advances. In some industries the technology of only five years ago is now outdated. For example, the rapid increase in the use of personal computers and computer-based information systems has revolutionized the publishing industry. Before the advent of personal computers, that industry was dominated by large firms with expensive printing presses. Personal computers have enabled small firms to enter this industry and compete effectively in terms of service and price. Apple, Compaq, Tandy, and IBM have made major commitments to the desktop publishing market.

Determining the Performance Gap

performance gap The difference between what the organization aspires to do to take advantage of its opportunities and what it actually does.

The next step in the change process is to determine the performance gap. The **performance gap** is the difference between what the organization aspires to do to take advantage of its opportunities and what it actually does. Matt Bohn, director of quality control for Hoechst Celanese Chemical Company's plant in North Carolina, posed five questions to his staff to evaluate the performance gap facing them:

1. What is your vision of the external changes (government rules, customers, competitors) affecting our business in the next five years?
2. Where are these now, and where are these taking the business?
3. What new comparative advantages (products, distribution channels, pricing) do we need to build into our thinking to cope with these changes?
4. How are we going to get there?
5. What can go wrong?

As Bohn and his employees answered these questions, pressure to change came from *within* his team. Not all performance gaps are brought about by competitors or governmental rules. A performance gap may occur when new technical breakthroughs are made. And a gap may persist for some time before it is recognized. (In fact, it may never be recognized.) Furthermore, when a performance gap—no matter what its cause—is recognized, it must have significant consequences for the firm to warrant narrowing or bridging it. The following Insight looks at how Richard Nicolosi closed a large performance gap at Procter & Gamble to more closely align his division's products with demands from customers.

CLOSING THE PERFORMANCE GAP AT PROCTER & GAMBLE

INSIGHT

From 1956 until about the mid-1970s, Procter & Gamble's Paper Products Division had little competition for its high-quality products, such as Pampers. But by the late 1970s, that had changed: Market share in the disposable diaper market fell from 75 percent in the mid-1970s to 52 percent in 1984. What had happened?

During good times, the Paper Products Division had become heavily bureaucratic. All decisions were made at the top. Middle-level managers were concerned with their own departmental goals and projects. Almost all information about customer wants and needs came through highly quantitative marketing research. The technical departments were rewarded for cost savings and the commercial departments for volume. The two groups hardly ever talked to each other.

This is what Richard Nicolosi found when he was appointed vice president of the division in 1984. After studying the operations for three months, he charted a new strategy—one that moved it from being a low-cost producer to being a high-quality producer. Teams of employees were created that cut across major product lines (such as diapers, tissues, towels). Authority and responsibility were pushed down to these teams so that they could make decisions. Layers of hierarchy were eliminated. Nicolosi created new-brand teams to instill a sense of entrepreneurship in the division. Managers were rewarded when they successfully introduced and marketed new products, such as Ultra-Pampers and Luvs Deluxe.

All employees were asked—and wanted—to contribute to the success of the division. What are the results? Since mid-1985 sales are up more than 40 percent and profits are up 66 percent.[15]

Diagnose Organizational Problems

The aim of the diagnostic step of the change process is to identify the nature and extent of the problem before taking action. The caution that *diagnosis should precede action* may seem obvious, but its importance is often underestimated. All too often the change process is started prematurely—early in the diagnostic step—depending on who does the diagnosis and the methods chosen for analyzing the problem. Harassed and results-oriented managers often impatiently push for solutions before the problem itself is clear.

Most organizational problems have multiple causes. There is seldom a simple and obvious one. As part of the diagnostic step, a manager might begin by asking these questions:

1. What specific problems have to be corrected?
2. What are the causes of these problems?
3. What must be changed to solve these problems?
4. What forces are likely to work for and against these changes?
5. What are the objectives of these changes, and how will they be measured?

A variety of data-gathering techniques—including attitude surveys, conferences, informal interviews, and team meetings—have been used successfully to diagnose problems. The purpose of these techniques is to gather data that aren't biased by a few dominant persons in the organization or by consultants.[16]

Interpersonal problems usually require the use of attitude surveys, perhaps handled by outside consultants who conduct interviews and analyze the data. Attitude surveys usually tap the feelings of employees effectively. This technique enables management to evaluate employee attitudes about pay, types of work, and working conditions. Survey responses should be recorded anonymously so employees can express their real feelings without fear of reprisal. Attitude surveys can provide insight into many potential problems. Managers or consultants should formulate key questions covering a wide variety of work-related factors.

Identify Sources of Resistance

Few organizational changes are complete failures. But few go as smoothly as managers would like, since efforts often run into various forms of resistance.[17] Experienced managers are all too aware of these. Some managers don't even initiate needed changes because they feel incapable of successfully carrying them off. Many managers could be helped by taking the time to think through what causes people to resist change.

Some people resist change because they fear they'll be unable to develop the new skills and behaviors required of them. A major obstacle to organizational change is often managers' inability to change their own attitudes and behaviors as rapidly as their organizations require.[18] Even when managers understand the need for change, they are sometimes unable to change. In addition to this fear, people—and sometimes even whole organizations—tend to resist change for five reasons: vested interests, misunderstanding or lack of trust, differences in assessment of the situation, limited resources, and interorganizational agreements. Let's take a closer look at each of these.

People who have a *vested interest* in maintaining the status quo often resist change. Downsizing, cost cutting, and restructuring by many organizations in the 1980s to improve their performance seem to have carried over into the 1990s. Much of this downsizing has hurt product quality, alienated customers, and actually cut productivity growth. As we discussed in an earlier chapter, employees who are anxious about where the ax will fall next will spend all their time trying to make sure it doesn't fall on them. Wary of losing their jobs, these employees become reluctant to take risks or innovate.

People resist change when they don't understand its implications. Unless the manager quickly addresses it, any misunderstanding or lack of trust builds resistance. This type of resistance often takes a manager by surprise, because a lot of managers assume employees resist change only when it isn't in their best interests. For example, the manager of a 200-person office recently attended a seminar on improving the quality of work life. Day care centers were discussed. Upon returning to work, the manager decided to set up an employee day care center on the company's premises. The rumor mill went into high gear. One rumor had it that a company-sponsored day care center would require all parents to use it. Another rumor claimed that it was simply a way to get employees to work longer hours. The manager, completely surprised by this reaction, dropped the idea.

Employees may also resist change if they and their managers assess the situation differently. Some managers initiate change believing that anyone with the same information would make the same decision. This assumption is not always correct. The president of a steel company was shocked to learn that a large order had been lost in the factory. Had it not been discovered, the loss could have severely hurt the company's profitability. Within a week the president had outlined a new set of communication and coordination procedures linking marketing, sales, and manufacturing. As soon as top management announced the new procedures, they met massive resistance from employees in sales and marketing who had assessed the problem differently. Several managers in these departments actually threatened to quit if this reorganization was implemented.

Although some organizations emphasize stability, others would prefer to change but have limited resources to carry out any changes. General Electric's alliance with Samsung saved General Electric millions of dollars that it would have had to invest in a new plant and equipment to compete effectively in microwave manufacturing. In 1983 it cost General Electric $218 to make a microwave oven, compared to Samsung's $155. Figuring the number of ovens produced per day per person showed even a more glaring difference: General Electric got four units per person per day, and Samsung got nine. So, instead of sinking millions of dollars into the microwave business, General Electric invested its money in plastics and medical equipment, where it had a global competitive advantage.[19]

Labor contracts are the most common examples of interorganizational agreements that limit options for change. Actions once considered major rights of management (for example, to hire and fire, assign personnel to jobs, and promote) have become subjects of negotiation. Advocates of change may also find their plans delayed because of agreements with competitors, suppliers, public officials, or contractors. Although agreements are sometimes ignored or violated, the legal costs of settlement can be expensive.

Ways to Overcome Resistance   Not all resistance to change is bad. Resistance may encourage management to reexamine its proposals. Employees can operate as a check-and-balance mechanism to ensure that management properly plans and implements change. If justifiable resistance causes management to screen its proposed changes more carefully, it may result in more thoughtful management decisions.

Resistance to change will never cease completely. However, managers can learn to lessen and overcome such resistance. Four commonly used methods are identified in Table 21.2. One method for overcoming resistance to change is through education and communication. This method is ideal when resistance is based on inadequate or inaccurate information and analysis, and the resisters are the ones who must carry out the change.[20] The following Insight describes how Mike Walsh used education and communication to overcome resistance to change at Union Pacific.

TABLE 21.2

Methods for Dealing with Resistance to Change

Method	Commonly Used In Situations	Advantages	Drawbacks
Education and communication	When there is a lack of information or inaccurate information and analysis.	Once persuaded, people will often help with the implementation of the change.	Can be very time-consuming if lots of people are involved.
Participation and involvement	When the initiators do not have all the information they need to design the change, and others have considerable power to resist.	People who participate will be committed to implementing change, and any relevant information they have will be integrated into the change plan.	Can be very time-consuming if participators design an inappropriate change.
Negotiation and agreement	When someone or some group will clearly lose out in a change, and that person or group has considerable power to resist.	Sometimes it is a relatively easy way to avoid major resistance.	Can be too expensive in many cases if it alerts others to negotiate for compliance.
Manipulation and cooptation	When other tactics will not work or are too expensive.	It can be a relatively quick and inexpensive solution to resistance problems.	Can lead to future problems if people feel manipulated.

Source: Adapted from J. P. Kotter and L. A. Schlesinger, "Choosing Strategies for Change," *Harvard Business Review,* March-April 1979, 111.

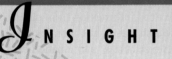

MIKE WALSH AT UNION PACIFIC

INSIGHT

When Mike Walsh took over the reins at Union Pacific in 1986 he found that the railroad was being run not as well as a model train set. The railroad had watched as truckers captured more and more of the market for everything except commodity freight. The marketing, engineering, and operating departments seldom communicated with one another. That had negative results. The machinery was dated. Customers rejected boxcars as faulty more than 10 percent of the time. Trains were derailed when newly welded track expanded in the sun. Work crews passed up savings of $600 million because of a lack of direction from supervisors. Nine layers of management stood between Walsh and the manager responsible for train operations in a territory. A supervisor had to get permission from Omaha (Union Pacific headquarters) to spend more than $1000.

Walsh asked all employees to help him turn around the railroad. He formed teams that devised measures on how well UP performed its jobs, such as moving trains on time, picking up and delivering goods, repairing locomotives, and sending invoices. He used statistical quality control measures to accurately assess the railroad's quality. Teams of managers visited customers to find out how the railroad was serving them. Up until this time, employees had resisted change because they believed that change would eliminate jobs. It wasn't until Walsh educated them on changes in the transportation industry that resistance decreased. Walsh had his teams look outward to see how other companies excelled in key areas for Union Pacific. For customer service, they studied American Express; for telephone processing, Marriott; and for reservations, American Airlines.[21]

FIGURE 21.3

Effect of Participation on Resistance to Change

The greater the amount of employee participation, the less the resistance to a change.

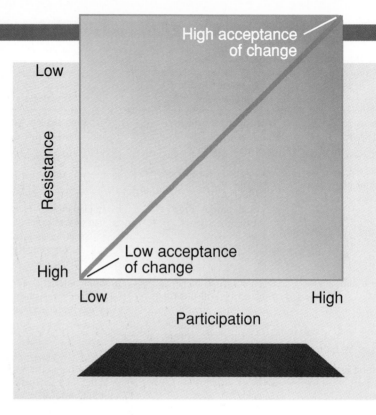

Managers often meet with less resistance to change when they allow participation and involvement, that is, when potential resisters are involved in aspects of the design and implementation of the proposed changes. Figure 21.3 suggests an inverse relationship between participation and resistance: the greater the participation, the less the resistance.

Many managers have strong feelings about participation. Some managers feel that change efforts should always include participation; others feel that this is usually a mistake. Participation works best when those proposing change need information from others to design and implement the change. This is the situation Walsh was in at Union Pacific. Research shows that participation leads to commitment.[22] Nevertheless, participation can have its drawbacks, as described in Chapters 14 and 16. If participation is not carefully managed, it can lead to a poor solution. It can also be very time-consuming. When change must be made quickly and will probably be resisted in any event, involving others may simply not be worth the effort.

Another way to deal with resistance is to negotiate and offer incentives or rewards to potential or active resisters. This method of dealing with resistance is especially appropriate when someone clearly is going to lose as a result of the change. For example, at Oryx,

Mike Walsh *overcomes resistance* at Union Pacific by lending an ear to the rank and file at a November "town hall" meeting in St. Louis.

cooptation A political maneuver for overcoming resistance that involves people in the decision-making process only to get their endorsement or their lack of resistance.

an oil and gas producer, the company eliminated rules, procedures, reviews, and reports that had little to do with finding more hydrocarbons. As the price of oil still dropped, it had to cut 1500 managerial jobs from its work force. Those who remained accepted wage and benefits concessions. They were committed to the changes and began to look for ways to further increase Oryx's efficiency.[23]

In some situations managers may try to manipulate others in an attempt to change them. This normally involves selective use of information. One common form of manipulation is cooptation. **Cooptation** is a political maneuver that involves people in the decision-making process to get their endorsement or, at least, their lack of resistance. Coopting a group involves giving one of its leaders a role in the change process. This is not a form of participation because those who are proposing the change do not really want advice from those coopted. However, people who feel that they have been tricked into not resisting, are not being treated fairly, or are being lied to, may respond negatively to a change. Many managers have found that, by coopting subordinates, they have ultimately created more resistance to the change than if they had chosen another tactic. The manager will face a whole new set of problems if those who were coopted use their ability and influence to propose changes that are not in the best interests of the organization.

Choosing a Method to Overcome Resistance Five factors need to be considered in selecting a method to overcome resistance to change.

1. *Amount and types of resistance anticipated.* All other things being equal, the greater the anticipated resistance, the more difficult it will be to overcome it. The communication and involvement methods in Table 21.2 are probably the most appropriate for combating strong resistance.

2. *Power of resisters.* The greater the power of the resisters, the more the proponents of change must involve the resisters. Conversely, the stronger the proponent's position, the greater the opportunity there is to use negotiation.

3. *Location of needed information and commitment.* The greater the need for information and commitment from others to help design and implement change, the more the advocates of change should use the education and participation methods. Gaining vital information and commitment from others requires time and their involvement.

4. *Stakes involved.* The greater the short-run potential for damage to the organization's performance and survival if the situation is not changed, the greater the need for managers to negotiate and/or use manipulation to overcome resistance.

5. *Short-term and long-term effects.* Accurate assessment of the first four factors still leaves the manager with the choice between short-term and long-term effects. Forcing change on people can have many negative effects, both in the short and the long runs. The communication and negotiation methods can often overcome initial resistance. These methods can lead to long-term benefits. The involvement method can lessen both short-term and long-term resistance. The cooptation method may be quickest in the short run but can lead to long-term resistance.

Set Objectives for the Change Effort

For change to be effective, objectives should be set before the change effort is started. If possible, the objectives should be (1) based on realistic organizational and employee needs, (2) stated in clear and measurable terms, (3) consistent with the organization's policies, and (4) attainable. For example, if an objective of a change program is to help first-line managers reduce machine downtime, one of the organization's obligations is to train these managers adequately in machine operation and maintenance prior to the initiation of the program. Top management must also clearly explain the need for the change and just how it will help attain the objective and should delegate maintenance responsibility to the first-line managers.

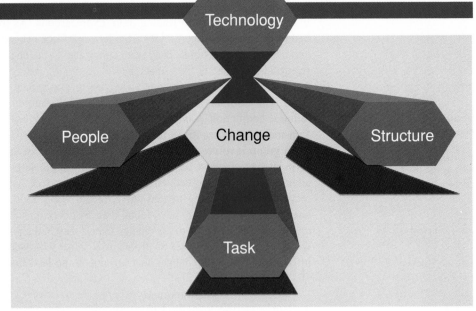

Approaches to Organizational Change

Managers and team leaders can take four different approaches to change. These approaches are all interrelated, such that using one approach will have an impact on the other approaches.

Source: From H. Leavitt, ''Applied Organizational Change in Industry: Structural, Technological and Humanistic Approaches,'' in J. G. March (ed), *Handbook of Organizations* (Chicago: Rand McNally, 1965), 1145. Used with permission.

Search for Change Approaches

The next step in planned organizational change is to look for practical approaches. Successful change can be approached only through modification of certain factors in an organization. The four interrelated approaches—technology, structure, task, and people—are identified by the factors they seek to change. These approaches to organizational change are shown in Fig. 21.4. A more detailed discussion of them is found later in this chapter. A change in any one of the four factors usually affects the others. For example, at GM, Chrysler, and Ford, robots are used to spray-paint cars, weld parts of chassis together, load and unload materials from storage bins, inspect engine blocks, and guide and repair other robots. This technology approach has several important implications for changes in the structure, people, and tasks of the organization:

▶   Robots can perform repetitive tasks more efficiently than people can. Fewer employees, managers,and levels in the organization are needed (impact on structure).

▶   As the cost of labor rises, it is often cheaper for a company to buy a robot than to hire people. A new breed of employee—robotic engineers, hydraulic and electronic experts—is increasingly needed (impact on people).

▶   Many jobs will be redesigned to take advantage of what robots can do (impact on tasks).

Methods involved in each of the four approaches to change are listed in Table 21.3. A technology approach focuses on change in workflows, production methods, materials, and information systems. Mike Walsh used this approach to achieve an integrated management information system to monitor over 10,000 miles of track throughout the Union Pacific rail system. A structure approach emphasizes internal structural changes: realigning departments, changing who makes the decisions, and merging or reorganizing departments that sell the company's products. A task approach concentrates on changing specific job responsibilities and activities. This approach could increase or decrease the quality of the work experience for employees and their job performance. A people ap-

TABLE 21.3

Change Approaches and Methods of Implementing Them

Approach	Methods
Technology	Introduce information technology, automation, and/or computerization
Structure	Change organizational structure Modify formal reward systems Redelegate authority and responsibilities
Task	Introduce job enrichment programs Establish quality groups and/or self-managed work groups
People	Study and act on survey feedback Implement team building and career planning programs

proach is usually aimed at improving individual skills and organizational effectiveness by means of training and development programs. For managers, the people approach would focus on improving the skills needed to perform one or more of the ten managerial roles (see Chapter 1).

Implement the Change

The next step in the change process is to implement and reinforce the change over a period of time. The ability to sustain change depends primarily on how well the organization reinforces newly learned behaviors during and after the change effort.[24] That is, employees should be properly rewarded for learning new behaviors. Organizational rewards can enhance the implementation process. A combination of money and pats on the back reinforces new behaviors, and if employees come to view the rewards as fair, they are likely to develop and maintain preferences for those behaviors. Effective implementation of change is also enhanced when the people being asked to change their behaviors have been allowed to participate in the designing of the change program.

Follow Up the Change

In the follow-up step managers face the problem of deciding whether the change process has been successful.[25] This determination measures the trend in improvement over time, based on the level of satisfaction, productivity, new-product development, market share or other dimension before the change process begins; the size of the improvement or decline; and the duration of the improvement or decline. Before implementing the change program, management should have set up objectives and benchmark levels to use in measuring the program's success. At Whirlpool Corporation there has been a major emphasis on quality. As a benchmark against which it could measure its quality improvement, Whirlpool used service calls per 1000 appliances. It decided that service calls must drop to 50 percent for its quality program to be considered successful. Achievement of other objectives, such as job satisfaction, level of commitment, job performance, or turnover, should also be determined. The effectiveness of a change program should not be determined by measuring only attitudes or performance. An index made up of both attitudinal and performance objectives and accomplishments should be used.

Ideally, managers should check the effectiveness of changes continuously. This kind of evaluation is usually too costly and time-consuming.[26] Most managers make assessments at predetermined time intervals. One set of measurements should be made immediately after a change is implemented. For example, if a people approach to change was used, the levels of employee attitudes, knowledge, skills, and job satisfaction would be measured against the predetermined objectives for these characteristics. To avoid a poor assessment based on only temporary changes in attitudes, another set of measurements should be made later, after the immediate effect of the change has worn off. This second set of measurements will often indicate attitudinal changes that the first one didn't reveal. At the time of the first set of measurements, the organization hadn't yet had the opportunity to reinforce (or try to end) newly developed employee attitudes.

APPROACHES TO ORGANIZATIONAL CHANGE AND INNOVATION

The change approaches and methods of implementing them that we present in this section expand on our earlier discussion. Since we have discussed some of the methods associated with these approaches in previous chapters (such as job enrichment in Chapter 13 and structural changes in Chapter 11), we won't discuss them at length here. Without a ready-made formula for determining which approaches or methods to use, managers must rely on clues from the organization's customers and employee behavioral changes generally.

Technology Approach

At the turn of the century, Frederick Taylor changed the workplace with his ideas of scientific management (see Chapter 2). His basic aim was to increase organizational efficiency through scientific principles. In the 1990s, information technology is changing the management of organizations just as Taylor once did.[27] In Chapters 19 and 20 we discussed how the application of information technology offered by computers, software, and telecommunications is affecting the management and operations of many organizations. In this section we look at information technology as a tool that managers can use to redesign or support new business processes, such as transportation, marketing, sales, manufacturing, and human resources. Texas Instruments, IBM and US Sprint, among other companies, are finding it necessary to develop more flexible, team-oriented communications based on information technology. IBM has urged its managers to improve the quality of its manufacturing operations by looking at the entire process, rather than a particular task. The following Insight shows how IBM used information technology to change its manufacturing process for typewriters and printers.

THE INFORMATION REVOLUTION AT IBM

*I*NSIGHT
When IBM launched a $350 million overhaul of its Lexington, Kentucky plant in 1983, the plant had been cranking out Selectric typewriters for twenty-two years. All of its 4200 workers had been making this product. IBM had been able to dominate the market for full-sized typewriters, holding a 44 percent share for years. Foreign competition, however, forced IBM to either change the way it manufactured these typewriters or lose its market share.

The key to the change came in IBM's use of information technology. Every new product has a manager who oversees both its design and manufacture, assisted by an engineering team of employees drawn from the plant's various departments. This team designs the product to assure that it can be made with automated pro-

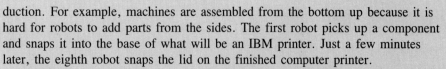

duction. For example, machines are assembled from the bottom up because it is hard for robots to add parts from the sides. The first robot picks up a component and snaps it into the base of what will be an IBM printer. Just a few minutes later, the eighth robot snaps the lid on the finished computer printer.

IBM's current typewriters have only one-fifth as many parts as Selectrics did. Screws and bolts are not used. To avoid having to adjust the robots when switching from one model to another, IBM puts as many of the same parts as possible in different models. Most printers and typewriters use the same frames and paper-feeding assemblies. As a result, the company can economically make products in small lots. Sometimes it makes only ten Spanish-language typewriters for Argentina during a production run.

The results of the application of information technology have been dramatic for IBM. Quality is far better than normal. The plant is posting 10 percent annual gains in productivity. Labor plus overhead is now less than a third of total expenses, down from about 50 percent. More than 80 percent of the components used are made in the United States. Over one-third of the components are now exported to competitors.[28]

Structure Approach

Organizational performance can often be improved by restructuring the organization. Managers give the following reasons for using a structural approach to change:

▶ The pressure of competition on profits puts a premium on efficient structure of an organization. Overlapping departments have to be combined, product divisions consolidated, and marginal functions eliminated.

▶ Maintaining or increasing market share in the booming international market may require a change from export departments to international divisions, international corporations, or even multinational corporations.

▶ Mergers and acquisitions may generate strong pressures for reorganization in parent companies, as well as in newly acquired subsidiaries.

▶ Technological advances may require new organizational arrangements to capitalize on their ultimate potential for improving performance. This was the case at IBM.

One company that has successfully restructured itself to meet the challenges of operating in a global marketplace is Unilever. It is ranked as the 18th largest industrial corporation in the world with sales of over $36 billion dollars. This British and Dutch company, famous for its soap and brands such as Lipton Tea and Ragu spaghetti sauce, underwent major structural changes since 1950 on the way to its current success. The Global Link highlights how Unilever changed its structure.

Task Approach

Whenever a job is changed—whether because of new technology, internal reorganization, or managerial whim—tasks also change. Recall from Chapter 13 that changing specific jobs with the intent of increasing both the quality of the work experience and productivity is called job enrichment. Let's briefly review its main characteristics.

Job enrichment has four unique aspects. First, it changes the basic relationships between employees and their work. Job enrichment is based on the assumption that work itself may be a powerful motivator, increasing satisfaction and productivity. Sometimes work may be satisfying only lower-order employee needs (physiological or security), and

GLOBAL
Link

UNILEVER'S NEW STRUCTURE

Like many other companies, Unilever built its international operations under the assumption that a consistent structure was needed across countries. Managers of foods or chemicals or detergents all reported to strong independent national managers, who in turn reported through regional directors to the board. About 1950, the company began to recognize a need to change this geographically determined structure with methods that would capture potential savings and transfer management practices learned in one location to another. To meet these needs, a few product groups were formed at the corporate center. The assumption of the need for organizational consistency ensured that all businesses followed some basic principles, but the number of product groups grew to ten by 1977.

By the mid-1970s, events caused this approach to be changed. Global economic disruption caused by the oil crisis dramatically highlighted substantial differences in the company's businesses and markets. It forced top management to recognize the need to change its organizational structure and administrative processes again. Standardization and coordination paid high dividends in the chemical and detergent businesses, for example. But important differences in local tastes and national cultures hurt packaged foods, such as Lipton Tea. As a result, the ten product-integrated groups eventually began to diverge as the company tried to shake off the consistency assumption. To be profitable, the detergent business must be managed in a more globally integrated manner than the packaged foods business. But not all tasks need to be managed in a coordinated manner. For example, there is little need for organizing by geography in research and development or for global coordination of sales management. Sales and marketing need not be managed in this way in all national markets. Marketing strategies for export sales can be highly coordinated. For closed markets, such as India and Brazil, they can be managed locally. This flexible and differentiated management approach stands in marked contrast to Unilever's earlier blanket commitment to a decentralized company.

Then it became clear that Europe's highly competitive markets and closely linked economies meant that Unilever companies operating in that region required more coordination and control than those in Latin America. Little by little, management increased the product-coordination groups' role in Europe until they had direct responsibility for all companies in their businesses. Elsewhere, however, national management maintained its role, and product coordinators acted only as advisors.

Unilever has moved from an organization that was structured and managed consistently among all divisions to a much more differentiated one: differentiating by product, then function, and finally by geography.

Adapted from C. A. Bartlett and S. A. Ghosbal, "Managing Across Borders: New Organizational Responses, Part II," *Sloan Management Review*, Fall 1987, 43–53; A. Armenakis, S. G. Harris, and K. W. Mossholder, "Creating Readiness for Large-Scale Change," unpublished working paper, Auburn University, April 1991.

CalComp asked employees to help them redesign and *enrich* their own jobs.

job enrichment provides a method for employees to move toward satisfaction of higher-order needs (esteem or self-actualization).

Second, job enrichment directly changes employees' behaviors in ways that gradually lead to more positive attitudes about work and the organization and a better self-image. Because enriched jobs usually increase feelings of autonomy and personal freedom, employees are likely to develop attitudes that support the new job-related behaviors.

Third, job enrichment offers numerous opportunities for initiating other organizational changes. Technical problems are likely to develop when jobs are changed, which offers management an opportunity to refine the technology used. Interpersonal problems almost inevitably arise between managers and subordinates and sometimes among co-workers who have to relate to one another in different ways. These situations offer opportunities for developing new skills and teamwork.

Finally, job enrichment can humanize an organization. Individuals can experience the psychological lift that comes from developing competence in their work and doing a job well. Individuals are encouraged to grow and push themselves.

In Chapter 13 we discussed the most popular job enrichment model. In Chapter 16 we discussed quality circles and self-managing teams. The following Insight builds on those earlier discussions.

SIMPLER DESIGN LEADS TO BIG PROFITS AT CALCOMP

INSIGHT

Most manufacturing experts agree that before any piece of new equipment is ordered, the shop floor should be simplified and streamlined. Gains from this are frequently so large that automation is not needed. CalComp learned its lesson the hard way. In a last-ditch effort to save the company, top managers finally turned to redesigning the tasks its workers performed.

CalComp builds plotters and prints computer drawings for engineers and architects. For an investment of around $300,000 it has achieved some great results. Since 1985, profits are up 50 percent, quality has increased 40 percent, and sales have risen 62 percent. In addition, production costs have fallen 30 percent and inventory costs have dropped by 90 percent.

To achieve these results, CalComp asked its employees to help redesign how they performed their jobs. It scrapped its traditional assembly line. Instead, employees are grouped in U-shaped compact areas where they can see and talk to one another. This not only improved communications but reduced the distance a product travels as it's pushed from station to station. Quality control was eliminated as a separate function. Instead, each person is responsible for checking the work received. Whenever anyone spots a major defect, work stops until the cause is found and fixed.

CalComp's latest plotter has only 95 parts, compared to 494 in its older model. And the product development cycle was cut from thirty-six months to eighteen. Engineers and employees are already talking with suppliers about how to shorten this cycle even more. Because all employees are involved in making decisions, absenteeism and turnover rates are very low.[29]

People Approach

Technology, structure, and task approaches try to improve organizational performance by changing the way work is done. These approaches are based on the belief that employees will be more productive in an appropriate work situation. People approaches, on the other hand, attempt to change the behavior of employees indirectly by focusing on changing their skills, attitudes, perceptions, and expectations. New attitudes, skills, and expectations may, of course, encourage employees to seek changes in the organization's structure, technology, or tasks.

Methods to change job-related behaviors and attitudes can be directed at individuals, groups, or the entire organization. Many of these methods are commonly grouped under a broad label—organization development methods.[30] **Organization development (OD)** is a planned, long-range behavioral science strategy for understanding, changing, and developing an organization's work force in order to improve its effectiveness. Although OD methods frequently include structural, technological, and task changes, their primary focus is on changing people. Typical OD methods include survey feedback, team building, conflict resolution, and improvement of interpersonal relations. Managers and team leaders can use these methods and others to resolve problems and conflicts within or between work groups.

organization development (OD) A planned long-range behavioral-science strategy for understanding, changing, and developing an organization's work force in order to improve its effectiveness.

OD Values   Organization development emphasizes three major sets of values that make it a unique approach to organizational change. These are as follows:

▶ *Values toward people.*   People have a natural desire to grow and develop. Organization development aims to overcome obstacles to individual growth, which will enable employees to give more to the organization. It stresses treating people with dignity and respect, behaving genuinely rather than playing games, and communicating openly.

▶ *Values toward groups.*   Acceptance, collaboration, and involvement in a group lead to expressions of feelings and perceptions. Hiding feelings or not being accepted by the group diminishes the individual's willingness to work constructively toward solutions to problems. Openness can be risky, but it can usually help people effectively plan solutions to problems and carry them out.

▶ *Values toward organizations.*   The way groups are linked strongly influences their effectiveness. Organization development recognizes the importance of starting change at the top and gradually introducing it throughout the rest of the organization. As one manager put it, ''Successful change is like a waterfall. It cascades from the top to the bottom.'' The links between the top and the bottom are accomplished through groups.

OD Methods   There are many OD methods, but we can look at only two of the more commonly used ones: survey feedback and team building.

survey feedback An organization development method that allows managers and employees to provide feedback about the organization and receive feedback about their own behaviors.

Survey feedback   **Survey feedback** is an organization development method that allows managers and employees to provide feedback about the organization and receive feedback about their own behaviors.[31] This information becomes the basis for group discussion and the stimulus for change. Accurate feedback from others about

FIGURE   21.5

Fort Worth Museum of Science and History

Instructions: We would like you to describe the environment in which you work. By environment, we mean the fundamental internal character of the museum that sets the pattern for how things get done. It is the core values and rules of the game that have evolved over the years. These values and rules have been shaped daily by both the content and style of top management. Make your descriptions as objectively and factually as possible. THERE ARE NO RIGHT OR WRONG ANSWERS. Please read each statement and assign it a number using the following scale. Your first reaction is probably the best response. DO NOT SIGN YOUR NAME.

9	Most characteristic
8	Quite characteristic
7	Fairly characteristic
6	Somewhat characteristic
5	Neutral
4	Somewhat uncharacteristic
3	Fairly uncharacteristic
2	Quite uncharacteristic
1	Most uncharacteristic

Statements:

____	High performance expectations	____	Fitting in
____	Emphasis on quality	____	Being careful
____	Being competitive	____	Paying attention to detail
____	Being highly organized	____	Having a clear, guiding philosophy
____	Being decisive		

Source: John Slocum, Cox School of Business, Southern Methodist University, Dallas, Texas, 1991.

behaviors and job performance is one of the primary characteristics and values on which organization development is based.

Feedback is obtained via a questionnaire, which is developed and distributed to all employees, who complete it and turn it in anonymously. The questionnaire shown in Figure 21.5 was designed by top managers to measure the corporate culture of Fort Worth's Museum of Science and History. The data obtained from such a questionnaire are summarized, usually by a consultant or someone from the organization's human resources department. The summarized data are then used in group problem-solving activities. Group meetings are chaired by a manager or team leader. The manager's job is to help the group to interpret the data, make plans for constructive change, and prepare the results for distribution to others in the organization. If the manager and team members decide that additional data are needed, another questionnaire could be developed.

Team building **Team building** is an organization development method designed to help teams operate more effectively by testing and improving their structure, processes (leadership, communication, conflict resolution), and member satisfaction.[32] Every organization depends on cooperation among employees to get work done effectively. Groups of people must work together to accomplish organizational objectives and to solve problems. Managers must carefully define the problems to be addressed and the extent to which they are related.

team building An organization development method that helps teams operate more effectively by testing and improving their structure, processes, and member satisfaction.

FIGURE 21.6

Team-Building Program

The six stages through which a team-building program takes a group.

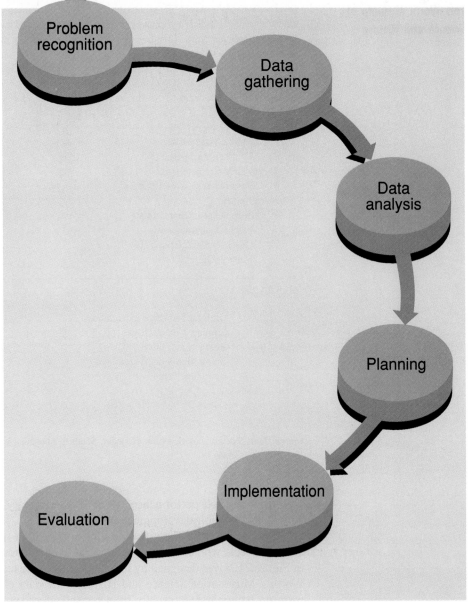

Source: W. G. Dyer, *Team Building: Issues and Alternatives,* 2nd ed. (Reading, Mass.: Addison-Wesley, 1987) 53.

Team building normally begins at the top of an organization and extends downward. Ideally, it focuses on solving problems within a group or department. Team-building sessions may last from half a day to several days. Ordinarily, a team-building program will follow a pattern similar to that shown in Figure 21.6. The program begins when someone recognizes a problem. Data are then gathered and analyzed to diagnose the problem and its cause(s). Following the diagnosis, the team starts planning and problem solving. The solutions are then implemented and the results are openly evaluated by the team.

The following Insight relates how Vonda Henderson effectively used team building. She had a high level of commitment, involved her subordinates, and enlisted their participation in a decision to take action.

*I*NSIGHT Vonda Henderson, a vice president at Trison Properties Management, had just returned from an executive development program. During the program, she learned things about her own management style that bothered her. She received feedback that she was too hard-driving and results-oriented. She also deliberately cut off others who expressed viewpoints different from her own. Henderson knew that things were not going well in her department. Absenteeism and turnover rates were high, and projects were not being completed on time or within budget. After thinking about these problems, Henderson decided to act.

She called a meeting of her staff and outlined her concerns. First, she described conditions in the department that bothered her: The accounting reports for some major tenants were late and sometimes inaccurate; some key people had recently quit or asked for transfers; attendance at weekly staff meetings was low. She also described the feedback about her management style that she had received during the executive development program.

Henderson then pointed out her dilemma. On the one hand, she wanted to improve the department's performance. On the other hand, the feedback she had received indicated that she might be part of the problem. Without open discussion, the group might not identify the basic problems. A plan for improving the situation was badly needed.

Henderson asked for her subordinates' help. She suggested, "I propose that we spend two or three days away from the office looking intensively at the issues I have raised today. Each of us should come prepared to give his or her ideas about the basic problems affecting our work, what causes these problems, and what we might do about them. If we put all our information together, we might come up with some interesting new solutions." The staff discussed the proposal at length and then agreed to go ahead with the meeting.[33]

Assessment of OD Methods Survey feedback is a highly successful OD method. It has been used in a variety of organizations, including the United States Navy, schools, hospitals, museums, and businesses. Survey feedback works best when it is used as a bridge between the diagnosis of organizational problems and the implementation of a people approach to change. There is little evidence to suggest that survey feedback alone will result in changes in individual behavior or organizational effectiveness. Survey feedback, however, enables managers to collect data from a large number of employees and to feed that information back to them for purposes of solving organizational problems.

Team building has been very successful for several reasons. First, it focuses mainly on feelings and attitudes of group members. These can be stumbling blocks to a change effort unless they are adequately addressed. Second, when off-site team meetings are held, as suggested in the Insight, organizational effectiveness can be improved because people can focus their attention on interpersonal issues. Finally, team building can improve group performance, particularly for tasks that are complex, unstructured, and require a group decision.

CHAPTER SUMMARY

1. Changes in work force characteristics and changing attitudes of employees and organizations toward one another present four basic challenges for managers: (1) Replacing the mechanistic approach to management with a more flexible approach; (2) adapting to increased use of participative management; (3) allowing individuals and groups to develop their own ideas; and (4) replacing large, central-

ized organizations with small, flexible, strategic business units that can take advantage of global competition.

2. Planned organizational change consists of the following steps:
Assessing changes in the environment.
Determining whether a performance gap exists and, if so, its nature and magnitude.
Diagnosing organizational problems.
Identifying sources of resistance to change, both individual and organizational.
Setting clear, realistic, and attainable objectives for change.
Searching for a change strategy that will accomplish the stated objectives.
Implementing the change.
Following up the change and determining whether it has been successful.

3. Change may be resisted for five reasons: (1) employees have vested interests in maintaining the status quo, (2) employees don't understand the purpose behind the change, (3) employees and management assess the problem differently, (4) the organization lacks the necessary resources, or (5) the change runs counter to interorganizational agreements. There are at least four methods for overcoming resistance, and effectiveness depends on five situational factors.

4. Depending on the nature of the problem, managers can use any of a variety of different approaches to change, including technology approach, structure approach, task approach, and people approach.

QUESTIONS FOR DISCUSSION AND APPLICATION

1. What environmental changes are requiring today's managers to change the way they operate?

2. John Sculley, president and CEO of Apple Computer, states that future organizations need to be designed according to "third-wave" concepts that require organizations to be flexible, to allow dissent, and to not be bureaucratically structured. Evaluate the wisdom of third-wave concepts for organizations of the 1990s.

3. **From Where You Sit:** Why do you resist change?

4. **From Where You Sit:** Based on your knowledge of the ways that people and organizations resist change, evaluate the following remark that Charlie Brown made to Snoopy: "Once a dog, always a dog."

5. Respond to the following statement: "A system that performs a certain function or operates in a certain way will continue to operate in that way regardless of the need or changed conditions."

6. Sometimes changes in people are hard to notice. What problems does this present for the manager?

7. Evaluate the following statement: "We trained hard, but it seemed that every time we were beginning to form up into teams, we would be reorganized. We tend to meet any new situation by reorganizing, and what a wonderful method it can be for creating the illusion of progress while producing confusion, inefficiency, and demoralization" (Petronius, 210 B.C.).

8. How long do you think a manager should wait to declare change successful or unsuccessful? Why?

9. **From Where You Sit:** Suppose you saw this on a bulletin board:

If you want to change people
it has to be toward a vision that's positive for them,

that taps important values,
that gets them something they desire,
and it has to be presented in a compelling
way that they feel inspired to follow.

What implications does this saying have for managers and team leaders who want to plan and achieve effective change?

How Innovative Are You?

Instructions:

To find out how innovative you are, respond to eighteen statements using the scale below. Remember that there is no right or wrong answer. Rather, the intent is helping you explore your attitudes.

SA = Strongly Agree
A = Agree
? = Undecided
D = Disagree
SD = Strongly Disagree

1. I try new ideas and new approaches to problems. SA A ? D SD

2. I take things or situations apart to find out how they work. SA A ? D SD

3. I can be counted on by my friends to find a new use for existing methods or existing equipment. SA A ? D SD

4. Among my friends, I'm usually the first person to try out a new idea or method. SA A ? D SD

5. I demonstrate originality. SA A ? D SD

6. I like to work on a problem that has caused others great difficulty. SA A ? D SD

7. I plan on developing contacts with experts in my field located in different companies or departments. SA A ? D SD

8. I plan on budgeting time and money for the pursuit of novel ideas. SA A ? D SD

9. I make comments at meetings on new ways of doing things. SA A ? D SD

10. If my friends were asked, they would say I'm a wit. SA A ? D SD

11. I seldom stick to the rules or follow protocol. SA A ? D SD

12. I discourage formal meetings to discuss ideas. SA A ? D SD

13. I usually support a friend's suggestion on new ways to do things. SA A ? D SD

14. I probably will not turn down ambiguous job assignments. SA A ? D SD

15. People who depart from the accepted organizational routine should not be punished. SA A ? D SD

16. I hope to be known for the quantity of my work rather than the quality of my work when starting a new project.

SA A ? D SD

17. I must be able to find enough variety of experience on my job or I will leave it.

SA A ? D SD

18. I am going to leave a job that doesn't challenge me.

SA A ? D SD

Scoring:

Give yourself the following points for each circled response:

SA = 5 points
A = 4 points
? = 3 points
D = 2 points
SD = 1 point

Interpretation

Total your scores for all responses to get a grand total. The higher the score, the more willing you are to be innovative and to welcome change. A score of 72 or greater is high; a score of 45 or less is low. People who aren't innovators have a tendency to maintain the status quo. Innovative people like to create planned changes in their organizations to increase performance.

To: William Lopez
From: Tito Molina, Team Leader — New
        Manufacturing Process

I have just returned from visiting NCR's new plant in
Atlanta, Georgia. With a new manufacturing process,
NCR is now able to turn out better-quality products at
lower costs. What NCR has done is change the way it
manufactures terminals used at checkout counters.
Before, it used to develop a product following a
series of steps. Like us, NCR used to start with
design and engineering and then let contracts for
various materials, parts, and services before finally
going to full-scale production. Each step in the
process was dependent on the other. Changes in the
design, especially after production started, caused
major delays and cost overruns.

Now terminals can be completed with 85 percent fewer
parts and assembled in two minutes. Now when NCR
starts a project, engineers, software, hardware,
purchasing, manufacturing, and sales all work together
in teams and compare notes constantly.

You know how we do things around here. When we get a
new product, the research team works on it and then
gives it to the design department. Design engineers
craft a blueprint and a hand-built model. Then they
throw the design over the wall to manufacturing, where
our production engineers struggle to bring the
blueprint into reality. Then the purchasing
department calls for bids on the necessary materials
and equipment. Sometimes it takes more than a year
just to get all the parts. Worst of all, a design
problem may turn up after all these wheels are in
motion. Then everything grinds to a halt until yet
another so-called engineering change order is made.

I would like you to give some thought to our adopting
a change similar to that put in place by NCR.

Question: Assume you are William Lopez and basically agree with the points outlined in this
memo from Molina. Write Molina a memo outlining your thoughts about achieving such a
change in your company. What must happen if this change is to be effective?

Firms in Europe Try to Find Executives
Who Can Cross Borders in a Single Bound

By Bob Hagerty

When Vittorio Levi decided to leave the warmth of Italy for a job in Sweden, everyone told him he was crazy.

Scandinavians may dream of working in a Mediterranean climate, but Italians aren't supposed to be willing to go north. Nonetheless, Mr. Levi says he made the right choice when he joined Oy Nokia's Stockholm-based computer division, where he became president early last year.

Expatriate executives are no novelty, of course. As more companies try to compete globally, more executives are crossing borders—not just as a brief detour but as a critical, and sometimes inevitable, stage in their careers. That trend is particularly pronounced in Europe, where plans for a unified market after 1992 are spurring companies to reorganize.

Responsibilities are rapidly shifting from national to regional or pan-European units. At the same time, companies want to stay in touch with local tastes. So they need managers who can think big while understanding local nuances.

Mastering that tricky mix often means hiring what some companies call Euromanagers: people skilled at dealing with a variety of cultures and at bringing a diverse team together. And that means hiring and promoting more foreigners.

"You need as much cultural mix and diversity and experience as possible . . . if you are running a global company," says Bob Poots, personnel director for the European division of London-based Imperial Chemical Industries PLC. ICI's executive ranks were predominantly British 20 years ago; now, only 74 of the company's top 150 executives world-wide are British.

That sort of change isn't easy to effect. The problem, headhunters and personnel managers say, is that Europe has a shortage of good senior executives who are willing to move. Tax and pension hassles, family ties and simple chauvinism keep many top managers in their own back yards.

"It's easy to say 'Euromanager,'" notes Brian F. Bergin, president of the European division of Colgate-Palmolive Co. "In fact, [hiring them] is an extremely difficult task. But it's happening."

To help realign its management, Colgate appointed a pan-European human-resources director, Peter Dessau, a Dane who moved to Brussels in 1989. His job is to encourage mobility among managers in the U.S. company's European units.

Colgate quizzed all of its top European managers about what kind of executive works best in an international setting. Among the main attributes, Mr. Dessau says, is flexibility in managing. "You don't always go by the book," he says.

ICI's Mr. Poots says he looks for people who are good at getting along with colleagues at home. "That skill travels remarkably well," he says. Any problems an executive has in dealing with colleagues, he figures, will be magnified in a foreign setting, where much more effort is needed to build understanding and trust.

Unilever Group, the Anglo-Dutch food and soap giant, shies away from bossy executives. "We tend to look for people who can work in teams and understand the value of cooperation and consensus," says Floris Maljers, chairman of Unilever NV, the group's Dutch arm.

Some recruiters want candidates who have learned at least one foreign language besides English. Even if the foreign language won't be needed much in a particular job, having learned it "shows you are willing to dive into someone else's culture," says Marc Swaels, a Brussels-based partner for Korn/Ferry International, a U.S. executive-search firm.

1. In today's global economy, would a Euromanager necessarily be more successful in creating or responding to change? Can you envision a situation where these managers might be successful? Where they might fail?

2. Assume you work for a small manufacturer that is thinking of expanding into Eastern Europe. Would you advise your company president to hire a European manager, an Eastern European manager, or an American manager? What would be the strengths and drawbacks of each?

3. Imagine your company president is of the mechanistic management school. How would you convince him or her to consider a Euromanager?

HEWLETT-PACKARD RETHINKS ITSELF

It's amazing that Bob Frankenberg ever got anything done at all. Until last year this Hewlett-Packard (HP) general manager dealt with no fewer than thirty-eight in-house committees. They decided everything from what features to include in a new software program to what city would be best for staging a product launch. Just coming up with a name for the company's NewWave Computing software took nearly a hundred people on nine committees seven months.

By the late 1980s, an unwieldy bureaucracy had bogged down the HP Way. A web of committees, originally designed to foster communication between HP's operating groups, had pushed up costs and slowed down development. The fifty-two-year-old company's entrenched culture was built around the HP Way, a philosophy of democracy and mutual respect that promoted consensus. But, critics say, the culture placed too much emphasis on rapport among executives and failed to penalize those who missed new markets.

By the spring of 1990, John Young, HP's CEO, realized that things had gotten out of hand. The message came through loud and clear when a manager warned him that HP's most important project, a series of high-speed workstations being developed under the code name Snakes, was slipping a year behind schedule because of the company's burdensome bureaucracy. Workstations, which are one of the computer industry's highest-growth product areas, are so important to HP's computer strategy that in 1989, in an uncharacteristically bold move, the company paid nearly $500 million to buy the ailing market pioneer, Apollo Computer Inc. HP wanted Apollo's customers and its engineers, who had expertise in the new RISC technology. But over the course of a bumpy merger, development schedules slipped, and some Apollo customers began jumping ship.

No wonder the normally even-tempered Young grew furious when he learned about the Snakes delay, which was caused by endless meetings about technical decisions. "I think I may have come unglued that day," says Young. "It was a pretty clear signal to me." Young immediately attacked the problem by removing the Snakes project's 200 engineers from the HP management structure so they could work on the project free of routine administrative tasks.

The crisis convinced Young that big changes had to be made throughout the company. He called in founder and chairman David Packard to discuss a major revamping of the corporate structure. Packard, who remains HP's single largest shareholder, began meeting frequently with Young to discuss changes. The cure was the company's most drastic reorganization in ten years. Young announced it in October 1990, just as HP was finishing a surprisingly poor fourth fiscal quarter. Earnings plunged 18 percent, dragging down the full-year net by 11 percent, to $739 million on sales of $23.2 billion.

Young wiped out HP's committee structure and flattened the organization. To cut costs, HP had already launched an early retirement program. Young's revamp divided the computer business into two main groups: One handles personal computers, printers, and other products sold through dealers, and the second oversees sales of workstations and minicomputers to big customers. In place of the single corporate sales force established in the mid-1980s, each of the two computer units has its own sales and marketing team. "The results are incredible," says Frankenberg, who now deals with three committees instead of thirty-eight. "We are doing more business and getting product out quicker with fewer people."

The overhaul has another benefit: It should pave the way for the ascent of a new generation of managers. Young and five of the other top eleven executives are expected to retire within the next four years. The new structure gives Young, who took HP's reins in 1978 when its founders retired from day-to-day operations, a chance to evaluate the company's younger lieutenants. They now report directly to him and Chief Operating Officer Dean O. Morton, whose main job is slashing HP's overhead and overseeing its extensive quality-control program.

The reorganization is helping to speed things up, but HP still proceeds rather cautiously by industry standards. "HP is a very conservative company, and computers are a market in which people are practicing guerrilla warfare," says ASK Computer Systems Inc. CEO Sandra Kurtzig, who resells HP computers with her company's manufacturing software. "The nice guys don't necessarily win."

1. How did HP determine its performance gap?
2. What approaches to change and innovation did HP use to achieve its new structure?
3. How successful do you think HP changes will be?

Chapter 22

Entrepreneurship and

Small Business*

Steve Jobs

What You Will Learn

1 What entrepreneurs are and how they develop.

2 Personal attributes and behaviors associated with successful entrepreneurs.

3 Planning issues associated with starting and managing your own business.

4 Opportunities and problems of operating a family business.

5 Characteristics of organizations that encourage intrapreneurship.

6 **Skill Development:** Whether you have what it takes to be an entrepreneur.

*This chapter was contributed by Frank Hoy, Dean, College of Business, University of Texas at El Paso.

"Jobs helped create a whole industry."

Steven P. Jobs, Now of Next

The 1980s were boom years for entrepreneurship in the United States. The number of new enterprises that sprang up during each year of the decade exceeded anything that *any* economy had ever experienced. Young company builders, especially those in high technology (such as Jim Manzi of Lotus, Sandra Kurtzig of Ask Computers, Jean Madar of Jean Philippe Fragrances, Bill Gates of Microsoft, Remedios Diaz Oliver of American International Container, and Ken Olson of DEC) became national heros. They not only introduced new products and services but also pioneered new ways of running businesses. Searching for the person who typified this innovative spirit, the magazine *INC.* named Steven Jobs "Entrepreneur of the Decade" for the 1980s.

Together with Steve Wozniak, Jobs founded Apple Computer in 1977. He made the cover of *Time* at age 26. This honor was conferred in recognition of more than his starting a business from scratch and "growing" it into a billion-dollar corporation. Jobs also helped create a whole industry by making computers affordable to individuals and accessible to people with no computer expertise.

In the early days of Apple, Jobs opposed bringing in experienced managers. He feared they would impose policies that would stifle creativity. Eventually, after concluding that the company had outgrown his own entrepreneurial skills, Jobs brought in John Sculley, a seasoned manager from PepsiCo Foods, to head Apple. Initially a successful team, Sculley and Jobs later butted heads over manufacturing and marketing directions for the firm. Sculley wanted uniform policies and directions, whereas Jobs wanted each product (Apple, McIntosh, Lisa, and so on) to be governed by rules and directions tailored to its own needs. Jobs, the brightest star of this decade of entrepreneurship, has his down side, too. He has been variously described as brash, abrasive, a dreamer, a perfectionist, and extraordinarily demanding. In response to these characteristics and to the need to meet the demands of the business more effectively, Sculley at last forced Jobs out of Apple.

Jobs spent the next three years channeling his entrepreneurial energies into developing a workstation for the higher-education market. In 1988 he announced his new company and product: Next. The design of the Next computer reflects active involvement of both engineers and consultants from higher education. Jobs set three goals for Next:

▶ Make the best computers in the world for individuals.
▶ Hire really bright people and give them lots of responsibility right away.
▶ Through bonus plans, share the company's success with those who help build it.

Despite Jobs's entrepreneurial vision, the success of Next has been mixed. On the positive side, Next machines are powerful desktop publishing machines that show the user exactly how a page will look on paper. But although Next's graphics software gets high marks, the machine performs sluggishly and offers only black-and-white graphics. Software development has also lagged behind. Others claim that the machine performs as well as engineering workstations from Sun Micro-Systems or Hewlett-Packard, but the Next system costs several thousand dollars more than these. Jobs claims that Next will quickly introduce new models to overcome these problems.[1]

Why have a chapter on entrepreneurship in a textbook about management? Some people believe that entrepreneurs are born, not made or shaped by any text. Others contend that entrepreneurs may be good at creating a business, but they can't manage one. Both sets of critics cite Steven Jobs as an example. After all, nobody taught Jobs and his partner Steve Wozniak how to start Apple Computer. And Jobs *was* forced out of Apple after it grew too large for him to manage.

incubator organization A company that spawns entrepreneurs.

Yet taking a closer look at Jobs may lead us to different conclusions. Jobs and Wozniak formed the company only after their idea for Apple Computer was rejected by Wozniak's employer, Hewlett-Packard. It isn't unusual for individuals to become entrepreneurs only after finding that they can't accomplish their objectives within a large organization. In fact, this happens so frequently that Arnold Cooper at Purdue University has coined the term **incubator organization** for companies that spawn entrepreneurs. An incubator can also be a building in which fledgling companies can rent space while getting a start, but Cooper uses the word to describe organizations where entrepreneurs worked before starting their own companies. His studies show that people tend to start businesses in the same general geographic areas as their incubator organizations and to use the skills and knowledge they learned while working in those organizations.[2] Perhaps entrepreneurship *can* be taught.

Was Steve Jobs more an entrepreneurial leader than a manager? How large must a company become for entrepreneurs to call themselves managers? Jobs held the reins until Apple reached more than $1 billion in sales. This would suggest that along the way, he developed some of the leadership skills we discussed in Chapter 14, such as visioning, empowerment, and intuition. And shortly after making the entrepreneurial plunge at Apple, Jobs recognized his business limitations and began learning about successful management practices. For example, he toured Japanese plants—not just to observe their production techniques, but also to learn from their management practices. Jobs also believes he has learned a great deal about effective management from his experience in starting and introducing Next's products. Perhaps entrepreneurs of all types, in companies of any size, can indeed be managers.

Another reason for dealing with the topic of entrepreneurship in a management text is sheer numbers. You may well be involved in an entrepreneurial venture when you graduate. The 1980s saw new ventures being started in record numbers. In 1989, almost 900,000 new companies were formed in the United States—compared with 200,000 in 1965 and only 90,000 in 1950. In addition to these 900,000, more than 300,000 entrepreneurs started their own businesses for the first time. Forecasters predict a high level of organizational births throughout the 1990s. In particular, an explosion in venture creation activity among women, immigrants, and members of minority groups is anticipated. New ventures on the part of female entrepreneurs rose from 24 percent of all start-ups in 1975 to 33 percent in 1988. Entrepreneurship has also resulted in several million new businesses being formed throughout the world, including nations such as China, Hungary, and Poland.[3] Does this mean we experienced a boom in "born entrepreneurs" a generation ago? No. More people simply came to view business ownership as a realistic career option and began learning how to achieve it.

ENTREPRENEURS: BORN OR MADE?

entrepreneur One who creates a new business activity.

Entrepreneur is the label usually given to someone who creates new business activity in the economy. In the broadest sense, an entrepreneur is exactly what this book talks about: a manager. The entrepreneur manages resources in order to create something new or innovative—generally a business.

New mothers Anita Dimondstein and Joan Cooper started their now-booming children's clothing business by distributing a single product: imported soft wool diaper covers.

Managers within large corporations also engage in entrepreneurial activity when they develop new product lines or establish new companies to enter markets they had not penetrated before. For their enterprises to survive, however, entrepreneurs typically have to manage their limited resources in different ways from managers of large organizations. In the following sections, we will outline what seem to be emerging as the management styles and characteristics of successful and of unsuccessful entrepreneurs.

The term *entrepreneur* is often used interchangeably with *small business owner*. The many ways in which people become small business owners include purchasing companies, inheriting them, buying franchises, and other means.

1. Some people who want to be in business for themselves are lucky enough always to have known what kind of business they wanted to run. They have systematically gone about gaining appropriate experience and acquiring the capital necessary to start their own companies.

2. Others have opportunities thrust on them. Perhaps they are the heirs to family firms. Some authorities estimate that over 90 percent of the small companies in the United States are family firms. Approximately 30 percent of family firms successfully pass from one generation to the next.[4]

3. Still others may learn about an owner's willingness to sell just at a time when they are mentally and financially prepared to take on the risk. A number of small business owners were employees of these firms. They were in the right place at the right time when the previous owners were seeking buyers.

4. And as the case of Apple Computer illustrates, some entrepreneurs spin off from larger organizations. Co-founder Steve Wozniak originally proposed the idea of a personal computer to his boss at Hewlett-Packard. Only after the idea was rejected did Wozniak team up with Steven Jobs to start Apple. Their initial investment was only $2000.[5]

Early Experiences

Let's consider our stereotypic entrepreneur: the small, independent business owner. The U.S. Small Business Administration (SBA) draws the line at 500 employees to distinguish small from large firms. By that standard, over 95 percent of the approximately 20 million businesses in the United States are small. There are therefore millions of people in business for themselves, each possessing a unique set of personal characteristics and experiences. Researchers have studied samples of business owners for years to determine whether any characteristics or experiences consistently set these owners apart from the rest of the population.

From the very beginning, the family environment has been shown to affect the development of an entrepreneur.[6] For example, first-born female children tend to be more entrepreneurial than females born as later children, perhaps because the first child receives special attention and thereby develops more self-confidence. There also is strong evidence that entrepreneurs tend to have had self-employed parents. The independent nature and flexibility shown by the self-employed mother or father is ingrained at an early age. Such parents are supportive and encourage independence, achievement, and responsibility.

Today's entrepreneurs are, on average, younger and better educated than those of years past. Some earlier business founders substituted on-the-job experience for education. Today it is not unusual for entrepreneurs to develop their business ideas—and even start their companies—while still in college.

▶ Phil Knight, a long-distance runner at the University of Oregon, and his coach, Bill Bowerman, discussed the poor quality of American-made running shoes. Two years after receiving his graduate degree, Knight entered into partnership with Bowerman to establish Nike, Inc.

▶ Linda Richardson actually started her first business in high school—selling makeup. During college, she formed companies to make and sell handbags and to distribute antique jewelry. After graduation, she attempted more traditional careers in education and banking, but eventually her entrepreneurial spirit reasserted itself, and she opened a bank sales training company.

▶ As a marketing class project at Harvard, Daniel Fylstra invested $500 to create Personal Software. The company introduced VisiCalc, the first personal computer planning and budgeting software package to be a major commercial success.

▶ Jody Gessow, owner of three Atlanta-based businesses, was featured in *People* magazine as the youngest travel broker in the nation. At the time, he was a student at Emory University and had a partner studying at the University of Virginia.[7]

What Do Successful and Unsuccessful Entrepreneurs Do?

We all have in mind an image of the successful entrepreneur. Words such as *create, innovate, risk,* and *grow* come to mind. The successful entrepreneur values independence and creativity, has the ability to find market opportunities that others may have overlooked, can't stand the "red tape" that often strangles large organizations, and has a vision that can be sold to potential employees and investors. Entrepreneurs position themselves well in markets that are shifting or untapped. For example, Julie and Bill Brice founded "I Can't Believe It's YOGURT!" because they saw yogurt as a substitute for ice cream—something that the major ice cream manufacturers (such as Borden, Blue Bell, and Sealtest) did not foresee. They also capitalized on the public's obsession with low-calorie foods.

Not all new ventures, however, are success stories. Thousands fail each year. According to Dun & Bradstreet and other credit-reporting agencies, the majority of failures can be traced to poor management practices.[8] Many failing owners do not have the right attitude toward hard work. There is no substitute in the small firm for hard work, which must often include 60-hour-plus weeks. One investor remodeled a vacant service station, filled it with cases of beer, hired a few part-time college students at minimum wage to collect the customers' money, and sat back to wait for the profits to roll in. They never did. The owner's absence and failure to exert control led to low sales, theft, and general physical deterioration of the business.

Hard work isn't enough, however. It is also necessary to "work smart" and use time effectively. Some of the managers who put in the most hours lose their businesses because their efforts were misdirected. A typical example is the inventor who spent all his or her time trying to sell a new product rather than hiring someone with marketing expertise to manage sales. This wise move would have freed the inventor to spend time back in the workshop doing what he or she did best.

Unsuccessful entrepreneurs also fail to plan and don't prepare for expansion. They don't recognize that their role must change along with changes in their organization. As a company grows from a one-person enterprise to a team effort to an organization requiring multiple levels of management, the entrepreneur must be flexible enough to change managerial styles. The owner starts out as an operator, moves into the role of a manager, and gradually evolves into a leadership position. But each role requires different patterns of behavior.

Poor and reckless money management can cripple an organization right from the start. There are many symptoms. Too much capital may have been put into fixed assets such as land, buildings, or equipment. Record keeping may be sloppy and haphazard. The owner may be taking out too much money in salary. Cash flow problems may be caused by poor credit-granting practices or by faulty inventory management. All these factors may spell doom for a business just as it is on the verge of success.

Many of these causes of small business failure are brought home in the following Insight. The idea for the service was fine, but several key managerial practices were never implemented.

AMERCARD COMPANY—AN ENTREPRENEURIAL ''MISS''

INSIGHT

Amercard Company looked like a ''can't miss'' proposition. In the early 1980s, a period of recession and double-digit inflation, Amercard offered a service that benefited both customers and independent businesses. Even so, this company opened in the spring and folded in the fall.

The Amercard plan was simplicity itself. For $25, a consumer obtained an identification card that participating retailers honored by granting a discount of at least 5 percent on all purchases. Only one retail outlet of any particular type (one jewelry shop, one shoe store, and so on) was affiliated with Amercard in any geographic area. Amercard circulated a bimonthly newsletter to its members informing them what stores were participating. More than fifty retailers initially honored the new discount card, and many reported noticeable increases in business volume. Yet by September, the merchants saw use of the card dropping off.

What had gone wrong? Amercard had run short of funds and was unable to publish its newsletter. Inadequately trained sales personnel weren't successful in marketing additional cards or in signing up more retailers for the program. Stores stopped subscribing to the program when they found the cards were no longer bringing in new customers. Within months, Amercard was out of business.

Owners of Amercard underestimated the amount of money they needed to get their business off the ground. They failed to recognize that a good idea doesn't necessarily sell itself. The principals gave their attention to running the office and to developing long-range plans. They left the retail clients and the discount card holders to the sales force. The salespeople worked part-time for commission. They had no training and so failed to recognize the importance of following up on their sales. Amercard owners gave them almost no supervision, expecting the commissions to be adequate incentives for good work. Although most of us could have predicted Amercard's bankruptcy on the basis of this lack of effective management, it is easy to lose perspective when dealing with the demands of running a business.

CHARACTERISTICS OF ENTREPRENEURS

Many studies of entrepreneurs have been conducted over the years.[9] Those entrepreneurs who succeed have been found to share a variety of characteristics and behaviors, which are listed in Table 22.1. Let's look at some of these attributes that are associated with successful entrepreneurship.

Characteristics of Successful Entrepreneurs

Personal Attributes	Behaviors
Need for achievement	Technically competent
Desire for independence	Willing to delegate
Not motivated to work in large organizations	Hard-working; task-oriented
Ambition	Effective leader
Self-confidence	Self-starter
Future-oriented	Decisive and methodical
High reward expectations	Reliable
Tolerance for ambiguity	Good accountant
Self-sacrificing	

Source: Adapted from B. C. Vaught and F. Hoy, "Have You Got What It Takes to Run Your Own Business?" *Business,* July–August 1981, 4; D. L. Sexton and N. Bowman-Upton, "Female and Male Entrepreneurs: Psychological Characteristics and Their Role in Gender-Related Discrimination," *Journal of Business Venturing,* 1990, 5: 29–36; J. Main, "A Golden Age for Entrepreneurs," *Fortune,* February 12, 1990, 120–125.

Key Personal Attributes

It is possible, though not easy, to change one's personal attributes. These characteristics tend to be deeply ingrained and are formed over a lifetime. Some personal attributes that are clearly related to entrepreneurial success may well be worth the effort to develop. In addition many theorists believe that personal attributes follow from behavioral changes. If this is true, engaging in entrepreneurial behavior may itself lead to the development of desired motivations and ways of thinking.

need for achievement
Desire to perform at a high level of excellence or to succeed in competitive situations.

Need for Achievement Heading the list in Table 22.1 is the **need for achievement:** a person's desire either to perform at a high level of excellence or to succeed in competitive situations. High achievers prefer to be as fully responsible for attaining their goals as possible, tend to set moderately difficult goals to achieve, and want immediate feedback on how well they performed a task. David McClelland and others have conducted extensive research into three human needs: the needs for power, affiliation, and achievement. Their findings indicate that only perhaps 5 percent of the American population is characterized by a predominant need to achieve. Yet this need is consistently found among samples of successful entrepreneurs.[10] Entrepreneurs direct their efforts toward goal accomplishment. When they reach their objectives, they set higher objectives still. They measure their success in terms of their ability to achieve objectives. Entrepreneurs learn to set challenging but achievable objectives for themselves and for their businesses. Objectives that are too high *and* those that are too low don't work. Low objectives breed complacency; objectives too high to achieve breed frustration.

Desire for Independence Small business entrepreneurs are often people who seek independence from others. As a result, they generally are not motivated to perform well in large, bureaucratic organizations. They have internal drive, are confident of their own abilities, and possess high levels of self-respect. They may be ambitious without being concerned about their social images.[11]

Self-Confidence A successful track record of accomplishment does much to improve an entrepreneur's self-confidence and self-esteem. Self-confidence enhances one's self-image as a successful entrepreneur. It enables one to be optimistic in representing the firm to employees and customers. Expecting and rewarding high performance from employees is personally reinforcing, and it also provides a role model for others in the company. Most people want an optimistic and enthusiastic

Clemon Wesley, founder of TEXCOM, a telecommunications service firm, bemoans the fact that "Schools teach African Americans to go out and get 8-to-5 jobs. Very little suggests to them that they might want to start their own businesses."

leader—someone they can look up to. Given the uncertainties in running an entrepreneurial organization, having an "upbeat" attitude is essential.

Future Oriented Successful entrepreneurs are future-oriented and money-oriented. They have high expectations of reward, and they use rewards (such as salary and status) as indicators of their achievements. They are optimistic but still have a reasonably objective outlook on the world in which they work. They are tolerant of the uncertainties they face on a daily basis.

Self-Sacrificing Finally, successful entrepreneurs have to be self-sacrificing. They recognize that nothing worth having is free. This means giving up that four-week vacation, that Saturday golf game, or that occasional trip to the mountains. Success has a high price tag, and they are willing to pay.

Some people's personal attributes fit the entrepreneurial mold so well that entrepreneurship itself becomes a career for them. Rather than managing a business solely for income or growth, these individuals use their companies as springboards to start or acquire other ventures. This is known as the **corridor principle.**[12] For such individuals, opening a business is like entering a passageway. As they walk along, they see new corridors that they may choose. Had they not entered the first one, they would never have learned of the others. The entrepreneur encounters many business opportunities that would otherwise have been hidden. Linda Richardson, whom we described earlier, offers one example of a person who exploits the corridor principle. Another is Robert Ontiveros, CEO of Bi-State Packaging.

corridor principle The principle that the entrepreneur will encounter many business opportunities that she or he would never have encountered otherwise.

ROBERT ONTIVEROS, PROFESSIONAL ENTREPRENEUR

*I*NSIGHT After six years of experience in selling bulk packaging, Robert Ontiveros decided to go into business for himself. The strategy he developed for his company, Bi-State Packaging, Inc., was to target *Fortune* 500 companies with track records of working with minority enterprises. His first two customers were John Deere and Caterpillar, corporations with which he had established contacts during his years in sales.

Unfortunately, Ontiveros found he had tied himself to the wrong industry. In the early 1980s, the farm implement business went into a deep recession, and Bi-State's volume dropped by 80 percent. Ontiveros hit the road, working trade shows. The U.S. Hispanic Chamber of Commerce proved to be a valuable network, leading to contracts with Adolph Coors and Eastman Kodak. By 1990, Bi-State's revenues hit the $10 million mark.

Ontiveros discovered he could win contracts with large corporations by adding products or services for them. Eventually, this expansion led to his creating and spinning off new ventures. The first new company was R & O Specialties, Inc. R & O began as a repair service for John Deere and Caterpillar. It was soon performing sandblasting, painting, packaging, and shipping services for parts manufacturers. Subsequently, Ontiveros started another enterprise that does special consumer packaging for customers that include Philip Morris, General Foods, and Eastman Kodak. He attributes his success to the relationships he has established. In addition to long-time customers such as John Deere and Caterpillar, Ontiveros works with the same attorney and banker with whom he started. He selected his uncle to run R & O Specialties. As they face the 1990s, Ontiveros and his venture team are determined to maintain leadership in technology in order to be low-cost producers.[13]

In summary, the key personal attributes we've discussed show that small business entrepreneurs have positive self-images. They believe in themselves and in their company's ability to succeed. This ''I can do it'' attitude permeates everything they do.

Key Behaviors

We all adopt patterns of behavior that become habits, and such habits are certainly easier to change than personal attributes. But taking on some of the behaviors associated with successful small business entrepreneurship can still cause discomfort if one is not prepared. It is important, for example, before launching an entrepreneurial effort, to have any necessary technical skills and to be confident about one's effectiveness in interpersonal relations and decision making.

Technical Skills As shown in Table 22.1, entrepreneurs demonstrate high levels of technical competence. They typically bring some related experience to their business ventures. For example, owners of successful automobile dealerships have usually acquired a significant amount of technical knowledge about selling and servicing automobiles before they open their dealership. Some people believe successful entrepreneurs are lucky. In reality, successful entrepreneurs have developed the skills, experience, and resources they need to take advantage of opportunities.[14] The following Global Link explains how some smaller companies have positioned themselves for seizing international opportunities by developing their technical skills.

Interpersonal Skills To take advantage of opportunities, entrepreneurs must also be very good managers. Those who are successful have acquired the skills necessary to manage both the human and the financial resources of their firms. Like Steven Jobs of Next, they must be willing to delegate to their subordinates the authority these people need to get the job done. At the same time, they must be willing to accept the responsibility for their decisions and actions. Soliciting constructive feedback is part of the management process.

Successful entrepreneurs are extremely hard-working and task-oriented, yet they have learned how to temper this drive and dedication with the interpersonal skills of effective leaders. They are self-starters who usually support their subordinates and

INTERNATIONAL VENTURING

Consider Silicon Valley entrepreneur Robert L. Chen, president and founder of AOT Corporation in Milpitas, California. When he first visited Sharp Corporation in Nara, Japan, in 1983, he had high hopes. A Japanese contact had arranged for him to present his company's semiconductor test to Sharp's top managers. But when Chen arrived, he was met by a low-level engineer who revealed his indifference to Chen's product during a brief conversation in the corporation's lobby.

Chen didn't give up. He found a more helpful Japanese go-between, who two years later managed to get him in the door in a very Japanese way. Chen offered to Sharp's senior managers a free ''seminar'' on the technical aspects of his products. He began building rapport with the company's executives. At about the same time, the value of the U.S. dollar started to plunge. This helped Chen's cause. Four years after that initial meeting with the engineer, AOT Corporation made its first sale to Sharp. Chen now counts the Japanese giant among a growing list of Asian buyers.

For the little company, exporting takes perseverance that strains even the toughest businessperson. Once outside the security of U.S. or Canadian borders, small companies find themselves in perilous waters.

Beyond the obstacles to getting a foot in the door, financing is often very difficult to arrange. Bernard van der Land, a Georgia-based personal computer exporter, reports losing $1 million in solid, letter-of-credit-backed orders to the Middle East and Africa last year because he couldn't get U.S. banks to finance equipment purchases by his company, Ashford International. Unlike bankers in Europe and Asia, U.S. lending officers typically don't understand small exporters and can't be bothered with them. Bernard van der Land says his bank demanded the impossible of a tiny trading company: assets to back the loans. After trying to make arrangements with a variety of U.S. banks, van der Land, a native of Holland, found a Middle Eastern bank that was willing to finance his export orders.

Even such basics as metric measurements and labeling can cause headaches because many employees aren't familiar with them. Jerry Allison, who runs AJC International, a food-exporting company in Atlanta, says he lost close to a million dollars last year when Taiwan blocked the import of American turkeys. Allison had a shipment sitting in a Taiwan port at the time; he had to sell it at a loss elsewhere in Asia. Allison says he has customers waiting in the Middle East who will buy frozen chicken legs and wings, but these products are required to have labels detailing all ingredients in Arabic. Allison says he has trouble finding a domestic manufacturer willing to bother with this detail.

Source: Adapted from J. R. Schiffman, ''Venturing Abroad,'' *Wall Street Journal*, February 24, 1989, R30.

Dan Hillis's dream as a student at MIT was to build parallel-processing supercomputers. His design—made a reality at Thinking Machines Corp.—is now an industry standard.

programs enthusiastically. Not insignificant to these behaviors are highly developed communications skills.[15]

Joseph Rod Canion, president of Compaq Computer Corporation, is one of the most successful entrepreneurs in the United States. In February 1982, he and his partners formed a company to realize their vision of developing the world's first portable computer. Canion, who has directed the operation since its beginning, is responsible for Compaq's phenomenal growth. Compaq Computer became the fastest company on record to be listed among the *Fortune* 500. It was also the first entrepreneurial company to reach $100 million in sales in its first year. The following account shows that Canion possesses many characteristics of the successful entrepreneurial leader—especially a variety of interpersonal skills.

Canion was a Texas boy whose tinkering led him into engineering studies at the University of Houston and, from there, into a 15-year engineering career at Texas Instruments. When he, Jim Harris, and Bill Murto (two Texas Instruments colleagues) decided to branch out on their own, they had about six months' savings in the bank. The trio approached several venture capital firms with the idea of manufacturing a portable computer compatible with IBM PCs. Canion envisioned a product that would not become obsolete and that would enable computer users to do new things without giving up old applications. He and his partners argued that portables using IBM standards would have the broadest applications-software base. According to the venture capitalist who lent them the money, "Rod came to me with a vision of building a new company which would not only be rewarding, but fun to build. Rod and his partners were committed to make this company grow."

Compaq's success can be traced to the plan that Canion and his partners formulated. They reasoned that if all parties knew where the company was going, then it would be backed by a cohesive, aggressive, and enthusiastic group of dedicated employees. Accordingly, management makes sure that employees, stockholders, dealers, and suppliers all know precisely what objectives the company is pursuing. The glue that holds Compaq together is Canion's belief in teamwork. "The system, culture, and attitude of teamwork is what makes the company so stable and strong. People have to put their ego in a closet." To foster this spirit, there are no private parking spaces, and all employees—including the founders—fly coach, not first class.[16]

Like other successful entrepreneurs, Canion is a risk taker who has a knack for pulling together the concept, the financing, and the right people. He accepts risks, but thanks to his education and past business experience, the risks he takes are well calculated ones.

Decision-Making Skills Successful small business entrepreneurs are good at making critical decisions affecting their operations. They are decisive and methodical—as opposed to impulsive—in reaching their decisions. They think with their heads more than their hearts. Decisions are right, in their minds, if they lead to accomplishment of the task.[17]

Most entrepreneurs don't have the time or the inclination to develop quantitative decision models for solving specific operational problems. They must learn to approach operations from the standpoint of a satisficer (see Chapter 6), not a maximizer. Few organizational problems can be solved perfectly. And not many problems can be solved in a way that absolutely prevents their recurrence sometime in the future.

Many problems that an entrepreneur encounters on a day-to-day basis are behavioral in nature. Employees and customers interpret situations from their own unique perspectives. In some cases, a problem may exist *only* in the mind of an employee or customer, but to that employee or customer, the problem is very real. For instance, the owner of a small parts-manufacturing firm witnessed the constant recurrence of a scheduling problem between the production-control manager and the manufacturing superintendent. Several meetings and procedural changes later, the "problem" still existed. Only in-depth interviews with the two men conducted by an outside consultant exposed the real, human problem: The older superintendent resented the younger production-control specialist telling him what to manufacture and when. The moral: Entrepreneurs won't make the right decisions if they can't diagnose the problem accurately.

BECOMING AN ENTREPRENEUR

The owners of Amercard Company, as we noted earlier had an exciting idea and an entrepreneurial spirit. But these alone weren't enough to make their venture a success. They returned to school and decided to invest more time in planning before starting another enterprise.

Research has shown that successful entrepreneurs typically do more planning before going into business than those who fail.[18] One tool that helps them do so is the *business plan*. A **business plan** is a step-by-step blueprint that enables the entrepreneur to move in an orderly fashion from the idea stage to making the new business a reality. A business plan also provides prospective investors with information about the new business. Table 22.2 outlines the major components of a business plan.

Some of the questions that entrepreneurs must answer in their business plan are:

1. What kind of business should I own?
2. Should I start or buy a business?
3. What and where is the market for my product or service?

business plan Outline of the steps an enterprise will follow to turn ideas into reality.

TABLE 22.2		
Components of a Business Plan	**Business Concept**	Description of the product or service.
		Market identification, target customers, and descriptive and economic data on demand.
		Competition defined and market analysis completed.
		Marketing strategy clearly articulated.
		Location information on business, facilities, outlets, and service.
		Management, leading entrepreneur profile, key employees.
	Financial Support	Planned financial needs and sources of capital, debt, and personal equity positions.
		Supporting documentation of financial plans:
		▶ Projected income statement (profit-and-loss operating statement)
		▶ Projected cash flow statement
		▶ Projected balance sheet
		▶ Breakeven analysis of sales quantity
	Incidental Information	Customer surveys, market information, forecasts of demand and sales.
		Personal data sheets on owners, lead entrepreneurs, key skilled managers.
		Support information on materials purchasing, vendors, quotes, and prices.
		Facility plans, layouts, manufacturing requirements, equipment needs.
		Credit reports, bids, contracts, and other appendices helpful to investors.

Source: Adapted from D. H. Holt, *Management: Principles and Practices,* 2nd ed (Englewood Cliffs, N.J.: Prentice-Hall, 1990), 692.

4. How much will it cost to own the business, and where will I get the money?
5. What skills will I need to manage a changing or a family enterprise successfully?

Let's take a closer look at each of these questions.

Kinds of Businesses

People become business owners for a variety of reasons. Some want to practice a hobby or craft, and others enter businesses owned by family members. Still other entrepreneurs choose an industry on the basis of their assessment of the growth and profit potential in that industry.[19] One way to think about business opportunities is to classify them as lifestyle, smaller profitable, or high-growth ventures.[20]

1. *Lifestyle ventures.* Independence, autonomy, and control are the overriding goals of the entrepreneur.
2. *Smaller profitable ventures.* Cash flow and profits are more important goals, as long as they don't jeopardize the entrepreneur's ability to control the firm.
3. *High-growth ventures.* Significant levels of sales and profits are sought; outside investment and eventual buyout are expected.

As we have noted, new ventures frequently spring from an incubator organization, where entrepreneurs acquire skills and knowledge that they subsequently use in their own businesses. When deciding what type of business to own, people should begin by examining what abilities, interests, and contacts they will bring to their future company. Prospective entrepreneurs should subject various alternatives to scrutiny according to such criteria as the income forecast from business earnings, the initial investment required, and the intensity of the competition. This analysis often turns up existing businesses that they may purchase. Business magazines, such as those listed at the end of this chapter, can be a good source of new-venture ideas.

Starting or Buying a Business

Prospective entrepreneurs who have the option to "start or buy" begin by weighing the advantages and disadvantages of each strategy. Sometimes, of course, the decision is made *for* them, because they don't have the financial resources necessary to purchase an existing company.

Here are some questions to answer in planning whether to *start* a business:

▶ Is there a way to begin the enterprise in stages or with a limited investment?
▶ Can the company be run as a home-based business?
▶ Is it possible to continue working for someone else and put in time on your own business after hours?
▶ To what extent can you draw on relatives to help you, perhaps simply by answering the phone while you work at your regular job?

Suzanne and Ross Greiner, now 14 and 11, launched their enterprise from the family kitchen. They shaped their mom's homemade, nonstaining chalk into shapes and sold them first at bazaars, eventually to major toy chains.

franchise A business run by an individual to whom a *franchisor* grants the right to market a certain good or service.

turnkey operation A business (such as a franchise) that can be opened quickly.

A middle ground between starting your own business and buying an existing independent business is to run a franchise. A **franchise** is a business run by a person to whom a *franchisor* grants the right to market a good or service. The *franchisee* pays the franchisor a franchise fee and a percentage of the sales. The franchisee often receives financial help, training, guaranteed supplies, a protected market, and technical assistance in site selection, accounting, and operations management. Franchises are sometimes referred to as **turnkey operations.** This term reflects the fact that an entrepreneur can open a franchise immediately, virtually by turning a key in the lock. More than 500,000 new franchise outlets were opened in 1990.[21] McDonalds, Domino's Pizza, Jiffy Lube, AAMCO Transmissions, Jenny Craig Diet Centers—all use franchises to market their goods and services. Whoever buys a franchise buys a brand name that enjoys recognition among potential customers. Franchise operators, however, are their own bosses. Of course, they can't run their businesses exactly as they please; they usually have to conform to standards set by the franchisor, and sometimes they must buy the franchisor's goods and services. But it is for this reason that many people want to operate a franchise in the first place.

Buying an existing firm is more complex and requires determining exactly what you are getting for your money. There are undoubtedly some hidden problems that the previous owner may not reveal—and may not even be aware of. Also, many a new owner has thought that she or he was buying goodwill, only to have the previous owner open a competing firm and lure away the established clientele. The prospective buyer is wise to specify, in the purchase agreement, restrictions limiting the previous owner's ability or right to compete with the new owner. Restrictions may limit the types of businesses that the previous owner can operate in a certain region or for a stipulated period of time.

Learning about businesses available for purchase and negotiating the terms of purchase often involve the assistance of experts. Bankers, accountants, attorneys, and other professionals may be aware of an opportunity to buy a business before it hits the market. A business broker may help find a firm and act as intermediary for the sale. Usually, an attorney prepares or reviews the sale documents.

The Market

The forecasting techniques described in Chapter 9 are often overlooked in planning for business ownership. Entrepreneurs are frequently so excited about their business ideas that they assume others will feel the same way. Their market research may consist of asking the opinion of a few friends or relatives about the salability of their product or service.

Help in targeting and analyzing markets is available to the prospective entrepreneur from numerous sources. The federal government compiles an enormous amount of data on products, industries, consumers, and other market-related categories. The business development programs supported by the U.S. Small Business Administration, such as the Service Corps of Retired Executives (SCORE) and Small Business Development Centers (SBDC), can help entrepreneurs sort through the data.

How should a business plan address the issue of the target market? A list of typical questions derived from a business plan (see Table 22.2) is given in Table 22.3. These questions focus on the attractiveness of the market and on the firm's ability to capture some share of the market.

Sources and Uses of Funds

Just as entrepreneurs are likely to overestimate their income, they tend to underestimate their costs. The new-venture plan should identify anticipated costs of opening the business, such as deposits, fixtures, incorporation fees, and so on. It should also project, month by month, the expenses that can reasonably be expected for the first one to three years. These include the costs of goods or services sold and the expenses of operating the firm.

TABLE   22.3

Market Issues Facing the Entrepreneur

1. Who exactly is your market? Describe the characteristics (age, sex, profession, income, and so on) of your various market segments.
2. What is the present size of the market?
3. What percentage of the market will you have?
4. What is the market's growth potential?
5. How will you *attract, expand,* and *keep* this market?
6. How are you going to *price* your service, product, or merchandise to make a fair profit and, at the same time, be competitive?
7. What special advantages do you offer that may justify a higher price?
8. Will you offer credit to your customers? If so, is this really necessary? Can you afford to extend credit? Can you afford bad debts?

Source: North Georgia Regional Small Business Development Center, *"How to Start and Manage a Business"* Workbook (Athens, Ga.: University of Georgia, 1990).

The entrepreneur must plan for obtaining funds to handle expenses, such as those associated with the start-up phase, that can't be covered by business revenues. Initial sources are most likely to be the entrepreneur and other members of the venture team, followed by family and friends.[22] Beyond these sources, a sound business plan becomes critically important to demonstrate to potential lenders and investors the viability of the proposed enterprise.

Lisa Tosi and Richard Altwarg are an entrepreneurial couple who took strategic planning seriously before they started their venture. The following Insight profiles their company's start-up. Note, too, the personal attributes and behaviors that helped them make their company successful.

PORTRAIT OF A PLANNED START-UP

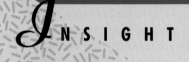

INSIGHT

Lisa Tosi and Richard Altwarg met when they were undergraduate students at Oberlin College. Lisa was an economics major; Richard specialized in East Asian studies. Both energetic and independent, Lisa and Richard decided they had complementary skills that would make them good business partners. They also concluded that their interests and expertise would enable them to take advantage of new trade relationships between the United States and the People's Republic of China (PRC).

In the following excerpt from their business plan, Lisa and Richard explain how they recognized an opportunity that others had missed.

During the late 1970s and early 1980s, a host of trading firms were started which intended to capitalize on the "opening" of China's economy to the West. The intent of most of these firms was to work within China's bureaucratic import/export trading system to sell foreign-produced goods to the immense Chinese market. What sounded good in theory, however, has not worked in practice for many of the companies intending to sell to the Chinese.

When the doors to China were opened, the central planning authorities never intended to allow their markets to be overrun with imported goods, causing chaos in what was a relatively stable, albeit extremely inefficient, domestic economy. Rather, the intention was to expand China's *export* market and bring foreign capital investment into China in order to modernize and strengthen the domestic economy.

Lisa and Richard decided that the best way to avoid the mistakes many other organizations had made was through *countertrade*. They planned to sell textile-manufacturing equipment to the Chinese and to accept finished products as payment. They would then market these products as wall coverings in the United States and other markets. This idea was intended to build on experience Richard acquired when he was employed by a New York textile importer. During this time, Lisa completed her master's degree in business at Michigan State University.

After graduating, Lisa accepted a position with General Motors. She supported Richard while he worked in China to establish relationships and honed his language skills. By now, the couple had married and believed the time was right to strike out on their own.

China International Trade Associates Ltd. (CITA) was formed in February 1987. Lisa and Richard soon found that their countertrade plan wasn't viable. They had developed a broader vision for their company, however. According to their business plan,

> CITA principals understood that in order to be successful in the China trade, it was advisable to work *within* the Chinese structure, capitalizing on existing Chinese advantages to help it develop export markets. In turn, as is the Chinese way, when trading authorities in the PRC require foreign-produced products (notably machinery), they are most inclined to turn to trading partners which have been working with them over the long run to help them to accomplish their own goals.

CITA shifted its attention to ceramic tiles, a strategy explained in the plan as follows:

> The company has been working closely with Chinese factories and U.S. distributors to develop quality, low-cost ceramic tile lines for sale in North America.
>
> CITA intends to use the ceramic tile sales as a profit base that will provide the company with the funds required to expand into other markets and trading activities. This will capitalize on the firm's unique ability to work within the Chinese system to bring low-cost, quality products to Western markets and provide real assistance to firms which produce products that are appropriate for sale to the Chinese.

Lisa and Richard carefully investigated the U.S. market for ceramic tiles and identified key competitors. They exhaustively analyzed and projected expenses and determined that they could penetrate the market with a low-cost strategy.

CITA lost money in each of its first three years, bottoming out at a loss of over $100,000 on $226,000 in revenues in 1988. By 1990, however, CITA was truly a multinational company, making sales in Canada, the United Kingdom, and Germany. Projections for 1991 are $660,000 in income on nearly $3 million in sales.[23]

In retrospect, Lisa and Richard could have done many things differently, including starting with a different initial product—one with which they could have made more money more rapidly. They also discovered that many aspects of their plan had to be changed in response to unforeseen events. Nevertheless, they found their plan most valuable in helping them organize their thoughts and plot a course of action. It also served them well as a document in their efforts to raise the money they needed from outside investors and lenders. Many of these outsiders, encouraged by the understanding of the business that they obtained by reviewing the plan, contributed not just funds but also critical managerial skills (in communication and in technical and conceptual areas) to the venture in its formative years.

Shanghai-born entrepreneurs Henry Yuen and Daniel Kwoh figured out a way to simplify programming a VCR. Their product, VCR Plus, allows viewers to tape by punching in the short code printed in many TV listings.

Lisa and Richard put together a venture team the members of which offered a broad range of skills and expertise that CITA was able to draw on. Serving on the board of directors were two attorneys, a professor of management, and a university vice president for finance. Also active in the company was Lisa's sister, Kathy Tosi, who had earned an MBA in marketing.

Growth Pressures on Entrepreneurs

Entrepreneurs such as Rod Canion, Steven Jobs, and Robert Ontiveros often find that as their businesses grow, they feel more and more pressure to lead their organizations by using formal methods. Howard Stevenson of Harvard has identified six dimensions on which the behaviors of entrepreneurial and of formal organizations differ: strategic orientation, commitment to opportunity, commitment to resources, control of resources, management structure, and compensation policy.[24] These six dimensions are displayed in Table 22.4.

To illustrate how these six dimensions can help you understand the key differences between an entrepreneurial and a formal organization, let's consider the experience of Gail Ray, founder of Personal Computer Rentals. Following this Insight, we will analyze her company's behavior in terms of Stevenson's dimensions.

TABLE 22.4

Business Dimensions of Entrepreneurial and Formal Organizations

Business Dimension	Entrepreneurial Organization	Formal Organization
Strategic orientation	Seeks opportunity	Controls resources
Commitment to opportunity	Revolutionary and of short duration	Evolutionary and of long duration
Commitment to resources	Lack of stable resource needs and bases	Systematic planning systems
Control of resources	Lack of commitment to permanent new ventures	Power, status, and financial rewards for maintaining the status quo
Management structure	Flat with many informal networks	Clearly defined authority and responsibility
Compensation policy	Unlimited; based on team's accomplishments	Short-term driven; limited by investors

Source: Adapted from H. H. Stevenson, M. J. Roberts, and H. I. Grousbeck, *New Business Ventures and the Entrepreneur,* 3rd ed. (Boston, Mass.: Irwin, 1989), 18–19; H. H. Stevenson and J. C. Jarillo, ''A Paradigm of Entrepreneurship: Entrepreneurial Management,'' *Strategic Management Journal,* 1990 Summer Special Issue, *11:* 17–27.

INSIGHT

It is hard to imagine a more entrepreneurial endeavor than PCR, Personal Computer Rentals, when Gail Ray founded it in 1983. She was the stereotypic "one-woman band." She met with customers, negotiated with suppliers, picked up equipment, delivered and installed it, answered the phone, and handled correspondence. She did anything and everything to get her company off the ground.

Ray hit on the idea for PC rentals while working in sales for IBM. She frequently received calls from people who wanted to lease equipment. In emergency situations, they were willing to pay almost anything. Because IBM chose not to get into the business of leasing personal computers, Ray saw an opportunity. Her instincts proved correct, and she was immediately swamped with orders as she tried to run her business from the file room of her accountant's office.

Ray was encouraged by her initial backer, Edward Miranda, a stockbroker, to expand through franchising. But before it could become a national company, PCR had to get its own house in order. Gail hired Bruce Minker to manage rentals in 1984. Bruce found what he later described as a "seat-of-the-pants operation." Everything from equipment purchases, to marketing, to collections was handled on an *ad hoc* basis. Minker and Ray overcame the disorganization by putting in long hours and scrutinizing every detail. PCR sold its first franchise in 1985.

It was immediately obvious that growth required more financing. Banks were not interested in making loans to unproven ventures in industries that have high failure rates. With the help of Miranda, Ray was able to get more equity investors. In 1987 the company was sold to a group of venture capitalists who made PCR their only investment, renaming their own company PCR International.

Ray continues to build the company, stressing marketing and letting accounting catch up. She has even forged deals whereby competitors rent her products as she moves toward her goal of 100 franchises.[25]

Looking at the dimensions listed in Table 22.4 reveals how well a venture such as PCR in its early stages fits the pattern of an entrepreneurial organization. Gail Ray sought an opportunity that larger corporations ignored or were not in a position to seize. Actually, her first idea was to start a chain of personal computer service centers. She abandoned that plan when she learned that Xerox intended to do the same thing. She expected competition in the rental business from retail chains such as Computerland. Her timing turned out to be an advantage, though, because the retail market hit a saturation point in the early 1980s, and the big retailers had to concern themselves with controlling their existing resources and could not expand into rentals.

Ray's management of PCR showed a focus on market potential. She refused to be restricted by limited resources. She was even willing to sacrifice ownership of the company in order to obtain the resources necessary to finance PCR's growth. Gail recognized that she was giving up the security offered by IBM for the risks associated with business ownership. She also recognized that the rewards could be virtually limitless. She and her investors foresee a time when they will sell off the enterprise for an enormous return.

Managing a Family Business

The two foregoing Insights not only highlight planning and growth but also illustrate the interactions of families and businesses. The success of CITA Ltd. shows how family members can work together effectively. Intimate knowledge of one another's strengths and weaknesses helped Richard, Lisa, and Kathy decide who was best able to take on certain responsibilities or make particular decisions. On the other hand, the strains of business ownership contributed to the breakup of Gail Ray's marriage.

These examples reflect a shift from the traditional pattern of the ''mom and pop'' business where pop was usually the boss. More family businesses now involve true co-ownership. For both the marriage and the business to succeed, couples should

1. Decide who is responsible for what. Jobs in companies just starting up should not be too narrowly defined. Couples should recognize each other's areas of expertise to determine who is best able to make each decision.

2. Draw up a legal agreement on disposing of the business. Investors and other outsiders have an interest in husband and wife being in accord on this outcome.

3. Agree on whether and when to sell the business.

4. Decide whether the business will employ other family members and, if so, what hiring criteria will be used.

5. Settle fights as they come up. If your spouse does something on the job that makes you angry, it won't be corrected if it isn't brought out in the open.

6. Establish a board of advisers. Sometimes outsiders are needed to mediate a conflict or at least to provide a fresh perspective.[26]

Of course, family businesses aren't restricted to spousal relationships. Often the greatest management problems that firms face are intergenerational. The issues that most family businesses have to address at some time in their existence may be classified as survival or operational. Survival issues may arise only once in the lifetime of the owners and the enterprise, but the way they are resolved may determine whether the firm will continue to exist. Examples of such issues include

1. Equitable estate treatment
2. Preparing for ownership transfer
3. Minimizing estate taxes
4. Ensuring the financial security of the senior generation
5. Selecting and developing a successor

Operating issues are not so critical, but they may occur daily. And left unattended, they may become survival issues. Examples include

1. Suppressing or avoiding conflict among family members
2. Retaining nonfamily members
3. Handling unproductive family members
4. Participating in executive decisions[27]

If you are employed in a family firm, these issues affect you regardless of whether you are a family member. They influence the survival prospects of the company, opportunities for career advancement within the company, the level of employee motivation and morale, the competitiveness of the firm, and the general quality of work life. Given the high percentage of American businesses that are family-owned and -managed, these issues should not be taken lightly.

Jan Massie started her basement business—C&C Creations, a children's clothing manufacturer and distributor—when her sons were infants.

CORPORATE INTRAPRENEURSHIP

Many large organizations themselves are beginning to conclude that entrepreneurial behaviors can achieve growth and profits. Corporate entrepreneurship, once considered a contradiction in terms, is becoming more and more widespread.

Consider for a moment *why* an organization exists. There is some mission—some objectives to be accomplished—that requires the efforts of more than one person. At the very least, a business has the objective of satisfying customers so that it can make profits over the long run.

Fundamental to organizing is dividing up the work. Managers may think they have organized successfully when they have brought different interests together, minimized conflict, increased stability, and reduced uncertainty. Imagine now the effects that those organizing efforts have on prospective entrepreneurial tendencies. Is the climate conducive to change? Will disruption be tolerated? Is redirection possible?

Large organizations are often formally structured for efficiency. They manage existing activities in such a way as to ensure that these activities will continue. As we noted in Chapter 21, this approach is often at odds with innovation and change. What can be done to encourage entrepreneurship when a company needs to be revitalized? The answer lies in changes—perhaps even a revolution—in an organization's practices. Over time, companies develop cultures (see Chapter 16) that become infused with traditions, norms, rituals, and values. Employees come to take the working environment for granted. Individual efforts to foster change may be met with resistance.

intrapreneur A manager who turns new ideas into profitable activities within an existing organization.

Gifford Pinchot III coined the term **intrapreneur** to describe managers within organizations who figure out how to turn ideas into profitable realities.[28] Typical of Pinchot's intrapreneurs is Arthur Fry, the 3M chemical engineer who invented Post-it Note Pads (see the 3M Insight, Chapter 21). Jacques Robinson and Howard R. Stevenson, Jr., who teamed up to rejuvenate General Electric's video products division, are also intrapreneurs. Robinson provided the risk-taking environment in which Stevenson was able to design circuitry that brought the quality of standard television sets up to the level of computer monitors. This made it more practical to use ordinary sets with home computers, video games, and video cameras.

The introduction of the IBM personal computer represents another intrapreneurial activity. IBM gave the assignment of developing the PC to Philip Estridge, but he and his group violated many time-honored IBM traditions. They used outside suppliers to speed up development and hold down costs, rather than depending solely on other IBM divisions. And they marketed PCs directly through retailers, rather than relying on IBM's sales organization. Estridge was able to accomplish his mission only with the support of top management.

Characteristics of Intrapreneurs

There are certain personal attributes that one must possess if one is to be a successful intrapreneur within the organizational environment. Let's review three of these qualities.

Vision As we showed in Chapter 14, the person who is going to establish a new intrapreneurial venture must have dreams. In order to establish this new venture, the individual will have to sell his or her dream to others. Arthur Fry did this at 3M with his Post-it Note Pads.

Flexibility to Build Teams By challenging the beliefs and assumptions of the organization, the intrapreneur has an opportunity to create something new. This person must encourage teamwork. And she or he must be a diplomat skilled in crossing departmental lines, structures, and reporting systems. Intrapreneurial activities can cause some disruption, particularly in large organizations where each manager's "turf" has been staked out carefully over the years. One of the keys to success in team building is to avoid open conflicts. Hulki Aldikacti, the intrapreneur at GM who created Pontiac's Fiero, was especially good at keeping the team's discussions focused on the product, not on personalities.

Persistence Frustrations occur throughout the establishment of any new entrepreneurial venture. The intrapreneur needs a strong group of supporters who will encourage him or her. Only through persistence will the intrapreneur overcome obstacles and achieve success.

Key Intrapreneurial Activities

Top management can foster an entrepreneurial culture by eliminating obstacles and providing incentives for intrapreneurship. Companies that redirect themselves through such innovations have the following characteristics:

▶ *Commitment from senior management.* Don't expect changes unless top-level managers are committed to supporting them. This support must include a willingness to tolerate failure. Top managers must regularly communicate their commitment to entrepreneurial activities—and back up their words with actions.[29]

▶ *Flexible organization structure.* Entrepreneurial organizations are structured for fast action. Management gives information—and the authority to make decisions—to those best positioned to react to changing market conditions. These people are often first-line managers. Intrapreneurial organizations frequently have profit centers. They may have internal new-venture teams or task forces, such as 3M does, that are in an incubator.[30]

▶ *Autonomy of the venture team.* Closely aligned with flexibility is maintaining a hands-off policy in day-to-day management of the team charged with implementing an innovation. Successful internal entrepreneurs, such as Arthur Fry at 3M, are usually volunteers who are allowed considerable leeway in their actions.[31]

▶ *Competent and talented people who exhibit entrepreneurial behaviors and attitudes.* His or her willingness to volunteer is not sufficient reason to assign someone to a venture team. Competent volunteers usually have experience in, or have received training for, new-venture creation. Some companies conduct formal training programs; others establish mentor or coaching relationships. Most intrapreneurs have at least one failure before achieving successes that more than offset the early losses.[32]

▶ *Incentives and rewards for risk taking.* Intrapreneurs do not risk their careers and undergo the frustration of forcing change solely for the satisfaction of seeing their ventures spring to life. Successful venturers should be generously compensated. Intrapreneurship should not be a dead-end activity; it should be linked with an identifiable career path of advancements. This is especially important in that it helps ensure that the entrepreneur's next new venture won't be a spinoff from the company![33]

▶ *An appropriately designed control system.* Nothing is more stifling to an entrepreneurial activity than bureaucratic controls. Nevertheless, despite the potential contradiction between strong controls and the entrepreneurial spirit, senior management cannot give up its accountability for new-venture projects. Controlling internal innovations means collecting and analyzing data that enable management to predict, to a reasonable degree, where the venturing team is headed. It also involves ensuring that the team understands the difference between entrepreneurial behavior and irresponsible risk taking. Obstacles that inhibit entrepreneurial management are generally structural, deeply ingrained within the firm. Unfortunately, those obstacles are often considered good management practices.[34]

Karl Bays is an executive who didn't just encourage intrapreneurship within Baxter Travenol. He "bet the company on a new direction" when he spotted the opportunity.

$\mathcal{I}$ **N S I G H T**

Karl Bays accepts the label of entrepreneur. He is especially proud of his decision to take what he called "the ultimate risk." As CEO of American Hospital Supply Corp., a successful marketer of hospital supplies, he merged his firm into Baxter Travenol Laboratories to create a fully integrated health-care organization.

Bays joined the company right out of college, attracted by American's feeling of entrepreneurship. The company grew steadily in what Bays described as a low-risk industry. He became president of American in 1970 at the age of 35, and the 15 years of his leadership saw company sales increase sevenfold.

Much of the growth occurred through acquisition. American acquired over 100 companies while Bays was CEO. He believes the key to operating these firms successfully was allowing them to remain entrepreneurial. He made sure that someone in every acquired company had full accountability, responsibility, and authority to make decisions. Key financial and market data were regularly reported to him. Bays says that his "experience has been that somebody has to feel that their whole reason for living—or at least their reason for showing up at work—is to see that venture through." As the acquired ventures grew, however, Bays observed that the transition from a small to a medium-sized company was often extremely difficult. He teamed founders with professional managers to smooth the transition.

By the mid-1980s, the competition American faced was fierce. The federal government changed the funding mechanism for Medicare. Corporations changed their medical-benefits programs. Health maintenance organizations (HMOs) proliferated. At an organizational meeting in 1985, Bays said to his managers, "Business history tells us, when industries change as dramatically as ours, a few companies emerge more powerful and with greater long-term growth potential than others. They're the ones that move boldly, take or create opportunities, and are willing to adapt and change." Four months later, Bays negotiated the deal to sell American to Baxter Travenol.

As chairman of the board of Baxter Travenol, Bays recognized that the most difficult problem facing the new entity was not merging systems, but merging cultures. Both parties had been successful, but Baxter had a highly centralized structure, American a highly decentralized one. Bays sought to move the organization ahead to new successes while retaining an entrepreneurial philosophy.[35]

Integrating Intrapreneurship into an Organization

Karl Bays provides an excellent example of how one organization was able to integrate intrapreneurship into a company. But as Steven Jobs found out, this isn't always an easy task. There appear to be four challenges that top managers must solve in order for an organization to have a lot of intrapreneurial activity.[36] First, top management must allow entrepreneurial activities to flourish as a part of the organization's normal day-to-day operations. These islands of intrapreneurial activity, which Peters and Waterman call **skunkworks** in their book *In Search of Excellence,* often violate formal review and reporting policies.[37] Top management must create cultures wherein these violations are tolerated, if not rewarded. When this occurs, employees are able to focus their attention on nonroutine and innovative tasks.

skunkworks Islands of intrapreneurial activity within an organization.

Second, intrapreneurship should generate ideas that turn into products or services that the organization can sell. The challenge every team faces is to shape ideas into commercially successful ventures. Organizations with intrapreneurial teams, such as Hallmark's Technology and Innovation Center and Kodak's Office of Innovation, have people who are sufficiently committed to these ideas to transform them into profitable ventures for the firm.

When Lois Benjamin-Bohm lost her husband and children in a car accident, running the moving business she and her husband had founded helped convince her to "get on with life."

Third, rewards need to be tied to performance of the intrapreneurial unit. This link encourages team members to work harder and compete more effectively; they reap the benefits of their efforts directly. Compensation is usually in the form of salary. However, incentives should be established to reward cooperation with other departments in the organization, as well as to reward those other departments that cooperate with and support the intrapreneurial project.

Fourth, in order for these activities to occur, top management must provide excellent and appropriate leadership. People are recruited to intrapreneurial activities by charismatic leaders. Shared norms and values are crucial; they create a spirit that fosters innovative activity within the organization.[38]

CHAPTER SUMMARY

1. An entrepreneur is someone who creates new business activity in the economy. Entrepreneurship is not only the creation of an independent venture; it can also occur within large corporations. However, shepherding a new venture to success requires different skills than those regularly used by managers in large, complex organizations.

2. Among the attributes that characterize successful entrepreneurs are the need for achievement, a desire for independence, self-confidence, future orientation, and a capacity for self-sacrifice. Key behaviors include technical competence, strong interpersonal skills, and decision-making ability.

3. Entrepreneurs can improve their chances for success by creating a business plan and following it. A prospective entrepreneur must consider a number of issues:

   ▶ What kind of business to own
   ▶ Whether to start a business or buy one
   ▶ Whether there is an adequate market for the product or service
   ▶ Where start-up funds will come from and how they will be used
   ▶ What skills will be needed to run the company successfully

4. Operating a family business leads to some unique opportunities *and* some special problems. The issues that family members must decide include who is responsible for what jobs and whom to hire. They must also reach agreement on legal matters and establish a board of advisors.

5. *Intrapreneurship* is a term used to describe an existing organization's involvement in a new activity. As such, it is more closely associated with a process than with a personality. Companies that are successful in new activities are characterized by commitment from senior management, flexible organization structures, autonomous venture teams, competent and talented internal entrepreneurs, incentives and rewards for risk taking, and appropriate control systems.

QUESTIONS FOR DISCUSSION AND APPLICATION

1. What does it take to be successful in starting an entrepreneurial business? Why do so many entrepreneurs fail?

2. Which attitudes and behaviors listed in Table 22.1 are more useful in managing an entrepreneurial company than in being an entrepreneur?

3. A recent survey published by *INC.*, a magazine widely read by entrepreneurs, revealed the following data. In 1990, many of the 600 fastest-growing entrepreneurial firms didn't even exist a decade before. Over 40 percent of these firms are in computer-related fields. Why has this industry—unlike, say, those producing energy-related or consumer goods—been such a hotbed of entrepreneurial activity?

4. Can managers in public-sector organizations be entrepreneurs? Why or why not?

5. **From Where You Sit:** If a friend of yours asked your advice on starting a new business, what would you say?

6. Why have such companies as 3M and Kodak, among others, been successful in spawning so many intrapreneurs?

7. **From Where You Sit:** Get together with several friends and try to come up with an idea for a new business. What kinds of resources do you need? What barriers must you overcome?

8. **From Where You Sit:** Suppose you're working for an organization and, during the normal course of your job, you discover a market for a new product or service. Your organization presently doesn't offer such a product or service. You share your idea with your neighbor, who thinks it would be a great money maker. In fact, your neighbor knows someone who would probably lend you the money to start your own organization. What would you do? If you start the organization, what ethical problems might you have to wrestle with (see Chapter 5)?

9. What are some roadblocks to opening up a new business in a foreign country?

10. What are some problems that entrepreneurs face as their ventures grow and become successful?

11. **From Where You Sit:** Using the information given in Tables 22.2 and 22.3, write a business plan for a photocopying service that you could locate near your school.

Do You Have What It Takes to be an Entrepreneur?

Wondering whether *you* have what it takes to succeed as an entrepreneur? No one can predict your success. But studies of successful entrepreneurs have revealed some characteristics that many have in common—including family backgrounds, motivations, and personality traits. Northwestern Mutual Life Insurance Company in Milwaukee has prepared this quiz to help give you an idea whether you'll have a headstart or a handicap if you go into business for yourself. Add or subtract from your score as you respond to each item.

1. Significantly high numbers of entrepreneurs are children of first-generation U.S. citizens. If your parents were immigrants, score plus 1. If not, score minus 1.

2. Successful entrepreneurs were not, as a rule, top achievers in school. If you were a top student, subtract 4. If not, add 4.

3. Entrepreneurs were not especially enthusiastic about participating in group activities in school. If you enjoyed group activities—clubs, team sports, double dates—subtract 1. If not, add 1.

4. Studies of entrepreneurs show that, as youngsters, they often preferred to be alone. Did you prefer to be alone as a youngster? If yes, add 1. If no, subtract 1.

5. Those who started an enterprise during childhood—lemonade stands, family newspapers, greeting card sales—or ran for elected office at school can add 2 because enterprise usually can be traced to an early age. Those who didn't initiate enterprises, subtract 2.

6. Stubbornness as a child seems to translate into determination to do things one's own way—certainly a hallmark of proven entrepreneurs. So, if you were a stubborn child—that is, you wanted to learn the hard way—then add 1. If not, subtract 1.

7. Caution may involve an unwillingness to take risks, a handicap for those embarking on previously uncharted territory. Were you cautious as a youngster? If yes, subtract 4. If no, add 4.

8. If you were daring, add 4.

9. Entrepreneurs often speak of pursuing different paths—despite the opinions of others. If the opinions of others matter to you, then subtract 1. If not, add 1.

10. Being tired of a daily routine is often a precipitating factor in an entrepreneur's decision to start an enterprise. If an important motivation for starting your own enterprise would be changing your daily routine, add 2. If not, subtract 2.

11. If you really enjoy work, are you willing to work long nights? If yes, add 2. If no, subtract 6.

12. If you would be willing to work "as long as it takes" with little or no sleep to finish a job, add 4.

13. Entrepreneurs generally enjoy their activity so much they move from one project to another—non-stop. When you complete a project successfully, do you immediately start another? If yes, add 2. If no, subtract 2.

14. Successful entrepreneurs are willing to use their savings to start a project. If you would be willing to spend your savings to start a business, add 2. If not, subtract 2.

15. If you would be willing to borrow from others, too, add 2. If not, subtract 2.

16. If your business failed, would you immediately work to start another? If yes, add 4. If no, subtract 4.

17. If you would immediately start looking for a good paying job, subtract 1.

18. Do you believe entrepreneurs are "risky"? If yes, subtract 2. If no, add 2.

19. Many entrepreneurs put long-term and short-term goals in writing. If you do, add 1. If you don't, subtract 1.

20. Handling cash flow can be critical to entrepreneurial success. If you believe you have more knowledge and experience with cash flow than most people, then add 2. If not, subtract 2.

21. Entrepreneurial personalities seem to be easily bored. If you are easily bored, add 2. If not, subtract 2.

22. Optimism can fuel the drive to press for success. If you're an optimist, add 2. Pessimists subtract 2.

Your Entrepreneurial Quotient

A score of 35 or more: You have everything going for you. You ought to achieve spectacular entrepreneurial success (barring acts of God or other variables beyond your control).

A score of 15 to 34: Your background, skills, and talents give you excellent chances for success in business. You should go far.

A score of zero to 14: You have a head start of ability and/or experience in running a business and ought to be successful in opening an enterprise of your own if you apply yourself and learn the necessary skills to make it happen.

A score of −15 to −1: You might be able to make a go of it if you ventured on your own, but you would have to work extra hard to compensate for a lack of built-in advantages and skills that give others a "leg up" in beginning their own businesses.

A score of −43 to −16: Your talents probably lie elsewhere. You ought to consider whether building your own business is what you really want to do because you may find yourself swimming against the tide if you make the attempt. Another work arrangement—such as working for someone else, or developing a career in a profession or an area of technical expertise—may be far more congenial to you and, therefore, allow you to enjoy a lifestyle appropriate to your abilities and interests.

To: Dana Noble, President, Dana's Fried Catfish
From: Andres Paris, Loan Officer
Re: Application for New Business Loan

It is with regret that I inform you that the bank's loan committee has rejected your application for a working-capital loan. Although your proposed business has merit, there were a number of factors that led to the committee's decision:

1. It is not the bank's policy to make uncollateralized loans to new ventures.
2. The committee believes that the expenses in your forecast are seriously underestimated. For example, you make no provision for advertising or other promotion for your restaurant. Also, we believe your wage estimates are low. The figures indicate that you do not anticipate experiencing any turnover of your personnel, ever having to pay overtime, or hiring any temporary workers.
3. Your management team (you, your son, and your sister) does not have experience in the restaurant industry, nor have any of you marketed products or services to consumers.

Although bank guidelines prohibit us from approving your loan application at this time, the committee did find merit in parts of your plan. Specifically, your market analysis was thorough and well documented. You clearly identified your target and included appropriate demographic information. Your proposed location was also well researched. As you know, location is critical to the success of a new restaurant.

If you decide to pursue this venture, we encourage you to aquire experience in the industry and continue your feasibility research. You should also consult an attorney, an accountant, and other experts familiar with this industry. We hope you will consider our bank for your future needs.

1. What do you think was the primary reason why the loan request was rejected?
2. What steps would you take at this point if you were Dana Noble?
3. What kinds of qualifications should a venture team have in order to operate an independent restaurant successfully? How could Dana Noble ensure that her team had those qualifications?

Minority-Owned Business's Surge of '80s Is Threatened

BY DOROTHY GAITER

Guy Louise-Julie used to sell facsimile machines for somebody else. In 1986 he tried to sell one to his neighbor, Clarence Williams, a founder of the Connecticut Minority Purchasing Council. Mr. Williams sugguested that he think about setting up his own business.

With the council's guidance and $10,000 in savings, Mr. Louise-Julie and his wife, Ann, started Fairfax Communications Co., which sells and services fax machines. The Milford, Conn., company now has six employees, 600 clients, and annual revenue of about $600,000.

The Connecticut business owners were part of the black entrepreneurial explosion of the 1980s. The U.S. Census Bureau's most recent figures show that the number of black-owned businesses soared to 424,000 in 1987, up 38% from 1982. That was almost three times the 14% overall growth in the number of U.S. companies.

That trend is being threatened by the economic downturn and legal and budgetary assaults on programs that help create and nurture minority businesses. A Supreme Court ruling has cast a cloud over 236 state and municipal programs that aid women and minorities. And the recession is certain to claim marginal companies, many of them black-owned.

Nevertheless, patterns in the rise of minority entrepreneurship are leading many specialists to conclude that, on balance, special-assistance programs for minorities are making a significant contribution.

"Businesses do better in states that have active minority-business programs or a governor or mayor with a strong commitment to minority procurement," says John F. Robinson, president of the National Minority Business Council, a New York not-for-profit group that helps minorities get contracts and training.

Not surprisingly, black capitalism took deepest root in states with booming economies and large black populations. But authorities said that private and government-sponsored programs were a factor, too. . .

In Connecticut, where a decade-old support system was bringing together black entrepreneurs, sympathetic state officials and corporations willing to invest in minority enterprises, the number of black-owned businesses surged through the mid-1980s. A strong state economy helped, too.

"As the economy was booming, opportunities opened for firms in general, but for black-owned firms in particular," says Joseph McGee, Connecticut's economic development commissioner. Blacks lobbied officials for help in promoting black startups.

As a result, he says, the state has effective programs in place to encourage minority-purchasing. He cites the Connecticut Minority Purchasing Council, a not-for-profit advocacy group that is one of 48 such groups nationwide. Allying itself with minority-business advocates, Connecticut in 1976 established one of the nation's first set-aside programs.

Some analysts question the effectiveness of set-asides, and the potential for abuse is great: Blacks have been used as fronts to qualify companies for minority-only contracts. But supporters say the benefits of the programs outweigh the drawbacks.

For the Louise-Julies and their Fairfax Communications, there was one particular hurdle that minority start-ups often face: a lack of connections. That's where the Connecticut Minority Purchasing Council helped.

The council, based in Bridgeport, besides offering advice on everything from writing a business plan to answering the telephone professionally, gives fledgling businesses a head start by putting them in contact with big companies committed to increasing purchases from minority-owned firms. More than one-third of Fairfax's revenue comes from contracts with big firms that are council members.

Cities as well as states are lending a hand to minorities and women. New York City, for example, has a program to provide counseling to start-up firms. One beneficiary is Pearl Hedgspeth, who set out on her own after 20 years of teaching shorthand, typing and word-processing. Miss

Hedgspeth had always tried to find jobs for her students, and decided to parlay that experience into a business. So she took business courses, attended seminars, rented space—and several years ago founded Temporary Solutions Inc., a provider of temporary office help.

The city's business mentoring program paired her with Rosann Levy, marketing director and partner with her husband in an accounting firm. Mrs. Levy helped work out a business plan and sharpen the firm's image. The city also paid most of a financial consultant's fee. On an initial investment of $7,000, Miss Hedgspeth's revenue grew to $350,000 last year. The city program doesn't guarantee success—her company now is slumping with the struggling economy. "But it helps," she says.

1. Can an entrepreneur starting up a business protect himself or herself against unreliable government funding? How?

2. If you were a minority businessperson trying to start up a new company today, would you seek government help? What are some of the pitfalls?

3. Explain the drawbacks and benefits of New York City's mentoring program.

BLOCKBUSTER VIDEO

In the late 1970s, an unsuccessful Hollywood actor named George Atkinson ran a small storefront operation, renting movies not under copyright and projectors in the old Super Eight home-movie format. After reading about the Betamax, which Sony Corp. introduced in the United States in 1976, Atkinson borrowed $10,000 from a high school buddy and purchased one copy each of the 50 modern movies then available on videocassette. He placed his first ad in the *Los Angeles Times:* "Movies for Rent." Like so many apparently "revolutionary" developments, the video rental industry began with an incremental marketing innovation.

Almost everyone, from studio executives to Wall Street investors, ignored the movie rental business. The electronics industry viewed home video as a transition to something completely different: laser disks, which were then selling for around $10 each. But as videocassette recorder (VCR) prices dropped—from $1300 when they were introduced to about $199 for today's sale-priced machines—the video rental market boomed. It topped $1 billion in 1983. And by the beginning of the 1990s, 56 percent of America's 89 million households with TV sets also had VCRs, up from 10 percent in 1983.

The retail business attracted anyone who could raise a few thousand dollars to buy tapes and to rent space for a store. Blockbuster Video began as an outgrowth of a computer services company that was seeking to diversify. Founder David Cook conceived the video superstore idea in 1985. He stocked the shelves in his first store in Dallas, Texas, with at least 8000 tapes—4 times as many as the average storefront operation.

"There were a lot of stores running around calling themselves 'superstores,' but they weren't," Cook recalls. "We spent nearly a year defining the tape library, re-searching sources, designing a distribution system, writing the software and coming up with the design for the prototype store."

Cook wrote a computer program to track inventory and speed the check-out process via bar-coding technology. But in 1987 he needed cash.

Enter Wayne Huizenga, John Melk, and Donald Flynn. They spent a couple of days looking over Blockbuster's books and getting a crash course in the tape rental business. Rather than buying a single Blockbuster franchise, they decided to buy the company.

"Blockbuster's concept was unique and different," Huizenga says. "There wasn't anything proprietary in the system, but it was clearly unique. It was Blockbuster's concept to display the tapes 'live' on the shelf, rather than behind a counter. There was a three-day rental policy, which I liked. They also had a distribution center with the computer tied in to keep the inventory under control. It was further ahead than any of the other video companies available at that time."

Blockbuster is an aggressive TV advertiser, hoping to position the company in the minds of American video consumers.

"What we're really vying for is a piece of the customer's time," says Huizenga. "Does that customer want to spend his time in the movie theater or watching network television or watching his favorite video? And we're trying to convince the consumer that the extra hour, hour-and-a-half, he has to spend is best spent watching a Blockbuster video."

Entrepreneurship was not new to Huizenga. He had started a one-truck garbage business in Fort Lauderdale, Florida, and turned it into the Chicago-based Waste Management Corp. Waste Management is now the nation's largest publicly owned garbage collection company.

1. Is Wayne Huizenga an entrepreneur?
2. What key personal attributes and behaviors does he exhibit?
3. Can an entrepreneur both start a company and manage a large organization? Is Huizenga an exception, or is he the rule?
4. What planning issues would you have to address if you were thinking of buying a Blockbuster franchise?

References

Chapter 1

1. Richard Brandt, "Microsoft May Have Macro Worries," *Business Week,* March 25, 1991, p. 30; Brenton Schlender, "How Bill Gates Keeps the Magic Going," *Fortune,* June 18, 1990, pp. 82–89.

2. J. P. Kotter, "What Leaders Really Do," *Harvard Business Review,* May-June 1990: 106.

3. S. S. Sherman, "Smart Ways to Handle the Press," *Fortune,* June 19, 1989, 69–75.

4. Interview with Al Casey, former President and Chief Executive Officer, American Airlines, November 1990, Dallas, Texas.

5. P. Moser, "The McDonald's Mystique," *Fortune,* July 4, 1988, 112–116.

6. Adapted from S. Overman, "Different World Brings Challenge," *HR Magazine,* June 1990, 52–55.

7. H. Mintzberg, *The Nature of Managerial Work* (New York: Harper & Row, 1973); L. Kurke and H. E. Aldrich, "Mintzberg was Right: A Replication and Extension of Managerial Work," *Management Science,* 1983, *29:* 975–984; R. Stewart, "Studies of Managerial Jobs and Behavior: The Ways Forward," *Journal of Management Studies,* 1989, *26:* 1–10; E. F. Jackofsky, J. W. Slocum, Jr., and S. McQuaid, "Cultural Values and the CEO: Alluring Companions," *Academy of Management Executive,* 1988, *2:* 39–49.

8. R. A. Kerin, V. J. Mahajan, and P. R. Varadarajan, *Contemporary Perspectives on Strategic Market Planning* (Boston: Allyn and Bacon, 1990), 428.

9. D. Hellriegel, J. W. Slocum, Jr., and R. W. Woodman, *Organizational Behavior,* 5th ed. (St. Paul, Minn.: West Publishing, 1989), 31–32.

10. Adapted from B. Burlington and C. Hartman, "Cowboy Capitalist," *Inc.,* January 1989, 54–69.

11. A. I. Kraut, P. R. Pegrego, D. D. McKenna, and M. D. Dunnette, "The Role of the Manager: What's Really Important in Different Management Jobs," *Academy of Management Executive,* 1989, *3:* 286–293.

12. Adapted from H. Evans, "Paying Dues," *C V Magazine,* November-December 1989, 58–59.

13. Adapted from A. Taylor, III, "How a Top Boss Manages His Day," *Fortune,* June 19, 1989, 95–100. *See also* J. Sonnenfeld, *The Hero's Farewell: What Happens When CEOs Retire.* (New York: Oxford University Press, 1988).

14. L. R. Offerman and M. K. Gowing, "Organizations of the Future," *American Psychologist,* 1990, *45:* 95–108.

15. A. M. Morrison and M. A. VonGlinow, "Women and Minorities in Management," *American Psychologist,* 1990, *45:* 200–208; J. Castro, "Get Set: Here They Come," *Time Special Issue, Women: The Road Ahead,* Fall 1990, 50–52; W. B. Johnston "Global Work Force 2000: The New World Labor Market," *Harvard Business Review,* March-April 1991, 115–129. K. Dychtwald, *Age Wave* (New York: Bantam Books, 1990).

16. J. M. Bardwick, *The Plateauing Trap* (New York: American Management Association, 1986).

17. K. S. Cameron, S. J. Freeman, and A. K. Mishra, "Best Practices in White-Collar Downsizing: Managing Contradictions," *Academy of Management Executive,* 1991, *5:* 57–73.

18. J. J. Turnage, "The Challenge of the New Workplace Technology for Psychology," *American Psychologist,* 1990, *45:* 171–178.

19. W. L. Mohr and H. Mohr, *Quality Circles: Changing Images of People at Work* (Reading, Mass.: Addison-Wesley, 1983).

20. P. Hirsch, *Pack Your Own Parachute* (Reading, Mass.: Addison-Wesley, 1987); P. R. Nienstedt, "Effectively Downsizing Management Structures," *Human Resource Planning,* 1989, *12:* 155–165.

21. D. Lei and J. W. Slocum, Jr., "Global Strategic Alliances: Payoffs and Pitfalls," *Organizational Dynamics,* Winter 1991, 44–62.

22. R. L. Katz, "Skills of an Effective Administrator," *Harvard Business Review,* January-February 1974: 90–101.

23. W. B. Wriston, "The State of American Management," *Harvard Business Review,* January-February 1990: 78–83.

24. Adapted from S. Thiederman, "Overcoming Cultural and Language Barriers," *Personnel Management,* August 1989, 78–83.

25. K. R. Harrigan, *Strategies for Joint Ventures* (Lexington, Mass.: Lexington Books, 1985).

26. W. Bennis and B. Nanus, *Leaders: The Strategies for Taking Charge* (New York: Harper & Row, 1985).

27. M. Walton, *The Deming Management Method* (New York: Dodd, Mead, 1986); J. B. McGuire and T. Schneeweis, "Perceptions of Firm Quality: A Cause or Result of Firm Performance," *Journal of Management,* 1990, *16:* 167–180.

Skill-Building Exercise. Adapted from E. Raudsepp, "Will You Find Management Fulfilling?" *Female Executive,* July-August 1990, 57, 59.

Manager's Memo. Adapted from G. DeGeorge, "Can Barry Gibbons Put the Sizzle Back in Burger King?" *Business Week,* October 22, 1990, 60–61; *1990 Application Guidelines, Malcolm Baldrige Quality Award* (Gaithersburg, Md.: United States Department of Commerce and National Institute of Standards and Technology, 1990).

In the News. Alicia Swasy, "At Procter & Gamble, Change Under Artzt Isn't Just Cosmetic," *Wall Street Journal,* March 5, 1991.

Management Case. Adapted from D. T. Dingle, "The Manager of Tomorrow—Today," *Black Enterprise,* March 1990, 43–50.

Chapter 2

1. Adapted from D. A. Wren, "Years of Good Beginnings: and 1936," in D. A. Wren and J. A. Pearce, II (eds.), *Papers Dedicated to the Development of Modern Management* (Starksville, Miss.: Mississippi State University, Academy of Management Proceedings, 1986), 1–4; D. A. Wren, "Management History: Issues and Ideas for Teaching and Research," *Journal of Management,* 1987, *13:* 239–250.

2. M. Weber, *The Theory of Social and Economic Organization,* trans. by A. M. Henderson and T. Parsons (New York: Free Press, 1947). See also A. Kieser, "Organizational, Institutional, and Societal Evolution: Medical Craft Guilds and the Genesis of Formal Organizations," *Administrative Science Quarterly,* 1989, *34:* 540–564.

3. D. A. Nadler and M. Tushman, *Strategic Organization Design* (Glenview, Ill.: Scott, Foresman, 1988).

4. R. P. Hummel, *The Bureaucratic Experience* (New York: St. Martin's Press, 1987); J. M. Jermier, J. W. Slocum, Jr., L. W. Fry, J. Gaines, "Organizational Subcultures in a Soft Bureaucracy: Resistance Behind the Myth and Facade of an Official Culture," *Organization Science,* 1991, 170–194.

5. J. L. Cotton, D. A. Vollrath, K. L. Froggatt, M. L. Lengnick-Hall, and K. R. Jennings, "Employee Participation: Diverse Forms and Different Outcomes," *Academy of Management Review,* 1988, *13:* 8–22; J. A. Raelin, "An Anatomy of Autonomy: Managing Professionals," *Academy of Management Executive,* 1989, *3:* 216–228.

6. G. Morgan, *Images of Organizations* (Beverly Hills, Calif.: Sage, 1986); W. R. Nord and S. Tucker, *Implementing Routine and Radical Innovations* (Lexington, Mass.: Lexington Books, 1987).

7. Adapted from K. Labich, "Big Changes at Big Brown," *Fortune,* January 18, 1988, 56–64; D. Machalaba, "Up To Speed: UPS Gets Deliveries Done by Driving Its Workers," *Wall Street Journal,* April 22, 1986, 1ff; J. A. Sonnenfeld, "A Year of Living Differently," *Harvard Business School Bulletin,* June 1987, 47–50; R. W. King, "UPS Isn't about to Be Left Holding the Parcel," *Business Week,* February 13, 1989, 69.

8. F. W. Taylor, *Scientific Management* (New York: Harper & Row, 1947), 66–71.

9. H. Fayol, *General and Industrial Management* (London: Pitman and Sons, 1949).

10. H. Koontz, "The Management Theory Jungle Revisited," *Academy of Management Review,* 1980, *5:* 175–188.

11. M. P. Follett, "Dynamic Administration," in H. Metcalf and L. F. Urwick (eds.), *Dynamic Administration: The Collected Papers of Mary Parker Follett* (New York: Harper & Row, 1942).

12. C. Barnard, *The Functions of the Executive* (Cambridge, Mass.: Harvard University Press, 1938).

13. E. Mayo, *The Social Problems of an Industrial Civilization* (Boston: Harvard University, Graduate School of Business, 1945); R. Greenwood, A. Bolton, and R. Greenwood, "Hawthorne: A Half Century Later: Relay Participants Remember," *Journal of Management,* 1983, *9:* 217–231.

14. J. A. Sonnenfeld, "Shedding Light on the Hawthorne Studies," *Journal of Occupational Behavior,* 1985, *6:* 111–130.

15. J. L. Massie, "Management History," in J. G. March (ed.), *Handbook of Organizations* (Chicago: Rand McNally, 1965), 387–422.

16. Adapted from D. F. Harvey, *Strategic Management and Business Policy,* 2nd ed. (Columbus, Ohio: Merrill, 1988), 434–458; P. Sellers, "Tandem: A

Rose among the Technology Thorns," *Fortune,* August 28, 1989, 42*ff;* J. B. Levine, "Why Tandem Struggles while Its Markets Sizzle," *Business Week,* August 22, 1988, 88*ff;* Tandem Computers, *Annual Reports,* 1986, 1987, 1988; Tandem Computers, *Form 10-K,* 1989.

17. W. R. Nord, A. P. Brief, J. M. Atieh, and E. M. Doherty, "Work Values and the Conduct of Organizational Behavior," in B. M. Staw and L. L. Cummings (eds.), *Research in Organizational Behavior* (Greenwich, Conn.: Jai Press, 1988), 1–42.

18. M. S. Poole and A. H. Van De Ven, "Using Paradox to Build Management and Organization Theories, *Academy of Management Review,* 1989, *14:* 562–578.

19. Adapted from H. Altman, "A Business Visionary Who Really Delivered," *Nation's Business,* November 1982, 57*ff;* K. Fitzgerald, "Federal Express Looks for Help Overseas," *Advertising Age,* July 3, 1989, 21*ff;* M. B. Solomon, "Federal, JAL Join Other Airlines to Consider Automatic Global Network," *Traffic World,* September 15, 1989, 22–23; "Federal Income Drops for Quarter and Year, Higher Costs Blamed," *Traffic World,* July 24, 1989, 36; D. Foust, "Mr. Smith Goes Global," *Business Week,* February 13, 1989, 66–68, 72.

20. G. A. Forgione, *Quantitative Management* (Hinsdale, Ill.: Dryden Press, 1990).

21. H. L. Tosi, Jr. and J. W. Slocum, Jr., "Contingency Theory: Some Suggested Directions," *Journal of Management,* 1984, *10:* 9–26.

22. L. W. Fry, "Technology-Structure Research: Three Critical Issues," *Academy of Management Journal,* 1984, *27:* 221–246.

23. J. Woodward, *Industrial Organization: Theory and Practice,* 2nd ed. (London: Oxford University Press, 1980).

24. H. Mintzberg, *Mintzberg on Management: Inside Our Strange World of Organizations* (New York: Free Press, 1989), 106–109, 279–280; E. Jacques, "In Praise of Hierarchy," *Harvard Business Review,* 1990, *68*(1): 127–133.

In the News. Ron Suskind, "Back to the Past: New England Banker, Sticking to Old Ways, Avoided Rivals' Woes," *Wall Street Journal,* February 19, 1991, A1, A6.

Management Case. Adapted from M. Keller, *Rude Awakening: The Rise, Fall and Struggle for Recovery of General Motors* (New York: Morrow, 1989); T. Maxon, "Heartbeat of a Joint Venture," *American Way,* February 15, 1990, 28–34.

Skill-Building Exercise. Professor Robert Keller, College of Business, University of Houston, Houston, Tex. (1991). Used by permission.

Chapter 3

1. Developed from K. Nickel, "Can This Man Really Deliver?" *Fortune,* August 14, 1989, 87–88.

2. D. A. Heenan, "Congress Rethinks America's Competitiveness," *Business Horizons,* May-June 1989, 11–16.

3. A. Marcus and G. Rands, "The Challenges for Business from the 'New Environmentalism'," in *Corporate Conservation Council, the Natural Environment: Issues for Management* (Washington, D.C.: National Wildlife Federation, Fall 1990), 45.

4. Ibid., 46–48; D. Kirkpatrick, "Environmentalism: The New Crusade," *Fortune,* February 12, 1990, 44–50, 52, 54.

5. T. S. Bateman and C. P. Zeithaml, *Management: Function and Strategy* (Homewood, Ill.: Irwin, 1990), 215.

6. J. S. Leonard, "The Changing Face of Employees and Employment Regulation," *California Management Review,* Winter 1989, 29–38.

7. *The Aging Work Force* (Washington, D.C.: American Association of Retired Persons, 1990).

8. J. Dreyfuss, "Getting Ready for the New Work Force," *Fortune,* May 23, 1990, 165, 168, 172, 180, 181.

9. Developed from R. E. Schmid, "Latinization of America," *Bryan–College Station Eagle,* March 23, 1990, 7B; J. L. Simon, "The More the Merrier," *Forbes,* April 2, 1990, 77–81.

10. G. Hofstede, "The Cultural Relativity of the Quality of Life Concept," *Academy of Management Review,* 1984, *9:* 389–398.

11. S. Ronen and O. Shenkar, "Clustering Countries on Attitudinal Dimensions: A Review and Synthesis," *Academy of Management Review,* 1985, *10:* 435–454.

12. G. W. England, "Organizational Goals and Expected Behavior of American Managers," *Academy of Management Journal,* 1967, *10:* 107–117; B. W. Becker and P. E. Connor, "On the Status and Promise of Values Research," *Management Bibliographies & Reviews,* 1986, *12:* 3–17.

13. G. W. England, O. P. Dhingra, and N. C. Agarwal, "The Manager and the Man: A Cross-Cultural Study of Personal Values," *Organization and Administrative Sciences,* 1974, *5:* 1–97; C. S. McCoy, *Management of Values: The Ethical Difference in Corporate Policy and Performance* (Marshfield, Mass.: Pitman, 1985).

14. G. Hofstede, *Culture's Consequences: International Differences in Work-Related Values* (Beverly Hills, Calif., and London: Sage, 1980).

15. G. Hofstede, "National Cultures in Four Dimensions: A Research-Based Theory of Cultural Dimensions among Nations," *International Studies of Management and Organization,* 1983, *13:* 1–2, 46–74.

16. Adapted from N. J. Adler, "Women in Management Worldwide," *International Studies of Management and Organizations,* Fall-Winter, 1986–87, 3–32; N. J. Adler, "Pacific Basin Managers: A Gaijin, Not a Woman," *Human Resource Management,* 1987, *26:* 169–191.

17. E. F. Jackofsky, J. W. Slocum, Jr., and S. J. McQuaid, "Cultural Values and the CEO: Alluring Companions?" *Academy of Management Executive,* 1988, *2:* 39–49; G. Hofstede and M. H. Bond, "The Confucius Connection: From Cultural Roots to Economic Growth," *Organizational Dynamics,* Spring 1988, 5–21.

18. J. Thompson, *Organizations in Action* (New York: McGraw-Hill, 1967).

19. S. Greenfeld, R. C. Winder, and G. Williams, "The CEO and the External Environment," *Business Horizons,* November-December 1988, 20–25.

20. J. R. Lang and D. E. Lockhart, "Increased Environmental Uncertainty and Changes in Board Linkage Patterns," *Academy of Management Journal,* 1990, *33:* 106–128.

21. P. F. Drucker, *Managing in Turbulent Times* (New York: Harper & Row, 1980), 3, 153, 154.

22. Developed from N. M. Carter, "Small Firm Adaptation: Responses of Physicians' Organizations to Regulatory and Competitive Uncertainty," *Academy of Management Journal,* 1990, *33:* 307–333.

23. M. E. Porter, *Competitive Strategy: Techniques for Analyzing Industries and Competitors* (New York: Free Press, 1980); M. E. Porter, *Competitive Advantage: Creating and Sustaining Superior Performance* (New York: Free Press, 1985).

24. B. D. Henderson, "The Anatomy of Competition?" *Journal of Marketing,* Spring 1983, 7–11.

25. A. A. Marcus, "Airline Deregulation: Why the Supporters Lost Out," *Long Range Planning,* 1987, *20*(1): 90–98.

26. K. Labich, "Should Airlines Be Reregulated?" *Fortune,* June 19, 1990, 82–90.

27. Developed from P. Sellers, "What Customers Really Want," *Fortune,* June 4, 1990, 58–68; S. Phillips, A. Dunkin, J. B. Treece, and K. H. Hammonds, "King Customer," *Business Week,* March 12, 1990, 88–94.

28. D. Jones Yang and M. Oneal, "How Boeing Does It," *Business Week,* July 9, 1990, 46–50.

29. D. Ulrich and J. B. Barney, "Perspectives in Organizations: Resource Dependence, Efficiency, and Population," *Academy of Management Review,* 1984, *9:* 471–481.

30. M. Beaucamp, "No More Weekend Stands," *Forbes,* September 17, 1990, 191–192.

31. Developed from M. Gianturco, "The Supernets Are Coming!" *Forbes,* February 20, 1989, 112–116; B. R. Schlender, "Who's Ahead in the Computer Wars," *Fortune,* February 12, 1990, 59–66; "Computer Software: An Infant Industry Becomes a Regional Leader," *Pacific Northwest Executive,* January 1990, 9–11.

32. M. Zeleny, "High Technology Management," *Human Systems Management,* 1986, *6:* 109–120. *See also* R. M. Henderson and K. B. Clark, "Architectural Innovation: The Reconfiguration of Existing Product Technologies and the Future of Established Firms," *Administrative Science Quarterly,* 1990, *35:* 9–30.

33. M. Zeleny, "High Technology Management," *Human Systems Management,* 1986, *6:* 109–120; T. Suzuk, "High Standard Automobile Society of the 21st Century," *Digest of Japanese Industry and Technology,* 1989 (250), 2–10.

34. D. D. Davis, "Technological Innovation and Organizational Change," in D. D. Davis and Associates (eds.), *Managing Technological Innovation* (San Francisco: Jossey-Bass, 1986), 1.

35. G. Gilder, *The Quantum Revolution in Economics and Technology* (New York: Simon & Schuster, 1989); E. H. Harbison, Jr., "Society and Technology," *World Link,* January-February 1990, 28–30.

36. M. S. Gerstein, *The Technology Connection* (Reading, Mass.: Addison-Wesley, 1987), 112. *See also* J. F. Rockart and J. D. Short, "IT in the 1990s: Managing Organizational Interdependence," *Sloan Management Review,* Winter 1989, 7–17.

37. M. S. Gerstein, *The Technology Connection,* p. 13. *See also* J. Morone, "Strategic Use of Technology," *California Management Review,* Summer 1989, 91–110; Y. Sankar, *Management of Technology Change* (New York: Wiley, 1990).

38. B. Bozeman, *All Organizations Are Public* (San Francisco: Jossey-Bass, 1987).

39. M. H. Bazerman and R. J. Lewicki, "Contemporary Research Directions in the Study of Negotiations in Organizations: A Selective Overview," *Journal of Occupational Behavior,* 1985, *6:* 1–17.

40. Adapted from P. Ravesies, "U.S. Investment in China's Energy Development: Prospects and Pitfalls," *Texas A&M Business Forum,* Fall 1987, 33–38. Used with permission.

41. G. Keim and B. Baysinger, "The Efficacy of Business Political Activity: Competitive Consideration in a Principal-Agent Context," *Journal of Management,* 1988, *14:* 163–180.

42. J. H. Birnbaum, "Chief Executives Head to Washington to Ply the Lobbyist's Trade," *Wall Street Journal,* March 19, 1990, A1, A6.

43. S. Levitan and M. Cooper, *Business Lobbies: The Public Good and the Bottom Line* (Baltimore: Johns Hopkins University Press, 1984).

44. E. Schurenberg and L. Luciano, "The Empire of AARP," *Best of Business Quarterly,* Spring 1989, 16–25.

45. G. Hamel, Y. L. Doz, and C. K. Prahalad, "Collaborate With Your Competitors—And Win," *Harvard Business Review,* January-February 1989, 133–139.

46. B. Barys and A. B. Jemison, "Hybrid Arrangements as Strategic Alliances: Theoretical Issues in Organizational Combinations," *Academy of Management Review,* 1989, *14:* 234–249.

47. D. Lei and J. W. Slocum, Jr., "Global Strategic Alliances," working paper: Southern Methodist University, 1990.

48. R. M. Kanter, "Becoming PALS: Pooling, Allying, and Linking Across Companies," *Academy of Management Executive*, 1989, *3*: 183–193.

49. I. F. Kesner and D. R. Dalton, "Boards of Directors and the Checks and (Im)Balances of Corporate Governance," *Business Horizons*, September-October 1986, 17–23.

50. P. L. Rechner, "Corporate Governance: Fact or Fiction?" *Business Horizons*, July-August 1989, 11–15; I. F. Kesner, "Shareholders and the Issue of Corporate Governance: The Silenced Partner," *Business Horizons*, July-August 1989, 16–21.

Skill-Building Exercise. Developed from M. Enez and P. C. Earley, "A Cross-Cultural Look at Acceptance and Value Orientation as the Determinants of Goal-Setting Effectiveness." Paper presented at the annual meeting of the International Association of Applied Psychology, Edinburgh, Scotland, 1982. Also, G. Hofstede, *Cultural Consequences: International Differences in Work-Related Values* (Beverly Hills, Calif.: Sage, 1980).

Manager's Memo. From D. N. Frey, "Reflections on Business and Technology," *Business in the Contemporary World*, October 1988, 71–79.

In the News. Joan E. Rigdon, "Kodak Zooms In on Pro Photographers," *Wall Street Journal*, February 27, 1991, pp. B1, B3.

Management Case. From B. Ives and R. O. Mason, "Can Information Technology Revitalize Your Customer Service?" *Academy of Management Executive*, November 1990, 58–59.

Chapter 4

1. Developed from G. Anders, "Going Global: Vision versus Reality," *Wall Street Journal*, September 22, 1989, R20–R21; J. O'Toole, "Beyond 1992: The Global Competitors," *Business Forum*, Fall 1989, 11–14; M. McNamee and P. Magnusson, "Think Globally, Survive Locally," *Business Week*, November 26, 1990, 50–51.

2. E. T. Yon, "Corporate Strategy and the New Europe," *Academy of Management Executive*, August 1990, 61–65.

3. "The Global Giants," *Wall Street Journal Reports*, September 21, 1990, R27–R30.

4. A. Phatak, *International Dimensions of Management*, 2nd ed. (Boston: Kent, 1988), 9–12; M. Leontiades, *Multinational Business Strategy: Techniques and Guidelines for Management* (Lexington, Mass.: Lexington Books, 1984).

5. J. M. Rains, "International Trade: The Key to Prosperity for the United States and Texas," *Texas A&M Business Forum*, Fall 1987, 9. *See also* C. Vlachoustsikos, "How Small- to Mid-sized U.S. Firms Can Profit from Perestroika," *California Management Review*, Spring 1989, 91–112; R. Howard, "Can Small Business Help Countries Compete?" *Harvard Business Review*, November-December 1990, 88–96.

6. Adpated from P. M. Lee, "Over There: The Exporting Challenge," *Small Business Reports*, January 1990, 39–42.

7. Y. Tsurumi, *Multinational Management: Business Strategy and Government Policy*, 2nd ed. (Cambridge, Mass.: Ballinger, 1984), 234–240.

8. J. J. Boddewyn, R. S. Soehl, and J. Picard, "Standardization in International Marketing: Is Ted Levitt in Fact Right?" *Business Horizons*, November-December 1986, 69–75.

9. J. Main, "How to Go Global—and Why," *Fortune*, August 28, 1989, 71.

10. Tsurumi, *Multinational Management*, 239–240; S. Ghoshal and C. A. Barlett, "The Multinational Corporation as an Interorganizational Network," *Academy of Management Review*, 1990, *15*: 603–625.

11. Main, "How to Go Global—and Why," 72.

12. A. J. Morrison, *Strategies in Global Industries: How U.S. Businesses Compete* (Westport, Conn.: Quorum, 1990).

13. D. J. Lecrew, "Factors Influencing Your Success at Countertrade," *International Executive*, July-August 1989, 34–38.

14. D. Lei and J. W. Slocum, Jr., "Global Strategic Alliances," Working Paper, Southern Methodist University, 1990.

15. P. S. Chan and R. T. Justis, "Franchise Management in East Asia," *Academy of Management Executive*, May 1990, 75–85.

16. L. Kraar, "Your Rivals Can Be Your Allies," *Fortune*, March 27, 1989, 67–76.

17. Lei and Slocum, "Global Strategic Alliances"; K. Ohmae, "The Global Logic of Strategic Alliance," *Harvard Business Review*, March-April 1989, 143–154; B. Gomes-Casseres, "Joint Ventures in the Face of Global Competition," *Sloan Management Review*, Spring 1989, 17–26; L. E. V. Nevaer and S. A. Deck, *Strategic Corporate Alliance* (Westport, Conn.: Quorum, 1990).

18. Developed from O. Port and T. Mason, "What's Behind the Texas Instruments–Hitachi Deal," *Business Week*, January 16, 1989, 93, 96; T. Steinert-Threlkeld, "Texas Instruments Aiming for Success on a Global Scale," *Dallas Morning News*, October 28, 1989, 1F, 3F.

19. G. S. Yip, "Global Strategy . . . In a World of Nations?" *Sloan Management Review*, Fall 1989, 29–41.

20. Adapted from H. Sugiura, "How Honda Localizes Its Global Strategy," *Sloan Management Review*, Fall 1990, 77–82.

21. J. McCormick and N. Stone, "From National Champion to Global Competitor," *Harvard Business Review*, May-June 1990, 127–135; D. Lei and B. Slater, "The Evolution of Global Strategy," *International Executive*, May-June 1990, 27–31; K. Ohmae, *The Borderless World: Power and Strategy in the Interlocked Economy* (New York: Ballinger, 1990).

22. Developed from J. Main, "How to Go Global—and Why," *Fortune*, August 28, 1989, 70–76; R. Siman and G. Button, "What I Learned in the Eighties," *Forbes*, January 8, 1990, 99–114; N. Tichy and R. Charan, "Citicorp Faces the World: An Interview with John Reed," *Harvard Business Review*, November-December 1990, 135–144; C. J. Loomis, "Citicorp's World of Troubles," *Fortune*, January 14, 1991, 90–99.

23. R. S. Ahlbrandt, Jr. (ed.), *Managing in a Global Competitive Environment* (Pittsburgh, Pa.: Joseph M. Katz Graduate School of Business, University of Pittsburgh, 1989); H. Vernon Wortzel and L. H. Wortzel, *Global Strategic Management: The Essentials* (New York: Wiley, 1990).

24. S. Nasar, "Competitiveness: Getting It Back," *Fortune*, April 27, 1987, 217–223; U.S. Small Business Administration, *Small Business in the American Economy* (Washington, D.C.: U.S. Government Printing Office, 1988); "Who Owns U.S.?" *Time*, December 10, 1990, 23.

25. R. Cardinali, "Trade with Canada under the FTA," *Business*, April-June 1989, 49–52; A. M. Rugman and A. Verbeke, "Corporate Strategy after the Free Trade Agreement and Europe 1992," paper presented at the Joint Canada-Germany Symposium on Regional Integration in the World Economy: Europe and North America, Kiel, Germany, March 1, 1990.

26. J. Urquhart and G. Lamphier, "Canada," *Wall Street Journal Reports*, September 21, 1990, R32, R35, R36.

27. Cardinali, "Trade with Canada under the FTA," 50.

28. Much of this section is developed from H. Weilhrich, "Europe 1992: What the Future May Hold," *Academy of Management Executive*, May

1990, 7–18. *See also* P. Brimelow, "The Dark Side of 1992," *Forbes*, January 22, 1990, 85–89; J. F. Magee, "1992: Moves Americans Must Make," *Harvard Business Review*, May-June 1989, 78–84; S. Tully, "The Coming Boom in Europe," *Fortune*, April 10, 1989, 108–114; J. A. Quelch, R. D. Buzzel, and E. R. Salama, *The Marketing Challenge of 1992* (Reading, Mass.: Addison-Wesley, 1990).

29. P. Fuhrman, "Your Market, Not Your Money," *Forbes*, September 17, 1990, 68–69.

30. M. M. Nelson, "Sticking Points: Is the 1992 Timetable for European Integration Too Optimistic?" *Wall Street Journal Reports*, September 21, 1990, R37–R38.

31. E. Calonius, "Federal Express's Battle Overseas," *Fortune*, December 3, 1990, 137–140.

32. M. E. Porter, "The Competitive Advantage of Nations," *Harvard Business Review*, March-April 1990, 73. *See also* M. E. Porter, *The Competitive Advantage of Nations* (New York: Free Press, 1990).

33. S. A. Lenway, C. K. Jacobson, and J. Goldstein, "To Lobby or to Petition: The Political Environment of U.S. Trade Policy," *Journal of Management*, 1990, *16*: 119–134; S. A. Lenway, *The Politics of U.S. International Trade: Protection, Expansion, and Escape* (Marshfield, Mass.: Pitman, 1985).

34. M. Fitzpatrick, "The Definition and Assessment of Political Risk in International Business: A Review of the Literature," *Academy of Management Review*, 1983, *8*: 249–254; D. A. Schmidt, "Analyzing Political Risk," *Business Horizons*, July-August 1986, 43–50.

35. D. Haendel, *Foreign Investments and the Management of Political Risk* (Boulder, Colo.: Westview, 1979); W. D. Coplin and M. K. O'Leary, *Introduction to Political Risk Analysis* (Croton-on-Hudson, N.Y.: Policy Studies Association, 1983).

36. W. D. Coplin and M. K. O'Leary, "World Political Risk Analysis for 1987," *Planning Review*, January-February 1987, 34–40.

37. L. Smith, "Fear and Loathing of Japan," *Fortune*, February 26, 1990, 50–60.

38. P. Chaote, "Political Advantage: Japan's Campaign for America," *Harvard Business Review*, September-October 1990, 87.

39. E. A. Finn, Jr., "Sons of Smoot-Hawley," *Forbes*, February 6, 1989, 38–40.

40. Coplin and O'Leary, "World Political Risk Analysis for 1987."

41. Adapted from G. Rayfield, "General Motors Political Risk Ratings: Assessment of a Track Record," in J. Rogers (ed.), *Global Risk Assessments: Issues, Concepts, and Applications*, Book 3 (Riverside, Calif.: Global Risk Assessment, 1988), 172–186.

42. R. Jacob, "Export Barriers the U.S. Hates Most," *Fortune*, February 27, 1989, 88–89. *See also* T. Agman and C. R. Hekman (eds.), *Trade Policy and Corporate Decisions* (New York: Oxford University Press, 1990).

43. P. Berman and R. Khalaf, "The Fanjuls of Palm Beach: The Family with a Sweet Tooth," *Forbes*, May 14, 1990, 56–69.

44. P. Magnusson, "Will We Ever Close the Trade Gap?" *Business Week*, February 27, 1989, 86–92.

45. *Investment Mission Program for U.S. Business Executives* (Washington, D.C.: Overseas Private Investment Corporation, 1987).

46. G. W. Stocking and M. W. Watkins, *Cartels or Competition?* (New York: Twentieth Century Fund, 1984), 3.

47. J. Rossant, "Why OPEC's Luck May Run Out," *Business Week*, February 26, 1990, 48.

48. J. L. Bower and E. A. Phenman, "Benevolent Cartels," *Harvard Business Review*, July-August 1985, 124–132.

49. D. B. Yoffie and H. V. Milner, "An Alternative to Free Trade or Protectionism: Why Corporations Seek Strategic Trade Policy," *California Management Review,* Summer 1989, 111–131.

50. N. H. Jacoby, P. Nehemkis, and R. Ells, *Bribery and Extortion in World Business* (New York: Macmillan, 1977), 90.

51. J. A. Fadiman, "A Traveler's Guide to Gifts and Bribes," *Harvard Business Review,* July-August 1986, 122–136; T. Donaldson, *The Ethics of International Business* (New York: Oxford University Press, 1989).

52. G. C. Greanias and D. Windsor, *The Foreign Corrupt Practices Act: Anatomy of a Statute* (Lexington, Mass.: Lexington Books, 1982).

53. H. Tong and P. Willing, "What American Managers Should Know and Do about International Bribery," *Baylor Business Studies,* January 1983, 7–19.

54. P. R. Harris and R. T. Moran, *Managing Cultural Differences,* 2nd ed. (Houston: Gulf, 1987); J. E. Austin, *Managing in Developing Countries: Strategic Analysis and Operating Techniques* (New York: Free Press, 1990); V. Terpstra and K. David, *The Cultural Environment of International Business* (Cincinnati, Ohio: South-Western, 1991).

55. E. S. Kras, *Management in Two Cultures* (Chicago, Ill.: Intercultural Press, 1988), 60–61.

56. R. L. Tung, *Business Negotiations with the Japanese* (Lexington, Mass.: Lexington Books, 1983).

57. L. Smith, "Fear and Loathing of Japan," *Fortune,* February 26, 1990, 50–60; T. E. Weinshall, *Cultural and Management: Managing in Cultures of Different Countries* (New York: Walter de Gruyter, 1990).

58. G. Hofstede, "National Cultures in Four Dimensions," *International Studies of Management and Organizations,* 1983, *13:* 46–74.

59. T. Yans, "Asia in the World, Japan in Asia," *Sumitomo Quarterly,* Winter 1989, 4–8; C. Rapoport, "Understanding How Japan Works," *Fortune,* Fall 1989 (Pacific Rim issue), 14–18.

60. J. Hodgson, *The Wondrous World of Japan* (Washington, D.C.: American Enterprise Institute, 1978), 3.

61. B. J. Campbell, "The Meaning of Work: American and Japanese Paradigms," *Asia Pacific Journal,* September 1985, 1–9; M. E. Mendenhall and G. Oddu, "The Cognitive, Psychological and Social Contexts of Japanese Management," *Asia Pacific Journal of Management,* September 1986, 24–40.

62. A. Dunphy, "Convergence/Divergence: A Temporal Review of the Japanese Enterprise and Its Management," *Academy of Management Review,* 1987, *12:* 445–459; R. A. Cosier and D. R. Dalton, "Search for Excellence, Learn from Japan—Are These Panaceas or Problems?" *Business Horizons,* November-December 1986, 63–68.

63. T. W. Kang, *Gaishi, the Foreign Company in Japan* (New York: Basic Books, 1990); J. R. Lincoln, "Employee Work Attitudes and Management Practice in the U.S. and Japan: Evidence from a Large Comparative Survey," *California Management Review,* Fall 1989, 89–106.

64. J. Hoer and L. Nathans Spiro, "Culture Shock at Home: Working for a Foreign Boss," *Business Week,* December 17, 1990, 80–84. See also S. Moffat, "Should You Work for the Japanese," *Fortune,* December 3, 1990, 107–120.

65. T. Oh, "Japanese Management—A Critical Review," *Academy of Management Review,* 1975, *1:* 13–25; H. Konoshita, "Matsushita's Basic Business Principles," *Management Japan,* Spring 1983, 26–32.

66. B. Keys and T. Miller, "Japanese Management Theory Jungle," *Academy of Management Review,* 1984, *9:* 342–353.

67. "The Switch Is On in Japan," *Fortune,* May 21, 1990, 144.

68. F. Gibney, *Japan: The Fragile Super Power* (Tokyo: Tuttle, 1975), 206.

69. W. C. Kester, *Japanese Takeovers: The Global Quest for Corporate Control* (Boston: Harvard Business School Press, 1990).

70. Developed from *Productivity & Employment: Challenges for the 1990s,* BLMR 132 (Washington, D.C.: U.S. Department of Labor, 1989), 26–27.

71. C. Rapoport, "How the Japanese Are Changing," *Fortune,* Fall 1990 (Pacific Rim issue), 15–22.

72. B. Buell, "Japan's Silent Majority Starts to Rumble," *Business Week,* April 23, 1990, 52–54; U. C. Lehmer, "Japanese May Be Rich but Are They Satisfied with Quality of Life?" *Wall Street Journal,* January 9, 1990, A1, A12.

73. S. Master, "Japan Divided Between Old, New Culture," *Battalion,* February 13, 1989, 1.

74. Characteristics used in this instrument developed from E. S. Kras, *Management in Two Cultures* (Yarmouth, Me.: Intercultural Press, 1988); and P. Casse and S. Deol, *Managing Intercultural Negotiations* (Washington, D.C.: Setnar International, 1985).

75. Developed from L. Grabowsky, "Globalization: Reshaping the Retail Marketplace," in *Retail Issues Newsletter,* published by Arthur Andersen & Company in conjunction with the Center for Retailing Studies, Texas A&M University, November 1989, 1–5.

76. "Transcontinental Industries (Malaysia) Ltd: A Case Study." Developed by J. Melvin Miller, Ph.D., Wing Commander P.T.C., Shastri (I.A.F., Ret.), 1980.

Chapter 5

1. Developed from C. Ralston, "Personal and Professional Aspects of Ethics," *Pacific Northwest Executive,* October 1988, 5–7.

2. "Taking 'Em For a Ride," *Time,* November 19, 1990, 85.

3. W. C. Frederick, K. Davis, J. E. Post, *Business and Society: Corporate Strategy, Public Policy, Ethics,* 6th ed. (New York: McGraw-Hill, 1988), 52.

4. C. E. Harris, Jr., *Applying Moral Theories* (Belmont, Calif.: Wadsworth, 1990), 7–11. *See also* O. C. Ferrell and J. Fraedrich, *Business Ethics: Ethical Decision Making and Cases* (Boston: Houghton Mifflin, 1991).

5. E. Bowen, "Looking to Its Roots," *Time,* May 27, 1987, 26–29; *Business Week/*Harris Poll: Is an Antibusiness Backlash Building?" *Business Week,* July 20, 1987, 71; K. Gudridge and J. A. Byrne, "A Kinder, Gentler Generation of Executives?" *Business Week,* April 23, 1990, 86–87; M. N. Vamos and S. Jackson, "The Public Is Willing to Take Business On," *Business Week,* May 29, 1989, 29; A. Farnham, "The Trust Gap," *Fortune,* December 4, 1989, 56–78.

6. B. Z. Posner and W. H. Schmidt, "Ethics in American Companies: A Managerial Perspective," *Journal of Business Ethics,* 1987, *6:* 383–391. *See also* M. T. Brown, *Working Ethics: Strategies for Decision Making and Organizational Responsibility* (San Francisco: Jossey-Bass, 1991).

7. A. Bhide and H. H. Stevenson, "Why Be Honest if Honesty Doesn't Pay," *Harvard Business Review,* September-October 1990, 126.

8. D. J. Wood, *Business and Society* (Glenview, Ill.: Scott, Foresman, 1990); R. T. DeGeorge, *Business Ethics,* 3rd ed. (New York: Macmillan, 1990).

9. R. Sacasas and A. Cava, "Laws, Ethics, and Management: Toward an Effective Audit," *Business Forum,* Winter 1990, 18–21; B. D. Fisher, "Positive Law as the Ethic of Our Time," *Business Horizons,* September-October 1990, 28–39.

10. A. H. Ringleb, R. E. Meiners, and F. L. Edwards, *Managing in the Legal Environment.* St. Paul, Minn.: West Publishing, 1990), 395.

11. Developed from J. Frug, "Why Courts Are Always Making Law," *Fortune,* September 29, 1989, 247–248; E. G. David and L. S. Hamilton, "Challenges to Employment at Will: A Survey of the Natural Gas Transmission Industry," *Employee Responsibilities and Rights Journal,* 1989, *2:* 109–119; S. A. Culbert and J. J. McDonough, "Wrongful Termination and the Reasonable Manager: Balancing Fair Play and Effectiveness," *Sloan Management Review,* Summer 1990, 39–46.

12. This section draws heavily from *Corporate Ethics: A Prime Business Asset* (New York: Business Roundtable, 1988).

13. Developed from *Corporate Ethics,* 35–36.

14. J. B. Cullen, B. Victor, and C. Stephens, "An Ethical Weather Report: Assessing the Organization's Ethical Climate," *Organizational Dynamics,* Autumn 1989, 50–62; B. Victor and J. B. Cullen, "The Organizational Bases of Ethical Work Climates," *Administrative Science Quarterly,* 1988, *33:* 101–125; B. J. Reilly and M. J. Kyj, "Ethical Business and the Ethical Person," *Business Horizons,* November-December 1990, 23–27.

15. L. Kohlberg, "Stage and Sequence: The Cognitive-Developmental Approach to Socialization," in D. A. Goslin (ed.), *Handbook of Socialization Theory and Research* (Chicago: Rand McNally, 1969), 347–380.

16. Descriptions of the stages based on L. Kohlberg, "The Cognitive-Developmental Approach to Moral Education," in P. Scharf (ed.), *Readings in Moral Education* (Minneapolis, Minn.: Winston Prisa, 1978), 36–51; G. D. Boxter and C. A. Rarick, "Education and Moral Development of Managers: Kohlberg's Stages of Moral Development and Integrative Education," *Journal of Business Ethics,* 1987, *6:* 243–248.

17. G. F. Cavanagh, *American Business Values,* 2nd ed. (Englewood Cliffs, N.J.: Prentice-Hall, 1984), 135.

18. W. A. Kahn, "Toward an Agenda for Business Ethics Research," *Academy of Management Review,* 1990, *15:* 311–328; L. K. Trevino, "Ethical Decision Making in Organizations: A Person-Situation Interaction Model," *Academy of Management Review,* 1986, *11:* 601–617; L. K. Trevino and S. A. Youngblood, "Bad Apples in Bad Barrels: A Causal Analysis of Ethical Decision-Making Behavior," *Journal of Applied Psychology,* 1990, *75:* 378–385.

19. Developed from G. F. Cavanagh, D. J. Moberg, and M. Velasquez, "The Ethics of Organizational Behavior," *Academy of Management Review,* 1981, *5:* 363–374. *See also* F. N. Brady, *Ethical Managing: Rules and Results* (New York: Macmillan, 1990).

20. J. S. Mill, *Utilitarianism* (Indianapolis, Ind.: Bobbs-Merrill, 1957; originally published 1863).

21. J. Q. Wilson, "Adam Smith on Business Ethics," *California Management Review,* Fall 1989, 59–72; B. Z. Posner and W. H. Schmidt, "Values and the American Manager: An Update," *California Management Review,* Spring 1984, 202–216.

22. A. Etzioni, "Humble Decision Making," *Harvard Business Review,* July-August 1989, 122–126.

23. R. Perloff, "Self-Interest and Personal Responsibility Redux," *American Psychologist,* 1987, *42:* 3–11.

24. M. Velasquez, D. V. Moberg, and G. F. Cavanagh, "Organizational Statesmanship and Dirty Politics: Ethical Guidelines for the Organizational Politician," *Organizational Dynamics,* Autumn 1983, 65–80; S. Block, R. Page, and N. Marguiles, "Perspectives on the Implementation of Employee Rights Programs," *Employee Responsibilities and Rights Journal,* 1988, *1:* 247–261.

25. Cavanagh, *American Business Values,* 2nd ed., 143; F. J. Aguilar, *The Moral Imperative: Corporate Ethics and the General Manager* (Boston: Harvard Business School Press, 1991).

26. J. R. Pierobon, "Passengers to Get Access to Airlines' On-Time Data," *Houston Chronicle,* Sep-

tember 3, 1987, Section 1, 2. *See also* R. F. Laden-son, "Free Expression in the Workplace: Does the Public-Private Distinction Matter?" *Employee Responsibilities and Rights Journal,* 1988, *1:* 91–99.

27. J. Rothfeder, "Is Nothing Private?" *Business Week,* September 4, 1989, 74–82.

28. D. W. Ewing, "Your Right to Fire," *Harvard Business Review,* March-April 1983, 32–34*ff.*

29. J. P. Near, "Whistle-Blowing: Encourage It!" *Business Horizons,* January-February 1989, 2–6; F. B. Bird and J. A. Waters, "The Moral Muteness of Managers," *California Management Review,* Fall 1989, 73–88.

30. J. D. Aram, *Managing Business and Public Policy: Concepts, Issues, and Cases* (Boston: Pitman, 1983), 21.

31. J. Locke, *Concerning Civil Government* (London, England: J. M. Dent, 1924), 180.

32. Adapted from D. J. Fritzche and H. Becker, "Linking Management Behavior to Ethical Philosophy: An Empirical Investigation," *Academy of Management Journal,* 1984, *27:* 166–175. Used with permission.

33. J. Rawls, *A Theory of Justice* (Cambridge, Mass.: Harvard University Press, 1971); J. Greenberg, "A Taxonomy of Organizational Justice Theories," *Academy of Management Review,* 1987, *12:* 9–22.

34. C. D. Fisher, L. F. Schoenfeldt, and J. B. Shaw, *Human Resource Management* (Boston: Houghton Mifflin, 1990), 488–489.

35. Rawls, *A Theory of Justice,* 111–112. *See also* E. W. Miles, J. D. Hatfield, and R. C. Huseman, "The Equity Sensitivity Construct: Potential Implications for Worker Performance," *Journal of Management,* 1989, *4:* 581–588: M. Sashkin and R. L. Williams, "Does Fairness Make a Difference?" *Organizational Dynamics,* Autumn 1990, 56–71.

36. R. Folger and M. A. Konovsky, "Effects of Procedural and Distributive Justice on Reactions to Pay Raise Decisions," *Academy of Management Journal,* 1989, *32:* 115–130; J. R. Meindl, "Managing to Be Fair: An Exploration of Values, Motives, and Leadership," *Administrative Science Quarterly,* 1989, *34:* 252–276.

37. Ewing, "Your Right to Fire," 38.

38. Ewing, "Your Right to Fire," 34.

39. Adapted from Fritzsche and Becker, "Linking Management Behavior to Ethical Philosophy." Used with permission.

40. M. E. Guy, *Ethical Decision Making in Everyday Work Situations* (Westport, Conn.: Quorum, 1990); R. E. Freeman (ed.), *Business Ethics: The State of the Art,* vol. 1 (New York: Oxford University Press, 1990).

41. W. D. Litzinger and T. E. Schaefer, "Business Ethics Bogeyman: The Perpetual Paradox," *Business Horizons,* March-April 1987, 21.

42. M. Friedman, "A Friedman Doctrine: The Social Responsibility of Business Is to Increase Its Profits," *New York Times Magazine,* September 13, 1970, 32*ff. See also* P. F. Hodapp, "Can There Be a Social Contract with Business?" *Journal of Business Ethics,* 1990, *9:* 127–131.

43. Friedman, "A Friedman Doctrine," 126.

44. R. Coye and J. Belohlav, "Disciplining: A Question of Ethics?" *Employee Rights and Responsibilities Journal,* 1989, *2:* 155–162; R. Folger, "Managerial Responsibilities and Procedural Justice," *Employee Responsibilities and Rights Journal,* 1989, *2:* 79–90.

45. Developed from R. King, Jr., "Fair—To Whom?" *Forbes,* November 28, 1988, 116–124.

46. F. Luthans, R. M. Hodgetts, and K. R. Thompson, *Social Issues in Business,* 6th ed. (New York: Macmillan, 1990); J. W. Kuhn and D. W. Shriver, Jr., *Beyond Success: Corporations and Their Critics in the 1990s* (New York: Oxford University Press, 1991).

47. P. F. Drucker, "The New Meaning of Corporate Social Responsibility," *California Management Review,* Winter 1984, 62.

48. A. B. Carroll, *Business & Society: Ethics and Stakeholder Management* (Cincinnati, Ohio: South-Western, 1989).

49. J. R. Aram, "The Paradox of Interdependent Relations in the Field of Social Issues in Management," *Academy of Management Review,* 1989, *14:* 266–283.

50. K. L. Kraft and J. Hage, "Strategy, Social Responsibility and Implementation," *Journal of Business Ethics,* 1990, *9:* 11–19; J. B. McGuire, A. Sundgren, and T. Schneeweis, "Corporate Social Responsibility and Firm Financial Performance," *Academy of Management Journal,* 1988, *31:* 854–872.

51. D. A. Garvin, "Can Industry Self-Regulation Work?" *California Management Review,* Summer 1983, 37–52.

52. Developed from R. Gibson, "McDonald's Will Put Nutritional Data for Menu on Wall Posters, Tray Liners," *Wall Street Journal,* June 11, 1990, B4; J. Castro, "One Big Mac, Hold the Box," *Time,* June 25, 1990, 44.

53. E. M. Epstein, "Business Ethics, Corporate Good Citizenship and the Corporate Social Policy Process: A View from the United States," *Journal of Business Ethics,* 1989, *8:* 583–595.

54. Developed from S. P. Sethi, "A Conceptual Framework for Environmental Analysis of Social Issues and Evaluation of Business Response Patterns," *Academy of Management Review,* 1979, *8:* 63–74. Used with permission.

55. Body shop examples are from S. Greengard, "Face Values," *US Air Magazine,* November 1990, 89–97.

56. O. Beaty and O. Harari, "Divestment and Disinvestment from South Africa: A Reappraisal," *California Management Review,* Summer 1987, 31–50.

57. *Corporate Ethics: A Prime Business Asset,* 65–76.

58. R. A. Buchholz, *Business Environment and Public Policy,* 3rd ed. (Englewood Cliffs, N.J.: Prentice-Hall, 1989), 471.

59. E. Bowen, "Looking to Its Roots," *Time,* May 27, 1987, 26.

Skill-Building Exercise. Scenario 1: From *The Harris Survey,* published by James R. Harris, Department of Marketing and Transportation, 108 Tichemar Hall, Auburn University, Auburn, Ala. 36849-5246; Scenario 2: B. Z. Posner and W. H. Schmidt, "Ethics in American Companies: A Managerial Perspective," *Journal of Business Ethics,* 1987, *6:* 383–391; and Scenario 3: D. J. Fritzsche and H. Becker, "Linking Management Behavior to Ethical Philosophy: An Imperical Investigation," *Academy of Management Journal,* 1984, *27:* 1, 172–173. Used with permission.

Manager's Memo. Adapted from L. K. Trevino, *The Influences of Vicarious Learning and Individual Differences on Ethical Decision Making in the Organizations: An Experiment,* doctoral dissertation (Texas A&M University, 1987), 158.

In the News. Ron Winslow, "Cost Control May Harm Dialysis Patients," *Wall Street Journal,* February 20, 1991, B1, B5.

Management Case. Adapted from "Rex Jordan case." Copyright © 1981 by Brigham Young University. Prepared by Professor Clinton L. Oaks as a basis for class discussion.

Chapter 6

1. Adapted from R. Sacasas and A. Cava, "Law Ethics and Management: Toward an Effective Audit," *Business Forum,* February 1990, 18–21.

2. This case is based on the facts and legal arguments presented in Crinkley v. Holiday Inns, 844 F.2d 156 (4th Cir. 1988).

3. K. R. MacCrimman and R. N. Taylor, "Decision Making and Problem Solving," in M. D. Dunnette (ed.), *Handbook of Industrial and Organizational Psychology* (Chicago: Rand McNally, 1976), 1397–1453. *See also* D. A. Cowan, "Developing a Classification Structure of Organizational Problems: An Empirical Investigation," *Academy of Management Journal,* 1990, *33:* 366–390.

4. J. Fierman, "Why Women Still Don't Hit the Top," *Fortune,* July 30, 1990, 40–62; J. Ciabattori, "Managing Nine Critical Career Turning Points: Results of a National Survey," *Working Woman,* October 1987, 87–94*ff.*

5. J. B. Levine, "Keeping New Ideas Kicking Around," *Business Week Innovation,* 1989, 128.

6. R. J. Hogarth, *Judgment and Choice: The Psychology of Decision* (New York: Wiley, 1987); J. G. March, "Ambiguity and Accounting: The Elusive Link between Information and Decision Making," *Accounting, Organizations and Society,* 1987, *12:* 153–168.

7. Developed from R. Henkoff, "Cost Cutting: How to Do It Right," *Fortune,* June 9, 1990, 40–49.

8. O. Port, "Back to Basics," *Business Week,* special issue on innovation, 1989, 16.

9. M. Mallory, "Profits on Everything but the Kitchen Sink," *Business Week,* special issue on innovation, 1989, 122.

10. O. Port, "Back to Basics," 17.

11. R. Mitchell, "Masters of Innovation," *Business Week,* April 10, 1989, 58–64. *See also* D. L. Sexton and N. Bowman-Upton, *Entrepreneurship: Creativity and Growth* (New York: Macmillan, 1991).

12. P. M. Senge, "The Leader's New Work: Building Learning Organizations," *Sloan Management Review,* Fall 1990, 20. *See also* L. G. Bolman and T. E. Deal, *Reframing Organizations: Artistry, Choice, and Leadership* (San Francisco: Jossey-Bass, 1991).

13. M. W. McCall, Jr., R. E. Kaplan, and M. L. Gerlach, *Caught in the Act: Decision Makers at Work,* Technical Report No. 20, Center for Creative Leadership, Greensboro, N.C., August 1982. *See also* P. Hawken, "Problems, Problems," *Inc.,* September 1987, 24–25; M. Murray, *Decisions: A Comparative Critique* (Marshfield, Mass.: Pitman, 1985).

14. Adapted from E. Larson, "Strange Fruits," *Inc.,* November 1989, 81–90.

15. Larson, "Strange Fruits," 90.

16. R. N. Taylor, *Behavioral Decision Making* (Glenview, Ill.: Scott, Foresman, 1984).

17. D. Bell, *Risk Management* (New York: Cambridge University Press, 1988); A. Fiegenbaum and H. Thomas, "Attitudes toward Risk and the Risk-Return Paradox: Prospect Theory Explanations," *Academy of Management Journal,* 1988, *31:* 85–106.

18. J. Saddler, "Small Concerns Face Big Impact from Bill," *Wall Street Journal,* April 4, 1990, A15.

19. M. W. McCall, Jr., and R. E. Kaplan, *Whatever It Takes: The Realities of Managerial Decision Making,* 2nd ed. (Englewood Cliffs, N.J.: Prentice-Hall, 1990).

20. M. H. Bazerman, *Judgment in Managerial Decision Making,* 2nd ed. (New York: Wiley, 1990).

21. K. E. Boulding, "Irreducible Uncertainties," *Society,* November-December 1982, 17.

22. K. R. MacCrimmon and D. A. Wehrung, *Taking Risks: The Management of Uncertainty* (New York: Free Press, 1988). *See also* C. Handy, *The Age of Unreason* (Boston: Harvard Business School Press, 1991).

23. M. D. Richards, *Setting Strategic Goals and Objectives* (St. Paul, Minn.: West, 1986).

24. A. Kupfer, "An Outsider Fires Up a Railroad," *Fortune,* December 18, 1989, 133–146.

25. E. A. Locke and G. P. Latham, *A Theory of Goal Setting and Task Performance* (Englewood Cliffs, N.J.: Prentice-Hall, 1990).

26. Developed from *The World Expects Excellence from Merck* (Rahway, N.J.: College Relations, Merck & Co., 1987); *Merck & Co., Inc., 1989 Annual Report*.

27. S. Smith, "America's Most Admired Corporations," *Fortune*, January 29, 1990, 58–63*ff*; A. L. Sprout, "America's Most Admired Corporations," *Fortune*, February 11, 1991, 52–82.

28. R. Stewart, *Choices for the Manager* (Englewood Cliffs, N.J.: Prentice-Hall, 1982).

29. I. I. Mitroff, *Stakeholders of the Organizational Mind* (San Francisco: Jossey-Bass, 1983); D. Miller, *The Icarus Paradox: How Exceptional Companies Bring about Their Downfall* (New York: Harper, 1990).

30. J. C. Worthy, *William C. Norris: Portrait of a Maverick* (Cambridge, Mass.: Ballinger, 1987); W. C. Norris, *New Frontiers for Business Leadership* (Minneapolis, Minn.: Dorm Books, 1983).

31. L. Driscoll, "Risks Are One Thing, Losses Are Another," *Business Week*, November 26, 1990, 58.

32. P. C. Nutt, *Making Tough Decisions: Tactics for Improving Managerial Decision Making* (San Francisco: Jossey-Bass, 1989).

33. H. J. Church, V. M. Smith, and B. H. Schell, "Managerial Problem Solving: A Review of the Literature in Terms of Model Comprehensiveness," *Organizational Behavior Teaching Review*, 1988–1989, *13*(2): 90–106; H. J. Brightman, *Problem Solving: A Logical and Creative Approach* (Atlanta: Business Publishing Division, Georgia State University, 1980), 161–192.

34. S. Kiesler and L. Sproull, "Managerial Response to Changing Environments: Perspectives on Problem Sensing from Social Cognition," *Administrative Science Quarterly*, 1982, *27*: 548–570; M. G. Bowen, "The Escalation Phenomenon Reconsidered: Decision Dilemmas or Decision Errors?" *Academy of Management Review*, 1987, *12*: 52–66.

35. M. Ray and R. Myers, *Creativity in Business* (Garden City, N.Y.: Doubleday, 1986), 94.

36. R. M. Hogarth and M. W. Reder (eds.), *Rational Choice: The Contrasts between Economics and Psychology* (Chicago: University of Chicago Press, 1987).

37. E. F. Harrison, *The Managerial Decision-Making Process*, 3rd ed. (Boston: Houghton Mifflin, 1987).

38. J. G. March and H. A. Simon, *Organizations* (New York: Wiley, 1958).

39. K. E. Goodpaster and T. R. Piper (eds.), *Managerial Decision Making and Ethical Values* (Boston: Harvard Business School Press, 1990).

40. Developed from T. F. O'Boyle, "GE Refrigerator Woes Illustrate the Hazards in Changing a Product," *Wall Street Journal*, May 7, 1990, A1, A6.

41. B. M. Bass, *Organizational Decision Making* (Homewood, Ill.: Irwin, 1983).

42. W. A. Agor, "How Top Executives Use Their Intuition to Make Important Decisions," *Business Horizons*, January–February 1986, 49–53; Suresh Srivastva and Associates, *The Executive Mind: New Insights on Managerial Thought and Action* (San Francisco: Jossey-Bass, 1983).

43. H. A. Simon, *Reason in Human Affairs* (Stanford, Calif.: Stanford University Press, 1983); H. A. Simon, "Making Management Decisions: The Role of Intuition and Emotion," *Academy of Management Executive*, 1987, *1*: 57–64; J. E. Martin, G. B. Kleindorfer, and W. R. Brashers, Jr., "The Theory of Bounded Rationality and the Problem of Legitimation," *Journal for the Theory of Social Behavior*, 1987, *17*: 63–82.

44. W. S. Silver, "The Status Quo Tendency in Decision Making," *Organizational Dynamics*, Spring 1990, 34–46.

45. J. M. Roach, "Simon Says: Decision Making Is a 'Satisficing' Experience," *Management Review*, January 1979, 8–9.

46. C. Saunders and J. W. Jones, "Temporal Sequences in Informational Acquisition for Decision Making: A Focus on Source and Medium," *Academy of Management Review*, 1990, *15*: 29–46.

47. Developed from R. M. Hogarth and S. Makridakis, "Forecasting and Planning: An Evaluation," *Management Science*, 1981, *27*: 117–120. *See also* M. A. Neale and M. H. Bazerman, *Cognition and Rationality in Negotiation* (New York: Free Press, 1991).

48. H. Mintzberg, *Mintzberg on Management: Inside Our Strange World of Organizations* (New York: Free Press, 1989).

49. J. Pfeffer, *Power in Organizations* (Boston: Pitman, 1981); D. Krackhardt, "Assessing the Political Landscape: Structure, Cognition, and Power in Organizations," *Administrative Science Quarterly*, 1990, *35*: 342–369.

50. L. E. Greiner and V. E. Schein, *Power and Organizational Development* (Reading, Mass.: Addison-Wesley, 1988); K. G. Provan, "Environment, Department Power and Strategic Decision Making in Organizations: A Proposed Integration," *Journal of Management*, 1989, *15*: 21–34.

51. D. Yates, Jr., *The Politics of Management* (San Francisco: Jossey-Bass, 1985); E. M. Eisenberg and M. G. Witten, "Reconsidering Openness in Organizational Communication," *Academy of Management Review*, 1987, *12*: 418–426.

52. Developed from N. C. Roberts and P. J. King, "The Stakeholders' Audit Goes Public," *Organizational Dynamics*, Winter 1989, 63–79.

Skill-Building Exercise. Reprinted from J. William Pfeiffer and Leonard D. Goodstein (eds.), *The 1982 Annual for Facilitators, Trainers, and Consultants* (San Diego, University Associates, 1982). Used with permission.

Manager's Memo. Developed from K. M. Eisenhardt, "Speed and Strategic Choice: How Managers Accelerate Decision Making," *California Management Review*, Spring 1990, 39–54; K. M. Eisenhardt and L. J. Bourgeois III, "Politics of Strategic Decision Making in High-Velocity Environments: Toward a Midrange Theory," *Academy of Management Journal*, 1988, *31*: 737–770.

In the News. Asra Q Nomahl, "NWA Weighs Sale of Routes, Merger Option," *Wall Street Journal*, February 11, 1991, A3.

Management Case. Developed from W. H. Starbuck and B. L. T. Hedberg, "Saving an Organization from a Stagnating Environment," in H. B. Thoreli (ed.), *Strategy + Structure = Performance* (Bloomington, Ind.: Indiana University Press, 1977), 249–258. *See also* P. C. Nystrom and W. H. Starbuck, "To Avoid Organizational Crises, Unlearn," *Organizational Dynamics*, Spring 1984, 53–65.

Chapter 7

1. Developed from J. J. Curran, "Why Investors Make the Wrong Choices," *Fortune/1987 Investor's Guide*, 1987, 63*ff*; J. J. Curran, "Why Investors Misjudge the Odds," *Fortune/1989 Investor's Guide*, 1989, 85–97; A. Tversky and D. Kahneman, "Rational Choice and the Framing of Decisions," in R. M. Hogarth and M. W. Reder (eds.), *Rational Choice: The Contrast between Economics and Psychology* (Chicago: University of Chicago Press, 1987), 67–94.

2. L. L. Lapin, *Statistics for Modern Business Decisions* (Chicago: Harcourt Brace Jovanovich, 1990).

3. E. F. Harrison, *Managerial Decision-Making Process*, 3rd ed. (Boston: Houghton Mifflin, 1987); G. F. Chacko, *The Systems Approach to Problem Solving* (New York: Praeger, 1989).

4. P. C. Nutt, *Making Tough Decisions: Tactics for Improving Managerial Decision Making* (San Francisco: Jossey-Bass, 1989).

5. D. N. Dickson (ed.), *Using Logical Techniques for Making Better Decisions* (New York: Wiley, 1983).

6. List of benefits developed from D. C. Funder, "Errors and Mistakes: Evaluating the Accuracy of Social Judgment," *Psychological Bulletin*, 1987, *101*: 75–90; V. L. Huber, "Managerial Applications of Judgmental Biases and Heuristics," *Organizational Behavior Teaching Review*, 1985–1986, *10*(4), 1–20; Curran, "Why Investors Misjudge the Odds."

7. E. Feigenbaum, P. McCorduck, and H. P. Nii, *The Rise of the Expert Company: How Visionary Companies Are Using Artificial Intelligence to Achieve Higher Profits and Productivity* (New York: Time Books, 1989).

8. C. Perrow, *Complex Organizations: A Critical Essay*, 3rd ed. (New York: Random House, 1986).

9. Editors of Time-Life Books, *Understanding Computers: Artificial Intelligence* (Alexandria, Va.: Time-Life Books, 1986), 120. *See also* S. H. Kim, *Designing Intelligence: A Framework for Smart Systems* (New York: Oxford University Press, 1991).

10. D. Pigford and G. Baur, *Expert Systems for Business and Applications* (Cincinnati, Ohio: South-Western, 1990).

11. E. Turban, *Decision Support and Expert Systems*, 2nd ed. (New York: Macmillan, 1990).

12. E. Turban and T. J. Mock, "Expert Systems: What They Mean to the Executive," *New Management*, Summer 1985, 45–52; D. Leonard-Barton, "The Case for Integrative Innovation: An Expert System at Digital," *Sloan Management Review*, Fall 1987, 7–19.

13. O. Port, "Smart Factories: America's Turn?" *Business Week*, May 8, 1989, 142–148.

14. Time-Life Books, *Understanding Computers*, 10.

15. B. Sheil, "Thinking about Artificial Intelligence," *Harvard Business Review*, July–August 1987, 94.

16. T. L. Powers, "Break-Even Analysis with Semifixed Costs," *Industrial Marketing Management*, 1987, *16*: 35–41.

17. S. R. Watson and D. M. Buede, *Decision Synthesis: The Principles and Practice of Decision Analysis* (New York: Cambridge University Press, 1987).

18. J. W. Ulvila and R. V. Brown, "Decision Analysis Comes of Age," *Harvard Business Review*, September–October 1982, 131.

19. U. B. Godin, "Solving Decision-Tree Analysis Using PS or Lotus," *Industrial Engineering*, April 1987, 20–27; J. F. Magee, "Decision Trees for Decision Making," in D. N. Dickson (ed.), *Using Logical Techniques for Making Better Decisions* (New York: Wiley, 1983), 54–72.

20. This section is based on L. W. Boone and A. T. Hollingsworth, "Creative Thinking in Business Organizations," *Review of Business*, Fall 1990, 3–12. *See also* J. Henry (ed.), *Creative Management* (Newbury Park, Calif.: Sage, 1991).

21. W. C. Miller, *The Creative Edge: Fostering Innovation Where You Work* (Reading, Mass.: Addison-Wesley, 1987), 90–91.

22. Miller, *The Creative Edge*, 7.

23. A. F. Osborn, *Applied Imagination*, 3rd rev. ed. (New York: Scribner's, 1963). *See also* J. R. Evans, *Creative Thinking in the Decision and Management Sciences* (Cincinnati, Ohio: South-Western, 1991).

24. E. deBono, *Masterthinkers Handbook* (New York: Mica Management Resources, 1987).

25. T. M. Amabile and S. S. Gryskiewicz, *Creativity in the R&D Laboratory*, Technical Report 30 (Greensboro, N.C.: Center for Creative Leadership, 1987); G. Nadler and S. Hibino, *Breakthrough Thinking* (Rocklin, Calif.: Prima, 1990).

26. A. B. Van Gundy, Jr., *Techniques for Structured Problem Solving* (New York: Van Nostrand Reinhold, 1981), 92–101.

27. Osborn, *Applied Imagination*, 124. *See also*

L. A. Witt and M. N. Beorkrem, "Climate for Creative Productivity as a Predictor of Research Usefulness and Organizational Effectiveness in an R&D Organization," *Creativity Research Journal*, 1989, *2:* 30–40.

28. Osborn, *Applied Imagination,* 229–290.

29. Osborn, *Applied Imagination,* 155–158.

30. R. Schank and P. Childers, *The Creative Attitude: Learning to Ask and Answer the Right Questions* (New York: Macmillan, 1988); L. G. Bolman and T. E. Deal, *Reframing Organizations: Artistry, Choice, and Leadership* (San Francisco: Jossey-Bass, 1991).

31. Osborn, *Applied Imagination,* 156.

32. T. M. Amabile and N. D. Gryskiewicz, "The Creative Environment Scales: Work Environment Inventory," *Creativity Research Journal,* 1989, *2:* 231–253.

33. C. Gregory, *The Management of Intelligence: Scientific Problem Solving and Creativity* (New York: McGraw-Hill, 1967).

34. Developed from B. W. Mattimore, "Mind Blasters," *Success,* June 1990, 46–47. MindLink was co-developed by Synectics, Inc. of Cambridge, Massachusetts.

35. R. A. Burgelman and L. R. Sayles, *Inside Corporate Innovation* (New York: Free Press, 1986); M. Sinetar, "Entrepreneurs, Chaos, and Creativity—Can Creative People Really Survive Large Company Structure?" *Sloan Management Review,* Winter 1985, 57–62.

Skill-Building Exercise. L. P. Martin, "Inventory of Barriers to Creative Thought and Innovative Action," reprinted from J. Williams Pfeiffer (ed.), *The 1990 Annual: Developing Human Resources* (San Diego, Calif.: University Associates, 1990), 138–141. Used with permission.

Manager's Memo. Developed from D. H. Lyman, "Being Creative," *Training & Development Journal,* April 1989, 45–49; R. W. Woodman and L. F. Schoenfeldt, "Individual Differences in Creativity," in J. A. Glover, R. R. Ronning, and C. R. Reynolds (eds.), *Handbook of Creativity* (New York: Plenum, 1989), 77–91.

In the News. G. Pascal Zachary, "Apple's Sculley Looks for a Breakthrough," *Wall Street Journal,* March 15, 1991, B1.

Management Case. V. L. Huber, "Managerial Applications of Judgmental Biases and Heuristics," *Organizational Behavior Teaching Review,* 1985–1986, *10*(4): 16–17. Used with permission.

Chapter 8

1. Developed from D. J. Morrow, "Iacocca Talks on What Ails Detroit," *Fortune,* February 12, 1990, 68–72; J. B. Treece and W. Sellner, "The Flashing Signal at Chrysler: Danger Dead Ahead," *Business Week,* June 18, 1990, 44–46; P. Ingrassia and B. A. Stertz, "With Chrysler Ailing, Lee Iacocca Concedes Mistakes in Managing," *Wall Street Journal,* September 17, 1990, A1, A8; J. B. White and J. Mitchell, "Detroit Rolls Out Old Play: Quotas," *Wall Street Journal,* January 14, 1991, B1.

2. A. Taylor, III, "Can American Cars Come Back?" *Fortune,* February 26, 1990, 62–65.

3. S. C. Certo and J. P. Peter, *Strategic Management: Concepts and Applications,* 2nd ed. (New York: Random House, 1991); D. M. Reid, "Operationalizing Strategic Planning," *Strategic Management Journal,* 1989, *10:* 553–567.

4. Ingrassia and Stertz, "With Chrysler Ailing, Lee Iacocca Concedes Mistakes in Managing," A1.

5. R. Henkoff, "How to Plan for 1995," *Fortune,* December 31, 1990, 70–77.

6. Treece and Zellner, "The Flashing Signal at Chrysler," 44–46; B. A. Stertz and P. Ingrassia, "Chrysler Plans to Lift Cost-Cutting Goal to $2.5

Billion, Maintain Stock Payout," *Wall Street Journal,* September 4, 1990, A3.

7. Stertz and Ingrassia, "Chrysler Plans to Lift Cost-Cutting Goal," A3; D. Woodruff and A. Bernstein, "Chrysler Headache No. 2: The UAW," *Business Week,* October 8, 1990, 40.

8. C. W. L. Hill and G. R. Jones, *Strategic Management: An Integrated Approach* (Boston: Houghton Mifflin, 1989).

9. Treece and Zellner, "The Flashing Signal at Chrysler," 44.

10. G. C. Sawyer, *Business Policy and Strategic Management* (New York: Harcourt Brace Jovanovich, 1990).

11. R. T. Lenz, "Managing the Evolution of the Strategic Planning Process," *Business Horizons,* January-February 1987, 34–39; D. H. Gray, "Uses and Misuses of Strategic Planning," *Harvard Business Review,* January-February 1986, 89–97.

12. Y. Allaire and M. E. Firsirotu, "Coping with Strategic Uncertainty," *Sloan Management Review,* Spring 1989, 7–16.

13. W. F. Dinsmore, "Strategic Dilemmas in Strategic Planning," in H. E. Glass (ed.), *Handbook of Business Strategy: 1989/1990 Yearbook* (Boston: Warren, Gorham & Lamont, 1989), 5-1–5-10.

14. H. H. Bean, "Strategic Discontinuities: When Being Good May Not Be Enough," *Business Horizons,* July-August 1990, 10–14; D. Ulrich and M. F. Wiersema, "Gaining Strategic and Organizational Capability in a Turbulent Environment," *Academy of Management Executive,* 1989, *3:* 115–122.

15. A. B. Fisher, "Is Long-Range Planning Worth It?" *Fortune,* April 23, 1990, 281–284.

16. G. S. Day and L. Fahey, "Putting Strategy into Shareholder Value Analysis," *Harvard Business Review,* March-April 1990, 156–162.

17. D. P. Slevin and J. G. Covin, "Juggling Entrepreneurial Style and Organizational Structure—How to Get Your Act Together," *Sloan Management Review,* Winter 1990, 43–53.

18. "Does G.E. Really Plan Better?" *MBA,* 1975, *9:* 42–45.

19. R. Henkoff, "How to Plan for 1995," *Fortune,* December 31, 1990, 71.

20. D. M. Reid, "Operationalizing Strategic Planning," *Strategic Management Journal,* 1989, *10:* 553–567; D. D. McConkey, "Planning for Uncertainty," *Business Horizons,* January-February 1987, 40–43.

21. D. D. McConkey, *How to Manage by Results* (New York: AMACOM, 1983), 116; J. R. Emshoff, *Managerial Breakthroughs: Action Techniques for Strategic Change* (New York: AMACOM, 1990), 75–105.

22. M. Hovde, "When Does Diversification Pay?" in H. E. Glass (ed.), *Handbook of Business Strategy: 1989/1990 Yearbook* (Boston: Warren, Gorham & Lamont, 1989), 8-1–8-10.

23. M. Leontiades, *Strategies for Diversification and Change* (Boston: Little, Brown, 1980). *See also* R. E. Hoskisson and M. A. Hitt, "Antecedents and Performance Outcomes of Diversification: A Review and Critique of Theoretical Perspectives," *Journal of Management,* 1990, *16:* 461–509.

24. W. J. Hampton and J. Rossant, "Now, for Chrysler's Next Trick," *Business Week,* March 23, 1987, 32–33.

25. *1989 General Motors Public Interest Report* (Detroit, Mich.: General Motors Corporation, 1990).

26. J. W. Fredrickson, *Perspectives on Strategic Management* (New York: Harper, 1990); F. R. David, *Strategic Management,* 3rd ed. (New York: Macmillan, 1991).

27. S. Waddock, "Core Strategy: End Result of Restructuring?" *Business Horizons,* May-June 1989, 49–55; P. C. Haspeslagh and D. B. Jemison, *Managing Acquisitions: Creating Value through Corporate Renewal* (New York: Free Press, 1990).

28. *Daimler-Benz 1989 Annual Report* (Federal Republic of Germany, 1990); A. Taylor, III, "Daimler-Benz Conglomerates," *Fortune,* October 27, 1986, 84–86.

29. W. H. Newman, J. P. Logan, and W. H. Hegarty, *Strategy: A Multi-Level, Integrative Approach* (Cincinnati, Ohio: South-Western, 1990); B. D. Henderson, "The Origin of Strategy," *Harvard Business Review,* November-December 1989, 139–143.

30. *Ford Motor Company 1989 Annual Report* (Dearborn, Mich.: Ford Motor Company, 1990), 7.

31. B. Gomes-Casseres, "Joint Ventures in the Face of Global Competition," *Sloan Management Review,* Spring 1989, 17–26.

32. G. S. Day, *Market Driven Strategy: Processes for Creating Value* (New York: Free Press, 1990); J. A. Pearce, II, and J. W. Harvey, "Concentrated Growth Strategies," *Academy of Management Executive,* 1990, *4:* 61–68.

33. *Ford Motor Company 1989 Annual Report,* 12–13.

34. R. Henkoff, "How to Plan for 1995," *Fortune,* December 31, 1990, 76.

35. *Daimler-Benz 1989 Annual Report,* Bonn, Germany, 4–7.

36. T. J. Wheelen and J. D. Hunger, *Strategic Management and Business Policy,* 3rd ed. (Reading, Mass.: Addison-Wesley, 1990).

37. *Honda Motor Company Ltd. 1989 Annual Report* (Japan: 1990), 12–13.

38. *General Motors Corporation 1989 Annual Report* (Detroit, Mich.: General Motors Corporation, 1990), 12. *See also* E. Koerner, "Technology Planning at General Motors," *Long Range Planning,* 1989, *22*(2): 9–19.

39. G. S. Day and L. Fahey, "Putting Strategy into Shareholders Value Analysis," *Harvard Business Review,* March-April 1990, 156–162; J. A. Pearce and R. B. Robinson, *Strategic Management: Formulation, Implementation, and Control,* 4th ed. (Homewood, Ill.: Irwin, 1991).

40. Developed from *Ford Motor Company 1989 Annual Report,* 2.

41. G. Benveniste, *Mastering the Politics of Planning* (San Francisco: Jossey-Bass, 1989); E. W. Johnson, "An Insider's Call for Outside Direction," *Harvard Business Review,* March-April 1990, 46–48, 52–55.

42. A. E. Pearson, "Six Basics for General Managers," *Harvard Business Review,* July-August 1989, 94–101. *See also* E. J. Zajac and M. H. Bazerman, "Blind Spots in Industry and Competition Analysis: Implications of Interfirm (Mis)perceptions for Strategic Decisions," *Academy of Management Review,* 1991, *16:* 37–56.

43. M. E. Porter, *Competitive Strategy: Techniques for Analyzing Industries and Competitors* (New York: Free Press, 1980); M. E. Porter, *Competitive Advantage: Creating and Sustaining Superior Performance* (New York: Free Press, 1985). *See also* J. F. Porac and H. Thomas, "Taxonomic Mental Models in Competitor Definition," *Academy of Management Review,* 1990, *15:* 224–240.

44. J. B. Treece, "Shaking Up Detroit," *Business Week,* August 14, 1989, 74–80. *See also* R. E. Cole, "U.S. Quality Improvement in the Auto Industry: Close but No Cigar," *California Management Review,* Summer 1990, 71–85.

45. J. B. White, "GM Slashes Dividend by 47%, Launches a Sweeping Program to Reduce Costs," *Wall Street Journal,* February 6, 1991, A3.

46. L. Kraar, "Japan's Gung-Ho U.S. Car Plants," *Fortune,* June 30, 1989, 97–108; A. Taylor, III, "Japan's New U.S. Car Strategy," *Fortune,* September 10, 1990, 65–80.

47. M. Keller, "The Japanese Can Take 50% of the U.S. Car Market," *Fortune,* March 26, 1990, 36–38.

48. Porter, *Competitive Strategy,* 24–27. *See also* V. H. Fried and B. M. Oviatt, "Michael Porter's Missing Chapter: The Risk of Antitrust Violations," *Academy of Management Executive,* 1989, *3:* 49–56.

49. Porter, *Competitive Strategy,* 27–28.

50. Developed from D. C. Smith, "Whatever Happened to Teamwork?" *Ward's Auto World,* July 1989, 35–41. *See also* R. G. Newman, "The Second Wave Arrive: Japanese Strategy in the U.S. Auto Parts Market," *Business Horizons,* July-August 1990, 24–30.

51. Developed from A. Taylor, III, "The New Drive to Revive GM," *Fortune,* April 9, 1990, 52–61; P. Ingrassia and J. B. White, "GM's New Chairman: Still an Innovator?" *Wall Street Journal,* April 4, 1990, B1, B5.

52. J. B. Treece, "War, Recession, Gas Hikes . . . GM's Turnaround Will Have to Wait," *Business Week,* February 4, 1991, 94–96.

53. R. Reed and R. J. DeFillippi, "Causal Ambiguity, Barriers to Imitation, and Sustainable Competitive Advantage," *Academy of Management Review,* 1990, *15:* 88–102; W. H. Davidson, "The Role of Global Scanning in Business Planning," *Organizational Dynamics,* Winter 1991, 4–16.

54. G. D. Smith, D. R. Arnold, and B. G. Bizzel, *Business Strategy and Policy,* 3rd ed. (Boston: Houghton Mifflin, 1991), 170–190.

55. Developed from *General Motors Corporation 1990 Annual Report*; P. Ingrassia and J. B. White, "GM's New Boss Runs into Many Problems—But Little Opposition," *Wall Street Journal,* February 8, 1991, A1, A4; P. Fuhrman, "A Tale of Two Strategies," *Forbes,* August 6, 1990, 42.

56. K. Ohmae, *Triad Power: The Coming Shape of Global Competition* (New York: Free Press, 1985).

57. S. Onkvisit and J. J. Shaw, "Competition and Product Management: Can the Product Life Cycle Help?" *Business Horizons,* July-August 1986, 51–62; C. R. Anderson and C. P. Zeithaml, "Stage of the Product Life Cycle, Business Strategy, and Business Performance," *Academy of Management Journal,* 1984, *27:* 5–24.

58. P. Ingrassia and K. Graven, "Japan's Auto Industry May Soon Consolidate as Competition Grows," *Wall Street Journal,* April 24, 1990, A1, A12.

59. Porter, *Competitive Strategy,* 34–46.

60. "Niche Markets—An Opportunity for Canadian Business," *Federal Industries Annual Report—1986* (Winnipeg, Manitoba): Federal Industries Ltd., 1987), 42–49. *See also* D. A. Aaker, "Managing Assets and Skills: The Key to Sustainable Competitive Advantage," *California Management Review,* Winter 1989, 91–106.

61. J. B. Treece, "How Ford and Mazda Shared the Driver's Seat," *Business Week,* March 26, 1990, 94–95.

62. S. Solo, "Japan's New Cars," *Fortune,* December 4, 1989, 82–86; C. Rapport, "Mazda's Bold New Global Strategy," *Fortune,* December 17, 1990, 111–113.

63. P. Wright, "A Refinement of Porter's Strategies," *Strategic Management Journal,* 1987, *8:* 93–101; T. G. M. van Asseldonk, "Porter Quantified," in H. E. Glass (ed.), *Handbook of Business Strategy 1989/1990* (Boston: Warren, Gorham & Lamont, 1989), 12-1–12-14.

64. B. Tesfay, "Policy and Strategy for Corporate Social Responsibility," in H. E. Glass (ed.), *Handbook of Business Strategy* (Boston: Warren, Gorham & Lamont, 1989), 7-1–7-5.

65. Adapted from J. F. Akers, "Ethics and Competitiveness—Putting First Things First," *Sloan Management Review,* Winter 1989, 69–71.

Skill-Building Exercise. H. H. Johnson, "Marzilli's Fine Italian Foods: An Introduction to Strategic Thinking," in J. W. Pfeiffer (ed.), *The 1989 Annual: Developing Human Resources* (San Diego, Calif.: University Associates, 1989). Used with permission.

Manager's Memo. R. T. Peterson, "Small Business Adoption of the Marketing Concept versus Other Business Strategies," *Journal of Small Business Management,* January 1989, 38–46.

In the News. Frank Edward Allen, "Governors Group to Urge 200 Firms to Cut Waste by Using Less Packaging," *Wall Street Journal,* March 15, 1991, B2.

Management Case. Adapted from "Sharpco: Singing the Small Business Blues," by A. A. Sharplin (2340 Lake Street, Lake Charles, LA 70601), 1989. Used with permission.

Chapter 9

1. Developed from S. Schnaars, *Megamistakes: Forecasting and the Myth of Rapid Technological Change* (New York: Free Press, 1988); R. Bailey, "Sweet Technology, Sour Marketing," *Forbes,* May 1, 1989, 140; P. Elmer-DeWitt, "Back to the Velvet-Roped Lines," *Times,* January 9, 1989, 49.

2. R. Bailey, "Sweet Technology, Sour Marketing," 140.

3. J. L. Webster, W. E. Reif, and J. S. Bracker, "The Manager's Guide to Strategic Planning Tools and Techniques," *Planning Review,* November/December 1989, 4–12, 47, 48.

4. F. W. Barnett, "Four Steps to Forecast Total Market Demand," *Harvard Business Review,* July-August 1989, 28–30, 34, 36, 38.

5. T. J. Gordon, "Futures Research: Did It Meet Its Promise? Can It Meet Its Promise?" *Technological Forecasting and Social Change,* 1989, *36:* 21–26.

6. J. F. Coates, "Forecasting and Planning Today Plus or Minus Twenty Years," *Technological Forecasting and Social Change,* 1989, *36:* 15–20.

7. S Makridakis, "Management in the 21st Century," *Long Range Planning,* 1989, 22(2): 37–53.

8. W. Wipple, III, "Evaluating Alternative Strategies Using Scenarios," *Long Range Planning,* 1989, 22(3): 82–86; H. Boshoff, "Testing Plans against Alternative Futures," *Long Range Planning,* 1989 (5), 69–75.

9. R. Henkoff, "How to Plan for 1995," *Fortune,* December 31, 1990, 70–78; T. Mack, "Time, Patience, and Money," *Forbes,* August 21, 1989, 60–61.

10. C. L. Jain, "Delphi—Forecast with Experts' Opinions," *Journal of Business Forecasting,* Winter 1985–1986, 22–23.

11. A. L. Delbecq, A. H. Van de Ven, and D. H. Gustafson, *Group Techniques for Program Planning: A Guide to Nominal Group and Delphi Processes* (Glenview, Ill.: Scott, Foresman, 1976).

12. D. Roman, "Technological Forecasting in the Decision Process," *Academy of Management Journal,* 1970, *13:* 127–138.

13. J. F. Preble and P. A. Rau, "Combining Delphi and Multiple Scenario Analysis for Planning Purposes," *Journal of Business Strategies,* Fall 1986, 12–21.

14. C. Orpen, "The Relative Accuracy of Individual, Group, and Delphi Process Strategic Forecasts," in W. D. Guth (ed.), *Handbook of Business Strategy: 1986–1987 Yearbook* (Boston: Warren, Gorham & Lamont, 1986), 19-1–19-9; R. L. Bunning, "The Delphi Technique: A Projection Tool for Serious Inquiry," in J. E. Jones and J. W. Pfeiffer (eds.), *The 1979 Annual Handbook for Group Facilitator* (La Jolla, Calif.: University Associates, 1979), 174–181.

15. T. H. Naylor (ed.), *Simulation Models in Corporate Planning* (New York: Praeger, 1979); P. A. Luker, "Computer Simulation: A Developer's Perspective," *Academic Computing,* Spring 1987, 18–21, 67.

16. K. K. Wieger, "A Computer for the Defense," *Forbes,* February 19, 1990, 158–159.

17. T. H. Naylor and H. Schauland, "Experience with Corporate Simulation Models—A Survey," in R. Hussey (ed.), *The Truth about Corporate Planning: International Research into the Practices of Planning* (Elmsford, N.Y.: Pergamon, 1983), 549–563.

18. A. M. Law, "Introduction to Simulation: A Powerful Tool for Analyzing Complex Manufacturing Systems," *Industrial Engineering,* May 1986, 46–63; S. W. Haider and J. Banks, "Simulation Software Products for Analyzing Manufacturing Systems," *Industrial Engineering,* July 1986, 98–103.

19. W. G. Wild, Jr., and O. Port, "The Video 'Game' Is Saving Manufacturers Millions," *Business Week,* August 17, 1987, 82–84; M. I. Reiman and A. Weiss, "Sensitivity Analysis for Simulations via Likelihood Ratios," *Operations Research,* 1989, *37:* 830–844.

20. Developed from C. U. Lambert, J. M. Lambert, and T. P. Cullen, *Cornell H.R.A. Quarterly,* August 1989, 15–20.

21. "The Forecasters Flunk," *Time,* August 27, 1984, 42–44.

22. R. Bailey, "Them That Can, Do, Them That Can't, Forecast," *Forbes,* December 26, 1988, 94, 98, 100; D. Wechsler Linden, "Dreary Days in the Dismal Science," *Forbes,* January 21, 1991, 68–71.

23. R. O. Mason, "A Dialectical Approach to Strategic Planning," *Management Science,* 1969, *15:* B402–B414.

24. C. Schwenk and H. Thomas, "Formulating the Mess: The Role of Decision Aids in Problem Formulation," *Omega,* 1983, *11:* 239–252.

25. I. I. Mitroff, *Break-Away Thinking* (New York: Wiley, 1988).

26. M. N. Chanin and H. J. Shapiro, "Dialectical Inquiry in Strategic Planning: Extending the Boundaries," *Academy of Management Review,* 1985, *10:* 663–675.

27. I. I. Mitroff, *Stakeholders of the Organizational Mind* (San Francisco: Jossey-Bass, 1983).

28. Adapted from R. O. Mason, I. I. Mitroff, and V. P. Barabba, "Creating the Manager's Plan Book: A New Route to Effective Planning," in A. J. Rowe, R. O. Mason, and K. E. Dickel (eds.), *Strategic Management and Business Policy: A Methodological Approach* (Reading, Mass.: Addison-Wesley, 1982), 82–86. Adapted and used with permission.

29. C. Schwenk, "A Meta-Analysis on the Comparative Effectiveness of Devil's Advocacy and Dialectical Inquiry," *Strategic Management Journal,* 1989, *10:* 303–306; P. C. Nutt, *Making Tough Decisions: Tactics for Improving Managerial Decision Making* (San Francisco: Jossey-Bass, 1989).

30. C. Schwenk, *The Essence of Strategic Decision Making* (Lexington, Mass.: Lexington Books, 1988).

31. C. R. Schwenk, "Devil's Advocacy and the Board: A Modest Proposal," *Business Horizons,* July-August 1989, 22–27.

32. G. S. Odiorne, *MBO II: A System for Managerial Leadership for the 80s* (Belmont, Calif.: Fearon Pitman, 1979).

33. P. Mali, *MBO Updated* (New York: Wiley, 1986).

34. W. C. Giegold, *Objective Setting and the MBO Process,* vol. II (New York: McGraw-Hill, 1978).

35. M. D. Richards, *Setting Strategic Goals and Objectives,* 2nd ed. (St. Paul, Minn.: West Publishing, 1986).

36. Developed from T. J. Rodgers, "No Excuses Management," *Harvard Business Review,* July-August 1990, 84–98; S. B. Kaufman, "The Goal System That Drives Cypress." Reprinted with permission, *Business Month* magazine, July 1987. Copyright; C.W. 1987 by Business Month Corporation, 38 Commercial Wharf, Boston, MA 02110.

37. E. A. Locke and G. P. Latham, *A Theory of Goal Setting and Task Performance* (Englewood Cliffs, N.J.: Prentice-Hall, 1990).

38. H. Levinson, "Management by Whose Objectives?" *Harvard Business Review,* July-August 1970, 125–135.

39. H. Weihrich, *Management Excellence: Productivity through MBO* (New York: McGraw-Hill, 1985).

40. R. D. Pritchard, P. L. Roth, S. D. Jones, P. J. Galgay, and M. D. Watson, "Designing a Goal-Setting System to Enhance Performance: A Practical Guide," *Organizational Dynamics*, Summer 1988, 69–78.

41. P. M. Wright, "Goals as Mediators of the Incentive-Performance Relationship: A Review and NPI Theory Analysis," *Human Resource Management Review*, 1991, 1, 1–22; T. R. Mitchell and W. S. Silver, "Individual and Group Goals When Workers Are Interdependent: Effects on Task Strategies and Performance," *Journal of Applied Psychology*, 1990, 75: 185–193.

42. G. L. Morrisey, P. J. Below, and B. L. Acomb, *The Executive Guide to Operational Planning* (San Francisco: Jossey-Bass, 1988).

43. L. W. Fry and D. Hellriegel, "The Role and Expectancy Participation Model: An Empirical Assessment and Extension," *Journal of Occupational Behavior*, 1987, 8: 295–309.

44. Adapted from J. P. Muczyk and B. C. Reimann, "MBO as a Complement to Effective Leadership," *Academy of Management Executive*, 1989, 3: 131–138.

45. Y. Y. Kim and K. I. Miller, "The Effects of Attributions and Feedback Goals on the Generation of Supervisory Feedback Message Strategies," *Management Communication Quarterly*, 1990, 4: 6–29.

46. W. C. Giegold, *Performance Appraisal and the MBO Process*, vol. III (New York: McGraw-Hill, 1978).

47. J. S. Kane and K. A. Freeman, "MBO and Performance Appraisal: A Mixture That's Not a Solution," *Personnel*, December 1986, 26–36.

48. M. C. McConkie, "A Clarification of the Goal Setting and Appraisal Processes in MBO," *Academy of Management Review*, 1979, 4: 29–40.

49. Developed from A. W. Schrader and G. T. Seward, "MBO Makes Dollar Sense," *Personnel Journal*, July 1989, 32–37.

50. J. N. Kondrasuk, "Studies in MBO Effectiveness," *Academy of Management Review*, 1981, 6: 419–430; J. P. Muczyk and B. C. Reimann, "MBO as a Complement to Effective Leadership," *Academy of Management Executive*, 1989, 3: 131–138.

51. J. P. Muczyk, "Dynamics and Hazards of MBO Application," *Personnel Administrator*, May 1979, 51–62.

52. W. A. Randolph and B. Z. Posner, *Effective Project Planning and Management: Getting the Job Done* (Englewood Cliffs, N.J.: Prentice-Hall, 1988); H. Kerzner, *Project Management: A Systems Approach to Planning, Scheduling, and Controlling* (New York: Van Nostrand Reinhold, 1989).

53. A. B. Badiru, *Project Management Tools for Engineering and Management Professionals* (Norcross, Ga.: Institute of Industrial Engineers, 1991); J. R. Meredith and S. J. Mantel, Jr., *Project Management: A Managerial Approach*, 3rd ed. (New York: Wiley, 1989).

54. R. W. Miller, "How to Plan and Control with PERT," in D. N. Dickson (ed.), *Using Logical Techniques for Making Better Decisions* (New York: Wiley, 1983), 33–53.

55. W. D. Randolph and B. Z. Posner, "What Every Manager Needs to Know about Project Management," *Sloan Management Review*, Summer 1988, 65–73; J. D. Wiest and F. K. Levy, *A Management Guide to PERT/CPM*, 2nd ed. (Englewood Cliffs, N.J.: Prentice-Hall, 1977).

56. "Code of Ethics for the Project Management Profession," *PM Network*, February 1991, 32.

57. Developed from G. Slutsker, "Good-bye Cable TV, Hello Fiber Optics," *Forbes*, September 19, 1988, 174–179.

Skill-Building Exercise. Adapted from H. Sims and E. Slusher, "Attributes of Job Objectives: A Multivariate Approach, in W. R. Allen and P. Weissenberg (eds.), *Proceedings of the Eastern Academy of Management*, 1977, 25–30. Used with permission.

Manager's Memo. W. B. Johnston and A. E. Packer, *Workforce 2000: Work and Workers for the Twenty-first Century* (Indianapolis, Ind.: Hudson Institute, 1987); R. S. Fosler, W. Alonso, J. A. Meyer, and R. Kern, *Demographic Change and the American Future* (Pittsburgh, Pa.: University of Pittsburgh Press, 1990).

In the News. David Stipp, "Life-Cycle Analysis Measures Greenness, But Results May Not Be Black and White," *Wall Street Journal*, March 28, 1991, B1–B5.

Management Case. Adapted from D. Stoffman, "Locking Up Profits," *Canadian Business*, February 1987, 103–109. Case within this article was prepared by Stephen Tax under the direction of Walter Good, professor of management studies at the Unversity of Manitoba, Winnipeg, Canada. Used with permission.

Chapter 10

1. Adapted from R. K. Berlin, "Bumpy Flight at McDonnell Douglas," *Fortune*, August 28, 1989, 79–80.

2. W. H. Starbuck and P. C. Nystrom, "Why the World Needs Organizational Design," *Journal of General Management*, 1981, 6: 3–17; G. P. Huber and R. R. McDaniel, "The Decision-Making Paradigm of Organizational Design," *Management Science*, 1986, 32: 572–589.

3. K. White, *Understanding the Company Organization Chart* (New York: American Management Association, 1963).

4. R. B. Duncan, "What Is the Right Organization Structure?" *Organizational Dynamics*, Winter 1979, 59–80.

5. J. Child, *Organization: A Guide to Problems and Practice*, 2nd ed. (London: Harper & Row, 1984); D. P. Slevin and J. G. Covin, "Juggling Entrepreneurial Style and Organization Structure—How to Get Your Act Together," *Sloan Management Review*, 1990, 31(2): 43–54.

6. J. D. Daniels and L. H. Radebaugh, *International Business: Environments and Operations*, 5th ed. (Reading, Mass.: Addison-Wesley, 1989); R. N. Osborn and C. C. Baughn, "Forms of Interorganizational Governance for Multinational Alliances," *Academy of Management Journal*, 1990, 33: 503–519.

7. H. Mintzberg, *Structure in Fives: Designing Effective Organizations* (Englewood Cliffs, N.J.: Prentice-Hall, 1983).

8. *Harris Corporation Annual Report*, 1990.

9. S. Davis and P. Lawrence, *Matrix* (Reading, Mass.: Addison-Wesley, 1977); D. Nadler and M. Tushman, *Organization Design* (Glenview, Ill.: Scott, Foresman, 1988); L. R. Burns, "Matrix Management in Hospitals: Testing Theories of Matrix Structure and Development," *Administrative Science Quarterly*, 1989, 34: 349–368.

10. Adapted from W. F. Joyce, "Matrix Organization: A Social Experiment," *Academy of Management Journal*, 1986, 29: 536–561.

11. G. P. Huber, "A Theory of the Effects of Advanced Information Technologies on Organizational Design, Intelligence, and Decision Making," *Academy of Management Review*, 1990, 4: 47–71.

12. P. D. Collins and F. Hull, "Technology and Span of Control Revisited," *Journal of Management Studies*, 1986, 23: 143–164; V. K. Kiam, "Growth Strategies at Remington," *The Journal of Business Strategy*, January-February 1989, 22–26.

13. P. M. Blau, "The Hierarchy of Authority in Organizations," *American Journal of Sociology*, 1967, 68: 453–467.

14. C. Barnard, *The Functions of the Executive* (Cambridge, Mass.: President and Fellows of Harvard University, 1938).

15. C. R. Leana, "Predictors and Consequences of Delegation," *Academy of Management Journal*, 1986, 29: 754–774.

16. L. A. Allen, *The Professional Manager's Guide* (Palo Alto, Calif.: Louis A. Allen, 1981).

17. L. P. Jennergren, "Decentralization in Organizations," in P. C. Nystrom and W. H. Starbuck (eds.), *Handbook of Organizational Design* (New York: Oxford University Press, 1981), 39–59.

18. G. P. Huber, C. C. Miller, and W. H. Glick, "Developing More Encompassing Theories about Organizations: The Centralization-Effectiveness Relationship as an Example," *Organization Science*, 1990, 1: 1–40.

19. J. Kerr and J. W. Slocum, Jr., "Managing Corporate Cultures through Reward Systems," *Academy of Management Executive*, 1987, 2: 99–108; T. E. Deal and A. A. Kennedy, *Corporate Cultures* (Reading, Mass.: Addison-Wesley, 1982); E. H. Schein, "Organizational Culture," *American Psychologist*, 1990, 45: 109–119; W. J. Duncan, "Organizational Culture: 'Getting a Fix' on an Elusive Concept," *Academy of Management Executive*, 1989, 3: 229–238.

20. "Corporate Culture," *Business Week*, October 27, 1980, 148–160; B. Dumaine, "Those High Flying PepsiCo Managers," *Fortune*, April 10, 1989, 78–86.

21. V. Govindarajan, "A Contingency Approach to Strategy Implementation at the Business Unit Level: Integrating Administrative Mechanisms with Strategy," *Academy of Management Journal*, 1988, 31: 828–853.

22. N. Tichy and R. Charan, "Speed, Simplicity, Self Confidence: An Interview with Jack Welch," *Harvard Business Review*, September-October 1989, 112–121.

23. D. Gerwin, "Relationships between Structure and Technology,"in P. C. Nystrom and W. H. Starbuck (eds.), *Handbook of Organization Design* (New York: Oxford University Press, 1981), 3–38.

Skill-Building Exercise. Adapted from J. F. Viega and J. N. Yanouzas, *The Dynamics of Organization Theory* (St. Paul, Minn.: West Publishing, 1979), 158–160.

In the News. Richard L. Hudson and Guy Collins, "Revamp at Olivetti Has Yet to Add Up: Computer Maker's Chief Says Turnaround Is at Hand," *Wall Street Journal*, March 12, 1991, A14.

Management Case. R. H. Waterman, Jr., *The Renewal Factor: How the Best Get and Keep the Competitive Edge* (New York: Bantam, 1987).

Chapter 11

1. Adapted from T. Richman, "Mrs. Fields' Secret Ingredient," *Inc.*, October 1987, 67–72; J. I. Cash, *Mrs. Fields Cookies* (Boston, Mass.: Publishing Division, Harvard Business School, 1989), case no. 9-189-056.

2. D. A. Nadler and M. Tushman, *Organization Design* (Glenview, Ill.: Scott, Foresman, 1988); R. L. Daft, *Organizational Theory*, 3rd ed. (St. Paul, Minn.: West Publishing, 1989).

3. A. D. Chandler, *Strategy and Structure* (Cambridge, Mass.: MIT Press, 1962).

4. G. P. Huber and R. R. McDaniel, "The Decision-Making Paradigm of Organizational Design," *Management Science*, 1986, 32: 572–589; G. P. Huber, "A Theory of the Effects of Advanced Information Technologies on Organizational Design: Intelligence and Decision Making," *Academy of Management Review*, 1990, 15: 47–61.

5. D. R. Wholey and J. Brittain, "Characterizing Environmental Variation," *Academy of Management Journal*, 1989, 32: 867–882; G. G. Dess and D. W. Beard, "Dimensions of Organizational Environ-

ments," *Administrative Science Quarterly,* 1984, *29:* 52–73; F. J. Milliken, "Three Types of Uncertainty about the Environment: State, Effect and Response Uncertainty," *Academy of Management Review,* 1987, *24:* 125–142.

6. E. Romanelli, "Environments and Strategies of Organization Start-Up: Effects on Early Survival," *Administrative Science Quarterly,* 1989, *34:* 369–387; R. Whittington, "Environmental Structure and Theories of Strategic Choice," *Journal of Management Studies,* 1988, *25:* 520–536.

7. Adapted from P. Gumbel, "Muscovites Queue Up at American Icon," *Wall Street Journal,* February 1, 1990, A12; K. Maney and D. Rinehart, "Here Comes the Bolshoi Mac," *USA Weekend,* January 26–28, 1990, 4–5; J. F. Love, *McDonald's: Behind the Arches* (New York: Bantam, 1986); P. Moser, "The McDonald's Mystique," *Fortune,* July 4, 1988, 112–116.

8. M. E. Porter, *The Competitive Advantage of Nations* (New York: Free Press, 1990); M. Yasai-Ardekani, "Effects of Environmental Scarcity and Munificence on the Relationships of Context to Organizational Structure," *Academy of Management Journal,* 1989, *32:* 131–156.

9. Adapted from J. Cook, "Entrepreneurial Power," *Forbes,* March 19, 1990, 83–90.

10. T. Burns and G. M. Stalker, *The Management of Innovation* (London: Tavistock, 1961), 119–122. *See also* A. Zanzi, "How Organic Is Your Organization?" *Journal of Management Studies,* 1987, *24:* 125–142; J. A. Courtright, G. T. Fairhurst, and L. E. Rogers, "Interaction Patterns in Organic and Mechanistic Systems," *Academy of Management Journal,* 1989, *32:* 773–802.

11. P. R. Lawrence and J. W. Lorsch, *Organization and Environment* (Homewood, Ill.: Irwin, 1967).

12. J. Child, "Information Technology, Organization, and Response to Strategic Challenges," *California Management Review,* 1988, *30*(1): 33–50.

13. J. D. Thompson, *Organizations in Action* (New York: McGraw-Hill, 1967), 51–67.

14. P. K. Mills, *Managing Service Industries* (Cambridge, Mass.: Ballinger, 1986); D. E. Bowen, C. Siehl, and B. Schneider, "A Framework for Analyzing Customer Service Orientations in Manufacturing," *Academy of Management Review,* 1989, *14:* 75–95; L. R. Offermann and M. K. Gowing, "Organizations of the Future," *American Psychologist,* 1990, *45:* 95–108.

15. B. Ives and R. O. Mason, "Can Information Technology Revitalize Your Customer Service?" *Academy of Management Executive,* 1990, *4:* 53–61; R. Larsson and D. E. Bowen, "Organization and Customer: Managing Design and Coordination Services," *Academy of Management Review,* 1989, *14:* 213–233; S. E. Jackson and R. S. Schuler, "Human Resource Planning: Challenges for Industrial/Organizational Psychologists," *American Psychologist,* 1990, *45:* 223–239.

16. Adapted from *Holiday Corporation Annual Report,* 1990.

17. C. Gresov, "Exploring Fit and Misfit with Multiple Contingencies," *Administrative Science Quarterly,* 1989, *34:* 431–453.

18. S. W. Gellerman, "In Organization, as in Architecture, Form Follows Function," *Organizational Dynamics,* Winter 1990, 57–68.

19. J. R. Galbraith, "Organization Design," in J. W. Lorsch (ed.), *Handbook of Organizational Design* (Englewood Cliffs, N.J.: Prentice-Hall, 1987), 343–357.

20. J. R. Galbraith, *Organization Design* (Reading, Mass.: Addison-Wesley, 1977).

21. R. E. Walton, *Up & Running: Integrating Information Technology and the Organization* (Boston: Harvard Business School, 1989), 33–49; "How Mrs. Fields Cookies Crunches Its Numbers," *Business Week,* February 5, 1990, 82A.

22. J. Carlzon, *Moments of Truth* (Cambridge, Mass.: Ballinger, 1987).

23. T. Finholt and L. S. Sproull, "Electronic Groups at Work," *Organization Science,* 1990, *1:* 41–64.

24. L. Fahey and V. K. Narayanan, *Macroenvironmental Analysis for Strategic Management* (St. Paul, Minn.: West Publishing, 1986).

25. J. P. Newport, Jr., "American Express: Service That Sells," *Fortune,* November 20, 1989, 80–94.

26. J. R. Kimberly, R. H. Miles, et al., *The Organizational Life Cycle* (San Francisco: Jossey-Bass, 1980); I. Adices, "Organizational Passages—Diagnosing and Treating Lifecycle Problems of Organizations," *Organizational Dynamics,* Summer 1979, 3–25.

27. Adapted from *The Franchise Program: I Can't Believe It's Yogurt* (Dallas, Tex.: I Can't Believe It's Yogurt, 1990); S. Friedlander, "Cold Cash," *Continental Profile,* October 1988, 27, 40–41; D. Fugard, "Yogurt's Sweet to Alumni," *The Daily Campus,* April 15, 1988, 1.

Skill-Building Exercise. Adapted from R. T. Keller, *Type of Management System* (Houston, Tex.: Department of Management, University of Houston, 1990).

In the News. Judith Valente, "Sour Notes: In Clash Between Art and Efficiency, Did Steinway Pianos Lose?" *Wall Street Journal,* March 27, 1991, A1–A7.

Management Case. Adapted from B. Soporito, "Woolworth to Rule the Malls," *Fortune,* June 5, 1989, 145–156; D. Henriques, "Cut to the Quick," *American Way,* October 1, 1989, 126–128; W. Lavin and A. T. Hollingsworth, "Woolworth Corporation: A Case of Creativity in Action," *Review of Business,* Fall 1990, 39–46.

Chapter 12

1. Adapted from "How Does Japan Inc. Pick Its American Workers?" *Business Week,* October 3, 1988, 84–88.

2. R. S. Schuler and V. L. Huber, *Personnel and Human Resource Management,* 4th ed. (St. Paul, Minn.: West Publishing, 1990), 42–66. *See also* C. D. Fisher, "Current & Recurrent Challenges in HRM," *Journal of Management,* 1989, *15:* 157–180.

3. B. Schneider and N. Schmitt, *Staffing Organizations,* 2nd ed. (Glenview, Ill.: Scott, Foresman, 1986); S. L. Rynes and A. E. Barber, "Applicant Attraction Strategies: An Organizational Perspective," *Academy of Management Review,* 1990, *15:* 286–310.

4. B. Dumaine, "Those High Flying PepsiCo Managers," *Fortune,* April 10, 1989, 78–86.

5. For an excellent summary of these laws, see J. A. Belohlay and E. Ayton, "Equal Opportunity Laws: Some Common Problems," *Personnel Journal,* April 1982, 282–285; and R. H. Faley and L. S. Kleinman, "Misconceptions and Realities in the Implementation of Equal Employment Opportunity," in R. S. Schuler, S. A. Youngblood, and V. L. Huber (eds.), *Readings in Personnel and Human Resource Management,* 3rd ed. (St. Paul, Minn.: West Publishing, 1988), 151–191.

6. J. Ledvinka, *Federal Regulation of Personnel and Human Resource Management* (Boston: Kent, 1982).

7. J. Dreyfuss, "Get Ready for the New Work Force," *Fortune,* April 23, 1990, 165–181, W. B. Johnston, "Global Work Force 2000: The New Labor Market," *Harvard Business Review,* March–April 1991, 115–129.

8. Dreyfuss, "Get Ready for the New Work Force," 168; R. R. Thomas, Jr., "From Affirmative Action to Affirming Diversity," *Harvard Business Review,* March–April 1990, 107–117.

9. A. M. Morrison and M. A. VonGlinow, "Women and Minorities in Management," *American Psychologist,* 1990, *45:* 200–208.

10. S. E. Jackson, R. S. Schuler, and J. C. Rivero, "Organizational Characteristics as Predictors of Personnel Practices," *Personnel Psychology,* 1989, *42:* 727–786.

11. M. J. Feuer, R. J. Niehaus, and J. A. Sheridan, "Human Resource Forecasting: A Survey of Practice & Potential," *Human Resource Planning,* 1988, *7*(2): 85–97.

12. J. P. Kirnam, J. A. Farley and K. F. Geisinger, "The Relationship between Recruiting Source, Applicant Quality, and Hire Performance: An Analysis by Sex, Ethnicity, and Age," *Personnel Psychology,* 1989, *42:* 293–308.

13. Adapted from *HR Reporter,* June 1988, 1–2.

14. Schuler and Huber, *Personnel and Human Resource Management,* 488.

15. N. Alster, "What Flexible Workers Can Do," *Fortune,* February 13, 1989, 62.

16. B. M. Meglino, A. S. DeNisi, S. A. Youngblood, and K. J. Williams, "Effects of Realistic Job Previews: A Comparison Using an Enhancement and Reduction Preview," *Journal of Applied Psychology,* 1988, *73:* 259–266; R. A. Dean and J. P. Wanous, "Effects of Realistic Job Previews on Hiring Bank Tellers," *Journal of Applied Psychology,* 1984, *69:* 61–68; R. J. Vandenberg and V. Scarpello, "The Matching Method: An Examination of the Processes Underlying Realistic Job Previews," *Journal of Applied Psychology,* 1990, *75:* 60–67.

17. M. S. Singer and C. Sewell, "Applicant Age and Selection Interview Decisions: Effect of Information Exposure on Age Discrimination in Personnel Selection," *Personnel Psychology,* 1989, *42:* 135–154; M. M. Harris, "Reconsidering the Employment Interview: A Review of the Recent Literature and Suggestions for Future Research," *Personnel Psychology,* 1989, *42:* 691–726.

18. Personal interview with David Anderson, President, ECCO Chemicals, Inc., February 1991.

19. H. M. Weiss and S. Adler, "Personality and Organizational Behavior," in B. M. Staw and L. L. Cummings (eds.), *Research in Organizational Behavior,* Vol. 6 (Greenwich, Conn.: Jai Press, 1984), 1–50.

20. A. Kupfer, "Is Drug Testing Good or Bad?" *Fortune,* December 19, 1988, 133–140; D. L. Gebhardt and C. E. Crump, "Employee Fitness and Wellness Programs in the Workplace," *American Psychologist,* 1990, *45:* 262–271; D. R. Ilgen, "Health Issues at Work," *American Psychologist,* 1990, *45:* 273–283; J. M. Grant and T. S. Bateman, "An Experimental Test of the Impact of Drug-Testing Programs on Potential Job Applicants' Attitudes and Intentions," *Journal of Applied Psychology,* 1990, *75:* 127–131.

21. K. Bishop, "Ex-Employee Wins Drug-Test Case," *New York Times,* October 31, 1987, 33; W. H. Wagel, "A Drug Screening Policy That Safeguards Employees' Rights," *Personnel,* February 1988, 10–11.

22. F. N. Kerlinger, *Foundations of Behavioral Science Research* (New York: Holt, Rinehart and Winston, 1986).

23. N. Schmitt, J. R. Schneider, and S. A. Cohen, "Factors Affecting Validity of a Regionally Administered Assessment Center," *Personnel Psychology,* 1990, *43:* 1–12; R. Klimoski and M. Brickner, "Why Do Assessment Centers Work?" *Personnel Psychology,* 1987, *40:* 243–260.

24. B. B. Gaugler, D. B. Rosenthal, G. C. Thornton, III, and C. Bentson, "Meta-Analysis of Assessment Center Validity," *Journal of Applied Psychology,* 1987, *72:* 493–511; G. M. McEvoy and R. W. Beatty, "Assessment Centers and Subordinate Appraisals of Managers: A Seven-Year Examination of

Predictive Validity," *Personnel Psychology,* 1989, *42:* 37–68.

25. Adapted from "Pepsi's Expectations," *HR Reporter,* July 1987, 4–5.

26. S. Zedeck and K. L. Mosier, "Work in the Family and Employing Organization," *American Psychologist,* 1990, *45:* 240–251; J. H. Greenhaus, S. Parasuraman, C. S. Granose, S. Rabinowitz, and N. J. Beutell, "Sources of Work-Family Conflict among Two-Career Couples," *Journal of Vocational Behavior,* 1989, *34:* 133–158.

27. H. J. Bernardin, "Increasing the Accuracy of Performance Measurement: A Proposed Solution to Erroneous Attributions," *Human Resource Planning,* 1989, *12:* 239–250.

28. Personal communication with H. Sutherland, Assistant Manager, Human Resources Department, Brooklyn Union Gas Company, February 1991.

29. E. E. Lawler, III, *Strategic Pay* (San Francisco: Jossey-Bass, 1990); S. L. Minken, "Does Lump-Sum Pay Merit Attention?" *Personnel Journal,* June 1988, 77–83.

30. M. Settle, "Up through the Ranks at McDonnell Douglas," *Personnel,* December 1989, 17–22.

31. J. Main, "Look Who Needs Outplacement," *Fortune,* October 9, 1989, 85–92; C. R. Leana and D. C. Feldman, "When Mergers Force Layoffs: Lessons about Managing the Human Resource Problems," *Human Resource Planning,* 1989, *12:* 123–140.

32. H. J. Bernardin and R. W. Beatty, *Performance Appraisal: Assessing Human Behavior at Work* (Boston: Kent-Wadsworth, 1984); H. H. Meyer, "A Solution to the Performance Appraisal Feedback Enigma," *Academy of Management Executive,* 1991, *5:* 68–76.

33. V. L. Huber, M. A. Neale, and G. B. Northcraft, "Judgment by Heuristics: Effects of Ratee and Rater Characteristics and Performance Standards on Performance-Related Judgments," *Organizational Behavior and Human Decision Processes,* 1987, *40:* 149–164.

34. Adapted from C. O. Longenecker, H. P. Sims, Jr., and D. A. Gioia, "Behind the Mash: The Politics of Employee Appraisal," *Academy of Management Executive,* 1987, *1:* 183–193.

35. S. J. Carroll, Jr., and C. E. Schneier, *Performance Appraisal Review (PAR) Systems* (Glenview, Ill.: Scott, Foresman, 1982).

36. G. Latham and K. Wexley, *Improving Productivity through Performance Appraisal* (Reading, Mass.: Addison-Wesley, 1981).

37. F. J. Landy and J. L. Farr, "Performance Rating," *Psychological Bulletin,* 1980, *88:* 72–107; K. R. Murphy and J. I. Constans, "Behavioral Anchors as a Source of Bias in Rating," *Journal of Applied Psychology,* 1987, *72:* 573.

38. Adapted from "Making Dreams Come True," *HR Reporter,* January 1987, 2–3.

39. "Overcoming the Illiteracy Barrier," *Bulletin to Management,* April 1987, 3–4.

40. Conversation with Gary McPherson, Personnel Manager, Missiles Division, LTV, February 1991.

41. A. D. Phillips, "Taking a Good Look at Development," *Issues and Answers,* Summer 1990, 1–5; M. Lombardo, M. McCall, and D. DeVries, *Looking Glass, Inc.* (Greensboro, N.C.: Center for Creative Leadership, 1991).

Skill-Building Exercise. Adapted from J. W. Pfeiffer, "What's Legal? Investigating Employment-Interview Questions," *The 1989 Annual: Developing Human Resources* (San Diego, Calif.: University Associates, 1989), 23–37.

Manager's Memo. Adapted from M. Magnus, "Personnel Policies in Partnership with Profit," *Personnel Journal,* September 1987, 105–106.

In the News. Dana Milbank, "Managers Are Sent to 'Charm Schools' to Polish up Their Interpersonal Skills," *Wall Street Journal,* December 14, 1990, B1–B3.

Management Case. Adapted from B. G. Posner, "Growing Your Own," *Inc.,* June 1989, 131–132.

Chapter 13

1. Adapted from C. Farrell and J. Hoerr, "ESOPs: Are They Good for You?" *Business Week,* May 15, 1989, 116–123; D. Kirkpatrick, "How the Workers Run Avis Better," *Fortune,* December 5, 1988, 103–114. *See also* J. L. Pierce and C. A. Furo, "Employee Ownership: Implications for Management," *Organizational Dynamics,* Winter 1990, 32–45; J. L. Pierce, S. A. Rubenfield, and S. Morgan, "Employee Ownership: A Conceptual Model of Process and Effects," *Academy of Management Review,* 1991, *16:* 121–144.

2. B. G. Posner, "Divided We Fall," *Inc.,* July 1989, 105.

3. M. G. Evans, "Organizational Behavior: The Central Role of Motivation," *Journal of Management,* 1986, *12:* 203–222.

4. For reviews of the literature, see F. J. Landy and W. S. Becker, "Motivation Theory Reconsidered," in L. L. Cummings and B. M. Staw (eds.), *Research in Organizations,* vol. 9 (Greenwich, Conn.: Jai, 1987), 1–38.

5. A. Bennett, "Pay for Performance," *Wall Street Journal,* April 18, 1990, R8.

6. Adapted from J. A. Trachtenberg, "The Dream of a Lifetime," *Forbes,* October 1, 1984, 250, 254; A. Stern, "Domino's: A Unique Concept Pays Off," *Dun's Business Month,* May 1986, 50–51; J. Jakubovics, "Domino's Pizza Founder Really Delivers," *Management Review,* July 1989, *78:* 11–13.

7. A. H. Maslow, *Motivation and Personality,* 2nd ed. (New York: Harper & Row, 1970).

8. J. Weber, L. Driscoll, and R. Brandt, "Farewell, Fast Track," *Business Week,* December 10, 1990, 192–200.

9. E. L. Betz, "Two Tests of Maslow's Theory of Need Fulfillment," *Journal of Vocational Behavior,* 1984, *24:* 204–220; J. Rauschenberger, N. Schmitt, and J. E. Hunter, "A Test of the Need Hierarchy Concept by a Markov Model of Change in Need Strength," *Administrative Science Quarterly,* 1980, *25:* 654–670.

10. T. A. Stewart, "Do You Push Your People Too Hard?" *Fortune,* October 22, 1990, 121–128.

11. F. Herzberg, B. Mausner, and B. Snyderman, *The Motivation to Work* (New York: Wiley, 1959).

12. M. A. Campion and P. W. Thayer, "Job Design Approaches, Outcomes and Trade-Offs," *Organizational Dynamics,* Winter 1987, 66–79; D. J. Brass, "Technology and the Structuring of Jobs: Employee Satisfaction, Performance and Influence," *Organizational Behavior and Human Decision Processes,* 1986, *35:* 216–240.

13. J. R. Hackman and G. R. Oldham, *Work Redesign* (Reading, Mass.: Addison-Wesley, 1980).

14. Adapted from J. Kapstein and J. Hoerr, "Volvo's Radical New Plant," *Business Week,* August 28, 1989, 92–93.

15. Y. Fried and G. R. Ferris, "The Validity of the Job Characteristics Model: A Review and Meta-Analysis," *Personnel Psychology,* 1987, *40:* 287–322; J. B. Cunningham and T. Eberle, "A Guide to Job Enrichment and Redesign," *Personnel,* February 1990, 56–61; P. E. Spector and S. M. Jex, "Relations of Job Characteristics from Multiple Data Sources with Employee Affect, Absence, Turnover Intentions, and Health," *Journal of Applied Psychology,* 1991, *76:* 46–53.

16. R. B. Goldman, *A Work Experiment: Six Americans in a Swedish Plant* (New York: Ford Foundation, 1976).

17. K. Ropp, "Candid Conversations," *Personnel Administrator,* October 1987, 49.

18. V. H. Vroom, *Work and Motivation* (New York: Wiley, 1964).

19. R. Stayer, "How I Learned to Let My Workers Lead," *Harvard Business Review,* November-December 1990, 66ff.

20. L. W. Porter and E. E. Lawler, III, *Managerial Attitudes and Performance* (Homewood, Ill.: Irwin, 1968).

21. J. Case, "The Open-Book Managers," *Inc.,* September 1990, 105–107.

22. B. M. Staw, "Organizational Psychology and the Pursuit of the Happy/Productive Worker," *California Management Review,* Summer 1986, 40–53; R. D. Arvey, T. J. Bouchard, N. L. Segal, and L. M. Abraham, "Job Satisfaction: Environmental and Genetic Components," *Journal of Applied Psychology,* 1989, *74:* 187–192.

23. D. A. Nadler, J. R. Hackman, and E. E. Lawler, III, *Managing Organizational Behavior* (Boston: Little, Brown, 1979), 32.

24. J. E. Ellis, "Feeling Stuck at Hyatt? Create a New Business," *Business Week,* December 10, 1990, 195.

25. J. P. Wanous, T. L. Keon, and J. C. Latack, "Expectancy Theory and Occupational/Organizational Choices: A Review and Test," *Organizational Behavior and Human Performance,* 1983, *32:* 66–86; M. C. Kernan and R. G. Lord, "Effects of Valence, Expectancies, and Goal-Performance Discrepancies in Single and Multiple Goal Environments," *Journal of Applied Psychology,* 1990, *75:* 194–203.

26. N. J. Perry, "Here Come Richer, Riskier Pay Plans," *Fortune,* December 19, 1988, 51.

27. J. S. Adams, "Toward an Understanding of Equity," *Journal of Abnormal and Social Psychology,* 1963, *67:* 422–436. *See also* R. P. Vecchio, "Models of Psychological Inequity," *Organizational Behavior and Human Performance,* 1984, *34:* 266–282; R. Cropanzano and R. Folger, "Referent Cognitions and Task Decision Autonomy: Beyond Equity Theory," *Journal of Applied Psychology,* 1989, *74:* 293–299; and R. W. Griffith, R. P. Vecchio, and J. W. Logan, Jr., "Equity Theory and Interpersonal Attraction," *Journal of Applied Psychology,* 1989, *74:* 394–401.

28. A. Farnham, "The Trust Gap," *Fortune,* December 4, 1989, 56–78; M. Sashkin and R. L. Williams, "Does Fairness Make a Difference?" *Organizational Dynamics,* Autumn 1990, 56–71.

29. J. Greenberg, "Employee Theft as a Reaction to Underpayment Inequity: The Hidden Costs of Pay Cuts," *Journal of Applied Psychology,* 1990, *75:* 561–568.

30. Adapted from G. B. Crystal, "Seeking the Sense in CEO Pay," *Fortune,* June 5, 1989, 88–104. *See also* R. L. Heneman, D. B. Greenberger, and S. Strasser, "The Relationship between Pay-for-Performance Perceptions and Pay Satisfaction," *Personnel Psychology,* 1988, *41:* 745–759; H. L. Tosi, Jr., and L. R. Gomez-Mejia, "The Decoupling of CEO Pay and Performance: An Agency Theory Perspective," *Administrative Science Quarterly,* 1989, *34:* 169–189; M. C. Jensen and K. J. Murphy, "CEO Incentives—It's Not How Much You Pay, but How," *Harvard Business Review,* May-June 1990, 138–153.

31. B. F. Skinner, *Beyond Freedom and Human Dignity* (New York: Knopf, 1971).

32. F. Luthans and R. Kreitner, *Organizational Behavior Modification* (Glenview, Ill.: Scott, Foresman, 1984).

33. Adapted from Farnham, "The Trust Gap," and A. Crouch and U. Nimran, "Office Design and the Behavior of Senior Managers," *Human Relations,* 1989, *42:* 139–156.

34. Adapted from W. Dierks and K. McNally, "An Arkansas Bank Is Putting B. F. Skinner's Theory into

Practice with Surprising Success," *Personnel Administrator,* March 1987, 61–65.

35. W. C. Hamner, "Using Reinforcement Theory in Organizational Settings," in H. L. Tosi, Jr., and W. C. Hamner (eds.), *Organizational Behavior and Management,* 3rd ed. (New York: Wiley, 1982), 534–542.

36. R. Kreitner and F. Luthans, "A Social Learning Approach to Behavioral Management: Radical Behaviorists Mellowing Out," *Organizational Dynamics,* Autumn 1984, 47–65.

In the News. Udayan Gupta, "Cutting Payrolls Without Axing Any Employees," *Wall Street Journal,* March 26, 1991, B1–B2.

Management Case. Adapted from B. Dumaine, "Business Secrets of Tommy Lasorda," *Fortune,* June 3, 1989, 130–135.

Chapter 14

1. Adapted from K. Labich, "Hot Company, Warm Culture," *Fortune,* February 27, 1989, 74–78; "Today's Leaders Look to Tomorrow," *Fortune,* March 26, 1990, 36.

2. J. P. Kotter, "What Leaders Really Do," *Harvard Business Review,* May-June 1990, 103–111. *See also* J. P. Kotter, *Leadership Differs from Management* (New York: Free Press, 1990).

3. B. Dumaine, "Who Needs a Boss?" *Fortune,* May 7, 1990, 54–55.

4. K. Labich, "The Seven Keys to Business Leadership," *Fortune,* October 24, 1988, 58–64.

5. R. E. Byrd, "Corporate Leadership Skills: A New Synthesis," *Organizational Dynamics,* Summer 1987, 34–43.

6. J. A. Byrne, R. Grover, and R. D. Hof, "Pay Stubs of the Rich and Corporate," *Business Week,* May 7, 1990, 56–108.

7. J. R. P. French, Jr., and B. H. Raven, "The Bases of Social Power," in D. Cartwright and A. Zanders (eds.), *Group Dynamics: Research and Theory,* 2nd ed. (New York: Harper & Row, 1960), 607–623; T. R. Hinkin and C. A. Schriesheim, "Development and Application of New Scales to Measure French and Raven (1959) Bases of Social Power," *Journal of Applied Psychology,* 1989, *74:* 561–567.

8. R. M. Kanter, "Power Failure in Management Circuits," *Harvard Business Review,* July-August 1979, 67. *See also* T. R. Hinkin and C. A. Schriesheim, "Relationships between Subordinate Perceptions of Supervisory Influence Tactics and Attributed Bases of Power," *Human Relations,* 1990, *43:* 221–238; C. A. Schriesheim, T. R. Hinkin, and P. M. Podsakoff, "Can Ipsative and Single-Item Measures Produce Erroneous Results in Field Studies of French and Raven's (1959) Five Bases of Power? An Empirical Investigation," *Journal of Applied Psychology,* 1991, *76:* 106–114.

9. G. A. Yukl, *Leadership in Organizations,* 2nd ed. (Englewood Cliffs, N.J.: Prentice-Hall, 1989), 12–53; G. A. Yukl and C. M. Falbe, "The Importance of Different Power Sources in Downward and Lateral Relations," paper presented at Society of Industrial and Organizational Psychology, Miami, April 1990; R. Lachman, "Power from What? A Reexamination of Its Relationships with Structural Conditions," *Administrative Science Quarterly,* 1989, *34:* 131–151.

10. P. F. Drucker, *The New Realities: In Government, in Politics, in Economics and Business, in Society and World View* (New York: Harper & Row, 1989).

11. Adapted from L. Brokow and C. Hartman, "Managing the Journey," *Inc.,* November 1990, 45–54; R. Stayer, "How I Learned to Let My Workers Lead," *Harvard Business Review,* November-December 1990, 66–69, 72–76, 80–83.

12. B. M. Bass, *Stogdill's Handbook of Leadership* (New York: Free Press, 1981), 43–96; R. G. Lord,

C. L. DeVader, and G. M. Alliger, "A Meta-Analysis of the Relations between Personality Traits and Leadership Perceptions: An Application of Validity Generalization Procedures," *Journal of Applied Psychology,* 1986, *71:* 402–410.

13. D. A. Kenny and S. J. Zaccaro, "An Estimate of Variance Due to Traits in Leadership," *Journal of Applied Psychology,* 1983, *68:* 678–685; J. R. Meindl, "Managing to Be Fair: An Exploration of Values, Motives and Leadership," *Administrative Science Quarterly,* 1989, *34:* 252–276.

14. D. McGregor, *The Human Side of the Enterprise* (New York: McGraw-Hill, 1960), 33–58.

15. Adapted from P. Nulty, "America's Toughest Bosses," *Fortune,* February 27, 1989, 40–54.

16. R. M. Stogdill, *Handbook of Leadership* (New York: Free Press, 1974).

17. For a review of the Ohio State leadership studies, see S. Kerr, C. A. Schriesheim, C. Murphy, and R. M. Stogdill, "Toward a Contingency Theory of Leadership Based on Consideration and Initiating Structure," *Organizational Behavior and Human Performance,* 1974, *12:* 68–82.

18. R. Likert, *New Patterns of Management* (New York: McGraw-Hill, 1961); R. Likert, *The Human Organization* (New York: McGraw-Hill, 1967).

19. R. R. Blake and J. S. Mouton, *The Managerial Grid* (Houston, Tex.: Gulf Publishing, 1965).

20. F. E. Fiedler, *A Theory of Leadership Effectiveness* (New York: McGraw-Hill, 1967); F. E. Fiedler, "The Effectiveness of the Contingency Model of Training: A Review of the Validation of Leader Match," *Personnel Psychology,* 1979, *32:* 45–62.

21. L. H. Peters, D. D. Hartke, and J. T. Pohlmann, "Fiedler's Contingency Theory of Leadership: An Application of the Meta-Analysis Procedures of Schmidt and Hunter," *Psychological Bulletin,* 1985, *97:* 224–285.

22. F. E. Fiedler and M. M. Chemers, *Leadership and Effective Management* (Glenview, Ill.: Scott, Foresman, 1974).

23. P. Hersey and K. H. Blanchard, *Management of Organizational Behavior,* 5th ed. (Englewood Cliffs, N.J.: Prentice-Hall, 1988).

24. K. H. Blanchard, *Leadership and the One-Minute Manager* (Escondido, Calif.: Blanchard Training & Development, 1985).

25. Adapted from B. Dumaine, "Who Needs a Boss?" *Fortune,* May 7, 1990, 52–58.

26. C. L. Graeff, "The Situational Leadership Theory: A Critical View," *Academy of Management Review,* 1983, *8:* 285–291; W. Blank, J. R. Weitzel, and S. G. Green, "A Test of Situational Leadership," *Personnel Psychology,* 1990, *43:* 579–598.

27. R. J. House and T. R. Mitchell, "Path-Goal Theory of Leadership," *Journal of Contemporary Business,* Autumn 1974, 81–98.

28. For a critical review of House's theory see G. A. Yukl, "Managerial Leadership: A Review of Theory and Research," *Journal of Management,* 1989, *15:* 251–290; R. T. Keller, "A Test of the Path-Goal Theory of Leadership with Need for Clarity as a Moderator in Research and Development Organizations," *Journal of Applied Psychology,* 1989, *74:* 208–212.

29. V. H. Vroom and P. W. Yetton, *Leadership and Decision Making* (Pittsburgh, Pa.: University of Pittsburgh Press, 1973); V. H. Vroom and A. G. Jago, *The New Leadership* (Englewood Cliffs, N.J.: Prentice-Hall, 1988).

30. D. Tjosvold, W. C. Wedley, and R. H. G. Field, "Constructive Controversy: The Vroom-Yetton Model and Managerial Decision Making," *Journal of Occupational Behavior,* 1985, *7:* 125–138; R. H. G. Field and R. J. House, "A Test of the Vroom-Yetton Model Using Manager and Subordinate Reports," *Journal of Applied Psychology,* 1990, *75:* 362–366.

31. J. M. Kouzes and B. Z. Posner, *The Leadership*

Challenge (San Francisco, Calif.: Jossey-Bass, 1990); W. G. Bennis and B. Nanus, *Leaders: The Strategies for Taking Charge* (New York: Harper & Row, 1985); A. Zaleznik, "The Leadership Gap," *Academy of Management Executive,* 1990, *4:* 7–22.

32. B. M. Bass, *Leadership and Performance beyond Expectations* (New York: Free Press, 1985); B. M. Bass, "From Transactional to Transformational Leadership: Learning to Share the Vision," *Organizational Dynamics,* Winter 1990, 19–31; F. J. Yammarino and B. M. Bass, "Transformational Leadership and Multiple Levels of Analysis," *Human Relations,* 1990, *43:* 975–995.

33. N. M. Tichy and M. A. Devanna, *The Transformational Leader* (New York: Wiley, 1986). For related work see J. M. Howell and P. J. Frost, "A Laboratory Study of Charismatic Leadership," *Organizational Behavior and Human Decision Processes,* 1989, *43:* 243–269.

34. J. Main, "How to Win the Baldridge Award," *Fortune,* April 23, 1990, 101–116.

35. Adapted from J. P. Kotter, "What Leaders Really Do," *Harvard Business Review,* May-June 1990, 106.

Skill-Building Exercise. Taken and modified with permission from C. A. Schriesheim, "A Preliminary Report on New-Individually-Worded Initiating Structure and Consideration Scales." Unpublished manuscript, Ohio State University and University of Miami, 1991.

Manager's Memo. *Special Report on Leadership* (Boston: Forum Corporation, 1991).

In the News. George Anders, "Back to Biscuits: Old Flamboyance Is Out as Louis Gerstner Remakes RJR Nabisco," *Wall Street Journal,* March 21, 1991, A1–A6.

Management Case. Adapted from C. Knowlton, "How Disney Keeps the Magic Going," *Fortune,* December 4, 1989, pp. 111–132; G. Hector, "Yes, You Can Manage Long Term," *Fortune,* November 21, 1988, pp. 64–76; R. Turner, "Disney Chairman's 1989 Pay Totals Under $10 Million," *Wall Street Journal,* January 16, 1990, p. A 16; G. E. Willigan, "The Value-Adding CFO: An Interview with Disney's Gary Wilson," *Harvard Business Review,* January-February 1990: 84–95.

Chapter 15

1. Adapted from B. Stack, "Survival Tactics: When the Facility Must Close Down," *Management Review,* May 1990, 54–57.

2. H. Mintzberg, *The Nature of Managerial Work* (New York: Harper & Row, 1973), 58–93.

3. R. C. Huseman, J. Lahiff, and J. M. Penrose, *Business Communications: Strategies and Skills,* 3rd ed. (Hinsdale, Ill.: Dryden, 1988), 32.

4. Huseman, *et al.,* 33.

5. C. L. Bovee and J. C. Thill, *Business Communication Today* (New York: Random House, 1986).

6. A. Mehradbian, *Non-Verbal Communications* (Chicago: Aldine, 1972).

7. S. Ornstein, "Organizational Symbols: A Study of Their Meaning and Influences on Perceived Psychological Climate," *Organizational Behavior and Human Decision Processes,* 1986, *38:* 207–229; F. Steele, *Making and Managing High-Quality Workplaces: An Organizational Ecology* (New York: Teachers College, Columbia College, 1986).

8. Adapted from J. W. Gibson and R. M. Hodgetts, *Organizational Communication: A Managerial Perspective* (Orlando, Fla.: Academic, 1986), 99.

9. S. Ornstein, "The Hidden Influences of Office Design," *Academy of Management Executive,* 1989, *3:* 144–147; J. Fulk, C. W. Steinfield, J. Schmitz, and J. G. Power, "A Social Information Processing Model of Media Use in Organizations," *Communication Research,* 1987, *14:* 529–552.

10. K. Turnquist, "Dress for Success Only Changes Name, Not Style," *Dallas Times Herald,* November 11, 1989, E-6; P. C. Morrow, "Physical Attractiveness and Selection Decision Making," *Journal of Management,* 1990, *16:* 45–60.

11. M. McCaskey, "The Hidden Messages Managers Send," *Harvard Business Review,* 1979, *57*(6): 146–147; R. Harrison, *Beyond Words: An Introduction to Nonverbal Communications* (Englewood Cliffs, N.J.: Prentice-Hall, 1974), 132–133.

12. Adapted from F. H. Katayama, "How to Act Once You Get There," *Fortune, Special Issue, Asia in the 1990s,* Fall 1989, 87–88.

13. L. E. Penley, E. R. Alexander, I. E. Jernigan, and C. J. Henwood, "Communication Abilities of Managers: The Relationship to Performance," *Journal of Management,* 1991, *17:* 57–76; K. G. Smith and C. M. Grimm, "A Communication-Information Model of Competitive Response Timing," *Journal of Management,* 1991, *17:* 5–24.

14. L. K. Trevino, R. H. Lengel, and R. L. Daft, "Media Symbolism, Media Richness, and Media Choice in Organizations," *Communication Research,* 1987, *14:* 553–574.

15. T. Peters, *Thriving on Chaos: Handbook for a Management Revolution* (New York: Knopf, 1987); P. M. Fandt and G. R. Ferris, "The Management of Information and Impressions: When Employees Behave Opportunistically," *Organizational Behavior and Human Decision Processes,* 1990, *45:* 140–158.

16. H. B. Vickery, III, "Tapping into the Employee Grapevine," *Association Management,* January 1984, 56–63; B. A. Baldwin, "Gossip and the Grapevine," *USAir Magazine,* January 1991, 96–100.

17. D. Kirkpatrick, "The New Executive: Unemployed," *Fortune,* April 8, 1991, 36–42, 46–48.

18. R. C. Huseman and E. W. Miles, "Organizational Communication in the Information Age: Implications of Computer-Based Systems," *Journal of Management,* 1988, *14:* 181–204; T. R. Zenger and B. S. Lawrence, "Organizational Demography: The Differential Effects of Age and Tenure on Technical Communications," *Academy of Management Journal,* 1989, *32:* 353–376; P. S. Goodman, L. S. Sproull, and Associates, *Technology and Organizations* (San Francisco: Jossey-Bass, 1990).

19. Adapted from G. L. Miles, "At Westinghouse, E-Mail Makes the World Go 'Round," *Business Week,* October 10, 1988, 110. *See also* P. G. Keen, "Telecommunications and Organizational Choice," *Communication Research,* 1987, *14:* 588–606; B. Ziegler, "How Confidential Is a Company's Electronic Mail?" *Plano Star Courier,* August 26, 1990, 13B.

20. R. W. Rasberry and L. F. Lemoine, *Effective Managerial Communication* (Boston: Kent, 1986), 168–170.

21. D. Kunde, "Engendering a Change," *Dallas Morning News,* January 13, 1991, H1–H3.

22. M. Sit, "Corralling the Corporate Ego," *Boston Globe,* April 15, 1990, A27–A31.

23. J. Main, "How 21 Men Got Global in 35 Days," *Fortune,* November 6, 1989, 71–74.

24. Personal interview with Gary McPherson, Personnel Manager, LTV Missiles and Electronics Group, April 4, 1991, Grand Prairie, Texas.

25. Summarized from *Ten Commandments of Good Communications* (New York: The American Management Association, 1955). *See also* L. Mikulecky, "Basic Skill Impediments to Communication Between Management and Hourly Employees," *Management Communication Quarterly,* 1990, *3:* 452–473.

Skill-Building Exercise. Reprinted by permission from G. E. Burton, *Exercises in Management* (Boston: Houghton Mifflin, 1990), 199–202.

In the News. Claudia H. Deutsch, "The Multimedia Benefits Kit: To Explain a New Plan, Citicorp Turns to Software, Videos, and Even a Hotline," *Wall Street Journal,* October 14, 1990, p. 25.

Chapter 16

1. Developed from B. Dumaine, "Who Needs a Boss?" *Fortune,* May 7, 1990, 52–60; J. Hoerr, "The Payoff from Teamwork," *Business Week,* July 10, 1989, 56–62.

2. Hoerr, "The Payoff from Teamwork."

3. C. Hendrick (ed.), *Group Processes and Intergroup Relations* (Beverly Hills, Calif.: Sage, 1987).

4. David Fearon, correspondence with the authors, January 11, 1991.

5. W. C. Swap and associates (eds.), *Group Decision Making* (Beverly Hills, Calif.: Sage, 1984).

6. D. Cole, "Meetings That Make Sense," *Psychology Today,* May 1989, 14–16.

7. A. Fuhreman, S. Drewschler, and G. Burlingame, "Conceptualizing Small Group Process," *Small Group Behavior,* 1984, *15:* 427–440.

8. L. Hirschhorn, *Managing in the New Team Environment: Skills, Tools, and Methods* (Reading, Mass.: Addison-Wesley, 1991).

9. A. Zander, *The Purposes of Groups and Organizations* (San Francisco: Jossey-Bass, 1985).

10. Hoerr, "The Payoff from Teamwork"; Dumaine, "Who Needs a Boss?"

11. K. Labich, "Making Over Middle Managers," *Fortune,* May 8, 1989, 58–64; T. Mack, "Energizing a Bureaucracy," *Forbes,* September 17, 1990, 76, 80.

12. S. Cohen, "More Businesses Turn to Self-managed Work Teams," *Bryan–College Station Eagle,* December 2, 1990, 1C, 3C; E. Olsen, "Building Teams That Never Drop the Ball," *Success,* November 1990, 40–44.

13. K. K. Smith, "The Movement of Conflict in Organizations: The Joint Dynamics of Splitting and Triangulation," *Administrative Science Quarterly,* 1989, *34:* 1–20.

14. R. W. Napier and M. K. Gershenfeld, *Groups: Theory and Experience,* 4th ed. (Boston: Houghton Mifflin, 1989).

15. W. F. Whyte and K. K. W. Whyte, *Making Mondragon* (Ithaca, N.Y.: ILR Press, 1988).

16. C. J. G. Gersick, "Marking Time: Predictable Transitions in Task Groups," *Academy of Management Journal,* 1989, *32:* 274–309; H. G. Dimock, *Groups: Leadership and Group Development* (San Diego, Calif.: University Associates, 1987).

17. B. W. Tuckman and M. A. C. Jensen, "Stages of Small Group Development Revisited," *Group and Organization Studies,* 1977, *2:* 419–427.

18. W. L. French and C. H. B. Bell, Jr., *Organization Development: Behavioral Science Interventions,* 4th ed. (Englewood Cliffs, N.J.: Prentice-Hall, 1990); G. M. Parker, *Team Players and Team Work* (San Francisco: Jossey-Bass, 1990).

19. C. Kormanski, "A Situational Leadership Approach to Groups Using the Tuckman Model of Group Development," in L. D. Goodstein and J. W. Pfeiffer (eds.), *The 1985 Annual: Developing Human Resources* (San Diego, Calif.: University Associates, 1985), 217–225.

20. G. C. Homans, *The Human Group* (New York: Harcourt, Brace, 1950); G. C. Homans, *Social Behavior: Its Elementary Forms* (New York: Harcourt, Brace, 1961). *See also* S. Worchel, W. Wood, and J. A. Simpson, *Group Process and Productivity* (Newbury Park, Calif.: Sage, 1991).

21. J. C. Chilberg, "A Review of Group Process Designs for Facilitating Communication in Problem-Solving Groups," *Management Communication Quarterly,* 1989, *3:* 51–70.

22. L. Hirschhorn, "Professionals, Authority and Group Life: A Case Study of a Law Firm," *Human Resource Management,* 1989, *28:* 235–252.

23. J. R. Gibb, *Trust: A New Theory of Personal and Organizational Development* (Los Angeles: Guild of Tudors Press, 1978); S. Allcorn, "Understanding Groups at Work," *Personnel,* August 1989, 28–35.

24. M. Sinetar, "Building Trust into Corporate Relationships," *Organizational Dynamics,* Winter 1988, 73–79.

25. G. H. Morris, S. C. Gaveras, W. L. Baker, and M. L. Coursey, "Aligning Actions at Work: How Managers Confront Problems of Employee Performance," *Management Communication Quarterly,* 1990, *3:* 303–333.

26. M. E. Gist, E. A. Locke, and M. S. Taylor, "Organizational Behavior: Group Structure, Process, and Effectiveness," *Journal of Management,* 1987, *13:* 237–257.

27. N. Josefowitz and H. Gadon, "Hazing: Uncovering One of the Best-Kept Secrets of the Workplace," *Business Horizons,* May-June 1989, 22–26.

28. D. C. Feldman, "The Development and Enforcement of Group Norms," *Academy of Management Review,* 1984, *9:* 47–53. *See also* J. L. Pearce and R. H. Peters, "A Contradictory Norms View of Employer-Employee Exchange," *Journal of Management,* 1985, *11:* 19–30.

29. M. Henderson and M. Argyle, "The Informal Rules of Working Relationships," *Journal of Occupational Behaviour,* 1986, *7:* 259–275.

30. A. Zander, *Effective Social Action by Community Groups* (San Francisco: Jossey-Bass, 1990).

31. G. N. Powell, "One More Time: Do Female and Male Managers Differ?" *Academy of Management Executive,* August 1990, 68–75; J. S. Hunsaker and P. L. Hunsaker, *Strategies and Skills for Managerial Women* (Cincinnati, Ohio: South-Western, 1990).

32. Developed from W. Konrad, "Welcome to the Woman-Friendly Company," *Business Week,* August 6, 1990, 48–55; J. Fierman, "Why Women Still Don't Hit the Top," *Fortune,* July 30, 1990, 40–42*ff;* A. S. Baron, "What Men Are Saying about Women in Business: A Decade Later," *Business Horizons,* July-August 1989, 51–53.

33. M. K. Moch and J. M. Bartunek, *Creating Alternative Realities at Work: The Quality of Life Experiment at FoodCom* (New York: Harper, 1990).

34. S. Cohen, "More Businesses Turn to Self-Managed Work Teams," *Bryan–College Station Eagle,* December 2, 1990, 1C, 3C; E. J. Ost, "Team-Based Pay: New Wave Strategic Initiative," *Sloan Management Review,* Spring 1990, 19–27.

35. Dumaine, "Who Needs a Boss?"

36. J. L. Cotton, D. A. Vollrath, K. L. Froggatt, M. L. Lengnick-Hall, and K. R. Jennings, "Employee Participation: Diverse Forms and Different Outcomes," *Academy of Management Review,* 1988, *13:* 8–22; C. R. Leana, E. A. Locke, and D. M. Schweiger, "Fact and Fiction in Analyzing Research on Participative Decision Making," *Academy of Management Review,* 1990, *15:* 137–146.

37. N. R. F. Maier, "Assets and Liabilities in Group Problem-Solving: The Need for an Integrative Function," *Psychology Review,* 1967, *74:* 239–249.

38. J. P. Wanous and M. A. Youtz, "Solution Diversity and the Quality of Group Decisions," *Academy of Management Journal,* 1986, *29:* 149–159.

39. P. G. Friedman, "Upstream Facilitation: A Proactive Approach to Managing Problem-Solving Groups," *Management Communication Quarterly,* 1989, *3:* 33–50.

40. G. Whyte, "Groupthink Reconsidered," *Academy of Management Review,* 1989, *14:* 40–56; J. P. Wanous, A. E. Reichers, and S. D. Malik, "Organizational Socialization and Group Development: Toward an Integrative Perspective," *Academy of Management Review,* 1984, *9:* 670–683.

41. T. G. Plax and L. F. Cecchi, "Manager Decisions Based on Communication Facilitated in Focus Groups," *Management Communication Quarterly,* 1989, *2:* 511–535; R. Y. Hirokawa, "Why Informed

Groups Make Faculty Decisions," *Small Group Behavior,* 1987, *18:* 3–29.

42. Developed from J. Hoerr, "The Payoff from Teamwork," *Business Week,* July 10, 1989, 56–62; J. Hoerr, "Work Teams Can Rev Up Paper-Pushers, Too," *Business Week,* November 28, 1988, 64–72.

43. G. DeSanctis and R. B. Gallupe, "A Foundation for the Study of Group Decision Support Systems," *Management Science,* 1987, *33:* 589–609.

44. A. P. Hare, "Group Size," *American Behavioral Scientist,* 1981, *24:* 695–708; R. Albanese and D. D. Van Fleet, "Rational Behavior in Groups: The Free-Riding Tendency," *Academy of Management Review,* 1985, *10:* 244–255.

45. G. E. Manners, Jr., "Another Look at Group Size, Group Problem-Solving and Member Consensus," *Academy of Management Journal,* 1975, *18:* 715–724.

46. W. M. Fox, *Effective Group Problem Solving* (San Francisco: Jossey-Bass, 1987); R. W. Napier and M. K. Gershenfeld, *Making Groups Work: A Guide for Group Leaders* (Boston: Houghton Mifflin, 1983).

47. P. L. Townsend and J. E. Gebhardt, "The Quality Process: Little Things Mean a Lot," *Review of Business,* Winter 1990/1991, 3–7.

48. E. R. Ruffner and L. P. Ettkin, "When a Circle Is Not a Circle," *SAM Advanced Management Journal,* Spring 1987, 9–15.

49. L. Fitzgerald and J. Murphy, *Installing Quality Circles: A Strategic Approach* (San Diego, Calif.: University Associates, 1982), 113–115; S. G. Goldstein, "Organizational Dualism and Quality Circles," *Academy of Management Review,* 1985, *10:* 504–517; G. W. Meyer and R. G. Scott, "Quality Circles. Panacea or Pandora's Box?" *Organizational Dynamics,* Spring 1985, 35–50.

50. M. L. Marks, "The Question of Quality Circles," *Psychology Today,* March 1986, 36–46.

51. E. E. Lawler III and S. A. Mohrman, "Quality Circles: After the Honeymoon," *Organizational Dynamics,* Spring 1987, 42–54; B. G. Dale and J. Lees, "Quality Circles: From Introduction to Integration," *Long Range Planning,* 1987, *20*(1): 78–83.

52. E. E. Lawler III, *High Involvement Management* (San Francisco: Jossey-Bass, 1986); V. C. M. Frazer and B. G. Dale, "A Further Study of Quality Circle Failures in British Manufacturing Companies," *Quality Assurance,* March 1986, 7–12; J. Brockner and T. Hess, "Self-Esteem and Task Performance in Quality Circles," *Academy of Management Journal,* 1986, *29:* 617–623.

53. A. Honeycutt, "The Key to Effective Quality Circles," *Training-Development Journal,* May 1989, 81–84.

54. Developed from "Quest for Quality: Florida Power & Light Wins the Deming Prize," *The Service Economy,* July 1990, 6–8.

55. W. J. Duncan, "Organizational Culture: 'Getting a Fix' on an Elusive Concept," *Academy of Management Executive,* 1989, *3:* 229–236.

56. E. H. Schein, *Organizational Culture and Leadership* (San Francisco: Jossey-Bass, 1985); B. Schneider (ed.), *Organizational Climate and Culture* (San Francisco: Jossey-Bass, 1991).

57. A. Farnham, "The Trust Gap," *Fortune,* December 4, 1989, 56–78.

58. R. H. Kilmann, M. J. Saxton, R. Serpa, and associates, *Gaining Control of the Corporate Culture* (San Francisco: Jossey-Bass, 1985).

59. W. G. Dyer, *Cultural Change in Family Firms* (San Francisco: Jossey-Bass, 1986); A. M. Kantrow, "The Constraints of Corporate Tradition (New York: Harper & Row, 1987).

60. E. F. Jackofsky, J. W. Slocum, Jr., and S. Mc-Quaid, "Cultural Values and the CEO: Alluring Companions," *Academy of Management Executive,* 1988, *22:* 39–49; G. Hofstede, B. Neuijen, D. D. Ohayu, and G. Sanders, "Measuring Organizational

Cultures: A Qualitative and Quantitative Study across Twenty Cases," *Administrative Science Quarterly,* 1990, *35:* 286–316.

61. J. A. Oliver and E. J. Johnson, "People Motives Redefine Customer Service," *HR Magazine,* June 1990, 119–121; R. Howard, "Values Make the Company: An Interview with Robert Haas," *Harvard Business Review,* September-October 1990, 132–144.

62. Excerpted from F. G. Rodgers with R. L. Shook, *The IBM Way.* Copyright © 1986 by Francis G. Rodgers and Robert L. Shook. Reprinted by permission of Harper & Row. *See also* J. Dreyfuss, "Reinventing IBM," *Fortune,* August 14, 1989, 30–38.

63. R. Pascale, "The Paradox of 'Corporate Culture': Reconciling Ourselves to Socialization," *California Management Review,* Winter 1985, 26–41.

64. A. E. Reichers, "An Interactionist Perspective on Newcomer Socialization Rates," *Academy of Management Review,* 1987, *12:* 278–287; N. J. Allen and J. P. Meyer, "Organizational Socialization Tactics: A Longitudinal Analysis of Links to Newcomers' Commitment and Role Orientation," *Academy of Management Journal,* 1990, *33:* 847–858.

65. Pascale, "The Paradox of 'Corporate Culture,'" 31.

66. J. D. Sherman, H. L. Smith, and E. R. Mansfield, "The Impact of Network Structure on Organizational Socialization," *Journal of Applied Behavioral Science,* 1986, *22:* 53–63.

67. R. Pascale, "Fitting New Employees into the Company Culture," *Fortune,* May 28, 1984, 28.

68. H. M. Trice and J. M. Beyer, "Studying Organizational Cultures through Rites and Ceremonials," *Academy of Management Review,* 1984, *9:* 653–669; J. B. Shaw, "A Cognitive Categorization Model for the Study of Intercultural Management," *Academy of Management Review,* 15(4): 626–645.

69. J. M. Beyer and H. M. Trice, "How an Organization's Rites Reveal Its Culture," *Organizational Dynamics,* Spring 1987, 5–24.

70. F. G. Rodgers, 183–195.

71. H. M. Trice and J. M. Beyer, "Cultural Leadership in Organizations," *Organization Science,* 1991, *2:* in press.

72. T. E. Deal and A. A. Kennedy, *Corporate Cultures: The Rites and Rituals of Corporate Life* (Reading, Mass.: Addison-Wesley, 1982), 87–88. *See also* D. K. Denton and B. L. Wisdom, "Shared Vision," *Business Horizons,* July-August 1989, 67–69.

73. This section is substantially based on J. Kerr and J. W. Slocum, Jr., "Managing Corporate Culture through Reward Systems," *Academy of Management Executive,* 1987, *1:* 98–108. *See also* W. Ouchi, *Theory Z* (Reading, Mass.: Addison-Wesley, 1981).

74. J. Sculley, *Odyssey: Pepsi to Apple . . . A Journey of Adventures, Ideas, and the Future* (New York: Harper & Row, 1987).

75. Developed from K. Labich, "Hot Company, Warm Culture," *Fortune,* February 27, 1989, 74–78.

76. Developed from B. Dumaine, "Those High Flying PepsiCo Managers," *Fortune,* April 10, 1989, 78–86; P. Sellers, "Pepsi Keeps On Going after No. 1," *Fortune,* March 11, 1991, 61–70; S. N. Chakravarty, "How Pepsi Broke into India," *Forbes,* November 27, 1989, 43–44.

77. B. Dumaine, "Creating a New Company Culture," *Fortune,* January 15, 1990, 127–132; T. H. Fitzgerald, "Can Change in Organizational Culture Really Be Managed?" *Organizational Dynamics,* Autumn 1988, 5–15; J. B. Barney, "Organizational Culture: Can It Be a Source of Sustained Competitive Advantage?" *Academy of Management Review,* 1986, *11:* 656–665.

78. D. R. Denison, *Corporate Culture and Organizational Effectiveness* (New York: Wiley, 1990); R. H. Waterman, Jr., *The Renewal Factor* (New York: Bantam, 1987).

79. B. A. Turner (ed.), *Organizational Symbolism* (Hawthorne, N.Y.: Walter de Gruyter, 1990); J. A. Raelin, *The Clash of Cultures* (Boston: Harvard Business School Press, 1986).

80. P. Gagliardi, *Symbols and Artifacts: Views of the Corporate Landscape* (Hawthorne, N.Y.: Walter de Gruyter, 1990); P. J. Frost, L. F. Moore, M. R. Loomis, C. C. Lundberg, and J. Martin (eds.), *Organizational Culture* (Beverly Hills, Calif.: Sage, 1985).

81. D. C. Limerick, "Managers of Meaning: From Bob Geldof's Band Aid to Australian CEOs," *Organizational Dynamics,* Spring 1990, 22–33; G. C. Pati and R. A. Saltimore, "The Resurrection of a Rust-Belt Service Organization," *Organizational Dynamics,* Summer 1989, 33–49.

82. J. J. Keller, "Bob Allen Is Turning AT&T into a Live Wire," *Business Week,* November 6, 1989, 140–152; W. B. Tunstall, "The Breakup of the Bell System: A Case Study in Cultural Transformation," *California Management Review,* Winter 1986, 110–124.

83. J. Main, "Waking Up at AT&T: There's Life after Culture Shock," *Fortune,* December 24, 1984, 67.

84. D. J. Garsombke, "Organizational Culture Dons the Mantle of Militarism," *Organizational Dynamics,* Summer 1988, 46–56.

Skill-Building Exercise. From W. G. Dyer, *Team Building: Issues and Alternatives* (Reading, Mass.: Addison-Wesley, 1987), 69–71. Copyright © 1987. Team Development Scale by William G. Dyer. Reprinted with permission.

In the News. Joann S. Lublin, "'Green' Executives Find Their Mission Isn't a Natural Part of Corporate Culture," *Wall Street Journal,* March 5, 1991, B1–B4.

Management Case. Adapted from J. Weiss, M. Wahlstrom, and E. Marshall, "The Consolidated Life: Caught between Corporate Cultures," *Journal of Management Case Studies,* 1986, *2:* 238–243. Elsevier Science Publishing Co., Inc., 52 Vanderbilt Ave., N.Y., N.Y. 10017. Used with permission.

Chapter 17

1. Developed from R. R. Thomas, Jr., "From Affirmative Action to Affirming Diversity," *Harvard Business Review,* March-April 1990, 107–117; B. Mandell and S. Kohler-Gray, "Management Development That Values Diversity," *Personnel,* March 1990, 41–46.

2. B. Mandell and S. Kohler Gray, *Ibid.,* p. 43.

3. M. A. Rahim (ed.), *Theory and Research in Conflict Management* (Westport, Conn.: Praeger, 1990).

4. M. Kohn, *No Contest: The Case Against Competition* (Boston: Houghton Mifflin, 1987); L. Greenhalgh, "The Case Against Winning in Negotiation," *Tuck Today,* Spring 1987, 30–35.

5. D. Tjosvold, *The Conflict-Positive Organization: Stimulate Diversity and Create Unity* (Reading, Mass.: Addison-Wesley, 1991).

6. R. A. Cosier and C. R. Schwenk, "Agreement and Thinking Alike: Ingredients for Poor Thinking," *Academy of Management Executive,* 1990, *4:* 69–74; R. A. Cosier and D. R. Dalton, "Positive Effects of Conflict: A Field Assessment," *International Journal of Conflict Management,* 1990, *1:* 81–92.

7. R. Kahn, D. Wolfe, R. Quinn, and J. Snoek, *Organizational Stress: Studies in Role Conflict and Ambiguity* (New York: Wiley, 1964).

8. R. Merton, *Social Theory and Social Structure,* 2nd ed. (Glenview, Ill.: Free Press, 1957).

9. M. F. Kets de Vries, "Leaders Who Self-Destruct: The Causes and Cures," *Organizational Dynamics,* Spring 1989, 5–17; M. Van Sell, A. P. Brief, and R. S. Schuler, "Role Conflict and Role Ambiguity: Integration of the Literature and Direc-

tions for Future Research," *Human Relations,* 1981, *34:* 43–71.

10. A. R. Cohen and D. L. Bradford, "Influence Without Authority: The Use of Alliances, Reciprocity, and Exchange to Accomplish Work," *Organizational Dynamics,* Winter 1989, 5–17.

11. G. Yukl and C. M. Falbe, "Influence Tactics and Objectives in Upward, Downward, and Lateral Influence Attempts," *Journal of Applied Psychology,* 1990, *75:* 132–140.

12. R. G. Netemeyer, M. W. Johnston, and S. Burton, "Analysis of Role Conflict and Role Ambiguity in a Structural Equations Framework," *Journal of Applied Psychology,* 1990, *75:* 148–157.

13. R. H. Frank, *Passions Within Reason: The Strategic Role of the Emotions* (New York: Norton, 1988).

14. D. A. Whetten, "Coping with Incompatible Expectations: An Integrated View of Role Conflict," *Administrative Science Quarterly,* 1978, *23:* 254–271.

15. D. T. Hall and J. Richter, "Career Gridlock: Baby Boomers Hit the Wall," *Academy of Management Executive,* 1990, *4:* 7–22.

16. D. T. Hall, "Promoting Work/Family Balance: An Organization-Change Approach," *Organizational Dynamics,* Winter 1990, 5–18; J. H. Greenhaus and N. J. Beutell, "Sources of Conflict Between Work and Family Roles," *Academy of Management Review,* 1985, *10:* 76–88; L. H. Chusmir and C. S. Koberg, "Development and Validation of the Sex Role Conflict Scale," *Journal of Applied Behavioral Science,* 1986, *22:* 397–409.

17. B. Mandill and S. Kohler-Gray, "Management Development That Values Diversity," *Personnel,* March 1990, 42.

18. L. Falkenberg, "Improving the Accuracy of Stereotypes Within the Workplace," *Journal of Management,* 1990, *16:* 107–118.

19. Developed from R. Lacays, "Between Two Worlds," *Time,* March 13, 1989, 58–67; D. Kirkpatrick, "Is Your Career On Track?" *Fortune,* July 2, 1990, 38–48.

20. Developed from R. Walton and R. McKersie, *A Behavioral Theory of Labor Negotiations: An Analysis of a Social Interaction System* (New York: McGraw-Hill, 1965); R. Kilmann and K. Thomas, "Four Perspectives on Conflict Management: An Attributional Framework for Organizing Descriptive and Normative Theory," *Academy of Management Review,* 1978, *3:* 59–68.

21. T. P. Paré, "Passing on the Family Business," *Fortune,* May 7, 1990, 81–85; R. Koselka, F. Meeks, and L. Saunders, "Family Affairs," *Forbes,* December 11, 1989, 212–218.

22. R. R. Blake and J. S. Mouton, *Solving Costly Organizational Conflicts* (San Francisco, Calif.: Jossey-Bass, 1984); M. Deutsch, *The Resolution of Conflict: Constructive and Destructive Processes* (New Haven, Conn.: Yale University Press, 1973).

23. R. E. Walton, *Managing Conflict,* 2nd ed. (Reading, Mass.: Addison-Wesley, 1987).

24. R. Koselka, F. Meeks, and L. Saunders, "Family Affairs," *Forbes,* December 11, 1989, 212–218.

25. K. K. Smith, "The Movement of Conflict in Organizations: The Joint Dynamics of Splitting and Triangulation," *Administrative Science Quarterly,* 1989, *34:* 1–20.

26. Developed from J. Dutton and R. E. Walton, "Interdepartmental Conflict and Cooperation: Two Contrasting Studies," in J. W. Lorsch and P. R. Lawrence (eds.), *Managing Group and Intergroup Relations* (Homewood, Ill.: Richard D. Irwin and the Dorsey Press, 1972), 285–304.

27. A. C. Filley, *Interpersonal Conflict Resolution* (Glenview, Ill.: Scott, Foresman, 1975); R. R. Blake and J. S. Mouton, *Solving Costly Organizational Conflicts* (San Francisco: Jossey-Bass, 1984).

28. E. Van de Vliert and B. Kabanoff, "Toward Theory-Based Measures of Conflict Management," *Academy of Management Journal,* 1990, *33:* 199–209; R. Likert and J. G. Likert, *New Ways of Managing Conflict* (New York: McGraw-Hill, 1976); C. W. Lee, "Relative Status of Employees and Styles of Handling Interpersonal Conflict: An Experimental Study with Korean Managers," *International Journal of Conflict Management,* 1990, *1:* 327–340.

29. K. W. Thomas, "Conflict and Conflict Management," in M. D. Dunnette (ed.), *Handbook of Industrial and Organizational Psychology* (Chicago: Rand McNally, 1976), 889–935. *See also* G. Yukl and C. M. Falbe, "Influence Tactics and Objectives in Upward, Downward, and Lateral Influence Attempts," *Journal of Applied Psychology,* 1990, *75:* 132–140.

30. K. W. Thomas and R. H. Kilmann, "The Thomas–Kilmann Conflict Mode Instrument," in O. W. Cole (ed.), *Conflict Resolution Technology* (Cleveland: Organization Development Institute, 1983), 57–64.

31. P. B. Link, "How to Cope with Conflict Between the People Who Work for You," *Supervision,* January 1990, 7–9; B. Richardson, "The Zero-Sum Management Disease and the Von Thunen Prescription," *Business Horizons,* November-December 1984, 15–20.

32. Adapted from Allen R. Cohen and David L. Bradford, "Influence Without Authority: The Use of Alliances, Reciprocity, and Exchange to Accomplish Work," *Organizational Dynamics,* Winter 1989, 5–6.

33. *Ibid.,* 4–17.

34. N. C. Roberts, "Organizational Power Styles: Collective and Competitive Power Under Varying Conditions," *Journal of Applied Behavioral Science,* 1986, *22:* 443–458.

35. B. Kabanoff, "Conflict Management Styles: Why Is Compromise So Favourably Viewed?" *Australian Journal of Management,* 1989, *14:* 29–48.

36. R. J. Nobile, "Putting Out Fires with a No-Smoking Policy," *Personnel,* March 1990, 5–10.

37. M. Williams, "How I Learned to Stop Worrying and Love Negotiating," *Inc.,* September 1987, 132.

38. R. L. Pinkley, "Dimensions of Conflict Frame: Disputant Interpretations of Conflict," *Journal of Applied Psychology,* 1990, *75:* 117–126; R. A. Baron, S. P. Fortin, R. L. Frei, L. A. Hauver, and M. L. Shack, "Reducing Organizational Conflict: The Role of Socially-Induced Positive Affect," *International Journal of Conflict Management,* 1990, *1:* 133–152.

39. R. E. Walton, *Managing Conflict,* 2nd ed. (Reading, Mass.: Addison-Wesley, 1987); C. Brown and M. Reich, "When Does Union–Management Cooperation Work? A Look at NUMMI and GM–Van Nuys," *California Management Review,* Summer 1989, 26–44.

40. J. D. Blair, G. T. Savage, and C. J. Whitehead, "A Strategic Approach for Negotiating with Hospital Stakeholders," *Health Care Management Review,* 1989, *14*(1): 13–23; H. Prein, "A Contingency Approach for Conflict Intervention," *Group and Organization Studies,* 1984, *9:* 81–102.

41. J. A. Wall, Jr., *Negotiation: Theory and Practice* (Glenview, Ill.: Scott, Foresman, 1985); G. I. Nierenberg, *The Complete Negotiator* (New York: Nierenberg and Zeif, 1986).

42. L. Greenhalgh, "I Would Abandon Business Contracts," *Fortune,* March 26, 1990, 49. *See also* W. R. Pendergast, "Managing the Negotiation Agenda," *Negotiation Journal,* April 1990, 135–145.

43. T. D. Williams, "Making Cooperative Negotiations Work," *Arbitration Quarterly of the Northwest,* Spring 1990, 1–9; D. A. Lax and J. K. Sebenius, *The Manager as Negotiator: Bargaining for Cooperation and Mutual Gain* (New York: Free Press, 1987).

44. W. L. Ury, J. M. Brett, and S. B. Goldberg, *Getting Disputes Resolved* (San Francisco: Jossey-Bass, 1989).

45. R. P. Nielsen, "Generic Win–Win Negotiating Solutions," *Long Range Planning,* 1989, *22*(5): 137–143.

46. Developed from P. B. Link, "How to Cope with Conflict Between People Who Work for You," *Supervision,* January 1990, 7–9; J. R. Allison, "Five Ways to Keep Disputes Out of Court," *Harvard Business Review,* January-February 1990, 166–168, 172–177; R. Karambayya and J. M. Brett, "Managers Handling Disputes: Third-Party Roles and Perceptions of Fairness," *Academy of Management Journal,* 1989, *32:* 687–704.

47. F. B. Bird and J. A. Waters, "The Moral Muteness of Managers," *California Management Review,* Fall 1989, 73–88.

48. Adapted from J. H. Barnett and M. J. Karson, "Personal Values and Business Decisions: An Explanatory Investigation," *Journal of Business Ethics,* 1987, *6:* 371–382.

49. T. R. Mitchell and W. G. Scott, "America's Problems and Needed Reforms: Confronting the Ethic of Personal Advantage," *Academy of Management Executive,* 1990, *4:* 23–35; S. A. Culbert and J. J. McDonough, "Wrongful Termination and the Reasonable Manager: Balancing Fair Play and Effectiveness," *Sloan Management Review,* Summer 1990, 39–46.

50. H. Seyle, "The Stress Concept Today," in I. L. Kutash, L. B. Schlesinger, and Associates (eds.), *Handbook on Stress Anxiety* (San Francisco: Jossey-Bass, 1980), 127–143.

51. H. Seyle, "The Stress Concept Today," p. 128. *See also* J. Seeman, "Toward a Model of Positive Health," *American Psychologist,* 1989, *44:* 1099–1109.

52. J. C. Quick and J. D. Quick, *Organizational Stress and Preventive Management* (New York: McGraw-Hill, 1984), 1–14.

53. T. A. Stewart, "Do You Push Your People Too Hard?" *Fortune,* October 22, 1990, 121–128; C. W. Downs, G. Driskill, and D. Wuthnow, "A Review of Instrumentation on Stress," *Management Communication Quarterly,* 1990, *4:* 100–126; M. T. Matteson and J. M. Ivancevich, *Controlling Work Stress* (San Francisco: Jossey-Bass, 1987), 32–52.

54. J. R. Kofodimos, "Why Executives Lose Their Balance," *Organizational Dynamics,* Summer 1990, 58–73; J. C. Quick, D. L. Nelson, and J. D. Quick, *Stress and Challenge at the Top: The Paradox of the Successful Executive* (New York: Wiley, 1990).

55. Developed from T. Cox, *Stress* (Baltimore, Md.: University Park Press, 1978); S. J. Modic, "Surviving Burnout: The Malady of Our Age," *Industry Week,* February 20, 1989, 29–34.

56. H. F. Stallworth, "Realistic Goals Help Avoid Burnout," *HR Magazine,* June 1990, 169–171.

57. S. A. Joure, J. S. Leon, D. B. Simpson, C. H. Holley, and R. L. Frye, "Stress: The Pressure Cooker of Work," *Personnel Administrator,* March 1989, 92–95.

58. R. S. Bhagat, "Effects of Stressful Life Events on Individual Performance Effectiveness and Work Adjustment Processes within Organizational Settings: A Research Model," *Academy of Management Review,* 1983, *8:* 660–671; G. F. Koeske and R. D. Koeske, "Construct Validity of the Maslach Burnout Inventory: A Critical Review and Reconceptualization," *Journal of Applied Behavioral Science,* 1989, *25:* 131–144.

59. R. T. Golembiewski, R. Munzenrider, and D. Carter, "Phases of Progressive Burnout and Their Work Site Covariants: Critical Issues in OD Research and Praxis," *Journal of Applied Behavioral Science,* 1983, *19:* 461–481.

60. Adapted from J. Grossman, "Burnout," *Inc.,* September 1987, 89–96.

61. D. L. Nelson, J. C. Quick, and J. D. Quick,

"Corporate Warfare: Preventing Combat Stress and Battle Fatigue," *Organizational Dynamics,* Summer 1989, 65–79; P. J. Rosch, "Stressbusters," *Parade Magazine,* July 22, 1990, 12–13.

62. Developed from R. S. Eliot and D. L. Breo, *Is It Worth Dying For?* (New York: Bantam, 1984); R. Williams, *The Trusting Heart: Great News About Type A Behavior* (New York: Random House, 1989); D. O'Reilly, "New Truths About Staying Healthy," *Fortune,* September 25, 1989, 58–66; D. Swanbrow, "The Paradox of Happiness," *Psychology Today,* July-August 1989, 37–39.

63. M. Friedman and R. Roseman, *Type A Behavior and Your Heart* (New York: Knopf, 1974), 84. *See also* H. J. Eysenck, "Health's Character," *Psychology Today,* December 1988, 28–35.

64. A. A. McLean, *Work Stress* (Reading, Mass.: Addison-Wesley, 1979), 69.

65. R. A. Baron, "Personality and Organizational Conflict: Effects of the Type A Behavior Pattern and Self-Monitoring," *Organizational Behavior and Human Decision Processes,* 1989, *44:* 281–296.

66. N. Nykodym and K. George, "Stress Busting on the Job," *Personnel,* July 1989, 56–59; B. O'Reilly, "Is Your Company Asking Too Much?" *Fortune,* March 12, 1990, 39–46; D. S. Allen, "Less Stress, Less Litigation," *Personnel,* January 1990, 32–35.

67. J. S. House, *Work Stress and Social Support* (Reading, Mass.: Addison-Wesley, 1981), 23–24.

68. D. Etzion, "Moderating Effect of Social Support on the Stress–Burnout Relationship," *Journal of Applied Psychology,* 1984, *69:* 615–622; S. Jayaratne and W. A. Chess, "The Effects of Emotional Support on Perceived Job Stress and Strain," *Journal of Applied Behavioral Science,* 1984, *2:* 141–153.

69. M. Roberts and T. G. Harris, "Wellness at Work," *Psychology Today,* May 1989, 54–58; F. S. Rodgers and C. Rodgers, "Business and the Facts of Family Life," *Harvard Business Review,* November-December 1989, 121–129.

70. Developed from N. Templin, "Johnson & Johnson 'Wellness' Program for Workers Shows Healthy Bottom Line," *Wall Street Journal,* May 21, 1990, B1, B4: M. Roberts and T. G. Harris, "Wellness at Work," *Psychology Today,* May 1989, 54–58.

Skill-Building Exercise. Adapted from A. A. Zoll, III, *Explorations in Managing* (Reading, Mass.: Addison-Wesley, 1974). Based on a format suggested by Allen A. Zoll, III. Reprinted with permission.

Manager's Memo. Developed from D. T. Hall, "Moving Beyond the 'Mommy Track': An Organization Change Approach," *Personnel,* December 1989, 23–29; J. Smolowe, "When Jobs Clash," *Time,* September 23, 1990, 82–83.

In the News. Thomas F. O'Boyle, "Fear and Stress in the Office Talk Toll," *Wall Street Journal,* November 6, 1990, B1–B3.

Management Case. This case was prepared by J. David Hunger of Iowa State University, Thomas L. Wheelen of University of South Florida, and Richard M. Ayers, FBI Academy. Revised August 1989. Although the case recounts events that actually occurred, the names are changed. Copyright © 1989 by Thomas L. Wheelen, J. D. Hunger, and Richard M. Ayers.

Chapter 18

1. Adapted from F. Rice, "Why Kmart Has Stalled," *Fortune,* October 9, 1989, 79–80; R. F. Lusch, "Retail Control Systems for the 1990's," *Arthur Andersen Retailing Issues Letter,* January 1990; B. Saporito, "Is Wal-Mart Unstoppable?" *Fortune,* May 6, 1991, 50–59.

2. J. Rothfeder, M. Galen, and L. Driscoll, "Is Your Boss Spying on You?" *Business Week,* January 15, 1990, 74–75.

3. H. Mintzberg, *Mintzberg on Management* (New York: Free Press, 1989); J. A. Alexander, "Adaptive Change in Corporate Control Practices," *Academy of Management Journal,* 1991, *34:* 162–193.

4. G. W. Dalton, "Motivation and Control in Organizations," in G. W. Dalton and P. R. Lawrence (eds.), *Motivation and Control in Organizations* (Homewood, Ill.: Irwin, 1971), 1–35.

5. W. G. Ouchi and J. B. Johnson, "Types of Organizational Control and Their Relationship to Emotional Well Being," *Administrative Science Quarterly,* 1978, *23:* 293–317; S. Kerr and J. W. Slocum, Jr., "Controlling the Performances of People in Organizations," in P. C. Nystrom and W. H. Starbuck (eds.), *Handbook of Organizational Design: Remodeling Organizations and Their Environments* (New York: Oxford University Press, 1981), 116–135.

6. Adapted from K. J. Euske, *Management Control: Planning, Control, Measurement and Evaluation* (Reading, Mass.: Addison-Wesley, 1984), 44–45.

7. J. P. Walsh and J. K. Seward, "On the Efficiency of Internal and External Corporate Control Mechanisms," *Academy of Management Review,* 1990, *15:* 421–458.

8. T. W. Ferguson, "Motorola Aims High, So Motorolans Won't Be Getting High," *Wall Street Journal,* June 26, 1990, A19.

9. Adapted from D. N. Clayton, "Sniffing Out Fraud," *Mortgage Banking,* December 1989, 30–33.

10. V. Govindarajan and J. Fisher, "Strategy, Control Systems, and Resource Sharing: Effects on Business-Unit Performance," *Academy of Management Journal,* 1990, *33:* 259–285; M. Goold and J. J. Quinn, "The Paradox of Strategic Controls," *Strategic Management Journal,* 1990, *11:* 43–57.

11. T. Lowe and J. L. Machin, *New Perspectives on Management Control* (New York: Macmillan, 1987).

12. E. E. Lawler III and J. G. Rhode, *Information and Control in Organizations* (Pacific Palisades, Calif.: Goodyear, 1976).

13. Personal interview with John Semyan, partner, Tuttle, Neidhart & Seymon, Inc., July 1991.

14. W. J. Bruns, Jr., and F. W. McFarlan, "Information Technology Puts Power in Control Systems," *Harvard Business Review,* September-October 1987, 89–94.

15. Adapted from D. Machan, "Great Hash Browns, But Watch Those Biscuits," *Forbes,* September 19, 1988, 192–196.

16. W. G. Ouchi, "Markets, Bureaucracies, and Clans," *Administrative Science Quarterly,* 1980, *25:* 128–141.

17. For an excellent review of self-managed teams, see C. C. Manz and H. P. Sims, Jr., *SuperLeadership: Leading Others to Lead Themselves* (New York: Simon & Schuster, 1989).

18. Adapted from J. Hoerr, "The Cultural Revolution at A. O. Smith," *Business Week,* May 29, 1989, 66–68.

19. G. W. Florkowski, "The Organizational Impact of Profit Sharing," *Academy of Management Review,* 1987, *12:* 622–636.

20. J. Dearden, "Measuring Profit Center Managers," *Harvard Business Review,* September-October 1987, 84–88.

21. Adapted from A. D. Sharplin, "Lincoln Electric Company Case," *Forbes,* June 5, 1982, 51–52.

22. P. K. Mills, *Managing Service Industries* (Cambridge, Mass.: Ballinger, 1986).

23. S. Eilon, "Analysis of Corporate Performance," *Business and Economic Review,* Summer 1987, 20–29; V. Govindarajan and J. Fisher, "Strategy, Control Systems, and Resource Sharing: Effects on Business-Unit Performance," *Academy of Management Journal,* 1990, *33:* 259–285.

24. Personal conversation with Howard Johnson, J. C. Penney Corporation, Dallas, Texas, April 13, 1991.

25. B. Sord and G. Welsch, *Managerial Planning and Control* (Austin, Tex.: University of Texas Press, 1964), 93–99.

26. P. A. Pyhrr, *Zero-Based Budgeting: A Practical Tool for Evaluating Expense* (New York: Wiley, 1973).

27. D. Davis, "SMR Forum: Computers and Top Management," *Sloan Management Review,* Spring 1984, 63–67.

28. J. Rothfeder, M. Galen, and L. Driscoll, "Is Your Boss Spying on You?" *Business Week,* January 15, 1990, 74–75; B. Dumaine, "Corporate Spies Snoop to Conquer," *Fortune,* November 7, 1988, 68–76; M. McDonald, "They've Got Your Numbers," *Dallas Morning News,* April 7, 1991, F1.

29. Adapted from R. Gelbspan, "Critics Rip Electronic Monitoring," *Houston Chronicle,* December 6, 1987, Sec. 1, p. 15; C. Kleiman, "Spying through Computers," *Bryan–College Station Eagle,* December 27, 1987, 3E; H. J. Chalykoff and T. A. Kochan, "Computer-aided Monitoring: Its Influence on Employee Job Satisfaction and Turnover," *Personnel Psychology,* 1989, *42:* 807–834.

30. M. R. Carrell and C. Heavrin, "Before You Drug Test . . . ," *HR Magazine,* June, 1990, 64–68; K. R. Murphy, G. C. Thornton III, and D. H. Reynolds, "College Students' Attitudes toward Employee Drug Testing Programs," *Personnel Psychology,* 1990, *43:* 615–632; F. J. Tasco and A. J. Gajda, "Substance Abuse in the Workplace," *Compensation and Benefits Management,* Winter 1990, 140–144; M. A. McDaniel, "Does Pre-employment Drug Use Predict On-the-Job Suitability?" *Personnel Psychology,* 1988, *41:* 717–730.

31. "Preventing Crime on the Job," *Nation's Business,* July 1990, 36–37; N. H. Snyder and K. E. Blair, "Dealing with Employee Theft," *Business Horizons,* May-June 1989, 27–34.

32. R. C. Hollinger and J. P. Clark, *Theft by Employees* (Lexington, Mass.: Heath, 1983).

Skill-Building Exercise. Adapted from L. R. Jauch, S. A. Coltrin, A. G. Bedeian, and W. F. Glueck, *The Management Experience: Cases, Exercises, and Readings,* 4th ed. (Chicago, Ill: Dryden Press, 1986), 254–255.

In the News. Alix M. Freedman, "Campbell Chef Cooks Up Winning Menu," *Wall Street Journal,* February 15, 1991, B1–B6.

Management Case. Adapted from "Regina Co. Files Suit Seeking $25 Million from Ex-Chairman," *Wall Street Journal,* February 10, 1989, B4; A. Rothman, "Two Ex-Officers of Regina Plead Guilty of Fraud," *Wall Street Journal,* February 9, 1989, A14; A. Rothman, "How a Vacuum Salesman Got Swept Out," *Wall Street Journal,* November 11, 1988, B3; J. A. Byrne, "How Don Sheelen Made a Mess that Regina Couldn't Clean Up," *Business Week,* February 12, 1990, 46–50.

Chapter 19

1. Developed from J. Bartimo, "TI Bets Most of Its Marbles on Chips," *Business Week,* January 29, 1990, 73–74; T. Steinert-Threlkeld, "Texas Instruments Aiming for Success on a Global Scale," *Dallas Morning News,* October 28, 1989, 1F, 3F; J. Mitchell, "TI's Pulse," *Dallas Morning News,* July 28, 1987, H1, H2.

2. J. W. Verity, P. Coy, and J. Rothfeder, "Taming the Wild Network," *Business Week,* October 8, 1990, 142–148.

3. H. J. Leavitt and T. L. Whisler, "Management in the 1980's," *Harvard Business Review,* November-December 1958, 41–48.

4. M. Khosrowpour, "The Changing Role of Information Technology Services," *Review of Business,* Spring 1990, 11–15; J. Kanter, "New Tools, New Rules," *Information Strategy: The Executive's Journal,* Winter 1990, 51–54.

5. L. M. Applegate, J. I. Cash, Jr., and D. Q. Mills, "Information Technology and Tomorrow's Manager," *Harvard Business Review,* November-December 1988, 131; B. J. Risman and D. Tomaskovic-Devey, "The Social Construction of Technology: Microcomputers and the Organization of Work," *Business Horizons,* May-June 1989, 71–75.

6. P. F. Drucker, "The Coming of the New Organization," *Harvard Business Review,* January-February 1988, 45–53; R. E. Umbaugh, "ISM Interviews . . . Peter F. Drucker," *Journal of Information Systems Management,* Winter 1987, 91–96.

7. S. L. Huff, "Information Technology and the Future Organization," *Business Quarterly,* Summer 1989, 94–96; D. K. Rossetti and F. A. DeZoort, "Organizational Adaptation to Technology Innovation," *SAM Advanced Management Journal,* Autumn 1989, 29–33; L. M. Applegate, J. I. Cash, Jr., and D. Q. Mills, "Information Technology and Tomorrow's Manager," *Harvard Business Review,* November-December 1988, 129; P. Hodges, "The Application Decade Begins," *Datamation,* January 15, 1990, 23–30; "Information Technology and the Changing Workplace: An Interview with Shoshana Zuboff," *Personnel,* June 1989, 26.

8. T. C. E. Cheng, "Toward a Policy Framework for Business Information Resources Management," *IMDS,* January-February 1987, 5–8.

9. G. W. Fairholm, "A Reality Basis for Management Information Systems Decisions," *Public Administration Review,* 1979, *39:* 176–179.

10. R. H. Gregory and R. L. Van Horn, "Value and Cost of Information," in J. D. Couger and R. W. Knapp (eds.), *Systems Analysis Techniques* (New York: Wiley, 1974), 473–489. *See also* J. C. Wetherbe, *Systems Analysis for Computer-based Information Systems* (St. Paul: West Publishing, 1979), 37–39.

11. C. A. O'Reilly III, "Individuals and Information Overload in Organizations: Is More Necessarily Better?" *Academy of Management Journal,* 1980, *23:* 684–696.

12. M. J. McCarthy, "No Place to Hide," *Wall Street Journal Reports,* November 9, 1990, R23–R25.

13. "Managing Information Technology Separates Winners From Losers," *Management Review,* July 1989, 9–10; R. Lane and R. Hall, "Yes, There Is a Way to Measure MIS Investments," *Business Monthly,* August 1989, 73.

14. R. M. Stair, Jr., *Computers in Today's World* (Homewood, Ill.: Irwin, 1986).

15. Developed from D. A. Armstrong, "How Rockwell Launched Its EIS," *Datamation,* March 1, 1990, 69–72; T. H. Davenport, and J. E. Short, "The New Industrial Engineering: Information Technology and Business Process Redesign," *Sloan Management Review,* Summer 1990, 11–17.

16. "Information Systems Services: Keys to Success in the '90s," *Fortune,* special advertising section, June 4, 1990, unpaginated.

17. E. M. von Simson, "The 'Centrally Decentralized' IS Organization," *Harvard Business Review,* July-August 1990, 55–62.

18. E. Dyson, "Coordination Technology," *Forbes,* August 8, 1988, 96.

19. T. J. O'Leary and B. K. Williams, *Computers and Information Systems,* 2nd ed. (Redwood City, Calif.: Benjamin-Cummings, 1989), 434.

20. R. W. Stone, "The Use of Expert Systems in Service Industries: Financial Services Examples," *Review of Business,* Spring 1990, 17–20; D. B. Hertz, *The Expert Executive: Using AI and Expert Systems for Financial Management, Marketing, Production, and Strategy* (New York: Wiley, 1988); D. Pigford and G. Baur, *Expert Systems for Business: Concepts and Applications* (Cincinnati, Ohio: South-Western, 1990).

21. M. H. Meyer and K. F. Curley, "Putting Expert Systems to Work," *Sloan Management Review,* Winter 1991, 21–31.

22. G. P. Huber, "Issues in the Design of Group Decision Support Systems," *MIS Quarterly, 8(3),* 1984, 195–204.

23. F. Ackerman, "The Role of Computers in Group Decision Support," in C. Eden and J. Radford (eds.), *Tackling Strategic Problems: The Role of Group Decision Support* (Newbury Park, Calif.: Sage, 1990), 132–141.

24. J. L. Whitten, L. D. Bentley, and T. I. M. Ho, *Systems Analysis & Design Methods* (St. Louis, Mo.: Times Mirror/Mosby College, 1986), 50–56; J. C. Henderson, "Plugging into Strategic Partnership: The Critical IS Connection," *Sloan Management Review,* Spring 1990, 7–18.

25. J. C. Carter and F. N. Silverman, "Establishing a MIS," *Journal of Systems Management,* July 1980, *31:*15.

26. G. A. Gorry and M. S. Scott Morton, "SMR Classic Reprint: A Framework for Management Information Systems," *Sloan Management Review,* Spring 1989, 49–61; R. N. Anthony, *Planning and Control Systems: A Framework for Analysis* (Boston: Harvard Business School Division of Research Press, 1965).

28. D. A. Armstrong, "How Rockwell Launched Its EIS," *Datamation,* March 1, 1990, 69–71.

29. R. G. Murdick, "MIS Development Procedures," *Journal of Systems Management,* 1970, *21(12):* 36–39.

30. R. L. Heckman, "Managing the Risks of Investing in Information Technology," *Bankers Magazine,* November-December 1989, 18.

31. W. Adriaans and J. T. Hoogakker, "Planning an Information System at Netherlands Gas," *Long Range Planning,* 1989, *22(3):* 64–74.

32. R. A. Rademacher, "Critical Factors for System Success," *Journal of Systems Management,* June 1989, 15–17; M. J. Cerullo, "Information Systems Success Factors," *Journal of Systems Management,* December 1980, 11; H. C. Lucas, Jr., *Why Information Systems Fail* (New York: Columbia University Press, 1975); D. Robey, "User Attitudes and Management Information System Use," *Academy of Management Journal,* 1979, *22:* 527–538.

33. J. Main, "At Last, Software CEOs Can Use," *Fortune,* March 13, 1989, 77–83.

34. J. W. Verity, P. Coy, and J. Rothfeder, "Taming the Wild Network," *Business Week,* October 8, 1990, 141–148.

35. R. L. Ackoff, "Management Misinformation Systems," *Management Science,* 1967, *14:* 18–21.

36. L. A. Mainiero and R. L. DeMichiell, "Minimizing Employee Resistance to Technological Change," *Personnel,* July 1986, 32–37; R. D. Hodge, "Integrating Systems," *Journal of Systems Management,* August 1989, 18–20.

37. R. Aeh, "Technology Integration, Agents of Change and a New IS Culture," *Journal of Systems Management,* October 1989, 20–26; J. Main, "Computers of the World Unite!" *Fortune,* September 24, 1990, 115–122.

38. D. K. Rossetti and F. A. DeZoort, "Organizational Adaptation to Technology Innovation," *SAM Advanced Management Journal,* Autumn 1989, 29–33; P. Faerstein, "Fighting Computer Anxiety," *Personnel,* January 1986, 12–17; A. K. Baronas and M. R. Louis, "Restoring a Sense of Control during Implementation: How Users Involvement Leads to System Acceptance," *MIS Quarterly,* March 1988, 89–94.

39. L. A. Mainiero and R. L. DeMichiell, "Minimizing Employee Resistance to Technological Change," *Personnel,* July 1986, 32–37; G. W. Dickson and J. K. Simmons, "The Behavioral Side of MIS," *Business Horizons,* August 1978, 68.

40. S. Kiesler, J. Siegel, and T. W. McGuire, "Social Psychological Aspects of Computer-Mediated Communication," *American Psychologist,* 1984, *39:* 1123–1134.

41. C. Argyris, "Management Information Systems: The Challenges to Rationality and Emotionality," *Management Science,* 1971, *17:* B-281.

42. D. K. Rossetti and F. A. DeZoort, "Organizational Adaptation to Technology Innovation," *SAM Advanced Management Journal,* Autumn 1989, 29–33; C. Brod, "Managing Technostress: Optimizing the Use of Computer Technology," *Personnel Journal,* 1982, *61:* 754; C. Brod, "How to Deal with Technostress," *Office Administration and Automation,* August 1984, 28*ff.*

43. S. Caminiti, "What the Scanner Knows about You," *Fortune,* December 3, 1990, 51–52.

44. M. J. McCarthy, "No Place to Hide," *Wall Street Journal Reports,* November 9, 1990, R23–R25.

Skill-Building Exercise. Adapted from T. J. O'Leary and B. K. Williams, *Computers and Information Systems,* 2nd ed. (Redwood City, Calif.: Benjamin-Cummings, 1989), 55.

In the News. Michael W. Miller, "Data Mills Delve Deep to Find Information about U.S. Consumers," *Wall Street Journal,* March 14, 1991, A1–A12.

Management Case. Developed from D. Kunde, "In The Chips: Frito-Lay Data System Feed Ideas for Boosting Sales to Employees," *Dallas Morning News,* July 29, 1990, H1–H2; J. Main, "Computers of the World, Unite!" *Fortune,* September 24, 1990, 115–122; R. Johnson, "In The Chips," *Wall Street Journal Reports,* March 22, 1991, B1–B2.

Chapter 20

1. Adapted from D. T. Kearns, "Leadership through Quality," *Academy of Management Executive,* May 1990, 86–89.

2. L. L. Krajewski and L. R. Ritzman, *Operations Management: Strategy and Analysis,* 2nd ed. (Reading, Mass.: Addison-Wesley, 1990), 2.

3. Kearns, "Leadership through Quality," 88. *See also* D. E. Bowen, R. B. Chase, T. G. Cummings, and associates, *Service Management Effectiveness* (San Francisco: Jossey-Bass, 1990).

4. D. W. Fogerty, J. H. Blackstone, and T. R. Hoffman, *Production and Inventory Management* (Cincinnati, Ohio: South-Western, 1990); E. E. Adams, Jr., "Towards a Typology of Production and Operations Management Systems," *Academy of Management Review,* 1983, *8:* 353–375.

5. Krajewski and Ritzman, *Operations Management: Strategy and Analysis,* 2–5.

6. Committee for Economic Development, *Productivity Policy: Key to the Nation's Economic Future* (New York: Committee for Economic Development, 1983), 23.

7. P. Petre, "Lifting American Competitiveness," *Fortune,* April 23, 1990, 56–66; J. Carey, "The Myth That America Can't Compete,"*Business Week,* June 15, 1990, 44–48; S. C. Cohen and J. Zysman, *Manufacturing Matters: The Myth of the Post-Industrial Economy* (New York: Basic Books, 1987).

8. H. E. Edmondson and S. C. Wheelwright, "Outstanding Manufacturing in the Coming Decade," *California Management Review,* Summer 1989, 70–90; O. Port, "The Productivity Paradox," *Business Week,* June 6, 1988, 100–113.

9. R. L. Harmon and L. D. Peterson, *Reinventing the Factory: Productivity Breakthroughs in Manufacturing Today* (New York: Free Press, 1990).

10. D. H. Ciscel and L. S. Lewis, "The Meaning of Productivity," *Mid-South Business Journal,* April 1987, 17–20.

11. J. L. Riggs and G. H. Felix, *Productivity by Objectives* (Englewood Cliffs, N.J.: Prentice-Hall, 1983).

12. Adapted from S. Samiee, "Productivity Planning and Strategy in Retailing," *California Management Review,* Winter 1990, 54–76.

13. L. J. Krajewski and L. P. Ritzman, *Operations Management: Strategy and Analysis,* 2nd ed. (Reading, Mass.: Addison-Wesley, 1990); J. R. Evans, D. R. Anderson and T. A. Williams, *Applied Production and Operations Management,* 3rd ed. (St. Paul, Minn.: West Publishing, 1990); N. Gaither, *Production and Operations Management,* 4th ed. (New York: Dryden Press, 1990).

14. Krajewski and Ritzman, *Operations Management: Strategy and Analysis,* 15–25.

15. W. J. Spencer, "Research to Product: A Major U.S. Challenge," *California Management Review,* Winter 1990, 45–53.

16. R. L. Long, *New Office Information Technology: Human and Managerial Implications* (London: Croom Helm, 1987).

17. J. A. Lopez, "Cellular Phone Concerns Step Up Effort to Get Ordinary Concerns On the Line," *Wall Street Journal,* September 24, 1990, B1.

18. Developed from S. Advokat, "Office Gear on the Go," *Nation's Business,* November 1989, 56–60; L. Therrien, "The Rival Japan Respects," *Business Week,* November 13, 1989, 108–118.

19. J. B. Quinn, T. L. Doorley, and P. C. Paquette, "Beyond Products: Services-Based Strategies," *Harvard Business Review,* March-April 1990, 58–60ff; M. Hammer, "Reengineering Work: Don't Automate, Obliterate," *Harvard Business Review,* July-August 1990, 104–112.

20. J. M. Hill, "New Families of Identification Systems Feature Modularity and Growing Standardization," *Industrial Engineering,* September 1986, 52–54.

21. J. B. Quinn, T. L. Doorly, and P. C. Paquette, "Technology in Services: Rethinking Strategic Focus," *Sloan Management Review,* Winter 1990, 79–87; D. G. Luckett, "On the Computerization of Finance," *Business Horizons,* November-December, 1989, 42–46.

22. Adapted from J. B. Quinn and P. C. Paquette, "Technology in Services: Creating Organizational Revolutions," *Sloan Management Review,* Winter 1990, 67–78.

23. P. C. Goodman, L. S. Sproull, and associates, *Technology and Organizations* (San Francisco: Jossey-Bass, 1990).

24. J. Baranson, *Robots in Manufacturing: Key to International Competitiveness* (Mt. Airy, Md.: Lomand Publications, 1983).

25. B. D. Nordwall, "Reconfigurable Robot, Vision Systems Key to Improved Industrial Productivity," *Aviation Week & Space Technology,* May 21, 1990, 111–115.

26. D. E. Whitney, "Real Robots Do Need Jigs," *Harvard Business Review,* May-June 1986, 110–116.

27. R. H. Mitchell and V. A. Mabert, "Robotics for Smaller Manufacturers: Myths and Realities," *Business Horizons,* July-August 1986, 9–16.

28. A. Tanzer and R. Simon, "Why Japan Loves Robots and We Don't," *Forbes,* April 6, 1990, 148–153.

29. L. Kuzela, "Here Comes the Automated Manager," *Industry Week,* November 20, 1989, 45–46.

30. Tanzer and Simon, "Why Japan Loves Robots and We Don't."

31. G. Bylinsky, "Invasion of the Service Robots," *Fortune,* September 14, 1987, 81–88; Y. Shirai, "Advanced Robot Technology Project," *Techno Japan,* September 1986, 4–17.

32. G. I. Susman, J. W. Dean, Jr., and S. Joon Yoon, "Advanced Manufacturing Technology and Organizations: A Study of 185 Pennsylvania Firms in Six Metal-Working Industries," Center for the Management of Technological and Organizational Change, Pennsylvania State University, University Park, August 1988.

33. B. Gold, "Computerization in Domestic, and International Manufacturing," *California Management Review,* Winter 1989, 129–143.

34. O. Port, "Smart Factories: America's Turn?" *Business Week,* May 8, 1989, 142–148.

35. Developed from O. Port, "A Smarter Way to Manufacture," *Business Week,* April 30, 1990, 110–117; D. Brousell and C. Sivula, "NCR's Exley: Build Bridges to Open Systems," *Datamation,* May 15, 1990, 68–70.

36. D. Lei and J. D. Goldhar, "Multiple Niche Competition—The Strategic Use of CIM Technology," *Manufacturing Review,* forthcoming _____; B. Avishai, "A CEO's Common Sense of CIM: An Interview with J. Tracy O'Rourke," *Harvard Business Review,* January-February 1989, 110–117.

37. P. F. Drucker, "The Engineering Theory of Manufacturing," *Harvard Business Review,* May-June 1990, 94–102.

38. D. Gerwin, "Manufacturing Flexibility in the CAM Era," *Business Horizons,* January-February 1989, 78–84; R. Venkatesan, "Cummins Engine Flexes Its Factory," *Harvard Business Review,* March-April 1990, 120–127.

39. D. Kearns, "Leadership through Quality," *Academy of Management Executive,* May 1990, 87.

40. F. F. Reichheld and W. E. Sasser, Jr., "Zero Defections: Quality Comes to Services," *Harvard Business Review,* September-October 1990, 105–111; S. W. Brown, E. Gummesson, B. Edvardsson, and B. Gustavsson, *Service Quality: Multidisciplinary and Multinational Perspectives* (Lexington, Mass.: Lexington Books, 1991).

41. B. T. Gale and R. D. Buzzell, "Market Perceived Quality: Key Strategic Concept," *Planning Review,* March-April, 1989, 6–12.

42. P. Sellers, "What Customers Really Want," *Fortune,* June 4, 1990, 58–68.

43. D. Kearns, "Leadership through Quality," 86.

44. J. Castro, "Making It Better," *Time,* November 13, 1989, 78–81.

45. L. S. Vansina, "Total Quality Control: An Overall Organizational Improvement Strategy," *National Productivity Review,* 1989/90, *9:* 59–73.

46. J. Main, "How to Win the Baldridge Award," *Fortune,* April 23, 1990, 101–116; N. J. De Carlo and W. K. Sterett, "History of the Malcolm Baldridge National Quality Award," *Quality Progress,* March 1990, 21–27.

47. P. E. Plesk, "Defining Quality at the Marketing/Development Interface," *Quality Process,* June 1987, 28–36; M. J. Austin and W. B. Newsom, "Can Service Performance Be Accurately Measured Using Manufacturing Methods?" in D. F. Ray (ed.), *Southern Management Association Proceedings* (Mississippi State, Miss.: Southern Management Association, 1987), 307–309.

48. D. A. Garvin, "What Does Product Quality Really Mean?" *Sloan Management Review,* Fall 1984, 25–39; D. A. Garvin, "Competing on the Eight Dimensions of Quality," *Harvard Business Review,* November-December 1987, 101–109.

49. W. E. Deming, *Out of the Crises* (Cambridge, Mass.: MIT Center for Advanced Engineering Study, 1986).

50. H. M. Wadsworth, K. S. Stephens, and A. B. Godfrey, *Quality Control* (New York: Wiley, 1986).

51. J. Oberle, "Quality Gurus: The Men and Their Message," *Training,* January 1990, 47–52.

52. M. Walton, *The Deming Management Method* (New York: Dodd, Mead, 1986).

53. D. Halberstam, "Yes We Can," *Parade Magazine,* July 8, 1984, 5.

54. W. J. Duncan and J. G. Van Matre, "The Gospel According to Deming: Is It Really New?" *Business Horizons,* July-August 1990, 3–9; W. W. Scherkenbach, *The Deming Route to Quality and Productivity: Roadmaps and Roadblocks* (Milwaukee: American Society for Quality Control, 1986).

55. C. Boisseau, "Family-Run Firm in Houston Wins National Award," *Houston Chronicle,* October 11, 1990, B1, B5; J. Main, "How to Win the Baldridge Award," *Fortune,* April 23, 1990, 101–116.

56. *1990 Application Guidelines: Malcolm Baldridge National Quality Award* (Washington, D.C.: United States Department of Commerce, 1990).

57. R. Henkoff, "What Motorola Learns From Japan," *Fortune,* April 24, 1989, 157–168.

58. Developed from J. Main, "How to Win the Baldridge Award," *Fortune,* April 23, 1990, 101–116; K. R. Bhote, "Motorola's Long March to the Malcolm Baldridge National Quality Award," *National Productivity Review,* 1989, *8:* 365–375; W. Wiggenhorn, "Motorola U: When Training Becomes an Education, *Harvard Business Review,* July-August 1990, 71–83.

59. P. Gupta, J. D. Macry, E. Pena, and G. Westerman, "A Systematic Approach to SPC Implementation," *Quality Progress,* April 1987, 22–25.

60. G. Preston, "Management Aspects of Statistical Process Control Implementation," *Quality Assurance,* March 1987, 5–9.

61. K. T. Krantz, "How Velcro Got Hooked on Quality," *Harvard Business Review,* September-October 1989, 34–38ff.

62. J. Main, "The Battle for Quality Begins," *Fortune,* December 24, 1980, 29. *See also* S. A. Hopkins, "Have U.S. Financial Institutions Really Embraced Quality Control?" *National Productivity Review,* 1989, *8:* 407–420.

63. Adapted from L. L. Berry, V. A. Zeithaml, and A. Parasuraman, "Five Imperatives for Improving Service Quality," *Sloan Management Review,* Summer 1990, 29–38; V. A. Zeithaml, A. Parasuraman, and L. L. Berry, *Delivering Quality Service: Balancing Customer Perceptions and Expectations* (New York: Free Press, 1990).

64. D. W. Fogerty, J. H. Blackstone, Jr., and T. R. Hoffman, *Production and Inventory Management,* 2nd ed. (Cincinnati, Ohio: South-Western, 1990).

65. R. B. Chase and N. J. Aquilano, *Production and Operations Management: A Life Cycle Approach,* 5th ed. (Homewood, Ill.: Irwin, 1989).

66. J. D. Wisner, "The MRP–JIT System: A Recent Manufacturing Phenomenon," in S. J. Hartman (ed.), *Proceedings of the Southwest Division of the Academy of Management* (Dallas, Tex.: Southwest Division of Academy of Management, 1990), 199–202.

67. P. Duchessi, C. M. Schaninger, D. R. Hobbs, "Implementing a Manufacturing Planning and Control Information System," *California Management Review,* Spring 1989, 75–90; G. Merli, *Total Manufacturing Management: Production Organization for the 90's* (Cambridge, Mass.: Productivity Press, 1990).

68. U. Karmarkar, "Getting Control of Just-in-Time," *Harvard Business Review,* September-October 1989, 122–131.

69. R. J. Schonberger, *World Class Manufacturing* (New York: Free Press, 1986); T. F. Lyons, A. R. Krachenberg, and J. W. Henke, Jr., "Mixed Motive Marriages: What's Next for Buyer-Supplier Relations?" *Sloan Management Review,* Spring 1990, 29–36.

70. R. Landeros and R. M. Monczka, "Cooperative Buyer/Seller Relationships and Firms Competitive Posture," *Journal of Purchasing and Materials Management,* Fall 1989, 9–18; D. M. Lascelles and B. G. Dale, "The Buyer-Supplier Relationship in Total Quality Management," *Journal of Purchasing and Materials Management,* Summer 1989, 10–19.

71. D. N. Burt, "Managing Suppliers Up to Speed," *Harvard Business Review,* July-August, 1989, 127–135; A. Ansari and B. Modarress, *Just-In-Time Purchasing* (New York: Free Press, 1990).

72. J. A. Klein, "The Human Costs of Manufacturing Reform," *Harvard Business Review,* March-April 1989, 60–61ff.

73. Adapted from G. Schwind, "Chrysler Windsor: A Plant in a Hurry to Turn Out Vans in a Hurry," *Materials Handling Engineering,* November 1984, 50–54.

Manager's Memo. Adapted from Daniel Stoffman, "Learning the Hard Way," *Canadian Business,* July 1987, 79–81. Used with permission.

In the News. Joseph B. White, "'Value Pricing' is Hot as Shrewd Consumers Seek Low-Cost Quality," *Wall Street Journal,* March 12, 1991, A1–A9.

Management Case. Adapted from L. J. Krajewski and L. P. Ritzman, *Operations Management,* 54–58. Copyright © 1987, Addison-Wesley Publishing Co., Inc., Reading, Mass. Adapted and reprinted with permission.

Chapter 21

1. Adapted from R. Mitchell, "Mining the Work Force for Ideas," *Business Week,* special edition on innovation, 1989, 121; P. F. Drucker, "The Emerging Theory of Manufacturing," *Harvard Business Review,* May-June 1990, 94–102.

2. J. Weber, "A Culture That Just Keeps Dishing Up Success," *Business Week,* special edition on innovation, 1989, 120.

3. P. M. Senge, *The Fifth Discipline* (New York: Doubleday, 1990). *See also* J. G. March, "Exploration and Exploitation in Organizational Learning," *Organization Science,* 1991, *2:* 71–88; G. P. Huber, "Organizational Learning: The Contribution Processes and the Literature," *Organization Science,* 1991, *2:* 88–115; K. E. Weick, "The Nontraditional Quality of Organizational Learning," *Organization Science,* 1991, *2:* 116–124; M. D. Cohen, "Individual Learning and Organizational Routine: Emerging Connections," *Organization Science,* 1991, *2:* 135–139.

4. J. Main, "The Winning Organization," *Fortune,* September 26, 1988, 50–51; S. Andrews, "America's Most Powerful Businessman: What Citi's John Reed Sees That Other Bankers Don't," *Manhattan, Inc.,* May 1990, 61–69.

5. J. Fierman, "Why Women Still Don't Hit the Top," *Fortune,* July 30, 1990, 40*ff.* An entire issue of the *Journal of Business Ethics,* April/May 1990, was dedicated to exploring issues facing women in organizations: see, for example, A. Gregory, "Are Women Different and Why Women Are Thought to Be Different," 257–266; and C. Andrews, C. Coderre, and A. Denis, "Stop and Go: Reflections of Women Managers on Factors Influencing Their Career Development," 361–368.

6. D. Kirkpatrick, "Is Your Career on Track?" *Fortune,* July 2, 1990, 39*ff;* D. C. Feldman, "Careers in Organizations: Recent Trends and Future Directions," *Journal of Management,* 1989, *15:* 136–156.

7. J. Dreyfuss, "Get Ready for the New Work Force," *Fortune,* April 23, 1990, 165*ff;* D. Kunde, "Gold Watch Loses Allure in Changing Workplace," *Dallas Morning News,* July 31, 1990, D1*ff.*

8. P. Hirsch, *Pack Your Own Parachute: How to Survive Mergers, Takeovers, and Other Corporate Disasters* (Reading, Mass.: Addison-Wesley, 1987); B. Burrough and J. Helyar, *Barbarians at the Gate* (New York: Harper & Row, 1990).

9. J. A. Raelin, "An Anatomy of Autonomy: Managing Professionals," *Academy of Management Executive,* 1989, *3:* 216–228; R. Drazin, "Professionals and Innovation: Structural-Functional versus Radical Structural Perspectives," *Journal of Management Studies,* 1990, *27:* 245–264.

10. G. Pinchot, III, *Intrapreneuring* (New York: Harper & Row, 1985); R. D. Hisrich, "Entrepreneurship/Intrapreneurship," *American Psychologist,* 1990, *45:* 209–222.

11. S. Tully, "Doing Business in One Germany," *Fortune,* July 2, 1990, 79*ff;* G. Hamel and C. K. Prahalad, "Managing in a Global Environment: Strategic Intent," *McKinsey Quarterly,* Spring 1990, 62–74; R. Dale, "The Changing Map of Europe," *Europe,* July/August 1990, 9–11; D. Lei and J. W. Slocum, Jr., "Global Strategic Alliances: Payoffs and Pitfalls," *Organizational Dynamics,* Winter 1991, 44–62; R. L. Tung, "Handshakes across the Sea: Cross-Cultural Negotiating for Business Success," *Organizational Dynamics,* Winter 1991, 30–43.

12. R. E. Hoskisson and T. A. Turk, "Corporate Restructuring: Governance and Control Limits of the Internal Capital Market," *Academy of Management Review,* 1990, *15:* 459–477; C. Hamel, Y. L. Doz, and C. K. Prahalad, "Collaborate with Your Competitors and Win," *Harvard Business Review,* January-February 1989, 133–139.

13. I. C. Magaziner and M. Patinkin, "Fast Heat: How Korea Won the Microwave War," *Harvard Business Review,* January-February 1989, 83–92; R. M. Steers, Y. K. Shin, and G. R. Ungson, *The Chaebol* (New York: Ballinger, 1989).

14. W. R. Grace, *10-K Report,* December 31, 1990.

15. Adapted from J. P. Kotter, "What Leaders Really Do," *Harvard Business Review,* May-June 1990, 110.

16. A. H. Van de Ven and G. P. Huber, "Longitudinal Field Research Methods for Studying Processes of Organizational Change," *Organization Science,* 1990, *1:* 213–220; R. A. D'Aveni and J. W. Cassell, "Crisis and Content of Managerial Communications: A Study of the Focus of Attention of Top Managers in Surviving and Failing Firms," *Administrative Science Quarterly,* 1990, *35:* 634–657.

17. J. Sculley, *Odyssey* (New York: Harper & Row, 1987).

18. P. F. Drucker, *The New Realities: In Government and Politics/In Economics and Business/In Society and World View* (New York: Harper & Row, 1989).

19. Magaziner and Patinkin, "Fast Heat," 83–92.

20. J. P. Kotter and L. A. Schlesinger, "Choosing Strategies for Change," *Harvard Business Review,* March-April 1979, 106–114; J. M. Howell, "Champions of Change: Identifying, Understanding, and Supporting Champions of Technological Innovations," *Organizational Dynamics,* Summer 1990, 40–57.

21. Adapted from A. Kupfer, "An Outsider Fires Up a Railroad," *Fortune,* December 18, 1989, 133*ff.*

22. R. Beckhard and R. T. Harris, *Organizational Transitions,* 2nd ed. (Reading, Mass.: Addison-Wesley, 1987).

23. Interview with Harold Ashby, Vice-President of Human Resources, Oryx Corporation, Dallas, Texas, April 1991.

24. E. F. Huse and T. G. Cummings, *Organizational Development and Change,* 4th ed. (St. Paul, Minn.: West Publishing, 1989); A. M. Pettigrew, "Longitudinal Field Research on Change: Theory and Practice," *Organization Science,* 1990, *1:* 266–292.

25. A. H. Van de Ven and M. S. Poole, "Methods for Studying Innovation Development in the Minnesota Innovation Research Program," *Organization Science,* 1990, *1:* 313–335; A. Van de Ven, H. L. Angle, and M. S. Poole, *Research on the Management of Innovation* (New York: Harper Business, 1990).

26. M. Beer and E. Walton, "Developing the Competitive Organization: Interventions and Strategies," *American Psychologist,* 1990, *45:* 154–161; M. Jelinek and C. B. Schoonhoven, *The Innovation Marathon* (Cambridge, Mass.: Basil Blackwell, 1990).

27. T. H. Davenport and J. E. Short, "The New Industrial Engineering: Information Technology and Business Process Design," *Sloan Management Review,* Summer 1990, 11–25.

28. Adapted from Davenport and Short, "The New Industrial Engineering"; Z. Schiller, "Big Blue's Big Overhaul," *Business Week,* special edition on innovation, 1989, 147.

29. Adapted from P. E. Cole, "Simpler Designs, Simpler Factories," *Business Week,* special edition on innovation, 1989, 150.

30. For a comprehensive list of organization development methods, see Huse and Cummings, *Organizational Development and Change.* See also I. L. Goldstein, *Training in Organizations: Needs Assessment, Development and Education* (Pacific Grove, Calif.: Brooks-Cole, 1989).

31. R. B. Dunham and F. J. Smith, *Organizational Surveys* (Glenview, Ill.: Scott, Foresman, 1979).

32. W. G. Dyer, *Team Building: Issues and Alternatives,* 2nd ed. (Reading, Mass.: Addison-Wesley, 1987).

33. Adapted from Dyer, *Team Building,* 33–35.

Skill-Building Exercise. Adapted from J. E. Ettlie and R. D. O'Keefe, "Innovative Attitudes, Values, and Intentions in Organizations," *Journal of Management Studies,* 1982, *19,* 176.

Manager's Memo. Adapted from O. Port, "A Smarter Way to Manufacture," *Business Week,* April 30, 1990, 110–117.

In the News. Bob Hagerty, "Firms in Europe Try to Find Executives Who Can Cross Borders in a Single Bound," *Wall Street Journal,* January 25, 1991, B1–B2.

Management Case. Adapted from B. Buell, "Hewlett-Packard Rethinks Itself," *Business Week,* April 1, 1991, 76–79.

Chapter 22

1. Adapted from G. Gendron and B. Burlingham, "The Entrepreneur of the Decade," *Inc.,* April 1989, 114–128; R. Brandt, "So Far, So-So for Steve Jobs's New Machine," *Business Week,* January 29, 1990, 76–77; "Steve Jobs to Announce What's Next for Next Inc." *Dallas Morning News,* September 18, 1990, D-21.

2. A. C. Cooper, "The Role of the Incubator Organizations in the Founding of Growth-Oriented Firms," *Journal of Business Venturing,* 1985, *1:* 75–86.

3. R. D. Hisrich, "Entrepreneurship/Intrapreneurship," *American Psychologist,* 1990, *45:* 209–222.

4. J. L. Ward, *Keeping the Family Business Healthy* (San Francisco, Calif.: Jossey-Bass, 1988).

5. B. Uttal, "Behind the Fall of Steve Jobs," *Fortune,* August 5, 1985, 20–24; J. Sculley, *Odyssey* (New York: Harper & Row, 1987).

6. J. Case, "The Origins of Entrepreneurship," *Inc.,* June 1989, 51–63; M. Hennig and A. Jardim, *The Managerial Woman* (Garden City, N.Y.: Anchor Press/Doubleday, 1977).

7. "Sagas of Five Who Made It," *Time,* February 15, 1982, 42–44; G. Carroll, "Business Moguls on Campus," *Georgia Trend,* September 1985, 60–66; G. Gregg, "Women Entrepreneurs: The Second Generation," *Across the Board,* January 1985, 10–18.

8. C. C. Ryans, *Managing the Small Business* (Englewood Cliffs, N.J.: Prentice-Hall, 1989); *Economic Report to the President: Council of Economic Advisors* (Washington, D.C.: U.S. Government Printing Office, 1990).

9. R. D. Hisrich and M. P. Peters, *Entrepreneurship: Starting, Developing, and Managing a New Enterprise* (Homewood, Ill.: BPI/Irwin, 1989); W. B. Gartner, "What Are We Talking About When We Talk About Entrepreneurship?" *Journal of Business Venturing,* 1990, *5:* 15–28.

10. D. C. McClelland, "Characteristics of Successful Entrepreneurs," *Journal of Creative Behavior,* 1987, *21* (3): 219–233; R. B. Johnson, "Toward a Multidimensional Model of Entrepreneurship: The Case of Achievement Motivation and the Entrepreneur," *Entrepreneurship Theory and Practice,* 1990, *14*(3): 39–54.

11. J. W. Carland, F. Hoy, W. R. Boulton, and J. C. Carland, "Differentiating Entrepreneurs from Small Business Owners: A Conceptualization," *Academy of Management Review,* 1984, *9:* 354–359.

12. R. C. Ronstadt, *Entrepreneurship* (Dover, Mass.: Lord, 1984).

13. Adapted from M. J. Mackowski, "Robert Ontiveros, B-State Packaging," *Hispanic Business,* April 1990, 44.

14. J. J. Kao, *Entrepreneurship, Creativity, and Organization* (Englewood Cliffs, N.J.: Prentice-Hall, 1989).

15. R. W. Torrence, *In the Owner's Chair* (Englewood Cliffs, N.J.: Reston, 1986).

16. Adapted from "Rod Canion," *Personal Computing,* April 1985, 94–101; S. Kindel, "Rod Canion: Compaq Computer," *Financial World,* April 5, 1988, 51; J. E. David, "Rod Canion," *Business Week,* April 18, 1986, 200.

17. F. Hoy and D. Hellriegel, "The Kilmann and Herden Model of Organizational Effectiveness Criteria for Small Business Managers," *Academy of Management Journal,* 1982, *25:* 308–322.

18. W. R. Sandberg and C. W. Hofer, "Improving New Venture Performance: The Role of Strategy, Industry Structure, and the Entrepreneur," *Journal of Business Venturing,* 1988, *3:* 5–28; K. Eisenhardt and C. B. Schoonhoven, "Organizational Growth: Linking Founding Team, Strategy, Environment, and Growth among U.S. Semiconductor Ventures, 1978–1988," *Administrative Science Quarterly,* 1990, *35:* 504–529.

19. D. D. Bowen and R. D. Hisrich, "The Female Entrepreneur: A Career Development Perspective," *Academy of Management Review,* 1986, *11:* 393–407; A. Jacobowitz and D. C. Vidler, "Characteristics of Entrepreneurs: Implications for Vocational Guidance," *Vocational Guidance Quarterly,* 1982, *30:* 252–257.

20. Ronstadt, *op. cit.*

21. "Domestic Franchising," *Statistical Abstracts of the United States, 1990* (Washington, D.C.: U.S. Bureau of the Census, 1991). *See also* J. Katz and W. B. Gartner, "Properties of Emerging Organizations," *Academy of Management Review,* 1988, *13,* 429–441; A. Peterson and R. P. Dant, "Perceived Advantages of the Franchise Option from the Franchisee Perspective," *Journal of Small Business Management,* 1990, *28*(3): 46–61.

22. D. L. Sexton and N. B. Bowman-Upton, *Entrepreneurship* (New York: Macmillan, 1991).

23. Personal interview with F. Hoy, Atlanta, Georgia, September 1990.

24. H. H. Stevenson, "A Perspective on Entrepreneurship," Harvard Business School Note 9-384-131, 1983; H. H. Stevenson, M. J. Roberts, and H. I. Grousbeck, *New Business Ventures and the Entrepreneur,* 3rd ed. (Boston: Irwin, 1989).

25. Adapted from K. McDermott, "Going It Alone," *D & B Reports,* March/April 1989, 31–35.

26. F. Hoy, quoted in H. Ezell, "A New Breed of 'Mom and Pop' Shops," *Atlanta Journal and Constitution,* November 28, 1990, C8.

27. F. Hoy, "Universities 'Discover' Family Business," *Atlanta Small Business Monthly,* September 1989, 2.

28. G. Pinchott, III, *Intrapreneurship* (New York: Harper & Row, 1985); J. S. DeMott, "Here Come the Intrapreneurs," *Time,* February 5, 1985, 36–37.

29. R. J. Ellis and N. T. Taylor, "Specifying Intrapreneurship," in N. C. Churchill, J. A. Hornaday, B. A. Kirchhoff, O. J. Krasner, and K. H. Vesper (eds.), *Frontiers of Entrepreneurship Research* (Wellesley, Mass.: Babson College, 1987), 527–541.

30. D. B. Merrifield, "Industrial Survival via Management Technology," *Journal of Business Venturing,* 1988, *3:* 171–185; M. A. Hitt, R. E. Hoskisson, and R. D. Ireland, "Mergers and Acquisitions and Managerial Commitment to Innovation in M-Form Firms," *Strategic Management Journal,* 1990 Summer Special Issue, *11:* 29–48.

31. R. M. Kanter, "Supporting Innovation and Venture Development in Established Companies," *Journal of Business Venturing,* 1985, *1:* 47–60; J. G. Covin and D. P. Slevin, "New Venture Strategic Posture, Structure, and Performance: An Industry Life Cycle Analysis," *Journal of Business Venturing,* 1990, *5:* 123–133.

32. D. F. Muzyka, "The Management of Failure: A Key to Organizational Entrepreneurship," in B. A. Kirchhoff, W. A. Long, V. E. McMullan, K. H. Vesper, and W. E. Wetzel, Jr. (eds.), *Frontiers of Entrepreneurship Research* (Wellesley, Mass.: Babson College, 1988), 501–518.

33. W. DeSarbo, I. C. MacMillan, and D. L. Day, "Criteria for Corporate Venturing: Importance Assigned by Managers," *Journal of Business Venturing,* 1986, *2:* 329–350; D. F. Kuratko, R. V. Montagno, and J. S. Hornsby, "Developing an Intrapreneurial Assessment Instrument for an Effective Corporate Entrepreneurial Environment," *Strategic Management Journal,* 1990 Summer Special Issue, *11:* 49–58.

34. D. J. Cohen, R. J. Graham, and E. B. Shils, "LaBrea Tar Pits Revisited: Corporate Entrepreneurship and the AT&T Dinosaur," in J. A. Hornaday, E. B. Shils, J. A. Timmons, and K. H. Vesper (eds.), *Frontiers of Entrepreneurship Research* (Wellesley, Mass.: Babson College, 1985), 621–635.

35. K. D. Bays, "The Force of Entrepreneurship." Speech delivered at the Sol C. Snider Entrepreneurial Center, Wharton School, University of Pennsylvania, May 7, 1987.

36. A. H. Van de Ven, "Central Problems in the Management of Innovations," *Management Science,* 1986, *32:* 590–607; E. G. Rule and D. W. Irwin, "Fostering Intrapreneurship: The New Competitive Edge," *Journal of Business Strategy,* May/June 1988, 44–47.

37. T. J. Peters and R. H. Waterman, Jr., *In Search of Excellence* (New York: Harper & Row, 1982).

38. J. S. Conant, M. P. Mokway, and S. D. Wood, "Management Styles and Marketing Strategies: An Analysis of HMOs," *Health Care Management Review,* 1987, *12*(4): 65–75; A. D. Meyer, G. R. Brooks, and J. B. Goes, "Environmental Jolts and Industry Revolutions: Organizational Responses to Discontinuous Change," *Strategic Management Journal,* 1990 Summer Special Issue, *11:* 93–110.

Skill-Building Exercise. "Tally Your Chances of Making It on Your Own," *USA Today,* May 11, 1987, 10E.

In the News. Dorothy Gaiter, "Minority-Owned Business's Surge of the '80s Is Threatened," *Wall Street Journal,* March 13, 1991, B2.

Management Case. Adapted from M. Bane, "How Neat It Is," *American Way,* July 15, 1989, 64–68; E. Calonius, "Meet the King of Video," *Fortune,* June 4, 1990, 208; "Blockbuster's POS Focuses on Three Goals: Moves Customers Quickly, Tracks Title Demand, Analyzes Preferences," *Chain Store Age Executive,* January 1990, 88*ff.*

ability An individual's mastery of the skills required to do a job.

acceptance theory of authority Barnard's theory, which states that employees will choose to follow management's orders if they understand what is required, believe the orders to be consistent with organizational goals, and see a positive benefit to themselves in carrying them out.

accountability The expectation that each employee will accept credit or blame for results achieved in performing assigned tasks.

achievement-oriented leadership A leadership style characterized by setting challenging goals, expecting others to perform at their highest level, and showing confidence that they'll meet this expectation.

act utilitarianism The branch of the utilitarian ethical approach that emphasizes the result of providing the greatest good for the greatest number (in other words, the end justifies the means).

adaptive decision A choice made in response to a combination of moderately unusual and only partially known problems and alternative solutions.

administrative management A traditional management system that focuses on managers and their actions rather than on overall organizational structure or workers.

affective conflict Conflict that arises because people's feelings or emotions are incompatible.

affiliation needs The needs for friendship, love, and belonging, which occupy the third level of Maslow's hierarchy.

affirmative action program A legally mandated program intended to ensure that a firm's hiring procedures guarantee equal employment opportunity as specified by the law.

affirmative social responsibility concept The idea that the organization should be the initiator of actions that benefit the environment, the stakeholders, and the general public.

alliance The uniting of two or more organizations, groups, or individuals to achieve common objectives with respect to a particular issue.

alliance strategy Strategy pursued when two or more organizations unite in order to attain common objectives.

artificial intelligence (AI) The ability of a properly programmed computer system to perform functions normally associated with human intelligence, such as comprehending spoken language, making judgments, and learning.

assessment center A human resource selection tool that simulates job situations in order to assess potential employees' performance.

assumption A prediction that an important future event, over which an organization has little or no control, will or will not occur.

authority The right to decide and act.

authority structure The organizational structure that determines the rights of employees to make decisions of varying importance at different levels within the organization.

automation The use of devices and processes that are self-regulating and operate independently of people within a defined range of conditions.

availability analysis A study that determines whether minorities' and women's representation in an organization is proportionate to their numbers in the relevant labor market.

avoidance reinforcement An attempt to avoid unpleasant consequences by maintaining desired behaviors.

avoidance style The tendency to withdraw from conflict or remain neutral.

backward integration The purchase of one or more of its suppliers by a larger organization as a cost-cutting strategy.

bar coding Information encoded as black bars of varying widths alternating with spaces, which can be read by an optical scanner into a computer.

behavioral models Theories of leadership that focus on differences in the actions (behaviors) of effective and ineffective leaders.

behavioral viewpoint One of the four major viewpoints of management, which focuses on helping managers deal effectively with the human side of organizations.

benchmarking The process of measuring an organization's goods, services, or practices against those of its toughest competitors.

benefits Pensions, health and life insurance, vacations, sick leave, child care, and similar nonmonetary remuneration for employees.

birth stage The first stage of the organizational life cycle, in which the organization is created.

bounded rationality model The decision-making model that emphasizes the limitations of the individual's rationality.

brainstorming An unrestrained flow of ideas within a group, with all critical judgments suspended, in order to come up with possible solutions to a problem.

brainware The objectives, the application, and the justification of hardware/software deployment, or what to employ, when, and why.

breakeven analysis A decision-making aid that looks at the various relationships between levels of sales (revenues) and costs in order to determine the point where total sales equal total costs.

bribe An improper payment made to obtain a special favor (not illegal in some countries).

budgeting The process of categorizing proposed expenditures and linking them to objectives.

bureaucratic controls Methods of managerial control that are formal, rigid, and structured.

bureaucratic management A traditional management system that relies on rules, set hierarchy, a clear division of labor, and firm procedures and that focuses on the overall organizational structure.

burnout Emotional exhaustion, depersonalization, and decreased accomplishment brought about by continuous work distress.

business-level strategy Strategy that guides the operations of a single business, outlining how it will compete.

business plan Outline of the steps an enterprise will follow to turn ideas into reality.

cartel An alliance formed among producers engaged in the same type of business in order to limit or eliminate competition.

centralization of authority A management approach that is characterized by authority concentrated at the top of an organization or department.

central tendency A rating error that occurs when a manager rates all employees as average, even when their performance varies.

certainty The condition that exists when individuals are fully informed about a problem, the alternative solutions are obvious, and the possible outcomes of each solution are known.

chaebol A South Korean business group consisting of large, globally diversified companies owned and managed by family members.

changing environment An organizational environment that is unpredictable because of frequent shifts in products, technology, competitive forces, markets, or political forces.

channel The path a message follows from sender to receiver.

charismatic authority The authority exerted by a person because of special personal qualities or powers others perceive in him or her.

chief information officer (CIO) A top-level manager who is responsible for fulfilling an organization's information-processing needs and coordinating all of its information systems.

clan culture A type of organizational culture based on extensive socialization and widely shared values and norms.

closed system A system that does not interact with its environment according to the systems viewpoint of management.

clout Pull or political influence within an organization.

coaching style A leadership style characterized by expanding two-way communication and helping maturing employees build confidence and motivation.

coercive power A type of power based on followers' fear of punishment by the leader.

cognitive ability test A written test that measures general intelligence, verbal ability, numerical ability, reasoning ability, and so forth.

cognitive conflict Conflict that arises because ideas or thoughts are perceived as incompatible.

cohesiveness The group trait that indicates the strength of the members' desire to remain in the group and their commitment to it.

collaborative situation In the contingency model of conflict, the situation that exists when the parties have many more shared goals than conflicting goals.

collaborative style The tendency to identify the causes of conflict, share information, and seek a mutually beneficial solution.

collectivism Hofstede's value dimension that measures the tendency of group members to focus on the common welfare and feel loyalty toward one another (the opposite of *individualism*).

commission agent A broker (an individual or a firm) who represents businesses in foreign transactions in return for a percentage of each transaction's value.

communication The transfer of information and understandings from one person to another via meaningful symbols.

communication feedback The receiver's response to the sender's message.

communication skills The abilities to send and receive information, thoughts, feelings, and attitudes.

communication system Any form of information technology that allows information to be transmitted between individuals or organizations.

comparative financial analysis An evaluation of a firm's financial condition for two or more time periods or in comparison to similar firms.

compensation The wages or salaries, stock options, bonuses, and other monetary items paid to employees in exchange for their labor.

compromise style The tendency to effect agreement by sacrificing some of one's own interests.

computer-aided design (CAD) The first part of a CAM process, involving special software that instructs a computer to display detailed configurations on a screen.

computer-aided manufacturing (CAM) A wide variety of computer-based technologies used to produce goods.

computer monitoring The use of special software to collect highly detailed quantitative information on employees' performance for management.

concentric diversification Growth strategy that involves a company's acquiring or starting a business related to it in terms of technology, markets, or products (sometimes called *related diversification*).

conceptual skills Thinking and planning abilities that depend heavily on the ability to view the organization as a whole made up of interrelated parts.

conditional value (CV) The outcome (payoff) for the combination of a particular state of nature and a specific strategy.

conflict Opposition arising from disagreements due to incompatible objectives, thoughts, or emotions within or among individuals, teams, departments, or organizations.

conflict management Interventions designed to reduce (or, in some cases, to increase) conflict.

conglomerate diversification Growth strategy that involves a company's adding unrelated goods or services to its product line.

considerate leadership style Leadership style identified by the Ohio State model and characterized by concern for employees' well-being, status, and comfort.

content approach The category of theories of motivation that assumes employees are motivated by the desire to fulfill inner needs.

contingency models Theories of leadership that hold that the situation is critical in determining the best leadership style.

contingency planning The process of identifying alternative future possibilities and then developing an action plan for each of them.

contingency viewpoint One of the four viewpoints of management, which contends that different situations require different practices and allows the use of the other viewpoints separately or in combination to deal with various problems.

continuous improvement The overall effect of a large number of small, incremental improvements resulting from streams of adaptive decisions made over time.

contrast error Interviewer error that occurs when an interviewee's rating is based on a comparison with the preceding interviewee.

control The methods and mechanisms used to ensure that behaviors and performance conform to an organization's objectives, plans, and standards.

controlling The process by which a person, group, or organization consciously monitors performance and takes corrective action.

cooptation A political maneuver for overcoming resistance that involves people in the decision-making process only to get their endorsement or their lack of resistance.

coordination The formal and informal procedures that integrate the activities performed by separate groups in an organization.

core value A value that is central to an organization's culture and is likely to reflect a work-related value of the society, or part of the society, in which the organization operates.

corporate culture The norms, values, and practices that characterize a particular organization.

corporate-level strategy Any strategy that guides the activities of an organization having more than one line of business.

corrective control model A six-step process that allows managers to detect and correct deviations from an organization's objectives, plans, and standards.

corrective controls Organizational controls intended to change unwanted behaviors and make performance conform to established standards or rules.

corridor principle The principle that the entrepreneur will encounter many business opportunities that she or he would never have encountered otherwise.

cost leadership strategy The business-level strategy that emphasizes competing with all other firms in an industry by providing a good or service at a price as low as or lower than theirs.

countertrade A variation on straightforward exporting (or importing) in which the export sale of goods or services is linked to the import purchase of other goods or services.

creativity The ability to visualize, foresee, generate, and implement new ideas.

critical path The path through a PERT network with the longest elapsed time, which determines the length of the entire project.

culture The shared characteristics (such as language, religion, heritage) and values that distinguish one group of people from another.

customer monitoring Systematic efforts by an organization to obtain feedback from customers concerning the quality of goods and services.

data Raw facts and figures.

decentralization of authority A management approach characterized by a high degree of delegated authority throughout an organization or department.

decision making The process of defining problems and choosing a course of action from the alternatives generated.

decision support system (DSS) A complex set of computer programs and equipment that allows users to analyze, manipulate, format, display, and output data in different ways.

decision tree A decision-making aid that breaks a problem down into a sequence of logically ordered smaller problems and identifies relationships among present choices, states of nature, and future choices.

decoding Translating encoded messages into a form that is meaningful to the receiver.

delegating style A hands-off leadership style characterized by giving responsibilities for carrying out plans and making task decisions to the highly mature employees.

delegation of authority The process by which managers assign the right to act and make decisions in certain areas to subordinates.

Delphi technique A forecasting aid based on a consensus of a panel of experts arrived at in steps.

demographics The characteristics of people composing work groups, organizations, countries, or specific markets.

departmentalization Subdividing work and assigning it to specialized groups within an organization.

development program Program designed to improve employee's conceptual and human relations skills in preparation for future jobs.

devil's advocacy method The process by which one person or team critiques a preferred plan or strategy in order to surface and challenge its assumptions.

dialectical inquiry method A process for systematically examining strategic planning issues from two or more opposing points of view in order to analyze the underlying assumptions.

differentiation The measure of the difference that exists among departments with respect to structure, tasks, and managerial orientation.

differentiation strategy The business-level strategy that emphasizes competing with all other firms in an industry by offering a product that customers perceive to be unique.

directive behavior One-way communication from leader to followers.

directive leadership A leadership style characterized by telling employees what's expected of them and how to perform their tasks.

directive style A leadership style characterized by the giving of clear instructions and specific directions to immature employees.

disseminator role The informational role that managers play when they share knowledge or data with subordinates and other members of the organization.

distress Unpleasant, detrimental, or disease-producing stress.

distributive justice principle The ethical principle that says that individuals should not be treated differently on the basis of arbitrary characteristics (such as gender or race).

distributive variable In the contingency model of conflict, the degree to which the goals of those in conflict are perceived as incompatible.

disturbance handler role The decisional role played by managers when they deal with problems and changes beyond their immediate control, such as a strike or a supplier's bankruptcy.

diversification Characteristic that reflects the number of different goods and/or services a company produces and the number of different markets it serves.

division of labor The process of dividing duties into simpler, more specialized tasks to promote efficiency.

dominant-business firm A company that provides goods or services to various segments of a particular market.

downsizing The process of letting employees go in an attempt to improve an organization's efficiency.

downward channel A channel of communication that managers use to send messages to employees or customers.

dual-career couple Any couple in which both the husband and the wife are employed outside the home.

economic order quantity The optimal quantity to order to achieve the lowest total inventory costs.

economy of scale The decrease in per-unit costs as the volume of goods and/or services produced increases.

electronic mail (E-mail) Communication system that allows users to transmit textual messages through their networked terminals or personal computers.

emotion A subjective reaction, or feeling.

employee-centered leadership style Leadership style identified by the University of Michigan model and characterized by encouraging employees to participate in decision making and making sure they are satisfied with their work.

employee effort The amount of energy—physical and/or mental—exerted to perform a job.

empowerment Being able to share influence and control with followers.

encoding Translating thoughts or feelings into a medium—whether written or oral—that conveys the meaning intended.

entrapment Luring an individual into committing a compromising or illegal act.

entrepreneur One who creates a new business activity.

entrepreneur role The decisional role played by managers when they design and implement a new project, enterprise, or even a business.

environment All external forces and the influences, direct and indirect, they have on the decisions and actions of an organization.

environmental uncertainty The element of risk due to the ambiguity or unpredictability of certain factors external to an organization (such as government regulation).

equity model A process model of motivation that is concerned with individuals' beliefs about how fairly they're treated compared with their peers.

esteem needs The needs for self-respect, personal achievement, and recognition from others, which occupy the fourth level of Maslow's hierarchy.

ethics A set of rules that define right and wrong conduct and that help individuals distinguish between fact and belief, decide how issues are defined, and decide what moral principles apply to the situation.

eustress Pleasant or constructive stress.

executive support system (ESS) Any information technology that integrates managers and other professionals into an organization's information flow.

expectancy The belief that effort will lead to first-order outcomes.

expectancy theory A process model of motivation which states that people choose among alternative behaviors according to their expectation that a particular behavior will lead to one or more desired outcomes.

expected value (EV) The weighted-average outcome for each strategy in a payoff matrix.

experienced meaningfulness The physiological state that's a measure of the degree to which employees perceive their work as valuable and worthwhile.

experienced responsibility The psychological state that's a measure of the extent to which employees feel personally responsible for the quality of their work.

expert power A type of power based on a leader's specialized knowledge.

expert system (ES) A computer-based system that is designed to function like a human expert in solving problems within a specific area of knowledge.

export department The department within an organization that handles all aspects of export operations and acts as liaison between foreign customers and management.

export manager Manager who actively searches out foreign markets for a firm's goods and services, representing only the one firm and working with a small staff.

exporting strategy Strategy pursued when an organization maintains facilities in its home country and transfers goods or services abroad for sale in foreign markets.

external system The part of Homans systems model that consists of outside conditions that exist before and after the group is formed.

extinction A technique that is actually an absence of any reinforcement, either positive or negative, following an incidence of undesired behavior.

extortion The obtaining of payment in response to some kind of threat.

extrapolation The projection of some tendency from the past or present into the future.

extrinsic reward Reward supplied by the organization, such as pleasant working conditions, fair salary, or job security.

facsimile (fax) machine A communication system that reproduces documents at a remote location.

fairness principle The ethical principle that requires employees to support the rules of the organization when they are just and the employees have voluntarily accepted benefits provided by the organization.

feedback Any form of information about a system's status and performance according to the systems viewpoint of management.

femininity Hofstede's value dimension that measures the tendency to be nurturing and people-oriented (the opposite of *masculinity*).

Fiedler's contingency model A leadership model that suggests successful leadership depends on matching the situation and the leader's style.

figurehead role The interpersonal role played by managers when they represent the organization at ceremonial and symbolic functions.

financial controls Methods of managerial control that are intended to prevent the misallocation of financial resources and provide timely financial information.

first-line manager Manager directly responsible for the production of goods or services.

first-order outcome Any work-related behavior—such as performance, creativity, reliability, tardiness—that is the direct result of the effort an employee expends on a job.

fixed interval schedule Reinforcement schedule that provides reinforcement at fixed time intervals such as weekly or twice monthly.

fixed ratio schedule Reinforcement schedule that provides reinforcement after a fixed number of desired behaviors has occurred.

flextime Practice of allowing employees to vary their arrival and departure times to suit their needs.

focus strategy The business-level strategy that emphasizes competing in a specific industry niche by offering either a unique product or a low-cost product.

forcing style The tendency to use power to make others agree with one's position.

forecasting Predicting, projecting, or estimating future events or conditions in an organization's environment.

formal group An organizational group whose purpose and tasks relate directly to the attainment of stated organizational objectives.

forward integration Growth strategy that involves a company's entering the businesses of its customers.

franchise A business run by an individual to whom a franchisor grants the right to market a certain good or service.

franchising strategy Strategy pursued when a parent organization (the franchisor) grants another company or individual (the franchisee) the rights to use its name and produce a product or service in return for a fee.

functional departmentalization Type of departmentalization that groups employees according to their areas of expertise and the resources they draw on to perform a common set of tasks.

functional foremanship System developed by Taylor to link each foreman's area of specialization to that foreman's scope of authority.

functional-level strategy Strategy that consists of guidelines for managing a firm's functional areas.

functional manager Manager who supervises employees with specialized skills in a single area of operation, such as accounting, personnel, payroll, finance, marketing, or production.

gain-sharing plan A program that passes on the benefits of increased productivity, cost reductions, and improved quality through regular cash bonuses to employees.

Gantt chart A visual progress report that identifies individual work stages in a project's execution and a deadline for completion of each stage.

general environment Those external factors, such as inflation rate and population demographics, that usually affect indirectly all or most organizations in the economy (also called the macroenvironment).

general manager Manager responsible for the overall operations of a complex unit such as a company or a division.

general objective Objective that provides broad direction for managerial decision making in qualitative terms.

generic strategies model A framework of three basic business-level strategies that can be applied to a variety of organizations in diverse industries.

global strategy A complex strategy for achieving international involvement by operating with worldwide consistency and standardization through highly independent international subsidiaries.

goal conflict Conflict that arises because desired objectives and preferred outcomes differ.

grapevine The organization's informal communication system.

graphic rating method A method of performance appraisal that evaluates employees on a series of performance dimensions along a five- or seven-point scale.

grease payment A small payment used to get lower-level government employees to speed up required paperwork (allowed under the U.S. Foreign Corrupt Practices Act of 1977).

group Two or more individuals who come into personal and meaningful contact on a continuing basis.

group control The norms and values that group members share and maintain through rewards and punishments.

group decision support system (GDSS) A set of software, hardware, and language components that support a team of people engaged in a decision-related meeting.

group social structure The pattern of interactions and relationships in a group, determined primarily by members' contributions to achieving the group's objectives, acceptance of the group norms, and personal characteristics.

groupthink An agreement-at-any-cost mentality that results in ineffective team decision making and poor solutions.

growth-need strength The extent to which a person desires a job that provides personal challenges, sense of accomplishment, and learning (personal growth).

halo effect Interviewer error that occurs when the interviewer judges a candidate's overall potential on the basis of a single characteristic, allowing it to overshadow other characteristics.

hardware The physical components and their logical layout that are the means for carrying out a task to achieve an objective.

Hawthorne effect The fact that when workers receive special attention, their productivity is likely to improve whether or not working conditions actually change.

Hersey and Blanchard's situational leadership model Contingency model that suggests that the levels of directive and supportive behaviors of leaders will vary based on the level of maturity of the employee or team.

hierarchical structure The organizational structure that determines the amount of power and authority given to each position within the organization.

hierarchy of needs Maslow's content model of motivation that suggests people have a complex set of needs arranged on five levels, which they attempt to meet, from the bottom (most basic) up.

hierarchy of objectives The formal linking of objectives between and across organizational levels in order to achieve the objectives of the organization as a whole.

horizontal channel A channel that managers use when communicating across departmental lines.

horizontal integration Growth strategy that involves a company's acquiring of a competitor.

House's path-goal model A contingency model of leadership that states that effective leaders clarify the paths, or means, by which employees can attain both high job satisfaction and high performance.

human relations viewpoint Another name for the *behavioral viewpoint*.

human resource management The process of analyzing and managing an organization's human resource needs to ensure satisfaction of its strategic objectives.

human resource planning Forecasting a firm's human resource needs and planning the steps to be taken to meet them.

hygiene factors The extrinsic factors of a job that, when positive in nature, maintain a reasonable level of job motivation but do not necessarily increase it; working conditions, company policies, supervision, co-workers, and salary and job security.

incubator organization A company that spawns entrepreneurs.

individual differences Personal needs, values, attitudes, and interests that people bring to their jobs.

individualism Hofstede's value dimension that measures the extent to which a culture expects people to take care of themselves and/or individuals believe they are masters of their own destiny (the opposite of *collectivism*).

individual self-control Control mechanisms operating consciously and unconsciously with each person.

informal group A group that develops because of the shared day-to-day activities, interactions, and sentiments of its members and for the purpose of meeting their own needs.

information Useful knowledge derived from data.

information richness The information-carrying capacity of a channel of communication.

information technologies (ITs) Any devices or systems that help individuals or organizations assemble, store, transmit, process, and retrieve data or information.

initiating-structure leadership style Leadership style identified by the Ohio State model and characterized by active planning, organizing, controlling, and coordinating of subordinates activities.

innovative decision A choice that is based on the discovery, identification, and diagnosis of an unusual and ambiguous problem and the development of unique or creative solutions.

input According to the equity model of motivation, what an employee gives to a job—such as time, effort, education—in order to obtain a desired outcome.

inputs The physical, human, material, financial, and information resources that enter the transformation process and leave it as outputs, according to the systems viewpoint of management.

instrinsic reward Reward derived by the individual from a job, such as self-recognition, performance, or personal growth.

instrumentality The perceived link between first-order outcomes and the achievement of second-order outcomes.

integrated system A network of information systems that provides closer links among functional areas within an organization and direct information exchanges with customers and suppliers.

integration The measure of similarity among various departments with respect to their goals and structure.

integrative variable In the contingency model of conflict, the degree to which the goals of those in conflict are perceived as compatible.

integrator An employee or manager who facilitates communication among departments through bypassing formal lines of communication within the hierarchy.

intermediate strategy A positioning strategy somewhere between a process-focus and a product-focus strategy.

internal system The part of Homans systems model that includes the activities, interactions, sentiments, and norms that group members develop over time.

international corporation A corporation with significant business interests (importing, exporting, production, marketing) that cut across national boundaries. It is sometimes an international division within each product group.

international division A division within an organization that handles not only international marketing and finance tasks, but also manufacturing operations in one or more foreign countries.

interpersonal conflict Disagreements over objectives, policies, rules, or decisions and incompatible behaviors that create anger, distrust, fear, resentment, or rejection.

interpersonal skills The abilities to lead, motivate, manage conflict, and work with others.

interrole conflict Conflict that occurs when role pressures associated with membership in one group conflict with those associated with membership in another.

intersender role conflict Conflict that results when pressures from one role sender are incompatible with those from another role sender.

intrapreneur An employee who develops a new product and a new market for his or her organization and who turns new ideas into profitable activities within an existing organization.

intrasender role conflict Conflict caused by receiving mixed messages from a single role sender.

intuition The abilities to scan a situation, anticipate changes, take risks, and build trust.

inventory The amount and type of raw materials, parts, supplies, and unshipped finished goods an organization has on hand at a given time.

inventory control The operations management decision area concerned with setting inventory levels, obtaining feedback about changes in them, and signaling the need for action to avoid insufficient or excess inventory.

inventory costs The expenses associated with maintaining inventory, including ordering costs, carrying costs, shortage costs, and set-up costs.

job analysis A breakdown of the tasks and responsibilities of a specific job and the personal characteristics, skills, and experience necessary for their successful performance.

job characteristics The dimensions of a job that determine its limitations and challenges.

job description A detailed outline of a position's essential tasks and responsibilities.

job-enrichment model An extension of the two-factor model for motivation that emphasizes ways to change specific job characteristics in order to satisfy more of employees' higher-level needs.

job specification A listing of the personal characteristics, skills and experiences a worker needs to carry out a job's tasks and assume its responsibilities.

joint venture A partnership between two (or more) firms to create another business to produce a product or service.

justice approach The ethical approach that judges decisions and behavior by their consistency with an equitable and impartial distribution of benefits and costs among individuals and groups.

just-in-time (JIT) system An inventory control system that delivers the smallest possible quantities to each stage of the transformation process at the latest possible time without affecting operations.

knowledge of results The psychological state that's a measure of the extent to which employees receive feedback about how well they are performing.

knowledge workers Employees whose jobs involve the creation, processing, and/or distribution of information.

lateral relations An information-processing strategy by which decision making is put in the hands of those with access to the information needed to make the decision.

law A value or standard of society that is enforceable through the courts.

leader-member relations The extent to which a leader is accepted by the group.

leader position power The extent to which a leader has legitimate, coercive, and reward power.

leader role The interpersonal role that managers play when they direct and coordinate the activities of subordinates to accomplish organizational objectives.

leadership The ability to influence, motivate, and direct others in order to attain desired objectives.

leadership-participation model A contingency model of leadership that provides a set of rules to determine the amount and form of participative decision making that should be encouraged in different situations.

leading The managerial function of communicating with and motivating others to perform the tasks necessary to achieve the organization's objectives.

lead time The time elapsed between placing of an order and receiving the finished goods.

least preferred co-worker (LPC) According to Fiedler's contingency model, the employee with whom a leader can work least well.

legend A well-known story about some significant person or event based on historical fact but embellished with fictional details.

legitimate power Type of power based on a leader's formal position in the organization's hierarchy.

leniency A common, often intentional, rating error that occurs when a manager rates all employees in a group higher than they deserve for any of a number of reasons.

leveraged buyout The acquisition of a company, financed through borrowing, by a small group of investors.

liaison role The interpersonal role played by managers when they deal with people outside the organization.

licensing strategy Strategy pursued when an organization (the

licensor) makes certain resources available to another company (the licensee) in return for a fee (royalty).

line authority The authority to direct and control immediate subordinates who perform activities essential to achieving organizational objectives.

listening Paying attention to a message, as distinguished from merely hearing it.

lobbying An attempt to influence government decisions by providing relevant officials with information on the anticipated effects of legislation or regulatory rulings.

local area network (LAN) Communication system consisting of computers linked within a limited geographical area.

low-interdependency situation In the contingency model of conflict, the situation that exists when the parties interact little and have few shared or conflicting goals.

machine controls Methods of managerial control that use instruments or devices to prevent or correct deviations from desired results.

management Planning, organizing, leading, and controlling the people working in an organization and the ongoing set of tasks and activities they perform.

management by objectives (MBO) A philosophy of and approach to management that guides the planning process by helping managers integrate strategic and tactical plans.

management information system A type of executive support system that provides managers with up-to-date financial, market, human resource, or other information about the status of the organization, its parts, or its environment.

manager A person who allocates human and material resources and directs the operations of a department or an entire organization.

managerial grid model A behavioral model of leadership that identifies five leadership styles that combine differing proportions of concern for production and concern for people.

market control The use of price competition to evaluate the output and productivity of an organization.

market culture A type of organizational culture based on impersonal relationships that are established via negotiated terms of exchange.

market development strategy A business-level growth strategy that seeks new markets for current products.

market penetration strategy A business-level strategy that seeks growth in current markets with current goods or services.

masculinity Hofstede's value dimension that measures the degree to which the acquisition of money and things is valued and a high quality of life for others is not (the opposite of *femininity*).

materials resource planning II (MRP II) A computerized information system for managing dependent-demand inventories and scheduling stock replenishment orders.

matrix departmentalization Type of departmentalization based on multiple authority and support systems.

maturity Subordinate's ability to set high but attainable goals and accept responsibility for reaching them.

maturity stage The final stage of the organizational life cycle, in which the organization is large, mechanistic and it operates in a stable environment.

measurable behavior Work-related behavior that can be quantified (number of units produced, percentage of defective units, and such).

measuring by attribute A total quality control method that assesses characteristics as either acceptable or unacceptable.

measuring by variable A total quality control method that assesses characteristics for which there are quantifiable standards (such as diameter or weight).

mechanistic structure Organizational structure in which activities are broken down into specialized tasks and decision making is centralized at the top.

merit pay plan A compensation plan designed to pay people according to their job performance.

message That body of verbal (oral and written) symbols and nonverbal cues that represents the information the sender wants to convey to the receiver.

middle manager A manager who receives broad, overall strategies and policies from top managers and translates them into specific objectives and plans for first-line managers to implement.

midlife stage The third stage of the organizational life cycle, in which the organization has become large, successful, and bureaucratic.

mission The organization's reason for existing; the identification of what business it's in.

mixed conflict situation In the contingency model of conflict, the situation that exists when there are many shared goals and many conflicting goals.

monitor role The informational role played by managers when they seek, receive, and screen information that may affect the organization.

moral principles The impartial general rules of behavior that are of great importance to a society and, along with the values they represent, are fundamental to ethics.

moral rights approach The ethical approach that judges decisions and behavior by their consistency with fundamental human rights and privileges.

motivation Any influence that elicits, channels, or sustains people's behavior.

motivator factors The intrinsic factors of a job that, when present, should create high levels of motivation: challenge of the work, responsibility, recognition, achievement, and advancement and growth.

multidomestic strategy Strategy pursued when a firm adjusts its products and practices to individual countries or regions, treating each uniquely.

multinational corporation (MNC) A corporation that views the *whole* world as its market, assessing problems and planning production and marketing strategies with that view in mind (also called global corporation or transnational corporation).

multiple scenarios Written descriptions of several alternative futures.

natural duty principle The ethical principle that requires that decisions and behavior be based on certain universal obligations (not to injure another, for example).

need A strong feeling of deficiency in a particular aspect of a person's life that creates an uncomfortable tension, which the person attempts to reduce.

need for achievement Desire to perform at a high level of excellence or to succeed in competitive situations.

negotiation The process by which two or more individuals or groups having common and conflicting interests or objectives present and discuss proposals in an attempt to reach an agreement.

negotiator role The decisional role played by managers when they meet with individuals or groups to discuss differences and reach some agreement.

Nenko system The pattern of organizational characteristics that form the basis for managerial practices found in most large-scale Japanese organizations.

networking The process by which computers communicate with one another.

niche A narrowly defined market segment that many competitors may overlook, ignore, or have difficulty serving.

nonroutine service technology Technology used by an organization that operates in a complex and changing environment and services customers or clients who are unaware of their needs or imprecise about their problems.

nonspecific response An emotional, physical, and/or cognitive response that the one who experiences it cannot control.

nonverbal messages Messages transmitted through facial expressions, movements, body position, and physical contact rather than by means of words.

norm An informal rule of behavior that is widely shared and enforced by members of a group.

normative decision making Any prescribed step-by-step process individuals may use to help them make decisions.

objective A specific result or outcome to be attained; indicates the direction in which decisions and actions should be aimed.

objective probability The likelihood that a specific outcome will occur based on hard facts and figures.

open network A computer-based information system that enables parts of highly dispersed service operations (including customers) to interact readily.

open system A system that interacts with its external environment, according to the systems viewpoint of management.

operational objective Objective that states in quantitative terms what is to be achieved, for whom, and within what time period.

operations management The systematic direction, control, and evaluation of the entire range of processes that transform inputs into finished goods or services.

organic controls Methods of managerial control that are flexible and rely on self-management abilities of groups and individuals.

organic structure Organizational structure that stresses teamwork, open communications, and decentralized decision making.

organization Any structured group of people brought together to achieve certain goals that the individuals alone could not achieve.

organizational control Control over an organization stemming from its formal strategies and mechanisms for pursuing its objectives.

organizational culture The organizations's personality, the way of thinking and doing things in it which is shared by most of its members and which must be learned by new members if they are to survive and progress.

organizational life cycle A sequence of major stages of development (usually birth, youth, midlife, and maturity) through which any organization evolves.

organizational practices The rules, personnel policies, managerial practices, and reward systems of an organization.

organizational socialization The systematic process by which an organization brings new members into its culture.

organizational structure A formal system of working relationships that both separates tasks (clarifies who should do what) and integrates tasks (tells people how they should work together).

organization chart A diagram showing the reporting relationships of functions, departments, and individual positions within an organization.

organization design The process of determining the structure and authority relationships for an entire organization.

organization development (OD) A planned long-range behavioral-science strategy for understanding, changing, and developing an organization's work force in order to improve its effectiveness.

organizing The managerial function of creating a structure of relationships among employees that will enable them to carry out management's plans and meet overall objectives.

orientation A formal or informal program that introduces new employees to their job responsibilities, their co-workers, and company policies.

Osborn's creativity model A three-phase problem-solving process that involves finding facts, ideas, and solutions and helps overcome blockages to creativity and innovation.

outcome A reward obtained from work, such as a promotion, a challenging assignment, and friendly co-workers.

outplacement activities A series of counseling services offered to terminated employees to minimize the length of their period of unemployment.

outputs The results of the transformation process, according to the systems viewpoint of management.

panel interview A job interview conducted by a group of the organization's current employees.

partial productivity The ratio of output to a single input, usually labor, capital, materials, or energy.

participative leadership A leadership style characterized by team participation in the decision-making process.

payoff matrix A decision-making aid in the form of a table (matrix) identifying possible states of nature, probabilities, and outcomes (payoffs) associated with the alternative strategies being considered.

perceived effort reward The individual's perception of the amount of effort on which certain rewards depend.

perceived equitable reward The amount of reward employees believe they should receive relative to what other employees receive.

perception The meaning ascribed to a message.

performance The level of the individual's work achievement that comes only after effort has been exerted.

performance appraisal The process of systematically evaluating each employees's job-related strengths and weaknesses and determining ways to improve his or her performance.

performance gap The difference between what the organization aspires to do to take advantage of its opportunities and what it actually does.

performance test A test that requires job candidates to perform simulated job tasks.

personality The unique blend of characteristics that define an individual.

person–role conflict Conflict that results from differences between the pressures exerted by one's role(s) and his or her needs, attitudes, values, or abilities.

PERT network The diagram showing the sequence and relationships of the activities and events needed to complete a project.

physiological needs The most basic human needs—for food, clothing, shelter—which occupy the lowest level in Maslow's hierarchy.

place departmentalization Type of departmentalization that groups all functions for a geographic area (place) under one manager.

planning The formal process of (1) choosing an organizational mission and overall objectives for both the short run and the long run, (2) devising divisional, departmental, and even individual objectives based on organizational objectives, (3) choosing strategies and tactics to achieve those objectives, and (4) deciding on the allocation of resources.

political model The model that describes the decision-making process in terms of the particular interests and objectives of powerful stakeholders e.g. customers, government.

political risk The probability that political events or actions will negatively affect the long-term profitability of an investment.

politics The maneuvering that employees engage in when seeking selfish goals that are opposed to the goals of others in the organization.

pooled interdependence The type of technological interdependence in which there is little sharing of information or resources among individuals and/or departments.

Porter-Lawler expectancy model The process model of motivation that states job satisfaction is the result rather than the cause of performance.

positioning strategy The method chosen by an organization for managing the resource flow in the transformation process.

positive reinforcement A technique that offers rewards to increase the likelihood that a desired behavior will be repeated.

power The ability to influence or control individual, departmental, divisional, or organizational decisions and outcomes.

power distance Hofstede's value dimension that measures the degree to which influence and control are unequally distributed among individuals within a particular society.

preventive controls Organizational controls intended to reduce errors and thereby minimize the need for corrective action.

principle of selectivity The idea that a small number of characteristics always account for a large number of effects (also known as Pareto's law).

probability The percentage of times a specific outcome would occur if a particular decision were made a large number of times.

problem-solving team A formal group of hourly and salaried employees, often volunteers, who meet to discuss ways to improve quality, productivity, and the work environment.

process approach The category of theories of motivation that assumes employees choose certain behaviors in order to meet their personal goals.

process-focus strategy A positioning strategy that organizes the physical layout of the equipment and work force around each operation in the transformation process.

product development strategy A business-level growth strategy that seeks to develop new or improved goods or services for current markets.

product differentiation Something unique in terms of quality, price, design, brand image, or customer service that gives a product an edge over the competition.

product-focus strategy A positioning strategy that organizes the physical layout of the equipment and work force around a few outputs.

product life cycle model A model of business-level strategy that emphasizes planning according to the life cycle phase of the firm's goods or services.

product or service departmentalization Type of departmentalization that divides the organization into self-contained units, each capable of designing and producing its own goods or services.

production-centered leadership style Leadership style identified by the University of Michigan model and characterized by setting standards, organizing and paying close attention to employees' work, and interest in results.

profit-sharing plan A program that provides employees with supplemental income based on the profitability of an entire organization or a selected subunit.

program evaluation and review technique (PERT) A project management aid that shows diagrammatically the sequence of activities and events required to reach an overall project objective.

project A one-time activity with a well-defined set of desired results.

projection A psychological mechanism used to place blame for problems on someone or something else.

project management The processes, techniques, and concepts used to run a project and achieve its objectives.

project manager A manager who coordinates activities across departments and shares authority with both functional and product managers in a matrix organizational structure.

protected group A category of people who are specifically covered by federal antidiscrimination laws on hiring and employment.

protectionism Various international political mechanisms designed to help firms avoid (or reduce) potential (or actual) competitive or political threats to an industry—for example, tariffs, quotas, subsidies, cartels.

proxemics The study of the way people use physical space to convey messages about themselves.

punishment A technique that attempts to discourage undesirable behavior by the application of negative consequences whenever it does occur.

quality According to the external view, achievement of the results that customers value and expect.

quality circle Meeting at which workers and first-line managers discuss how to improve the way their jobs are done.

quality improvement team A group of employees who meet regularly to find ways to achieve both quality in fact and quality in perception.

quota A restriction in the quantity of a country's imports or exports, usually intended to guarantee domestic manufacturers a certain percentage of the domestic market.

ranking method A performance appraisal method that compares employees doing the same or similar work.

ratio analysis A method of financial comparison that involves selecting two significant figures, expressing their relationship as a proportion or fraction, and comparing its value for two time periods or with ratios of similar organizations.

rational-legal authority An authority structure, defined by Max Weber, based on impersonal rules and laws that apply to all employees.

rational model The decision-making model that consists of a series of steps managers or teams should follow to increase the likelihood that their decisions will be logical and well-founded.

realistic job preview A screening technique that clearly shows candidates a job's tasks, or requirements.

receiver The person who receives and decodes (or interprets) the sender's message.

reciprocal interdependence The type of technological interdependence in which all individuals and departments are encouraged to work together and to share information and resources in order to complete a task.

recruitment The process of searching, both inside and outside an organization, for employees to fill vacant positions.

referent power A type of power based on followers' personal identification with the leader.

reinforcement theory Behavior theory of motivation that holds that behavior is a function of its consequences (rewards or punishments).

related-business firm A company that provides a variety of similar goods and/or services to a number of markets.

relationship-oriented leader A leader concerned about employees feelings and welfare.

reliability   The measure of the degree to which a test provides consistent scores.

replacement chart   A diagram showing each position in an organization's management hierarchy, with the name of each incumbent and the names of candidates eligible to replace him or her.

representation   Membership in an outside organization for the purpose of furthering the interests of the member's organization.

resource allocator role   The decisional role managers play when they choose among competing demands for money, equipment, personnel, and so forth.

responsibility   An employee's obligation to perform assigned tasks.

reward   A job outcome that an employee desires.

reward power   A type of power based on a leader's ability to reward followers.

Ringi system   A bottom-up form of decision making used in many Japanese organizations; involves reaching a consensus among all parties affected by a decision.

risk   The condition that exists when individuals can define the problem, specify the probability of certain occurrences, identify alternative solutions, and state the probability that each solution will lead to desired results.

ritual   A relatively elaborate and planned set of dramatic expressions carried out through a special event.

robots   Reprogrammable, multifunctional manipulators that can perform repetitive tasks efficiently.

role   An organized set of behaviors, which for managers may fall into the category of interpersonal, informational, or decisional.

role ambiguity   Confusion created by inadequate or unclear information or by uncertainty about the consequences of one's behavior.

role conflict   Conflict resulting from a person's being subjected to strong and inconsistent pressures or expectations.

role episode   Role senders' attempts to influence the behavior of the focal person and the responses of that focal person, which in turn influence the future expectations of the role senders.

role expectations   Views held by others about what an individual should or should not do.

role perception   The employee's belief that certain tasks should be performed—certain roles should be played—in order to perform a job successfully.

role pressure   Attempts on the part of role senders to induce the focal person to meet their expectations.

role set   The collection of roles occupied by other individuals that are directly related to the role of the person in question.

routine decision   A standardized choice made in response to a relatively well-defined and known problem and solution.

routine service technology   Technology used by an organization that operates in a relatively stable environment and services customers who are relatively sure about their needs.

rule   The specification of a course of action that must be followed in dealing with a particular routine problem.

rule utilitarianism   The branch of the utilitarian ethical approach that relies primarily on the following of predefined rules or standards in order to obtain the greatest good for the greatest number.

satisfaction   An attitude determined by the difference between the rewards employees receive and those they believe they should have received—the smaller the difference, the greater the satisfaction.

satisficing   The practice of selecting an acceptable (that is, easier to identify, less controversial, or otherwise safer) objective or alternative solution.

scalar principle   The basic principle of organizational coordination that states that a clear and unbroken chain of command should link every person in the organization with someone a level higher, to the top of the organization chart.

scenario   A written description of a possible future that is used as a forecasting aid.

scientific management   A traditional management system that focuses on improving the efficiency of individual worker–machine relationships.

second-order outcome   The result, good or bad, brought about by a first-order outcome (behavior).

security needs   The fairly basic human needs for safety, stability, and absence of pain, threat, and illness, which occupy the second level of Maslow's hierarchy.

selective perception   The process of screening out information that one wishes or needs to avoid.

self-actualization needs   Needs related to personal growth, self-fulfillment, and the realization of one's full potential, which occupy the highest level of Maslow's hierarchy.

self-managing team   A formal group of employees who work together on a daily basis to produce an entire good (or major identifiable component) or service and perform a variety of managerial tasks connected with their jobs.

self-understanding   Being able to recognize one's strengths and compensate for one's weaknesses.

semantics   The study of the way words are used and the meanings they convey.

sender   The source of information and initiator of the communication process.

sequential interdependence   The type of technological interdependence in which the flow of information and resources between individuals and/or departments is serialized.

similarity error   Interviewer error caused by a bias in favor of candidates that look or act like the interviewer.

simulation   A model, for representation, of a real system that describes the behavior of the system in quantitative and/or qualitative terms.

single-business firm   A company that provides a limited number of goods or services to one segment of a particular market.

skills   Abilities related to performance that are not necessarily inborn and that fall into four groups for managers: technical, interpersonal, conceptual, and communication.

skills inventory   A detailed file maintained for each employee that lists his or her level of education, training, experience, length of service, current job title and salary, performance history, and personal demographics.

skunkworks   Islands of intrapreneurial activity within an organization.

slack resources   Extra resources, such as materials, money or time, that an organization stockpiles in order to be prepared to respond to environmental changes.

smoothing style   The tendency to minimize or suppress differences and to emphasize common interests.

social audit   An attempt by an organization to identify, measure, evaluate, report on, and monitor the effects it is having on its stakeholders and society as a whole, which are not covered in its financial reports.

socialization   The process by which people learn the beliefs and values held by an organization (or the broader society).

software   The collection of rules, guidelines, and algorithms necessary for using particular hardware properly.

span of management   The basic principle of organizational coordination that refers to the number of people reporting directly to any one manager must be limited.

specialization   The process of identifying particular tasks and assigning them to individuals or teams who have been trained to do them.

special-purpose team A formal group of employees from various departments or even two organizational levels that is empowered with responsibility to handle any of a number of possible special situations.

spokesperson role The informational role managers play when they provide others, especially those outside the organization, with information that is to be taken as the official position of the organization.

stable environment An organizational environment characterized by little change in products, technology, competitive forces, markets, or political forces.

staff authority The authority to direct and control subordinates who support line activities through advice, recommendations, research, technical expertise.

staffing The process by which organizations satisfy their human resource needs by forecasting future needs, recruiting and selecting candidates, and orienting new employees.

stakeholder Anyone having potential or real power to influence an organization's decisions or actions (for example, a shareholder, important customer, or union member).

stakeholder control Control over an organization exerted by outsiders, such as stockholders, customers, or government agencies.

stakeholder social responsibility concept The idea that managers have obligations to identifiable groups that are affected by or can affect achievement of an organization's goals (such as important customers, shareholders, employees).

standardization The process of developing an organization's procedures in such a way that employees perform their jobs in a uniform and consistent manner.

standard operating procedure (SOP) A series of rules that must be followed in a particular sequence when dealing with a certain type of routine problem.

standards Criteria against which qualitative and quantitative characteristics are evaluated.

state of nature The conditions, situations, and events that individuals cannot control but that may in the future influence the outcomes of their decisions.

statistical process control The use of statistical methods and procedures to determine whether production operations are being done correctly to detect any deviations, and to find and eliminate their causes.

status Social rank in a group.

stereotyping Making assumptions about an individual solely on the basis of her or his belonging to a particular gender, race, age group, or the like.

strategic business unit (SBU) A division or subsidiary of a firm that serves a distinct product-market segment.

strategic planning The process of deciding on and analyzing the organization's mission, overall objectives, general strategies, and major resource allocations.

strategy Major course of action that an organization plans to take in order to achieve its objectives.

stress The individual's emotional, physical, and cognitive response to excessive demands.

stressor Any situation that places special demands on the individual.

subjective probability The likelihood that a specific outcome will occur, based on an individual's personal judgment and beliefs.

subsidy A direct or indirect payment by the government to its country's firms that makes selling or investing abroad cheaper and thus more profitable.

substitute good or service A good or service that can easily replace another.

subsystem One of possibly many lower levels within a larger system.

supporting style A leadership style characterized by active two-way communication and support of mature employees' efforts to use their skills.

supportive behavior Two-way communication between leader and followers.

supportive leadership A leadership style characterized by a friendly, approachable demeanor and concern for employees' well-being.

survey feedback An organization development method that allows managers and employees to provide feedback about the organization and receive feedback about their own behaviors.

system An association of interrelated and interdependent parts.

systems viewpoint One of four major viewpoints of management, which represents an approach to solving problems within the framework of inputs, transformations, and outputs.

tactical planning The process of making detailed, short-term decisions concerning what to do, who will do it, and how to do it.

tariff A government tax on goods or services entering a country.

task environment The external forces, such as customers or labor unions, that have a direct effect on an organization.

task-oriented leader A leader concerned with getting the job done.

task structure The degree to which the job is organized.

team A group organizationally empowered to participate in decision making, exercise influence over how their objectives are met, and, often, establish many of those objectives.

team building An organization development method that helps teams operate more effectively by testing and improving their structure, processes, and member satisfaction.

technical skills The ability to apply specific methods, procedures, and techniques in a specialized field.

technological interdependence The degree of coordination required between individuals and departments to transform information and raw materials into finished products.

technology The knowledge, tools, techniques, and actions used to transform materials, information, and other inputs into finished goods or services.

teleconferencing Use of a video-based communication system to conduct meetings between people in different locations.

theory x A set of negative assumptions about team members that leads to a directive leadership style.

theory y A set of positive assumptions about team members that leads to a participative leadership style.

time-and-motion study A study that identifies and measures a worker's physical movements, analyzes the results, and deletes movements that slow down production.

top manager A manager who is responsible for the overall direction and operations of an organization.

total-factor productivity A measure of economic efficiency, the ratio of outputs to total inputs used.

total quality control An organizational strategy that makes quality a responsibility of all employees.

traditional authority An authority structure, defined by Max Weber, based on tradition or custom.

traditional quality control Inspection of products during or at the end of the production process.

traditional social responsibility concept The idea that management should serve the interests of shareholders, that is, maximize shareholders' profits and long-term interests.

traditional viewpoint The oldest of the four major viewpoints of management; stresses the manager's role in a strict hierarchy and focuses on efficient and consistent job performance.

training Improving an employee's skills to the point where he or she can do the current job.

trait Individual personality characteristic that can affect a person's job performance.

traits model Theories of leadership based on the assumption that certain physical, social, and personal characteristics are inherent in leaders.

transformation process The technology used to convert inputs (physical, human, material, financial, and information resources) into outputs according to the systems viewpoint of management.

transformational leadership A style of leadership that provides extraordinary motivation to employees by appealing to their higher ideals and moral values and inspiring them to think about problems in new ways.

turbulent environment An external environment that is very complex, includes many forces that are constantly changing, and is both ambiguous and unpredictable.

turnkey operation A business (such as a franchise) that can be opened quickly.

two-factor model Herzberg's theory of motivation, which states that distinct kinds of experiences produce job satisfaction (motivator factors) and job dissatisfaction (hygiene factors).

Type A behavior pattern Chronic, aggressive struggle to achieve more in less time, in opposition to the efforts of others if necessary.

Type B behavior pattern Contemplative, nonagressive pursuit of realistic objectives.

uncertainty The condition that exists when an individual cannot clearly define the problem, identify alternative solutions, or assign probabilities to outcomes.

uncertainty avoidance Hofstede's value dimension that measures the degree to which individuals or societies attempt to avoid the ambiguity, riskiness, and indefiniteness of the future.

union shop A company whose agreement with labor stipulates that all employees covered by the contract must be union members or join the union within sixty to ninety days of being hired.

unity of command principle The basic principle of organizational coordination that states that an employee should have only one boss.

unrelated-business firm A company that provides diverse goods and services to many different markets.

upward channel A channel of communication by which subordinates send information to superiors.

utilitarian approach The ethical approach that judges the effect of decisions and behavior on others, with the objective of providing the greatest good for the greatest number of people.

valence The value or weight an individual attaches to a first- or second-order outcome, which can motivate behavior and influence decisions.

validity The measure of the degree to which a test measures what it's supposed to measure.

value From a competitive perspective, the relationship between quality and price.

value congruence Being able to understand the organization's guiding principles and employees' values and reconcile the two.

value of reward The importance that a person places on benefits to be obtained from a job.

value system Multiple beliefs (values) that are compatible and supportive of one another.

variable interval schedule Reinforcement schedule that provides reinforcement at irregular intervals of time.

variable ratio schedule Reinforcement schedule that provides reinforcement after a varying number of desired behaviors occur during an unspecified amount of time.

vertical information system An information-processing strategy managers can use to send information efficiently up and down the levels of an organization.

vision Being able to imagine a different and better situation and ways to achieve it.

wellness program Program instituted by an organization to promote the physical and psychological health of employees.

whistleblower An employee who reports to an outside authority violations of laws by his or her employer.

wide area network Communication system consisting of computers linked over great distances.

win–lose conflict situation In the contingency model of conflict, the situation that exists when the parties have many more conflicting goals than shared goals; that is, when one person's gain is another's loss.

work-force analysis A listing of all of a firm's job titles and salary rates and a breakdown by sex and ethnic/racial background of the total number of people holding each job title.

youth stage The second stage of the organizational life cycle, in which the organization competes successfully and is formalizing its design.

zero-based budget (ZBB) A financial method of justifying activities and programs in terms of efficiency and organizational priorities, based on looking at the activities and programs as if they were entirely new.

zone of indifference The intangible area within which fall the decisions or orders a subordinate will accept without question.

CREDITS

CHAPTER 1: p. 4, © Philip Saltonstall/ONYX; **p. 5,** Courtesy of Microsoft Corporation; **p. 8,** Courtesy of Westinghouse Electric Corporation; **p. 15,** © Joseph McNally/SYGMA; **p. 25,** © Steven Pumphrey. **CHAPTER 2: p. 38,** CULVER PICTURES, INC.; **p. 39,** (left) CULVER PICTURES, INC., (right) Courtesy of The Coca-Cola Company; **p. 40,** Courtesy of Rockwell International Corporation; **p. 42,** CULVER PICTURES, INC.; **p. 49,** THE BETTMANN ARCHIVE; **p. 55,** Courtesy of The Promus Companies Incorporated; **p. 59,** Courtesy of Federal Express; **p. 60,** Courtesy of Boeing Computer Services. **CHAPTER 3: p. 74,** UPI/BETTMANN NEWSPHOTOS; **p. 75,** Lara Hartley; **p. 78,** Courtesy of Alyeska Pipeline Services Company; **p. 82,** Fujifotos/THE IMAGE WORKS; **p. 88,** Courtesy of L.L. Bean, Inc. **CHAPTER 4: p. 104,** © Gregory Edwards/Honeywell; **p. 105,** Courtesy of Campbell Soup Company; **p. 110,** © Arthur Meyerson; **p. 117,** Courtesy of Unisys Corporation; **p. 124,** Maclean's. **CHAPTER 5: pp. 144 and 145,** Lara Hartley; **p. 147,** UPI/BETTMANN NEWSPHOTOS; **p. 157,** © John Chiasson/GAMMA-LIAISON; **p. 165,** © Paul Fusco/MAGNUM; **p. 167,** © Ben Boblett. **CHAPTER 6: pp. 180 and 181,** Lara Hartley; **p. 186,** © Gregory Heisler; **p. 189,** Courtesy of Quad/Graphics; **p. 197,** Courtesy of Texas Utilities Company; **p. 200,** Courtesy of Fisher-Price. **CHAPTER 7: pp. 216 and 217,** Lara Hartley; **p. 220,** Courtesy of Siemens Corporation; **p. 223,** Lara Hartley; **p. 231,** © Ed Kashi; **p. 234,** Courtesy of Harris Corporation. **CHAPTER 8: pp. 244 and 245,** Courtesy of Chrysler Corporation; **p. 249,** © Ray Ng; **p. 250,** Courtesy of Browning-Ferris; **p. 256,** Courtesy of Siemens Corporation. **CHAPTER 9: p. 280,** Jacket, Copyright © 1989 by Macmillan, Inc. Reproduced by permission of The Free Press, a Division of Macmillan, Inc. Photo by Lara Hartley; **p. 281,** Reproduced with permission of AT&T; **p. 289,** Courtesy of Bethlehem Steel Corporation; **p. 299,** Mark Antman/THE IMAGE WORKS; **p. 303,** Courtesy of The Walt Disney Company. **CHAPTER 10: p. 318,** Mike Greenlar/THE IMAGE WORKS; **p. 326,** Bob Daemmrich/THE IMAGE WORKS; **p. 332,** Tom Wojnowski, Ford Motor Company; **p. 343,** © Steve Niedorf. **CHAPTER 11: p. 354,** © Pat Casey Daley; **p. 355,** Lara Hartley; **p. 359,** Courtesy of The Dial Corporation; **p. 362,** Tom Wojnowski, Ford Motor Company; **p. 368,** (left) Courtesy of St. Francis Hospital, The Heart Center, Long Island, New York, (right) Reproduced with permission of AT&T. **CHAPTER 12: pp. 388 and 389,** Courtesy of Diamond-Star Motors; **p. 393,** © Michael Abramson; **p. 405,** © John Harding; **p. 408,** © Andy Freeberg; **p. 411,** © John S. Abbott. **CHAPTER 13: pp. 428 and 429,** Courtesy of Avis, Inc.; **p. 434,** Andrew Sacks/Time Magazine; **p. 435,** © Gary Hannabarger; **p. 449,** © Allen Dean Steele/Allsport; **p. 452,** © Andy Freeberg. **CHAPTER 14: p. 466,** © Michael Melford; **p. 467,** Courtesy of Herman Miller, Inc.; **p. 475,** © Steve Woit; **p. 478,** © Charles Thatcher; **p. 487,** © Breton Littlehales/Giannini & Talent. **CHAPTER 15: p. 504,** Cary Wolinsky/STOCK BOSTON; **p. 505,** Reproduced with permission of AT&T; **p. 509,** Sharon Risedorph/Courtesy of STUDIOS Architecture; **p. 513,** © Reuven Kopitchinski; **p. 516,** (left) IMAGE WORKS ARCHIVES, (right) Courtesy of Async Voice Services; **p. 521,** Ulrike Welsch/PHOTO RESEARCHERS, INC. **CHAPTER 16: pp. 534 and 535,** Courtesy of Texas Instruments Incorporated; **p. 537,** Deere & Company Annual Report 1989; **p. 548,** Courtesy of McDonnell-Douglas Corporation; **p. 550,** Courtesy of IBM Corporation; **p. 558,** Bob Daemmrich/THE IMAGE WORKS. **CHAPTER 17: pp. 578 and 579,** Courtesy of Digital Equipment Corporation; **p. 581,** © Alex Meyboom; **p. 600,** Topham/THE IMAGE WORKS; **p. 603,** Courtesy of Hewlett-Packard Company. **CHAPTER 18: pp. 616 and 617,** Wal-Mart Stores, Inc.; **p. 627,** © Mark Joseph; **p. 632,** Courtesy of Hilton Hotels Corporation; **p. 637,** Courtesy of Bethlehem Steel Corporation. **CHAPTER 19: p. 648,** Courtesy of Texas Instruments Incorporated; **p. 649,** Michael Stuckey/COMSTOCK; **p. 653,** © Steven Pumphrey; **p. 655,** Courtesy of Digital Equipment Corporation; **p. 646,** Deere & Company Annual Report 1989; **p. 659,** © Andy Freeberg; **p. 665,** Courtesy of Rockwell International Corporation; **p. 669,** Bill Taufic/Mead Corporation. **CHAPTER 20: pp. 678 and 679,** Courtesy of Xerox Corporation; **p. 683,** © Gerry Gropp/SIPA PRESS; **p. 687,** © Gregory Heisler; **p. 702,** Courtesy of E.I. du Pont de Nemours and Company. **CHAPTER 21: p. 714,** © Mitch Kezar; **p. 715,** Courtesy of 3M; **p. 718,** © Nina Barnett; **p. 720,** Courtesy of 3M; **p. 726,** © David Klutho; **p. 733,** © Alan Levenson. **CHAPTER 22: pp. 746 and 747,** Courtesy of NeXT Computer, Inc.; **p. 749,** © Christopher Springman; **p. 753,** © Charles Freeman; **p. 756,** © Seth Resnick; **p. 758,** © Stephen Collector; **p. 762,** © Alan Levenson; **p. 764,** © Charles Lemay/GAMMA-LIAISON; **p. 768,** © Emmett Martin.